THE OXFORD HANI

URBAN
PLANNING

THE OXFORD HANDBOOK OF

URBAN PLANNING

Edited by

RACHEL WEBER

and

RANDALL CRANE

OXFORD

UNIVERSITY PRESS

OXFORD
UNIVERSITY PRESS

Oxford University Press is a department of the University of Oxford.
It furthers the University's objective of excellence in research, scholarship,
and education by publishing worldwide.

Oxford   New York
Auckland   Cape Town   Dar es Salaam   Hong Kong   Karachi
Kuala Lumpur   Madrid   Melbourne   Mexico City   Nairobi
New Delhi   Shanghai   Taipei   Toronto

With offices in
Argentina   Austria   Brazil   Chile   Czech Republic   France   Greece
Guatemala   Hungary   Italy   Japan   Poland   Portugal   Singapore
South Korea   Switzerland   Thailand   Turkey   Ukraine   Vietnam

Oxford is a registered trade mark of Oxford University Press
in the UK and certain other countries.

Published in the United States of America by
Oxford University Press
198 Madison Avenue, New York, NY 10016

© Oxford University Press 2012

First issued as an Oxford University Press paperback, 2015.

Library of Congress Cataloging-in-Publication Data
The Oxford handbook of urban planning / edited
by Randall Crane and Rachel Weber.
p. cm.
Includes bibliographical references and index.
ISBN 978-0-19-537499-5 (hardcover); 978-0-19-023526-0 (paperback)
1. City planning—Handbooks, manuals, etc.
2. City planning—United States—Handbooks, manuals, etc.
I. Crane, Randall.   II. Weber, Rachel.
HT166.O94 2012
307.1'216—dc23
2011034086

CONTENTS

....

PART III   HOW AND WHAT DO WE PLAN? THE MEANS AND MODES OF PLANNING

A. PLAN MAKING

B. FRONTIERS OF PERSISTENT AND EMERGENT QUESTIONS

PART IV   WHO PLANS, HOW WELL, AND HOW CAN WE TELL?

A. Planning Agents

B. Making Good Plans

ABOUT THE CONTRIBUTORS

Lisa K. Bates is Assistant Professor of Urban Studies and Planning at Portland State University.

Victoria A. Beard is Associate Professor of Planning, Policy and Design at the University of California, Irvine.

Eran Ben-Joseph is Professor of Landscape Architecture and Planning at the Massachusetts Institute of Technology.

Eugénie L. Birch is the Lawrence C. Nussdorf Professor of Urban Research at the University of Pennsylvania.

Marlon G. Boarnet is Professor of Public Policy at the University of Southern California.

Thomas J. Campanella is Associate Professor of City and Regional Planning at the University of North Carolina, Chapel Hill.

John I. Carruthers is Program Director of the Sustainable Urban Planning Program at The George Washington University.

Karen Chapple is Associate Professor of City and Regional Planning at the University of California, Berkeley.

Igal Charney is a Lecturer in the Department of Geography and Environmental Studies at the University of Haifa.

Jason Corburn is Associate Professor of City and Regional Planning at the University of California, Berkeley.

Randall Crane is Professor of Urban Planning at the University of California, Los Angeles.

Elizabeth Currid-Halkett is Assistant Professor of Policy, Planning and Design at the University of Southern California.

J. R. DeShazo is Associate Professor of Public Policy at the University of California, Los Angeles.

Margaret Dewar is Professor of Urban and Regional Planning at the University of Michigan.

Yonn Dierwechter is Associate Professor of Urban Studies at the University of Washington Tacoma.

Ann-Margaret Esnard is Professor of Urban and Regional Planning at Florida Atlantic University.

Susan S. Fainstein is Professor of Urban Planning and Design at Harvard University.

Norman Fainstein is Professor Emeritus of Sociology and Urban Studies at Connecticut College.

John Forester is Professor of City and Regional Planning at Cornell University.

John Friedmann is an Honorary Professor at the School of Community and Regional Planning at the University of British Columbia.

Jennifer Girourd is a Graduate Student in Sociology at Brandeis University.

David R. Godschalk is Emeritus Professor of City and Regional Planning at the University of North Carolina, Chapel Hill.

Elisabeth M. Hamin is Associate Professor of Regional Planning at the University of Massachusetts, Amherst.

Charles Hoch is Professor of Urban Planning and Policy at the University of Illinois, Chicago.

Lewis D. Hopkins is Emeritus Professor of Urban and Regional Planning and Landscape Architecture at the University of Illinois, Urbana-Champaign.

Annette M. Kim is Associate Professor of Urban Studies & Planning at the Massachusetts Institute of Technology.

Kevin J. Krizek is Associate Professor of Planning, Design and Civil Engineering at the University of Colorado, Boulder.

John D. Landis is the Crossways Professor of City and Regional Planning at the University of Pennsylvania.

David M. Levinson is Associate Professor of Civil Engineering at the University of Minnesota.

Na Li is a recent PhD graduate of the University of Massachusetts, Amherst.

Elizabeth Macdonald is Associate Professor of City and Regional Planning, Landscape Architecture and Urban Design at the University of California, Berkeley.

Peter Marcuse is Professor of Urban Planning at Columbia University.

Linsey Marr is Associate Professor of Civil and Environmental Engineering at Virginia Tech.

Juan Matute is Director of the Luskin Center for Innovation's Climate Change Initiative at the University of California, Los Angeles.

Faranak Miraftab is Associate Professor of Urban and Regional Planning at the University of Illinois, Urbana-Champaign.

Vinit Mukhija is Associate Professor of Urban Planning at the University of California, Los Angeles.

Brenda Parker is Assistant Professor of Urban Planning and Policy at the University of Illinois, Chicago.

Ananya Roy is Professor of City and Regional Planning at the University of California, Berkeley.

Brent D. Ryan is Assistant Professor of Urban Studies & Planning at the Massachusetts Institute of Technology.

Tore Sager is Professor at the Norwegian University of Science and Technology in Trondheim.

Lisa Schweitzer is Associate Professor of Policy, Planning and Design at the University of Southern California.

Carmen Sirianni is the Morris Hillquit Professor of Labor and Social Thought at Brandeis University.

Yan Song is Associate Professor of City and Regional Planning at the University of North Carolina, Chapel Hill.

Emily Talen is Professor at the School of Geographical Sciences and Urban Planning and School of Sustainability at Arizona State University.

J. Phillip Thompson is Associate Professor of Urban Politics at the Massachusetts Institute of Technology.

Andy Thornley is a Professor of Urban Planning at the London School of Economics, Regional and Urban Planning Studies Programme.

Karen Umemoto is Professor of Urban and Regional Planning at the University of Hawaii at Manoa.

Matthew D. Weber is a Graduate Student in Urban and Regional Planning at the University of Michigan.

Rachel Weber is Associate Professor of Urban Planning and Policy at the University of Illinois, Chicago.

Vera Zambonelli is a Graduate Student in Urban Planning at the University of Hawaii at Manoa.

THE OXFORD HANDBOOK OF

URBAN PLANNING

PART I

INTRODUCTION

CHAPTER 1

PLANNING AS SCHOLARSHIP: ORIGINS AND PROSPECTS

RACHEL WEBER AND RANDALL CRANE

…guessing directions, they sketch
transitory lines rigid as wooden borders
on a wall in the white vanishing air
—Margaret Atwood, "The City Planners," 1990

PLANNING SCHOLARSHIP

URBAN planning is a relatively young academic discipline and, despite its storied genes, lacks an extensive, established canon on which to rest its laurels. Its youth affords it the flexibility to take on varied guises: an upstart social science; a boundary-spanning source of professional knowledge; and a fraternity of generalists, problem-solvers, and idealists, many being migrants from other, more traditional disciplines.

Yet the absence of a singular disciplinary tradition often obscures commonalities between scholars within the field. Because of its multiple identities, the field often breaks down along distinct problem-oriented lines: studying housing or transportation can be more important to one's identity as a scholar than the disciplinary parameters of the planning profession (e.g., Glazer, 1974). That said, we propose that planning research habitually embodies at least four indicative, overlapping orientations:

- *Built and natural environments.* Frederick Law Olmsted Jr. famously defined city planning in 1913 as the "intelligent control or guidance…of the physical form of the city, in its entirety." In this still compelling view, planning is fundamentally a normative effort defined by its focus on the hows, whys, and ways of place-making. While many fields aim to better understand poverty, traffic, governance, or environmental resource conflicts, planning is distinctive in its focus on how the complexity of urban place and space informs and affects these phenomena. Even today, when space can be more virtual than tangible, it arguably remains the first planning focus and lens.

- *Complex, interdependent problems.* As its core task, planning addresses the complex, messy, and often unsolvable "wicked" problems of urbanism, growth and decline, and the social conflicts that confound places, individuals, and organizations. These challenges are multidimensional, interrelated, and often deeply problematic. Above all, much like the cities and places they seek to both explain and repair, they are neither simply described nor understood.

- *Implementation and practice.* In contrast to many other disciplines for which the problems of cities and their hinterlands are an object of study, the principle purpose of planning is to do something about them. The questions that urban planners ask and the perspectives that they bring to these issues are, if not entirely unique, distinctively solutions-oriented. An overarching concern for practice, implementation, and affirmative change distinguishes planning from the other social sciences and enriches the intellectual content of research conducted under its auspices.

- *Change.* Like the hypothetical planner in the lines quoted above, practicing planners try to "guess directions," anticipate the future, and create physical plans, processes, and institutions that can induce, respond to, and manage change. Unlike the ironic stance taken by Attwood in the poem, they are united by a confidence that efforts to anticipate and prepare for change should be taken as part of the collective or shared purpose of improving cities. Some construct detailed models and imagine alternative scenarios in order to predict the future consequences of present actions. Others gather data and build theories to more accurately represent real-time transformations in neighborhoods and regions.

Cohesion around these orientations has allowed planning research to grow from a subset of urban-oriented topics within many different but traditional disciplines to the distinctive use of those disciplines to confront the challenges of modern cities, rich and poor. However, the advantages of scholarship about the field of spatial planning are often underappreciated. In the chapters that follow, the authors highlight the unique strengths of urban planning research. The *Handbook* organizes this state-of-the-art research by its leaders and emerging young scholars to sample the breadth of insight among diverse disciplinary outlooks. It broaches established topics of planning scholarship in a manner that emphasizes both cross-cutting themes and fresh approaches. We avoid rehashing existing knowledge, accepted wisdom, and constraining orthodoxies.

While offering a source of information, commentary, and expertise relevant to practitioners, this volume is not intended to offer best practices or translate innovative academic thinking for them. The American Planning Association's *Planning and Urban Design Standards* (American Planning Association 2006), as well as the ICMA's two "Green Books," *The Practice of Local Government Planning* (Hoch, Dalton, and So 2000) and *Local Planning: Contemporary Principles and Practice* (Hack et al. 2009), are excellent references for planning commissioners, planners, and professionals in related fields such as environmental and land-use law, architecture, and government. These handbooks describe the mainstream practices of planning and city management.

By contrast, this handbook offers planning academics and scholars in such allied fields as architecture, geography, economics, and public administration detailed literature reviews, conceptual musings and theoretical frameworks. The following thirty-eight chapters demonstrate the breadth, substance, and significance of the multiple spatial, historical, economic, physical, and social policy contexts in which cities have developed. Each chapter represents an original contribution tailor-made for the volume. They report the latest research on these topics in a manner that is accessible to an academic audience from the social sciences, policy sciences, and design and legal professions. No comparable compendium of contemporary urban planning research currently exists.

The remainder of this chapter further considers this volume's significance, intellectual structure, organizational scheme, and content.

THE EVOLUTION OF PLANNING

People flock to cities in pursuit of prosperity even as they contend with severe resource shortages, segregation, and polarized labor markets. While few would claim that the problems plaguing contemporary cities are greater in number or magnitude than in the past, more individuals are certainly affected by those problems today owing to contemporary urbanization patterns. In 2010, 3.5 billion or 51 percent of the world's population lived in urban areas, compared to 29 percent sixty years ago (United Nations 2010).

Attention to urban problems accompanies this geographic shift. The modern nation state in the nineteenth century thrived on unprecedented urbanization and the expansion of a market economy. The administration of growing and moving populations inspired new tools for social order and control, foremost among these bureaucratic reforms tied to an impersonal, secular, and calculating rationality (Simmel 1950; Weber 1978; Flyvbjerg 1998; Mitchell 2002). The powers of engineering that made warfare, trade and travel predictable and swift inspired the imaginations of reformers. The promise of health, security, and welfare, once the prerogative for elites, could be provided to the urban masses through enlightened and efficient municipal planning and management (see Corburn this volume for a discussion of the roots of urban planning in sanitary and health reforms). Notes Webber (1969) "The solutions to the problems plaguing the industrial city could be solved through the rational application of moral reform." New crises—wars, natural disasters, epidemics, poverty—only posed anew and with greater urgency "the question of how 'reason' might gain ascendancy over the insentient forces that seemed increasingly to dominate the institutions of Western society" (Friedmann and Hudson 1974, 6).

The progressive movement nurtured planning institutions that tapped and expanded the roles of professionals as administrators and consulting experts subjecting political corruption and economic exploitation to the norms of purposeful collective decisions responsive to a public interest. The focus of these reformers, for the most part, was spatial; the field of urban planning grew out of the urban land "nexus," and taming disorderly urban growth and its attendant social and environmental problems became the focus of this young profession. Scholars have offered detailed historical accounts of how urban space emerged as a legitimate sphere of governance (Boyer 1983; Fishman 1977; 2000; Hall 2002; see also Ben-Joseph this volume). They track and critique how professions such as landscape architecture, engineering, economics, and sociology shaped the emerging field of city planning, especially as an institutional reform located between the administrative and political functions of government. Western imperialism exported many of the tenets of modern spatial planning to colonies around the world where they were grafted on to and appropriated through indigenous traditions of city building (King 1976).

Plans became the legal and moral artifacts that represented the principles, goals, and expert advice of their authors and sponsors. Plans were initially comprehensive in scope, focused on the city as a synthetic object of concern, a system "whose parts would lose meaning if separated from the whole" (Beauregard 1990, 211). After the 1920s, the synthetic focus on the physical city gradually lost out to more diffuse and bureaucratic policy approaches to the subject, such as technical standards and land use regulations. Planners became specialists operating within their own functionally segregated areas of expertise, cut off both from grand visions and from the moral sentiment that motivated them. Later advances in computing technologies allowed for further rationalization of planning approaches (Michael 1965; see also Landis and Esnard, this volume).

The growing professional distance and faith in methods led mainstream planning to ignore or misinterpret the racial conflict and economic polarization occurring in urban regions. In the 1960s, attempts to reshape the profession to be an advocate for those most harmed by the concentrations of public and private power—namely low-income residents, immigrants, people of color—surfaced as a challenge to the ongoing bureaucratization process.

In the United States, urban planning developed more independent professional coherence and integrity during the latter half of the twentieth century. This was a fertile period of planning scholarship, capturing the great tensions between competing paradigms of urban governance and reacting to professional planning's greatest accomplishments and failures. The postwar era saw the wholesale clearance of working-class neighborhoods, the coordination feats involved in laying thousands of miles of highways, the ambitious plans to end urban poverty, and grassroots efforts to build community. And during this turbulent period, the visibility of planners and the demands on the scholarly field of urban planning grew. Specialized educational offerings for this young profession expanded in the 1950s, and the first PhD program was developed during this time (Perloff 1957; Teitz 1984).

The profession has ventured well beyond its traditional boundaries since those origins, integrating such diverse subfields as geospatial analysis and community organizing. Since the profession began its accreditation process, over eighty universities in the North America have adopted graduate urban planning degrees programs.

The field of urban planning has experienced something of a rebirth in the last decade; urban planning programs are experiencing a record number of applicants and are graduating an unprecedented number of professionals. The profession is expected to grow at an above average rate of 19 percent between 2008 and 2018 (Bureau of Labor Statistics 2010). This popularity could be due in part to a growing awareness of the hazards of unplanned growth, concerns about natural environments and economic injustice, and belief that planning can smooth transitions as society becomes more urbanized (Michael 1965). The status of academic planning also reflects the ascendance of the policy sciences and the value of applied knowledge in the face of continued urban development challenges. The field's pragmatism has allowed planning scholars entrée to the worlds of policymaking at all scales of government. Though never unimportant, systematic study of the ways in which cities and their administrations work, and fail to work, has gained renewed intellectual currency in a world where the promises of prosperity often fall short.

The Conflicted Status of Planning
in the Academy

Owing to its youth and practical relevance, planning holds an awkward place within the academy, one that deserves further exploration and explication through an undertaking such as this one. Planning is one of those "schools of the minor professions" (Glazer 1974) marked by the conflicts that emerge in the absence of the legitimacy of a major profession, a singular grounding in specific technique, and fixed and unambiguous ends (Teitz 1984).

Its dual nature as both craft (how to plan) and intellectual field (why and for whom to plan) can be viewed as a liability. Planning aspires to be both legible and useful to those outside the academy and valued by the analytical standards of the academy. As such, academic planning finds itself trapped between competing instrumentalities of knowledge. It is often dismissed as overly concerned with the application of existing knowledge for external constituencies and normative to the sake of being biased (Scott and Roweis 1977). Other, more established academic disciplines claim to focus instead on the development of new knowledge for its own sake.

Such generalizations are unfair and have invited a torrent of analytic hair splitting about the nature of applied knowledge. The permeable walls between academe and the profession have many supporters. On one hand, constant engagement with practitioners allows planning scholars to theorize practice with an appreciation for its nuances, politics, and pathologies (Schön 1983). As Tore Sager notes in this volume "Planning is an institutionalized social technology for systematizing knowledge pertinent for a particular kind of collective action and for marshalling the power required for its implementation" (PAGE 26). On the other hand, planners' generalist knowledge and problem-focused orientation are often sought out by practitioners who as fellow problem solvers know no allegiance to a single academic discipline. Planners develop knowledge that informs the practical judgments of a wide range of decision makers.

Planners have also had to contend with intellectual and professional assaults on the profession's basic premises: that planned processes and outcomes are superior to unplanned ones and that planning can, in fact, reflect some kind of public interest (for a review of the latter, see Campbell and Marshall 2002). Critiques of planning have a longstanding and diverse ideological pedigree. As archetypical producers of technocratic knowledge, those in central planning have been accused by scholars ranging from Frederich von Hayek (1944, 1994) to Peter Gordon (see, for example, Gordon and Richardson 2001) of misrepresenting individual preferences (e.g., for living in sprawling suburbs), falsely claiming to reflect consensus on the nature of public interests, and distorting the operation of markets. These critiques are not just voiced in the halls of academe but also, more loudly, in city council meetings, policy debates, and development conflicts around the world. Libertarian activists, such as the Institute for Justice and the Wise Use movement in the United States, have made similar arguments against the abuse of government's power to sap individual freedoms and undermine rights to private property.

Other critiques of planning—coming from left-leaning scholars such as Michel Foucault (1979) and James Scott (1998)—have challenged the abstracting logics of state planning. They argue that the interpretations of space and human behavior that derive from abstractions such as maps and statistics (i.e., the tools of the planning trade) devalue local knowledge, homogenize idiosyncrasies, and inevitably lead to failed policies. Unlike the neo-Hayekians, it is not state intervention that is anathema to their views; rather, the "rational" practices and tactics of governance—ones that could be used in the private, public, or third sectors—that are the root of the problem. When efforts to change human settlement patterns attempt to be comprehensive or do not accept the cognitive limits of their "societal guidance" efforts (Etzioni 1967), the futility of such efforts is exposed. Only recognition of the tacit knowledge and material experiences of nonexperts—acknowledged somewhat by the turn toward communicative action and participatory planning—could undo some of the damage wrought by planning's grandiose attempts to improve the human condition.

While offering important insights into the multi-partisan resistance to planning, both critiques tend to overstate the power that contemporary planners possess. Indeed a strong anti-expert sentiment has kept public-sector technicians relegated to advice giving—at least in the North American context. Fears about planners ruling the world may be less realistic than the more radical critique of planning, which accuses planners not of having too much power but of sitting on the sidelines while capitalism extends its reach (somewhat confirmed by the political case analyses of Altshuler 1966). The squalid, unhealthy, unsustainable, and expensive conditions of cities are less a by-product of planning's wrong-headed interventions, these critics point out, than of its short-term political impotence and its long-term inability to address the contradictions and dislocations of capital accumulation (Scott and Roweis 1977).

Academic planners are aware of these shortcomings, and some of the field's loudest critics have themselves found homes within the discipline. This is testament to the field's willingness to embrace diverse views and its interest in confronting controversy. Critique and disagreement contribute to intellectual ferment within the field, a ferment that we attempt to represent and engage in the following compilation. Indeed, the *Handbook* is intended not just to bring together in one volume an inclusive statement of the varied frameworks and substantive foci within the field of urban planning but to focus on the debates surrounding them.

THE HANDBOOK ORGANIZATION

The *Handbook* is organized into three sections. These sections concern the three fundamental lines of inquiry most apparent in urban planning scholarship today: the role and purpose of planning, its practice and content, and its impact.

Part II. Why Plan?

The *Handbook* begins with a discussion of the discipline's motivations and goals. Planning in a mixed-market economy is most often justified by the presence of market failures. Competing land uses abutting each other (negative externalities), retail market opportunities foregone by businesses because of racial stereotyping (information asymmetries), and overconsumption of natural resources (public goods) are all accepted motivations for planning interventions by even by the staunchest free marketer. However, the market-failure perspective provides only one, very functional explanation for the evolution of planning. Other more historical or institutional accounts of the field's genesis and rationale are considered here.

Planners make judgments in the context of great uncertainties and competing interests, and they are motivated by a variety of values and beliefs. These values often conflict within the same plan. Can one plan be aesthetically pleasing, fiscally productive, and environmentally sustainable? Certain principles nonetheless constitute a repertoire that frequently guides plans, and their definition and operationalization are discussed in this section.

Part III. How and What Do We Plan?

This section addresses grounded and normative questions of practice, as well as the field's clashing philosophical roots in both Enlightenment-era rationalism and American pragmatism. Issues of expertise, technique, and communication have engaged planning theory for the last century. This section also focuses on the different activities that constitute contemporary planning.

Research is presented in two forms. One form concerns *methods*, which in planning are distinctive in their problem- and solution-orientation as well as their variety and mix. The second form surveys a number of *traditional* and *emerging* *issues* that are both intellectually challenging and popularly visible, such as economic development, housing, smart growth and climate-change planning, with an emphasis on research gaps and new results. These topics raise similar intellectual challenges that span different subfields of planning: that is, risk, uncertainty, limited knowledge, value differences, inequality, power, and accountability.

IV. Who Plans, How Well, and How Can We Tell?

This third section addresses the issues of agency and outcomes. Who ultimately holds power over the shape of places? Whereas the city planning function traditionally has been located in local government, actual control over city building may reside more with private developers who possess both the overriding self-interest and the financial capital to initiate change. Recently there has been more attention paid to those ways in which individuals transform places, not by virtue of their role in any state apparatus but acting through civil society or on their own through creative and informal forms of appropriation.

The products of planning include not just the documents we call plans, the blueprints that guide physical development in a neighborhood or region, but also the physical and political infrastructure that creates opportunities for agglomeration and exchange—the essence, according to Sennett (1992), of urbanity. Authors in this section discuss different ways of evaluating the outcomes of planning and the value of plans. Planners distinguish themselves from economists and policy analysts by devoting their attention not just to the creation of public benefits but also to the allocation of those benefits. The chapters in this section address the state–market–civil society relations and the politics of planning that determine winners and losers.

Handbook Themes: Contemporary Intellectual Currents

Whereas the organizational structure of the *Handbook* is dictated by the fundamental questions of why, how, what, and who, the content follows the intellectual contours of the field by way of less conventional paths and categories, summarized below.

We intersperse work by the field's established and junior scholars, and consciously choose not to reify the conventional boundaries that divide planning into functions or sectors such as transportation, historic preservation, growth management, and land use. We are not dismissing the canon; after all, the work gathered here still expresses concern for the same old problems of space, complexity and coordination, the knowledge-practice relationship, and comprehensiveness. But in this volume the authors propose some innovative frameworks for understanding old problems as well as introduce readers to new topics and approaches within the field.

These approaches reflect changed thinking and the influential intellectual trajectories within the applied social sciences at the beginning of the twenty-first century. For example, several of the chapters break down the dualisms that separate states from markets, focusing instead on civil society, third-sector organizations, and informal planning practices. Several of the chapters adopt communicative and constructivist epistemologies, demonstrating, for example, how expert knowledge must be made and established rather than assumed by virtue of its superior technical acumen. Several chapters challenge accepted assumptions about urban relationships and dynamics by looking at the empirical record, typically one that blends complex spatial modeling with unique data sources.

In particular we see some convergence between the chapters on a few general points: planning is contingent on place and culture, planning is increasingly hybrid, planning expertise is socially constructed, and even the most sensible appearing solutions call for validation.

Planning Is a Locally, Culturally, and Temporally Contingent Practice

Because academic planning is often explicitly self-conscious and normative (i.e., what planning ought to be, what it should aspire to do, how it can do its job better), it treats the practice of planning as decision making and guidance that somehow floats above the rest of society. The field's roots in architecture and engineering encouraged the notion that there can be one-size-fits-all standards and algorithms that are universally valid. But despite its idealist roots, urban planning is not a "transcendental activity, which contains certain principles that are appropriate for all time" (Cooke 1983, 10). Much of the new planning scholarship directly addresses the contingencies of place, time, and identity.

Chapters by Annette Kim and co-authors Yonn Dierwechter and Andy Thornley locate the planning function within the specific institutional networks of complex societies. These authors are not focused on what planning should be or what it should do. Planning, they argue, can best be viewed as a set of institutions and practices that are constrained by power relations between states, markets, and civil society, and these relations are highly variable across time and space. Their chapters lead to critical questions for any planning scholar: What does planning actually accomplish in different places? Why is it important in some historical eras and places and less so in others? What are the connections between planning and the other critical societal and political functions of the state?

Planning acquires its distinct characteristics based on forces that lay both inside and outside its realm of control. John Friedmann describes some of the contextual variables that alter the nature of planning in different settings: unitary versus federal states; strong central states versus strong regional states; liberal democracies versus authoritarian states; active participation in civic affairs by an organized civil society versus a civil society that is largely disengaged; preponderance of regulatory versus developmental planning; a legal system based on common law versus statutory law. Authors of several of the chapters would likely add to this list the degree to which communities are relatively diverse or homogenous, given that identity affects citizenship and political enfranchisement and, therefore, planning processes and outcomes.

Planning processes are also dependent on local conditions, including the health of property markets, the degree of trust between actors or the sources of funding. Margaret Dewar and Matthew Weber's chapter points out how little the field has to say about planning in areas that are not growing but instead are experiencing severe population and economic decline, disinvestment, and abandonment. They seek to fill in this absence by presenting frameworks, as opposed to specific tools, for addressing urban shrinkage. Even the field's defining normative principles—as Elizabeth MacDonald shows in her chapter on beauty or when Peter Marcuse discusses the meaning of justice—are defined and pursued in historically and culturally specific ways. John Carruthers's chapter on the public financing of urban growth is highly specific, making general patterns and thus practices difficult to justify.

If we approach the function, processes, and goals of planning contextually, then the artifacts planners produce should command the same kind of orientation. Brent Ryan proposes that planners treat plans like works of art that can be deconstructed through historically informed readings, pointing out how they represent ideas about design, public space, and city-suburban relations in vogue at the time. Contemporary land-use controls and building codes can also be read in this manner although, in his chapter on the topic, Eran Ben-Joseph is more concerned with whether the disconnect between these historically specific regulatory regimes contained in these codes and planning goals such as efficiency and sustainability can ever be breached. Emily Talen wants to argue that sustainable planning is a straightforward consequence of contemporary principles of sustainability, but getting from one to the other often proves elusive. Lisa Schweitzer and Linsey Marr give the critical example of air quality policy, and the clear disadvantages of advice based on imperfect knowledge. J. R. DeShazo and Juan Matute expand this example by showing how regulation for climate change depends on local planning goals and structures, and yet remains experimental because of that local dependence.

These local features not only shape the nature of the planning function but also influence other actors whose behaviors are circumscribed and influenced by planning. For example, Igal Charney emphasizes the importance of place—particularly the distinct regulatory environments, development cultures, and constellations of actors—that alter the power of the real estate profession across geographies.

Despite their attentiveness to the idiosyncrasies of place and time, the chapters in the *Handbook* still draw heavily from a contemporary North American planning tradition, one in which cities have developed quickly, local authorities regulate land use, and property rights are strong. This bias is intended to suggest neither a global planning monoculture nor the convergence of individual traditions along an Anglo-American model (through, for example, imperialism or the dissemination of "best practices" through international planning consultancies). As Friedmann acknowledges in his chapter, institutional change has proceeded at such different rates and according to such different logics as to make a one-world planning culture a utopian or dystopian idea. At the same time, however, one cannot deny the increasingly similar development trajectories between places that for centuries managed to retain a local distinctiveness. In their chapter comparing urban redevelopment patterns in the United States and Western Europe, Norman Fainstein and Susan Fainstein isolate a set of recent political and economic dynamics that serve to integrate local conditions with global transformations.

Still, many authors in this volume use cases from non-Western countries to contrast or challenge the notion of American exceptionalism. Individual contributors such Ananya Roy, Victoria Beard, Vinit Mukhija, and Faranak Miraftab consider their topics in places where planning research questions are particularly acute, such as the fast-growing countries of China, Brazil, Indonesia, South Africa, and India. Several authors examine them in the transitional economies of Europe and Asia where state-market relations were radically restructured after the fall of communism. Others explore boundaries between functions and responsibilities in different cases as well as their historical evolution.

The Boundaries between States, Markets, and Third-Sector Organizations Have Broken Down

Debates about the whether states or markets do a better job of allocating resources and regulating the built environment seem musty in the twenty-first century. Hybrid forms of governance—contracting out, self-regulation, partnerships—cast a new light on planning. Once bound inexorably to the apparatus of local government, planning activities and functions can now be found in other sites and organizations, many of which are in the so-called third sector, or what some refer to as "civil society." Karen Chapple, for example, shows how the subfield of community economic development has not only become increasingly separate from planning but also, to a much greater extent, its implementation occurs outside of government agencies through a variety of nonprofit, labor, and business organizations. Elizabeth Currid-Halkett treats "the arts" as a planning sector increasingly driving regional economies rather than the other way around. These shifts in professional structure are both opportunistic and strategic on the part of practicing planners and are a response to the defunding of the local state.

As Carmen Sirianni and Jennifer Girouard explain in their chapter on the civics of planning, planning becomes an issue of coordination across a variety of stakeholders and associations, each of whom struggles for control and decision-making power. Creating frameworks for effective governance depends on designing civic engagement into planning processes that meet certain normative standards (inclusiveness, accountability, balance of power). Such norms permit, the authors note, "expanded scope for civic actors to make decisions, engage in coproduction and multiple forms of collaboration, but within a framework where they are accountable to other partners, and especially to relevant government authorities, elected by the larger polity or serving as administrators of statutes passed by democratic legislatures" (This volume, 682). They must also meet instrumental standards such as relative effectiveness and the efficient use of time and resources.

Other contributors question the degree to which civil society can include those poor households and individuals unable to make claims as fully enfranchised citizens. Ananya Roy points out that citizen participation is difficult in settings of urban informality, an alternative urban order where low-income individuals exist in tenuous spaces of ambiguous legal standing. "Formalized" state planning, economic production, and citizen involvement are rare, and so structured interactions between discrete sectors (e.g., states collaborating with markets) are less plausible. Instead, poor households develop forms of everyday practice and self-provisioning outside the organized labor force, formal economy, and state that allow them to survive in underresourced cities. Informality, she argues, should imply neither stigma nor absence of governmentality as much as a different way of organizing space and negotiating citizenship. Vinit Mukhija gives examples of successful improvements of slums, not via traditional top-down planning strategies but by residents themselves.

Faranak Miraftab and J. Phillip Thompson also describe the relationship between citizenship and formal state structures as central to planning. In her chapter, Miraftab expresses doubts about the extent to which formal political avenues and state-sanctioned rights and entitlements matter to achieving improvements in the lives of marginalized households. The only options in the cases of undocumented workers in small Midwestern towns or slum dwellers in the townships of South Africa that she studied were to fashion new forms of citizenship that afforded them inclusion in public institutions and in public spaces. Similarly, Thompson points out the materialist roots of racial discrimination and acknowledges the wide divide between what is promised through formal channels and what is actually provided—particularly in those communities that have suffered historically from discrimination and political marginalization. "Insurgent" citizenship and communal politics, which includes everything from anti-eviction campaigns to door-to-door organizing, often achieves more programmatic outcomes for such communities than professional planners and formal political channels are able to provide.

Planners Construct Expert Knowledge in Different Ways

In this volume, authors engage the issue of expertise in myriad ways. For example, Brenda Parker observes that the official historical narratives of the planning discipline obscure the ways in which ordinary citizens—namely women—contributed to its institutionalization. By ignoring women (and individuals of color who made similar kinds of underappreciated contributions), these narratives downplay the role that local knowledge and "street science" play in both the formation of the field and its contemporary functioning.

To engage effectively in urban planning, citizens need the authorization and scope to utilize local knowledge associated with "good processes." Some authors, such as Jason Corburn, stress that expertise needs to become a resource shared by both planner and the subject of plans. Ann-Margaret Esnard describes investments in data visualization systems that are sophisticated yet usable by the public so that knowledge can be co-produced. John Forester advocates for planning processes that are expert enabled rather than expert led or expert dominated. Shaping future action in a world of interdependent stakeholders depends less on choosing the right alternative up front than in creating spaces where consensus and the political will to implement can be generated. Elisabeth Hamin and Li Na note that planners act more like mediators in emotionally charged preservation battles where landscapes are connected to memory and there is a highly individualized sense of place. Doing so effectively requires not methods or tools for validating historic truths but, rather, the ability to create venues for story-telling and oral history. Similarly Karen Umemoto's chapter on the principle of diversity emphasizes that multicultural communities are constantly negotiating planning goals, principles, and strategies to find shared meanings.

Tore Sager explains that Condorcet's jury theorem shows that plural planning, even if composed of imperfectly informed lay participants, is likely to choose the better alternatives than will expert-devised solutions. Lew Hopkins also examines the research into collective action, collaborative problem solving, and preference aggregation, and he finds evidence that good processes tend to produce better plans. Good processes, for example, increase the likelihood that plans will be used and, therefore, influence decisions and future actions.

Others acknowledge the importance of citizen input and political participation, particularly when it comes to identifying goals. Planning methods tell us little about the comparative advantages of alternative distributions of resources *ex ante*, and so citizens often deal with this issue politically and through debate.

However, some authors also stress the importance of deepening planners' expertise through more sophisticated and scientific methods to identify the best means of managing expectations and increasingly complex environments. They, either explicitly or implicitly, are reluctant to give up the notion of comprehensive planning that has shaped the field to date. Tackling the issue of shelter, for example, Lisa Bates discusses methods of housing planning that involve simulations of market trends and modeling the effects of planning interventions to better characterize distinct market segments and address future needs. John Landis assesses many of the primary tools of expertise—planning models—as well as their evolution and success. Tom Campanella and David Godschalk argue that many of the planning models examined by Landis need to be refined to accommodate the occasional disaster, no matter how rare, and to adjust to a steady state or decline in land consumption.

The use of planning expertise is no more straightforward than public participation. Charlie Hoch demonstrates that plan making requires individuals to reconcile radically different domains of knowledge—namely, design artistry and scientific competence. Whereas design has the potential to guides future development toward beauty, scientific analysis offers predictability and control through the precise application of methical analysis and evaluation. Hoch argues that planners use practical reasoning and judgment to digest scientific evidence that can inform and tame imaginative designs about future alternatives.

The views represented in this volume reflect different opinions on the proper balance of local, scientific, aesthetic, and practical judgment that do not always converge perfectly with one another. Despite some evidence, as Hopkins notes, that opportunities for human judgment and political ownership tend to complement the use of analytical methods, the tensions between participation and expertise, and between different kinds of expert judgment, still electrifies the field.

"Superior" Outcomes Associated with Planning Need to be Empirically Validated Rather than Suggested

Much of the canon of planning theory can be described as normative assertions about the benefits of planning (e.g., in reducing uncertainty through collective action) and the improvements to democratic institutions that would aid those most disenfranchised. Plans should result in positive outcomes by communicating useful and usable information to intended audiences so as to influence decisions and change the behavior of those aware of it.

However critics have punctured the optimism associated with planning—pointing to failures ranging from urban renewal in the United States to neo-colonial forms of social engineering in the Global South. That planning can be associated with improvement in the lives of the poor and vulnerable cannot be assumed.

Kevin Krizek and David Levinson consider the apparently intuitive planning goal of accessibility, and find it sometimes unintuitive and yet still useful as a planning measure and objective, if done with care. Mirroring both the general move toward empiricism, positivism, and scientific validation in the social sciences, on one hand, and a new communicative orientation, on the other, planning research increasingly has sought to explore these seemingly unassailable statements about the value of planning. Are planning outcomes really superior to those from unplanned processes? Are residents of New Urbanist communities happier or better off? Does transportation planning reduce commute times? These questions do not ask if planning goals such as beauty or sustainability are worth pursuing—questions that can be evaluated before or after outcomes are realized. Instead, they examine if plans really will help or did help in achieving them.

Yan Song's chapter on the classic archenemy of planning—sprawl—and its prince on a white horse, smart growth, takes stock of both presumptions and finds them inadequate. Even while we have learned much about the costs and benefits of alternative urban forms, as John Carruthers surveys, there may be more still we do not know, making constructive advice to the profession a risky business indeed. Marlon Boarnet's chapter on the influence of land use on travel, perhaps the most active research literature in planning journals over the past fifteen years, argues both that substantial progress has been made in how to think about and thus study this set of issues and that we remain shorthanded by the state of that scholarship. Lew Hopkins's chapter addresses these challenges of plan evaluation from a wider vantage point. He points out that analysts interested in whether outcomes conformed to plan intent have found inconclusive results. In contrast, those who have used in-depth case studies and statistical inference have found planning to be effective in influencing actions and outcomes (i.e., the plans have "performed" in that people have used the information in them). Sometimes, however, these outcomes may be unintended and undesirable. These questions also pertain to the agents of planning; for example, are people who know how to plan really better problem solvers than those who lack such skills?

Empirical planning studies can be used to support or counter the cynicism about the claims of improvement and betterment that planners have historically made. Eugénie Birch's encyclopedic chapter of case studies in urban planning makes it easy to see why so much planning research has gravitated toward "best practices" that describe the "context, chronology, key actors, and crucial decision points" (this volume, 274) that authors claim are responsible for the positive outcomes observed. In some instances, the cases she describes make compelling arguments for the value of planning interventions (e.g., Moving to Opportunity) and in others, they reveal the complexity that good plans encounter when their sponsors attempt implementation. They also reveal the difficulties in doing statistically valid evaluations of planning, which requires the controlled experiments that scholars rarely encounter in public life. Nonetheless, the results of case research are often accessible and convincing to practitioners, and they wend their way into policy reforms, much as William Whyte's study of public plazas (1980) led to a rewrite of New York City's zoning ordinance.

CONCLUSION

Stripped down, planning scholarship is a manifest concern with the collective and individual problems of cities, looking forward. In that spirit, this *Handbook* considers a good many parts of the who, what, where, and how of urban planning. It covers both theories about planning purpose, role, process, and practice, as well as the phenomena with which contemporary planning has been most concerned.

Yet this *Handbook* also conceals the diversity of scholarship in the field; our first proposed outline for the volume was nearly twice as long. Even in a book of this size and scope, it is inevitable that certain critical topics get left out. For example, we would have liked to include chapters on property rights, infrastructure, planning histories, and regional governance. While the final chapters are not meant as fully representative of the creative thought within planning research, they do make for an excellent introduction to the range of issues currently under investigation by leading and emerging scholars in the field. Each of the chapters presents key debates within the author's respective field, a summary of what the scholarship reveals to date, and a long list of research questions left inadequately examined, together with strategies for further examining them.

The profession of planning faces enormous challenges across the world. Public employees, collective schemes for financing public goods, and systems of expert knowledge are all under attack. And yet, as the *Handbook* reveals, we are at a point of "lift-off" in the field's intellectual development. Perhaps the contested nature of the planning's context and objects of inquiry enriches the scholarship and gives it a sense of urgency. What is clear is that the complex relationship between the scholarship and profession of planning blurs the boundaries between theory and practice, between basic and applied research, and it provides fertile ground for the hybrid, undisciplined approaches found in this volume.

ACKNOWLEDGMENTS

The editors gratefully acknowledge J. R. DeShazo, the Director of the Ralph & Goldy Lewis Center for Regional Policy Studies at UCLA, and the College of Urban Planning and Public Affairs at the University of Illinois, Chicago for financial support of this *Handbook*, and permission granted by the *Journal of the American Planning Association* to reuse substantial portions of the chapters by Boarnet, Kim, and Ryan that first appeared there. We also thank Jennifer Benoit and David Mason for help preparing individual chapter manuscripts, and Charles Hoch for comments on this chapter.

REFERENCES

Altshuler, A. 1966. *The City Planning Process: A Political Analysis.* Ithaca, NY: Cornell University Press.

American Planning Association. 2006. *Planning and Urban Design Standards.* Hoboken, NJ: John Wiley.

Beauregard, R. 1990. "Bringing the City Back In." *Journal of the American Planning Association* 56(2): 210–14.

Boyer, M. C. 1983. *Dreaming the Rational City: The Myth of American City Planning.* Cambridge, MA: MIT Press.

Bureau of Labor Statistics. 2010. *Occupational Outlook Handbook.* Available at: http://www.bls.gov/oco/ocos057.htm.

Campbell, H., and R. Marshall. 2002. "Utilitarianism's Bad Breadth? A Re-evaluation of the Public Interest Justification for Planning." *Planning Theory* 1(2): 163–87.

Cooke, P. 1983. *Theories of Planning and Spatial Development.* London: Hutchinson.

Etzioni, A. 1967. "Toward a Theory of Societal Guidance." *American Journal of Sociology* 73(2): 15–50.

Fishman, R. 1977. *Urban Utopias in the Twentieth Century: Ebenezer Howard, Frank Lloyd Wright, and Le Corbusier.* New York: Basic Books.

Fishman, R. 2000. *The American Planning Tradition: Culture and Policy.* Baltimore: Johns Hopkins University Press, and Washington, DC: Wilson Center Press.

Foucault, M. 1979. *Discipline and Punish: The Birth of the Prison.* New York: Vintage.

Flyvbjerg, B. 1998. *Rationality and Power: Democracy in Practice.* Chicago: University of Chicago Press.

Friedmann, J., and B. Hudson. 1974. "Knowledge and Action: A Guide to Planning Theory." *Journal of the American Institute of Planning* 40(1): 2–16.

Glazer, N. 1974. "The Schools of the Minor Professions." *Minerva* 12:346–64.

Gordon, P. and H. Richardson. 2001. "The Sprawl Debate: Let Markets Plan." *Publius* 31 (3): 131–149.

Hack, G., E. Birch, P. Sedway, and M. Silver, eds. 2009. *Local Planning: Contemporary Principles and Practice.* Washington, DC: International City/County Management Association.

Hall, P. 2002. *Cities of Tomorrow: An Intellectual History of Urban Planning and Design in the Twentieth Century.* London: Blackwell.

Hayek, F. 1944/1994. *The Road to Serfdom.* Chicago: University of Chicago Press.

Hoch, C., L. Dalton, and F. So, eds. 2000. *The Practice of Local Government Planning,* 3rd ed. Washington, DC: International City/County Management Association.

King, A. 1976. *Colonial Urban Development: Culture, Social Power and Environment.* New York: Routledge.

Michael, D. 1965. "Urban Policy in the Rationalized Society." *Journal of the American Institute of Planning* 31(4): 283–88.

Mitchell, T. 2002. *Rule of Experts: Egypt, Techno-Politics, Modernity.* Berkeley: University of California Press.

Perloff, H. 1957. *Education for Planning: City, State and Regional.* Baltimore: Johns Hopkins University Press.

Schön, D. 1983. *The Reflective Practitioner. How Professionals Think in Action.* London: Temple Smith.

Scott, A., and S. Roweis. 1977. "Urban Planning in Theory and Practice: A Reappraisal." *Environment and Planning Part A* 9: 1097–19.

Scott, J. 1998. *Seeing Like a State.* New Haven, CT: Yale University Press.

Sennett, R. 1992. *The Uses of Disorder: Personal Identity and City Life.* New York: Norton.

Simmel, G. 1950. "The Metropolis and Mental Life." In *The Sociology of Georg Simmel,* Kurt Wolff, ed. 409–424 New York: The Free Press.

Teitz, M. 1984. "Planning Education and the Planning Profession." *Journal of Planning Education and Research* 3:275–77.

United Nations. 2010. *World Population Prospects: The 2006 Revision and World Urbanization Prospects: The 2007 Revision.* Population Division of the Department of Economic and Social Affairs, United Nations Secretariat. Available at: http://esa.un.org/unup; accessed July 24, 2010.

Weber, M. 1978. *Economy and Society: An Outline of Interpretive Sociology,* edited by Guenther Roth and Claus Wittich. Berkeley: University of California Press.

Webber, M. 1969. "Planning in an Environment of Change. Part II: Permissive Planning." *Town Planning Review* 39(4): 277–95.

Whyte, W. 1980. *The Social Life of Small Urban Spaces,* Washington, DC: The Conservation Foundation.

PART II

WHY PLAN?
INSTITUTIONS
AND VALUES

A. DELIVERING PUBLIC GOODS

CHAPTER 2

COLLECTIVE ACTION: BALANCING PUBLIC AND PARTICULARISTIC INTERESTS

TORE SAGER

1. INTRODUCTION

THE purpose of this chapter is to explore important motivations for urban planning, putting emphasis on legitimation, the concept of public interest, and the communicative (collaborative) mode of planning. Reasons for planning that follow from the various forms of market imperfections are covered elsewhere and will not be dealt with here (see also Moore 1978). Arguments for public planning can spring from qualities of the process leading up to the plan or from qualities of the substance of the plan itself. This chapter deals mainly with procedural motives for planning, while substantive motives are discussed in other chapters in this volume dealing with sustainability, accessibility, preservation, and the like.

In preparation of the public interest theme, this introduction offers a brief account of planning as uncertainty reduction—a quality that every stakeholder and the public at large seem to expect from planning. The next section's discussion of social conflict or harmony—strife or consensus—takes the reader into the contemporary planning debate on the public interest and related themes. The main

positions are surveyed, and extensive dialogue is identified as communicative planning theory's solution to the problem of public interest. Inclusive dialogue also gives
legitimacy, which is an underresearched concept in planning theory dealt with in
a separate section. Clear justification of planning is surely needed, and planning in
turn helps to legitimize political decisions. A more comprehensive answer to the
question of why planning should be communicative is sought in the penultimate
section by analyzing the legitimizing potential for communicative planning of
drawing on a broad knowledge base, aiming to empower participants, and contributing to deliberative democratic action.

    Planning is an institutionalized social technology for systematizing knowledge
pertinent for a particular kind of collective action and for marshaling the power
required for its implementation. Various theoretical frameworks for the application of this technology have been tried in different places and periods, such as
synoptic (rationalistic) planning (Banfield 1959), disjointed incremental planning
(Lindblom 1959), advocacy planning (Davidoff 1965), and communicative (collaborative) planning (Forester 1989; Sager 1994). These modes—suggested ways or
manners in which planning should be done—are all meant to strengthen democracy in various ways, and thus serve the public interest by improving procedures
leading to that common goal. Synoptic planning aims to enhance democracy by
using experts and scientific method to enrich the knowledge base of majority decisions. Disjointed incrementalism serves democracy by arranging for every important interest or value to have its watchdog (Lindblom 1959, 85). Furthermore:

> It reduces the stakes in each political controversy, thus encouraging losers to
> bear their losses without disrupting the political system. It helps maintain the
> vague general consensus on basic values (because no specific policy issue ever
> centrally poses a challenge to them) that many people believe is necessary for
> widespread voluntary acceptance of democratic government. (Lindblom 1979,
> 520)

Incremental planning avoids bringing democratically made decisions into disrepute by shunning any policies "whose scope is such that if they miscarry, the evils
will exceed the remedial power of existing institutions" (Braybrooke and Lindblom
1963, 239). Advocacy planning makes local popular government more inclusive
by giving voice to marginalized groups whose interests would not otherwise be
conveyed to political decision makers. Communicative planning aims to advance
deliberative democracy by exploring the potential for broad, workable agreement
on planning matters, in any case making deliberation inclusive and thorough
before a planning issue is decided somehow. This mode of planning also helps
democracy produce fair outcomes by striving to reduce the influence of systematically biased power relations on the dialogically determined recommendations.
In many countries where government reflecting "the will of the people" has become
a strong tradition supported by nearly everybody, participatory public planning is
a candidate for being in the "public interest," suitably defined.

    No matter which of the above planning modes have inspired a particular pro-
cess, attention is likely to be directed to goals, alternatives, and consequences in

different phases of the future-oriented work. This means–ends analysis deals with substantive aspects of the plan (rather than the process), and the point is uncertainty reduction, which is a general and primary function of planning. Uncertainty forces actors to prepare for several future scenarios of which only one will be realized. This is costly because all preparation requires resources. Uncertainty also complicates the planning process, as disagreement easily arises about which scenario is the most realistic, and hence how resources should be allocated. Low uncertainty is usually desired by all parties to collective action, and this helps the candidacy of some plans for being in the "public interest."

2. CONFLICT OR HARMONY, STRIFE OR CONSENSUS?

This section outlines the different views of society that are often behind planning theorists' contrasting attitudes toward the usefulness of the public-interest concept. The conflict–harmony debate emerged in sociology in the 1950s. There was a tendency to divide social theories into two contrasting classes on the basis of their descriptions of social processes. Harmony theories emphasize the persistence of shared values and norms as the fundamental characteristics of society. Conflict theories accentuate the dominance of some groups over others and often regard conflicts between social groups as natural and inevitable (Bernard 1983).

The harmony view of society is consistent with the idea of conflict being due to social anomalies, to abnormal or pathological conditions. Conflict is seen as superficial and caused by misunderstanding, misconceptions, insufficient information, and deficient communication. In contrast, those who hold a conflict view of society regard conflict as fundamental. It is seen as a normal form of human interaction, which might even have positive functions in society (Coser 1956). It is to be expected, then, that harmony and conflict theories correspond to very dissimilar views on planning. Advocacy planning is perhaps the purest expression of the social conflict perspective. The harmony approach is in many cases applied to large-scale synoptic planning based on economics and welfare theory. This approach is usually phrased in aggregate terms—the common good, the welfare of society—neglecting opposing groups and competing interests.

The conflict–harmony debate continues to put its mark on planning theory. Around the turn of the millennium, it is reflected in discussions between (often Habermasian) proponents of communicative planning theory and their (often Foucauldian) critics. Communicative planning theory is criticized for its alleged bracketing of power and exaggerated reliance on consensus building. The main arguments against consensus building as a generic and central planning practice are listed below. No attempt is made here to distinguish between more and less substantiated claims.

- Consensus is always shallow and does not respect difference (Hillier 2003, 43; McGuirk 2001, 213; Pløger 2004, 87).
- Consensus is a threat to freedom (Flyvbjerg 1998, 229; Tewdwr-Jones and Allmendinger 1998, 1979). The privilege to engage in conflict is part of freedom, and therefore attempts to vanquish conflict suppress freedom.
- Consensual discourse necessarily involves the exclusion of some voices and the foreclosure of certain possibilities; it might silence rather than give voice (Hillier 2003, 53; Pløger 2004, 87; Tewdwr-Jones and Allmendinger 1998, 1979).
- Consensus is utopian: "In such a heavily politicised arena as planning, consensus is completely utopian—there will always be winners and losers—and it will never be possible for all individuals to abandon their political positions and act neutrally" (Tewdwr-Jones and Allmendinger 1998, 1982).

The consensual approach to planning cannot succeed as an emancipatory and empowering project, according to the critics. This view is to a large extent inspired by Foucault's (1980) thinking about power and Mouffe's (1999, 2000) theory of agonistic pluralism: the shallowness of consensus is due to language games and different community life forms, causing participants hailing from different communities to sometimes talk at cross-purposes. "Any agreement they come to would then be more the product of power politics or clever rhetoric than real consensus" (Kapoor 2002, 464). Another main argument of Mouffe's (1999, 755) is that "[p]olitics aims at the creation of unity in a context of conflict and diversity; it is always concerned with the creation of an 'us' by the determination of a 'them.'" Reaching the Habermasian "ideal speech situation" is impossible in these circumstances; meaning can emerge only by advancing one point of view at the expense and exclusion of other viewpoints, rendering the establishment of any discourse authoritarian.

Mouffe (1999, 755) stresses the importance of "distinguishing between two types of political relations: one of *antagonism* between enemies, and one of *agonism* between adversaries [italics in original]....An adversary is a legitimate enemy, an enemy with whom we have in common a shared adhesion to the ethico-political principles of democracy." Strife is the expressive form of agonism (Pløger 2004, 75). Power, persuasion, and strategic behavior are intrinsic to agonistic relations, and hence strife cannot be ended by appeals to mutual understanding and the force of the best argument. Instead, a pluralist democracy is one in which there are constant conflicts of interest and renegotiation of social identity, and— according to followers of Mouffe such as Hillier (2003) and Pløger (2004)—this is therefore the social condition that urban planning should be designed to deal with. Kapoor (2002) sees the Habermas-Mouffe debate "as a stand-in for the modern-postmodern argument, with Habermas defending reason, legitimacy, justice, universality, Mouffe defending antagonism, pluralism, contingency" (2000, 466).

In general, the idea of a public interest holds a stronger position among those believing that stable consensus solutions to difficult planning problems can often be worked out than among those who argue on theoretical grounds that any consensus will necessarily be shallow and thus unstable. The next section surveys some problems and possibilities of employing the concept of public interest in urban planning.

3. The Concept of Public Interest as a Support for Public Planning

From early on, the planning profession felt the need for a concept that can describe clearly what planners are aiming at. In the tradition of harmony theories, the public interest has been such a concept, and (effective from June 1, 2005), the AICP Code of Ethics and Professional Conduct states as a first principle for planners that "our primary obligation is to serve the public interest" (American Planning Association [APA] 2005). The concept is held by Klosterman (1980) to provide a meaningful, empirically verifiable, and rationally defensible criterion for evaluating public policies. It is not my concern to marshal support for this view, but I take the position that the public interest concept can be helpful if defined so as to not require everybody's agreement on a policy. This section points to some difficulties with the concept of public interest. It also discusses what the public interest might mean in communicative planning, as the ensuing sections will primarily deal with that mode of planning.

The concept of public interest is controversial and has weaknesses that have been acknowledged for several decades (see references in Campbell and Marshall 2002, 170). It is feared that articulation of a public interest masks difference and heterogeneity and therefore represents a potentially oppressive idea, similar to the critique of consensus. Moreover, the concept might mystify rather than clarify. "For example, it is frequently used as a device to cast an aura of legitimacy over the final resolution of policy questions where there are still significant areas of disagreement" (Campbell and Marshall 2000, 308). Conceptual weaknesses do not place the public interest in a special position, though. There is hardly any concept or theory in the social sciences that cannot be meaningfully criticized from some relevant perspective. The disclosure of weaknesses in the definition of a concept should not necessarily lead to its rejection. For example, planning theorists never stopped using the concept of power, even though its content remains unclear and its definitions are legion. The same is true for the concept of planning; already around 1970, enough definitions had been proposed to warrant a separate bibliography (McCloskey 1971).

Perhaps one reason for the strong wish in some camps (especially among those skeptical to consensus in planning matters) to abandon the public interest concept is the propensity to ascribe too much importance to it. Critics may fear that once a project, plan, or policy is found to be in the public interest, no objection will be taken seriously, and the proposal in question will be implemented. However, the public interest does not provide the final answer regarding the desirability of a collective action. Contrasting views on social harmony and conflict make composite justification of plans imperative. Even proponents of the public interest concept agree to this, and Klosterman (1980, 330) concedes that conformity with the public interest is not the only consideration that goes into deciding what to do: "The collective interest of the community may conflict with, and on occasion be overridden by, the dictates of justice and individuals' legal and moral rights of free speech, due process, and equal protection."

Surveys of the ideas of the public interest in planning are offered by Campbell and Marshall (2002) and Alexander (2002). These authors choose substantive/procedural as the main distinction between different concepts of the public interest, and both differentiate subjective and objective points of view corresponding to different assumptions about the way in which individual interests relate to the interests of everyone taken together. "If an individual is considered to be the only judge of what is in his or her interest, this constitutes a subjective view.... Under an objective idea of individual interest, on the other hand, it is quite possible to argue that a person can be wrong about what he or she defines as his or her interest" (Howe 1992, 233). The subjective/objective distinction is linked to paternalism later in this chapter.

Substantive definitions of the public interest assume the existence of a normative standard outside of the processes of politics and planning by which to judge public policy, and they are outcome-focused and thus make demands on the contents of the plan. This is in contrast to approaches relying on procedural norms and rules by which the public interest can somehow be discovered. Substantive definitions cannot require unanimity if they are to be useful in practice, as there will always be somebody disagreeing with planning proposals. The basic problem is that any limited consensus opens the possibility that what is decided on is a plan that serves the particularistic interest of a very large majority. Is it possible to distinguish between a plan with 90 percent support that is in the public interest and another plan backed by 90 percent that serves a particularistic interest? Benditt (1973, 300) offers a line of reasoning that helps us get around this difficulty.

> (I)f a particular action or policy is in the public interest because it will provide enough to eat for anyone who meets its conditions, no one can claim that such a policy is not in the public interest on the ground that he himself, being rich, is unlikely to benefit from it. Its being in the public interest has nothing to do

with whether everyone will actually get some of the results of it. It has to do with whether having enough to eat is an interest of everyone's and with whether the serving of this interest is social in nature.

Benditt's example "enough to eat" is a likely candidate for a generalizable interest, since it is hard to insist in a public debate that others should starve because the debater in question would not benefit from the arrangements catering to them. Planning-related examples are nevertheless needed in order to check whether Benditt's reasoning is relevant to planning practice. Consider "uncertainty reduction" as a candidate for a public interest (compare the introduction to this chapter), and let uncertainty include all forms of risk. It is expected that people protect themselves against some sorts of uncertainty by private insurance contracts. A plan protecting people against loss following the risk of bicycle theft, for example, is therefore not likely to be in the public interest. The risks of flooded residential areas, an avalanche hitting public roads, and a landslide undermining railway tracks are a different matter. It is in the interest of everybody to be protected against accidents brought about by these forces, and in most places such protection is defined as a public task. The fulfillment of this criterion is what causes some plans to secure roads against rocks and snow to be in the public interest. This conclusion is not changed by protests from a road user who will soon be moving to another part of the country and thus will not receive any safety gain from the planned measures. His support is not needed for the plan to be in the public interest.

The basis of the public interest concept is the belief that indicators of the collective will can be constructed that are broader and more integral to a community or society than any particularistic interest. If there is no entity with a will of its own above the individual, then individual interests must be aggregated in order to express the public interest. It is not always possible to do this in a consistent and logical manner when preferences are strongly diverging (Arrow 1963; Sager 2002). One way to create a wider range of permissible preference aggregations is to apply public interest indicators that accept decreasing welfare for some people (that is, to relax the Pareto condition). This is much like using definitions of the public interest that do not require unanimity.

Habermasian dialogue does not require acknowledgment of community or society as entities with interests of their own that are separate from individual interests. The demand for inclusive dialogue upholds the requirement that the judgment of each individual is to count when sorting out the best arguments and thus in the articulation of the public interest. Now, the result does not emerge by formal aggregation and calculation but instead by communication. This does not solve all logical problems (Sager 2002, 2005), although the possibilities of identifying a consistent collective will are improved (Dryzek and List 2003).

What seems to be worth doing together, according to communicative planning theorists, is determined by what the parties can agree on in a dialogical process. Hence, collective action should not be determined by an "objective" notion of the public interest that is independent of the outcome of dialogue. Quite to the contrary, with the very demanding requirements that have to be fulfilled by a communicative process in order for it to be dialogical in the Habermasian sense adopted by most communicative planning theorists, it might not be unreasonable to *define* consensual outcome of dialogue as being in the public interest. After all, everyone concerned should take part, freely and equally, in the cooperative search for truth, where nothing coerces anyone except the force of the better argument (Pellizzoni 2001). This is "a speech situation that satisfies improbable conditions: openness to the public, inclusiveness, equal rights to participation, immunization against external or inherent compulsion, as well as the participants' orientation toward reaching understanding (that is, the sincere expression of utterances)" (Habermas 1999, 367). In ideal conditions, then, the public interest can be discovered discursively through participatory practice.

The debate on the public interest concept continues also in the general literature on public administration (Box 2007; Lewis 2006; Morgan 2000). A potentially fruitful use of the concept is to apply the public interest as a utopian standard in critical analysis, much like Habermas's (1999, 367–68) "ideal speech situation" or Rawls's (1972, 136–42) fairness as conceived by individuals behind a veil of ignorance. As Cooper (1998, 77) asserts, the public interest should stand "as a kind of question mark before all official decisions and conduct." The pursuit of the public interest leads planners to "broaden the discussion, the time frame, and the roster of participants; public interest is a process—an exploration—rather than an immutable or even identifiable conclusion" (Lewis 2006, 699). The hope is that devotion to a purpose that is broader than any particularistic interest will lead planners toward a more democratic and fair practice, whether or not there exist planning-relevant interests shared by everybody.

Although planners can do without the exact term "the public interest," many planners find it hard to discard the idea that public planners should serve "society," defined so as to reflect their felt commitment beyond any particularistic interest. Healey (2006), for example, often avoids the controversial public interest phrase while articulating its content in alternative terms. She writes about "an aggregate interest," "our shared interests," and our "common concern, though immensely various in its forms" (2006, 124–25). The widespread reluctance to let go of the underlying idea (Alexander 2002; Campbell and Marshall 2002; Moroni 2004) is due to the usefulness of the public interest in legitimizing public planning and to politicians' need to call on impartial planning input when attempting to legitimize their decisions.

A critique of institutions that are meant to serve society impartially is implicit in the attack on the public interest. It is hard to see how science, analytic methods, laws, norms, and social organizations can be neutral if the public interest is a chimera. If every interest is particularistic, any mental or physical construct must serve such an interest, and institutions and organizations that are claimed to serve us all need to be unmasked and at least partly stripped of authority. To the extent that this happens, purportedly common institutions, like urban planning, lose legitimacy. Legitimation is briefly analyzed in the next section.

4. LEGITIMACY AND PLANNING

Sustainable systems for collective action need legitimacy. This section analyzes the legitimation needs of public planning and the role of the public interest concept in satisfying them. The discussion is structured around three ways to address the legitimation issue. First, it is argued that legitimacy of planning follows for a large part from the legitimacy of the political system it serves. Second, there is a special need to legitimize the power of planners to influence the decision-making system they render assistance. Third, the role of technocratic legitimation is mentioned.

Legitimation is the process of explaining and justifying the validity of an institutional order (Ansell 2004, 8706). Political legitimacy refers to the moral and normative principles by which governing bodies justify their right to demand compliance, obedience, or allegiance. Public planning is legitimate only when planners can invoke sources of authority beyond and above themselves. A planning agency enjoys legitimacy when acceptance of its authority is general among people in its area of jurisdiction and those people consider their obedience as a just commitment. In this line of reasoning, legitimation of planning does not really rest on the public interest. A decision is legitimate if it was made by the right legitimate authority and if the procedural rules of this authority were observed.

Legitimation as dealt with here is both about planners' justifications for their professional activities and about politicians' use of planning to raise acceptance of decisions. These aspects of legitimation are mutually dependent, as legitimacy of planning increases with democratically elected politicians' demand for planning and the ability of politicians to legitimize decisions by invoking skillful preparation and expert advice increases with the authority of the planning profession.

Preparing for the decisions to be made by democratically elected politicians has both substantive and procedural aspects. On the substantive side, it means providing information on plausible options for place making and their consequences. On the procedural side, it means, among other things, organizing the planning process in such a way that all interested parties feel they have been listened to. The political decision on a plan is more readily legitimized the more inclusive and deliberative the process and the more comprehensive the option seeking and the impact assessment—that is, the better the preparation. The politicians can then credibly assert that the knowledge required for taking rational action was available to them at the time of decision.

It would be too simplistic to think that the main task of providing analyses and recommendations to political principals leaves the planners powerless. In fact, planners have agenda-setting power that can, in many cases, affect the final outcome (Hammond 1986). This leverage follows from option seeking, impact assessment, and comparative evaluation of plans. In addition, planners have power to form the planning process, and broad agreement on the outcome of an inclusive process will put considerable pressure on the decision-making politicians to follow suit. The legitimacy of the power generated by those activities cannot come from the democratic system of representation and voting. They are an external influence on this democratic system and must tap legitimacy from another source. This is an important reason that the public interest concept is still used by many planning theorists despite its weaknesses. Appeal to the public interest helps legitimize the aspects of planning that are not only passively serving but also actively influencing democratic decision making.

"Legitimacy is particularly important in democracies since a democracy's survival is ultimately dependent on the support of a majority of its citizens" (Dogan 2004, 111). Without the granting of legitimacy by the people, a democracy would lose its authority. In democratic theory, legitimacy is directly ascribed to the planning system by the citizens in addition to being indirectly produced when planning serves the legitimate political system. When the population endorses democracy, the planning system gains legitimacy if it is believed to further the higher principles of a democratic society—for example, self-determination, freedom of speech, and governmental accountability to the people.

The procedural aspects of planning support participation and sharing of information, while the substantive aspects cater to place making—that is, the production side of planning that balances expert proposals for physical design with bureaucratic and political considerations of urban development. The legitimacy of planning therefore results from a mixture of technocratic and democratic legitimation. Under a wide variety of political systems and planning processes, planners prepare for the building of roads, management of traffic, and protection of the natural environment, as well as the construction of attractive and safe residential areas and well-functioning city centers. This expertise is the basis for Mueller's (1973, 135) outline of technocratic legitimation:

> [T]echnocratic legitimation...does not accord any significance to the beliefs of the citizen or to morality per se. This legitimation grants to political institutions an autonomy and detachment from the public that seems to be as indisputable as the moral principles of traditional legitimacies. Deprived of moral and consensual referents, technocratic legitimation is completely "secularized" and establishes legitimacy either (1) through the manipulation of public opinion or (2) through the provision of material compensations.

The production side of planning contributes to material compensations by preparing for public service delivery and collective goods provision as mentioned above (Lowry 1994, 102). Material compensation (economic growth) is important to most politicians in neoliberal societies. It is a priority of neoliberal politics to fight alleged waste in the public sector in order to keep taxes down and increase private purchasing power. In many societies with mixed-market economies, there is constant pressure to shift from planned solutions drawn up in bureaucratic hierarchies to solutions implemented in competitive or contested markets. When democratic legitimacy is weak, politicians risk losing decision areas to the market. They therefore explore every source of legitimacy, including public planning (Sager and Sørensen 2011), vacillating between restricting the mandate of planning and exploiting its capacity for grounding political decisions. Dialogical values can help to produce public goods in a democratic and efficient manner (Sager 2007), but the next section nevertheless draws attention to three other reasons for communicative planning.

5. Legitimizing Communicative Planning as a Democratic Institution

This section highlights three particular characteristics of communicative planning that facilitate its legitimation as a social technology serving democracy: pooling information and judgments from many different participants, fighting forms of power that undermine their autonomy, and linking local planning processes to a political system of deliberative democracy. It is shown how these features help communicative planning resist particularistic interests and improve the basis for place-making forms of collective action. Issues of cost and public expense are ignored here in order to cultivate legitimizing aspects of the planning mode.

John Friedmann's theoretical breakthrough came with the realization that planning theory should analyze how knowledge is transformed into action (1998, 248). Planning is a technology that systematizes knowledge in preparation for collective action and it marshals the power required for implementation. As it was gradually realized that all affected parties posit some kind of valuable knowledge, forms of participatory and communicative planning emerged—for example, transactive planning championed by Friedmann (1973) himself. Different ways to interpret and systematize knowledge, and different views on the relative importance of knowledge types, led to a range of more or less open and inclusive processes.

Friedmann clearly thought that the concept of power deserves a prominent place in planning theory, but he did not explicitly introduce it in his overview of planning approaches (1987, 51–85) in order to underscore that power is necessary to transform knowledge into action (Sager 1995). Power is a prerequisite for the balancing act brought to the fore in the title of this chapter. It is needed for making particularistic interests yield to interests that most people have in common, and vice versa. In the following, we take a closer look at the advantages of planning communicatively by drawing attention to three key terms, one for each of the elements in the knowledge-power-action nexus: the Condorcet jury theorem, paternalism, and deliberative democracy. The argument is that communicative planning is a more legitimate way of defining what is in the interest of the public, for the following three reasons:

- Many people representing all interests affected by the planning are drawn into dialogue, thus increasing the likelihood that decisions are right and fair.

- The expressed preferences of one interest group cannot be set aside by another group for paternalistic reasons.
- Votes, if they are required, follow arguments put forward in inclusive debate where efforts are made to level power differentials.

5.1 Knowledge: The Condorcet Jury Theorem

Even deliberative democrats worry that citizen ignorance and disinterest in political matters might mess up the governing potential of public dialogue (Habermas 2006). This section brings forward a theorem that gives reason for optimism. Assume that there are questions in planning matters that have right and wrong answers, with the correct solution set by authorities external to the single planning process. For example, is traffic safety likely to be more improved by a roundabout (traffic circle) than by an unregulated intersection at a specific location? Is it cheaper to use electricity or another heating system to keep a particular new residential area warm? Can a city terminal covering X acres be built with sufficient capacity to serve the number of public transit passengers set as a political goal by the city council? Planning alternatives with potential for being in the public interest in the substantive sense have to be based on the correct technical-economic answers, and the question is whether they are likely to be identified in dialogue between lay participants. This is a timely question, as most people are unfamiliar with planning matters and cannot be expected to hold clear ideas of causal relationships between means and ends in public planning. According to the Condorcet jury theorem, it is nevertheless likely ($p > 0.9$) that an assemblage of, say, fifty imperfectly informed lay participants (each with 0.6 probability of being right) will collectively opt for the best of two alternatives (List and Goodin 2001). The theorem states that majorities are more likely than any single individual to select the better of two alternatives when there is uncertainty about which of the two best serves the purpose. More accurately, the Condorcet jury theorem (Black 1958; McLean and Hewitt 1994) says that if each individual is somewhat more likely than not to make the better choice between some pair of alternatives, and each individual has the same probability of being correct in this choice, then (with each voter voting independently) the probability of the group majority being correct increases as the number of individuals increases, toward a limiting value of 1.

There is a classical debate over the question of whether we want political outcomes to be right or whether we want them to be fair (List and Goodin 2001). The outcomes of communicative planning are expected to be fair when the dialogue observes the principle of universalization: that all affected can accept the consequences and side effects that the decisions can be anticipated to have for the satisfaction of everyone's interests (and these consequences are preferred to those of known alternative options; Eriksen and Weigård 2003, 54–85). However, it would presumably be much easier to convince political decision makers that communicative planning is a practice worth supporting if it can also be effectively argued that local dialogical forums have a high probability for selecting the right or best option according to generally accepted standards external to the process—for example, that such forums are likely to identify and select the plan with the most stimulating economic impacts on society when it is agreed that this is the superior goal. This is where the Condorcet jury theorem is helpful.

Condorcet's theorem has been generalized in several directions and has proved to be valid in decision-making conditions that are quite realistic for communicative planning. For example, a jury theorem still holds even if individuals have varying competence—that is, "not every member of the jury has exactly the same probability of choosing the correct outcome: all that is required is that the mean probability of being right across the jury be above one-half" (List and Goodin 2001, 283). Furthermore, a similar theorem is valid even if there are (certain sorts of) interdependencies between the judgments of different electors (Ladha 1992) and even when plurality voting over many options takes place instead of majority voting over two options (List and Goodin 2001). Importantly, Miller (1986) shows that a straightforward extension of the Condorcet jury theorem can be applied to cases in which individual interests conflict.

"Best" or "right" planning solutions must often yield to alternatives that are technically or economically merely "good enough" but that are considered superior for political reasons. It may nevertheless be advantageous to use a participatory planning approach that has a high probability of recognizing the best option and selecting it when political criteria are also satisfied. The literature on the jury theorem suggests that "policy choices made by majority rule tend to be far more accurate than one would expect based on survey evidence of voter knowledge" (Congleton 2007, 208). The statistical mechanism behind the Condorcet jury theorem—the law of large numbers—works more effectively when the number of participants in planning dialogue increases and when the competence of the interlocutors is enhanced (Gabel and Shipan 2004). The exchange of arguments in inclusive debate free from repression educates the interlocutors and makes it more likely that each of them identifies the best alternative. The conclusion is that the Condorcet jury theorem offers a strong argument for democratic practices such as communicative planning, and there are procedures embedded in that mode of planning that in turn strengthen the argument further.

5.2 Power: Paternalism

"Paternalism" can be defined as the interference of a state or an individual with another person against his or her will, and is justified by a claim that the person interfered with will be better off or protected from harm (Dworkin 2005, 1). Exertion of power in the form of paternalism raises the question of what is the trade-off between regard for the welfare of others and respect for their right to make their own decisions. Planning theorists have worried about too much paternalism in planning (Arnstein 1969, 217; Silva 2005, 313) and even too little (Fainstein 2000,

457). Paternalism is common in emergency preparedness planning, for example (Jennings 2008). Such disaster planning often forces some people to protect themselves in ways of which they do not approve today, in order to make them better off in the future should an anticipated type of emergency occur. For example, people can be prohibited from building new houses on land prone to flooding, and housing cooperatives can be forced to construct air-raid shelters even when they would prefer not to. There are very few, if any, in-depth studies of paternalism in planning except for the industrial paternalism of company towns (Alanen and Peltin 1978; Oberdeck 2000). These mainly historical studies do not, however, define paternalistic acts as being against the will of the "beneficiary."

Paternalistic interference is premised on the objective idea of individual interest and the conviction that people are not—or not always—the best judge of their own interests. This conviction is a challenge to communicative planning in particular, as it questions the ability of local citizens to reach rational consensus. In contrast, the planning profession has a tradition for claiming rationality in some sense. So the debate on paternalism in planning raises the question of how members of the self-proclaimed rational elite should be allowed to treat people they consider to be endowed with less rational intellects. How should persons be treated when assumed to be less than fully rational? Can they demand autonomy in planning matters? Is paternalistic action okay as long as those interfered with come to subsequently approve of it (Kasachkoff 1994)? Who decides whether an opponent is rational when, after all, everybody deviates from the behavior of the rational agent of rational choice theorists (Kahneman 1994; Sen 1977). In the discourse on environmentalism, Meyer (2008, 221) recognizes the attitude that: "*We*—the informed, engaged, public spirited—wish to protect *you* the uninformed, apathetic, or egoistic, from the consequences of your environmentally destructive ways" [italics in original]. This attitude is not linked to any mode of planning in particular.

Communicative planning theory takes a clear stance against paternalism and tries to do what is necessary to fight it by advising that all affected parties be brought to the table and take part in deliberative decision making. Communicative planners nevertheless have to be on guard to avoid one paternalist conviction in particular: *We know that it is in your best interest to be included in the planning process and participate in the debate on plans concerning your local community.* Thoughtful consideration for others' welfare, on the one hand, and concern for their autonomy, on the other, is easily brought out of balance in participatory processes, as paternalism that pulls more stakeholders and citizens into the dialogue serves the communicative planners and their principals. The reason is that planning processes are more useful for legitimation purposes when everybody takes part.

The principle of autonomy is that "competent adults should be left free to make their own decisions about how to live their lives based on their own preferences, religious beliefs, conceptions of justice and virtue, beliefs about honor and dignity, and views about what's prudentially best for them" (Scoccia 2008, 354). Communicative planning theory assumes that, in the course of dialogue on the issue at hand, people come to know what is in their own best interest. Planners might disagree with local citizens on what is to be done, but the communicative planner should not implement actions that overrule another's preferences with the main intention of making the recalcitrant participant better off. The primary motive must be better living conditions for consenting persons. The central problem of paternalism in democratic politics is "that in a democracy all actions of the state have ultimately to be approved by the people, and yet one of the conditions of a paternalistic act is that it is not sanctioned by the individual whom the act is supposed to benefit at the time of the intervention" (New 1999, 81). Paternalism is directly opposed to autonomy and self-determination, and communicative planning theory is about ways to remove this form of power from the planning process.

5.3 Action: Deliberative Democracy as Legitimate Collective Action

Deliberation is a process of careful and informed reflection on facts and opinions, generally leading to a judgment on the matter at hand (King 2003, 25). Deliberative democracy means that the affairs of an association are governed by the public deliberation of its members (Cohen 1989, 17). Communicative planning aims for extensive deliberation through inclusive dialogue and thus supports deliberative democracy where the association is a municipality or another political-administrative unit responsible for public planning. The communicative mode can make use of several techniques for organizing small-group deliberation in mini-publics composed of ordinary citizens, such as citizen's panels and consensus conferences (Goodin and Dryzek 2006).

There are very different approaches to the making of collective decisions—for example, formal aggregation of individual preferences, voting systems, interest-based negotiation, and consensus building public deliberation. List (2006) distinguishes between two (extreme) types of deliberation, focusing on *what* choices should be made and *why* those choices should be made, respectively. The "minimal liberal" account of how to make decisions responds to the *what* question. This approach holds that "collective decisions should be made only on practical actions or policies and that the reasons (or justifications) underlying those decisions should be kept private" (2006, 362–63). The "comprehensive deliberative" account answers the *why* question. This approach emphasizes "the importance of giving reasons for collective decisions, where those reasons should themselves be collectively decided" (2006, 363). These approaches to collective decision making have different legitimation potentials.

Several distinguished scholars on deliberative democracy link the public interest, legitimation, and deliberation. Cohen (1989, 25), for example, holds that "the interests, aims, and ideals that comprise the common good are those that survive deliberation, interests that, on public reflection, we think it legitimate to appeal to in making claims on social resources." Bohman (1998, 402) maintains that all forms of deliberative democracy must refer to the ideal of public reason, "to the requirement that legitimate decisions be ones that 'everyone could accept' or at least 'not reasonably reject.'" Benhabib (1996, 69) sees legitimacy itself as a common good that can be produced only if the institutions of the polity "are so arranged that what is considered in the common interest of all results from processes of collective deliberation."

In the political sphere, unanimity engenders legitimacy but is most often unrealistic, as it requires communicative rationality beyond what people are capable of. "The criterion of communicative rationality is that we pursue our goals *to the extent this receives qualified acceptance from others*, in other words, the maximising of interests is subordinated to and conditioned by a communicatively obtained agreement" (Eriksen and Weigård 2003, 45, italics in original). Moreover, as Dryzek (2001) and Manin (1987, 341) observe, most democratic theories are concerned not only with legitimacy but also with efficiency. These are two reasons deliberative democracy settles for decision-making procedures that combine communicative and strategic rationality (introducing, for example, majority voting and negotiation). The need to relinquish "the ideal speech situation," and instead combine modified Habermasian dialogue with instrumental rationality and means-ends thinking, is equally pressing in communicative planning. Misuse of power that engenders systematic communicative distortion cannot be effectively opposed unless planners act strategically as well as communicatively (Sager 2006).

The scope of strategic-communicative hybrid models has recently been explored by communication theorists (Black 2008; White 2008). One aim is to study how types of strategic communication (discussion, purposeful storytelling) can facilitate disinterested dialogue. Another aim is to construct a theoretical basis for legitimizing at least partially those institutions that are grounded in openly strategic action—for example, markets (White 2008, 11). Less reliance on consensus is part of this pragmatic (re)orientation of communicative planning theory. For instance, discursive legitimacy should not require a comprehensive deliberative approach that implies agreement on why a particular decision should be made. Workable agreement on public plans will have to do, making use of the insight that assent can be secured for courses of action for different reasons (Dryzek 2001, 661).

By forming communicative planning as an integral part of deliberative democracy, we can achieve effective legitimacy of planned collective action. Public deliberation is vital because the planning decisions imposed by governments demand justification to those burdened by the plans; and justification must appeal to evidence and argument acceptable to the citizens. Deliberative democracy is an ideal of popular sovereignty, according to which legitimacy is ultimately assessed in terms of the judgments of those that are governed and have access to the public deliberations (King 2003, 26). "As political decisions are characteristically imposed on *all*, it seems reasonable to seek, as an essential condition for legitimacy, the deliberation of *all* or, more precisely, the right of all to participate in deliberation" (Manin 1987, 352, emphasis in original). A legitimate decision does not represent

the will of all, but results from the potentiality of the deliberation of all. If participation is not inclusive, and if the representative system is less than perfect, suspi-
cion will linger that the conclusions from deliberation serve particularistic rather
than public interests.

6. Conclusion: Linking Legitimacy and the Public Interest

This chapter has discussed some important—and mainly noneconomic—motives
for planning as collective action. Legitimacy of such action requires that public
and particularistic interests be balanced, and it is common that planners check
this balance by empirically exploring the potential for workable agreements on
planning issues.

Planners' transformation of *knowledge* into *action* is mediated by *power*. The
knowledge base and the likelihood of good decisions are augmented by pooling
the information of many participants (the Condorcet jury theorem). Paternalistic
forms of power are counteracted by enhancing the self-determination of the local
citizenry through public dialogue. Finally, planning as collective action achieves
stronger legitimacy through inclusive deliberation.

The above legitimizing knowledge-power-action features of communicative
planning theory intertwine and create a new opening for the public interest concept. Assume that inclusive deliberation and dialogue sometimes produce informed
agreement without offensive intimidation and pressure. Assent is informed when
even imperfectly knowledgeable participants are more likely to be right than
wrong. Then the mechanism of the Condorcet jury theorem is functioning, and
there is little reason to believe that a workable agreement would be due to misguided conception of facts. Moreover, antipaternalist planners cannot easily appeal
to the notion of "false consciousness" and contend that the agreement is due to lay
people being ideologically duped, while they, the planners, see through the smoke-
screen and know what is really in the best interest of the participants. There will be
cases, then, in which the agreed planning solution is best regarded as transcending
particularistic interests and can reasonably be interpreted as being in the public
interest.

References

Alanen, A. R., and T. J. Peltin. 1978. "Kohler, Wisconsin: Planning and Paternalism in
    a Model Industrial Village." *Journal of the American Planning Association* 44(2):
    145–59.

Alexander, E. R. 2002. "The Public Interest in Planning: From Legitimation to Substantive Plan Evaluation." *Planning Theory* 1(3): 226–49.

American Planning Association. 2005. *AICP Code of Ethics and Professional Conduct.* Available at: http://www.planning.org/ethics/ethicscode.htm; accessed November 25, 2008.

Ansell, C. K. 2004. "Legitimacy: Political." In *International Encyclopedia of the Social and Behavioral Sciences,* edited by N. J. Smelser and P. B. Baltes, 8704–706. Amsterdam: Elsevier.

Arnstein, S. R. 1969. "A Ladder of Citizen Participation." *Journal of the American Institute of Planners* 35(4): 216–24.

Arrow, K. J. 1963. *Social Choice and Individual Values.* New York: John Wiley.

Banfield, E. C. 1959. "Ends and Means in Planning." *International Social Science Journal* 11(3): 361–68.

Benditt, T. M. 1973. "The Public Interest." *Philosophy and Public Affairs* 2(3): 291–311.

Benhabib, S. 1996. "Toward a Deliberative Model of Democratic Legitimacy." In *Democracy and Difference,* edited by S. Benhabib, 67–94. Princeton, NJ: Princeton University Press.

Bernard, T. J. 1983. *The Consensus-Conflict Debate.* New York: Columbia University Press.

Black, D. 1958. *The Theory of Committees and Elections.* Cambridge, UK: Cambridge University Press.

Black, L. W. 2008. "Deliberation, Storytelling, and Dialogical Moments." *Communication Theory* 18(1): 93–116.

Bohman, J. 1998. "The Coming of Age of Deliberative Democracy." *Journal of Political Philosophy* 6(4): 400–25.

Box, R. C. 2007. "Redescribing the Public Interest." *Social Science Journal* 44(4): 585–98.

Braybrooke, D., and C. E. Lindblom. 1963. *A Strategy of Decision.* New York: Free Press.

Campbell, H., and R. Marshall. 2000. "Moral Obligations, Planning, and the Public Interest: A Commentary on Current British Practice." *Environment and Planning Part B: Planning and Design* 27(2): 297–312.

Campbell, H., and R. Marshall. 2002. "Utilitarianism's Bad Breath? A Re-evaluation of the Public Interest Justification for Planning." *Planning Theory* 1(2): 163–87.

Cohen, J. 1989. "Deliberation and Democratic Legitimacy." In *The Good Polity,* edited by A. Hamlin and P. Pettit, 17–34 Oxford: Basil Blackwell.

Congleton, R. D. 2007. "Informational Limits to Public Policy: Ignorance and the Jury Theorem." In *Public Choice and the Challenges of Democracy,* edited by J. C. Pardo and P. Schwartz, 206–19. Cheltenham, UK: Edward Elgar.

Cooper, T. L. 1998. *The Responsible Administrator,* 4th ed. San Francisco: Jossey-Bass.

Coser, L. 1956. *The Functions of Social Conflict.* New York: Free Press.

Davidoff, P. 1965. "Advocacy and Pluralism in Planning." *Journal of the American Institute of Planners* 31(4): 596–615.

Dogan, M. 2004. "Conceptions of Legitimacy." In *Encyclopedia of Government and Politics,* 2nd ed., vol. 2, edited by M. Hawkesworth and M. Kogan, 110–19. London: Routledge.

Dryzek, J. S. 2001. "Legitimacy and Eeconomy in Deliberative Democracy." *Political Theory* 29(5): 651–69.

Dryzek, J. S., and C. List. 2003. "Social Choice Theory and Deliberative Democracy: A Reconciliation." *British Journal of Political Science* 33(1): 1–28.

Dworkin, G. 2005. "Paternalism." In *Stanford Encyclopedia of Philosophy*. Available at: http://plato.stanford.edu/entries/paternalism/; accessed January 12, 2009.

Eriksen, E. O., and J. Weigård. 2003. *Understanding Habermas. Communicative Action and Deliberative Democracy*. London: Continuum.

Fainstein, S. S. 2000. "New Directions in Planning Theory." *Urban Affairs Review* 35(4): 451–78.

Flyvbjerg, B. 1998. "Habermas and Foucault: Thinkers for Civil Society?" *British Journal of Sociology* 49(2): 210–33.

Forester, J. 1989. *Planning in the Face of Power*. Berkeley, CA: University of California Press.

Foucault, M. 1980. *Power/Knowledge*. Brighton, UK: Harvester Press.

Friedmann, J. 1973. *Retracking America. A Theory of Transactive Planning*. Garden City, NY: Anchor Press/Doubleday.

Friedmann, J. 1987. *Planning in the Public Domain: From Knowledge to Action*. Princeton, NJ: Princeton University Press.

Friedmann, J. 1998. "Planning Theory Revisited." *European Planning Studies* 6(3): 245–53.

Gabel, M. J., and C. R. Shipan. 2004. "A Social Choice Approach to Expert Consensus Panels." *Journal of Health Economics* 22(3): 543–64.

Goodin, R. E., and J. S. Dryzek. 2006. "Deliberative Impacts: The Macro-Political Uptake of Mini-Publics. *Politics and Society* 34(2): 219–44.

Habermas, J. 1999. *On the Pragmatics of Communication*, edited by M. Cooke. Cambridge, UK: Polity Press.

Habermas, J. 2006. "Political Communication in Media Society: Does Democracy Still Enjoy an Epistemic Dimension? The Impact of Normative Theory on Empirical Research." *Communication Theory* 16(4): 411–26.

Hammond, T. H. 1986. "Agenda Control, Organizational Structure, and Bureaucratic Politics." *American Journal of Political Science* 30(2): 379–420.

Healey, P. 2006. *Collaborative Planning. Shaping Places in Fragmented Societies*. Basingstoke, Hampshire, UK: Palgrave Macmillan.

Hillier, J. 2003. "Agonizing over Consensus: Why Habermasian Ideals Cannot be 'Real.'" *Planning Theory* 2(1): 37–59.

Howe, E. 1992. "Professional Roles and the Public Interest in Planning." *Journal of Planning Literature* 6(3): 230–48.

Jennings, B. 2008. "Disaster Planning and Public Health." In *From Birth to Death and Bench to Clinic: The Hastings Center Bioethics Briefing Book for Campaigns, Journalists and Policymakers*, 41–44. Garrison, NY: Hastings Center.

Kahneman, D. 1994. "New Challenges to the Rationality Assumption." *Journal of Institutional and Theoretical Economics* 150(1): 18–36.

Kapoor, I. 2002. "Deliberative Democracy or Agonistic Pluralism? The Relevance of the Habermas-Mouffe Debate for Third World Politics." *Alternatives* 27(4): 459–87.

Kasachkoff, T. 1994. "Paternalism: Does Gratitude Make it Okay?" *Social Theory and Practice* 20(1): 1–23.

King, L. A. 2003. "Deliberation, Legitimacy, and Multilateral Democracy." *Governance* 16(1): 23–50.

Klosterman, R. 1980. "A Public Interest Criterion." *Journal of the American Planning Association* 46(3): 323–33.

Ladha, K. K. 1992. "The Condorcet Jury Theorem, Free Speech, and Correlated Votes." *American Journal of Political Science* 36(3): 617–34.

Lewis, C. W. 2006. "In Pursuit of the Public Interest." *Public Administration Review* 66(5): 694–701.

Lindblom, C. E. 1959. "The Science of 'Muddling Through.'" *Public Administration Review* 19(2): 79–88.

Lindblom, C. E. 1979. "Still Muddling, Not Yet Through." *Public Administration Review* 39(6): 517–26.

List, C. 2006. "The Discursive Dilemma and Public Reason." *Ethics* 116(2): 362–402.

List, C., and R. E. Goodin. 2001. "Epistemic Democracy: Generalizing the Condorcet Jury Theorem." *Journal of Political Philosophy* 9(3): 277–306.

Lowry, K. 1994. "The Legitimation of Planning." *Planning Theory* 10/11:99–109.

Manin, B. 1987. "On Legitimacy and Political Deliberation." *Political Theory* 15(3): 338–68.

McCloskey, M. C. 1971. "Planning and Regional Planning – What Are They? An Annotated Bibliography of Definitions." Exchange Bibliography No. 174. Monticello, IL: Council of Planning Librarians.

McGuirk, P. M. 2001. "Situating Communicative Planning Theory: Context, Power, and Knowledge." *Environment and Planning Part A* 33(2): 195–217.

McLean, I., and F. Hewitt. 1994. *Condorcet: Foundations of Social Choice and Political Theory*. Brookfield, VT: Elgar.

Meyer, J. M. 2008. "Populism, Paternalism and the State of Environmentalism in the U.S." *Environmental Politics* 17(2): 219–36.

Miller, N. R. 1986. "Information, Electorates, and Democracy: Some Extensions and Interpretations of the Condorcet Jury Theorem." In *Information Pooling and Group Decision Making*, edited by B. Grofman and G. Owen, 173–92. Greenwich, CT: JAI Press.

Moore, T. 1978. "Why Allow Planners to Do What They Do? A Justification from Economic Theory." *Journal of the American Institute of Planners* 44(4): 387–98.

Morgan, D. F. 2000. "The Public Interest." In *Handbook of Administrative Ethics*, 2nd ed., edited by T. L. Cooper, 151–78. New York: Marcel Dekker.

Moroni, S. 2004. "Towards a Reconstruction of the Public Interest Criterion." *Planning Theory* 3(2): 151–71.

Mouffe, C. 1999. "Deliberative Democracy or Agonistic Pluralism." *Social Research* 66(3): 745–58.

Mouffe, C. 2000. *The Democratic Paradox*. London: Verso.

Mueller, C. 1973. *The Politics of Communication*. New York: Oxford University Press.

New, B. 1999. "Paternalism and Public Policy." *Economics and Philosophy* 15(1): 63–83.

Oberdeck, K. J. 2000. "From Model Town to Edge City: Piety, Paternalism, and the Politics of Urban Planning in the United States" (review essay). *Journal of Urban History* 26(4): 508–18.

Pellizzoni, L. 2001. "The Myth of the Best Argument: Power, Deliberation and Reason." *British Journal of Sociology* 52(1): 59–86.

Pløger, J. 2004. "Strife: Urban Planning and Agonism." *Planning Theory* 3(1): 71–92.

Rawls, J. 1972. *A Theory of Justice*. Oxford: Oxford University Press.

Sager, T. 1994. *Communicative Planning Theory*. Aldershot, UK: Avebury.

Sager, T. 1995. "Teaching Planning Theory as Order or Fragments?" *Journal of Planning Education and Research* 14(3): 166–73.

Sager, T. 2002. *Democratic Planning and Social Choice Dilemmas*. Aldershot, UK: Ashgate.

Sager, T. 2005. "Planning Through Inclusive Dialogue: No Escape from Social Choice Dilemmas." *Economic Affairs* 25(4): 32–35.

Sager, T. 2006. "The Logic of Critical Communicative Planning: Transaction Cost Alteration." *Planning Theory* 5(3): 223–54.

Sager, T. 2007. "Dialogical Values in Public Goods Provision." *Journal of Planning Education and Research* 26(4): 497–512.

Sager, T., and C. H. Sørensen. 2011. "Planning Analysis and Political Steering with New Public Management." *European Planning Studies* 19(2): 217–41.

Scoccia, D. 2008. "In Defense of Hard Paternalism." *Law and Philosophy* 27(4): 351–81.

Sen, A. K. 1977. "Rational Fools: A Critique of the Behavioural Foundations of Economic Theory." *Philosophy and Public Affairs* 6(4): 317–44.

Silva, C. N. 2005. "Urban Planning and Ethics." In *Encyclopedia of Public Administration and Public Policy*, Update Supplement, edited by J. Rabin, 311–16. New York: Facts on File.

Tewdwr-Jones, M., and P. Allmendinger. 1998. "Deconstructing Communicative Rationality: A Critique of Habermasian Collaborative Planning." *Environment and Planning Part A* 30(11): 1975–89.

White, W. J. 2008. "The Interlocutor's Dilemma: The Place of Strategy in Dialogic Theory." *Communication Theory* 18(1): 5–26.

CHAPTER 3

URBAN PLANNING AND REGULATION: THE CHALLENGE OF THE MARKET

YONN DIERWECHTER AND ANDY THORNLEY

1. INTRODUCTION

FOR a long time, discussions in planning studies have focused on how to improve the physical development of urban and regional environments. But even as the urban literature has its own, distinctive bloodlines and theoretical contributions, broader debates about the appropriate political economy of modern society have invariably contrasted "planning" with the "market." The end of state socialism and the rise of neoliberalism once appeared to have consigned these debates to the dustbin of history. But the recent financial crisis in the global economy has resurrected classical concerns that capitalist markets do not perform well without economic planning and state regulation. In this chapter, we take the view that "big" shifts in state–market relations are important for understanding urban planning discourses, which too often are isolated from larger questions of political ideology, global economic conditions, and geographical variations in national culture (Albrechts 1991). Our approach here is therefore historical and geographical in nature, as we believe a review of past shifts in state–market relations in different countries should be a central theme in all contemporary scholarship.

Urban planning per se is the publicly mediated attempt to make interrelated decisions that collectively shape concrete spatial development patterns at various institutional scales. In theory, such decisions reflect deliberately worked out schemas for change; in practice, planning often occurs through projects influenced by deep cultural values and diverse economic interests.[1] Urban planning is therefore political because values and interests clash—and are furthermore infused with problems of uneven power (Altshuler 1965; Reade 1987; Forester 1989; Flyvbjerg 1998). But democratic governments "not only 'power,'" as Hugh Heclo has observed, "they also puzzle" (cited in Skocpol 1985, 11). In consequence, urban planning ultimately implies a specialized form of "collective puzzlement" about the social organization of space—whether we see this with Marxists as a fix for hegemonic capital or with more mainstream observers as a precarious consensus among competing actors.

At the heart of this collective puzzlement is the broader conundrum of state–market relations—the knotty question of just how (and for whom) the state at various levels of authority should intervene in private market activities (including "private" planning). This is especially so, as these activities involve land development projects and built-environmental transformations that impact a range of interests living in close proximity. Should the state simply provide basic regulatory frameworks and information for private market actors in order to ensure smoother capital accumulation—for example, the protection of private property rights from negative externalities—as economic liberals such as Milton Friedman (1962) argued and his libertarian followers still demand? Or, in contrast, should the state, as many if not all planning scholars and practitioners believe, deploy public regulations and investments to realize more positive societal values? The latter might include cultural, social, and ecological aspirations like *in loco* class/race integration, poverty alleviation, and ozone protection, all of which require much more assertive state controls over private-sector actors, who are usually less interested in collective or "global" concerns.[2]

Different ideologies provide different answers to these questions. But ideologies invariably wax and wane in history, and are themselves conditioned by substantial cultural variations across regulatory spaces (between national societies, of course, but also *within* them).[3] As Karl Mannheim (1940, 239), the Hungarian sociologist of knowledge and a major planning philosopher at mid-century, originally put it, "thought adapts itself to the needs of society." Needs are unevenly expressed by various groups and, moreover, often change, especially during periods of economic and social crisis; societies around the world also remain remarkably diverse in cultural terms, even as they each experience the increasingly common pressures of economic globalization, the latent hyper-mobility of capital, and the concomitant challenges to national regulatory capacities. Thus, as discussed here, intellectual debates about the "proper" role of public planning in regulating (and/or positively supplementing) private market activities are best understood in historical and geographical contexts rather than as abstract philosophical statements conducted outside the crisis-induced pressures of time and place.

Urban planning requires social and political legitimacy, which it only gains from being embodied in accepted laws and regulations. Its strength and scope will therefore depend, in our view, on the broader *ideology* regarding the role of the state and how much it should (and can) intervene in market processes—something that varies over time and between places. In John Friedmann's (1987) view, urban planning involves the translation of ideas into action; hegemonic ideas are thus strongly constitutive rather than weakly reflective of state–market relationships. This does not deny other important aspects of the overall state–market debate in planning studies, such as recent discussions of "institutional design" (Alexander 2005), which have started to question the whole concept of state–market dichoto-mies by offering useful insights into the "transaction costs" actors must pay to make governance decisions (Webster 1998; Buitelaar 2004). Indeed, we consider these more recent themes below. But institutions, however designed to lower or raise such costs, are fundamentally "shared mental constructs" (Lai 2005, 9)—constructs that we maintain here are influenced by the macro nature of broader ideological developments.[4]

The modern profession of urban planning is usually traced to the late nine-teenth century, but the focus in this chapter is on more recent phases in the broader ideological debate. Following our main argument, we locate key shifts in the tempo-ral flow of ideological developments in and across real places, particularly Europe and the United States. The first phase took place just before World War II, a period of severe economic and political crisis for the overall liberal capitalist order. This was a time of rich discussion in the West, as elsewhere, about the role of the state, and that ultimately laid the intellectual foundation for many national planning systems. Indeed, this "Great Debate" helped occasion a major shift to a second key phase—from a laissez-faire mentality before World War II to one that involved considerable state involvement after the war, often within the broader framework of the "welfare state." In the long aftermath of World War II, though, as markets returned to health, a third phase emerged. This phase, which arguably reached its zenith in the 1990s and early twenty-first century, involved pervasive questioning of the postwar "settlement" and a return to greater market freedom. That said, the most recent debates in planning studies highlight the ambiguities and complexities largely missing in these earlier phases, a development that may also reflect ideo-logical efforts to accommodate now globalized markets with a renewed respect for the indispensable services of the territorial state.

While the past is important in its own right, the global economic crisis pre-cipitated in 2008 makes this a particularly interesting moment to reconsider the role of planning in regulating land and development markets. It is possible that, in many countries, recent changes in the state's overall role in the broader economy will lead to the renewed acceptance of an ideology of greater intervention gener-ally, a development few planning scholars of state–market relations thought likely a few years ago (Healey 2003). For the last twenty years or so, the dominant ideology around the globe has championed minimum regulation of the market. The financial sector especially has been largely left to light-touch, self-regulatory monitoring. This neoliberal approach appears to have collapsed as a coherent ideology as world governments across the world now introduce various packages of involvement, from stronger regulation to outright state control. Major ideological shifts, should they occur, will therefore impact the scope and degree of urban planning intervention as in the past, though differently in different countries and probably in unexpected ways. The debates reviewed here, starting with the "Great Debate" of the 1930s and '40s, have thus rightly returned to the front burner of comparative planning studies.

2. The "Great Debate"

The economic crisis of the interwar years led to the first major debate over the relationship between the state and the market. From this broader debate regarding the merits of laissez-faire versus economic planning came a changed view of the role of the state. The New York Stock Market crash of 1929 and the worldwide Great Depression of the 1930s led to high unemployment levels in many countries. The very fabric of democratic capitalism was under threat. This precipitated greater state involvement of one sort or another, which in turn opened the way for a more comprehensive approach to planning regulation and laws, although it is also important to keep in mind the practical variations across countries with differing political cultures.

In the United States, for example, most individuals arguably still lacked a deep "sense of the state," as H.G. Wells observed in 1906, perhaps owing to the absence of a pre-modern state apparatus associated with the monarchical polities of Europe (Skowronek 1982). All the same, the American state's regulatory capacities developed inexorably in direct response to international and domestic crises (e.g., the U.S. Civil War, the depression of the 1890s); industrial class and ethnic conflicts; and growing urban-economic complexity.[5] During the New Deal, what would eventually be called Keynesian approaches catapulted reformers from the "outcast" periphery of society to the center of "a new state" (Skowronek 1982, 165).

Franklin D. Roosevelt introduced the New Deal, encompassing more state control of the economy, major social programs, and public works epitomized by the Tennessee Valley Authority and the Works Progress Administration. These developments suggest, we would argue, a decisive shift in ideology concerning the appropriate role of the state, although figures like Rexford Tugwell—who originally tried to build Garden Cities across the country as head of FDR's Resettlement Administration—felt this did not go far enough; others thought the commercial rather than the social-democratic nature of the New Deal allowed for an easy reversal after the Second World War (see Cullingworth 1993). Certainly, major urban planning intellectuals of this period, notably Lewis Mumford (1938, 1961), lamented the missed opportunities of the tumultuous 1930s, although Mumford's theoretical focus on neo-anarchistic cultural renewal in what he brilliantly envisioned as a "republic of regions" made him deeply suspicious of both the overcorporatization of the American economy and the centralizing bureaucratization of this so-called new American state.

But even as American commitments to social redistribution and public control over market activities were (and remain) more tepid than in other countries, the central regulatory and legislative achievements of the New Deal state—Social Security, collective bargaining, banking and securities reform, unemployment insurance, farm subsidies, home mortgage support, ecological conservation, and regional resource planning—nonetheless occasioned once-unimagined state involvement in the free market. As Blum (1982, 30) later put it: "sheer liberalism...could no longer serve as the basis for a society that had grown rich and complex." While the United States would never develop a national planning system for either urban development or the overall economy comparable to those in Europe, urban planning historians have identified the crucial importance of the New Deal era, whether interpreted sympathetically or critically, in the ongoing state institutionalization and public acceptance of local and even state-level planning regimes within a heretofore economically liberal, market-oriented polity (e.g., Altshuler 1965; Scott 1969; Friedmann and Weaver 1980).

In some European countries, the disruptive legacies of World War I in the 1920s and the even greater severity of the Depression during the 1930s led to wholesale dissatisfaction with democratic capitalism. On the right, the economic turmoil in Germany, Spain, and Italy produced fascist regimes; on the left, the communist alternative was being developed in Russia. Despite their differences, a strong state approach in all of these countries involved substantially more collective planning and public works programs than seen in, for instance, the United States or the United Kingdom. This set a challenge to leading democratic capitalist countries. The sheer physical impact of World War II on European shores, moreover, was far greater and added other elements to the state–market debate. Considerable propaganda was disseminated during the war years to maintain morale, and the foundations were laid for the subsequent postwar "welfare state." Planning was a central element in this process, riding the overall expansion of state power universally experienced in the liberal democracies during the Depression and World War II.

For example, in Britain, Thomas Sharp published his best-selling Penguin paperback in 1940 called *Town Planning*, in which he noted:

> It is no overstatement to say that the simple choice between planning and non-planning, between order and disorder, is a test-choice for English democracy. In the long run even the worst democratic muddle is preferable to a dictator's dream bought at the price of liberty and decency. But the English muddle is nevertheless a matter for shame. We shall never get rid of its shamefulness unless we plan our activities. And plan we must—not for the sake of our physical environment only, but to save and fulfill democracy itself. (143)

Karl Mannheim (1954) went even further after the war, developing the theme of freedom *through* planning. So the search was on to find a way in which planning could bring order and efficiency to the physical environment without resorting to fascism or communism. If this were to happen in a democratic environment, then the old capitalist system would need to be modified. A new market–state relationship was needed. The formulation of this new relationship drew upon the fertile ideas that emanated from the "Great Debate" of the prewar years—a debate between supporters of the free market and those advocating economic planning (i.e., planning focused on the national economy).

A key moment in this debate was the publication in 1936 of the *General Theory* by John Maynard Keynes. After the stock market crash of 1929 there was a widespread view among industrialists, businessmen, and civil servants that stability was needed in the economic system and that the state should intervene in the market in order to ensure this was achieved. Keynes was able to put forward ideas on how this might be done. His ideas had a great influence on politicians around the world. For example, in Britain a major political debate took place between the supporters of the free market and those advocating a role for the state in economic affairs. The young Harold Macmillan, later to become a Conservative prime minister, wrote *The Middle Way* (1938), in which he advocated the "new doctrine" of close cooperation between the state and economic interests.

Another key figure, Karl Polanyi, was in England at the time and started to write his influential analysis of the economic system. *The Great Transformation* was eventually published in 1944. In this work, he blamed the economic crisis on a wrong-minded utopian attempt to restore nineteenth-century economic liberalism after World War I. His message was that market forces often lead to destruction unless carefully regulated. He exposed the tensions between a self-regulating market system and the imperative that leads to national protectionism and social objectives. These messages underlie the current crisis and the responses to it. A similar tension can be identified within the planning system as it tries to promote social and environmental goals within the context of a land and property market. The "welfare state" approach that was adopted in many countries after 1945 was a response to the national and social imperative identified by Polanyi, and it gave planning the potential to pursue more wide-ranging ambitions.

However, while writers such as Keynes and Polanyi were producing their economic analyses, an opposing strand of thinking was also developing. This view is probably most famously expressed in the work of Friedrich Hayek (1944), in his best-known book, *The Road to Serfdom*. His aim was to oppose socialism as he saw it developing at the time, but Hayek presented his arguments broadly to show the problems inherent in any kind of state intervention or collectivism. His views were based on the belief that the principles of liberalism were fundamental, and he sought to show why they were a necessary basis for a good society. Socialism, which involves central planning for the national economy, he saw as inappropriate for modern society because it involves such great complexity that it cannot be fully understood and controlled. Any "plans" result in oversimplicity, have detrimental side effects, and slow down innovation. This problem of complexity can be avoided by focusing on individual action in the market and following traditional rules that have evolved slowly over generations.[6]

Although this view of minimal regulation can be said to have lost the argument at the time, the ideas continued to be developed by Hayek and others, such as Milton Friedman. Their day came in the 1980s, when the view was the central approach taken by many national governments, most notably in the United States and United Kingdom, but also in New Zealand and Australia. The ideas still have resonance—paradoxically Hayek is widely read in China today. These themes will be addressed again later in this chapter, but first we discuss how the role and function of planning evolved in the postwar period.

3. The Postwar "Settlement"

Many Western countries in the postwar era experienced consensus among economic interests and an agreement on ideology. This was the postwar settlement period in which the welfare state was established. Some commentators even talked about the "end of ideology" (Bell 1960). The accepted view was that the state and diverse economic interests could work together to maximize their own interests and those of society generally. It was in this climate that many countries established their first comprehensive planning systems, with the inherent powers to intervene in development and land markets. In many ways, this can be regarded as the moment when the planning system was at its ideological and practical strongest, carrying public support and encompassing a wide range of accepted purposes and roles. These roles included not mere regulation but also positive intervention for the public good (in Britain, for example, development rights were nationalized). Planning was given the umpire, or balancing, role mediating between competing interests, and was seen as one mechanism that helped prevent a return to prewar economic and class conflicts.

In this climate, it was accepted that planning could serve a wide range of purposes (Foley 1960; Klosterman 1985). These purposes varied from country to country and also evolved to a certain degree during the following decade. That is, immediately after the war many countries had to focus on rebuilding their cities when resources were scarce. The public sector took a leading role in managing this effort. However, in time a market returned to the development process, and the private sector became the leading actor again. This shifted the balance in planning from being state led to that of regulating the market. However, the consensus view of planning as a balancing function ensured that it retained wide-ranging powers in most countries until the economic crisis of the 1970s.

These powers encompassed quite different aspects. There were those provisions that regulated the market, ensured that it operated efficiently, limited its adverse neighborhood effects, and contributed to the provision of public goods that the market did not supply. This was seen as enabling the good management of cities, regions, and rural areas. There were, then, those purposes concerned with the appearance of the physical environment, such as the design of buildings and the preservation of historic areas or good landscapes. Then, thirdly, there were the social objectives, such as ensuring equity across communities, contributing to the improvement of deprived areas, and maintaining social cohesion.

Different values lay behind the three aspects: the first focused on efficiency, the second on visual attractiveness, and the third reflected the ideology of the welfare state. The pursuit of these different values sometimes reinforced each other, but also sometimes caused conflicts—for example, when protection of land from development for aesthetic or environmental reasons hindered economic development and created a scarcity of building land. However, such contradictions in goals were contained during the postwar settlement; the consensus was that planning could provide a secure basis for society as a whole and contribute to the general economic prosperity.

McAuslan (1980), drawing on the British experience, has described this precarious co-existence of different values in an alternative way. He talks about the three ideologies of planning law that lie alongside each other in uneasy tension. There is the legal system, which is based on the prime ideology of protecting private property; there are the public laws oriented to the public interest and involving market regulation; and there are the more recent attempts to give people legal rights to more direct participation. Planning is on the frontline in this struggle between the legal rights of ownership and the public interest and public participation, as well as having a central position in balancing the roles of market and state.

This description of the strong role for planning in the postwar settlement is based mostly on the European experience. Naturally, the situation in the United States was different. Until the twentieth century, few public actions at any level were initiated to control private development so as to ameliorate, for instance, worsening urban housing and neighborhood conditions. This was arguably a practical consequence of three main factors: the country's longstanding ideology of laissez-faire economics; the weakness of municipal authorities in the liberal constitutional order; and more generally, the anti-urban origins of American culture (Krueckeberg 1983/1997, 2–4). But eventually the largest cities—like New York, Chicago, and Philadelphia—necessarily began to manage urban development more deliberately, using basic tools and techniques such as comprehensive sewerage systems, zoning ordinances, building codes, and multichaptered "master plans" to harness, service, and ultimately shape the urban land markets.

Public involvement in private development dynamics was, therefore, increasingly deemed an appropriate responsibility of the state, though planning as a more ambitious mechanism to protect the public interest focused disproportionately on protecting single-family residential areas from unwanted uses and on giving security to real estate developers. The main purpose of planning in the United States was to help achieve the American Dream (Haar & Kayden 1989) and, rather than positively interfering with private property, to provide order and stability to home ownership. Certainly other values were present, such as ensuring adequate provision of public amenities like integrated parks. And after the 1960s, a few state governments, notably Oregon and Florida, started to mandate local planning efforts in a manner that represented what Bossleman and Callies called "a quiet revolution" in U.S. planning history (see Dierwechter 2008).

But in too many places, American planning was merely a localized form of "bad neighbor" control and an alternative to using the law of nuisance. Society accorded a stronger "governance" role to the legal processes protecting property rights, which tended to block broader efforts to create a national planning "system" (Cullingworth 1993).[7] In contrast to Europe, with its centralized and bureaucratized approach to administering the postwar planning system, U.S. planning remained a local responsibility in most places until the 1970s, albeit with notable spatial variations in application and state assertiveness regarding issues of redistribution (e.g., Clavel 1985). The postwar settlement in Europe thus built more directly upon the ideas of those writers in the Great Debate who argued for extensive state involvement. The central premise was that a more co-operative relationship between the state and the market would benefit both sides. In the United States, this attitude was not as prevalent. In McAuslan's terms, the ideology of property law tended to dominate the ideology of public-interest law.

However, in the 1970s, a new theoretical approach was propounded by some U.S. authors—for example, C. E. Lindblom (1977). He suggested that in a liberal democracy there are two main interrelated centers of authority: the democratically accountable government and the asset-owning private sector. They need each other. The government does not have the resources, particularly risk capital, to undertake ventures, while the private sector requires legitimacy to support its need for stability. The environment is stable, lessening the uncertainties for investment. This symbiosis thus leads to the concept of a public–private partnership, which became a central concept from this time on. It was to apply largely to specific development projects and can still be seen in arrangements such as the Urban Development Corporations and the Public Benefit Corporations. But the balance of power between public and private within this type of arrangement can and does vary over time and from place to place. From the 1980s on, the power balance tipped toward the market. After gaining institutional ground for decades, planning was now under attack, both ideologically and practically.

4. PLANNING UNDER ATTACK

The 1960s was a time of considerable social unrest and social criticism. There were urban riots and student protests in many countries. In this climate, the planning system also came under attack. One of the early critics was Jane Jacobs, whose well-known book *The Death and Life of Great American Cities* came out in 1961.

The opening sentence stated that "this book is an attack on current city planning and rebuilding"; in it Jacobs focused particularly on comprehensive redevelopment schemes and urban motorways. She claimed that planners were imbued with old and irrelevant principles, such as zoning for separate land uses, and were contributing to the economic decline of American cities. She contrasted the appeal of everyday community life with the monotonous world of the planners. She saw the vitality of cities as stemming from their diversity, which was being destroyed by strict zoning. So Jacobs believed that planners were unable to deal with the complexity of cities and were using simplistic solutions.

This message was central to Hayek's argument for the free market, and it is interesting to note that Jacobs's work was featured on the reading list for civil servants circulated by the right-wing Thatcher government in its first year of office (Thornley 1993). Another message from Jane Jacobs is less well known. She blamed the large corporations, such as insurance companies, banks, and pension funds, for also destroying the city's diversity by building large, monotonous, single-block developments. However, it was not long before planners were adopting a more flexible approach to urban development, and the late 1960s and early 1970s were marked by a concern for meeting social needs, correcting inequality, and offering more opportunities for public participation.

Planning was also thoroughly attacked by the Marxist left (see Foglesong 1986). From this perspective, the planning system was an agent in maintaining the capitalist system. It was claimed that, despite the stated objectives of serving the public interest, or the beliefs of planners themselves, the system was structurally dominated by market interests (see, for example, Fainstein et al. 1983; Reade 1987). They argued that planning provided a mythical justification that market forces and dominant interests were being kept in check, but the reality was different (Harvey 1985). That is, planning legitimized the existing capitalist system and the inequality of power in society. This critique had considerable purchase at the time in academic quarters and also in some urban regeneration projects. However, it did little to impact planning systems; it was the critique from the opposite end of the political spectrum that was to have an effect in the 1980s.

The 1970s brought another global economic crisis. In 1971, the United States pulled out of the Bretton Woods Accord and floated the dollar; and in 1973, OPEC raised oil prices and the U.S. stock markets crashed. This was the first economic crisis to have a long-lasting and global effect since the Great Depression. Once more, the debate over the relationship between the state and the market became a major issue. This time, there was a reaction against the significant postwar role of the state and a mounting campaign for greater market freedom. Hayek's work was revisited and taken up, for example, by economists such as Milton Friedman (1962; Friedman and Friedman1980). Hayek had also been expanding his own ideas (1960, 1982). A body of work was therefore developing that portrayed the answer to the economic crisis as greater market freedom and withdrawal of state interference. The view was that the state had become too powerful, was open to corrupting influences, and was also financially unable to meet the increasing demands of the welfare state. Individuals acting in the marketplace were a safeguard against overambitious governments operating with political bias. The welfare state was seen as having become wrongly imbued with ideological permanence. Hayek in his later work stressed the vagueness and ambiguity of concepts such as social justice that underlay the welfare state. These ideas had a major influence on politicians, especially in the United States and Britain (Thornley 1993). As a result, there was a shift in the approach to urban policy and planning. We illustrate this through the British case where the move to this New Right was particularly clear, and it involved a major shift in ideology away from the welfare state that had become so widely accepted as normal.

The new approach gained political purchase in Britain when Margaret Thatcher won the national election in 1979 on a New Right platform. Immediately there was an attack on the role of planning, which had been central since the Second World War. Now, planning had to justify any interventionist role. Whereas the assumption before was that development would not be allowed unless acceptable within the planning system, the Thatcher government said that all development should be allowed unless a very strong argument could be made against it. Removing the burdens on economic initiative was the mantra, and this meant that regulations and restrictions on development had to be removed wherever possible. The statutory plans that provided a framework for individual decisions regarding development were reduced and special planning-free zones were established in certain areas. The opportunities for public participation in the planning process were also circumscribed. As a result, planning was no longer to perform all the functions it had undertaken previously. All social objectives were removed. It was assumed that more economic freedom would enhance economic growth, and social issues would be dealt with through "trickle down" effects. However, planning was not completely abolished. Even with this laissez-faire approach, it was believed that planning could help the efficiency of the market. So controlling for bad-neighbor effects, providing some "public goods" not possible through the market, and offering information about the future to suggest more certainly for investment were all seen as still necessary.

As noted earlier, a potential second aspect of planning was to safeguard visual attractiveness and the environment. This proved problematic for the New Right ideology. Developers were urging the relaxation of environmental constraints, and the logic of the ideology supported such a move. However, at the same time there were many people whose property values and quality of life were maintained by such controls. These people were generally the more wealthy citizens who nonetheless were supporters of Mrs. Thatcher's political party.

The answer to this dilemma was to create a dual planning system. In some areas with good-quality environments and where many of these supporters lived, the strong controls over development were retained on the grounds of conservation. Elsewhere, the general approach for greater development freedom prevailed. This New Right ideology dominated the planning system in Britain for about a dozen years. However, gradually its ability to maintain a dual system started to fail. Environmental sustainability was becoming a significant global issue, and this concern took legal expression in directives from the European Union. Britain had to conform to these directives; simultaneously, public opinion was moving in this direction as well. Hence, greater constraints were imposed on development, thereby compromising the "purity" of the ideology. Once the intervention was introduced, why not expand it for other purposes in the public interest or that had long-term implications?

In 1997, there was another political shift in power, and the Labour Party under Tony Blair came to the fore with an ideology more accepting of state intervention, claiming that "trickle down" economics had not worked. But before that had happened, the idea of economic freedom dominated the period and had shifted the balance between market and state by greatly restricting the role of planning. Indeed, planning had become largely a regulatory function oriented toward improving the efficiency of the development process. Although this approach dominated Britain from 1979 to the mid-1990s, it was also evident in other countries, sometimes in later periods. It can be viewed as at the opposite end of the spectrum from the planning system that had operated after the Second World War in those countries that establish a strong welfare state.

5. BEYOND THE DICHOTOMY: DIVERSE PLANNING CULTURES IN A CONVERGING WORLD?

Arguably, since the mid-1990s or so, planning debates about state–market relations have sought to go beyond the dichotomy often implied in these previous phases by rethinking institutions and cultures in what appears to be a converging world. We therefore address these more recent themes in this final section before offering general conclusions.

Noting that state–market relations in the land and property development process are a critical but often neglected issue, Patsy Healey (2003, 6), for example, highlighted the growing problems of clarity, legitimacy, and accountability as "the negotiation of the 'public interest' and the relative roles of the 'state' and the 'market' [in Europe] are worked out at the project level." Here, the twin issues of flexibility and discretion are for her in constant tension, with geographically more extensive and longer term goals associated classically with comprehensive strategic spatial planning (cf. Healey 1992). For Healey, such issues require "rethinking the complex and multi-layered nature of land and property development processes" (2003, 6).[8]

The most significant ideas in this new round of state–market rethinking is the theoretical work of Ernest Alexander (2001, 2008), who has tried to recover the seemingly threadbare concept of a "Third Way" (though see Webster 1998 and Buitelaar 2004 for work that focuses especially on property rights). For Alexander (2008, 120), contemporary theoretical critiques of/within planning studies—for example, Habermasian concerns with rational technocratic planning; various Marxian approaches that ultimately embed planning within state capitalist hegemony; and Foucaultian, Lacanian, and Deluezoguarttarian efforts at postmoderm deconstruction—"all fall short of offering a plausible alternative paradigm to old-fashioned progressive modernism, which deduced rational planning from liberal social-democracy." These diverse critiques, however valuable in changing taken-for-granted perceptions of social reality (e.g., Purcell 2008), are for Alexander unable to supplant neoliberalism, with its conceptual basis in traditional liberal political theory and neoclassical (post-Keynesian) economics.

Alexander's (2001) argument deploys integrated transaction cost theory. From this perspective, policy prescriptions based on abstract liberal-market approaches, in particular, are far too simple theoretically to be useful practically. While regulatory complexity tempts many to call for freeing up the market, the reality is that planning and markets, in his view, are no longer analytically or empirically distinguishable—a variation on the mixed-economy themes going back to the 1930s. "The false dichotomy between them," he concludes, "is based on a widely held association between planning and public intervention and governmental or state regulation and action, as opposed to private enterprise in the supposedly unplanned market" (1–2). Accordingly, the key policy question is not whether or not to plan but to consider the most effective form (or mix of forms) of governance.

Rather than call for more civic participation or more private markets—standard lines of policy thinking on both the progressive left and the libertarian right—policy questions of institutional design are explored with respect to exchanges between parties, "from simple exchanges of goods and services for money, to other transactions involving the promise of action of value by one party in exchange for money, goods, services or other valued resources, or for the promise of reciprocal action of economic or other value" (Alexander 2001, 1–2). Rather than hypothetical ideals, either procedural or spatial, more analytical emphasis should be placed on *remediability* and *discriminating alignment*, which lead to questions about the institutional design necessary to support land-use and environmental management systems able to confront the awesome territorial challenges of the urban region. By focusing narrowly on transactions, *remediability* compares alternative feasible forms of governance, while *discriminating alignment* matches the specific attributes of state and nonstate transactions with alternative governance structures.

While this now fashionable focus on institutions—rather than on state or market per se—resonates with parallel developments in other fields, notably neo-Weberian work in political science, economic sociology, and even social psychology (Skowronek 1982; and see Kim, this volume), little work in planning studies has explored effectively the differential capacities of various societies to build institutions capable of *remediability* or of *discriminating alignment*. Yet institutions are themselves "part and parcel of particular, historically contingent configurations of social and economic power" (Skowronek 1995, 92). And as Fukuyama (1995) has shown in his work on the crucial role of trust, such configurations are shaped by deeper norms and ethical habits—that is, "culture" (which includes ideas and ideologies).[9]

In this sense, future work in planning studies that seeks to transcend state–market dichotomies will have to consider in much more detail the various ways in which institutional choices are shaped by what Sanyal (2005) and others have called the "cultures of planning" (see Friedmann, this volume).[10] Whether this can be done via Alexander's concepts of transaction costs and institutional design remains to be seen, as far more robust efforts, to use Healey's (2003) ideas, are needed to integrate institutional economics and cultural politics—for example, with planning studies. This work has barely started, and surely represents a new frontier in urban planning scholarship.

Specifically, new work on planning cultures that helps to illuminate institutional choices should first engage with authors who have identified different models of the market–state relationship—or different "cultures of capitalism" as a whole, as they are sometimes called (e.g., Hutton 1995; Esping Anderson 1990). The idea is that there are many variations in the way the capitalist system operates around the world, based on differing national value systems, and these shape the institutional choices. Hutton, for example, identifies different models to illustrate this point—although these models should be viewed as ideal types rather than descriptions of reality. One model, which can be labeled the "free market" model, minimizes the role of the state and seeks the greatest freedom for the market. In this model, economic and social cohesion is obtained from optimizing growth, from which all requirements can be met. Innovation is maximized and the individual pursuit of short-term profits will generate overall social gains. Planning in this model has a minimal role, and it is difficult to develop arguments for social intervention or long-term approaches. This model is often identified with the United States and can also be seen in Thatcherist ideology.

A second concept has sometimes been called the "social market" model. In this approach partnership is a key concept, and the state, market, and people work together; the capitalist market is not a natural force that results from individuals pursuing their own end, but has to be consciously organized and monitored, a point that both revisits Karl Polanyi and anticipates Alexander. The Scandinavian nations and Germany are seen as countries that have, at times, taken this approach furthest. This culture of capitalism stresses the longer term, consensus, and social harmony. As a result, planning can have an important function.

A third model is one that has been implemented in Asia, and in particularly in Japan. Here, the state plays a significant role but not in quite the comprehensive manner of the social market model. The state is particularly focused on national economic growth and is often labeled the "developmental state." State intervention is high, but it is oriented almost exclusively to this national economic goal; there is close partnership and co-operation between and among politicians, business, and bureaucrats. Planning is strong where it can contribute to this national economic objective, but in other areas—such as housing, quality of the urban environment, or encouraging public participation—the state does not play a significant role. Thus, although nearly all countries now have a capitalist system with the market playing a leading role, there can be considerable differences in the degree to which traditions and national value systems allow the state to act as a mediator. In addition, some countries maintain traditions and values while others have a more volatile history. Also, sometimes a particular model is imposed from outside—for example, through conquest or colonialism.

But future work in planning studies that seeks to transcend the state–market dichotomies cannot simply dissect various cultures of capitalism; such work should also consider strong tendencies toward systemic convergence. This idea rests on two arguments. The first is that, as the market process has become globalized since the 1980s, a common experience has been imposed on all nations, leading to a common planning response. The second argument looks at convergence through the other half of the equation—the state—suggesting that, for example, the formation of the European Union has supplanted the role of individual nation-states and this has led to a common European approach to planning. While other world regions have not experienced this level of supra-national political and administrative integration, many planning problems, such as global warming, will almost certainly require new levels of territorial authority, both below and above the national scale of regulation.

Economic globalization is generally regarded to have taken hold in the late 1980s (e.g., Scholte 2000). Through improved telecommunications and computer technology, and cheaper and more frequent air travel, the links between countries and cities have increased dramatically. The market economy has become more interconnected, as clearly demonstrated in the financial crisis of 2008. People, information, services, finance, culture, and ideas move on a rapid, global scale aided by the internet. Castells (1996) has suggested that these global flows have resulted in a "network society" in which location is no longer so important.

What does this globalization mean for the relationship between the state and the market, and does it lead to a homogenized planning response? There is one, quite dominant school of thought that claims that globalization is an inevitable and beneficial stage of capitalism this is a view put forward by business gurus in the United States and at the World Bank. This approach looks like the laissez-faire views of the past writ large: globalization will promote maximum world economic growth and the benefits of this will trickle down to even the less developed countries. One of the key parts of this argument is that, as a result of globalization, economic decision makers are freed from the constraints of the nation-state, as they can locate anywhere in a borderless world (Ohmae 1990). National and city leaders respond to this message by trying to capture a piece of this global pie. They see themselves in a very competitive situation in which they have to do everything they can to attract, globally footloose economic interests. City marketing is everywhere, advertising incentives to attract investment, including providing physical benefits

like airports, transport, and quality office space or soft incentives such as tax or
planning exemptions.

In such a climate one would expect planning to be weakened in relation to
market demands, and the development and investment projects that cities pursue might look very similar. Waterfront financial districts with hotels and smart
restaurants, designed by the same international architects (Olds 2001) are an illustration of this response. However, there are other writers who, although accepting that economic globalization has occurred, do not accept its inevitability. They
claim that it can be politically manipulated and shaped, and rather than being
a single process, it is made up of many complex elements. In this scenario, the
state and planning do have a role. Rather than the nation-state evaporating, it is
restructuring—decentralizing some roles to regional and city levels but maintaining other roles and even taking on new ones. Some politicians can draw upon
national traditions and culture, or popular reaction from civil society, to extract
public benefits from the various processes involved in economic globalization—or
even reject some aspects. One of the themes in this literature is that, rather than
the "hollowing out of the nation state," there is a process of "rescaling" (Held et al.
1999; Brenner 1999). The state itself becomes more complex and can respond in
different ways.

So where politicians have adopted the response of solely catering to the demands
of global economic interests, one could argue that there has been a convergence in
the planning approach. That's an approach in which the market dominates and
planning at best extracts some public benefits. Then, competition is fierce between
cities and politicians are loath to impose regulations lest they lose investment to
their competitors. However, if politicians view the globalization process as more
complex, then opportunities might exist for proactive planning—for example,
supporting local economic growth or greater local R&D efforts.

Also, just as the trickle-down claim is challenged in the laissez-faire model,
it can be challenged in relation to globalization. If this challenge is accepted, then
making a case for planning interventions as a response to social needs is enhanced.
Many authors point to the increased social polarization developing in world cities
where economic globalization has had the greatest impacts (e.g., Sassen 1991). Such
polarization carries the danger of social unrest, and many cities have experienced
urban riots in recent years. It can be argued that, in the longer term, it is better to
intervene in the market to prevent any instability that can arise when such intervention is lacking. Of course, the events of 2008 show that there can also be economic instability in the way that the global financial system operates, and this also
points to a need for greater state regulation.

We have noted that one of the discussions within the globalization debate concerns the way that the nation-state, historically the center of a country's power,
has restructured its role. Some of its functions might be decentralized to a lower
tier, such as a region or city, while other functions are abrogated to a higher level,
such as the European Union (EU). One of the questions raised is whether the EU
has taken on certain planning functions that have led to greater conformity in any

approach to planning. The essential role of the EU is to ensure a level playing field within its boundaries, and this would not be achieved if some countries had a more lenient planning regime than others. So, the logic of this argument would be to harmonize national planning systems.

Over the years there have been a number of moves toward a common EU approach to planning issues. These have included the Directive on Environmental Impact Assessment, a spatial policy for the whole EU area, and a number of urban policy experiments aiming at identifying good practices. The first of these has had to be incorporated into each national planning system, but the spatial policy and urban policies have not been mandatory, although they have provided a framework for the allocation of the EU's own grants. Even though some people have imagined a convergence of planning systems, this has not happened to any significant extent.

The reasons for this can be found in the strength of the legal and administrative structures. There are different legal and institutional traditions and histories across Europe within which planning operates (see Newman and Thornley 1996). These differences are greater than the push toward a common approach. For example, the legal case-by-case common-law system of Britain and Ireland can be contrasted with the written Napoleonic system in most of Europe. Similarly, there are administrative differences in degree of central control, decentralization, and regional federalism. Such differences shape the planning systems in each country. It can be said that there are opportunities to harmonize the planning systems among countries that share similar legal and administrative frameworks, but not across such extremes of difference.

These differences in frameworks mean that if a country takes a particular position regarding planning and the regulation of the market, there is room to impose this position, regardless of EU philosophy. In fact, this can be said to have occurred in the Thatcher period in Britain. Nevertheless, there is general agreement within the EU that a free-market regime is not the best way forward and that some form of social intervention by the state, whether national or at the EU level, is necessary. Many of the EU grant programs are aimed at alleviating the adverse effects of the market on socially deprived groups or poorer areas within EU. As mentioned earlier, the purpose of the EU is to establish a free market across Europe and to harmonize the way nation-states relate to that market; at the European level, the EU could be regarded as following a "social market" approach to its own relationship with the market.

6. SUMMARY

In this chapter, we have argued that recognizing the major shifts in state–market relations is important for understanding urban planning. We have seen significant variation in ideological views regarding the ideal relationship between the market and the state. Planning plays a pivotal role in this relationship and is therefore a contentious activity. It is not surprising that the broader ideological context has a strong impact on the planning function. At one extreme, the market is viewed as the favorable mechanism for creating an ideal society and planning should not interfere in its operation—in fact, the major function of planning is seen as that of improving the operation of this market. Maximizing economic growth and innovation will create the conditions whose benefits will trickle down to everyone else. At the other extreme, the limitations of the market are stressed—such as a lack of concern for long-term issues, an inability to create certain public goods, and a lack of beneficial evidence for trickle-down effects.

The historical and geographical coverage here has shown the periods and places where the laissez-faire approach has dominated, such as the early United States or the Thatcher period in Britain. The use of planning as a mechanism to "manage" capitalism in a more positive way can also be detected here—for example, in the post-World War II settlement. There have, of course, been variations on these as a result of some strong national traditions and political cultures. For example, Sweden had a short-lived period of deregulation in the early 1990s, while France has maintained a strong central state. In other cases, such as in modern China, different approaches can be seen to operate alongside each other. The national ideological and cultural context thus shapes approaches to urban planning.

But global economic conditions also tend to have a strong impact on the market–state relationship. There have been three global economic crises: the interwar Great Depression, the crisis of the 1970s, and the current financial crisis. In each case, a major debate has arisen about the role of the state in planning decisions. During the Great Depression, the advocates of laissez-faire argued against the economic planners, with the latter winning the day after the war. The result was a significant role for planning, often within a welfare state framework. However, the crisis of the 1970s led to a backlash and a return to market dominance. In most parts of the world, regulation of all kinds was minimized, reinforced by the competitive imperative that globalization was seen to bring.

Now there is another crisis, a renewed debate and maybe another U-turn. In closing, then, we believe that new work in the field should not only consider more intently the role of political ideology, global economic conditions, and geographical variations in cultural values in shaping the theory and practice of urban planning; it should also consider how such factors influence the practical capacity of various societies to produce new kinds of governing institutions that rely on both state regulatory power and market dynamism to improve the urban condition. Such work will need to present new ways to examine the differential effects of varying cultural conditions on the broader processes of systemic convergence associated with economic globalization. That is certainly a tall order, but also an exciting prospect for a new generation of planning scholars.

NOTES

1. "The crucial distinction between planning and [everyday] decision making," Shih-Kung Lai (2002, 32, emphasis added) has put it, "is that planning considers a set of *related decisions at the same time* while decision making chooses from a set of alternatives the best based on some criterion." That said, planning practice varies from simply managing the coexistence of individual development projects, as in Flanders and indeed much of the United States, to what Albrechts, Healey, and Kunzmann (2003) call a *spatial* approach to spatial planning, which foregrounds the future schema rather than the present projects.

2. Economists like Milton Friedman are not necessarily hard-hearted, but argue instead that "global" concerns associated with positive planning practices are best pursued through voluntary cooperative exchange and the universal pursuit of individual self-interest. Their classical hero is Adam Smith; however, as the conservative political philosopher Francis Fukuyama (1995) has pointed out, economic libertarians usually reference *The Wealth of Nations*, ignoring Smith's more "cultural" works, such as *The Theory of Moral Sentiments*. According to Fukuyama, Smith embedded economic practices in broader cultural values and ethical habits, a move that reduces the theoretical power of ahistorical and placeless rational-utility maximizing individuals so crucial to the explanatory assumptions of neoclassical economic theories of urban development.

3. Even in the UK, with a relatively more "unitary" planning system than in the federated American context, Healey (1992, 411) noted at the beginning of the 1990s considerable geographical variation: "In some places, a strategic plan-based approach was being taken, in others the public sector led a process of urban regeneration. Elsewhere, the system was used merely to facilitate market-led development." Thornley (1993) similarly documents the rise of "economic efficiency" under Thatcherism over and above the environmental and community values that operated only in "specific geographical areas" of the country. Clavel (1985) has documented (if not theorized) an important minority of "progressive" planning regimes within the United States, whose government officials deploy their local planning systems to engage in redistributive policy and meaningful participatory democracy—something he argued is unusual in the American context.

4. For example, as Ihlanfeldt (2009, 74–75) argues in the U.S. context, there is paradoxically little positive evidence that comprehensive planning of land markets is particularly effective in improving quality of life and reducing sprawl, yet state legislatures around the country now increasingly mandate the local development of comprehensive plans because they believe this to be true. (For his part, concludes that in Florida, local comprehensive planning does contribute decisively to enhanced community welfare, mainly by enhancing the demand side of the housing stock by addressing market externalities.)

5. The market-driven rawness of turn-of-the-century Chicago, for instance, invited a visiting Max Weber to famously liken the city to a "human being with his skin removed" (cited in Dierwechter, 2008, 16). In this sense, the City Beautiful Movement, associated with the Chicago World's Fair and often considered the first major planning movement within the U.S., was an effort to put the "skin back on" such cities, focusing on aesthetic achievements and publicly owned lands, but not yet direct regulation over private-sector development. "Rawness" had to do with the limited presence of the state. "During the first half of the nineteenth century," Donald Krueckeberg (1983/1997, 2–4) observes, virtually no governmental actions were initiated to control or redirect private development in order to ameliorate worsening housing and living conditions."

6. According to contemporary writers on planning and urban development working broadly within this tradition, for example, "governments should intervene in private markets only where there are serious market failures" (Swanstrom, 2001, 481). This includes land markets, which experience market failures in two main areas: the inadequate provision of public goods and spillover effects. The core liberal tenets that inform the welfare economics framework are suspicious of purposeful interventions by state authorities, particularly where these involve positive aspirations beyond basic organization of land markets. Urban planning is, in the classic liberal schema, dangerously coercive. "If the goals of collaborative planning are to be achieved, then," the libertarian critic of urban planning, Mark Pennington (2002, 187) argues, "far from extending the range of state activities, there should be a reduction in the role of the social democratic planning and the extension of private markets."

7. The U.S. Senate proposed, as a regulatory "bookend" to the landmark National Environmental Policy Act of 1969, the National Land Use Policy Act (NLUPA). As John Nolon (1996) notes, NLUPA was adopted by a substantial majority in the Senate but it twice failed to pass in the House of Representatives. While national planning legislation continued to have political momentum in the early 1970s, Nixon's Watergate scandal killed it—and the U.S. still lacks an integrated national approach to land-use planning and spatial policy comparable to Britain or the Netherlands. Had the House passed NLUPA, the role of the state in private land development arguably would have be different.

8. As one example of such state-market complexity in practice, Stan Majoor (2008) calls attention to major publicly organized changes in Ørestad, located near Copenhagen. Though similar to mega-projects elsewhere, which tend to reflect "competitiveness-oriented constraints" on both the central state and local municipality, Majoor nonetheless maintains that this mega- project has also exhibited legitimate efforts to implement what he calls "progressive planning ideals," such as democracy and social justice, on the one hand, and socially mixed neighborhoods and environmentally qualities, on the other.

9. Economists operating within traditions of methodological individualism tend to emphasize how institutions constrain individual moral choices, rather than how collective moral and ethical habits constrain, shape, and indeed establish institutions. As an illustration, Hiser (2003, 7), in his piece in *Planning and Markets*, argues that "Institutional structure is seen as sets of rules that constrain people's moral choices." This hypothesis ignores the sociological and historical questions of how and why specific institutional structures form in the first place—or why they vary between societies.

10. Sanyal's edited book compares planning across countries in the developed and developing world, using the organizing idea of "planning culture," which is defined as "the collective ethos and dominant attitude of planners regarding the appropriate role of the state, market forces, and civil society in influencing social outcomes" (2005, xxi). Though arguably reflective of neo-Weberian assumptions about the "autonomous" role of the state in society, Sanyal accepts that planners' roles are conditioned by broader factors both within and outside the nation-state, such as history, legal traditions, and structures of governance. Most of the contributions to the volume show that to understand planning culture in a particular place requires setting it within the processes of socioeconomic and political change. Thus, in his chapter, Leaf (2005) illustrates the considerable complexity in China, concluding that globalization and the introduction of the market economy have had a significant impact on Chinese cities and institutions, but that this has been

overlaid on traditionalist structures of governance. Often traditionalism wins out, which means that no universal market–state relationship exists across the country. Banerjee (2005) explores the Indian case and develops the premise that planning culture is based on history and the contingency of institutions, while Cowherd (2005), in his excellent chapter on Indonesia, similarly explores the path from colonialism to economic liberalism. He suggests that planning culture has changed from a Dutch-influenced one to an American one. These three contributions illustrate the earlier premise that planning is conditioned by its broader context and the power battles that might be taking place. These can be external interests embedded in globalization, marketization, or colonialism, or local power elites.

References

Albrechts, L. 1991. "Changing Roles and Positions of Planners." *Urban Studies* 28(1): 123–13.

Albrechts, L. Patsy Healey, and Klaus R. Kunzmann. 2003. "Strategic Spatial Planning and Regional Governance in Europe." *Journal of the American Planning Association* 69(2): 113–30.

Alexander, E. 2001. "Why Planning vs. Markets Is An Oxymoron: Asking The Right Question." *Planning and Markets* 4(1): 1–6. Available at: *http://www-pam.usc.edu/volume6/v6i1a2s1.html*; accessed October 23, 2009.

Alexander, E. 2005. "Institutional Transformation and Planning: From Institutionalization Theory to Institutional Design." *Planning Theory* 4(3): 209–23.

Alexander, E. 2008. "Between State and Market: A Third Way of Planning." *International Planning Studies* 13(2): 119–32.

Altshuler, A. 1965. *The City Planning Process: A Political Analysis*. Ithaca, NY: Cornell University Press.

Banerjee, T. 2005. "Understanding Planning Cultures: The Kolkata Paradox." In *Comparative Planning Cultures*, by B. Sanyal, 145–63. New York and London: Routledge.

Bell, D. 1960. *The End of Ideology*. Glencoe, IL: Free Press. Repr. Cambridge, MA: Harvard University Press, 2000.

Blum, J. 1982. *The Progressive Presidents: Theodore Roosevelt, Woodrow Wilson, Franklin Roosevelt, Lyndon Johnson*. Toronto: Norton.

Brenner, N. 1999. "Globalization as Reterritorialisation." *Urban Studies* 36(7): 431–51.

Buitelaar, E. 2004. "A Transaction-cost Analysis of the Land Development Process." *Urban Studies* 41:2539–53.

Castells, M. 1996. *The Information Age*. Oxford: Blackwell.

Clavel, P. 1985. *The Progressive City*. Thousand Oaks, CA: Sage.

Cowherd, R. 2005. "Does Planning Culture Matter? Dutch and American models in Indonesian Urban Transformations." In *Comparative Planning Cultures*, by B. Sanyal, 165–92. New York and London: Routledge.

Cullingworth, J. B. 1993. *The Political Culture of Planning: American Land Use Planning in Comparative Perspective*. New York and London: Routledge.

Dierwechter, Y. 2008. *Urban Growth Management and Its Discontents: Promises, Practices and Geopolitics in U.S. City-Regions*. New York: Palgrave-Macmillan.

Esping-Anderson, G. 1990. *The Three Worlds of Welfare Capitalism*. Cambridge, UK: Polity Press.

Fainstein, S. S., N. I. Fainstein, R. Child-Hill, D. Judd, and M. P.Smith. 1983. *Restructuring the City: Political Economy of Urban Development*. New York: Longman.

Flyvbjerg, B. 1998. *Rationality and Power*. Chicago: University of Chicago Press.

Foglesong , R. 1986. *Planning the Capitalist City*. Princeton, NJ: Princeton University Press.

Forester, J. 1989. *Planning in the Face of Power*. Berkeley, CA: University of California Press.

Foley, D. 1960. "British Town Planning: One Ideology or Three?" *British Journal of Sociology* 11:211–31.

Friedman, M. 1962. *Capitalism and Freedom*. Chicago: University of Chicago Press.

Friedman, M., and R. Friedman. 1980. *Free to Choose*. Harmondsworth, UK: Penguin.

Friedmann, J. 1987. *Planning in the Public Domain*. Princeton, NJ: Princeton University Press.

Friedmann, J., and C. Weaver. 1980. *Territory and Function*. Berkeley, CA: University of California Press.

Fukuyama, F. 1995. *Trust*. New York: Free Press.

Haar, C. M., and J. S. Kayden, eds. 1989. *Zoning and the American Dream*. Chicago: American Planning Association.

Harvey, D. 1985. "On Planning the Ideology of Planning." In *Urbanization of Capital*, by David Harvey, 165–84. Oxford. UK: Basil Blackwell.

Hayek, F. 1944. *The Road to Serfdom*. London: Routledge. Repr. London: Routledge, 2001.

Hayek, F. 1960. *The Constitution of Liberty*. London: Routledge.

Hayek, F. 1982. *Law, Legislation and Liberty*. London: Routledge. Reprint of 3-vol. 1st ed., 1973, 1976, 1979.

Healey, P. 1992. "The Reorganization of State and Market in Planning." *Urban Studies* 29(3/4): 411–34.

Healey, P. 2003. Editorial. *Planning Theory and Practice* 4(1): 5–7.

Held, D., A. McGrew, D. Goldblatt, and J. Perraton. 1999. *Global Transformations: Politics, Economics and Culture*. Cambridge, UK: Polity Press.

Hiser, R. 2003. "Moral Consequences of Institutional Structure Planning and Markets." *Planning and Markets* 6(1): 7–13. Available at: *http://www-pam.usc.edu/volume6/v6i1a2s1.html*; accessed October 23, 2009.

Hutton, W. 1995. *The State We're In*. London: Cape.

Ihlanfeldt, K. 2009. "Does Comprehensive Land-Use Planning Improve Cities?" *Land Economics* 85(1): 74–86.

Jacobs, J. 1961. *The Death and Life of Great American Cities*. New York: Random House.

Keynes, J. M. 1936. *General Theory of Employment, Interest and Money*. London: Macmillan. Repr. Houndsmill, UK, and New York: Palgrave Macmillan, 2007.

Klosterman, R. E. 1985. "Arguments For and Against Planning." *Town Planning Review* 56(1): 5–20.

Krueckeberg, D., ed. 1983/1997. *Introduction to Planning History in the United States*. New Brunswick, NJ: Center for Urban Policy Research.

Lai, Henry Wai-Chung. 2005. "Neo-institutional Economics and Planning Theory." *Planning Theory* 4(1): 7–19.

Lai, Shih-Kung. 2002. "Information Structures Exploration as Planning for a Unitary Organization." *Planning and Markets* 5(1): 32–41.

Leaf, M. 2005. "Modernity Confronts Tradition: The Professional Planner and Local Corporatism in the Rebuilding of China's Cities." In *Comparative Planning Cutures*, by B. Sanyal, 91–111. New York and London: Routledge.

Lindblom, C. E. 1977. *Politics and Markets.* New York: Basic Books.

Macmillan, H. 1938. *The Middle Way.* London: Macmillan.

Majoor, S. 2008. "Progressive Planning Ideals in a Neo-liberal Context; The Case of Orestad Copenhagen." *International Planning Studies* 13(2): 101–17.

Mannheim, K. 1940. *Man and Society in an Age of Reconstruction.* New York: Harcourt Brace.

Mannheim, K 1954. *Ideology and Utopia: An Introduction to the Sociology of Knowledge.* London: Routledge & Kegan Paul.

McAuslan, P. 1980. *The Ideologies of Planning Law.* Oxford: Pergamon.

Mumford, L. 1938. *The Culture of Planning.* New York: Harcourt Brace.

Mumford, L. 1961. *The City in History.* New York: Harcourt Brace.

Newman, P., and A. Thornley. 1996. *Urban Planning in Europe: International Competition, National Systems and Planning Projects.* London and New York: Routledge.

Nolon, J. 1996. "The National Land Use Policy Act." *Pace Environmental Law Review* 13: 519–23.

Ohmae, K. 1990. *The Borderless World.* New York: Harper Business.

Olds, K. 2001. *Globalization and Urban Change: Capital, Culture, and Pacific Rim Mega-projects.* New York: Oxford University Press.

Pennington, M. 2002. "A liberal HAYEKIAN critique of collaborative planning." In *Planning Futures: New Directions in Planning Theory,* edited by P. Allmendinger, 187–205. London: Routledge.

Polanyi, K. 1944. *The Great Transformation: The Political and Economic Origins of our Time.* Boston: Beacon Press. Repr. Boston: Beacon Press, 2001.

Purcell, M. 2008. "Resisting Neoliberalization: Communicative Planning or Counter-Hegemonic Movements?" *Planning Theory* 8(2): 140–65.

Reade, E. J. 1987. *British Town and Country Planning.* Milton Keynes, UK: Open University Press.

Sanyal, B. 2005. *Comparative Planning Cultures.* New York and London: Routledge.

Sassen, S. 1991. *The Global City: New York, London, Tokyo.* Princeton, NJ: Princeton University Press.

Scholte, J. A. 2000. *Globalization: A Critical Introduction.* Basingstoke, UK: Palgrave/Macmillan.

Scott, M. 1969. *American City Planning Since 1990.* Berkeley, CA: University of California Press.

Sharp, T. 1940. *Town Planning.* Harmondsworth, UK: Penguin.

Skocpol, T. 1985. "Bringing the State Back In: Strategies of Analysis in Current Research." In *Bringing the State Back In,* edited by P. Evans et al., 3–43. Cambridge, UK, and New York: Cambridge University Press.

Skowronek, S. 1982. *Building a New American State.* Cambridge, UK, and New York: Cambridge University Press.

Skowronek, S (1995) "Order and Change." *Polity* 28(1): 91–96.

Swanstrom T. 2001. "What We Argue about When We Argue about Regionalism." *Journal of Urban Affairs* 29(5): 479–96.

Thornley, A. 1993. *Urban Planning under Thatcherism: The Challenge of the Market,* 2nd ed. London: Routledge.

Webster, C. 1998. "Public Choice, Pigouvian and Coasian Planning Theory." *Urban Studies 35(1): 53–75.*

CHAPTER 4

THE EVOLUTION OF THE INSTITUTIONAL APPROACH IN PLANNING

ANNETTE M. KIM

WE have witnessed unimaginable change: American consumers recycling and buying green, pedestrians and bikes taking over Times Square, the end of the cold war and entrepreneurs and private corporations proliferating in Russia and China, a popularly elected black president. To people in the 1970s and 1980s, each of those occurrences would have seemed impossible—laughable, even. They would have involved too many fundamental changes in our institutions: our norms, our ingrained habits, our political interests, and our economic interests, not to mention our laws and regulations. How did these changes come to pass?

Many have tried to explain these changes; one emerging idea is that they involved a phenomenon spreading among everyday people. While it is true that national recessions usually bring about a change in political party dominance and that race relations in the United States have been evolving, Obama's election has also been attributed to grassroots networking and social media, to celebrity support, to easy media coverage, and to the way his campaign was able to package his narrative (Briscoe et al. 2008). While planners have long been advocating for more public space for bikes and pedestrians, and the 1991 ISTEA act provided significant federal subsidies, cities did not take advantage of them unless there was enough local support and advocacy (Handy and McCann 2011). And in trying to explain how China's strong-arm government has been able to change and grow the economy so quickly, scholars are now pointing to factors beyond the state—to an underreported social phenomenon (Ho 2005).

The question of institutional change is core to planning. In our pursuit of prosperous, just, healthy, and beautiful cities, planners must inevitably turn their attention to institutions. Knowledge about institutions is central to urban planning endeavors because planning is more than a scholarly enterprise, but it is oriented on the premise of action, intervening in the world for the greater good. An institutionalist perspective recognizes that planning is not so much about action as about *interaction*. In other words, finding ways to improve economic growth, sustainability, or livability—to name a few common contemporary goals of planning—ultimately requires coordination of actors and organizations that are mediated through institutions.

Now, more than ever, planners and planning scholars are referring to the importance of institutions in their work and research. For example, in reviewing recent issues of some of the major planning journals, one finds planners invoking "institutions" to refer to:

- collaboration (Wang and Lee 2007)
- contracts (Whittington and Dowall 2006)
- culture (Holloway et al. 2000)
- government (Doig 1993; Blumenberg 2002; Buitelaar and Lagendijk 2007)
- governance (Goetz et al. 2003; Leach 2006; Zierhofer 2007)
- industries or economic sectors (Peterson 1997)
- localities (Henry and Pinch 2001; Salet and Thornley 2007)
- market structure (Wojcik 2005)
- norms (Holloway et al. 2000)
- policy (Holloway et al. 2000)
- regulation (Wojcik 2005; Buitelaar and Lagendijk 2007; Litman 2008)
- rules and laws (Salet 2002)
- organizations (Bebbington and Kothari 2006)
- power (Clark and Jones 2001)
- representation (Clark and Jones 2001)
- social networks and information flows (Clark and Jones 2001; Tompkins, Adger, and Brown 2002)
- universities (Bannon 1999; Mitchell 2001)

This chapter discusses the concept of institutions and explains why it is of central importance to planning. The definition of what an institution is and how to study it has undergone major overhauls in the last thirty to forty years. The institutional turn needs to be understood as part of a larger trend in the social sciences. As such, I will outline the intellectual history of institutions and describe current events that surround the resurgence of this vital concept. Although disparate new institutionalist projects across the social sciences were often at odds with one another, planning as an interdisciplinary enterprise has been particularly adept at incorporating the various concepts for its purposes. With several decades of new institutionalist research to build on, we can also outline some of the major limitations and gaps in this approach and discuss some promising directions going forward.

1. Why the Exuberance in Institutionalism?

Planning has often been conceived of as an enterprise framed in dualities: state versus market, public versus private, top-down versus bottom-up, incremental versus rational, and so on. While nearly every piece of writing so framed acknowledges that real situations are more complicated and that the dualities are only meant to be used for analytic ease, their predominance nonetheless creates some major pitfalls. For one, overly strong dualities or over-reliance on dualities work to miss whole swathes of society and concerns. For example, it is hard to fit in or not marginalize civil associations in a public versus private duality or climate change in a state versus market duality. So, one of the reasons for moving toward an institutional approach in planning is to increase the realism of modeling problems and to pluralize the objectives of planning, as well as to open up the field of explanatory variables considered for understanding situations and possible solutions. But, in addition to widening the phenomena considered, an institutional approach helps to integrate the dualities. Often, the very problems in planning do not reside in the false choice between state/market or public/private, but in the question of how they work together. As we travel in this section through the different stages and quarters of institutionalism, as the definition of what an institution is expands, we will see each turn coming as a critique of the inadequacy of pre-existing paradigms to explain current events and concerns.

By the 1970s, neoclassical economic theory had gained increasing currency in policymaking and, meanwhile, the field of economics had become increasingly abstracted into mathematical modeling. The dominant role of economics in the social sciences was further bolstered, initially, by the fall of the Berlin wall when confidence and support for a private-market economic system was high and being used to determine an increasing number and array of public resource and planning decisions. The model of the market economy was based on assumptions about predictable, natural human behavior, and so the institutions that were needed to shape that behavior and make the market function properly were clear. Legal property rights to protect wealth and promote investment, access to capital through banks, and the free flow of market information were key. In terms of urban planning practice, neoclassical notions of institutional reform included the privatization of state-owned property, the devolution of planning responsibilities and fiscal decisions down to local government, and the proliferation of public–private partnerships. Some planners and many economists argued that if only people were freed from the grabbing hands of the state, markets would happen and function naturally, since optimizing people have always privately engaged in trading (Beito et al. 2002).

In time, however, it became apparent that it was not so easy to form market economies. Many of the transition economies that were pursuing the prescribed list of reforms were having major difficulties with unemployment and inflation. Furthermore, decades of lackluster reform efforts in developing countries underscored that functional market economies were not so inevitable. Meanwhile, other economies were growing rapidly despite, or perhaps because of, heavy state intervention. Interest in "new institutional" economics spread during the 1980s and 1990s primarily because core theories in the fields were not explaining well the world around us.

New institutional economics modified the neoclassical model, which lacked an appreciation for how institutions are an integral part of making markets work. An enduring definition of "institution" is North's (1991, 97) "humanly devised constraints that structure political, economic and social interaction." The social constraints are important in helping to make behaviors more predictable. The revelatory corollary for economists, but foundational for sociology, is that we do not just make any choice that benefits us personally, but society has sway over the individual, influencing his or her behavior. While this insight has the far-reaching implication that there may be many kinds of considerations pulling us in different directions, the earlier new institutional economics literature moved modestly from the neoclassical model conceiving of primarily business institutions. Its work was to show its own discipline how these institutions mattered. Instead of taking institutions as a given, their variation and how they impacted behavior and the economy became a focus of inquiry. The property-rights group of new institutional economists focused on how formal institutions such as different legal and banking systems and policies helped or hindered market functions (Hart 1995). The transaction-cost group expanded the definition of institutions to also include the details of what makes business feasible, such as contracts, insurance, and brokers (Williamson 1996). So conceived, institutions exist to help offset the real-world costs of finding one another, obtaining information, conducting negotiations, and mitigating risks. The absence or underdevelopment of these institutions could help to explain why markets were more complicated to build than previously thought. Whether laws or contracts, institutions are conceived of as a design choice that could be redesigned. The new institutional economics approach was easily adopted by more positivistic planners trying to analyze how infrastructure, land, and other publicly managed systems could improve efficiency and welfare gains (Alexander 1992; Lai and Webster 2003; Moulaert 2005; Whittington and Dowall 2006).

Some schools in the other social science disciplines, particularly sociology and political science, roundly criticized the economics rational choice model of institutions and human behavior. Essentially, the biggest omission in the economic story of institutions is power. Instead of being motivated by narrow conceptions of economic self-interest, human behavioral motivations are more complex, ranging from desires to be social to desires to dominate. Furthermore, institutions are not the amalgation of individual choices but, rather, the product of inherently social and political processes. Instead of viewing institutions as exogeneous constraints upon agents, they are embedded in the agents who also help to reproduce them.

While there are many critiques of the neoclassical economics model, there have also been sharp differences between the "old" and "new" institutionalists in economic sociology and political economy. Others have more carefully discussed the fuller group of scholars in each school and the distinctions between them (DiMaggio and Powell 1983; Hirsch and Lunsbury 1997; Granovetter 2002; Moulaert 2005), but here I draw some generalizations to be able to discuss some of the major philosophical and methodological differences in their conceptualizations of institutions and their implications for planners. The earlier generation of institutionalists, such as Thorstein Veblen and John Commons, were political economists who drew attention to how major organizations within the economy—such as firms, bureaus, industries, or labor—had their own interests and logics. Instead of assuming common, apolitical motivations, their analysis identified different interests, key agents, social networks, and alliances to understand why the organizations formed, varied, and changed. It also focused on how commitment to the organization was socialized into its members.

More recently, economic sociologists have moved in two different directions. Some sociologists have focused on power, conceiving institutions from a broader, historical point of view and examining how social structures have shaped cognitive scripts that in turn shaped behavior and organizations. For example, Bourdieu (1977) showed how pervasively colonialism affected Algerians' diminished aspirations, which ultimately compromised their choices. Others analyzed the similarities between organizational forms and the ways in which they began to mimic one another (DiMaggio and Powell 1983). Still others focus on the importance of social networks and the spreading of information. A lively debate ensued between "oversocialized sociologists," who saw people as hopelessly handcuffed by dark, structural forces, and "interactionists," who focused on the mechanics without seeing the interests of power being the more relevant story (Granovetter 1985; Collet 2003; Bourdieu 2005).

This debate became heated and more compelling because current events were challenging old theories (Burawoy 2001; Eyal et al. 2001). With the end of the cold war and the collapse of the socialist economic systems around the world, a new globalized world system was forming and it needed to be understood. Planning theorists made important intellectual contributions by critically mapping the links between global, national, and local institutions, and between first and third worlds, with a critical lens (Castells 1996; Storper 1997; Roy 2010). Socialist studies became comparative economies—and actually a comparison of capitalisms. And it seemed there was quite a lot of variation to observe between the transition countries who had pursued similar market-oriented institutional reforms. For example, in some cases, capitalism was forming under a communist political system, without a propertied bourgeoisie, or with oligarchs (Eyal et al. 1998; Woodruff 2000). Furthermore, the Western democracies had major differences in how labor, corporations, and government entities interacted (Hall and Soskice 2001). In some ways, it was obvious that variations in capitalism should occur, since the transitions were located in very different places with different histories, endowments, and legacies.

Given the important variations, early planning theory's dualities (private versus public, market versus state) are clearly outdated. They do not explain the strange bedfellows in the world and the variations between places. Some proposed moving to a market–state–civil society triad (Richardson and Gordon 1993). Some planning researchers and theorists called upon planners to adopt a new institutionalist approach in order to better ground their analysis (Alexander 1992; Innes 1995; Healey 1999; Whittington and Dowall 2006). However, as Verma (2007) notes, most of the theoretical development about institutions came from the other social sciences.

One major exception, however, is the insight from regional planners about the persistent importance of local institutions, even in a rapidly globalizing world. People had first assumed that with increased globalization, financial capital, and the elites who manage it, could capriciously move around the world to the latest areas of comparative advantage, leaving those who were not part of the elite networks stuck in vulnerable places on the ground. However, regional scholars countered that a locality's comparative advantage was based on more than natural resources, infrastructure, and costs savings. It included institutions such as tacit knowledge that are based on face-to-face interactions grounded in a local culture of embedded routines, habits, and norms (Saxenian 1996; Storper 1997). Since space still mattered, planning had much it could contribute to our understanding of globalization processes. In terms of practice, economic development planning emphasized the promotion of regional clustering and specialization with synergistic interdependencies. Associations, networking, training, and finance programs were used to try to facilitate the sharing of information, creation of productive norms and relationships, and innovation (Henry and Pinch 2001). The hopeful message of this research was that cities could play a proactive role in making spatially oriented economic development investments promoting soft assets to make themselves more globally competitive (Florida 2002). Ironically, the challenge was to not ultimately resort to a boilerplate institutionalist approach, which would run counter to the original premise that localities had important specificities (Amin 1999).

This review of the intellectual trajectory of new institutionalism accounts for the wide-ranging conceptions of planning institutions listed at the beginning of the chapter. Despite the disparate new institutionalisms, what they have in common is still significant. They all emphasize the socially constructed nature of institutions. The implications of this are profound. If they are created, then they are not naturally occurring, even though some institutional literature tried to argue that certain types of legal or economic institutions are based on natural human instincts. If they are socially created, this opens up the recognition of a plurality of possible institutional frameworks, as we can empirically observe. Social construction also implies that institutions can be reconstructed and significant social change is possible. This is particularly exciting for planning, which pursues normative goals of improving society. However, if these are institutionalism's strengths, they are also connected to its weaknesses.

2. Problems with New Institutionalism

2.1 Lack of Conceptual Clarity

A major difficulty with new institutionalism is that many disciplines with fundamentally different philosophies about human behavior, worldviews, and methods are using the same term to mean very different things. It has been like a frontier territory upon which anyone can stake a claim with the flimsiest of tents. Feel free to make your own personal definition. Markusen (1999) offers an amusing critique of its fuzzy concepts, indicated by the proliferation of new vocabulary ending with -isms, -ologies, and -izations.

More problematic, until recently any clear interdisciplinary dialogue about institutions was rare. At the millennium, scholars from several disciplines recognized the need for the social science equivalent of a unifying theory outlining the relationship between institutions and individuals. Granovetter (2002) summed it up well when he proposed that this theory needs to integrate how social norms, instrumental self-interest, trust, and power jointly motivate and shape economic action. Furthermore, this theory needs to be dynamic enough to explain institutional change.

2.2 Lack of Policy Relevance

Some scholars have argued that by focusing on disembodied processes and language rather than on people, planning theory obfuscates agency and responsibility (Mandelbaum 1985; Markusen 1999). Furthermore, planning theory's objects of study have increasingly become planners themselves and planning processes. Navel-gazing fails to address urgent issues such as how spatial planning can disenfranchise segments of the population, destroy the environment, and exacerbate racial/ethnic divisions. Critics claim that part of the problem is that most planning theoreticians are American and European and still parochially assume the preoccupations and political institutions of the "northwest." They advocate a Global

South planning theory, which would focus on basic material concerns such as land (Connell 2007; Sanyal 2008; Watson 2008; Yiftachel 2006).

Even though the new regional planning had policy implications that gained a wide audience, some questioned its usefulness. Many of the studies focused on the unique characteristics of a successful place in order to mine causal factors so that other cities and regions could try to mimic their dynamic. But, how many Silicon Valleys can there be in the world? Markusen further argues that an over-emphasis on endogenous factors may overlook the policy-relevant role that larger scale institutions play. For example, in Silicon Valley, large defense-contract invest-ment in the electronics industry may have laid the foundation for its future success. National governments can better coordinate the macroeconomic conditions that localities cannot determine, such as increasing demand through public spending, expansion of credit, and creating linkages. More recent studies interested in plan-ning at multiple scales investigate the links between multinational, national, and local institutions.

2.3 Uncritical of Power

Some have argued that new institutional economics and some economic sociolo-gists' emphasis on organizational issues and micro-analysis of economic interac-tions obfuscates the more sinister structural forces at play. The social networks available to people are not randomly distributed. Institutions such as norms and habits are not innocuous elements of culture but, rather, are reinforced by the social structure and governmental and financial institutions to constrain and condition people with lower social positions to make choices that are not in their best interest (Burawoy 2001; Collet 2003; Bourdieu 2005). Institutionalism does not pay enough attention to the role of elites in dominating the institutional order (Jessop 2001; MacLeod 2001). The institutions that they study may be the product of strategic forces, and focusing narrowly on the institutional mechanisms only helps to reify them. Or less normatively, without considering the power imbalances, our under-standing of a situation may be incomplete and lead us to biased conclusions. For example, the rosy case studies of cooperative yet competitive regional economies do not mention that the industries have poor labor standards and records of social responsibility (Markusen 1999).

However, an examination into the uniqueness of local institutions does not require one to overlook the larger power dynamics. Indeed, they need to be thor-oughly considered in order to identify the relevant institutions and dynamics behind outcomes. To deny local specificities would mean that structuralists would be slipping into another conceptual hegemony where elites dominate absolutely, end of story. Empirical observations show that the story is not so simple. For exam-ple, studies show that old Communist Party members did not benefit economi-cally in the transition. In central Europe, it was the young and educated, as well as those who were able to form alliances with the new politocracy and opinion-making intellectual elites, who tended to become wealthier, not the former political elites (Svejnar 1996; Eyal et al. 1998). In China, too, while cadre members might have enjoyed some market power at the beginning of transition, financial returns to political elites declined as the market expanded (Nee 1989). Other examples include the underreported cases in which the politically disenfranchised have been able to increase their property rights standing and land compensation by making alliances in intergovernmental conflicts (Abramson, 2011; Kim, 2011; Po, 2011; Sorensen, 2011; Webster & Zhao, 2011; Whiting, 2011) . How institutions and power interact to affect the material conditions of those being planned is a complex subject that deserves further study.

More recent treatments of power appreciate that the most powerful individuals and groups in society have a limit on how much they can coerce society into normalizing change. Current frameworks examine not only power but also the resistance to power as part of an ongoing social reconstruction process (Silbey and Ewick 2003). And part of this negotiation of power happens in the cognitive realm when power's legitimacy is contested. Communicative, critical, and discursive planning theories are pertinent here. In their view, planners are part of the institutional framework; through their personal interactions, relationships, and mundane activities, they condition and influence others by how they frame situations. We can be a cog in the wheel of institutional reproduction or we can shed light on how our discursive practices reify power relations and suggest alternative knowledge and discourses (Forester 1993; Weber 2002).

2.4 Does Not Explain Institutional Change

Institutional literature has primarily focused on examining current institutions to explain the conditions we observe. Ideas about how institutions change are as yet underdeveloped. Most economists conceive of institutions as emerging, declining, and changing as a response to changing costs and benefits in the economic environment. Agents in society find that they need a change in institutions in order to take advantage of new opportunities (Demsetz 1967). Economic models assumed that society is a single, rational agent that will choose institutions based on some aggregated social optimum. More realistically, political economists tweak the model to explain that in other cases we see suboptimal outcomes because of the relative benefits to powerful elites and the mechanisms they use to maintain political power (Acemoglu and Robinson 2008).

Instead of viewing processes of institutional change as a rational design choice, evolutionary economics uses Darwinian concepts of variation, replication, and selection of social technologies that occur through processes of individual and collective learning. Also, using a longer term perspective, path-dependent models of institutional change posited that institutions are constrained by the vestiges of previous institutions. For example, eastern European transition countries' industries communication and production networks were shaped by Soviet-era relationships between state-owned enterprises and local government (Stark and Bruszt 2001). The comparative historical political scientists have made significant contributions in this regard by combining situated, nuanced understandings of local institutions and histories with a comparative analytical framework to identify some causal factors (Skocpol 1979; Thelen 1999; Hall and Soskice 2001).

However, a key question is how constrained societies are by their pasts. One depressing implication could be that some places have the right institutional endowments and others do not and are headed down inescapable paths (Diamond 1999; Pomeranz 2001; Fritsch 2004). Unlike the framework of new institutional economists who vested agents with the ability to choose optimal designs, in a heavily structured worldview, discontinuous, major economic change is not possible except through evolutionary processes so gradual that particular administrations or generations make little impact. But, the reality is that we have seen amazing cases of major economic reorganization that produced rapid economic growth (Rodrik, Subramanian, and Trebbi 2004). In particular, these economic success stories require us to return some degree of agency and importance to the role of state planners (Evans, Skocpol, and Rueschemeyer 1985; Amsden 1989). However, while allowing the state back into the market is important, it is only a partial answer. Just as there are authoritarian states with an export-oriented development agenda whose economies have not grown, there are democratic regimes that have also grown remarkably (Rodrik and Wacziarg 2005). Furthermore, ethnographic studies of major economic growth cases suggest that it was not the state alone but its engagement of a widespread social phenomenon that precipitated institutional change (Ho 2005; Kim 2008).

3. LATEST DIRECTIONS: BEYOND NEW INSTITUTIONALISM

Exciting points of convergence have been emerging across the disciplines that can lead us out of the disparate new institutionalisms and better illuminate the process of institutional change. As the previous section discussed, the different social science disciplines had little to do with each other in the first iteration of new institutionalism. However, now there has been the beginnings of meaningful communication between some of the leading figures in economics and sociology in turning their attention to the critical role of cognition (North 2005; Greif 2006; Nee and Swedberg 2007).

One of the reasons for the turn to cognition is that there are important questions left unanswered. Greif (2006) points out that when fellow economists refer to rules and laws as institutions because they provide some bounds on agent behavior through credible commitment of enforcement, this pushes the real question back to what is motivating the behavior of the enforcer. From where does the larger dynamic between agent and enforcer emanate? He suggests that norms, beliefs, and culture are the microfoundations that build institutions such as law or finance.

Douglass North is another proponent of the cognitive realm as an area needing research. He reserves economics' rational agent model for relatively stable, competitive market situations when rules might be known and followed. However, in times of major institutional change involving novel situations, multiple agents, collective action, and high uncertainty, even the most rational of agents can no longer follow their normal decision-making processes. He advocates the development of "cognitive institutionalism" that incorporates how agents learn new paradigms (Denzau and North 1994; Mantzavinos, North, and Sharig 2004; North 2005).

Some sociologists are also making the call for the cognitive turn. In cases of major institutional change, old cognitive frameworks are challenged and reconstructed, leading to new behaviors and actions. These cases represent opportunities for reflective cognitive processes as opposed to habitual, automatic processes (DiMaggio 1997). Cognition is a difficult sell in sociology because structuralists have derided past sociological attempts to conceptualize the mental realm by reducing culture to shared values, norms, and attitudes rather than viewing culture as a resource that is put to strategic use by elites. However, a little room for interdisciplinary openness was created by the unpredictable results of the transition countries (Eyal et al. 2001).

Another reason for the cognitive turn is the tremendous growth in the field of the cognitive neurosciences, with its advances in technology and research. Humans have advanced neural systems that are specialized for channeling attention, detecting causal structures in their environment, processing that information into abstract form, and adapting behavior accordingly. Much of cognitive science research does not lend itself to the social sciences because it either examines the behavioral idiosyncrasies of individuals or universal, physiological functioning. But, some of it can be helpful in detailing the mechanisms of the social-construction process of institution building and also can have profound implications for practice. Interestingly, cross-cultural research in cognitive development provides evidence that there are few universal psychological processes, in part because human development is so intimately tied to how societies make meaning of their world in a particular place and time (Rogoff 1990). An approach currently being taken by such disciplines as cross-cultural psychology, social psychology, cultural anthropology, and cognitive sociology explores how society interacts with agent cognition, thereby dispensing with the old structure-versus-agency duality.

The social cognition approach is particularly relevant to planning because planners study interactions and transactions between people. Planning's economic development literature has identified the need to promote learning, adaptive mindsets, and a reflexive rationality (Sabel 1994; Jessop 2001). This is advocated, however, without the employment of cognitive science research that is showing us how we learn and change our ways of thinking (Amin 1999).

Take the issue of attention, for example. Perception of new information is not automatic. Most policies and development projects assume attention to the information and institutional paraphernalia that the project is producing. They also assume that it will mean the same thing to each society. But research has shown that we do not pay attention to everything, but that our attention is shaped by our peers and the socially esteemed. This is related to the process of vicarious learning. One of the most powerful ways we acquire and adopt new information and practices is by watching other people whom we are predisposed to pay attention to and who are within our social circles. These insights could be important in helping to keep economic development strategies from adopting boilerplate clustering and capacity-building programs. It suggests that there might be limited value in training programs through lectures by strangers or the introduction of specific institutional paraphernalia such as associations. Instead, a different set of questions would need to be answered. Who is supposed to be learning exactly and to whom do they pay attention? What are the relationships present in a particular society through which people might learn vicariously? How would people in the project have the opportunity to observe and interact with one another? Answering such questions might explain the difference between ineffectual policies and meaningful institutional change, in which new ideas have entered people's consciousness and been absorbed into social relations so that new behaviors and expectations result, reifying the change in institutions (Kim 2008).

The process of social cognition has many similarities with consensus building and planning theory's contemporary interest in communicative action. The move toward social cognition theory is an extension of this trend, in two regards. One is that the scale of social change addressed by social cognition is broader. While bringing people physically together in a forum can help build bridges between people who had misconceptions about a project or did not trust each other (Forester 1987; Healey 1992; Innes 1996; Susskind, McKearnan, and Thomas-Larmer 1999), the unimaginable changes we started this chapter with are much larger in scale. Significant changes happen outside of meetings. So although both communicative rationality and social cognition emphasize the importance of socialization and communication (Forester 1993), social cognition also advocates engaging preexisting social networks, as well as celebrities and other leaders who influence people's choices.

Another major difference between social cognition and communicative rationality is that Habermasian ideal speech assumes people are hyper-conscious and articulate, whereas many studies have shown that the majority of communication is neither verbal nor textual. Social cognition emphasizes the role of the visual. It also emphasizes what is happening on the recipient's—not the speaker's—end. Recipients may not be sitting down trying to listen, but they may pick up observations and ideas communicated through example, in unofficial settings. This has profound implications for planners in terms of (a) where effective practice should take place, (b) the kinds of people and technologies they should be engaging, and (c) the kinds of symbols that will communicate and resonate.

4. CONCLUSION

Despite the myriad definitions and deficiencies, the focus on the role of institutions at the end of the twentieth century, across the social science disciplines, has been important and promising for planning for two reasons. First, all of the new institutionalisms discuss how institutions are socially constructed rather than naturally occurring. Their socially constructed nature helps to explain why we see such variation around the world. Second, as a corollary, because they are constructed, they can also be reconstructed. Change is possible.

However, the new institutionalist projects must further study how institutions change, how power relations are renegotiated in this process, and how these cognitive, social construction processes might be connected with material conditions and outcomes that can inform current planning practice. A research agenda should:

a. Conduct empirical research into how power has interacted with positive, institutional innovations. One strategy for doing this would be to extend the scope of our studies beyond innovations in businesses and economic development to include labor, the displaced, and the disenfranchised. If we studied instances of institutional change where there have been movements away from elite domination, our findings might suggest planning implications.

b. Develop research that capitalizes upon and contributes to cognitive science research in order to find out how we might more effectively promote learning and social change. The challenge will be to disentangle socially contingent factors from neurologically functioning factors and understand how they interact. Unfortunately, the two have been conflated in neuroscience research design—a misconception that applied social sciences like planning could address. Given the recent criticisms of planning theory, this research agenda should connect these social, cognitive processes to material, spatial impacts.

c. Question the methodology of institutional analysis. Usually, methods involve a case study or, sometimes, quantitative analysis, where the tested variable is an institution or institutional factor. Is institutional analysis, then, any different from other methods? Like the theory, the methods could benefit from conceptual clarification.

Planning practice that aims toward large institutional changes rather than incremental ones should incorporate the empirical lessons of contemporary history and the latest findings in cognitive science. Furthermore, if we retain our strengths in empirical research grounded in real places, and multiscalar, interdisciplinary analysis, then planning practice and research can make policy-relevant contributions to our understanding of social cognition change. Knowledge about the social cognition process can help planners to more effectively engage in fundamental change.

NOTE

A substantially similar version of this chapter appeared in the *Journal of the American Planning Association* as Kim (2011), and is reproduced here with permission.

REFERENCES

Abramson, D. (2011). Transitional property rights and local developmental history in China. *Urban Studies,* 48(3): 529–551.

Acemoglu, D., and J. A. Robinson. 2008. "Persistence of Power, Elites, and Institutions." *American Economic Review* 98(1): 267–93.

Alexander, E. R. 1992. "A Transaction Cost Theory of Planning." *Journal of the American Planning Association* 58(2): 190–200.

Amin, A. 1999. "An Institutionalist Perspective on Regional Economic Development." *International Journal of Urban and Regional Research* 23(2): 365–78.

Amsden, A. H. 1989. *Asia's Next Giant: South Korea and Late Industrialization.* New York: Oxford University Press.

Bannon, M. J. 1999. "Dublin Town Planning Competititon: Ashbee and Chettie's 'New Dublin-A Study in Civics.'" *Planning Perspectives* 14(2): 145–62.

Bebbington, A., and U. Kothari. 2006. "Transnational development networks." *Environment and Planning Part A* 38(5): 849–66.

Beito, D. T., P. Gordon, et al. 2002. "Toward a Rebirth of Civil Society." In *The Voluntary City: Choice, Community, and Civil Society,* edited by D. T. Beito, P. Gordon, and A. Tabarrok, 33–34. Ann Arbor, MI: University of Michigan Press.

Blumenberg, E. 2002. "Planning for the Transportation Needs of Welfare Participants: Institutional Challenges to Collaborative Planning." *Journal of Planning Education and Research* 22:152–63.

Bourdieu, P. 1977. *Outline of a Theory of Practice.* New York: Cambridge University Press.

Bourdieu, P. 2005. *The Social Structure of the Economy.* Malden, MD: Polity Press.

Briscoe, D., E. Clift, K. Connolly, P. Goldman, D. Stone, N. Summers, and E. Thomas. November 17, 2008. "How He Did It." *Newsweek,* 152(20): 38–49.

Buitelaar, E., and A. Lagendijk. 2007. "A Theory of Institutional Change: Illustrated by Dutch City-Provinces and Dutch Land Policy." *Environment and Planning Part A* 39:891–908.

Burawoy, M. 2001. "Neoclassical Sociology: From the End of Communism to the End of Classes." *American Journal of Sociology* 106(4): 1099–120.

Castells, M. 1996. *The Rise of the Network Society.* Cambridge, MA: Blackwell.

Clark, J. R. A., and A. Jones. 2001. "Territorial Policies and Transformative Politics? Agri-environmentalism in Central Spain." *Environment and Planning Part A* 33(11): 2049–69.

Collet, F. 2003. "Economic Social Action and Social Network Influences." Discussion around Mark Granovetter Sociology of Economic Life, European Sociological Association Conference, Murcia, Spain.

Connell, R. 2007. *Southern Theory: The Global Dynamics of Knowledge in Social Science.* Sydney: Allen and Unwin.

Demsetz, H. 1967. "Toward a Theory of Property Rights." *American Economic Review* 57(May): 347–59.

Denzau, A. T., and D. C. North. 1994. "Shared Mental Models: Ideologies and Institutions." *Kyklos* 47(1): 3–31.

Diamond, J. 1999. *Guns, Germs, and Steel: The Fates of Human Societies*. New York: Norton.

DiMaggio, P. J. 1997. "Culture and Cognition." *Annual Review of Sociology* 23:263–87.

DiMaggio, P. J., and W. W. Powell. 1983. "The Iron Cage Revisited: Institutional Isomorphism and Collective Rationality in Organizational Fields." *American Sociological Review* 48(2): 147–60.

Doig, J. W. (1993). "Expertise, Politics, and Technological Change." *Journal of the American Planning Association* 59(1): 31–44.

Evans, P., T. Skocpol, and D. Rueschemeyer, eds. 1985. *Bringing the State Back In*. New York: Cambridge University Press.

Eyal, G., I. Szelenyi., E. Townsley, et al. 1998. *Making Capitalism without Capitalists: The New Ruling Elites in Eastern Europe*. New York: Verso.

Eyal, G., I. Szelenyi, E. Townsley, et al. 2001. "The Utopia of Postsocialist Theory and the Ironic View of History in Neoclassical Sociology." *American Journal of Sociology* 106(4): 1121–28.

Florida, R. L. 2002. *The Rise of the Creative Class and How It's Transforming Work, Leisure, Community and Everyday Life*. New York: Basic Books.

Forester, J. 1987. "Planning in the Face of Conflict: Negotiation and Mediation Strategies in Local Land Use Regulation." *Journal of the American Planning Association*, 53(3): 303–314.

Forester, J. 1993. *Critical Theory, Public Policy, and Planning Practice: Toward a Critical Pragmatism*. Albany, NY: State University of New York Press.

Fritsch, M. 2004. "Entrepreneurship, Entry and Performance of New Business Compared in Two Growth Regimes: East and West Germany." *Journal of Evolutionary Economics* 14:525–42.

Goetz, E. J., K. Chapple, B. Lukerman, et al. 2003. "Enabling Exclusion: The Retreat from Regional Fair Share Housing in the Implementation of the Minnesota Land Use Planning Act." *Journal of Planning Education and Research* 22:213–25.

Granovetter, M. 1985. "Economic Action and Social Structure: The Problem of Embeddedness." *American Journal of Sociology* 91(11): 481–510.

Granovetter, M. 2002. "A Theoretical Agenda for Economic Sociology." In *The New Economic Sociology: Developments in an Emerging Field*, edited by M. F. Guillen, C. Randall, P. England, and M. Meyer, 35–60. New York: Russell Sage Foundation.

Greif, A. 2006. *Institutions and the Path to the Modern Economy*. New York: Cambridge University Press.

Hall, P. A., and D. Soskice. 2001. *Varieties of Capitalism*. New York: Oxford University Press.

Handy, S., and B. McCann. 2011. "The Regional Response to Federal Funding for Bicycle and Pedestrian Projects." *Journal of the American Planning Association* 77(1): 27–38.

Hart, O. 1995. *Firms, Contracts, and Financial Structure*. Oxford: Oxford University Press.

Healey, P. 1992. "Planning through Debate: The Communicative Turn in Planning Theory." *Town Planning Review*, 63(2): 143–162.

Healey, P. 1999. "Institutionalist Analysis, Communicative Planning, and Shaping Places." *Journal of Planning Education and Research* 19:111–21.

Henry, N., and S. Pinch. 2001. "Neo-Marshallian Nodes, Institutional Thickness, and Britain's 'Motor Sport Valley': Thick or Thin?" *Environment and Planning Part A* 33(7): 1169–83.

Hirsch, P. M., and M. Lunsbury. 1997. "Ending the Family Quarrel: Toward a
    Reconciliation of "Old" and "New" Institutionalism." *American Behavioral Scientist*
    40(4): 406–18.

Ho, P. 2005. *Institutions in Transition: Land Ownership, Property Rights and Social
    Conflict in China*. New York: Oxford University Press.

Holloway, S. L., G. Valentine, N. Bingham, et al. 2000. "Institutionalising Technologies:
    Masculinities, Feminities, and the Heterosexual Economy of the IT Classroom."
    Environment and Planning Part A 32(4): 617–33.

Innes, J. 1995. "Planning Theory's Emerging Paradigm: Communicative Action and
    Interactive Practice." *Journal of Planning Education and Research* 14(3): 183–89.

Innes, J. 1996. "Planning Through Consensus Building: A New View of the
    Comprehensive Planning Ideal." *Journal of the American Planning Association*
    62:460–72.

Jessop, B. 2001. "Institutional Re(turns) and the Strategic-Relational Approach."
    Environment and Planning Part A 33(7): 1213–35.

Kim, A. M. 2008. *Learning to Be Capitalists: Entrepreneurs in Vietnam's Transition
    Economy*. New York: Oxford University Press.

Kim, A. M. 2011. "Unimaginable Change: Future Directions in Planning Practice and
    Research About Institutional Reform." *Journal of the American Planning Association*
    77(4): 328–37.

Kim, A. M. 2011. Talking back: The role of narratives in Vietnam's recent land
    compensation changes. *Urban Studies*, 48(3): 493–508.

Lai, L. W.-C., and C. Webster. 2003. *Property Rights, Planning, and Markets*.
    Northampton, MA: Edward Elgar.

Leach, W. D. 2006. "Adaptive Governance and Water Conflict: New Institutions for
    Collaborative Planning." *Journal of the American Planning Association* 72(4): 514.

Litman, T. 2008. "Institutions and Sustainable Transport: Regulatory Reform in
    Advanced Economies." *Journal of the American Planning Association* 74(3): 381–82.

MacLeod, G. 2001. "Beyond Soft Institutionalism: Accumulation, Regulation, and Their
    Geographical Fixes." *Environment and Planning Part A* 33:1145–67.

Mandelbaum, S. J. 1985. "The Institutional Focus of Planning Theory." *Journal of
    Planning Education and Research* 5(3): 3–9.

Mantzavinos, C., D. C. North, and S. Shariq. 2004. "Learning, Institutions, and
    Economic Performance." *Perspectives on Politics* 2(1): 75–84.

Markusen, A. 1999. "Fuzzy Concepts, Scanty Evidence, Policy Distance: the Case for
    Rigour and Policy Relevance in Critical Regional Studies." *Regional Studies* 33(9):
    869–84.

Mitchell, W. J. 2001. "Where I'm @." *Journal of the American Planning Association* 67(2):
    144–45.

Moulaert, F. 2005. "Institutional Economics and Planning Theory: A Partnership
    between Ostriches?" *Planning Theory* 4(21): 21–32.

Nee, V. 1989. "A Theory of Market Transition: from Redistribution to Markets in State
    Socialism." *American Sociological Review* 54(5): 663–81.

Nee, V., and R. Swedberg. 2007. *On Capitalism*. Palo Alto, CA: Stanford University Press.

North, D. 2005. *Understanding the Process of Economic Change*. Princeton, NJ: Princeton
    University Press.

Peterson, M. A. 1997. "The Limits of Social Learning: Translating into Action." *Journal of
    Health Politics, Policy, and Law* 22(4): 1077–114.

Po, L.-C. 2011. Property rights reforms and changing grassroots governance in China's urban–rural peripheries: The case of Changping district in Beijing. *Urban Studies*, 48(3): 509–528.

Pomeranz, K. 2001. *The Great Divergence: China, Europe, and the Making of the Modern World Economy.* Princeton, NJ: Princeton University Press.

Richardson, H. W., and P. Gordon. 1993. "Market Planning: Oxymoron or Common Sense?" *American Planning Association Journal* 59(3): 347–52.

Rodrik, D., A. Subramanian, and F. Trebbi. 2004. "Institutions Rule: The Primacy of Institutions over Geography and Integration in Economic Development." *Journal of Economic Growth* 9: 131–65.

Rodrik, D., and R. Wacziarg. 2005. "Do Democratic Transition Produce Bad Economic Outcomes." *American Economic Review, Papers and Proceedings* 95(2): 50–55.

Rogoff, B. 1990. *Apprenticeship in Thinking: Cognitive Development in Social Context.* New York: Oxford University Press.

Roy, A. 2010. *Poverty Capital: Microfinance and the Making of Development.* New York: Routledge.

Sabel, C. 1994. "Learning-by-Monitoring: The Institutions of Economic Development." In *Handbook of Economic Sociology,* edited by N. J. Smelser and R. Swedberg, 137–65. Princeton, NJ: Princeton University Press.

Salet, W. G. M. 2002. "Evolving Institutions." *Journal of Planning Education and Research* 22(1): 26–35.

Salet, W. G. M., and A. Thornley. 2007. "Institutional Influences on the Integration of Multilevel Governance and Spatial Policy in European City-Regions." *Journal of Planning Education and Research* 27:188–98.

Sanyal, B. 2008. "Critical about Criticality." *Critical Planning* 15:143–60.

Saxenian, A. L. 1996. *Regional Advantage.* Cambridge, MA: Harvard University Press.

Silbey, S. S., and P. Ewick. 2003. "Narrating Social Structure: Stories of Resistance to Legal Authority." *American Journal of Sociology* 108(6): 1328–72.

Skocpol, T. 1979. *States and Social Revolutions: A Comparative Analysis of France, Russia, and China.* New York: Cambridge University Press.

Sorensen, A. 2011. Evolving property rights in Japan: Patterns and logics of change. *Urban Studies,* 48(3): 471–491.

Stark, D., and L. Bruszt. 2001. "One Way or Multiple Paths: For a Comparative Sociology of East European Capitalism." *American Journal of Sociology* 106(4): 1129–137.

Storper, M. 1997. *The Regional World: Territorial Development in a Global Economy.* New York: Guilford.

Susskind, L., S. McKearnan, and J. Thomas-Larmer. 1999. *The Consensus Building Handbook: A Comprehensive Guide to Reaching Agreement.* Thousand Oaks, CA: Sage.

Svejnar, J. 1996. "Enterprises and Workers in the Transition: Econometric Evidence." *American Economic Review* 86(2): 123–27.

Thelen, K. 1999. "Historical Institutionalism in Comparative Politics." *Annual Review of Political Science* 2:369–404.

Tompkins, E., W. N. Adger, and K. Brown. 2002. "Institutional Networks for Inclusive Coastal Management in Trinidad and Tobago." *Environment and Planning Part A* 34(6): 1095–111.

Verma, N. 2007. Institutions and Planning: An Analogical Inquiry. *Institutions and Planning.* Oxford: Elsevier.

Wang, J.-H., and C.-K. Lee. 2007. "Global Production Networks and Local Institution Building: The Development of the Information-Technology Industry in Suzhou, China." *Environment and Planning Part A* 39(8): 1873–88.

Watson, V. 2008. "Down to Earth: Linking Planning Theory and Practice in the 'Metropole' and Beyond." *International Planning Studies* 13(3): 223–37.

Weber, R. 2002. "Extracting Value from the City: Neoliberalism and Urban Redevelopment." *Antipode* 34(3): 519–40.

Webster, C., and Y. Zhao. Forthcoming. "Land Dispossession and Enrichment in China's Suburban Villages." *Urban Studies*.

Whiting, S. (2011). Values in land: Fiscal pressures, land disputes, and justice claims in rural and peri-urban China. *Urban Studies*, 48(3): 553–568.

Whittington, J., and D. E. Dowall. 2006. "Transaction-Cost Economic Analysis of Institutional Change Toward Design-Build Contracts for Public Transportation." Institute of Urban and Regional Development, Working Paper Series, University of California, Berkeley.

Williamson, O. 1996. *Mechanisms of Governance*. Oxford: Oxford University Press.

Wojcik, C. G. L. 2005. "Path Dependence and Financial Markets: The Economic Geography of the German Model, 1997–2003." *Environment and Planning Part A* 37(10): 1769–91.

Woodruff, D. M. 2000. "Rules for Followers: Institutional Theory and the New Politics of Economic Backwardness in Russia." *Politics and Society* 28(4): 437–82.

Yiftachel, O. 2006. "Re-engaging Planning Theory? Towards 'South-eastern' Perspectives." *Planning Theory* 5(3): 211–22.

Zierhofer, W. 2007. "Representative Cosmopolitanism: Representing the World Within Political Collectives." *Environment and Planning Part A* 39(7): 1618–31.

CHAPTER 5

VARIETIES OF PLANNING EXPERIENCE:

TOWARD A GLOBALIZED PLANNING CULTURE?

JOHN FRIEDMANN

How are cities of recent memory being planned? There are thousands of stories that could be told; I will tell only two of them as an introduction to my theme, which is the variety of planning cultures existing in the world today. The first story is about planning in Yaroslavl, Russia, and the second is about Rotterdam, the Netherlands.[1] I call them "probes" into their respective planning cultures rather than complete profiles. Following these stories, I will try to draw out some of the things we may learn from them. The chapter then proceeds to address three topics: the concept of a planning culture; why studying planning cultures is a worthwhile undertaking; and whether globalization is likely to lead to their convergence upon a single global culture of planning. Finally, I discuss some issues in the methodology for the study of planning cultures.

1. Yaroslavl, Russia

The transition from a centrally planned to a market economy occurred more abruptly in Russia than it did in the People's Republic of China, where the Communist Party continues in power.[2] Under the Soviet regime and until the beginnings of perestroika in the late 1980s, city planning was rigidly bureaucratized and, as Blair Ruble (1995) describes it, "enigmatic." City general plans, and the process leading up to them, were treated as classified documents. Physical planning was understood to be a problem of urban design and was handled by enormous planning institutes based in Moscow, Leningrad, and the capital cities of the union republics. Every city had to have such a plan: between 1945 and 1977, for example, the Russian Socialist Federative Republics (SFSR) completed 720 general plans. Typically, these plans projected a thirty-year future for a city. But because they were drafted by planners who had little if any direct knowledge of the cities for which they were planning, their idealized futures found only limited practical application.

What kept Soviet cities functioning were informal bureaucratic processes. For example, in the medium-size city of Yaroslavl, located some 150 miles northeast of Moscow, "the massive Avtodizel Motor Works opened schools, hospitals, and rest homes while constructing some thirty-five thousand apartments for its workers, largely with ministerial funds from Moscow that never passed through city coffers—or city control" (Ruble 1995, 107). Nothing illustrates better the sea-change that happened with the collapse of the Soviet system than the attempt of Avtodizl to build new workers' cottages in a popular wooded park on the banks of the Volga River. Now obliged to seek city council approval, and to almost everyone's astonishment, the Motor Works failed in this attempt at a "land grab" (Ruble 1995, 125).

During the Yeltsin post-Soviet regime in Russia, planning was radically decentralized, leaving local communities with a greater say over the directions of future growth...or decline. In Yaroslavl's case, the city invited the Moscow-based Central Scientific Research and Design Institute for City Construction to prepare a new city-wide development plan based on alternative projections about future demographic change. In discussions with the city council—a first—the idea that Yaroslavl might have a declining population in the future was rejected, however. Even as this planning effort was going forward, the regional (*oblast*) administration appointed by President Yeltsin launched its own planning scheme, bypassing city authorities. The consulting firm brought in by the *oblast* was a private venture, located in Moscow and headed by a former Russian prime minister who had good political connections with central ministries. Their proposal was for a new international airport on the city's outskirts. Although nothing seems to have come of this "plan," it illustrates how, in the transition period, the "Soviet-era tradition of establishing large-scale economic goals continued, leaving the details of consequent physical and social patterns for architects and city planners to worry about later on" (Ruble 1995, 120). It also reveals something about the politics of local development, where city and region might go in opposite directions (with or without mutual consultation).

At least during the early period of the "transition," much time was spent in developing the new structure of local institutions through which planning might become effective. "The absence of zoning regulations," writes Ruble, "posed an immediate concern to city officials.... [C]ity officials did not know how to proceed with regulating privately owned property. New owners, for their part, firmly believed that title would transfer total authority over a particular building or site. Bitter fights erupted" (Ruble 1995, 122). But even as the city struggled to establish a new planning order, it had to confront entirely unforeseen problems ranging from the threatened bankruptcy of older Soviet enterprises like Avtodizel, the arrival of refugees from Russia's war-torn zone in Chechnya, mounting unemployment, serious soil pollution with heavy metals, a change in the political regime with the ascent of President Putin, growing social inequalities, inter-ethnic tensions, and large-scale corruption. Planning may have been opened up to public debate. But the city of Yaroslavl, with its woefully inadequate financial means, inexperienced in self-development under a capitalist system of "primitive accumulation," and beset by a new politics of money—Ruble's account of Yaroslavl's travails is tellingly entitled *Money Sings*—faces an uncertain future where the ingenuity of its leaders to improvise solutions is probably more important than the future-gazing of planning experts based in Moscow.

2. ROTTERDAM, NETHERLANDS

Having reclaimed much of their country from the sea, the Dutch, it is said, have a "soft spot" in their hearts for planning (Faludi and Van der Valk 1994). Rather than delve into the institutional setting of city and regional planning, however, the following brief account will focus on a dimension of planning in the Netherlands that has become increasingly popular over the past two decades: the management of so-called mega-projects. In addition to incremental zoning and the persistent attempts to chart the future of cities through a general plan that covers the entire territory of a municipality or region, and that embodies the restraining hand of government, mega-projects are undertaken in an entrepreneurial spirit to break through the routines of the everyday to build spectacular urban spaces that will, it is hoped, enhance a city's competitiveness in global capital markets. Because mega-projects often exceed the fiscal capacity of municipalities, the local state is obliged to seek partners in the corporate sector and the central government. As a rule, a newly formed public–private partnership (PPP) of this sort will bypass routine planning procedures, creating its own organizational framework with varying degrees of autonomy, and, it might be added, with varying degrees of transparency and accountability. Frequently, it will also bring on board world-class architects who are expected to give memorable visual form to the undertaking.

The Rotterdam Central Station project is one of these.[3] In the mid-1990s, it was identified as one of the six "strategic" projects that would lend heightened international profile to this major port city. Envisioned was a large area surrounding the central railway station that would be given over to commercial developments particularly in the service and leisure sectors in the hope of revitalizing the city center. The station itself would be converted into an intermodal transport node. To get this project under way, a partnership was formed involving the City of Rotterdam, the Dutch railway company (NS), and two private property developers who had a long-term relationship with both the site and the city. A British design firm, Alsop Architects, was selected to redesign the entire area. The projected redevelopment period would extend for up to eighteen years, with three goals in mind: (1) the improvement and enlargement of the railway station, (2) an improvement of the interface between the station and the rest of the city, and (3) a property development program covering an area of 650,000 square meters. A plan was discussed to set up a joint Land Development Corporation that would amalgamate all of the plans, buildings, and rights in a common enterprise, but this was eventually abandoned. Instead, the original project was divided into two subprojects, each with its own organization: the railway terminal and transport node (with the railway company NS in the driver's seat), and a profit-oriented real estate venture guided by the city council.

After years of work, a master plan was published in April 2001. And then the sky fell down. In March of the following year, a new political party, calling itself Leefbar Rotterdam ("Livable Rotterdam") and led by the charismatic Pim Fortuyn (who was tragically murdered two months later), received 30 percent of the vote in municipal elections and fundamentally changed the coalition of forces that had supported the project. Together with two smaller political parties, Livable Rotterdam had succeeded in dethroning the Social Democrats who had governed the city since the end of World War II. A new set of values and ideals was coming to the fore. The Rotterdam Central Station project had been part of a strategy that would turn Rotterdam into a "world city." The basic idea was to market the city to global capital, based on the argument that competitive economic growth was essential if the social needs of the city were to be met. But in 2002, the newly formed city council could not be convinced of this logic. A document published in September of that year shows a change in the privileged position of strategic projects, and so also in the position of city marketing in the political domain. With more than half of the budget devoted to it, the new emphasis was to be on safety in the streets. The old railway station was declared a heritage building; a "homegrown" architect was enlisted for the project, replacing the British firm Alsop; and the budget for the project was cut in half, from 875 to 410 million euros.

In this instance, globalization did not eliminate the local; it strengthened it. The new council majority represented the interests of small businesspeople and petit bourgeois in the city who were feeling disoriented, their livelihood threatened by the seemingly irreversible forces of globalization. It was this majority that the formerly hegemonic Social Democrats, in their eagerness to put Rotterdam on the global map, had chosen to ignore.

3. Discussion

What can we learn from these two probes into the realities of planning practice in Russia and the Netherlands? Russia was in transition from a centrally planned to a market economy where "money sings," and with decentralization, cities like Yaroslavl were now in position to challenge state-owned enterprises such as the powerful Avtodizel Motor Works. A "land grab" that would have converted a popular riverside park into a massive housing development (35,000 apartments!) outraged the local council members, and so they stopped it. We also learn that despite the new localism, the city was still completely dependent on the nation's capital for professional planning services. The council had contracted for a long-term development plan with one of the old planning institutes in Moscow, given different assumptions of future population growth but rejecting the most likely option, a decline in population.[4] Like local councils everywhere, they could only imagine their city expanding. That, too, must have been in the mind of the *oblast* authorities, who dreamed of a nearby international airport, hoping that a former Russian prime minister, who now worked as a private consultant, would lobby for this new airport venture with relevant ministries in Moscow. But nothing came of this. The city and *oblast* were at loggerheads about this project, or at least failed to consult with each other, even though the project would have had major implications for Yaroslavl. Meanwhile, the council had to deal on an emergency basis with refugees from the war in Chechnya, some of whom may have been ethnic Russians, but for whom there were neither local jobs nor housing.

Rotterdam evokes a different story. The city has a thriving European port and is a multicultural mecca for new immigrants, many from Islamic countries. Though the Dutch have a reputation for being a tolerant nation, by the end of the century they seemed to have reached the limits of their tolerance, as this ancient port city, rebuilt after its near-total devastation during World War II, was slated to undergo another transformation that threatened to destroy its character as a treasured place in the collective heart of its citizens. With American-style neoliberalism the reigning ideology in most parts of the world, and cities anxiously competing for footloose global capital, Rotterdam's city council, dominated by Social Democrats, decided to engage in this competitive game, forming a partnership with the national railway system and two private developers for a redevelopment program that, in the course of nearly two decades, would have transformed the central city beyond recognition. As is often the case with projects on this scale, its design was removed from the ordinary planning process, proceeding without public input. The Central Railway Station was preserved from destruction, and the money saved was put to use to improve safety on the streets.

Both of these stories relate dramatic events, and the planning cultures of the two cities continue to be adjusted to changing external conditions. They also tell us that the planning cultures of Yaroslavl and Rotterdam are completely different, with the insolvent Russian city dependent, as it had always been, on planning expertise from Moscow, while the Dutch Euro-port city has a lively democratic politics grounded in a civil society that turned its full attention to projects in the public sphere: mega-projects, immigration, safety, and place making.

4. WHAT IS PLANNING CULTURE?

So far, I have avoided defining the term "planning culture," hoping that my stories would be sufficient to suggest its general meaning. In today's entrepreneurial world, master planning or its equivalent may still be ritually practiced, but the really interesting stories involve some sort of development planning focused on large-scale projects: airports and seaports, subways and skytrains, bridges and tunnels, gigantic theme parks and shopping malls, waterfront reclamation schemes, urban redevelopment and new towns, world expo sites and Olympic venues, and so on, all of which are designed with an eye toward luring global venture capital as well as well-heeled tourists in what is perceived to be a competitive game with high stakes.[5] Every city wants to stand out and be noticed. But this obsession with city marketing rides roughshod over low-income neighborhoods (Angotti 2008); and in developing countries such as India, the result is often a dual city where perhaps two-thirds of the population is living in poorly served informal settlements, while elites close themselves off in the upscale city of condos and gated communities (Nair 2005; see also chapters by Roy and Miraftab, this volume).

The idea of a planning culture was put into circulation in the early 1990s by the Frankfurt (Germany) city councilor Martin Wentz, who was charged with planning affairs in his city (Wentz 1992). Soon after, the idea was projected onto an international canvas by three European planners and academics who undertook a four-country survey of planning experts covering Germany, Switzerland, France, and Italy (disP 1993; Keller, Koch, and Selle 1996). Underlying their research was a concern with the growing interest of the European Union in promoting transnational planning, especially at the regional scale. If European planning systems were significantly different from each other, institutionally and legally, it was important to discover the nature of these differences. A decade later, the first major statement on planning cultures in the United States was an edited collection by Sanyal, *Comparative Planning Cultures* (2005). In contrast to his European antecedents, Sanyal, a professor at the Massachusetts Institute of Technology, adopted not only a global perspective but also included empirical, historical, and institutional studies that offer us glimpses of the varieties of planning experience throughout the world.[6] It may be instructive to look at how various authors represented in this volume approach their subject.

Wisely, the editor had left it to each author to interpret both the meaning of planning culture and how to undertake its study. There are a number of excellent books that describe what might be called a *national* planning culture, although their authors do not invoke the concept that is chiefly useful in comparative studies (Sandercock 1990; Sorensen 2002). Both are represented in the Sanyal volume with essays, respectively, on Australia and Japan. Sandercock provides a definition that many will find helpful:

> I conceptualize planning culture as an ensemble of people, ideas, social values, institutions, politics, and power. Each of these ingredients has a history. Anatomizing only the present-day manifestations of planning culture in Australia would be both partial and misleading. It would be partial to ignore the paths to the present, the shaping of the here and now, and the different forms that planning has taken in other historical eras and making the present seem inevitable and "natural." And it would be misleading in suggesting a *national* culture, which may miss more that is of interest, in terms of regional differences, than it catches in its desire to pin down the larger picture. One rich form of "anatomy" of a planning culture would be an ethnographic study, in the belly of the beast, from inside one of the state planning bureaucracies. (Sandercock 2005, 310)[7]

The wide reach of Sandercock's definition serves her purpose well, and reveals professional planning activities as only a tiny rivulet in the building of the country's cities, with much larger roles reserved for politics and markets. But she acknowledges an alternative methodology—an ethnography—in the very "belly of the beast" of the planning bureaucracies of the several states that in the Australian federation enjoy considerable autonomy in the spatial ordering of their respective territories. André Sorensen, who for the most part follows Sandercock's lead, also uses an historical approach to studying the evolving national planning culture of Japan.

Both authors insist on the importance of the *longue durée* that allows the reader to become aware of the changes in planning cultures that are always in motion but that, in the extended present of most studies, are rendered virtually invisible. Nor are they the only authors with an historical sensibility: Diane Davis (Mexico City), Philip Booth (France and Britain), Tridib Banerjee (Kolkata), and Robert Cowherd (Indonesia) all return us to the past in order to arrive at the present or near-present.[8]

The national approach is only one point of entry, however, into the worlds of planning culture. Urban case studies, such as of Banerjee's Kolkata, Davis's Mexico City, and in comparative perspective, Ng's study of Hong Kong and neighboring Shenzhen, is another way of coming to grips with our subject. In a dramatic map (Ng 2005, 114), Ng reminds us that these two very different urban ecologies are feeding off each other while remaining divided by a policed border that requires entry and exit visas. She, too, adopts an historical perspective, albeit in condensed form. Today, the former British colony of Hong Kong, whose official name is now the Hong Kong Special Administrative Region, has become part of the People's Republic, but it was granted considerable autonomy and a political system that is far more open than is the case for mainland cities. Shenzhen, too, prospers under special conditions within China. A virtual city-state, Shenzhen was carved out of

Guandong Province, enjoying privileges not granted to other cities in the Pearl River Delta, while Hong Kong continues in its laissez-faire tradition despite its political incorporation into the People's Republic. A notable Shenzhen reform was the joining up of land management functions with those of planning, which elsewhere in China are accountable to different central ministries in Beijing. Ng also reports that here are even the beginnings of a more consultative planning process, which in the rest of China is still all but unknown.

In the concluding part of her chapter, Ng comments on Hong Kong's planning. In the absence of a coordinative development plan, the land-use development strategy produced by the Planning Department can be no more than the "sum of its parts" (Ng 2005, 135). Coordination is difficult, if not impossible. Moreover, "the communities in Hong Kong pay...little attention to planning matters" (2005, 136). Most people are focused chiefly on the economic advantage they can derive from planning initiatives, neglecting social and environmental issues. In this sense, she says, Hong Kong is a "one dimensional city" (2005, 139). By contrast, Shenzhen is a "plan-rational city" where coordinative planning continues to play a central role in the management of development (2005, 138–43). The Shenzhen Special Economic Zone was built according to basic parameters laid down by successive master plans. By comparison to Hong Kong, Ng concludes, "where land use planners seem to play an established and subservient role in the development process, planners in Shenzhen...have more room to try out and learn new modes of governance. On the other hand, it appears that private sector interests in both cities have more channels to influence policy outcomes than do average community members" (2005, 142).

A complementary essay on China's planning culture is by Michael Leaf.[9] His case focuses on the Street Committee (*jiedao*) of Jinhua, a once poor neighborhood on the outskirts of Guangzhou City, the provincial capital of Guandong (Leaf 2005, 100–102).[10] To someone unfamiliar with China, his story may seem strange. By the early 1960s, the Jinhua neighborhood had established 145 collectively owned factories, providing jobs for many local residents. The Street Committee served as a kind of CEO for the neighborhood when it created the Jinhua Industrial Corporation in 1980 and two years later the Jinhua Labor Service Corporation. By 1990, the latter owned 85 light manufacturing enterprises that produced for both export and the domestic market, returning an annual profit of nearly $2 million. Before long, its business interests expanded into other areas, and its labor force is no longer just of local residents but also includes 40 percent migrant workers. As a further initiative, the Street Committee established the Jinhua Neighborhood Bank, which engages in a variety of financial activities, including the buying and selling of government securities and acting as an agency for issuing industrial securities. Jinhua's collective entrepreneurship has made local residents wealthy and has completely altered the neighborhood's physical appearance.

Leaf argues that

> China's shift to a market economy has in effect strengthened lower-level administrative units, as the administrative functions of the *jiedao* have

become increasingly reinforced by its economic activities. The corporate
nature has thus become further entrenched through the rise of market forces.
The...interpenetration of state and society that it implies can be seen here in
the functional integration of what in other market economies are seen as public
and private sectors. (2005, 101–102)

Leaf points out that Jinhua's story is not unique. He refers to it as a form of
local corporatism that empowers local leadership at the same time that it leads
to a fine-grained interpenetration of citizenship and membership in a corporate
organization.

This overlap of roles is widespread throughout China, where functional distinctions are often blurred, thus allowing for flexible and often personalistic
decision making that affords opportunities for corruption.[11] Leaf contrasts local
corporatism with the high modernism of physical planning in China, which has
flourished since the mid-1980s. In his own words,

> On the one hand, one finds the nation-wide promulgation of standardized
> rules governing urban spatial development, while...a new sense of local
> entrepreneurialism, spurred on by administrative and fiscal decentralization,
> emphasizes local difference in order to competitively attract outside
> investment.... The challenge for planners is thus enormous, because urban
> investment decision making will be shaped by formal regulatory structures
> and by less transparent negotiations that all too often obviate formal planning
> channels. (2005, 105)

This contradiction is reinforced by a bureaucratic division of labor, where plan
making is the responsibility of "institutes" that are often attached as profitable
business ventures to universities, the China Academy for Urban Planning and
Design located in Beijing, and provincial governments, while the enforcement of
these "scientific" but actually quite formulaic plans is left to the municipal planning bureaucracy and its district offices. Given the hyper-rapid growth of Chinese
cities over the past thirty years, which continuously sprints ahead of even the most
"rational" of master plans, it should be fairly obvious that formulaic planning is
chiefly a ritual practice to convey an impression of stately order, and that the actual
process of developmental decision making is on a project-by-project basis that
involves rule breaking more often than it does not.

It is hard to pin down the nature of China's planning culture. A recent book
by Thomas Campanella, *The Concrete Dragon: China's Urban Revolution* (2008),
argues convincingly that China is reinventing the city as a "landscape of consumption" characterized by speed, scale, spectacle, sprawl, segregation, and sustainability. To encounter Shanghai's skyline at night is to be almost convinced that "the
future is already here." One has to suppose that its spectacular appearance is a
result of some sort of "planning" because that is the word we have; but if so, who
are the planners and what is the process that yields such astounding results? Short
of climbing into the belly of the beast, as Sandercock would have us do, it is impossible to say, though Michael Leaf has certainly touched on some relevant aspects.

Shanghai works as a city, the whole somehow coheres, and the stories of its growth are many. But we still lack a language to talk about its actual planning system.[12]

The many case studies in Sanyal's book give us a panoramic view of planning cultures as seen from different perspectives. Some of them are focused on planning as officially constituted; others take a broader approach that has city building at the center of its vision, allowing for a multiplicity of actors and their responses to historical challenges. In all of them, key roles are assigned to the state at its various levels of presence, the corporate sector, and where civil society is actively engaged, also representatives from the organized community. Planning in this view is like a drama with multiple actors performing partially scripted roles while improvising their responses to each other. A few years ago, I suggested a concise definition of "planning culture" as "the ways, both formal and informal, that spatial planning...is conceived, institutionalized, and enacted" (Friedmann 2005, 184). Today, although I find this definition unnecessarily focused on professional planning, it can still serve us because it points us in the direction of empirical, historically grounded studies of planning. How planning in given circumstances is institutionalized is part of the question to be researched. Nation, region, and city are the relevant arenas of action, though in a globalized world, extra-national forces (such as the behavior of financial markets and international accords) also play significant roles. The underlying assumption is that planning, unlike civil engineering, is not a universal "science" or "discipline," but a culturally contingent form of practice. This formulation raises two further questions: why is an understanding of "cultural contingency" important; and what is the likelihood of a convergence of planning cultures in the course of the next few decades?

5. WHY STUDY PLANNING CULTURES?

Given the still nebulous character of the concept, one might well ask what the fuss is all about and why planners should spend precious time to learn more about planning cultures. I will propose three reasons for doing so.

Planners who are steeped in their own national cultures and have studied planning at a national university may not even be aware that what they take for granted at home may not, in fact, be universally acknowledged. Or, put another way, they may not even be conscious of living in a culturally specific environment, just as all of us are usually not aware of the air we breathe until the moment we are deprived of it. But when we move into a different work environment— and this may be no farther away than simply traveling from city A, where we have practiced planning for twenty years, to city B, say from Los Angeles to Vancouver, or even within the same country, from Vancouver to Toronto, parachuting down after only a short flight—we may quickly come to realize that our taken-for-granted modes of working in city A will no longer be appreciated in city B, and we may be politely informed to change our ways. An interest in planning cultures may therefore serve to sensitize our awareness to differences in how planning is actually practiced around the world.

A deeper understanding of planning cultures will also teach planners, especially the younger members of our profession, a greater sense of realism about how planning interacts with other societal actors in different places, each contributing in its own quite specific way to city building and regional development. This will help us in our educational practices, which necessarily are centered on acquiring planning knowledge and skills even as they underplay the actual roles of state, corporate capital, and civil society actors, their dynamic interaction, the institutions through which interaction takes place, and the shifting locus of power. It will also make planners who normally live for much of the time in a normative future appreciate the actual power plays of the day, as well as give them a historical perspective on how we arrived in the present. Studying the dynamics of the planning culture of different cities (or countries) will contribute to this educational enterprise.

A third reason for studying planning culture is that planning in a globalizing age cannot afford to be provincial. Ideas do travel, and we are now in an era of world planning congresses (Shanghai, Mexico City, Perth), annual joint European and American planning conferences, professional journals (in English) that address a wider audience than we enjoy at home (*European Planning Journal, Planning Theory and Practice, dispP, International Development Planning Review, China City Planning Review*), overseas consultancies, and a growing number of international students in our planning schools. The flow of words is going in all directions, and we need to try to make ourselves understood. This is not an easy task. Part of the difficulty resides in the fact that when we speak to audiences at home, we can make assumptions about background, common understandings, and values that will be lacking when we communicate with those unfamiliar with coded information of this kind. In a global discourse, this can lead to serious misunderstandings and confusion. For this reason, we need to educate ourselves in the variety of planning languages and practices to which many of us are increasingly exposed.

It could be argued that one of the results of this flood of words circling the planet is that globalization brings the furthest reaches of the world nearer to our own, and that this ever-shrinking world will inevitably result in a gradual convergence of planning cultures. What is the likelihood of this occurring? I will try to answer briefly with an analogy. If cities were like a hotel, say a Marriott, with only superficial differences from city to city, or country to country, then perhaps yes, we would all be living like jet-setters, unmoored from our place-specific lives, our expenses paid for by a global corporation. But I don't believe this is a realistic model.

The literature on planning cultures clearly reveals systematic differences among cities arrayed along different structural dimensions. Here are a few of them: unitary versus federal states; strong central states versus strong regional states; liberal democracies versus authoritarian states; active participation in civic affairs by an organized civil society versus a civil society that is largely disengaged; preponderance of regulatory versus developmental planning; a legal system based on common law versus statutory law; rich countries/cities versus poor; and infinitely varied forms of local governance arrangements. In actuality, these and other structural features that are likely to influence the way planning is done are superimposed on each other in any given locality, where they are interwoven with local formal and informal practices.[13] Observed planning processes are therefore infinitely varied and socially embedded, with verbal accounts that will depend on the perspective adopted and the literary skills of the observer.

This is one reason for my skepticism about a one-world planning culture: it is a utopian conception. There is another version of pro-convergence thinking, however, that focuses on the transplanting of planning ideas (Healey and Upton 2010). This is a more complex story because the very idea of modern spatial planning is a Western conception initially exported to British, French, American, and Japanese colonies, where they were grafted on to indigenous traditions of city building (Ward 2010; see also King 1984). Following World War II, with the dissolution of these imperial adventures, Western "experts" were sent abroad to the newly independent states to advise them on a variety of planning issues. And of course there were extensive borrowings.

This is a long story with varying outcomes. To summarize briefly, most "expert" advice in the postcolonial era either failed to take hold because political priorities differed, or the political timing was wrong, or the proposed idea was interpreted in ways that the visiting expert might have puzzled over, or the idea was briefly adopted as a semiotics of modernity before being "naturalized" in ways that occasionally would lead to bizarre urbanistic realizations. And, of course, frequent regime changes in postcolonial societies didn't help, so that continuity in urban policies was and continues to be a rare phenomenon (Friedmann 2010).

7. A Note on Methodology

If this chapter should lead the reader to undertake empirical research on planning cultures, how should he or she proceed? There is, of course, no recipe for this, and any researcher would begin this task with certain objectives in view that would be crucial in deciding on an approach. Nevertheless, throughout this chapter I have given some pointers that I have found useful in my own work, and I will try to rearticulate them here.

There are many dimensions of planning, and although planning culture remains somewhat vague as a concept, the concrete realities of planning practice in a given city or region are anything but. It is a question—and here I repeat Leonie Sandercock's pungent phrase once more—of getting into the "belly of the beast," of getting close to where the action is. This suggests case studies of actual planning practices and observing them in minute detail over a period of time. In choosing a "case," some special event or project is probably the best way to discover its unique character, as was the Rotterdam story at the beginning of this chapter. Preferably, the case selected should be of local planning, but tracing its linkages to multiple scales would form an essential part of the analysis.

Every case requires a context, however, and to ensure that the researcher becomes aware of its distinctive character, two sorts of context are necessary. The first is the national context (or provincial, in Canada)—that is, the institutional and legal basis for planning, the story of its origins, its political-administrative setting, the social background and personality of those actively engaged in the process, the role of outsiders such as international aid agencies, the professional status of planners as opposed to other actors (developers, lawyers, bureaucrats), the role (if any) of mobilized civil society, and so forth. A good model to follow would be André Sorensen's study on the history of Japanese planning (2002).

The second context would be given by a comparison case, as was the juxtaposition in this chapter of planning toward the end of the millennium in Russia and the Netherlands. There are very few planning studies that are explicitly comparative (e.g., Newman and Thornley 2005). Comparative study is fraught with difficulties, yet it is only by contrasting how planning is done in one city with planning practices in another, so as to heighten the contrast, preferably in a different country, that the specificities—the unique cultures of planning in both—will become visible to the observer.

Notes

1. These stories are adapted from Friedmann 2005.
2. This story is a summary of Ruble 1995.
3. This account is based on Kooijman and Wigmans 2003.
4. In 1994, the Russian Federation had a population of 148 million; this is projected to decline to 111 million by mid-century (United Nations Population Fund 2007).
5. For a critical view of city marketing and a proposal for an assets-based development, see Friedmann 2007.
6. The idea of comparative planning studies was catching on in the new millennium, though all of them studiously avoided the term "planning culture." See Herrschel and Newman 2002, and Newman and Thornley 2005. Healey (2007) should also be mentioned here, with her in-depth studies of strategic planning in Amsterdam, Milan, and Cambridge, England. Meanwhile, in Germany, Klaus Selle, at the University of Aachen, has promoted a network discussion on the concept of planning culture; see the commentary by Altrock (2009), which is looking for conceptual clarification but is lacking the underpinning of empirical studies.
7. "State" in this sentence refers to the "provincial" states of the Australian federation. State planning in Australia is much more powerful than planning by the small municipalities that make up the large metropolitan regions of the country, such as Sydney and Melbourne.

8. Unless otherwise noted, all authors mentioned here and in the following paragraphs refer to essays in Sanyal (2005).

9. For a fuller account of China's planning culture, see his subsequent essay (Leaf 2006).

10. Street committees (or "street offices," as they are sometimes called in English) are the lowest level of state administration in urban areas. It is also important to point out that all urban land is state land that in principle cannot be alienated.

11. This overlap has been called "amphibious" (Ding 1994), and refers, as Leaf (2005, 98) points out, "not only to the institutional integration of state and society, but to the ambiguities surrounding the differentiation between...public sector and private sector."

12. A clue for such a language might be to journey into Shanghai's own cultural history. See Yue 2006.

13. In a private comment on this paragraph, Leaf points out that "most if not all these dichotomies are merely shorthand for grey-scales that themselves interact in complex...ways, thus making the systematic comparative interpretation of planning cultures a messy business indeed."

References

Altrock, U. 2009. "Planungskultur—Notizen zu einer anhaltenden Diskussion." In PND online. Available at: www.planung-neu-denken.de; accessed January 2009.

Angotti, T. 2008. New York for Sale: Community Planning Confronts Real Estate. Cambridge, MA: MIT Press.

Campanella, T. J. 2008. The Concrete Dragon: China's Urban Revolution. New York: Princeton Architectural Press.

Ding, X. L. 1994. "Institutional Amphibiousness and the Transition from Communism: The Case of China." British Journal of Political Science 24:293–318.

disP 1993. Special issue on planning cultures in Europe, edited by D. A. Keller, M. Koch, and K. Selle. Zurich: ORL-Institute ETH. [In German]

Faludi, A., and A. J. Van der Valk. 1994. Rule and Order: Dutch Planning Doctrine in the Twentieth Century. Dordrecht: Kluwer Academic Publishers.

Friedmann, J. 2005. "Globalization and the Emerging Culture of Planning." Progress in Planning 64:183–234.

Friedmann, J. 2007. "The Wealth of Cities: Towards an Assets-based Development of Newly Urbanizing Regions." Development and Change (Forum) 38:987–98.

Friedmann, J. 2010. "Crossing Borders: Do Planning Ideas Travel?" In Planning Ideas and Planning Practices, edited by P. Healey and R. Upton, 313–28. London: Routledge.

Healey, P. 2007. Urban Complexity and Spatial Strategies: Towards a Relational Planning for Our Times. London: Routledge.

Healey, P., and R. Upton, eds. 2010. Crossing Borders: International Exchangbe and Planning Practices. London and New York: Routledge.

Herrschel, T., and P. Newman. 2002. Governance of Europe's City Regions: Planning, Policy, and Politics. London: Routledge.

Keller, D. A., M. Koch, and K. Selle. 1996. "'Either/or' and 'And': First Impressions of a Journey into the Planning Cultures of Four Countries." Planning Perspectives 11:41–54.

King, A. D. 1984. The Bungalow: The Production of a Global Culture. London: Routledge.

Kooijman, D., and G. Wigmans. 2003, "Managing the City: Flows and Places at Rotterdam Central Station." *City* 7:301–26.

Leaf, M. 2005. "Modernity Confronts Tradition: The Professional Planner and Local Corporatism in the Rebuilding of China's Cities." In *Comparative Planning Cultures*, edited by B. Sanyal, 91–112. New York: Routledge.

Leaf, M. 2006. "The 'Third Spring' of Urban Planning in China: The Resurrection of Professional Planning in the Post-Mao Era." *China Information* 20:553–85.

Nair, J. 2005. *The Promise of the Metropolis: Bangalore's Twentieth Century.* New York: Oxford University Press.

Newman, P., and A. Thornley. 2005. *Planning World Cities: Globalization and Urban Politics.* New York: Palgrave Macmillan.

Ng, M. K. 2005. "Planning Cultures in Two Chinese Transitional Cities: Hong Kong and Shenzhen." In *Comparative Planning Cultures*, edited by B. Sanyal, 113–44. New York: Routledge.

Ruble, B. A., 1995. *Money Sings: The Changing Politics of Urban Space in Post-Soviet Yaroslavl.* Cambridge, UK: Cambridge University Press.

Sandercock, L. 1990. *Property, Politics, and Urban Planning: A History of Australian City Planning, 1890–1990*, 2nd ed. New Brunswick, NJ: Transaction. Originally published as *Cities for Sale.*

Sandercock, L. 2005. "Picking the Paradoxes: A Historical Anatomy of Australian Planning Cultures." In *Comparative Planning Cultures*, edited by B. Sanyal, 309–30. New York: Routledge.

Sanyal, B., ed. 2005. *Comparative Planning Cultures.* New York: Routledge.

Sorensen, A. 2002. *The Making of Urban Japan: Cities and Planning from Edo to the Twenty-First Century.* London and New York: Routledge.

Sorensen, A. 2005. "The Developmental State and the Extreme Narrowness of the Public Realm: The Twentieth Century Evolution of Japanese Planning Culture." In *Comparative Planning Cultures*, edited by B. Sanyal, 223–58. New York: Routledge.

United Nations Population Fund. 2007. *State of the World Population: Unleashing the Potential for Growth.* New York: United Nations Population Fund.

Ward, S. V. 2010. "Transnational Planners in a Post-colonial World." In *Crossing Borders: International Exchange and Planning Practices*, edited by P. Healey and R. Upton, 47–72. London and New York: Routledge.

Wentz, M., ed. 1992. *Planungskulturen.* Frankfurt: Campus Verlag.

Yue, M. 2006. *Shanghai and the Edges of Empire.* Minneapolis: University of Minnesota Press.

B. PRINCIPLES
AND GOALS

CHAPTER 6

BEAUTY

ELIZABETH MACDONALD

1. INTRODUCTION

GIVEN a choice of routes to get to a destination, might a person consciously pick to travel along one versus another for purely aesthetic reasons, assuming time and distance variables were the same? Given a choice to sit facing a line of trees in a park, an elevated highway structure, or a fast-moving arterial street, wouldn't most people face the park even if the sun might be in their eyes? Why were seemingly thousands of main streets in American cities planted with trees during the early part of the twentieth century, and why are tree-lined streets so fondly remembered? Why do communities desire, even require, public art in public spaces? Why do tourists and local people alike find a walk on the Golden Gate Bridge, looking eastward toward San Francisco a compelling thing to do? Given a choice, why do people visit one city or neighborhood rather than another, if the purpose is just to experience a place? Why do people flock to the Trevi Fountain in Rome? The answers to "why" questions like these are many, the variables that may prompt replies are complex, but certainly beauty or lack thereof has a lot to do with the answers to all of them.

People value beautiful environments. This is evidenced most directly by widespread efforts to protect and visit scenic landscapes, and the general appreciation of photographic images or paintings of them. But people also value *urban* beauty, both large and small instances of it: attractive cityscape vistas, verdant parks, handsome buildings, entrancing water fountains, tree-lined streets, well-hewn public art, well-crafted paving—the list goes on. For different people, this valuing is felt differently. It may be conscious or unconscious, able to be verbally articulated or simply intuited, but it is there.

In keeping with its perceived importance, beauty has long been a motivation for city planning, though its primacy as a value on which to base planning practice, and as a subject matter for planning research and theory, has ebbed and flowed during the modern era. The desire to create beautiful things has been a key motivator of human action throughout history—think of the works of art and craft across time and cultures—and this desire has always been applied to cities and the elements of urban form. Throughout the world, beauty has long been sought in opulent religious and civic buildings, in the grand estates of ruling and wealthy families, and in the well-crafted houses of ordinary people. In recent centuries, in parts of the world where ideas of civil society have promulgated the creation of an expanded public realm, beauty has also been sought for prominent public places and parks. Today, city planners and urban designers put pen to paper (or fingers to computer keyboard) to think through and graphically represent future urban places where people will live and go about their lives in a physical context. This is often done within the context of community planning processes that gather citizens' input on what future is desired. Whatever the action—a city plan, a neighborhood plan, a neighborhood park, a public plaza, a civic building, an urban streetscape, design guidelines for private development—doing it well is usually associated with some notion of beauty, though the term itself may not be used, as well as other driving motivations. Why would any community members or local planners—whether they define themselves as social planners, land-use planners, transportation planners, or physical planners—consciously want to create something ugly in their community?

Local planning directives—embodied in plans and the goals, objectives, and policies contained in them—articulate what a community thinks will make a "good city." They are usually accompanied by some description of the physical attributes thought most likely to achieve the desired ends and also result in attractive places. In essence, most adopted plans represent a *joining* of social concerns and physical design concerns resulting from planning processes that allow both planning "experts" and community members many opportunities to get notions of beauty into the mix. While in many cities social and economic concerns are more to the fore in city plans than are physical design concerns, a desire for urban beauty can usually be found embedded in at least some objectives, policies, and physical form proposals. In other cities, achieving beauty is an explicitly stated objective along with other concerns.

What follows in this chapter is, first, a brief history of beauty as a driving force in city building and professional city planning activities from the pre-modern era up to the present day. The necessary brevity combined with the large time span means that this history can only be a whirlwind tour, hitting some of the highlights. Those highlights include the centrality of beauty as a city planning concern from the pre-modern era to the 1920s, the narrowed definition of beauty that came with the functionalism that drove "modernist" planning practice from the 1920s to the 1960s, the near banishing of beauty as a city planning value from the 1960s to the 1980s resulting from ill-conceived modernist planning practices promoted in part in its name, and the recent reemergence of beauty as a strengthening planning value because of growing concerns for environmental quality. Following this history, we consider several theoretical frameworks that lend insight into why beauty in cities is important and then move on to key concerns voiced about beauty in contemporary planning practice. We end with a discussion of future research needs.

2. Beauty as a Motivation for City Design and City Planning

Today's ideas of what makes for beauty in cities draw upon many centuries of thought and practice, and consequentially many different types and arrangements of urban forms are purported to be associated with creating beauty. To understand and appreciate today's complex weave of urban beauty concepts, it is helpful to know something of this history.

2.1 The Pre-Modern Era

Though somewhat arbitrary, as most time-era distinctions usually are, for the sake of brevity it is necessary to place city design and planning prior to the mid-nineteenth century into a single pre-modern era, in this case defined as the era before the modern city planning profession emerged.

For sure, early cities—large, dense, permanent settlements of people—reflected many concerns; power, defense, water supply, basic sanitation, salubrious climate, food production and agricultural surrounds, and access were among the many considerations. But so were they concerned with beauty. Today, preserved towns and city quarters that date from the medieval period are valued for their picturesque qualities that include narrow, winding streets interspersed with places, both large and small, fronted by churches and other large public buildings whose towers and domes rise above the surrounding dense urban fabric, creating striking visual counterpoints. In *The City in History*, Lewis Mumford (1961, 297) extols the visual beauty of medieval towns and asks "is it not mainly for their beauty, indeed, that people still make pilgrimages to them?" Unlike others who might assume that the beauty found in medieval cities is the result of unplanned organic processes alone, he concluded that their beauty was intentionally created:

> One cannot leave the medieval city, in its unity and diversity, without asking a
> final question about its planning: how far was it pursued as a conscious effort to
> achieve order and beauty? In formulating an answer, it is easy to overestimate
> both spontaneity and accidental good looks, and to forget the rigor and system
> that were the fundamental qualities in the education of both scholar and
> craftsmen. The esthetic unit of the medieval town was not achieved any more
> than its other institutions without effort, struggle, supervision, and control. (311)

The Renaissance, a European artistic period spanning from roughly the fourteenth to seventeenth centuries that drew upon rediscoveries of classical Greek and Roman culture, was concerned in major ways with order, balance, and harmony—qualities that philosophers had long deemed associated with beauty. In city building, these concerns were expressed in symmetrically composed public spaces having regular geometric shapes and surrounded by buildings of uniform height having similar façades (Kostof 1992, 161) composed of classic elements in their proper relation to each other—arches, columns, pediments, friezes, architraves, cornices, and the like. As well, pleasing proportions were deemed important: the Renaissance theorist Alberti recommended that a good public square should be twice as long as it was wide (Kostof 1992, 137). The subsequent Baroque period, prevalent in Europe during the late sixteenth to early eighteenth centuries, introduced a new aesthetic of dynamic movement and asymmetrical balance. In cities, this was expressed in new systems of diagonal streets, often overlaid on earlier street patterns, which were punctuated at their ends by striking focal points, such as civic or religious buildings or statuesque works of public art (Kostof 1991, 215).

Order and harmony were also concerns of Renaissance-era city planning in North America, best evidenced by the symmetrically designed central squares and regular building façade of towns built in the Southwest according to the Spanish Laws of the Indies regulations (Kostof 1991, 114; Kostof 1992, 137), of which Santa Fe and Sonoma remain as prime examples. The dynamic Baroque aesthetic was best expressed in the plan for Washington, D.C., which comprises diagonal avenues connecting the seats of government and public monuments (Kostof 1991, 211).

However, the urban form most ubiquitously adopted in early American city building was the regular grid plan, no doubt because of the kinship of this easily laid out form with the emerging American values of thrift, equality, and rapid progress. According to John Reps (1965, 314), "The gridiron plan stamped on an identical brand of uniformity and mediocrity on American cities from coast to coast.... We now view most of these gridiron plans with distaste. Their lack of beauty, their functional shortcomings, their overwhelming dullness and monotony, cause us to despair." Today's observer might well agree, but would also give thanks that in most cases the blocks of early American grid towns were of a human, walkable scale—central Portland, with its 200 by 200-foot blocks, stands out as a prime example—and that this quality itself establishes a fortunate framework upon which community aspirations for urban beauty can be overlaid.

2.2 The 1850s to the 1920s

The modern city planning profession began to form around the middle of the 1800s, and beauty became one of its central values—indeed, it was one of the key motivators for the profession's emergence. An awakened desire for urban beauty as a counterpoint and antidote to the nineteenth-century industrialization of cities and its perceived ugliness became, for a time, a rationale for civic improvement, as well as the inspiration for grand city designs. Ideas about the importance of city beauty and how to best achieve it were developed and put into practice by a diverse group of architects, landscape architects, surveyors, social theorists, and city bureaucrats—including in Europe, George Eugene Haussmann, Ildefons Cerda, and Camillo Sitte; and in America, Fredrick Law Olmsted and Daniel Burnham—supported by the various popular civic movements their ideas inspired, including the Urban Parks Movement, the Civic Arts Movement, and the City Beautiful Movement (Sitte 1945; Robinson 1904, 1907; Olmsted 1870/2007; Kostof 1991, 1992).

This was a period of bringing nature to the city by way of urban parks and tree-lined boulevards and parkways—nature was held as undeniably beautiful, as well as necessary for health. This was the time, also, of Ebenezer Howard and his influential garden city idea, which postulated that industrial cities had become too large, ugly, and unhealthful and that a system of smaller cities distributed throughout the countryside was necessary (Howard 1902). Garden cities were supposed to combine the best aspects of cities and the best aspects of nature and so contribute a better quality of urban life. These ideas spurred the start of the New Towns Movement in England, and morphed into the idea of creating garden suburbs at the expanding edges of large cities. In sum, the idea of creating beauty in cities by incorporating nature took hold in multiple ways.

It was also a period of bringing amenities and embellishments to the public realm of cities in the form of street lights, fountains, gardens, and civic center ensembles of classically inspired buildings. As well, it was a period of grand urban form gestures, including the building of broad diagonal streets and the creation of splendid urban vistas. While professional designer-planners may have been concentrating on grand gestures, ordinary people living in cities sought beauty in everyday, seeable, experiential ways. In America, the Urban Parks Movement, originally spurred by the success of New York's Central Park (designed by Frederick Law Olmsted) evolved into a community-led movement focused on the creation of small neighborhood parks. The civic arts and beautification movement was also largely promoted by community groups (Robinson 1904, 1907). Children in city elementary schools celebrated Arbor Day, often with the planting of a tree on school grounds, and some city schools had gardens and periodic lessons in cultivation and planting.

2.3 The 1920s to the 1960s

Modernism was embraced by city planners and architects toward the beginning of the twentieth century and held firm sway over the city planning profession from the 1920s to the early 1960s. During this period, beauty came to be associated with the modernist doctrine of "form follows function" that was curiously at odds with the long-held philosophical belief that aesthetics was independent of usefulness, which will be discussed later. Modernist city design, exemplified by the projects of Swiss architect Le Corbusier, embraced engineering-led functionalism and efficiency. Traditional, locally inspired building design was rejected in favor of homogenized and unornamented "international style" design and industrially manufactured materials. Old cities were to be demolished and rebuilt as ideal modern cities with tall buildings, serviced by elevated highway systems, and set in vast open spaces—the so-called tower in the park concept.

Unfortunately, all too often the modernist city design vision did not translate well into reality. While some extraordinary modernist buildings and urban ensembles were built by talented designers, a host of mundane modernist buildings, consisting of unadorned structures with repetitive façades set in a sea of parking lots, scar many urban environments.

Most problematically, in America many city "beautification" projects inspired by modernism were associated with large-scale publicly sponsored urban redevelopment projects. These projects were typically located in poor inner-city areas and involved building demolition, land consolidation, and the construction of wide roadways and elevated highways—all of which severely disrupted neighborhoods. Redevelopment was promoted on the pretense of ridding cities of unsafe and unsanitary "slums" and was supported by readily available federal funding. Both physical planners interested in creating more attractive cities and social planners interested in bettering the housing conditions of low-income people advocated for redevelopment. Among other things, the argument was made that orderly modernist urban forms would result in more healthful urban life. This argument was proved wrong when numerous modernist high-rise public housing projects became crime-ridden, dangerous places.

In 1961, Jane Jacobs's seminal book *The Death and Life of American Cities* presented a stunning critique of redevelopment and articulated the many valuable attributes of traditional urban neighborhoods. At the same time, "just hold on there" community members and progressive planning professionals began arguing that many areas slated for redevelopment, like San Francisco's Western Addition, were not unsanitary or poorly built (three-story, first-growth redwood structures unsound?) in their eyes and experience, and that "slum clearance" really amounted to racism. All this led to community distrust of planning activity and, within the academy, a loss of confidence in physical planning.

2.4 The 1960s through the 1980s

The labeling of city planners as physical determinists, who believed that the physical environmental has a determining influence on human behavior, and the concurrent discrediting of determinism by social science academics, who discerned a more complex interaction between people and their environment, took a large toll on the credibility of the planning profession. As a result, concerns for physical planning and "design" became suspect within the field and the emphasis turned to community planning, economic development, and advocacy planning. From the 1960s through the 1980s, beauty was dismissed as an inappropriate value on which to base planning practice because of its association with power, elitism, and physical determinism, and it was largely banished from mainstream planning concerns.

However, the planning subfield of urban design emerged during this time as a place where planners who remained concerned with urban form and physical planning sought refuge from the increasingly hostile-to-physical planning and increasingly social-science–based mainstream planning field. Within the urban design subfield, physical beauty remained a concern, though ways of referring to it tended to be oblique. Theoretical emphasis shifted from a direct focus on how to create beautiful cities to issues of place making and imageability, concepts which will be discussed later.

2.5 The 1990s to the Present

By the early 1990s, physical form started to once again become a central concern of the city planning field. This shift was spurred on by the increasing widespread concern for environmental quality inspired by the growing environmental movement. Embedded within concerns for *urban* environmental quality are concerns for environmental justice, environmental conservation and restoration, and sustainability, as well as concerns for identifying and enhancing appropriate environmental character. Central normative ideas include the desirably of trying to achieve environmental balance, harmony, and fittingness.

The practitioner-led New Urbanism movement, which began in the early 1990s and has since gained momentum, has developed a framework of normative theory that reasserts the value of physical planning and well-designed urban form, including beautiful form, for creating sustainable and livable communities. According to Peter Calthorpe (Katz 1994, xx), "The New Urbanism offers an alternative future for the building and re-building of regions. Neighborhoods that are compact, mixed-use and pedestrian friendly, districts of appropriate location and character, and corridors that are functional and beautiful can integrate natural environments and man-made communities into a sustainable whole." While some are alarmed that the New Urbanism smacks of physical determinism and so dismiss it out of hand, others view the New Urbanism's concern with physical form as reflecting *environmental possibilism*, an idea deriving from human-environment studies that posit that since there is a complex two-way relationship between people and the environments they inhabit, environments designed in certain ways offer more possibility of eliciting certain behaviors and, in this case, have more potential to achieve better environmental outcomes.

3. THEORETICAL FRAMEWORKS FOR UNDERSTANDING THE IMPORTANCE OF BEAUTY IN CITIES

Theoretical frameworks that help give understanding of why beauty in urban environments is important come from the fields of philosophy and psychology, as well as urban design. In particular, key insights can be gained from environmental aesthetics, environmental psychology, place theory, and imageability studies.

3.1 Environmental Aesthetics

Aesthetics is the field of philosophy that studies the ways in which people perceive the environment through their senses; in short, it is about knowledge derived from the senses. The concept of beauty has always been deeply embedded in ideas of aesthetics, often expressed in terms of visual pleasure. The classical notion of beauty, developed in large part by Plato and Aristotle, deemed its essential components to be balance, harmony, proportion, and order. Plato, in particular, felt that beauty lay in form rather than in content and that an object's beauty was independent of its usefulness. During the Renaissance, aesthetics and beauty were understood to be two of the six normative disciplines, the others being ethics, logic, goodness, and truth. By the eighteenth century, aesthetics had evolved into the science of sensory cognition, and by the nineteenth century, the focus of concern had narrowed to encompass just nature and art. By the early twentieth century, the focus had narrowed further, encompassing just art. In the late twentieth century, this narrowing was reversed, with the emergence of the field of environmental aesthetics (Carlson 2002). Spurred by the growing public concern for environmental quality, this field is concerned with the aesthetic appreciation of everyday environments, including both natural environments and those that are human made or human influenced, such as cityscapes, neighborhoods, and urban parks.

Within environmental aesthetics, two basic philosophical positions have emerged. The *engagement approach* postulates that, unlike the aesthetics of art appreciation which involves both distance between the observer and the object being observed and some knowledge of art history and traditions, aesthetic appreciation of everyday environments is characterized by the observer's total immersion in the environment and consists of immediate sensory perception. Various kinds of individual feeling responses are stressed, such as arousal, affection, awe, wonder, and mystery. There is no attempt to theorize what constitutes appropriate aesthetic appreciation; rather, the emphasis is on personal response and enjoyment.

The *cognitive approach* offers a perspective that is perhaps more comfortable for today's urban planners, steeped as they are in social science traditions that seek to generalize from "scientific" evidence and to base notions of appropriate courses of public action on those generalizations. The central idea is that aesthetic appreciation is "guided by the nature of the objects of appreciation and thus that knowledge about their origins, types and properties is necessary for serious, appropriate aesthetic appreciation" (Carlson 2002, 4). In other words, whether or not a tree-lined urban street is deemed aesthetically pleasing may be guided in part by a person's knowledge as to whether or not the trees are native species or at least appropriate species for the local climate.

In sum, theories of environmental aesthetics suggest that aesthetic appreciation is innate to the human experience because people are sentient beings immersed in physical environments. Because many people live in cities, and so mostly experience urban environments in their daily lives, urban beauty is valued because of the enjoyment it gives, whether that enjoyment is intellectualized or not.

3.2 Environmental Psychology

Environmental psychology focuses on the interrelationships between environmental settings and human behavior. Of particular interest relevant to the subject of beauty are theories concerned with environmental preference and environmental contributions to health that focus on the psychological effects of viewing nature, including urban nature.

Notably, more and more evidence is accumulating that people's well-being increases significantly as a result of contact with physical environments deemed to have high aesthetic value. In general, preference studies show that urban environments deemed most aesthetically pleasing are those in which natural elements, such as trees, landscaping, and water, are highly visible (Ulrich 1986). Research that has investigated the impacts of environmental settings on individual health and well-being have linked contact with nature—including views of natural elements, particularly trees—to stress reduction, faster healing from illness or injury, lower blood pressure, and higher task performance, such as better performance on academic tests (Maller et al. 2005). As well, research has found that the presence of natural elements visible from one's home can contribute to greater personal happiness, a greater feeling of security, and a greater propensity to socialize with others outdoors (Kuo 2003).

Numerous theories aimed at explaining the human affiliation with nature have been developed within the environmental psychology field. Of particular interest is *Attention Restoration Theory*, which is concerned with how to restore the mind from *directed attention fatigue*, which occurs as a result of overconcentration on tasks, particularly the intensive mental tasks that make up so much of modern work (Kaplan 1995). Such fatigue is a key ingredient in human error and ineffectiveness, and it results in reduced ability to perceive information, understand situations, and make decisions. One way to restore attention is by giving the mind a break and focusing on something that provokes involuntary attention, or fascination. *Attention Restoration Theory* posits that natural settings offer four essential properties that contribute to restoration: being away, extent (i.e., sufficient content and structure to occupy the mind for a period long enough to allow directed attention to rest), fascination (i.e., encouragement of a moderate level of effortless attention), and compatibility (i.e., support for a wide range of activities that coincide with the inclinations of the people who want to visit the place (Herzon, Maguire, and Nebel 2002). This theory is supported by physiological evidence. Research investigating the effects of viewing nature on brain activity has found that psychological response to nature involves feelings of pleasure, sustained attention or interest, "relaxed wakefulness," and dilution of negative emotions like anger and anxiety. In addition, while viewing nature, nervous system activity is reduced and the brain is relieved of "excess" circulation. Natural experiences seem to be able to strengthen the right hemisphere of the brain and restore harmony to the brain functions overall.

The findings of environmental psychology give strong credence to long-held ideas that including nature in cities not only creates beauty but also contributes to people's well-being. Further research is needed to understand people's aesthetic preferences for built form, if it is possible to generalize about the types of built forms that people consider beautiful, and whether or not views of aesthetically pleasing built environments have positive impacts on health.

3.3 Sense of Place and Imageabilty

Additional theories that give insight into the importance of beauty focus on sense of place and imageability—concepts that have been explored by urban designers, as well as researchers in other fields.

In the 1960s, researchers in geography, landscape architecture, architecture, and urban design, concerned with the increasing homogeneity, monotony, and lack of deep meaning of mid-twentieth-century cities, began investigating issues of place as a means of identifying more meaningful possibilities for urban form. The research explored relationships between people and the physical environments in which they dwell. The concept of "sense of place" evolved and was associated with the Latin concept of *genius loci*, which roughly translated means "the spirit of a place" (Norberg-Schulz 1976). In his seminal book *Place and Placelessness*, geographer Edward Relph (1976) identified meaningful experience, a sense of belonging, human scale, fit with local physical and cultural contexts, and local significance as the important qualities of place. Placelessness, on the other hand, is associated with an overriding concern for efficiency, mass culture, and anonymous, interchangeable environments. Concerned largely with how city design could reinforce a regional sense of place, landscape architect Michael Hough (1990) explored the role of landscape design in creating place identity, particularly the use of local plant materials, and creating a city form that worked with and respected topography.

Within place theory, ideas of harmony and balance have emerged as particularly important, harkening back to early philosophical ideas of what constitutes beauty. Designers concerned with sense of place ask themselves the question, "What does this place want to be?" While places having a "sense of place" may not all be physically beautiful, many would argue that they have a beauty that derives from being inspired by local landscapes and existing built form, and with "fitting in" to their local context.

The desire to create meaningful places inspired urban designers to explore the urban form elements critical to place making. Influential research by urban designer Kevin Lynch (1960) explored the importance of visual qualities for making cities both legible and memorable. He identified five elements of urban form important for imageability—paths, edges, districts, nodes, and landmarks—and postulated that designing with these elements in mind gave urban designers a tool kit for creating more perceptually satisfying urban environments. Emphasizing these physical elements within citywide and neighborhood level plans—indeed, structuring plans around them—was deemed an appropriate way to contribute to creating "good city form." While the visual qualities of imageability, legibility, and memorability may not equate directly with beauty, that there is a relationship seems intuitive.

4. Concerns Regarding Beauty as a City Planning Value

Today, two main issues tend to be raised regarding beauty as a city planning value, and debates can be contentious. The first issue is how important beauty should be relative to social, economic, and mobility issues. The second issue is the apparent subjectivity of individual aesthetic judgment, which leads to uncertainty about what can be generalized about beauty and hence uncertainty about what forms of beauty will be widely appreciated.

4.1 The Relative Importance of Beauty as a Planning Concern

Beautiful things have long been associated with wealth, and this association makes social planners uneasy. On the other hand, urban designers take the position that beauty in large and small forms is a positive attribute whose presence contributes to the quality of people's everyday lives, that a beautiful urban public realm spreads wealth to the whole community, and that therefore the pursuit of a beautiful public realm is an important planning purpose. (Note that the emphasis is on the public realm, which is a focus of planning-based urban design.)

Maslow's (1968) hierarchy of human needs teaches that basic physiological needs, such as needs for warmth, comfort, safety, and security, must be satisfied before higher level needs, such as needs for affiliation, esteem, and self-fulfillment, can be addressed. Therefore, it is very appropriate that things like the provision of affordable housing and public services that promote social equity and give access to employment opportunities, such as comprehensive public transit systems, are first-order city planning concerns. However, it can be argued that a test of a civilized society is how well all human needs are met, including the higher order needs with which beauty seems to be associated (Carmona et al. 2003, 107). Furthermore, experience suggests that all development can be pursued with an eye toward design quality, and hence beauty, and that this approach doesn't necessarily mean higher costs but, rather, more care in design decision-making (Carmona et al. 2003, 235).

Gentrification concerns are often raised against the pursuit of urban beauty. For instance, in debates that question the importance of proposals such as street trees in low-income areas—for reasons of aesthetics, shade, and protection from vehicle traffic—there is often an argument made against them on the grounds that they will foster gentrification, forcing out lower income people. Aside from embracing the idea that beauty has value, and is valued, this raises the obvious question of why lower income people should not have pleasant streets. Might not other mechanisms, besides an ugly public realm, be used to maintain affordability and reduce social displacement?

4.2 The Subjectivity of Aesthetic Judgment

"Beauty is in the eye of the beholder," goes the old saying, implying that it is all a matter of subjective taste. While this may hold true for art appreciation, notable plan preparation processes suggest that people in local communities may hold some common aesthetic values for their city.

In preparing the San Francisco Urban Design Plan the professional city staff, after considerable research that included outreach to citizens, other design professionals, businesses, and various movers and shakers, put forth eighty-seven illustrated urban design principles—truths—dealing with the physical qualities of San Francisco (San Francisco Department of City Planning 1971). They were under four major headings: city pattern, conservation, major new development, and neighborhood environment. Some examples:

- Street layouts and building forms which do not emphasize topography reduce the clarity of the city form and image.
- Landscaped pathways can visually and functionally link large open spaces to neighborhoods.
- The consistent use of one type of tree, planted in regular intervals, can impart a sense of order and continuity appropriate to major streets.

- Uninterrupted grid streets in flat areas often result in monotonous vistas.
- Large buildings impair the character of older, small-scale areas if no transition is made between small-scale and large-scale elements.
- Historic buildings represent crucial links with past events.
- Blocking, constriction or other impairment of pleasing street views of the Bay or Ocean, distant hills, or other parts of the city can destroy an important characteristic of the unique setting and quality of the City.

Few or none of the principles speak directly to beauty, but aesthetic values are certainly reflected, and without directly saying so, the plan's authors were certainly trying to keep and create urban beauty as related to their and citizen's values and perceptions of San Francisco's unique sense of place. Few of the principles had been explicitly expressed before, but once expressed and presented in many meetings—including presentations in elementary schools to see if the principles were easily understood—they were agreed to. Indeed, the most common response was, "of course" (A. Jacobs 1980, 214). The plan's authors held that the principles, after all, did not come out of the blue. Concerns for beauty, for sure with other issues as well, had been made clear with the so-called freeway revolt of the mid-1960s and with an outcry against the Fontana Towers apartments that blocked water views along San Francisco's north waterfront, bringing about a forty-foot height limit for future development along the waterfront. The urban design principles, to a considerable extent, merely stated and showed clearly what had been consciously and subconsciously held aesthetic values of residents. Once stated and shown, the principles served as well as an educational tool, making explicit, at least for that generation, what had been unconsciously felt and understood.

Place-specific urban form principles, such as the ones articulated in the San Francisco Urban Design Plan, which derive from both the natural landscape and historical built form and are meaningful to local communities, can be at all levels of urban scale: the region, the city, the district, the neighborhood, the corridor, the building site. This approach to determining what is constitutes urban beauty in a particular place remains a promising approach for city planning efforts.

In the end, however, it must also be acknowledged that urban beauty is in part a matter of art, and that with art there is always some subjectivity. On this matter, Kevin Lynch (1981, 104), as he so often did, put things well:

> [C]ommonly understood rules of evaluation—may be possible in regard to purely practical objects such as foundations of bridges, but are inappropriate for esthetic forms. Here we rely on the inscrutable inner knowledge of the artist or the critic, or we retreat to "I know what I like." The beauty of a great city is a matter of art, not of science—an intensely private affair, incommunicable in prosaic language.... Esthetic experience is a more intense and meaningful form of that same perception and cognition which is used, and which developed, for extremely practical purposes. Theory must deal with the esthetic aspects of cities, even though it may be a more difficult part of its task. Indeed, it must deal with function and esthetics as one phenomenon. Some of the complex, subjective qualities of places will escape us; others can be discussed and even agreed upon.

5. Future Research Needs

There are many research needs related to beauty and the city planning field. Perhaps most important are studies that seek to find connections between urban beauty, in large and small forms, and the quality of people's everyday life. What effect does living in a city or town that has a beautiful public realm have on individual well-being and community-mindedness? What principles about urban form related to beauty are commonly agreed to? What effect does a city's or town's beauty have on the community's economic well-being, and what are the best methods for ensuring that economic benefits are widely distributed to the whole community? What aspects of city beauty are most likely to contribute to positive public effects?

References

Carlson, Allen. 2002. "Environmental Aesthetics." In *Routledge Encyclopedia of Philosophy*, edited by E. Craig. Available at: www.rep.routledge.com/article/M047SECT6; accessed March 31, 2009.

Carmona, Matthew, Tim Heath, Taner Oc, and Steve Tiesdell. 2003. *Public Places/Urban Spaces: The Dimensions of Urban Design*. Oxford: Architectural Press.

Herzon, T. R., C. P. Maguire, and M. B. Nebel. 2002. "Assessing the Restorative Components of Environments." *Journal of Environmental Psychology* 23:159–70.

Hough, Michael. 1990. *Out of Place: Restoring Identity to the Regional Landscape*. New Haven, CT: Yale University Press.

Howard, Ebenezer. 1902. *Garden Cities of To-Morrow*. London: S. Sonnenschein.

Jacobs, Allan. 1980. *Making City Planning Work*. Washington, DC: American Planning Association.

Jacobs, Jane. 1961. *The Death and Life of Great American Cities*. New York: Modern Library.

Kaplan, Stephen. 1995. "The Restorative Benefits of Nature: Toward an Integrative Framework." *Journal of Environmental Psychology* 15:169–82.

Katz, Peter. 1994. *The New Urbanism: Toward an Architecture of Community*. New York: McGraw-Hill.

Kostof, Sprio. 1991. *The City Shaped*. Boston: Little, Brown.

Kostof, Sprio. 1992. *The City Assembled*. Boston: Little, Brown.

Kuo, Frances E. 2003. "The Role of Arboriculture in a Healthy Social Ecology." *Journal of Arboriculture* 29(3): 148–54.

Lynch, Kevin. 1960. *The Image of the City*. Cambridge, MA: MIT Press.

Lynch, Kevin. 1981. *Good City Form*. Cambridge, MA: MIT Press.

Maller, Cecily, Mardie Townsend, Anita Pryor, Peter Brown, and Lawrence St. Leger. 2005. "Healthy Nature Healthy People: 'Contact with Nature' as an Upstream Health Promotion Intervention for Populations." *Health Promotion International* 21(1): 45–54.

Maslow, A. 1968. *Towards a Psychology of Being*. New York: Van Nostrand.

Mumford, Lewis. 1961. *The City in History: Its Origins, Its Transformations, and Its Prospects*. New York: Harcourt, Brace & World.

Norberg-Schulz, Christian. 1976. "The Phenomenon of Place." *Architectural Association Quarterly* 8:4.

Olmsted, Frederick Law. 1870/2007. "Public Parks and the Enlargement of Towns." In *The Urban Design Reader*, edited by Michael Larice and Elizabeth Macdonald. New York: Routledge.

Relph, Edward. 1976. *Place and Placelessness*. London: Pion.

Reps, John William. 1965. *The Making of Urban America: A History of City Planning in the United States*. Princeton, NJ: Princeton University Press.

Robinson, Charles Mulford. 1904. *Modern Civic Art; or, The City Made Beautiful*, 2nd ed. New York: G.P. Putnam.

Robinson, Charles Mulford. 1907. *The Improvement of Towns and Cities; or, The Practical Basis of Civic Aesthetics*, 3rd ed. New York: G.P. Putnam.

San Francisco Department of City Planning. 1971. *The Urban Design Plan for the Comprehensive Plan of San Francisco*. San Francisco: Department of City Planning.

Sitte, Camillo. 1945. *The Art of Building Cities; City Building According to its Artistic Fundamentals*. New York: Reinhold.

Ulrich, Roger S. 1986. "Human Responses to Vegetation and Landscapes." *Landscape and Urban Planning* 13:29–44.

CHAPTER 7

SUSTAINABILITY

EMILY TALEN

> "The truth of the matter is that we simply do
> not know enough about our cities to chart
> their replanning or justify necessary controls."
> —Melville Branch Jr., *The Planners Journal*, 1941

IT has been seventy years since Melville Branch cautioned planners to wait before they acted. But on the subject of sustainability, the truth about cities has mostly been settled in much the same way that the truth about global warming has mostly been settled (Pooley 2010). To be sustainable means to last, to endure—and for planners, that means that cities, towns, and other human habitats should seek to reduce their consumption of resources and increase their resilience and adaptability.

Of course, this agreement declines as one attempts to get more specific. What does the notion of a less-consuming, resilient, and adaptive urbanism mean in terms of metrics and parameters? What is the degree of compactness and diversity necessary, for example, and at what point do these conditions cease to be important? What perverse and unintended outcomes are created when various attempts to be sustainable are implemented? What are the limits to accommodating natural processes in urban places, such that the human connectivity required for resilience is left intact? How can social diversity, which for so long had been dealt with via geographic dispersion, now be condensed? Should cities be bounded, in the tradition of Ledoux, Howard, and Kropotkin, or is a gradual leveling off of urbanism more sustainable? How should we integrate crop production, cars, college campuses, energy sources, or employment centers within our sustainable urban ideal? And what of the processes involved? How are sustainable cities to be promoted through the haze of an American public confused about nature (Cronon 1996), a public participation system often characterized as raucous and dysfunctional (Campanella 2011), and a sprawl building machine accustomed to reaping huge profits on the very antithesis of the sustainable city (Leinberger 2008)?

This chapter attempts to sort through this complex array of sustainability issues and provide a forward-looking basis for future planning scholarship. For, despite the remaining indeterminacies, I believe some consensus on what the sustainable human habitat looks like is finally congealing. On that basis, this chapter will take a stand on what is known and unknown, what we seem to agree on and what we don't, what should be put to rest and what should be pursued full force.

The chapter is in two parts. First, I overview what I believe to be consensus thinking concerning what sustainable places are. Citing key literature, I review the generalized principles of sustainable cities, moving from a broader review toward a more specific definition. I begin with the basic principles, and then spell out what those principles might mean for the physical form and pattern of cities. I then lay out the debates and gray areas. Although planners largely agree what a sustainable place should be on a certain level, there continue to be entrenched disagreements about the parameters, effects, and implementation strategies necessary.

Admittedly, my approach is based on a definite point of view—so it is necessary to explain that the discussion that follows rests on two core ideas. First, my belief is that sustainability in planning is made richer, and more meaningful, if it does not attempt to escape objectives, values, and normative thinking. There are definite goals, and it is often necessary to judge whether something contributes to those goals or not. Related to this, not every position planners take with respect to the question of sustainability can be answered through quantitative analysis. For example, a high-quality public realm is essential for sustainable cities because it makes possible a diversity of uses and people in close proximity (Talen 2008). But it would not be desirable, nor even possible, to design a public space based on the results of a regression analysis.

Second, the ideas presented in this chapter are based on a particular definition of planning as a field whose primary interest is the built environment—cities, towns, and places; their civic spaces and physical infrastructure; and their relationship to the natural world. In this I agree with Thomas Campanella, who recently argued that planning ought to return to its roots as a "grounded, tangible, place-bound matter of orchestrating human activity on the land" (2011, 151). Where planning is defined as analysis devoid of this connection, the topic of sustainability in planning—in my view—loses meaning.

This is not to say that sustainability in an urban context includes nothing more than the physical and infrastructure qualities of built form. In particular, institutional strategies like recycling programs, local governance, and civic participation are considered important for promoting sustainable cities (Newman and Jennings 2008; Farr 2008; Roseland 2005). And always, green building and infrastructure technologies—efficiencies in structural design, energy use, and materials, as well as green infrastructure—are an important part of the task of sustainable city building. But it is important to hone in on the physical form of cities for two very practical reasons. First, some aspects of sustainability, even when focused on cities, are fully within the purview of other, nonplanning fields. For example, institutional practices like recycling and civic participation can be, and often are, handled by public policy or, increasingly, by sustainability science. Second, there is no other constituency besides urban planning specifically devoted to urban pattern and form. It is within their purview more than any other field to identify sustainable practice when it comes to how land is developed and occupied.

1. What We (Mostly) Know about Sustainable Places

Most urban planners would now argue that, in principle and in broad terms, we know what a sustainable place is supposed to be and what the economic, social, health, and environmental benefits of it are. Berke and Manta-Conroy (2000, 23) define sustainable development as "a dynamic process in which communities anticipate and accommodate the needs of current and future generations in ways that reproduce and balance local social, economic and ecological systems, and link local actions to global concerns." This is the planning version of "sustainability" from the oft-cited Brundtland Report: "Sustainable development is development that meets the needs of the present without compromising the ability of future generations to meet their own needs" (World Commission on Environment and Development [WCED] 1987, 43). Of relevance to planning is the idea that sustainability involves adopting a life-style "within the planet's ecological means" to ensure that development does not compromise the needs of future generations and to ensure that population growth is "in harmony with the changing productive potential of the ecosystem" (43). Urban planners have translated this to mean that cities must endure environmentally, economically, and socially, balancing what have come to be known as the three "E"s: environment, economy, and equity (Berke 2002, 30; see also Campbell 1996). The book *Sustainable Urbanism* by Doug Farr (2008, 10) provides an even more explicit interpretation: "Sustainable urbanism is an integration of walkable and transit-served urbanism with high-performance buildings and high performance infrastructure." Thus, the sustainable city is more than just green buildings and pervious pavement; it involves the design of walkable communities along with the connections to transit, food, and amenity they require (Brown, Southworth, and Stovall 2005; Sanchez 1999; Wu and Murray 2005).

Planners seem especially in agreement about what an *unsustainable* city looks like. Sprawl is defined as "low density, noncontiguous, automobile dependent" development (Bengston, Fletcher, and Nelson 2004, 271), and researchers have become adept at measuring and defining it (Freihage et al. 2001), quantifying its costs and effects (Burchell et al. 2005; Hirschhorn 2005; Williamson 2010), and unraveling its underlying causes (Glaeser and Kahn 2003; Burchfield et al. 2006). Sprawl has been implicated as a factor in some of the most serious problems facing American society, including global warming (Gonzalez 2009), social inequity (Squires 2002; Pendall 2000), environmental degradation (Benfield, Terris, and Vorsanger 2001; Ewing 2005), and public health problems (Frumkin 2004). More popular literature like *Green Metropolis* by David Owen (2009) or even Edward Glaeser's *Triumph of the City* (2011) continue to make the case for dense urban places—expounding the environmental, social, and economic benefits of living smaller, driving less, lowering energy costs, strengthening social connections, and fostering networks of economic interdependence.

The environmental side of sustainability in planning is often prioritized. While planners agree that sustainability requires a holistic view "that includes equal concern for environmental, economic, and social sustainability" (Daniels 2009, 185; see also Newman and Jennings 2008), the environmental perspective dominates. Thus, urban transport is to be energy efficient, solar power is to be promoted where possible, water is to be used efficiently—in short, cities are to be redefined as "eco-technical systems" (Girardet 2004). Cities are going "green," and Routledge's comprehensive four volumes entitled *Sustainable Urban Development* (Vreeker, Deakin, and Curwell 2008; Cooper and Symes 2008; Deakin et al. 2007; Curwell, Deakin, and Symes 2005) is principally devoted to environmental assessment. Out of this larger environmental focus, many subtopics have evolved that are of particular relevance to urban planners, such as the relationship between sustainability and technology (Sharples, Bougdah, and Zunde 2008), sustainability and architecture (Thomas and Garnham 2007), and even "sustainable Olympic Games" (Pitts and Liao 2008).

The ability of planners to measure the sustainable qualities of urban form has advanced significantly over the past two decades (e.g., Breheny 1992; Frey 1999; Mazmanian and Kraft 1999; Williams, Burton, and Jenks 2000; Clemente et al. 2005; Wheeler 2005; Jenks and Dempsey 2005; Jabareen 2006; Farr 2008; van der Ryn and Calthorpe 2008; Miles and Song 2009). This literature attests to a high degree of consensus about what a sustainable place is supposed to be: sustainable places are walkable and compact, have diverse uses and mixed housing types, and have well-designed public spaces around which diverse uses and housing types are anchored. These qualities run counter to a previous generation of city building that promoted segregated land uses, superblock "projects," socially insular and physically disconnected housing, and car-dependent subdivisions and shopping malls.

We can summarize the key principles that promote sustainable places from an environmental point of view. Cities must (a) lower vehicle miles traveled (VMTs), limiting carbon emissions by looking for ways to reduce reliance on fossil fuels (cars) and increase reliance on clean transportation (e.g., bus rapid transit, light rail); (b) lower energy costs by lowering infrastructure, like highways, and utility lines, which in turn results in lower transmission loss; and (c) limit damage to natural environments by lowering impervious surfaces and runoff, compacting development, and lowering disruption of biodiversity and natural habitat (Ewing et al. 2008). Sustainable industrial and energy systems, food production, and mitigation of heat-island effects are also essential. Sustainable places promote "green streets" that handle storm water within their rights-of-way; contain visible, green infrastructure; and maximize street trees to improve air quality, reduce temperature, and absorb storm water (Low 2010). Sustainable places support passive solar design, sustainable storm-water practices, organic architecture, the harnessing of waste heat, and the protection of biodiversity corridors. There are also sustainable activities, regulations, and development approval processes (Lubell, Feiock, and Handy 2009) that promote eco-industrial park development, bicycle ridership programs, point systems for green architecture, or the use of sustainability indicators (see Portney 2003).

That's just the environmental side. To endure economically, sustainable places need to foster diverse economic networks of interconnected relations, a view that Jane Jacobs famously advocated in *The Death and Life of Great American Cities* (1961) and that Richard Florida (2005), Edward Glaeser (2011), and many others have expanded upon. The basic idea is this: "the combinations of mixtures of activities, not separate uses, are the key to successful urban places" (Montgomery 1998, 98). Allan Jacobs and Donald Appleyard (1987, 117) wrote a widely cited manifesto in which they argued that diversity and the integration of activities were necessary parts of "an urban fabric for an urban life." The maximizing of "exchange possibilities," both economic and social, is viewed as the key factor of urban quality of life (Greenberg 1995), and now, sustainability. What counted for Jane Jacobs was the "everyday, ordinary performance in mixing people," forming complex "pools of use" that would be capable of producing something greater than the sum of their parts (1961, 164–65). More empirically, the mixture of land uses has been shown to encourage nonautomobile-based modes of travel such as walking and bicycling (Cervero 1996), which in turn are seen as having a positive impact on public health (Frank et al. 2006; Moudon et al. 2006; Giles-Corti and Donovan 2003). Mixed uses have been shown to be associated with lower congestion levels and lower commuting time (Ewing et al. 2003).

The connection between sustainability and diversity is that a diverse community is, presumably, better able to take care of itself. The book *Building Sustainable Urban Settlements* (Romaya and Rakodi 2002), for example, lists "mixed land uses" first under its set of principles for building settlements that are considered sustainable. The "richly differentiated neighborhood" is more "durable and resilient" against economic downturn, in other words (Scott 1998, 138). The optimal scale of this diversity is generally small, since a "close-grained" diversity of uses provides "constant mutual support," rendering planning "the science and art of catalyzing and nourishing these close-grained working relationships" (Jacobs 1961, 14). The separation of urbanism into components, like land-use categories, miles of highways, square footage of office space, or park acreage per capita, work against this, leading to, as Lewis Mumford had earlier termed it, the "anti-city" (1968, 128). Large-scale modernist urbanism "from Soviet bureaucracy to L.A. freeways to the

Cabrini Green housing project" is generally viewed as antithetical to diversity, and as such, "spectacularly wrong" (Walljasper 2007).

Diversity also contributes to resilience by offering opportunity. Nondiversity offers little hope for future expansion, in the form of either personal growth or economic development. Additionally, nondiverse places are not able to support the full range of employment required to sustain a multifunctional human settlement (Ledebur and Barnes 1993). Diversity of income and education levels means that the people needed for service employment, including local government workers (police, fire, schoolteachers), and those employed in the stores and restaurants that cater to a local clientele, will not have to travel from outside the community to be employed there (Orfield 2002; Rusk 2001).

This brings us to the third dimension—that of social sustainability. As with economic sustainability, diversity is seen as a key variable. Socially diverse neighborhoods are believed to be essential for broader community well-being, resiliency, and social equity goals (for example, Turner and Berube 2009; Popkin, Levy, and Buron 2009; Talen 1998; Murray and Davis 2001). A socially diverse city—one that avoids differentiation of social groups into segregated housing enclaves—ensures better access to resources for all social groups, providing what is known as the "geography of opportunity" (Briggs 2005). Diversity can also help build social capital of the bridging kind by widening networks of social interaction. Where there is less social diversity and more segregation, there is likely to be less opportunity for the creation of these wider social networks. This could be a significant disadvantage for segregated neighborhoods, and could even have the effect of prolonging unemployment (Grannoveter 1983; see also Nyden, Maly, and Lukehart 1997; Putnam 2000).

Recent revelations that suburban poverty rates are higher than urban poverty rates have produced calls for more economically integrated neighborhoods throughout metropolitan regions (Berube and Kneebone 2006). These social-mixing goals (for a summary, see Sarkissian 1976; Talen 2008) can all be tied to sustainability: to raise the living standards of lower income residents, to encourage aesthetic diversity and cultural cross-fertilization, to increase equality of opportunity, and to maintain stable neighborhoods, whereby one can choose to move up or down in housing expenditure and remain in the same area. Diversity is also believed to foster a more active use of neighborhood space at different times of the day, providing a natural form of community surveillance. Supporting this are findings that a mix of neighborhood public facilities plays a role in reducing crime (Colquhoun 2004; Peterson, Krivo, and Harris 2000).

A kind of meta-principle for sustainable urban places is compactness. There is general agreement that cities that are more dense and compact and less sprawling and land consumptive are likely to be more sustainable in environmental and economic terms (Newman and Kenworthy 1996). All of the environmental principles of sustainability suggest or even require it, although there is no defined threshold, and it may be necessary to provide a continuum of levels of compactness or density (Duany and Talen 2002). While compact cities do not necessarily lead to shorter commute times (Gordon, Richardson, and Kumar 1989), there is solid evidence that compact urban form is connected to lower energy consumption (Andrews 2008). Ewing et al. (2008) estimate that each increment of compact development reduces both CO_2 emissions and fuel consumption by 20 to 40 percent. Compactness means that there will be fewer highways, greater transit feasibility, greater opportunities for combined heat and power, and lower pumping requirements for water and sewer.

The level of density required for sustainability is unknown, although low-density development, variously defined, has been linked to higher infrastructure costs (Speir and Stephenson 2002), increased automobile dependence (Cervero and Wu 1998), and increased air pollution (Stone 2008). Density is seen as an essential factor in maintaining walkable, pedestrian-based access to needed services and neighborhood-based facilities (Kunstler 1994; Newman and Kenworthy 2006). Planners' commitment to a denser form of urbanism is supported by research that shows increasing preference for "traditionally designed communities" (Handy et al. 2008), and there are predictions that demand for denser urban neighborhoods is likely to grow in the coming decades (Leinberger 2008; Nelson and Lang 2007).

Another dimension of sustainable places is accessibility, a longstanding component of theories of good (i.e., sustainable) urban form (see in particular Jacobs 1961; Lynch 1981; Jacobs and Appleyard 1987). A sustainable settlement pattern is regularly defined as one that increases access between residents, their places of work, and the services they require (Dittmar and Ohland 2003). Accessibility is tied to the principles of smart growth (Song and Knaap 2004; Talen 2002) and active living environments (Heath et al. 2006; Norman et al. 2006), and measures of access have been used extensively in the past few years as part of an effort to evaluate the built environment for health effects (see, for example, Moudon and Lee 2003; Greenwald and Boarnet 2002).

Transportation scholars like to point out the difference between access and mobility, or the idea that the costs involved in getting between two places is different from the opportunities available from a given location (Crane 2008; Levinson and Krizek 2005). For sustainability, a focus on planning for accessibility over planning for mobility is especially important (although the two are often confused), since maximizing the ability to get around by car (mobility) is a different, and usually less sustainable, approach from maximizing accessibility overall (Handy 2005).

Walkable access to services is an essential part of the sustainability equation. It is common for sustainable urban form to be defined by the degree to which it supports the needs of pedestrians and bicyclists over car drivers (Moudon and Lee 2003). Streets that are pedestrian oriented are believed to have an effect not only on quality of place but also on the degree to which people are willing to walk, which in turn has important health outcomes (Forsyth et al. 2008). Researchers have argued that activity levels can be increased by implementing small-scale interventions in local neighborhood environments (Sallis, Bauman, and Pratt 1998), and a whole catalog of design strategies are now used to make streets more pedestrian oriented (Institute of Transportation Engineers 2005).

Connectivity, a related concept, refers to the degree to which local environments offer points of connection and contact (to people and resources) at a variety of scales and for multiple purposes. This quality promotes sustainability in that higher connectivity is believed to lead to higher levels of interaction between residents and the environment, society, and cultural and economic activity—all of which are believed to improve neighborhood stability in the long term. Social connection on the neighborhood scale is seen as a pedestrian phenomenon (Michelson 1977), and networks of "neighborly relations" are related to interconnected pedestrian streets and the internal neighborhood access those street networks provide (Grannis 2009). Opportunities for interaction and exchange are maximized by increasing the number of routes (streets, sidewalks, and other thoroughfares and pathways) and access points throughout an area (Salingaros 1998; Hillier and Hanson 1984; Alexander 1965). From an urban-form point of view, increasing connectivity translates to gridded street networks, short blocks, streets that connect rather than dead-end, central places where multiple activities can coalesce, and well-located facilities that function as shared spaces (Carmona et al. 2003). It is generally agreed that large-scale blocks, cul-de-sacs, and dendritic (treelike) street systems are less likely to provide good connectivity (Trancik 1986).

Finally, sustainable places are associated with what could be termed polycentric or multinucleated urbanism—the idea that urban development should be organized around nodes of varying sizes (see Frey 1999). Whereas sprawl tends to be spread across the landscape uniformly, sustainable urban form has a discernible hierarchy to it—from regional growth nodes to neighborhood centers or even block-level public spaces. On the largest scale, centers may be conceived as regionally interconnected "urban cores," with higher intensity growth converging at transportation corridors. At the neighborhood level, nodes support sustainable urban form by providing public space around which buildings are organized. It is not a place where all shopping and social interaction necessarily occurs, nor does it need to be literally at the center of a population. By providing a common destination for surrounding residents, such spaces support other aspects of sustainable urbanism, such as increases in surrounding density, mixed housing type anchored by a centralized space, or the viability of neighborhood-based retail.

2. DEBATES AND GRAY AREAS

Sustainability in planning is a matter of degree. While the direction of association is mostly agreed upon—sustainable places are compact, diverse, connected, and so on—the specific parameters of these principles are not. Thus, studies of the connection between, say, urban form and travel behavior (Boarnet and Crane 2001; see also Boarnet, this volume), or between urban form and health (Frank, Engelke, and Schmid 2003), may admonish planners for failing to see the full complexities involved in linking particular forms to sustainability outcomes, but they are unlikely to call for the wholesale reversal of the basic idea that compact, diverse, walkable urbanism supports sustainability. Between business-as-usual sprawl development of the "nineteen real estate product types" that define suburbia (Leinberger 2008) and urban planners seeking a more diverse and compact urbanism, there is a significant divide. Debates center on *how much* compactness, walkability, and diversity of land use (Frey, 1999; Jenks, Burton, and Williams 1996; Williams, 2005), not *whether* compactness and diversity are important goals. And while it is entirely possible to discuss the level of social sustainability—in terms of equity, justice, and social capital—that might be achieved by alternative sustainable urban forms, these too are a matter of degree (Ancell and Thompson-Fawcett 2008; Bramley and Power 2005).

The parameters of every one of the dimensions discussed above can be debated. On the question of density, for example, it is possible to debate what level of density is sustainable, and under what conditions. When is a place merely "dense sprawl" as opposed to walkable urbanism? What lot sizes correlate with a density sufficient enough to support transit, and under what conditions does this relationship change? How many units of what building type produce a sustainable outcome? Some suggest that the data show a leveling off of sustainable benefits at about 100 persons to the hectare (about 20 units to the acre; see Mehaffy et al. 2009), but how does this square with Glaeser's (2011) contention that even the density proposed by Jane Jacobs (150 units per acre) was too low?[1]

Related to these parametric issues, there is the problem of partially realized sustainability principles—a phenomenon that, in particular, puts a significant strain on social equity (Jenks, Burton, and Williams 1996; Burton 2002). For example, some have recently questioned the idea that sustainability for affordable housing residents is necessarily beneficial (Pendall and Parilla 2011; Schwartz 2011). One issue is that neighborhoods can be walkable in terms of urban-form dimensions like small block size and land-use diversity, but such neighborhoods might not be the ones that offer the most employment access, the lowest crime, or the best schools. Research that is just now surfacing (for example, Pendall and Parilla 2011; Been et al. 2010) seems to indicate that what residents value most is low poverty and low crime, and that walkable, well-serviced, "sustainable" urban form is of secondary importance. In some neighborhoods, access to nearby parks and transit stops might coincide with higher crime risks, and land-use mix might represent a higher likelihood of living near a variety of undesirable land uses. In other words, the indicators of walkability that are appreciated in higher income neighborhoods do not necessarily have the same value in neighborhoods where crime, poor quality of amenities, and undesirable land uses are prevalent (Talen and Koschinsky 2011). Again, this is a problem of incomplete realization of sustainability goals—neighborhoods that are walkable but crime ridden can hardly be viewed as fully "sustainable."

The question is whether partial success in implementation is better or worse than doing nothing. Ancell and Thompson-Fawcett (2005, 427) raise a legitimate question about whether intensifying parts of a city make a city more sustainable:

"if this results in diminished opportunities for lower-income groups to live in the central city, is such intensification necessary or sufficient as a basis for social sustainability with respect to planning for housing?" (See also Bunce 2009.) One response is that this might be more a matter of failed or incomplete implementation than of failed principle.

Implementation of sustainability principles is a tall order in the United States, requiring fundamental change to existing policies and regulations that have for decades promoted the opposite of sustainable urbanism—that is, sprawl. These include housing policies, transportation regulations, federal expenditures, water policy, and immigration, to name only a few (Wiewel and Persky 2002; Wolch 2004; Frece 2008). There have been thorough explorations of the inefficiencies, social inequities, and added costs of conventional zoning codes (Dowall 1984; Levine 2005), which have been deemed anything but sustainable (Krier 2009). Of course, even where policy is directed at growth management (Landis 2006), or smart growth (Sartori, Moore, and Knaap 2011; see also Song, this volume), the effects of these policies are not always in line with sustainability. This may be why it has been said that it is during implementation of sustainability principles that "tensions inherent in the idea of sustainable development itself" are exposed (Owens and Cowell 2002, 28; see also Batty 2006).

These questions—of degrees, parameters, perverse effects, partial realization, and policy implementation—are all vital issues in sustainability scholarship (and warrant a fuller discussion than this chapter can provide). But in the remainder of this chapter, I want to explore two additional debates that I believe are of special relevance for planning scholars interested in the topic of sustainability: process versus form, and city versus nature.

The first concerns the tension between flexibility and open-ended process versus preconceived forms and concrete visions expressed as ideal models of urban form. In his book *The Original Green*, Steven Mouzon (2010) makes the argument that cities, to be sustainable, must embody a number of specific design principles, from walkable streets, to preservation of the embodied energy of historic buildings, to design that encourages the use of public space and the civic interaction that results (see also Duany, Speck, and Lydon 2009). For some, the specific design qualities needed to enhance sustainability at this level should be more open ended and flexible.

In lieu of this kind of normative approach, common among New Urbanists, some argue that sustainability in planning should instead be about managing "the continuous processes of change" (Brown 2006, 100). Brown notes that this was the perspective of the revered urban planner Kevin Lynch, who wrote in *Good City Form* (1981, 116):

> The good city is one in which the continuity of this complex ecology is
> maintained while progressive change is permitted. The fundamental good is
> the continuous development of the individual or the small group and their
> culture: a process of becoming more complex, more richly connected, more
> competent, acquiring and realizing new powers—intellectual, emotional,
> social, and physical.

Planners who agree with this view are not likely to promote "a steady state with respect to human-environment relations," and will instead devote their energies to promoting the best possible process.

Process and form need not necessarily be in opposition. Many New Urbanists contend that both are needed, relying on the charrette process to implement their model of sustainable urban form (Lenertz and Lutzenhiser 2006). But many planners, while they would agree with the basic outlines of what a sustainable place should look like, are far more interested in ensuring a sustainable process than a preconceived form. Phil Berke (2008, 393) summed up the objectives in a special issue on green communities in the *Journal of the American Planning Association*: "collaborative planning processes aimed at strengthening and mobilizing social networks to support green community initiatives, requirements and incentives that stimulate greener community and household behaviors, and new assessment tools for green building rating, and greenhouse gas inventory and analysis." In other words, process, procedure, and assessment rather than specific urban form ideals. Largely this entails prioritizing resident views: "it is important to avoid undertaking research with pre-conceived notions as to whether impacts of urban compaction such as smaller houses are negative or positive, and instead to let the residents speak for themselves" (Ancell and Thompson-Fawcett 2008, 440). In a similar vein, some have argued that sustainability is being thwarted by bureaucracies that are ill-prepared to deal with the reality that "sustainable development is political rather than analytical," and that overly pragmatic policy solutions (i.e., urban design ideals) might forever frustrate the value-laden complexity of sustainability (Batty 2006, 38).

In the architecture field, models of sustainable urban form that appear to be universalist (such as those of the New Urbanists) are rejected. Architects are especially "skeptical of the assumption that a single approach, model, or list of best practices can be universally applied," arguing instead for a "much needed transdisciplinary conversation to emphasize the long-term consequences of our actions, not their ideological or disciplinary purity" (Moore 2010). Reviewing why one city is better able to develop sustainably than another rests on "particular dispositions toward politics, nature, and technology," not on "a single abstract model" (Moore 2007, 248).

An even more fundamental debate concerns the relationship between cities and nature, which can be described as "human versus nature duality" (Talen and Brody 2005). There is a long history to this in urban planning, and the recent focus on sustainability elevates its importance. It originated with the regionalism of early twentieth-century botanist Patrick Geddes, who viewed metropolitan development as dependent upon knowledge of the large-scale, regional complexities of the landscape and the human response to that landscape. However, early regionalists believed no synthesis between *existing* metropolitan development and nature was possible. This imbalance, which was explicitly outlined by MacKaye (1928) in *The New Exploration*, came to epitomize the view that large metropolitan areas were the antithesis of environmental conservation (Duany 2002).

Now, there is recognition that sustainable cities require that economic, environmental, and social needs be balanced and interconnected (Daly and Cobb 1989; Rees 1989; Van der Ryn and Calthorpe 1991). Sustainability is believed to be based on the idea that it is necessary to find the proper balance between human-made and natural environments, the "warp and woof that make up the fabric of our lives" (Van der Ryn and Cowan 1995, 3). According to Beatley and Manning (1997), this constitutes a new brand of environmental thinking. Under what is sometimes branded "the new urban ecology" (Collins et al. 2000), cities are no longer viewed as necessarily detrimental, but are in fact part of the solution to environmental problems.

For the most part, however, this is a rhetorical position. Historian William Cronon explored the deeply ingrained American ethos of separating human and natural worlds in the book *Uncommon Ground: Rethinking the Human Place in Nature* (1996), and argued that wilderness, the "ideological underpinning" of the environmentalist movement, is a highly problematic concept because it is viewed as something wholly separate from ourselves. Even the opening line of the Union of Concerned Scientists' *Warning to Humanity* (1992, 1) included the premise of separation. It begins: "Human beings and the natural world are on a collision course."

The metrics of environmentalism do little to resolve this duality. Planners have translated urban impacts using concepts like "carrying capacity" to promote the idea that metropolitan development should not consume resources faster than they can be renewed (Meadows et al. 1972), while the "ecological footprint" is used to measure sustainability by calculating the amount of resources consumed (Wackernagel and Rees 1996), but these methods fail to fully account for the trade-offs and benefits of compact urban form, among other things (Fiala 2008). In essence, the ecological footprint may foster human versus nature duality because of its emphasis on establishing a causal link between cities and accelerated global ecological decline.

What may be the most lucid example of human–nature duality in planning is the way in which the "greening" of human places is interpreted as something unilaterally positive for the environment, regardless of broader impacts (Kunstler 1994; Low 2010; Mouzon 2010). There may be a failure to recognize that metropolitan development patterns that appear "natural" in the suburban landscape actually disrupt natural systems. In fact, maintaining green spaces may be harmful both in direct ways (through soil compaction, irrigation, and the need for chemical treatment) and in indirect ways (increasing atmospheric pollution through increased automobile use caused by spreading out the urban pattern; Duany and Brain 2004). In short, interweaving green spaces through human settlement may sometimes be more harmful than not when viewed on a larger scale. Somewhat ironically, the most environmentally sound pattern of human settlement—in some cases—may be the one with lower rather than higher levels of green space.

This tension between cities and nature has been identified by Godschalk (2004) and others as the "green cities conflict." It is essentially a conflict over the degree to which natural versus human connectivity is to be prioritized (see Duany,

Plater-Zyberk, and Speck 2000 vs. Beatley and Manning 1997). New Urbanism has been criticized for failing to accommodate more environmental sensitivity (Beatley 2005; Berke 2002), and this often boils down to their focus on maintaining urban connectivity. New Urbanists argue that environmental regulations may inadvertently thwart compact urban development, including suburban retrofits.

In addition to these technical issues, the human versus nature duality manifests itself in politics. Sustainable development can engage a complex array of political views that range from "free market" environmentalism to ecofeminism, animal rights, and bioregionalism. The three-way conflict between environmentalism, economic development, and social justice—green cities, growing cities, and just cities, as Campbell (1996) refers to them—is present in all of these approaches, and each manifests a human versus nature duality to varying degrees. Proposals include "greening the market" (Hawken 1993), liberal environmentalism in the tradition of John Rawls (Clark 2000), ecosocialist theory that searches for "collective conscious control by humans of their relationship with nature" (Pepper 1993), or the biological rooting of culture through "reinhabitation" (Alexander 1990).

In many of these applications, there remains a fundamental, lingering duality that conceptualizes an environmental crisis in human versus nature terms. This is unlikely to advance social justice. While Harvey (2000, 232) promotes the idea that "our collective responsibilities to human nature and nature need to be connected in a far more dynamic and co-evolutionary way across a variety of spatiotemporal scales," the translation to concrete action—from compact urban form to recycling—is easily discounted as the "residues of a utopian environmentalism" found in the "landscapes of capitalism" (Harvey 2000, 231).

3. CONCLUSION

The debates and gray areas outlined above frame some of the most interesting aspects of sustainability in the planning field. We might know what sustainable urbanism is in broad terms, but scholarship is still needed to define more specific parameters, understand and work to offset perverse effects, and figure out ways to more effectively implement the essential objectives. The definition of the sustainable city is, in principle, resolved; the question is how to get there and how to stay on target. Should our strategy involve a reliance on the right process that guides city building toward a more sustainable outcome, or via a stronger articulation of what the sustainable city is supposed to be? Should we look to an urban development approach that prioritizes natural systems, or one that allows natural systems to be trumped in some cases in order to promote urban connectivity and compactness?

There is an interesting overlap between the two debates discussed above. Ultimately, the need to balance process versus form and the need to integrate city versus nature may ultimately converge in our approach to sustainable urban planning. It could be argued that creating visually explicit models of future development *and* providing an inclusive process are both needed to help resolve the human versus nature duality problem. An explicit, but inclusive process that allows flexibility and the exploration of alternative proposals is needed not only to ensure that development actually addresses human–nature integration but also does so in a way that makes sense to people.

Planners need to find a balance between visualized ideals and inclusive process, and between the unequivocal protection of nature and the corresponding human claim to land development. In both cases, there is a need to bring the language of integration into sharper focus. In sustainable planning, actions are supposed to balance natural, economic, and social concerns. Sustainability challenges us to make every decision supportive, and integrative, of each realm.

NOTE

1. Although Glaeser makes this claim, Jane Jacobs's view on density was not this exact. She advocated maximizing density as long as it did not undermine the diversity of building types and ages.

REFERENCES

Alexander, Christopher. 1965. "A City Is Not a Tree." *Architectural Forum* 122 (April): 58–62 and (May): 58–61.

Alexander, D. 1990. "Bioregionalism: Science or Sensibility?" *Environmental Ethics* 12(Summer): 161–73.

Ancell, Sarah, and Michelle Thompson-Fawcett. 2008. "The Social Sustainability of Medium Density Housing: A Conceptual Model and Christchurch Case Study." *Housing Studies* 23(3): 423–41.

Andrews, C. J. 2008. "Greenhouse Gas Emissions along the Rural-Urban Gradient." *Journal of Environmental Planning and Management* 51(6): 847–70.

Batty, Susan E. 2006. "Planning for Sustainable Development in Britain: A Pragmatic Approach." *The Town Planning Review* 77(1): 29–40.

Beatley, Timothy. 2005. *Native to Nowhere: Sustaining Home and Community in the Global Age.* Washington, DC: Island Press.

Beatley, Timothy, and Kristy Manning. 1997. *The Ecology of Place.* Washington, DC: Island Press.

Been, Vicki, Mary Cunningham, Ingrid Gould Ellen, Adam Gordon, Joe Parilla, Margery Austin Turner, Sheryl Verlaine Whitney, Aaron Yowell, and Ken Zimmerman. 2010. "Building Environmentally Sustainable Communities: A Framework for Inclusivity." A paper of the What Works Collaborative. Available at: http://www.urban.org/UploadedPDF/412088-environmentally-sustainable-communities.pdf; from September 14, 2010.

Benfield, F. Kaid, Jutka Terris, and Nancy Vorsanger. 2001. *Solving Sprawl: Models of Smart Growth in Communities Across America.* New York: Natural Resources Defense Council.

Bengston, D. N., J. O. Fletcher, and K. C. Nelson. 2004. "Public Policies for Managing Urban Growth and Protecting Open Space: Policy Instruments and Lessons Learned in the United States." *Landscape and Urban Planning* 69(2–3): 271–86.

Berke, Philip. 2002. "Does Sustainable Development Offer a New Direction for Planning? Challenges for the Twenty First Century." *Journal of Planning Literature* 17(1): 22–36.

Berke, Philip R. 2008. "The Evolution of Green Community Planning, Scholarship, and Practice." *Journal of the American Planning Association* 74(4): 393–408.

Berke, Philip, and Maria Manta-Conroy. 2000. "Are We Planning for Sustainable Development? An Evaluation of 30 Comprehensive Plans." *Journal of the American Planning Association* 66(1): 21–34.

Berube, Alan, and Elizabeth Kneebone. 2006. *Two Steps Back: City and Suburban Poverty Trends 1999–2005*. Washington, DC: Brookings Institution. Available at: www.brookings.edu/metro/pubs/20061205_citysuburban.htm.

Boarnet, Marlon, and Randall Crane. 2001. *Travel by Design: The Influence of Urban Form on Travel*. New York: Oxford University Press.

Bramley, G., and S. Power. 2005. "City Form and Social Sustainability." Working paper, Sustainable Urban Form Consortium, Edinburgh, June.

Breheny, Michael, ed. 1992. *Sustainable Development and Urban Form*. London: Pion.

Briggs, Xavier De Souza, ed. 2005. *The Geography of Opportunity. Race and Housing Choice in Metropolitan America*. Washington, DC: Brookings Institution Press.

Brown, David F. 2006. "Back to Basics: The Influence of Sustainable Development on Urban Planning with Special Reference to Montreal." *Canadian Journal of Urban Research* 15(1, Suppl.): 99–117.

Brown, Marilyn A., Frank Southworth, and Therese K. Stovall. 2005. *Towards a Climate-Friendly Built Environment*. Arlington, VA: Pew Center for Global Climate Change.

Bunce, Susannah. 2009. "Developing Sustainability: Sustainability Policy and Gentrification on Toronto's Waterfront." *Local Environment* 14(7): 651–67.

Burchell, Robert, Anthony Downs, Barbara McCann, and Sahan Mukherji. 2005. *Sprawl Costs: Economic Impacts of Unchecked Development*. Washington, DC: Island Press.

Burchfield, Marcy, Henry G. Overman, Diego Puga, and Matthew A. Turner. 2006. "Causes of Sprawl: A Portrait from Space." *Quarterly Journal of Economics* 121(2): 587–633.

Burton, Elizabeth. 2002. "Measuring Urban Compactness in UK Towns and Cities." *Environment and Planning Part B: Planning and Design* 29:219–50.

Campanella, Thomas. 2011. "Jane Jacobs and the Death and Life of American Planning." In Reconsidering Jane Jacobs, edited by Max Page and Timothy Mennel, 141–60. Chicago: APA Planners Press.

Campbell, Scott. 1996. "Green Cities, Growing Cities, Just Cities? Urban Planning and the Contradictions of Sustainable Development." *Journal of the American Planning Association* 62(3): 296–312.

Carmona, Matthew, Tim Heath, Taner Oc, and Steve Tiesdell. 2003. *Public Places, Urban Spaces: The Dimensions of Urban Design*. Oxford: Architectural Press.

Cervero, Robert. 1996. "Mixed Land-Uses and Communting: Evidence from the American Housing Survey." *Transportation Research* 30(5): 361–77.

Cervero, R., and K-L. Wu. 1998. "Sub-Centering and Commuting: Evidence from the San Francisco Bay Area, 1980–90." *Urban Studies* 35(7): 1059–76.

Clark, John. 2000. "Political Ecology." In *Environmental Philosophy: From Animal Rights to Radical Ecology* edited by Michael E. Zimmerman, 343–64. Upper Saddle River, NJ: Prentice-Hall.

Clemente, O., R. Ewing, S. Handy, R. Brownson, and E. Winston. 2005. *Measuring Urban Design Qualities—An Illustrated Field Manual.* Princeton, NJ: Robert Wood Johnson Foundation. Available at: www.activelivingresearch.org/index.php/Tools_and_Measures/312.

Collins, J., A. Kinzig, N. B. Grimm, W. Fagan, J. Wu, and E. Borer. 2000. "A New Urban Ecology." *American Scientist* 88:416–25.

Colquhoun, Ian. 2004. *Design Out Crime: Creating Safe and Sustainable Communities.* London: Architectural Press.

Cooper, Ian, and Martin Symes. 2008. *Sustainable Urban Development, Vol. 4: Changing Professional Practice.* London: Routledge.

Crane, Randall. 2008. "Counterpoint: Accessibility and Sprawl." *Journal of Transport and Land Use* 1(1): 13–19.

Cronon, William, ed. 1996. *Uncommon Ground: Rethinking the Human Place in Nature.* New York: W.W. Norton.

Curwell, Steven, Mark Deakin, and Martin Symes. 2005. *Sustainable Urban Development. Vol. 1: The Framework and Protocols for Environmental Assessment.* London: Routledge.

Daly, Herman E., and John B. Cobb Jr. 1989. *For the Common Good: Redirecting the Economy toward Community, the Environment, and a Sustainable Future.* Boston: Beacon Press.

Daniels, Thomas L. 2009. "A Trail Across Time: American Environmental Planning From City Beautiful to Sustainability." *Journal of the American Planning Association* 75(2): 178–93.

Deakin, Mark, Gordon Mitchell, Peter Nijkamp, and Ron Vreeker, eds. 2007. *Sustainable Urban Development. Vol. 2: The Environmental Assessment Methods.* London: Routledge.

Dittmar, Hank, and Gloria Ohland. 2003. *The New Transit Town: Best Practices in Transit-Oriented Development.* Washington, DC: Island Press.

Dowall, D. E. 1984. *The Suburban Squeeze.* Berkeley, CA: University of California Press.

Duany, Andres. 2002. Introduction. Special issue dedicated to the transect. *Journal of Urban Design* 7(3): 285–92.

Duany, Andres, and David Brain. 2004. "Regulating as if Humans Matter: The Transect and Promise of Post-Suburban Planning. In *Regulating Place: Standards and the Shaping of Urban America*, edited by Eran Ben-Joseph and Terry S. Szold, 293–332. New York: Routledge.

Duany, Andres, Elizabeth Plater-Zyberk, and Jeff Speck. 2000. *Suburban Nation: The Rise of Sprawl and the Decline of the American Dream.* New York: North Point.

Duany, Andres, Jeff Speck, and Mike Lydon. 2009. *The Smart Growth Manual.* New York: McGraw-Hill.

Duany, Andres, and Emily Talen. 2002. "Transect Planning." *Journal of the American Planning Association* 68(3): 245–66.

Ewing, Reid H. 2005. *Endangered by Sprawl: How Runaway Development Threatens America's Wildlife.* Washington, DC: National Wildlife Federation, Smart Growth America.

Ewing, Reid, Keith Bartholomew, Steve Winkelman, Jerry Walters, and Don Chen. 2008. *Growing Cooler: The Evidence on Urban Development and Climate Change.* Washington, DC: Urban Land Institute.

Ewing, R., T. Schmid, R. Killingsworth, A. Zlot, and S. Raudenbush. 2003. "Relationship between Urban Sprawl and Physical Activity, Obesity and Morbidity." *American Journal of Health Promotion* 18(1): 47–57.

Farr, Douglas. 2008. *Sustainable Urbanism: Urban Design with Nature*. Hoboken, NJ: John Wiley.

Fiala, N. 2008. "Measuring Sustainability: Why the Ecological Footprint Is Bad Economics and Bad Environmental Science." *Ecological Economics* 67(4): 519–25.

Florida, R. 2005. *Cities and the Creative Class*. London and New York: Routledge.

Forsyth, Ann, Mary Hearst, J. Michael Oakes, and M. Kathryn Schmitz. 2008. "Design and Destinations: Factors Influencing Walking and Total Physical Activity." *Urban Studies* 45(9): 1973–96.

Frank, Lawrence, Peter Engelke, and Thomas Schmid. 2003. *Health and Community Design: The Impact of the Built Environment on Physical Activity*. Washington, DC: Island Press.

Frank, L. D., J. F. Sallis, T. L. Conway, J. E. Chapman, B. E. Saelens, and W. Bachman. 2006. "Many Pathways from Land Use to Health: Associations between Neighbourhood Walkability and Active Transportation, Body Mass Index, and Air Quality. *Journal of the American Planning Association* 72(1): 75–87.

Frece, John W. 2008. *Sprawl & Politics: The Inside Story of Smart Growth in Maryland*. Albany, NY: State University of New York Press.

Freihage, Jason, Stephen Coleman, Royce Hanson, George Galster, Harold Wolman, and Michael R Ratcliffe. 2001. "Wrestling Sprawl to the Ground: Defining and Measuring an Elusive Concept." *Housing Policy Debate* 12(4): 681–717.

Frey, Hildebrand. 1999. *Designing the City: Towards a More Sustainable Urban Form*. London: Taylor & Francis.

Frumkin, Howard. 2004. *Urban Sprawl and Public Health: Designing, Planning, and Building for Healthy Communities*. Washington, DC: Island Press.

Giles-Corti, B., and R. J. Donovan. 2003. "Relative Influences of Individual, Social Environmental and Physical Environmental Correlates of Walking." *American Journal of Public Health* 93(9): 1583–89.

Girardet, Herbert. 2004. *Cities People Planet: Liveable Cities for a Sustainable World*. Hoboken, NJ: Wiley-Academy.

Glaeser, Edward L. 2011. *Triumph of the City: How our Greatest Invention Makes Us Richer, Smarter, Greener, Healthier, and Happier*. New York: Penguin.

Glaeser, Edward L., and Matthew E. Kahn. 2003. "Sprawl and Urban Growth." NBER Working Paper Series w9733. Available at: http://ssrn.com/abstract=412880.

Godschalk, David R. 2004. "Land Use Planning Challenges: Coping with Conflicts in Visions of Sustainable Development and Livable Communities." *Journal of the American Planning Association* 70(1): 5–14.

Gonzalez, George A. 2009. *Urban Sprawl, Global Warming, and the Empire of Capital*. Albany, NY: State University of New York Press.

Gordon, Peter, Harry W. Richardson, and Ajay Kumar. 1989. "The Spatial Mismatch Hypothesis: Some New Evidence." *Urban Studies* 26:315–26.

Grannis, Rick. 2009. *From the Ground Up: Translating Geography into Community through Neighbor Networks*. Princeton, NJ: Princeton University Press.

Granovetter, Mark S. 1983. "The Strength of Weak Ties: A Network Theory Revisited." *Sociological Theory* 1:201–33.

Greenberg, Mike. 1995. *The Poetics of Cities: Designing Neighborhoods that Work*. Columbus, OH: Ohio State University Press.

Greenwald, M. J., and M. G. Boarnet. 2002. "Built Environment as a Determinant of Walking Behaviour." *Transportation Research Record* 1780: 33–42.

Handy, Susan. 2005. "Planning for Accessibility, in Theory and in Practice." In *Access to Destinations*, edited by D. Levinson and K. Krizek, 131–48. London: Elsevier.

Handy, S., J. F. Sallis, D. Weber, E. Maibach, and M. Hollander. 2008. "Is Support for Traditionally Designed Communities Growing? Evidence from Two National Surveys." *Journal of the American Planning Association* 74(2): 209–21.

Harvey, David. 2000. *Spaces of Hope*. Berkeley, CA: University of California Press.

Hawken, Paul. 1993. *The Ecology of Commerce: A Declaration of Sustainability*. New York: Harper-Business.

Heath, Gregory W., Ross C. Brownson, Judy Kruger, Rebecca Miles, Kenneth E. Powell, Leigh T. Ramsey, and the Task Force on Community Preventive Services. 2006. "The Effectiveness of Urban Design and Land Use and Transport Policies and Practices to Increase Physical Activity: A Systematic Review." *Journal of Physical Activity and Health* 3(Suppl. 1): S55–76.

Hillier, B., and J. Hanson. 1984. *The Social Logic of Space*. Cambridge, UK: Cambridge University Press.

Hirschhorn, Joel S. 2005. *Sprawl Kills: How Blandburbs Steal Your Time, Health and Money*. New York: Sterling & Ross.

Institute of Transportation Engineers. 2005. *Context Sensitive Solutions in Designing Major Urban Thoroughfares for Walkable Communities*. Washington, DC: Institute of Transportation Engineers.

Jabareen, Yosef Rafeq. 2006. "Sustainable Urban Forms: Their Typologies, Models and Concepts." *Journal of Planning Education and Research* 26(1): 38–52.

Jacobs, Allan, and Donald Appleyard. 1987. "Toward an Urban Design Manifesto." *Journal of the American Planning Association* 53:112–30.

Jacobs, Jane. 1961. *The Death and Life of Great American Cities*. New York: Vintage.

Jenks, Mike, Elizabeth Burton, and Katie Williams, eds. 1996. *The Compact City: A Sustainable Urban Form?* London: Spon.

Jenks, Mike, and Nicola Dempsey, eds. 2005. *Future Forms and Design for Sustainable Cities*. London: Architectural Press.

Krier, Leon. 2009. *The Architecture of Community*. Washington, DC: Island Press.

Kunstler, James Howard. 1994. *Geography of Nowhere*. New York: Touchstone.

Landis, John. 2006. "Growth Management Revisited." *Journal of the American Planning Association* 72(4): 411–30.

Ledebur, L. C., and W. R. Barnes. 1993. *All in it Together: Cities, Suburbs and Local Economic Regions*. Washington, DC: National League of Cities.

Leinberger, Christopher. 2008. *The Option of Urbanism*. Washington, DC: Island Press.

Lenertz, Bill, and Aarin Lutzenhiser. 2006. *The Charrette Handbook*. Chicago: APA Planners Press.

Levine, Jonathan. 2005. *Zoned Out: Regulation, Markets, and Choices in Transportation and Metropolitan Land-Use*. Washington, DC: Resources for the Future.

Levinson, D., and K. Krizek, eds. 2005. *Access to Destinations*. London: Elsevier.

Low, Thomas E. 2010. *Light Imprint Handbook: Integrating Sustainability and Community Design*. Miami, FL: Civic by Design.

Lubell, Mark, Richard Feiock, and Susan Handy. 2009. "City Adoption of Environmentally Sustainable Policies in California's Central Valley." *Journal of the American Planning Association* 75(3): 293–308.

Lynch, Kevin. 1981. *Good City Form*. Cambridge, MA: MIT Press.

MacKaye, Benton. 1928. *The New Exploration: A Philosophy of Regional Planning*. New York: Harcourt, Brace.

Mazmanian, D. A., and M. E. Kraft. 1999. *Toward Sustainable Communities: Transition and Transformations in Environmental Policy.* Cambridge, MA: MIT Press.

Meadows, Donella H., Dennis L. Meadows, Jorgen Randers, and William Behrens III. 1972. *The Limits to Growth.* New York: Signet.

Mehaffy, Michael, Sergio Porta, Yodan Rofe, and Nikos Salingaros. 2009. "Urban Nuclei and the Geometry of Streets: The 'Emergent Neighborhoods' Model. *Urban Design International* 15(1): 22–46.

Michelson, W. H. 1977. *Environmental Choice, Human Behavior, and Residential Satisfaction.* New York: Oxford University Press.

Miles, R., and Y. Song. 2009. "'Good' Neighborhoods in Portland, Oregon: Focus on Both Social and Physical Environments." *Journal of Urban Affairs* 31(4): 491–509.

Montgomery, John. 1998. "Making a City: Urbanity, Vitality and Urban Design." *Journal of Urban Design* 3(1): 93–116.

Moore, Steve A. 2007. *Alternative Routes to the Sustainable City: Austin, Curitiba and Frankfurt.* Lanham, MD: Rowman & Littlefield.

Moore, Steve A., 2010. *Pragmatic Sustainability: Theoretical and Practical Tools.* London: Routledge.

Moudon, A. V., and C. Lee. 2003. "Walking and Bicycling: An Evaluation of Environmental Audit Instruments." *American Journal of Health Promotion* 18(1): 21–37.

Moudon, Anne Vernez, Chanam Lee, Alien O. Cheadle, Cheza Garvin, Donna Johnson, Thomas L. Schmid, Robert D. Weathers, and Lin Lin. 2006. "Operational Definitions of Walkable Neighborhood: Theoretical and Empirical Insights." *Journal of Physical Activity and Health* 3(1): 99–117.

Mouzon, Stephen A. 2010. *The Original Green: Unlocking the Mystery of True Sustainability.* Miami: New Urban Guild Foundation.

Mumford, Lewis. 1968. *The Urban Prospect.* New York: Harcourt Brace Jovanovich.

Murray, Alan T., and Rex Davis. 2001. "Equity in Regional Service Provision." *Journal of Regional Science* 41(4): 577–600.

Nelson, Arthur C., and Robert E. Lang. 2007. "The Next 100 Million." *Planning* 73(1): 4–6.

Newman, Peter, and Isabella Jennings. 2008. *Cities as Sustainable Ecosystems: Principles and Practices.* Washington, DC: Island Press

Newman, Peter W. G., and Jeffrey R. Kenworthy. 1996. "The Land Use–Transport Connection: An Overview." *Land Use Policy* 13(1): 1–22.

Newman, Peter W. G., and Jeffrey R. Kenworthy. 2006. "Urban Design to Reduce Automobile Dependence." *Opolis: An International Journal of Suburban and Metropolitcan Studies* 2(1): 35–52.

Norman, Gregory J., Sandra K. Nutter, Sherry Ryan, James F. Sallis, Karen J. Calfas, and Kevin Patrick. 2006. "Community Design and Access to Recreational Facilities as Correlates of Adolescent Physical Activity and Body-Mass Index." *Journal of Physical Activity and Health* 3(Suppl. 1): S118–128.

Nyden, Philip, Michael Maly, and John Lukehart. 1997. "The Emergence of Stable Racially and Ethnically Diverse Urban Communities: A Case Study of Nine U.S. Cities." *Housing Policy Debate* 8(2): 491–533.

Orfield, Myron. 2002. *American Metropolitics: The New Suburban Reality.* Washington, DC: Brookings Institution Press.

Owen, David. 2009. *Green Metropolis: Why Living Smaller, Living Closer, and Driving Less Are the Keys to Sustainability.* New York: Riverhead.

Owens, S., and R. Cowell. 2002. *Land and Limits: Interpreting Sustainability in the Planning Process.* London and New York: Routledge.

Pendall, Rolf. 2000. "Local Land Use Regulation and the Chain of Exclusion." *Journal of the American Planning Association* 66(2): 125–42.

Pendall, Rolf, and Joe Parilla. 2011. "Comment on Emily Talen and Julia Koschinsky's 'Is Subsidized Housing in Sustainable Neighborhoods? Evidence from Chicago's 'Sustainable' Urban Form and Opportunity: Frames and Expectations for Low-Income Households." *Housing Policy Debate* 21(1): 33–44.

Pepper, David. 1993. *Ecosocialism: From Deep Ecology to Social Justice*. London: Routledge.

Peterson, Ruth D., Lauren J. Krivo, and Mark A. Harris. 2000. "Disadvantage and Neighborhood Violent Crime: Do Local Institutions Matter? *Journal of Research in Crime and Delinquency* 37:31–63.

Pitts, Adrian, and Hanwen Liao. 2008. *Sustainable Olympic Games: Strategies for Design and Development*. London: Routledge.

Pooley, Eric. 2010. *The Climate War: True Believers, Power Brokers, and the Fight to Save the Earth*. New York: Hyperion.

Popkin, Susan J., Diane K. Levy, and Larry Buron. 2009. "Has HOPE VI Transformed Residents' Lives? New Evidence from the HOPE VI Panel Study." *Housing Studies* 24(4): 477–502.

Portney, Kent E. 2003. *Taking Sustainable Cities Seriously*. Cambridge, MA: MIT Press.

Putnam, R. D. 2000. *Bowling Alone. The Collapse and Revival of American Community*. New York: Simon and Schuster.

Rees, William E. 1989. *Planning for Sustainable Development*. Vancouver, British Columbia: UBC Centre for Human Settlements.

Romaya, Sam, and Carole Rakodi. 2002. *Building Sustainable Urban Settlements: Approaches and Case Studies in the Developing World*. London: ITDG Publishing.

Roseland, Mark. 2005. *Toward Sustainable Communities: Resources for Citizens and Their Governments*. Gabriola Island, British Columbia: New Society Publishers.

Rusk, David. 2001. *Inside Game/Outside Game: Winning Strategies for Saving Urban America*. Washington, DC: Brookings Institution Press.

Salingaros, Nikos A. 1998. "Theory of the Urban Web." *Journal of Urban Design* 3:53–71.

Sallis, J. F., A. Bauman, and M. Pratt. 1998. "Environmental and Policy Interventions to Promote Physical Activity." *American Journal of Preventive Medicine* 15:379–97.

Sanchez, T. 1999. "The Connection between Public Transit and Employment – The Cases of Portland and Atlanta." *Journal of the American Planning Association* 65:284–96.

Sarkissian, S. 1976. "The Idea of Social Mix in Town Planning: An Historical Overview." *Urban Studies* 13(3): 231–46.

Sartori, J., T. Moore, and G. Knaap. 2011. *Indicators of Smart Growth in Maryland*. College Park, MD: National Center for Smart Growth Research and Education, University of Maryland.

Schwartz, Alex. 2011. Comment on Emily Talen and Julia Koschinsky's "Is Subsidized Housing in Sustainable Neighborhoods?" *Housing Policy Debate* 21(1): 29–32.

Scott, James C. 1998. *Seeing Like a State: How Certain Schemes to Improve the Human Condition Have Failed*. New Haven, CT: Yale University Press.

Sharples, Stephen, Hocine Bougdah, and Joan Zunde. 2008. *Environment, Technology and Sustainability*. London: Routledge.

Song, Yan, and Gerrit-Jan Knaap. 2004. "Measuring Urban Form. Is Portland Winning the War on Sprawl?" *Journal of the American Planning Association* 70(2): 210–25.

Speir, C., and K. Stephenson. 2002. "Does Sprawl Cost Us All? Isolating the Effects of Housing Patterns on Public Water and Sewer Costs." *Journal of the American Planning Association* 68(1): 56–70.

Squires, Gregory D. 2002. *Urban Sprawl: Causes, Consequences & Policy Responses.* Washington, DC: Urban Institute Press.

Stone Jr., B. 2008. "Urban Sprawl and Air Quality in Large U.S. Cities. *Journal of Environmental Management* 86:688–98.

Talen, Emily. 1998. "Visualizing Fairness: Equity Maps for Planners." *Journal of the American Planning Association* 64(1): 22–38.

Talen, Emily. 2002. "Pedestrian Access as a Measurement of Urban Quality." *Planning Practice and Research* 17(3): 257–78.

Talen, Emily. 2008. *Design for Diversity. Exploring Socially Mixed Neighborhoods.* London: Elsevier.

Talen, Emily, and Jason Brody. 2005. "Human vs. Nature Duality in Metropolitan Planning." *Urban Geography* 26(8): 684–706.

Talen, Emily, and Julia Koschinsky. 2011. "Is Subsidized Housing in Sustainable Neighborhoods? Evidence from Chicago." *Housing Policy Debate* 21(1): 1–28.

Thomas, Randall, and Trevor Garnham. 2007. *The Environments of Architecture: Environmental Design in Context.* London: Routledge.

Trancik, Roger. 1986. *Finding Lost Space.* New York: Van Nostrand Reinhold.

Turner, Margery Austin, and Alan Berube. 2009. *Vibrant Neighborhoods, Successful Schools: What the Federal Government Can Do to Foster Both.* Washington, DC: Urban Institute.

Union of Concerned Scientists. 1992. *World Scientists' Warning to Humanity.* Cambridge, MA: Union of Concerned Scientists. Available at: http://www.ucsusa.org/.

Van der Ryn, Sim, and Peter Calthorpe. 1991. *Sustainable Communities: A New Design Synthesis for Cities, Suburbs and Towns.* San Francisco: Sierra Club Books.

Van der Ryn, Sim, and Peter Calthorpe. 2008. *Sustainable Communities: A New Design Synthesis for Cities, Suburbs and Towns.* Gabriola Island, British Columbia: New Catalyst Books.

Van der Ryn, Sim, and Stuart Cowan. 1995. *Ecological Design.* Washington, DC: Island Press.

Vreeker, Ron, Mark Deakin, and Steven Curwell, eds. 2008. *Sustainable Urban Development. Vol. 3: The Toolkit for Assessment.* London: Routledge.

Wackernagel, Mathis, and William Rees. 1996. *Our Ecological Footprint: Reducing Human Impact on the Earth.* Gabriola Island, British Columbia: New Society Publishers.

Walljasper, Jay. 2007. *The Great Neighborhood Book: A Do-it-Yourself Guide to Placemaking.* Gabriola Island, British Columbia: New Society Publishers.

Wheeler, Stephen M. 2005. *Planning for Sustainability: Creating Livable, Equitable, and Ecological Communities.* London: Routledge.

Wiewel, Wim, and Joseph J. Persky. 2002. *Suburban Sprawl: Private Decisions and Public Policy.* Armonk, NY: M.E. Sharpe.

Williams, K., ed. 2005. *Spatial Planning, Urban Form and Sustainable Transport.* Aldershot, UK: Ashgate.

Williams, Katie, Elizabeth Burton, and Mike Jenks. 2000. *Achieving Sustainable Urban Form.* London: Spon.

Williamson, Thad. 2010. *Sprawl, Justice, and Citizenship: The Civic Costs of the American Way of Life.* New York: Oxford University Press.

Wolch, Jennifer. 2004. *Up Against the Sprawl: Public Policy and the Making of Southern California.* Minneapolis: University of Minnesota Press.

World Commission on Environment and Development (Brundtland Commission). 1987. *Our Common Future.* Oxford: Oxford University Press.

Wu, C., and A. Murray. 2005. "Optimizing Public Transit Quality and System Access: The Multiple-Route, Maximal Covering/Shortest-Path Problem." *Environment and Planning Part B: Planning and Design* 32:163–78.

CHAPTER 8

JUSTICE

PETER MARCUSE

1. Why Is Justice Relevant to Planning?

STRIVING for justice is an intuitively attractive goal.[1] But justice is a complex concept, debated for centuries by philosophers, political scientists, sociologists, and many people in their ordinary lives. Is it relevant to planning? The assumption that it is should not be lightly made. If an architect is asked to design a building for a client, she is not asked to judge whether the client deserves the building or who needs that location the most; why should a planner thus tasked be any different? The planning profession's Code of Ethics, at least in the United States, tiptoes around the subject; it speaks of planners "serving the public interest," does not define the public interest, and refers to social justice only once, and both references are as an "aspiration," and not as a "rule" whose violation may lead to adverse action.

And if it did define justice, what would the Code mean by it? Intuitively, justice has to do with a sense of fairness in the distribution of what is valuable in life; like pornography, one may not be able to define injustice, but one knows it when one sees it.

There are several good reasons why planners should be concerned with justice:

- Planning is an action of government that necessarily affects the distribution of goods, services, and more generally life opportunities among individuals and groups, and justice is a necessary criterion for such distribution.
- Planners' actions focus on the distribution of space, and thus the distribution of its benefits and costs, among individuals and groups, and justice concerns the proper criteria for such distribution.[2]

- Planners necessarily analyze the causes and effects of their work on existing conditions over time, and thus must deal with the causes of unjust distributions.
- History, and planning's own history, tells us so. A major current in planning's historical role has been the expansion of the just distribution of the benefits of the built environment.
- The Codes of Ethics of most professional associations of planners have included obligations that are part of the concerns of justice in their aspirations and sometimes in their mandates.

Each of these points is taken up in the course of the following discussion. It necessarily begins by addressing some frequent confusions. There are many forms of justice; with which is planning primarily concerned?

2. WHICH JUSTICE?

2.1 Justice as Professional Obligation vs. Justice as Moral Aspiration

As citizens and as moral human beings, most would feel that we have obligations to act justly; certainly most religions call for just action in daily life. We thus all might claim an "aspiration" to do justice. The question for planners is whether their obligation *as planners* goes beyond this moral aspiration, and if so, exactly what that means. Whether, for instance, an applicant for a zoning change should be granted special standing because he or she is a veteran is essentially a moral question, as to which planners can claim no special competence and have no special responsibility. Whether affirmative benefits based on past racial discrimination are a planner's concern is a different question; racial discrimination is so integrally tied to past public policies, and specifically to policies for which planners have played a key role, that indeed they must take it into consideration in their work.

2.2 Social Justice versus Individual Justice (Planning versus Law)

Individual justice—legal justice of the kind that occupies the judicial system—looks at the impact of a planning action on specific individuals and judges it by standards prescribed by law. Social justice is the broader category that examines the impact of planning proposals on the public generally. The two will frequently conflict. While the procedure for obtaining individual justice needs to be of concern to planners as itself a component of social justice, it is social, rather than individual, justice that is among the goals of planning.

Social justice overrides individual justice. Thus, if a zoning action restricts gas stations to one of four corners of an intersection, the owner of a second corner may complain about unjust treatment and seek a lawyer. But if the restriction is for a public benefit, its individual injustice is not a direct concern of planners (P. Marcuse 1988). More broadly, it is ultimately the planning argument for affirmative action, conceding that it may override individual justice. It is likewise the argument for bailing out all banks in trouble, even though some banks may be individually unjustly enriched in the process. The opposite policy would, of course, pose the same conflict of principles.

Social justice is the concern of planners, individual justice is the concern of lawyers. Justice among private individuals or groups of private individuals is the concern of lawyers; the justice of public actions is the concern of planners. The distinction is fundamental, and is a basic matter of definitions. As Del Vecchio (1953, 1) says: "Justice...is held to consist in conformity with law, but it is also asserted that law must conform to justice." He resolves the issue by distinguishing between legal justice and ethical justice. The distinction in fact goes back to a largely parallel formulation by Aristotle, in one of the foundational discussions of justice in modern philosophy, the *Nicomachean Ethics* (Aristotle 1911, 106), in which he made the distinction between distributive social justice and corrective justice. It is in a passage raising several issues of importance also taken up below:

> Now of the Particular Justice...one species is concerned in the distributions of honour, or wealth, or such other things as are to be shared among the members of the social community (because in these one man as compared with another may have either an equal or an unequal share). And the other [species of Justice] is that which is Corrective in the various transactions between man and man.[3]

It is a distinction adopted here: between distributive justice and corrective justice, the public interest and individual justice, between legal and ethical justice, or, in the formulation generally used here, between social justice and individual justice. If justice is only conformity to law, there is no reason for this chapter; planners simply cede any concern with justice to lawyers or the framers of law. But what, then, is the meaning of "ethical" justice? It certainly sounds like a tautology.

The tension between legal justice and justice as a component of public policy parallels in many ways the tension between regulatory and systemic planning approaches, and between the view of justice as a system of individual rights and justice as the outcome of social processes. It should be clear that both forms of justice are desirable, and that the defense of individual justice, individual rights, is also a matter of social justice. The balance is one that is particularly prominent today in debates over such issues as torture or freedom of speech. But the social importance of individual rights is beyond the scope of this chapter.[4]

2.3 Government versus "The Market"

If planners, then, must be concerned with social justice, they must necessarily advocate for governmental action to advance it. The private market does not function, and is not intended to function, to do so. Injustice is not a "market failure"; it is simply not a concern of markets.[5] If the market in fact has produced a just result, there is no injustice to be addressed; it is the specific role of government to do that which the private market does not do, or does badly. If there is a question whether government action is less just in its effects than what the private market does, then of course the government action should not be undertaken. It should be within the competence (and obligation) of planners to make sure this does not happen.

Much of the discussion of justice in philosophy, carried over into everyday usage, speaks of justice as a standard of conduct between or among individuals, without reference to the manner of enforcement of such standards. For planners, it is axiomatic that their concern for justice *as planners* is with those forms of justice and injustice with which government is concerned. Justice in parents' treatment of their children, for instance, or on the private noncommercial sports field, or in dealing with competition or envy or jealously in personal relations, is not a concern of government as we generally see it today. These are matters of individual, not social, justice. But they may nevertheless involve government; "individual justice" does not mean private justice, independent of a governmental role. The line is clearly fluid: at what point does the corporal punishment of a child by a parent become child abuse? At what point is lobbying a planning commission for a land-use change a matter of free enterprise, and at what point should it be regulated? Are political contributions a private matter, or of concern to government?

It follows that planners' concern for justice is linked to their view of the appropriate role of government. The concern of the planner for social justice suggests support for zoning changes that move toward a just distribution of the benefits of land-use regulation; but whether individual property owners should receive compensation for the effects of a zoning change is not a matter of individual justice. In general, the planning profession prefers limited rights of compensation so as to avoid obstacles to socially just zoning practices.

But the extent to which government should be concerned with individual versus social justice can be controversial. It relates to planners' conceptions of the proper role of government. In one of the major problems confronting planners today—escalating mortgage foreclosures impacting whole communities—the extent to which government should protect individuals who have entered into fraudulently sold mortgages, or individuals who have met unemployment or illness preventing them from making payments, or those who have simply been greedy in knowingly taking out mortgages of a size exceeding their ability to repay, hinges not only on conceptions of justice but also on conceptions of the appropriate role of government. Planners' position on that question will be influenced by their roles, not only as planners but also as citizens, as parents, as businesspeople, as thinkers, and as moral human beings (P. Marcuse 1976).

2.4 Inputs vs. Outputs

If justice is concerned with the criteria for the distribution of goods and services, about which goods and services are we talking?

To begin with, the concern is with the distribution of outputs, not of inputs. In one key case in New York City, the mayor, relying on analyses and recommendations of planners, was found not to have distributed the resources of the park department unjustly when he provided equal maintenance to Crotona Park, a heavily used park in a poor area of dense multifamily housing undersupplied with open space, and to Van Cortlandt Park, a more lightly used park in a better-off neighborhood of single-family houses, even though the need was greater in Crotona Park. The case measured inputs, not outputs, and that was found adequate by law.[6] Planners are, however, called on to plan outputs, to deal with results, and to propose efforts, or inputs, according to their contribution to results. If the result is unjust, that is a concern of planners; however, the distribution of inputs may be judged by strictly legal criteria.

3. How Should Justice Be Defined?

3.1 Justice as Historically Defined

One view sees justice as it exists in reality i.e., realistic justice. It is the view that is recounted in Plato's famous dialogue in *The Republic,* in which Thrasymachus argues that justice is always the will of the stronger (Plato 2002, 24). Broadly speaking, it is the realist view of justice, defining justice as the way disputes are in fact resolved in the real world. Justice as a value, or an independent aspiration of planning, thus becomes irrelevant; justice is what the system says it is. Sometimes the emphasis on justice as a political process comes close to this view, if it concludes that the planner should subordinate him or herself to that process, rather than inject his or her substantive views of what justice demands (Catanese 1988). In any event, such a definition suggests planners need not concern themselves with justice as a goal of their work; they can simply accommodate themselves to the way justice is determined by others.

There is a broader aspect to the realist view of justice, however, that needs to be noted. For if the stronger impose justice as they will, they also define it as they will. The definition of justice has a *historical dimension.* It is tempting to believe that all of the above discussion moves toward an absolute concept of justice—one good for all times and all places. But that is hardly a defensible proposition. When Thrasymachus tells Socrates, "justice is what the powerful say it is," he is reporting a simple historical truth. Slavery offended no one's sense of injustice in Socrates'

Greece, was bitterly contested in United States history, is probably rejected in most of the world today as unjust. The concept of wage slavery, however, continues to divide people and classes. Disasters awaken other and more commitments to justice than do periods of prosperity. Major social movements have had an influence in redefining what justice is: the women's movement, Justice for Janitors, the civil rights movement, the human rights movement, the labor movement, the gay and lesbian rights movement, and many others over the course of history. The definitions of justice are contested not only on philosophical and logical and practical grounds but also based on self-interest, status, and tradition.

But planners are not passive instruments to implement others' reality. Planners' actions influence reality, as well as reflect its pressures. And planning's own history is rooted in concerns for justice. The debate about the role of justice in planning goes far back in the history of planning and the origins of planning as a profession with a particular calling. Leonardo Benevolo traces it back to 1848, with a growing split between consideration of planning as a means of promoting the efficient functioning of the existing urban system and a utopian espousal of social ideals held to be inherent in planning (Benevolo 1967). In 2009, on the centennial of the founding of the first conference on city planning in the United States, articles in the *Journal of the American Planning Association*'s celebratory issue alluded to similar cleavages in approach in 1909, at the founding of the profession (P. Marcuse 2011).[7] Planners need actively to define how they wish to understand and implement justice in their activities.

3.2 Justice as the Negative of Injustice

Justice may often appear as a constraint in planning rather than as a goal of planning, if a concern is to avoid an injustice rather than to pursue justice. And such situations may in fact present fewer problems of definition, be less difficult to explain and deal with, than the broader question of how to achieve full justice. John Stuart Mill, for instance, said flatly: "justice, like many other moral attributes, is best defined by it opposite" (Levi 1963, 286).

Take the case of racial discrimination or segregation. There would (it is hoped) today be little dispute that segregating any specific population group, imposing a ghetto, is wrong and unjust. There will be much less agreement on what integration is, however: what a fully nondiscriminatory space would look like, or even what forms of separation are consistent with justice—immigrant enclaves? religious communities? retirement communities? any separation based on race? (see P. Marcuse 2005). Racial discrimination is unjust; is a just allocation simply the absence of racial discrimination, or equal treatment in every way? And what if remedying one cause of injustice creates a different form of injustice, as remedying injustice against minorities may cause an injustice to some members of a majority? Unfortunately, while avoiding injustice is certainly an initial and indispensable obligation of planners, it is a minimum obligation.

For planners, in practice, this is nevertheless a reassuring approach. For rarely is a planner confronted with a situation in which achieving the ideal is a realistic possibility. Much more often, it is a question of weighing alternatives, judging which approaches an ideal the most closely. And for that purpose, the exact definition of the ideal is not necessary, but simply which of two alternatives comes closest to it. And if there is an agreement as to which of the alternatives is furthest from the opposite of the ideal, that is enough. Consensus in practice is much more likely to be reached on how to reduce injustice than on how to achieve full justice.

Yet planners are professionally charged with taking a long-term view in their planning, balancing costs against benefits and various benefits against each other, and viewing issues comprehensively, not piecemeal. For those purposes, avoiding injustices on an ad hoc basis is not sufficient; a fuller definition of justice is required.

3.3 Justice as Procedure

One stream of thought avoids entirely the effort to give justice a substantive meaning and focuses on the procedure through which it is reached. For a lawyer, the procedural question is simple: have the procedural requirements established by law been followed? If the answer is yes, that ends the matter, and Justice has been done.

For planners concerned with social justice, however, a procedural definition of justice is clearly insufficient. The planner adopting a procedural definition of social justice must at least begin by examining the nature of the process by which the rules to be applied were fashioned, and that examination cannot itself be guided by purely procedural standards, as a lawyer might do. Going beyond due process means relying on a fuller meaning of just procedure: a democratically established procedure. If campaign financing and effective lobbying have granted or denied certain land uses in a certain location, for instance, no interpretation of the law passed as the result of such a tainted political process may be considered just, no matter how proper the procedure used for its implementation.

If the process was fully democratic, it can be argued that the planner must then abandon consideration of whether its results conflict with the planner's own views of a substantively just result. If it was not democratic, then part of the remedy is in improving the democratic process. But improving the democratic process is not what most planners today are trained to do.

So then, what is democratic needs to be defined, and there are many approaches to that vexing question. Within theories of procedural justice, two strands among them have attracted much attention from planners. One is communicative planning; the other, John Rawls's *Theory of Justice* (1971/1999). A third, Mark Purcell's (2008) examination of direct democracy, has not received the attention it deserves.

Communicative planning stresses the key role of communication for democracy—communication which must be free, rational, without the imposition of power (see Fischer and Forester 1993; Forester 1989). Rawls's theory can be interpreted as supporting the view of justice as procedure in his definition of justice as what would result from a "decision made behind a veil of ignorance"; here, justice is defined as what people would decide if they did not know where their own interests lay (1971/1999). It is provocative, but is several steps removed from practical application. Purcell's (2008) emphasis on democratic procedures draws on policies such as participatory budgeting pioneered in Brazil and emulated elsewhere, but proposes more radical arrangements to achieve real democracy. The implications of each of these three complex lines of thinking need to be incorporated into any thorough definition of justice for planners, in which the relationship of democracy to justice needs to be worked through.

But the apparent conflict between justice and democracy is a nonstarter for planners in practice. Planners need to adhere to a concept of justice developed from their own history and practice and logically thought through, even where public processes lead in a different direction. The concern is sometimes expressed that planners are preempting the role of elected officials, and/or that they are substituting their own values for those that have been established by citizens in democratic and participatory fashion. But the concern is misplaced. In the first place, few decisions can be defended as being made in truly democratic fashion—that is, by fully informed free citizens not subject to any form of manipulation, intimidation, or coercion, and in the absence of power (Tilly 2005, 2005; Purcell 2008; H. Marcuse 1964). Where there is in practice a conflict between what is presented as a democratic decision and what is a planner's carefully arrived at conception of what social justice would require, the planner can do no more than attempt to expose the factors that have prevented full democratic consideration. The planner then has done all a planner can do, and that is the second reason the concern is unnecessary: planners are not decision makers, and in the very limited areas in which they do have decision-making power, they have it only as a matter of delegation from those elected, and the possibility of reversing their decisions democratically is generally available.[8]

The classic example has to do with race. Many planning decisions are made in a context in which racism plays a significant role (see Manning Thomas and Ritzdorf 1997; P. Marcuse 2002). When a suburban, largely white, higher income community refuses to zone for multifamily housing, with a racially exclusionary result, racial prejudice is often thinly concealed. And of course historically racial prejudice was decisive in many communities in which it rested on a majority consensus. Justice requires a planner to oppose racially exclusionary zoning, whether a procedural or a substantive definition of justice, such as is suggested below, is used.

If a *procedural* definition of justice is used, racial exclusionary policies are linked to racially distorted procedures and can be condemned on that ground. Whether the issue is past bias in development, or bias in drawing district lines or in apportionment, or bias in the accessibility of information, or actual bias in elections, a biased result will emerge from a biased procedure. A public decision made based on racial discrimination in the electoral process cannot be just because justice requires a just distribution of the right to participate in electoral politics also, and it places limits on what a majority can do that interferes with the basic rights of a minority. If, on the other hand, a *substantive* definition of justice is used, racial exclusion violates the standards of just distribution of the benefits of the built environment.

Thus, there is no principled tension between procedural and substantive definitions of justice, no tension between democracy and justice. Any decision made through the exercise of power, or without full transparency and information, cannot be just, because justice requires a just distribution of power and information. Formal but unjust democracy cannot be used as an excuse for unjust actions. The intricacies of achieving democracy so as to maximize its likelihood of achieving just results are an unavoidable challenge to planners. When, and only when, we have full democracy in the sense both Habermas (1984) and Purcell (2008) describe, it will be time to worry about a conflict between views of justice. Until then, the search for democracy and justice will go hand in hand.

3.4 Justice as Nondiscrimination

Negative discrimination against any disadvantaged group based on race, or gender, or other irrelevant and toxic criteria, is unjust. It cannot be justified by any of the standards for just distribution discussed below: contribution, effort, need, agreement. But all distributions avoiding that injustice are not thereby necessarily just. Nor is affirmative discrimination unjust—that is, discrimination for the benefit of a disadvantaged group and thus against an advantaged group—if to overcome the effects of present or past negative discrimination. Clearly just affirmative discrimination may result in unjust (but not, in our definition, negative, because it is applying to an advantaged, rather than a disadvantaged, group) discrimination against others, and action to remedy that injustice may also be appropriate. The rules both of proportionality and of hierarchy, discussed below, must be respected.

The point here, however, is simple: while negative discrimination is always unjust, the absence of negative discrimination does not make an action just; nondiscrimination is not an adequate definition of justice for planners.

3.5 Justice as Just Distribution

Justice as a standard by which *distribution* can be judged is perhaps the most common understanding of the concept, both in common usage and in centuries of philosophic discussion. Such a distributional definition of course requires further specification of a number of elements. Aristotle is not of much help here; in the passage quoted earlier, he speaks of "the distributions of honor, or wealth, or such other things as are to be shared among the members of the social community (because in these one man as compared with another may have either an equal or an unequal share)." But what "other things"?

The pragmatic answer suggested here proposes three rules:

1. *A rule of hierarchy*, in which the importance of the multiple and potentially conflicting criteria for distribution are rank-ordered (What Distribution?).
2. *A rule of primacy*, in which the "things that are to be shared" are identified and their importance is balanced against the importance of others (The Distribution of What?).
3. *A rule of proportionality*, in which the extent to which criteria are met needs to be balanced against the importance of the criteria (Beyond Distributional Justice?).

4. WHAT DISTRIBUTION?

A television reporter, in what has become known as "Santelli's rant," made headlines and generated acrimonious debate for weeks, reporting from the floor of the Chicago Board of Trade:

> CNBC's Rick Santelli and the traders on the floor of the CME Group express outrage over the notion they may have to pay their neighbor's mortgage, particularly if they bought far more house than they could actually afford.[9]

The issue is, of course, the distribution of the benefits of the stimulus package and the assistance being offered to homeowners caught in the subprime mortgage foreclosure crisis. Santelli sharply posed at least two questions as to the criteria for a just distribution: need (is facing foreclosure—the need for housing—a just basis for a claim for public assistance?); and desert (did those claiming assistance deserve that assistance?).

As Aristotle pointed out, not everyone agrees what a just distribution is. What is offered here is an attempt to clarify what alternate criteria might be used, with a suggestion that perhaps reflects an evolving consensus on their position in a hierarchy.

4.1 Distribution Based on Equality

"All human beings are created equal" is probably a formulation that would meet with near-universal agreement today. But it is clear that the statement is false.

People at birth are very unequal, in strength, abilities, parentage, and position. But it is not intended as a statement of fact, but rather as a statement of a legal precept, which provides all people with "certain inalienable rights, including the right to life, liberty, and the pursuit of happiness." Justice requires equality in the distribution of those rights—clearly political rights—to be guaranteed by government whose "just powers are derived from the consent of the governed." The equality that justice requires is not an equal distribution of goods and services but an equality in three ways: the political sphere, in the extent to which each individual's consent to the powers of government can be exercised; and in the economic sphere, in the extent to which each individual has available the means to sustain life and pursue happiness; and in the cultural sphere (for lack of a better term), in which each individual is entitled to the same respect for his or her individual characteristics as each other individual. In the political sphere, it means an equality of legal rights; in the economic sphere, it means an equality in the extent to which the necessities of life are available; and in the cultural sphere, it means full respect for individuality and difference.

For planners, the absolute level of equality in the distribution of goods and services is a factor that justice requires be taken into account because it affects the extent to which justice in the distribution of those goods and services can be achieved. Justice does not require equality in the quality or size of the housing that all people occupy. But if the level of inequality is too great, if the rich consume too much of the land, or building materials, or labor required for the poor also to have housing they should have, planners must address this problem. Over and above equality in meeting the necessary conditions for life, liberty, and the pursuit of happiness, the goal of just planning is not equality in luxury housing, but such a distribution of all housing that all just needs can be met, which may well require a reduction in the level of inequality in housing. The point becomes apparent in considering the just distribution of space: all people are not justly entitled to equal space in their housing, but if one group relegates to itself too much space for its own use, not enough space or space in locations appropriate to their just needs may be available to others.

Equality, then, is not an adequate criterion of distributive justice. It is so often used as equivalent to the goal of justice because it allows for a clear, quantifiable, and intuitively acceptable standard by which to evaluate the justice of a particular plan or proposal. That is valid as to political rights, the provision of necessities, and societal respect. But beyond that, equality is only a surrogate for justice.

4.2 Distribution Based on Need

How should need be defined? We are used to the phrase "safety net," meaning some minimum level of life support that government should provide to everyone. How those minimums are defined varies—for example, in Germany it is phrased for housing as so-and-so many square meters of space per person, adequate plumbing, and so on; the United States uses very specific measures of quality in defining "substandard" in the annual census, and in approving housing for various subsidies. To a very moderate extent those standards reflect variations in needs among individuals; large families, for instance, have greater needs for space than small ones, and the handicapped have specific design needs. Thus, the provision of what we might call "safety net goods" (including services) is necessarily relevant to the particular circumstances of each individual.

The level at which safety net goods are provided should also be relative to the ability of society to provide such goods. If two societies provide the same level of safety net goods but one is far richer than the other, with a far greater level of inequality, a question of justice is involved. The rule of proportionality applies here. The debate over what proportion of redistribution is required to provide a just level at which safety net goods are provided is a debate planners should be prepared to engage in, seeking a just proportion between, for example the taxation of the rich and the abolition of poverty for the poor.

Thus, social justice demands the provision of minimal safety net goods, but it requires more. John Rawls (1971/1999) uses the phrase "primary goods" to define the appropriate level of provision required by justice—which I will discuss in turn.

4.3 Distribution Based on Desert

After human needs are met, justice may be judged by whether a given distribution is deserved, and desert may be judged by effort or by contribution. Most people who have been through school know that some teachers grade on effort, others grade on results. In considering what just distribution might require, other qualities, such as morality, might be considered. When we say a person "deserves" a particular benefit, all such criteria—effort, result, fault, morality—might be considered. Take the case of justice in helping homeowners facing mortgage foreclosure:

Effort: If a person facing foreclosure is unemployed and not looking for work, and his or her chances of being able to avoid foreclosure with adequate earnings from an available job were good, should that person be helped despite the lack of effort to help him or herself?

Result: Is a person earning too little to afford adequate housing (i.e., low income) because, for instance, that person has a disability, or is an industry with high unemployment or low wages, disqualified from receiving assistance?

Fault: If a person has bought a house knowing he or she could not afford to make the payments on it, so that it is his or her "fault" that foreclosure is looming, should the person be helped? In the opposite case, is a person who was tricked into buying a home he or she could not afford entitled to special consideration?

Morality: If a person already has everything he or she needs for a decent or better
standard of living (i.e., high income), and buys a larger house than he or
she needs, should that person be helped even if the default in payments
is because of, say, ill health or unemployment?

Clearly, opinions vary widely and passionately about the answers to these questions, as the controversy over Santelli's rant demonstrates. Planners face not only
the decisions among these potentially conflicting criteria (a person without fault
in the purchase but making little effort, or a person having enough but tricked into
buying over his or her head). They also face the question of how to implement a
rule that would take each factor into account. Pragmatically, thus, the answer in
justice might be:

- A clear and necessarily formal requirement of effort
- No disqualification for low income, but rather assistance and subsidy
- No disqualification for fault, and civil remedies for being tricked
- A necessary disqualification from receipt of assistance based on some
  income and wealth limits

These are obviously controversial answers. The answers to *result* and *morality*
are accepted as meeting the requirements of justice for planners, giving need priority, but those criteria as well as considerations of effort and fault require the application of the rule of proportionality: the answers will not be "yes" or "no," but "to
some extent." The planner pursuing justice should press answers along the above
lines, but in any case has the responsibility of clarifying the alternative positions
and encouraging informed debate on them.

4.4 Distribution Based on Reasonable Expectation

Distribution based on reasonable expectation is the very heart of contract law and
thus plays a major role in individual justice. Party A entering into a contract with
party B should have the reasonable expectation that party B will perform its part of
the bargain, provided party A performs its part. That holds true whether party A
needs what is expected or whether it deserves it by any ethical standard. Contract
claims will generally be claims of individual justice, but they may also be principles
of social justice. Residents in New Orleans living in areas protected by levies built
by the U.S. Corps of Engineers may reasonably expect those dykes to be adequate
for their protection, and as a matter of social justice be entitled to help when those
expectations are disappointed.

Using the standard of expectation, however, the criteria of need and desert also
apply. A banker or broker may reasonably expect a mortgagee to pay off a mortgage contract, but if that contract was entered into by a person with inadequate
income but nevertheless trying hard, justice may require the expectation to be

disappointed. Even the law, under the doctrine of unjust enrichment, allows deviation from contract terms where key elements of individual justice are involved.

5. The Distribution of What?

5.1 Space

If there is a single benefit over whose distribution planners have influence, it is the use of space and the built environment—what some speak of as "the urban." David Harvey's *Social Justice and the City* (1973) placed that issue firmly in the planning discourse, and the complexities of the subject have been extensively debated (see also Lefebvre 1967/1996 and P. Marcuse et al. 2009). The result is that not only matters of zoning, of building codes, of housing policy are matters of justice of concern to planners but also the related questions of transportation, environmental quality, location of public facilities and services—and the decision-making processes by which policies in these areas are determined. A simple question such as conflicts over the design and use of public space, on the one hand, for middle-class and family-oriented users and, on the other hand, for the homeless (say, benches designed for sitting and uncomfortable for sleeping, or not?) shows the need for clarity on the criteria of justice. The distribution of space, which underlies so much of the quality of life for residents, needs to be planned with considerations of just distribution well in the foreground.

5.2 Goods and Services

The issue of distributional justice is not relevant to the distribution of all goods and services. Not everyone has a just claim to gold watches or the services of a butler. John Rawls (1971/1999) has used the category of "primary goods" to denote those to which the principles of justice should apply, and that seems reasonable. The minimal level of goods and services necessary to maintain a healthful life are "safety net goods," and there is common agreement that justice requires they at least be available to all.

But safety net goods are a penurious definition of what a person's needs are. Today a safety net supporting what our societies can afford to provide would be much bigger than what is required for physical health. As for income and wealth, Rawls's concept proposes that the requirement be a minimal distribution adequate to provide the opportunity for individual and social development in accordance with the social standards of the dominant society. That leaves open two questions:

are those standards absolute or are they relative to time and place? And how is the standard of individual and social development to be conceptualized?

5.3 Respect

Distribution based on respect is a somewhat awkward formulation of the intuitive injustice felt when a person or group is discriminated against because of any essential characteristic of that person, whether inherent or ascribed: race, gender, sexual orientation, and disability are among the obvious. But nondiscrimination is a negative; the correlative might be called respect, and was referred to above as requiring equality in the cultural sphere.[10] It is too often overlooked by planners, even in working through the requirements of just distribution. Actions have symbolic as well as physical consequences, social meanings that vary widely from group to group, historical implications that depend on different histories. Policies relating to the use of public spaces, to historic preservation, to public art, and to arrangements for public participation are classic examples of instances in which justice requires respect for difference as well as just distribution of more tangible assets.

5.4 Power

The distribution of power is itself the key determinant of the extent of justice in a society, and certainly in planning practices. The definition of a just distribution of power is not difficult in the political theory of democracy (although democracy is a complex concept and beyond the scope of this discussion); its principle is the absolute equality of political rights and political powers. How it is achieved is, of course, not easy question, but it too must be addressed by planners.

6. Beyond Distributional Justice?

6.1 Remedying the Causes of Injustice

Whatever definition is used, if justice is held desirable, and if justice can be achieved by specific measures subject to the influence of planners, then supporting movement in that direction would be an obligation of planners.[11] So if the analysis of problems in the housing sector suggests that a different distribution of housing subsidies will come closer to what is held to be justice, effort in that direction is indicated. If, however, the analysis suggests that housing is unjustly distributed

because landowners are enabled to capture privately the benefit of socially created increases in land values, then something more than a distributional concept is
required, something that takes into account the effect of the system that produces
the unjust distribution. The claim for distributional justice is pressed on its own
merits, but to be coherent it must then be linked to a claim for other outcomes that
may be grounded on the value of justice as fair distribution but that goes beyond
that claim, extending its reach to nondistributional causes and goals.

The question of the causes of distributional injustice is a social scientific one, in
that sense, an objective one that well-grounded analysis can clarify. Thus, it may be
considered an extension of the pursuit of justice that planners be well educated in
the social sciences and apply their understanding to any given problem. Education
plays an important role here, as does what Susan Fainstein and Scott Campbell
(2011) have categorized as "urban theory." While it may well be true that "science
has nothing substantive to say on what is right, just, or good for human beings"
(Miller 2008, 10), social science does have something to say about the causes of
those conditions otherwise determined to be right, just, or good, and it should be
used—in the interests of justice.

6.2 Justice as One Value among Others

Justice is not always the dominant concern in planning. To take a simple example,
in formulating a building and zoning code, it is conventional to set aside the power
to grant variances for hardship to a zoning appeals board of some type and to
give it broad discretionary power to determine when regulations should be varied because of hardship. How shall "hardship" be defined? Theoretically, along
standards of justice. But ask any developer whether he or she would rather have
decisions made along the line of justice determined by such a board, or have them
clearly set forth in the ordinance, even if less just in some outcomes, and clarity
will be preferred over justice in many if not most instances. For this particular
case, the individual value that is preferred is certainty—or more generally formulated, efficiency. What other values might be given precedence, or at least require
consideration in addition to justice, in planning? One could list them (other lists
are of course possible), and most are addressed in other chapters in this volume:

- sustainability[12]
- diversity[13]
- beauty[14]
- peace[15]
- efficiency[16]
- freedom[17]
- growth[18]
- sustainability
- ecological health

- community
- democracy
- the expansion of capabilities[19]
- happiness[20]

It is, of course, possible to define justice as resting on any one or all of these other values. In the discussions around the Just City, for instance, the implicit tendency is to use "Just" as a concept including many of these concepts by definition (see P. Marcuse et al. 2009). Such a usage blurs the specific meaning of "justice" as it is commonly understood or as it is defined here. Nor are these other values co-equal to each other.

The difficulty can be seen in one widely spread formulation, which shows a triangle of values—Equity, Environment, Economy, sometimes known as the three Es of planning—with Sustainable Development being the desired combination of the three. Sustainability is sometimes replaced by Ecology or Environment and is focused on the health of the natural ecosystem, although the term itself may be taken as a reminder to planners that the durability of their projects needs always to be taken into account (see Campbell 1996; Moomaw 1996; Daily 1997).The values listed differ, they are not in a hierarchical relationship to each other, and the resolution is simply a call for balance among them. Interestingly, justice does not appear in any of these triangles.

No simple abstract formula can resolve the relationship among these and other goals. It is important, however, to distinguish among the types of values with which planning does deal. Some values are instrumental only—*instrumental values*—and speak to the evaluation of differing means to other ends; some values are ends in themselves—*substantive values*—valuable because they contribute to ultimate ends; and, perhaps, it is possible to formulate an ultimate end for planning, a single, *ultimate value.*

7. How Should We Advance Justice in Planning?

Can the organized planning profession advance the cause of justice in planning? One practical answer might be to address more directly the issues of justice in the professional Code of Ethics, the rules and aspirations governing planners' conduct. Specifically, three steps might be involved: first, stating the commitment to justice clearly and spelling out its practical meaning for planners; second, making that commitment a binding obligation of planners; and third, supporting planners who run into difficulty for adhering to such a commitment.

The commitment to justice in general can already be read as implied in the existing provision of the American Institute of Certified Planners' (AICP) Code of Ethics and Professional Conduct (set forth in the chapter appendix) that:

> Our primary obligation is to serve the public interest [see entry under "public interest"].... We shall seek social justice by working to expand choice and opportunity for all persons, recognizing a special responsibility to plan for the needs of the disadvantaged and to promote racial and economic integration. We shall urge the alteration of policies, institutions, and decisions that oppose such needs.

But that is as far as it goes. It speaks of an "allegiance to a conscientiously attained concept of the public interest that is formulated through continuous and open debate," but no debates about proposals to make explicit in the Code the meaning or consequences of that commitment have yet taken place. As we come to the end of a long and perhaps torturous examination of the meaning of justice for planners, it is understandable that formulating conscientiously the necessary concepts is a difficult and painstaking undertaking, but it cannot be abandoned if the commitment is serious.

Consider one simple example. Race has played a major role in the history of planning, yet there is no forthright statement in the Code demanding racial justice, stating an obligation of planners to work against racial segregation. Does the aspiration that planners "promote racial and economic integration" make it unethical for a planner to support a zoning code that excludes multifamily housing in an overwhelmingly white community where the evidence suggests a racial motivation for opposition to affordable housing? Should it make it unethical to support large-lot zoning?

A warning about the costs of ignoring such action comes from South Africa. There, the planning discipline has been widely perceived to have been (and in many cases has been) an instrument to implement the ideology of apartheid.[21] In 1997, however, representatives of the Council testified before the Truth and Reconciliation Commission: "[T]he present Council considers that previous Councils...were negligent in the sense that they did not see fit to confront the imbalances, discrimination and injustices prevalent during those years."[22]

There are other cases where a formal statement of the meaning of justice in planning might be developed. Should there be standards for the accessibility and use of public space? Attention to the job-creation potential of alternative land uses? Insistence on the availability of technical assistance to community groups on planning issues? Opposition to measures reducing the availability of affordable housing in favor of luxury housing? Of course, all of these are complex issues, but they are worthy of debate in the context of requirements imposed on planners to show that at least they have been seriously considered and efforts conscientiously made to find their resolution in practice.

Beyond spelling out in words the commitment to justice, making that commitment effective involves putting the strength of the profession behind it. In the present Code, the aspirations are explicitly not enforceable.[23] What can be required of planners is obviously not success in, say, achieving integration, or providing affordable housing, or promoting job creation; what is required is that they conscientiously try. It is unlikely that many charges of unethical conduct will be brought where there is the least evidence of effort. Most likely, the existence of an enforcement mechanism will be most effective in supporting a planner who argues the interests of justice to a hostile or unconcerned client, or employer, or public. Conceivably, charges might be appropriate where a planner knowingly uses his or her effort to develop a plan violating the commitment. Appropriate procedures can be devised to make sure injustice is not done in the pursuit of justice, and the recent revision of the AICP Code (Section C) already shows how much care is possible in this direction.

A third practical step the profession can take to advance its commitment to justice in planning is to establish a "Whistle-Blowers Support Fund," which would recognize the fact that an enforced obligation to the principles of justice can, under some circumstances, lead to a loss of work or discharge from a job; for example, a planner may be ethically unable to take a particular job or may be fired from a job for protesting against the injustice of a task the job entails.

Appendix: AICP Code of Ethics and Professional Conduct

Adopted March 19, 2005
Effective June 1, 2005
Revised October 3, 2009 (available at www.planning.org/ethics/ethicscode.htm)

...

Section A contains a statement of aspirational principles that constitute the ideals to which we are committed. We shall strive to act in accordance with our stated principles. However, an allegation that we failed to achieve our aspirational principles cannot be the subject of a misconduct charge or be a cause for disciplinary action.

Section B contains rules of conduct to which we are held accountable. If we violate any of these rules, we can be the object of a charge of misconduct and shall have the responsibility of responding to and cooperating with the investigation and enforcement procedures. If we are found to be blameworthy by the AICP Ethics Committee, we shall be subject to the imposition of sanctions that may include loss of our certification.

...

The principles to which we subscribe in Sections A and B of the Code derive from the special responsibility of our profession to serve the public interest with compassion for the welfare of all people and, as professionals, to our obligation to act with high integrity.

...

A. Principles to Which We Aspire

1. Our Overall Responsibility to the Public

Our primary obligation is to serve the public interest and we, therefore, owe our allegiance to a conscientiously attained concept of the public interest that is formulated through continuous and open debate. We shall achieve high standards of professional integrity, proficiency, and knowledge. To comply with our obligation to the public, we aspire to the following principles:

a) We shall always be conscious of the rights of others.

b) We shall have special concern for the long-range consequences of present actions.

c) We shall pay special attention to the interrelatedness of decisions.

d) We shall provide timely, adequate, clear, and accurate information on planning issues to all affected persons and to governmental decision makers.

e) We shall give people the opportunity to have a meaningful impact on the development of plans and programs that may affect them. Participation should be broad enough to include those who lack formal organization or influence.

f) We shall seek social justice by working to expand choice and opportunity for all persons, recognizing a special responsibility to plan for the needs of the disadvantaged and to promote racial and economic integration. We shall urge the alteration of policies, institutions, and decisions that oppose such needs.

g) We shall promote excellence of design and endeavor to conserve and preserve the integrity and heritage of the natural and built environment.

h) We shall deal fairly with all participants in the planning process. Those of us who are public officials or employees shall also deal evenhandedly with all planning process participants.

2. Our Responsibility to Our Clients and Employers

We owe diligent, creative, and competent performance of the work we do in pursuit of our client or employer's interest. Such performance, however, shall always be consistent with our faithful service to the public interest.

a) We shall exercise independent professional judgment on behalf of our clients and employers.
b) We shall accept the decisions of our client or employer concerning the objectives and nature of the professional services we perform unless the course of action is illegal or plainly inconsistent with our primary obligation to the public interest.
c) We shall avoid a conflict of interest or even the appearance of a conflict of interest in accepting assignments from clients or employers.

3. Our Responsibility to Our Profession and Colleagues

We shall contribute to the development of, and respect for, our profession by improving knowledge and techniques, making work relevant to solutions of community problems, and increasing public understanding of planning activities.

a) We shall protect and enhance the integrity of our profession.
b) We shall educate the public about planning issues and their relevance to our everyday lives.
c) We shall describe and comment on the work and views of other professionals in a fair and professional manner.
d) We shall share the results of experience and research that contribute to the body of planning knowledge.
e) We shall examine the applicability of planning theories, methods, research and practice and standards to the facts and analysis of each particular situation and shall not accept the applicability of a customary solution without first establishing its appropriateness to the situation.
f) We shall contribute time and resources to the professional development of students, interns, beginning professionals, and other colleagues.
g) We shall increase the opportunities for members of underrepresented groups to become professional planners and help them advance in the profession.
h) We shall continue to enhance our professional education and training.
i) We shall systematically and critically analyze ethical issues in the practice of planning.
j) We shall contribute time and effort to groups lacking in adequate planning resources and to voluntary professional activities.

. . .

NOTES

1. This chapter owes a major debt to the ongoing interaction of the author, both in person and through writings, with Susan Fainstein, with the co-editors of *Searching for*

the Just City, with David Harvey, and with my colleagues and students at Columbia University's Urban Planning Program.

2. The issue of spatial justice is not addressed further in this chapter, but see the new journal *Justice Spatiale/Spatial Justice*. Recent conferences include the Spatial Justice Symposium (University of Paris, Nanterre, March 2008); the Conference on the Right to the City (Technical University of Berlin, November 2008); and the Conference on Justice and the American Metropolis (Washington University in St. Louis, May 2008).

3. *Nicomachean Ethics*, Book V, 1130b–1131a (Aristotle 1911, 106).

4. As is the issue of retributive justice, the claim in criminal justice cases is of an injured party for just punishment of the offender. Planners will rarely be involved in such cases. Whether fines should be imposed on violators of land-use regulations may, but probably should not, raise issues of retribution, such as when neighbors argue that a developer who deliberately violated the zoning ordinance in building over height limits should be required to demolish below those limits as a result of his knowing violation. The impact of penalties on future behavior is an appropriate concern of planners, as a matter of their understanding of the way developers work, but it is not a matter of justice. It involves predicting the effect of the penalty as a social science matter, not a question of value judgments as to whether the penalty is just. Whether the violator is being punished in view of the moral gravity of his or her offense is also not a matter of justice for the planner but, rather, a matter of corrective justice outside the particular competence of planners.

5. The term "social market" often used in postwar Germany and some other countries is not so much a modification of a normal capitalist economy as a limitation on its scope. The concept of a socialist market, or market socialism, suggests that there may be forms or definitions of markets that might include relevance to justice within their operating rules, but they do not contend such markets are today operating in any capitalist economy (Bardhan and Roemer 1993; Ollman 1998).

6. The complaint alleged:

> The maintenance of Crotona Park is almost nonexistent. What was once one of the major parks in the city is now a mass of broken glass and litter strewn about. Most of the benches and fencing are broken and non-usable. Numerous abandoned automobiles often litter the roads running through the park for days. Little or no attempt has been made to clean up the park despite numerous requests by residents of the community On the contrary, Van Courtland Park, Pelham Bay Park and Bronx Park are kept in near spotless condition. During warm weather seasons, numerous park personnel can be seen removing the litter created by weekend crowds. Within a couple of days, these parks are spotless.

The city responded:

> Not disputing the allegations concerning the deplorable condition of Crotona Park, he maintained that this was not the consequence of any lack of effort by the City. He asserted that, on the contrary, the municipal effort at Crotona was as good as or better than that at other Bronx parks. Although Crotona contained only 146.59 acres in contrast to the much larger acreage of the three other parks, a far greater number of park personnel was assigned to Crotona. He attributed the failure of the City's maintenance efforts to the high degree of vandalism at Crotona Park and Pool.

(*Beale v. Lindsay*, 468 F2d 287, U.S. Second Circuit Court of Appeals (1972), available at http://openjurist.org/468/f2d/287.)

7. P. Marcuse (2011) separates the account into three currents—conformist, reformist, and radical.
8. Leave aside the point that in real life people are not ignorant of who they are or what position in society they hold. Rawls never supposed they were; he only used the formulation to logically derive his two principles, which he did indeed intend for practical application.
9. See http://www.cnbc.com/id/15840232?video=1039849853. Another video of the full "rant" is on Youtube: http://www.youtube.com/watch?v=bEZB4taSEoA.
10. Iris Marion Young, bell hooks, Nancy Fraser, Amartya Sen, and Martha Nussbaum are among those who have contributed significantly to the understanding of this issue.
11. The concern for causes is one of the major omissions in Rawls's *Theory of Justice*, but then Rawls was not writing for planners.
12. This is perhaps the most prominent buzzword in planning today, largely relying on the definition in Bruntland 1987.
13. For an excellent provocative discussion, see Fainstein 2005.
14. After all, this was the primary goal of the City Beautiful Movement, a critical participant in the birth of professional planning in the United States.
15. At least in the sense of personal security, this is a growing aim of many planning proposals, both in the context of racial tensions as after the "race riots" of the late 1960s, and after the attack of 9/11.
16. Arguably the primary motivating idea behind the City Scientific Movement in early-twentieth-century planning.
17. Freedom or liberty as an overriding goal is heavily considered in political philosophy, and Isaiah Berlin (1969/2002) has pressed the point that freedom to, as well as freedom from, is necessary. Freedom to might be the formulation planners would employ as a goal in their work. It may be well argued that freedom from is an instrumental goal, and freedom to is the ultimate goal it serves.
18. Perhaps the most widely accepted end of much urban planning today, with competitive position accepted as desirable because of its necessary contribution to economic growth.
19. A concept first popularized in Nussbaum and Sen 1993.
20. In classical philosophy, going back at least as far as Aristotle, perhaps the most frequently formulated term for the goal of the good society.
21. South African Council for Town and Regional Planners, Position Statement, August 1995.
22. South African Council for Town and Regional Planners, Submission to the Truth and Reconciliation Commission, September 1997, p. 2.
23. In the words of the person charged with the application of the Code, the aspirations "are not technically enforceable," but they are not enforceable in any other way either, unlike the other "rules" of the Code. See http://www.planning.org/ethics/pdf/farmeraddress.

References

Aristotle. 1911. *Nicomachean Ethics*, edited by J. A. Smith. London: Everyman's Library, J. M. Dent.
Atkinson, Anthony Barnes. 1983. *Social Justice and Public Policy*. Cambridge, MA: MIT Press.

Bardhan, Pranab K., and John E. Roemer. 1993. *Market Socialism: The Current Debate.* New York: Oxford University Press.

Barusch, Amanda S. 1994. *Older Women in Poverty: Private Lives and Public Policies.* New York: Springer.

Benevolo, Leonardo. 1967. *The Origins of Modern Town Planning*, translated by Judith Landry. London: Routledge and Kegan Paul.

Berlin, Isaiah. 1969/2002. "Two Concepts of Liberty." In *Four Essays on Liberty*, by Isaiah Berlin. London: Oxford University Press.

Brenner, Neil, and Roger Keil, eds. 2006.*The Global Cities Reader.* London and New York: Routledge.

Bridge, Gary, and Sophie Watson, eds. 2002. *The Blackwell City Reader.* Malden, MA: Blackwell.

Bruntland Commission. 1987. *Our Common Future, Report of the World Commission on Environment and Development.* World Commission on Environment and Development. Published as Annex to General Assembly document A/42/427, Development and International Co-operation: Environment, August 2.

Bryant, Bunyan, ed. 1995. *Environmental Justice: Issues, Policies, and Solutions.* Washington, DC: Island Press.

Campbell, Scott. 1996. "Green Cities, Growing Cities, Just Cities? Urban Planning and the Contradictions of Sustainable Development." *Journal of the American Planning Association* 62:296–312.

Capeheart, Loretta, and Dragan Milovanovic. 2007. *Social Justice: Theories, Issues, and Movements.* New Brunswick, NJ: Rutgers University Press.

Catanese, Anthony J. 1988. *Urban Planning.* New York: McGraw-Hill.

Clough-Riquelme, Jane, and Nora Bringas Rábago, eds. 2006. *Equity and Sustainable Development: Reflections from the U.S.-Mexico Border.* San Diego: Lynne Rienner.

Daily, Herman. 1997. *Beyond Growth: The Economics of Sustainable Development.* Boston: Beacon Press.

Darke, Jane, Sue Ledwith, and Roberta Woods, eds. 2000.*Women and the City: Visibility and Voice in Urban Space.* Basingstoke, UK: Palgrave.

Del Vecchio, Giorgio. 1953 *An Historical and Philosophical Essay.* New York: Philosophical Library.

Fainstein, Susan S. 2005. "Cities and Diversity: Should We Want it? Can We Plan for it?" *Urban Affairs Review* 41(1): 3–19.

Fainstein, Susan. 2009. "Planning and the Just City." In *Searching for the Just City*, edited by Peter Marcuse, James Connolly, Johannas Novy, Ingrid Oliva, Cuz Potter, and Justin Steil, 19–38. New York and London: Routledge.

Fainstiein, Susan, and Scott Campbell. 2011. *Readings in Urban Theory*, 3ⁿᵈ ed. Hoboken, NJ: John Wiley.

Fischer, Frank, and John Forester. 1993. *The Argumentative Turn in Policy Analysis and Planning.* Durham, NC: Duke University Press.

Forester, John. 1989. *Planning in the Face of Power.* Berkeley, CA: University of California Press.

Habermas, Jürgen. 1984. *The Theory of Communicative Action*, translated by Thomas McCarthy. Boston: Beacon Press.

Harvey, David. 1973. *Social Justice and the City.* Baltimore: John Hopkins University Press.

Hawkins v. Shaw. 1972. U.S. Court of Appeals, Fifth Circuit. 461 F. 2d 1171.

Krumholz, N., and J. Forester. 1990. *Making Equity Planning Work.* Philadelphia: Temple University Press.

Lefebvre, Henri. 1967/1996. "The Right to the City." In *Writings on Cities*, edited by
    Eleonore Kofman and Elizabeth Lebas, 63–184. London: Blackwell.

Levi, Albert William. 1963. *The Six Great Humanistic Essays of John Stuart Mill.*
    Chapter 5, "Utilitarianism." New York: Washington Square Press.

Manning Thomas, June, and Marcia Ritzdorf. 1997. *Urban Planning and the African
    American Community: In the Shadows.* Thousand Oaks, CA: Sage.

Marcuse, Herbert. 1964. *One-Dimensional Man.* Boston: Beacon Press.

Marcuse, Peter. 1976. "Professional Ethics and Beyond: Values in Planning." *Journal of the
    American Institute of Planners* 42(3): 264–74. Repr. 1980 in *Urban Planning*, edited by
    Donald Hagman. Minneapolis: West; and 1985 in *Ethics in Planning*, edited by Martin
    Wachs. New Brunswick, NJ: Center for Urban Policy Research, State University of
    New Jersey Press.

Marcuse, Peter. 1988. "Are Planners Judges?" *Land Use Law*, September, 3–5.

Marcuse, Peter. 2002. "The Shifting Meaning of the Black Ghetto in the United States."
    In *Of States and Cities: The Partitioning of Urban Space*, edited by Peter Marcuse and
    Ronald van Kempen, 109–42. Oxford: Oxford University Press.

Marcuse, Peter. 2005. "Enclaves Yes, Ghettos No: Segregation and the State." In
    Desegregating the City: Ghettos, Enclaves, and Inequality, edited by David Varady.
    Albany, NY: State University of New York Press.

Marcuse, Peter, James Connolly, Johannes Novy, Ingrid Olivo, Cuz Potter, and Justin
    Steil, eds. 2009. *Searching for the Just City: Debates in Urban Theory and Practice.*
    London and New York: Routledge.

Marcuse, Peter. 2011. "The Three Historic Currents of City Planning." In *The New
    Blackwell Companion to the City*, edited by Gary Bridge and Sophie Watson, 643–55.
    Oxford: Wiley-Blackwell.

Miller, Eugene. 2008. "Philosopher's Progress." *The Good Society* 17(1): 10.

Moen, Phyllis, Donna Dempster-McClain, and Henry A. Walker, eds. 1999. *A Nation
    Divided: Diversity, Inequality and Community in American Society.* Ithaca, NY:
    Cornell University Press.

Moomaw, W. R. 1996. "Managing Urban Sustainability." *Environmental Impact
    Assessment Review* 16(4–6): 425–27.

Nussbaum, Martha, and Amartya Sen. 1993. *The Quality of Life.* Oxford: Clarendon
    Press.

Ollman, Bertell. 1998. *Market Socialism: The Debate Among Socialists.* London and
    New York: Routledge.

Plato. 2002. The Republic. In *Philosophy: A Text with Readings*, translated by M.
    Velasquez. Belmont, CA: Wadsworth Publishing.

Purcell, Mark. 2008. *Recapturing Democracy: Neoliberalization and the Struggle for
    Alternative Urban Futures.* New York: Routledge.

Rawls, John. 1971/1999. *A Theory of Justice.* Cambridge, MA: Belknap Press.

Sanchez, Thomas W., and Marc Bernman. 2007. *The Right to Transportation: Moving to
    Equity.* Washington, DC: APA Planners Press.

Stimpson, Catharine R., Elsa Dixler, Martha J. Nelson, and Kathryn B. Yatrakis. 1981.
    Women and the American City. Chicago: University of Chicago Press.

Tilly, Charles. 2005. *Trust and Rule.* London: Cambridge University Press.

Wachs, M. 1985. *Ethics in Planning.* New Brunswick, NJ: Center for Urban Policy
    Research, State University of New Jersey Press.

CHAPTER 9

....

ACCESS

....

KEVIN J. KRIZEK AND
DAVID M. LEVINSON

1. INTRODUCTION

....

ANNUALLY, traffic-weary residents across the United States eagerly wait for the arrival of their news source to learn about the latest congestion report card from the Texas Transportation Institute. This Urban Mobility Report makes headlines, especially in places with worsening congestion. Even smaller areas, possibly not yet victims what some might consider serious traffic, lament their annual increase in levels of congestion, yet secretly enjoy their emerging big-city status. Traffic engineers, planners, and politicians take more than feigned interest because, to date, such ratings are the only available measure to assess progress toward a concern central to livability that is front and center in the minds of many residents.

Traffic congestion is a serious issue, undoubtedly, particularly in major metropolitan areas worldwide. But is congestion the problem or the solution? Taylor (2003) argues that traffic congestion is a solution to the problem of how to allocate scarce road space. (In contrast, economists argue for road pricing to allocate road space, but clearly there are factors limiting its widespread deployment.) Even if we agree that congestion wastes time, is minimizing congestion the most appropriate public policy goal (Taylor 2003)? Do measures of congestion provide the basis for policy prescriptions? We argue elsewhere (Levinson and Krizek 2008) that mobility (or lack thereof because of inadequate networks or congestion) is an element of the larger goal—ensuring accessibility.

Recent years have witnessed more than a handful of conferences or workshops whose central themes focused on the concept of accessibility. For example, the University of Minnesota sponsored two conferences, producing an array of recent scholarly publications on the topic in 2004 (Levinson and Krizek 2005) and

2007 (Axhausen 2008; Bruegmann 2008; Crane 2008; Lo, Tang, and Wang 2008; Ottensmann and Lindsey 2008; Scott and Horner 2008); in 2007, the European Science Foundation hosted a workshop, How to Define and Measure Access and Need Satisfaction in Transport (Becker, Bohmer, and Gerike 2008). The Network on European Communications and Transport Activities Research (NECTAR) continues to sponsor activities focusing on accessibility. Accessibility has even been touted as a civil rights issue (Sanchez 1999).

As judged by the level of discussion, mention, and focus in specialized workshops, interest in accessibility is high. Previous writings have focused on defining the concept of accessibility generally, starting from Hansen (1959), but also involving other extensions (Dalvi 1979; Ingram 1971; Kau 1979; Rutherford 1979), measuring the concept using different approaches (Handy and Niemeier 1997), various data needs (Krizek 2008),[8] or its use in explaining behavior (Levinson and Krizek 2005; Levinson 1998).

This chapter recommends that policy decisions be based on important and reliable performance measures. Robust measures that simultaneously assess the performance of the transportation *and land use* dimensions of cities, however, are mostly missing from such discussions (Levinson 2003). At the heart of the proposed approach lies the concept of accessibility: the ability of people to reach the destinations that they need to visit in order to meet their needs. A focus on accessibility—rather than congestion or mobility— would produce a more complete and meaningful picture of metropolitan transport and land use.

This chapter aims to articulate a clear role for measures of metropolitan accessibility and to demonstrate the utility of these measures in informing and influencing policy. It reviews necessary definitions, comments on the nature of past research, and suggests strategies to adapt such research into means. It endeavors to place accessibility in a position of prominence as a performance measure; thus, this chapter has four parts and functions, as follows:

- To describe the use and measurement of accessibility for metropolitan areas,
- To appraise the current state of knowledge and literature,
- To identify issues about measurement,
- To offer prescriptions for resolving those issues, given political contexts, and
- To point to future directions.

2. DEFINITIONS

Accessibility has been a familiar concept in the transportation planning field since the 1950s, when it was defined as the ease of reaching desirable destinations

(Hansen 1959). What has been widely labeled as the "Hansen measure" represented one of the first efforts by planners to develop measures that linked land use and activity systems with the transportation networks serving them. Hansen presented a hypothetical model showing how differences in accessibility—constructing an express highway—could be used as the basis for a residential land-use model. In this context and others (Patton and Clark 1970), highways (and other transportation infrastructure) provide accessibility that affect location decisions.

In these applications, accessibility weights opportunities (e.g., the quantity of an activity as measured by employment) by impedance (e.g., a function of travel time or cost). Within this framework, accessibility is typically described by the following equation:

$$A_i = \sum_{j-1}^{n} O_j f\left(C_{ij}\right)$$

where A_i = accessibility from a zone (i) to the considered type of opportunities (j)

O_j = opportunities of the considered type in zone j (e.g., employment, shopping, etc.)

C_{ij} = generalized (or real) time or cost from i to j

$f\left(C_{ij}\right)$ = Impedance function (exponential or power functions are most often used)

Accessibility applies within cities and between cities. The matrix depicted in table 9.1 suggests one organizational schema. Most focus in the planning community has been on access for passengers to various daily activities. But access from a city to other cities is important in explaining the growth of areas as a whole; furthermore, industry depends on easy access to goods both within the metropolitan area (to distribute to customers and suppliers) and to other cities.

New modes of transportation change each city's relative (and absolute) positioning for each type of accessibility, and this in turn helps drive the rise and fall of cities. Cities built in earlier times that could not, or did not, adapt to new modes fell by the wayside; cities that were well located in one era may be redundant in another,

Table 9.1 Matrix of Accessibility

	Intra-metropolitan				Inter-metropolitan
Passenger	Car	Bus	Bike	...	Walk
Jobs					
Stores					
...					
Workers					
Freight					

faster era when primary cities need not be so close. The same applies within cities, and as intrametropolitan transportation modes change, neighborhoods that were once exclusive or attractive lose their relative advantage, and new developments rise in their wake.

Accessibility's identifying characteristic, the *ease of reaching destinations*, is often considered a suitable definition and contains two important tenets. There is the land-use side of the coin—the desirability of what can be reached—and there is the transportation side, or by what mode and how fast. The term *accessibility* is often countered with the term *mobility*, often defined as the "ease of movement."

Such benefits are perhaps best illustrated through examples. Imagine traveling to (or through) the prairie province of Manitoba in Canada. The traveler meets with the basic services required for daily living (i.e., food stores, shelter, employment opportunities); these services are mostly distributed across the landscape in a manner befitting relatively low density development. The result is an environment with relatively limited services but also (usually) free-flowing traffic. Traffic congestion fails to exist, and when the roads are free of snow and mud, levels of mobility are quite high. People can get what they need, assuming auto-based travel, but the array of choices of things to get is relatively limited, so they are less likely to get what they want.

Contrast the above situation with the island of Manhattan in New York City. Often thought of as the congested heart of the largest city in the United States, its overall attraction, both culturally and economically, suffers little nonetheless. The reason is relatively simple. An endless array of services and opportunities exist for consumption, accompanied by several options as available transportation modes. Despite its high levels of congestion, New York City thrives because of the extreme ease with which it enables residents and visitors to reach varied and valuable destinations.

The above exemplifies how nearby destinations produce high accessibility even with low mobility. Conversely, where origins and destinations are spread broadly, even great mobility does not ensure high accessibility. The two concepts can be readily distinguished through an understanding of the meaning of a change in each: an improvement in mobility reduces the time-plus-money cost of travel per mile, while an improvement in accessibility reduces the time-plus-money cost per (value of) destination. Land is more expensive in Manhattan than Manitoba, suggesting the market values accessibility more than mobility.

3. APPRAISAL

The above concepts appear straightforward—and they are from the bird's-eye perspective. More than a half-century's worth of study on related issues provides a solid foundation to understand some inherent interactions between land use and transportation. Measures of accessibility have historically subscribed to one of three categories: gravity-based measures, cumulative opportunity measures, and behavioral measures (Handy and Niemeier 1997). Even some of the more advanced measures (Miller 1999) derive from these three categories.

However, an examination of the literature suggests that different aspects of how accessibility is measured (e.g., how to measure attributes, how to measure travel cost, how to value or weight for various considerations) are considerably more complicated. Below, we appraise a half-dozen key dimensions of past work for their usefulness in informing contemporary planning issues. Without being exhaustive, this list provides the reader with a starting point for wading through existing knowledge.

1. The concept of accessibility was initially developed for automobile travel. To the extent that accessibility has been employed in past mainstream transportation planning circles, such measures have also typically been auto based (Handy and Clifton 2001: Iacono, Krizek, and El-Geneidy 2009). The past decade has witnessed considerable attention on developing measures that more fully capture walking and transit (and sometimes even cycling), but these efforts are still in their infancy and where they are pursued, are usually conducted for limited geographic areas (e.g., a particular neighborhood or a corridor).

2. The overwhelming majority of studies focus on access to employment. The emphasis on employment accessibility is understandable, given its link to other important aspects of urban structure, such as choice of residential location and social exclusion (Preston and Rajé). However, access to other types of destinations, such as retail, are also important because they strongly influence various dimensions of travel behavior, such as trip frequency (Daly 1982), destination choice (Handy 1993), mode choice, and trip or tour complexity (Hanson and Schwab 1987). They also affect the price people will pay for land; areas with higher accessibility to desirable activities will be more expensive. The market (the collection of individual buyers and sellers) has an opinion on what is desirable, which can be ascertained through tools such as hedonic models for the price of real estate. Higher access levels to activities such as shopping and recreation are also thought to improve the general quality of life. Land price implicitly incorporates the value the market places on a variety of goods that may be available across a metropolitan area into a single measure of attractiveness, but also contains other factors. Decomposing this into its constituent elements is difficult. And, where nonemployment measures have been researched, their context has usually been limited to specialized purposes such as parks and schools.

3. There is an enormous difference in how things are measured for dimensions such as spatial separation between origins and destinations (e.g., crow flies versus network distance), travel time, and composite travel cost. For example, travel cost typically only considers either time or distance, but rarely money.

4. Measures of accessibility are almost always divorced from political realities. Different types of activities and services are associated with different sets of restrictions. Being located in a particular jurisdiction determines which government services one can legally access. Access to police, fire, and schools, for example, depends on jurisdictional residence. Other types of activities (jobs, shops) are open to the free market (at least within national borders), and while still subject to the capability (how far one can reach) and coupling (who one wants to reach it with) constraints of time geography (Hägerstrand 1970), are not as limited by authority constraints.

5. As with sprawl and smart growth, the language (and sometimes the literature) associated with accessibility often suffers, as not everyone employs the same dictionary; it can be confusing and pliable. For example, accessibility planning has traditionally focused on access to emergency services and/or to services for people with disabilities. Today it has expanded in scope to consider the impacts of limited access on outcomes, such as economic status, diet, social isolation, and health care. Rarely in colloquial settings does it resemble the definition we present above, and the terms are often adapted depending on one's purpose (the American Disabilities Act (ADA) is a classic example, suggesting that various destinations need to be accessible for a variety of users, but in the ADA sense accessibility refers to physical ability to enter, rather than geographically able to reach). That said, there is growing agreement among transportation scholars that accessibility refers specifically to the ability (can I get there from here?) or ease (how hard is it to get there from here?) of reaching destinations, while mobility simply represents the ease of moving on the network (Levinson and Krizek 2005). In that view, accessibility is about getting places and doing things, while mobility is just about the cost of travel.

6. Finally, despite the wealth of research and breadth of different ways of measuring different aspects, the culmination lacks a "unified theory" for measuring geographic accessibility; the accessibility we employ has been called Type 1 accessibility by Batty (2009), in contrast with Type 2 and Type 3 measures that concern the connectedness of physical infrastructure but not the value of the destinations. Despite a half-century of study, many of the above issues continue to get in way. These issues are further complicated by recent developments such as how to best account for the rapid increase in electronically mediated interaction, information and communication technology, and new "virtual" environments.

4. IMPLEMENTATION

While the concept of accessibility has received support among the academic community, its application as a planning concept has been less widespread, with just a few concrete examples to point to (Handy 2005). The reasons for limited use are myriad and not limited to the lack of: (a) consensus on a preferred and comprehensive measure (by purpose or by mode); (b) detailed, reliable and widely available travel or land use data (Krizek 2008)⁺ (c) consensus in understanding the different purposes for which the measures will be employed; and (d) relatively straightforward strategies for putting it all together. Below, we describe some of the difficulties, and based on experience developing robust and metropolitan-scale measures in the Minneapolis-St. Paul metropolitan area (El-Geneidy and Levinson 2007), prescribe strategies to address them.

To Where?

As mentioned, most measures of accessibility center on the ease of reaching employment. This is understandable given the prominent role economic activity plays in the health of cities. But in the spirit of quality of life, diversity of goods and services, and health, we see access to food, low-cost goods, parks and recreation, and medical care as important subjects to be measured (among others). Even nominally similar destinations may not be perceived equally; see Box 9.1 on Taste.

Box 9.1 Taste

Imagine a hypothetical residential neighborhood that has the following services all within 800 meters: deli, movie theatre, grocery store, veterinary, coffee shop, and a restaurant. According to most metrics of accessibility, such an environment would score exceptionally high; residents have a full array of opportunities all within convenient walking distance. Consistent with conventional theory, more places in the metropolitan area along the line of the above would be preferred over fewer places. (Too much choice may increase search and mental transaction costs however, and not be as desirable as a simple "more is better" rule would suggest, e. g., see Barry Schwartz's *Paradox of Choice*). Overall the market is likely to score a place with more access higher, (with concomitant higher rents), though for any individual, their preference structure values proximity to some different mix of destinations. Sometimes these individual-level constraints require accounting for consumer tastes. For example, most people seek access to a grocery store, but for some people that means finding the closest location for milk, while for others only a gourmet food store will suffice.

By What Mode?

Broadening the scope of accessibility to include additional types of destinations and active transportation modes such as walking and cycling has been proposed as an objective worthy of further study in the land-use transportation field (Handy and Clifton 2001; Handy 1993). Other than Iacono, Krizek, and El-Geneidy (2009), to date there have been few examples computing nonmotorized accessibility measures for entire metropolitan areas (as opposed to smaller neighborhoods). Issues including, but certainly not limited to, lack of reliable data, computational power, and knowledge of nonmotorized travel behavior have prevented widespread application of such measures.

Using Which Function?

At least three general functions have been extensively employed in past efforts. These include the cumulative opportunities function, the traditional Hansen function, and the log-sum function.

Despite their historic popularity, attraction-accessibility measures have some significant weaknesses. These measures assume that the ordering of alternatives is irrelevant to the individual; this is clearly not the case when individuals have less than complete knowledge and must acquire information through a search process. Attraction-accessibility measures also deny the possibility of a hierarchical decision process where individuals mentally cluster individual choices into aggregates (e.g., making a choice between downtown versus suburban shopping malls prior to choosing individual stores). Finally, attraction-accessibility measures can be difficult to interpret. For example, researchers often interpret the Hansen measure as a gauge of "potential interaction"; however, it is unclear exactly what this means beyond simple ordinal relationships (e.g., "A has more potential interaction than B"; Miller 1999). We do not know whether (or under what conditions) there are increasing or decreasing returns to accessibility. We imagine one is better than zero, or two is better than one, but is access to three almost identical stores significantly more valuable than two? The increment in value might be diminishing at some point.

5. POLICY

Having discussed some important theoretical underpinnings and outstanding intellectual issues in measuring accessibility, we turn to describing how accessibility measures can best inform and influence policy in metropolitan areas.

In community planning initiatives, the goal of enhanced accessibility has generally garnered a welcome seat at the table (Handy 2005), alongside a laundry list of aspirations and platitudes, such as increased mobility, decreased congestion, and reduced greenhouse gas emissions.

However, despite a seeming consensus among land-use transportation scholars and practitioners about the merits of accessibility as a performance measurement tool, the concept has not yet been widely adopted. A fundamental issue is that accessibility measures come in all different shapes and sizes. Some are more theoretical and robust in their complexity. Others are more practical and applicable with readily available data. The advantages of each depend on the intent and purpose. Furthermore, data requirements have been relatively burdensome, thereby rendering the concept difficult to effectively measure. Faster computational speeds and increasingly available land-use data that are both detailed and reliable, however, help relax these constraints. The current outstanding challenge when approaching such a goal in metropolitan and policy confines now centers on the type—and value—of measures that would be used.

We suggest that accessibility measures have enormous potential to provide an appropriate performance measurement tool to guide both physical changes, such as future land-use decisions and transportation investments, and policy changes, such as road pricing. But for such a measure to gain the currency it deserves in the policy process, it needs to be straightforward and appealing to users and politicians.

These stipulations require several criteria to be filled—criteria not unlike those described for measures of effectiveness in analyzing the goals or success of different policy initiatives (Levinson and Krizek 2008). Key to the particular pursuit of measuring and furthering accessibility is that the measures be clearly understood by both residents and policy decision makers. Toward this end, we suggest that five criteria be satisfied. We label these the "Five Cs" of effective accessibility measures, and each are briefly discussed as follows.

Cumulative—Accessibility measures need to scale well. They need to apply to a particular address, a neighborhood, or an entire region.

Comparable—Accessibility measures need to inform multiple modes on the same continuum and on the same scale. In other words, it is ideal to have the associated varying networks, varying travel speeds, and varying impedance functions be as consistent as possible. Comparing an accessibility measure for walking that focuses particular attention on experiential elements (e.g., urban design amenities) with an accessibility measure for auto based solely on travel time presents outstanding challenges.

Clear—For the measures to have appeal to various constituents, they need to be understood by them. They need to be transparent in terms of where the data came from, how they were calculated, and what they mean. Politicians and citizens have a hard time relating to phenomena such as log-sum measures or negative exponential distance decay curves.

Comprehensive—Accessibility measures need to be able to clearly capture just certain domains of interest—restaurants, for example—or be able to aggregate different types of land uses.

Calculable—It is best for measures to employ data that are readily accessible, available for an entire metropolitan area, and specific enough to capture the fine-grain calculations required for pedestrian travel.

The above criteria ultimately limit the utility of some of the more theoretical, nuanced, or even robust and extended measures that have appeared in the literature over the past decades. As much as researchers support continued exploration of how more complex measures could and should be applied to policy environments, there are competing demands—demands which often cannot be realized. Satisfying the above Five Cs of effective accessibility measures leads us to recommend the *cumulative opportunity* measures of accessibility.

Several advantages of this measure for this purpose stand out. It is a straightforward measure for people to understand; the number of destinations within a set amount of travel time is a concept most can relate to. It scales well; it can be used in a straightforward manner for a single point or an entire metropolitan area. It compares well; it can be used in the same manner to compare different modes, different neighborhoods, and even different metropolitan areas.

Of course, a number of definitional considerations still need to be fully ironed out. Even the most straightforward of measures can be made complicated by attending to all sorts of details. For example, how should destinations be measured (e.g., by establishment, employees, floor area, or something else)? How detailed should transit schedules be consulted (e.g., what time of day, how many transfers)? What time cut-off for waiting for transfers should be imposed (20 minutes, longer or shorter)? Should more than one time band be used?

A prescribed measure we endorse would be computed using a cumulative opportunity measure that: (a) uses 20 minutes as a baseline measure for comparative purposes; (b) is performed for specific subunits for a region (e.g., transportation analysis zones to measure auto accessibility, census blocks for other modes); (c) measures various types of destinations (e.g., jobs, retail, food, health care) independently or in an aggregated manner; and (d) does so using actual measures of the phenomena rather than modeled estimates.

Accessibility measures are typically thought of in terms of locational (*x-y*) attributes. Their value from a policy perspective, however, is when the measures are detailed in nature, but can be scaled up to represent broader areas using a weighted average for the area under inquiry. One could present a weighted accessibility score for a particular latitude and longitude location or a subarea (e.g., a transportation analysis zone, or block) or an accessibility measure for an entire neighborhood, community or even metropolitan area using the following equation:

$$A_{area} = \left(\Sigma A_{sub\text{-}area} * P_{sub\text{-}area} \right) / P_{area}$$

A = Accessibility Measure (for a particular area such as a neighborhood, district or even metropolitan area)

P = Weight (e.g., population of the disaggregate unit area)

Figures 9.1, 9.2, and 9.3 illustrate the accessibility to jobs by walking, bicycling, and transit for 1995, 2000, and 2005, respectively, in the Twin Cities Metropolitan Area (Minnesota). The bar charts, compiled using the above equation, parsimoniously depict the number of jobs that can be reached in 20 minutes of travel time by each mode. As can be seen, walking is slower than biking or transit, and thus has overall a lower level of accessibility. Over time accessibility is increasing, primarily because of the redistribution and growth of land use, and in part because of changes to the transportation network. The visual map depiction combined with the bar chart—which could be computed for any geographic area—provide a clear, useful, and robust story for accessibility in the region that planners, high level policy analysts and decision makers can easily relate to.

6. DIRECTIONS

For many years, normative work looking at cities and transportation has focused on strategies to modify transportation phenomena or behavior: how to encourage

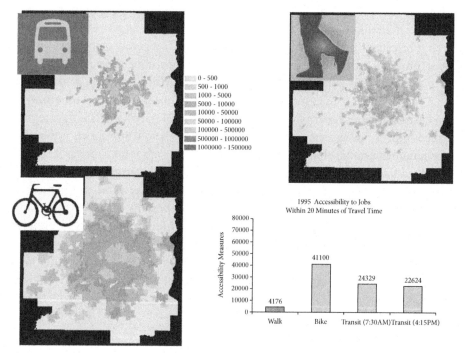

Figure 9.1 1995 Total Employment.

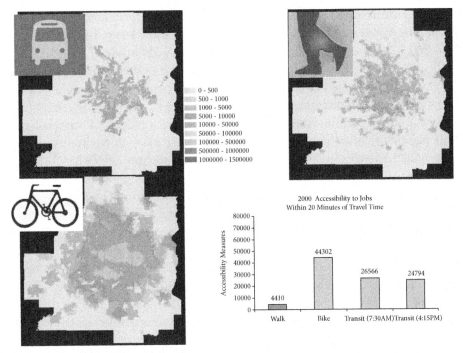

Figure 9.2 2000 Total Employment.

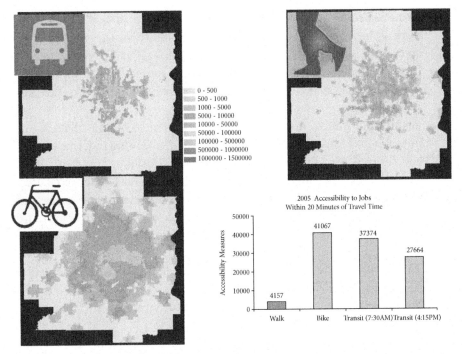

Figure 9.3 2005 Total Employment.

residents to drive less, use transit more, or spur walking. (In contrast with mid-twentieth century policy, which favored more driving and less transit, and spurned walking). These normative strategies are often pursued outside of an appreciation of the policies and economic forces that have shaped these behaviors. Furthermore, the ways of thinking about policy prescriptions are bereft of appropriate measurement methods or standards.

For example, considerable research seeks improved models of travel behavior. This research furthermore tries to draw close associations to environmental outcomes; alternatively, research might seek to put more accurate dollar figures on various intangibles, and so on. The intent is that such research will enhance policy-making. Implicit in this line of reasoning is that a shortcoming of past transportation policies was primarily attributable to a lack of accuracy in this kind of knowledge. By reducing uncertainty in these areas, it is thought, more effective policies could be uncovered. But weaknesses in the policies may derive from sources other than gaps in predicted outcomes. One major weakness in current policy is a misdefinition of the problem as one aims to maximize mobility rather than maximize accessibility.

This chapter recommends that problem definitions can be reformed to bring them in line with current transportation goals (and thus develop metrics that are closer to measures of benefits identified in economic theory, which are often too idealized to realize) and also identifies several important issues.

The concept of accessibility operationalized using cumulative opportunities measures offers a compelling, attractive and alternative basis for policies related to the built environment. Such measures are:

- Easily scaled to be regional in scope. A shortcoming of much of the past work at the neighborhood scale is that accessibility measures, while robust and sometimes detailed, cannot be easily scaled up to the regional level.
- Inclusive as desired. Depending on local data sources (most of which are rich and widely available), measures can easily be as inclusive or exclusive as need be.
- Readily interpreted. Accessibility is rarely presented in units that are easily interpreted. Measures rarely have any absolute meaning in terms of costs or benefits or other values such as convenience. Thus, they are often normalized over a certain range and interpreted in purely relative terms (Batty 2009). Relativity helps users grasp differences between various places or neighborhoods, but many are yearning for a concrete unit of measurement. Cumulative opportunities measures rectify this problem.

In this application we view the process of developing consistent accessibility measures for both motorized and nonmotorized (active transportation) modes as both an accomplishment and an invitation for future work by both practitioners and academics.

There remain many questions that do not have satisfactory answers. Does accessibility have increasing or diminishing returns? How do different people value different types of accessibility? Accessibility as a property of location can be capitalized in land value. Many hedonic models of real estate aim to disentangle locational attributes from structural attributes, but most use crude, and incomplete, measures of accessibility when doing so. Distance to CBD is a useful surrogate, but is insufficient as an accessibility measure. We lack experience of implementing decision criteria dominated by accessibility (e.g., how different proposed transportation projects rank by their accessibility contribution), so have yet to see how political realities confront this posited decision tool for investment. We do not know how well accessibility describes the economies of agglomeration that make cities valuable, but with a comparison of metropolitan economic product and metropolitan accessibility, we may be able to discover the macroeconomic value of metropolitan organization.

The late Mel Webber of the University of California, Berkeley, often asserted that the ideal city is "one that maximizes access among its interdependent residents and establishments." This chapter aimed to crystallize metrics to sufficiently capture the degree to which Mel Webber's ideal city is achieved. The bottom line is that accessibility measures help planners and others better differentiate between policy variables they can control—such as trip cost or development approvals—and how individual travelers weigh and select among destinations (which planners can do little to control). Implementation of this framework would, at a minimum, permit a more straightforward comparison of access in different communities, in a given community over time, or across alternative future scenarios. A more standardized definition of what to measure is thus valuable.

References

Axhausen, K. 2008. "Accessibility Long Term Perspectives." *Journal of Transport and Land Use* 1(2): 5–22.

Batty, M. 2009. "Accessibility: In Search of a Unified Theory." *Environment and Planning Part B: Planning and Design* 36:191–94.

Becker, U., J. Bohmer, and R. Gerike, eds. 2008. *How Define and Measure Access and Need Satisfaction in Transport.* Dresden: Dresdner Institut fur Verkehr und Umwelt e. V.

Bruegmann, R. 2008. "Sprawl and Accessibility." *Journal of Transport and Land Use* 1(1): 5–11.

Crane, R. 2008. "Counterpoint: Accessibility and Sprawl." *Journal of Transport and Land Use* 1(1): 13–19.

Dalvi, M. Q., "Behavioural Modelling, Accessibility, Mobility, and Need: Concepts and Measurement." In *Behavioural Travel Modelling*, edited by D. A. Hensher and P. R. Stopher, 639–53. London: Croom Helm.

Daly, A. J. 1982. "Estimating Choice Models Containing Attraction Variables." *Transportation Research* B16(1): 5–15.

El-Geneidy, A., and D. Levinson. 2007. "Mapping Accessibility Over Time." *Journal of Maps* :76–87.

Hägerstrand, T. 1970. "What About People in Regional Science?" *Papers in Regional Science* 24(1): 6–21.

Handy, S. L. 1993. "Regional versus Local Accessibility—Implications for Nonwork Travel." *Transportation Research Record* 1400:58–66.

Handy, S. L. 2005. "Planning for Accessibility: In Theory and in Practice." In *Access to Destinations*, edited by D. M. Levinson and K. J. Krizek, 131–47. Amsterdam: Elsevier.

Handy, S. L., and K. J. Clifton. 2001. "Evaluating Neighborhood Accessibility: Possibilities and Practicalities." *Journal of Transportation and Statistics* 4(2/3): 67–78.

Handy, S. L., and D. A. Niemeier. 1997. "Measuring Accessibility: An Exploration of Issues and Alternatives." *Environment and Planning Part A* 29(7): 1175–94.

Hansen, W. 1959. "How Accessibility Shapes Land Use." *Journal of the American Institute of Planners* 25(1): 73–76.

Hanson, S. A., and M. Schwab. 1987. "Accessibility and Intraurban Travel." *Environment and Planning Part A* 19(6): 735–48.

Iacono, M., K. J. Krizek, and A. El-Geneidy. 2009. "Measuring Non-motorized Accessibility: Issues, Alternatives, and Execution. *Journal of Transport Geography* 18:133–40.

Ingram, D. R. 1971. "The Concept of Accessibility: A Search for an Operational Form." *Regional Studies* 5:101–107.

Kau, J. B. 1979. "The Functional Form of the Gravity Model." *International Regional Science Review* 4(2): 127–36.

Krizek, K. J., ed. 2008. "Exploiting Parcel Level Data to Create Detailed Measures of Accessibility." In *How Define and Measure Access and Need Satisfaction in Transport*, edited by J. B. U. Becker and R. Gerike. Dresden: Dresdner Institut fur Verkehr und Umwelt e. V.

Levinson, D. 1998. "Accessibility and the Journey to Work." *Journal of Transport Geography* 6(1): 11–21.

Levinson, D. 2003. "Perspectives on Efficiency in Transportation." *International Journal of Transport Management* 1:145–55.

Levinson, D. M., and K. J. Krizek, eds. 2005. *Access to Destinations.* Amsterdam: Elsevier.

Levinson, D., and K. J. Krizek. 2008. *Planning for Place and Plexus: Metropolitan Land Use and Transport.* New York: Routledge.

Lo, H. K., S. Tang, and D. Z. W. Wang. 2008. "Managing the Accessibility on Mass Public Transit: The Case of Hong Kong." *Journal of Transport and Land Use* 1(2): 23–49.

Miller, H. J. 1999. "Measuring Space-time Accessibility Benefits within Transportation Networks: Basic Theory and Computational Procedures." *Geographical Analysis* 31:187–212.

Ottensmann, J. R., and G. Lindsey. 2008. "A Use-Based Measure of Accessibility to Linear Features to Predict Urban Trail Use." *Journal of Transport and Land Use* 1(1): 41–63.

Patton, T. A., and N. Clark. 1970. "Towards an Accessibility Model for Residential Development." In *Analysis of Urban Development*, edited by. Tewksbury Symposium, Department of Civil Engineering, Melbourne.

Preston, J., and F. Rajé. 2007. "Accessibility, Mobility and Transport-related Social Exclusion." *Journal of Transport Geography* 15(3): 151–60.

Rutherford, G. S. 1979. "Use of the Gravity Model for Pedestrian Travel Distribution." *Transportation Research Record* 728:53–59.

Sanchez, T. W. 1999. "The Connection between Public Transit and Employment." *Journal of the American Planning Association* 65(3): 284–96.

Scott, D., and M. Horner. 2008. "Examining the Role of Urban Form in Shaping People's Accessibility to Opportunities: An Exploratory Spatial Data Analysis." *Journal of Transport and Land Use* 1(2): 89–119.

Taylor, B. Rethinking Traffic Congestion. *Access*, University of California Transportation Center, Vol. 21, 2002, pp. 8-16.

CHAPTER 10

PRESERVATION

NA LI AND ELISABETH M. HAMIN

1. INTRODUCTION

THE twentieth century witnessed historic preservation expanding from a hand-ful of scattered efforts to salvage elite houses to an organized social movement. For instance, the restoration of Colonial Williamsburg, Virginia, in the 1930s required the cooperation of a federal agency, the National Park Service, with civilian expertise across various disciplines, such as architecture, history, land-scape architecture, historic archaeology, and planning. The preservation of Charleston, South Carolina, resulted from the first zoning ordinance for his-toric preservation in the United States. These sorts of interdisciplinary efforts allowed preservation to tap into the cultural politics of governmental and pri-vate civic organizations. They have achieved admirable progress as "one of the broadest and longest-lasting land-use reform efforts" (Page and Mason 2004, 3), although they have typically been considered separate from much of the "bread and butter" of planning, such as zoning and other land-use regulation. The practice of historic preservation in the United States extends back to the nine-teenth century, but it gained official recognition as a field in the 1960s, arguably when the National Historic Preservation Act was passed in 1966. In recent years, preservation planning has moved from a staid, traditionalist field toward an emerging practice that embraces, we argue, a subtly revolutionary approach that encourages an appreciation of the shared, diverse, conflicting, and emotional characters of landscapes.

To achieve this momentum preservation planning's domain of interest has shifted from individual structures to wider landscapes, neighborhoods, and sites of production, with greater emphasis on public participation. Actors of all sorts have become engaged in sometimes fierce contests over whose history to preserve, which stories to tell and which to keep quiet, and what counts as authentic. These questions require more deliberative processes that engage and value the opinions of nonexperts and a narrative approach allowing the walk-through of histories and multiple senses of place. Historic preservation has become an integral part of a larger planning practice, one that uses the tools of wider participatory methods of planning and that contributes to a greater depth of emotional attachment and place identity in planning. Historic preservation has come of age. This chapter explores these transitions with a focus on professional practices in the United States.

2. TRADITIONAL PRESERVATION PLANNING

Appreciating the changes that have taken place in preservation planning requires an understanding of its roots. In 1965, Charles Hosmer published one of the first scholarly accounts of preservation planning. In it, he identified major reasons why preservation should be undertaken: patriotic inspiration, local and civic pride, the need for exhibition areas, family pride, commercial objectives, and architectural or aesthetic enjoyment (1965, 3). These reasons were based on forensic evidence of the basic accomplishments of the early preservers—namely, large numbers of historic landmarks that are still with us today. The pioneers of the preservation movement convinced some Americans to accept the idea of spending money for the seemingly profitless activity of saving a few buildings that contributed to the study of history or the appreciation of beauty.

By the 1980s, a substantial body of academic work had coalesced around the critical history, theory, and practice of preserving buildings, exemplified by the work of James Fitch (1982) and William Murtagh (1988).[1] These perspectives became legal doctrine with the landmark 1978 case *Penn Central Transportation Co. et al* v. *New York Co. et al.* In it, Justice William J. Brennan Jr. observed:

> [A] widely shared belief that structures with special historic, cultural, or architectural significance enhance the quality of life for *all*. Not only do these buildings and their workmanship represent the lessons of the past and embody precious features of our heritage, they serve as examples of quality for today. "Historic conservation is but one aspect of the much larger problem, basically an environmental one, of enhancing—or perhaps developing for the first time—the quality for people." (Stipe 2003, 183)[2]

As a social movement, organized through interlocking constituencies with shared commitments at local, state, national, and international levels, historic preservation came to be pursued in concert with urban development in Western Europe and North America (Page and Mason 2004; Heathcott 2006). In the United States, the first half of the twentieth century witnessed the growing professional legiti-macy of the field. Page and Mason (2004, 11) argue that "urban planner" and even "real estate developer" were just other names for "preservationist," especially in the prewar era, because they took a constructive approach in shaping development to fit the old urban fabric. As a result, preservation stepped beyond its curatorial boundaries into the social arena.

Yet from the heroic efforts of Ann Pamela Cunningham to save Mount Vernon from gradual decay in 1853,[3] or the first zoning ordinance to encourage preservation in Charleston, South Carolina, in 1931,[4] and the failed attempt in 1963 to save Penn Station in New York City, traditional preservation planning has emphasized the end results—the preserved buildings and sites—with little thought to the quality of the process. Indeed, the process was largely expert driven and centered on preventing imminent demolition of the structures asso-ciated with the rich and powerful, leading to a conservative image of preser-vation as embedded in the status quo and averse to change. Kevin Lynch, for instance, points out that "preservation has usually been the work of established middle- and upper-class citizens. The history enshrined in museums is cho-sen and interpreted by those who give the dollars" (1972, 30). Preservationists are viewed as the "keepers of the moribund, if not downright dead" (Bookspan 2001, 8).

3. LIMITS TO THE TRADITIONAL APPROACH

As daring and passionate as these earlier theoretical and judicial inquiries were, their authors primarily aimed to define preservation as a taken-for-granted social good (Heathcott 2006; Thomas 2004). They believed that preserving monumental structures unquestionably contributed to "the quality of life for all." The significant changes in social order and theory beginning in the 1960s, however, slowly trick-led into historic preservation, with an awareness that standard practices left the question of "good for whom?" unasked and, therefore, the fundamental premise of being a public good on shaky ground. The core issues of preservation began to open up: what is *historic* at a particular time and place? If preservation is largely driven by nostalgic, patriotic, and intellectual fervor, which version of history should be preserved? Who is actually involved in defining what is "historically significant"? What and who is missing from the preserved landscapes? Underlying and uniting these questions, we find three limits to the traditional approach to preservation planning: first, the painstaking pursuit of historic authenticity; second, the pres-sure to save a fixed and singular version of historic narratives; and third, the lack of attention to the intangible aspects of the built environment, particularly memory and sense of place.

3.1 Authenticity: A Cherished Professional Myth

The idea of authenticity makes people nervous. The public generally expects accurate history, a clear story that matches a singular truth, so preservation is expected to provide a physical touchstone for the basic effort to tell the truth about the past. But history is always a representation, a textual reconstruction of the past, and never a direct reflection of it (Barthel 1996). History is subject to the bias of both the narrator and the audience. As such, authenticity becomes an inapproachable goal of historical inquiry. The attempt to tell the truth about the past seems a socially responsible endeavor, but when we seek truths, our capacity to deal with messy, contested, and interpretive history is diminished. Interpretation turns out to be more relevant and usable. Given the complexity of history's multiple layers, this apparently simple conceptual parameter of truth seeking does not, in fact, render much practical guidance in specific preservation situations.

Indeed, the very quest for authenticity alters the nature of the past. Interpreting the past unavoidably moves beyond immediate concerns, as we deal with creations begun some time ago, often before our own epoch, and we seek to save and interpret remnants for future generations. It may be more productive instead to seek to understand what different social actors involved in these debates—preservationists, politicians, developers, and publics—think is authentic and why authenticity matters to them (Barthel 1996). Lowercase truth, and perhaps multiple truths, that move toward the goal of authenticity without expecting ever to arrive may be a more feasible goal in the public planning process.

If authenticity is neither possible nor necessary, which version of history is the one to preserve? How is the selection process intertwined in political and power struggles? How does faith in authenticity clash with interpretive flexibility, which may encourage the unwanted outcome—that is, a fabrication of heritage (Lowenthal 1998, 1996)? At its worst, this flexibility can lead to invented or imagined traditions selected for their potential to be sold and consumed, often going by the catch-all label of "heritage." More commonly, heritage as practiced in communities becomes local history selectively perceived and explained through a rosy glow. Lowenthal (1996), for example, believes that heritage, at its best, is an act of *faith* since the very act of interpretation changes the residues of history. Despite this, he argues for the social and spiritual benefits of heritage, finding that "heritage underpins and enriches continuities with those who came before and those who will come after us" (2008, 12).

A central and helpful aspect of heritage is that, as practiced, it tends to make the common more visible. In preservation planning this comes forth through an increasing willingness to preserve sites of work and of production, as well as sites of middle- and upper-class consumption. Preservation of old industrial landscapes such as those in the Cuyahoga Valley National Recreation Area, which includes derelict steel mill structures, or similar parks in the Rühr Valley in Germany, demonstrate ways that preservation practice can honor working-class histories.

In these cases, the industrial structures no longer function. Equally interesting are cases where, in order for the landscape to be preserved in its most meaningful form, it must continue to be a site of production and work. The most obvious examples are heritage farms and forests that evolved through active human management, such as Areas of Outstanding Natural Beauty in England and Wales (Anderson 1990). In these, for both aesthetic and preservation purposes, the organizational goal is to maintain the landscape in its traditional functions and ecology, and that requires continued human intervention to keep up. A key challenge in these cases is that retaining the landscape requires retaining the cultural management practices of the past, or at least simulating their effects. In these cases, the intimate connection between human and landscape is the focus of preservation, more so than the structures themselves. This is the sort of preservation project that requires engagement with longstanding local communities because the practices that created the landscape need to be documented, continued, and taught to new generations in order for the essential qualities of it to continue (Hamin 2001).

3.2 Single History, Visible Narrative: But What Is Missing?

A simplified historic narrative by definition excludes other interpretations, particularly contested ones. Marginalized social and cultural groups, whose histories may be less uplifting, run a great risk of having their history be largely rendered into oblivion, intentionally or unintentionally, and disappearing from the urban landscape (Dubrow and Goodman 2003). Taking up the challenge of connecting the tangible and intangible values associated with places, Dubrow and Goodman argue that the answer to the fundamental question *Why preserve?*[5] lies in the curatorial promise of preservation to archive an otherwise lost historical consciousness. Lee (2003) traces the trajectory of cultural and ethnic diversity awareness in terms of its role in shaping the future of historic preservation and demonstrates how the expansion of cultural limits beyond the traditional mainstream has benefited the profession and the nation as a whole.[6] The importance of this inclusiveness is irrefutable—how can we understand Williamsburg, Virginia, without viewing the slave quarters there?[7] Understanding why certain groups are typically ignored or stand outside of the preservation agenda becomes one of the central tasks of a progressive historical preservation project.

Urban preservation in communist countries vividly illustrates the ideological conflicts of representing a particular version of history.[8] The rapid redevelopment of traditional urban neighborhoods in China, for instance, which results in the destruction of historic vernacular neighborhoods, is largely a result of the sheer concentration of power or absolute political will and a culture that celebrates progress (Li 2010). Support for local historic places conveniently slips outside the agenda, and the resulting built environment poorly represents any sense of the long histories of those places. Worse than the loss of the physical structures, the spirit of the place, or in Anthony Tung's words (2001, 414), the "city's capacity to tell its past" gets ruptured. Consequently, collective memories in those places are deliberately suppressed or ignored (Bodnar 1992). This intentional jettisoning of problematic pasts and preserving of sanctified ones is, of course, not limited to post-communist cultures, and instead forms some of core debate that surrounds preservation in emotionally charged locales.

3.3 Culture and Memory: Multiple Senses of Place

Despite an increasing awareness of the social, instead of purely physical, dimensions of preservation there still has been fairly limited scholarly attention what makes built environments contested, emotional, and political—that is, the role of collective memory and specific cultural protocols.

Collective memory, acting as the meeting ground between the past and the present, connects the physical world with a gamut of cultural, social, individual, and community values and offers insights into the retrospective version of the past through shared frames of understanding. By constructing and sustaining the essence of urban places, collective memory can help us make intellectual and personal connections with physical landscapes. Meanwhile, a sense of history embedded in collective memory locates us in time and space, "connecting our personal experiences and memories with those of a larger community, region, and nation," as Glassberg (2001, 7) explains powerfully in his *Sense of History*. He argues that a perspective on the past is at the core of who a community is and the places they care about (Glassberg 2001). Once the interplay of remembering and forgetting is translated into physical form, it makes a fixed and sometimes permanent imprint on the landscapes, which in turn shapes the public understanding of the past. This mutually evolving process can spark or inhibit collective imagination, and it can make a strong psychological statement about the past, present, and future. Given different interpretations of the same past, however, the process can be deeply fraught with politics and often involves emotional conflicts. This is why the meanings of a place evolve with constant negotiations of multiple stakeholders, so instead of sense of place, we deal with senses of place.

Memory shapes our perceptions of urban environments, and the environments help us to remember, and re-experience, our histories. "Memory locates us, as part of a family history, as part of a tribe or community, as a part of city-building and nation-making. Loss of memory is, basically, loss of identity" (Sandercock 2003, 402). Dolores Hayden (1995) argues that "place memory encapsulates the human ability to connect with both the built and natural environments that are entwined in the cultural landscape" (Hayden 1995, 46). Boyer also suggests, in *The City of Collective Memory,* that urban landscapes should actively represent collective memory to evoke "a better reading of the history written across the surface and hidden in forgotten subterrains of the city" (1995, 21). She quotes Halbwachs and Coser (1992, 137-38):

> Now space is a reality that endures, since our impressions rush by, one after another, and leave nothing behind in our mind, we can understand how we can recapture the past only by understanding how it is, in effect, preserved by our physical surroundings. It is to space—the space we occupy, traverse, have continual access to, or can at any time reconstruct in thought and imagination— that we must turn our attention. Our thoughts must focus on it if this or that category of remembrances is to reappear.

But the individual reflection from seeing or experiencing a building is a fairly weak form of remembering; a stronger, culturally lasting memory requires that we experience and share socially those memories evoked by the built environment. The city and its architecture provides a collective set of memory spots that enable people to create meaning to reproduce, recall, and retain their history through informal and collective actions. In this line of reasoning, buildings alone cannot preserve memory; the social practices behind it do.

It is to these practices that this chapter now turns, first exploring the more general connections between planning and current approaches to preservation and then turning to contemporary understandings of key characteristics of good preservation process (which, we will argue, is also good planning process).

4. Planning and Preservation

Planning for preservation connects the past, the present, and the future. Mandelbaum (2000) explains that the first cognitive act of planners is to impose order upon the future—that is, What do you want of it? But he also argues that historic reflection is good for planning as a profession (Mandelbaum 1985). History has an important function in forming a community identity, as well as broadening the horizon of self-defined groups. Becker's (1932) insight that history is myth making, an unconscious and necessary effort on the part of society to understand what it is doing in light of what it has done and what it hopes to do, bears particular relevance to preservation planning, given that planners as a group tend to be action driven and future oriented.

Abbot and Adler (1989) advocate using historical analysis as a planning tool, arguing that planners can benefit from *thinking historically* in very specific ways— without dwelling in the archives or even immersing themselves in the growing scholarly literature on planning history. Thinking like a historian can equip planners with a sense of time and proportion, or more accurately, a sense of the complexity of issues at hand.[9] This history need not be solely human history; understanding geologic history, for instance, helps to explain why development occurs where it does and where it can reasonably expand in the future.

Silver (1991) suggests that the urban American South affords an exemplary case of historic preservation's contributing to the broader processes of planning and revitalization. He notes that while preservationists in southern cities are often portrayed as "the backward-looking guardians of a vanishing culture" (69), their deep attachment to the contested and emotionally charged history evoked in their built environment supplied an important justification for city planning and contributed directly to the implementation of planning strategies. Private urban preservation organizations developed the techniques of neighborhood conservation that became the mainstay of publicly backed housing improvement programs in most cities, which according to Silver, provided a valuable counterpoint to the dominant clearance approach to city planning.

Recent economic changes have encouraged the integration of planning with preservation. Cities pursuing the "creative class" (Florida 2005) often try to capitalize on their own unique histories. Given these strong connections between economic development, local identity, and historic sense of place, community planning can begin, rather than end, with the identification of a place's unique character and strengths (Hester 1984; Hamin 2007). Thus, for reasons both theoretical and practical, historic preservation planning is becoming a closer ally to comprehensive and economic development planning.

4.1 Communicative Democracy

It is because of history's narrative quality and particularities, its emotional content and economic value, that preservation planning needs to rely on highly communicative processes. Done well, it allows for layered, multiple-voice outcomes, with many stories told rather than one "consensus" outcome. The process itself can be liberating; "a *politics* that values active individual engagement over group, ideology, and institution may be built by listening for and to the deepest needs that individuals present, in places that presently elude pundits and pollsters, as they use the past to sustain and change the course of their lives and the world" (Rosenzweig and Thelen 1998, 207).

Doing this, however, is difficult. In "Expanding the Language of Planning," Sandercock et al. (1999) explore how cultural differentiation and change continually reinvent the city as new immigrants, or those who begin to speak up for the first time, challenge existing narratives and normative categories. Confronting *otherness* and articulating the cultural values and social identities challenge planners working in culturally diverse communities, but those are also essential parts of their role as planners (Umemoto this volume; Thompson 2003). Specific cultural norms, values, and ways of knowing and interpreting form the basis of judgment and shape the quality of social interaction. So, when a planner enters a community, he or she enters an invisible cultural setting replete with temporal and spatial significance, culture, history, and memory.

A second significant challenge is to the culture of professionalism itself. Finding the "truth" in history accords well with the way we are trained as professionals—that is, to interpret, preserve, and plan as objectively as possible, weighing different facts and interests to develop a plan (Dalton 1986). It is deceptively easier to objectify and rationalize historic environments and employ a set of criteria for evaluation and inventory. Seeking an abstract authenticity dilutes our attention to the messy emotional, sensual, and protean nature of history, ignoring the role that power plays in selecting what to preserve or to demolish. And indeed, as noted above, many community members ask for the "truth" of history (or the plan), so that it takes a strong planner to admit that he or she does not know the truth, that it cannot be revealed, because in a contested situation only many truths exist.[10]

In popular history, as well as in some aspects of planning, these truths often emerge as stories. Sandercock (2003) argues that story has a special importance in planning that has neither been fully understood nor sufficiently valued. In order to imagine the space, life, and languages of the city, to make them legible, we translate them into narratives. The way we narrate the city becomes constitutive of urban reality, affecting the choices we make and the ways we then might act. She concludes that planning is performed through story in myriad ways—in process, as a catalyst for change, as a foundation, in policy, in pedagogy, and in explanation and critique, as well as justification of the status quo and as moral exemplar. Throgmorton (1996) contends that planning itself is an enacted and future-oriented narrative in which the participants are both characters and joint authors; preservation planning would appear to conform to his definition, but even more so as the narrative arc encompasses a longer time frame.

Local residents often bring forward their histories as stories, and these provide crucial insight into what a community needs to preserve, as well as the multiplicity of a site or neighborhood's possible meanings. At its best, this historical storytelling can help in forming *open moral communities* that allow multiple stories—diverse and often incommensurable narratives to emplot both the past and the future (Mandelbaum 2000). The power of emplotment is subtle, but real. An example is the reinterpretation of history and future undertaken by Deborah and Frank Popper (1987), in their work on the Great Plains where the story of the Buffalo Commons provides an entirely new vision of a restored, preserved, still working but very different region. The local resonance of their proposed narrative of the Buffalo Commons, according to them, is partly from the skill and good luck of finding a highly resonant metaphor with which residents can connect. If this were not appropriate to the residents' sense of history, it would not have that resonance in the first place (Popper and Popper 1999).

But once preservation touches sites of contest, planning processes need to be much more explicitly concerned with accommodating, allowing, and managing emotions. Forester (1999) is pioneering in demonstrating the emotional demands of planning in an ambiguous and politicized world, where emotional sensitivity can work as a source of knowledge and recognition, as well as a moral vision. Forester (1999) and Baum (1999) both pursue this line of thought in exploring how dialogue can be transformative learning. Forester explains that deliberative rituals, brainstorming sessions, or search conferences can be safe places for participants to explore new roles and identities along with new norms and agreements.

Individuals often behave *irrationally* when communicating emotional or contested issues, but they may communicate strategically, presenting issues that are more likely to win converts rather than the issues that lie at the center of their concerns (Hamin 2003). The powerful may have little interest in a real dialogue (Flyvbjerg 2002). Those who have experienced the pain and shame of historical difficulties or oppression may feel neither comfortable nor safe uttering their experience. In these processes we are likely to find, as Abram (2000) rightly argues, that the requirements that Innes (1995) sets for the consensus-building process— that is, the willingness of all parties to put aside power differentials, to be sincere, and to find solutions at the discussion table—are in practice not achievable, since they suggest that either the power relations are negligible or that the interests are superficial. In emotionally and historically fraught situations with diverse publics, moving beyond consensus building may well be necessary. A narrative approach to process management may help overcome these issues and achieve the goals of a culturally sensitive historical preservation that brings forward multiple stories and multiple histories, and that assures retention of multiple senses of place.

5. CONCLUSION

Edward Chappell (2007) suggests that preservationists should sharpen their focus on the use of vernacular architecture, generally defined as ordinary buildings and landscapes, for public history because vernacular structures often provide the most tangible evidence for how people lived in the past or live today. This renewed attention to the ordinary and the marginalized can bridge the gap between insiders and outsiders, accommodating the multiple interpretations of history.

A more diverse and inclusive interpretation of history brings a new awareness of what (and who) is invisible in the official representation (Barthel 1996; Page and Mason 2004). Interpreting and preserving the past often involves negotiations and renegotiations of meanings and values through signs, symbols, artifacts, landscapes, and narratives. In fact, sites of collective memory extend the temporal and spatial range of communication and are inevitably situational. "In effect the physical durability of landscapes permits it to carry meaning into the future so as to help sustain memory and cultural traditions" (Foote 2003, 33). The process also can be a personal and collective journey of historical inquiry, which assists us in asking more important or urgent questions about the assumed historic truths or the themed cultural landscapes of various scales. Landscape-scale vernacular architecture more easily accommodates these multiple stories than does a focus on individual sites of the rich and famous. Including these multiple stories requires a highly participatory public process that builds on local historical narratives.

We acknowledge, however, that such participatory processes can experience roadblocks in particular locales and cultures.[11] In some Asian communities, for example, protocols such as respect for and obedience to elders and community leaders present barriers to public participation. In such cases, emotional sensitivity based on understanding of the power structures and cultural norms within a particular community becomes critical. Even within the same general culture, the public arrives at the planning table with a variety of agenda, cultural values, and personal priorities, which are often different from what professionals bring. Therefore, the challenge here is twofold: first, how to communicate and balance the competing values through storytelling, and second, how to accomplish this in a culturally diverse setting.

In less-contested landscapes, preservation initiatives may be more open to participatory processes (Hamin, Geigis, and Silka 2007; Hester 1984). An example is the election process recommended by the Commonwealth of Massachusetts to prioritize local landscapes to preserve. Different groups of community residents undertake identification of locally meaningful landscapes, explore why these landscapes matter to them, and then design the practices that can maintain them. Another dedicated stakeholder group with representation from each of these groups resolves any conflicts and develops the final plan (Bischoff 2007). This sort of effort can make purists a bit queasy, however, as it can easily move toward packaging attractive, even imaginary, "heritages" for tourist consumption, as described earlier in this essay. A trained public historian can provide some checks and balances.

In more complex, contested situations, such as sites of trauma or great injustice, planners should move toward a format of storytelling and oral history. Providing small venues for storytelling may serve to highlight different histories and the connections to the built form that are most meaningful for different groups. Making space and time for stories in the public planning process can be a part of regular participation, but it needs a conscious effort on the part of the planners to overcome the tendency toward more traditional top-down approaches that may not reach the most marginalized groups.

Collecting oral histories of marginalized groups provides an academically tested means of engaging storytelling in the process, and this is particularly helpful to those unlikely to speak up in public meetings (Lynd 1993; Hayden 1995; Shopes 2002). Unlike official sources that typically present a single interpretation, the symbolic and intended meaning of oral history makes it accumulative through generations and open to multiple interpretations. This goal requires more time in the field for the planner or else managing volunteers to do the interviews. But giving residents a chance to tell their own stories at their own pace, and using their own structure, will provide a much richer interpretation of local history than is available through the brief and formally designed frame of an official public meeting.

J. B. Jackson's life-long passion for vernacular landscapes precisely illustrates how a landscape rich in collective memories and history brings personal connection with time and space (1984, 152):

> A landscape without visible signs of political history is a landscape without memory or forethought. We are inclined to think that the value of monuments is simply to remind us of origins. They are much more valuable reminders of long-range, collective purpose, of goals and objectives and principles. As such even the least sightly of monuments gives a landscape beauty and dignity and keeps the collective memory alive.

We began this chapter by arguing that preservation planning has moved in scale from individual site to neighborhood, farm, and workplace; it has broadened its concern from the elite to the vernacular, from architecture to landscape; it has become an avenue for economic development rather than its antithesis. But with all of this comes challenges, including the management, accommodation, and sensitive treatment of emotional histories. Historic preservation thus becomes, in some ways, one of the most complicated planning venues, because the value of preservation increases as a site elicits emotions, fragile histories, relationships among communities, people, and the land. The intention of contemporary historic preservation is both modest and grand: to preserve landscapes that are perhaps less aesthetic yet representative of various periods of urban development, that make an emotional connection with the lives of the community members that lived through their history, and who remember their history in that place. This includes an honest record of the social and environmental disparities among different groups, from the extraordinarily opulent to those of relatively meager means, including a community's difficult and troubling chapters. A culturally sensitive narrative approach (Li 2010) can help us reconnect these disparate points on the urban landscape, critically and reflectively.

ACKNOWLEDGMENTS

Our thanks go to Richard Taupier, David Glassberg, and Marla Miller for their valuable contributions to this chapter. Rachel Weber was extraordinarily helpful as an editor, and we thank her for that.

NOTES

1. In his comprehensive review essay, Joseph Heathcott (2006) listed important works that have contributed to preservation study, including Art Ziegler, *Historic Preservation in Inner City Areas* (1971); Deirdre Stanforth with photographs by

Louis Reens, *Restored America* (1975); Tony Wrenn and Elizabeth Malloy, *America's Forgotten Architecture* (1976); Nathan Weinberg, *Preservation in American Towns and Cities* (1979); Richard Reed, *Return to the City* (1979); and the influential *Readings in Historic Preservation*, edited by Norman Williams Jr., Edmund Kellogg, and Frank Gilbert (1983).

2. See *Penn Central Transportation Co. et al. v. New York City Co. et al.*, 438 US.104, 107–108 (1978).

3. See the National Women's History Museum's Web site for sources on Ann Pamela Cunningham, http//www.nwhm.org/education-resources/biography/biographies/ann-pamela-cunningham.

4. For an overview of preservation efforts in Charleston, see the National Park Service's Web site on Charleston at http//www.nps.gov/nr/travel/charleston/preservation.htm.

5. See Stipe (2003) for more on the question of why we should preserve at all.

6. Despite some counter-examples, such as the 1966 National Historic Preservation Act to include some ethnic minority interests in the massive urban renewal projects of the time, the emphasis remains on the visible elites in minority groups rather than the vernacular environment associated with the culturally and socially marginalized. In 1943, Congress added the George Washington Carver National Monument in Diamond, Missouri, to the National Park System. According to Lee (2003), this action may have been an acknowledgment of the sacrifices that African Americans were making to the war effort.

7. See the Web site for Colonial Williamsburg, http//www.history.org/Almanack/places/hb/hbslave.cfm.

8. Cities such as Beijing and Moscow are typical in this genre.

9. The sense of complexity that we may gain from studying history can perhaps better be utilized through scenario building than through attempts to produce quantified forecasts. History makes us aware of the interrelations of technical, economic, social, cultural, and political factors. Scenario building in one sense is history in reverse; focused on the future, it utilizes the same combination of disparate pieces of information within a broad context to create an understandable narrative of event (Abbott and Adler 1989).

10. There are, in addition, challenges that enter into all public communicative processes. Examples include questions such as, What should we do with stakeholders we disagree with or find reprehensible? How hard should we push regarding stories that victims do not necessarily want told? In the interest of space, we will not seek to answer these, and only suggest that they are appropriate parts of the dialogue in historic preservation planning.

11. Raymond Williams (1966) explored this pattern in the following aspects: the middle classes over less powerful groups; the male gender and heterosexuality as against women or sexual minorities; majority lifestyles over diverse, multicultural complexities; cities over the countryside, or overarching bioregional realities; the artifacts of high culture, including architecture, over history, archeology, and cultural landscapes; "settler" culture over indigenous cultures and values in postcolonial settings; in general, "dominant" culture over the claims of "residual" or "emergent" culture. Instead of a broad analysis of integrating culture into different social inquiries, we focus on history and its cultural implications in intangible aspects of urban places.

REFERENCES

Abbott, C., and S. Adler. 1989. "Historical Analysis as a Planning Tool." *Journal of the American Planning Association* 55(4): 467–73.

Abram, S. A. 2000. "Planning the Public; Some Comments on Empirical Problems for Planning Theory." *Journal of Planning Education and Research* 19(4): 351–57.

Anderson, Margaret A. 1990. "Areas of Outstanding Natural Beauty and the 1949 National Parks Act." *Town Planning Review* 61(3): 311–39.

Barthel, D. L. 1996. *Historic Preservation, Collective Memory and Historical Identity.* New Brunswick, NJ: Rutgers University Press.

Baum, H. S. 1999. "Forgetting to Plan." *Journal of Planning Education and Research* 19(1): 2–14.

Becker, C. 1932. "Everyman His Own Historian." *American Historical Review* 37(2): 221–36.

Bischoff, A. 2007. "Historic Landscape Preservation: Saving Community Character." In *Preserving and Enhancing Communities: A Guide for Citizens, Planners, and Policymakers,* edited by E. M. Hamin, P. Geigis, and L. Silka, 221–330. Amherst, MA: University of Massachusetts Press.

Bodnar, J. E. 1992. *Remaking America: Public Memory, Commemoration, and Patriotism in the Twentieth Century.* Princeton, NJ: Princeton University Press.

Bookspan, S. 2001. "Preservation, Memory, and Values." *Public Historian* 23(1): 5–8.

Boyer, M. C. 1994. *The City of Collective Memory, its Historical Imagery and Architectural Entertainments.* Cambridge, MA: MIT Press.

Casey, E. S. 1987. *Remembering: A Phenomenological Study.* Bloomington, IN: Indiana University Press.

Chappell, E. A. 2007. "Viewpoint, Vernacular Architecture and Public History." *Buildings & Landscapes, Journal of the Vernacular Architecture Forum* 1:1–12.

Dalton, L. 1986. "Why the Rational Paradigm Persists—The Resistance of Professional Education and Practice to Alternative Forms of Planning." *Journal of Planning Education and Research* 5(3): 147–53.

Dubrow, G. L., and J. B. Goodman. 2003. *Restoring Women's History through Historic Preservation.* Baltimore: Johns Hopkins University Press.

Fitch, J. M. 1982. *Historic Preservation, Curatorial Management of the Built World.* New York: McGraw-Hill.

Florida, R. 2005. *The Flight of the Creative Class: The New Global Competition for Talent.* New York: HarperCollins.

Flyvbjerg, B. 2002. "Bringing Power to Planning Research, One Researcher's Praxis Story." *Journal of Planning Education and Research* 21(4): 353–66.

Foote, K. E. 2003. *Shadowed Ground, America's Landscapes of Violence and Tragedy.* Austin: University of Texas Press.

Forester, J. 1999. *The Deliberative Practitioner: Encouraging Participatory Planning Processes.* Cambridge, MA: MIT Press.

Glassberg, D. 2001. *Sense of History, The Place of the Past in American Life.* Amherst, MA: University of Massachusetts Press.

Halbwachs, M., and L. A. Coser. 1992. *On Collective Memory, Heritage of Sociology.* Chicago: University of Chicago Press.

Hamin, E. M. 2001. "Western European Approaches to Landscape Protection." *Journal of Planning Literature* 16(3): 339–58.

Hamin, E. M. 2003. *Mojave Lands: Interpretive Planning and the National Preserve.* Baltimore: Johns Hopkins University Press.

Hamin, E. M., P. Geigis, and L. Silka. 2007. *Preserving and Enhancing Communities: A Guide for Citizens, Planners, and Policymakers.* Amherst, MA: University of Massachusetts Press.

Hayden, D. 1995. *The Power of Place: Urban Landscapes as Public History.* Cambridge, MA: MIT Press.

Heathcott, J. 2006. "Curating the City, Challenges for Historic Preservation in the Twenty-First Century." *Journal of Planning History* 5(1): 75–83.

Hester, R. T. 1984. *Planning Neighborhood Space with People,* 2nd ed. New York: Van Nostrand Reinhold.

Hosmer, C. B. 1965. *Presence of the Past: A History of the Preservation Movement in the United States before Williamsburg.* New York: Putnam.

Innes, J. E. 1995. "Planning Theory's Emerging Paradigm: Communicative Action and Interactive Practice." *Journal of Planning Education and Research* 14(3): 183–89.

Jackson, J. B. 1984. *Discovering the Vernacular Landscape.* New Haven, CT: Yale University Press.

Lee, Antoinette J. 2003. "The Social and Ethnic Dimensions of Historic Preservation." In *A Richer Heritage: Historic Preservation in the Twenty-First Century,* edited by R. E. Stipe, 385–403. Chapel Hill, NC: University of North Carolina Press.

Li, N. 2010. "Preserving Urban Landscapes as Public History: The Chinese Context." *The Public Historian* 32(4): 51–61.

Lowenthal, D. 1996. *Possessed by the Past: The Heritage Crusade and the Spoils of History.* New York: Free Press.

Lowenthal, D. 1998. "Fabricating Heritage." *History & Memory* 10(1): 5.

Lowenthal, D. 2008. "Authenticities Past and Present." *CRM: The Journal of Heritage Stewardship* 5(1): 6–17.

Lynch, K. 1972. *What Time Is this Place?* Cambridge, MA: MIT Press.

Lynd, S. 1993. "Oral History from Below." *Oral History Review* 21(1): 1–8.

Mandelbaum, S. J. 1985. "Historians and Planners, The Construction of Pasts and Futures." *Journal of the American Planning Association* 51(2): 185–88.

Mandelbaum, S. J. 2000. *Open Moral Communities.* Cambridge, MA: MIT Press.

Murtagh, W. J. 1988. *Keeping Time: The History and Theory of Preservation in America.* Pittstown, NJ: Main Street Press.

Page, M., and R. Mason. 2004. *Giving Preservation a History: Histories of Historic Preservation in the United States.* New York: Routledge.

Popper, D. E., and F. J. Popper. 1987. "The Great Plains, From Dust to Dust." *Planning* 53(12): 12–18.

Popper, D. E., and F. J. Popper. 1999. "The Buffalo Commons: Metaphor as Method." *Geographical Review* 89(4): 491–510.

Rosenzweig, R., and D. P. Thelen. 1998. *The Presence of the Past: Popular Uses of History in American Life.* New York: Columbia University Press.

Sandercock, L. 2003. "Out of the Closet: The Importance of Stories and Storytelling in Planning Practice." *Planning Theory & Practice* 4(1): 11–28.

Sandercock, L., P. Healey, K. R. Kunzmann, and L. Mazza. 1999. "Expanding the 'Language' of Planning: A Meditation on Planning Education for the Twenty-first Century/Comments." *European Planning Studies* 7(5): 533–61.

Shopes, L. 2002. "Oral History and the Study of Communities, Problems, Paradoxes, and Possibilities." *Journal of American History* 89(2): 588–98.

Silver, C. 1991. "Revitalizing the Urban South: Neighborhood Preservation and??" *Journal of the American Planning Association* 57(1): 69–84

Stipe, R. E. 2003. *A Richer Heritage: Historic Preservation in the Twenty-first Century.* Chapel Hill, NC: University of North Carolina Press.

Thomas, R. G. 2004. "Taking Steps Toward a New Dialogue: An Argument for an Enhanced Critical Discourse in Historic Preservation." *Future Anterior* 1(1): 11–15.

Thompson, S. 2003. "Planning and Multiculturalism: A Reflection on Australian Local Practice." *Planning Theory & Practice* 4(3): 275–93.

Throgmorton, J. A. 1996. *Planning as Persuasive Storytelling: The Rhetorical Construction of Chicago's Electric Future.* Chicago: University of Chicago Press.

Tung, A M. 2001. *Preserving the World's Great Cities: The Destruction and Renewal of the Historic Metropolis.* New York: Clarkson Potter.

Umemoto, K. 2001. "Walking in Another's Shoes: Epistemological Challenges in Participatory Planning." *Journal of Planning Education and Research* 21(1): 17–31.

Williams, R. 1966. *Culture and Society, 1780–1950.* Harmondsworth, UK: Penguin Books.

CHAPTER 11

CULTURAL DIVERSITY

KAREN UMEMOTO AND VERA ZAMBONELLI

THERE is a paradox in the world today in regard to the diversity of languages, cultures, and ways of life that exist on this planet. Cities and regions around the globe have become more diverse, experiencing the cumulative effects of global migration. People gather from different regions of the world to live within the same locale under a shared system of governance. Cultural diversity is seen in cities and rural towns, large and small, particularly across industrialized and industrializing countries. Yet, on the global scale, the world is losing cultural diversity, with the disappearance of entire knowledge systems and ancient traditions. Traditional customs and place-specific ways of living are decreasing in variation. This is seen most clearly in what has been termed "language death," which refers to the extinction of many languages and dialects.[1]

Planners find themselves at the intersection of this paradox. On the local and regional level, planners and policymakers confront the challenges that increasing cultural diversity brings. Differences abound in language, communication styles, social protocols and familial traditions, normative values, and overall epistemic lenses. These variations are oftentimes overlaid by stark inequities in the quality of life. How can we, as Iris Marion Young (1995) asked, take advantage of cultural difference as a resource rather than a liability to enrich civic life for a more equitable and just future? Concurrently, the diminishing range of cultural diversity across the planet poses a distinct challenge. The loss of cultural knowledge systems and traditions themselves can be understood as an issue of equity and social justice. Hence, the challenge of diverse groups living together within a shared geography and system of governance coexists with the issues of cultural preservation and the right to autonomous development, particularly for indigenous peoples whose traditions and knowledge systems are most seriously threatened.

Both are vital issues and pose important challenges to planners and policymakers, as well as to us all.

It is critical for planners to understand the nature and dynamics of cultural diversity, which signifies different ways that people see, experience, and act upon their surroundings, and how such diversification challenges existing planning systems. As Sandercock (2003) writes, while planning systems have historically expressed the norms of the culturally dominant group, expecting ethnic or racial minorities to assimilate, new models and social movements have pressed for change. Planners and planning systems are often called upon to respond to planning controversies involving ethnically or racially charged divisions. Some involve public expressions of prejudice and xenophobia, and some may include proposals based on cultural practices that may even be incompatible with planners' own beliefs and values. Hence, as Sandercock advocates, there is a need for an epistemology of multiplicity, which entails not only different ways of knowing,[2] but also a norm of openness and self-reflection. She argues for ways of bridging understanding, building relationships across cultural divides, and mediating epistemically embedded conflicts to overcome historic prejudices while appreciating the uniqueness of groups and individuals. This is crucial because planning is concerned with forging a collective future. Planners who understand how differences manifest themselves, and how different standpoints have evolved in relation to one another, can better facilitate the dialogue necessary to devise plans that people can agree are just or reasonable (Umemoto 2001).

This chapter is intended to orient practitioners and scholars to issues and concepts pertinent to planning in a culturally diverse society. We focus primarily on ethnic and racial diversity for the purposes of this chapter, acknowledging that there are related dimensions of diversity such as gender, class, age, religion, sexual orientation, physical ability, and others that are equally important and closely intertwined. We begin with an overview of schools of thought that inform planning approaches within multicultural settings. We then explore some of the major issues and challenges that cultural diversity brings for planners and the planning profession within the context of democratic governance. Here, we draw somewhat more heavily from U.S. cases, as that is the country context we are most familiar with and comfortable writing about, with adequate confidence in our experiential and secondary knowledge. We close by sharing what we believe are pertinent questions for future research.

1. Cosmopolitanism, Multiculturalism, and Self-determination

There are several normative models of governance that have been suggested for culturally diverse cities and societies within a multicultural milieu. For heuristic purposes, we provide a brief overview of three major strands of discourse that place the nature and importance of culture[3] at their center: cosmopolitanism, multiculturalism, and self-determination.

The idea of *cosmopolitanism* has regained currency as those such as Kwame Anthony Appiah (2006, xiii) pose the challenge: "to take minds and hearts formed over the long millennia of living in local troops and equip them with ideas and institutions that will allow us to live together as the global tribe we have become." Cosmopolitanism has been used in many ways—to describe a sociocultural condition, a philosophical worldview, a political project toward building transnational institutions, a political project for recognizing multiple identities, an attitudinal or dispositional orientation, and a mode of practice and competence (Vertovec and Cohen 2002).[4] As a social descriptor, cosmopolitanism refers to a socio-cultural condition emerging from globalization that is "celebrated for its vibrant cultural creativity as well as its political challenges to various ethnocentric, racialized, gendered and national narratives" (Vertovec and Cohen 2002, 9). As a philosophy or worldview, largely following Kant, cosmopolitanism is projected to inspire us all to be "citizens of the world, creating a worldwide community of humanity committed to common values" (Vertovec and Cohen 2002, 10). Cosmopolitan values of egalitarianism and equitable distribution of resources are seen to garner a general practice of fairness and generosity (Appiah 2006; Binnie et al. 2006; Entrikin 1999). In the field of planning, Sandercock (1998b, 2003) posed the notion of "cosmopolis" as "a construction site of the mind, a city/region in which there is genuine connection with, and respect and space for, the cultural Other, and the possibility of working together on matters of common destiny, the possibility of a 'togetherness in difference'" within a multicultural milieu (Sandercock 1998b, 7).

Cosmopolitan thinking points to the pursuit of a more equitable global order with new institutions of global governance, a global civil society, and transnational political movements for justice that transcend national residency. Yet, cosmopolitanism's view of one's relation to the nation-state varies widely. Some suggest a political project featuring the notion of the "cosmopolitan patriot"—those who may set roots in different places, even different nations, among different peoples at various times, while retaining loyalty to a single nation-state (Appiah 1998). Others project a political subject who seeks to transcend the national scale altogether by putting globality at the heart of political imagination, action, and organization (Beck 1998; Vertovec and Cohen 2002). In the latter, cosmopolitanism subsumes concerns over nationality, race, or ethnicity within the notion of global citizenship, in all its diversity. Proponents describe its orientation as "universality plus difference," seeking a balance between the universal and particularistic through exchange and dialogue (Appiah 2006). From this perspective, some see the weakening of loyalties to a single nation-state and the contingencies of identities in the age of globalization as a virtue in a postmodern society. Here, human rights and the notion of cosmopolitan justice cross national boundaries and inhabitants negotiate difference as an everyday practice of urban life (Turner 2000).

When understood as an attitude or disposition, cosmopolitanism means having an open mind toward the other, a "desire for, an appreciation of, cultural diversity and the ability to move comfortably and being at ease everywhere" (Vertovec and Cohen 2002, 13). As a mode of practice and competence, it involves the individual ability to navigate different cultures and their respective systems of meanings, which may also result from a more consumer-oriented notion of exchange. In fact, through the massive transfer of cultural commodities from food and fashion to music and artwork, people are exposed to other cultural customs, habits, and lifestyles. To what extent this exposure and modes of consumption lead to a fundamental change in attitude toward the cultural other is hard to determine (Vertovec and Cohen 2002). This particular consumption-oriented representation of cosmopolitanism has been criticized for its slant toward the glamorous life of world travelers and global elites, to the extent that it overlooks its vernacular expressions in the everyday life of ordinary people (Werbner 1999).

The term *multiculturalism* became more prominent in planning and policy discourse in the 1960s and 1970s, as new social movements began mobilizing for justice around issues of ethnicity, race, gender, sexuality, and nationality in Western industrialized nations. These movements challenged the primacy of class to focus on the processes of racial formation and alternative policies and institutions that would expand equality and democracy for historically marginalized communities of color (Callard 2004; Omi and Winant 1986). Like cosmopolitanism, multiculturalism as a term has been used in several ways: as a demographic descriptor, a programmatic or political model, an ideological viewpoint, and a set of social practices (Inglis 1996; Martinello 1998; Wieviorka 1998). Empirically, it referred to the emerging social condition of ethnic and racial diversification of many cities and regions as global migration changed demographic patterns. But more important, it upheld cultural pluralism or the equal flourishing of various cultures as a societal value, seeking to protect the unique and evolving characteristics of the range of cultural groups within and across societies.

This was a departure from the idea of the monocultural nation-state in which minority groups were expected to assimilate to the norms, belief systems, language, and identity of the "national" (usually majority) group, often through various nation-building policies (Tiryakian 2003; Kymlicka 2003). Multiculturalism, in principle, upholds the right of individuals and groups to maintain their cultural identity and heritage beyond their national identity. Politically, this means supporting social policies such as language rights and cultural and historic preservation. Multiculturalists also acknowledge past injustices with allowance for their remediation. Others go further to postulate a society where respective cultures are not only maintained but also are freely shared and adopted by others, including the host or dominant cultural group. Taylor's (1994) view of deep diversity maintains that citizens are different in different ways and may embrace various forms of multicultural membership in the larger state.

Proponents of multiculturalism differ in regard to the application of policy principles of universalism versus particularism, often steeped in ideological positions. Those who subscribe to "liberal multiculturalism" seek to integrate the different groups into the mainstream by universally granting individual citizenship while tolerating, in the private realm, certain particularistic cultural practices. In contrast, "pluralist multiculturalism" allows for the formal enfranchisement of different groups along cultural lines within a communitarian political order (Hall 2000, 210).[5] One of the main critiques of multiculturalism as a political and policy framework is its risk of "essentializing" culture and identities and "freezing" them in a particular moment in time within institutional codes. Ethnic minority communities are not integrated collective social actors with clear-cut boundaries (Hall 2000) and a policy emphasis on ethnic boundaries may negate the "recognition of the many other sources of identity formation based on experiences of gender, age, education, class, and consumption, which are shared with other groups and which cut across ethnic lines" (Amin 2002, 977). Proponents of culturally specific policies, however, maintain that many historical inequities, as well as unique attributes specific to groups based ethnic and racial distinctions, remain relevant for consideration in planning and policy in order to ensure effectiveness, equality, and social justice.

Like most models, both meet up with political realities that complicate their application to real-life settings. Kymlicka (2003, 157) stressed the importance of the fit between a particular model of the multicultural state and the characteristics of the intercultural citizen—that is, "someone who is curious rather than fearful about other peoples and cultures; someone who is open to learning about other ways of life, and willing to consider how issues look from other people's point of view, rather than assuming that their inherited way of life or perspective is superior; someone who feels comfortable interacting with people from other backgrounds, and so on." Martiniello (1998, 915) emphasizes the social practice of multiculturalism, examining how individuals and groups, "confronted with cultural and identity diversity in their daily life, manage or not the social interaction with the other." Neither model would work smoothly without broad consensus as to their appropriateness. At the same time, it can be argued that policies may be necessary to nurture such social attitudes in the first place for either model to be realized.

Some scholars and social justice advocates transcending the academic discourses of cosmopolitanism and multiculturalism have gathered under the slogan of the "right to the city" (Dikec 2002; Isin 2000; Lefebvre 1996; McCann 2002; Mitchell 2003; Purcell 2002). This includes the right to claim presence in the city, democratizing its spaces and engaging residents fully in civic life as subjects rather than objects. Harvey (2008, 23) insists the "freedom to make and remake our cities and ourselves" as a human right must entail the democratic management over urban development. An undergirding principle is the idea that every individual who contributes to urban life should have a say in its operations and planning for the future. The notion privileges lived engagement in a given place over formal status, cultural identity, or group association. For example, it is less important that one is a legal citizen of the nation and more important that one is engaged in the life of a designated locale as the basis for the right to shape its spaces and participate in its governance. This echoes longstanding calls among communities of color and low-income communities for new forms of urban decision making and the inclusion of a diverse range of stakeholders in the process. The geographic unit of "the city" is the primary boundary of identification and allocation of rights and resources. It also outlines the boundaries of obligation to engage with others in civic affairs.

While the above conceptual approaches address the coexistence of diverse groups in a shared space, indigenous peoples have long voiced their calls for *self-determination* as distinct peoples. Since the time of colonization or conquest, indigenous peoples around the world have resisted domination in both overt and covert forms. During the latter part of the twentieth century, many indigenous groups and tribal nations began to either regain their independence or more forcefully assert their desires for sovereignty within their postcolonial settler states. Decolonizing efforts include political recognition as distinct peoples with rights to nationhood, the promotion of different political models of self-determination, the revival and promotion of traditional and contemporary cultural beliefs and practices, and the acquisition of conquered lands for cultural use despite the absence of sovereign rule. During the 1980s and 1990s, indigenous movements gained greater international momentum, with the establishment of the UN Voluntary Fund for Indigenous Populations (1985), the adoption of International Labor Organization (ILO) Convention No. 169 on Indigenous and Tribal Peoples in Independent Countries (1989), the establishment of the Permanent Forum on Indigenous Issues (2000), the proclamation of the International Year of the World's Indigenous People (1993), the Proclamation of the International Decades of the World's Indigenous People (1995 and 2005), and passage of the Declaration on the Rights of Indigenous Peoples (2007).

According to the United Nations' State of the World's Indigenous Peoples report (2009), there are more than 370 million indigenous peoples in some ninety countries worldwide. Among the most pressing issues surveyed is the high level of impoverishment and ongoing land dispossession, particularly in developing regions. Language loss and the related loss of cultural wisdom and identity related to the impact of globalization, as well as the commodification of indigenous cultures, is leading to the extinction of whole cultural systems. Land dispossession and environmental degradation have eroded subsistence practices, adding to poverty, preventable diseases, and malnourishment. Other health and educational disparities have also been part of the widening divide in well-being in many societies, with indigenous populations suffering from among the worst health and educational indicators, even in industrialized countries.

From a global perspective, we are confronted with the question of what role governments and public agencies have in respecting or supporting efforts to preserve and protect the diverse range of world cultures through planning and policy. For indigenous groups within settler states such as the United States, Australia, New Zealand, and Canada, there are ongoing dialogues to define and realize self-determination while many continue pressing governments to fulfill their obligations on broken treaties. Models of self-determination range from land succession and independent rule to nation-within-a-nation arrangements or granting of rights that afford a degree of political self-determination, such as in the case of Greenlandic Home Rule, the Sami Parliament, or Nisga'a Self-Government. Many indigenous groups continue their work to define and strengthen internal governance structures and protocols. Deep differences in worldviews remain between industrialized modern states and land-based indigenous peoples, many of whom retain subsistence practices. Planning with indigenous communities and tribal nations represents an opportunity to address historic and contemporary claims, bridge enduring chasms, and build greater understanding of traditional wisdom and practices that can inform the future.

2. Dilemmas of Diversity in Planning

Planning confronts a multitude of philosophical questions concerning the roles of the state and civil society organizations in a culturally diverse society. One question is the role of planning in acknowledging the depth and range of difference that the condition of cultural diversity has brought while providing means for intercultural civic engagement. Wieviorka (1998, 1) put it this succinctly in this way: "Cultural differences are not only reproduced, they are in the constant process of being produced which means that fragmentation and recomposition are a permanent probability. In such a situation, the problem is how to broaden democracy in order to avoid at one and the same time the tyranny of the majority and the tyranny of the minorities." For planners, the specific challenge is to facilitate ways that people living and working in the same geographic space can chart a future that respects cultural difference while finding shared meaning, values, and principles. The meanings of equality, social justice, reciprocity, freedom, and liberty vary across publics yet are also socially constructed through changing experiences and dialogue. Transformative planning approaches aim to facilitate the co-creation of a shared future through nurturing mutual respect and an understanding of deep differences, as well as a shared humanity.

Planning regarding the coexistence of different ethnic, racial, and other forms of cultural community within the same political space encompasses the interrelated issues of process, structure, and substance. *Process* refers to the ways by which planning and policy decisions are deliberated among multiple and often conflicting publics. Deliberation takes places within a larger political economic *structure* that, in part, mediates the ways in which various publics can exert their influence with and over others. Philosophical debates surround the *substance* of policies and rules, particularly as issues concerning racial and ethnic groups have been historically (and problematically) dichotomized within the frame of "universalism" versus "particularism." These are described in fuller detail below.

2.1 The Planning Process in a Multicultural Milieu

Planners play a critical role in the democratic process by facilitating the establishment of policies, administrative rules, and procedures by which individuals,
organizations, and firms co-exist and interrelate. Planners confront fragmented
publics who come to differ on issues ranging from land use and infrastructure
to redevelopment and social policy. Responsibilities often fall on planners to help
differing parties understand the source and nature of their disagreements and,
ideally speaking, raise the substance of deliberation to the level of principles and
values such that parties at odds have a better chance of finding common ground.
One of the greatest challenges is to facilitate deliberation among people who share
different "ways of knowing." The concern here is how to acknowledge different
epistemic lenses without falling into the "relativist trap" where all points of view
are equally legitimate within their own paradigmatic universe, making it nearly
impossible to find shared judgment as to what is right or wrong, good or bad,
better or worse.

Planning theorists have drawn upon communicative action theory to argue
that, while there may be different knowledge and value systems at work, satisfactory agreement may be found through deliberative planning. In practical form,
deliberative planning is presented as a method of civic engagement in decision
making based on reasoned discourse where the conditions of interaction—mutually respectful, inclusive, transparent, honest, impartial—lead to empathy, social
learning, and mutual transformation toward collaborative solutions to defined
problems (Sager 1994; Forester 1989; Hajer and Wagenaar 2003; Throgmorton 1996;
Innes 1995; Verma and Shin 2004; Healey 1993, 1997, 1999). Theorists believe that
the exchange of ideas can allow participants to transcend the relativism of their
different perspectives (Healey 1999) and increase the likelihood that they can settle
on solutions they feel are just and desirable (Saarikoski 2002).[6] They argue that
deliberative planning practice could lead to emancipatory knowledge, illuminating the many sides of reality and uncovering the workings that reinforce existing
power relations. This would make way for more just decision making that would
satisfy a broader constituency.

Proponents and critics note the potential shortcomings and pitfalls of deliberative planning theory and practice that have particular relevance to ethnic, racial,
and other groups that have been historically oppressed or disadvantaged.[7] Some
critics have excavated the complex realities of power politics that stand in the way
of deliberative practice (Allmendinger and Tewdwr-Jones 2002; Fischler 2000;
Flyvbjerg 1998; Forester 1989, 1999; Huxley 2000; Lauria and Soll 1996; McGuirk
2001). They point out that deliberative planning theory assumes that all stakeholders value political decisions made according to the exchange of informed and
reasoned arguments. In reality, however, not all entities give equal consideration
to different interests and perspectives. And even if public conversations appear
to conform to ideal conditions for deliberative planning, it is difficult to monitor
the transparency of planning processes, given the behind-the-scenes deal making

that often occurs. Furthermore, individuals are associated with social, political, economic, and cultural groups, hence making it difficult to extricate themselves from the networks and power grids to which they have attachments (Hillier 1998; Sager 2006). This is especially so where the reach of competitive networks of global capital overshadows the less powerful within local, collaborative decision-making processes (Brand and Gaffikin 2007).

Thus, the challenge remains as to how deliberative planning processes can be structured and facilitated to level the playing field to the extent possible to hear all voices with equal respect to each. Leonie Sandercock, John Forester, and others have argued for planners to facilitate the types of dialogue through which people can tell their stories in ways that lead to deeper understanding and appreciation of the unique histories and sensibilities that diversity brings. They have described occasions when well-structured and well-facilitated dialogue, mediation, and engagement in collaborative work allowed individuals to transcend cultural boundaries and create deep understanding and agreement (Forester 2009; Sandercock 2003). There are, of course, many obstacles to overcome, even if conditions are close to ideal. These include overcoming racial, class, gender, and other forms of prejudice and discriminatory attitudes, as well as facilitating an equal hearing among those with different native languages and communication styles, educational backgrounds, levels of privilege, perceived status, and norms of public discourse (Umemoto and Igarashi 2009).

2.2 Structures of Planning and Issues of Citizenship

Aside from facilitated processes, there are institutional and structural constraints that affect the ability of groups to participate democratically in plan making. Popular debates rage over who has a right to participate, what is required to have influence, and for whom the planning should be done. From the launching of the modern system of nation-states as major actors in global relations, national citizenship and nationalism became the dominant organizing form and ideology of societies. At the nation-state level, citizenship as a set of rights and obligations structured the allocation of resources and ability to participate in governing functions, such as voting in elections, holding public office, and serving on official bodies such as juries or planning commissions. In some nations, such as Japan, foreigners, with the exception of a few groups, are prohibited from acquiring Japanese citizenship and have little or no means to participate in planning and governance. Other countries, like Canada, have more liberal naturalization laws where, over time, one can gain citizenship rights. These legal structures that formed through political struggle unique to each nation-state continue to include and exclude different groups in planning. For residents who are not yet naturalized or who are undocumented, there is fear of legal prosecution if participation in civic affairs puts them in an official spotlight. Legal status also affects whether others perceive them as having a legitimate right to have their claims heard.

We can see how different nations have addressed citizenship rights and protections for culturally distinct groups differently. Canada, Australia, and Sweden are among Western democratic systems that have national policies that, to varying degrees, support the evolution of unique characteristics of cultural groups. For example, a Charter for Rights and Liberties was incorporated into the Canadian Constitution in 1982. This development can be traced back to the social movements among Francophones in Quebec, who strove, among other efforts, to preserve French in addition to English as an official language of the state. This led to legislation on language, culture, and education, as well as protections against discrimination and for equality of opportunity in the labor market. In Australia, there was no national charter, but instead a range of policies and agencies devoted to redress the social and educational disadvantage of the indigenous Aboriginal and immigrant populations. Sweden adopted a multiculturalism policy in 1975 based on three principles of equality—in the quality of life for minority groups relative to the general population, the freedom of choice in ethnic identity and specifically Swedish identity, and assurances that everyone benefits in the labor market from working together (Ålund and Schierup 1991). Switzerland and Belgium are multicultural states with more than one official language, with regional bodies that manage civic affairs in those respective languages. Other countries, such as the United States, Aotearoa (New Zealand), and Mexico have instituted official recognition of some indigenous populations and have shifted away from "acculturation and assimilation" programs and toward recognizing some of their demands for group rights and privileges. And various nations have anti-discriminatory laws to protect minorities, women, persons with disabilities, gays, lesbians, and bisexual and transgendered persons in the areas of housing, employment, and service provision. This is not a critique of different systems. Rather, it is to highlight several contrasting governance models that shape the structure of planning participation and power among the ethnic and racial groupings within them.

Beyond legal citizenship rights, a major issue affecting the hearing of diverse voices in planning processes is the concentration of power in urban and regional politics. As economic globalization gave rise to an international elite, often with little personal connection or loyalty to the places in which they exert influence, the poor (disproportionately comprised of ethnic and racial minorities), undocumented residents, and those indigenous to those places have had a diminishing say in public affairs (Bauman 2000). There is a difference between formal citizenship and substantive citizenship, the latter referring to the ways that resource allocation is discursively woven into negotiations of national belonging (K. Anderson 2000). Even among citizens, not all are treated equally. Countless stories of social injustice and disenfranchisement continue to be told, such as in cases of forced displacement of ethnic communities through urban renewal and gentrification (LeGates and Hartman 1982; Thomas 1997; Wilson 1966); the neglect of inner city neighborhoods, including their crumbling physical and social infrastructure; the siting of public nuisances such as landfills in communities of color (Bullard 1990; Bullard et al. 2008); or redlining by financial institutions to discourage reinvestment in low-income and minority communities (Squires 1997). A rise in influence of financially elite sectors, combined with the devaluation of vulnerable groups within broader discourses of citizenship, has hastened the erosion of democratic, participatory planning among the most vulnerable populations across the globe (Munck 2002).

2.3 Substance of Planning and Issues of Justice

Related to the role of the state is the issue of justice and the processes through which justice is defined and achieved. How should planning address disagreements that arise within democracies when there may be conflicting views of justice among groups that may be rooted in different cultural belief systems, values, or preferences? How should planning address historic inequities and transgressions? And should planning consider ways to redress them toward reaching a more equitable society? While the aforementioned schools of thought and assertions of the "right to the city" treat as a given the general view that planning should accommodate cultural diversity, there are unresolved questions as to how this can or should be achieved. Several policy debates shape the way the field of planning approaches these questions.

One debate in social policy has been posed along the political principles of universalism versus particularism. In the United States, for example, there were policies that targeted certain groups as being eligible for certain protections or services, such as the elderly or war veterans. The civil rights movement of the 1960s advanced equal rights for racial groups that were historically disadvantaged owing to the legacy of colonization, slavery, and exploitative treatment. Born were affirmative action and other programs that provided assistance and support for African Americans, Latinos, Native Americans, Native Alaskans, Native Hawaiians, and, in some cases, Asian Americans, in areas from housing to employment and education. The justification for such targeted programs was an acknowledgment that the free-market system left to its own devices would not correct historic inequities; state intervention was necessary to level the playing field upon which individuals could compete. From the 1970s, however, these policies were slowly reversed under the cry of "reverse discrimination" and calls for "universalism" (Gamson and Modigliani 1994). Some, meanwhile, argued against a polarization of the two concepts and proposed the idea of "targeting within universalism" in order to enhance the stability and success of important universal programs, yet address particular social needs among selected groups such as those historically marginalized (Skocpol and Fiorina 1999).

The polarization of the debate between universalism and particularism in ideological terms spurred a belief among some segments of society that designing policies and plans tailored to the needs or preferences of specific ethnic, racial, and other groups was antithetical to the principles of liberal democracy, including individual equality, liberty, and freedom. Conservatives appropriated the banner of universalism in a discursive strategy to reassert assimilationist views and to oppose place-making activities among nonwhite ethnic and racial groups. "English only," anti-immigration, and anti-affirmative action campaigns intensified throughout the 1980s and 1990s. Fear of cultural diversity manifested itself in physical planning controversies, with opposition to non-English-language signage, permitting of certain ethnic architecture, and official designations of ethnic "towns" as such.[8] Within this context, many communities of color continued to undertake initiatives to create places that asserted their self-defined cultural identities and to maintain programs that addressed their unique group needs (Boyd 2008; Schneekloth and Shibley 1995; Toji and Umemoto 2003).

A second and related debate in planning was framed around the idea of equality of *process* juxtaposed with the idea of equality of *outcomes*. Some have argued that planning should primarily ensure equality in the planning process so that all groups have a voice in shaping plans, as reflected in the literature on deliberative and communicative planning theory. Others have argued that this is not enough; planners and policymakers should do more to ensure that plans contain mechanisms to correct inequities, regardless of what input comes through the planning process. Fainstein (2005, 2006, 2010b) argues that planning should lead to outcomes that are just; it is not enough to focus solely on process, given inherent structural and institutional biases and inequities. While the debate has often counterposed process and outcomes, the two are not in contradiction (the creation of truly inclusive and deliberative processes should ideally lead to a greater degree of just outcomes) and just outcomes are difficult to achieve without inclusive processes (who is to define justice among multiple publics if not with the representation of people themselves?).

3. CONTEMPORARY PLANNING CONTROVERSIES

Issues of process, structure, and substance can be seen in contemporary planning controversies. We can understand planning controversies concerning communities of difference to be of at least three main types: (a) pursuit of equality and human rights, (b) tolerance for difference, and (c) the right of groups to perpetuate and evolve unique cultural traditions and ways of life.

The protection of equal and human rights includes protection against discrimination based on cultural or other difference. For some, this includes dealing with the legacies of past injustices. Many acknowledge that planning has often contributed to the exacerbation of inequality by either design or neglect. One of the most serious instances in the industrialized cities has been the forced relocation and removal of ethnic enclave communities under the campaign labels of "urban renewal" and "redevelopment" (Carmon 1999; Fainstein 2010a; Marris 1962; Nickel

1995; Weiss 1980). Starting in earnest in the 1960s, many ethnic enclaves, especially those located near growing financial centers, were razed and replaced by high-rise hotels and corporate offices. Others were displaced for the construction of monuments, stadiums, highways, and international showcases, such as with the building of Olympic facilities in Australia (Andersen 1999). Communities that once consisted of vital social networks of support and integration were destroyed. Some neighborhoods successfully resisted displacement, standing their ground and charting their own course for development (Heskin 1991; Medoff and Sklar 1994). Related to this is the longstanding issue of racial residential segregation, a pattern that continues despite the elimination of racial covenants owing to the persistence of illegal discriminatory practices in the housing market among landlords, lenders, and sellers (Brimicombe 2007; Cristaldi 2002; Ellis, Wright and Parks 2004; Massey and Denton 1993; Smets and Uyl 2008).

Other planning arenas that involve the pursuit of equity and social justice include environmental justice movements opposing facilities seen as hazardous or undesirable. Waste landfills, refineries, and prisons, for example, are often placed in or near predominantly low-income, minority neighborhoods (Bullard 1990; Bullard et al. 2008). Calls for equity also surround government responses to natural disasters, such as in the case of Hurricane Katrina in Louisiana, in which predominantly low-income and African-American victims faced disparities in impacts along with obstacles to accessing emergency and rebuilding assistance (Hartman and Squires 2006; Pastor et al. 2006). Within the planning profession itself, calls for equality have included the training and hiring of professionals who come from those communities that have been historically underrepresented (American Planning Association 2005). In fact, there is increasing recognition within the profession that those who comprise the planning profession have not mirrored the diversity of the populations they serve.[9] Efforts to address these failings are ongoing.

A second type of planning controversy involves the call for tolerance and the right of cultural expression in the built and lived environment. Demographic change involves the entrance of newcomers, the exodus of old-timers, and usually the combination of both. It demands a social adjustment among neighbors who may not have past experience living or working alongside new acquaintances who may be culturally different. Even in places with relatively stable populations, longstanding conflicts between ethnic, racial, tribal, or other groups may simmer in the midst of coexistence. While planners are trained to think about physical infrastructure needs, we are less prepared as a professional group to address social infrastructure needs. When newcomers display their business signs in their native non-English language, when neighbors relandscape their front yards to raise vegetables or animals as they did in their places of origin, or when new ethnic towns create architectural symbols to make their presence visible, there is sometimes a backlash of anger or resentment among longtime residents. These types of planning controversies test the level of tolerance for cultural specificity in the private and public spheres with respect to others' rights and preferences. Inevitably, this has implications for the range of alternatives considered in planning, as well as the ways through which local planning ordinances allow people of different cultural backgrounds to express themselves within the physical and social environment.

This is closely related to a third area of controversy: the right of cultural groups to maintain and nurture an identity, epistemology, and lifestyle that may differ from the mainstream society or other groups. In planning and social policy, controversy over this set of rights can center on bilingual education programs that allow people to maintain their native language, the preservation of sacred spaces for the practice of non-Western religious and spiritual beliefs, the maintenance of ethnic enclave communities as centers of cultural activity and association, special access to land and natural resources for the preservation of cultural and subsistence practices, or the allowance of traditional burial practices and protection of burial objects, especially among indigenous groups. Many planning controversies entail characteristics of all three types of controversy. For example, the establishment and naming of ethnic enclaves such as "Little Saigons" and "Chinatowns" envelop expressions among ethnic groups for political recognition while requiring support or at least tolerance by others sharing or traversing those spaces. In many indigenous communities, this means increasing community self-sufficiency and protecting land and natural resources that may be the bases for a broad range of cultural practices and, for many, subsistence lifestyles (Lane and Hibbard 2005).

In divided societies, ethnic conflict over land, land use, and governance often manifest themselves in heated planning controversies at the local level. Bollens (1998) illustrates how urban policy and planning can exacerbate social tensions or facilitate the mediation of group-based identity conflict. Cities can be important sites for peace building in post-conflict societies among groups that have battled for generations. And practitioners can see planning projects as opportunities for the clarification of abstract concepts such as democracy and fairness as it affects people in the most practical and direct ways. Among the lessons Bollens gleans from cases of planning in conflicted societies is the importance of engagement in equity planning, sensitivity to land uses having historical and cultural salience within neighborhoods or regions, protection and promotion of a collective public sphere responsive to diverse identity groups, and the diffusion of knowledge that would enhance peace building, not only in planning but also in other spheres of public and private life. Additionally, intergroup conflict can be highly personalized and fraught with distrust, real and perceived value differences, and conflicting interpretations. Informal processes are equally important alongside formal ones to work through differences (Hou and Kinoshita 2007).

Today, there remains a strong push toward assimilation in most Westernized nations to the dominant group culture, as hybridized as that may be. And there remains sharp polarization between those who take the philosophical stance of assimilation and those who support some model of pluralism (with a small "p") or self-determination in prescribing what is best for a people or society. These planning controversies along with countless others continue to define the theoretical debates as well as the practical ones.

4. Questions for Future Pursuit

There are infinite questions worthy of scholarly and practical pursuit, but our selection of concluding questions is driven by a deep concern for how we are all to get along and get along in a just and fair society. There are locales that are fraught with ethnic and racial strife, while others are less adversarial and some relatively harmonious. Planners usually do not think of themselves as shaping race or ethnic relations in the city. Nor do they necessarily assume responsibility to help preserve the diversity of cultures that exist on this planet. Maybe these are unfair expectations. But our hope is that this set of concerns will begin to occupy our minds as we think about the future of planning research and practice.

We end with a short list of salient questions in seeking a just and convivial society where we can all thrive equally and together.

    a. How does planning shape identity formation and intergroup relations?
    b. What is the role of planning in helping to achieve better intergroup relations and greater equality and justice in a multicultural milieu, understanding different histories and circumstances?
    c. What are the theoretical and ethical implications of recognizing multiple publics that may share different epistemic lenses on the world? And in practical terms, what are ways we can recognize multiple publics without falling down the slippery slope of moral relativism?
    d. What are the prospects for transformative planning to engage people in a process of learning how to see the world through the lens of others? What does this process look like? How can such processes lead to a greater measure of social justice as experienced by multiple publics?
    e. How can we identify, codify, and routinize collaborative, transformative processes in addressing issues of cultural diversity in planning and governance?

There are a growing number of scholars who are probing these questions, and this chapter is built upon many of their works. But there is much more to be done.

Notes

1. It is estimated that half of the world's 6000 languages may disappear by the end of the century (Crystal 2000).
2. Sandercock (2003) suggests multiple ways of knowing, including knowing from dialogue, from experience, through seeking out local knowledge of the specific and the concrete, though learning to read symbolic, nonverbal evidence, through contemplation, and through action.
3. Let us briefly clarify our use of the term "culture" for this chapter. We borrow the meaning from anthropology, referring to culture as a system of human knowledge, belief, social interaction, and behavior that is shared among a group of people such that there is a common "lens" through which people see and interpret the world around them. In referring to cultural groups here, we are mainly focused on ethnic

groups, though recognizing that those who may share a distinct lens on the world may also share other boundary markers, be they place-based, generational, racial, ethnic, tribal, religious, familial, or other distinction or combination of distinctions. Cultural identities are shaped in one's association with multiple and overlapping groups, and the salience of any one boundary marker is often situational, though some such as race, ethnicity, and class may be more central. This interpretive definition of culture reflects the turn in anthropology from a focus on attitudes, norms, and behaviors of groups to the systems of belief and thought that shape them.

4. It is important to note that cosmopolitanism as a philosophical orientation has parted from its popular use, as the neoliberal managerial class has appropriated the term in place-marketing urban development, as illustrated in the cases of Manchester, Singapore, and elsewhere (Binnie et al. 2006; Yeoh 2004; Young, Diep, and Drabble 2006). City boosters promote a "cosmopolitan" city with ethnic arts, restaurants, and cultural activities that appeal to a diverse professional class, but at the exclusion of the undesirable "other" who would upset their version of the utopian vision.

5. The different theoretical positions are exemplified, respectively, in the work of Kymlicka (1995) and Parekh (2000), who write of rights to differ within the political community. In *Multicultural Citizenship* (1995), Kymlicka argues that certain "collective rights" of minority cultures are consistent with liberal democratic principles, although no single formula can be applied to all groups, and that the needs and aspirations of immigrants are very different from those of indigenous peoples and national minorities. Parekh (2000) argues for a pluralist perspective on cultural diversity and posits that identities are socially constructed with only a minimal set of features in common. Thus, he argues for a dialogic interplay between human commonalities and cultural difference.

6. The topic of incorporating a diverse array of voices into planning processes and finding "just solutions" and "common ground" are longstanding concerns in the planning literature (see Forester 1989; Krumholz and Clavel 1994; Krumholz and Forester 1990; Friedmann 1981; Healey 1997; Heskin 1991; Sandercock 1998a, 1998b; Schön 1983).

7. Debates over these concerns among communicative planning theorists have run parallel to similar debates among deliberative democracy theorists in political science (Abelson et al. 2003; Ackerman and Fishkin 2004; Beierle 1999; Fishkin 1991, 1995; Fung 2001, 2004; Fung and Wright 2001; Gastil 2000; Gastil and Levine 2005; Mansbridge 1980; Neblo 2005; Ryfe 2005; Smith and Wales 2000; Sulkin and Simon 2001).

8. While there is no compendium of racially charged incidents surrounding ethnic community developments, some descriptions may be found in hate-crime reports issued by agencies and organizations such as the U.S. Federal Bureau of Investigation, Human Rights First, and various state and county Human Relations Commissions.

9. In the United States, the American Planning Association Diversity Task Force, in its 2005 report entitled "Increasing Diversity in the Planning Profession," recognized that less than 10 percent of APA members were racial minorities while persons of color represented over 30 percent of the general population.

REFERENCES

Abelson, J., P. Forest, J. Eyles, P. Smith, E. Martin, and F. Gauvin, F. 2003. "Deliberations about Deliberative Methods: Issues in the Design and Evaluation of Public Participation Processes. *Social Science and Medicine* 57:239–51.

Ackerman, B., and J. Fishkin. 2004. *Deliberation Day.* New Haven, CT: Yale University Press.

Allmendinger, P., and M. Tewdwr-Jones. 2002. "The Communicative Turn in Urban Planning: Unraveling Paradigmatic, Imperialistic and Moralistic Dimensions." *Space & Polity* 6(1): 5–24.

Ålund, A., and C. U. Schierup. 1991. *Paradoxes of Multiculturalism: Essays on Swedish Society.* Research in Ethnic Relations Series. Brookfield, VT: Avebury.

American Planning Association Diversity Task Force. 2005. *Increasing Diversity in the Planning Profession: A Report on the 2004 Minority Planning Summit and Recommendation for Future Action.* Chicago: American Planning Association.

Amin, A. 2002. "Ethnicity and the Multicultural City: Living with Diversity." *Environment and Planning Part A* 34: 959–80.

Andersen, A. 1999. *Economic Impact Study of the Sydney 2000 Olympic Games.* Centre for Regional Economic Analysis. Sydney: University of Tasmania.

Anderson, K. 2000. "Thinking 'Postnationally': Dialogue Across Multicultural, Indigenous and Settler Spaces." *Annals of the Association of American Geographers* 90:381–91.

Appiah, A. 1998. "Cosmopolitan Patriots." In *Cosmopolitics*, edited by P. Cheah and B. Robbins, 91–114. Minneapolis: University of Minnesota Press.

Appiah, A. 2006. *Cosmopolitanism: Ethics in a World of Strangers.* New York: W.W. Norton.

Bauman, Z. 2000. *Globalization: The Human Consequences.* New York: Columbia University Press.

Beck, U. 1998. "Cosmopolitan Manifesto." *New Statesman* 127:1–3.

Beierle, T. 1999. "Using Social Goals to Evaluate Public Participation in Environmental Decisions." *Policy Studies Review* 16:75–103.

Binnie, J., J. Holloway, S. Millington, and C. Young, eds. 2006. *Cosmopolitan Urbanism.* New York: Routledge.

Bollens, S. A. 1998. *Urban Peace Building in Divided Societies.* Boulder, CO: Westview.

Boyd, M. R. 2008. *Jim Crow Nostalgia: Reconstructing Race in Bronzeville.* Minneapolis: University of Minnesota Press.

Brand, R., and F. Gaffikin. 2007. "Collaborative Planning in an Uncollaborative World." *Planning Theory* 6(3): 282–313.

Brimicombe, A. 2007. "Ethnicity, Religion and Residential Segregation In London." *Environment and Planning Part B: Planning and Design* 34:884–904.

Bullard, R. 1990. *Dumping in Dixie: Race, Class, and Environmental Quality.* Boulder, CO: Westview.

Bullard, R., P. Mohai, R. Saha, and B. Wright. 2008. "Toxic Wastes and Race at Twenty: Why Race Still Matters After All of These Years." *Environmental Law* 38(2): 371–411.

Callard, F. 2004. "Iris Marion Young." In *Key Thinkers on Space and Place*, edited by P. Hubbard, R. Kitchin, and G. Valentine, 337–43. London: Sage.

Carmon, N. 1999. "Three Generations of Urban Renewal Policies: Analysis and Policy Implications." *Geoforum* 30(2): 145–58.

Cristaldi, F. 2002. "Multiethnic Rome: Toward Residential Segregation?" *GeoJournal* 58(2–3): 81–90.

Crystal, D. 2000. *Language Death.* New York: Cambridge University Press.

Dikec, M. 2002. "Police, Politics, and the Right to the City." *GeoJournal* 58(2–3): 91–98.

Ellis, M., R. Wright, and V. Parks. 2004. "Work Together, Live Apart? Geographies of Racial and Ethnic Segregation at Home and at Work." *Annals of the Association of American Geographers* 94(3): 620–37.

Entrikin, J. N. 1999. "Political Community, Identity and Cosmopolitan Place." *International Sociology* 14:269–82.

Fainstein, S. 2005. "Planning Theory and the City." *Journal of Planning Education and Research* 25:121–30.

Fainstein, S. 2006. "Planning and the Just City." Paper presented at conference on "Searching for the Just City," Graduate School of Architecture, Planning and Preservation, Columbia University, New York, April 29.

Fainstein, S. 2010a. "Redevelopment Planning and Distributive Justice in the American Metropolis." Social Science Research Network. Unpublished manuscript. Available at: http://papers.ssrn.com/sol3/papers.cfm?abstract_id=1657723; accessed November 4, 2011.

Fainstein, S. 2010b. *The Just City*. Ithaca, NY: Cornell University Press.

Fischler, R. 2000. "Communicative Planning Theory: A Foucauldian Assessment." *Journal of Planning Education and Research* 19:358–68.

Fishkin, J. 1991. *Democracy and Deliberation: New Directions for Democratic Reform*. New Haven, CT: Yale University Press.

Fishkin, J. 1995. *The Voice of the People: Public Opinion and Democracy*. New Haven, CT: Yale University Press.

Flyvbjerg, B. 1998. "Empowering Civil Society: Habermas, Foucault and the Question of Conflict." In *Cities for Citizens: Planning and the Rise of Civil Society in a Global Age*, edited by M. Douglass and J. Friedmann, 185–211. New York: John Wiley.

Forester, J. 1989. *Planning in the Face of Power*. Berkeley, CA: University of California Press.

Forester, J. 1999. *The Deliberative Practitioner: Encouraging Participatory Planning Processes*. Cambridge, MA: MIT Press.

Forester, J. 2009. *Dealing with Differences: Dramas of Mediating Public Disputes*. New York: Oxford University Press.

Friedmann, J. 1981. *Planning as Social Learning*. Berkeley, CA: Institute of Urban and Regional Development.

Fung, A. 2001. "Accountable Autonomy: Toward Empowered Deliberation in Chicago Schools and Policing." *Politics & Society* 29:73–103.

Fung, A. 2004. *Empowered Participation: Reinventing Urban Democracy*. Princeton, NJ: Princeton University Press.

Fung, A., and E. O. Wright. 2001. "Deepening Democracy: Innovations in Empowered Participatory Governance." *Politics & Society* 29:5–41.

Gamson, W. A., and A. Modigliani. 1994. "The Changing Culture of Affirmative Action." In *Equal Employment Opportunity: Labor Market Discrimination and Public Policy*, edited by P. Burstein, 373–94. Hawthorne, NY: Aldine de Gruyter.

Gastil, J. 2000. *By Popular Demand: Revitalizing Representative Democracy Through Deliberative Elections*. Berkeley, CA: University of California Press.

Gastil, J., and P. Levine, eds. 2005. *The Deliberative Democracy Handbook: Strategies for Effective Civic Engagement in the Twenty-First Century*. San Francisco: Jossey-Bass.

Hajer, M. A., and H. Wagenaar, eds. 2003. *Deliberative Policy Analysis: Understanding Governance in the Network Society*. New York: Cambridge University Press.

Hall, S. 2000. "Conclusion: The Multi-Cultural Question." In *Un/settled Multiculturalisms: Diasporas, Entanglements, "Transruptions,"* edited by B. Hesse, 209–41. New York: Zed Books.

Hartman, C. W., and G. D. Squires. 2006. *There Is No Such Thing As a Natural Disaster: Race, Class, and Hurricane Katrina*. New York: Routledge.

Harvey, D. 2008. "The Right to the City." *New Left Review* 53:23–40.

Healey, P. 1993. "The Communicative Work of Development Plans." *Environment and Planning Part B: Planning and Design* 20(1): 83–104.

Healey, P. 1997. *Collaborative Planning: Shaping Places in Fragmented Societies.* Vancouver: University of British Columbia Press.

Healey, P. 1999." Institutionalist Analysis, Communicative Planning, and Shaping Places." *Journal of Planning Education and Research* 19:111–21.

Heskin, A. D. 1991. *The Struggle for Community.* Boulder, CO: Westview.

Hillier, J. 1998. "Beyond Confused Noise: Ideas Toward Communicative Procedural Justice." *Journal of Planning Education and Research* 18(1): 14–24.

Hou, J., and I. Kinoshita. 2007. "Bridging Community Differences Through Informal Processes: Reexamining Participatory Planning in Seattle and Matsudo." *Journal of Planning Education and Research* 26:301–14.

Huxley, M. 2000. "The Limits to Communicative Planning." *Journal of Planning Education and Research* 19:369–77.

Inglis, C. 1996. "Multiculturalism: New Policy Responses to Diversity." Management of Social Transformations, UNESCO Policy Paper 4. Available at: http://www.unesco.org/most/pp4.htm; accessed November 4, 2011.

Innes, J. 1995. "Planning Theory's Emerging Paradigm: Communicative Action and Interactive Practice." *Journal of Planning Education and Research* 14:183–89.

Isin, E. F. 2000. "Introduction: Democracy, Citizenship and the City." In *Democracy, Citizenship and the Global City*, edited by E. F. Isin, 1–21. London and New York: Routledge.

Krumholz, N., and P. Clavel, P. 1994. *Reinventing Cities: Equity Planners Tell Their Stories, Conflicts in Urban and Regional Development.* Philadelphia: Temple University Press.

Krumholz, N., and J. Forester. 1990. *Making Equity Planning Work: Leadership in the Public Sector, Conflicts in Urban and Regional Development.* Philadelphia: Temple University Press.

Kymlicka, W. 1995. *Multicultural Citizenship: A Liberal Theory of Minority Rights.* Oxford: Oxford University Press.

Kymlicka, W. 2003. "Multicultural States and Intercultural Citizens." *Theory and Research in Education* 1(2): 147–69.

Lane, M. B., and M. Hibbard. 2005. "Doing It for Themselves: Transformative Planning by Indigenous Peoples." *Journal of Planning Education and Research* 25:172–84.

Lauria, M., and M. J. Soll. 1996. "Communicative Action, Power, and Misinformation in a Site Selection Process." *Journal of Planning Education and Research* 15(3): 200–11.

LeGates, R. T., and C. Hartman. 1982. "Gentrification-Caused Displacement." *Urban Law.* 14:31–55.

Lefebvre, H. 1996. *Writings on Cities*, selected, translated, and introduced by E. Kofman and E. Lebas. Oxford, UK: Blackwell.

Mansbridge, J. 1980. *Beyond Adversary Democracy.* Chicago: University of Chicago Press.

Marris, P. 1962. "The Social Implications of Urban Redevelopment." *Journal of the American Institute of Planners* 28(3): 180–86.

Martiniello, M. 1998. "Wieviorka's View on Multiculturalism: A Critique." *Ethnic and Racial Studies* 21(5): 9–11.

Massey, D. S., and N. A. Denton. 1993. *American Apartheid.* Cambridge, MA: Harvard University Press.

Mccann, E. J. 2002. "Space, Citizenship, and the Right to the City: A Brief Overview." *GeoJournal* 58:77–79.

Mcguirk, P. M. 2001. "Situating Communicative Planning Theory: Context, Power and Knowledge." *Environment and Planning* 33:195–217.

Medoff, P., and H. Sklar. 1994. *Streets of Hope: The Fall and Rise of an Urban Neighborhood*. Cambridge, UK: South End Press.

Mitchell, D. 2003. *The Right to the City: Social Justice and the Fight for Public Space*. New York: Guilford.

Munck, R. 2002. "Globalization and Democracy: A New 'Great Transformation'?" *Annals of the American Academy of Political and Social Science* 581(May): 10–21.

Neblo, M. 2005. "Thinking Through Democracy: Between the Theory and Practice of Deliberative Politics." *Acta Politica* 40(2): 169–81.

Nickel, D. 1995. "The Progressive City? Urban Redevelopment in Minneapolis." *Urban Affairs Review* 30:355–77.

Omi, M., and H. Winant. 1986. *Racial Formation in the United States: From the 1960s to the 1980s*. New York: Routledge & Kegan Paul.

Parekh, B. 2000. *Rethinking Multiculturalism: Cultural Diversity and Political Theory*. Cambridge, MA: Harvard University Press.

Pastor, M., R. Bullard, J. Boyce, A. Fothergill, R. Morello-Frosch, and B. Wright. 2006. *In the Wake of the Storm: Environment, Disaster, and Race After Katrina*. New York: Russell Sage Foundation.

Purcell, M. 2002. "Excavating Lefebvre: The Right to the City and Its Urban Politics of the Inhabitant." *Geojournal* 58:99–108.

Ryfe, D. M. 2005. "Does Deliberative Democracy Work?" *Annual Review of Political Science* 8:49–71.

Saarikoski, H. 2002. "Naturalized Epistemology and Dilemmas of Planning Practice." *Journal of Planning Education and Research* 22(1): 3–14.

Sager, T. 1994. *Communicative Planning Theory: Rationality Versus Power*. Aldershot, UK: Avebury.

Sager, T. 2006. "The Logic of Critical Communicative Planning: Transaction Cost Alteration." *Planning Theory* 5(3): 223–54.

Sandercock, L. 1998a. *Making the Invisible Visible: a Multicultural Planning History*. Berkeley, CA: University of California Press.

Sandercock, L. 1998b. *Towards Cosmopolis: Planning for Multicultural Cities*. New York: John Wiley.

Sandercock, L. 2003. *Cosmopolis II: Mongrel Cities of the 21st Century*. New York: Continuum.

Schneekloth, L. H., and R. G. Shibley. 1995. *Placemaking: The Art and Practice of Building Communities*. New York: John Wiley.

Schön, D. A. 1983. *The Reflective Practitioner: How Professionals Think in Action*. New York: Basic Books.

Skocpol, T., and M. P. Fiorina, eds. 1999. *Civic Engagement in American Democracy*. Washington, DC: Brookings Institution Press.

Smets, P., and M. D. Uyl. 2008. "The Complex Role of Ethnicity in Urban Mixing: A Study of Two Deprived Neighbourhoods in Amsterdam." *Urban Studies* 45(7): 1439–60.

Smith, G., and C. Wales. 2000. "Citizens' Juries and Deliberative Democracy." *Political Studies* 48(1): 51–65.

Squires, G. D. 1997. *Insurance Redlining: Disinvestment, Reinvestment, and the Evolving Role of Financial Institutions*. Washington, DC: Urban Institute Press.

Sulkin, T., and A. F. Simon. 2001. "Habermas in the Lab: A Study of Deliberation in an Experimental Setting." *Political Psychology* 22(4): 809–26.

Taylor, C. 1994. "The Politics of Recognition." In *Multiculturalism: Examining the Politics of Recognition*, edited by A. Gutmann, 25–73. Princeton, NJ: Princeton University Press.

Thomas, J. M. 1997. *Redevelopment and Race: Planning a Finer City in Postwar Detroit.* Baltimore, MD: John Hopkins University Press.

Throgmorton, J. 1996. "Impeaching" Research: Planning as Persuasive and Constitutive Discourse." In *Explorations in Planning Theory*, edited by L. M. S. Mandelbaum and R. Burchell, 345–64. New Brunswick, NJ: Center for Urban Policy Research, Rutgers.

Tiryakian, E. A. 2003. "Assessing Multiculturalism Theoretically: E Pluribus Unum, Sic Et Non." *International Journal on Multicultural Societies* 5(1): 20–39.

Toji, D., and K. Umemoto. 2003. "The Paradox of Dispersal: Ethnic Continuity and Community Development Among Japanese Americans." *APA Nexus: Asian Americans and Pacific Islanders Policy, Practice and Community* 1(1): 22–45.

Turner, B. S. 2000. "Liberal Citizenship and Cosmopolitan Virtue." In *Citizenship and Democracy in a Global Era*, edited by A. Vandenberg, 18–32. Basingstoke, UK: Palgrave Macmillan.

Umemoto, K. 2001. "Walking in Another's Shoes: Epistemological Challenges in Participatory Planning." *Journal of Planning Education and Research* 21(1): 17–31.

Umemoto, K., and H. Igarashi. 2009. "Deliberative Planning in a Multicultural Milieu." *Journal of Planning Education and Research* 29(1): 39–53.

United Nations. 2009. "State of the World's Indigenous Peoples." New York: United Nations.

Verma, N., and H. Shin. 2004. "Communicative Action and the Network Society: A Pragmatic Marriage?" *Journal of Planning Education and Research* 24(2): 131–40.

Vertovec, S., and R. Cohen. 2002. *Conceiving Cosmopolitanism: Theory, Context and Practice.* New York: Oxford University Press.

Weiss, M. 1980. "The Origins and Legacy of Urban Renewal.: In *Urban and Regional Planning in an Age of Austerity*, edited by J. F. P. Clavel and W. Goldsmith, 53–80. New York: Pergamon.

Werbner, P. 1999. "Global Pathways, Working Class Cosmopolitans and the Creation of Transnational Ethnic Worlds." *Social Anthropology* 7(1): 17–35.

Wieviorka, M. 1998. "Is Multiculturalism the Solution?" *Ethnic and Racial Studies* 21(5): 881–910.

Wilson, J. Q. (Ed.). 1966. *Urban renewal: The record and the controversy.* Cambridge, MA: MIT Press.

Yeoh, B. S. A. 2004. "Cosmopolitanism and its Exclusions in Singapore." *Urban Studies* 41(12): 2431–45.

Young, C., M. Diep, and S. Drabble, 2006. "Living with Difference? The "Cosmopolitan City" and Urban Reimaging in Manchester, UK." *Urban Studies* 43(10): 1687–714.

Young, I. M. 1995. "Difference as a Resource for Democratic Communication." In *Deliberative Democracy: Essays on Reason and Politics,* edited by J. Bohman and W. Rehg, 383–406. Cambridge, MA: MIT Press.

CHAPTER 12

RESILIENCE

THOMAS J. CAMPANELLA AND DAVID R. GODSCHALK

1. INTRODUCTION

A resilient city is able to survive a traumatic blow to its physical infrastructure, its economy, or its social fabric. A resilient city bends but does not break; it absorbs impacts without shattering. Even if the bridges and roads are ruined and the buildings toppled, the resilient city's core institutions survive; its social fabric holds; and in time, its economy rebounds—all, ideally, without undue infusions of aid or assistance from external actors, such as the federal government. Urban resilience is an elusive state that resists easy metrics or qualification. It can be difficult or even impossible to gauge a city's true rebound capacity until an actual disaster is at hand. A city's degree of resilience can also change over time; the same kind of event can yield very different outcomes depending on prevailing socioeconomic conditions. The blackouts of 1969 and 1977 in New York City are a case in point. The initial events were virtually identical. The first blackout occurred during an economic boom, when the city was in robust overall health; strangers aided one other in the streets and the city was enveloped by a sense of collective goodwill and common purpose. The second blackout, in 1977, occurred in a time of economic decline and rising poverty and lawlessness in the city. The hale spirit and communalism of 1969 was gone, and the city was wracked instead by looting and vandalism. For many, the 1977 "Night of Terror" was the nadir of New York's long downward spiral in the postwar era.

Urban resilience is determined by a complex web of interlocking factors that resist easy measurement or visualization. A city can build a dazzling new sports stadium or airport, and the finished product will look great on the evening news or in annual reports. Banking up a city's rebound capacity, on the other hand, cannot be so easily imaged or sold. Planners can work for years to boost a city's immune system with seemingly little to show taxpayers or the press corps. Urban resilience is also difficult to achieve quickly. A city cannot purchase or implement resilience per se, but it can bolster incrementally the various systems and infrastructures—both physical and social—deemed essential to metropolitan functionality and well-being. In this sense, a resilient city is much like a person in good health, whose strong heart and robust immune system are the result of years of careful attention to diet and exercise. Building up urban resilience requires similar commitment, like a person working out daily to keep fit and healthy. Though the benefits of such conditioning may not been immediately apparent, a sudden trauma or catastrophe will quickly reveal a city's level of fitness. The resilient city, like a well-conditioned body, will fend off infectious agents and recover swiftly from illness or trauma.

In the following chapter we describe and analyze some of the key elements that can augment a city's fitness, adaptability, and resilience. The chapter begins with a historical survey of urban resilience through the ages, examines the present status of policies and programs aimed at building resilience, and concludes with a series of essential lessons for enhancing future resilience.

2. URBAN RESILIENCE IN HISTORY

Cities are extraordinarily resilient entities, capable of rebounding from even horrific devastation. History is filled with examples of urban disasters both natural and human-made—of cities burned, flooded, shaken, pummeled by artillery, and infected by dread disease. But despite these horrors, virtually no major city has been permanently ruined in the last 300 years. Even in the ancient world, cities were rarely abandoned in the wake of a catastrophic event. There was, of course, Pompeii, buried forever by an eruption of Mount Vesuvius; Monte Albán, near Oaxaca in modern Mexico, was crushed for good by the Spanish; and in the Xingu region of the Brazilian Amazon, a vast network of quasi-urban settlements that flourished 1,500 years ago mysteriously vanished and was quickly reclaimed by jungle.[1] Jared Diamond describes the early settlements on Easter Island and Norse Greenland that lost resilience, declined, and eventually died out.[2] The mythic city of Atlantis has yet to be found, let alone lost. But these are history's exceptions, not the rule. Even the storied destruction of Carthage by the Romans after the Third Punic War was not permanent. The Centurions may have leveled the city and spread salt on its fields to render it barren. But the Romans themselves resurrected the city during the reign of Augustus, eventually making Carthage the administrative hub of their African colonies.

More typical are stories of durability and resilience. For reasons that are not fully clear, cities become effectively indestructible after the eighteenth century, and this in spite of humankind's increasing ability to destroy and the increasingly larger populations living in known danger zones. No city has been permanently lost due to either warfare or natural disaster in the last several hundred years, with the sole exception of St. Pierre, Martinique, whose 30,000 inhabitants were annihilated by a volcanic eruption in 1901. Lisbon endured a triple blow in 1755—an earthquake followed by fire and a tsunami that, together, killed some 60,000 people and destroyed nearly all of the city's buildings; yet Lisbon recovered and would go on to become one of Europe's great cities. Chicago was incinerated in 1871 but resurrected itself seemingly overnight and mightier than before. Galveston, Texas, rebounded from a catastrophic hurricane in 1900—still the deadliest natural disaster in American history—even if it was largely displaced as a major port by Houston. San Francisco lifted itself up from the ashes and rubble of its own catastrophe six years later. Each of these cities suffered appalling destruction of life and property; each was forever changed by the catastrophe, sometimes radically. Yet each survived and even flourished. Even the twentieth century—with its industrial warfare, wholesale genocide, and unprecedented urban devastation—has failed to take a city. Hiroshima, Tokyo, Warsaw, Dresden, Berlin, Beirut—all were subjected to terrible devastation, yet all are with us still. So too are Tangshan and Mexico City, cities leveled by powerful earthquakes in 1976 and 1985, respectively. Even benighted New Orleans has rebounded to some degree, though it is a very different city from the one struck by Hurricane Katrina.

To what can we ascribe this extraordinary capacity for resilience among cities in the modern era? The reasons are many and complex. Partly it has to do with the rise of the nation-state, which has a vested interest in the well-being of its constituent cities. Notwithstanding Washington's infamous snub of New York City during the 1975 fiscal crisis—"Ford to City: Drop Dead," reported the *Daily News*—a nation will usually go to great lengths to help a city in need, for good public relations if nothing else: a country that can do little for one of its own cities telegraphs a message of weakness to the world. This is never more so than when the city in distress is the seat of national government; the capital represents the nation on the global stage and must be protected at all cost. The advent of fee-simple property ownership in the eighteenth century also helped make urban sites more "sticky" and less prone to abandonment. Parcel boundaries and property lines—recorded in plats and deeds and other legal documents—may not seem all that robust, but they represent a virtually indestructible system of spatial organization; providing the documents themselves survive somewhere, lot lines can easily be redrawn, even atop the ashes of a city rubbed out by a nuclear blast. Other factors have contributed to the persistence of urban places in the modern era. By the end of the eighteenth century, many cities must have passed a magical tipping point in terms of sheer amount of built matter; there was simply too much investment on the ground to warrant total abandonment, even in the face of a terrible disaster. Ancient cities were small and compact; pulling up the stakes and moving to a fresh site was relatively easy. Related to this is embedded infrastructure. Concrete foundations and deeply buried utilities can often survive a major catastrophe, and they virtually guarantee that new roads and buildings will be erected in the very same place. Finally, there is the rise of the modern insurance industry, which is fundamentally conservative and resistant to change. Insurance awards are generally based on what was lost, where it was lost; property owners are typically urged to rebuild in situ and as before—and as speedily as possible.

Barring a direct asteroid strike, no disaster will fully wipe out a city; but even a minor disaster can profoundly alter the fate and future of an urban place. Therein lies the rub of urban resilience: we can rest assured that our cities will survive; the question is *how well* they survive. Related to this is the fact that a city can be rebuilt, even heroically, without fully recovering. This is because true urban resilience involves much more than roads and buildings and other physical things. As Vale and Campanella argue in *The Resilient City: How Modern Cities Recover From Disaster*, "The process of building is a necessary but, by itself, insufficient condition for enabling recovery and resilience." Broken highways can be mended; office towers can be repaired; and communications systems can be patched back together. But a city is more than the sum of its buildings. It is also a complex of intermingled social and cultural networks—the messy magical human "software." Recovering *this* city "fundamentally entails reconnecting severed familial, social and religious networks of survivors"—a process that cannot be imposed, but must be cultivated from below, "network by network, district by district, not just building by building." This requires painstaking reconstruction of the "myriad social relations embedded in schools, workplaces, childcare arrangements, shops, places of worship, and places of play and recreation." It is a terrible thing for a city's buildings to be reduced to rubble; but it is much worse when a city's communal institutions and social fabric is also torn asunder. Indeed, a city can be brought to its knees without hardly even touching the buildings.[3]

This is what happened in Wilmington, North Carolina, in the wake of the race riot of 1898. Wilmington was then the largest and most economically vital city in the state. It was also home to a majority African-American population, and was known as "one of the best cities for blacks in the American South." Blacks were well represented among the city's mercantile elite, and the *Daily Record* was among the only black newspapers in America at the time. Moreover, blacks and whites got along relatively well. By the 1880s, however, whites agitating against Reconstruction launched a "white supremacy campaign" to neutralize the racially mixed political coalition then in power—the Republican Populist Fusion. On November 10, 1898, a band of whites burned the *Daily Record* and began a killing spree that left scores, possibly hundreds, of blacks dead. Thousands of black residents fled the city. The city's elected officials were replaced by a cabal of segregationists. Remaining blacks were soon banished from every form of occupation and public office. Though only a few buildings were destroyed, the race riots ruined Wilmington's unique and vibrant social fabric, while the departure of black businessmen and skilled craftsmen brought the city's economy to a halt. Wilmington survived, but it never fully recovered and sank into a century of irrelevance. Only with the extension of Interstate 40 from Raleigh in the 1990s was the city revived.[4]

The Basque city of Guernica in northern Spain offers another insight into how social factors can alter the mechanics of recovery. Guernica was subjected to an infamous act of violence in 1937, when Franco sought Hitler's assistance in bombing this center of Basque autonomy into submission. Hitler obliged, seeing it as a chance to perfect saturation and dive-bombing techniques he would later use in England, Poland, and elsewhere. On a busy market day in late April the town was pulverized by the Luftwaffe's Condor Legion, causing extensive loss of life. The bombing became known to the world largely as the subject of Picasso's monumental painting, *Guernica*, which was exhibited at the 1937 Paris World's Fair. Less than a decade later, the entire city center of Guernica had been meticulously rebuilt—on orders by none other than Franco himself. But only in outward appearance did the city seem healed. In fact, Guernicans resisted the forced reconstruction of the city by the hated Franco regime. In this case, the physical infrastructure was restored to good order, but on terms that chafed against the will of the local citizenry. Full recovery of the city—its emotional and psychological healing—did not take place until well after Franco's death in 1975.[5]

Just as a city is more than the sum of its buildings, it may also be only as resilient as its citizens. Resilient citizens have enabled urban resilience throughout history. At the outset of the Second World War, a "Blitz spirit" enabled Londoners to carry on in spite of daily—and nightly—bombardment by the German Luftwaffe. Even the class divide seemed breached; the defiant cry of "We can take it!" echoed from the East End to Coventry. "Some of the damage in London has been pretty heartbreaking," wrote filmmaker Humphrey Jennings in the fall of 1940, "but what an effect it has had on the people!...What warmth—what courage! What determination...a curious kind of unselfishness is developing."[6] To some extent this street-level resilience was romanticized and exaggerated by the media, and it is true that many people simply fled the bombs. (London's population sank by about 20 percent, and industrial boroughs like Shoreditch and Stepney lost as many as 50 percent of their residents in the wake of the Blitz.) On the other hand, government ministers had been convinced that the bombs would cause widespread chaos and a collapse of morale; they were happily proven wrong. Traces of the Blitz spirit were seen in New York after the terrorist attacks of September 11, 2001. The impromptu candlelight vigils and informal monuments to the lost and fallen brought the vast and often fractious city together in an extraordinary way; for months the city had the social cohesion and warmth of a small town. The great Tangshan, China, earthquake of July 1976 unleashed a force 400 times as powerful as the Hiroshima atomic bomb. Ninety-seven percent of the city's residential buildings were destroyed and at least 240,000 people killed. Yet China and the Tangshan people pulled together and rebuilt the city in less than a decade, and without the aid of any foreign nation. Local citizenry rallied to rebuild, giving real meaning to the Chinese Communist Party's official earthquake rhetoric: *Kang Zhen Jiu Zhai*—"Resist the earthquake and rescue ourselves."[7]

A very different form of resilient citizenry emerged in the aftermath of the Mexico City earthquake of 1985. A major catastrophe often reveals the fault lines in a society, exposing the inequalities of race and class. It can also reveal long-concealed abuses of authority. The Mexico City earthquake not only rattled the city's buildings but also shook the very legitimacy of the political system and its leadership. As Diane Davis describes it in *The Resilient City*, the earthquake exposed a raft of official corruption and abuses—in some cases quite literally: new government buildings pulverized by the earthquake were found to be of substandard construction quality, and the exposed cellars of ruined police stations contained evidence of torture. These revelations galvanized the capital's "resilient citizens" to demand political accountability and a reordering of reconstruction priorities. "Within days of the earthquake," writes Davis, "people began to organize on their own and reclaim the city for themselves by taking over the business of recovery and reconstruction without assistance from government authorities. Their efforts ensured that certain activities were recovered or restored, ranging from housing to medical services." The grassroots mobilizing triggered by the disaster led, in turn, to lasting political reforms, new political leadership, and a successful movement to secure affordable housing.[8]

The devastating blow inflicted by the floods following Hurricane Katrina to New Orleans led many to predict that the city would be effectively lost. Not only was much of the city's physical infrastructure ruined, so was its social fabric. Tens of thousands of New Orleanian families scattered to the four winds in the wake of the flood. More affluent residents had packed up and left town well ahead of the storm. But members of the impoverished, largely African-American underclass lacked the means to get out and were largely abandoned by the tragically inept evacuation efforts on the part of state and local officials. The poorest of the poor were thus left to their own devices. Many, of course, never made it out alive. This was a demographic group already burdened by numerous and intractable socio-economic problems long before Katrina formed over the Atlantic. The immune system of these people was already down, so to speak, much the way a person battling the flu will have lowered resistance to a secondary infection. To be resilient, an urban population needs to have a certain threshold level of communal wellness, cohesion, and self-esteem—something that the poorest of the New Orleanian poor largely lacked.

But it is not a matter of poverty alone. The citizen activists of Mexico City were poor; so too were the residents of industrial East London pounded by Nazi bombs. The Vietnamese population in New Orleans at the time of Hurricane Katrina was also poor, but it benefited mightily from strong social cohesion and an ethic of self-determination born out of adversity (many of the older residents had fled Vietnam after the fall of Saigon in 1975).[9] The Vietnamese enclave in New Orleans East was hard hit by the storm and subsequent floods; homes and stores and restaurants were destroyed. But the social fabric of the community held fast, and few looked outward to the government for help. As the *New York Times* reported:

> [the Vietnamese] formed neighborhood groups to rebuild, using the [Mary
> Queen of Vietnam Roman Catholic Church] as headquarters. One team repairs
> and decontaminates the houses. Others arrange tetanus shots to prevent illness,

and acupuncture sessions to ease stress. Another team buys food to make spicy stews and rice for the families who visit for the day to check on property. Friends and family members drive one another to work, church or even back and forth to cities in Texas where they have temporarily settled. Now they are working on a plan with the Federal Emergency Management Agency to place a core group of Vietnamese into trailers in the neighborhood, planting the seeds of resettlement.[10]

Of course, New Orleans did not simply disappear from the map. It lives on, but in an altered state. Many former residents of the Ninth Ward and neighboring districts simply chose to abandon what, to them, had become a deeply dysfunctional city, home of the highest murder rate in America. New Orleans had effectively failed its most needy citizens—failed to give them good educations, failed to provide them decent jobs, failed to protect them from gang violence, failed even to give them a lift out of harm's way. Thus, it came as no surprise that the first broad survey of hurricane victims—conducted in October 2005 using data from the American Red Cross—found that 39 percent of New Orleans residents, some 50,000 households, mostly poor and black, had no plans to return to the city.[11] This is a staggering number, easily the largest single movement of Americans since the "Great Migration" of African Americans in the post-World War II era. By January 2006, about one-third of the city's pre-Katrina population of 455,000 had returned, and a year later—on the second anniversary of the disaster—only about half had made their way back.[12] The loss of these residents, many of whom had deep family roots in New Orleans, throws a real warp in the New Orleans recovery picture. These people were part of the lifeblood of the Big Easy, and they carried with them—in their traditions and cuisine and mannerisms and habits of speech—a kind of urban genetic code that made New Orleans what it was. This code has been splicing itself into hundreds of local cultures across the country since the Katrina diaspora, enriching places far beyond Louisiana. But mostly it was a loss for New Orleans.

The ongoing struggle to bring New Orleans back from the brink provides a rich glimpse into the mechanics of postdisaster recovery and reconstruction. It would require a separate chapter to describe the tangled web of planning initiatives drafted and promoted by a diversity of commissions, governmental agencies, quasi-governmental authorities, and well-intentioned actors from the design professions, the business community, universities, and the public at large. The city's near total lack of a priori planning for such a disaster, along with seemingly insurmountable political realities, has made recovering New Orleans an enormous task, indeed. As Olshansky and colleages have written, "Neither the FEMA, the state of Louisiana, nor the city of New Orleans was prepared for the task of rebuilding a city after a catastrophic urban disaster." New Orleans also lacked, in the best of times, "a system for citizen involvement in governance," and it possessed "no pre-existing plan for the city's future." Not long after the flood, Mayor Ray Nagin actually *reduced* the city's planning staff by two-thirds. Indeed, most of the home rebuilding, clean-up, and community organizing work was carried out not by the government but by a variety of emergent grassroots, faith-based, and university organizations that descended on the region in a cloud of goodwill. "Clearly, this experience has confirmed much of what we know about postdisaster recovery, including the importance of previous plans and planning capacity, citizen involvement, information infrastructure and data clearinghouses, and external resources. It has also confirmed that recovery is a complex and often chaotic process, requiring nimble institutions and creative ways of harnessing the power of emergent organizations."[13] As Olshansky et al. conclude, the real benchmark of urban resilience is how quickly and how effectively the recovery process "returns the area to a state equal to or better than before the disaster."[14] By this standard, New Orleans can hardly be termed a model of urban resilience. Entire neighborhoods remain derelict, and according to the 2010 census, only about 75 percent of the pre-Katrina population now lives in the city, an estimated 343,829 people.

As sobering as the Katrina experience has been, prospects for urban resilience in the years ahead may be even more daunting. We are just beginning to understand and respond to the new specter of fundamental climate change, coupled with the likelihood of declining oil supplies, global pandemics, terror attacks, sea level rise, and other threats. The twentieth-century governmental policy apparatus constructed to cope with hurricanes, floods, and other natural hazards will require major reform in order to guide twenty-first-century cities toward a more resilient future. The next section briefly reviews the current state of urban readiness and identifies changes needed to maintain a sustainable future balance.

3. Resilient Cities Today and Tomorrow

While cities continue to age and change in response to population movements and development activities, one of the biggest challenges to present and future resiliency is likely to spring from devastating impacts of climate change.[15] This challenge spans all areas of urban planning, from infrastructure to housing, health, transportation, and land use. The United Nations forecasts that some 50 million people will become environmental refugees by the end of this decade due to forecasted storm surges and floods, sea level rise, ice storms, floods, wildfires, droughts and other natural hazards.[16] Coupled with climate change are anticipated major increases in world population, projected by the United Nations to increase by 2.5 billion between 2007 and 2050,[17] and anticipated passing of the world's peak oil supply by 2020.[18] While the bulk of those affected are likely to live in the developing countries, or the so-called Global South, many people in developed countries—the Global North—will find that these changes demand major shifts in their living environments and behavior patterns if their cities are to remain resilient.

Implementing the changes will require a range of innovative management and urban design responses by both governments and the design professions.

Two types of necessary responses have been identified: (1) *avoiding* the unmanageable impacts (preparing for climate change), and (2) *managing* the avoidable impacts (slowing climate change). Avoiding the unmanageable impacts is achieved through *adaptation* of urban development patterns and lifestyles to respond to the new realities of unprecedented increases in greenhouse gases that trigger environmental changes such as alterations in weather and ecosystems and increases in pollution. Managing the avoidable impacts is achieved through *mitigation* of the greenhouse gas impacts themselves by decreasing the amounts of carbon dioxide and other heat-trapping gases entering the atmosphere. These definitions have arisen out of contemporary efforts to deal with climate change. Semantics can be confusing, however. The term "mitigation" has a long history in the field of emergency management, where it refers to predisaster actions to reduce damage and injury from natural hazards, a definition that includes *both* adaptation and mitigation measures.[19]

While the definitions separate adaptation (bowing to the inevitable by smart development that reduces vulnerability to climate change effects) from mitigation (proactive efforts to reduce greenhouse gas emissions), in fact the actions taken under both banners are often similar, as in the case of emergency management. For example, redirecting urban sprawl to increase sustainable development is seen as both an adaptive response and a mitigation response in the 2006 Climate Change Adaptation and Mitigation Action Plan of Durban, South Africa.[20] Durban mapped its risks to sea level rise, flooding, and drought, and targeted its resilience measures by risk levels in its economic urban core, its large informal settlements, its rural drought belt, and its major transportation routes. The city is improving drainage, increasing the height of shoreline stabilization structures, building water retention ponds, and maintaining wetlands. It is revising its land-use zones to prevent building in the high-risk areas. And it is educating its population on how to reduce the human health effects of a flood.

The Durban case highlights the many dimensions that a resilient city strategy must deal with, including physical urban form and development processes, environmental hazards and resources, infrastructure and transportation facilities, economic activities and employment areas, social and institutional relationships, and demographic conditions. It is not enough to consider only one aspect of this integrated system, as New Orleans discovered in the Katrina tragedy where levees alone provided little social or environmental resilience. Ideal resilient cities are sustainable networks of strong and flexible physical systems, natural environments, human communities, and economic enterprises.[21] Resilient physical systems build in redundancy and diversity, so that if one part of a lifeline system fails there are other parts to keep it operating; think of substituting an alternative transportation or communication channel for a broken one. Resilient natural environments replenish their resource bases and adapt to changing impacts, so that their carrying capacity is not exceeded; think of maintaining healthy wetlands that absorb floods and storm surges. Resilient human communities are collaborative and inter-dependent, so that communication flows are maintained in times of stress; think of neighborhoods and institutions that trust and rely on each other in the face of disasters. Resilient economic enterprises are adaptable and foresighted, so that they maintain reserve capacity to accommodate for disaster losses; think of cor-porations that employ sound risk-management strategies. Learning and planning together, these networks continuously evolve toward higher degrees of resiliency.

In practice, resilient city strategies must be crafted to reflect the unique condi-tions of each urban area. The largest divide falls between cities of industrialized nations of the Global North, which are well established and growing slowly under effective regulations, and cities in developing countries of the Global South, which must cope with rapid growth owing to the wholesale migration of rural popula-tions seeking to better their lives. In the North, feasible government policies link-ing development to climate change targets are under way (see box 12.1; see also DeShazo and Matute this volume). In the Global South, lack of financial resources and legal authority limits the effectiveness of governmental intervention into set-tlement activity. Bangladesh, for example, has earned the dubious distinction as the world's capital for natural disasters, thanks to its vulnerable natural environ-ment coupled with poverty, corruption, and inadequate infrastructure.[22]

The U.S. experience in mitigating the impacts of natural hazards offers a case study that can shed light on creation of resilient cities coping with climate change. National policy is described in the Stafford Act, which establishes an intergov-ernmental system led by the Federal Emergency Management Agency (FEMA) to provide funding and technical assistance to state and local governments, which must prepare hazard-mitigation plans to become eligible for aid. When a disaster strikes, the affected state government requests a Presidential Disaster Declaration in order to receive federal aid. Over time, the federal policy has evolved from a focus on postdisaster response and recovery to one on predisaster mitigation plan-ning and action, as defined in the Disaster Mitigation Act of 2000, which contain both requirements and incentives. In order to be eligible for federal disaster aid, state and local emergency management agencies must prepare and adopt hazard-mitigation plans. Best-practice procedures and lessons have been derived for local emergency management[23] and post-disaster recovery.[24]

A large body of research by U.S. disaster scholars has analyzed the effective-ness of hazard-mitigation efforts. They have found that the bulk of mitigation expenditures have been directed toward *structural* actions (physical improvements such as levees, building elevation and strengthening, etc.). A smaller amount has been allocated to *process* mitigation that seeks to strengthen social and economic resiliency through planning, community outreach, and education, though some analysts have pointed out the importance of process mitigation to creating resilient cities.[25] They conclude that, in general, U.S. natural-hazard mitigation has been effective. For example, a 2005 national study for Congress of the aggregate costs and benefits of natural-hazard mitigation found that every federal dollar spent on mitigation results in four dollars in damages avoided, or a benefit-cost ratio of four

---

Box 12.1 Smart Growth and Climate Change in California[i]

California's climate change smart growth bill, Senate Bill 375, signed in October 2008, seeks to reduce greenhouse gas emissions by curbing urban sprawl, reducing commute times, and encouraging infill development.* Essentially a growth-management law that ties transportation funding to growth patterns, the bill asks each California region to create a preferred growth scenario to meet regional greenhouse gas reduction targets derived from the statewide reduction goal. Each metropolitan planning organization (MPO) must prepare a "sustainable communities strategy," which will be the land-use allocation in the regional transportation plan. The strategy is to identify land-use patterns and housing needs and set forth a forecasted development pattern, which, when integrated with the transportation network and policies, will reduce greenhouse gas emissions from automobiles and light trucks to achieve the approved reduction targets. Implementation is delegated to the regions and land-use regulation authority remains with the cities and counties.

The California sustainable communities strategy is distinguished from the smart-growth strategies of other states, such as Florida, Maryland, New Jersey, Oregon, and Washington, by its specific linkage of greenhouse gas reduction targets with growth-management techniques. While the smart-growth programs of other states may in fact help to mitigate climate-change impacts, they are not measured by the effectiveness of their actions in reducing greenhouse gases, as the California program requires.

California also provides funding for growth management planning. Its Regional Blueprint Planning Grants Program aims to build capacity for regional collaboration to plan for future growth and reduce sprawl. One of its key goals is to foster a more efficient land-use pattern that supports improved mobility and reduced dependency on single-occupant vehicle trips; accommodates an adequate supply of housing for all incomes; reduces impacts on valuable habitat, productive farmland, and air quality; increases resource use efficiency; and results in safe and vibrant neighborhoods.

[i]From David R. Godschalk, Raymond Burby, and Philip Berke, "Coping with Climate Change through Land Use Planning," Unpublished paper (Chapel Hill: Department of City and Regional Planning, University of North Carolina, 2008).

---

to one.[26] State-level studies have concluded that mitigation programs of structural strengthening generally have been effective, but that revising land-use policies has been less effective, owing to vested property rights.[27] Research on the impact of different policy styles on mitigation performance has concluded that collaborative approaches are more effective than state mandates.[28] Analyses of the role of public participation in hazard mitigation have concluded that it is important, but difficult, to involve citizens in comprehensive mitigation planning, owing to the perception that it is a technical activity.[29] However, some citizen groups are aware of the need to increase resilience with respect to natural hazards. See for example, the seismic resilience strategy under development by the San Francisco Planning

---

Box 12.2 SPUR Resilient City Policy Paper

The 1906 San Andreas Fault earthquake and fire caused over 3,000 deaths, destroyed over 28,000 buildings, and left about 225,000 homeless in Northern California. If the 1906 earthquake were to happen today on the San Andreas Fault, it could cause some 800 to 3,400 deaths, damage more than 90,000 buildings, and displace 160,000 to 250,000 households. It would cost between $90 and $120 billion to repair the damaged buildings, and damage to utilities and transportation systems would increase losses by another 5 percent to 15 percent. The total price tag for a repeat of the 1906 earthquake could reach $150 billion—about four times the total losses from the 1994 Northridge earthquake and ten times the losses from the 1989 Loma Prieta earthquake.

In anticipation of a repeat earthquake disaster, the San Francisco Planning and Urban Research Association (SPUR) has defined the resilient city in terms of seismic mitigation policies.* SPUR defines *seismic resilience* as the ability of the city to contain the effects of earthquakes when they occur, carry out recovery activities in ways that minimize social disruption, and rebuild following earthquakes in ways that mitigate the effects of future earthquakes.

SPUR proposes *performance goals* to restore everyday life in the wake of an earthquake disaster. Their goals, which are organized in three phases, are: initial response (1–7 days), mid-term planning (7–30 days), and long-term reconstruction (several years); these add specific target times to the recovery objectives set forth in the city's earthquake plan. For example, in the immediate phase, 90 percent of water, power, and wastewater systems should be operational and 90 percent of major transportation routes open for at least emergency response. In the mid-term phase, all utility systems and transportation routes should be restored to 95 percent of pre-event levels, public transportation running at 90 percent capacity, and airports open for general use at 95 percent capacity. In the long-term phase, within four months, temporary shelters should be closed, 95 percent of community retail services and 50 percent of nonworkforce support businesses should be reopened. And within three years, all business operations and city services should be restored to pre-earthquake levels.

SPUR also expands the city's performance standards for buildings and lifeline systems. They note that virtually all of the public-sector efforts are devoted to emergency response, and propose a focus on pre-disaster hazard mitigation to ensure that buildings and infrastructure do not fail in the future.

*SPUR. The Resilient City: A New Framework for Thinking About Disaster Planning in San Francisco. Available at: http://www.spur.org/policy; accessed 22 November 2011.

and Urban Research Association (SPUR), a nonprofit group in San Francisco (see box 12.2).

Most scholars agree that, while it has been effective with some notable exceptions such as Hurricane Katrina, U.S. disaster policy still needs strengthening and reform.[30] They note that emergency management institutions have been weakened in the aftermath of the 9/11 terrorist attack on New York City by the rush to concentrate on terrorism, rather than on natural hazards. Rebuilding capacity will require new federal, state, and local policies, plans, and actions to further improve a relatively robust natural-hazard mitigation capability.

Unfortunately, no similar widespread awareness or action planning is yet in place to increase U.S. resilience in the face of climate change. This serious vacuum results from a lack of clear nationwide leadership, standards, and funding. The U.S. federal government has not enacted a significant law to deal with the impacts of climate change on urban areas. To fill this vacuum, a number of states are beginning to develop climate action plans, but most are stated in general terms and fail to provide adequate funding or specific requirements.[31] The California state program, a leader, has been discussed here, but most other states lag well behind. Moreover, most of the present programs focus on mitigating greenhouse gases, but do not deal with the need for cities to adapt to climate-change impacts. However, there is a workable template for adaptation guidelines to be found in the smart-development movement, led by the design profession under the banner of New Urbanism.[32]

Smart development draws together concerns for creating sustainable and livable cities that respond to twenty-first-century challenges. As the statement from a 2008 urban design conference summed up:

> Changing climate patterns and diminishing supplies of inexpensive oil require us to design our cities in radically different ways. Reducing energy usage and carbon emissions is necessary to limit global warming, address severe weather events and rising sea levels, and face the threats of reduction of food production, loss of biodiversity, and dependence on unreliable energy supplies.[33]

As compared with natural-hazard mitigation governmental programs, which are focused on management, smart-development efforts focus on urban design, calling on architects, planners, landscape architects, and developers to incorporate green features and sustainable structures in their plans for buildings and neighborhoods. The result is to expand on and broaden the concept of sustainable development, generally seen as balancing the needs of economic development, environmental preservation, and social equity—the three "e's."

For the past two decades, the concept of sustainable development has been defined by the Brundtland Report as "development that meets the needs of today without compromising the ability of future generations to meet their own needs."[34] However, Janis Birkeland challenges this definition as based on the simplistic idea that negative impacts and trade-offs are necessary accompaniments of economic growth--a vicious circle.[35] The Brundtland Report assumed that sustainability was simply industrial growth with fewer impacts, marginalizing ecology and framing sustainability as resource efficiency and equitable distribution. Birkeland advocates a radical new concept of sustainable design in which cities and buildings are eco-productive and socially satisfying as well as eco-efficient. Under her Positive Development model, cities would *increase* the earth's ecological health, habitats, and carrying capacity through renaturalizing the built environment—a "virtuous circle." Designers would create cities that offer greater life quality, health, amenities, and safety for all without sacrificing resources or money, increasing both the public estate and the ecological base. Through both new development and eco-retrofitting of existing urban areas, cities would become generators of sustainability, rather than consumers of resources, judged not only by the degree to which they generate zero waste but also the amount that they contribute to net positive outcomes. Some heartening evidence that the concept of net positive development is taking hold can be found in designs for buildings and neighborhoods that contribute power to the grid, restore the natural functions of wetlands and aquifers, and generate jobs and wealth enhancement for poor and minority residents. While still very limited, this approach could be one harbinger of the future resilient city.

4. Conclusions: Lessons for Resilience and Directions for Research

What does history tell us about urban resilience in the face of past disasters? What are the implications for future resilient cities threatened by climate change, as well as peak oil and population growth, of the U.S. experience with natural-hazard mitigation? What are the implications from the literature on urban design and sustainable development? We conclude with some summary thoughts on overall lessons for resilience and adaptation and on future directions for resilience research and scholarship.

Lesson 1. History reveals that cities have an extraordinary capacity for rebounding from major disasters, and in the modern era, virtually no major city has been permanently lost or abandoned in the wake of catastrophe. On the other hand, contemporary cities and metropolitan regions face challenges that our ancestors could hardly have imagined. The cold-war threat of atomic annihilation may be gone, but we now have the specter of rogue nuclear weapons and "dirty bombs" in the hands of terrorists. Fast-mutating new viruses like SARS and swine flu have already threatened our cities with pandemic disease, and they could turn world cities like Hong Kong, Guangzhou, and Mexico City into ghost towns. The permeable borders of our global village assure the rapid diffusion of contagious disease. Unprecedented immigration and population growth, the threat of climate change and sea level rise, and the coming end of cheap oil also threaten the world's cities in new and troubling ways.

Lesson 2. The United States has developed the world's most robust and systematic governmental policy framework for anticipating and responding to natural hazards—the predominant twentieth-century threat to urban resilience. In its present form, however, this framework is inadequate to cope with the forecast impacts of climate change, peak oil, and other major twenty-first century threats. Still, its approach to nationwide *predisaster planning* provides a model for other countries and cities around the world. This model combines knowledge generated by scientific risk analysis with actions designed to build social, environmental, and economic resilience in advance of probable threats. It implements the resulting plans through a combination of governmental requirements and incentives, as well as organizational and individual activities. Worldwide efforts to set limits on carbon emissions provide one example of the necessary planetary scope of future efforts; more aggressive positive urban development policies and programs will be needed at the scale of metropolitan regions.

Lesson 3. Smart planning and development, geared to national, regional, and local contexts, are critical to achieving future resilient cities. Smart development in the Global North will differ from that in the Global South, owing to different demands and capabilities. But the essential elements are similar: (1) careful analysis of potential future risks; (2) widespread communication of mitigation and adaptation guidelines; (3) agreement on region-wide standards for positive development; (4) creation of resilient development plans that knit together social, environmental, and economic actions; and (5) forceful program implementation backed up by real-time outcome monitoring. Achieving true resiliency will demand significant levels of investment, as well as significant behavioral changes. Land use and physical planning and design, environmental conservation programs, and economic development initiatives must generate net positive returns in order to counter the negative impacts of future threats.

Given these broad conclusions, what are the relevant questions for tomorrow's resilience researchers? In this current age of uncertainty about not only the scientific projections of climate change but also the efficacy of planning responses, careful, continuing research will play a critical role in bringing evidence to the often roiling debates over what is actually happening and what we should do about it. This turbulent situation presents an unprecedented opportunity for research contributions to our understanding about the effectiveness of new planning strategies, the promise of new theoretical paradigms, and the need for new planning roles. While debates over the reality of climate change and the impact of human activities on it undoubtedly will continue,[36] we suggest that planning researchers focus on topics where their expertise gives them an advantage in framing and analyzing the issues central to planning theory and practice. Here are some recommendations:

New Planning and Implementation Strategies. At the federal level, climate change response is in gridlock.[37] State and local responses to climate change range from disappointingly deliberate (e.g., sea level rise) to promisingly proactive (e.g., reducing greenhouse gas emissions), depending on the difficulty of mitigation and adaptation involved.[38] The present status is difficult to grasp because there are lots of initiative scattered over many jurisdictions. Research is needed to categorize the various strategies into credible typologies and to analyze their effectiveness. In order to derive comparative findings, it will be important to agree on standardized indicators of feasibility (political, economic, engineering, etc.), equity, and sustainability of outputs, and outcomes. Researchers, such as Adam Rose,[39] are beginning to analyze the economic implications of proposed solutions, but there remains much work to be done in the areas of land use, transportation, housing, and environmental management.

New Planning Theory Paradigms. Some authors believe that responding to climate change demands a new planning paradigm. Given the long time horizons and wide bands of uncertainty in climate change projections, they argue for an incremental approach informed by continuous monitoring of both scientific findings and observable trends. For example, Ray Quay has called for "anticipatory governance" based on a flexible decision framework that uses a range of possible futures to guide decisions and prepare for change.[40] Others cite the use of modeling tools, coupled with citizen workshops, to create future land-use scenarios and to evaluate their effectiveness in reducing greenhouse gas emissions, as a way to build the community consensus necessary for behavior change.[41] Community-based research and case studies are needed to explore the theoretical implications of the new practices.

New Planning Roles. Planners need to become more activist in order to lead communities toward resilient futures. The traditional role of planners as visionary advocates of desirable futures has been eclipsed by their responsibilities as bureaucrats in governmental systems. Creativity has been submerged in the day-to-day operations of permit processing, zoning changes, and subdivision approvals. Success as a bureaucrat is too often measured in terms of job security, particularly in times of political conflict. The new planners will need to be consensus builders, but they will also need to be leaders in interpreting and acting on the stability-shattering changes their communities are expected to face. Research on municipal climate action plans suggests that planning departments so far have played a minor role in their development.[42] New research is needed to identify the successes of innovative and activist planning roles.

The bottom line is this: *urban resiliency is an urgent matter.* Planning must adapt to an era of fierce volatility in which the old assumptions of stable social, economic, and environmental systems no longer hold. The questions are critical. Can cities weather the impacts of climate change? Can we create effective institutions and planning approaches to respond to the threats ahead? Can smart-development approaches be implemented on a global basis? We are at a historic juncture and the answers matter greatly.

NOTES

1. See, for example, David Grann, "The Lost City of Z," *The New Yorker,* September 19, 2005.

2. Jared Diamond, *Collapse: How Societies Chose to Fail or Succeed* (New York: Viking, 2005).

3. Lawrence J. Vale and Thomas J. Campanella, eds., *The Resilient City: How Modern Cities Recover from Disaster* (New York: Oxford University Press, 2005), 335–337, 347.

4. David S. Cecelski and Timothy B. Tyson, eds., *Democracy Betrayed: The Wilmington Race Riot of 1898 and Its Legacy* (Chapel Hill: University of North Carolina Press, 1998), 16–20, 37–39.

5. Julie B. Kirschbaum and Desirée Sideroff, "A Delayed Healing: Understanding the Fragmented Resilience of Gernika," in *The Resilient City: How Modern Cities Recover from Diaster* (New York: OUP, 2005) 159–76.

6. James Heartfield, "Revisiting the Blitz Spirit." Available at: http://www.spiked-online.com/index.php/site/article/869/.

7. Beatrice Chen, "'Resist the Earthquake and Rescue Ourselves': The Reconstruction of Tangshan after the 1976 Earthquake," in *The Resilient City: How Modern Cities Recover from Disaster* (New York: OUP, 2005) 235–53.

8. Diane E. Davis, "Reverberations: Mexico City's 1985 Earthquake and the Transformation of the Capital," in *The Resilient City: How Modern Cities Recover from Disaster* (New York: OUP, 2005) 261–72.

9. As one man put it, "My mother walked from North Vietnam to South Vietnam pregnant with my sister in 1954 when the communists forced the French out of the north. She fled communism to get to freedom and freedom of religion. My parents fled South Vietnam in 1976 to get to America, the land of freedom, freedom of choice, and freedom of religion. My parents are gone now but after Hurricane Katrina we had but one option: to rebuild without complaint. The government would never have saved us as well as we could save ourselves." Quoted in John E. Carey, "The Unspeakable Truth: Katrina, New Orleans and Culture," *Peace and Freedom,* August 30, 2007.

10. Christine Hauser, "Sustained by Close Ties, Vietnamese Toil to Rebuild," *New York Times,* October 20, 2005.

11. Susan Page, "Evacuees Shun Going Home," *USAToday,* October 13, 2005.

12. Robert B. Olshansky, Laurie A. Johnson, Jedidiah Home, and Brendan Nee, "Planning for the Rebuilding of New Orleans," *Journal of the American Planning Association* 74, no. 3 (Summer 2008): 273. For a more detailed account, see Robert B. Olshansky and Laurie A. Johnson, *Clear as Mud: Planning for the Rebuilding of New Orleans* (Chicago: APA Planners Press, 2010).

13. Ibid., 274, 279, 284.

14. Ibid., 274.

15. For a comprehensive summary of anticipated impacts, see Thomas R. Karl, Jerry M. Melillo, and Thomas C. Peterson, eds. *Global Climate Change Impacts in the United State* (New York: Cambridge University Press, 2009).

16. Cited in Neal R. Pierce and Curtis W. Johnson, with Farley M. Peters, *Century of the City: No Time to Lose* (New York: Rockefeller Foundation, 2008), 106.

17. Cited in Thomas L. Friedman, *Hot, Flat, and Crowded: Why We Need a Green Revolution and How It Can Renew America* (New York: Farrar, Straus and Giroux, 2008), p. 28.

18. Cited in Peter Newman, Timothy Beatley, and Heather Boyer, *Resilient Cities: Responding to Peak Oil and Climate Change* (Washington, DC: Island Press, 2009), 22.

19. See the types of potential measures discussed in David R. Godschalk, "Mitigation," chapter 6 in W. L. Waugh Jr. and K. Tierney, eds., *Emergency Management: Principles and Practice for Local Government* (Washington, DC: ICMA Press, 2007).

20. See Neal R. Pierce and Curtis W. Johnson, with Farley M. Peters, *Century of the City: No Time to Lose* (New York: Rockefeller Foundation, 2008), chapter 3, "Climate Change Resilience: An Urgent Action Agenda."

21. See David R. Godschalk, "Urban Hazard Mitigation: Creating Resilient Cities," *Natural Hazards Review*, August 2003, 136–43. See also D. R. Godschalk, A. Rose, E. Mittler, K. Porter, and C.T. West, "Estimating the Value of Foresight: Aggregate Analysis of Natural Hazard Mitigation Benefits and Costs," *Journal of Environmental Planning and Management* 52, no.6 (September 2009): 739–56.

22. Pierce and Johnson, *Century of the City*, 119.

23. Waugh and Tierney, "Emergency Management."

24. J. Schwab, K. C. Topping, C. C. Eadie, R. E. Deyle, and R. A. Smith, *Planning for Post-Disaster Recovery and Reconstruction*, PAS Report 483/484 (Chicago: American Planning Association, 1998).

25. Godschalk et al., "Estimating the Value of Foresight."

26. Multihazard Mitigation Council (MMC) of the National Institute of Building Sciences (NIBS), *Natural Hazard Mitigation Saves: An Independent Study to Assess the Future Savings from Mitigation Activities* (Washington, DC: NIBS, 2005).

27. See R. E. Deyle, T. S. Chapin, and E. J. Baker, "The Proof of the Planning Is in the Platting: An Evaluation of Florida's Hurricane Exposure Mitigation Planning Mandate," *Journal of the American Planning Association* 74, no. 3 (2008): 349–70; P. R. Berke, D. J. Roenigk, E. J. Kaiser, and R. J. Burby, "Enhancing Plan Quality: Evaluating the Role of State Planning Mandates for Natural Hazard Mitigation," *Journal of Environmental Planning and Management* 37, no. 2 (2006): 155–169; S. D. Brody, "Are We Learning to Make Better Plans? A Longitudinal Analysis of Plan Quality Associated with Natural Hazards," *Journal of Planning Education and Research* 23, no. 2 (2003): 191–201; R. J. Burby and L. C. Dalton, "Plans Can Matter! The Role of Land Use Plans and State Planning Mandates in Limiting the Development of Hazardous Areas," *Public Administration Review* 54, no. 3 (1998): 229–38; A. Nelson and S. French, "Plan Quality and Mitigating Damage from Natural Disasters: A Case Study of the Northridge Earthquake with Planning Policy Considerations," *Journal of the American Planning Association* 68, no. 2 (2002): 194–207.

28. P. J. May and R. J. Burby, "Coercive versus Cooperative Policies: Comparing Intergovernmental Mandate Performance," *Journal of Policy Analysis and Management* 15, no. 2 (1996): 171–201.

29. S. D. Brody, D. R. Godschalk, and R. J. Burby, "Mandating Citizen Participation in Plan-Making: Six Strategic Planning Choices," *Journal of the American Planning Association* 69, no. 3 (2003): 245–64; and D. R. Godschalk, S. D. Brody, and R. J. Burby, "Public Participation in Natural Hazard Policy Formation: Challenges for Comprehensive Planning," *Environmental Planning and Management* 46, no. 5 (2003): 733–54.

30. See, for example, R. T. Sylves, *Disaster Policy and Politics: Emergency Management and Homeland Security* (Washington, DC: CQ Press, 2008); K. J. Tierney, "Testimony on Needed Emergency Management Reforms," *Journal of Homeland Security and Emergency Management* 4, no. 3 (2007); and David R. Godschalk, Timothy Beatley,

Philip Berke, David J. Brower, and Edward J. Kaiser, *Natural Hazard Mitigation: Recasting Disaster Policy and Planning* (Washington, DC: Island Press. 1999).

31. For an overview of state and local climate action plans, see the EPA climate change Web site, http://www.epa.gov/statelocalclimate/; accessed November 22, 2011. See also the Pew Trust Center on Global Climate Change, http://www.pewclimate.org/; accessed December 20, 2008.

32. See the Web site of the Congress for the New Urbanism, www.cnu.org.

33. Symposium on Re-Imagining Cities: Urban Design After the Age of Oil, Symposium, University of Pennsylvania, Philadelphia, November 6–8, 2008. http://penniur.upenn.edu/research/initiatives/re-imagining-cities; accessed November 22, 2011.

34. World Commission on Environment and Development, Report of the Brundtland Commission, *Our Common Future* (Oxford: Oxford University Press, 1987).

35. Janis Birkeland, *From Vicious Circles to Virtuous Cycles Through Built Environment Design* (London: Earthscan, 2008).

36. Although the overwhelming predominance of scientific opinion is clear that warming is occurring and that it is influenced by human activities, discussion of these issues is ongoing. See, for example, the Web sites, http://www.climatedebatedaily.com, and http://en.wikipedia.org/wiki/Global_Warming. For a planning oriented view, see Randall Crane and John Landis, "Planning for Climate Change: Assessing Progress and Challenges," *Journal of the American Planning Association* 76, no. 4 (2010): 389–401.

37. See Ryan Lizza, "As the World Burns: How the Senate and the White House Missed Their Best Chance to Deal with Climate Change," *The New Yorker*, October 11, 2010, 70–83.

38. As of 2010, only a handful of local governments in California and Maryland have developed plans to adapt to sea level rise, while scores of localities (such as Chicago, whose Climate Action Plan contains 452 action steps) have developed proactive climate action plans.

39. Adam Rose, *The Economics of Climate Change Policy: International, National and Regional Mitigation Strategies* (Northampton, MA: Edward Elgar, 2009).

40. Ray Quay, "Anticipatory Governance: A Toll for Climate Change Adaptation," *Journal of the American Planning Association* 76, no. 4 (2010): 496–511.

41. See Patrick Condon, Duncan Cavens, and Nicole Miller, *Urban Planning Tools for Climate Change Mitigation* (Cambridge, MA: Lincoln Institute of Land Policy, 2009).

42. Ellen Bassett and Vivek Shandas, "Innovation and Climate Action Planning: Perspectives from Municipal Plans," *Journal of the American Planning Association* 76, no. 4 (2010): 435–50.

PART III

HOW AND WHAT DO WE PLAN? THE MEANS AND MODES OF PLANNING

A. PLAN MAKING

CHAPTER 13

....

MAKING PLANS

....

CHARLES HOCH

1. INTRODUCTION

....

IN this chapter I will argue that urban planners learn to make plans by studying plans and how they are made. Professional planners use explicit principles
and norms to form and guide the formal theory or method of plan-making.
I roughly cluster these traditions into two domains of plan-making craft: design
artistry and scientific competence. Professionals also draw upon cultural inheri-
tance, personal experience, and communication with others to identify the relevance and meaning of the values that inform their plans These features tap a tacit
and widespread human cognitive capacity that I nickname "small 'p' planning."
I argue that conceptions of professional plan making that recognize this resource
avoid exaggerated and exclusive expertise.

The historical roots of the planning profession included the collaborative
efforts of architects, landscape architects, and civil engineers making plans to beau-
tify industrial urban centers with public parks, plazas, and civic centers, as well
as transport plans to alleviate traffic congestion using roadway and rail improvements. The collaboration was necessary because the objects for the plans—cities
and regions—do not possess the limits of a building or surrounding landscape
where physical design enjoins blueprints to guide future construction. Second,
they are composed at the broad scale of the municipality or district, where diverse
sponsorship requires attention to complex and often conflicting conceptions for
the future appearance and use of urban space. These challenges remain today, even
as urban design analysts offer an astonishing array of principles to guide future
development (Lynch 1981; Alexander et al. 1987; Calthorpe 1993, Van der Ryn and
Cowan 1996; Carmora et al. 2003; Gindroz et al. 2003; Barnett 2003; Lang 2005).

Professional practitioners of the engineering and social sciences adopted analytical concepts and tools to city plan making. On the one hand, scientific analysis offers predictability and control through the precise application of methodical
analysis and evaluation—for instance, demographic analysis to estimate population change for local places (Myers 1992). On the other hand, science relies on
the tolerance, patience, doubt, and prudence of a community of analysts testing
hunches about the patterns and causes of urban change (Latour 1988). Hope that
scientific prediction might enable improved urban control has proved elusive and
even misguided. Many technical and physical features of urban construction and
infrastructure benefit from scientific precision, but the lessons of scientific collaboration and the discipline of joint inquiry currently animate plan making.
Ironically, the rational planning model promulgated optimistically in the 1950s
(Black 1990) continues to invite criticism even as plan makers still adapt sets of scientific tools to conceive and test plan beliefs and proposals (Hopkins 2001; Berke
and Godschalk 2006; Hoch, So, and Dalton 2000; Healy et al. 1997).

Professional planners employ knowledge that combines design and science
to represent select urban relationships as images, descriptions, narratives, arguments, and models that sponsors and clients can use to comprehend the relationship between purpose and context, comparing alternative futures. The interests
and hopes of the sponsors and clients shape plan-making design and analysis in
ways that defy easy summary. In this chapter, I frame current professional plan
making as a kind of practical judgment. Instead of designing attractive places as
architects do or analyzing predictable urban patterns as social scientists do, professional planners compose future settlements using the evidence of science to inform
and tame imaginative designs about future alternatives. These plans inform the
intentions people hold about the future of a settlement—intentions susceptible to
deliberate persuasive change.

How do we combine knowledge from such different domains? I believe we rely
on practical reasoning and judgment (Hoch 2002, 2007). Professional plan making taps the resources of practical judgment to represent and interpret the relationships among sponsorship, clientele, and the professional interplay of artistic
and scientific composition. Here, the conventional amateur arts of speaking, writing, enumerating, and visualizing provide the scaffolding for composing plans.
Professional training and practice applies more specialized knowledge and skills to
this scaffold, improving the validity, resiliency, and relevance of the plan making
craft that it supports. This conception of professional planning presumes that most
people already know how to make plans, but that professionals learn to improve
this skill and put it to use advising diverse audiences of stakeholders how to
anticipate and prepare for future urban change (Hoch 1994).

How do we combine design arts and scientific analysis to improve the quality
of the composition activity used to make urban plans?[1] We all learn to plan reflectively as we acquire and use language to shape our futures with others. We plan
outings, meetings, and gatherings. We anticipate and coordinate where to pitch
a tent, hold a meeting, or otherwise keep a promise in diverse social contexts and

settings. We use plans to turn desires and preferences into practical commitments that we can follow until we lose interest, conditions change, or a satisfactory outcome ensues.

We should not confuse plan making with desires that fuel goals or decisions that turn goals into action. Plan making offers counsel between desire and decision. Plans include deliberate reflection about what to do, but do not compel or otherwise require decisions or choices. Plans inform intentions. As such, they may be ignored, dropped, revised, amended, or even adopted to help fit goals to context, purpose to place, means to an end, or some other purpose-laden situation that allows forethought and anticipation.

What happens when we face conflicting desires and goals? How do we create personal plans when we find ourselves facing competing attractions? We need to reconcile goal diversity; otherwise, any planning effort will fail at the outset. There are two considerations. First, planning does not resolve differences in basic desires or commitments to antagonistic goals. Plans do not motivate, they mediate. Planning can reconcile differences among competing interpretations about the relevance and meaning of current desires and goals—as long as these interpretations remain open to such reconsideration because the plan audience has yet to make a commitment to any one or combination. As we deliberate with ourselves or others about different plans, we offer advice about imagined future outcomes and effects. We may anticipate risky and uncertain threats to desires and goals, and we see what differences these might make for different situations. We may project disruptions to familiar institutions or practices, and assess future effects in seeking and reaching disparate goals.

Second, as we represent future situations and outcomes, we use knowledge to help us create and compare different goal-choice sets. We may review the quality and meaning of competing desires and goals, as well as prepare more useful and valid plans to judge imagined effects. Often, we deliberate with others and use the knowledge we acquire together to adjust how we coordinate our trajectories for the future. Plan-making knowledge includes comprehension of diverse purposes, using ideas about urban change to form and assess these trajectories.

The chapter draws upon the research and insights of cognitive science to construct a naturalistic account of planning (Mumford, Schultz, and Van Doorn 2001). This naturalistic account sidesteps the expectations associated with rational decision making. Instead of seeking a theoretical foundation to support how professionals make plans, we need to pay more attention to studying and describing how we plan. We develop theoretical ideas within the context of practical inquiry. From this viewpoint, we always meet the practical demands for planning before we tackle the epistemic demands of rationality. We may plan well even as our plans do not meet the standards of rationality. Instead of treating Herbert Simon's concept of "satisficing" as a poor version of rationality, we may instead consider it as a prerequisite for practical judgment (Simon 1957; Gigerenzer 2000). So, as professional planners turn their attention to order complex urban relationships, I argue that they use craft to filter and assimilate knowledge obtained by design and scientific disciplines.

2. Plan-Making Goals

Planners compose and present combinations of goals demonstrating how selecting one or another will yield a different outcome. Plan makers frequently overlook this aspect of goal setting and problem framing. Selecting and comparing goal sets includes constructing a frame of reference and specific measures to describe relevant change across space and over time. The plan maker considers the desires, needs, and goals of the sponsor and client to frame intentions that focus on only a limited portion of the complex relationships that compose a neighborhood or a city.

These comparisons introduce provisional concepts used to imagine the plausible effects of a specific imagined or simulated future tied to a unique combination of current beliefs and goals. Urban plans cannot offload the back and forth of revision without ignoring complex interactions. The meaning of traffic congestion, water conservation, and park location may begin with options that project current standards, but iterative comparisons of different goals and beliefs yield different effects for the future.

As we make plans for an urban district, an institution, or a region, we comprehend the relevance of the goals that fuel interest and involvement with the plan by drawing comparisons that inform judgments about the meanings and importance of these goals. Many of the goals may exclude one another. For example, congestion relief from increased transit use accompanies a reduction in trip-chaining convenience. Tax relief for homeowners means less revenue for park district expansion. Other goals may complement one another, as when roadway improvements increase access to retail business, enhance the flow of through traffic, and encourage private investment in adjacent property. The more clearly, thoroughly, and fairly plan makers conduct this assessment, the more those involved will understand the meaning of the plan. In this sense, value judgments give focus and meaning to plans, even as they make the plan more politically relevant.

A plan anticipates building a joint intention toward the future. This means that stakeholders of a plan expect it may help them decide what action to take toward the future. The plan provides a tool for interpreting the meaning of distant and expansive goals in terms of intermediate steps. The client may change the goals and the plan as people, conditions, or their interactions change; plans must be provisional, otherwise they could not offer practical guidance of this sort. Finally, there may, and will likely, exist many plans for the same settlement or place.

Urban planners taught to value comprehensive planning may confuse breadth of practical relevance and scope with a unitary or exclusive authority (Kelly, Becker, and So 1999). Critics of urban planners and planning who complain that plans do not include implementation authority misconstrue how plans work. Plans persuade people to act by informing their intentions, whether as public officials, community organizers, homeowners, activists, investors, or builders. These actions may fail or succeed in accomplishing the purposes of the plan. If people follow the plan, it worked. If ensuing consequences produce a disaster, then a review might find that the plan offered bad advice (Hall 1982). But it may also be that other personal or institutional failures contributed to the disaster (Dormer 1997). And plans may be good even if the immediate consequences prove unimpressive (Petroski 2007; see also Hopkins, this volume).

Often, critics of urban plan making will cynically dismiss the effort and its product as a pointless and wasteful exercise. This may prove a legitimate criticism if the people involved (including professional planners) do not sincerely, truthfully, competently, and legitimately work together to foster commitment to the plan (Forester 1989). But it may be a dismissive attack by those who hope to obtain their purposes without attending to the purposes of others (Flyvberg 1998). Other times, people have learned one scheme for resolving certain problems that fits their organizational or community context, and they do not want to consider another option. Their commitment to a strategy or plan makes it difficult to consider a plan that might encompass other desires and goals (Innes and Booher 1999a). There are many reasons not to plan. Planners need to understand these reasons in order to anticipate and prepare for criticism.

3. Plan-Making Knowledge

When we make "small 'p' plans," we rely upon our common sense knowledge of the world, for example, to map out a travel route for an efficient commute home, draw up a shopping list for a trip to the supermarket, or prepare a recipe for a meal. If explored carefully enough, however, even these "simple" activities prove more complex than we presume. Human evolution has selectively favored "small 'p' planning" aptitude (Mithen 1996; Seabright 2004; Arp 2008). The tacit cognitive planning skill that we take for granted becomes obvious when we suffer physical damage that immobilizes motor skills or brain capacity. Putting things in order and then following the order we make relies upon an extraordinary set of complex hard-wired processes. Physical therapists create detailed plans for helping injured people learn how to recover their "common sense" judgment about balance, distance, grasping, and the like after the trauma of an accident or the ravages of a serious illness, thereby regaining the use of a previously "automatic" plan-making capacity.

When we make urban plans, we cannot rely directly on the intuitive sensibility of our own bodies but must turn, instead, to the complex mediation of social and institutional relationships. We may borrow ideas and experiences from individual plan making to inform how we make these plans, but our intuitions cannot grasp the institutional and organizational complexity of modern urban societies. We must rely upon representations created jointly or by others. For instance, we create organizational models to map out relationships of influence and responsibility.

By the middle of the twentieth century, the creation of planning commissions and departments as units of municipal and county government in the United States offered organizational vehicles for plan making. As urban renewal, public housing, water quality, economic development, environmental conservation, and a host of publicly fostered improvement policies obtained popular support, the institutional relationships needed to organize and manage the pursuit of these policies grew as well. Making plans offered a way to coherently comprehend and order these efforts.

Urban planning relies on representations of what people believe and do in interactive settings across scale (from the block to the region). Planners use different forms of inquiry combining social and environmental science, design arts, and theoretical and moral reflection to observe, compose, analyze, and justify representations of these settings. These modes of inquiry and associated vocabularies each focus attention on a portion of these relationships.

When professional planners represent urban change, they selectively frame and organize different representations used to order these shifting relationships based on the purpose of the plan. This relevance criterion helps guide the use of different disciplinary concepts and tools. The purpose often includes multiple interests and goals, some explicitly presented while others less so. When two individuals set a time to meet and discuss a contract, they select a time and place to come together, evoking for one another a common frame of reference that usually is based on familiar memories: "Let's meet at Jena's Grill." The terms of the contract discussion may involve a different, less tacit process, as the demands of the agreement require preparation and study; the ensuing results remain elusive and unsettled, open to deliberation. Casting the same distinctions at the large scale, we can imagine institutional and organizational arrangements framing the context where the partners to a plan (professionals, sponsors, and clients) meet and deliberate. The different institutional steps taken to develop an inchoate desire or interest into a plan produce a plan-making process that organizes the information used to conceive the plan. Robert Walker (1941), an urban planning reform proponent, argued against the segmenting of planning into a functional bureaucratic slot, and argued for its location as an activity sponsored by the local government executive to coordinate and guide the deployment and organization of specialized services. Later critics point out the limits of centralization and offer instead institutional designs that foster more democratic forms of deliberation (Innes and Booher 1999b).

The ensuing viewpoints, unlike the intention-building features of communication and participation among stakeholders, shape the symbolic products used to describe and analyze the change. For instance, census tract boundaries describe the enumeration districts used to aggregate the household information obtained at the ten-year survey. But plan makers use the census tract to represent a neighborhood, a traffic destination, a policy impact area, or something else relevant to a specific audience.

Professional planners draw upon two kinds of knowledge to organize the representation of urban complexity: theory and method. This distinction describes

the curriculum for planning education and encompasses a large portion of the
disciplines used to inform how planners represent urban change.

3.1 Theory

Theory includes the beliefs used to describe and analyze complex urban relationships. Planners use theory to answer questions about the reasons and causes for
urban order and change. In making a plan, planners compose these answers as
narratives, explanations, and arguments about changes in the pattern of urban
activity and form that provide the plot line for stories and models that then describe
and simulate alternative futures. Professional planners draw largely from theory
in the social sciences, engineering sciences, and design arts—theory that emerges
from different disciplines: economics, sociology, psychology, political science,
geography, anthropology, civil engineering, environmental engineering, architecture, landscape architecture, and urban design (Hoch, So, and Dalton 2000). The
theoretical knowledge that may prove useful for making plans often exceeds the
grasp of any one professional precisely because many different disciplines offer
relevant knowledge about order and change for distinct sets of urban relationships.
Transmitting the knowledge needed to make plans for complex urban settlement
accurately and reliably requires many professionals working together, combining
diverse theoretical insights to foster joint comprehension. This proves difficult to
do. Planners need be undisciplined enough to gather, sort, and combine disciplinary insights without insisting or imposing the norms of inquiry used to enforce the
boundaries of specialized inquiry. Theory holds out the promise of binding these
viewpoints together, but the varieties of theoretical discourse rarely enjoin consensus (Healey and Hillier 2008).[2]

Many theoretical ideas may inform plan making. The first planning professionals were architects and engineers who sought to remedy the social and economic
ills of industrial cities using major infrastructure projects and civic improvements
to impress order and beauty upon chaotic, ugly urban squalor (Scott 1969; Fairfield
1993). Later, the social sciences provided a crucial resource for professional urban
planners and their critics. The Regional Plan for New York provides perhaps the
earliest prototype for the region-wide comprehensive plan as conceiving territorial
order across a metropolitan landscape that combines economic, physical, social,
and legal ideas (Johnson 1996). Thereafter, the concentrated complexity of modern
cities inspired utilization of theories from many disciplines and fields. Ironically,
this wealth of knowledge about the many dimensions of change and order poses
a challenge for practical plan making. What disciplinary theory should guide the
interpretation of desire and need? If more than one, what combination merits
selection and use? Other chapters in this book provide insight into these different
approaches.

Some analysts argue that we need to turn to a distinct planning theory to guide
our choices. For instance, they argue for a rationality that systemically encompasses

the separate disciplines (Faludi 1986), justifies a particular social or economic theory (Blakely and Green Leigh 2010; Lewis 2003; Green and Haines 2007), or prescribes a certain kind of governance (Sager 2002; Healey et al. 1997). A pragmatic approach side steps this search for a theoretical foundation and conceives of plan making as a kind of practical judgment. The desires, needs, and purposes that animate these plans emerge from the pragmatic view as disruptions to meaningful patterns of continuity that give pause for reflection.

We begin plan making as we identify and describe the frustrated desires, unmet needs, and unclear goals for those people and organizations whose futures include imagined outcomes that might reconcile and resolve these ruptures. The accomplished urban planner draws upon knowledge from diverse disciplines and fields to make sense of a complex situation, whether it's a congested intersection, neighborhood displacement, flood hazard, or corrupt contracting. The pragmatist envisions the cognitive knowledge used to identify and describe problematic situations as a kind of toolkit (Briggs 2008).

3.2 Method

Theory and method complement one another. For example, economists use econometric models based on a specific theory of market demand to analyze housing choices and then use the results to build a model that might forecast future demand. In this way, the why and how of market changes complement one another.

Professional planners learn to use tools developed from the different sciences and design arts, too. These tools describe the aspects of urban relationships that planners believe are relevant for future change and susceptible to purposeful intervention. Professionals tend to specialize in some set of methods usually organized around topical clusters of urban relationships. For instance, a transportation planner might combine knowledge from civil engineering with knowledge from economics and environmental science to represent the value of complex environmental features tied to specific kinds of transportation improvements. The planner might consider using cost-benefit analysis or agent-based modeling to animate urban change (Kitchen 2007).

Methods need be tamed both by the relevance of the inquiry—the purpose guiding the plan—and the knowledge combination so as to offer practical advice about future actions. The planner needs be sure to use any disciplinary tool correctly, but avoid adopting (projecting) the disciplinary beliefs and standards where the tool works best. For instance, this might be adopting economic base analysis to project local impacts on municipal employment, using national park standards to estimate a shortfall in local park land requirements, or estimating future activity levels for a redevelopment site using trend analysis.

Theory and method include vast amounts of knowledge about urban relationships, but the conventions of inquiry for each cannot serve as the point of departure for plan making. The demands for adequate research, theoretical insight, or critical design within disciplinary traditions can keep someone from taking the first practical step in plan making. The demands of sponsors and clients holding different expectations for the future, and insisting on timely advice, provide the catalyst for plan making. Urban planners start with the practical desires and goals that focus public attention on a problem, making and offering practical advice that clients may use to consider alternative solutions. So, planners need to make sure that their representations offer relevant practical knowledge. Plan making works more like a craft than a science, more like an SUV than a sports car.

Composing an urban plan helps us move beyond the pointless seesaw of wish fulfillment on one side (if we just stick with goal-oriented fantasy) and causal inevitability on the other (if we stick with one concept of causal attribution about underlying urban complexity). Instead, we compose plans as we foster commitment to the plan among the relevant clients and create representations of urban complexity that offer alternatives that the clients can willingly and successfully use to assess the prospects for the future and modify current policy and practice. But how do planners compose relevant, valid, and useful advice?

4. Composing Plans

Plans order urban complexity in ways that inform the choices we make about current polices, practices, and behavior. The population projection, the economic forecast, the land-use suitability assessment, and other similar studies do not uncover the truth of the city, but they provide ordered relationships that plausibly frame future conditions—frames that rely on judgments combining future expectations, prior assumptions, and current observations. We compose these frames with specific audiences in mind. That is how planners can interpret the meaning of the goals and plausibly relate these goals to the contextual conditions of a specific situation. We do not make the plan for a universal, godlike audience but, rather, for specific audiences (Mandelbaum 2000). So, when we compose judgments that frame future conditions, we anticipate the responses and use these to modify our expectations, assumptions, and observations. The objectivity of our work flows from the quality of this composition rather than from any imagined capacity to form judgments exclusive of a specific audience. But how do we compose plans?

The model of inquiry that has a professional planner engaging in scientific or moral discovery in order to compose a plan will likely lead to trouble. The planner needs to approach the task with ideas about relevant futures already in mind, but with ideas that offer provisional sketches of future outcomes sensitive to a divergence of outlook and subject to modification and rejection. Planners offer alternatives to raise questions that help frame the problem and develop the contours for the plan that will include knowledge of urban relationships that can tame and channel unrealistic, misinformed, or mistaken beliefs about urban complexity.[3]

When we envision and imagine representations that describe future changes, and the outcomes these changes might produce, we adopt different orientations. These orientations combine client purpose and theoretical ideas into an integrated product. They include precedent, protocol, prototype, and policy. The orientations need not be mutually exclusive. People can combine orientations to improve the quality and depth of efforts to prepare a plan and to judge the quality of the plans they read. But for purposes of this analysis, I emphasize the differences, as follows:[4]

> *Precedent* looks backward to prior efforts whose authority proved useful and legitimate (prestigious or popular) in shaping plans. The framework tells its user to adapt the precedent to current conditions as a guide for projecting beliefs about future designed changes to these conditions (Heritage Plans).
>
> *Protocol* describes current "best practice" abstracted into plan-making rules, conventions, and guidelines that others should copy and adapt to new situations. The frame presumes little ambiguity and uncertainty across relevant urban locales to make copying useful and acceptable (State Planning Law).
>
> *Prototype* involves invention of new forms of representation that transpose ambiguous hopes and beliefs into plausible future visions or tools for constructing them. Prototypes go beyond trial-and-error increments to include imaginative scenarios. For instance, planning support visualization efforts do not simply illustrate a problem; they make possible conceptions of relationships previously difficult or even impossible to envision. These new simulations, models, projections, or images enable us to adapt old means to new ends, new means to old ends, or both (Myers 2001).
>
> *Policy* turns complex problems into complex action proposals that represent plausible options for the future.[5] The stakeholders agree about facts and causes, yet hold different expectations about future effects. The policy plan compares the meanings of alternative moral and political trajectories, seeking to test their contributions to these effects. Plans to end homelessness, remedy regional employment disparities, and ensure water conservation work in this fashion.

I will describe how each orientation interprets the complexity and ambiguity of purpose with concepts and ideas, thereby taming the uncertainty of future effects.

4.1 Precedent: Prior Experience in a Particular Context

When we begin a plan, we often start where others left off in earlier plan-making efforts, or we look to the efforts of others in trying to do a plan for a community that shares many characteristics with our own. Additionally, we may look to the precedents set by other professionals, firms, or groups with plan-making experience. For instance, the American Planning Association (APA) promotes "best practices" for different planning activities. These consist mainly of completed plans that have produced valued consequences. The meaning of the consequences flows from an attention to narrative details about the history of effects that accompanied similar efforts in the past.[6] This is what Seymour Mandelbaum (2000) describes as "story." But design and narrative overlap and interplay in plan making as human purposes transform space and time into place and journey.

Precedent proceeds inductively, starting with observation and attention to details and comparing across cases to uncover patterns of variation and association—difference and similarity, as these relate to specific change efforts. Designers often learn to conceive plans by analyzing how earlier plans worked in a specific place and time. What elements of form and fit might be carried forward in time and applied to a new place? These elements constitute the precedent that inspires current effort (Barnett 2003; Lang 2005). When we use precedent, we can still recognize the author in the authorization it provides for its user. We use elements of Olmstead's Central Park or Bernnini's Piazza Navonna. The 1909 Plan of Chicago used European precedent to describe residential and civic space for that industrial city's future.

As we combine these precedents, we consider how well prior analysis, tools, conceptions, and activities inform our beliefs and expectations about current relationships—those we select for attention and believe susceptible to change. Precedent emphasizes continuity with prior experience and action, using the past to explicitly reference a future organized in familiar and desirable terms.

4.2 Protocol: A Convention of Prior Inquiry

We usually do not start from scratch but, rather, by adapting an existing practice that other, more experienced (e.g., veteran) and more powerful (e.g., supervisor) planners have used to make plans. But there are many other, less sweeping protocols often embedded in specific institutional histories or regional occupational traditions. The protocol differs from precedent, in consisting of conventions, customs, rules, or principles. Some protocols may have stood the test of time, but others might be the product of recent consensus, legislative mandate, or judicial ruling (Brody 2003). Protocols often draw upon precedent, but the specific features of the precedent disappear. For instance, we adopt park standards or parkway standards as described in the ordinance, regulations, guidelines, or textbook, not by studying the original.

Protocols draw upon conceptual ideals, images, blueprints, or other sources for deductive insight. The most generic protocol is the framework for the rational plan (e.g., goals, analysis, alternatives, evaluation, implementation), the social science model emulating urban behaviors (e.g., transportation mode split model), or other abstract conceptions of order borrowed from current knowledge. This type represents a vast domain divided up by disciplinary specialization (e.g., economics, geography) and practical technique (cost-benefit analysis, geographic information systems). The textbook on land-use planning by Berke and Godschalk (1996) offers an excellent example.

Protocols have gained popular footing among planners because they encourage copying for ease of use. The protocol also complements the demands of modern institutional life, where consistency with regulatory rules or institutional conventions matches the predictable patterns and sequences of organizational activity (Dalton and Burby 1994). But often, planning problems demand attention to relationships and attributes that do not fit current practices. For instance, institutional conventions and personal habits work well because they resist change. So, we tend to use protocols for situations where we expect change to be modest and uncertainty to be low (Pendall 2001). Many plans look so much alike because their makers copied one another. This works until the rate of change accelerates or gets lumpy.

4.3 Prototypes: Innovations Linking New Ideas to Unfamiliar Contexts

We can make a plan to show others how new ideas make certain kinds of complexity legible, tractable, beautiful, and the like. Prototypes draw upon the knowledge of precedent and protocol, but they do not rely upon these sources for composing the plan. Utopian plans represent perhaps the strongest example of such prototypes; these are plans that include detailed descriptions of future designs and their expected effects, offering surprising, unfamiliar, and novel responses to urban change. For example, the super-block design for worker housing became a popular prototype for new town development in the twentieth century. Olmsted invented the urban pastoral landscape that profoundly shaped the organization and function of urban parks across the United States. Tax-increment financing was invented to get around public finance approval and was adapted over time into a redevelopment tool for guiding private investment. So, prototypes break with prior beliefs and provoke a critical yet practical revision of beliefs about an alternative for the future.

Designers and theorists compose an imagined product that demonstrates how a newly imagined design of physical arrangement, structural form, functional operation, institutional order, organizational process, or some other arena of the urban complex will provide a comprehensible order that tames complexity in a new way (McHarg 1969). The plan as prototype generates comprehension of how the future might appear after the new idea takes shape as imagined (Wheeler 2008). Often, prototypes emerge by mixing disciplinary insights in imaginative juxtapositions or combinations. The pragmatic conception of "abduction" best describes this activity: instead of offering inductive consistency or deductive coherence, the protocol uses plausible relevance to fit concept to task.

Prototypes can be tied to the rational comprehensive protocol, but they may also adopt or invent other protocols (e.g., adversarial, negotiated, brokered, etc.). Prototypes may be imagined and tested in the context of certain problem definitions. We might, for instance, cast a prototype as a scenario or a simulation of future urban features and relationships (Hopkins and Zapata 2007).

4.4 Policy: Solution Sets in Search of Problem Settings

We can make a plan by paying attention to the kinds of tools we know how to use and that have worked well in the past. We look in our toolkit seeking ideas for how to compose a response to complex urban relationships. Plan makers describe complex uncertainties using policy tools and solutions they trust. This counterintuitive yet widespread approach tends to emphasize beliefs about the efficacy of a method or tool. The more complex the urban setting, and the more diverse the audience, the greater the risk a methodical solution will not work.

Familiarity with a policy solution set such as knowledge of a protocol offers a consistent way to frame urban complexity for a plan. Scanning, selecting, and comparing different solutions offer a proactive way to anticipate and frame a response to specific aspects of urban complexity (McGahey and Vey 2008). For instance, we know how to improve the efficiency of local capital-improvement programs, so we focus on the economic problems facing infrastructure maintenance in a local municipality (Porter 2007). We know how to use tax increment finance (TIF) districts to stimulate local commercial reinvestment, so we focus attention on the property-tax revenue capacity of a local jurisdiction. In the strong instances, we might engage in a kind of reverse engineering: we identify a familiar set of future outcomes that we associate with the successful use of our planning tool, and then work backward through the tool's relevant features, framing the problem to fit with our beliefs about a solution (Mitchell 2008). A weaker version adopts the familiar tool as a kind of diagnostic device to provisionally frame possible solutions in ways that address aspects of local complexity (Arnott, Rave, and Schob 2005). Social scientists, engineers and architects often succumb to the temptation of taking a policy approach because their attachments to the discipline and its conventions blind them to those features of complexity that escape the grasp of the tools they know best (Dormer 1997; Petroski 2007).

The meaning and priority of an orientation depends on the practical situation the plan maker faces. The orientations describe the conduct of plan making and not the ideal types.

5. CONCLUSION

I have emphasized a conception of plan making in this chapter that purposely avoids longstanding debates about collective decision making and governance or about rationality and theoretical foundations. Treating plan making as a practical tool that informs intention means that we can understand how we do plans without having to settle theoretical disagreements about political agreement or rational expectations. These interesting and fruitful debates too often distract us from considering the many ways that plans work to translate desires into intentions that may, in turn, inspire us and others to act together in more or less rational ways.

At the very outset of the plan, as participants articulate their desires, needs, and goals, they set out their expectations of the future. For each of us, the future we know in the present inhabits an imagined world that we create. The planner draws upon knowledge from theory and method to inform the conversations, discussions, and debates that ensue at the very beginning of the plan-making effort. The planner constructs descriptions of the future based on that theory and prior experience, composing sketchlike futures that take account of stakeholder goals. These imaginary alternatives allow stakeholders to grasp the contours of difference that their views might make for varying versions of the future.

Plan-making composition does not challenge the purposes that people hold directly but, rather, seeks to describe the meaning of these diverse purposes within the context of complex relationships tied to relevant future consequences. The claims of precedent might shift over time to become a durable protocol. Innovative prototypes may be refined into precedents. Policy-relevant outlooks may pop up wherever and whenever practical solutions offer an opportunity for useful and coherent action guides.

The craft of plan making offers an important resource for those people and agencies taking responsibility for the future of urban settlements. Urban planners succeed if their sponsors and clients listen to the advice offered in a plan, and they celebrate if the clients take the advice to heart. It is too much to expect that clients will act upon the plan so as to obtain outcomes exactly as described, however. The metaphor of the architectural blueprint places too great a burden on the practice of urban planning. The complexity of changing expectations and urban relationships makes this unrealistic and undesirable. Plans do help people and organizations anticipate and adapt, not to predict and control. Learning to improve how we compose plans contributes to the quality of the judgments that people and institutions can make.

NOTES

1. Raphaël Fischler (2000) offers an excellent review of different conceptions of rational planning in a review of case studies: instrumental, interpretive, and practical. This chapter adopts a pragmatic conception of planning that steps around the rationality issue by insisting that the difference between what is learned from theory and practice is more a matter of degree than of kind. We do not need theory as a foundation, but as

a kind of conceptual critique that holds action accountable to the standards of science, morals, art, and any other important cultural norms.

2. While many people insist that planners be multidisciplined, this imposes an impractical demand on professionals. The time and effort needed to acquire disciplinary knowledge precludes any one individual's acquiring multiple disciplines. Professionals need to learn instead how to learn and adapt the knowledge of different disciplines as part of the practical judgment used to make plans. Hence, the term "undisciplined" focuses attention on the detachment needed to grasp the meaning of disciplinary ideas for purposes outside the discipline.

3. Planning is not "applied social science" precisely because the cognitive organization of planning knowledge includes practical expectations at the outset of inquiry. We can adapt knowledge from many different sources to make plans, but no one of these sources—even powerful scientific inquiry—adequately substitutes for planning judgment. How we conduct scientific research does not provide a model for how we conduct urban plan making.

4. There may be more than four, and these four may be more clearly distinguished than I am able to do at this time. I am trying to develop a vocabulary to help describe how people in complex institutional settings conceive the form and meaning of practical advice about an uncertain future. If we avoid the rational–irrational trap, then our attention shifts to the varieties of organized ways that people use.

5. I am self-consciously avoiding disciplinary distinctions here. We may acquire our academic expertise as historian, geographer, economist, engineer, architect, and so on. But these boundaries rarely play a prominent role in the practical art of plan making.

6. The "best practice" approach too often substitutes mimesis for irony, sacrificing the critical contextual details of historical narrative for relatively superficial similarities between past and present. Casting the debate between academic theory and practitioner practicality is not helpful, especially as those promoting this misleading stereotype want to convince practitioners that the particular version of practical best practice they are selling works everywhere with ease.

REFERENCES

Alexander, Christopher, Hajo Neis, Artemis Anninou, and Ingrid King, 1983. *A New Theory of Urban Design*. Centre for Environmental Structure Series vol. 6, New York: Oxford University Press.

Arnott, Richard, Tilmann Rave, and Ronnie Schob. 2005. *Alleviating Urban Traffic Congestion*. Cambridge, MA: MIT Press.

Arp, Robert. 2008. *Scenario Visualization: An Evolutionary Account of Creative Problem Solving*. Cambridge, MA: MIT Press.

Barnett, Johnathan. 2003. *Redesigning Cities: Principles, Practice Implementation*. Chicago: APA Planners Press.

Baum, Howell S. 1983. *Planners and Public Expectations*. Cambridge, MA: Schenkman.

Bennet, Edward, and Daniel Burnham. 1909. *The Plan of Chicago*. Chicago: The Commercial Club of Chicago.

Berke, Phillip, and David Godschalk. 2006 *Urban Land Use Planning*. Urbana, IL: University of Illinois Press.

Black, Alan. 1990. "The Chicago Area Transportation Study: A Case Study of Rational Planning." *Journal of Planning Education and Research* 10(1): 27–37.

Blakely, Edward, and Nancey Green Leigh. 2010. *Economic Development: Theory and Practice*. Thousand Oaks, CA: Sage.

Briggs, Xavier. 2008. *Democracy as Problem Solving: Civic Capacity in Communities across the Globe*. Cambridge, MA: MIT Press.

Calthorpe, Peter. 1993. *The Next American Metropolis: Ecology, Communities, and the American Dream*. New York: Princeton Architectural Press.

Carmora, Matthew, Tim Heath, Taner Oc, and Steve Tiesdell. 2003. *Public Places Urban Spaces: The Dimensions of Urban Design*. London: Elsevier.

Dalton, Linda. 1989. "Emerging Knowledge about Planning Practice." *Journal of Planning Education and Research* 9(1): 29–44.

Dalton, Linda, and Ray Burby. 1994. "Amandates, Plans and Planners: Building Local Commitment to Development Management." *Journal of the American Planning Association* 60(4): 444–61.

Dormer, Dietrich. 1997. *The Logic of Failure: Recognizing and Avoiding Error in Complex Situations*. Reading, MA: Addison-Wesley.

Fairfield, John D. 1993. *The Mysteries of the Great City: The Politics of Urban Design, 1877–1937*. Columbus, OH: Ohio State University Press.

Faludi, Andreas. 1986. *Critical Rationalism and Planning Methodology*. London: Routledge, Kegan and Paul.

Fischler, Raphaël. 2000. "Case Studies of Planners at Work." *Journal of Planning Literature* 15(2): 00–00.

Flyvbjerg, Bent. 1998. *Rationality and power*. Chicago: University of Chicago Press.

Forester, John. 1989. *Planning in the Face of Power*. Berkeley, CA: University of California Press.

Gigerenzer, Gird. 2000. *Adaptive Thinking: Rationality in the Real World*. New York: Oxford University Press.

Gindroz, Ray, Donald K. Carter, Paul Ostergaard, Rob Robinson, and Barry J. Long. 2003. *The Urban Design Handbook*. New York: W.W. Norton.

Green, Gary Paul, and Anna Haines. 2007. *Asset Building and Community Development*. Thousand Oaks, CA: Sage.

Hall, Peter. 1982. *Great Planning Disasters*. Berkeley, CA: University of California Press.

Healey, Patsy. 2007. *Urban Complexity and Spatial Strategies*. London: Routledge.

Healey, Patsy, A. Khakee, A. Motte, and B. Needham, eds. 1997. *Making Strategic Spatial Plans: Innovation in Europe*. London: UCL Press.

Hillier, Jean, and Patsy Healey. 2008. *Critical Essays in Planning Theory*, vols. 1–3. Hampshire, England: Ashgate.

Hoch, Charles. 1994. *What Planners Do: Power, Politics, and Persuasion*. Chicago: APA Planners Press.

Hoch, Charles. 2002. "Evaluating Plans Pragmatically." *Planning Theory* 1(1): 53–75.

Hoch, Charles. 2007. "Making Plans: Representation and Intention." *Planning Theory* 6(1): 15–35.

Hoch, Charles, Frank So, and Linda Dalton, eds. 2000. *The Practice of Local Government Planning*. Washington, DC: International City Managers Association.

Hopkins, Lew. 2001. *Urban Development: The Logic of Making Plans*. Washington, DC: Island Press.

Hopkins, Lew, and Marisa Zapata. 2007. *Engaging the Future: Forecasts, Scenarios, Plans and Projects*. Cambridge, MA: Lincoln Institute of Land Policy.

Innes, Judith, and David Booher. 1999a. "Consensus Building and Complex Adaptive Systems: A Framework for Evaluating Collaborative Planning." *Journal of the American Planning Association* 65(4): 412–23.

Innes, Judith, and David Booher. 1999b. "Metropolitan Development as a Complex System: A New Approach to Sustainability." *Economic Development Quarterly* 13(2): 141–56.

Johnson, David A. 1996. *Planning the Great Metropolis: The 1929 Regional Plan of New York and its Environs* London: Spon, Chapman & Hall.

Kelly, Eric Damien, Barbara Becker, and Frank So. 1999. *Community Planning: An Introduction to the Comprehensive Plan*. Washington, DC: Island Press.

Kitchen, Ted. 2007. *Skills for Planning Practice*. Houndmills, Basingstroke, UK: Palgrave MacMillan.

Lang, John. 2005. *Urban Design, A Typology of Procedures and Products*. London: Elsevier.

Latour, Bruno.1988. *Science in Action: How to Follow Scientists and Engineers through Society*. Cambridge, MA: Harvard University Press.

Lewis, W. Arthur. 2003. *Development Planning*. London: Routledge

Lynch, Kevin. 1981. *A Theory of Good City Form*. Cambridge, MA: MIT Press.

Mandelbaum, Seymour. 2000. *Open Moral Communities*. Cambridge, MA: MIT Press.

McGahey, Richard M., and Jennier S. Vey, eds., 2008. *Retooling for Growth: Building a 21st Century Economy in America's Older Industrial Areas*. Washington, DC: Brookings Institution Press.

McHarg, Ian. 1969. *Design with Nature*. Garden City, NY: Natural History Press.

Mitchell, Jerry. 2008. *Business Improvement Districts and the Shape of American Cities*. Albany, NY: State University of New York Press.

Mithen, Steven. 1996. *The Prehistory of the Mind: The Cognitive Origins of Art and Science*. London: Thames and Hudson.

Mumford, Michael D., Rosemary A. Schultz, and Judy R. Van Doorn. 2001. "Performance in Planning: Processes, Requirements, and Errors. *Review of General Psychology* 5(3): 213–40.

Myers, Dowell. 1992. *Analysis with Local Census Data: Portraits of Change*. Boston: Academic Press.

Myers, Dowell. 2001. "Symposium: Putting the Future in Planning." *Journal of the American Planning Association* 67(4): 365–67.

Pendall, Rolf. 2001. "Municipal Plans, State Mandates, and Property Rights: Lessons from Maine." *Journal of Planning Education and Research* 21:154–65.

Petroski, Henry. 2007. *Success Through Failure: The Paradox of Design*. Princeton, NJ: Princeton University Press.

Porter, Douglas. 2007. *Managing Growth in America's Communities*. Washington, DC: Island Press.

Sager, Tore. 2002. *Democratic Planning and Social Choice Dilemmas: Prelude to Institutional Planning Theory*. Hampshire, England: Ashgate.

Schön, Donald. 1983. *The Reflective Practitioner: How Professionals Think in Action*. New York: Basic Books.

Scott, Mel. 1969. *American City Planning Since 1890*. Berkeley, CA: University of California Press.

Seabright, Paul. 2004. *The Company of Strangers: A Natural History of Economic Life*. Princeton, NJ: Princeton University Press.

Simon, H. A. 1957. *Models of Man: Social and rational.* New York: John Wiley.

Van der Ryn, Sim, and Stuart Cowan. 1996. *Ecological Design.* Washington, DC: Island Press.

Walker, Robert. 1941. *Planning Function in Urban Government* Chicago: University of Chicago Press.

Wheeler, Stephen M. 2008. "State and Municipal Climate Change Plans: The First Generation." *Journal of the American Planning Association* 74(4): 481–96.

CHAPTER 14

CITIES, PEOPLE, AND PROCESSES AS PLANNING CASE STUDIES

EUGÉNIE L. BIRCH

Since urban planning focuses on creating communities of lasting value, the use of case studies to illustrate the various elements needed to achieve this goal comes naturally to many researchers. Whether looking at the finished product or the knowledge required to foster the public and private decision making for the desired outcome, case studies are an appropriate research strategy for this practice-based discipline. As with other clinical fields like medicine or law, advancing knowledge calls for laboratory work. While the human body (or an animal substitute) or a courtroom is the physician's or lawyer's lab, the city (or the urban environment) is the urban planner's lab. In these arenas, knowledge results from studies that translate to and from practice, adding to theory that, in turn, informs other studies and practice. The associated lab-based techniques for planners take many forms, ranging from statistical analysis of large databases to assessments of smaller units or cases. This research rarely encompasses controlled experiments requiring random assignment samples, but tends to engage in quasi-experimental or comparative projects, often case-based work.

The discussion that follows examines three topics. They are the nature of case-study research and its application to urban planning; patterns in the use of case-study research in urban planning; and some effects of case-study research on urban planning. Table 14.1, Some Examples of Case Study Research Arranged Chronologically by Type, serves as a guide to the numerous references in the text.

Table 14.1 Some Examples of Case Study Research Arranged Chronologically and by Type

Single Case (Single authors, holistic)	Multiple Case (Single authors, holistic)	Multiple Case (Single or multiple authors, embedded)	Multiple Case ("mini," Single authors)	Multiple Case (Edited)
	Meyerson and . Banfield (1995), Politics, Planning and Public Interest			
Gans (1959), Urban Villagers, Group and Class in Life of Italian Americans	Lewis (1959), Five Mexican Families, Case Studies on Culture of Poverty			
J. Jacobs (1961), Death and Life of Great American Cities	Glazer and Moynihan (1963), Beyond the Melting Pot, The Negroes, Puerto Ricans, Jews, Italians and Irish in New York City	Meyerson (1963), Face of the Metropolis		
Altshuler (1966), City Planning Process, A Political Analysis		Freiden (1964), The Future of Old Neighborhoods	Marris and Rein (1967), Dilemmas of Social Reform, Poverty and Community Action in United States	
Gans (1967), The Levittowners, Ways of Life and Politics in a New Suburban Community				
Suttles (1968), Social Order of the Slum, Ethnicity and Territory in the Inner City				

Rodwin (1969), *Planning Urban Growth and Regional Development: The Experience of the Guayana Program of Venezuela*	Lewis (1968), *La Vida, A Puerto Rican Family and the Culture of Poverty in San Juan and New York*	Hall (1966), *World Cities*	
Rainwater and Yancy (1967), *Moynihan Report and Politics of Controversy*			
Rainwater (1970), *Behind Ghetto Walls, Black Family Life in a Federal Slum*	Pressman and Wildavsky (1973), *Implementation, How Great Expectations in Washington Are Dashed in Oakland*		Bell and Tyrwhitt (1972), *Human Identity in the Urban Environment*
Newman (1972), *Defensible Space People and Design in Violent City*			
Caro (1974), *The Power Broker, Robert Moses and the Fall of New York*	Barnett (1974), *Urban Design as Public Policy, Practical Methods for Improving Cities*		Greer and Greer (1974), *Neighborhood and Ghetto, The Local Area in Large-Scale Society*

(Continued)

Table 14.1 (Continued)

Single Case (Single authors, holistic)	Single Case (Single authors, embedded)	Multiple Case (Single authors, holistic)	Multiple Case (Single or multiple authors, embedded)	Multiple Case ("mini", Single authors)	Multiple Case (Edited)
A. Jacobs (1978), Making City Planning Work					
Whyte (1980), Social Life of Small Urban Spaces		Hall (1980), Great Planning Disasters	Jamieson and Doig (1982), The Politics of Urban Regional Development		
		Garreau (1991), Edge City, Life on the New Frontier	Forester (1989), Planning in the Face of Power		
		Frieden and Sagalyn (1989), Downtown Inc.			
Haar (1996), Suburbs Under Siege, Race, Space and Audacious Judges	A. Jacobs (1995), Great Streets	Fainstein (1994), The City Builders, Property, Politics and Planning in London and New York	Sassen (1991), The Global City, New York, London, Tokyo	Blakely and Snyder (1997), Fortress America, Gated Communities in the United States	Porter (1997), Managing Growth in America's Communities
Kayden (1996), Privately Owned Public Space: The New York City Experience		Newman (1996), Creating Defensible Space			

Flyvbjerg (1998), *Rationality and Power, Democracy in Practice*	Abu-Lughod (1999), *New York, Chicago, Los Angeles, America's Global Cities*	Hoch (1994), *What Planners Do: Power, Politics and Persuasion*	Bernick and Cervero (1997), *Transit Villages in the 21st Century*	Healey et al. (1997), *Making Strategic Plans: Innovations in Europe*
Cohen and Taylor (2000), *American Pharaoh, Mayor Richard J. Daley, His Battle for Chicago and the Nation*	Flyvbjerg, Bruzelius, and Rothengatter (2003), *Megaprojects and Risk, An Anatomy of Ambition*	Buron et al. (2002), *HOPE VI Resident Tracking Study, A Snapshot of the Current Living Situation of the Original Residents from Eight Sites*	Beatley (2000), *Green Urbanism, Learning from European Cities*	Simmonds and Hack (2000), *Global City Regions, Their Emerging Forms*
Klinenberg (2002), *Heatwave, A Social Autopsy of Disaster in Chicago*	Orfield (2002), *American Metropolitics, The New Suburban Reality*	Altshuler and Luberoff (2003), *Mega-Projects, The Changing Politics of Urban Public Investment*	Garvin (2002), *The American City, What Works What Doesn't*	Ozawa (2004), *The Portland Edge, Challenges and Successes in Growing Communities*
Anderson (1999), *Code of the Street, Decency, Violence and Moral Life of the Inner City*	Faga (2006), *Designing Public Consensus, The Civic Theater of Community Participation for Architects, Landscape Architects, Planners and Urban Designers*	Popkin (2004), *Three City Study of the Moving to Opportunity Program*	Lang and LeFurgy (2007), *Boomburgs, The Rise of America's Accidental Cities*	Sanyal (2005), *Comparative Planning Cultures*
Sagalyn (2003), *Times Square Roulette Remaking the City Icon*				

(Continued)

Table 14.1 (Continued)

Single Case (Single authors, holistic)	Single Case (Single authors, embedded)	Multiple Case (Single authors, holistic)	Multiple Case (Single or multiple authors, embedded)	Multiple Case ("mini," Single authors)	Multiple Case (Edited)
Gilfoyle (2006), *Millennium Park, Creating a Chicago Landmark*		Hall and Pain (2006), *The Polycentric Metropolis, Learning from Mega-City Regions in Europe*	Dunham-Jones and Williamson (2009), *Retrofitting Suburbia, Urban Design Solutions to Redesigning Suburbs*		Perry and Wiewel (2005), *The University as Urban Developer, Cases and Analysis*
Gordon (2008), *Mapping Decline St Louis and the Fate of the American City*		Brown (2009), *America's Waterfront Revival, Port Authorities and Urban Redevelopment*	Ingram et al. (2009), *Smart Growth Policies: An Evaluation of Programs and Outcomes*		Vale and Campanella (2005), *The Resilient City, How Modern Cities Recover from Disaster*
Bloom (2008), *Public Housing That Worked, New York in the Twentieth Century*		Rosentraub (2010), *Major League Winners, Using Sports and Cultural Centers as Tools for Economic Development*	Calame and Charlesworth (2009), *Divided Cities, Belfast, Beirut, Jerusalem, Mostar and Nicosia*		Massey and Sampson (2009), *The Moynihan Report Revisited, Lessons and Responses After Four Decades*
Orfield and Luce (2010), *Planning and the Future of the Twin Cities*			Briggs et al. (2010), *Moving to Opportunity, An Experiment to Fight Ghetto Poverty*		

1. THE NATURE OF CASE-STUDY RESEARCH AND ITS APPLICATION TO URBAN PLANNING

Case studies fall into three general categories according to Robert Yin, the authoritative compiler of case-study research methods (Yin 2009, 47–52). The first category, *exploratory,* seeks to understand a problem or questions in general. The second, *descriptive,* details phenomena from which to draw lessons. The third, *explanatory,* endeavors to develop causal relationships. Sometimes a researcher begins a project intending to undertake one kind of case study and ends up with another. For example, Lee Rainwater, in the preface to *Behind Ghetto Walls, Black Family Life in a Federal Slum* (1970, vii), explained "This…study began as a study of the problems in a public housing project, Pruitt Igoe in St. Louis [descriptive], and ended as a study of the dynamics of socioeconomic inequality [explanatory]."

Or, a researcher may use a case study to disprove a theory. Oxford University professor Bent Flyvbjerg (2006, 228) reported that he approached his study of Aalborg, Denmark, thoroughly ingrained through university instruction in the belief that planning decisions would be transparent, inclusive, and in service of the free market, but when observed in the field, he found the opposite. This experience led him to refine the Yin typology, enumerating four nonexclusive kinds of case studies: "extreme" or "deviant," chosen to dramatize a point; "critical," selected to verify or disqualify a particular condition; "maximum variation," used to show the range of types of phenomenon; and/or "paradigmatic," created to highlight general qualities, rules or behaviors of the subject in question (Flyvbjerg 2006, 232). To this list, Yin later added two other types: "revelatory," offering insights not previously available; and "longitudinal," covering a span of time (Yin 2009, 47–52).

1.1 Application to Urban Planning

Case-study research in urban planning revolves around such questions as uncovering phenomena to be considered in formulating urban public policy; describing the decision-making processes in urban planning; and providing exemplars of what the authors consider best practices, frequently focusing on urban design or physical development. (An extensive discussion of these types of studies follows in the section of this chapter entitled "Patterns of Case-Study Research in Urban Planning.")

As with all research, whether case study or quantitative database analysis, a research design involves four decisions: (1) what question(s) to ask; (2) what data will answer the question(s); (3) how to collect the data; and (4) how to analyze the data. The characteristics that differentiate case-study research are in the answers to questions below.

What Questions?

In general, the scientific method guides the planning scholar. He or she couches research in one or more hypotheses or propositions related to current theory. She can develop questions only after acquiring some prerequisite knowledge: a firm grounding in existing literature pertaining to the immediate area of study, aware-ness of contributions from associated disciplines, and familiarity with what is hap-pening "on the ground" or in practice. Only then can he hone in on the key issues, gaps, or discrepancies that shape the project. In addition, the researcher articulates the anticipated findings as a means to structure the design and the subsequent discussion of the findings.

In case-study research, an iterative process is quite normal—that is, after com-pleting the research, the author may revise his or her questions. In *Divided Cities, Belfast, Beirut, Jerusalem, Mostar and Nicosia,* authors Jon Calame and Esther Charlesworth (2009) originally posited that urban managers who prevented spar-ring (and more dangerous activities like killing) by partitioning off discordant areas in ethnically and religiously divided cities would not cause permanent dam-age but, rather, achieve peace. They found, however, something quite different: while managers gained respite by separating antagonists, they ruined the social contract among residents because they were masking, not curing, "a profound, longstanding problem in a short-term temporary way" (5).

What Data?

To determine data needs, the researcher identifies the study's goals and defines its objectives and time frame. At the same time, he or she decides whether to pursue a single or multiple case(s) based on the nature of the work (e.g., exploratory, descrip-tive, or explanatory) and a judgment about the effectiveness of specified types of case(s) (e.g. representative, extreme, and/or with variation) in answering the ques-tions. For example, Mark Rosentraub (2010, 13), in *Major League Winners, Urban Change and New Destinies for Downtowns,* chose his cases as representative with variation, noting, "This book is about the balance achieved by successful leadership in several different cities and the positive economic outcomes that took place... [in order to identify] the opportunities available to other cities." In contrast, *Divided Cities* authors Calame and Charlesworth (2009, 2) selected extreme cases in order to "expose what lies in store for a large and perhaps growing class of cities on a tra-jectory toward polarization and partition between rival communities."

Above all, researchers have a clear understanding of the "unit of analysis" (what they are going to study e.g., a group, a process, a development project) and the boundaries (or time frame e.g., specified decades, months, etc.) to be covered. For example, in *The Future of Old Neighborhoods,* Bernard Frieden (1964) questioned current thinking on "gray areas" that dismissed these older central-city districts as economically and socially obsolete by identifying, tracking, and proving the use-fulness of inexpensive housing in such neighborhoods in New York, Los Angeles, and Hartford between 1950 and 1960. In *Mega-Projects: The Changing Politics of*

Urban Public Investment, Alan Altshuler and Daniel Luberoff (2003, 2) wanted to explore the trajectory of "the political impulses that generated mega-projects of the 1950s and 1960s," so they concentrated on "three inter-related mega-projects: highways, airports and rail transit systems…during the second half of the twentieth century" to gauge decision-making processes in each.

At the very least, regardless of the number or type of cases included in the research design (as is discussed below), the data will include a chronology of events relevant to the subject under study, a step that includes reviewing primary and secondary documents, identification of the key actors or stakeholders, quantitative and descriptive information that helps establish the context of the case, interviews of people who can clarify various elements of the case, site visits and/or personal observation of meetings or other events relevant to the case, and collection of assessment information that will assist in judging the outcomes of the case.

1.2. The Single Case

The decision to have one, or more than one, case is closely related to the goals of a given study. A single case, while offering depth, calls for careful marshaling of information to tell a story that has broad application as is illustrated in the examples below. While researchers have the luxury of making deep probes and being immersed in one place, they still have to organize the material to demonstrate its contribution to theory—that is, its ability to produce knowledge that may be applied elsewhere.

For example, Martin Meyerson and Edward Banfield (1955, 11), in *Politics, Planning and the Public Interest: The Case of Public Housing in Chicago*, investigated "how some important decisions were reached in a large American city." In their research design, they established clear criteria for their unit of analysis, "decisions," by choosing a *certain kind* (the siting of public housing); a certain *type* ("we take into account decisions only if, and only insofar as they have to do with 'politics,' 'planning,' or 'the public interest'")—concepts that they define in a twenty-six-page appendix; and a certain *class*, noting that, at the time, siting was not only "big business," but also "suggestive for certain classes of issues" such as a sewage disposal plant, a tuberculosis sanatorium, a superhighway, or even a church or a school (14, 303–329,12). In establishing the broad application of their work, they were bold ("many other governments resemble that of Chicago") but circumspect:

> The reader should be cautioned, however, against inferring that the political history of public housing in other cities has been identical with that of Chicago…the Chicago experiences should sensitize the reader to certain influences and relationships which are likely to be found, although not in the same form, in most other cities. In short, acquaintance with what happened in Chicago may give the student of the public housing issue some indication of *what to look for in other cities*. [italics added] (11–12)

Many other studies of public housing siting and its effects ensued, including Arnold Hirsch's (1983) *Making of the Second Ghetto: Race and Housing in Chicago 1940–1960* and Lawrence Vale's (2000) *From Puritans to the Projects: Public Housing and Public Neighbors.* A more recent single case study, Nicholas Dagen Bloom's (2008) *Public Housing That Worked, New York in the Twentieth Century* dissected the New York experience between 1934 and 2008. Like Meyerson and Banfield, Bloom seeks to show the reader a different story than his predecessors, one that includes, but goes beyond, siting to explore management policies as an explanatory force for the success of public housing in a large American city.

In the single-case arena, several works take one city as the unit of analysis and explore the outcomes of different public policies in that city. Examples are Colin Gordon's (2008) *Mapping Decline, St. Louis and the Fate of One American City,* which looks at St. Louis to study the effects of a single type of action: evolving housing and renewal policies over decades. Similarly, Birch and Wachter's (2006) *Rebuilding Urban Places After Disaster, Lessons From Katrina,* reviews one city, New Orleans, and but investigates the role of the several different types of policies—economic to educational—in aiding recovery efforts.

1.3 The Single Embedded Case

A researcher may choose another approach: the single case with embedded subunits that receive more or different attention, in order to illustrate a phenomenon that has variation within it. This method goes beyond a simple numerical count or statistical attempt to create causal relationships used by many social scientists pursuing complex problems to add nuances and depth to the overall case or argument that the author is presenting. In the late 1950s, anthropologist Oscar Lewis (1959) formulated the "culture of poverty" theory based on studying five Mexican families. He argued that the poor had "a way of life that is passed down from generation to generation," that contributed to their economic and social marginality (Lewis 1959, xlii–lii). He tested this idea using an embedded single case in *La Vida: A Puerto Rican Family and the Culture of Poverty in San Juan and New York* (1965) by focusing on one family that contained five households—three living in Puerto Rico and two in New York City. In this manner, he captured the varied forms of behavior associated with the "culture of poverty" concept and argued that it was a behavioral type that had several manifestations depending on household composition and location.

Similarly, when political scientist Alan Altshuler (1965), studied city planning in the Twin Cities (Minneapolis/St Paul), in *The City Planning Process: A Political Analysis,* he used the embedded single case study. While he focused on "the city planning process," he analyzed how city planning decisions were made in creating four types of plans (a comprehensive plan for Minneapolis, a land-use plan and hospital site for St. Paul, and an interstate freeway routing plan for the two cities). In using several examples or subunits as evidence, he challenged reigning planning theory (rational decision making), arguing that it was an ineffective model because it neglected to account for local political behavior. Jeffrey Pressman and Aaron Wildavsky (1973) would follow the same approach in *Implementation, How Great Expectations in Washington Are Dashed in Oakland*, a study of the U.S. Economic Development Administration's employment programs in Oakland California that tracked the expenditure of a $23 million allocation for four types of infrastructure investments (airport, marine terminal, industrial park, and roads) in case studies of the individual projects to test the outcomes, measured as job creation. Here, the authors focused on such issues as individual program achievements and explanations for their failure to meet projected goals.

Urban design researchers also make use of the embedded single case study. For Jonathan Barnett (1974), in *Urban Design as Public Policy*, New York City zoning is the overall topic and its city-shaping power is the concern. He documented the effects of two newly invented devices—the plaza bonus and the special district—and showed how they played out in various development projects. For Allan B. Jacobs (1995), in *Great Streets*, the "street" is the unit of analysis and fifteen exemplary thoroughfares in Europe and North America distinguished by their dimensions and patterns of use are the subunits.

In a more recent study, *Heatwave, A Social Autopsy of a Disaster in Chicago*, sociologist Eric Klinenberg (2002) used an embedded single case study that employed mixed methods to question whether the more than 485 heat-related deaths in six days in Chicago in July 1995 affected everyone equally. (Notably, this crisis produced more than twice as many deaths as the Great Chicago Fire of 1871.) Through statistical analysis, he discovered that impoverished, elderly minorities had the highest rates; but with further scrutiny, he saw that poor, elderly black men suffered disproportionately. To explain this phenomenon, he then studied comparative spatial data—place of residence and crime rates—to conclude that the black victims who lived in high-crime neighborhoods remained in their overheated apartments, while others, especially low-income Hispanics whose neighborhoods were safer, were less housebound and, consequently, had lower mortality rates.

1.4 The Multiple Case

A researcher selects a multiple case study design to show repeated patterns, variation in patterns, and exceptional examples of patterns to achieve balance (geographic, size, etc.) among exhibited patterns and to offer more ample descriptions and explanations of complex phenomena, all in the effort to enhance generalization from the data (Stake 2006, v; Yin 2009, 54). Two examples are Peter H. Brown's (2009) *America's Waterfront Revival, Port Authorities and Urban Redevelopment* and Mark S. Rosentraub's (2010), *Major League Winners, Using Sports and Cultural Centers as Tools for Economic Development*. Here, each author employed four (Brown) to five (Rosentraub) cases to illustrate types of urban planning in postindustrial cities.

In each of these cases, the authors developed hypotheses about their subjects from a combination of research, observation, interviews, and experience. Brown, as a former city employee, had noticed that the Philadelphia Port Authority had a surplus of land owing to its relocation of facilities to accommodate container-ization, and he decided to investigate how this change had affected how it and other port authorities perceive their missions, hypothesizing that they had become urban developers. Rosentraub, through research for an earlier book, *Major League Losers, The Real Cost of Sports and Who's Paying for It?* (1999), detected a change in municipal approaches to the construction of sports facilities, hypothesizing that some appeared to be using stadiums as anchors for reinvention and growth.

1.5 The Embedded Multiple Case

Like the embedded single case, the embedded multiple case presents several cases dealing with a particular question, with additional attention given to other details within the cases. For example, when Larry Buron and colleagues (2002) under-took *HOPE VI Resident Tracking Study, A Snapshot of Current Living Situation of the Original Residents from Eight Sites*, they selected a large sample of residents from projects in varying degrees of completion (two completed and fully reoc-cupied, four partially reoccupied, and two under construction) to review four fea-tures (the residents' housing conditions, neighborhood quality, social environment and employment, and hardship and health). They tested the basic assumptions of the HOPE VI program—notably, that original residents' lives, as judged by the four elements, would be improved. However, since the cases were so varied with regard to their progress, the treatment of residents was also varied—factors that the researchers discussed in detail.

1.6 The "Mini" Multiple Case

In contrast to these approaches, Edward J. Blakely and Mary Gail Snyder's (1997) *Fortress America: Gated Communities in the United States* and Robert E. Lang and Jennifer B. LeFurgy's (2007) *Boomburgs: The Rise of America's Accidental Cities* offered many "mini" case studies to describe a new settlement type that they each identify by studying empirical data. Blakely and Snyder focus on gated communi-ties that numbered more than 20,000 at the time of their research (7); Lang and LeFurgy, on "boomburgs"—large (100,000 population) incorporated places, not core cities, that were housing one-in-nine suburban dwellers and having double-digit growth between 1970 and 2000 (6, 19). Each team explored a large question— Blakely and Snyder studied the nature of community (29); Lang and LeFurgy looked at the dynamics of metropolitan change (20)—by marshaling "mini" cases that con-tributed to the description of the overall case (gated community or boomburg), as well as analysis of the phenomenon under study. In this fashion, they captured the issues in the types of places by developing a "mosaic" that formed each case study. For example, in their exploration of the pace and quality of boomburg development, Lang and LaFurgy identified future build-out as an issue. They used survey research to tally their places' plans (ranging from promoting compact development to resisting densification) and provided brief examples of each.

1.7 Edited Multiple Case Studies

Finally, some scholars produce edited collections of case studies. Lawrence J. Vale and Thomas J. Campanella (2005), in *The Resilient City, How Modern Cities Recover From Disaster,* used eight cases to identify the characteristics found in places that survive natural and manmade disasters; and Bishwapriya Sanyal (2005, xxi), in *Comparative Planning Cultures,* has his contributors generate "thick descriptions of planning practices in various countries" in order to "demonstrate whether there are core cultural traits...which differentiate planning efforts in different nations." In these types of collections, the editors take responsibility for comprehensive cross-case analyses. Vale and Campanella provided a well-argued concluding chapter that not only used the cases to present a model of the stages of recovery (from emergency to reconstruction) but also commented on key characteristics of the recovery process, ranging from observations about every place experiencing physical recovery of one sort or another to conclusions about opportunism and opportunity as well as governmental and human resilience (2005, 335–53). Sanyal took a different tack, employing a long introductory chapter to set up the cases and then let the cases tell the story (2005, 3–63).

  As can be seen from this description of the design of case-study research, the choice of cases and their number depend on the authors' abilities to demonstrate that their research designs answer their questions credibly. There is no "right" answer to whether one or more than one case is appropriate. Researchers with a social science inclination tend to select multiple cases, believing that more examples will offer greater proof of the existence of a given phenomenon. Their training, often based in quantitative analysis, supports this approach. Researchers with an inclination toward history or ethnography tend to gravitate to the single case, believing that rich description will enable the reader to apply the resulting knowledge to his or her circumstances with a deeper understanding of the context and conditions of the case.

What Data Collection Methods?

As part of the design for a project, the investigator conceives a research protocol outlining the types of data sought and the methods of collection. Having such a protocol ensures that other researchers can replicate (or critique) the approach, and in the case of multiple case studies, assures uniform treatment of each. The objective

is to develop a portrait or tell a story about each case by collecting basic descriptive data, developing a chronology, and identifying key actors and actions. Data
can come from many sources, including censuses, specially generated surveys, participant observation, interviews, review of primary and secondary documents, field
work, and/or mapping and spatial analysis employing GIS or other methods.

For example, the contributing authors to *The University as Urban Developer,
Cases and Analysis,* edited by David C. Perry and Wim Wiewel (2005), used primary
and secondary documents, interviews, personal accounts, and maps to tell their
stories. Saskia Sassen (1991), in *The Global City, New York, London, Tokyo,* relied
heavily on databases from the International Monetary Fund, U.S. Department of
Labor, United Nations Centre on Transnational Corporations, Organization for
Economic Cooperation and Development, Metropolitan Government of Tokyo,
United Kingdom Department of Employment, and other organizations.

How to Analyze the Data?

Having gathered the data for the cases, the researcher returns to the original questions and/or propositions to interpret the evidence, the most important and creative function of any research project. As mentioned earlier, case approaches allow
researchers to reformulate their questions as information-gathering progresses. In
some quantitatively based multiple-case projects, often those related to program
evaluation, the researcher has set up measurable outcomes and can discuss them.
For example, when Briggs, Popkin, and Goering (2010), in *Moving to Opportunity,
The Story of an American Experiment to Fight Ghetto Poverty,* organized the study
to cover five cases and to report on whether families who moved from de facto
segregated public housing to racially integrated communities fared better in terms
of housing quality, employment, and education than those who chose other alternatives (staying in public housing, moving within the city, etc.), they established
a "controlled" experiment that allowed for quantitative analysis of the outcomes.
(They found, however, that so many unanticipated factors influenced the outcome
that they had to qualify their findings with descriptive explanations.) In other
studies with little or no quantitative data, the researcher assesses features or characteristics, or he or she identifies patterns that bear on the original research questions. Brown (2009), Rosentraub (2010), and Calame and Charlesworth (2009) are
examples of this type of assessment.

Depending on the type of case study or studies that have emerged, researchers
will report exploratory, descriptive, revelatory, or explanatory findings, aiming to
demonstrate elements that contribute or disprove the theoretical framework on
which the study is based. They offer an "analytical" (not statistical) generalization—that is, the mounting of the empirical findings of one or more case studies
to prove, disprove, or amplify previously developed theory. A necessary goal is to
produce results capable of replication because only through replication is theory
robust (Yin 2009, 38, 54). Single case analysis is straightforward, as the researcher
analyzes the evidence to point out key aspects of the case, leading to general assertions; multiple case analysis calls for cross-case observations relative to the general

questions, again pointing out the commonalities and differences (Gerring 2007). Focusing on a single place, Ram Cnaan (2006, 274–92) explored religious congregations in Philadelphia to demonstrate the pros and cons of their contributions to social welfare in disadvantaged neighborhoods. Using an embedded, multiple case study approach, Sassen (1991) marshaled evidence to argue that the rise of global cities as centers of finance represented a shift in their definition and role from hosting manufacturing and production to enabling or financing such functions worldwide, asserting "It is this combination of a new industrial complex that dominates economic growth and sociopolitical forms through which it is constituted and reproduced that is centered in major cities and contains the elements of a new type of city, the global city" (Sassen 1991, 338).

Most cases in urban planning aim to inform the future, while some—notably the explanatory and paradigmatic—attempt to predict or affect future decision making directly. Briggs, Popkin, and Goering's (2010) *Moving to Opportunity* is an example of the latter, while Beatley's (2000) *Green Urbanism, Learning from European Cities* is an example of the former. A common impetus is a desire to identify qualities that contribute to the creation of communities of lasting value. One example is *The Portland Edge: Challenges and Success in Growing Communities*, edited by Connie Ozawa (2004, 304), who writes:

> The purpose of this volume was not simply to tell "The Portland Story." We had hoped that by doing so, however, we would add to larger discussions about how to recover, sustain and create strong communities. We offer no recipes... nonetheless it is clear that the level of livability in Portland is no accident.... [W]e have identified a few key ingredients of a strong community.

A more recent effort is Joan Fitzgerald's (2010) *Emerald Cities, Urban Sustainability and Economic Development*, which endeavors to blend European and U.S. cases to provide inspiration for formulation of a national policy on the subject.

2. PATTERNS IN THE USE OF CASE-STUDY RESEARCH IN URBAN PLANNING

As evident from table 14.1, urban planning scholarship has relied heavily on case studies over the last fifty years. Organized according to six types of approaches ranging from single cases to edited multiple case study collections, the table supports five observations beyond the general statement that, regardless of discipline, urban researchers use cases extensively. First, many urban planning scholars employ case studies as a vehicle to translate knowledge into action. Second, case study approaches allow urban planning scholars to provide the evidence, depth, and detail about place that other methods do not capture. Third, case study authors have taken on a wide range of roles, from participant observer to dispassionate analyst. Fourth, revisiting a phenomenon over time occurs in urban planning case-study research. Fifth, the professional biography stands out as a distinct type of case study for urban planners and deserves attention in the future.

Case Studies Serve as Vehicles for Translating Knowledge into Action

Planning scholars either explicitly articulate their motivation to inform or improve urban planning or implicitly do so through their work. Further, case studies provide "road maps" regarding context, chronology, key actors, and/or crucial decision points, offering readers searching for models or solutions to the same or similar problems a means to compare and test their own situations. While there is never any "best way" to translate knowledge to action, at the very least, case-study research adds a layer of information or best practices to assist decision makers, who will also rely on other types of information, whether it comes from quantitative research, experience, professional group interactions, or other means.

Examples of the value of case studies are found in the work of Herbert Gans (1959), Jane Jacobs (1961), William Whyte (1980), and Mark Rosentraub (2010), who have uncovered information that changed perceptions about the urban environment or activities occurring in cities. Martin Meyerson and Edward Banfield (1955);, Bent Flyvbjerg (1998); Brent Flyvbjerg, Nils Bruzelius, and Wernter Rothengatter (2003); and Lynne Sagalyn (2003) have successfully shown the behaviors and actions of key actors in urban planning activities, while Martin Meyerson (1963), Jonathan Barnett (1974), Jerold Kayden (2000), Timothy Beatley (2000), Alexander Garvin (2002), and Ellen Dunham-Jones and June Williamson (2009) provide exemplars for improving physical planning. Barbara Faga (2006) describes participatory processes and Allan Altshuler (1965), Charles Hoch (1994), and John Forester (1989) contribute ideas about practitioner operations. Hoch (1994) has full-scale portraits of typical planners, while Forester's (1989, 163–208) contributions with regard to cases are restricted to a final chapter, "Supplement on Planning Education: Teaching Planning Practice." Finally, Timothy Beatley (2009), who provided a firm foundation for "green urbanism," defined the knowledge-to-action process as "telling stories—innovative efforts at moving cities and urban neighborhoods in the direction of sustainability, at finding ways to build economy, reconnect to place and environment, and at once to enhance quality of life and reduce ecological footprints."

Case-study approaches allow urban planning scholars to provide information about place that other methods would not capture. Since case-study authors examine the physical manifestations of a wide variety of urban phenomena, they offer contextual details about places that are often lacking in purely quantitative studies. Depending on the subject under study, they may explain the geography (e.g., terrain, climate), locational characteristics (e.g., street layout, neighborhood or housing conditions), or the interplay of demographic factors and place (e.g., segregation) that are explanatory or have an effect on the outcomes. When Lynne Sagalyn (2003) dealt with the redevelopment of New York City's Times Square, in *Times Square Roulette*, she detailed relevant characteristics of the area (e.g., parcel size, ownership patterns, zoning requirements, accessibility to transportation, land values), its location in the NYC theater district, and other factors that influenced subsequent public and private decision making that explained the success of this particular development project. Similarly, Timothy Gilfoyle (2006) deconstructed the spatial aspects (e.g., location, acreage) that affected the events and decisions that resulted in the design and creation of Chicago's famed Millennium Park. Others have shown the physical imprint of pressing social, economic, and environmental issues. For example, legal scholar Charles Haar (1996, 2005) explored both the ramifications of the Mt. Laurel I and II cases on New Jersey settlement patterns owing to court remedies for residential racial discrimination and outlined the physical effects of legal efforts on the cleanup of Boston Harbor. Capturing urban ethnic strife, John Calame and Esther Charlesworth (2009) mapped its varied expression is such forms as walls, gated districts, and other elements in the cities of Belfast, Beirut, Jerusalem, Mostar, and Nicosia. Some examine existing or potential public policy related to transportation, land use, regional planning, growth management, and the potential for political alliances. Michael Bernick and Robert Cervero (1997) and Cervero (1998) surveyed transit-oriented development; Douglas Porter (1997) covered U.S. regional planning efforts; Patsy Healey (2007 looked at innovative planning in several countries in Europe; and Myron Orfield (2002) demonstrated the economic and social commonalities among suburbs in a study of twenty-five metro areas.

Case-Study Author Roles Range from Witness to Dispassionate Analyst

The presence of the author as a witness takes different forms. Jonathan Barnett (1974) and Allan Jacobs (1978) represent first-person, active participants who are "reflective practitioners," taking time to scrutinize their practical experiences and share the results. Schön (1983), Herbert Gans (1959, 1967), Oscar Lewis (1959, 1965), Gerald Suttles (1968), and Elijah Anderson (1999) are participant observers, inhabiting the communities they are studying in order to understand them. Jane Jacobs (1961) also lives in the community and uses her daily experiences to articulate desirable urban qualities. Unlike the sociologists, she does not focus on ethnographic concerns but, rather, on the effects of the physical environment on behavior and well-being. More remote are Lee Rainwater (1970), Joel Garreau (1991), Peter Brown (2009), and Ellen Dunham-Jones and June Williamson (2009), who use field observations to supplement work that relies on many other forms of data and that places them at arm's length from their subjects.

Some Case Study Authors Revisit Phenomena

An author or co-authors may engage in longitudinal case studies that show how a phenomenon fares over time. For example, in the 1970s, Oscar Newman (1972) crafted "defensible space" design principles to reduce crime in public housing. More than twenty years later, sponsored by the U.S. Department of Housing and Urban Development, he (1996) evaluated their application in a three-case study project. Two years after the publication of the notorious "Moynihan Report" or *The Negro Family, The Case for National Action* (U.S. Department of Labor 1965), Lee Rainwater and William Yancy (1967) looked at the stir it had created. (The Moynihan Report asserted that high levels of black male unemployment negatively affected family lives and led to a "tangle of pathology" that undermined black society.) Fifty years later, Douglas Massey and Robert Sampson (2009, 12) reassessed the uproar again, arguing that the fallout contributed to avoidance and consequent lack of rigorous analysis of the "unpleasant realities of ghetto life," consequently leaving the conservative explanation (welfare dependence created the observed pathologies) unchallenged for more than twenty years until William Julius Wilson (1987), in *The Truly Disadvantaged,* provided an alternative explanation (structural changes in the economy). Other works followed Wilson's, breaking the blockade of silence by liberal scholars.

The Professional Biography as a Type of Case Study Needs More Attention

Life stories focusing on people's careers illustrate the environment, character, and decision-making patterns of leaders who have shaped urban places. Exemplary are Robert Caro's (1974) biography of Robert Moses, a subject recently revisited by Hillary Ballon and Kenneth Jackson (2007) in a massive exhibit and catalogue *Robert Moses and the Modern City: The Transformation of New York*; Adam Cohen and Elizabeth Taylor's (2000) study of the first Mayor Richard Daley of Chicago, M. Jeffrey Hardwick's (2004) portrait of Victor Gruen and Nicholas Dagen Bloom's (2004) tracing of developer James Rouse's career highlighting his role in the creating Columbia, Maryland, festival malls and the Enterprise Foundation. Notably, there is a dearth of biographies of mid-twentieth-century city planners, including Kevin Lynch, Martin Meyerson, Lloyd Rodwin, Harvey Perloff, and others (Birch 2011), leaving an important gap to be filled by scholars in the future.

An important note here is that journalists often write professional biographies that differ in tone and analysis from those written by scholars. The journalist's approach tends to focus on the immediate story more than the context, while the scholars give much attention to placing the subject in a larger picture of his or her times. In the journalist group are Caro's book on Moses and Buzz Bissinger's (1997) portrait of Mayor Ed Rendell in *A Prayer for a City*; among the scholar-generated offerings are Nicholas Dagen Bloom's (2004) *Merchant of Illusion* (James Rouse) and Wendell Pritchett's (2008) *Robert Clifton Weaver and the American City: The Time and Life of an Urban Reformer*. Edited biographical collections are another version of this approach. Representative are Donald Krueckeberg's (1983, 1994) pioneering work that includes portraits of more than twenty leaders and Scott Gabriel Knowles's (2009) recent book on Edmund Bacon, featuring several authors with different perspectives on a single person.

3. Some Effects of Case-Study Research on Urban Planning

The impact of case-based research becomes evident with the passage of time, allowing for the dissemination and application of findings. Two types of outcomes are evident, displayed as follows: (1) the translation of the new knowledge into practice; and (2) the stimulation of new research. Examples of the translation of the new knowledge into practice are evident in many arenas. William H. Whyte's (1980) *Social Life of Small Urban Spaces*, a study of public plazas in New York City, and Jane Jacobs's (1961) *Death and Life of Great American Cities*, an explanation of urban design successes also focused on New York City (primarily Greenwich Village) achieved widespread readership and reshaped city planning practice in New York and beyond. For example, New York City rewrote the public plaza sections of its zoning ordinance in response to Whyte's findings as did many other cities (Kayden 1996; Birch 1986).

Both textbooks and practice are infused with concepts that first saw life in case study monographs. Martin Meyerson and Edward Banfield's (1955) exploration of urban decision making in *Politics, Planning and the Public Interest* advanced planning theory, especially with regard to a nuanced definition of the public interest, that value that planners, through their code of ethics, pledge to pursue. Similarly, Alan Altshuler (1965) turned the rational planning model on its head. Herbert Gans's (1959) *The Urban Villagers, Group and Class in the Life of Italian Americans* transformed ideas about community life in slums, a theme that has been deepened through the ongoing work of other ethnographers like Elijah Anderson. Bernard Frieden (1964) *The Future of Old Neighborhoods* helped put a halt to slum clearance and successfully promoted rehabilitation. The zoning techniques that Jonathan Barnett (1974) put forward in *Urban Design as Public Policy* have been replicated in cities throughout the United States.

An example of the second type of outcome, stimulation of new research, is the seminal work of Sir Peter Hall (1966) in *World Cities*. Attributing the term "world cities" to Scottish scholar Patrick Geddes, Hall (7–9) was the first writer to operationalize the concept by defining world cities as places "in which a disproportionate part of the world's business is conducted,…[that are] national centers not merely of government but also of trade,…centers of population [with]…significant portion of the richest of the community, [and]…the locus of manufacturing and luxury goods, entertainment and culture." Hall selected seven places, or "world cities," to examine, analyzing the drivers of growth, current problems, and their solutions, and arguing that they represented the wave of the future whose stories provided lessons for urban planners. He chose the case studies from places that varied by function (political and financial capitals), by spatial arrangement (nuclear and polycentric), and by geographic location (Europe, Asia, North America). He found that "in every city…growth brings problems; but those problems may vary in intensity according especially to the internal disposition of functions and land uses within metropolitan regions" (234). From the data, Hall identified, quite presciently as it turns out, two categories of concern: the spread of the suburbs and the future of the downtown (237–42). He thus alerted his readers to what to "look for in other cities" (as Meyerson and Banfield [1955, 12] had suggested a decade earlier in discussing the usefulness of case studies) and established an important agenda for subsequent research.

In the years to follow, scholars would flesh out the concerns highlighted by Hall in three significant streams of inquiry. The first focused on suburbs and sprawl, the next on downtowns, and the last on large-scale regions. The suburban literature spanned early studies that gauged the effects of suburbs on social behavior, such as William H. Whyte's (1956) *The Organization Man,* based on Park Forest, Illinois; and Herbert Gans's (1967) *The Levittowners Ways of Life and Politics in a New Suburban Community,* focused on community life in one of the nation's first, postwar, mass-produced subdivisions, Ann Forsyth's (2005) *Reforming Suburbia, The Planned Communities of Irvine, Columbia and The Woodlands* explored three master-planned places. Later works addressed public policies designed to shape suburbs as exemplified by Gregory K. Ingram and colleagues' (2009) *Smart Growth Policies: An Evaluation of Programs and Outcomes,* which employed quantitative measures supplemented by mulitiple case studies, and Myron Orfield and Thomas F. Luce Jr.'s (2010, xiii) *Region, Planning the Future of the Twin Cities,* which combined in-depth data analysis represented graphically in a number of GIS maps "to think more clearly about the socio-economic polarization that is occurring in the region," and to decide what to do about it.

The second stream explored downtowns, especially the decentralization of central business district functions. *Edge City, Life on the New Frontier* by Joel Garreau (1991) redefined the idea of downtown through the investigation of nine "new urban centers" characterized by five elements (5 million square feet of leasable office space; 600,000 square feet of leasable retail space; more jobs than bedrooms) and perceived as one place, nonexistent thirty years ago. About a decade later, *Edgeless Cities* by Robert E. Lang (2003, 2) challenged Garreau, employing multiple "mini" case studies to identify a new pattern of places that are downtowns "in *function* in that they contain office employment but not in *form* because they are scattered…contain isolated office buildings or small clusters of buildings of varying densities over vast swabs of metropolitan space." Other works have focused on the actual downtown concept and its changing activities. These studies, as they were published over time, sequentially referenced their predecessors to demonstrate change. They include John Rannells's (1956) *The Core of the City*, which tracked traditional central business district (CBD) functions in Philadelphia; Bernard Frieden and Lynne B. Sagalyn's (1989) *Downtown Inc., How America Rebuilds Cities*,which portrayed changing retail formats in Pasadena, Boston, San Diego, Seattle, and St. Paul; Roberta Gratz and Norman Mintz's (2000) *Cities Back from the Edge;* and Eugenie L. Birch's (2005) *Who Lives Downtown?*, with their many small case examples, that show the new residential and entertainments components of the twenty-first century 24/7 downtown.

The third stream examines large-scale regions. The literature is extensive, but four recent works are representative: Roger Simmonds and Gary Hack (2000, 3, 183–93), in *Global City Regions, Their Emerging Forms*, compared eleven large-scale places closely linked by economic activity but exhibitingcontrasting features, including infrastructure, regional organization and cultures of governance. Peter Hall and Kathy Pain's (2006) *The Polycentric Metropolis, Learning from Mega-City Regions in Europe*, showcased eight places that have become mega-city regions in work that is closely related to thinking about mega-regions in the United States, fostered by Jonathan Barnett and colleagues (2007) in *Smart Growth in a Changing World,* Catherine Ross (2009) in *Megaregions, Planning for Global Competitiveness* and Arthur Nelson and Robert Lang (2011) in *Megapolitan America.*

As it turns out, Hall's three streams of inquiry are closely related. The suburban work informs state and local dialogues on community life, sprawl, and urban design. Public and private decision makers are shaping downtown investments based on researchers' findings. The study of large-scale places is now influencing national policy discussions in such infrastructure discussions as those revolving around high-speed rail, as a recent scan of the America 2050 (http://www.america2050.org/) and the U.S. Federal Rail Administration (http://www.fra.dot.gov/Pages/2325.shtml) Web sites indicate.

4. CONCLUSION

Urban planning scholars employ case-study research widely to pursue a range of questions related to the field, including analyzing urban behaviors in the political arena, in neighborhoods, and in other places and providing exemplars of best practices in physical planning. They have done so for more than fifty years. And as they have worked, they have evolved several types of approaches, ranging from the single case monograph to the multiple case edited collection. In the process, they have pursued rigorous and replicable research designs whose formats have been repeated in the work of successive case-study researchers and whose protocols have been formalized in case-study textbooks (Yin 2009; Seale et al. 2008; Stake 2006). An analysis of representative studies reveals several patterns, including an effort to develop cases that translate knowledge into action, that pay attention to "place" or the physical dimensions of a question, and have a tendency to revisit and reevaluate a phenomenon that has been studied at an earlier time. Important gaps in case study research such as in the special format, biography, exist. Finally, case-study research has yielded important outcomes, influencing both practice and ongoing research.

References

Abu-Lughod, J. 1999. *New York, Chicago, Los Angeles, America's Global Cities.* Minneapolis: University of Minnesota Press.

Altshuler, A. 1965. *The City Planning Process, A Political Analysis.* Ithaca, NY: Cornell University Press.

Altshuler, A., and D. Luberoff. 2003. *Mega-Projects, The Changing Politics of Urban Public Investment.* Washington, DC: Brookings Institution Press.

Anderson, E. 1999. *Code of the Street, Decency, Violence and Moral Life in the Inner City.* New York: W.W. Norton.

Ballon, H., and K. Jackson. 2007. *Robert Moses and the Modern City: The Transformation of New York.* New York: W.W. Norton.

Barnett, J. 1974. *Urban Design as Public Policy, Practical Methods for Improving Cities.* New York: McGraw-Hill.

Barnett, J., F. Benfield, P. Farmer, S. Poticha, R. Yaro, and A. Carbonell. 2007. *Smart Growth in a Changing World.* Chicago: APA Planners Press.

Beatley, T. 2000. *Green Urbanism, Learning from European Cities.* Washington, DC: Island Press.

Beatley, T. 2009. "Tim Beatley: Telling Stories of Green Urbanism." Available at: http://blog.islandpress.org/tim-beatley-telling-the-stories-of-green-urbanism; accessed January 8.

Bell, G., and J. Tyrwhitt. 1972. *Human Identity in the Urban Environment.* Harmondsworth, Hammersmith, UK: Pelican.

Bernick, M., and R. Cervero. 1997. *Transit Villages in the 21st Century.* New York: McGraw-Hill.

Birch, E. 1986. "The Observation Man, ." *Planning Magazine*, March, 4–8.

Birch, E. 2005. *Who Lives Downtown?* Washington, DC: Brookings Institution Press.

Birch, E. 2011. "Reviving the Art of Biography: The Emblematic Life of Martin Meyerson. *Journal of Planning History* 10(3): 175–79.

Birch, E., and S. Wachter, eds. 2006. *Rebuilding Urban Places After Disaster, Lessons from Katrina.* Philadelphia: University of Pennsylvania Press.

Bissinger, B. 1997. *A Prayer for the City.* New York: Random House.

Blakely, E., and M. Snyder. 1997. *Fortress America, Gated Communities in the United States.* Washington, DC: Brookings Institution Press.

Bloom, N. 2004. *Merchant of Illusion, James Rouse America's Salesman of the Businessman's Utopia.* Columbus: Ohio State University Press.

Bloom, N. 2008. *Public Housing That Worked, New York in the Twentieth Century.* Philadelphia: University of Pennsylvania Press.

Briggs, X., S. Popkin, and J. Goering. 2010. *Moving to Opportunity, The Story of an American Experiment to Fight Ghetto Poverty.* New York: Oxford University Press.

Brown, P. 2009. *America's Waterfront Revival, Port Authorities and Urban Redevelopment.* Philadelphia: University of Pennsylvania Press.

Buron, L. S. Popkin, D. Levy, L. Harris, and J. Khadduri. 2002. *HOPE VI Resident Tracking Study: A Snapshot of the Current Living Situation of the Original Residents from Eight Sites.* Washington, DC: Urban Institute.

Calame, J., and E. Charlesworth. 2009. *Divided Cities, Belfast, Beirut, Jerusalem, Mostar and Nicosia.* Philadelphia: University of Pennsylvania Press.

Caro, R. 1974. *The Power Broker, Robert Moses and the Fall of New York.* New York: Random House.

Cervero. R. 1998. *The Transit Metropolis, A Global Inquiry.* Washington, DC: Island Press.

Cnaan, R. 2006. *The Other Philadelphia Story, How Local Congregations Support Quality of Life in Urban America.* Philadelphia: University of Pennsylvania Press.

Cohen, A., and E. Taylor. 2000. *American Pharaoh, Mayor Richard J. Daley, His Battle for Chicago and the Nation.* Boston: Little Brown.

Dunham-Jones, E., and J. Williamson. 2009. *Retrofitting Suburbia: Urban Design Solutions for Redesigning Suburbs.* Hoboken, NJ: John Wiley.

Faga, B. 2006. *Designing Public Consensus, The Civic Theater of Community Participation for Architects, Landscape Architects, Planners and Urban Designers.* Hoboken, NJ: John Wiley.

Fainstein, S. 1994. *The City Builders, Property, Politics and Planning in London and New York.* London: Blackwell.

Fitzgerald, J. 2010. *Emerald Cities Urban Sustainability and Economic Development.* New York: Oxford University Press.

Flyvbjerg, B. 1998. *Rationality and Power, Democracy in Practice.* Chicago: University of Chicago Press.

Flyvbjerg, B. 2006. "Five Misunderstandings about Case-Study Research." *Qualitative Inquiry* 12(2): 219–45.

Flyvbjerg, B., N. Bruzelius, and W.Rothengatter. 2003. *Megaprojects and Risk, An Anatomy of Ambition.* Cambridge, UK: Cambridge University Press.

Forester, J. 1989. *Planning in the Face of Power.* Berkeley, CA: University of California Press.

Forsyth, A. 2005. *Reforming Suburbia, The Planned Communities of Irvine, Columbia and The Woodlands.* Berkeley and Los Angeles: University of California Press.

Frieden, B. 1964. *The Future of Old Neighborhoods.* Cambridge, MA: MIT Press.

Frieden, B., and L. Sagalyn. 1989. *Downtown Inc., How America Rebuilds Cities.* Cambridge, MA: MIT Press.

Gans, H. 1959. *The Urban Villagers, Group and Class in the Life of Italian Americans.* Philadelphia: University of Pennsylvania, Insitute for Urban Studies.

Gans, H. 1967. *The Levittowners, Ways of Life and Politics in a New Suburban Community.* New York: Pantheon Books.

Garreau, J. 1991. *Edge City, Life on the New Frontier.* New York: Doubleday.

Garvin, A. 2002. *The American City, What Works, What Doesn't.* New York: McGraw-Hill.

Gerring, J. 2007. *Case Study Research Principles and Practices.* New York: Cambridge University Press.

Gilfoyle, T. 2006. *Millennium Park, Creating a Chicago Landmark.* Chicago: University of Chicago.

Glazer, N., and D. Moynihan. 1963. *Beyond the Melting Pot, The Negroes, Puerto Ricans, Jews, Italians and Irish in New York.* Cambridge, MA: MIT Press.

Gordon, C. 2008. *Mapping Decline, St. Louis and the Fate of the American City.* Philadelphia: University of Pennsylvania Press.

Gordon, D. 2006. *Planning Twentieth Century Capital Cities.* London: Routledge.

Gratz, R., and N. Mintz. 2000. *Cities Back from the Edge.* Hoboken, NJ: John Wiley.

Greer, S., and A. Greer, eds. 1974. *Neighborhood and Ghetto, The Local Area in Large-Scale Society.* New York: Basic Books.

Haar, C. 1996. *Suburbs Under Siege, Race, Space and Audacious Judges.* Princeton, NJ: Princeton University Press.

Haar, C. 2005. *Mastering Boston Harbor Courts, Dolphins& Imperiled Waters.* Cambridge, MA: Harvard University Press.

Hall, P. 1980. *Great Planning Disasters.* Berkeley, CA: University of California Press, 1980.

Hall, P. 1966. *The World Cities.* New York: McGraw-Hill.

Hall, P., and K. Pain. 2006. *The Polycentric Metropolis, Learning from Mega-City Regions in Europe.* London: Earthscan.

Hardwick, M. 2004. *Mall Maker, Victor Gruen, Architect of an American Dream.* Philadelphia: University of Pennsylvania Press.

Healey, P. 2007. *Urban Complexity and Spatial Strategies,Toward a Relational Planning for Our Times.* London: Routledge.

Healey, P., A. Khakee, A. Motte, B. Needham. 1997. *Making Strategic Plans: Innovations in Europe* London: UCL Press.

Hirsch, A. 1983. *Making the Second Ghetto: Race and Housing in Chicago 1940–1960.* New York: Cambridge University Press.

Hoch, C. 1994. *What Planners Do: Power, Politics and Persuasion.* Chicago: APA Planners Press.

Ingram, G., A. Carbonell, Y. Hong. and A. Flint eds.. 2009. *Smart Growth Policies: An Evaluation of Programs and Outcomes.* Cambridge, MA: Lincoln Institute of Land Policy.

Jacobs, A. 1978. *Making City Planning Work.* Chicago: American Society of Planning Officials.

Jacobs, A. 1995. *Great Streets.* Cambridge, MA: MIT Press.

Jacobs, J. 1961. *The Death and Life of Great American Cities.* New York: Random House.

Jamieson, M., and J. Doig. 1982. *The Politics of Regional Development.* Berkeley, CA: University of California Press.

Kayden, J. 2000. *Privately-Owned Public Space: The New York City Experience.* Hoboken, NJ: John Wiley.

Klinenberg, E. 2002. *Heatwave, A Social Autopsy of Disaster in Chicago.* Chicago: University of Chicago Press.

Knowles, G., ed. 2009. *Imagining Philadelphia, Edmund Bacon and the Future of the City.* Philadelphia: University of Pennsylvania Press.

Krueckeberg, D., ed. 1983. *The American Planner, Recollections & Biographies.* New York: Methuen.

Krueckeberg, D. ed.1994. *The American Planner, Biographies & Recollections,* 2nd ed. New Brunswick, NJ: Center for Urban Policy Research.

Lang, R. 2003. *Edgeless Cities, Exploring the Elusive Metropolis.* Washington, DC: Brookings Institution Press.

Lang, R., and J. LeFurgy. 2007. *Boomburgs, The Rise of America's Accidental Cities.* Washington, DC: Brookings Institution Press.

Lang, R. and A. Nelson. 2011. *Megapolitan America*. Chicago: APA Planner Press.

Lewis, O. 1959. *Five Mexican Families: Case Studies in the Culture of Poverty*. New York: Basic Books.

Lewis, O. 1965. *La Vida, A Puerto Rican Family in the Culture of Poverty—San Juan and New York*. New York: Random House.

Marris, P., and Rein, M. 1967. *Dilemmas of Social Reform, Poverty and Community Action in the United States*. London. Routledge and Kagan Paul..

Massey, D., and R. Sampson.eds. 2009. "The Moynihan Report Revisited: Lessons and Reflections After Five Decades." *Annals of the American Academy of Political and Social* Science e 621: 6–314.

Meyerson, M. 1963. *Face of the Metropolis*. New York: Random House.

Meyerson, M., and E. Banfield. 1955. *Politics, Planning and the Public Interest, The Case of Public Housing in Chicago*. Glencoe, IL: Free Press.

Newman, O. 1972. *Defensible Space*. New York: Macmillan.

Newman, O. 1996. *Creating Defensible Space*. Washington, DC: U.S. Department of Housing and Urban Development.

Orfield, M. 2002. *American Metropolitcs, The New Suburban Reality*. Washington, DC: Brookings Institution Press.

Orfield, M., and T. Luce. 2010. *Region, Planning the Future of the Twin Cities*. Minneapolis: University of Minneapolis Press.

Ozawa, C., ed. 2004. *The Portland Edge, Challenges and Success in Growing Communities*. Washington, DC: Island Press.

Perry, D., and W. Wiewel, eds. 2005. *The University as Urban Developer, Cases and Analysis*. Armonk, NY: M.E. Sharpe.

Pressman, J., and A. Wildavsky. 1973. *Implementation, How Great Expectations in Washington Are Dashed in Oakland or Why It's Amazing that Federal Programs Work At All*. Berkeley and Los Angeles, University of California Press.

Popkin, S., 2004. "Three City Study of the Moving to Opportunity Program." Available at: http://www.urban.org/projects/mto.cfm.

Porter, D. 1997. *Managing Growth in America's Communities*. Washington, DC: Island Press.

Pritchett, W. 2008. *Robert Clifton Weaver and the American City, The Life and Times of an Urban Reformer*. Chicago: University of Chicago Press.

Rainwater, L. 1970. *Behind Ghetto Walls, Black Family Life in a Federal Slum*. Chicago: Aldine.

Rainwater, L., and W. Yancy. 1967. *The Moynihan Report and the Politics of Controversy*. Cambridge, MA: MIT Press.

Rannells, J. 1956. *The Core of the City, A Pilot Study of Changing Land Uses in the Central Business Districts*. New York: Columbia University.

Rodwin, L. 1969. *Planning Urban Growth and Regional Development: The Experience of the Guayana Program of Venezuela*. Cambridge, MA: MIT Press.

Rosentraub, M. 2010. *Major League Winners, Using Sports and Cultural Centers as Tools for Economic Development*. London: CRC Press Taylor & Francis Group.

Rosentraub, M. 1999. *Major League Losers. The Real Cost of Sports and Who's Paying for It*. New York: Basic Books.

Ross, C., ed. 2009. *Megaregions, Planning for Global Competitiveness*. Washington, DC: Island Press.

Sagalyn, L. 2003. *Times Square Roulette, Remaking a City Icon*. Cambridge, MA: MIT Press.

Sanyal, B., ed. 2005. *Comparative Planning Cultures.* New York: Routledge.

Sassen, S. 1991. *The Global City, New York, London, Tokyo.* Princeton, NJ: University of Princeton Press. Add Lang,R. and A. Nelson. 2011. *Megapolitan America.* Chicago: APA Planner Press.

Schon, D. 1983.*The Reflective Practitioner, How Professionals Think in Action.* New York: Basic Books.

Seale, C., G. Coto, J. Gubrium, and D. Silverman. 2008. *Qualitative Research Practice.* Los Angeles: Sage.

Simmonds, R., and G. Hack, eds. 2000. *Global City Regions, Their Emerging Forms.* London: Spon.

Stake, R. 2006. *Mulitiple Case Study Analysis.* New York: Guilford.

Suttles, G. 1968. *The Social Order of the Slum, Ethnicity and Territory in the Inner City.* Chicago: University of Chicago Press.

U.S. Department of Labor. 1965. *The Negro Family, The Case for National Action.* Washington, DC: Office of Policy Planning and Research.

Vale, L. 2000. *From Puritans to the Projects: Public Housing and Public Neighbors.* Cambridge, MA: Harvard University Press.

Vale, L., and T. Campenella, eds. 2005. *The Resilient City, How Modern Cities Recover from Disaster.* New York: Oxford University Press.

Whyte, W. 1956. *The Organization Man.* New York: Simon and Schuster.

Whyte, W. 1980. *The Social Life of Small Urban Spaces.* New York: Project for Public Spaces.

Wilson, W. 1987. *The Truly Disadvantaged, The Inner City, The Underclass and Public Policy.* Chicago: University of Chicago Press.

Yin, R. 2009. *Case Study Research,* 4th ed. Los Angeles: Sage.

CHAPTER 15

FROM GOOD INTENTIONS TO A CRITICAL PRAGMATISM

JOHN FORESTER

1. How Can Planners Be Communicative? As Handmaidens, Whiners, or Facilitative Leaders?

Do we want planning to be uncommunicative—to be mute? Hardly. No one advocates that. Do we want planning to be just talk, talk, talk—while the powerful make self-serving decisions, while neo-nasty, brutish, and short liberalism rolls along (Bengs 2005)? Hardly. No one advocates that, either. But saying that planning has an importantly communicative, performative character tells us nothing until we appreciate how in actual practice(s) planning can reproduce or challenge established inequalities and inequities, can disempower or empower vulnerable populations, can encourage stakeholders' resignation and inaction, or instead enable their public learning and practical action. So we need to explore, in actual cases, whether and how planners might serve as handmaidens to enable old boys' deal making or, instead, perform as facilitative leaders to stage power-sensitive, results-oriented public deliberations.

To say that planning is communicative, then, is trivial. But what demands critical analysis, both theoretically and practically in real cases, is just *how* planning can communicatively empower or disempower stakeholders, include or exclude issues, recognize or dismiss values and interests, craft public-serving outcomes or squander public opportunities—and more, as we shall see.

To be critical and not just rediscover breathlessly that planning is political, we need to do more, too: we need to distinguish practical critique from righteous complaint. For how much longer can we continue to rediscover urban injustice and racism before we assess how we might more effectively counteract them? How often do we have to rediscover "power" before both practically and theoretically addressing how to engage and deploy power to better our cities? How many more times do we have to rediscover the ugliness and viciousness of racial and class discrimination before we will demand of supposedly "critical" accounts of planning that they castigate less and instead do the real work of critique to educate us more—not just to finger-point to identify inequalities, inequities, and injustices, but also to suggest practical and institutional responses, whether via policy changes or social movements or local organizing, or all of these and more?

So, we need to put aside the misleading question, "Communicative planning or not?" and turn to the pressing political and practical questions of just *how* any planning worth worrying about might ever be powerfully communicative (not mute!), powerfully effective practically as well as politically, thus critically sensitive to real power and exclusion, ugliness and injustice too (Healey 2012; Sager 2012). It's simply not enough, theoretically or practically, to point to injustice or ugliness or inefficiency without addressing "what is to be done?"—strategies of response.

Toward that end, I will argue, we need to move far beyond planning analyses and theories that are primarily aspirational, goal oriented, or teleological to a more nuanced, performative, practice-centered approach or paradigm (Hoch 2007). Taking the demands of change-oriented practice seriously can move us beyond more conventional good intentions (Justice! Beauty! Efficiency! Sustainability!), however noble and well-meaning, and help us assess and evaluate actual planning practices more astutely and robustly than we have so far.

Our object here can neither be the sweeping scope of "the city" or "urban development" in their full complexity, nor deeply contested theories of social or political justice, but the practical, spatially focused work, even the vocation, that we broadly call "planning." We will find it difficult enough to assess how diverse planners might really work to improve human spaces and places, and we should leave to others in fields of history, geography, and sociology even broader accounts of urban change and historical development (Fischer 2009). Because history teaches us that distributive outcomes often shift politically as objects of conflict, contestation, and contradiction—that's why struggles over urban policy, for example, matter—we should distrust facile distinctions between "process" and "outcome" and focus instead on critically engaged practices producing results over time.

So, by looking through the window of an urban transportation planning case in what follows, we can learn, I will argue, about planning in smaller communities too; and the elements of the case can help us to understand and even to evaluate planning in other fields—health and housing, environmental and economic development, community development planning, and more.[1] Still, I will present no general model, no universal solution—just a web of concepts, even variables, that we need to consider, I will suggest, to evaluate many complex public planning processes, especially as these might seek to right injustice or challenge exclusion or established power or "hegemony," or, of course, in many cases, fail miserably to do that (Innes 2004; Innes and Booher 2010; Healey 2012).

2. THE PRIVILEGING OF DOMINANT GOALS: GOOD INTENTIONS AREN'T ENOUGH

We can begin by sketching several aspirational views of planning that students of the field routinely seem to counter-pose to communicative planning accounts. We can group five of these views, we shall see, under the category of "good intentions." These perspectives upon planning seem to privilege the noble intentions of each kind of planning, even if telling us about that good intention might tell us very little, if anything, about *how* such planning might really work in any actual political world in terms of implementation or performance, coalition building, or even strategy. We can briefly identify five candidate "good intentions," and perhaps soon see that having an intention or goal does not tell us much about how to accomplish that goal—any more than wanting to be financially secure tells us how to be financially secure. These five objects of good intentions often capture planners' attention: Beauty, Justice, Plurality, Equity, Rationality.

We can defer to the planning historians to map out the controversial views that internally animate each of these ambiguous ends of planning. For our purposes here, we do not need to choose whether Le Corbusier's views of beauty teach us more about the possibilities of planning than do John Root's and Daniel Burnham's. We do not need to choose, here, whether Peter Marcuse's notion of "the Right to the City" or Susan Fainstein's redistributive appeal to "the Just City" will ultimately be more compelling as a formulation of "justice" as a privileged end of planning efforts (Fischer 2009). Similarly with desires to honor "plurality": Leonie Sandercock makes a compelling case that gives a progressive, multicultural cast to the thinner liberalism of Charles Lindblom writing decades earlier, and perhaps to John Dewey's writing decades even earlier. Notice that despite their differences, of course, none of these authors argues for ugly cities; none argues for unjust cities, and none argues for intolerant or racist cities.

Similarly, Paul Davidoff captured our field's imagination with an appeal to legalistically inspired advocacy planning, an approach readapted under the banner of equity planning by Norman Krumholz—even as, to be sure, neither Davidoff nor Krumholz was "against" beauty, justice, or plurality. Not least of all, however, should we forget that goal of "rational comprehensiveness," of trying to make cities work functionally as complex, interrelated systems: to have transport and water and sewer and housing systems integrally connected to parks and employment centers and school systems (Sternberg 2000). So "rationality," too, has claimed planners' and planning students' attention for decades: cities present us with notorious interconnected complexities that planners ignore at their own and at city residents' and neighbors' substantial risk.

Each of these five views honors a praiseworthy, if unfortunately quite ambiguous, end. Who, after all, other than a cranky few, can be against Beauty, Justice, Plurality, Equity, or Rationality—as long as we have no small cadre of experts pushing their particular interpretations of these goals down our throats? That condition turns out, of course, to be important. Thus, the joke about the two drinkers at the bar: one leans over to the other and sagely observes, "Democracy's the theory that government by thirty fools is better than government by one fool."

Each of these laudable goals and aspirations, these privileged good intentions, orients us toward generally desirable, if also vague, ambiguous, and contested, ends—ends about which we can have important differences of interpretation, ends which we must then somehow (fairly? wisely? expertly?) debate, learn about, and further refine.

Each of these aspirational views of planning seems particularly at home in the university, too, for the critical enterprise of scholarship might help us to refine what's possible: what Beauty can mean and be, what policy choices Justice might pose, what Plurality requires, how we can assess Equity and Inequity, how we can understand the reach of a Comprehensive Rationality. What's beautiful, what's just, what's tolerant, what's equitable, what's rational? What these dominant goals or intentions really *might* mean, what they require—even as less vague visions of possible "outcomes" or aspirations—seems the province not of some mere public "process" but, rather, of the insightful judgment of expert designers who know Beauty when they see it, of political theorists who understand what Justice demands, of liberal defenders of diversity who truly understand Plurality, of expert legal-aid (or planning-aid) advocates who know whose needs deserve Advocacy, or, of course, of the expert-systems analysts, building and refining large-scale formal, presumably "rational" models. This might all be fine in the university—though not even there should epistemology preempt ethics; not even there should debates about the ambiguities of goals preempt, displace, and suppress the practical claims and judgments of what really ought to be done now, ambiguity and all. We not only need to study beauty and justice, but we also need evolving, critical, and pragmatic institutional and political processes to decide how actually to achieve some human semblance of beautiful, just, tolerant, equitable, and rational urban outcomes today, not just tomorrow, and not just 'theoretically.'

We can debate the pros and cons of each intention, each privileged goal—and we can have vibrant debates in each of these related fields in the university, the arts, and cultural and political life—*but what then?* If Fainstein's view of justice differs from Marcuse's, and theirs differ from Yiftachel's, what then? How can we not just espouse such aspirations but assess, practically and theoretically too, how we might ever actually achieve such ends? We have to connect any debates about ends—all noble, all surely important, of course—to practical analysis of opportunities for change, for organizing, for actually getting from an aspirational "there" to real results "here" (Rorty 1988).

So any critical planning theory must be a power-sensitive, institutionally astute, organizationally creative, practice-oriented planning theory. But here our more aspirational planning theories have too often remained relatively silent. We have lots of work to do.

This matters for planning, of course, only if we care as much about *doing* planning as we care about *knowing* what we want planning to achieve. For *doing planning means more than having goals*, even critically informed goals. For as crucial as having good goals might be, we might all see that wanting to eat still falls more than a bit short of actually eating. Wanting justice falls short of doing justice, much less achieving justice. Wanting beautiful cities falls short of achieving beautiful cities. So, if we care about ever realizing the goals of planning, we need also to analyze critically several issues of politically situated, practical place-making *performance*: how policymakers and community members, how legislative bodies or social movement groups, might ever achieve these goals as they confront threats of power, ugliness, complexity, intolerance, uncertainty, and more in our cities and regions.

2.1 A Critical-Pragmatic Paradigm: Challenging "First Knowledge, then Action"

We might make progress in moving beyond and building upon these aspirational views if we see that each of these approaches nests comfortably under John Friedmann's paradigmatic formulation of planning understood as the link between knowledge and action (Friedmann 1987). Friedmann's magnum opus gives us, as he ambitiously put it, a mapping of two hundred years of planning thought—of the ways that social scientists, philosophers, and political theorists have thought about the knowledge required in planning and the range of actions that such knowledge subsequently makes possible. But at the same time that Friedmann wrote this major review which subtly put "epistemology first"—first knowledge, then action—a pragmatic sea change was under way in twentieth-century philosophy and social science.[2]

In a striking series of books, Richard Bernstein (1978, 1983) mapped these philosophical developments, but no one captured the practical implications better than C. W. Churchman, life-long student of Kant and American pragmatist Edgar A. Singer as well. Churchman—a lucid proponent of pragmatism who had a deep respect for the significance of ends—might have asked us to consider critically the messy and contested histories and prior demands and actions that have made each of today's aspirations to Beauty, Justice, Plurality, Equity, and Rationality so plausibly pressing in the first place. In his wry and ironic way, Churchman might simply have pointed out that these ideals can really matter today because so many of yesterday's social and political-economic actions have endangered or threatened today's and tomorrow's beautiful, just, diverse (and so on) outcomes, just as many more of today's political and social *actions* threaten these ends as well. Only in the university do we have the deceptive luxury to think about knowledge first, action second, he might well have argued, as *The Systems Approach and Its Enemies* (1979) essentially does.

If action and knowledge interact inevitably as chicken and egg—neither comes first—we need to reformulate our view of real planning in a political world to depend less on good intentions, to depend less on knowledge first and action second. We might develop, instead, a view of planning that can help us to evaluate *both* planning processes and planning goals, planning in both its doing and its desired end results.

So let's try to consider planning less as the link of abstracted knowledge to concrete action, and more, instead, as a way of redirecting future action in a world of interconnected and interdependent stakeholders who have been already acting on—placing demands on—each other's destinies. We can borrow Larry Susskind's (2006) apt phrasing here and call this planning work "facilitative leadership" for it works to reshape the interdependence of diverse stakeholders, or better, perhaps, in cities and regions, we can say, it "enables spatial diversity by managing interdependence" (Forester 2009).

3. FACILITATIVE LEADERSHIP: ENABLING SPATIAL DIVERSITY VIA MANAGING INTERDEPENDENCE

To develop this view, let's first consider a brief story of planning bus routes in Calgary, Canada, as told by Larry Sherman, architect and planner, part-time professor and consultant. This story provides a nuanced view of the work of facilitative leadership—no tale of rocket science, no extraordinary or heroic epic, but a realistic view of both common problems and practical moves in response that we can find instructive and useful, as well (Forester 2005, 2011).

3.1 Larry Sherman's Story of Planning Bus Routes in Calgary

Interested in the micro-politics of planning in the face of conflict, I had been exploring the development of Sherman's career, in particular as he had responded at different times and in different places to the challenges of involving stakehold-ers with differing interests and values as he planned. He had worked as a young architect-planner in Philadelphia during the Model City days of the 1960s. Soon after that he found himself working on a hospital design with various staff milling around a plastic model of what might affordably be built. In a striking passage, he observed:

> The interesting thing that was going on was that they began to have a dialogue of their own. The more they started talking about their problems with how they put those chips on the model, the more I realized they were negotiating among themselves for solutions right then and there. They were the staff of the hospital—and I said to myself, "If *they're* negotiating, then what the heck am I doing?" and then I realized, "I'm *facilitating*—I'm not designing the hospital yet—I'm mediating their attempts to solve *their* problems."
> ...they would create these options, and people were talking about them—but it was very important that all the stakeholders made the meeting, and they did. Then from there we'd go on, and we'd design it. I began to put these experiences together, and I thought that somehow the architect, urban designer, and urban planner also needed somehow to become a facilitator, to help people have constructive dialogue. (Forester 2011)

This "Aha!" experience deepened his sense of work as a designer rather than displacing it. He went on, significantly: "For me, it all added up to make a lot of sense—this was a dimension of urban planning and design that I wanted to be a part of. I didn't switch and become a mediator. I do mediation to do better plan-ning and architecture."

Sherman's last thought here bears repeating for emphasis: "I didn't switch and become a mediator. I do mediation to do better planning and architecture." He argues that he saw no necessary conflict or choice to make between the practices of doing planning and architecture and doing mediation: the mediation work could, he learned, help refine and improve his work of doing planning and architecture. So I wanted an example: the proof would be in the pudding.

To illustrate the way his professional practice had evolved and developed, Sherman turned to a transportation-planning example in Canada. Let's consider not only the outcome in this case but also the multidimensional character and complexity of the planning challenges faced. He continues:

> This brings me to a turning point, the Calgary Transit case. One of my earli-est projects involved transportation planning for the city of Calgary. Our firm had planned the fixed rail transit in the northwest sector of the city, and we'd designed all the stations. All the feeder bus lines in the city were based on the terminus being at a certain place.
> When the City Council got the money to extend the transit line farther out, they needed to then re-plan all the feeder bus systems to the terminus, to the end of the line. This way you could have a feeder bus system to the end of the line, and then efficiently get downtown for the rest of the work trip.
> Council, in this case, did not trust the transit planners to go to the public and conduct a participation program on a fairly massive scale of re-jigging all

the bus lines, because they simply didn't think staff had the people skills to do that. So, in parallel with the planning work that our firm was doing with Calgary Transit, I was hired to facilitate a public process to see if I could get some kind of involvement of the public on what this plan should be.

Notice that even from this short introduction, we can infer that "planning" might be performed by at least four different planners: (i) the city's transportation planners appear, in the City Council's eyes, to lack certain "people skills," so, Sherman explains, (ii) as a part of his architecture and planning firm, he has been hired by the city to "conduct a participation program," with (iii) members of the affected public who might function as lay planners to shape the public transport investments that will affect them, distributed as they are spatially in the areas whose land-uses are typically planned by (iv) the city's land-use planning staff. Planning, Sherman shows us, may very well *not* simply be the institutional province of just public authorities or private firms or citizens' groups.

He continues by beginning to tell us what he did:

> We had the first public meeting, and we invited representatives of 24 neighbor-hoods associations, the major hospital, the major university, the five shopping centers that were served by this system and the special interest groups, such as seniors and schools, that had big stakes in this bus system. We invited them all to a public meeting.
>
> I insisted that the transit planners and our own technical planners not make a presentation to begin with. Instead, we started out by talking about process and not about the technical issues—especially because technical issues can initially intimidate the public in something technical like transportation planning.
>
> I decided that the transportation planners should not be allowed to come on as technical experts until the public needed them. *When* the public perceived a need to learn more about technical transportation planning, then I had a relationship develop between the two.

Sherman tells us that he thought carefully about *how* to involve the public and the transportation experts, in a shared planning process, together. He did not simply announce a meeting for whomever might show up; he did not, we see, simply defer to the transportation experts to have them, experts that they were, introduce the transportation problems facing the neighborhoods. Sherman did, we see, consider carefully who might be asked or encouraged to participate. He did, he carefully points out, consider the effects of timing—to shape the consequences of who actually might speak first in the public meetings he convened.

But all this happened at the request of a public authority, the City Council. He goes on:

> The way I encouraged that relationship was that I went to the City Council and asked them to give me the parameters within which they would accept a plan generated by the community. They gave me the limits, and the limits were fiscal. They said, "The community can make any plan for the buses that they want to, but they can't spend one dollar more than the present transit subsidy to this area."

Sherman's authority came not only from his own expertise or his firm's reputation or his collaboration with the transportation planners or his invitation to affected stakeholders, but also from the City Council. Given the Council's mandate and limits, he returned to the stakeholders. He says:

> I went back and told them that at the second meeting. They said, "Well, how can we do that?"
>
> I said, "Well, for example, if you double service on one route, then you're going to have to divide it on other routes."
>
> They said, "How are we ever going to keep track of this?"
>
> I said, "Why don't you ask the transportation experts who are here?"
>
> The [experts] stepped up and said, "Well, this is what 'level of service' means, and this is what 'headways' mean, and we can develop a little laptop program that will balance the budget for you as you propose changes."
>
> So that was the union that was made. They then went off, and worked on this together.
>
> For me, it was an example of joint fact-finding—where they jointly generated the information that they had to have—because they needed to.

Notice that Sherman had convened a process that included affected parties and professional experts as well. He'd clarified the political and financial constraints and the planning tasks that lay ahead too. He also reminded participants that their ideas and proposals would not be theirs alone. He continued:

> Then, at the end of that process, I reminded them that they needed to go back to their constituent groups—they needed to have their plan ratified. They all had to go back and present it to their neighborhood groups. Some of them had to help each other out, because by now they all had a stake in the plan that balanced the budget and gave them the kind of transit service that they wanted throughout their whole district.
>
> They were the constituent representatives. Each constituent group had a representative that came to these meetings. We had about 35 people coming to these meetings to do this planning.
>
> We would take maps and mark them and do all the kinds of things that people do around land use and transportation planning. We would divide the groups up into neighborhoods, and there would be a few groups that would be in one district or neighborhood of the area. They would start to lay out where they thought the routes should be. Then they would lean over and start to talk with the next table because the two maps had to mesh, because you had bus lines that had to connect.

Sherman tells us that the process involved stakeholders acting not simply for themselves but for groups whom they "represented" as well. Those groups differed from one another, though, by membership, location, priorities, and more. In the meetings, too, the neighborhoods worked to align their individually planned bus routes so they would meet properly at their borders:

> Sometimes the lines would mesh, and sometimes they didn't, and the transportation experts, *the technical people,* would then have to help them when it didn't

work. Then together they would negotiate the best route for a bus that would serve their interests and that *also* worked for Calgary Transit.

This process, we see, faced the challenges of surfacing (and reconciling!) both the interests of particular neighborhoods—as represented by neighborhood stakeholders—and the concerns of the Calgary Transit staff, the publicly employed professionals responsible for watching out for the (transportation) welfare of the city as a whole. The parties here were interdependent with substantial differences of interests, backgrounds, expertise, and more; how could they now deal with their differences and produce a plan together?

But, Sherman suggests, coming up with such an operational "plan" was hardly the end of the planning story. Sherman hardly understood his role as surfacing ideas and encouraging "participation" and then walking away with little concern for subsequent implementation. On the contrary, he suggests, participation involves more than "having a say," and planning in turn involves more than plan making. He went on:

> Finally, they had a total plan of all these different routes that worked out. Then I had to remind them that first of all they had to go back and get it ratified by each constituent group—but after that, *I then had to take this plan and present it to City Council, because Council would actually make the decision,* not these people. They had simply been asked to recommend the plan.

Plans don't implement themselves, and Sherman suggests, planning that does not anticipate adoption for implementation might be less than useful planning, especially when urban systems need protection or improvement, when city residents need better services in better places. This Calgary process, accordingly, was both timely and results oriented:

> Every two weeks we would have a public meeting. We did the whole plan in 6 weeks. We had another 6 weeks of ratification meetings with the neighborhoods because it was hard to get them scheduled. In twelve weeks we had the whole thing done and I was back at City Council—but not only was I back at Council in 12 weeks, but I was back in 12 weeks with a plan that represented the interests and support of all of these stakeholder groups! The stakeholders groups all agreed. They had invented it—they had worked on it and come to consensus.

Their process, Sherman tells us, produced not only a functional plan, not only a timely plan, not only a plan that grew from a "participatory process," but one with the political "support" of the neighborhoods, and not just the enthusiasm of the thirty-five representatives. Sherman takes pains, it seems, to stress that the stakeholder groups had not so much been the recipients of a carefully drawn up plan as they had been the owners of that plan because they had "invented" it themselves, albeit with the advice of the technicians from the city's staff. "They had worked on it and come to consensus," Sherman says, clearly telling us that the neighborhoods had forged a working agreement on bus routes, a working agreement crafted with expertise—even if they had surely not erased their other differences of class and

income, gender and race, values and interests. All those other differences and lines
of cleavage remained, but on bus routes and their transport future, they had managed to carve out a working consensus to press City Hall to implement.

Sherman explains what happened next:

> So I made my presentation to the Council, and then Council asked if there were
> any comments from the public. One lady stood up, and she wore a yellow lapel
> flower. She said, "Members of the Council, I don't want to take a lot of your time,
> but you'll notice that there are 35 people in the chambers today, and they all have
> yellow flowers in their lapels. They all represent organizations and institutions
> that participated in putting together this plan and recommending it to you"—
> and I'll quote her; she said, "And we don't want you futzing with our plan!"

So the neighborhood representatives had come prepared. They did not simply
sign a petition. They did not write individual letters. They showed up at the City
Council meeting, and they showed up together, wearing visible signs of their working agreement—and together as a political coalition they hoped to provide the City
Council with a clear sense of direction.

Sherman describes his own "Aha!" here, his own realization of the significance
of what had happened:

> I realized then the power of the consensus when it was presented back to a
> political body like City Council. I realized that the City Council could accept
> this without having to play referee, without creating winners and losers. At the
> same time, they could feel as though they had control over the product because
> they had set the parameters at the very beginning. So it wasn't as if they'd waited
> until the end and then said, "We don't like your plan, and we can't afford it,"
> because they had said this is what we can do.
>
> This was a very big breakthrough for me. I went back through other work
> that I'd done, including the hospital design and city planning, and I realized
> that when the public, when the group, the stakeholder group, could agree on
> something, then it has a huge power with the people who make the decisions.
>
> It's very difficult for people with authority to go against the stakeholders
> if the stakeholders can agree among themselves with what the plan is, as long
> as the plan is reasonable. If the members of the hospital—to use the example
> from earlier—could agree on the use of space, it was pretty hard for the archi-
> tects or the Province who was going to fund it to say, "No, that's not a very good
> plan." These were the people that were going to use the place, and that was very
> important.

The lesson that Sherman draws here concerns power and authority, influence and
implementation: "I realized," he says, "that when the public…the stakeholder
group could agree…then that it has a huge power with the people who make the
decisions." Sherman makes no universal claim for all cases, just a general statement that coalitions of affected stakeholders—who actually agree on a carefully
developed plan of action—can have significant power with public decision makers
to support that plan. That much hardly makes the news, but the work of *coalition
building among affected stakeholders* might now assume greater significance as we
think about planning practice.

Sherman has recounted a case here that involved both affected citizens and professional experts—powers-that-be including the City Council and a range of neighborhood or stakeholder organizations, as well as large and small meetings along the way. Notice that this transportation planning effort, however, seems to fit awkwardly, if at all, with a single-minded search for Beauty or Justice, Equity or Plurality, or even a more comprehensive Rationality. Nevertheless, Sherman's work of facilitative leadership seems ordinary enough—it was not characterized by some obviously unique or terribly special social, political, or extra-ordinary influence. So, how should we understand this planning case, if none of the prominent "good intentions" views seems to do it much justice? We can reframe this question—how we might insightfully understand the complexities of planning in this case—by identifying the concepts that seem central, even "necessary," if we hope to make practical and political sense of this case.

4. Theoretical Constituents of Communicative Planning and Facilitative Leadership

4.1 Interdependence, Process Design, and Representation

We learn about the complexity of Sherman's transportation case as the story unfolds. We see that as the City Council intended to extend their transit line, "they needed to then re-plan all the feeder bus systems to the terminus, to the end of the line." The planning effort began not from a blank slate but from needs created by public investment decisions—"Council got the money to extend the transit line"—and the functional requirements of technological systems already in space and place, since, "This way you could have a feeder bus system to the end of the line, and then efficiently get down[town] for the rest of the work trip." The planning challenge, we learn very quickly, required not just imagination and expertise and creativity but also recognizing systemic and practical *interdependence*. Everything that follows addresses that functional and political interdependence, as we shall see.

Sherman speaks of his role in traditional terms: "I was hired to facilitate a public process," to "get some kind of involvement of the public on what this plan should be." He identifies at least three objectives here: His role will be to "facilitate" a process, and we will learn from the story what he means by that. That process will be a "public" one, in which "some kind of involvement of the public" provided a richly ambiguous goal. Not least of all, though, that process will be deeply value laden, deeply normative if not prescriptive, speaking to "what this plan should be." So his work presented him very early on with what we might call the challenge of "process design." Sherman had not just to interpret the ambiguities of "facilitation" and "public involvement," but also to shape what they might really mean in this place—to say nothing of handling some publics getting involved in saying what the resulting plan for the bus system "should be." He had his objectives in mind, but what was he now *to do*? What expertise would he bring to bear and who would he now try to get involved?

Sherman's story quickly becomes specific and detailed, helping us to learn what kind of public involvement he had in mind: "We had the first public meeting, and we invited representatives of 24 neighborhoods associations, the major hospital, the major university, the five shopping centers that were served by this system and the special interest groups, such as seniors and schools, that had big stakes in this bus system."

That diffuse "public" now becomes one of those with "big stakes in this bus system," neighborhood associations, the hospital and university, the five shopping centers "served by this system," and "special interest groups" like "seniors" and "schools." We have too little information, of course, to know who else might have been involved, and that question we even now share with Sherman: what form of *representation* might actually transform a general "public" into a specific group of actual individuals—working representatives who might speak for broader groups and interests, who might bring their knowledge and cares and worries, who might lend their ideas and creativity, whose anger might fuel efforts to improve city systems, whose distrust might encourage greater transparency? Moving from an ambiguous idea of a process of public involvement, Sherman had to make practical, inevitably imperfect decisions about which stakeholder groups to involve or even invite or address as he launched the planning process at hand.

4.2 Expertise, Power, and Difference

If in one breath, though, Sherman mentions stakeholder "representatives," in the next he speaks directly to another problem he faced: the role of *expertise* and, even more practically, the role of the actual transportation experts who might be involved in the work at hand. Were citizen stakeholders and technical experts like oil and water? As a profession, planning has often been haunted by the joke that says, "A camel is a horse designed by a committee." Mention "public involvement" and not ten seconds will pass before one of us worries about expertise: "Do we want surgery performed by someone popular or someone with real training? Do we want our bridges designed by public committees or by licensed engineers?" and so on.

So Sherman takes pains to tell us immediately that he had to address not just "public involvement" but the professional "transit planners" and "our own technical planners," too. Clearly, Sherman had not reduced public involvement to a popularity contest, just as he had not reduced transportation planning to an exercise in technical problem solving or even social engineering.

Significantly, though, in the early public meetings of stakeholders and experts that Sherman had convened, he "insisted that the transit planners and our own technical planners not a make a presentation to begin with." Had he not faced some resistance here, of course, had this not been an uphill battle, he would not have needed to "insist." Telling us that "technical issues can initially intimidate the public in something technical like transportation planning," Sherman tells us, in effect, that he faced challenges of *power* as the stakeholders came together, not just in the selection of stakeholder groups in the first place but even in the details here of influencing who might speak first, how the official city transit planners might take part, set agendas, and "intimidate" members of the public (as traditional planning practices have done before). Professionals, he reminds us, have not only knowledge but also status and power, and in this case, Sherman recounts, he had to insist that these professionals speak second, not first.

But speaking second was hardly a second-class role, Sherman makes clear. The technical staff responded to practical and technical problems as they arose in the stakeholders' discussions. The experts could help to solve specific problems and keep the budget balanced. Sherman had struggled, and had seemed to find a practical way, to integrate broad public involvement with deep technical expertise: "So...they worked on this together...it was an example of joint fact-finding—where they jointly generated the information that they had to have—because they needed to."

So Sherman tells us not just about complexity and a diversity of issues involved, some technical and some less so, but also about the diversity of people involved: some will have technical training, some will not; some will approach technical issues with mastery and confidence, while others will find these issues intimidating. Some will be official agency staff and some will be citizen representatives with altogether other jobs, and so on. Where we have public involvement, then, Sherman suggests, we face both challenges of *inequality* and *power*, not as generalities but in the specifics of who to invite and who not, how to encourage their engagement in real meetings and how not, and more.

Power appears too, of course, in the way that Sherman considered the political and financial constraints he took as operative. As he put it, "I went to the City Council and asked them to give me the parameters within which they would accept a plan generated by the community. They gave me the limits, and the limits were fiscal."

Notice that Sherman views power here equally as a constraint and as an opportunity. He seems concerned at least as much with the limits as indicating what cannot be done as with their indicating what can be done, "the parameters within which they *would accept a plan* generated by the community." Power, he reminds us, enables as well as constrains, and so we might infer that we hardly do justice to new possibilities either by reducing our understanding of power to "limits" or by accepting apparent constraints too quickly. Power pervades planning processes, Sherman implies, and so planners will inevitably need to make judgments about the ways that diverse forms of power can not only limit planning outcomes but enable them as well.

But now the plot thickens. Sherman has assembled public, nonprofit, and private-sector representatives, along with technical experts. He sees the possibility of actual implementation, the actual City Council support of a resulting plan, if—and only if—the assembled representatives can bridge their *differences* in priorities and interests, values, and preferences. The representatives live, after all, in different places. Schools and shopping centers have different needs. Their neighborhoods vary as neighborhoods often do in terms of age and income and more: public involvement means dealing with differences, for such involvement would be wholly beside the point if any "public" was simply homogenous, all the same without differences of priorities, interests, values, and more. Not only, of course, do neighborhoods vary as their topography and locations and demographics vary, but Sherman points out that what promises to satisfy the interests of any one neighborhood might not appear as promising for the Calgary transit staff trying to look out for the interests of the larger city bus system.

4.3 Integrating Participation and Negotiation

In six weeks, Sherman says, this process had generated a plan, "a total plan of all these different routes that worked out," that met interests of the stakeholders and that met the approval of the technical staff as well. In another six weeks, Sherman and the participants faced the challenges of accountability and ratification by the constituent groups that the "representatives" had presumably represented in their discussions. So Sherman's story, curiously enough, *integrates* two concepts or concerns that the planning literature traditionally has kept quite—apparently unnecessarily!—separate: broad public involvement or *"public participation"* and interest-satisfying, *joint gains producing negotiations*. Encouraging participation without joint-gains negotiations would merely produce talk, talk, talk without interest-satisfying agreements. Encouraging negotiations without broader participation would merely produce deal making without accountability or transparency. So Sherman's story suggests a practical challenge—and the very real possibilities of meeting that challenge without recipes, panaceas, or cookie-cutter techniques: the challenge of integrating meaningful public participation with actually effective, joint gains producing negotiations—no small feat (Forester 2009, 2011).

4.4 Distinct, Yet Interwoven, Processes of Dialogue, Debate, and Negotiation

So Sherman's simple story might teach us, too, about what more generally (and unfortunately, vaguely) we might call "democratic deliberations," and about several important, practical processes that appear interwoven in such deliberations. If we listen closely, we might recognize within the deliberative practice that

Sherman has enabled the *distinct practices* and at times the *institutional processes of dialogue, debate, and negotiation*. Consider each briefly in turn.

Neighborhood and other stakeholder representatives had to talk to their constituents about their needs and interests, and convened together in this planning effort, they had to listen to one another. Here in the work of identifying needs and interests and listening to one another's priorities and making sense of one another's fears and frustrations, distrust and suspicions, hopes and expectations, we see elements of what we might call "moments of dialogue."

In other moments, as stakeholders made arguments, about which bus routes might be best, which might be most cost-effective, or which might meet the most important needs, we can see what we might call "moments of debate." But not least of all, of course, the stakeholder representatives and experts also need to make decisions, to compare their options and to make agreements upon what practically they can really implement, what they can really do now, and here we see an important move beyond dialogue, beyond debate, to actual "moments of negotiation."

In moments of dialogue, stakeholders answer the abiding questions of what in the world one another means by saying what they have, and planners might facilitate those discussions. In moments of debate, stakeholders and their supporters try to persuade others, justify positions, weaken the arguments of others, and establish ways of framing both threats and opportunities, and planners might moderate such debates. But in moments of negotiation, stakeholders go further, from understanding meaning and justifying arguments to forging agreements about what to do in practice, and here planners might not facilitate, not moderate, but practically mediate such negotiations (Forester 2009).

Sometimes stakeholders might devote whole meetings to dialogue, to listening to one another's concerns, or to debating, to clarifying a particular set of alternatives, or to negotiating a particular agreement that they need to settle now. Moments of dialogue, debate, and negotiation may intertwine in real time, or they can become distinct processes in themselves. In one meeting, for example, stakeholders might try to learn about one another as much as about the issues at hand, because their mutual ignorance hardly empowers them. In another meeting, or part of a longer session, stakeholders might explore relative strengths and weaknesses of competing arguments about safety or efficiency, or the adequacy of available databases or methods. In yet another meeting, the same stakeholders might focus on making decisions.

4.5 Structure and Process, Outcome and Micro-politics

Sherman's story takes us back and forth from the City Council chambers to public meetings with neighborhood and stakeholder representatives to the still smaller meetings of groups of those representatives sitting and standing around tables and land-use maps as they tried to plan with experts for their own neighborhoods. His story, then, weaves back and forth between the politics of planning at two levels, one more structural and one more processual or personally interactive. Structurally, his story leads us to ask about both formal and de facto relations of power and authority. Notice that Sherman identified stakeholders not only by subjective special interest but also by more objective, less psychological characteristics of spatial location, "neighborhoods," business ownership and function, "shopping centers," intensity of demand, "universities," and state power, "Calgary transit." However Sherman may have done this, the abiding point remains: even a relatively simple story of planning may well involve structural dimensions of state and business, investment, and location, as well as more "micro-political" interactions through which whatever planning gets done actually gets done.

4.6 Coalition Building and Consensus Building: Power and Legitimation

So, Sherman's account of his final presentation to the City Council has lessons for us, too. His role seems overshadowed, he seems quite content to suggest, by the stakeholders present. As he put it,

> One lady stood up, and she wore a yellow lapel flower. She said, "Members of the Council, I don't want to take a lot of your time, but you'll notice that there are 35 people in the chambers today, and they all have yellow flowers in their lapels. They all represent organizations and institutions that participated in putting together this plan and recommending it to you"—and I'll quote her; she said, "And we don't want you futzing with our plan!"

Sherman offers this not as a cute story of flower power in the City Council's chambers, but as a revelation of his own about power and organizing, power from the ground up, one we might take seriously ourselves. He continued,

> I realized then the power of the consensus when it was presented back to a political body like City Council. I realized that City Council could accept this without having to play referee, without creating winners and losers. At the same time, they could feel as though they had control over the product because they had set the parameters at the very beginning.

His realization here concerns both "power" and "consensus" equally, and we should not let the vagaries of "consensus" distract us from his point. Sherman does not appeal here to any harmony or stakeholder bliss, just to their real agreement in coalition on a practical and politically vetted plan of action. The consensus has power, he suggests, not primarily because of any pristine rationality but because of the legitimating power of the stakeholders having agreed to act in concert, to turn out together, to show their joint ownership of the plan, to present themselves as a practical coalition on this issue in this political setting, enabling in turn the City Council to "accept this" without the further rancor of "creating winners and losers" and even with the feeling as though they remained in control, even though the planning work, *with the agreement of the stakeholders*, had already been done for them.

302 HOW AND WHAT DO WE PLAN? THE MEANS AND MODES OF PLANNING

Sherman's point here, his own revelation, concerns not just the "power" of the Council but their needs (to maintain public support) and prerogatives as well:

> This was a very big breakthrough for me. I went back through other work that I'd done including the hospital design and city planning, and I realized that when the public, when the group, the stakeholder group, could agree on something, then that it has a huge power with the people who make the decisions.

Sherman's story does not provide a recipe for us, but it helps us to understand how bottom-up organizing of stakeholders can have political power—in ways that community organizers and action researchers have also argued. Sherman adds to the organizers' accounts, of course, a larger planning process in which power remains central to everything that happens—power not only as a source of constraint but crucially too as a source of real action demanded by affected stakeholders.

"But, but, but," one may object, "Sherman's story leaves the power of the City Council intact, unchallenged." Sherman's story does, indeed, but nothing in our analysis of that story precludes asking how coalitions of stakeholders might press the City Council, and indeed other influential investors, for more. Our analysis suggests that political power takes relational forms, that power can take a form of "fiscal constraint," on one hand, but also "stakeholder organization" and concerted action, on the other hand. By looking at planning through the window of a story like Sherman's, we see not just power's constraints but also its *empowering possibilities*, not just stakeholder participation as diffuse talk but also stakeholders' knowledge potentially integrated with professional expertise, not just participation as a promise of enabling voice but also the possibilities of broad public participation carefully integrated with mutual gain negotiations, and not least of all, not just the expression and demands of particular interests but also those interests reconciled with a larger sense of the good of the city as a whole. We see in this view of Sherman's simple case not an example of complaint about existing relations of power but an example of a critique of power relations that acts upon both limits *and* opportunities, political possibilities (Forester 2012a, forthcoming).

Theories, of course, do not solve problems, political or otherwise; people acting together do. The single-mindedness of the aspirational, single goal-oriented accounts of planning—privileging the dominant good intentions of Beauty or Justice, Plurality or Equity or Rationality—quickly becomes not a strength but a liability in the face of actual practical cases. For that reason we should take seriously an account of planning that asks us not to privilege one overriding goal, but to consider instead a normative and empirical web of crucially and practically related concepts: interdependence making problematic relations of power, stakeholder representation leading to challenges of process design; inequality implying diverse public differences, stakeholder involvement contingently integrated with practical negotiations, and not least of all, distinct but related processes and practices of dialogue, debate, and negotiation.

These related concepts constitute the framework or rough "paradigm" of what I propose to call, "critically pragmatic, communicative planning"—*not* because "communication" plays any central role (we never mentioned the term in this case example), but because work on deliberative politics and practices in planning seem easily labeled in this way (as if anyone wished to espouse "mute planning" instead). We would do better to speak *not* of "communicative planning" at all but of a critical pragmatism "enabling" or "democratizing" interdependence, either of which would characterize far better the practically complex and deeply political potentials and possibilities (if not, of course, the conventional practice) of planning today (Forester 1993, 2012b forthcoming).

Why bother, then, with such an analysis of planning? We should bother because this web of concepts and questions will help us to understand how planning might enable and democratize planning (or fail to do so) in far more specific ways than will the narrower accounts of privileged good intentions, no matter how much we prize, individually, Beauty or Justice or Plurality or Equity or Rationality. Not least of all, let us not exaggerate the role or agency of the planner as facilitative leader or mediator and minimize the significance of this web of central concepts, for as I have argued before, facilitative leaders or mediators no more make multi-stakeholder agreements than do midwives make babies!

We need to understand the web of theoretical constituents discussed above, not just a node here and there, as normative and empirical at once. So this analysis makes far more normative than prescriptive claims. Copying what Sherman did is of course not the point, and certainly not a general recommendation. But considering, both practically and theoretically, what Sherman took into account matters deeply—both ethically and normatively. So we need to understand power and interdependence, stakeholder involvement *and* negotiation, process design *and* the distinct practices of facilitating, moderating, and mediating. We need to stop trying to reduce planning to any one simple teleological goal and start trying instead to understand planning as a complex politically and morally entangled practice.

Planning means dealing with differences, and those differences will not be mute. As Sherman's simple story suggests, planners might not only listen to but also convene stakeholders—in different ways in different settings, to be sure. Not only might planners facilitate their dialogues, but they might also mediate their differences, again in different ways in different settings. In these ways, then, planners might not only enable interdependent stakeholders' practical agreements to produce material results, but they might do so to build power as well. We don't need to call that "critically pragmatic, communicative planning," but if we do, the richness of this analysis, showing both the limits of power in planning and the possibilities of building power too, should suffice to tell us why we will do well to bother with a form of communicative planning, given our competing, aspirational, but less critical and still less pragmatic, alternatives.

Acknowledgments

This essay was written during the author's sabbatical year as NICIS Scholar at the University of Amsterdam in 2008–2009. The author is both indebted to Larry Sherman for his generous, striking interview account and grateful for provocative comments from Heather Campbell, Patsy Healey, Tore Sager, Ernest Sternberg, Mark Purcell, Libby Porter, David Laws, and Ken Reardon.

Notes

1. I take planning theory to differ from urban theory, from theories of "urban development," just as I would distinguish theories of political campaigning (or political mobilization) from theories of political justice or regimes. Giving a good account of organizing and campaigning (or planning) will be difficult enough; giving an account of justice that supercedes that of John Rawls, for example, I will leave to those who, impatient with "process" but failing to see that outcomes rarely remain static, believe somehow that "planning theory" could account not only for urban planning as a political practice but also for urban development and even justice as well.
2. Charles Sanders Peirce and John Dewey began to reframe even the scientific enterprise as pragmatic, provisional, contingent, performative, not foundationally tied to "reality itself," whatever that might be (Bernstein 1978). Not long after, Wittgenstein overthrew his own early "picture theory" of language corresponding to brute objects, that "reality itself," and with other anti-foundationalists like Edmund Husserl, what later became "postmodernism" and theories of "social constructionism" began to take off.

References

Bengs, C. 2005. "Planning Theory for the Naïve?" *European Journal of Spatial Development.* Available at: http://www.nordregio.se/EJSD/debate050718.pdf (Debate and Miscellaneous, July).

Bernstein, Richard. 1978. *The Restructuring of Social and Political Theory.* Philadelphia: University of Pennsylvania Press.

Bernstein, Richard. 1983. *Beyond Objectivism and Relativism.* Philadelphia: University of Pennsylvania Press.

Churchman, C. West. 1979. *The Systems Approach and Its Enemies.* New York: Basic Books.

Fischer, Frank. 2009. "Discursive Planning: Social Justice as Discourse." In *Searching for the Just City: Debates in Urban Theory and Practice,* edited by Peter Marcuse, James Connolly, Johannes Novy, Ingrid Olivo, Cuz Potter, and Justin Steil, 52–71. New York: Routledge.

Forester, John. 1993. *Critical Theory, Public Policy and Planning Practice: Toward a Critical Pragmatism.* Albany, NY: State University Press of New York.

Forester, John. 2005. "Mediation and Collaboration in Architecture and Community Planning: A Profile of Larry Sherman." Profile approved, 2005. Department of City and Regional Planning, Cornell University.

Forester, John. 2009. *Dealing with Differences: Dramas of Mediating Public Disputes.* New York: Oxford University Press.

Forester, John. 2011. "Interface: Learning from Practice in the Face of Conflict: Integrating Technical Expertise with Participatory Planning (Critical Commentaries on the Practice of Planner-Architect Laurence Sherman)." *Planning Theory and Practice* 12(2): 287-310.

Forester, John. 2012a. Lessons From Practice Stories and Practitioners' Own Discourse Analyses (Or Why Only The Loons Show Up)." *Planning Theory and Practice* 13(1): forthcoming.

Forester, John. 2012b. "On the Theory and Practice of Critical Pragmatism: Deliberative Practice and Creative Negotiations." *Planning Theory.* Forthcoming.

Friedmann, John. 1987. *Planning in the Public Domain.* Princeton, NJ: Princeton University Press.

Healey, Patsy. 2012. "The Idea of 'Communicative' Planning: Practices, Concepts and Rhetorics." In *Planning Ideas that Matter,* edited by L. Vale, B. Sanyal, and T. Rosan. Boston: MIT Press.

Hoch, Charles. 2007. "Pragmatic Communicative Act Theory." *Journal of Planning Education and Research* 26:273-82.

Innes, Judith. 2004. "Consensus Building: Clarifications for the Critics." *Planning Theory* 3(1): 5-20.

Innes, Judith, and David Booher. 2010. *Planning with Complexity.* London: Routledge.

Marcuse, Peter. 2009. "Postscript: Beyond the Just City to the Right to the City." In *Searching for the Just City: Debates in Urban Theory and Practice,* edited by Peter Marcuse, James Connolly, Johannes Novy, Ingrid Olivo, Cuz Potter, and Justin Steil, 240-54. New York: Routledge.

Rorty, Amelie. 1988. *Mind in Action: Essays in the Philosophy of Mind.* Boston: Beacon Press.

Sager, Tore. 1994. *Communicative Planning Theory.* Aldershot, Hampshire, UK: Ashgate.

Sager, Tore. 2012. *Reviving Critical Planning Theory.* London: Routledge.

Sternberg, Ernest. 2000. "An Integrative Theory of Urban Design." *Journal of the American Planning Association* 66(3): 265-78. Repr. 2007 in *The Urban Design Reader,* edited by Matthew Carmona and Steve Tiesdell, 33-42. Oxford: Architectural Press.

Susskind, Lawrence. 2006. *Breaking Roberts' Rules.* New York: Oxford University Press.

CHAPTER 16

VISUALIZING INFORMATION

ANN-MARGARET ESNARD

THE latter half of the twentieth century beckoned a gradual shift in how planning was viewed. What was once seen as an activity whose success depended upon the form and appearance of the city evolved into an activity viewed as more complex and dynamically interactive. This realization led to new styles and processes of planning that used "scientific" methods of analysis and problem solving, increasingly enabled by powerful compact computers. Planners wanted to be certain that their counsel was reliable. What emerged was the rise of a "new professional class"—a technical intelligentsia that focused on the rationality of decisions (Friedmann 1987) and brought special skills to the analysis and solution of planning problems. Visualization tools (instruments used) and methods (techniques used) increasingly filled the planner's toolkit to (i) enhance and inform multiple planner roles and tasks (e.g., plan maker, regulator, mediator, advocate, technical analyst); (ii) facilitate participatory and communicative planning processes; (iii) integrate and interpret data from disparate sources and in a variety of formats; and (iv) facilitate iterative processes in the analysis and recursive exploration of data. As the availability and utility of information visualization tools has increased, so too have the roles of planners shifted toward creating information environments and interfaces that empower themselves and other participants (Langendorf 2001; Jankowski and Nyerges 2001; Berke et al. 2006).

Despite this optimistic rhetoric, the technician–theoretician tension lurks in the background. There are lingering questions and issues about rationality and positivist assumptions that the world is inherently ordered and can be managed to reduce uncertainty (Beauregard 1991; Hemmens 1992; Lake 1992).

Nowhere are these tensions more evident than in the use of geographic information systems (GIS) by planners and other social scientists. The GIS-related scholarly writings in the nineties provided a critical turning point cautioning against the promotion of a positivist epistemology and instrumental forms of decision making. Geography and planning scholars highlighted the need for expanding and diversifying theoretical frameworks and applied practices to respond to critical concerns about access, representation, epistemology, and power (Aitken and Michel 1995; Miller 1995; Pickles 1995; Sheppard 1995; Esnard and MacDougall 1997; Elwood 2006). Specifically, the late renowned planning scholar Britton Harris voiced concern in the early nineties that GIS entered planning practice "via routes that have bypassed planning theory and academic research" (Harris 1992, 151). In many ways the same holds true for the wide array of information visualization tools and methods that are being used and created by urban planners.

Against this backdrop, this chapter draws on a diverse set of fields (e.g., planning, geography, sociology, psychology, communication, computer science) to advance the state of knowledge about information visualization tools, planning applications, theoretical constructs, and dilemmas. The basic premise is that simply adding information visualization tools and methods to a planner's toolbox does not guarantee that new questions will be raised or new insights will be developed, or that use of visual information will lead to appropriate and inclusive planning processes and actions. This chapter focuses on highlighting implicit links and relationships between diverse influences, ideas, theories, practice, applications, and processes. What follows is a section that highlights the vast array of information visualization tools and methods used by urban planning practitioners and scholars. This provides the basis for an original typology that is applicable to the various roles and tasks of planners. Such typologies are useful because they help highlight the implicit links and relationships referred to above. Finally, looming and emergent dilemmas are presented with the intention of encouraging deliberation and action by both planning academicians and practitioners.

1. VISUALIZATION AND PLANNING

> "Visualization is the process of taking abstract ideas or
> data and translating them into easily understood and
> interpreted images to enhance planning, urban design and
> decision processes"
>
> —Herman and Synder 2006, 543

Visualization is a term with a number of meanings. In the broadest sense, it is a communicative process that relies on encoded meanings that can be transferred from creators and organizers of information to users and receivers of the same information (Shannon 1948). Visualization is facilitated by an array of tools and methods, including at least five broad and overlapping categories detailed below: (i) graphics; (ii) Web sites; (iii) maps; (iv) GIS; and (v) three-dimensional and simulation models. Combined, they contribute to intelligence gathering and knowledge creation at each stage of the planning process, and they offer functionality that can also be described as static (e.g., graphics and maps); interactive (e.g., Web sites and GIS), and dynamic (e.g., 3-D and Web-GIS).

1.1 Graphics

Graphicacy refers to fluency with graphs, maps, sketches, diagrams, and photographs. It is the most spatial of communication skills when compared to articulacy and numeracy (Monmonier 1993) and epitomizes the old adage that "a picture is worth a thousand words." Graphics can be used in various combinations to enhance visual thinking, reasoning, and communication (DiBiase 1990; MacEachren 1992), and to enhance and inform the planning process for a broad cross-section of society. Data graphics, communicated effectively, can do much more than simply substitute for small statistical tables; they are instruments for reasoning about quantitative information, and impact planning and decision-making processes (Dandekar 1982; Tufte 1983; Witzling and Greenstreet 1989).

It is commonplace to utilize a mixture of noncomputerized (e.g., sketching) and computerized (e.g., GIS) methods for planning and design. For example, Al-Kodmany (1999) reported on a study in which three different visualization tools (GIS, art/sketches, and photo manipulation) were employed during a participatory planning process in Chicago's Pilsen neighborhood. The author concluded that freehand sketching and GIS were most effective for problem identification and brainstorming, while photo manipulation using computer imaging was most useful for exploring solutions to previously defined design issues. The effectiveness seemed to have resulted from the fact that efforts were made to promote and maximize public input and participation in a creative way—that is, the artist provided an avenue for residents to actively participate in design creation by quickly capturing ideas and discussions in sketches, as well as a venue for traditional interactive participation. According to Al-Kodmany (2002), noncomputerized visualization tools such as pen-and-paper sketching, paper maps, photographs, and physical models draw forth high levels of participation and input from participants in a social learning environment, and are particularly effective when the audience includes varied interest groups and stakeholders with opposing interests. However, there are limitations and drawbacks that result from: (i) issues of feasibility and practicality of graphical creation methods such as sketching; (ii) the fact that static imagery does not invoke interaction or provide comprehensive contextual data; and (iii) inherent difficulties with transmitting complex information (Al-Kodmany 2002). Web-based technologies provide one means to overcome problems with the transmission and dissemination of comprehensive contextual data and to increase interactivity between planners and citizens.

1.2 Web Sites

Web sites, subsets of what Herman and Synder (2006) refer to as "community process tools," have become popular avenues for planning and plan making, and a low-cost mode of communication for participatory planning (Al-Kodmany 2002). They also provide a medium for hosting meetings, blogs and chat rooms; sharing important planning event information; and disseminating online surveys. Web sites are also used to elicit comments on planning projects and proposals and to disseminate plan proposals, documents, data, and policies in the pre- and post-plan adoption stages. Proposals and plans can be displayed and downloaded by the wider public, and this allows for more flexibility in the design of documents. For example, animated graphics, audio, and video clips, as well as text, can be included; and color maps and 3-D images critical to land-use planning can be disseminated at low cost to a planning department (Berke et al. 2006).

Web sites also enable academic research geared at improving planning practice, innovation, and improvisation. The *Visual Tools for Planners* website by Hopkins et al. (2008), a library of representations, is one that is worth noting. The website combines graphics, numbers, and stories with the intent to help people think systematically and creatively about relationships, changes, and patterns; to communicate across diverse perspectives of varying knowledge; and to innovate in the face of unusual challenges such as with catastrophic hurricanes (Hopkins et al. 2008).The website reflects the notion that the plan-making process is a dynamic and interdependent process (Hopkins 2001).

Overall, there are pros and cons to this information visualization and dissemination mode. According to Berke et al. (2006, 99),

> [On one hand]...this means that public access to planning proposals is no longer limited to those few citizens able to obtain a copy of a printed report or to attend a public workshop....[On the other hand]...relying on digital communications also decreases the face to face interaction between planners and the community, thus making the planning process more remote and impersonal and decreasing the accountability of planners to the public.

As municipal and regional planning entities deploy online data repositories to share their map and digital data holdings (especially GIS data) with the public, other concerns have surfaced. Research findings by Conroy and Evans-Cowley (2006, 383) show that that e-participation and e-government tools (including information tools such as GIS and maps) highlight the one-way flow of information, and that "the vast majority of the participation tools that are provided do not engage citizens beyond the role of information receiver." This is reinforced by Lanza and Prosperi's (2009) findings that local government Web sites, despite their ubiquity and utility, have basically become points of information, and that the real value of social learning and/or shared decision making is not realized.

Additionally, there have been concerns about sources of data and knowledge. One example is from environmental hazard planning. Community groups frequently have their own, distinct sources of data and local knowledge that should supplement (and in some instances replace) traditional planning data sets on these Web sites. Ambient air quality monitoring data, for example, do not portray major emission sources from bus depots and idling diesel buses parked in close proximity to residential units (Esnard, Gelobter, and Morales 2004). Also worth noting is Kellogg's (1999) example that street addresses serving as geographic identifiers of discharge points are misleading, given that some facilities span several parcels or even city blocks.

1.3 Maps

This section provides more details about maps, one of the most popular and intuitive planning information sources utilized for urban planning in the public, private, and nonprofit sectors. According to Monmonier (1993, 3), maps

> [H]ave an important place in scholarly writing. Historians, sociologists, and other humanists and social scientists often write about territories and neighborhoods, about global disputes and local conflicts, and about causes and correlations involving areal differences, regional clusters, and other spatial patterns. By helping readers visualize regions and comprehend relative distances and other geographic relationships, maps amplify an author's sentences and paragraphs. After all, a two-dimensional stage may be more efficient than a one-dimensional trail of words for recreating and explaining a two-dimensional event.

Maps are tools for analysis and discovery (Monmonier 1993, 12) and prompt insights, reveal patterns in data, and highlight anomalies. Maps also serve as powerful and impressionable metaphors, such as the first depictions of decadal changes in urban growth, which led to more questions and theorizing about urban sprawl. Such visual metaphors "have the greatest power to inform, educate, and persuade an individual and a culture" (Lester 2006, vii) or field.

At the basic level, maps are a fundamental source of information for planning and design activities (American Planning Association [APA] 2006, 527) and are extremely useful visual representations of space and place at different scales (Kelly and Becker 2000). They complement verbal descriptions and are employed to communicate, interpret, and explain spatial phenomenon. Planners rely on maps for depictions of fundamental characteristics of sites (e.g., soils, topography, slope); neighborhoods (e.g., census boundaries, districts, enterprise zones, parcels, parks, bus routes, schools, employment centers, demographics, zoning); and regions (e.g., municipal boundaries, planning districts, land use/land cover, transportation routes, wetland, waterbodies, flood zones). Maps that contrast current and future land-use patterns are usually the most visible part of community plans (Kelly and Becker 2000; Berke et al. 2006), although concerns have been voiced about the potentially flawed assumptions and judgments embedded in maps for areas that are likely to develop between the date of the plan and the planning horizon (Kelly and Becker 2000). Blob maps that indicate the general location of future uses (without setting out the precise boundaries of the area) are used to partially address the concerns about rigid future land use map boundaries in such developing areas.

> [A] mapped representation of the plan...is extremely useful in many ways. It provides a simple, visual representation of the future of the community to landowners, developers and interested citizens. It creates a sense of predictability. It provides guidance to those planning roads and utilities, allowing them to plan the extension of infrastructure to projected growth areas. It also provides guidance to those who may want to invest in agricultural operations, allowing them to choose land outside the growth areas and away from development pressures and potential conflicts with new neighbors. (Kelly and Becker 2000, 180)

Overall, well-designed maps can imply authority. As noted by MacEachren (1992,10) most people have a tendency "to treat both maps and computers as less fallible than the humans who make decisions based on them".

Despite their ubiquity and utility in urban planning, maps can aggravate and exacerbate problems when they are misused—the persuasive power of well-designed maps. The bias of mapmakers and the power of maps as instruments of persuasion and power have been well documented (MacEachren 1992; Wood 1992; Monmonier 1993; O'Looney 1997).

1.4 Geographic Information Systems

Individual maps are frequently overlaid in order to visually interpret patterns and relationships, an approach popularized by Ian McHarg (1969) in his book *Design with Nature*. GIS technologies have automated the map overlay process, and they provide a platform for integrating data from myriad sources, conducting spatial analyses, performing queries, visualizing impacts, and revealing patterns. GIS technologies have emerged as key visualization tools and powerful mediators of spatial knowledge in planning (Elwood 2006). In public planning agencies, GIS is used for spatially analyzing existing conditions and making development decisions based on a combination of spatial parameters. By combining a range of spatially referenced data and analytics tools, GIS technologies enable planners, policymakers, and the public to prioritize issues, understand them, consider them, and reach viable alternatives.

While any visualization technique risks being hijacked for some contrary political purpose, GIS is especially prone to abuse, given the many opportunities for (intentionally or unintentionally) injecting values and assumptions from the initial selection of data layers for one's analysis. An example is a planner using GIS to ascertain areas where polluting facilities are already located assuming that those communities would be more likely to accept additional plants than communities that had avoided this type of development (O'Looney 1997). This example demonstrates how GIS can be used to drive specific political agendas under the guise of value neutrality and technical rationality (Esnard 1998), and undermine plan making and good public policy in the process.

Web-GIS technologies enable nonexperts to take advantage of the analytical capabilities of GIS, increase accessibility to important information for community stakeholders, and facilitate public participation in the planning process. Such combinations of GIS with Internet technology can ideally provide a fully interactive, easily understandable decision-making tool to enhance the connectivity between government agencies, nongovernment organizations, and the general public. For example, to mitigate adverse effects from predicted climate change and sea-level rise, coastal counties are increasingly creating interactive Web-GIS planning tools, as well as 3D and simulation models to enable proactive future-oriented planning actions.

1.5 Three-dimensional (3-D) and Simulation Models

Traditionally, 3-D physical models were largely confined to design and architecture offices and studios, and used for site-planning projects. Over time, such models have replaced two-dimensional (2-D) drawings and made their way into charettes and other community-based planning forums to inform public choice. The 3-D digital modeling, virtual reality, and urban simulation methods have revolutionized visualization of scenes, plans, and architecture (Al-Kodmany 2002), and are increasingly packaged with planning support systems (PSS) to simulate urban futures and permit the evaluation of alternative scenarios (Klosterman 1997; Brail and Klosterman 2001). For example, 3-D visualization tools can show proposed buildings in the context of their actual surroundings and relationships among community elements (i.e., housing, transportation, land use, and the environment), and potential impacts of a development; increase public understanding of a proposed plan or ordinance; and engage the public by soliciting constructive feedback on draft plan concepts and recommendations (Herman and Synder 2006; Berke et al. 2006).

> [W]hen a realistic image of infill development is shown, it is not uncommon for people who are opposed to it to change their minds and launch into discussions about transit, mixed-use development, and other necessary components of a mixed-use project. (Herman and Synder 2006, 543)

San Diego's Association of Governments, for example, developed a set of smart-growth visualization tools to help illustrate how communities can be transformed by smart-growth development and transit-friendly design, and to provide ideas for discussion in local communities. The 2-D visual simulations showed existing conditions and potential changes based on smart-growth principles, and the 3-D visual simulations consisted of a 3-D digital model and animated fly-throughs of conceptual possibilities based on smart-growth principles. The Planning Commission for Hillsborough County in Florida implemented a similar interactive, Internet-based 3-D system. The intent, however, was geared toward communicating planning concepts and ideas with clarity, precision, and efficiency and with making plan amendments, maps, and other graphics available to planners, officials, and citizens via an Internet browser. However, the caution expressed for other information visualization tools and techniques is also warranted for Internet-based 3-D and simulation models. If used as the only avenue for communication, they can magnify concerns about access (to plug-ins and other additional programs that need to be downloaded) and expertise (i.e., the types and sources of knowledge used to represent communities).

2. TOWARD AN INFORMATION VISUALIZATION TYPOLOGY

The preceding sections highlighted the range of visualization tools and methods used by urban planning practitioners, scholars, and community advocates, as well as some limitations and concerns. These tools and methods can be grouped together through different kinds of classification exercises to highlight their similar and distinct functionalities.

Typologies (or classifications) provide value to urban planning academics and practitioners for a variety of reasons. For example, Yiftachel's (1989) typology of urban planning theories aimed to clarify academic planning theory discourse and debates, and make it more useful to practicing planners. Allmendinger's (2002) postpositivist typology of planning theories was, among other things, a response to two traditional planning theory dualisms: the procedural–substantive distinction and the theory–practice gap. Crewe and Forsyth (2003), although focused on landscape architecture, used typologies as a way to advance reflection and debate on implicit and invisible dimensions of the profession.

> Typologies provide a 'frame' for understanding much in the same way as a discourse—they convey a common understanding of subject area, methodologies, language and history of the developments of ideas and practice. Typologies are therefore useful if not essential to anyone involved in a subject area. (Allmendinger 2002, 78)

In the information visualization realm, we encounter typologies and taxonomies that link technologies, theoretical underpinnings, planning processes, and applications. For example, Peng (2001), using the context of Web-based public participation system development, presented a taxonomy based on different levels of information content and functionality (i.e., exploration, evaluation, scenario building, and forum), as well as different levels of services (i.e., representing the level of involvement of the public in the planning and decision-making process). The collaborative GIS cube presented by Dragiceciv and Balram (2006), and Balram, Dragicevic, and Feick (2009) offered a different perspective by juxtaposing levels of participation (ranging from private to public), map usage (ranging from none to high), and technology variables (ranging from nondigital to Internet/wireless modes) in the context of planning and decision-making theoretical frameworks (i.e., argumentative, collaborative, distributive, and collective theories). What we see, however, is a focus largely based on collaborative and participatory GIS technologies and a level of abstraction and sophistication that does not easily capture the full realm of information visualization tools and methods discussed in this chapter.

I propose a novel typology (figure 16.1) to fill this gap. It highlights implicit links and relationships between diverse influences, ideas, applications, and theories. It also identifies potential problems and concerns with different kinds of visualization. It is expandable and can easily be revised as new information visualization tools and methods emerge.

It builds on Batty et al.'s (1999) nuanced classification of backward and forward visualization, and Knigge and Cope's (2006) grounded visualization framework. According to Batty et al. (1999), *backward visualization* involves developing visual tools and imagery that support experts and professionals, while *forward visualization* supports a less informed constituency—the public at large, but more specifically, particular interest groups. Grounded visualization techniques (Knigge and Cope 2006), on the other hand, incorporate grounded theory (largely qualitative with an emphasis on building theories from data about the social world such that theories are "grounded" in people's everyday experiences and actions) and visualization (based on quantitative GIS).

3. GAPS AND DILEMMAS

What emerges from the above typology are four main gaps and dilemmas—three are implicit (cognition, local knowledge, and expertise) and one explicit (i.e., technical expertise). Some dimensions of these dilemmas will eventually be eliminated through technical and technological advances, but others (such as social cognition and local knowledge/expertise) merit ongoing research and theorizing, discussed in the following sections.

3.1 Cognition and Learning

Beyond applying factual knowledge to action, planning functions as an important societal lubricant by mediating and resolving desires in this often-unachievable collective fantasy that is in our social reality (Gunder 2004, 309).

One end goal of visualization is to evoke cognitive relationships in the viewer, and to develop mental images between visible and nonvisible forms, and between spatial and aspatial information (MacEachren 1992; MacEachren et al. 1992; Ramasubramanian and McNeil 2004). A second goal is to enable interactions that sustain and enrich the process of temporal knowledge building, and allow users to identify, explore, discover, and develop understandings of complex situations (Wise et al. 1995; Langendorf 2001).

In the urban planning context, our cognition and knowledge of the spatial environment is a function of several factors, including one's social position, the normative requirements attached to it (Orleans 1973), and the social realm in which planning and decision making occurs. Furthermore, planners rarely, if ever, solve problems or develop proposals and plans in isolation (Tweed 1998). Many plan-making tasks are group based and involve a significant amount of social interaction and information exchange. Yet we do not have sufficient knowledge about group processes in terms of information exchange and the role of prior knowledge (Nijhof and Kommers 1985). Theories of social cognition and behavior setting provide some clues worth noting. Social cognition theory partly explains human behavior in terms of a continuous reciprocal interaction among individuals behavioral and environmental influences (Bandura 2001), and theories of behavior settings emphasize the importance of dynamic and interactive real-life settings in which human behaviors take place (Barker 1968).

Additionally, we are dealing with relationships and engagement between people, tools, and methods (Gill and Borchers 2003) and changing/dynamic formulations and representations of knowledge. Overall, cognition in the complex and dynamic planning realm has made it difficult (despite advances in artificial intelligence) to replicate human thinking, reasoning, intelligence (Tweed 1998), and information exchange. Further research is needed on the covert modes of cognition in planning environments, as well as modes of knowledge building and knowledge exchange. The latter naturally raises questions about sources of knowledge and expertise, addressed in the following section.

3.2 Local Expertise and Knowledge

Displaying quantitative spatial data in a variety of ways may reveal patterns, and statistical analysis may reveal correlations, but it is often the case that explanations (and theory building) are grounded in the experiences of real people living under specific conditions, and they are in many ways the "experts," even if their explanations seem to be at odds with other sources of data (Greene 2008, 2028).

James Scott's (1998) *Seeing Like a State*, a social science classic, makes the distinction between state abstractions (like maps) and tacit, local knowledge. Scott critiques the use of maps, or what he referred to as "abridged maps," as part of a flawed top-down bureaucratic process that does not successfully represent the actual activity of the society they depict. Scott (1998, 6) further argues for the indispensable role

Contextual visualization: Provides factual spatial and nonspatial contexts to facilitate creating a sense of history and place (Langendorf 2001), and presents basic facts for plan-making and policy formulation at various scales and units of planning and analysis.

> Enabling information visualization tools and techniques: graphics, maps, GIS, Internet, Web-GIS, 3-D models and simulation models are all applicable but questions about the legitimacy of local knowledge can arise.

Communicative visualization: Aids in the communication of information and plans to various "publics," from developers to the affected community (Delaney 2000; Batty et al. 2001; Ramasubramanian and McNeil 2004). In that regard, information visualization is highly graphical and image intensive because images more easily than words can cross disciplinary, cultural, and language divides (Langendorf 2001). Visualization also helps overcome communication difficulties caused by the use of planning jargon and technical terms, and helps with movement away from the abstract to more concrete images (Herman and Synder 2006).

> Enabling information visualization tools and techniques: graphics, maps, GIS, Internet, Web-GIS, 3-D models and simulation models are all applicable, but questions about social cognition (in the planning and decision-making realm) can arise.

Advocacy and participatory visualization: Reinforces the goals of participation related to providing citizens with a voice in planning and decision making thereby improving plans, decisions, service delivery and overall community quality of life (Sanoff 2006).

> Enabling information visualization tools and techniques: the applicability of the information visualization tools are questionable based on issues of access, expertise and local knowledge.

Transactive visualization: Presents a venue for co-creation of alternative design and development scenarios, eliciting immediate feedback from diverse stakeholders on the quality and appeal of design and planning options, and assessing impacts during development reviews, comprehensive planning, and policy/regulatory (re)formulation (Brail and Klosterman 2001; Herman and Synder 2006).

> Enabling information visualization tools and techniques: graphics, maps, GIS, Internet, Web-GIS, 3-D models and simulation models are all applicable, but requires highly developed skills and expertise.

Figure 16.1 Information Visualization Typology

of practical knowledge, informal processes, and improvisation in the face of unpredictability, and he contrasts the high modernist views and practices of city planners and revolutionaries with critical views emphasizing process, complexity, and
open-endedness. By not embracing local context and local knowledge, planning
becomes sterile—what Scott refers to as "planning for abstract citizens," "planning
for generic subjects," and "planning for standardized citizens" (346). He explains,
however, that the lack of context and particularity is not an oversight but, rather,
it is the necessary first premise of any large-scale planning exercise. To the degree
that the subjects can be treated as standardized units, the power of resolution in the
planning exercise is enhanced, and "questions posed within these strict confines
can have definitive, quantitative answers" (Scott 1998, 346).

The confrontation between expertise and "lay" knowledge has been and
remains a looming concern for planning and visualization scholars (Alexander
2005; Rydin 2007; Alexander 2008). Aitken and Michel (1995) aptly described
issues of marginalization for groups attempting to enter the public discourse from
different political positions, grounded in local contexts, aesthetics, and emotions.
Rantanen and Kahila (2009) warn, however, that local knowledge is not just about
the qualitative. It is much more nuanced given that: (i) it is produced in diverse
interactions; (ii) it is very versatile and can be processed in different ways; and (iii)
it can be social when it includes experiential and situated knowledge of the local
contexts of actions and settings in one's environment. Further research is needed
on how local knowledge is assimilated in planning practices and decision making,
how to collect and connect local knowledges (Rantanen and Kahila 2009), and the
social process of knowledge production (Ramsey 2009).

The practical, technological, and societal problems with converting local,
behavioral, and experiential knowledge into GIS data remains an old challenge as
well (Harris, Weiner, and Levin 1995; Talen 2000; Esnard, Gelobter, and Morales
2004; Elwood 2006; Sieber 2006; Ramsey 2009; Rantanen and Kahila 2009). This
problem is applicable beyond GIS to a variety of visualization tools and techniques,
and it occurs partly because of the functional limitations of information visualization tools and techniques to handle local knowledge, as opposed to data.

The question should no longer be "How do we convert local knowledge derived
from social narratives into data?"; rather, it should be "When should we convert
local knowledge derived from social narratives into data?" Information visualization technologies work better for some phases of the planning process and for some
planning tasks—something I have attempted to address with the typology presented earlier. There are functional limitations to the techniques and technologies
in handling knowledge. Traditional face-to-face methods of communication and
dialogue must be weighted more heavily in certain circumstances.

Mixed-method research and techniques have emerged from similar theoretical
and epistemological concerns, and they capture the dynamic interplay between theory and practice, thinking and knowing, and acting and doing (Ramasubramanian
and McNeil 2004; Elwood 2006; Knigge and Cope 2006; Greene 2008). Mixed
methods have an orientation toward social inquiry that facilitates multiple ways

of seeing and hearing, multiple ways of making sense of the social world, multiple standpoints on what is important and to be valued and cherished, and multiple subjectivities, truths, and meanings (Greene 2008). It rests on an acceptance that there is partial knowledge from each method (one piece of the story), as well as on assumptions that there are multiple legitimate approaches to social inquiry (Knigge and Cope 2006; Greene 2008).

4. CONCLUSIONS

The ever-expanding reliance on information visualization cannot be overstated. There are ongoing advancements in the structuring of information architectures, interactivity planning in multisensory virtual reality environments, and methodologies for understanding complex patterns through visualization. Users, creators, and mediators of information spaces include a broad "public" who are increasingly using visualization tools in their explorations, knowledge building, decisions, and actions related to planning and decision making. While emergent mixed methodologies can help address some concerns about the representational (in)flexibility of GIS and other visualization tools, there are implicit dilemmas (practical, theoretical, technical) that have come into sharper focus for visualization scholars and practitioners. Some specific dilemmas addressed in this chapter include social cognition (in the planning and decision-making realms) and the confrontation between "expert" knowledge and "lay" knowledge. This has implications for renewed theorizing about the role of knowledge in planning (Friedmann 1987; Rydin 2007), and about modalities and mediators of information visualization and knowledge exchange. It seems especially fitting that the term "public participation GIS (PPGIS) was partially influenced by the planning profession" (Obermeyer 1998, 65), given the significant role that planners can play in democratizing data and information technology (Sawicki and Craig 1996, 520). Planners have a valuable role to play in resolving these dilemmas given the increasingly visible roles that they will continue to play in the creation and dissemination of information environments. This is not the time for them to remain on the sidelines.

REFERENCES

Aitken, S., and Michel, M. 1995. "Who Contrives the 'Real' in GIS? Geographic Information, Planning and Critical Theory." *Cartography and Geographic Information Systems* 22:17–29.

Alexander, E. R. 2005. "What Do Planners Need to Know? Identifying Needed Competencies, Methods and Skills." *Journal of Architectural and Planning Research* 22(2): 91–106.

Alexander, E. R. 2008. "The Role of Knowledge in Planning." *Planning Theory* 7(2): 207–10.

Al-Kodmany, K. 1999. "Using Visualization Techniques for Enhancing Public Participation in Planning and Design: Process, Implementation, and Evaluation." *Landscape and Urban Planning* 45(1): 37–45.

Al-Kodmany, K. 2002. "Visualization Tools and Methods in Community Planning: From Freehand Sketches to Virtual Reality." *Journal of Planning Literature* 17(2): 189–211.

Allmendinger, P. 2002. "Towards a Post-Positivist Typology of Planning Theory." *Planning Theory* 1(1): 77–99.

American Planning Association. 2006. *Planning and Urban Design Standards*. New York: John Wiley.

Balram, S., S. Dragicevic, and R. Feick. 2009. "Collaborative GIS for Spatial Decision Support and Visualization." *Journal of Environmental Management* 90: 1963–65.

Bandura, A. 2001. "Social Cognition Theory: An Agentic Perspective." *Annual Review of Psychology* 52:1–26.

Barker, R. G. 1968. *Ecological Psychology: Concepts and Methods for Studying the Environment of Human Behavior*. Stanford, CA: Stanford University Press.

Batty, M., D. Chapman, S. Evans, M. Haklay, S. Keuppers, N. Shiode, A. Smith, and P. Torrens. 2001. "Visualizing the City: Communicating Urban Design to Planners and Decision Makers." In *Planning Support Systems: Integrating Geographic Information Systems, Models, and Visualization Tools*, edited by R. K. Brail and R. E. Klosterman, 405–33. Redlands, CA: ESRI Press.

Batty, M., M. Dodge, B. Jiamg, and A. Smith. 1999. "Geographical Information Systems and Urban Design." In *Geographical Information and Planning*, edited by J. Stillwell, S. Geertman, and S. Openshaw, 43–65. Heidelberg, Germany: Springer.

Beauregard, R. A. 1991. "Without a Net: Modernist Planning and the Postmodern Abyss." *Journal of Planning Education and Research* 10(3): 189–94.

Berke, P. R., D. R. Godschalk, and E. J. Kaiser, with D. A. Rodriguez, D.A. 2006. *Urban Land Use Planning*, 5th ed. Urbana, IL: University of Illinois Press.

Brail, R. K., and R. E. Klosterman, eds. 2001. *Planning Support Systems: Integrating Geographic Information Systems, Models, and Visualization Tools*. Redlands, CA: ESRI Press.

Conroy, M. M., and J. Evans-Cowley. 2006. "E-Participation In Planning: An Analysis of Cities Adopting On-Line Citizen Participation Tools." *Environment and Planning Part C: Government and Policy* 24:371–84.

Crewe, K., and A. Forsyth.2003. "Landscapes: A Typology of Approaches to Landscape Architecture." *Landscape Journal* 22(1): 37–53.

Dandekar, H. C.1982. *The Planner's Use of Information*. Stroudsburg, PA: Hutchinson Ross.

Delaney, B. 2000. Visualization in Urban Planning: They Didn't Build LA in a Day. *Computer Graphics and Applications, IEEE* 20(3): 10–16.

Dibiase, D. 1990. "Visualization in the Earth Sciences." *Earth and Mineral Sciences Bulletin* 59(2): 13–18.

Dragicevic, S., and S. Balram. 2006. "Collaborative Geographic Information Systems and Science: A Transdisciplinary Evolution." In *Collaborative Geographic Information Systems*, edited by S. Balram and S. Dragicevic, 341–50. Hershey, PA: Idea Group.

Elwood, S. 2006. "Critical Issues in Participatory GIS: Deconstructions, Reconstructions and New Research Directions." *Transactions in GIS* 10(5): 693–708.

Esnard, A-M. 1998. "Cities, GIS and Ethics." *Journal of Urban Technology* 5(3): 33–45.

Esnard, A-M., and E. B. MacDougall. 1997. "Common Ground for Integrating Planning Theory and GIS Topics." *Journal of Planning Education and Research* 17: 55–62.

Esnard, A-M, M. Gelobter, and X. Morales. 2004. "Environmental Justice, GIS and Pedagogy." *Cartographica* 38(3&4): 53–61.

Friedmann, J. 1987. *Planning in the Public Domain: From Knowledge to Action.* Princeton, NJ: Princeton University Press.

Gill, S. P., and C. O. Borchers. 2003. "Knowledge in Co-Action: Social Intelligence in Collaborative Design Activity. *AI & Society* 17(3–4): 322–39.

Greene, J. 2008. "Is Mixed Methods Social Inquiry a Distinctive Methodology?" *Journal of Mixed Methods Research* 2(1): 7–22.

Gunder, M. 2004. "Shaping the Planner's Eco-Ideal: A Lacanian Interpretation of Planning Education." *Journal of Planning Education and Research* 23(3): 299–311.

Harris, B. 1992. "A View of Planning and Planning Education." *Journal of Planning Education and Research* 11:151–52.

Harris, T. M., D. Weiner, and R. Levin. 1995. "Pursuing Social Goals Through Participatory Geographic Information Systems: Redressing South Africa's Historical Political Ecology." In *Ground Truth: The Social Implications of Geographic Information Systems,* edited by J. Pickles, 196–222. New York: Guilford.

Hemmens, G. C. 1992. "The Postmodernists Are Coming, The Postmodernists Are Coming." *Planning* 58(7): 20–21.

Herman, J., and K. Synder. 2006. "Visualization." I In *Planning and Urban Design Standards, edited by the American Planning Assocation.* 543–51. New York: John Wiley.

Hopkins, L. D. 2001. *Urban Development: The Logic of Making Plans.* Washington, DC: Island Press.

Hopkins, L. D., A. Dasgupta, L. Kinsell, S. Strate, V. G. Pallathucheril, Y. W. Kim, and Y. Shao. 2008. *Visual Tools for Planners: Representing Possibilities of Change for Places, People, Economics and Ecosystem: A Handbook to Accompany the Visual Tools for Planners Website Project Team.* CiteSeerX online library, Pennsylvania State University; available at: http://citeseer.ist.psu.edu.

Jankowski, P., and T. Nyerges 2001. *Geographic Information Systems for Group Decision Making: Towards a Participatory Geographic Information Science.* New York: Taylor and Francis.

Kellogg, W. A. 1999. "Community-Based Organizations and Neighborhood Environmental Problem-Solving: A Framework for Adoption of Information Technologies." *Journal of Environmental Planning and Management* 42(4): 445–69.

Kelly, E. D., and B. Becker. 2000. *Community Planning: An Introduction to the Comprehensive Plan.* Washington, DC: Island Press.

Klosterman, R. E. 1997. "Planning Support Systems: A New Perspective on Computer Aided Planning." *Journal of Planning Education and Research* 17(1): 45–54.

Knigge, L., and M. Cope. 2006. "Grounded Visualization: Integrating the Analysis of Qualitative and Quantitative Data Through Grounded Theory and Visualization." *Environment and Planning* 38(11): 2021–37.

Lake, R. W. 1992. "Planning and Applied Geography." *Progress in Human Geography* 16(3): 414–21.

Langendorf, R. 2001. "Computer-Aided Visualization: Possibilities for Urban Design, Planning and Management." In *Planning Support Systems: Integrating Geographic Information Systems, Models, and Visualization Tools,* edited by R. K. Brail and R. E. Klosterman, 309–59. Redlands, CA: ESRI Press.

Lanza, V., and D. C. Prosperi. 2009. "Collaborative E-Governance: Describing and Pre-Calibrating the Digital Milieu in Urban and Regional Planning." In *Urban and Regional Data Management Systems*, edited by A. Krek, M. Rumor, S. Zlatanova, and E. M. Fendel, 373–83. London, U.K.: Taylor and Francis.

Lester, P. M. 2006. *Visual Communication: Images and Messages*. Belmont, CA: Thomson Wadworth.

Maceachren, A. M. 1992. "Visualizing Uncertain Information." *Cartographic Perspective* 13: 10–19.

Maceachren, A. M., with B. P. Butenfield, J. B. Campbell, D. W. Dibiase, and M. Monmonier. 1992. "Visualization." In *Geography's Inner Worlds: Pervasive Themes in Contemporary American Geography*, edited by R. F. Abler, M. G. Marcus, and J. M. Olson, 99–137. New Brunswick, NJ: Rutgers University Press.

McHarg, I. L. 1969. *Design with Nature*. Garden City, NY: Natural History Press.

Miller, R. P. 1995. "Beyond Method, Beyond Ethics: Integrating Social Theory into GIS and GIS into Social Theory." *Cartography and Geographic Information Systems* 22(1): 98–103.

Monmonier, M. 1993. *Mapping It Out: Expository Cartography for the Humanities and Social Sciences*. Chicago: University of Chicago Press.

Nijhof, W., and P. Kommers. 1985. "An Analysis of Cooperation in Relation to Cognitive Controversy." In *Learning to Cooperate, Cooperating to Learn*, edited by R. Slavin, S. Sharan, S. Kagan, R. H. Lazarowitz, C. Webb, and R. Schmuck, 125–72. New York: Plenum Press.

Obermeyer, N. J. 1998. "The Evolution of Public Participation GIS." *Cartography and Geographic Information Systems* 25(2): 65–66.

O'Looney, J. 1997. *Beyond Maps: GIS and Decision Making in Local Government*. Washington, DC: International City/County Management Association.

Orleans, P. 1973. "Differential Cognition of Urban Residents: Effects of Social Scale on Mapping." In *Image and Environment: Cognitive Mapping and Spatial Behavior*, edited by R. M. Downs and D. Stea, 115–30. New Brunswick, NJ: Aldine Transactions.

Peng, Z. 2001. "Internet GIS for Public Participation." *Environment and Planning Part B: Planning and Design* 28:889–905.

Pickles, J. 1995. *Ground Truth: The Social Implications of Geographic Information Systems*. New York: Guilford.

Ramasubramanian, L., and S. McNeil. 2004. "Visualizing Urban Futures: A Review and Critical Assessment of Visualization Applications for Transportation Planning and Research." *Proceedings of the City Futures Conference*, Chicago, July 9–10.

Ramsey, K. 2009. "GIS, Modeling and Politics: On the Tensions of Collaborative Decision Support." *Journal of Environmental Management* 90:1972–80.

Rantanen, H., and M. Kahila 2009. "The Softgis Approach to Local Knowledge." *Journal of Environmental Management* 90:1981–90.

Rydin, Y. 2007. "Reexamining the Role of Knowledge in Planning Theory." *Planning Theory* 6(1): 52–68.

Sanoff, H. 2006. "Participation." In *Planning and Urban Design Standards, edited by the American Planning Assocation*, 46–48. New York: John Wiley.

Sawicki, D. S., and W. J. Craig. 1996. "The Democratization of Data: Bridging the Gap for Community Groups." *Journal of the American Planning Association* 62:512–23.

Scott, J. 1998. *Seeing Like a State: How Certain Schemes to Improve the Human Condition Have Failed*. New Haven, CT: Yale University Press.

Shannon, C. E. 1948. "A Mathematical Theory of Communication." *Bell System Technical Journal* 27:379–423.

Sheppard, E. 1995. "GIS and Society: Toward a Research Agenda." *Cartography and Geographic Information Systems* 22(1): 5–16.

Sieber, R. E. 2006. "Public Participation Geographic Information Systems: A Literature Review and Framework." *Annals of the American Association of Geographers* 96(3): 491–507.

Talen, E. 2000. "Bottom-Up GIS: A New Tool for Individual and Group Expression in Participatory Planning." *Journal of the American Planning Association* 66:279–94.

Tufte, E. R. 1983. *The Visual Display of Quantitative Information.* Cheshire, CT: Graphics Press.

Tweed, C. 1998. "Supporting Argumentation Practices In Urban Planning and Design." *Computers, Environment and Urban Systems* 22(4): 351–63.

Wise, J. A., J. J. Thomas, K. Pennock, D. Lantrip, M. Pottier, A. Shur, and V. Crow. 1995. "Visualizing the Non-Visual: Spatial Analysis and Interaction with Information from Text Documents." In *Proceedings of the 1995 IEEE Symposium on Information Visualization,* 51–58. New York: Institute of Electrical and Electronics Engineers.

Witzling, L., and R. Greenstreet. 1989. *Presenting Statistics: A Manager's Guide to Persuasive Use of Statistics.* New York: John Wiley.

Wood, D. 1992. *The Power of Maps.* New York: Guilford.

Yiftachel, O. 1989. "Towards a New Typology of Urban Planning Theories." *Environment and Planning Part B: Planning and Design* 16(1): 23–39.

CHAPTER 17

....

MODELING URBAN SYSTEMS

....

JOHN D. LANDIS

THANKS to the advent of faster and more powerful computers; the increased avail-ability of spatial, demographic, and economic databases over the Internet; greater international interest (especially in Asia, where rapid urbanization is the rule); and a new emphasis on linking urban and environmental processes to promote sus-tainability, interest in urban models is exploding. Indeed, if there is a golden age of urban models, it is surely now. This chapter presents a survey of different types of urban models in planning use in North America, and to a lesser extent, in Europe, Asia, and South America.

I begin by discussing models in widespread professional use such as popula-tion projection models, economic base models, hedonic price models, and travel behavior models. I next move on to procedures such as land-use change and urban growth models that are just now emerging from their developer's heads and labo-ratories to find wider use as scenario-building tools. Last, I take a look at more aca-demic models, like the monocentric/polycentric city model, Tiebout's (1956) model of efficient public choice, and Schelling's (1969) model of spatial segregation. This last set, although not always useful for addressing everyday problems, provides powerful insights into the organization, structure, and dynamics of metropolitan areas and urban life.

Urban models lie at the intersection of a larger set of demographic, economic, and spatial patterning and change models. In the interests of being concise, I limit the subject of this chapter to those models of interest to planners—that is, to mod-els that yield practical advice for undertaking spatial or policy interventions in the real world. By choosing to focus on planning-related models, I leave out others, most notably Central Place Theory, Zipf's Law of the distribution of city sizes, real estate appraisal models, models of metropolitan comparative advantage, input-output models, and models of regional spatial equilibrium such as those proposed by Krugman, Fujita, and Venables (1999). For different reasons, I also leave out economic and transaction accounting models, such as fiscal impact assessment models, cost-benefit models, financial feasibility models, and legacy models such as Urban Dynamics (Forrester 1969). And because our focus is primarily in the urban sphere, I leave out environmental impact assessment models, environmental overlay models, air and water quality models, and climate change models. Despite these intentional omissions, the planning toolkit—and hence this overview chapter--remains quite full.

1. Model Forms and Functions

Planners use urban models for purposes of description, for explanation, and for prediction. Models used for *descriptive purposes* help us make sense of the world by identifying a few key drivers consistently associated with observable outcomes in a variety of contexts or situations. Descriptive models are intended to be indicative rather than comprehensive; as such, they tend to focus on a few key variables and relationships. The economic base model, for example, which describes how external income is recirculated in a local economy, is primarily a descriptive model. So, too, are urban density and bid-rent models, which describe the patterns of metropolitan densities and land prices primarily as a function of distance from employment centers.

Explanatory models connect one or more driver variables (also known as *exogenous* or *independent variables*) to an output or outcome variable of interest (also known as the *endogenous* or *dependent variable*). For example, we might be interested in how the combination of square footage, number of bathrooms, and house age precisely influences home prices. Alternatively, we might be interested in how neighborhood density, household income, and walking distance to the nearest bus stop influence the choice of commute mode. Explanatory models are especially useful when planners have some control over possible driver variables (e.g., transit frequency of service) and want to explore how intentional changes in the value of that variable (e.g., doubling bus frequencies) will affect specific outcomes (e.g., bus ridership).

Predictive models build on simple explanatory relationships to help us predict future outcomes or construct alternative future scenarios. Predictive models are typically composed of multiple and interacting drive variables whose values tend to unfold over time. If planning is about undertaking near-term interventions to generate alternative and hopefully better futures, then planners should have great use for predictive models. Some predictive models are normative, meaning that they identify *desirable future outcomes*. Other predictive models are positivist, meaning that they predict future outcomes *without evaluating their desirability*. While good predictive models are built on strong explanatory and descriptive relationships, the opposite is not necessarily true: a good descriptive model need not be explanatory or predictive.

Most explanatory and many predictive models take the following general form:

$$Y = f(X_1, X_2, X_3 \ldots X_n)$$

where: Y is a current or future outcome of interest; X_1 through X_n are explanatory or driver variables; and f indicates a linear or nonlinear mathematical function

The X, or independent variable(s), can be nominal, categorical, or interval in nature. In the case of regression models, the dependent, or Y variable, is typically an interval variable such as housing prices or trip volumes or average census tract densities. In the case of logistical regression (logit), the dependent variable is typically a category such as tenure choice (owner or renter) or mode choice (drive-alone or take public transportation or walk). Table 17.1 includes examples of common urban models that follow this form.

Some explanatory models and most predictive models are also *temporal*, meaning that the values of the dependent variable and (some of the) independent variables may trend over time. In the case of geographic information systems (GIS) or *spatial models*, the values of both the independent and dependent variables can also indicate locational characteristics such as co-location (one variable or attribute is spatially coincident with another) or proximity.

Most explanatory models are either deterministic or statistical. In the case of *deterministic* models, the relationships or associations (as indicated by the coefficients or weights attached to each independent variable, X) hold for each and every value of X and Y. In the case of *statistical* models, the relationships between the independent and dependent variables may vary along a statistical distribution. Finding the properties of these distributions requires a step known as coefficient estimation or *model calibration*.

Once estimated, coefficient values can be interpreted as explanatory weights. Positive coefficient values generally indicate that an increase in the value of X is associated with an increase in the value of Y; negative coefficient values indicate that an increase in the value of X is associated with a decrease in the value of Y. When all the X variables are scaled the same way, larger coefficient values indicate a bigger effect, while smaller values indicate lesser effects. When the X variables are scaled differently or the model is nonlinear, it may be necessary to rescale the coefficient values to compare their relative importance.

Importance is not the same as statistical significance. A coefficient may seem important based on a large coefficient value, but be statistically insignificant (meaning that there is a reasonable probability that the coefficient value might

Table 17.1 Examples of Common Urban Models with Independent ▶ Dependent Variable Structure

Model Type	Dependent Variable (Y)	Independent Variables (X)	Typical Unit of Analysis (Observation)	Estimation Method
Population Change	Net migration rate by age cohort	Population age and demographic characteristics; job and economic opportunities; cost of living	County	Linear Regression
Trip Generation	Number of trips generated by household or zone	Density and land use mix in zone; household demographic and economic characteristics; auto availability; ease of travel from/to zone.	Zone or individual household	Linear Regression
Choice of Travel Mode	Choice of mode (among several) for trip, by purpose, and origin-destination zone pair	Level of service (time and cost) among competing modes; traveler characteristics.	Trip activity, by purpose	Multinomial Logit
Urban Density Gradient	Population or housing density by location	Distance from central business district (CBD); age of development; availability of developable land	Average residential density by zone or census tract	Linear Regression
House Prices	Sale price of homes	Structural characteristics (size, age, design); locational characteristics (distance to roads and amenities); quality of neighborhood services; prior prices of similarly located homes	Recently sold homes	Linear Regression
Activity (Residential) Location	Choice of tenure, home, and neighborhood combination when moving	Household demographic and economic characteristics; types and prices of available homes in competing locations; household's work location.	Homes and neighborhoods in combination	Multi-nomial Logit
Land-Use Change	Site-level change from undeveloped to developed status, or change in density	Physical characteristics of site (slope); zoning and regulatory characteristics; access to roads and infrastructure; public service quality; supply of competing sites	Sites or parcels	Multi-nomial Logit

actually be zero). Alternatively, a coefficient may seem unimportant based on a small coefficient value, but be highly significant.

Statistical models can be combined in a variety of ways to try to model complex phenomena. In *path models* (estimated using a technique known as structural equation modeling), variables may be both endogenous and exogenous. In hierarchical or *multilevel models*, outcomes may occur in sequence, with a subsequent outcome dependent on a prior one. In sequential, recursive, or *iterative models*, the outcome value of one model equation becomes the input to another model equation.

Once properly specified and calibrated, models can be used for evaluation, forecasting, simulation, or impact assessment. In the case of an evaluation model, one or more of the X variables is a *policy variable* reflecting the inputs or characteristics of a government policy or strategic intervention. In the case of a forecasting model, current or future values of the X variables are used to calculate a forecast value of Y. In the case of a simulation model, alternative values of several X variables are used to simulate how an outcome would respond to a purposeful change in several X values. In the case of an impact assessment model, alternative values of several X values are traced through coupled models to determine whether small changes in the X variables translate into a large change from the status quo of Y.

Models are only as good as the data they are derived from, and in the case of urban models, the availability of high-quality data is getting better all the time. Historically, most urban models were cross-sectional, aggregate, and of low spatial resolution. By *cross-sectional*, I mean that it relies on data that cover multiple places or people, but for only a single point in time. By *aggregate*, I mean that it makes use of data that aggregate individual observations into community or census tract totals, rather than relying on the individual observations themselves. And by low *spatial resolution*, I mean that it is unable to precisely identify individual observations in space so that their locations can be compared in terms of proximity or distance.

All of this is now changing. Today's urban datasets often include observations from multiple time periods, enabling researchers to more precisely identify and model actual changes. Likewise, analysts and modelers are increasingly using real-time data to understand behavior on a minute-to-minute basis. The growing use of the Internet to collect survey data (and in the case of Internet companies, to assemble and mine large Internet transaction databases) now means planners have greater access to data on individual preferences and behaviors. This type of individual-level data is commonly referred to as *disaggregate* data. Last, the widespread use of remote-sensing technologies, especially GPS, now means that most observations can be geo-coded, or located in space, and quickly compared to other observations.

Still, some things don't change. To be regarded as reliable, models still need to be based on observations drawn from representative—or better yet, random—samples. The laws of statistics have yet to be repealed, so obtaining robust model results requires having a sufficient number of observations. Good models are *calibrated*, or estimated based on historical or current data. Better models are also *validated*, meaning that their results are checked for consistency using comparable data from other circumstance or time periods. Good modelers keep one eye on how their models fit the data—that is, on how their models predict the values of the dependent variable—but their other eye on whether the model coefficients (the estimated weights calculated for the independent variables) make intuitive and statistical sense. Above all, good modelers understand that the real value of modeling lies not in the apparent closeness of a particular prediction or the clever formulation of a particular variable, but in the power of models to shed new light, yield new insights, and serve as a vehicle for collective learning.

2. COMMON URBAN MODELS

Urban models come in every size and shape imaginable. Among the urban models of greatest interest to planners are: (i) population projection models; (ii) local economic base models; (iii) models of metropolitan form and density; (iv) hedonic price models; (v) activity location models; (vi) travel behavior models; (vii) land-use models; and (viii) filtering and spatial sorting models. Each of these model types is explained in summary form below and in table 17.2. At the end of each model summary, I offer a "quick take evaluation" on which models work best and why, as well as a short list of useful references.

2.1 Demographic and Population Projection Models

Planners use population models to project the amount and composition of population change for municipalities, counties, metropolitan regions, and in some cases, states. Three types of models are in common use for projecting future population: (1) step-down models, in which a population total for a larger area (e.g., a metropolitan area or county) is "stepped down" to a smaller area (e.g., a municipality or neighborhood) using a fixed or historical ratio; (2) trend models, in which an historical growth trend is projected forward into the future; and (3) cohort-component models, in which historical birth, death, and migration rates are projected forward by gender and age cohort. Step-down and trend models may be constructed for any geography for which decennial or annual census data is available.[1] Cohort-component models require age-specific birth, death, and migration rate data, and are typically limited in their use to counties and larger geographical units. Figure 17.1 graphically illustrates the workings of a cohort-component model.

Table 17.2 Types of Common Urban Models

Model Type	Appropriate Scale of Use	Useful for Description & Explanation?	Useful for Forecasting and Prediction?	Useful for Simulation & Scenario-building?	Useful for Evaluation?	Positive or Normative?
Population Projection (Cohort Component)	Multiple: County, state, nation	Yes, decomposes past population changes into birth, death, and migration components	Yes, can extend component trends into future	Yes, can vary component rates to explore alternative population totals	No	Positive
Economic Base and Multiplier	Multiple: Community → region	Yes, explains relationships between "basic" and "local-serving" sectors	No	Yes, by applying multipliers to prospective projects	Yes, ex ante	Positive
Urban Form, Density, and Housing and Land Prices	Metropolitan area	Yes, explains how transportation costs and location preferences determine density, land and housing prices, and land uses patterns as a function of distance from metro core	Somewhat, assuming past preferences are repeated in the future	No	Somewhat	Positive and Normative
Hedonic Price Models	Multiple: Community → metropolitan area	Yes, identifies key structural and location factors affecting property prices	No	Somewhat, can simulate effects of public policies and investments on houisng and property prices	No	Positive

(Continued)

Table 17.2 (Continued)

Model Type	Appropriate Scale of Use	Useful for Description & Explanation?	Useful for Forecasting and Prediction?	Useful for Simulation & Scenario-building?	Useful for Evaluation?	Positive or Normative?
Activity Location Models	Metropolitan area	Yes, identifies key determinants of housing, business, retail, and public facilities location decisions	Somewhat, assuming past preferences are repeated in the future	Yes, can simulate effects of public policies and investments on household and business locations	Ex ante	Positive and Normative
Travel Behavior Models	Metropolitan area	Yes, identifies determinants of travel behavior and patterns	Yes, by extending past preferences into the future	Yes, can simulate effects of public policies and investments on travel behavior and system performance	Ex ante	Positive
Land Use Change Models	City or metropolitan area	Yes, identifies key determinants of land use patterns and change	Yes, by extending past determinants into the future	Yes, can simulate effects of alternative public policies and investments on future land use patterns	Ex ante	Postive
Filtering and Spatial Sorting Models	Multiple Neigborhood → Metropolitan area	Yes, describes and explains movement of households across and within neighborhoods and housing types	No	Limited, may help identify instability points	No	Normative

Each type of population projection model has advantages and disadvantages and embeds particular assumptions. Step-down models require that past relationships between a larger geographical unit (e.g., a state) and a smaller one (e.g., a county) remain in force. Trend models assume that the factors and forces that drove past population change will continue to do so into the future—albeit, perhaps in a modified form. Cohort-component models, although generally more accurate than step-down or trend models, require considerably more data. They also require forecasters to make explicit assumptions about the drivers and nature of future migration rates and totals. The outputs of population projection models (especially cohort-component models) are frequently used with average or cohort-specific household formation and tenure rates to project future household, owner, and renter totals. Most well-constructed population projection models are likely to be reasonably reliable over a planning horizon of ten or fewer years. It is for longer planning horizons that they run into problems.

Quick-take Evaluation: Step-down and trend models obscure as much as they illuminate. If possible, take the extra time and effort necessary to collect good migration data, and go with the cohort-component model.

Quick References: *Research Methods in Urban and Regional Models* (Wang and vom Hofe 2007); *Community Analysis and Planning Techniques* (Klosterman 1990).

2.2 Economic Base and Multiplier Models

Economic base models are descriptive models that relate the amount and location of so-called "basic" jobs and businesses (business that produce goods and services for sale outside the local economy) to secondary or "local-serving" jobs and businesses (businesses that produce goods and services for local consumption).[2] The ratio of local-serving jobs to basic jobs (or local income to basic income) is known as the *multiplier.*

Local multipliers can be identified using simple job or sales ratios, using regression techniques, or, when at the regional level, through the use of input-output analysis. Once derived, multipliers are used by planners and economic development officials primarily for evaluation and simulation—that is, to calculate the job or public revenue benefits associated with a particular public or private investment (such as a convention center or sports arena) or job attraction program. Local income multipliers usually vary from 1 to 3, indicating that every dollar of income generated outside the local economy is re-circulated one to three times inside the local economy, generating additional jobs and income. Higher multipliers are usually identified with more powerful, resilient, and self-sufficient local economies. As is the case with any model-derived parameter—but especially job and income multipliers—poorly constructed models typically lead to erroneous results. Figure 17.2 graphically illustrates the workings of the economic base model.

Sex and Age Cohort	2005 Base Population	5-year Survival Rate	5-year Survivors + Births	5-year Migration Rate	2010 Forecast Population
Male:	856,865				1,036,527
Under 5 years	65,534	0.9910	69,200	1.0000	69,200
5 to 9 years	64,343	0.9991	64,946	1.2235	79,461
10 to 14 years	64,709	0.9991	64,283	1.2111	77,853
15 to 19 years	55,242	0.9922	64,649	1.1572	74,812
20 to 24 years	56,029	0.9922	54,809	1.2937	70,905
25 to 29 years	65,772	0.9916	55,590	1.3661	75,943
30 to 34 years	71,713	0.9916	65,219	1.2809	83,542
65 to 69 years	31,859	0.8654	34,812	1.1725	40,818
70 to 74 years	21,356	0.8654	27,572	1.0040	27,681
75 to 79 years	15,818	0.6795	18,482	0.9187	16,980
80 to 84 years	8,995	0.6795	10,749	0.9737	10,467
85 years+	5,507	0.4320	8,492	0.8988	7,632
Female:	834,348				1,021,781
Under 5 years	62,442	0.9931	69,200	1.0000	69,200
5 to 9 years	61,069	0.9990	62,008	1.2242	75,909
10 to 14 years	60,994	0.9990	61,006	1.2022	73,342
15 to 19 years	52,908	0.9968	60,932	1.1679	71,159
20 to 24 years	52,416	0.9968	52,740	1.2830	67,666
25 to 29 years	61,784	0.9966	52,249	1.3982	73,057
30 to 34 years	68,266	0.9966	61,573	1.2971	79,868
65 to 69 years	34,110	0.9071	38,771	1.2283	47,625
70 to 74 years	21,216	0.9071	30,940	0.9530	29,485
75 to 79 years	18,384	0.7662	19,244	0.9571	18,418
80 to 84 years	13,196	0.7662	14,086	1.0683	15,048
85 years+	8,709	0.3995	13,590	0.8527	11,588
Total	1,691,213				2,058,309
Source and Logic	American Community Survey	Based on state Vital Statistics reports	Initial population * 5-year survival rate ▸ down 1 row	Calculated as a residual from prior model; or from state data	5-year survivors * migration rate

Figure 17.1 Cohort-component model workings

5-year Survival Rate	5-year Survivors + Births	5-year Migration Rate	2015 Forecast Population	5-year Survival Rate	5-year Survivors + Births	5-year Migration Rate	2020 Forecast Population
			1,454,374				1,721,186
0.9910	85,354	1.0000	85,354	0.9910	106,390	1.0000	106,390
0.9991	84,588	1.2235	103,492	0.9991	84,588	1.2235	103,492
0.9991	84,510	1.2111	102,349	0.9991	103,396	1.2111	125,222
0.9922	84,431	1.1572	97,704	0.9922	102,254	1.1572	118,328
0.9922	83,769	1.2937	108,370	0.9922	96,938	1.2937	125,406
0.9916	83,112	1.3661	113,543	0.9916	107,521	1.3661	146,888
0.9916	82,414	1.2809	105,568	0.9916	112,588	1.2809	144,220
0.8654	64,140	1.1725	75,207	0.8654	73,731	1.1725	86,453
0.8654	55,510	1.0040	55,729	0.8654	65,087	1.0040	65,345
0.6795	48,041	0.9187	44,137	0.6795	48,231	0.9187	44,311
0.6795	32,646	0.9737	31,788	0.6795	29,993	0.9737	29,205
0.4320	10,410	0.8988	9,356	0.4320	25,643	0.8988	23,048
			1,251,476				1,535,143
0.9931	85,354	1.0000	85,354	0.9931	106,390	1.0000	106,390
0.9990	68,719	1.2242	84,124	0.9990	84,761	1.2242	103,762
0.9990	75,831	1.2022	91,165	0.9990	84,038	1.2022	101,031
0.9968	73,267	1.1679	85,566	0.9968	91,071	1.1679	106,358
0.9968	70,933	1.2830	91,008	0.9968	85,294	1.2830	109,433
0.9966	67,451	1.3982	94,312	0.9966	90,719	1.3982	126,847
0.9966	72,807	1.2971	94,440	0.9966	93,990	1.2971	121,917
0.9071	50,996	1.2283	62,641	0.9071	59,938	1.2283	73,624
0.9071	43,198	0.9530	41,167	0.9071	56,819	0.9530	54,147
0.7662	26,744	0.9571	25,596	0.7662	37,341	0.9571	35,738
0.7662	14,112	1.0683	15,076	0.7662	19,612	1.0683	20,952
0.3995	16,160	0.8527	13,779	0.3995	17,057	0.8527	14,544
			2,705,850				3,256,329
Based on state Vital Statistics reports	Initial population * 5-year survival rate ► down 1 row	Calculated as a residual from prior model; or from state data	5-year survivors * migration rate	Based on state Vital Statistics reports	Initial population * 5-year survival rate ► down 1 row	Calculated as a residual from prior model; or from state data	5-year survivors * migration rate

Figure 17.1 (Continued)

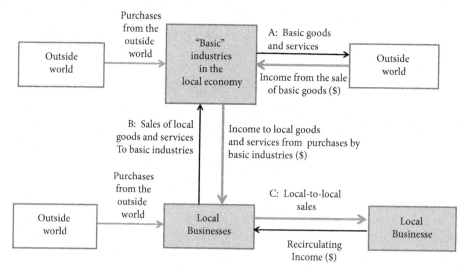

Figure 17.2 Schematic relationships in the economic base model

Quick-take Evaluation: The ways in which local economies function within global markets are changing so rapidly as to render economic base and multiplier models (and their results) relics of a bygone era. Still, as descriptive ways of thinking about how income enters and is recirculated within a local economy, they have their uses.

Quick References: Research Methods in Urban and Regional Models (Wang and vom Hofe 2007); *Economic Base Studies for Urban and Regional Planning in the Profession of City Planning: Changes, Images, and Challenges, 1950–2000* (Isserman 2000); "Why Regions Grow: A Review of Research on the Economic Base Model" (Krikelas 1992).

2.3 Models of Urban Form, Density, and Land and Housing Prices

Ever since the eighteenth century German geographer Joachim von Thünen explained why land prices decline predictably and nonlinearly as a function of distance from town centers, planners, geographers, and urban economists have been testing and using models of urban form and structure. Von Thünen's original land price model was updated by Clark (1951) to include density patterns; by Alonso (1964) to include multiple urban land uses; by Muth (1970) and Mills (1969) to include housing prices; and by Wheaton (1977, 1982) and others to include income, slums, redevelopment and multiple workplaces. Today, the combined land-price–density–land use–housing-price model is commonly referred to as the *bid-rent* or *density-gradient* model of urban structure. Urban areas in which there is a single, large job center are said to be *monocentric*, while urban areas with multiple and distributed job centers are said to be *polycentric*. Following Clark's early work, Ingram (1998), and Bertaud and Renaud (1997) and others have constructed bid-rent models in metropolitan areas throughout the world, and they found the model's underlying logic—involving the trade-off between access to jobs at the center, and privacy preferences for more land and a larger home at the fringe—to be near universal wherever land is allocated through market-like mechanisms. Figure 17.3 presents density gradients for the year 2000 for four U.S. metropolitan areas.)

Bid-rent models were originally developed for descriptive and explanatory purposes, but with a little tinkering, they can also be used to project future urban forms and land/housing prices, and to simulate how land and housing prices might respond to particular transportation investments or local land-use controls. Bid-rent models can also be used for normative purposes: to identify how particular market failures or government interventions could distort the private land market in ways that mis-allocate land uses and densities, or unnecessarily inflate land or housing prices.

Quick-take Evaluation: Although they tend to lack predictive power, bid-rent and density gradient models still provide powerful insights into the key drivers of changing urban forms. They also make it easy to compare two or more metropolitan areas at a glance.

Quick References: Urban Economics (O'Sullivan 2009); "Urban Spatial Structure" (Anas, Arnott, and Small 1998).

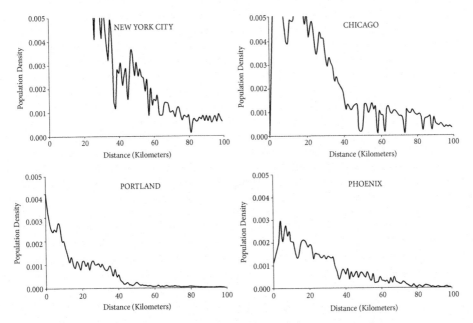

Figure 17.3 Comparative density gradients (base on 2000 Census data)

2.4 Hedonic Price Models

Hedonic price models are regression models that relate the sales price of a house or commercial building to its structural, locational, or accessibility characteristics (Rosen 1974; Sheppard 1999). Hedonic price models are widely used for property appraisal and property tax assessment purposes, as well as to construct housing price indices. Hedonic price models can be used for explanatory purposes (e.g., to identify the housing price premium associated with a particular neighborhood or design feature); and for policy evaluation or simulation purposes (e.g., to explore how the location of a new transit line might affect property values; or whether the price premium associated with a remodeled kitchen will exceed the remodeling cost).

Properly modified to include the price effects of interest rates or nearby properties, hedonic price models can also be used to *project* future housing or property prices. Provided that the local property market is active and competitive—meaning that there are enough transactions to build the model, and that neither property buyers nor sellers have undue influence over the other—hedonic price models are easy to build and interpret.

Table 17.3 is an example of how home sales prices in three San Francisco area counties varied in 1990, with various physical characteristics of the home, including distance to major highways and transit stops. In this example for Alameda County, California, each additional meter of distance from a major highway was associated with an average home value decline of $2.80 in 1990.

Quick-take Evaluation: Hedonic price models are very useful for short-term property appraisal and submarket delineation purposes, but because they do not incorporate the basic supply and demand factors driving most real estate markets, they are less useful for forecasting or policy analysis.

Quick *Reference: Hedonic Pricing Models: A Selective and Applied Review* (Malpezzi 2002).

2.5 Activity Location Models

Geographers and regional scientists have long studied how and why individual households and businesses choose preferred locations, and how those individual decisions add up to consistent spatial patterns of land uses, personal and business transactions, and travel behavior (Isard 1956). Activity location models can be subdivided into those that deal with household location choices and moving behavior, business location choices, retail location choices, and public facility siting:

- *Household Location and Mover Models:* Household location and mover models attempt to explain and predict where in a metropolitan area

Table 17.3 Example of Residential Hedonic Price Model Incorporating
Proximity to Major Transportation Facilities in Three San Francisco Bay
Area Counties, 1990

Dependent Variable: Home Sale Price in 1990 Independent Variables		Alameda County	Contra Costa County	San Mateo County
Home Characteristics	Square footage	110.62**	107.37**	145.71**
	Lot size	1.81**	2.51**	4.17**
	Number of bathrooms	3,768.88	297.03	27,397.66**
	Home age	91.63	2.08	-16.19
	Number of bedrooms	-5523.37**	-13,335.03	-27,134.33**
Census Tract Characteristics	Median HH Income	2.10**	2.21**	1.57**
	% White	-125,164	-886,249	808.02
	% Asian	-175,514**	-61,199	-256.26
	% Black	-214,791**	-1,381,145	-207.94
	% Hispanic	-225,039**	-143,943**	-147.49
	% Homeowner	-57,769**	-85,097**	-65,855.08**
Transportation Proximity Characteristics	Distance to Major Highway (meters)	2.80**	3.41**	4.41
	Distance to Rail Transit Stop (meters)	-2.29**	-1.96**	-2.61
	Adjacent to Major Highway (within 100 meters)	-108.43	631.86	-6,217.90
	Adjacent to Transit Line (within 100 meters)	5,240.62	10,484.16	-31,424.99**
Constant		182,376**	138,127	55,308
R-squared		0.80	0.76	0.64
Number of Observations		1,131	1,228	232

** indicates significant at
the $p < .05$ level

Source: Landis et al. 1995.

a given household will choose to locate based on its demographic
characteristics and income, and the availability and affordability of
desired housing types (Lerman 1976; Gabriel and Rosenthal 1989). Outside
the world of academia, planners have yet to find much practical use for

household location models. This is partly because the data required to build them are not commonly available, and partly because conventional modeling techniques cannot accommodate the almost infinite number of housing and neighborhood choices available to most movers. Recent developments in the area of agent-based modeling, however, hold promise for taking a fresh look at household mover and location behavior.

- *Business Location Models:* Business location models come in two flavors: those that explain why different businesses choose among competing metropolitan areas; and those that explain where a particular business might choose to locate within a single metropolitan area. Business location models enjoyed some popularity in the 1970s and 1980s (Bartik 1985) as communities tried to systematize their business attraction efforts, but have not been widely pursued in recent years. This may now be changing as comprehensive and GIS-based business location databases are becoming available at reasonable prices.[3]

- *Retail Location Models:* Ever since Harold Hotelling first presented his ice cream vendor on the beach model in 1929, geographers, modelers and retailers have all been building models to identify potential locations which maximize retail demand and market share. Most of today's retail location models are implemented in GIS and use some version of Huff's probabilistic gravity model formulation (Huff 1963) in which retailers seek to minimize their distance from all likely customers while also accounting for the locations (and store sizes) of particular competitors. Built and maintained by individual retailers and mall operators, the formulas these models generate are, like Colonel Sanders' secret recipe for fried chicken, understandably proprietary.

- *Public Facilities Siting Models.* Public facilities siting models seek to do much the same thing as retail location models: identify the set of preferred locations for a proposed public facility based on maximizing access to multiple client populations. Public facilities siting models were popular in the 1960s and 1970s, but their use has declined since as financial feasibility, environmental suitability, and parcel availability have all replaced public access as dominant siting criteria. The two areas in which these models are making a comeback is in locating police substations and neighborhood health facilities.

Quick-take Evaluation: Today's retail location models are pretty good, but are commonly proprietary, and do a poor job predicting store synergies. Household location models are improving, but still lack predictive power. Business and public facilities siting models remain underdeveloped.

Quick Reference: "Race, Immigrant Status, and Housing Tenure Choice" (Painter, Gabriel, and Myers 2001).

2.6 Travel Behavior Models

Travel behavior models are the most widely used of all urban models, especially by metropolitan olanning organizations (MPOs) to prepare federally mandated Regional Transportation Plans (RTPs). Most travel behavior models work by modeling travel behavior as a series of four sequential steps: trip generation; trip distribution, modal split (choice), and route assignment (figure 17.4).

- In the *trip generation* step, a set of ratios or regression models is used to relate the number and characteristics of population and jobs (organized into traffic analysis zones, or TAZs) to the number of trips emanating or terminating in each TAZ. This is typically done separately for each trip purpose.
- In the *trip distribution* step, a gravity model or similar approach is used to link individual trip origins and destinations (as produced from the trip generation step) into a complete set of origin-destination pairs.
- In the *mode split/mode choice* step, travel mode level of service (LOS) data are used to allocate trip numbers or shares (again, usually organized by purpose) to competing modes, or to determine the probability that an individual trip-maker will choose a certain mode.
- In the *route assignment step*, individual trips are assigned to particular routes (e.g., streets or mass transit routes) to minimize en-route travel times and congestion levels.

A number of high-quality travel behavior modeling packages are available commercially, including VISUM, Cube, and TransCad.[4] Once properly calibrated—which is no mean feat given their complexity, and spatial detail—these

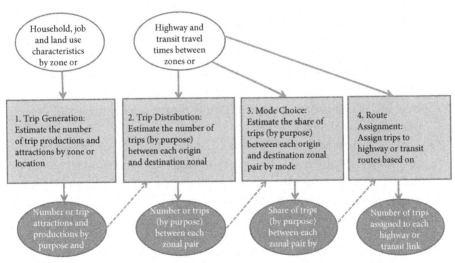

Figure 17.4 Four-step transportation model

models can be used for a wide range of multi-modal forecasting, simulation, facility planning, and alternative investment analyses.

Quick-take Evaluation: Because of the size and sophistication of the user community, today's travel behavior models are good and getting better. The modeling of walking, non-motorized trips, and congestion remain weak spots.

Quick Reference: *Urban Transportation Planning: A Decision-Oriented Approach* (Meyer and Miller 2001).

2.7 Urban Growth and Land-Use Change Models

Land-use change models, also known as urban growth models, help planners identify location-specific changes in urban land use patterns and densities as a function of population or economic growth, new infrastructure investments, and/or particular regulatory changes. Land-use change models can be categorized according to their spatial unit of analysis (e.g., zones vs. grid-cells vs. parcels vs. building or point locations); whether they are based on ad hoc rules or calibrated against observed behavior; and the nature of how different activities interact with each other in space.

- *Zonal, or spatial interaction models*, of which ITLUP, DRAM-EMPAL, and MEPLAN are perhaps best known, presume that households choose their locations to minimize their commute times; and that businesses choose their locations to minimize their total location costs, including worker commuting costs, the costs of assembling inputs, and the costs of delivering final goods and services to market.
- *Cellular automata models*, of which SLEUTH (Clarke, Hoppen, and Gaydos 1997) and LEAM are best known, allocate new population and business growth to individual grid cells based on conditions and constraints in neighboring grid cells (Figure 17.5 traces out the stylized operation of a cellular automata model.)
- *Agent-based models*, of which UrbanSim (Waddell 2002) is best known, allow individual households or businesses (e.g., "agents") to choose the locations which maximize their utility or profits subject to possible interactions with other agents.
- *Reduced form models*, of which the CUF-model family is best known (Landis and Zhang 1998), use linear or categorical regression techniques to relate the characteristics of individual parcels or grid cells and their neighborhoods to the likelihood of an observed land use or density change.

Among their virtues, land-use change models are very versatile and can be used for projection and planning purposes (e.g., where is the next increment of population

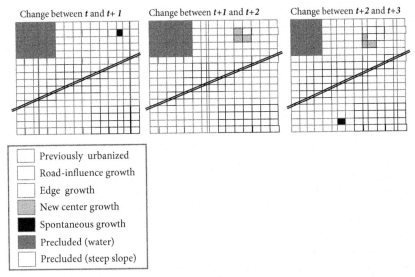

Change between *t* and *t+ 1*   Change between *t+1* and *t+2*   Change between *t+2* and *t+3*

- Previously urbanized
- Road-influence growth
- Edge growth
- New center growth
- Spontaneous growth
- Precluded (water)
- Precluded (steep slope)

Figure 17.5 Cellular automata model workings

growth most likely to go?); for policy evaluation and simulation purposes (e.g., how will the construction of a highway or designation of an urban growth boundary change development patterns?); or for impact assessment purposes (e.g., how will projected development affect local air quality or surface runoff?). On the downside, land-use change models are typically very complicated and take considerable effort to setup and run.

Quick-take Evaluation: Despite their complexity—or perhaps because of it-and with the possible exception of UrbanSim, none of these modeling approaches has demonstrated any real predictive power or ability to simulate original policies or planning interventions outside their calibration range.

Quick Reference: *Planning Support Systems for Cities and Regions* (Brail 2008).

2.8 Filtering and Spatial Sorting Models

Filtering describes the process by which households of different incomes sort themselves by house type, quality, and neighborhood. In the standard filtering model, the construction of new homes at the top of the housing quality "ladder" causes the prices (but not the quality) of slightly older homes to fall, enabling less wealthy people to "move up." This, in turn, frees up lesser quality homes, enabling the next income group to move up; and so on and so on. The end result of this process, at least in theory, is that higher quality housing gradually filters downward to lower income groups without the need for government subsidies (see figure 17.6). Like all models, filtering presents a highly-simplified view of the world. In practice, there are many real-world complications that prevent filtering from working as

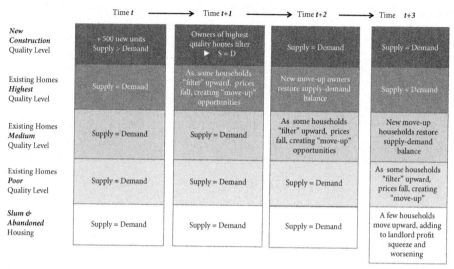

Figure 17.6 Filtering model workings

it might or should, including population growth at the top of the income ladder, discrimination, declining neighborhood quality and a lack of competition. As a result, filtering is best viewed as a descriptive or normative model rather than as an explanatory or predictive one.

Spatial *sorting models* try to replicate the processes by which different income, demographic, or racial/ethnic groups redistribute themselves in space. The most famous such models are Ernest Burgess's concentric ring model, Homer Hoyt's sector model, the Tiebout Model, and Thomas Schelling's residential segregation model. Burgess's concentric zone model and Hoyt's sector model were entirely descriptive and lack a clear explanatory or predictive logic. The Tiebout model, on the other hand, is profoundly normative, and the Schelling model is troublingly predictive.

- The *Tiebout model* attempts to solve the classic public choice problem of determining the optimal mix of public services and taxes by assuming that residents "vote with their feet" among different municipalities, each offering a unique mixture of public services and taxes. The result is metropolitan spatial sorting (or segregation) by taste and preference rather than explicitly by income or race. The normative implication of the Tiebout model—which requires accepting its underlying assumption of being able to costlessly shift communities—is that politically fragmented metropolitan areas may actually be more economically efficient than metro areas in which public services and taxes are regionally coordinated. The Tiebout model says little about metropolitan equity, however.

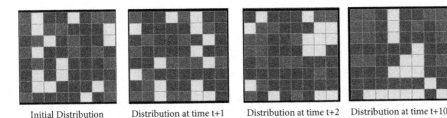

Initial Distribution   Distribution at time t+1   Distribution at time t+2   Distribution at time t+10

Figure 17.7 Schelling model workings

- The *Schelling model* is more descriptive and less normative. Given a set of neighborhoods composed of a majority group and a minority group (typically, as indicated by race), each with defined preferences for living among its own kind, the Schelling model identifies the dynamics by which the arrival of new minority residents will cause a previously integrated neighborhood to rapidly and irreversibly cascade into a completely segregated one. In Schelling's world, small changes to an initially stable system can quickly lead to large and irreversible changes (see figure 17.7).

Quick-take Evaluation: These models are more academic than practical, but they do provide powerful insights into how complex urban systems actually work and suggest that planners should probably be more modest and realistic in their ambitions for change.

Quick References: "Property Taxation and the Tiebout Model: Evidence for the Benefit View From Zoning and Voting" (Fischel 1992); "Tipping and Residential Segregation: A Unified Schelling Model" (Zhang 2011).

3. Urban Modeling Gaps—Toward a Research Agenda

Most of today's urban models were developed in a world in which data were scarce, dual-parent–one-worker households were in the majority, average household incomes were rising, bigger cars and suburban homes were what everyone aspired to, and growth was deemed uniformly desirable. It goes without saying that today's world is a good deal more complicated than that. Yet, for all the intervening improvements in data-mining techniques and statistical estimation, the conceptual basis of today's urban models has not advanced much since the 1960s and 1970s. This section explores some of the gaps between how urban change phenomena are represented and modeled, and how they are actually occurring in the contemporary world. In identifying these gaps, I begin to develop an urban modeling agenda for the future.

3.1 Demographic and Population Projection Models

The cohort component model and its offshoots are as entrenched as ever among population forecasters. And appropriately so. What's still up for grabs is how to incorporate undocumented migrants and distinguish short-term migration dynamics—for example, those attributable to an economic downturn—from longer term demographic and cultural trends. In the planning world, researchers are working to better connect age, race, and gender characteristics to household formation trends and estimates of housing and public service demand.

Birth and death rates, two of the cohort model's key driver rates, change slowly and in well-understood ways. Migration rates, the third piece, are less stable and can quickly rise or fall in response to shifting economic opportunities or changing immigration laws. At the national level, the Census Bureau takes great pains to track annual immigration into the United States, and to develop estimates of illegal migration. Comparable estimates are more problematic at the state and local levels where data are sparse, and where differences between boom-bust cycles and long-term trends are less apparent. This makes local population projections more volatile and in need of continuous updating.

On the modle output side, it used to be that cohort-specific household formation and tenure rates—the multipliers used to convert population projections into household and homeownership/rental projections—were also fairly predictable. Notwithstanding persistent differences by gender, race, and ethnicity, household formation and homeownership rates both rose with population age. This is still the case nationally, but it is no longer the case locally or at the metropolitan level, where local economic conditions and housing prices are differentially affecting household formation and homeownership, and where the growth of ethnic enclaves has reduced social and demographic convergence pressures. The implication of these shifts is that local demographers and planners need to learn much more about the composition, dynamics, and mobility of the multiple local populations they are planning for *before* undertaking their forecasts, with or without formal models.

3.2 Models of Urban Form—Polycentric Archetypes and Excess Commuting

More and more metropolitan areas worldwide are developing multiple centers and subcenters. In some places, Los Angeles and Phoenix, for example, multiple centers arose to compete with historically weak downtowns. In other places—Silicon places, Silicon Valley near San Francisco and Bellevue-Redmond near Seattle are good examples, subcenters grew as places of industrial or business specialization. In still other places—Tysons Corners outside of Washington, D.C., for example—new urban centers evolved out of well-placed shopping malls. In London and Paris, the secondary urban centers of Canary Wharf and La Defence emerged out of the minds of government planners and commercial real estate developers. Unlike monocentric urban forms, which follow a negative exponential pattern everywhere they occur (although not the same negative exponential pattern), there seems to be no single common pattern or archetype of polycentric urban form. Everything seems to vary city to city: the number of centers and subcenters, their sizes and locations their economic functions, and their mix of land uses. It's almost as if having been constrained to be monocentric for so much of urban history, newly polycentric urban areas have decided to eschew a common pattern of geographical and economic organization and just let everything hang out.

This lack of common patterning is both refreshing and disturbing. It is refreshing in the sense that urban areas should be free to pursue their own spatial destinies. Yet it is also disturbing because it means that the basic factors long thought to govern the existence and form of urban areas—the importance of agglomeration, the trade-off between centrality and privacy, and the mediating effects of major transportation infrastructure investments—are either declining in importance or are recombining in new ways and with different, locally important factors.

The monocentric model is not only comforting in its simplicity, it also provides normative criteria against which to evaluate efficient urban planning and management. In a monocentric frame, efficient urban growth is characterized by an upward shift in an area's density gradient or bid-rent curve (see figure 17.8). Should an area's growth occur instead in a manner in which its density gradient extends outward while flattening near the center (figure 17.9), the resulting and inefficient combination of increased traffic congestion, higher public and private service costs, and excess land consumption *can and should be deterred by good planning*. In a polycentric frame, we cannot yet draw similar conclusions about efficient versus inefficient growth.

Nowhere are the difficulties inherent in polycentric urban forms more apparent than in studies of *excess commuting* (Syoung 1995). Excess commuting is defined as the difference between the actual average commute time and the minimum average commute time required to get all workers from their home locations to their jobs. Because more workers can live closer to their jobs, in theory, there may be less excess commuting in polycentric metropolitan areas than in similarly sized monocentric ones. Empirically, however, this is not the case: controlling for differences in mode use and congestion, there is generally *more* excess commuting in polycentric urban areas.

Clearly, certain polycentric urban forms are preferable to others. Until we can identify such forms, *and develop testable models to explain their emergence and evolution*, planners will be at a disadvantage when undertaking metropolitan landuse and transportation plans or trying to coordinate local planning efforts.

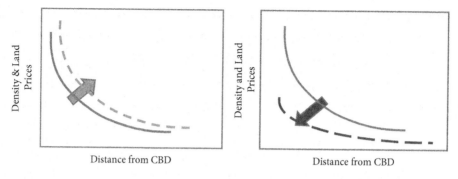

Figure 17.8 Efficient and Inefficient urban growth

3.3 Hedonic Price Models: How Much Is a Park Worth? Two Parks?

With municipal governments everywhere struggling to pay for desired public services, cities are increasingly turning to benefit assessment districts and other special district formats as a means of raising needed revenues. Benefit assessment districts are based on the idea that the localized benefits of additional services are capitalized into property values, and can therefore be partly or wholly recovered through appropriate taxes or fees. Properly setting such fees, as well as explaining them to suspicious property owners—requires being able to demonstrate how such benefits are monetized. This will require developing an improved generation of hedonic price models that can better incorporate and price neighborhood and environmental amenities.

3.4 Travel Behavior Modeling

The big advance in travel behavior modeling occurred in the late 1970s and early 1980s, when modelers started using discrete choice analysis to model the behavior of individual trip-makers rather than trip-making patterns across zones. This triggered a still ongoing effort to better incorporate individual decision-making processes into travel behavior models. Coming under the rubric of agent-based modeling and micro-simulation, these efforts have been focused in four areas.

- *Improving the land use transport connection.* Traditional travel demand models presume that the major effects of land use on travel behavior occur through zonal-level effects rather than via more localized influences. (Another way of saying this is that zones with a few land uses and higher average densities generate more trips than zones with more uses and lower densities.) Recent empirical studies as summarized by Ewing and Cervero (2010) suggest that this is not the case. These studies have catalogued the sizable effects of neighborhood-level densities, land use and neighborhood diversity, block and street geometry, and building design on trip generation rates, trip frequency and length, choice of access and travel mode, and even choice of destination. Collectively, this work suggests that these neighborhood-scale characteristics exert a major effect on travel behavior, and that by paying attention to them, sound community and neighborhood planning practices can substantially reduce the frequency and length of auto trips in an urban area.

- *Modeling tours.* Most travel behavior models assume that every trip has a unique purpose. In real life, however, people frequently combine or "chain together" different purposes in a single trip. Known as tours, these types of trips are often less time-consuming and more environmentally benign than conventional single-purpose trips. They are also difficult to simulate using today's travel behavior models, although the capabilities for doing so are improving.

- *Modeling pedestrian and bike trips.* Because most pedestrian and bicycle trips are for short distances, making them intra- rather than interzonal, conventional travel demand models tend to underestimate their frequency and minimize their importance. This bias is contrary to the results of empirical studies undertaken by urban designers and pedestrian and bike advocates, who find that good pedestrian, bike, and intermodal facility planning can result in significant increases in walking and bicycling for many different types of trips.

- *Micro-level traffic assignment procedures.* Ever been in a traffic jam caused by rubber-neckers or drivers who carelessly "block the box" at a critical intersection? These types of individual behaviors, while extremely common and disruptive to traffic, are difficult to simulate using conventional travel demand models. To deal with these problems, transportation modelers and traffic engineers are developing new and more sophisticated "micro-simulation" approaches—some in 3D—to monitoring traffic bottlenecks, modeling their cumulative effects on traffic flow, and testing alternative relief approaches.

- *Improved Air Quality and Traffic Safety Modeling.* Overuse of petroleum-powered private vehicles is bad for the environment and for public health and safety. Automobile use is a leading source of CO_2 and nitrogen oxides (the major component in smog); and diesel vehicles, mostly trucks and buses, account for a good share of particulate emissions in urban areas. Cars are also the cause of most pedestrian deaths and injuries. Today's urban transportation planning models provide only rudimentary connections between the configuration and performance of the urban transportation system and the spatial incidence and extent of environmental and safety spillovers. Before the models can be improved, additional research is necessary into the local *and* cumulative air quality and public safety impacts of new transportation investments, design modifications, and system usage patterns.

3.5 Urban Growth and Change Models

The advent of detailed spatial land use and environmental data in the late 1990s, and more recently, of annual population change data (through the American Community Survey) and geo-coded business databases (such as those available through ESRI's Business Analyst software package) are revolutionizing urban growth and change models, shifting them from modeling aggregate spatial or activity changes and toward modeling the behavior and interaction of individual agents.

3.6 The New Spatial Sorting

As recently as ten years ago, concerns over residential segregation focused entirely on race. Today, with black-white segregation indices falling in just about every U.S. metropolitan area, concerns over segregation are increasingly focusing on spatial sorting by income. Two types of sorting patterns seem to be emerging. The first is that poorer households are increasingly being shunted to the metropolitan fringe where housing is least expensive. (Although, depending on the metropolitan area, not necessarily *inexpensive*.) Because low-wage jobs are not decentralizing at the same rate, this is creating a growing imbalance between housing and job opportunities, causing trip lengths to rise, and exacerbating traffic congestion.

A second type of sorting pattern concerns gentrification and the mass displacement of long-time, lower income residents by higher income newcomers. Most of the research into this process, known as gentrification, has focused on changes to the demographic and physical character of the neighborhoods being gentrified. Far less work has been done on where those being displaced wind up, and whether their lives get better or worse. (Related research into those displaced by the federal HOPE VI program suggests cause for concern.) All of this is by way of noting that nearly ninety years after Ernest Burgess and Robert Park (1925) published their seminal descriptions of urban succession, fifty years after Charles Tiebout (1956) put forth his theory of municipal sorting, and more than thirty years since Thomas Schelling (1969) first analyzed how individual racial preferences combined to generate neighborhood sorting, planners still lack robust and predictive models for understanding spatial sorting and counteracting its potentially pernicious effects. We should get busy on this.

4. CONCLUSION: A LONGER VIEW

Three trends, now clearly on the horizon, will shape the longer term evolution of urban modeling. The first is the ever greater availability of high-quality, near-real-time data, especially land-use and urban activity data. The availability of these data will make it possible to specify, test, and deploy a wide range of land-use change and household and business activity location models; and to compare their results across multiple scales and locations. This, in turn, will lead to improved urban theory.

A second advance will occur through the confluence of agent-based modeling and behavioral economics. By combining the capabilities of agent-based models to simulate the interactions and emergent behavior potential of individual households, businesses, shoppers, travelers, landowners, land developers and service providers with the realistic assumptions of behavioral economics—that most people act as unevenly informed outcome satisficers rather than perfectly informed utility maximizers—urban models will become more realistic and more useful.

Last, but not least, the great interest in urban models of all types among Asian urban researchers and universities, coupled with Asia's continuing rapid urbanization, will mean that future urban models will be both more diverse and comparative.

NOTES

1. Wang and vom Hofe (2007, Chapter 3), and Kaiser, Godshalk, and Chapin 1995, (Chapter 5) provide two good planner-oriented overviews of demographic analysis and forecasting models.
2. Wang and vom Hofe (2007, Chapter 4) provide concise summaries of the economic base model and the derivation and use of employment and income multipliers.
3. ESRI's ArcGIS Business Analyst extension (http://www.esri.com/software/arcgis/ extensions/businessanalyst/index.html) includes procedures and census and business location data to undertake retail location and site selection studies.
4. Further information on VISUM, CUBE, and TransCAD is available at: http://www. ptvag.com/software/transportation-planning-traffic-engineering/software-system-solutions/visum (VISUM); http://www.citilabs.com/cube; and http://www.caliper.com/ TransCAD.

REFERENCES

Alonso, William. 1964. *Location and Land Use*. Cambridge, MA: Harvard University Press.

Anas, Alex, Richard Arnott, and Kenneth Small. 1998. "Urban Spatial Structure." *Journal of Economic Literature* 36:1426–64.

Bartik, T. J. 1985. "Business Location Decisions in the United States: Estimates of the Effects of Unionization, Taxes, and Other Characteristics of States." *Journal of Business and Economic Statistics* 3(1): 14–22.

Bertaud, Alain, and B. Renaud. 1997. "Socialist Cities without Land Markets." *Journal of Urban Economics* 41(1): 137–51.

Brail, Richard. 2008. *Planning Support Systems for Cities and Regions*. Cambridge, MA: Lincoln Institute of Land Policy.

Burgess, Ernest, and Robert Park. 1925. *The City: Suggestions for the Study of Human Nature in the Urban Environment.* Chicago: University of Chicago Press.

Clark, Colin. 1951. "Urban Population Densities." *Journal of the Royal Statistical Society Part A: General* 114(4): 490–96.

Clarke, Keith, Stephen Hoppen, and Len Gaydos. 1997. "A Self-Modifying Cellular Automaton Modle of Historical Urbanization in the San Francisco Bay Area." *Environment and Planning Part B: Planning and Design* 24:247–61.

Ewing, Reid, and Robert Cervero. 2010. "Travel and the Built Environment: A Meta Analysis." *Journal of the American Planning Association* 76(3): 265–94.

Fischel, William A. 1992. "Property Taxation and the Tiebout Model: Evidence for the Benefit View from Zoning and Voting." *Journal of Economic Literature* 30: 171–77.

Forrester, Jay. 1969. *Urban Dynamics.* Portland, OR: Productivity Press.

Gabriel, Stuart, and Stuart Rosenthal. 1989. "Household Location and Race: Estimates of a Multinomial Logit Model." *Review of Economics and Statistics* 71(2): 240–49.

Hotelling, Harold. 1929. "Stability in Competition." *Economic Journal* 39(15): 41–57.

Huff, David. 1963. "A Probabilistic Analysis of Shopping Center Trade Areas." *Land Economics* 39(1): 81–90.

Ingram, Gregory K. 1998. "Patterns of Metropolitan Development: What Have We Learned?" *Urban Studies* 35(7): 1019–35.

Isard, Walter. 1956. *Location and Space-economy; a General Theory Relating to Industrial Location, Market Areas, Land Use, Trade, and Urban Structure.* Cambridge, MA: MIT Press and John Wiley.

Isserman, Andrew. 2000. *Economic Base Studies for Urban and Regional Planning in the Profession of City Planning: Changes, Images, and Challenges, 1950–2000.* New Brunswick, NJ: Rutgers University, Center for Urban Policy Research.

Kaiser, Edward J., David Godshalk, and Stuart Chapin. 1995. *Urban Land Use Planning,* 4th ed. Chicago: University of Illinois Press.

Klosterman, Richard. 1990. *Community Analysis and Planning Techniques.* Savage Mills, MD.: Rowman and Littlefield.

Krikelas, Andrew. 1992. "Why Regions Grow: A Review of Research on the Economic Base Model." *Federal Reserve Bank of Atlanta Economic Review,* July, 16–29.

Krugman, Paul, Masahisa Fujita, and Anthony Venables. 1999. *The Spatial Economy— Cities, Regions and International Trade.* Cambridge, MA: MIT Press.

Landis, John, Subhrajit Guhathakurta, William Huang, and Ming Zhang. 1995. "Rail Transit Investments, Real Estate Values, and Land Use Change: A Comparative Analysis of Five California Rail Transit Systems." Monograph 48, Institute for Urban and Regional Development, University of California at Berkeley.

Landis, John, and Ming Zhang. 1998. "The 2nd Generation of the California Urban Futures Model: Part 1: Model Logic and Theory." *Environment and Planning Part B: Planning and Design* 25(5): 657–66.

Lerman, Steven. 1976. "Location, Housing, Automobile Ownership, and Mode to Work: A Joint Choice Model." *Transportation Research Record* 610:6–11.

Malpezzi, Stephen. 2002. *Hedonic Pricing Models: A Selective and Applied Review.* Madison: University of Wisconsin, Center for Urban Land Research.

Meyer, Michael, and Eric Miller. 2001. *Urban Transportation Planning: A Decision-Oriented Approach.* New York: McGraw-Hill.

Mills, Edwin S. 1969. "The Value of Urban Land." In *The Quality of the Urban Environment,* edited by H. Perloff, 231–53. Washington, DC: Resources for the Future.

Muth, Richard F. 1970. *Cities and Housing.* Chicago: University of Chicago Press.

O'Sullivan, Arthur. 2009. *Urban Economics,* 7th ed. New York: McGraw-Hill.

Painter, Gary, Stuart Gabriel, and Dowell Myers. 2001. "Race, Immigrant Status, and Housing Tenure Choice." *Journal of Urban Economics* 49:1.

Rosen, Sherwin. 1974. "Hedonic Prices and Implicit Markets: Product Differentiation in Pure Competition." *Journal of Political Economy* 82(1): 34–55.

Schelling, Thomas. 1969. "Models of Segregation." *American Economic Review* 59(2): 488–93.

Sheppard, Stephen. 1999. "Hedonic Analysis of Housing Prices." In *Handbook of Regional and Urban Economics,* edited by Paul Cheshire and Edwin Mills, 3:1595–637. Amsterdam: North-Holland.

Syoung, Kim. 1995. "Excess Commuting for Two-Worker Households in the Los Angeles Metropolitan Area." *Journal of Urban Economics* 38(2): 166–82.

Tiebout, Charles. 1956. "A Pure Theory of Local Expenditures." *Journal of Political Economy* 64(5): 416–24.

Waddell, Paul. 2002. "Modeling Urban Development for Land Use, Transportation, and Environmental Planning." *Journal of the American Planning Association* 68(3): 297–314.

Wang, Xinhao, and Ranier vom Hofe. 2007. *Research Methods in Urban and Regional Models.* Beijing: Tsinghua University Press.

Wheaton, William. 1977. "Income and Urban Residence: An Analysis of Consumer Demand for Location." *American Economic Review* 67:620–31.

Wheaton, William. 1982. "Urban Spatial Development with Durable but Replaceable Capital." *Journal of Urban Economics* 1:53–67.

Zhang, Junfu. 2011. "Tipping and Residential Segregation: A Unified Schelling Model." *Journal of Regional Science* 5(11): 167–93.

CHAPTER 18

CODES AND STANDARDS

ERAN BEN-JOSEPH

CODES, rules, and standards are part of a matrix of relations that influence the practice of urban planning and design. These forms of regulation provide an important and inescapable framework for development, from the laying out of subdivisions to the control of stormwater runoff. The subject of regulations leads to the source of how communities are designed and constructed—defining how they can and can't be built—and how codes, rules, and standards continue to shape the physical space where we live and work.

Codes and standards are used extensively to determine the minimum requirements in which the physical environment must be built and perform. But they are also legal and moral instruments through which professionals can guarantee the good of the public. Their influence emanates from and is applied at different levels of government: local governments define land-use controls, building codes are often nationally determined, and state and national environmental legislation affects local development practices.

Certainly, development codes assure a certain quality of performance, as do many construction standards that are designed to protect our health and safety. However, local governments often automatically adopt and legitimize these standards to shield themselves from lawsuits and from responsibility in decision making. Financial institutions and lenders also are hesitant to support a development proposal outside the mainstream, particularly when it does not conform to established design practices. This happens despite the fact that a mainstream, by-rote solution may be less desirable in its result than a new and creative approach.[1]

At present, the long, historical trend of regulation has reached a critical juncture. The expanded application of alternative development regulations and improved development outcomes, such as Form-Based Codes (FBC) and Leadership in Energy and Environmental Design for Neighborhood Development (LEED-ND), reflect a kind of societal learning that has resulted from the failures associated with conventional standards. A fresh set of choices is now available, driven by local empowerment, adaptation of place-based guiding principles, and renewed interest in urban form and design. Therefore, a discussion about standards and place is important not only to add to our understanding of contemporary practice but also to inform current efforts at improving planning. Standards help draw our attention toward the tangible and unassuming activities of planners—evaluating designs on the basis of the fixed rules specified in regulations and codes. This crucial role is of utmost importance to decision making at the local level. The simplicity, professional authority, and ease of using standards have meant that few, if any, communities have escaped their influence.

The search for a more equitable planning process and a more just urban environment could greatly benefit from a better understanding of the impact of standards on our built and natural environment. For example, how do standards and codes affect housing affordability, infrastructure provision, and environmental conditions? Do they support equitable distribution and opportunities for all? Do they allow and accommodate alternatives and nonprescribed solutions? Do they result in aesthetically pleasing and responsive design?

Little has been written regarding the actual physical results of codes and standards upon built form. This may be due in part to the nature of their format, their complex array of qualifications, and/or their perplexing idioms. Existing literature in this area addresses a range of aspects on the subject either as isolated case studies, such as building codes, or in general terms, such as the economic impacts of standards and regulations on infrastructure development. There is little discussion of the reasons for their widespread adaptation in the realm of city planning and design. The lack of attention may also reflect an underestimation of standards' influence on form and spatial quality.

While this chapter will only briefly touch upon the evolution, role, and impact of codes used by societies to create, control, and transform the built environment, the following selection of writings provides a more elaborate and in-depth discussion on the topic.

New Urbanists have been particularly vocal about the effect of codes on the built environment, drawing designers' attention back to codes and their influence on urban pattern and form. Three publications have specifically documented these impacts: Emily Talen's *City Rules: How Regulations Affect Urban Form*, Steve Tracy's *Smart Growth Zoning Codes: A Resource Guide*, and the Congress for the New Urbanism's *Codifying New Urbanism: How to Reform Municipal Land Development Regulations*. The state of form-based codes have been undertaken in the books *Form-Based Codes* and *The Smart Growth Manual*.[2]

In addition, the work of Mathew Carmona, Robert Imrie, and Emma Street shows how regulations (particularly in the UK) influence aspects of the creative practice and process in architecture and urban design. The book *Architectural*

Design & Regulation by Robert Imrie and Emma Street looks at how the work of architects is shaped by the rules and regulations relating to the conduct of the design process, including the building regulations and the risk management of projects. Articles such as "Design Codes: Their Use and Potential," by Matthew Carmona, Stephen Marshall, and Quentin Stevens; and "Design Codes," by Matthew Carmona and J. Dann assess the impact of codes and standards with regard to urban design.[3]

Finally, three books by the author of this chapter, *The Code of the* City, *Regulating Place,* and *Streets and the Shaping of Towns and Cities,* specifically focus on the influence of standards on urban form and place making. All three books offer an extensive look at the spatial implications of codes and standards in the realm of physical planning and neighborhood design.[4]

1. CODES AND STANDARDS—MODES AND MODELS

The term *standard* is generally defined as "a rule, principle, or means of judgment or estimation." It might also be seen as "a definite level of excellence, attainment, wealth,...or a definite degree of any quality, viewed as a prescribed object of endeavour or as the measure of what is adequate for some purpose."[5] One common usage and form of standards is found in the area of industrial production. In this context, standards are seen primarily as a tool to ensure the quality, safety, and manufacturing of goods, as well as to increase and maintain the compatibility of their use. Standards, therefore, assume both an archetypal and a procedural application: they establish the foundation for the design and production of artifacts by specifying the characteristics they should have, and guide decision making by offering criteria for their ongoing evaluation.[6]

Standards, again with two distinct functional applications, are also utilized in the realm of physical planning to set minimum requirements for the physical environment for the well-being of communities and society at large. This intent is apparent in the regulation and control over the design and planning of subdivisions. As stated by the International City Management Association: "Establishing minimum standards for subdivision improvements and design is the traditional way to protect purchasers, who generally lack the specialized knowledge to evaluate improvements and design."[7]

Discussions on the use of standards in urban planning generally fall into three categories: descriptive/directive, evaluative/normative, and historical/societal. Descriptive and directive text encompasses the most common literature on the subject. It is composed of numerous guidelines and manuals that either compare the standards used in different places or advocate and prescribe their application. These sets of text relate to the earliest elements of modern planning history. Originating in the desire to better the dreadful conditions of dense urban areas at the end of the nineteenth century and beginning of the twentieth century, they denoted the institutionalization of planning. In this fight for progress, provisions for parks and open space and control over housing quality became key weapons. Standards became the essential tool for solving the problems of health, safety, and morality. Assuming control over neighborhood patterns and form, standards shaped the largest segment of urban development in twentieth-century America— the suburbs.

These directive standards are of a specific type: quantitative in nature and specifying minimum values. Those created by the Federal Housing Administration (FHA), the American Public Health Association (APHA), and more recently, the American Planning Association (APA) are of primary importance, in terms of both their effects on planning practice and the residential neighborhoods themselves, as well as their theoretical meaning.[8] The FHA standards, for example, as contained in the Underwriter's Manual and in later publications, were developed to support federal intervention in depressed housing markets. They were a means of ensuring not only the health and safety but, above all, the marketability and durability of housing that was to be financed with loans guaranteed by the federal government. The APHA standards, on the other hand, were the product of a professional association whose members saw it as their duty to protect the health and welfare of residents. Thus, the APHA's *Planning the Neighborhood* offered professionals a set of standards they could use to create healthy residential environments—a set of standards that have effectively made their way into the toolboxes of many planners. The APA's standards reflect the growing need for new types of standards, with an eye on greater environmental and developmental balance. By publishing and promoting its 2002 *Growing Smart Legislative Guidebook*, the APA fostered the diffusion of new standards developed at the local level, which came, in part, as a response to the weaknesses of federally mandated standards and the growing concern over sprawl.[9]

The second series of discussions concern the specific objects and levels of standards. These critiques attempt to evaluate the effect of standards on urban development. Some discussions address the impact of various land-use regulations on housing costs, affordability, and exclusions.[10] Others attempt to calculate and compare development costs in relation to neighborhood patterns.[11] All try to use their findings to promote change and address normative prospects.

Dominating this discourse is the critique of standards associated with housing affordability. Numerous federal commissions, state committees, and private studies indicate that the typical regulatory envelope discourages efficiency and increases housing costs. For example, in 2002, the Congressional Millennial Housing Commission stated, "the nation faces a widening gap between the demand for affordable housing and the supply of it. The causes are varied—rising housing production costs in relation to family incomes, inadequate public subsidies, restrictive

zoning practices, adoption of local regulations that discourage housing development, and loss of units from the supply of federally subsidized housing."[12]

Many other studies point to a direct correlation between regulations and higher
housing prices. As acknowledged by the Advisory Commission on Regulatory
Barriers to Affordable Housing: "The cost of housing is being driven up by an
increasingly expensive and time-consuming permit approval process, by exclusionary zoning, and by well-intentioned laws aimed at protecting the environment
and other features of modern-day life."[13]

Finally, the third category of discourse considers standards in a historical and/
or sociological perspective. To this category belongs works that describe the context
in which standards have been developed and applied. Their emphasis on historical
processes, such as suburbanization, provides a unique framework for explaining
the emergence of specific urban planning standards and analyzing their impacts.[14]
To this group we can also include discussions of the creation and use of social
indicators as a mechanism to drive urban planning discourse.[15] These works tend
to question the values and premises of various standards and their hidden social
implications. Such studies help us understand the ideologies and political forces
driving the formulation of standards.

2. Brief Chronology of Urban Controls

Rules for the built environment are as old as the rise of the city-states in the valleys
of the Indus, Nile, Tigris, and Euphrates. As these cities expanded to become complex systems, laws became codified and social norms were turned into standardized practice. Regulating production and controlling and administrating land,
always a precious commodity, gave rise to governing techniques. The Egyptians,
subjected to the annual flooding of the Nile, created a benchmark system to readily
reestablish property lines once the water receded. Clay tablets and artistic representations dating back to the Sumerian culture of 1400 B.C. show records of land
measurements and plans of agricultural and built areas. In China, a unified land
measurement system was enacted by the self-styled first emperor Shin Huang-Ti in
221 B.C. Yet it seems clear that these technical codes bore a complex relationship to
the communities they attempted to order: They blended government control with
a recognition of the customs of the place.

While rules and norms of social conduct are commonly mentioned in trea-
tises of antiquity, little is actually known about rules for city planning. Evidence
from archeological excavations such as those in Kahun and Tell-El-Amarna in
Egypt suggest that these towns, built 3,000 to 4,000 years ago, were laid out in a
formal pattern with straight streets and small blocks filled with dwellings abutting each other. Wider avenues connected important civic buildings, and a clear

differentiation in the density and size of the housing is associated with each sector of the city. Other excavations, such as those in the Indus Valley, at Mohenjo-Daro and at Hapappa in Punjab, show that the valley had cities planned and built in rectangular blocks lined with two-story houses along broad, straight streets. Such evidence of the pervasive use of orthogonal arrangements tells of an enduring continuity of farm, village, and city. The farmer's custom of long narrow fields and right-angled boundaries carried easily to streets and squares. However, the innovative geometry of towns and cities was influenced more by the mechanics of supplying water and draining sewage than in the imposition of right-angled street corners.

Urban planning standards that emphasized rectangular subdivision to maintain social rank and function also played an important role in the ancient cities of the Far East, particularly those of China and Japan. One of the oldest descriptions of regulation for the construction of cities and their architecture are found in the *Zhouli* (*The Rites of Zhou*), one of the thirteen Confucian classics dating from the Chinese Zhou Dynasty of the second century B.C. These passages illustrate the fundamental principles and components of every Chinese imperial city. Although no specific dimensions were required (except for the width of the north–south streets), strict divisions along geometrical right-angled lines and specific usages were designated. The strong emphasis on geometrical, gridlike patterns was derived from religious and philosophical influences such as are found in Confucianism. For example, Confucianism's emphasis on the imperial system of power and the centrality of the emperor is reflected in the placement of the palace at the city's center. The square-shaped, symmetrical city, with houses located in different wards, often according to social ordering, was designed to reinforce the vision of the imperial core as the correct and moral ordering focus for society and daily life.

The need to control the growth of cities and to maintain public order was also part of the growing culture along the Aegean Sea. Aristotle and Plato tell us that around this time of expansion (350 B.C.), Greek cities began to pass by-laws relating to the policing and the securing of the public order of the markets, the agora (public square), and the streets. These were enforced by special officials—the Agoranomi—to control the markets and the agora, and the Astynomi to control the streets.[16] It is not surprising that in later years many of these common rules found their way into the by-laws of Roman municipalities. Both the ancient Greek and Roman cultures tried to manifest their high regard for civic life and city culture by bestowing duties as well as privileges upon their citizens. Roman city planning often followed a systematic layout of a gridlike pattern. Scholars have attributed this pattern to early agricultural land demarcation practices around Rome. These farming subdivisions, easily measured and controlled by their owners, influenced the laying out of Roman military camps and eventually shaped the regular forms of Roman colonial towns.[17]

In these towns, the grid was often reinforced by two main streets crossing at right angles to each other at the town's center. Some have argued that these streets—the *cardo* and the *decumanus*—were such an essential and widely used element of urban planning that they served as cornerstones for any new colonial expansion. Yet little written evidence exists to indicate that Romans had to follow strict rules or standards in planning their cities.[18] When the tendency to build higher houses left dark, narrow passages insufficient for wheeled traffic, Augustus (31 B.C.–A.D.14) responded by limiting the height of buildings to 66 feet, or no more than six stories. He also required that new construction along the *decumanus* (processional road) be limited to 40 feet in height, along the *cardo* (main road) to 20 feet, and on the *vicinae* (side road) to 15 feet. After Augustus, Nero (A.D. 54–68), stipulated new guidelines advocating that buildings should not exceed a height of two times the street's width.[19]

Still, it is unclear if these street-related standards possessed the force of law. The few actual rules relating to city buildings, as stated in Roman laws and charters, typically dealt with the unlawful destruction of buildings, and not with the design of streets. Such rules were more typical of the time—rules aimed at protecting citizens from damaging acts of others and perhaps, to protect the common value of town properties. Less usual were rules designated to standardize the design of cities.

In London, for example, fears of urban fires and harm associated with poorly constructed housing led to governmental building acts and the institutionalization of overseeing professions. In 1844, the passing of the first Metropolitan Building Act created a new category of surveyor—the district surveyor. For the purpose of sharing experience, securing uniformity of practice, and advancing sound principles of professionalism, aspiring or practicing surveyors had to pass an examination before their official appointment.[20]

The Building Act of 1844 can be considered one of the most comprehensive regulations of the time. It evolved from earlier ordinances that controlled party-wall thicknesses, building heights, and materials, and was mainly instituted after the Great Fire of London in 1666. Unlike these specific building guidelines, the 1844 Act established town planning principles.

Regulating street widths and building setbacks was seen as key for controlling growth and encouraging better living conditions by promoting light, air, cleanliness, and relief from congestion. Unfortunately, the physical manifestation of these acts often resulted in wide, straight, and uniform streets and buildings out of place and insensitive to the area's natural and social conditions.

The precedents of English surveys and European social statistical studies led the U.S. Congress to authorize an 1892 investigation into the conditions in American slums. By 1900, more than three thousand surveys had been produced, many of them by private organizations.[21] With the prevailing spirit of technology and science, rational planning and utilitarian ethics were summoned to guide public policy. Mounting pressure for professional solutions to cities' chaotic environments prompted the First National Conference on City Planning and the Problems of Congestion to be held in Washington, D.C., in 1909. This conference was the earliest formal expression of widespread professional interest in a systematic approach to solving the problems of America's urban environment.

The 1909 conference attracted the attention of senators and representatives. President William Howard Taft (1857–1930) showed his interest by consenting to make the opening address. This conference, and those that followed, laid the groundwork for city planning structure and formed its implementation techniques. Issues such as "The Best Methods of Land Subdivision" and "Street Widths and their Subdivision" established land-planning standards based on contemporary public health and housing concerns. They also set the base upon which the federal, state, and local governments erected zoning and subdivision regulations a few years later.

In this conference, and those that followed, participants struggled with the notion of control despite the lusty and unruly growth of cities. The nation's belief in the sanctity of land speculation, land ownership, and property rights seemed to stand in opposition to any control and regulation. In a speech titled "The Control of Municipal Development by the Zone System and its Application in the United States," Antrim Haldeman, the assistant engineer for the city of Philadelphia, remarked: "The necessity for limiting the right of the individual to do as he pleases has arisen from the exploitation of the property and rights of the public by private interests, and from the exigencies attending the intensive growth of great cities."[22]

In their search for a scientific model for the American city, these newly formed experts looked overseas. According to Fredrick Law Olmsted, Jr. (1870–1957), the president of the National Planning Conference and the first president of the American City Planning Institute (1917), the model was found in Prussia (Germany). After the Franco-Prussian War (1870–1871), many Prussian cities experienced uncontrolled buildup of inner-city factories and housing, followed by dangerous health hazards and pollution. Citizens protested the deteriorating environmental conditions. Thereupon, Prussian city officials responded with a zone system that assigned particular land uses to designated locations. The Prussian zone system also called forth new principles of design. In trying to avoid the evils of American land speculation, German planners rejected the American grid system and chose instead a hierarchical, varied street system to order the zones.

This notion of directing city development through design codes and regulations was widely admired in Britain, the United States, and Scandinavia. In England, the well-established Public Health Act, aimed at improving the health and sanitary conditions of British towns, granted regulatory powers to local authorities. Similar to the German law, these included stipulations for the physical design of the city, such as the arrangement and configuration of streets. The by-law for a street right-of-way of 60 to 70 feet rested upon the justification of access to light and air. The by-law also set basic configurations of street widths that remain the cornerstone of residential street standards used today.[23]

Although German zoning addressed problems of securing decent environments for both city centers and their growing edges, in the United States the adoption of the German precedent began with a concern for the city center, and only later moved outward to the suburban edge, where it took on a new direction.

Land speculation, uncontrolled growth, and shoddy building construction in the late nineteenth and early twentieth centuries raised concern over the acts of subdividing the land. Premature subdivision created an oversupply, leading to the instability and ultimate deflation of property values. Depreciation of economic value also led to tax delinquencies and widespread foreclosures. Partial development of tracts often resulted in conflicting property titles, misaligned streets, increased costs, and reduced provisions for public amenities. President Herbert Hoover (1874–1964), an engineer and firm believer in local control, was a strong proponent of regulatory priority. Already in 1922, as U.S. Commerce Department under-secretary, he promulgated the Standard Zoning Enabling Act (SZEA). Among its goals were "to lessen congestion in the streets; ... to prevent the overcrowding of land; [and] to avoid undue concentration of population."[24] In 1928, as president, Hoover introduced the Standard City Planning Enabling Act (SCPEA). In addition to serving as a tool for recording and conveying property, and setting forth models for local zoning, SCPEA emphasized the need for onsite improvements to support the demands created by the new subdivisions. Road layouts, block sizes and lots, sidewalks, and drainage facilities were addressed as ways to ensure minimum standards of construction, livability, and control of development itself.

By default, zoning took on its present function as a template for the creation of new urban and suburban districts. Zoning, with its strict separation of uses and its comprehensive and uniform dimensional standards, provided a powerful ideological motivation for urban renewal projects in the 1950s, as well as for suburban sprawl developments. This paradigm of control through zoning has practically remained intact for generations. Zoning, like many other codes, suffers from a common planning flaw—it envisions an ideal state without providing for changing market conditions or community priorities. Zoning tends to incorporate an overly simplistic notion of what constitutes an ordered environment—a notion that ignores how cities actually operate.[25]

3. Debate over Consequences and Impacts of Codes

Three important trends are crucial in forming an understanding of the impact of standards and codes on urban development and the need for modification:

- The global dispersion of uniform formulas and standards
- Deficient urban patterns appearing in forms of sprawl
- Limited responses by regulatory agencies despite numerous calls for reforms

With high rates of growth and expansion of the metropolitan fringe, concern over the adverse impacts of development continues to mount. Debate over the nature and type of growth has taken central stage in the professional and political arenas. Whatever position the debaters have taken, almost all agree that the current form of land-use regulations and their related codes are archaic and inadequate. The foundation of the trouble lies in the poor connection between land-use regulation systems and physical design. The rationale for regulating development based on the separation of uses, as devised by the Standard Zoning Enabling Act, does not address physical design beyond rudimentary dimensional requirements. The American model focuses on individual cases and parcels and neglects to address broader contextual issues. This type of model forces idiosyncratic rules, which it seeks to make uniform by the application of generic dimensional standards such as lot configurations and building setbacks.

The deficiencies of this model can be seen in its constant need for amending. Through the years, assortments of approaches have been overlaid on the existing system in an attempt to fit it to the realities of physical planning. Some examples include the establishment of multiple overlay districts by various jurisdictions, historic preservation ordinances, planned unit developments, neighborhood conservation districts, unified development ordinances, and traditional neighborhood development codes. This type of "bandaiding" has resulted not only in additional layers of regulations but also in unnecessary levels of complexity owing to the unmodified underlining approach.

Calls for regulatory reforms have been as numerous as the multitude of overlay ordinances. The critique of standards associated with housing affordability has dominated discussions and calls for change. Numerous federal commissions, state committees, and private studies indicate that the typical regulatory envelope discourages efficiency, is costly, and increases housing costs. Both 2003 and 2006 studies by the Pioneer Institute for Public Policy Research and the Rappaport Institute for Greater Boston concluded that, in Massachusetts, "excessive regulation by agencies and boards at both the state and local level has gotten to the point of frustrating the development of housing in Massachusetts. Both levels of government need to prune back the sprawling regulations and improve coordination among the different regulatory player."[26] Another statement by the U.S. Advisory Commission on Regulatory Barriers to Affordable Housing declares that, "the cost of housing is being driven up by in increasingly expensive and time-consuming permit approval process, by exclusionary zoning, and by well intentioned laws aimed at protecting the environment and other features of modern-day life."[27]

Challenges to the regulatory barriers associated with building affordable housing have also occurred in the international arena. Of particular interest is the attempt in reforming standards associated with international lending institutions, such as the World Bank, and creating reforms in practices such as slum upgrading. Reformers have repeatedly challenged existing practices where countries strive for standards that were a part of their colonial legacy or for standards that are imported at face value from the industrialized nations.[28] These reformers conclude that the key to solving the problem of urban shelter in developing countries lies in the relaxation of existing standards and regulations. They show that, in many instances, existing standards often impair livelihoods by not allowing the incorporation of alternative building materials such as soil or not allowing for incremental construction. According to several studies, less than half of the urban population in developing countries can afford to build according to the prevailing standards.[29]

Codes and standards associated with subdivision development have also resulted in an urban form characterized by excessive impervious surfaces and piped drainage systems. A joint study by American Rivers, the Natural Resources Defense Council, and Smart Growth America shows that this type of development increases runoff while decreasing the supply of potable water. Wide streets, excessive parking requirements, and increased pavement around setbacks contribute to loss of potential infiltration. Sewerage collection system standards for subdivisions are also so entrenched and widely accepted that alternative planning, sizing, and locations of the systems are seldom considered.[30] As early as 1967, the Urban Land Institute warned that "the basic parameters for sanitary sewer design were set at the turn of the century and, for the most part, have remained unquestioned since that time. Sewerage collection systems today are designed almost by rote, picking values off charts and conforming to standards which were in existence before the present generation of engineers was born."[31] Planners in particular feel inadequate in challenging proposals put forward to them because of perceived lack of expertise and a general attitude of not being able to address engineering criteria and parameters. The lack of public interest in the manner or methods of sewerage has perpetuated the use of outmoded methods.[32]

The desire for consistency, particularly in building construction, is understandable. As cities expanded and experienced the consequences of disease, fire, and structural collapse, they responded with evermore and complex laws. Early in the twentieth century, the insurance industry, endeavoring to reduce their losses, developed a model code for states and local governments to enact into law. This model, known as the National Building Code, was promulgated by the American Insurance Association to be a foundation upon which a legislative body could create its own regulations. The model code gained widespread popularity because it allowed local governments to adopt technical requirements without the difficulties and expense of research and the production of individual local codes. It also guaranteed compliance with insurance standards and disengagement of personal liability. Building codes and standards, particularly those associated with fire safety, are reasonably enforced through a uniform model. However, the expansion of these organizations and their universal codes into other areas of urban development is questionable. In 1994, the International Code Council (ICC) was established as a nonprofit organization dedicated to the development of a single set of national and international model construction codes, including standardized zoning. By the year 2000, ICC published an impressive array of codes containing an International Residential Code (IRC), an International Private Sewage Disposal Code (IPSDC), an International Property Maintenance Code (IPMC), an International Zoning

Code (IZC), and even an International Urban-Wildland Interface Code (IUWIC). By 2011, fifty states plus Washington, D.C., and more than 1,900 local jurisdictions have adopted some form of these codes. Out of these, over sixty jurisdictions have embraced the International Zoning Code.[33]

4. Ethos and Ecos—Toward Transformation of Intrinsic Tendencies

Although attempts to reform the regulatory envelope have been an integral part of the planning landscape for the past two decades, the rate of change has been so slow as to reinforce the claim that current standards have attained the power of a genetic code. Yet, for all their dominance, there is now strong evidence that new modes of governance and new processes of building can allow citizens and planners to find better alternatives. The forces for change are emerging from the rise of ecological and environmental concerns and the resurgence of physical planning and urban design.

In the past few decades, decisions regarding the built environment were often made by those far removed from understanding urban design and its impacts. The planning profession has generally been reluctant to champion physical design largely because of an ideological commitment to social science–based disciplines as the foundation for urban planning education and practice. This has resulted in the marginalization of urban design and physical planning to the point that it all but disappeared from urban planning curricula. Physical planning aspects have been turned over to others—and not even to architects or builders, but often left to developers to implement by following outdated formulas of local codes and regulations. This has not only created a one-dimensional approach to planning, from which it has yet to fully recover, but has also rendered planning practices inadequately prepared to deal with current environmental and development trends. In effect, planners have turned environmental concerns over to civil engineers.

The increasing prominence of ecology, sustainability, and lifestyle has brought physical planning and design to the fore. The question of how communities should be organized and planned to minimize their ecological footprint and impact has gained importance in regional planning efforts. Renewed emphasis on place and ways of living has refreshed the value of urban design. The New Urbanism movement, now a major force in urban planning practice and education, is a driving force behind the resurgence of emphasis on design and physical planning. Altogether, the reemphasis on physical planning has exposed the inadequacies of common regulatory mechanisms. This renewed bond between design and planning, between shaping space and its context, between the expert and the community, presents new opportunities: planners, architects, and engineers can now challenge existing regulatory practices based on their poor performance, provide place-based criteria responsive to the local and not the universal, streamline an exhaustive process, and turn obscurity into a clear vision that communities can grasp. Two examples of this new approach are form-based codes (FBC) and the Leadership in Energy and Environmental Design for Neighborhood Developments (LEED-ND).

5.1 Form-Based Codes

Form-based codes are often traced back to the early 1980s and the development of the Florida resort town of Seaside, designed by Andres Duany and Elizabeth Plater-Zyberk. In an attempt to avoid conventional zoning regulation and its inherent inability to address design and form, the team created a specific design code for the community. The code established basic physical parameters mapped to parcels and zones. The team then invited developers and architects to design their own distinctive buildings within the framework, while maintaining a certain vocabulary and pattern associated with the overall development. With the subsequent success and fame of Seaside came a growing interest in the tools used by the team and their possible application beyond the specific project. Plater-Zyberk continued to explore the potential for developing the code framework to suit other contexts, from small sites to large-scale regional planning.

The ensuing efforts by Plater-Zyberk and the Congress of New Urbanism (CNU) saw the development of related tools such as transect and form-based codes within what is often referred to as the SmartCode. The transect, for example, defines zones that provide location-based procedures for designing and planning. For human environments, this cross-section can be used to identify a set of habitats that vary by their level and intensity of urban character. These sectional habitats range from very rural to densely urban. For each one, a set of categories shows building, street, and civic space types, and each has appropriate characteristics for its location.[34]

Form-based codes focus on the public realm—primarily streets and public spaces—in order to shape physical form. The intended character of the streets and public spaces is codified to create rules for the building envelopes, which are part of the private realm. Since regulations applied to building form are secondary, the vision for the public realm has to be compelling and persuasive to generate collective support. Conventional zoning, which is based on principles of health, safety, and welfare, addresses basic physiological needs of inhabitants but assumes little responsibility for perceptual and psychological qualities of place. Form-based codes, by definition, assume this duality and are structured, as product and process, to address this intention. Thus, form-based codes represent a fundamentally different way of regulating land use, with a focus on physical form and a community's design vision rather than simply on buffering incompatible uses.

5.2 Rating and Directive Frameworks

Building on the success of the Leadership in Energy and Environmental Design (LEED) standards for green buildings, the U.S. Green Building Council (USGBC) has teamed with the Congress for the New Urbanism (CNU) and the Natural Resources Defense Council (NRDC) to create a rating system for whole neighborhood developments, known as LEED-ND.

One of the appealing features of the LEED systems in general, and what has in no small part contributed to their success, is the simplicity of the checklist. Architects and builders know that no matter where they working, their buildings are held to the same standards. This system works well for individual buildings—their outward design will change to complement the context, but the green technology that underlies the façade is not dependent on location. The USGBC has produced a document aimed at helping local public officials and policymakers use the system properly, whether they choose to integrate it into their zoning, use it to evaluate the quality of their existing code, or embrace it as the basis for providing structural or financial incentives to developers. The LEED-ND will be used most likely in three ways: to evaluate current policies and practices to reveal existing code barriers to sustainable development (such as high parking requirements or restrictions on solar panels); as a basis for structural incentives (such as density and height bonuses or expedited permitting); and as ideas for financial incentives (such as lower impact fees or qualifying for Tax Increment Financing).[35]

The newly implemented LEED standards for neighborhood development could be an effective and valuable tool for promoting more placed-based and well-designed communities. Its success, yet to be seen and assessed, will be due to the combination of an increasing public awareness of environmental issues, the clout of the LEED brand name, and the relative ease by which planners and developers will be able to recognize and reward good design by using a checklist. The standards do a relatively good job of capturing the elements of good green design that planning and design professions have recognized over the years, as reflected in a number of model communities.

In ways similar to the U.S. LEED-ND and form-based codes, other countries are also applying new sets of codes and standards for development. In the UK, for example, the Commission for Architecture and the Built Environment (CABE) has been producing various design guidelines, directives, and programs since the early 2000s. Many have been adopted and put into place around the country. An assessment of their actual value and usefulness in creating better, more appropriate design reveals interesting trends. Research shows that, indeed, design codes are valuable tools to deliver a range of more sustainable processes and built development outcomes. However, their value tends to be highest when applied to large sites (or multiple smaller related sites) being built over a long period of time. This, according to the assessment, reflects the key benefit of design codes—namely, their ability to coordinate the outputs of multiple teams and development phases across large sites in order to realize a design vision.[36]

5. Conclusion

Concerns over environmental conditions, depleting resources, and uncontrolled growth are prompting various organizations and government agencies to take a fresh look at their current models of operation. At the national and state level, several professional associations have endorsed local adjustments of fixed national standards. The Institute of Transportation Engineers (ITE), for example, has carried out a reexamination of their street standards. The American Planning Association (APA), in a major effort to provide new direction, has published a model regulatory book for smart growth, and together with the Congress of New Urbanism has advocated for reforming municipal land development regulation.[37] Cities and states such New York City, San Francisco, and Oregon have published and legislated manuals for Green Street Design and Best Practices for the Public Right-Of-Way.[38] Abroad, public agencies such as the Commission for Architecture and the Built Environment in the UK have championed design guidelines and standards dealing with sustainable neighborhoods and buildings.[39]

The utilization of rating as a mechanism for code change and innovation is the most promising tool for change. As can be seen in the LEED example, a fundamental aspect of rating systems is their ability to provoke creative development. The LEED and other rating systems give credit points for innovative building methods and thus incentivize improvement. The concept of rating a baseline or minimum standard, and then awarding credits for outperformance of those criteria, leads to change and innovation. For example, with energy criteria, if the minimum requirements are exceeded by a certain specified percentage, the project earns additional points. Such dynamic frameworks are more appealing than typical codes that often stay frozen in time. As suggested by some critics of the recently approved ICC Residential Green Building Code, these are often "obsolete before the ink is dry."[40]

Whether we utilize ranking systems such as LEED, form-based codes, or SmartCodes, it is important to realize that the purpose remains the same: to control and shape the places we build and inhabit. No doubt, regulations and codes will continue to exert influence on the built form of the global landscape. Designers, planners, and those who wish to shape the built environment cannot easily ignore their obligations to create and maintain places where rules do not oust the physical qualities that attract and anchor people. We must adhere to notions of "goodness" as a test for regulations and forming standards, and at the same time ensure that adequate flexibility is provided for ever-changing markets, lifestyle demands, and personal values. As we shape and reshape our regulatory regime, we must make certain that standards do not result in mediocrity in urban form or in the public realm.

Notes

1. For a discussion on the historical relations among codes, zoning, and the real estate market, see N. Marantz and E. Ben-Joseph, "The Business of Codes: Urban Design

Regulation in an Entrepreneurial Society," in *Urban Design in the Real Estate Development Process,* ed. S. Tiesdell and D. Adams (London: Blackwell, 2011).

2. Emily Talen, *City Rules: How Regulations Affect Urban Form* (Washington, DC: Island Press, 2011); Steve Tracy, *Smart Growth Zoning Codes: A Resource Guide* (Sacramento, CA: Local Government Commission, 2003); Paul Crawford, Congress for the New Urbanism, *Codifying New Urbanism: How to Reform Municipal Land Development Regulations* (Chicago: American Planning Association, 2004); Daniel Parolek, Karen Parolek, and Paul Crawford, *Form-Based Codes* (Hoboken, NJ: John Wiley, 2008); Andres Duany, Jeff Speck, and Mike Lydon, *The Smart Growth Manual* (New York: McGraw-Hill, 2009).

3. Robert Imrie and Emma Street, *Architectural Design & Regulation* (Chichester,West Sussex, UK: John Wiley, 2011); Matthew Carmona, Stephen Marshall, and Quentin Stevens, "Design Codes: Their Use and Potential," *Progress in Planning* 65 (2006): 209–89; Matthew Carmona and J. Dann, "Design Codes," *Urban Design* 101 (2007): 16–35.

4. Eran Ben-Joseph, *The Code of the City* (Cambridge, MA: MIT Press, 2005), *Regulating Place* (London and New York: Routledge, 2004), and *The Shaping of Towns and Cities* (Washington, DC: Island Press, 2003).

5. *Oxford English Dictionary,* online ed. (Oxford: Oxford University Press), www.oed.com.

6. For further discussion, see R. Fischler, "The Standardization of Urban Planning" (dissertation prospectus, University of California, Berkeley, 1991), 2.

7. F. So and J. Getzels, eds., *The Practice of Local Government Planning* (Washington, DC: International City Management Association, 1988), 201.

8. For example, see the underwriting handbook *Home Mortgages* (Washington, DC: Federal Housing Administration, 1935); Committee on Hygiene of Housing, *Planning the Neighborhood* (New York: American Public Health Association, 1948, 1960); Federal Housing Administration, "Subdivision Development," circular no. 5 (Washington, DC: FHA, 1935); Federal Housing Administration, "Planning Neighborhoods for Small Houses," technical bulletin no. 5 (Washington, DC: FHA, 1936; Federal Housing Administration, "Subdivision Standards," circular no. 5 (Washington, DC: FHA, 1937; Federal Housing Administration, "Planning Profitable Neighborhoods," technical bulletin no. 7 (Washington, DC: FHA, 1938); Federal Housing Administration, "Subdivision Standards," circular no. 5 (Washington, DC: FHA, l938); Federal Housing Administration, "Principles of Planning Small Houses," technical bulletin no. 4 (Washington, DC: FHA, 1936/1946).

9. American Planning Association, *Growing Smart Legislative Guidebook* (Chicago: APA Planners Press, 2002).

10. For example, C. Field and S. Rivikin, *The Building Code Burden* (Lexington, MA: Lexington Books, 1975); S. Seidel, *Housing Costs and Government Regulations: Confronting the Regulatory Maze* (New Brunswick, NJ: Rutgers University, Center for Urban Policy Research, 1978); K. Rosen and L. Katz, "Growth Management and Land Use Controls: The San Francisco Bay Area Experience," *Journal of Urban and Real Estate Economics* 9, no. 4 (1981): 321–44; A. Fischel, *Do Growth Controls Matter? A Review of Empirical Evidence on the Effectiveness and Efficiency of Local Government Land Use Regulation* (Cambridge, MA: Lincoln Institute for Land Policy, 1990); M. I. Luger and K. Temki, *Red Tape and Housing Costs: How Regulation Affects New Residential Development* (New Brunswick, NJ: CUPR Press, 2000); R. Pendall, "Local Land Use Regulation and the Chain of Exclusion," *Journal of the American Planning Association* 66, no.2 (2000):125–42; G. Knaap, S.

Meck, T. Moore, and R. Parker, "Do We Know Regulatory Barriers When We See Them? An Exploration Using Zoning and Development Indicators," *Housing Policy Debate* 18, no. 4 (2007): 711–49.

11. For example, W. L. Wheaton and M. J. Schussheim, *The Cost of Municipal Services in Residential Areas* (Washington, DC: U. S. Department of Commerce, 1995); Urban Land Institute, "The Effect of Large Lot Size on Residential Development," technical bulletin no. 32 (Washington, DC: ULI, 1958); Real Estate Research Corporation, Council on Environmental Quality, Department of Housing and Urban Development, *The Cost of Sprawl, Environment and Economic Costs of Alternative Residential Development Patterns at the Urban Fringe* (Washington, DC: U.S. Government Printing Office, 1974); P. Gordon and H. Richardson. "Are Compact Cities a Desirable Planning Goal?," *Journal of the American Planning Association* 63, no. 1 (1997): 95–106; Sierra Club, *Sprawl: The Dark Side of the American Dream* (San Francisco, CA: Sierra Club, 1998); R. Burchell, W. Dolphin, and C. Galley, *The Costs and Benefits of Alternative Growth Patterns: The Impact Assessment of the New Jersey State Plan* (New Brunswick, NJ: Rutgers University, Center for Urban Policy Research, 2000); J. Quigley and L. Rosenthal, "The Effects of Land Use Regulation on the Price of Housing: What Do We Know? What Can We Learn?," *Cityscape: A Journal of Policy Development and Research* 8, no. 1 (2005): 69–137.

12. "Meeting Our Nation's Housing Challenges," Report of the Bipartisan Millennial Housing Commission Appointed by the Congress of the United States, Washington, DC, May 30, 2002, 2.

13. Ibid., xiii.

14. For example, K. Jackson, *Crabgrass Frontier: The Suburbanization of America* (New York: Oxford University Press, 1985); M. Weiss, *The Rise of the Community Builder* (New York: Columbia University Press, 1987); (David Rusk, *Inside Game Outside Game: Winning Strategies for Saving Urban America.* (Washington, DC: Brookings Institution Press, 1999; R. Ewing, R. Pendall, and D. Chen, *Measuring Sprawl and Its Impacts* (Washington, DC: Smart Growth America, 2002); M. Southworth and E. Ben-Joseph, *Streets and the Shaping of Towns and Cities* (Washington, DC: Island Press, 2003); A. Duany, E. Plater-Zyberk, and J. Speck, *Suburban Nation: The Rise of Sprawl and the Decline of the American Dream* (New York: North Point Press, 2000).

15. For example, C. Baer, "Toward Design of Regulations for the Built Environment," *Journal of Environment and Planning B: Planning and Design* 24 (1997): 37–57; G. Sternlieb, *Housing Development and Municipal Costs* (New Brunswick, NJ: Rutgers University, Center for Urban Policy Research, 1973).

16. F. Haverfield, *Ancient Town-Planning* (Oxford: Clarendon Press, 1913), 37.

17. T. Adams, *Outline of Town and City Planning* (New York: Russell Sage Foundation. 1936), 60.

18. Haverfield, *Ancient Town-Planning*, 73.

19. Adams, *Outline of Town and City Planning*, 53.

20. F. Thompson, *Chartered Surveyors: The Growth of a Profession* (London: Routledge, 1968), 140.

21. C. Cristensen, "The American City: Concepts and Assumptions" (Ph.D. thesis, University of Minnesota, 1977).

22. A. Haldeman, "The Control of Municipal Development by the 'Zone System' and its Application in the United States," *Proceedings of the Fourth National Conference on City Planning*, Boston, MA, May 27–29, 1912, 173–88.

23. Southworth and Ben-Joseph, *Streets and the Shaping.*

24. Standard Zoning Enabling Act 3, 1926, reprinted in Edward H. Ziegler, *Rathkopf, The Law of Zoning and Planning,* 100–101, app. A (New York: C. Boardman, 1956).

25. J. Wickersham, "Jane Jacobs's Critique of Zoning: From Euclid to Portland and Beyond," *Environmental Affairs* 28, no. 4 (2001): 547–64.

26. C. Euchner, *Getting Home: Overcoming Barriers to Housing in Greater Boston* (Boston: Pioneer Institute for Public Policy Research, 2003). 42; E. L. Glaeser, J. Schuetz, and B. Ward, *Regulation and the Rise of Housing Prices in Greater Boston* (Cambridge, MA: Rappaport Institute for Greater Boston, Harvard University, and Pioneer Institute for Public Policy Research, 2006).

27. Luger and Temki, *Red Tape.*

28. See R. Gakenheimer and G. H. J. Brando, "Infrastructure Standards." In *Shelter, Settlement and Development,* ed. R. Lloyd (Boston: Allen and Urwin, 1987), 133–50; D. Dowall, "The Benefit of Minimal Land Development Regulation," *Habitat International* 16, no. 4 (1992): 15–26; S. Angel, *Housing Policy Matters: A Global Analysis* (New York: Oxford University Press, 2000); S. Yahya, E. Agevi, L. Lowe, A. Musandu-Nyamayro, O. Schilderman, and T. Mugova, *Double Standards Single Purpose: Reforming Housing Regulations to Reduce Poverty* (London: ITDG Publishing, 2001); S. Burra, "Towards a Pro-poor Framework for Slum Upgrading in Mumbai, India," *Environment & Urbanization* 17, no. 1 (2005): 67–88.

29. Yahya et al., *Double Standards,* 1.

30. American Rivers, Natural Resources Defense Council, and Smart Growth America, *Paving Our Way to Water Shortages: How Sprawl Aggravates the Effects of Drought* (Washington, DC: Smart Growth America, 2002).

31. J. Newville, *New Engineering Concepts in Community Development* (Washington, DC: Urban Land Institute, 1967), 27.

32. R. Tabors, S. Michael, and P. Rogers, *Land Use and the Pipe* (Lexington, MA: Lexington Books, 1976); International City Managers Association, *Local Planning Administration,* Municipal Management Series (Chicago: ICMA, 1941), 146; *Community Development: Extent of Federal Influence on "Urban Sprawl" Is Unclear* (Washington, DC: U.S. General Accounting Office,1999); Newville, *New Engineering Concepts,* 27.

33. See http://www.iccsafe.org/gr/Pages/adoptions.aspx, http://www.iccsafe.org/gr/ Documents/jurisdictionadoptions.pdf, http://www.iccsafe.org/gr/Documents/ stateadoptions.pdf; accessed November 10, 2011.

34. A. Duany and E. Talen, "Transect Planning," *Journal of the American Planning Association* 68, no. 3 (2002): 245.

35. USGBC 2008, 3–4.

36. For further reading on design codes, their use and assessment in the UK, see M. Carmona, R. Blum, L. Hammond, Q. Stevens, J. Dann, A. Karski, C. Pittock, S. Rowlands, and K. Stille, *Design Coding in Practice, An Evaluation* (London, Department for Communities and Local Government, 2006); M. Carmona et al., "Design Codes"; Carmona and Dann, "Design Codes"; M. Carmona, "Design Coding and the Creative, Market and Regulatory Tyrannies of Practice," *Urban Studies* 46, no. 12 (2009): 2643–67.

37. American Planning Association, *Growing Smart Legislative Guidebook* (Chicago: APA Planners Press, 2002); P. Crawford, *Codifying New Urbanism: How to Reform Municipal Land Development Regulations* (Chicago: APA Planners Press, 2004).

38. High Performance Infrastructure Guidelines Best Practices for the Public Right-of-Way, New York City, 2005; Design Trust for Public Space; City of Portland Green Street Construction Guide for Permit Applicants Contractors Sub-contractors.

39. For example, Commission for Architecture and the Built Environment (CABE), "Hallmarks of a Sustainable City," 2009; Commission for Architecture and the Built Environment (CABE), "Evaluating Housing Proposals Step by Step," 2008; Commission for Architecture and the Built Environment (CABE), "Sustainable Design, Climate Change and the Built Environment," 2007; Commission for Architecture and the Built Environment (CABE), "Building for Life Standard: A Better Place to Live," 2005. Available at: http://webarchive.nationalarchives.gov.uk/20110118095356/http://www.cabe.org.uk/publications

40. See: http://www.worldchanging.com/archives/009807.html (accessed 10 June 2010)

B. FRONTIERS
OF PERSISTENT
AND EMERGENT
QUESTIONS

CHAPTER 19

EVOLVING PERSPECTIVES ON THE ARTS, PLACE, AND DEVELOPMENT

ELIZABETH CURRID-HALKETT

THERE is no question that the postindustrial economy, beginning with the collapse of manufacturing in the 1970s, brought about a new emphasis on people, not things, and ideas, not natural resources. It is within this sea change that we have witnessed a keen interest in the role of the arts in economic development. But of course, like all development, whether turning iron ore into steel, ideas into semiconductors, or screenplays into films, the arts and their concentration in some places and not others is not so easy to explain. In fact, the arts are more unevenly distributed than just about any other industrial cluster (Power and Scott 2004; Scott 2000, 2005; Currid 2006).

Despite the seeming "winner take all" geography of the arts (e.g., New York fashion, London art, Hollywood films, and so forth), there is a vested interest among local and regional economies around the world in cultivating a rich artistic milieu. There is no question that the arts offer extraordinary benefits to the locales in which they reside. Primarily, their role has been viewed through four lenses: (1) as an amenity or consumption product that lures productive and highly skilled labor pools (Glaeser 2003; Glaeser, Kolko, and Saiz 2001; Florida 2002); (2) as a means for generating tourism dollars (Evans 2003); (3) as a way to brand place-specific products and imbue them with value (e.g., New York art, Hollywood films, and so forth; Molotch 1996, 2002; Scott 2005); and (4) as significant drivers of development, jobs, revenue, and innovation in their own right (Markusen and Schrock 2006b; Currid 2006) and a way to build local "distinction" over other places (Markusen and Schrock 2006a). The arts, just like other postindustrial sectors, contribute billions of dollars in tax revenues, hundreds of thousands of jobs, and drive huge sectors of the labor force. But unlike other industrial sectors, the arts contribute through both ad hoc and secondary markets. Tourism is not usually the first reason an art gallery opens, but inevitably people flock to New York, London, and Paris to see these cities' great paintings and sculpture. New York City's Fashion Week is primarily one of the most important industry events, which draws countless magazine editors, fashion critics, clothing store buyers, and designers, but also attracts thousands of other "hangers-on" who attend the shows as a pasttime and flock to the after-show parties at nightclubs and restaurants around the city. Similarly, the controversial "creative class theory" makes the case that highly skilled human capital (e.g., knowledge workers) are drawn to amenity- and consumer-rich environments, which the arts play a crucial role in cultivating (Florida 2002; Clark 2004).

First, we need a definition of "the arts." The arts mean many different things to different disciplines, which I will discuss in greater detail later in this chapter. While many would agree that the arts contribute cultural capital and are subjectively evaluated, the concise definition of the arts and their impact on society and the economy diverges across academic disciplines. For example, sociologists are interested in the symbolic capital of the arts (Bourdieu 1983), while economists are troubled with the market failure of the arts and intrigued by how cultural goods accrue cultural capital (Caves 2000). For economic development purposes, the arts can be defined as a set of occupations and industries that are innovation and taste driven, and that depend on perpetual innovation for their survival. Thus, while both software and fashion are innovative, the latter depends on a taste-driven, and thus subjective, process of evaluation. These art-based occupations and industries are relevant to urban development and redevelopment (and more generally, planning), owing to their perceived positive impact on increasing tourism, attracting human capital, and generating entertainment and cultural clusters—all of which are stated goals within the field of economic development. These goals are believed to contribute to the greater good of increasing jobs and raising revenue for a specified locale.

The arts matter to economic development, unquestionably. But they are also harder to pin down, harder to understand, harder to measure than other industrial sectors because of their tendency to cross-fertilize with other sectors, and their inclusion of higher numbers of freelancers, which makes the arts less well recorded in census and Bureau of Labor Statistics data (Markusen and King 2003). Equally significant, as scholars and practitioners we have a very limited understanding of how the cultural industries and artists work and how they make location decisions. Never is this so clear as in the very pedestrian observation that starving artists flock to the most congested and cost-prohibitive cities in the world, despite every economically rational alternative location that offers more work space and cheaper rent, so they could focus on their art rather than need to get a second job. And yet flock by the millions to central-city locales they do. Current research argues that this seemingly counterintuitive location pattern can be explained by artists' desire to participate in the same creative scene, hobnobbing with influential gatekeepers and trading ideas with one another (Currid 2007a, 2007b). Thus, incorporating the arts in economic development means understanding how these industries work, how we can measure their presence in regional and local economies, and how our study of other industrial clusters may inform our understanding of the arts, and vice versa.

As art and culture become important to development, scholars and practitioners have sought to understand the underlying processes and mechanisms that produce positive economic development outcomes. Some of the more recent work has attempted to gauge the impact of the arts on urban economies by establishing the size of these arts industries, their contribution to local and regional economies, and their impact on other industries (Center for an Urban Future 2002; Currid 2006; Alliance for the Arts 2007; Markusen and Schrock 2006b). However, such efforts are not uniform by region, categorization, or data source (e.g., What industries can be defined as artistic? Do we use U.S. Census or Bureau of Labor Statistics data?). Further, artists tend to engage in many industries other than the arts, providing skills to public relations, advertising, finance, and various other sectors. How do we capture these contributions?

In addition to these quantitative measurements, recent work has identified the qualitative mechanisms by which art "works" and the place-embedded mechanisms through which cultural production occurs. To understand how art works from a spatial perspective, interdisciplinary contributions must be considered. Scholars from geography, sociology, economics, along with those who study social network analysis, statistics, and geographic information systems (GIS) all offer important insights into the study of this relationship between art and place, and by extension the arts' contribution to economic development. After all, these are the underpinnings of how art and culture "happen" and how they contribute to urban and regional development. In order to attain a comprehensive view of the arts, planning research, thus, needs to understand and outline the processes of cultural activity and how they interact across and within these different spheres. Understanding the processes and establishing a systematic methodology for measuring the arts provide a deeper and more lucid perspective on how policy and planning might be directed toward art and culture.

While the research is copious, the challenges remain plentiful as well. This chapter will commence with a brief look at the research so far on the art and culture production system, looking at contributions from sociology, economics, and geography, and concluding with the current contributions of art and culture to planning and economic development. I will then address some of the challenges facing the field and give possible suggestions for where current research ought to go in our effort to understand the role of art and culture in our local and regional economies.

As art and culture are difficult to measure, and are often defined in various ways, we must establish a systematic methodology that allows for more thorough comparative analysis across cities and regions. This chapter will argue that the arts tend to use unconventional modes and institutions in their industrial activities (as outlined above), which hinders our research but also enables us to apply innovative techniques and theories from other disciplines in our efforts to study art and culture. I will provide some possible trajectories.

1. What We Know So Far

Thus far, what we do know is that art and culture exhibit a particular (and peculiar) "interactional mode" of industrial activity: they (the cultural workers and the firms) need to be around each other socially and informally, along with the traditional economic clustering linkages (Porter 1998) in order to network, attain jobs, valorize goods, and so forth (Becker 1982; Rantisi 2004; Currid 2007a, 2007b). In fact, the artist glorified as a "lone genius" and the art work (or music or fashion) hailed as "iconoclastic" obscure the intensely interactive world of producing art. Artists and cultural goods are products of important intermingling social and contextual dynamics that produce "art worlds" (Becker 1982).

We also know that these interactive, intermingling processes have acute spatial boundaries—they are significantly place specific. Both quantitatively and ethnographically, scholars have noted the dense physical concentration of the arts—more so than any other industrial clusters (Currid and Connelly 2008). The dense concentration enables the interactions that are so essential to the process of "producing art," which contributes to the overall cultural and creative milieu that is central to contemporary urban development. More precisely, art and cultural production tend to overconcentrate in some locales precisely because the process of producing art is most efficient and most innovative in dense milieus (Currid 2007a).

The cultural elements and the intermingling of social, economic, and geographical dynamics tend to get the short shrift in policy and planning despite their much-hailed importance. As many scholars studying industrial geography have noted, "being there" (Gertler 2003) counts for capturing the tacit knowledge and uncodified information that is traded, often spontaneously. Much of the postindustrial economic geography literature points to the significance of "untraded interdependencies" (Storper 1997), and the ability to have intensely flexible chains of production located within the same geographical place (Piore and Sabel 1984). Saxenian (1994), in her documentation of Silicon Valley, noted that it was the informal social networks and ad hoc "hang-out" venues where much idea trading and information exchange occurred. She argues that these social interactions are what enabled the Valley to usurp Boston's Route 128 as the global leader in technology, the latter having a more autarkic work culture.

Because art and culture are taste driven, such dynamics are even more acute. Many of the mechanisms by which cultural production occurs are peculiarly interactive and of a social nature. The need for proximity is more necessary than in other industries, partly because of the need to be part of the habitus (Bourdieu 1977) that creates and cultivates the taste and art world "conventions" (Becker 1982). The arts operate within the unique position of being both innovation and taste driven, and as such are intensely reliant on social interactions that determine economic outcomes. As such, scholars studying the arts as they relate to development and planning must also look at the sociological and economic explanations for how the arts work and why their industries might cluster where they do. In order to understand the arts spatially, we must look at the contributions across a wide range of nonspatial disciplines. Below I will assess the progress of scholarship on the arts and consider some of the seminal contributions to the study of the arts across a wide range of fields.

2. How Have the Arts Been Understood so Far?

2.1 Sociology of the Arts

The study of art and culture as an economic production system has its roots in sociology. As early as 1890, Veblen (1899/1994) coined the term "conspicuous consumption" to describe the phenomenon of using luxury goods to demarcate one's higher position in society. Cultural goods—whether artistic forks made of cheap materials (his famous example) or designer clothing—are a natural conduit for such signaling. Others, such as Simmel (1904), Robinson (1961), and Blumer (1969), have also pointed to the use of cultural goods as a function of capitalist society. Simmel went so far as to argue that fashion would not exist in a classless society, while Blumer posited "collective selection" (e.g., the masses picked the best cultural good) and Simmel and Veblen believed that the most elite echelons of society dictated style and trends. All of these authors acknowledged the ambiguity of taste and "good" art. Because art—whether paintings and sculptures or couture ball gowns—is not performance driven (we cannot quantitatively measure how "good" it is), we rely on various people and signals to help us form opinions about taste. Simmel (1904), Crane (1989), and later Caves (2000) believe that gatekeepers (e.g., art critics, magazine editors, and gallery owners) make these decisions, while others such as Blumer (1969) and Salganick, Dodds, and Watts (2006) believe that society as a whole makes collective decisions and ultimately arrives at a conclusion about what is good art. More to the point, art and culture are not so easy to gauge in terms of quality. Most distinctions are taste driven and even then, are regularly up for debate.

Despite this murkiness, sociologists, and increasingly economists, have pointed to the significance of "network effects" in both cultivating taste and creating market demand for particular cultural goods and services. DiMaggio (1987) and Elberse (2008) have argued that we socially consume cultural goods and tend to use art and culture as ways to assimilate and establish social networks. Rosen's (1981) and Adler's (1985) seminal articles on the phenomenon of "superstars," or stardom, posit that the selection of one cultural producer (e.g., musician, artist, and so forth) disproportionately over others is an efficient way to reduce user search costs. In a contemporary example of this, the average teenager's choice to download the pop music star Britney Spears's latest single from iTunes is partly because all of her friends have already downloaded this song. Why would this girl spend time finding another bubblegum pop musician of equal talent when the filtering process has already been conducted for her? Similarly, we tend to go to a particular movie because everyone else already is talking about it. Not only do we feel compelled to view it in order to talk about it at dinner parties and the water cooler, but we also then don't have to make the subjective choice about what movie to go to because everyone else has already selected the one worth seeing. In a controlled music experiment, Salganik, Dodds, and Watts (2006) found that when listeners were not aware of what other listeners ranked as their favorite song, there was no pattern to their ranking of songs, but when they were able to see how others had voted, there were clear winners. The researchers concluded that people's decisions about what "good" music is depends largely on the earlier choices of other listeners.

Important in these outcomes are the mechanisms by which such selection of "good" art occurs in the first place. Surely, part of this process is just luck and its ensuing cumulative advantage, in the way that Arthur (1998) elegantly describes in his discussion of the Polya urn, whereby that initial, arbitrary selection of a colored ball out of the urn and replacement with that same ball and another of the same color changes (and increases) the chances of selecting that colored ball again and again thereafter. Similarly, if a number of people consume the same cultural good, review it in the newspapers, talk about it at dinner parties, and so forth, then the chances that more people will continue this process increase. Cumulative advantage and network externalities matter in many industry innovations (consider, for example, Linux versus Microsoft or the dominance of the QWERTY keyboard). And art, despite its subjectivity, has its own processes of selecting cultural producers and goods. Becker (1982) in his famous book *Art Worlds*, has called these dynamics "conventions," whereby institutions, gatekeepers, and other industry-specific actors determine both the process and the criteria for evaluating art as good or bad. Bourdieu (1977) has used the term "habitus" to describe this environment or context through which such conventions are established. Within these art worlds, conventions are established through gatekeepers or aestheticians (or what Caves [2000] calls "certifiers"), institutions train artists in particular techniques, and outlets (whether galleries or cinemas or theaters) enable cultural goods to be consumed and evaluated by the public at large. These are the dynamics by which art (which includes art, fashion, music, and other cultural goods) is created, evaluated, and consumed. Or, as Becker (1982, 131) notes,

> Aestheticians study the premises and arguments people use to justify classifying things and activities as "beautiful" or "bad art." They construct systems with which to make and justify.... Critics apply aesthetic systems.... [T]hose judgments produce reputations for works and artists. Distributors and audience members take reputation into account when they decide what to support emotionally and financially, and that affects the resource available to artists to continue their work.

2.2 Cultural Economics

The economics of art has been examined in terms of not only the process of selecting cultural goods and "superstars" but also the debatable worth of arts' contribution to society outside the traditional measures of productivity and marginal return, or what Baumol famously called "the cost disease" (Baumol and Bowen 1966; Cowen 1996). As Baumol put it, the quantity of musicians necessary for performing a Beethoven string quartet now is the same as it was several hundred years ago and yet the cost of supporting the musicians has increased tenfold. Thus, the productivity and marginal cost associated with supporting the arts are not reciprocal.

While the arts have largely been studied for their "symbolic capital" (Bourdieu 1983), more recently there has been a vested interest in measuring the economic impact of the arts (Throsby 1994; Pratt 1997). Pioneered by Markusen and colleagues (Markusen and King 2003; Markusen et al. 2006), economists and economic developers have aimed to capture the number of jobs and amount of revenue generated by the arts. In major metropolitan areas, the arts and cultural industries are attributed with producing billions of dollars in revenue and utilizing significant proportions of the region's total workforce (Currid 2006; Alliance for the Arts 2007; Los Angeles Economic Development Corporation 2007; Americans for the Arts 2009; Arts Council of England 2004, among others). Florida (2002) argues that the arts contribute to the economy in indirect ways by acting as a lure for highly skilled labor drawn to places with a strong cultural milieu.

The idea of the arts as a viable aspect of a regional economic system should be unsurprising. On a macro level, huge industrial agglomerations of cultural productions, like Hollywood films and New York's art market, generate great numbers of jobs and cultural products that are sold in a global marketplace. In addition, these cultural juggernauts tend to operate much the same as do other types of industrial clustering, bringing in other economic sectors that both contribute and benefit from being nearby (Scott 2000, 2005; Currid 2007a). For example, the rise of Los Angeles's new media and video game industries is certainly a function of the city already having a sophisticated film industry that provides talented labor experienced in the skills needed for these new fields.

2.3 The Geography of Cultural Production

As urban planners and geographers, these latter lines of inquiry are of central importance. For planners, the critical question when discussing social and economic phenomena is, *Where* do all of these mechanisms occur? Where do these gatekeepers and institutions organize themselves? *Why* do we observe such dramatic and uneven geographical distribution of these social and economic dynamics? We know that these geographical nodes are quite finite in number. First, when studying art and culture, it is apparent that particular places tend to attract far more than their fair share of the cultural sectors. For example, despite the endless speculation over runaway film production, there is no other real center of film-making in the United States other than Hollywood (Christopherson and Storper 1986; Scott 2005). Innovation in films and the buzz about new movies happen in Hollywood, not Nashville or Vancouver. Fashion designers really do need to come to New York City if they want to grace the pages of *Vogue* (Rantisi 2004; Currid 2007a, 2007b).

Second, cultural industries appear to cluster more so than any other industry (Currid and Connolly 2008). It is largely believed that this concentration of cultural activity has a lot to do with the tremendous importance of proximity to the cultural industries—even more so than documented in other knowledge-intensive industries such as technology (see, for example, Saxenian 1994). The intense need for proximity appears to be for both the usual reasons of capturing tacit knowledge, sharing resources and so forth (see Gertler 2003) so as to be part of the habitus or art world that establishes the conventions and norms and has the gatekeepers of taste.

Recently, scholars have looked at some of the place-based micro-social mechanisms that are significant in producing art. Many of their findings relate to more general theories of economic action, including agglomeration economies (Marshall 1820/1920), reputation effects (Banerjee and Duflo 2000), and transaction costs (Williamson 1979, 1981). For example, much of the ability for artists to use their skills in related fields and to access the gatekeepers of culture comes from being in a significantly dense concentration of related workers who engage with the same institutions, events, and outlets that allow for social interaction to occur (Currid 2007a; Molotch and Treskon 2009; Currid and Williams 2010b). For example, one might be the greatest artist in the world, but without interacting with art dealers, art critics, and an audience, such a title is both meaningless and impossible to achieve. Reputation is attained by socially interacting with those gatekeepers who make such decisions about artists and their work.

Geographical concentration matters for the usual economies of scale and scope, but also (perhaps even more importantly) because cultural agglomerations like Hollywood, Paris, and New York are "star markets." They hold the key players responsible for both determining good art and funneling it through various channels to a global marketplace. We also know that much of this funneling process occurs through discrete social mechanisms that enable networking and engage gatekeepers, as found in Currid's (2007a, 2007b) study of the New York City arts economy. But most of these interactions are enabled by proximity. In other words, cultural producers and players in the art world must actually be in the same place, at the same time.

Additionally, artists rely on ad hoc labor networks, as do firms seeking freelancers for special projects. Often, the choice of one artist over another comes down to transaction costs. In other words, living in New York City enables an artist to attain ad hoc jobs in a way that he would not if he lived anywhere else. Since being there counts, artists tend to disproportionately concentrate in particular places that offer these opportunities.

Something else happens, too. In the process of artists' concentrating to attain the benefits of gatekeepers and other artists, these places attain a cultural "brand," whereby the products emerging from that geographic area are instilled with an advantage over similar products emerging from different locales. Or, as Molotch (2002, 684) puts it, "although more expensive than they would be if made elsewhere, [these products] would not be the same if made elsewhere," a point he also makes in his later work on the New York art market and the rise of the Chelsea art district (Molotch and Treskon 2009). Thus, cultural producers locate in particular places to gain the benefits of being in situ, among the people and institutions that are necessary for the establishment of "good art." In that process, these concentrations of cultural production become branded as centers of film, art, music, design, and so forth.

There is no need to become too academic here: one need only think of the seamless link between the words in phrases such as "Hollywood films" or "Parisian fashion" to observe this in action. The branding of place is, then, recursive. Success begets success, and the branding of Hollywood as the eminent center of filmmaking brings more actors, screenwriters, and directors to Hollywood. Or, as Power and Scott (2004, 7) put it, "Successful cultural-products agglomerations, as well, are irresistible to talented individuals who flock in from every distant corner in pursuit of professional fulfillment."

Place and the concentration of economic activity are essential to the production of art. Indeed, because determining "good" art is subjective, the industry requires a system of certification (Becker 1982). Lawyers can get degrees from good universities, intern at prestigious firms, and work 100 hour weeks to become partner in a law firm. Doctors, computer scientists, and other performance-driven professions are, at very base level, able to attain success through obvious sector channels. The taste-driven nature of the arts makes this task far more difficult. A music critic's positive concert review in the newspaper or a gallery owner's choice to exhibit an artist's work has more than a little element of arbitrariness. Thus, the best a cultural producer can do is "manipulate the probability" of success by interacting with the gatekeepers and institutions that valorize cultural goods. Cultural producers do this by physically locating themselves in the heart of the cultural world. In New York City, much of this occurs on the narrow island of Manhattan, but such activity occurs in neighborhoods like Chicago's Wicker Park (Lloyd 2005) or Los Angeles's West Hollywood (Currid and Williams 2010a, 2010b) as well.

2.4 The Arts in Economic Development

The branding of place, the cultivation of tourism, and the multiple direct and indirect revenue streams that are attained through the arts demonstrate that the arts have become a nexus in economic development (Currid 2009). It should come as no surprise, then, that clustering of cultural industries and their accompanying labor pools have become a central thrust of contemporary development and policy making. Cultural industry agglomeration both generates revenue in its own right and acts as a powerful magnet for other skilled labor (e.g., "the creative class"). In addition, the arts have been widely employed in development schemes aimed at kick-starting tourism (Fainstein and Judd 1999). The development of "theme park" (Sorkin 1992) or "tourist bubble" (Judd 1999) initiatives that aim to identify particular neighborhoods with artistic branding has aided in city development along with bringing in tourists dollars. The now famous example of Times Square, New York, demonstrates the way in which public–private partnerships (in this case, Disney and New York City) are able to both clean up and revitalize a neighborhood along with creating a global tourist hub (Fainstein 2001). No longer is Times Square a bastion of drug dealing and prostitution; now Disney's Lion King and Red Lobster restaurant hold court. Others have noted the importance of "high" culture institutions (Strom 2002) as important urban elixirs that also create tourism opportunities, most notably the "Bilbao effect," with reference to the Frank Gehry–designed Guggenheim museum established in Bilbao, Spain (Plaza 2006; Grodach 2008, 2010).

And thus we get to the heart of the connection between development and the arts. Increasingly, the arts can be seen as an important means of attracting the labor necessary for economic development, drawing tourists interested in the "commodified cultural experience" (Evans 2003) and in these processes becoming viable economic contributors in their own right. By achieving these goals, art and culture are also able to create one of the most fundamental elements of economic development: competitive advantage. In what Markusen and Schrock (2006) have called "distinctiveness," art and culture create a particular place-specific identity in an otherwise homogenized global economy. In other words, while law firms and financial services are present in every workforce, from San Francisco to Kansas City to New York, the industry that makes some cities different is their cultural identity. It is no surprise, then, that we see art districts in both big and small locales demonstrating the significance of their own pottery, art, or music scene. What we also observe is that, in all of these economic and social processes, geographical concentration—place—matters intrinsically. For cities and regions to optimize the economic impact of their arts, they must maintain a spatially-bound density of social and economic activity. Economic development schemes must support the social milieu that is so important to the economic and social mechanisms of cultural production.

3. Challenges to Data and Methods

This literature review demonstrates that there is a wide range of scholarship on the arts, ranging from sociological to economic theory and empiricism. Yet, this diversity of disciplines studying the arts also brings with it a confusing mix of terms and definitions applied to defining, studying, and measuring the arts. For theoretical exercises, these contributions have been insightful and thoughtful. But with regard to the practical matter of capturing how the arts relate to local, regional, and global economies and policies, our efforts have been less impactful. While there is no question that important research in the social sciences, ranging from sociology to economics to geography, has been conducted, there is also a lack of cohesion on how to measure the arts, the methodology to use, and even how "arts and culture" should be defined. Thus, our larger project of understanding the contribution of the arts to society and economy, and how the arts "work," cannot be fully achieved until we create a systematic means by which to study the arts. Of course, part of the problem is that the composition of the arts and their interactions with other economic processes are ambiguous. Cultural producers tend to contribute their skills in sectors as far-flung as finance and manufacturing; cultural producers also tend to merge their skills to produce different products. And the data we have on the arts fails to capture the contributions of individual artists or freelance workers, categories that fall underneath the usual measures. We also know that the dynamics so important to producing art happen informally, through spontaneous ad hoc social networks, and are almost impossible to capture in quantitative data. We rely on place-specific cases that, of course on some level, are limited in their ability to reveal aggregate patterns across places and sectors. Below, I will discuss some of the limitations of current research on the arts and culture, and offer some possibilities for new trajectories.

3.1 First, A Definition

If you ask a person on the street what the definition of "art and culture" is, the individual is likely to offer a more concise answer than are the multiple scholars who have devoted time to studying the industries and occupations that compose this sector. Because the arts are so important to so many different industries, and because certain sectors tend to have artistic components to them, it is hard for researchers to categorize and agree upon a working definition of the artistic occupations and culture industries. For example, UK research includes the media as a part of its "creative industries" research agenda (Bakhshi et al. 2007), while the Los Angeles Economic Development Corporation includes apparel manufacturing (LAEDC 2007) in its statistics. One of the most prolific scholars in the field, Ann Markusen, focuses primarily on the "pure arts," which includes musicians, fine artists, and writers, in her occupational perspective, an approach that Currid (2006, 2007a) also employs. On the far other end of the spectrum, Florida (2002) includes computer programmers and engineers in his definition of the "creative class." In this dizzying array of definitions, how can we ever begin to compare and contrast the research to formulate an aggregate picture of the artistic and cultural economy?

Scholars must create a working catalog of the occupations and industries that are part of the artistic and cultural economy. These definitions cannot be so general that they detract from the basic meaning of artistic production, however. In other words, we are aware that the arts contribute something different to regional economies from that which other knowledge-driven industries contribute, and thus the definition and categories must highlight the difference. In short, the catalog of definitions should be *artistic*. This is not to say that more commercialized artistic forms such as graphic design should not be included, but that computer programmers are not the same as fine artists, and their distinct contributions cannot be measured in the same breath. Artistic occupational categories should include those workers *who not only depend on perpetual innovation but also that this innovation is taste driven and subjective.* In other words, both engineers and fashion designers depend on creating "meaningful new forms" for their career survival, but the contributions of engineers can be measured easily in how well the bridge is built, the building infrastructure holds up over time, and so forth. A fashion design, on the other hand, has very little to do with simply how well the dress is made. When a fashion designer's work is reviewed on the pages of *Vogue,* it is not just because the suit is tailored well; the designer is also making an aesthetic contribution, which is largely subjectively judged. Similarly, we need it to create a catalog of working definitions for the industries that are considered artistic and cultural. This task is somewhat more difficult because artistic occupations often contribute to different sectors in unconventional ways, not exclusively to the cultural industries. Again, the litmus test should be whether the industry is not only innovation dependent but also aesthetically and taste driven.

3.2 Quantitative Data

Even after we establish an agreed-upon working definition of "art and culture," we still must figure out a systematic way to measure the contribution of the arts to local, regional, and national economies. We must decide upon the data sources necessary. Historically, the problem has been that scholars have selected data sources that are not always comparable with other researchers' analyses (e.g., firm versus worker data; U.S. Census versus Bureau of Labor Statistics (BLS); locally versus nationally collected). It is necessary, then, to decide upon what data sources are the most useful. As it turns out, one source is not good enough on its own. One of the most problematic aspects of understanding the economic contribution of the arts is that, by their very nature, industries in this sector tend to cross-fertilize with other artistic industries and with other sectors. Over 50 percent of artists work in nonartistic industries (Currid and Stolarick 2009), and almost 40 percent of artists work in commercial realms (Markusen et al. 2006). Most datasets, therefore, tell only part of the story. For example, Bureau of Labor Statistics Metro and County Business Patterns are a useful means of gauging company location patterns and general industry concentrations, but they tell us nothing about the occupational composition of these industries, which is often misleading for regional comparative analysis. Case in point: both New York City and Los Angeles are centers of fashion design. Looking at Bureau of Labor Statistics data, we see that Los Angeles appears significantly more concentrated than New York. But U.S. Census data and BLS Occupational Employment Statistics (OES) reveal a different picture: Los Angeles is more concentrated in fashion apparel manufacturing, but New York City holds a significant lead in fashion design. In terms of understanding the skills and economic dynamics of these regions (and how to develop arts policy and development), the BLS company data tell us very little. Yet the OES data have their own problems: while the data isolate occupational concentrations, they do not demonstrate the links between occupation and industry. Because artists tend to use their skills in many industries, the OES data fail to explain how these skills are being used within a particular region. As Massey (1984) pointed out, industry locates in many different locales, but the actual contribution to the industrial production system varies from place to place. Most associate the (rapidly declining) auto industry with Detroit, for example, but auto design innovation is actually located in the Los Angeles metropolitan region.

Census data tend to be more useful as they are self-reported and thus give an accurate gauge of freelance cultural producers who are not affiliated with particular firms and are thus otherwise not captured in BLS data. Further, the U.S. Census Public Use Microdata Sample (PUMS) data report occupations by industry and industry composition, both at the Public Use Microdata Area (PUMA) level (a geographic area of 100,000 people). But there are limits to the data here, as well. First, the most detailed U.S. Census data are decennial, which means that they can become outdated rather quickly. (BLS data are reported annually.) Second, because of confidentiality issues, census data are still only a sample of the entire population and thus may exhibit sampling errors when looked at a detailed level (either over- or underreporting industry-specific workers). Finally, while the PUMA geography is useful for densely populated areas like New York or Los Angeles, this geographic area is much less informative when considering more spread-out areas.

To accurately measure the artistic component of a local or regional economic system, data that enables researchers and practitioners to examine the interactions and links between industries and occupations are the most important. While not one data source is detailed enough to use, the combination of these types of occupational and industry datasets can provide a comprehensive view of the artistic composition of a region and can enable cross-checking of findings (Currid and Stolarick 2011). The standardization of data on the national level allows for comparative analysis across metropolitan areas within the United States.[1]

3.3 Ethnographic and Qualitative Approaches

While quantitative research approaches demonstrate and measure the importance of the arts to the economic system, they do not wholly explain one of the more perplexing but essential observations of this sector: Why is it that cultural industries tend to concentrate more than other industrial sectors or occupational groups? Becker (1982) was one of the first scholars to penetrate the artistic production system in order to understand how it "works." Since then, a number of scholars have looked at New York City (Rantisi 2004; Currid 2006, 2007a); Chicago (Lloyd 2005); Hollywood (Scott 2005); and Los Angeles (Molotch 1996), among others. This research has unpacked much of how the cultural industries operate, how cultural producers engage themselves with local economies, and how "art" in its broadest sense is evaluated and distributed to a larger market. However, one of the most obvious criticisms of the qualitative approach is that it inherently lacks a counterfactual.

For example, one cannot really study a different New York from the one that already exists, thus it is hard to pinpoint which aspects of New York City (e.g., density, "walkability," inelastic geography, building height, historical events, path dependency, and so forth) might explain the city's dominance in many cultural sectors. Related, does what we learn about New York City tell us anything about film in Los Angeles, country music in Nashville, and cultural industries and their home cities in general? In other words, place-specific studies tell us a lot about one place, but owing to their research design, they are limited in their transference to other places and other industries. Yet, the limits to the ethnographic approach are also its strengths. The richness of information given to us through the detailed study of a particular place cannot be underestimated for its impact on our understanding. It is useful, then, to study lots of places and begin to tease out the similarities in results. Even if the analysis of New York City does not square completely with the study of another locale, understanding how art works in New York may explain the city's dominance in cultural production over other places. The very fact that art works in a particular way in New York might be part of the explanation for its competitive advantage.

3.4 Unconventional Data

Social science research tends to understand the arts through census data, ethnography, and interviews. More recently, however, scholars have begun to employee unconventional datasets that enable them to understand some of the ways in which art generates value and how it geographically locates. One of the ways in which new data sources can be used is by attaching geographical tags to data not traditionally associated with spatial dynamics, or what Zook et al. (2004) have called "data shadows" (an approach now gaining momentum in the use of cell phone data). For example, a new form of data is constructed by attaching geographical codes (geo-coding) to photographs of arts-related social events in order to study social behavior patterns within the cultural industries (Currid and Williams 2010b). Still others have amassed huge databases of information about the location of amenities strongly linked to cultural centers or "entertainment machines" (Clark 2004; Silver, Clark, and Rothfield 2007). Because art and culture are so dependent on particular spatial qualities, the ability to combine unique data sources with geographical identification allows for new spatial dimensions in understanding the important variables in the concentration and location choices of the arts and cultural producers.

4. CONCLUSION

What is apparent in the study of art and culture is that the taste-driven nature of the cultural industries and producers depends significantly on interactional and proximate industrial activity, much of which is cultivated in informal social milieus. Further, these qualities are very much spatially dependent. Despite the nebulousness of these social and economic dynamics, there are nontrivial benefits to local and regional economies able to foster a cultural economy. Art and culture are attributed with attracting skilled labor, generating tourist dollars, and producing jobs and revenue in their own right.

Yet, simultaneously, they are some of the more opaque industries and occupations to measure and gauge in terms of composition and full contribution to the economy. Partly, this lack of clarity is due to the inherent nature of the arts to cross-fertilize with other industries, including nonartistic sectors. In addition, current research lacks a universally accepted definition of the art and culture sectors and occupations, and no singular data source offers comprehensive and complete information. If scholars can agree on how to define "art and culture," along with using the various mixed-method sources of data and information available, we will not only gain a panoramic perspective on how the arts work in various ways, but also we will be able optimize the impact of this important sector on our local and regional economies.

NOTE

1. Both the UK and France provide crosswalks between their industry and occupation data and the U.S. data to enable country comparison.

REFERENCES

Adler, M. 1985. "Stardom and Talent." *American Economic Review* 75(1): 208–12.

Alliance for the Arts. 2007. *Arts as an Industry: Their Economic Impact on New York City and New York State.* New York: Alliance for the Arts.

Americans for the Arts. 2009. *Arts & Economic Prosperity III: The Economic Impact of Nonprofit Arts and Culture Organizations and Their Audiences.* Washington, DC: Americans for the Arts.

Arthur, W. B. 1998. *Increasing Returns and Path Dependence in the Economy.* Ann Arbor: University of Michigan Press.

Arts Council of England. 2004. *Arts in London.* London: Arts Council of England.

Bakhshi, H., W. Hutton, Á. O'Keeffe, P. Schneider, and R. Andari. 2007. *Staying Ahead: The Economic Performance of the UK's Creative Industries.* London: The Work Foundation, National Endowment for Science, Technology, and the Arts.

Banerjee, A.V., and E. Duflo. 2000. "Reputation Effects and the Limits of Contracting: A Study of the Indian Software Industry." *Quarterly Journal of Economics* 115(3): 989–1017.

Baumol, W. J., and W. G. Bowen. 1966. *Performing Arts—The Economic Dilemma.* New York: Twentieth Century Fund.

Becker, H. 1982. *Art Worlds.* Berkeley, CA: University of California Press.

Blumer, H. 1969. "Fashion: From Class Differentiation to Collective Selection." *Sociological Quarterly* 10:275–91.

Bourdieu, P. 1977. *Outline of a Theory of Practice.* Cambridge, UK: Cambridge University Press.

Bourdieu, P. 1983. *The Field of Cultural Production.* New York: Columbia University Press.

Caves, R. 2000. *Creative Industries: Contracts between Art and Commerce.* Cambridge, MA: Harvard University Press.

Center for an Urban Future. 2002. The Creative Engine. New York City: Center for an Urban Future. Available at: http://www.nycfuture.org/images_pdfs/pdfs/CUFArtsReport1118. pdf; accessed November 2011.

Christopherson, S., and M. Storper. 1986. "The City as Studio: The World as Back Lot: The Impact of Vertical Disintegration on the Location of the Modern Picture Industry." *Environment and Planning Part D: Society and Space* 4:305–20.

Clark, T. N. 2004. *The City as an Entertainment Machine.* Oxford: Elsevier.

Cowen, T. 1996. "Why I Do Not Believe in the Cost Disease." *Journal of Cultural Economics* 20:207–14.

Crane, D. 1989. *The Transformation of the Avant-Garde: The New York Art World, 1940–1985.* Chicago: University of Chicago Press.

Currid, E. 2006. "New York as a global Creative Hub: A Competitive Analysis of Four Theories on World Cities." *Economic Development Quarterly* 20(4): 330–50.

Currid, E. 2007a. *The Warhol Economy: How Fashion, Art and Music Drive New York City.* Princeton, NJ: Princeton University Press.

Currid, E. 2007b. "How Art and Culture Happen in New York: Implications for Urban Economic Development." *Journal of the American Planning Association* 73(4): 454–67.

Currid, E. 2009. "Bohemia as Subculture; 'Bohemia' as Industry: Art, Culture and Economic Development." *Journal of Planning Literature* 23(4): 368–82.

Currid, E., and J. Connelly. 2008. "Patterns of Knowledge: The Geography of Advanced Services and the Case of Art and Culture." *Annals of the Association of American Geography* 98(2): 414–34.

Currid, E., and K. Stolarick. 2008. "The Occupation-Industry Mismatch: New Trajectories for Regional Analysis and Implications for Economic Development." *Urban Studies* 47(5): 337–62.

Currid-Halkett, E. and Stolarick, K. (2011). "The Arts: Not Just Artists (and vice versa): A Comparative Regional Analysis for Studying the Composition of the Creative Economy." In *The Handbook of Cities and Creativity*, edited by Charlotta Mellander, Ake E Andersson, and David E Andersson. London and New York: Elgar.

Currid, E., and S. Williams. 2010a. "Two Cities, Five Industries: Similarities and Differences Within and Between Cultural Industries in New York and Los Angeles." *Journal of Planning Education and Literature* 29(3): 322–35.

Currid, E., and S. Williams. 2010b. "The Geography of Buzz: Art, Culture and the Social Milieu in New York and Los Angeles." *Journal of Economic Geography* 10(3): 423–51.

DiMaggio, P. 1987. "Classification in Art." *American Sociological Review* 52(4): 440–55.

Elberse, A. 2008. "Should You Invest in the Long Tail?" *Harvard Business Review* 86(7/8): 88–96.

Evans, Graeme. 2003. "Hard-branding the Cultural City—From Prado to Prada." *International Journal of Urban and Regional Research* 27(2): 417–40.

Fainstein, S. 2001. *The City Builders: Property Development in New York and London, 1998–2000.* Lawrence, KS: University Press of Kansas.

Fainstein, S., and D. Judd. 1999. "Global Forces, Local Strategies and Urban Tourism." In *The Tourist City*, edited by Dennis Judd and Susan Fainstein, 1–20. New Haven, CT: Yale University Press.

Florida, R. 2002. *The Rise of the Creative Class: And How It's Transforming Work, Leisure, Community and Everyday Life.* New York: Basic Books.

Gertler, M. 2003. "Tacit Knowledge and the Economic Geography of Context, Or The Undefinable Tacitness of Being (There)." *Journal of Economic Geography* 3:75–99.

Glaeser, E. 2003. "The Rise of the Skilled City." Working paper, Harvard University, Cambridge, MA.

Glaeser, E, Jed Kolko, and Albert Saiz. 2001. "Consumer City." *Journal of Economic Geography* 1(1): 27–50.

Grodach, C. 2008. "Museums as Urban Catalysts: The Role of Urban Design in Flagship Cultural Development." *Journal of Urban Design* 13(2): 195–212.

Grodach, C. 2010. "Art Spaces, Public Space, and the Link to Community Development." *Community Development Journal* 45(4): 474.

Judd, D. 1999. "Constructing the Tourist Bubble." In *The Tourist City*, edited by Dennis Judd and Susan Fainstein, 35–53. New Haven, CT: Yale University Press.

Los Angeles Economic Development Corporation. 2007. Report on the creative economy of the Los Angeles region. Prepared for Otis College of Art and Design. Los Angeles. Available at: http://www.otis.edu/creative_economy/download/2007_Creative_Economy_Report.pdf.

Lloyd, R. 2005. *Neo-Bohemia: Art and Commerce in the Postindustrial City.* New York: Routledge.

Markusen, A., Sam Gilmore, Amanda Johnson, Titus Levi, and Andrea Martinez. 2006. "Crossover: How Artists Build Careers across Commercial, Nonprofit and Community Work." Project on Regional and Industrial Economics, Humphrey Institute of Public Affairs, University of Minnesota.

Markusen, A., and D. King. 2003. "The Artistic Dividend." Project on Regional and Industrial Economics, Humphrey Institued of Public Affairs, University of Minnesota.

Markusen, A., and D. Schrock. 2006a. "The Distinctive City: Divergent Patterns in Growth, Hierarchy and Specialization." *Urban Studies* 43(8): 1301–23.

Markusen, A., and D. Schrock. 2006b. "The Artistic Dividend: Urban Artistic Specialisation and Economic Development Implications." *Urban Studies* 43:1661–86.

Markusen, A, Gregory H. Wassall, Douglas DeNatale, and Randy Cohen. 2008. "Defining the Creative Economy: Industry and Occupational Approaches." *Economic Development Quarterly* 22(1): 24–45. [doi:10.1177/0891242407311862]

Marshall, A. 1890/1920. *Principles of Economics.* New York and London: Macmillian.

Massey, D. 1984. *Spatial Divisions of Labor.* New York: Methuen: New York.

Molotch, H. 1996. "L.A. as Design Product: How Art Works in a Regional Economy." In *The City: Los Angeles and Urban Theory at the End of the Twentieth Century,* edited by Allen J. Scott and Edward W. Soja, 225–75. Los Angeles: University of California Press.

Molotch, H. 2002. "Place in Product." *International Journal of Urban and Regional Research* 26(4): 665–88.

Molotch, H., and M. Treskon. 2009. "Changing Art: SoHo, Chelsea and the Dynamic Geography of Galleries in New York City." *International Journal of Urban and Regional Research* 33(2): 517–41.

Plaza, B. 2006. "The Return on Investment of the Guggenheim Museum Bilbao." *International Journal of Urban and Regional Research* 30(2): 452–67.

Piore, M. J, and C. F Sabel. 1984. The Second Industrial Divide: Possibilities for Prosperity. New York: Basic Books.

Porter Michael. 1998. "Clusters and the New Economics of Competition." *Harvard Business Review* 76(6): 77–90.

Power, D., and A. J. Scott. 2004. "A Prelude to Cultural Industries and the Production of Culture." In *Cultural Industries and the Production of Culture,* edited by Ed, Dominic Power, and Allen J. Scott, 3–16. London and New York: Routledge.

Pratt, Andy. 1997. "The Cultural Industries Production System: A Case Study of Employment Change in Britain, 1884–91." *Environment and Planning Part A* 29(11): 1953–74.

Rantisi, Norma. 2004. "The Ascendance of New York Fashion." *International Journal of Urban and Regional Research* 28(1): 86–107.

Robinson, D. 1961. "The Economics of Fashion Demand." *Quarterly Journal of Economics* 75:376–98.

Rosen, S. 1981. "The Economics of Superstars." *American Economic Review* 81(5):845–58.

Salganik, M., P. Dodds, and D. Watts. 2006. "Experimental Study of Inequality and Unpredictability in an Artificial Cultural Market." *Science* 311:854–56.

Saxenian, A. 1994. *Regional Advantage: Culture and Competition in Silicon Valley and Route 128.* Cambridge, MA: Harvard University Press.

Scott, A. 2000. *The Cultural Economy of Cities.* London: Sage.

Scott, A. 2005. *Hollywood: The Place, the Industry.* Princeton, NJ: Princeton University Press.

Silver, D., T. Clark, and L. Rothfield. 2007. "A Theory of Scenes." Working paper, Sociology Department, University of Chicago.

Simmel, G. 1904. "Fashion." *American Journal of Sociology* 52:541–48.

Sorkin, M. 1992. *Variations on a Theme Park: The New American City and the End of Public Space.* New York: Hill and Wang.

Storper, M. 1997. *The Regional World: Territorial Development in a Global Economy.* New York: Guilford.

Storper, M., and A. Venables. 2004. "Buzz: Face-to-Face Contact and the Urban Economy." *Journal of Economic Geography* 4(4): 351–70.

Strom, E. 2002. "Converting Pork into Porcelain: Cultural Institutions and Downtown Development." *Urban Affairs Review* 38(1): 3–21.

Throsby, D. 1994. "The Production and Consumption of the Arts: A View of Cultural Economics." *Journal of Economic Literature* 32(1): 1–29.

Veblen. T. 1899/1994. *The Theory of the Leisure Class.* New York: Penguin.

Williamson, O. E. 1979. "Transaction-Cost Economics: The Governance of Contractual Relations." *Journal of Law and Economics* 22(2): 233–61.

Williamson, O. E. 1981. "The Economics of Organization: The Transaction-Cost Approach." *American Journal of Sociology* 87(3): 548–77.

Zook, M., Martin Dodge, Yuko Aoyama, and Anthony Townsend. 2004. "New Digital Geographies: Information, Communication, and Place." In *Geography and Technology,* edited by S. D. Brunn, S. L. Cutter, and J. W.Harrington, 155–76. Netherlands: Kluwer Academic Publishers.

CHAPTER 20

....

RECONNECTING URBAN PLANNING AND PUBLIC HEALTH

....

JASON CORBURN

AT the turn of the twentieth century, a key debate that shaped the direction and focus of American urban planning was whether human health and the plight of the urban poor ought to be a principal concern of the emerging profession. Benjamin Clarke Marsh, Florence Kelley, Mary Simkhovitch and others who were part of the Committee on the Congestion of Population (CCP) in New York argued that planners ought to make the problems of congestion, including disease, and issues of social justice two key priorities of the emerging profession. Marsh would declare in his 1909 book, *An Introduction to City Planning*, that "no city is more healthy than the highest death rate in any ward or block and that no city is more beautiful than its most unsightly tenement" (Marsh, 1909/1974, 27). However, Frederick Law Olmsted Jr. would use his stature and leadership position at the first National Conference on City Planning and the Problems of Congestion to define the American field of planning as principally concerned with integrating the circulation of transportation, the design of public spaces, and the development of private land—not issues of human health and social justice.

While nineteenth-century work in both urban planning and public health[1] combined physical, economic, and social interventions aimed at improving the health of the least well-off, the fields increasingly moved toward single disease and individual behavior interventions and away from their social justice agendas throughout the twentieth century. One result of the disconnect between planning and public health is the growing urban health inequities—or the disproportionate burden of premature death and preventable and remediable disease for the poor and communities of color—in America and around the world (Galea, Freudenberg and Vlahov, 2005; Kjellstrom et al. 2007).[2] Yet, by the turn of the twenty-first century, urban planning was reengaging with public health; and conceptual and practical debates resurfaced over whether efforts to reconnect the fields should focus on specific diseases, hazards, and behaviors—such as obesity, sprawl, and physical inactivity—or on what has come to be understood as the "root causes" of poor urban health: the cumulative impacts of physical hazards, economic deprivation, social stressors, and a failure of public institutions and policies to address these issues (Department of Health and Human Services [DHHS] 2007; Wilkinson and Pickett 2009; Marmot 2004).[3] In 2010, the World Health Organization (WHO) dedicated World Health Day to the issues of urban health and called on the field of urban planning to redirect its resources and priorities to promote more healthy and sustainable cities (World Health Organization [WHO] 2010).

This chapter offers a brief but critical review of the connects and disconnects between the fields of urban planning and public health from the late nineteenth through the twentieth century, and argues that engaging with the histories of the fields offers contemporary planners insights for reconnecting planning with public health in the twenty-first century to tackle growing urban health inequities (Corburn 2007). I focus on key events, actors, and institutions that shaped theory and practice in each field, with a particular attention to urban health equity—or how each field addressed social, economic, and human health disparities between rich and poor, people of color and whites, and neighborhoods within cities. I identify at least three political challenges for reconnecting planning and public health, including an overemphasis on: (1) physical changes for improving social conditions, (2) scientific rationality, and (3) professionalization and fragmentation of the disciplines. Building on the historic review and these themes, the second section of the chapter suggests a set of research and practice challenges for moving toward "healthy urban planning" that will require continued critical engagement with the histories of the fields, along with new issue and problem framings, investigative and analytic techniques, and inclusive and deliberative public processes that together can generate new norms, discourses, and practice for greater health equity. In short, healthy urban planning will require new commitments to inject health and social justice into urban governance, where both the substantive content of what contributes to human well-being—the physical and social qualities that promote urban health—and the decision-making processes and institutions that shape the distributions of these qualities across places and populations are improved.

I. Early Connections between City Planning and Health, 1840s–1890s

Decades before the Marsh–Olmsted Jr. debate over the direction of American city planning, engineers, public health professionals, and city planners worked to address human health in cities. In the early decades of the 1800s, French epidemiologist Louis René Villermé highlighted that the wealthier the Parisian neighborhood, or *arrondisement*, the lower the mortality rate and likelihood of illness. By 1842, Edwin Chadwick would build on Villerme's work and publish the *Report on the Sanitary Conditions of the Labouring Population in Great Britain*, documenting that the "gentry and professional" classes lived longer than "laborers and artisans."

Miasma—filth or dirty air—was the leading theory of disease causation and sanitary commissions were created in European and American cities to clean up urban environments with the hope of arresting epidemics of infectious diseases (Duffy 1990). American sanitarians, such as John H. Griscom, New York City's Chief Sanitary Inspector, published *The Sanitary Conditions of the Laboring Population of New York* in 1845, and engineers, public health professionals, and planners worked to prevent disease and death by cleaning up urban environments. New drinking and wastewater systems were constructed, tenement housing was improved, and regular street cleaning and refuse removal became new functions of city management.

Sanitary engineers tended to address urban health issues by employing new technologies to remove waste by, for instance, piping it away from cities into rivers and oceans (Melosi, 2000). When removing the miasma did not seem to reduce disease, the sick were removed from society. *Contagion*, the belief in the direct passage of poison from one person to another, led to large quarantines of immigrants and justified state-sponsored interventions in the economy (Mullan 1989).[4]

Research and practice linking planning and public health during this era included the sanitary survey, park and playground planning, and the work of settlement houses. After a devastating yellow fever outbreak in and around Memphis in 1878, a sanitary survey was launched to describe every street, structure, and individual lot within the city to determine the environmental conditions that might "breed" diseases (Peterson 1979, 90). Progressive Era park and playground movements advocated for urban play spaces next to schools so that gymnasiums, reading rooms, and baths could all be used for children's recreation, literacy, and hygiene (Lubove 1974).[5]

The women of Hull House in Chicago, influenced by the burgeoning Chicago School of Sociology that initiated the study of the neighborhood effects on well-being, worked with residents to document unsanitary neighborhood and workplace conditions, and advocated on behalf of immigrants for new social policies (Hull-House Residents 1895).[6] The researchers at Hull-House, particularly Florence Kelley, borrowed methods from public health researchers in England at the time—namely, Charles Booth—to conduct some of the first community health surveys that included neighborhood mapping of both noninfectious and infectious diseases in the United States. Community health surveys that stratify data by class, ethnicity, and place remain an essential aspect of understanding the forces shaping urban health inequities today.

While there was widespread disagreement at this time over the definition, identification, and diagnosis of disease, there is some evidence of health inequities by income and ethnicity. For example, in 1892, the health commissioner of the city of Milwaukee noted that the wards with the greatest incidence of diphtheria were the immigrant communities that had not been connected to the sewer system (Leavitt 1982, 67). When a smallpox epidemic hit Milwaukee in 1894, there were over 400 cases in one south side, largely German and Polish immigrant ward, while most other wards in the city had fewer than fifteen cases (Leavitt 1982, 105).

By the end of the nineteenth century, many urban health interventions focused on physical removal of both "environmental miasmas"—such as garbage, waste-water and air pollution—and the "undesirable and sick" people. For sanitarians, the local solution to pollution was removal and dilution, but the downstream environmental health impacts were often ignored (Tarr 1996). Housing reformers were split between those advocating physical improvements, such as bathrooms, ventilation, and fire escapes, and those calling for the construction of safe and affordable housing. Many housing and sanitary reforms were grounded in the belief that technological and design innovations could not only improve living conditions but also make "immoral" slum-dwellers more orderly and healthy (Fairfield 1994).

2. GERM THEORY AND PLANNING "THE CITY SCIENTIFIC": 1900S–1940S

By the turn of the new century, it was well known in public health that both miasma and contagion failed to explain certain aspects of urban health, such as why, with ubiquitous filth, epidemics only occurred sometimes and in some places. By this time, the driving ideology in public health shifted to *germ theory*, which stated that microbes were the specific agents that caused infectious disease (Susser and Susser 1996). Medical treatment and disease management began to replace strategies of physically removing harms, and public health shifted to laboratory research and interventions aimed at eliminating bacteria, such as vaccinations and chlorination of municipal drinking water supplies. Data from the offices of vital statistics gathered between 1864 and 1923 in New York, Boston, Philadelphia, and New Orleans—cities that combined infrastructure improvements with treatment of water-borne bacteria—suggest a reduction in death rates from environmentally related diseases (table 20.1; Meeker 1972). However, the specific determinants behind declines in morbidity and mortality were controversial at the time and remain a central question for twenty-first-century public health (e.g., Link and Phalen 1996; Marmot 2004). For example, Thomas McKeown (1976) and others have argued that economic development, increases in per capita income, access to food, and improved nutrition—not public sanitation, vaccinations, and advances in medical technology—explain the decline in mortality between 1850 and 1935, and that public health ends are better served by broad-based efforts to redistribute the social, political, and economic resources that determine the health of populations rather than targeted interventions.

In 1906, W. E. B. Du Bois published *The Health and Physique of the Negro American* and used data from census reports, vital statistics, and insurance

Table 20.1 Disease-specific Death Rates for New
York, Boston, Philadelphia, and New Orleans,
1864–1913

Disease	Average Death Rate	
	1864–1888	1889–1913
Consumption	365	223
Stomach & Intestinal	299	196
Scarlet Fever	66	19
Typhoid & Typhus	53	25
Smallpox	40	2
Cholera	8	0
Diphtheria	123	58
Yellow Fever	14	1
Total for Group	964	524
Crude Death Rate	2570	1890

Source: Meeker 1972.

company records to generate some of the first documentation of the poor health status of African Americans living in both southern and northern cities in comparison to white Americans. Du Bois questioned whether improvements in science, technology, housing, and other services were benefiting all Americans, and he concluded that racial health disparities were a result of social conditions, not eugenic ideas of inherent racial inferiority that were commonly accepted at the time (Du Bois 1906). One-hundred years later, racial and ethnic health disparities persist and remain largely unaddressed (Satcher et al. 2005).

3. FRAGMENTATION OF URBAN HEALTH RESEARCH

Separate municipal bureaucracies emerged during this era to manage urban improvement schemes, such as water service delivery infrastructure, sewage systems, public housing, parks and recreation, school-based health, and others. One result was an increased fragmentation and segmentation of practice—and soon thereafter, research—into the aspects of urban living that promote health and well-being. The integrated place and health research methods, such as those of the settlement house workers, was increasingly replaced with laboratory-based investigations of how to eliminate the microbes suspected of contributing to infectious disease epidemics. Social scientists, planners included, were marginalized in urban health research, as clinicians, bacteriologists, and bench scientists began to dominate the field (Susser and Stein, 2009).

Yet, there were important exceptions to the segmentation and fragmentation of urban health research that act as important examples for reconnecting the fields today. For example, in 1912, the newly formed U.S. Children's Bureau—under the leadership of Julia Lathrop, a longtime Hull-House resident—sponsored the first substantial prospective epidemiologic study in the United States investigating how family socioeconomic status and nutritional access influenced infant mortality (Meckel 1990). Four years later, in 1916, Edgar Sydenstricker, a statistician with the U.S. Public Health Service, initiated a study of the health consequences of low wages, and would later partner with Joseph Goldberger to document that pellagra was a dietary deficiency disease whose incidence was driven by social disparities in access to food, as determined by wages, access to markets selling fresh produce, and ownership of garden plots (Goldberger, Wheeler, and Sydenstricker 1920). From 1921 to 1924, Sydenstricker conducted one of the first longitudinal studies of diseases among an urban population, in Hagerstown, Maryland. A groundbreaking study by the U.S. Public Health Service and the Milbank Memorial Fund in 1933 would use similar methods to track how the depression influenced morbidity in ten cities. These studies were some of the first urban health research to stratify data by occupational class and race, and they revealed that poorer health among black compared with white Americans was neither innate nor inevitable but instead reflected African Americans' greater exposure to poverty and occupational hazards (Perrott and Collins 1935; Holland and Perrott 1938). Yet, research designs where place, class, race, and other social factors were integrated, rather than being treated as nuisance variables, were the exception and not the rule in urban public health.

4. PUBLIC HEALTH, SOCIAL JUSTICE AND THE EMERGENCE OF AMERICAN CITY PLANNING

As American planners prepared for the first national conference, Marsh and the CCP argued that the field ought to more explicitly embrace a social justice agenda. In a 1908 article entitled "City Planning in Justice to the Working Population," Marsh argued that American planning ought to make "the right of the citizen to leisure, to health, to care in sickness, to work under normal conditions, and to live under conditions which will not impair his health or efficiency" a "foresight" rather than an afterthought (Marsh 1908, 1514). Frederick L. Ford, speaking at the First National Conference on City Planning and Problems of Congestion in 1909, on "The Scope of City Planning in the United States," noted that, "city planning, if it means anything, means the better preservation of health, and the protection of life and property, and therefore directly or indirectly affects the health, happiness, and prosperity of the people and the nation" (Ford 1910, 70). Olmsted Jr. (1910, 69) responded by articulating his three planning priorities:

> The first concerns the means of circulation—the distribution and treatment of the spaces devoted to streets, railways, waterways, and all means of transportation and communication. The second concerns the distribution and treatment of the spaces devoted to all other public purposes. The third concerns the remaining or private lands and the character of development thereon, in so far as it is practicable for the community to control such development.

As Peterson (2003, 249) has noted, "while Marsh battled for justice, Olmsted focused more on planning itself, especially ways to build it up as a technically effective field and to attract new professional support."[7] The comprehensive, rational, and aesthetically focused "City Beautiful" idea took hold, while the human health and social justice concerns of Marsh and the CCP largely fell off the agenda (Sloane 2006, 12). By the fifth National City Planning conference in 1913, entitled "The City Scientific," American planning had defined itself largely as a technocratic profession aimed at designing efficient cities (Fishman 2000).

5. THE LABORATORY IDEAL AND CITY PLANNING

Consistent with the emerging aesthetic and technocratic ideals of planning, tools to classify and segment city functions took hold and land-use zoning emerged as one such powerful tool. Local zoning ordinances were often couched as both protecting public health and benefiting private landowners. For example, in the landmark 1926 Supreme Court case *Village of Euclid, Ohio, et al. v. Ambler Realty Company*, zoning was characterized as promoting health: "the exclusion of buildings devoted to business, trade, etc., from residential districts, bears a rational relation to the health and safety of the community…by excluding from residential areas the confusion and danger of fire, contagion, and disorder, which in greater or less degree attach to the location of stores, shops, and factories" (272 U.S. 365, 392). Yet, there was little to no epidemiologic evidence at the time suggesting that health improvements would come about by physically separating land uses, and some have suggested that zoning tended to concentrate health hazards and perpetuate disadvantage in poor urban communities (Maantay 2001).

Yet, a "laboratory-like" view of urban improvement would take hold in planning, much like the shift in epidemiology from "street surveys" to laboratory-based microbiology brought about by germ theory. At least three early twentieth-century urban design schemes claimed to offer—much like laboratory science—a remedy for improving urban living that could be objectively applied with scientific precision almost anywhere, irrespective of local context. First, the Garden City ideal called for a series of human-scale urban areas in a region, linked by high-speed rail and roadways, that avoided the congestion plaguing large cities, preserved green space, and took advantage of the efficiencies of urban life (Hall 1996). Clarence Perry's Neighborhood Unit, where 5,000 to 6,000 people would live in single-family homes around a primary school with business located on the periphery, offered a similar urban improvement ideal (Perry 1929). A third scientific view of the city was the Chicago School concentric zone model popularized by Robert E. Park and Ernest W. Burgess (1925) in their sociological work, *The City.*[8] Figure 20.1 shows the similarities of these three conceptions of a rationally designed city.)

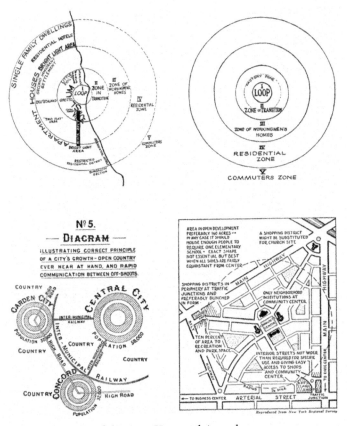

Figure 20.1 Representations of the City: Here and Anywhere
Sources: Top left: Park and Burgess Map of Chicago; top right: their generalized city map (1925, 51, 55). Bottom left: Ebenezer Howard's Garden City (Howard 1965); bottom right: Clarence Perry's Neighborhood Unit (Perry 1929)

By leaving out the distinctive virtues of particular places in a bid for universal applicability, these three representations of the city were intended to be credible and capable of being applied irrespective of time and place, social and physical geography, or political and administrative organization—mimicking many of the claims made by laboratory science of the time. The three urban design schemes were a distinct departure from the "field site" view of urban improvement, such as the street and workplace surveys and the interventions of the Progressive Era, which emphasized that the variegated characteristics of cities and places ought to act as the foundation of urban improvement schemes.

The laboratory-science view of cities was most forcefully expressed in the American Public Health Association's Committee on the Hygiene of Housing 1948 report, *Planning the Neighborhood*. The report outlined "the basic health criteria which should guide the planning of residential neighborhood environments" and that "no perfection in the building or equipment of the home can compensate for an environment which lacks the amenities essential for decent living" (American Public Health Association [APHA] 1948, v–vi). The APHA report also emphasized the need for explicit attention to poor areas and to link design with an attention to social inequality, noting that:

> The mere elimination of specific hazards in poor neighborhoods falls short of the real goal of planning an environment which will foster a healthy and normal family life...a sense of inferiority due to living in a substandard home may often be a more serious health menace than any insanitary condition associated with housing. (APHA 1948, vii)

In a cautionary lesson for contemporary planners, the APHA report's "healthy" neighborhood design guidelines were widely adopted by planners, architects, and policymakers, despite having almost no evidence of their efficacy from epidemiologic or practice-based research (Banerjee and Baer 1984).

6. THE BIOMEDICAL MODEL, HOUSING POLICIES, AND THE FRACTURED CITY: 1950S–1990S

By mid-century, the driving theory in public health would shift again to the *biomedical model* of disease. This model combined laboratory science with a focus on individuals and attributed morbidity and mortality to molecular-level pathogens brought about by lifestyles, behaviors, hereditary biology, or genetics. The biomedical model would provide public health with explanations for emerging chronic diseases, such as heart disease, and shifted research and interventions to personal health "risk factors," such as smoking, diet, and exercise (Susser and Susser 1996). At the same time, New Deal programs would help usher in the era of the "bureaucratic city," where a new set of impersonal public institutions, staffed by newly credentialed professionals, would help to increase disciplinary boundaries and further separate planning from public health (Duhl and Sanchez 1999).

As is well known by students of urban planning, a series of Federal Housing Administration policies would help to physically and socially fracture poor urban communities of color in the 1940s and 1950s by refusing to insure mortgages for older homes and razing poor communities of color under the guise of urban renewal (Fullilove 2004; Hirsh 1983). Planners and public health practitioners often justified the labeling of an area as blighted and thus subject to demolition by using the healthy housing and neighborhood guidelines recommended in the 1948 APHA *Planning the Neighborhood* and almost no efforts were made by health departments to *improve* existing housing to meet these subjective hygiene standards (Tiboni 1949; Twitchell 1943).

Yet, some public health officials denounced the narrow "hygiene of housing" view that was increasingly used to justify "negro removal" (Fullilove 2004). For example, E. R. Krumbiegel, the Commissioner of Health in the City of Milwaukee, criticized urban health professionals and engineers in 1951 for taking a "traditional physical and disease approach to the hygiene of housing," and pointed out that health departments are called upon to fix "the planning mistakes of the past" (Krumbiegel 1951, 500). Krumbiegel also noted that by concerning themselves with "the elimination of rodent infestations, the provision of a potable water supply on the dwelling premises, and the construction of suitable facilities for the disposal of sewage," health officers had not taken a "truly comprehensive" approach to improving housing that should include a "broader sociological viewpoint" (Krumbiegel 1951, 499).[9] The commissioner of public health in Springfield, Massachusetts, noted:

> Objectively speaking, health departments in many cities have found themselves in the hideous role of persecuting and harassing the poor. A health department that vigorously enforces housing and sanitary code regulations frequently compels an identical family to move, and then move, and then move again, sometimes within a few months of each move, and the poor family repeatedly and successively takes refuge in substandard housing…the sociopsychological cost of repeated moving to adults and children of the family are formidable and inhumane. (Bellin 1966, 778)

With the 1956 passage of the Federal Aid Highway Act and perpetuation of urban renewal, residents of many urban communities of color were also shut out from the health-promoting benefits of suburban living, such as home ownership, capital accumulation, access to better funded schools, and participation in the growing suburban economy.

7. SOCIAL RESISTANCE AND CRITICAL RESEARCH

Social movements in the 1950s and 1960s pushed back against the displacement and inequities perpetuated by federal housing and other urban policies. Social movements helped pass important legislation that would improve the health of all populations, but especially the urban poor and people of color, such as Medicaid and the civil rights laws. Krieger et al. (2008) have shown that between 1966 and 1980, the gap in premature (dying before age 65) and infant mortality between rich and poor, black and whites, in all U.S. counties declined. However, while absolute death rates continued to decline after 1980, the gap—or disparity—between rich and poor, whites and people of color, widened after 1980 and continued to grow more unequal every year through 2007 (Pear 2008). The reasons for the shift in the 1970s and 1980s remain unclear, but a combination of federal and municipal policies during this time, such as "benign neglect" and "planned shrinkage," which redirected resources away from inner cities to suburbs and withdrew fire, police, and other essential municipal services from designated "sick" urban neighborhoods, are suspected of contributing to the rise in socioeconomic inequities in health (Fried 1976; Wallace and Wallace 1998).[10]

Researchers took clues from activists and began to critically reengage with how the work of planners, policymakers, and other social scientists could help better explain the persistence of urban health inequities and suggest ameliorative strategies. In 1964, the now classic article by John Cassel, "Social Science Theory as a Source of Hypotheses in Epidemiologic Research," appeared in the *American Journal of Public Health* and called for more research into how social conditions act as determinants of health outcomes and for the use of "social theories to help define some of the general social processes that could be regarded as potentially deleterious to health" (Cassel 1964, 1486). In 1968, the journal *Science* would publish, "Public Health Asks of Sociology...," which also encouraged social scientists to join with epidemiologists and others to elucidate how the "psychosocial environment can act directly on the host as a disease-producing agent"(Rogers 1968, 507).

Planning and urban policymakers turned to improving neighborhoods, and the Office of Economic Opportunity funded Community Health Centers (CHC), the first two of which were located in Columbia Point, Boston, and Mound Bayou, Mississippi. The CHC model focused on providing both immediate care and preventive services for the poor, instead of treating people and sending them back into the living and working conditions that made them sick in the first place. According to Jack Geiger (2005, 7), a physician and leader of the health center movement, Community Health Centers aimed to take a holistic view of health—by "writing prescriptions for the building blocks of health" such as food, rent, jobs, and sanitation. The implications of these and other ideas in social medicine was that research and practice for urban health equity could no longer be easily separated, that no one discipline or methodology alone was capable of understanding the issues, and that social conditions acted not only as determinants of exposure to exogenous hazards but also as pathogens in their own right (Corburn 2009).

8. HEALTH INEQUITIES, CITIES AND SOCIAL EPIDEMIOLOGY

By the mid-1980s, academics, government agencies, and the World Health Organization (WHO) came together to create the Healthy Cities Program in order to reinvigorate the linkages between city planning and public health (Duhl and Sanchez 1999). Focused primarily in Europe, the Healthy Cities Program enrolled cities to draft "healthy city plans" and share examples of the opportunities and barriers for planning more healthy cities. By the 1990s, public health researchers began to reconceptualize explanations for the distribution of disease across populations in order to explain health disparities, energizing the field of social epidemiology (Berkman and Kawachi 2000). Social epidemiology, by emphasizing *distribution* as distinct from *causation*, pushed public health to reconsider how poverty, economic inequality, stress, discrimination, and social capital become "biologically embodied" and help explain persistent patterns of inequitable distributions of disease and well-being across different population groups and geographic areas (Krieger and Davey-Smith 2004). Place inequities—such as residential segregation, urban divestment, and environmental injustices[11]—began to be seen by epidemiologists as linked social determinants of health that may help explain distributions of death and disease across different population groups and places (Fitzpatrick and LaGory 2000). By the end of the century, the U.S. government issued its blueprint for public health, called Healthy People 2010, and made eliminating health disparities one of its top two priorities; and the fields of planning and public health began forging new connections to confront the forces that separated the fields over the past century (table 20.2).

9. TWENTY-FIRST CENTURY HEALTHY AND EQUITABLE URBAN PLANNING

Data on health inequities in the twenty-first century suggest that no matter the disease or cause of death, the poor and people of color are less healthy and die earlier,

Table 20.2 Key Events in American Urban Planning and Their Relationships to Health Equity

Years	Public health events	City planning & health events	Health equity issues/questions
1840s–1890s	Infectious disease epidemics in cities, such as yellow fever, typhoid, & cholera. Mortality differences documented by economic, social and physical conditions of city wards. Miasma—filth—and Contagion—direct passage of poison from one person to another—leading theories of disease. Sanitary Surveys	Metropolitan sanitary commissions & boards of health created Water & waste removal infrastructure, but industrial pollution seen as progress. Housing reform—ventilation, bathrooms and fire escapes. Settlement Houses—linked social, occupational, & neighborhood conditions. Parks, playground, & bathhouse movements	Filth was everywhere, but why did epidemics only occur sometimes and impact the poor most? Not clear where disease came from. Eugenics blamed disease & death rates for African Americans on inherent physical and biologic inferiority.
1900s–1940s	Germ theory- specific microbes lead to specific diseases—replaces miasma. Doctors & laboratory research replace sanitarians & engineers. Vaccinations & chemicals treat individuals & bacteria; environment & prevention moves to background. Neighborhood health centers combined health & social planning.	"City Beautiful" aesthetic Scientific & efficient plans based on laboratory principles & Taylorism. Zoning legitimized, in part, as protecting public health. Universal models to promote well-being, such as Neighborhood Unit, Garden City, & concentric zone. APHA publishes guidelines for healthy housing & neighborhoods.	Laboratory research seeks universal interventions inattentive to living conditions of poor and people of color. DuBois argues that social factors, not inherent inferiority, explain racial differences in health.
1950s–1990s	Biomedical model leading framework = health determined by individual biology, behavior, & genetics. Interventions aim to alter lifestyles & "risk" factors, such as smoking. Hygiene of housing reconsidered Chronic disease focus of profession; HIV/ AIDS afflicts people of color greatest. Healthy Cities Movement & social epidemiology.	Federal housing policies physically & socially fracture poor urban communities of color "planned shrinkage" removes services in low income neighborhoods. Social movements resist elitist, top-down planning. Federal environmental legislation, including NEPA. Suburban sprawl & health links explored.	Urban divestment, deindustrialization & racial residential segregation. Place inequities become concern of social epidemiologists to explain distribution of health inequities. Social epidemiology asks how society & aspects of place "get into the body?"

and the disparities are getting worse, not better. For example, the death rate in 2005 for African Americans was comparable with that of whites in 1975, and black-white disparities in mortality have been fairly stable over four decades (Satcher et al. 2005). Health inequities also persist across poor communities of color in cities. For example, in the predominantly poor, minority neighborhoods of the South Bronx, Harlem, and central Brooklyn in New York City, residents have rates of diabetes, asthma, mental illness, and people living with HIV/AIDS that are nearly double that of the rest of the city (Karpati et al. 2004). In Boston's predominantly African-American and Latino Roxbury neighborhood, asthma rates between 2003 and 2005 for children under five years of age were the highest in the city and more than double the city-wide average (Boston Public Health Commission 2007, 35). Infant mortality for African Americans living in the city of Compton, Los Angeles County, in 2004 was 17.3 deaths per 1,000 live births, the highest in the state of California and nearly two-and-a-half times greater than the rate for the United States (McCormick and Holding 2004). While little agreement exists over the causes of these place-based health inequities, according to Dr. Adam Karpati, assistant commissioner of the New York City Department of Health and Mental Hygiene, the concentration of health disparities in poor, African-American, and Latino neighborhoods is not likely due to disparities in access to health care, risky individual lifestyles, or genetic differences but, rather:

> They are due primarily to differences in the social, economic, and physical conditions in which people live and the health behavior patterns that arise in these settings. "Health disparities" are more than "health-care disparities"...one lesson from the health data is that disparities exist for almost every condition. This observation suggests that, regardless of the specific issue, poor health shares common root causes. It is important to remember, then, that strategies aimed at particular issues need to be complemented by attention to those root causes of poor health: poverty, discrimination, poor housing, and other social inequities. Fundamentally, *eliminating health disparities is about social justice*, which is the underlying philosophy of public health. (Karpati 2004, emphasis added)

10. TOWARD HEALTHY AND EQUITABLE URBAN GOVERNANCE

As this chapter has suggested, reconnecting planning and public health in the twenty-first century in order to eliminate health inequities requires continued critical engagement with the histories of the fields in order to inform research and practice today. Reconnecting the fields must also be attentive to the political—not just the scientific, technical, and physical design—challenges of *healthy urban governance* (Burris et al. 2007).[12] Healthy urban governance demands more than just governmental reform; it includes such political processes as identifying and framing new policy issues; generating appropriate standards of evidence; constituting some social actors as "experts"; adjudicating scientific uncertainty and different knowledge claims; securing public accountability for decisions; and implementing and monitoring policies.[13] Governance practices are, in short, the rules, norms, and processes for exercising power over collective actions and, when inattentive to social inequalities, often sort populations into unequal outcomes by upholding existing distributions of resources like political power, wealth, and knowledge (Healey 2009). I suggest that, in order to move toward healthy and equitable urban governance, planners must address a set of outstanding research questions, including:

1. What makes places healthy?
2. How to shift from problem to *solution* analyses?
3. How to make science policy more democratic and accountable to those most in need?

11. A Relational View of Healthy Places/Cities

Early leaders of the international healthy city movement Trevor Hancock and Len Duhl (1986) suggested that the healthy city is a place that is continually creating and improving the physical, social, and political environments while also expanding the community resources that enable individuals and groups to support each other in performing all the functions of life and in developing themselves to their maximum potential. Hancock and Duhl (1986, 23) go on to note that the healthy city:

> Must be experienced, and we must develop and incorporate into our assessment of the health of a city a variety of unconventional, intuitive and holistic measures to supplement the hard data. Indeed, unless data are turned into stories that can be understood by all, they are not effective in any process of change, either political or administrative.

This definition suggests that how the healthy city is conceptualized has much to do with the framing of research and interventions.

Donald Schön and Martin Rein (1994, 33), in their book, *Frame Reflection*, define a policy frame as "a way of selecting, interpreting, and organizing information to construct a policy argument." As Schön and Rein note, how policy issues are framed from the outset impacts the quality of solutions; defined too narrowly or too broadly, public policy solutions will suffer from the same defects. For example, a chemical testing policy focused on single chemicals cannot produce knowledge about the environmental health consequences of multiple exposures. The framing of the regulatory issue is more restrictive than the actual distribution of chemical-induced risks, and is therefore incapable of delivering optimal management strategies. Similarly, a policy that frames the healthy city as primarily a function of individual behaviors, the built environment, or access to clinical care may discourage policies that aim to address the social, economic, and environmental influences on well-being.

Yet, place is often underconceptualized in healthy urban planning research (Frumkin 2003). I argue that a relational view of place is necessary for capturing the complexity of how place characteristics influence human health. A relational view of place, borrowed from similar ideas of relational research in sociology, recognizes that the physical and social characteristics in space become a *place* when people assign meaning to these characteristics (Emirbayer 1997; Gieryn 2000; Willis and Trondman 2000). Thus, we might think of places as being doubly constructed: through material and physical building (the buildings, streets, parks, etc., of the "built environment") and through the assigning of meanings, cultural interpretations, narratives, perceptions, feelings, and imaginations. Yet, these meanings are contingent and contested, constantly being constructed and reconstructed as, for instance, new population groups and cultures move into a place. The contingent and contested characteristics of place meanings suggests an anti-essentialist view of places, or the notion that there is no one single set of place characteristics, meanings, or relations that will make all cities and neighborhoods healthy. The relational view also recognizes that there are multiple vulnerabilities in places—from poverty, discrimination, access to education, goods, services, and the like—that cumulatively promote health or contribute to illness. Yet, more research is needed to capture how differences in social processes, such as power, inequality, and collective action, influence the construction and reconstruction of the material forms and social meanings that tend to define places.

Importantly for research, the relationship-centered view of healthy urban places is an alternative to the single, independent variable-centered view of places used in most "neighborhood effects on health," "built environment and health," and "urban design and health" studies today. Most work on the built environment and health tends to turn characteristics of places, whether physical or social, into covariates in regression models (e.g., Fox, Jackson, and Barondess 2003; Handy et al. 2002), too often obscuring the subjective meanings people assign to make sense of their physical and social environments. A second weakness of much built environment and health work is that neighborhood characteristics (defined as static variables) are shown to either have a statistically significant influence on well-being or little or no influence at all, suggesting that individual biology, behaviors, or genes are to blame. Yet, this framing misses a key insight from public health—namely, that there are mutually reinforcing relationships between places and people. Both context and composition (or one's biology) matter, as do the institutions and processes that shape one's physical context and access to health promoting resources.

Another challenge for research into the relational view of healthy places is further articulating the mechanism(s) through which characteristics of the built and social environments get "into the body," or biologically embodied, to influence well-being (Krieger 2005). To date, much research continues to make implicit, although sometimes explicit, physically deterministic assumptions, such as suggesting that the presence or absence of a physical resource, such as a park, bicycle lane, or grocery store, is the primary determinant for why nearby populations are or are not physically active or eat healthy foods. This research misses the complexity and emerging understandings in the area of embodiment research—namely, that the histories of places and biographies of people, such as the legacy of racism and segregation in places, can and do leave an indelible biologic mark and influence health for generations.

Geronimus (2000) has suggested one embodiment hypothesis, arguing that chronic discrimination, stress, and exposure to home, neighborhood, and workplace hazards result in a persistent "weathering" on the bodies of the poor and people of color that denigrates the immune, metabolic, and cardiovascular systems and fuels the development or progression of infectious and chronic disease. This cumulative weathering, argues Geronimus, is at least partly to blame for health inequities and the persistence of disparities between differently situated population groups in the United States. Further study of the processes of embodiment are necessary, but the concept could act as an organizing principle for urban planning researchers, much as it has for some epidemiologists, sociologists, and anthropologists aiming to understand, and ultimately change, the institutions and policies that shape the characteristics of places and opportunities for people to live healthy lives.

12. APPRECIATIVE INQUIRY OR PRACTICE-BASED RESEARCH

As noted above, public health has a long history of documenting what is wrong with certain populations in terms of excess disease burden and premature mortality. Social epidemiologists have recently begun to ask what explains persistent patterns of poor health for certain population groups and places, but one weakness of this work is that results often come too late; statistically significant findings are revealed after populations are sick or dead. Similarly, research into the "built environment and health" is yet to balance the quest for methodologically perfected technical/quantitative evaluation with simultaneous attention to the policy translation of these findings. Healthy urban governance must draw on pragmatic traditions in planning (Healey 2009; Hoch 2007), practice-based research in medicine, and other similar methodologies to shift from problem to solution analyses.

Pragmatic appreciative inquiry and practice-based research demand employing the "fire-aim-ready" approach to analysis, where interventions are crafted and implemented knowing they are fallible and require close monitoring of progress and adjustment along the way. These same interventions need to be flexible enough to "learn" or adapt to new understandings, changing circumstances, and even new technologies. Environmental decision makers have been doing just this for decades in the management of complex ecosystems such as the Great Lakes, Columbia River basin, and Chesapeake Bay. Planners might look at the methods used by a new class of development economists, such as Ether Duflo of the Abdul Latif Jameel Poverty Action Lab at M.I.T., who has adopted the randomized experiment model from clinical trails of drugs to evaluate ongoing practice, rather than modeling likely behavior and outcomes before intervening (Parker 2010). Adaptive management may be more appropriate for problems such as addressing urban health inequities, where randomized experimentation may be impractical and unethical. How and where to apply strategies of intervention studies and adaptive management—which require teams of practitioners with diverse skill sets, systems to monitor progress, feedback loops to ensure monitoring results reach decision makers, and processes for social learning and adjusting practice—in urban health settings remain open and challenging questions.

Health impact assessment (HIA) is one practice that can allow planners to analyze the likely health impacts of a policy or plan while also monitoring interventions for how well they are promoting health. For example, the San Francisco Department of Public Health (SFDPH) has used HIA to assess a proposed living-wage ordinance, new housing proposals, and rezoning plans. During one HIA process, called the Eastern Neighborhoods Community Health Impact Assessment (ENCHIA), the SFDPH organized a participatory planning process that included over forty governmental and nongovernmental organizations for evaluating the positive and negative human health impacts from a proposed rezoning plan. During the ENCHIA process, stakeholders collaboratively defined the elements of a healthy place, discussed how land use does or does not influence these elements, and investigated how a set of rezoning proposals and potential alternatives might influence the health of the largely low-income, immigrant communities of the Mission District and South of Market neighborhoods in San Francisco (Corburn 2009).

One outcome of the ENCHIA process was the Healthy Development Measurement Tool (HDMT), an analytic method outlining the broad social indicators, land-use development goals, and quantitative and qualitative data for healthy urban development (www.thehdmt.org). The HDMT is now being used by the city's planning agency, private developers, and community-based organizations to evaluate the extent to which new development projects and land-use plans will promote health equity (Farhang et al. 2008). While no panacea, HIA is beginning to bring together government agencies, advocacy organizations, and researchers that rarely work together, suggesting that it may be a process for breaking down "disciplinary boundaries" and other institutional obstacles confronting efforts to reconnect planning and public health (Dannenberg et al. 2006).

13. Democratizing Urban Science Policy

Healthy urban governance will require a recasting of science, expertise, and evidence, much like those calling for a new social contract between science and society to address pressing issues of climate change and sustainability. This new paradigm calls for a shift away from experimental science, driven from inside existing disciplines with scientists working alone, to where the pursuit of science is more dispersed, context dependent, and problem oriented. The science underwriting the healthy city, like that for climate change and sustainability, is inherently political, since facts are uncertain, values in dispute, stakes high, and decisions urgent—contributing to what Funtowicz and Ravetz (1993) have called postnormal science ("normal" science is paradigmatic in the sense described by the philosopher of science Thomas Kuhn). In postnormal conditions, science crosses disciplinary lines; enters into previously unknown investigative territories; requires the deployment of new methods, instruments, protocols, and experimental systems; and involves politically sensitive processes and results. Questions arise in this postnormal situation that additional "fact finding" cannot answer, such as how to grapple with uncertainty and the likely distribution of benefits and harms, and democratic processes are necessary to offer responses to these trans-science issues.

14. Toward Healthful and Equitable City Planning

This chapter has aimed to both critically review the histories of American urban planning and public health and suggest strategies for reconnecting the fields around healthy and equitable research and practice. No one healthy planning intervention or design change will be sufficient to make urban places and populations more healthful. Instead, the field must reach across long entrenched institutional and disciplinary boundaries to forge a research and practice agenda around notions of healthful and equitable urban governance. The strategies offered here suggest more questions than answers, and work needs to be done to explore a wider range of possibilities for confronting the deeply entrenched norms, values, and institutional practices that currently act as barriers to healthy and socially just urban governance. Twenty-first-century healthful planning will require critical analyses and experimental interventions that continually ask what constitutes a healthy place; how this changes over time and varies across neighborhood, city, and region; and what strategies can address the multiple and overlapping material and social forces that continue to perpetuate urban health inequities?

NOTES

1. To be explicit, by "public health" I am referring to public policies, practices, and processes that influence the distribution of disease, death, and well-being for populations, or what the field generally calls "health promotion." I use the Institute of Medicine's (IOM; 2003, 46) definition of public health, which defines its mission as "fulfilling society's interest in assuring the conditions in which people can be healthy" and links many disciplines but rests upon the scientific core of epidemiology. The IOM also states that the framework of public health encompasses both activities undertaken within the formal structure of government and the associated efforts of private and voluntary organizations and individuals. When using the term "planning," I am describing public policies, practices, and processes that influence both urban populations and the built environment of the city. I conceive planning as much more than land use and design; I see it also as the organizing of information, forecasting and modeling complex systems, and structuring public processes that can include or exclude impacted populations.

2. According to Braveman (2006), health inequities refer to material, social, gender, racial, income, and other social and economic inequalities that are beyond the control of individuals and are therefore considered unfair and unjust.

3. The root causes of health inequities are defined by the World Health Organization (2008) as the social determinants of health (SDOH) and include such planning-related issues as persistent poverty, unemployment, toxic pollution, racial discrimination, poor education, substandard housing, violence, incarceration, access to grocery stores, and lack of medical and social services.

4. There are a number of examples during this era of state-sponsored quarantines targeted at immigrants. In 1892, the Port Authority of New York quarantined all passengers aboard ships arriving from Southern and Eastern Europe, where a cholera outbreak had occurred. By 1900, Chinese immigrants were regularly detained at Angel Island and interrogated for diseases such as bubonic plague. In 1916, during an epidemic of poliomyletis, New York City's Department of Health began forcibly separating children from their parents and placing them in quarantine. However, wealthy parents were allowed to keep their stricken children at home if they could provide a separate room and medical care for their child (Rosen 1993).

5. Public baths were another sanitarian approach to removing moral and physical miasma. A private charity, the New York Association for Improving the Condition of the Poor, is credited with building one of the first public baths for the poor, driven largely by the belief that slum dwellers needed to be cleansed of moral failures and physical dirt (Duffy 1990).

6. While the Settlement House movement embraced immigrants, it often refused to serve impoverished African Americans.

7. Olmsted's views also helped shape one of the first city planning texts published by Nelson Lewis (1916, 17–18), entitled *The Planning of the Modern City*, where Lewis would note:

> There are many who believe that the chief purposes of city planning are social, that the problems of housing, the provision of recreation and amusement for the people, the control and even the ownership and operation of all public utilities, the establishment and conduct of public markets, the collection and disposal

of wastes, the protection of public health, the building of hospitals, the care of paupers, criminals and the insane, and all of the other activities of the modern city are all a part of city planning. All of these, however, are matters of administration rather than of planning.

8. Their model, known as concentric zone theory and first published in *The City* (1925), predicted that cities would take the form of five concentric rings with areas of social and physical deterioration concentrated near the city center and more prosperous areas located near the city's edge. Concentric zone theory was one of the earliest models developed to explain the spatial organization of urban areas including the existence of social problems, such as unemployment and crime in certain districts of Chicago.

9. During the same era, the engineer-director of the Los Angeles Bureau of Sanitation, Charles L. Senn (1951, 512), also argued for attention to equity issues when developing coordinated health and planning policies, noting that what was missing from "healthy housing" programs was "suitable low-rent, public housing units for families which must be vacated from unfit dwellings" and that "the negative approach of condemnation must go hand-in-hand with the positive task of rebuilding our cities."

10. "Benign neglect" was proposed by Daniel Patrick Moynihan, Nixon's adviser on urban and social policy, in his 1970 memo reprinted in the *New York Times* on January 30, entitled "Text of the Moynihan Memorandum on the Status of Negroes."

11. Environmental injustice has at least three place-based dimensions: (1) there is a disproportionate concentration of hazardous pollutants and noxious facilities and a lack of amenities, such as parks and hospitals, in poor communities of color; (2) these same communities are excluded from decision-making processes where land-use decisions are made; and (3) government enforcement of existing environmental regulations is lax or nonexistent in poor communities of color (IOM 2003).

12. According to Tony Iton (2006, 124), director of the Alemeda County, California, Health Department:

> Decisions that governments and corporations make every day benefit some and burden others. Unfortunately, they often reinforce class, racial and gender inequities that contribute to unequal patterns of illness and premature death. Building a social movement that can advocate effectively for more equitable social policies is critical to changing our economic, physical and social environments so that they promote rather than threaten our health. In other words, tackling health inequities is unavoidably a matter of politics; of engaging in struggles over how we want our government to allocate resources, regulate corporate power, and implement the principles of democracy. It is also a matter of empowering communities and reshaping institutions to address the social and economic conditions that profoundly shape our health.

13. I interpret the often ambiguous but popular term "governance" from Oran Young (1996, 247), who suggests that it includes:

> the establishment and operation of social institutions or, in other words, sets of roles, rules, decision making procedures, and programs that serve to define social practices and to guide interactions of those participating in these practices... [G]overnance systems are arrangements designed to resolve social conflicts, enhance social welfare, and, more generally, alleviate collective action problems in a world of interdependent actors.

REFERENCES

American Public Health Association. 1948. *Planning the Neighborhood: Standards for Healthful Housing.*. Chicago: Public Administration Service, Committee on the Hygiene of Housing.

Banerjee, T., and W. Baer. 1984. *Beyond the Neighborhood Unit: Residential Environments and Public Policy.* New York: Springer.

Bellin, L. 1966. "Obligatory Alliance—The Urban Renewal Authority and the City." *American Journal of Public Health* 56(5): 776–84.

Berkman, L., and I. Kawachi, eds. 2000. *Social Epidemiology.* New York: Oxford University Press.

Boston Public Health Commission. 2007. *The Health of Boston.* Boston: Research Office.

Braveman P. 2006. "Health Disparities and Health Equity: Concepts and Measurement." *Annual Review of Public Health* 27:167–94.

Burris, S., T. Hancock, V. Lin, and A. Herzog. 2007. "Emerging Strategies for Healthy Urban Governance." *Journal of Urban Health: Bulletin of the New York Academy of Medicine* 84(1): 154–63.

Cassel, J. 1964. "Social Science Theory as a Source of Hypotheses in Epidemiologic Research." *American Journal of Public Health* 54:1482–88.

Corburn, J. 2007. "Reconnecting with Our Roots: American Urban Planning and Public Health in the 21st Century." *Urban Affairs Review* 42:688–713.

Corburn, J. 2009. *Toward the Healthy City: People, Places and the Politics of Urban Planning.* Cambridge, MA: MIT Press.

Dannenberg, A. L., R. Bhatia, B. L. Cole, C. Dora, J. E. Fielding, K. Kraft, D. McClymont-Peace, J. Mindell, C. Onyekere, J. A. Roberts, C. L. Ross, C. D. Rutt, A. Scott-Samuel, and H. H. Tilson. 2006. "Growing the Field of Health Impact Assessment in the United States: An Agenda for Research and Practice." *American Journal of Public Health* 96:262–70.

Department of Health and Human Services. 2000. "Healthy People 2010: Understanding and Improving Health." Available at: http://www.healthypeople.gov/Document/html/uih/uih_2.htm#goals; accessed December 13, 2007.

Department of Health and Human Services. 2007. "A Strategic Framework for Improving Racial/Ethnic Minority Health and Eliminating Racial/Ethnic Health Disparities." Available at: http://www.omhrc.gov:80/npa/templates/content.aspx?lvl=1&lvlid=13&id=79; accessed March 31, 2008.

Du Bois, W. E. B., ed. 1906. *The Health and Physique of the Negro American: Report of a Social Study Made Under the Direction of Atlanta University.* Atlanta, GA: Atlanta University Press.

Duffy, J. 1990. *The Sanitarians: A History of American Public Health.* Chicago: University of Illinois Press.

Duhl, L. J., and A. K. Sanchez. 1999. "Healthy Cities and the City Planning Process." Available at: http://www.who.dk/document/e67843.pdf; accessed July 29, 2007.

Emirbayer, M. 1997. "Manifesto for Relational Sociology." *American Journal of Sociology* 103:281–317.

Fairfield, J. D. 1994. "The Scientific Management of Urban Space: Professional City Planning and the Legacy of Progressive Reform." *Journal of Urban History* 20:179–204.

Farhang, L., R. Bhatia, C. Scully, et al. 2008. "Creating Tools for Healthy Development: Case Study of San Francisco's Eastern Neighborhoods Community Health Impact Assessment." *Journal of Public Health Management and Practice* 14(3): 255–65.

Fishman, R., ed. 2000. *The American Planning Tradition: Culture and Policy.* Washington, DC: Woodrow Wilson Center Press.

Fitzpatrick, K., and M. LaGory. 2000. *Unhealthy Places: The Ecology of Risk in the Urban Landscape.* London: Routledge.

Ford, F. L. 1910. "The Scope of City Planning in the United States." In *Proceedings of the First National Conference on City Planning,* May 21–22, 1909. Washington, DC: American Society of Planning Officials.

Fox, D. M., R. J. Jackson, and J. A. Barondess. 2003. "Health and the Built Environment." *Journal of Urban Health* 80(4): 534–35.

Fried, J. 1976. "City's Housing Administrator Proposes 'Planned Shrinkage' of Some Slums." New York Times, February 3, B1.

Frumkin, H. 2003. "Healthy Places: Exploring the Evidence." *American Journal of Public Health* 93:1451–56.

Fullilove, M. T. 2004. *Root Shock: How Tearing Up City Neighborhoods Hurts America and What We Can Do About It.* New York: Ballantine.

Funtowicz, S., and J. R. Ravetz. 1993. "Science for the Post-normal Age." *Futures* 25:739–55.

Galea, S., N. Freudenberg, and D. Vlahov. 2005. "Cities and Population Health." *Social Science and Medicine* 60:1017–33.

Geiger, J. 2005. "The Unsteady March." *Perspectives in Biology and Medicine* 48:1–9.

Geronimus, A T. 2000. "To Mitigate, Resist, or Undo: Addressing Structural Influences on the Health of Urban Populations." *American Journal of Public Health* 90:867–72.

Gieryn, T. 2000. "A Space for Place in Sociology." *Annual Review of Sociology* 26:463–96.

Goldberger, J., G. A. Wheeler, E. Sydenstricker. 1920. "A Study of the Relation of Family Income and Other Economic Factors to Pellagra Incidence in Seven Cotton-Mill Villages of South Carolina in 1916." *Public Health Reports* 35:2673–714.

Hall, P. 1996. *Cities of Tomorrow: An Intellectual History of Urban Planning and Design in the Twentieth Century,* rev. ed. Oxford: Blackwell.

Hancock, T., and L. Duhl. 1986. *Promoting Health in the Urban Context.* WHO Healthy Cities Papers No.1,World Health Organization, Copenhagen.

Handy, S. L., M. G. Boarnet, R. Ewing, and R. E. Killingsworth. 2002. "How the Built Environment Affects Physical Activity." *American Journal of Preventive Medicine* 23(Suppl. 2): 64–73.

Healey, P. 2009. "The Pragmatic Tradition in Planning Thought." *Journal of Planning Education and Research* 28:277–92.

Hirsh, A. R. 1983. *Making the Second Ghetto: Race and Housing in Chicago, 1940–1960.* Cambridge, UK: Cambridge University Press.

Hoch, C. 2007. "Pragmatic Communicative Action Theory." *Journal of Planing Education and Research* 26:272–83.

Hoehner, C. M., L. K. Brennan, R. C. Brownson, S. L. Handy, and R. Killingsworth. 2003. "Opportunities for Integrating Public Health and Urban Planning Approaches to Promote Active Community Environments." *American Journal of Health Promotion* 18(1): 14–20.

Holland, D. F., and G. S. J. Perrott. 1938. "Health of the Negro. Part II. A Preliminary Report on a Study of Disabling Illness in a Representative Sample of the Negro and White Population of Four Cities Canvassed in the National Health Survey, 1935–1936." *Milbank Memorial Fund Quarterly* 16:16–38.

Howard, E. 1965. *Garden Cities of To-Morrow.* Cambridge, MA: MIT Press.

Hull-House Residents. 1895. *Hull House Maps and Papers.* New York: Thomas Y. Crowell.

Institute of Medicine. 2003. *Unequal Treatment: Confronting Racial and Ethnic Disparities in Healthcare.* Washington, DC: National Academies Press.

Iton, A. 2006. "Tackling the Root Causes of Health Disparities through Community Capacity Building." In *Tackling Health Inequities Through Public Health Practice, National Association of County and City Health Officials,* edited by R. Hofrichter. Available at: www.naccho.org/topics/justice/upload/NACCHO_Handbook_hyperlinks_000.pdf; accessed December 20, 2010.

Karpati, A. 2004. Testimony before New York State Assembly Committee on Health and the Black, Puerto Rican and Hispanic Legislative Caucus, April 22. Available at: http://www.nyc.gov/html/doh/html/public/testi/testi20040422.html; accessed September 20, 2005.

Karpati, A., B. Kerker, F. Mostashari, T. Singh, A. Hajat, L.Thorpe, M. Bassett, K. Henning, and T. Frieden. 2004. "Health Disparities in New York City." New York City Department of Health and Mental Hygiene. Available at: www.nyc.gov/html/doh/downloads/pdf/epi/disparities-2004.pdf.

Kjellstrom, T., S. Mercado, D. Sattherthwaite, G. McGranahan, S. Friel, and K. Havemann. 2007. *Our Cities, Our Health, Our Future: Acting on Social Determinants for Health Equity in Urban Settings.* Kobe, Japan: World Health Organization, Centre for Health Development.

Krieger, J., and D. L. Higgins. 2002. "Housing and Health: Time and Again for Public Health Action." *American Journal of Public Health* 92(5): 758–68.

Krieger, N. 2005. "Embodiment: A Conceptual Glossary for Epidemiology." *Journal of Epidemiology and Community Health* 59:350–55.

Krieger, N., and G. Davey-Smith. 2004. "'Bodies Count,' and Body Counts: Social Epidemiology and Embodying Inequality." *Epidemiologic Reviews* 26:92–103.

Krieger, N., D. H. Rehkopf, J. T. Chen, P. D. Waterman, E. Marcelli, and M. Kennedy. 2008. "The Fall and Rise of U.S. Inequities in Premature Mortality: 1960–2002." *PLoS Medicine* 5(2). Available at: e46doi:10.1371/journal.pmed.0050046; accessed March 23, 2008.

Krumbiegel, E. R. 1951. "Hygiene of Housing: The Responsibilities of Public Health in Housing." *American Journal of Public Health Nations Health* 41:497–504.

Leavitt, J. W. 1982. *The Healthiest City: Milwaukee and the Politics of Health Reform.* Madison, WI: University of Wisconsin Press.

Lewis, N. 1916. *The Planning of the Modern City.* New York: John Wiley.

Link, B. G., and J. Phelan. 1996. "Understanding Sociodemographic Differences in Health—The Role of Fundamental Social Causes." *American Journal of Public Health* 86:471–73.

Lubove, R. 1974. *The Progressives and the Slums: Tenement House Reform in New York City, 1870–1917.* Westport, CT: Greenwood.

Maantay, J. A. 2001. "Zoning, Equity, and Public Health." *American Journal of Public Health* 91:1033–41.

Marmot, M. 2004. *The Status Syndrome: How Social Standing Affects our Health and Longevity.* New York: Henry Holt.

Marsh, B. C. 1908. "City Planning in Justice to the Working Population." *Charities and the Commons* 19:1514–18.

Marsh, B. C. 1909/1974. *An Introduction to City Planning: Democracy's Challenge to the American City.* New York: Arno Press.

McCormick, E., and R. Holding. 2004. "Too Young to Die. A Special Report." *San Francisco Chronicle* October 7. Available at: http://www.sfgate.com/cgi-bin/article.cgi?file=/c/a/2004/10/07/MNGII94D931.DTL.

McKeown, T. 1976. *The Modern Rise of Population.* New York: Academic Press.

Meckel R. A. 1990. *Save the Babies: American Public Health Reform and the Prevention of Infant Mortality 1850–1929.* Baltimore: Johns Hopkins University Press.

Meeker, E. 1972. "The Improving Health of the United States, 1850–1915." *Explorations in Economic History* 9:353–73.

Melosi, M. 2000. *The Sanitary City: Urban Infrastructure in America From Colonial Times to the Present*. Baltimore: Johns Hopkins University Press.

Mullan, F. 1989. *Plagues and Politics: The Story of the United States Public Health Service*. New York: Basic Books.

Olmsted Jr., F. L. 1910. "City Planning: An Introductory Address." *American Civic Association* 2(4): 1–30.

Park, Robert E., and Ernest W. Burgess. 1925. *The City*. Chicago: University of Chicago Press.

Parker, I. 2010. "The Poverty Lab." *New Yorker* 86(13): 78–89.

Pear, R. 2008. "Gap in Life Expectancy Widens for the Nation." *New York Times*, March 23.

Perrott, G. S. J., and S. D. Collins. 1935. "Relation of Sickness to Income and Income Change in Ten Surveyed Communities." Health and Depression Studies No. 1: Method of study and general results for each locality. *Public Health Reports* 50:595–622.

Perry, C. A. 1929. "City Planning for Neighborhood Life." *Social Forces* 8(1): 98–100.

Peterson, J. 1979. "The Impact of Sanitary Reform Upon American Urban Planning, 1840–1890." *Journal of Social History* 13:83–103.

Peterson, J. 2003. *The Birth of City Planning in the United States, 1840–1917*. Baltimore: Johns Hopkins University Press.

Porter, D. 1999. *Health, Civilization and the State: A History of Public Health From Ancient to Modern Times*. London: Routledge.

Rogers, E. S. 1968. "Public Health Asks of Sociology..." *Science* 159:506–508.

Rosen, G. 1971. "The First Neighborhood Health Center Movement—Its Rise and Fall." *American Journal of Public Health* 61:1620–37.

Rosen, G. 1993. *A History of Public Health*, rev. ed. Baltimore: Johns Hopkins University Press.

Satcher, D., G. E. Fryer, J. McCann, A. Troutman, S. H. Woolf, and G. Rust.(2005. "What If We Were Equal? A Comparison of the Black-White Mortality Gap in 1960 and 2000." *Health Affairs* 24(2): 459–64.

Schon, D., and M. Rein. 1994. *Frame Reflection: Toward the Resolution of Intractable Policy Controversies*. New York: Basic Books.

Senn, C. 1951. "Hygiene of Housing: Contribution of the American Public Health Association to Housing Evaluation." *American Journal of ublic Health* 41:511–15.

Sloane, D. C. 2006. "Longer View: From Congestion to Sprawl— Planning and Health in Historical Context." *Journal of the American Planning Association* 72:10–18.

Susser, M., and E. Susser. 1996. "Choosing a Future for Epidemiology I: Eras and Paradigms." *American Journal of Public Health* 86(5): 668–73.

Susser, M., and Stein, Z. 2009. *Eras in Epidemiology: The Evolution of Ideas*. NY: Oxford University Press.

Tarr, J. A. 1996. *The Search for the Ultimate Sink: Urban Pollution in Historical Perspective*. Akron, OH: University of Akron Press.

Tiboni, E. 1949. "Appraisal of Substandard Housing." *American Journal of Public Health* 39(4): 459–61.

Twitchell, A. 1943. "A New Method for Measuring Quality in Housing." *American Journal of Public Health* 33(6): 729–40.

Villiage of Euclid v. Ambler Realty Co. 1926. 272 U.S. 365. Available at: caselaw.lp.findlaw.com/scripts/getcase.pl?court=US&vol=272&invol=365; accessed April 2, 2008.

Wallace, D., and R. Wallace. 1998. *A Plague on Your Houses: How New York Was Burned Down and National Public Health Crumbled*. New York: Verso.

Wilkinson, and Pickett. 2009. *Spirit Level:Why Greater Equality Makes Societies Stronger*. NY: Bloomsbury Press.

Willis, P., and M. Trondman. 2000. "Manifesto for Ethnography." *Ethnography* 1:5–16.

World Health Organization. 2008. "Closing the Gap in a Generation: Health Equity through Action on the Social Determinants of Health." Final Report of the Commission on Social Determinants of Health. Geneva, World Health Organization.

World Health Organization.. 2010. "Urban Planning Essential for Public Health." Available at: http://www.who.int/mediacentre/news/releases/2010/urban_health_20100407/en/index.html.

Young, O. 1996. "Rights, Rules, and Resources in International Society." In *Rights to Nature: Ecological, Economic, Cultural and Political Principles of Institutions for the Environment*, edited by A.Hanna, C. Folke, and K. Maler, 245–64. Washington, DC: Island Press.

CHAPTER 21

SUBURBAN SPRAWL AND "SMART GROWTH"

YAN SONG

1. INTRODUCTION

CONCERNS over the consequences of urban sprawl in the U.S. metropolitan areas have, since the 1980s, led to increased advocacy for more compact and traditional urban development. Numerous planning agencies have initiated efforts to alter land development practices dominated by sprawl. Compact and traditional development has drawn increasing attention from land-use and environmental policymakers. Advocates for smart growth argue that neighborhoods referred as "compact" or "transit-oriented" can decrease automobile dependency, lessen air pollution, and reduce the amount of land affected by impervious surfaces such as roads and parking lots (Duany, Plater-Zyberk, and Speck 2000). Accordingly, an increasing number of state and local governments have adopted smart growth policies to encourage compact development in response to rising concerns about urban sprawl (Weitz 1999; Song 2005). States such as Maryland, Florida, and Oregon have adopted "smart growth" legislation that requires local governments to alter development practices dominated by low-density sprawl and create more compact urban areas and traditional neighborhoods. Local governments in these states and the other non–smart growth states have been experimenting with specific plans, policies, codes, and development standards to promote compact development and traditional neighborhoods since the 1990s. The smart growth agenda has also been endorsed by many different environmental organizations and interest groups. In practice, smart growth is a bundle of polices to reach goals such as land protection, denser and more compact developments, multimodal transportation, infill development, affordable housing, and sense of community (Ye, Mandpe, and Meyer 2005; Burchell, Listokin, and Galley 2000).

Recent studies show that smart growth has been limited in success so far (Ingram et al. 2009; Sartori, Moore, and Knaap 2011). Many communities have not embraced the smart growth programs. In places where smart growth has been implemented, no substantial progress has been made toward achieving smart growth goals. Within this context, it is critical to understand the determinants of adopting smart growth policies by local communities, since this knowledge can help us understand what factors are amenable to the sponsorship of alternative growth directions.

Several studies have been carried out to evaluate to what degree local cities and counties are adopting plan elements consistent with smart growth (Talen and Knaap 2003; Edwards and Haines 2007; Downs 2005; Pendall 2004). This set of analyses reveals that the majority of the U.S. communities are not fully embracing the smart growth agenda. For example, Talen and Knaap (2003) show that regulation at the local level in Illinois is not well focused on the implementation of smart growth principles. Smart growth tools used to promote more compact growth, infill development, or pedestrian-oriented development are generally nonexistent. The study by Pendall (2004) also casts some doubt on any expansion in the adoption of smart growth policy instruments. Using the results of national surveys of local governments administered in 1994 and 2003, Pendall identifies little change in the use of plans, zoning, or urban growth boundaries by those local governments.

In addition, it is crucial to evaluate the extent to which smart growth plans have been effective in bringing compact, pedestrian-oriented, multimodal, revitalized, and affordable outcomes. Different localities define smart growth in their own ways to achieve their particular missions and goals (Ye, Mandpe, and Meyer 2005). Downs (2005) finds out that approaches to smart growth vary across localities. Information on whether smart growth measures have achieved their goals and whether varied approaches have different levels of efficacy will be helpful in future policy design and implementation.

Surprisingly, given the high stakes of smart growth in recent years, systematic studies on the determinants of adoption of smart growth and the evaluation of outcomes of smart growth programs have been rare and are typically not comprehensive. In this chapter I discuss both issues. After providing a review of smart growth tools to set the necessary background for the discussion, I present an overview of our current knowledge base regarding the determinants of local adoption of smart growth tools. This is followed by an overview of the evaluations of the efficacy of smart growth in bringing compact, pedestrian-oriented, multimodal, affordable, and revitalized forms. Finally, I identify the understudied areas regarding smart growth adoption and outcomes. The purpose of these discussions is to help provide explanations of past efforts and offer better guidance for future policy development and evaluation.

2. ELEMENTS OF SMART GROWTH PLANS

The implementation of the principles of smart growth is accomplished through an array of tools. Many scholars and practitioners have described and categorized the sprawl-reduction tools adopted in local plans (Pendall 1999; Bengston, Fletcher, and Nelson 2004; Brody, Carrasco, and Highfield 2006; Talen and Knaap 2003). Based on the impacts of the locally adopted land-use controls on sprawl, Pendall (1999) identifies the land-use controls that shift the cost of development onto builders and away from the general public, those that mandate densities (such as zoning and urban containment systems), and those that rely on tax policies to fund services and infrastructure. Bengston, Fletcher, and Nelson (2004) group tools for managing urban growth into three broad categories: taking public ownership and management of land for land protection, enforcing regulations for development control, and designing incentives for behavior alteration. Talen and Knaap (2003) develop a typology of the different tools used to implement smart growth. They divide the various implementation strategies into four following categories: regional programs and policies managing urban growth on a regional scale, process-oriented policies requiring the development review process, spatial policies imposing spatially specific zones, and site-specific policies prescribing certain styles of development. Dierwechter (2008) draws largely on public documents produced and administered at various levels of governance and identifies four overarching principles of the smart growth paradigm: open space preservation, compact urban form, urban design, and public participation. A recent study by Ingram et al. (2009) focuses on evaluation of five smart growth goals, including compact development, protection of land resources, provision of transportation options, affordable housing, and positive fiscal impact.

This chapter employs a classification of smart growth tools (Wu and Cho 2007) that has the virtues of simplicity and is consistent with smart growth goals. The broad goals of smart growth are synthesized as (1) land protection, (2) compact and infill development, (3) multimodal transportation, (4) affordable housing, and (5) sense of community. It is necessary to note that these categories are not mutually exclusive. In other words, tools serving one goal might serve other goals as well. In what follows, tools categorized by the set of goals are briefly described in turn.

For the primary purpose of protecting land, public acquisition of land and conservation easement are carried out (Gustanski and Squires 2000). In many urban areas, land acquisition serves land preservation and other smart growth goals, and plays a significant role in shaping regional development form and managing urban growth (Hollis and Fulton 2002) by defining where not to grow (Bengston, Fletcher, and Nelson 2004; Daniels and Lapping 2005). Conservation easement (or conservation covenant) creates a legally enforceable land preservation agreement between a landowner and a government agency or a qualified land protection organization. The primary purpose of a conservation easement is to protect land from certain forms of development or use. Protection of land is achieved primarily by separating the right to subdivide and build on the land from the other rights of ownership. The landowner who gives up these "development rights" continues to privately own and manage the land and receives tax advantages.

To encourage compact developments that are denser in form and closer to an urban center in location, various tools have been developed. For examples, small-lot zoning or upzoning were extensively used in urban areas throughout Oregon in the 1970s and 1980s to encourage more intense development (Knaap and Nelson 1992). Clustering development is another planning tool targeting development density in specific areas (Arendt 1997; Brody, Carrasco, and Highfield 2006). Development impact fees, one type of development exactions, are used to help finance off-site impacts and infrastructure costs of development and to encourage more efficient development patterns (Heim 2001). Other strategies have been used to contain urban growth, including rate of growth controls, growth-phasing regulations, and urban containment policies. Rate of growth controls put an upper limit on the number of building permits issued annually. Growth-phasing regulations (i.e., adequate public facility ordinances, or APFOs, or "concurrency" in Florida) impose development caps by scheduling the timing of public improvements needed for development. Urban growth boundaries (UGB) and urban service areas (USA) are widely used as urban containment policies. An UGB is a dividing line drawn around an urban area to separate it from surrounding rural areas. Areas outside the boundary are zoned for rural uses, and inside are for urban use. A USA delineates the area beyond which certain urban services such as sewer and water will not be provided, prohibiting development in areas not served by these urban services.

A variety of infill incentives have been used by cities in an effort to direct development into areas that are already urbanized. One set of tools includes a waiver or reduction of development fees, subsidized land costs, tax exemptions or reductions, and improvements to infrastructure in a desired development zone, such as Priority Funding Areas (Howland and Sohn 2007). A two-rate property tax and value-capture technique are other approaches to promote infill and redevelopment in urban areas. The tools reduce the tax rate on assessed building values and increase the tax rate on assessed land values. By doing so, the tools tax away the speculative values of holding undeveloped property within the urban growth area, thus promoting urban infill (Rybeck 2004). In addition, transfer of development rights (TDRs) is a hopeful policy tool to promote a dense urban core. The TDRs separate the right to develop from the right to own, and create a market that allows the development rights to be transferred from sending zone to receiving zone. If the markets work well, targeted sending areas are protected from development, thereby maintaining them as open space, wildlife habitat, or scenic vistas and other uses; targeted receiving areas are more densely developed than would otherwise be the case (McConnell and Walls 2009).

To encourage multimodal transportation, smart growth promotes transit-oriented development (TOD) at the regional scale and New Urbanist design at the site level. Through alteration of land-use form and provision of a variety of transportation options; a dense network of interconnected streets, sidewalks, and paths; and most or all of the components of a person's daily routines in close proximity to home, New Urbanists hope to reorient American's travel behavior (Duany, Plater-Zyberk, and Speck 2000).

To increase the supply of affordable housing for low-income households, the density bonus—an incentive-based tool—permits developers to increase the square footage or number of units allowed on a piece of property if they agree to restrict the rents or selling prices of a certain number of the units for low-income or senior households. The additional cash flow from these bonus units offsets the reduced revenue from the affordable units. This tool works best in areas where growth pressures are strong and land availability is limited (Nolon and Bacher 2007). Another policy used to encourage affordable housing is local inclusionary zoning. Inclusionary zoning programs either require developers to make a certain percentage of the units within their market-rate residential developments available at prices or rents that are affordable to specified income groups, or offer incentives that encourage them to do so (Nolan and Bacher 2007).

In addition, smart growth is intended to foster a "sense of community," a feeling of belonging, emotional investment, positive human relationships, and safety. Through the New Urbanist design, the architectural syntax in New Urbanist projects aims to discourage social "conflict." People attribute part of the sociability experience to design factors, including front porches, proximity of houses to one another, and availability of common gathering spaces such as town center and parks (Duany, Plater-Zyberk, and Speck 2000; Steuteville 2001). New Urbanist neighborhoods also encourage design styles that lend increased safety. Having keen "eyes on the street" to watch for suspicious activity is cultivated from narrower lots, houses closer to the street, usable front porches, residential units mixed with commercial, and increased pedestrian activity. In contrast to the "fortress strategy," in which "outsiders" are unwelcome, New Urbanist neighborhoods attempt to create a safe environment by welcoming a continual flow of people, adding more connecting streets, creating smaller blocks and greater accessibility to the outside world, defining public and private space, ensuring informal surveillance of streets, and encouraging social interaction (Steuteville 2001).

Smart growth advocates often speak of the importance of smart growth goals and tools mainly in terms of a normative framework. In order for the programs to sustain and succeed, however, we need more systematic understandings of the determinants of adoption of smart growth and the evaluation of outcomes of smart growth programs. The next two sections summarize research findings in these two areas to date.

3. WHAT DO WE KNOW ABOUT THE DETERMINANTS OF ADOPTION OF SMART GROWTH TOOLS?

Several studies have investigated what factors determine the local adoption of a variety of smart growth tools, including O'Connell's (2008, 2009) study of the impact of local activism, education, homeownership, and race on smart growth policy adoption; Jeong's (2006) investigation of factors contributing to local adoption of impact fees; Brody, Carrasco, and Highfield's (2006) analysis of socioeconomic and demographic influences on the adoption of sprawl-reduction planning policies in comprehensive plans in Florida; Jepson's (2004) exploration of planners' roles in implementing sustainable development principles and techniques; Downs's (2005) arguments on the dimensions of smart growth actions that might not be widely accepted by the American public; and studies by several researchers (Berke, Song, and Stevens 2009; Song, Berke, and Stevens 2009; Stevens, Berke, and Song 2010) on how public participation and policy adoption style would affect the incorporation of hazard-mitigation techniques in developments. In what follows, I summarize the findings from the above studies on determinants of adoption of smart growth tools.

The state government's powers are essential for local adoption of smart growth tools. Without strong support from the state government, an overall smart growth strategy that encompasses most of the tools discussed above cannot be carried out by local governments (Downs 2005). In an undergoing study by Song, Stevens, and Berke (2011), the researchers explore the set of determinants involving more New Urbanist developments in American metropolitan areas. Controlling for other factors such as wealth and demographic and sociopolitical features, they find out that having a statewide smart growth program is a statistically strong predictor of achieving more New Urbanist developments in the metropolitan areas. In general, having a state program of smart growth demonstrates a clear set of high-priority goals, pressures the local governments to agree on the set of goals, and provides supportive and enabling conditions for local governments to plan and zone for alternative growth patterns (Ingram et al. 2009). Smart growth programs implemented by local governments with no state or regional coordination are unlikely to yield good outcomes because of the negative spillover effects from communities (Song 2007).

Stakeholder and public participation help to bolster both the strength of smart growth plans and their adoption (O'Connell 2009; Stevens, Berke, and Song 2010). Several studies reveal that the number of stakeholder groups involved in the planning process is positively correlated with the endorsement of smart growth tools to protect land from development. Song, Stevens, and Berke (2011) compare the number of groups included in the planning process between jurisdictions with and without New Urbanist developments. They find that localities with New Urbanist developments have statistically significant more public groups involved in the planning process. Apparently, broad stakeholder representation has an impact on acceptance and on subsequent adoption of smart growth tools, especially measures to protect land from unplanned developments. The stakeholder groups advocating smart growth include environmental groups, smart growth groups, and neighborhood associations. The groups raising opposition include realtors, developers, and groups presenting property rights (O'Connell 2009).

Several scholars have studied and confirmed the correlation between higher education and higher level of endorsement of smart growth tools (Brody, Carrasco, and Highfield 2006; O'Connell 2008). O'Connell observes that the population obtaining higher education and economic security is more supportive of smart growth. Song, Stevens, and Berke (2011) compare the education levels of jurisdictions with and without New Urbanist developments, and find that, in metropolitan areas with New Urbanist developments, 18 percent of residents have bachelor's degrees, while in areas without New Urbanist developments, only 10 percent of residents have that same level of education. The estimated difference of 8 percent between the two sets of metropolitan areas is statistically significant. It is possible that a population with higher education is more sensitive to the unwanted environmental consequences of urban development and is thus more willing to endorse smart growth principles. If the above reasoning is true, it confirms the importance of educating and persuading the general citizenship. Downs (2005)identifies three main groups that initiate the implementation of smart growth principles: nongovernmental environmentalists, planners and other public officials, and innovative private real estate developers. The above list does not include citizen groups such ashomeowners in suburban communities. This indicates that most of the pressure to adopt smart growth policies does not come from the citizenry at large, but from special interest groups. Thus, education and the persuasion of "ordinary citizens" are necessary to support the adoption of a new and different set of growth-related policies.

Sociopolitical conditions matter because they are reflected in the overall political and environmental persuasion of local decision makers and voters. In general, the more politically liberal and environmentally conscious the voters are, the more open to and permissive of smart growth they will be, and thus, the higher the level of adoption of smart growth tools, especially those tools promoting environment-friendly design. Song, Stevens, and Berke (2011) find that several sociopolitical variables, including the percentage of those who vote for the Democratic Party presidential candidate in the United States, and whether or not the community is a member of the International Council for Local Environmental Initiatives (ICLEI), are correlated with a higher level of endorsement of New Urbanism.

Finally, the local planning agency capacity, indicated by number of planners working on smart growth plans, influences the degree of local adoption of sprawl-reduction tools (Brody, Carrasco, and Highfield 2006). In addition to the number of planners, it is important to understand that the degree those planners promote local endorsement of smart growth can make a difference (Stevens, Berke, and Song 2008). That is, planners can be partisan participants in the land-use planning process and openly promote their own ideas and values; they can be technicians so that they limit their activities to producing the technical planning information and providing objective advice to decision makers; they can be mobilizers to actively notify and encourage citizen groups to provide support for and/or counteract opposition to particular planning efforts; and they can be lobbyists to defeat proposals they think are harmful, even if they need to challenge powerful interests in the process. Some initial evidence shows that, rather than using regulations to prohibit development in certain zones for land protection or urban form redirection, it might be more efficient if planners can negotiate with project developers regarding the location, form, and timing of developments (Stevens, Berke, and Song 2008).

The above findings provide initial evidence outlining the set of factors that contribute to greater acceptance of smart growth tools by local communities. These factors include state support, public participation and education, sociopolitical conditions, and local planning capacity.

4. WHAT DO WE KNOW ABOUT OUTCOMES OF SMART GROWTH PROGRAMS?

To date, only a few local communities have carried out evaluations of their smart growth programs. The scarcity of studies is surprising given the fact that, with strengthened evaluation and monitoring procedures, planning efforts and policies in general would be well served to discover the accomplishments and find areas needing improvement (Hoernig and Seasons 2004).

In this section, I summarize findings on the assessment of smart growth programs from the following sources: a survey of current practices of evaluating smart growth plans in a selected set of twenty U.S. cities, carried out through telephone interviews with senior-level planners (Song 2011); assessment studies of Oregon's land-use program in 2008 (Institute for Natural Resources 2008); Seattle's comprehensive plan in 2003 (City of Seattle 2003); Maryland's smart growth program (Sartori, Moore, and Knaap 2011); and a recent assessment of smart growth states by the Lincoln Institute of Land Policy (Ingram et al. 2009). The results are organized to explore whether smart growth programs have been effective in protecting land resources, containing urban growth, reorienting transportation, providing affordable housing, and fostering a sense of community. To facilitate assessments, evaluators have developed numerous indicators that can be used to measure the achievement level of the goals (Hoernig and Seasons 2004; Berke et al. 2006; Ingram et al. 2009).

4.1 Effective in Preserving Land Resources?

Evaluators carry out assessments of how much land resources, such as open space, farmland, and ecologically sensitive land, have been preserved. According to Ingram et al.'s (2009) study, at state level there is no evidence to support the smart growth states' outperformance in terms of protection of undeveloped areas in comparison to non–smart growth states. Sartori, Moore, and Knaap (2011) suggest that there is still a substantial amount of critical land that is not protected in the state of Maryland. At the local level, the city of Seattle (City of Seattle 2003) has developed an inventory of open spaces and employs the database to assess residents' proximity to preserved open spaces over time. That assessment indicates that there has been little progress made since 1994 on improving residents' access to preserved open spaces.

Several other studies do not have sufficient information to carry out an assessment. For example, the Institute for Natural Resources (2008) developed performance measures to assess whether the Oregon Land Use Program is helping the state meet its goals of preserving farm and forest lands at the local level. The study concluded that it is difficult to carry out a meaningful assessment, and suggested several ways in which the assessment can be improved. These methods include tracking the amount and quality of converted farmland, using spatial data to analyze land conversion trends, and assessing the causes and patterns of farmland loss. The review team also suggested that, in order to carry out better assessments, spatial data on soil quality and location of new permits are essential. These suggestions echo the findings of the Kiesecker et al. (2007) study. Kiesecker et al. examined temporal patterns of the set activities allowed under 119 conservation easements held by the Nature Conservancy (TNC), spanning eight states and twenty years (1984–2004). The researchers found out that recently established easements are more strategically planned, and thus perform better in protecting land resources. More important, the review team concluded that it is difficult to draw general conclusions regarding easement effectiveness because of a lack of systematic information on the amount and quality of land conserved. According to the Song (2011) interviews with planners from more than thirty-five U. S. cities, most cities lack a land information system to monitor progress on protecting land resources.

4.2 Effective in Promoting Dense, Compact, and Infill Developments?

The population and development density, location of new populations and employment, and land conversion locations and rates are common indicators of denser and more compact urban growth. Most studies find that smart growth localities have made positive progress toward redirecting their growth patterns and locations, although these studies have not been able to confirm whether changes in growth pattern and location are from smart growth measures or from market forces.

Ingram et al. (2009) demonstrate that in four selected smart growth states, marginal land consumption per new resident was lower, the share of new population locating in urban areas was higher, and population and employment decentralization was lower than in selected non–smart growth states. Song and Knaap (2004) and Song (2005) found that development densities are increasing in several U.S. metropolitan areas with or without smart growth programs. They conclude that either smart growth measures or market forces cause these increasing densities. Several scholars have assessed whether urban containment policies, such as UGB or USA, can slow the consumption of urban land, and they found that these policies are achieving their desired goal of shrinking urban sizes (Wassmer 2006; Wu and Cho 2007). By comparing the rate of land conversion for selected counties in Maryland during both pre–smart growth and post–smart growth time periods, and controlling for other determinants of land conversion, Shen and Zhang (2007) found that the smart growth policy has generally been successful in achieving its objective in infilling growth in desired zones such as priority funding areas. Through interviews with city planners, Song (2011) finds out that smart growth tools have been somewhat effective in relocating growth to desired locations. However, according to these planners, there is little information on the form of this relocated growth.

4.3 Effective in Re-orienting Transportation?

Smart growth programs propose both land-use and transportation policies to alter travel behavior. For example, the city of Seattle has established land-use approaches, such as designating urban villages; expanding its multimodal transportation facilities; and implementing a range of transportation programs such as the Employee Trip Reduction Program and the Car Smart program.

Across cities, efforts have been made on both metropolitan and neighborhood levels to redesign both the land-use and the transportation systems. Previous studies show that, at the metropolitan level, regional connectivity of a multimodal transportation system is constrained by economies of scale in the transportation infrastructure. At the neighborhood level, local ordinances appear to move neighborhoods toward more internal connectivity and are more pedestrian friendly in design (Song 2005; Song and Knaap 2004). However, the effects of changes in neighborhood design and urban form on travel behavior remain elusive (Boarnet and Crane 2001; Boarnet and Sarmiento 1998). In assessing if Portland's smart tools, such as UGB, have had any transportation impact, researchers find that the results remain inconclusive (Institute for Natural Resources 2008). In general, using land use and design tools to change travel behavior might not be as efficient as using transportation policies (Boarnet and Crane 2001).

A set of indicators has been developed to track the reorientation of transportation, and they typically include the distance and means of travel to work, transit ridership, supply of alternative transportation facilities, level of congestion, and public perception of the ease of getting around by bus, bicycle, and on foot. Sartori, Moore, and Knaap (2011) show that vehicle miles traveled (VMT), congestion, and car ownership have risen over time in Maryland, although the state has higher transit ridership than most other states. However, the higher ridership level may be attributable to historic investments in transit that predate the state's smart growth program. Ingram et al. (2009) analyze other indicators, such as work-trip transit ridership and changes in congestion, and they found that smart growth programs are associated with desirable transportation outcomes. Smart growth states have somewhat higher shares of work trips by transit, biking, and walking. Seattle (City of Seattle 2003) has developed a range of indicators to evaluate whether its plan has been effective in shifting travel behaviors. The city finds that, although it did not meet its goal of decreasing the percentage of solo driving from 59 percent in 1990 to 51 percent in 2000, it observed a slight increase in transit ridership over 1994 levels, mostly owing to its expansion of multimodal transportation facilities.

4.4 Effective in Promoting Affordable Housing?

There has always been debate about whether smart growth measures can improve housing affordability. Since there are many contributing factors that govern the levels and fluctuations of housing prices, it is difficult to conclude whether the UGB around Portland, for example, contributed to an increase in housing prices (Downs 2005). Furthermore, intense arguments are made about whether the increase in housing prices in smart growth localities is brought on by improved amenities or by the suppression of land and housing supply. Nevertheless, preliminary evaluation results seem to indicate that smart growth policies have the potential of causing housing prices to rise.

Seattle (City of Seattle 2003) employs indicators that include home-ownership rate, the number of low-income housing units, and the cost of housing to review its progress toward measuring housing affordability. The evaluation results show that home values and rents have increased faster than household income since 1994. The city implemented a multifamily housing tax exemption program that provided tax relief for developers of multifamily units in targeted zones. As a result, the city gained a large number of affordable units for low-income households. Nevertheless, in the 2001 residential surveys, 80 percent of respondents felt that housing had become less affordable in comparison to only 59 percent of respondents in 1999 (City of Seattle 2003).

Needless to say, it is difficult to attribute this decrease in housing affordability to smart growth. Sartori, Moore, and Knaap (2011) show that housing prices have inflated faster in Maryland than in many other states. Ingram et al. (2009) have compared housing affordability between smart growth and non–smart growth states, and their results indicate that, in the 1990s, smart growth states experienced a smaller increase in median housing prices and added a greater share of multifamily units. In addition, the smart growth states had higher shares of cost-burdened owners and renters than did the other selected states. Furthermore, they find out that smart growth programs that lack an affordable housing element have been associated with increases in housing cost burdens, especially for owners.

4.5 Effective in Enhancing a Sense of Community?

There is a scarcity of studies evaluating whether smart growth and/or New Urbanist developments have increased a sense of community. Possibly for the reason that "sense of community" is an elusive concept, most cities do not monitor any change in this sense of community (Song 2011). Seattle (City of Seattle 2003) monitors, over time, several proxy measures via surveys, and these measures include the percentage of residents who volunteer their time in communities and the percentage of residents who feel safe. The results show that there has been only slight improvement in any sense of safety between 1994 and 2001. Yang (2008) has evaluated how neighborhood satisfaction varies by urban form, finding that the influence of compact development and mixed uses on residents' quality of life varies depending on the context, and it is sensitive to the spatial scales at which urban form is examined.

As shown above, the evaluation and monitoring of the outcomes of smart growth programs by local communities is rare and typically not comprehensive. There are several reasons for this shortage in evaluations. First, smart growth policies are but one of many factors that influence urban development, making impact assessment a difficult task (Bengston, Fletcher, and Nelson 2004). Second, policies for redirecting any urban growth patterns often take a long time to implement. Without integrating the evaluation as part of the smart growth program, these programs are unlikely to be monitored until long after implementation.

5. CONCLUSION AND FUTURE RESEARCH AGENDA

In a time of looming uncertainties in the economic, energy, environment, and housing sectors, more cities are becoming conscious of the choices they make regarding growth and development patterns. In this chapter, I summarized research findings in two important smart growth research areas: determinants of smart growth adoption, and evaluation of smart growth's efficacy.

Although awareness of smart growth is greater than ever, active implementation of the program is taking place in less than a handful of locations. In places where smart growth has been implemented, no substantial progress has been made toward achieving the smart growth goals. The results of previous studies suggest that adopting and achieving smart growth goals are both extremely challenging, and that the obstacles to significant change in growth patterns remain formidable.

After more than two decades with the experiment, there are several reasons to qualify the lack of progress toward reaching smart growth goals in American cities. First, the public and the institutions are resistant to change. Many efforts and plans to increase densities, for examples, in smart growth areas have encountered determined public opposition. Furthermore, some local officials view the government's smart growth efforts as intrusive and thus have circumvented these goals. For there to be significant changes in growth patterns, there must be changes in values, preferences, and institutional settings (Knaap 2006). Second, smart growth policies have not overcomed public and institutional inertia with efforts such as sustaining public support, inviting incentives, and coordinating implementation. Smart growth exposure was often limited to its supporters but preempted by its adversaries. Although incentive approaches have gained notice because they are seen as an improvement over regulatory or command-and-control approaches, these incentives are typically insufficient to alter public behavior (Knaap 2006). In addition, individual smart growth tools, if designed without coordinated implementation across sectors and over space, might backfire and undermine smart growth's credibility (Knaap 2006). Third, it is possible that we need more time to discern any changes in altered growth patterns and effects brought about by smart growth policies.

Apparently, to redirect any growth patterns, further progress is needed in developing and refining the smart growth policies. In what follows, I highlight several future research needs.

How to Gain More Public and Institutional Support?

Previous studies have shown that smart growth is supported by a minority of groups and citizens with higher income and education and with more environmental consciousness. Smart growth needs to expand to include a much broader base. More comparative cases are essential to provide advocates with an understanding of what spawns local opposition, what spurs political and institutional momentum, how understanding is fostered across stakeholder groups, how best to give proper public notice concerning new policy tools, and how to form credible responses to public inquiries and critics. Studies on how Planning Supporting Systems (PSS) and GeoDesign techniques in general are particularly helpful in growing public group learning and consensus building (Deyle and Schively 2009). Furthermore, as it is unclear how the implementation of smart growth affects different groups, studies are needed to consider the income distribution consequences of smart growth policies.

Are Smart Growth Tools Working?

In pursuit of smart growth goals, it is essential that planners improve the efficacy of policies and tools (Ingram et al. 2009). Research questions can be grouped in three areas. First, are the existing tools effective in bringing about the intended changes? Studies have shown that, for example, land-use policies have not induced targeted changes in travel behavior (Boarnet and Sarmiento 1998; Handy, Cao, and Mokhtarian 2005); the New Urbanist movement has not improved its external transportation connectivity (Song and Knaap 2004); land acquisition programs have yet to succeed in preserving critical lands (Sartori, Moore, and Knaap 2011); and affordable housing programs have had very limited success (Sartori, Moore, and Knaap 2011). More studies, either case studies or statistical analyses, need to use careful research designs to account for confounding factors and trace the effects of smart growth tools.

Second, do some of the existing smart growth tools bring unintended effects? Some smart growth tools, for example, have unintentionally encouraged spillovers of low-density developments (Song 2007) or induced more developments surrounding ecologically sensitive lands (Song 2010). More studies are needed on how smart growth tools can be coordinated across sectors, space, and time so as to minimize unintended consequences. Third, future research should explain why some of the smart growth tools are not effective and should offer remedies. Lack of enforcement and/or funding support might be the obvious explanations for ineffective implementation of these tools; but more important, studies need to be carried out to expand and strengthen the use of these market instruments (Knaap 2006). For instance, the use of economic incentives large enough to affect decision making, and the design of new pricing mechanisms such as congestion pricing, might deserve more focus in the next stage of the smart growth movement.

How Is Smart Growth Progressing?

Research and practice in both the evaluation and the monitoring of smart growth progress is meager. A lot of work remains to be done in terms of evaluation and monitoring, and there are several areas for improvement. First, more efforts need to be made on data collection. For example, timely information on the amount and quality of land protected and the forms of new developments needs to be collected on a regular basis in order to facilitate evaluation. Second, evaluation and monitoring methods need to be refined to assess outcomes. Most evaluations have indicators to track progress toward smart growth goals, but these indicator systems, in terms of number, measurement, construction, aggregation, interpretation, and demonstration, need to be further developed to assist meaningful evaluation. In addition, to generate public support, the mechanisms for incorporating community participation into design need to be considered, helping planners gauge public satisfaction with specific policies (Smolko Strange, and Venetoulis 2006). Innovative instruments, such as the Sustainability Dashboard (Scipioni et al. 2009), need to be devised to demonstrate results to the general public. In fact, one of the goals of using indicators to track smart growth progress is to facilitate a dialogue among stakeholders. Furthermore, it is essential to recognize that the evaluation of smart growth programs can be a political undertaking. Studies on how to tailor the indicator system to consider these political realities, as well as community needs and the availability of local resources, will enhance local acceptance of the evaluation process (Wong 2006).

In conclusion, there is a vast need for more studies on how smart growth efforts will progress. There is reason to believe that, with new experiments, smart growth tools will become more politically feasible, more technically sound, and more economically efficient. From a research perspective, all of these new experiments will provide great opportunities to conduct interesting research and gain further insights into the efficacy of smart growth.

References

Arendt, R. 1997. "Basing Cluster Techniques on Development Densities Appropriate to the Area." *Journal of the American Planning Association* 63(1): 137–45.

Bengston, D. N., Jennifer O. Fletcher, and Kristen C. Nelson. 2004. "Public Policies for Managing Urban Growth and Protecting Open Space: Policy Instruments and Lessons Learned in the United States." *Landscape and Urban Planning* 69(2–3): 271–86.

Berke, P., M. Backhurst, M. Day, N. Ericksen, L. Laurian, J. Crawford, and J. Dixon. 2006. "What Makes Plan Implementation Successful? An Evaluation of Local Plans and Implementation Practices in New Zealand." *Environment and Planning Part B: Planning and Design* 33(4): 581–600.

Berke, P. R., Yan Song, and Mark Stevens. 2009. "Integrating Hazard Mitigation into New Urban and Conventional Developments." *Journal of Planning Education and Research* 28(4): 441–55.

Boarnet, M., and Randall Crane. 2001. "The Influence of Land Use on Travel Behavior: Specification and Estimation Strategies." *Transportation Research Part A: Policy and Practice* 35(9): 823–45.

Boarnet, M. G., and Sharon Sarmiento. 1998. "Can Land-use Policy Really Affect Travel Behaviour? A Study of the Link between Non-work Travel and Land-use Characteristics." *Urban Studies* 35(7): 1155–69.

Brody, S. D., Virginia Carrasco, and Wesley E. Highfield. 2006. "Measuring the Adoption of Local Sprawl: Reduction Planning Policies in Florida." *Journal of Planning Education and Research* 25(3): 294–310.

Burchell, R. W., David Listokin, and Catherine C. Galley. 2000. "Smart Growth: More than a Ghost of Urban Policy Past, Less Than a Bold New Horizon." *Housing Policy Debate* 11(4): 821–79.

City of Seattle. 2003. "Monitoring Our Progress: Seattle's Comprehensive Plan: The City of Seattle." Available at: http://www.seattle.gov/dpd/Planning/Seattle_s_Comprehensive_Plan/ReportsonGrowth/default.asp; accessed Oct 2009.

Daniels, T., and Mark Lapping. 2005. "Land Preservation: An Essential Ingredient in Smart Growth." *Journal of Planning Literature* 19(3): 316–29.

Deyle, R., and S. Carissa Schively. 2009. "Group Learning in Participatory Planning Processes: An Exploratory Quasiexperimental Analysis of Local Mitigation Planning in Florida." *Journal of Planning Education and Research* 29(1): 23–38.

Dierwechter, Y. 2008. *Urban Growth Management and Its Discontents: Promises, Practices, and Geopolitics in U.S. City-Regions.* London: Palgrave Macmillan.

Downs, A. 2005. "Smart Growth: Why We Discuss It More than We Do It." *Journal of the American Planning Association* 71(4): 367–78.

Duany, A., E. Plater-Zyberk, and J. Speck. 2000. *Suburban Nation: The Rise of Sprawl and the Decline of the American Dream.* New York: North Point Press.

Edwards, M. M., and Anna Haines. 2007. "Evaluating Smart Growth: Implications for Small Communities." *Journal of Planning Education and Research* 27(1): 49–64.

Gustanski, Julie Ann, and Roderick H. Squires. 2000. *Protecting the land: Conservation Easetments Past, Present, and Future.* Washington, DC: Island Press.

Handy, S., Xinyu Cao, and Patricia Mokhtarian. 2005. "Correlation or Causality Between the Built Environment and Travel Behavior? Evidence from Northern California." *Transportation Research Part D: Transport and Environment* 10(6): 427–44.

Heim, C. E. 2001. "Leapfrogging, Urban Sprawl, and Growth Management: Phoenix, 1950–2000." *American Journal of Economics and Sociology* 60(1): 245–83.

Hoernig, H., and Mark Seasons. 2004. "Monitoring of Indicators in Local and Regional Planning Practice: Concepts and Issues." *Planning Practice and Research* 19(1): 81–99.

Hollis, L. E., and W. Fulton. 2002. *Open Space Protection: Conservation Meets Growth Management.* Washington, DC: Center on Urban and Metropolitan Policy, Brookings Institution Press.

Howland, M., and Jungyul Sohn. 2007. "Has Maryland's Priority Funding Areas Initiative Constrained the Expansion of Water and Sewer Investments?" *Land Use Policy* 24(1): 175–86.

Ingram, G. K, Armando Carbonell, Yu-hung Hong, and Anthony Flint. 2009. *Smart Growth Policies: An Evaluation of Programs and Outcomes.* Cambridge, MA: Lincoln Institute of Land Policy.

Institute for Natural Resources. 2008. "The Oregon Land Use Program: An Assessment of Selected Goals." Oregon Department of Land Conservation and Development. Available at: http://ir.library.oregonstate.edu/xmlui/handle/1957/13920; accessed Oct 2009.

Jeong, Moon-Gi. 2006. "Local Choices for Development Impact Fees." *Urban Affairs Review* 41(3): 338–57.

Jepson, E. J. Jr. 2004. "The Adoption of Sustainable Development Policies and Techniques in U.S. Cities: How Wide, How Deep, and What Role for Planners?" *Journal of Planning Education and Research* 23(3): 229–41.

Kiesecker, J. M., Tosha Comendant, Terra Grandmason, Elizabeth Gray, Christine Hall, Richard Hilsenbeck, Peter Kareiva, Lynn Lozier, Patrick Naehu, Adena Rissman, M. Rebecca Shaw, and Mark Zankel. 2007. "Conservation Easements in Context: A Quantitative Analysis of Their Use by The Nature Conservancy." *Frontiers in Ecology and the Environment* 5(3): 125–30.

Knaap, G. J. 2006. "A Requiem for Smart Growth?" Working paper. Available at: http://www.smartgrowth.umd.edu/research/pdf/Knaap_Requiem_022305.pdf; accessed October 2009.

Knaap, G., and A. C. Nelson. 1992. *The Regulated Landscape: Lessons on State Land Use Planning from Oregon.* Cambridge, MA: Lincoln Institute of Land Policy.

McConnell, V., and Margaret Walls. 2009. "Policy Monitor: U.S. Experience with Transferable Development Rights." *Review of Environmental Economic Policy* 3(2): 288–303.

Nolon, J. R., and Jessica A. Bacher. 2007. "Local Inclusionary Housing Programs: Meeting Housing Needs." *Real Estate Law Journal* 36:73.

O'Connell, L. 2008. "Exploring the Social Roots of Smart Growth Policy Adoption by Cities." *Social Science Quarterly* 89(5): 1356–72.

O'Connell, L. 2009. "The Impact of Local Supporters on Smart Growth Policy Adoption." *Journal of the American Planning Association* 75(3): 281–91.

Pendall, R. 1999. "Do Land-Use Controls Cause Sprawl?" *Environment and Planning Part B: Planning and Design* 26(4): 555–71.

Pendall, R. 2004. "The Growth of Control?: Local Land Use Regulations and Affordable Housing Measures in Major U.S. Metropolitan Areas, 1994–2003." Conference paper, presented at the conference of *Association of Collegiate Schools of Planning,* Portland.

Rybeck, Rick. 2004. "Using Value Capture to Finance Infrastructure and Encourage Compact Development." *Public Works Management Policy* 8(4): 249–60.

Sartori, J., Terry Moore, and Gerrit Knaap. 2011. "Indicators of Smart Growth in Maryland." Available at: http://www.smartgrowth.umd.edu/research/pdf/ SartoriMooreKnaap_MDIndicators_010611.pdf; accessed January 20, 2011.

Scipioni, A., Anna Mazzi, Marco Mason, and Alessandro Manzardo. 2009. "The Dashboard of Sustainability to Measure the Local Urban Sustainable Development: The Case Study of Padua Municipality." *Ecological Indicators* 9(2): 364–80.

Shen, Qing, and Feng Zhang. 2007. "Land-Use Changes in a Pro-Smart-Growth State: Maryland, USA." *Environment and Planning Part A* 39:1457–77.

Smolko, R., Carolyn J. Strange, and Jason Venetoulis. 2006. *The Community Indicators Handbook: Measuring Progress Toward Healthy and Sustainable Communities.* Oakland: Redefining Progress.

Song, Y. 2005. "Smart Growth and Urban Development Pattern: A Comparative Study." *International Regional Science Review* 28(2): 239–65.

Song, Y. 2007. "The Spillover Effects of Growth Management: Constraints on New Housing Construction." In *Growth Management in Florida: Planning for Paradise,* edited by T. S. Chapin, C. E. Connerly, and H. T. Higgins, 155–67. Burlington, UK: Ashgate.

Song, Y. 2010. "Preservation Backfired? Open Space Acquisition and Its Impacts on Land Markets." In *Smart Growth through Public Land Acquisition: Realities and Prospects,* edited by T. Chapin and C. Coutts, 101–15. Burlington, UK: Ashgate.

Song, Y. 2011. "Smart Growth Plan Evaluation: Current Practices." Working paper. Cambridge, MA: Lincoln Institute of Land Policy.

Song, Y., P. R. Berke, and M. R. Stevens. 2009. Smart Developments in Dangerous Locations: A Reality Check of Existing New Urbanist Developments." *International Journal of Mass Emergencies and Disasters* 27(1): 1–24.

Song, Y., and Gerrit-Jan Knaap. 2004. "Measuring Urban Form: Is Portland Winning the War on Sprawl?" *Journal of the American Planning Association* 70(2): 210–25.

Song, Y., Mark S., and Phil B. 2011. "Where Do New Urbanist Developments Locate?" Working paper, Institutte for Environment, University of North Carolina at Chapel Hill.

Steuteville, R., ed. 2001. *New Urbanism: Comprehensive Report and Best Practices Guide,* 2nd ed. Ithaca, NY: New Urban Publications.

Stevens, M. R., Philip R. Berke, and Yan Song. 2008. "Protecting People and Property: The Influence of Land-Use Planners on Flood Hazard Mitigation in New Urbanist Developments. *Journal of Environmental Planning and Management* 51(6): 737–57.

Stevens, M. R., P. R. Berke, and Yan Song. 2010. "Creating Disaster-Resilient Communities: Evaluating the Promise and Performance of New Urbanism." *Landscape and Urban Planning* 94:105–15.

Talen, E., and Gerrit K. 2003. "Legalizing Smart Growth: An Empirical Study of Land Use Regulation in Illinois." *Journal of Planning Education and Research* 22(4): 345–59.

Wassmer, R. W. 2006. "The Influence of Local Urban Containment Policies and Statewide Growth Management on the Size of United States Urban Areas." *Journal of Regional Science* 46(1): 25–65.

Weitz, J. 1999. "From Quiet Revolution to Smart Growth: State Growth Management Programs, 1960 to 1999." *Journal of Planning Literature* 14(2): 266–337.

Wong, C. 2006. *Indicators for Urban and Regional Planning: The Interplay of Policy and Methods.* London and New York: Routledge.

Wu, JunJie, and Seong-Hoon Cho. 2007. "The Effect of Local Land Use Regulations on Urban Development in the Western United States." *Regional Science and Urban Economics* 37(1): 69–86.

Yang, Y. 2008. "A Tale of Two Cities: Physical Form and Neighborhood Satisfaction in Metropolitan Portland and Charlotte." *Journal of the American Planning Association* 74 (3): 307–23.

Ye, L., Sumedha M., and Peter B. M. 2005. "What Is 'Smart Growth?' Really?" *Journal of Planning Literature* 19(3): 301–15.

CHAPTER 22

PLANNING FOR IMPROVED AIR QUALITY AND ENVIRONMENTAL HEALTH

LISA SCHWEITZER AND LINSEY MARR

ACCORDING to the World Health Organization, about 800,000 people die prematurely each year from outdoor air pollution (Ezzati et al. 2002, 2003; Kunzli et al. 2000). Climate change, if unabated, promises to be another environmental health threat (Haines et al. 2006; Martens et al. 1999). Many planning studies concerned with walking, biking, transit, and sustainability assume that planners can help fight pollution and climate change. By changing urban form from sprawl to compact, many argue, people will depend less on automobiles (Bernick and Cervero 1997; Ewing and Cervero 2010; Goodchild 1994). If people depend less on their cars, vehicle emissions should be lower—or so the planning logic goes (Newman and Kenworthy 1999).

As we discuss in this chapter, the planning assumptions about emissions reductions, air quality, and climate change may reflect more wishful thinking and project marketing than effective air quality and climate planning. Planning research around air quality has settled into what we call "emissions talk"[1]—the tendency of planners, environmentalists, and architects to derive unvalidated, often overly optimistic forecasts of "tons of emissions saved" to advocate for pet projects, particularly rail projects. If planners are wrong about being able to curb car use overall with transit and land use—and there are reasons to believe that many planners and architects greatly oversell their ability to use infill and density to curb car use—emissions talk is a distraction from the more aggressive, regulatory action needed for effective environmental health interventions.

Planners have spent decades debating how urban form affects vehicle use, and yet the field has few clear findings, if any. Even if it is possible to reduce vehicle travel with urban design, the ensuing air quality outcomes for urban neighborhoods are much more difficult to predict than current planning studies acknowledge. Rather than grapple with the real social, scientific, and spatial complexities of environmental health, planning research, projects, and proposals instead offer up "emissions talk" around everything from sidewalks, to mixed use, to high-speed rail. The goal of planning analysis in air quality seldom, if ever, considers neighborhoods or people.

This chapter will cover four problems that follow from emissions talk in the planning research:

1. Overstating the impact that planning, land use, and transit have on reducing automobile use
2. Ignoring the subsequent uncertainty in emissions and, more importantly, local-area outcomes, based on those optimistic assumptions about travel demand
3. Treating emissions as an air quality outcome—and more importantly, the only air quality outcome—rather than dealing with environmental and climate health outcomes
4. Co-opting environmental justice arguments to use for planning project marketing and advocacy, such as using emissions talk to claim environmental benefits that may never materialize or take decades to materialize vis-à-vis neighborhoods and individuals currently struggling with respiratory health issues today

Incorrectly optimistic research surrounding planning and urban design as a means of regulating vehicle emissions may take the pressure off regulatory agencies, the industry, and the public to grapple with the higher stakes, higher cost methods to control emissions such as carbon taxes, fuel taxes, rationing, more costly vehicle controls, or outright vehicle bans and restrictions. If planning research can produce the veneer of emissions reductions from voluntary strategies like soft transportation control measures (TCMs), there are few reasons for regulators or politicians to take the political risks that are probably necessary to make using a car or wasting gas really hit voters and industry groups where they live.

Throughout this chapter, we contrast current planning and regulatory approaches with how community and environmental justice advocates frame air quality issues. The subsequent tensions generate new directions for planning research concerned with air quality.

1. Emissions Talk

"Emissions talk" appears just about everywhere in planning; it is so common to planning parlance that it can be difficult to see. The California High-Speed Rail (CalHSR) project provides a great example on its Web site, where environmental documents contend that high-speed rail between Sacramento in northern California and San Diego in the south will "eliminate over 12 billion pounds of the greenhouse gas emissions that cause global warming each year. That's equivalent to removing more than one million vehicles from our roads annually" (California High Speed Rail Authority 2007, 1).

For this project and others like it, emissions are the environmental payday—what taxpayers are going to pay billions for—so the emissions talk around the project had better look pretty good. And in the case of the CalHSR, look good it does: 12 billion pounds each year sounds like a substantial savings.

Yet, these are heroic environmental promises for a project that will not do anything for at least another two decades, perhaps longer. In addition to the long wait for future emissions reductions—which is a problem for climate change—the emissions talk skates over the assumptions and uncertainties of the environmental analysis, leaving critical readers with a lot of unanswered questions. Do the pounds of emissions savings promised in the future amount to a big part of the greenhouse gas (GHG) inventory, or just a small portion?[2] How much per pound do these emissions reductions cost? Are there easier and cheaper ways to get the same impact sooner? Emissions talk does not address these questions. The result is a dangerously limited dialogue around emissions, where planning researchers, practitioners, and the public treat emissions like an outcome, rather than what emissions really are: inputs into much greater and more complex physical and social systems that affect air quality and human health.

2. Uncertainty in Planning for Emissions

Planning for emissions reductions has a fairly lengthy history. In 1968, the U.S. Public Health service established the AP-42 guidelines as a means to help agencies estimate how much pollution comes from particular sources. Though these guidelines were originally designed for point sources like factories and refineries, regulatory agencies later measured emissions from vehicles' tailpipes to incorporate into models, such as MOBILE. When the Clean Air Act (PL 91-604 or CAA) passed the U.S. Congress in 1970, and the U.S. Environmental Protection Agency (EPA) became charged with enforcing the law, emissions factors, inventories, and accounting became the primary planning tool to figure out where pollutants come from in order to monitor progress and compliance. Nonetheless, probably the most important innovation in the CAA concerned the powers granted to the EPA to set health-based ambient standards based on ambient concentrations rather than emissions.

Along with emissions controls for vehicles and point sources, the CAA suggested transportation control measures (TCMs). The TCMs are intended to control vehicle emissions by discouraging auto use. The original language around TCMs included policies with strong restrictions on autos, such as gas rationing, parking charges, and tolls. Except for parking charges, the more restrictive policies have largely disappeared in favor of the more voluntary, "softer" TCMs, such as investment in alternatives to driving, including transit, walking, and biking, without explicit disincentives for driving (Harrington et al. 2003).

The softer TCMs—plying auto drivers with multiple cleaner alternatives—appear in virtually all major planning models, like transit-oriented development (TOD), smart growth, and New Urbanism (Jabareen 2006). Thus, in theory, planning models dovetail with air quality regulatory efforts to contain emissions from vehicles through TCMs.

2.1 Optimistic Vehicle Miles Traveled (VMT) Reductions

Academics and practitioners have tried to prove that TCMs are effective as air quality and climate strategies. Two recent reports perhaps best exemplify the optimism with which planning scholars have approached these issues: *Growing Cooler* (Ewing et al. 2008) and *Moving Cooler* (Cambridge Systematics 2009), both sponsored by the Urban Land Institute. We will discuss *Moving Cooler* later in the chapter. In *Growing Cooler*—which is predominately a literature review—the authors conclude that altering development plans away from baseline sprawl could save the United States as many as 79 million tons of CO_2 every year—again, more emissions talk.[3] This time, the emissions talk rests on unprecedented VMT reductions of 40 to 50 percent.

Other synthetic research by some of the authors of *Growing Cooler* suggests that 40 to 50 percent reductions are simply unrealistic. Two recent planning meta-analysis studies from the same researchers reflect this disturbing potential for planners to overestimate the efficacy of TCMs on emissions reductions. The first study pooled the land use–transport scenario modeling results that practitioners have produced to predict the outcomes of their compact development plans (Bartholomew and Ewing 2009). The U.S. regions in the study's sample were expecting compact development—without more aggressive policies like gas taxes or VMT fees—to dampen VMT growth in their regions by 17 percent, on average. This estimate is more conservative than the 40 to 50 percent reductions suggested in *Growing Cooler* (Ewing et al. 2008), but the latter study also considered regulatory measures like pricing in addition to the soft TCMs more common in the regional forecasts made by practitioners.

One implication of the study, however, is that regional plans cherry-pick the voluntary soft TCMs like supplying transit, walking, and biking infrastructure, probably because voluntary measures are more likely to be palatable to tax-averse voters and politicians. It is not clear, however, why. Perhaps voluntary TCMs are so much more popular because they compel less behavior change, and thus are potentially much less effective in reducing auto use.

The second meta-analysis, which extensively covers the empirical literature on travel behavior and land use, found that most built-environment variables did not exert a large effect on vehicle travel (Ewing and Cervero 2010). Nonetheless, the study's authors suggest that in combination, the land use and urban design variables currently showing little effect might exert a large effect on overall vehicle travel. They describe sketch planning factors that enable planners to assume vehicle travel will go down with built-environment changes in order to comply with climate-change planning. Regardless of the evidence, planners apparently can just go ahead and assume future efficacy.

Ewing and Cervero (2010) may not have found large effect sizes in the empirical research for any number of reasons, only one of which is that regions have not yet mastered the art of compact development. Another reason they may not have found a large effect size is, simply, that the effect sizes are, in reality, small—or much smaller than planners want them to be. It may be that New Urban developments, even compact developments, have little effect when plopped into regions where auto usage is already basically ubiquitous—in contrast with older cities like New York or London, which grew from walking cities into transit-oriented regions. Supplying the soft TCMs of transit, walking, and biking in auto-oriented contexts may not reduce auto travel much, but simply increase local travel by those alternatives—that is, by giving drivers more ways of getting around in addition to, rather than instead of, driving (Boarnet and Crane 2001; Crane 1996).

Researchers from outside of planning have felt much less need to hype the possibility that planning, land use, transit, or urban design produces emissions reductions. Epidemiologists and public health researcher Graham-Rowe et al. (2011) studied seventy-seven recent travel behavior analyses and found only twelve to be methodologically defensible. Of those twelve, only six found evidence of auto-use reduction. And none of the promising interventions is related to planning or urban design. Instead, they involved rather unexpected cognitive interventions—asking people to drive less and use less gas—and more direct inventions, such as having employers relocate workers.

Thus, the recent, high-profile reports that aggregate findings from multiple planning studies suggest the following:

- The planning and policy strategies needed to attain a 1 percent reduction in the yearly GHG inventory for the United States would have to produce a 40 to 50 percent reduction in VMT.
- Regions are forecasting a 17 percent reduction (on average) in VMT due to compact development, and most are forecasting futures based on the soft

TCMs like transit building and future land use, rather than things like pricing or tax floors, which penalize auto use outright and immediately.

- The empirical research suggests that compact development currently has only a slight effect on total VMT (Ewing and Cervero 2010), but planning researchers contend that the effect sizes could be larger if regions changed physically and pursued stronger disincentives to auto use—a potentially thorny implementation problem (Boarnet and Crane 2001).

As long as heroic claims for TCMs and planning dominate the dialogue while the empirical research shows little reason to be confident in those claims, planning research risks harming progress in climate change and air quality. By overestimating the potential contributions of land use, rather than discussing what approaches may lead to greater results, planners are promising more than they are likely to deliver in terms of air quality improvement. And these promises may give regulators, polluters, and developers an easy way to duck out of less popular or more costly, but more effective, strategies.

2.2 Emissions Estimation Uncertainty

In addition to propping up what may be politically palatable but weak climate and air quality strategies, faulty VMT forecasting and measurement contribute uncertainty to climate and air quality analyses, including emissions inventories. Estimating vehicle emissions is a dark art even with good-quality auto-usage estimates, let alone forecasts built on hoped-for policy and planning changes. In the research on mobile source emissions, it is possible to find uncertainty estimates ranging from 10 to 300 percent, depending on the pollutant and the context (on-road or nonroad; Miller et al. 2006). A critical review of emissions inventories claims that confidence in mobile source inventories ranges from low-medium for hazardous air pollutants from nonroad sources to high for NOx from on-road sources (Miller et al. 2006; National Academy of Science 2000; National Research Council 1991, 1994; U.S. Government Accounting Office 2001; Reis et al. 2009). On-road measurement studies found uncertainties of around 10 to 20 percent for NOx (a component of smog) to 50 percent for $PM_{2.5}$ (fine particulates; Dallmann and Harley 2010).

Though emissions inventories are often reported at the county, state, or national level on an annual basis, for actual modeling purposes, estimates are disaggregated spatially and temporally. Modeling grids typically require emissions at spatial resolutions of 1, 4, 12, 36, and/or 108 km and a one-hour temporal resolution. Each step in producing a gridded inventory for atmospheric modeling presents an opportunity for uncertainty to accumulate. Inconsistent methodologies can even lead to discrepancies in estimates prepared for the same geographical area and time (Gurjar et al. 2008).

Emissions estimates typically derive from multiplying an emission factor (e.g., grams of carbon monoxide emitted per mile driven) by an activity measure (e.g., number of miles driven). Obviously, if the activity measure is off, the emissions estimate will be off as well. However, the emissions factors also introduce uncertainty, particularly with mobile-source emissions. Emissions factors describe the amount of pollutant emitted per unit of activity performed (e.g., grams of particulate matter emitted per mile driven for a certain size car). Uncertainty in emissions factors for vehicles has occurred in the past because emissions factors derived from a small sample of vehicles failed to represent the on-road fleet. In addition, lab testing to derive emissions factors may not adequately represent real-world conditions, including transient startup and shutdown operations (Miller et al. 2006). These issues plague mobile-source estimation, whose emissions tend to be skewed toward a small percentage of "gross polluters" or "super emitters" on-road (Choo, Shafizadeh, and Niemeier 2007; Jiang et al. 2005; Mazzoleni et al. 2004; Sawyer et al. 2000; Singer and Harley 2000; Yanowitz, McCormick, and Graboski 2000; Zhang et al. 2008). Predicting emissions factors for future technologies is especially challenging.

The consensus in the air quality modeling literature is as follows: inaccuracy comes from multiple sources, in particular from poor quality travel-demand forecasts, limited fleet characteristic data, and lack of VMT measurement and validation, in addition to the scientific uncertainties from speciation and transport. This means that faulty planning data and analysis—from travel-demand forecasts, particularly—undermine the entire process.

Among what planning researchers have envisioned as an ideal future scenario, what practitioners can simulate using mechanistic models of the politically palatable strategies, and what existing research says about travel behavior, the state of the research is a morass of loud emissions talk and small empirical findings topped off with daunting uncertainties of emissions estimation.

A new direction for planning research—in addition to doing better studies of potential VMT reductions—would begin to place parameters on the uncertainties, including the validity of activity and emissions estimates. A host of techniques can be used to cross-validate emissions estimates with real-world conditions, including applying receptor models to observed concentrations (Buzcu-Guven and Fraser 2008; Cho et al. 2009; Song et al. 2008; Thornhill et al. 2009; Vivanco and Andrade 2006; Xiao et al. 2008; Ying, Lu, Allen, et al. 2008; Ying, Lu, Kaduwela, et al. 2008); incorporating inventories into air quality models and comparing predictions with atmospheric measurements or satellite observations (Boersma et al. 2008; Han et al. 2009); comparing pollutant ratios within the inventory to measured ambient ratios (Warneke et al. 2007; Zhang et al. 2008); conducting on-road studies for vehicle studies (Ban-Weiss et al. 2008); and applying inverse methods using three-dimensional air quality models (Kopacz et al. 2009; Kurokawa et al. 2009).

These and other independent estimates currently show that official emissions inventories may be severely under- or overestimated for criteria pollutants and air toxics (Dreher and Harley 1998; Fujita et al. 1992, 1995; Harley et al. 2001; Kasibhatla et al. 2002; Kean, Sawyer, and Harley 2000; Marr, Black, and Harley 2002; Mendoza-Dominguez and Russell 2001; Singer and Harley 2000). Planning researchers seeking new data and methods for studying the connections among urban form, travel, and emissions can draw on these state-of-the-art methods to bring new insights into a field of research dominated by unverifiable computer modeling methods.

3. RESEARCHING EXPOSURES

Unlike planning research, which has focused almost exclusively on emissions, air quality research in other fields has evolved in response to emerging science and social claims from environmental justice advocates in cities around the world. By 2000, health studies demonstrated geographic and temporal variations in pollutant concentrations (hotspots) and human health effects, particularly for urban communities of color (Brainard et al. 2002; Brunekreef and Holgate 2002; Brunekreef et al. 1999; Buzzelli et al. 2003; Dolinoy and Miranda 2004; Gwynn and Thurston 2001; Houston et al. 2004; Kinney, Thurston, and Raizenne 1996; Kunzli et al. 2000; Morello-Frosch and Jesdale 2006; Pastor, Sadd, and Morello-Frosch 2002). Studies also linked diesel particulates to different cancers (Hemminki and Pershagen 1994; Kinney et al. 2000). Community-based monitoring in Boston and Harlem, New York found unacceptably high levels of diesel particulates at street level undetected by regulatory agencies (Corburn 2003, 2005; Kinney et al. 2000; Loh et al. 2002). In response to these studies, localities have pursued place-based regulations, such as prohibitions against truck, bus, and train idling in specific places (Brodrick et al. 2002; Lutsey et al. 2004; Schweitzer, Brodrick, and Spivey 2008), and required cleaner-fuel vehicles at particular corridors and destinations, such as restricting the fleets eligible to serve particular areas, like the Ports of Long Beach and Los Angeles in southern California or London's low-emission vehicle (LEV) zone for its downtown.

Place-based monitoring and environmental justice activism in response to new health information have changed air quality and public health research to focus more on intraregional differences in air quality and far less on emissions. For urban residents, whether a region is in compliance with federal air quality standards or whether a project saves emissions may be far less important than the ambient air quality within their neighborhoods. Planners have largely missed out on these important changes in the research, and in so doing, they have yet to contribute to addressing the challenges that arise for planning and development from this new research.

Emissions and emissions talk can be, at best, a distraction and, at worst, a red herring when trying to understand human exposures, atmospheric conditions, and urban environments. As part of a recent collaborative effort among local governments, university researchers, and community members to provide science-based support for air quality policies, researchers performed model simulations to assess different emissions management strategies on $PM_{2.5}$ and ozone concentrations in the Shenandoah Valley in Virginia (Bansal 2008). Their model predicted that $PM_{2.5}$ concentrations would be reduced by 10 to 27 percent, depending on the time of year and location within the valley. Because emissions of greenhouse gases (GHG) and criteria pollutants such as nitrogen oxides and volatile organic compounds often stem from the same sources, such as cars, GHG strategies can, in theory, produce co-benefits for local neighborhoods. A bundle of ten policies, including TCMs, aimed primarily at reducing greenhouse gas emissions produced similar emissions reductions.

But not all types of air quality problems move together in the same way, nor do co-benefits necessarily help those local populations in the most need of environmental health improvements. One of the Shenandoah Valley's local major respiratory health issues concerns ozone. Even with all the emissions reductions, the simulations showed either no expected change in most seasons or only a small increase in ozone concentrations in the fall. In this case, GHG savings could lead to slightly worse local air quality—a finding that contradicts the idea that TCM strategies inevitably produce co-benefits for climate change and local environmental health. Co-benefits for local neighborhoods have been a thorny issue for states like California, trying to implement climate change regulation. Better analyses using multiple outcome measures in addition to emissions reductions can help avoid naive research findings that overstate climate and air quality progress.

Another recent modeling study, from California's Central Valley, illustrates the contradictions that can arise when research examines multiple outcomes for both people and emissions. In this study, atmospheric scientists forecasted emissions, concentrations, and human exposures to fine particulates resulting from four different twenty-year transportation and land-use scenarios for the San Joaquin Valley (Hixson et al. 2010). The simulation allocated 3 million new residents in the valley according to the standard saint-and-sinner development patterns (i.e., compact development versus sprawl) common to most planning analyses, including high-speed rail. From these assumptions, they modeled the effects all the way from emissions to concentrations to human exposures.

The results illustrate the tensions that arise around human settlement patterns and pollutant distributions. Fine particulate emissions increased by the lowest amount under compact growth, as expected. But human exposures went up under the same scenario by 10 to 15 percent over the base case. The low-density scenarios resulted in 11 percent lower exposures to organic carbon and 19 percent lower exposures to elemental carbon than current conditions in the valley. Sprawl may prompt more driving, but it also allows more people to breathe better air. In this analysis, cars only marginally contributed to the problems with exposures to fine particulates. Instead, increased urban densities placed people within the plume of agricultural sources.[4]

What if this study had been conducted using the typical approach from planning research? Charging forward with assumptions about VMT reductions and ignoring the agricultural sources of pollution, a typical land use–transport study would conclude that the Central Valley would be much better off pursuing compact development with its promise of fewer cars and less driving. Had Hixson et al. (2010) stopped with emissions, they would have found evidence—like most planning studies do—that compact development and TCMs support air quality goals. But by considering the whole geographic, atmospheric, and social environment of the region, they illustrated how compact development portends a trade-off between emissions savings and higher exposures.

These recent studies have provided fuel for sensationalistic coverage by an independent newspaper in Los Angeles, the *LA Weekly*, that described the city's transit-oriented developments (TODs) as "Black Lung Lofts"—rather than the healthy, livable communities so often envisioned by planners. The newspaper blamed the city's "density hawks"—people who advocate for greater densities in development no matter what the context—for pushing TODs in the wrong places (McDonald 2010). All the right ingredients are there for a compact development project: light rail, mixed use, and multifamily housing. Unfortunately, those also occur right next to some of the busiest freeways in the world. The resulting light rail running along the freeway rights of way, and the TODs attached to them, may simply be crowding relatively low-income families into affordable units near the worst line sources of pollutants within a region.

An empirical study of regions throughout the United States looked at the possibility that compact regions placed more people into close proximity to pollutants using three separate air quality outcome measures: (a) emissions, (b) ambient pollutant concentrations, and (c) exposures in both compact and sprawled regions (Schweitzer and Zhou 2010). These results mirrored the findings in the San Joaquin Valley and the Shenandoah Valley. Compact development was associated with lower levels of emissions per person within the regions, but higher human exposures to unhealthy pollutant levels in over 500 neighborhood locations throughout the United States. The research further found that exposures among vulnerable socio-demographic groups, like children and seniors in poor communities and communities of color, were higher in neighborhoods within compact regions than in sprawled regions.

Looking at this issue from a macro-scale perspective, human settlement patterns and exposure to future climate change effects need greater study right along with more work on neighborhood air quality. The planning research has stressed planning's contribution to preventing climate change on the assumption that urban infill and increased densities will lower emissions. Currently 35 million people around the world live on land that would be underwater with a one-meter increase in ocean levels, and many of those encompass downtown areas and city centers where planners advocate for higher densities. That is a lot of potential human exposure to climate effects to ignore, and creating even higher densities in urban areas within that coastal zone to pursue VMT reductions may be the worst possible strategy; inland densification for the same emissions reduction goals may make for better policy and planning. A recent article in the *Journal of the American Planning Association* is among the first to describe climate adaptation issues for planning (Bedsworth and Hanak 2010). Where people live within regions affects their exposure to climate effects and regional air quality problems. These are topics where planning research can offer invaluable insights if the field broadens its scope, methods, and approaches.

4. Guide for Future Planning Research

Just as many people argue that American cities became planned for cars instead of people, planning and regulation for air quality, too, has focused on emissions rather than on people or neighborhoods. When the research uses multiple goals and measures for air quality, the story surrounding how urban form affects neighborhoods becomes much more complicated than the emissions talk allows. Research outside planning tends to unsettle the neat logic that compact development and TCMs can support key air quality goals for the communities that planners wish to serve. Emissions talk is not good enough for planning research to deliver meaningful environmental change.

One problem concerns the knowledge and practices around emissions estimation. The problems with emissions estimation do not amount to the usual straw man complaints about forecasting inaccuracy. Rather, the estimates are very inaccurate, researchers from fields outside of planning have little guidance on just how wrong the emissions forecasts and inventories are, and poor VMT estimates and travel demand modeling are among the culprits in fostering uncertainties in emissions inventories and estimates.

Better planning research would help enlighten human activity impacts on emissions, and not just with driving. The distribution of land uses can have any number of effects on emissions. For example, the mixed land uses so celebrated in places like New York, while fostering emission-free walking trips, also dot the urban landscape with small-scale dry cleaners that can really add to the amounts of volatile organic compounds.

Instead of considering the latter issue, planners have focused on the former. Planning research has tended to use scenarios to show the range of what can seem, to the uninitiated, as equally likely development futures. This approach may be useful for visioning, but not for quantifying the uncertainties associated with the scenarios or how those uncertainties may propagate throughout subsequent emissions analyses. Research that reduces the uncertainty in predicting long-term urban futures, for both transport and land use, offers interdisciplinary research in atmospheric science and climate change tremendously valuable tools. Perhaps nothing can be done about the subjective nature of forecasts, but researchers should at least know what the confidence ranges are. The timing of development and changes in urban form—and how long those might take to produce effects on aggregate travel (if any)—requires renewed empirical analysis in planning and forecasting, especially in light of worldwide changes in development markets in the global recession.

Finally, planning research needs to pay attention to people in the air quality and climate change debate. Where people live relative to air quality problems and potential effects of climate change vary a lot within metropolitan regions, and at this stage of investigation, researchers cannot tell whether the potential emissions reductions from compact development outweigh the costs incurred by potentially increasing human exposures. Resolving this question would help planners look for strategic opportunities to deploy infill and greater densities in places where the neighborhood air quality is good and away from places where there are problems for either criteria pollutants or potential climate change effects—at least until those problems become resolved.

Even though GHG emissions are global, and urbanization could help to reduce emissions, locations are differentially vulnerable to climate change, and it is likely that some places within regions will be less vulnerable than others to the looming consequences of climate change if prevention becomes impossible. Understanding neighborhood environments within regions might enable planners to derive development strategies that enable adaptation. As it is now, the planning research and its focus on emissions reductions reflect a dominant mindset—that planning can serve to help prevent climate change by emissions reductions. That tendency toward optimism may limit planning's potential research and practice contributions. Research that looks at the big picture of differential exposures and neighborhood resilience might be able to forge strategies that are both adaptive and preventative—but only if planning research pays attention to and incorporates both science and community concerns.

The dual-purpose adaptation and prevention research mirrors the logic that planning can produce co-benefits with climate change prevention and local air quality improvements through emissions reductions. The atmospheric science and modeling research suggests contradictions in the logic when we look at multiple outcome measures, such as exposures and emissions together.

Co-benefits have been apparent in theory but uneven in particular contexts. These types of contradictory findings suggest that physical and human geography determine whether co-benefits or trade-offs occur. Planning research can offer numerous insights on the spatial aspects of potential co-benefits and benefits for both regions and neighborhoods—so long as the research takes seriously the complex nature of the human-environment trade-offs in play.

Planning researchers seem to have come to a consensus that soft TCMs and compact development alone are not going to produce major changes in VMT or fuel consumption with strategies that directly limit auto use and fuel consumption, like pricing and taxes. That said, these types of policies are already in place in various parts of the globe and, while effective in dampening the rate of VMT growth and supporting transit provision, still have not managed to stop VMT growth (Sperling and Gordon 2009). Productive planning research would follow from the more recent Urban Land Institute publication, *Moving Cooler* (Cambridge Systematics

2009).[5] The report analyzed "bundles" of strategies evaluated according to multiple criteria—the two most important being the time frame for implementation and the costs associated with implementation. This approach stresses the significance of a multipronged strategy toward emissions along with the acknowledgment that revamping cities according to the smart growth vision may produce results, but those are among the longer term strategies. Despite the relatively large claims made about the efficacy of bundled strategies for dampening auto use, fuel consumption, and emissions, there is remarkably little research that actually models the premise that multiple strategies can achieve climate and air quality goals.

Relatedly, *Moving Cooler* contains caveats about how feasible it will be to impose auto-restrictive policies such as gas tax floors, higher fuel taxes, or congestion pricing in places like the United States. If, as we have suggested throughout this chapter, localities cherry-pick the most palatable parts of climate and air quality plans, like soft TCMs, planning and policy research should address how and why some jurisdictions manage to pass restrictive auto policies while other places cannot do so. Soft TCMs, for example, may be politically popular precisely because they do not compel action or behavior, and in addition, they offer really nice urban amenities like walking districts and rail transit. Moreover, research on the outcomes of cherry-picking would help inform the debate and guide localities to avoiding problems like the "Black Lung Lofts" accusations. Which policies and planning strategies can get through the political process will determine implementation and outcomes, no matter how many carrots and sticks researchers can bundle together in theory or in a simulation.

This chapter's goal has been to expand planners' scope of the connections among land use, urban form, air quality, and community health. Indeed, planning research and practice have significant opportunities to contribute to working with the many issues at stake with urban environmental health, air quality, and climate change. In order to do so, however, the field has to recognize that there many issues other than the automobile and its emissions. Significant though those issues are, they are only one part of the story about environmental health—the beginning.

For those who believe that land development will change radically, and that those changes will affect how much fuel consumption occurs, this chapter may seem overly cynical, assigning a smaller role to planning and design than they merit in environmental health. Instead, this chapter is merely a call to complexity, one that planners can and should answer in the interest of being truly precautionary in our planning. More cynical would be to see no evil, hear no evil, and speak no evil about these uncertainties when failure to deliver on environmental health improvements results in continued human suffering.

NOTES

1. Here we allude to Mary Ann Glendon's concept of "rights talk"—the tendency of Americans to assert rights in political discussions in an attempt to trump or short-

circuit political deliberations in one's own favor. The constant assertion of rights, one after another, causes political discussion to devolve into irreconcilable swaps about whose rights are most important. In a similar vein, emissions talk dominates air quality and climate planning in troublesome ways.

2. To answer some of the questions we raise, the "billions of pounds" reported each year is an odd way of reporting GHG emissions reductions, which are usually reported in metric tons of carbon equivalent. The estimated emissions reductions from HSR would be 6 million metric tons of carbon equivalent, which are about 3.5 percent of the current transport GHG inventory and 1.25 percent of the total inventory for 2008 in California's inventory. The number would be impressive enough reported in the standard way, but the use of "billions" jazzes up the emissions talk and the project marketing nicely.

3. In this case, those 79 million tons amount to a little over 1 percent of the U.S. CO_2. Since the current U.S. federal administration has set a target of 17 percent reduction overall, it is possible to argue that this 1 percent is a significant portion of that goal.

4. Cleaning up those sources in the valley would change the outcomes here, but the timing and feasibility of those changes pose a different set of problems than that addressed by more walking and biking.

5. This report, *Moving Cooler*, produced by Cambridge Systematics in 2009, should not be confused with *Growing Cooler* by Ewing et al. (2008). Both were published by the Urban Land Institute.

References

Bansal, Gaurav. 2008. *Modeling the Effects of Local Air Pollution Control Measures on Air Quality in the Shenandoah Valley*. Harrisonburg, VA: ShenAir Institute.

Ban-Weiss, George A., John P. McLaughlin, Robert A. Harley, Melissa M. Lunden, Thomas W. Kirchstetter, Andrew J. Kean, Anthony W. Strawa, Eric D. Stevenson, and Gary R. Kendall. 2008. "Long-Term Changes in Emissions of Nitrogen Oxides and Particulate Matter from On-Road Gasoline and Diesel Vehicles." *Atmospheric Environment* 42(2): 220–32.

Bartholomew, Keith, and Reid Ewing. 2009. "Land Use–Transportation Scenarios and Future Vehicle Travel and Land Consumption: A Meta-Analysis." *Journal of the American Planning Association* 75(1): 13–27.

Bedsworth, Louise W., and Ellen Hanak. 2010. "Adaptation to Climate Change—A Review of Challenges and Tradeoffs in Six Sectors." *Journal of the American Planning Association* 76(4): 477–95.

Bernick, Michael, and Robert Cervero. 1996. *Transit Villages in the 21st Century*. New York: McGraw-Hill.

Boarnet, Marlon, and Randall Crane. 2001. *Travel by Design: The Influence of Urban Form on Travel*. Oxford: Oxford University Press.

Boersma, K. Folkert, Daniel J. Jacob, Eric J. Bucsela, Anne E. Perring, Ruud J. Dirksen, Ronald J. van der A, Robert M. Yantosca, Rokjin J. Park, Mark O. Wenig, Timothy H. Bertram, and Ronald C. Cohen. 2008. "Validation of OMI Tropospheric NO_2 Observations During INTEX-B and Application to Constrain NOx Emissions over the Eastern United States and Mexico." *Atmospheric Environment* 42(19): 4480–97.

Brainard, Julii S., Andrew P. Jones, Ian J. Bateman, Andrew A. Lovett, and Peter J. Fallon. 2002. "Modeling Environmental Equity: Access to Air Quality in Birmingham, England." *Environment and Planning Part A* 34(4): 695–716.

Brodrick, Christie-Joy, Timothy E. Lipman, Mohammad Farshchi, Harry A. Dwyer, Daniel Sperling, S. William. Gouse, D. Bruce Harris, and Foy G. King. 2002. "Evaluation of Fuel Cell Auxiliary Power Units for Heavy-Duty Diesel Trucks." *Transportation Research Part D: Transport and Environment* 7(4): 303–15.

Brunekreef, Bert, and Stephen T. Holgate. 2002. "Air Pollution and Health." *Lancet* 360(9341): 1233–42.

Brunekreef, Bert, Nicole A. H. Janssen, Jeroen de Hartog, Hendrik Harssema, Mirjam Knape, and Patricia van Vliet. 1997. "Air Pollution from Truck Traffic and Lunch Function in Children Living Near Motorways." *Epidemiology* 8(3): 298–303.

Buzcu-Guven, Birnur, and Matthew P. Fraser. 2008. "Comparison of VOC Emissions Inventory Data with Source Apportionment Results for Houston, Texas." *Atmospheric Environment* 42(20): 5032–43.

Buzzelli, Michael, Michael Jerrett, Richard Burnett, and Norm Finklestein. 2003. "Spatiotemporal Perspectives on Air Pollution and Environmental Justice in Hamilton, Canada, 1985–1996." *Annals of the Association of American Geographers* 93(3): 557–73.

California High Speed Rail Authority. 2008. "California High Speed Train System Environmental Protection." Available at: http://www.cahighspeedrail.ca.gov/WorkArea/DownloadAsset.aspx?id=876; accessed November 12, 2011.

Cambridge Systematics. 2009. *Moving Cooler: An Analysis of Transportation Strategies for Reducing Greenhouse Gas Emissions*. Washington, DC: Urban Land Institute.

Cho, Sunhee, Paul A. Makar, S. Win Lee, T. Herage, John Liggio, Shao-Meng Li, Brian Wiens, and L. Graham. 2009. "Evaluation of a Unified Regional Air-Quality Modeling System (AURAMS) Using PrAIRie2005 Field Study Data: The Effects of Emissions Data Accuracy on Particle Sulphate Predictions." *Atmospheric Environment* 43(11): 1864–77.

Choo, Sangho, Kevan Shafizadeh, and Deb Niemeier. 2007. "The Development of a Prescreening Model to Identify Failed and Gross Polluting Vehicles." *Transportation Research Part D: Transportation and Environment* 12(3): 208–18.

Corburn, Jason. 2003. "Bringing Local Knowledge into Environmental Decision Making: Improving Urban Planning for Communities at Risk." *Journal of Planning Education and Research* 22(4): 420–33.

Coburn, Jason. 2005. *Street Science: Community Knowledge and Environmental Health Justice*. Cambridge, MA: MIT Press.

Committee on Risk Assessment of Hazardous Air Pollutants. National Research Council. 1994. *Science and Judgment in Risk Assessment*. Washington, DC: National Academies Press.

Committee on Tropospheric Ozone Formation and Measurement. National Research Council. 1991. *Rethinking the Ozone Problem in Urban and Regional Air Pollution*. Washington, DC: National Academies Press.

Crane, Randall. 1996. "On Form Versus Function: Will the New Urbanism Reduce Traffic, or Increase It?" *Journal of Planning Education and Research* 15(2): 117–26.

Dallmann, Timothy R., and Robert A. Harley. 2010. "Evaluation of Mobile Source Emission Trends in the United States." *Journal of Geophysical Research-Atmospheres* 115(D14305): 1–12.

Davies, John, Michael Grant, John Venezia, and Joseph Aamidor. 2007. "Greenhouse Gas Emissions of the U.S. Transportation Sector: Trends, Uncertainties, and Methodological Improvements." *Transportation Research Record* 2017:41–46.

Dolinoy, Dana C., and Marie Lynn Miranda. 2004. "GIS Modeling of Air Toxics Releases From TRI-Reporting and Non-TRI-Reporting Facilities: Impacts for Environmental Justice." *Environmental Health Perspectives* 112(17): 1717–24.

Dreher, David B., and Robert A. Harley. 1998. "A Fuel-Based Inventory for Heavy-Duty Diesel Truck Emissions." *Journal of the Air and Waste Management Association* 48(4): 352–58.

Ewing, Reid, and Robert Cervero. 2010. "Travel and the Built Environment: A Meta-Analysis." *Journal of the American Planning Association* 76(3): 265–94.

Ewing, Reid, Keith Bartholomew, Steve Winkelman, Jerry Walters, and Don Chen. 2008. *Growing Cooler: The Evidence on Urban Development and Climate Change.* Washington, DC: Urban Land Institute.

Ezzati, Majid, Alan D. Lopez, Anthony Rodgers, Stephen Vander Hoorn, Christopher J. L. Murray, and the Comparative Risk Assessment Collaborating Group. 2002. "Selected Major Risk Factors and Global and Regional Burden of Disease." *Lancet* 360(9343): 1347–60.

Ezzati, Majid, Stephen Vander Hoorn, Anthony Rodgers, Alan D. Lopez, Colin D. Mathers, Christopher J. L. Murray, and the Comparative Risk Assessment Collaborating Group. 2003. "Estimates of Global and Regional Potential Health Gains From Reducing Multiple Major Risk Factors." *Lancet* 362(9380): 271–80.

Fujita, Eric M., Bart E. Croes, Charles L. Bennett, Douglas R. Lawson, Frederick W. Lurmann, and Hilary H. Main. 1992. "Comparison of Emission Inventory and Ambient Concentration Ratios of CO, NMOG, and NOx in California's South Coast Air Basin." *Journal of the Air and Waste Management Association* 42(3): 264–76.

Fujita, Eric M., John G. Watson, Judith C. Chow, and Karen L. Magliano. 1995. "Receptor Model and Emissions Inventory Source Apportionments of Nonmethane Organic Gases in California's San Joaquin Valley and San Francisco Bay Area." *Atmospheric Environment* 29(21): 3019–35.

Goodchild, Barry. 1994. "Housing Design, Urban Form, and Sustainable Development: Reflections on the Future Residential Landscape." *Town Planning Review* 65(2): 143–58.

Graham-Rowe, Ella, Stephen Skippon, Benjamin Gardner, and Charles Abraham. 2011. "Can We Reduce Car Use and, If So, How? A Review of Available Evidence." *Transportation Research Part A: Policy and Practice* 45(5): 401–18.

Gurjar, B. R., Tim M. Butler, Mark G. Lawrence, and Jos Lelieveld. 2008. "Evaluation of Emissions and Air Quality in Megacities." *Atmospheric Environment* 42(7): 1593–606.

Gwynn, R. Charon, and George D. Thurston. 2001. "The Burden of Air Pollution: Impacts Among Racial Minorities." *Environmental Health Perspectives* 109:501–06.

Haines, Andy, R. Sari Kovats, Diarmid Campbell-Lendrum, and Carlos Corvalan. 2006. "Climate Change and Human Health: Impacts, Vulnerability and Public Health." *Public Health* 120(7): 585–96.

Han, K. M., Chul Han Song, H. J. Ahn, R. S. Park, J. H. Woo, C. K. Lee, Andreas Richter, John P. Burrows, J. Y. Kim, and J. H. Hong. 2009. "Investigation of NOx Emissions and NOx- Related Chemistry in East Asia Using CMAQ-Predicted and GOME-Derived NO_2 Columns." *Atmospheric Chemistry and Physics* 9(3): 1017–36.

Harley, Robert A., Stuart A. McKeen, James Pearson, Michael O. Rodgers, and William A. Lonneman. 2001. "Analysis of Motor Vehicle Emissions During the Nashville/Middle Tennessee Ozone Study." *Journal of Geophysical Research-Atmospheres* 106(D4): 3559–67.

Harrington, Winston, Arnold Howitt, Alan J. Krupnick, Jonathan Makler, Peter Nelson, and Sarah J. Siwek. 2003. *Exhausting Options: Assessing SIP-Conformity Interactions.* Washington, DC: Resources for the Future.

Hemminki, Kari, and Göran Pershagen. 1994. "Cancer Risk of Air Pollution: Epidemiological Evidence." *Environmental Health Perspectives* 102(Suppl. 4): 187–92.

Hixson, Mark, Abdullah Mahmud, Jianlin Hu, Song Bai, Debbie A. Niemeier, Susan L. Handy, Shengyi Gao, Jay R. Lund, Dana C. Sullivan, and Michael J. Kleeman. 2010. "Influence of Regional Development Policies and Clean Technology Adoption on Future Air Pollution Exposure." *Atmospheric Environment* 44(4): 552–62.

Houston, Douglas, Jun Wu, Paul Ong, and Arthur Winer. 2004. "Structural Disparities of Urban Traffic in Southern California: Implications for Vehicle Related-Air Pollution Exposure in Minority and High-Poverty Neighborhoods." *Journal of Urban Affairs* 26(5): 565–92.

Jabareen, Yosef R. 2006. "Sustainable Urban Forms: Their Typologies, Models, and Concepts." *Journal of Planning Education and Research* 26(1): 38–52.

Jiang, Mei, Linsey C. Marr, Edward J. Dunlea, Scott C. Herndon, John T. Jayne, Charles E. Kolb, W. Berk Knighton, Todd M. Rogers, Miguel Zavala, Luisa T. Molina, and Mario J. Molina. 2005. "Vehicle Fleet Emissions of Black Carbon, Polycyclic Aromatic Hydrocarbons and Other Pollutants Measured by a Mobile Laboratory in Mexico City." *Atmospheric Chemistry and Physics* 5:3377–87.

Kasibhatla, Prasad, Avelino Arellano, Jennifer A. Logan, Paul I. Palmer, and Paul Novelli. 2002. "Top-Down Estimate of a Large Source of Atmospheric Carbon Monoxide Associated with Fuel Combustion in Asia." *Geophysical Research* Letters 29(19): 1900.

Kean, Andrew J., Robert F. Sawyer, and Robert A. Harley. 2000. "A Fuel-Based Assessment of Off-Road Diesel Engine Emissions." *Journal of the Air and Waste Management Association* 50(11): 1929–39.

Kinney, Patrick L., Maneesha Aggarwal, Mary E. Northridge, Nicole A. H. Janssen, and Peggy. Shepard. 2000. "Airborne Concentrations of $PM_{2.5}$ and Diesel Exhaust Particulates on Harlem Sidewalks: A Community-Based Pilot Study." *Environmental Health Perspectives* 108 (3): 213–18.

Kinney, Patrick L., George D. Thurston, and Mark Raizenne. 1996. "The Effects of Ambient Ozone on Lung Function in Children: A Reanalysis of Six Summer Camp Studies." *Environmental Health Perspectives* 104(2): 170–74.

Kopacz, Monika, Daniel J. Jacob, Daven K. Henze, Colette L. Heald, David G. Streets, and Qiang Zhang. 2009. "Comparison of Adjoint and Analytical Bayesian Inversion Methods for Constraining Asian Sources of Carbon Monoxide Using Satellite (MOPITT) Measurements of CO Columns." *Journal of Geophysical Research-Atmospheres* 114(D04305): 1–10.

Kunzli, Nino, Reinhard Kaiser, Sylvia Medina, Michael J. Studnicka, Olivier Chanel, Paul Filliger, Max Herry, Friedrich Horak, Valerie Puybonnieux-Texier, Philippe Quenel, Jurgen Schneider, Rita Seethaler, Jean-Christoph Vergnaud, and Heini Sommer. 2000. "Public-Health Impact of Outdoor and Traffic-Related Air Pollution: A European Assessment." *Lancet* 356:795–801.

Kurokawa, Jun-ichi, Keiya Yumimoto, Itushi Uno, and Toshimasa Ohara. 2009. "Adjoint Inverse Modeling of NO_x Emissions Over Eastern China Using Satellite Observations of NO2 Vertical Column Densities." *Atmospheric Environment* 43(11): 1878–87.

Loh, Penn, Jodi Sugerman-Brozan, Standrick Wiggins, David Noiles, and Cecilia Archibald. 2002. "From Asthma to Airbeat: Community-Driven Monitoring of Fine Particles and Black Carbon in Roxbury, Massachusetts." *Environmental Health Perspectives* 110(Suppl. 2): 297–301.

Lutsey, Nicholas, Christie-Joy Brodrick, Daniel Sperling, and Carolyn Oblesby. 2004. "Heavy-Duty Truck Idling Characteristics: Results from a Nationwide Truck Survey." *Transportation Research Record* 1880:29–38.

Marr, Linsey C., Douglas R. Black, and Robert A. Harley. 2002. "Formation of Photochemical Air Pollution in Central California 1. Development of a Revised Motor Vehicle Emission Inventory." *Journal of Geophysical Research-Atmospheres* 107(6): 4047.

Martens, Pim, R. Sari Kovats, Saskia Nijhof, Piebe de Vries, Matthew T. J. Livermore, David J. Bradley, Jonathan Cox, and A. J. McMichael. 1999. "Climate Change and Future Populations at Risk of Malaria." *Global Environmental Change* 9:S89–S107.

Mazzoleni, Claudio, Hampden D. Kuhns, Hans Moosmuller, Robert E. Keislar, Peter W. Barber, Norman F. Robinson, John G. Watson, and Djordje Nikolic. 2004. "On-Road Vehicle Particulate Matter and Gaseous Emission Distributions in Las Vegas, Nevada, Compared with Other Areas." *Journal of the Air and Waste Management Association* 54(6): 711–26.

McDonald, Patrick Range. 2010. "Black Lung Lofts." *LA Weekly*. Available at: http://www.laweekly.com/2010-03-06/news/black-lung-lofts/; accessed November 12, 2011.

Mendoza-Dominguez, Alberto, and Armistead G. Russell. 2001. "Emission Strength Validation Using Four-Dimensional Data Assimilation: Application to Primary Aerosol and Precursors to Ozone and Secondary Aerosol." *Journal of the Air and Waste Management Association* 51(11): 1538–50.

Miller, C. Andrew, George Hidy, Jeremy Hales, Charles E. Kolb, Arthur S. Werner, Bernd Haneke, David Parrish, H. Christopher Frey, Leonora Rojas-Bracho, Marc Deslauriers, Bill Pennell, and J. David Mobley. 2006. "Air Emission Inventories in North America: A Critical Assessment." *Journal of the Air and Waste Management Association* 56(8): 1115–29.

Morello-Frosch, Rachel, and Bill M. Jesdale. 2006. "Separate and Unequal: Residential Segregation and Estimated Cancer Risks Associated with Ambient Air Toxics in U.S. Metropolitan Regions." *Public Health Reports* 114(3): 386–93.

National Academy of Science. 2000. *Modeling Mobile-Source Emissions*. Washington, DC: National Academies Press.

Newman, Peter, and Jeffrey R. Kenworthy. 1999. *Sustainability and Cities: Overcoming Automobile Dependence*. Washington, DC: Island Press.

Pastor, Manuel, Jr., James L. Sadd, and Rachel Morello-Frosch. 2002. "Who's Minding the Kids? Pollution, Public Schools, and Environmental Justice in Los Angeles." *Social Science Quarterly* 83(1): 263–80.

Reis, Stefan, Rob W. Pinder, Meigen Zhang, G. Lijie, and Mark A. Sutton. 2009. "Reactive Nitrogen in Atmospheric Emission Inventories." *Atmospheric Chemistry and Physics* 9(19): 7657–77.

Sawyer, Robert F., Robert A. Harley, Steven H. Cadle, Joseph M. Norbeck, Robert Slott, and Humberto Bravo. 2000. "Mobile Sources Critical Review: 1998 NARSTO Assessment." *Atmospheric Environment* 34:2161–81.

Schweitzer, Lisa, Christie-Joy Brodrick, and Sue E. Spivey. 2008. "Truck Driver Environmental and Energy Attitudes: An Exploratory Analysis." *Transportation Research Part D: Transport and Environment* 13(3): 141–50.

Schweitzer, Lisa, and Jianping Zhou. 2010. "Neighborhood Air Quality, Respiratory Health, and Vulnerable Populations in Compact and Sprawled Regions." *Journal of the American Planning Association* 76(3): 363–71.

Singer, Brett C., and Robert A. Harley. 2000. "A Fuel-Based Inventory of Motor Vehicle Exhaust Emissions in the Los Angeles Area During Summer 1997." *Atmospheric Environment* 34(11): 1783–95.

Song, Jihee, William Vizuete, Sunghye Chang, David Allen, Yosuke Dimura, Susan Kemball-Cook, Greg Yarwood, Marianthi-Anna Kioumourtzoglou, Elliot Atlas, Armin Hansel, Armin Wisthaler, and Elena McDonald-Buller. 2008. "Comparisons of Modeled and Observed Isoprene Concentrations in Southeast Texas." *Atmospheric Environment* 42(8): 1922–40.

Sperling, Daniel, and Deborah Gordon. 2009. *Two Billion Cars: Driving Toward Sustainability.* New York: Oxford University Press.

Thornhill, D. A., A. E. Williams, Timothy B. Onasch, E. Wood, Scott C. Herndon, Charles E.
Kolb, W. Berk Knighton, Miguel Zavala, Luisa T. Molina, and Linsey C. Marr. 2009. "Application of Positive Matrix Factorization to On-Road Measurements for Source Apportionment of Diesel- and Gasoline-Powered Vehicle Emissions in Mexico City." *Atmospheric Chemistry and Physics Discussions* 9:27571–609.

U.S. Government Accounting Office. 2001. "Air Pollution: Should EPA Improve Oversight of Emissions Reporting by Large Facilities?" Report to the Ranking Minority Member, Committee on Government Reform, House of Representatives. Washington, DC: General Accounting Office.

Vivanco, Marta G., and Maria de Fatima Andrade. 2006. "Validation of the Emission Inventory in the Sao Paulo Metropolitan Area of Brazil, Based on Ambient Concentrations Ratios of CO, NMOG, and NOx and on a Photochemical Model." *Atmospheric Environment* 40(7): 1189–98.

Warneke, Carsten, Stuart A. McKeen, Jozef A. de Gouw, Paul D. Goldan, William C. Kuster, John S. Holloway, Eric J. Williams, Brian M. Lerner, David D. Parrish, Michael Trainer, Fred C. Fehsenfeld, Shuji Kato, Elliot L. Atlas, Angela Baker, and Donald R. Blake. 2007. "Determination of Urban Volatile Organic Compound Emission Ratios and Comparison with an Emissions Database." *Journal of Geophysical Research-Atmospheres* 112(D10S47): 1–13.

Xiao, Yaping, Jennifer A. Logan, Daniel J. Jacob, Rynda C. Hudman, Robert Yantosca, and Donald R. Blake. 2008. "Global Budget of Ethane and Regional Constraints on U.S. Sources." *Journal of Geophysical Research-Atmospheres* 113(D21306): 1–13.

Yanowitz, Janet, Robert L. McCormick, and Michael S. Graboski. 2000. "In-use Emissions From Heavy-Duty Diesel Vehicles." *Environmental Science Technology* 34(5): 729–40.

Ying, Qi, Jin Lu, Paul Allen, Paul Livingstone, Ajith Kaduwela, and Michael Kleeman. 2008. "Modeling Air Quality During the California Regional $PM_{10}/PM_{2.5}$ Air Quality Study (CRPAQS) Using the UCD/CIT Source-Oriented Air Quality Model—Part I. Base Case Model Results." *Atmospheric Environment* 42(39): 8954–66.

Ying, Qi, Jin Lu, Ajith Kaduwela, and Michael Kleeman. 2008. "Modeling Air Quality During the California Regional $PM_{10}/PM_{2.5}$ Air Quality Study (CRPAQS) Using the UCD/CIT Source-Oriented Air Quality Model—Part II. Regional Source Apportionment of Primary Airborne Particulate Matter." *Atmospheric Environment* 42(39): 8967–78.

Zhang, J., T. Wang, William L. Chameides, Carlos Cardelino, Donald R. Blake, and David G. Streets. 2008. "Source Characteristics of Volatile Organic Compounds During High Ozone Episodes in Hong Kong, Southern China." *Atmospheric Chemistry and Physics* 8(16): 4983–996.

CHAPTER 23

THE LOCAL REGULATION OF CLIMATE CHANGE

J. R. DESHAZO AND JUAN MATUTE

1. INTRODUCTION

RESEARCHERS and practitioners seek to measure the greenhouse gas (GHG) effects of urban and regional planning and policy in order to develop and implement policies to reduce GHG emissions. The success of these policies depends in part on how well we can measure GHG emissions from cities, counties, and substate regions. Yet researchers and practitioners lack a commonly accepted framework to define and measure GHG emissions at these scales. This is not due to a lack of interest in such a framework but, rather, in part to a difference in objectives between these two groups and the difficulties inherent in collecting appropriate data at the local level. In a growing body of literature, researchers have sought to measure the full life cycle of emissions within a community's geographic boundary to understand how consumption activities within these boundaries affect global GHG emissions (Kennedy et al. 2010; Ramaswami et al. 2008; Dodman 2009). Practitioners have sought measures of a jurisdiction's emissions appropriate for developing plans and effective policies to reduce those emissions. However, the methods needed to achieve these researchers' objectives diverge with those methods needed to accomplish practitioners' and regulators' objectives. We seek to refocus research on the core challenges to accurately and validly measure the GHG effects of local policies for purposes of regulation and policy evaluation.

In doing so, we argue that existing local government GHG measurement methods fail to support these local governments in their evaluation of policy design and the GHG reductions resulting from their policies. The discrepancy between the emissions a government is able to affect through policy and the emissions resulting from activities within its geography is most pronounced for local governments. Neither geographic-based GHG inventory methods nor entity-focused protocols are designed to evaluate the effectiveness of individual policies or a set of policies that a local government can implement to reduce GHG emissions. By failing to support policy evaluation, these methods also fail to support state and federal efforts to ensure local government compliance with GHG-reduction targets.

A measurement framework should have several capabilities to accurately measure the effectiveness of local policies. It should strive to be as accurate as possible, given locally available data. It must be able to isolate and control for regional effects that state or federal policies have on local emissions sources. It should be able to identify the spillover effects of policies of neighboring local governments. It should be able to identify and control for the effects of macroeconomic trends, which are beyond the influence of a local government but nevertheless affect emissions. It should be able to control for issues of data quality and trans-boundary economic transactions. A local GHG emissions inventory that differs from national methods only in terms of geographic boundary would not offer any of these abilities.

Inherent in any measurement framework are boundaries, or parameters, that define the GHG emissions sources to be included in the measurement. The use of boundaries in GHG emissions measurement sources has evolved over time to meet new measurement needs. Recent literature on urban and regional carbon management has focused on measuring the complete set of emissions associated with activities occurring within a defined geographic boundary. In doing so, researchers have focused on a set of emissions that go well beyond those that can be influenced through local policy. We agree that such a measurement framework is critical to understanding the second-order effects that community-based consumption has on the upstream and downstream productions of GHGs. However, we find that this framework does not support local measurement that is accurate, appropriate, and relevant to regulation and policy evaluation.

In this chapter, we outline the need for a measurement framework capable of crediting local governments with reductions they did produce, avoiding the mistaken crediting for emissions they did not produce, and the error in holding local governments accountable for emissions they cannot be reasonably expected to affect. Toward this end, we introduce a new inventory boundary, referred to as "policy effort," which we argue is necessary to meet new and emerging local GHG emissions measurement needs. After mounting this argument, we then describe the types of new methods that are needed in order to better measure the effectiveness of policies implemented by local governments. We highlight the need for a large amount of observational data, from different locations and different times, as well as the need for control variables in order to disentangle local policy effects from nonpolicy and extra-local effects. We focus on transportation emissions because accurately measuring GHG emissions from mobile sources and validly attributing these GHG emissions to specific jurisdictions or policies pose the greatest challenges for local emissions management.

2. Measuring the Performance of Local Policies

National GHG emissions inventory guidelines focus on identifying the sources and magnitudes of GHG emissions within a nation's borders (Intergovernmental Panel on Climate Change 2006). While local governments have historically focused on these measurement needs, new and emerging policies spur the need for GHG emissions measurement that goes beyond identifying sources and magnitudes. Multilevel GHG emissions reduction schemes, such as California's SB 375 regional targets for greenhouse gas emissions from transportation, necessitate accurate and valid ex-ante forecasts of policy performance. In response to these policies, local governments increasingly seek to evaluate the effects of the GHG reduction policies they implement, both ex-post and ex-ante. In this section, we illustrate that understanding ex-post policy effects, especially how these effects are sensitive to specific implementations and local conditions, is a critical step toward forecasting policy effects ex-ante.

Currently, our ability to measure the performance of local government policies depends greatly on the focus of those policies. Policies that focus on reducing GHGs from *municipal operations* can be reasonably measured ex-post. However, emissions from municipal operations comprise only a small portion of total community emissions (Randolph and Pitt 2008). Measuring the performance of policies targeting *community-wide emissions* is more challenging. As we explain below, the challenge here is in establishing boundaries and acquiring data of sufficient resolution to evaluate policy effects. A much thornier challenge awaits those who want to measure the performance of policies targeting GHG emissions in the community.

2.1 Defining Local Inventory Boundaries

All methods to measure GHG emissions assume a set of accounting principles that list which emissions will be included in the measurement. A common reporting format for GHG emissions measurement is the greenhouse gas inventory, which typically includes emissions from a defined set of sources for a calendar year. The

GHG emissions can also be measured from single sources for differing time periods—for example, the flow of emissions through a smokestack in kilograms per minute or the emissions associated with operating a light bulb for one day.

The set of accounting principles that establish the parameters for the emissions to be measured are known as boundaries. A variety of boundary dimensions have been introduced over time. *Geographic* boundaries define the physical locations of facilities or emitting activities to be included in the inventory. *Operational* boundaries define the scope of emissions to be included within the inventory. Operational boundaries were introduced through entity-based inventory methods[1] based on a need to integrate consumption-based approaches without double-counting the emissions. Unlike nations, entities have considerable influence over the activities that drive GHG emissions outside of their direct control. These scopes include direct emissions from combustion (scope 1), indirect emissions from imported energy use (scope 2), and indirect upstream and downstream emissions from other consumption-based activities (scope 3). Entity-based inventory methods also have introduced organizational boundaries, which are used to establish operational control over or ownership of the emitting facility or activity. Inventories are also defined by temporal boundaries and the gases that are to be included.[2]

Different inventory implementations require different boundaries that define the set of emissions. A *global* emissions inventory includes scope 1 emissions of certain gases from a given temporal boundary. A *national* inventory introduces a geographic boundary, usually defined by the geopolitical borders of the nation.[3] With the narrower geographic scope of the state or subnational inventory, the operational boundary is usually expanded to include both scope 1 and 2 emissions in order to account for electricity imports.

Scholars have documented several possible boundary definitions for consumption-based approaches to measure GHG emissions that are associated with a local government's activities. Kennedy et al. (2010, 4828) suggest three measures of local government emissions: "(i) actual emissions within the boundary of the city; (ii) single process emissions (from a life-cycle perspective) associated with the city's metabolism; and (iii) life-cycle emissions associated with the city's metabolism." The first measure includes those scope 1 (production-based) emissions in the Intergovernmental Panel on Climate Change's (IPCC) national inventory methodology. The second measure includes indirect scope 2 emissions from imported energy, but also scope 3 downstream emissions of landfill gas associated with a community's waste and fuel loaded at harbor and airports. The third measure includes the lifecycle emissions of fuels, energy embodied in food, construction materials, and other products consumed within the city.

A recent body of urban and regional carbon management literature focuses on defining the boundaries and developing the methods for the third measure of community emissions: lifecycle emissions. Many scholars view this method as the most appropriate measure of local emissions. Larsen and Hertwich (2009) contend that local governments should use a consumption-based perspective to create the carbon footprint for providing municipal services in order to understand the upstream emissions ramifications of purchasing decisions.

A separate body of literature has focused on using the first and second measures of local government emissions to determine the GHG reduction effects of various local, regional, and state policies. These include comprehensive studies by the Transportation Research Board (2009), Ewing et al. (2008), Cambridge Systematics (2009), and Granade et al. (2009). These studies describe the observed and forecasted effectiveness of policies to reduce GHG emissions. Included in these studies are state or national policies, such as a vehicle miles traveled (VMT) fee, energy efficiency standards, and renewable portfolio standards; regional policies such as transit system investments or congestion pricing; and local policies, such as parking restrictions, transit-oriented development, and green building standards.

There is a disconnect between the scholarly debate on how to measure a local government's GHG emissions and the practical matter of how to measure a policy's effects on GHG emissions. In section 3, we propose a new dimension for inventory boundaries—policy effort—that strengthens the connection between the two measurement methods and the bodies of literature.

2.2 Measuring the Effects of Policies to Reduce Emissions from Municipal Operations

The Local Government Operations Protocol[4] improves a local government's ability to measure the effects of policies that address GHG emissions from the operation of its municipal services. The Protocol guidance sets standards for the quality of input data, increasing inventory precision and making the finer changes in emissions levels more observable. It also establishes clearly defined boundaries, based on operational control, for emissions to be included in the inventory.

The Local Government Operations Protocol's reporting guidance results in a data resolution that is appropriate to evaluate policy performance. This reporting guidance requires local governments to, at a minimum, categorize their emissions into ten functional sectors.[5] Local governments should also report the key indicators that influence the emissions from each of these sectors. The combination of functional-level reporting and indicators allows researchers to normalize and compare local government emissions to identify best practices.

The Protocol also contains guidance for facility-level reporting of GHG emissions. Facility-level resolution allows the observation of year-to-year differences in facility emissions. By comparing observed changes in emissions for a facility that received a treatment with a facility that did not, local governments can better understand the effects of treatments, such as policies, projects, and programs, designed to reduce facility energy consumption and GHG emissions. Approaches to measuring GHG emissions from the greater community should incorporate the strengths of the Local Government Operations Protocol: accurate input data, high resolution, and clearly defined boundaries.

2.3 Current Policy Motivations for Community GHG Emissions Measurement

New state and federal policies highlight the need for ex-ante forecasts of GHG emissions. For instance, states and the federal government can use GHG emissions forecasts in their incentive programs. The U.S. Federal Transit Administration's TIGGER[6] program uses GHG reduction forecasts from transit vehicle operations as an evaluation criterion for transit capital funding. In the future, policymakers may seek to tie funding to forecasted reductions in community-scale GHG emissions.

State and national governments will also use GHG reduction forecasts as a critical tool in the implementation and enforcement of local or regional GHG reduction schemes. State and national governments may seek to implement such schemes to allocate a portion of their own reduction burden to local governments or to explicitly seek local policies that are complementary to state and national emissions reduction goals.

The state of California has implemented a regional GHG reduction scheme for light and medium-duty vehicles. With SB 375, the Sustainable Communities Planning Act, California seeks to allocate a portion of its statewide GHG emissions reduction burden[7] and encourage local land-use policies that do not erode those reductions achieved by statewide vehicle efficiency and low carbon fuel standards (SB 375 §1(b)). The California Air Resources Board, charged with implementing and enforcing SB 375, set regional targets on a per-capita basis. The California Air Resources Board enforces SB 375 by evaluating whether a region's policy commitments will allow it to achieve the prescribed reduction targets in 2020 and 2035. To do this, it relies on simulated forecasts of infrastructure and policy commitments[8] provided by each region's metropolitan planning organization.

These and other emergent policies prompt the need for measuring a policy's GHG reduction effectiveness. Some early-adopter governments were willing to implement policies without precise evidence of those policies' effectiveness. But now, partly in response to state and federal policies that seek local emissions reductions, more local governments seek to adopt policies to reduce community GHG emissions. The needs of these local governments will differ from those of the innovator local governments that have already developed and implemented local policies. These laggard local governments are likely to be more risk-averse and more sensitive to the monetary and nonmonetary costs of policy implementation than were innovators. Some of these later adopters will be reluctant to act, as they are only pursuing local GHG-reduction strategies in response to a state or federally imposed reduction target. Thus, these users will demand that measurement methods be both accurate and valid.

2.4 Challenges to Forecasting Future Policy Effects

In implementing and enforcing a local or regional scheme, the state or national government will require ex-ante forecasts of policy effects, as iterative policymaking based on periodic performance monitoring is not practical for some policies that have lagged effects. Consider the lagged effects in the approval and construction of a new transit line: several years will elapse between project approval and operation. Decades more may elapse until the ridership and land-use changes stimulated by the transit line reach equilibrium and the full GHG-related effects can be evaluated.

Existing methods to use ex-post measurement of policy effectiveness to generate ex-ante forecasts of policy effects are subject to high levels of uncertainty. Actual policy effects will be sensitive to local conditions, specific design, and applications. Existing research lacks this sensitivity, however. Consider the example of a city that looks to increase pricing of public parking so as to discourage single-occupant vehicle trips to a central business district. To forecast the policy's effects, planners will either use a model or the model's source material: empirical studies of how parking prices affect trip generation and VMT. The limited set of studies includes Deakin et al (1996), Shoup (2005, 2006), and multiple studies examined by Vaca and Kuzmyak (2005). From this limited set of studies, the planner will develop a method to calculate the VMT reduction effects of a given price increase, and then translate this VMT reduction figure into a GHG reduction.

However, many local conditions affect the sensitivity of local travel to a specific policy application. First, there may be a difference in the quality of transit service and pedestrian and bicycle networks between the planner's case and those in the studies. Residential density and income levels near the retail district may also differ. Additionally, the quality and proximity of alternative retail opportunities will influence actual VMT generated. A parking price increase may result in higher VMT reductions in a retail-oriented district than in an employment-oriented district, as shoppers have more destination options than employees have. Researchers must account for such effects in order to reduce the uncertainty in policy forecasts. In section 3, we propose a method to do just that.

2.5 Challenges in Attributing Community Transportation Emissions to Specific Policies

Several issues make measuring the effects of local policies far more challenging than measuring the effects of national policies. The first is that, while national geographic boundaries are roughly contiguous with the set of emissions that can be influenced through national authority, this is not the case at the local level. Locally, vehicles are free to travel between local jurisdictions, and policies at all jurisdictional levels can affect vehicle activity.

State governments that seek to hold local governments accountable for their GHG emissions will attempt to validly attribute emissions to local governments.

Local governments that seek to evaluate the performance of their actions will attempt to isolate and measure the effects of just their actions. Doing so requires that the inventory boundaries include only those emissions that can be validly attributed to a local government. However, the need for valid attribution complicates efforts to measure community-level GHG emissions. Valid attribution requires an understanding of the causal relationship between observed GHG emissions reductions and specific policies that have led to the reduction. Developing this understanding is difficult, as the proportion of GHG emissions a local government can affect with a given policy or set of policies varies by local authority, conditions, and specific properties of policy implementation.

A closer look at the attribution methods used to define the inventory boundaries in the transportation sector highlights how these boundary choices affect inventory results. Ganson (2008, 7–8, 9) uses a variety of boundaries to attribute local emissions from transportation:

1. GHGs from vehicles traveling within the geopolitical boundaries of the community
2. GHGs from all vehicle trips that end in the community
3. GHGs from all vehicle trips that begin in the community
4. One half each of methods 2 and 3.

These results can differ substantially. Figure 23.1 shows the totals for each of these attribution methods for Berkeley, California's 2005 transportation CO_2 inventory.

It is worth noting that none of these methods is capable of validly attributing emissions to a local government based on its authority to influence transportation through policymaking. A local government can better understand the magnitude of transportation emissions within its geopolitical boundaries using method 1. A local government could gain insight into how its transportation-demand management policies affect trip generation by using method 2 and tracking the changes

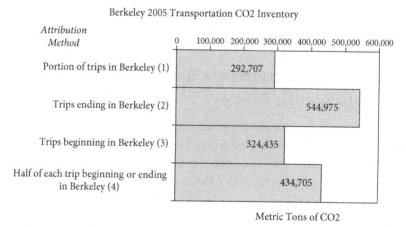

Figure 23.1 The Effects of Boundary Choice on Emissions
(Ganson 2008, 9)

over time. A local government could better understand how the city's transportation infrastructure investments affect mode choice for trips that begin in the city by using method 3. Method 4, which provides some limited insight into how local policies can affect emissions from both trip generation and trip attraction, does not establish a valid causal relationship between policies implemented by the local government and observed changes in emissions. In the next section, we propose a framework that is capable of overcoming these limitations.

3. MOVING THE FRONTIERS OF GHG MEASUREMENT FOR LOCAL PLACES

In this section, we describe potential approaches that are capable of meeting future policy and research needs. We have set forth above that current methods to inventory GHG emissions from within the geopolitical boundaries of a jurisdiction do not meet current needs for local GHG measurement. Researchers need new local measurement approaches to address and overcome these existing accuracy and attribution issues. The new approaches must allow researchers to determine the causal relationship between a policy and changes in GHG emissions. Without this ability, researchers and regulatory bodies will not be able to validly attribute GHG emissions to local governments.

In proposing a local measurement framework, we must first reexamine why stakeholders seek to measure GHG emissions from local government. Stakeholders seek to (1) identify the sources and (relative) magnitudes of local emissions; (2) compare the emissions between local governments (cross-sectional analysis); (3) compare the emissions for one local government by year (longitudinal analysis); and (4) seek to understand local policy effects; and (5) enforce multi-jurisdictional accountability schemes. Lifecycle approaches can be appropriate for (1) and (3) in understanding how local changes affect upstream and downstream emissions. Lifecycle approaches may also be appropriate for consumers to analyze the effects of their purchasing decisions. However, we assert that lifecycle analysis is not appropriate for (4) or (5), which depend on the policymaking authority of local governments.

3.1 Policy Effort: An Authority-Based Dimension for Local Inventory Boundaries

Determining a government's ability to affect emissions is important for policy analysis at all levels. However, its importance is more pronounced at the local level,

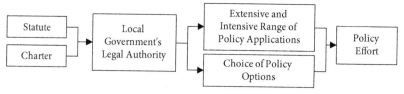

Figure 23.2 Deriving Policy Effort from Authority

where a there's a difference in the set of emissions attributable to activities within a geographic boundary and the set of emissions that local policy can affect.

A local government's legal authority determines the policies it can pursue to affect GHG emissions. These legal powers differ by country, state, or even city within a state. Legal authority defines not only the choices of policy options available but also the extent and application of each policy. These two factors combine to form our definition of *policy effort* (see figure 23.2).

We define *policy effort* as a point on a continuum of authority that ranges from laissez-faire to the full extent of legal authority to affect emissions (see figure 23.3). The quantity of emissions that can validly be attributed to a local government depends on the specific level of policy effort made. Accurate measures of policy effectiveness that are sensitive to a range of applications can define and compare the emissions quantities for any given level of policy effort through a scenario analysis (see section 3.3).

Each point on the continuum defines a set of bounds for extensive and intensive policy applications. Consider the simplified case of a regional government that has legal authority over a single policy option: congestion tolling for all on-road vehicles on regional highway and streets. In this case, congestion tolling policies can vary *extensively* (the number of roads to toll, how many lanes to toll on each) and *intensively* (the amount of the toll). The laissez-faire level of policy effort may be no congestion-based tolling of vehicles. An "ambitious but achievable" policy may result in the tolling of two lanes of each of the region's highways during peak hours, with carpools of three or more persons exempt from the toll. (For the sake of illustration, let's say this produces a 4 percent reduction in regional emissions from on-road transportation.) If the regional government exercises the full extent of its

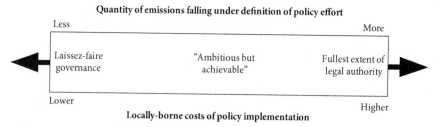

Figure 23.3 A Continuum of Policy Effort

legal authority, it implements congestion tolling on all highways and streets at all hours, which produces a 20 percent reduction in regional emissions from on-road transportation.

From this scenario analysis, we are able to determine the quantity of emissions attributable to this single-purpose regional congestion tolling authority. Under the "ambitious but achievable" definition of policy effort, 4 percent of regional transportation emissions would be attributed to the regional government. Under the "full extent" definition of the regional government's legal authority, 20 percent of emissions are attributed to the regional government. Under both definitions, all or a portion of these emissions may overlap with emissions that can validly be attributed to other levels of government and nongovernmental factors.

The framework outlined in figure 23.4 can be used to further classify local government emissions sources and examples of strategies to reduce GHG emissions by operational boundaries (scope), as well as the manner in which the emissions can be affected. The quantities of GHG emissions for each source or strategy would vary based on the level of policy effort.

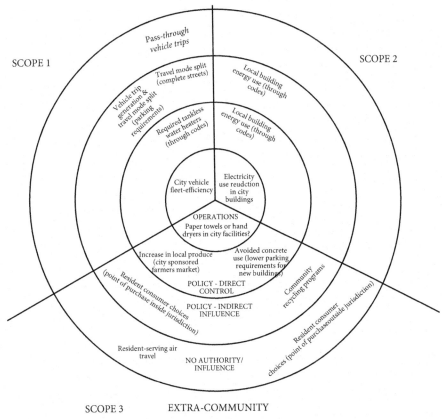

Figure 23.4 Local Emissions Sources and Strategies, Classified by Scope and Means of Influence

3.1 Policy Effort as a Political Decision

The definition of *policy effort* used to attribute emissions is ultimately a political decision made using ex-ante forecasts of policy effects. Policymakers must decide on the set of parameters that define how a local government utilizes its authority to affect emissions, understanding that, in many cases, there is a trade-off between the quantity of emissions reductions and the locally borne costs of implementation. California policymakers considered this trade-off in determining the emissions targets for SB 375. To set regional reduction targets, the California Air Resources Board used a scenario analysis to forecast possible reductions at various levels of local policy effort (California Air Resources Board 2010). The California Air Resources Board sought to determine the potential set of reductions as those which were both "ambitious" and "achievable" (Regional Targets Advisory Committee 2009b, 26).

3.2 Practical Challenges to Determining the Range of Potential Policy Effort

Local governments face many challenges in developing a valid GHG emissions attribution methodology. The first is that local governments are able to control or influence only a portion of the GHGs emitted within their geopolitical boundaries. In virtually all cases, local governments will lack the legal authority to affect 100 percent of emissions within their geographic boundaries. Consider the extreme case. A local government's municipal utility could provide 100 percent of the community's electricity needs through zero emissions generation. However, if the local government receives state transportation funding, it could not restrict road access to only electric vehicles that draw power from this zero emissions generation. In the more practical case, local and regional governments typically have authority over the provision of municipal services, land-use regulations, and some aspects transportation. Policies that affect vehicle and fuel technology are under the authority of the state[9] or federal government. Figure 23.5 below illustrates the transportation and land-use policies that typically fall under the authority of each level of government.

   The second challenge is that local policymaking can affect emissions outside of a jurisdiction's geographic boundaries. Subnational transportation networks are open, and vehicles can freely travel between geopolitical boundaries. Thus, a transportation policy implemented in one city may affect transportation emissions in a neighboring city. Consider the earlier example of the city that looks to increase the price to park in its central business district. A corresponding reduction in single occupant vehicle trips will reduce emissions within the geopolitical boundaries of the cities where trips originate or pass-through. However, the increase in parking price could also increase emissions in a neighboring city that experiences an increase in retail-oriented trips. Accounting for this unintended spillover of

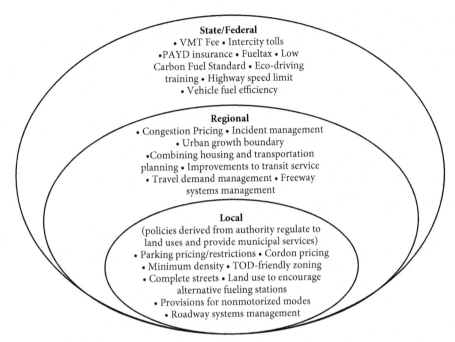

State/Federal
• VMT Fee • Intercity tolls
•PAYD insurance • Fueltax • Low
Carbon Fuel Standard • Eco-driving
training • Highway speed limit
• Vehicle fuel efficiency

Regional
• Congestion Pricing • Incident management
• Urban growth boundary
•Combining housing and transportation
planning • Improvements to transit service
• Travel demand management • Freeway
systems management

Local
(policies derived from authority regulate to
land uses and provide municipal services)
• Parking pricing/restrictions • Cordon pricing
• Minimum density • TOD-friendly zoning
• Complete streets • Land use to encourage
alternative fueling stations
• Provisions for nonmotorized modes
• Roadway systems management

Figure 23.5 Multiple Layers of Policy Influence Emissions in the Transportation Sector

emissions from one jurisdiction to another, or *emissions leakage*, is necessary to make claims that a city policy led to an absolute reduction in global GHG emissions. Accurately accounting for these spillover effects without before and after observations from the implementing and neighboring jurisdictions is prohibitively difficult.

A third challenge occurs if governments at multiple levels concurrently pursue GHG reduction policies. In this case, disentangling the effects of supra-local policy from local policy is difficult. For example, imagine that concurrently:

- The federal government introduces new sustainable communities lending standards that factor in a neighborhood's transportation costs into FHA-backed loans
- The state government implements a pay-as-you-drive insurance scheme, which increases the marginal cost of a mile driven
- The local government pursues a land-use plan that supports densification around transit stations

Observers may see reductions in travel demand and GHG emissions under this scenario. However, it would be impossible to attribute these reductions to a specific policy given a single local data point, such as project-level or community-level emissions. Attributing each policy's marginal contribution to any observed emissions reductions would likely require cross-sectional data to compare observations in different states and localities, controlling for various combinations of state and local policies. In a real-world scenario, the combination of many local, state, and federal policies implemented simultaneously would further complicate efforts to evaluate the effectiveness of any single policy, or to validly attribute the effects of a set of policies to a single jurisdiction. The GHG emissions measurement methodology California uses to determine SB 375 compliance controls for the current and future effects of two state policies, the Low Carbon Fuel Standard and the Pavley Vehicle Efficiency Standards, but does not control for other extra-local policies.

The fourth and final challenge is that some factors that influence emissions are not subject to the direct authority of governments. Governments at all levels have limited ability to influence certain factors, including:

- Economic activity influences the quantity of travel and energy demanded
- Market-based changes in fuel prices affect the quantity of fuel demanded
- Market-based changes in national, regional, or local real estate preferences
- Demographic changes that affect per capita travel through changes in housing and travel preferences

Researchers must address these four challenges in order to validly attribute observed changes in vehicle activity or GHG emissions to specific policies.

3.3 New Methods to Increase Spatial and Temporal Resolution of Data to Increase Measurement Accuracy

The use of spatially and temporally explicit activity data can lead to more accurate ex-post emissions measurement and ex-ante emissions forecasting. More accurate measurement is necessary to quantify the GHG emission reductions possible under a given level of policy effort. In sections 3.4 and 3.5, we detail the measurement methods needed to produce accurate, high-resolution emissions data. In sections 3.6 and 3.7, we look at how these measurement methods can support the evaluation necessary to validly attribute changes in behavior to a specific policy.

3.4 New Methods for Accurately Measuring Local Electricity Emissions

In many cases, state and local governments import electricity from outside of their jurisdiction. Accounting for these transfers requires the use of a consumption-based approach to measuring greenhouse gas emissions from subnational electricity use. To adjust for regional differences in electricity generation profiles, cities and regions in the United States use subregional emissions factors. Each year, the U.S. EPA publishes eGRID, a database of annual emission factors per megawatt hour of consumption for different electrical grid regions in the United States (U.S. Environmental Protection Agency 2010). For communities served by a regional grid network, the emission factor is based on the total end-user grid electricity consumption divided by the total production-based emissions for carbon dioxide, methane, and nitrous oxide.[10] This method implicitly accounts for electricity lost in transmission and due to other system inefficiencies.

However, common assumptions employed in consumption-based methods often introduce an imprecision not present with production-based methods. First, emission factors vary based on the time of day and day of year because the mix of electric-generating units deployed to meet electricity demand changes in real time. The U.S. EPA's eGRID emission factors express the annual average GHG emissions for electricity generated and delivered within a regional grid network.

The difference between real-time emission factors and annual average emission factors can be significant for some grid regions. In the UK, the National Grid Balanced Mechanism Reporting Services publishes emission factors at five-minute intervals (Real Time Carbon 2009). Over a 24-hour period, the average CO_2 emission factor in the UK was 451.9 grams/kWh (Real Time Carbon 2010). However, during this time emissions ranged from a low of 365.83 grams/kWh at 4:55 on September 20 to a high of 545.82 grams/kWh at 17:35 on September 20. Off-peak overnight emissions are between 25 and 33 percent lower than peak daytime emissions.

The use of regional average annual emission factors limits the ability to measure the GHG reduction effects of some local programs. Some strategies to reduce GHG emissions from electricity consumption may not reduce aggregate electricity demand but, rather, shift demand to a different time of day. For example, a local utility could develop an incentive program to shift some electricity demand from peak hours to off-peak hours. The primary goal of this program could be to displace peak electricity load, which is more expensive to deliver. Smart-grid connected appliances could automatically perform this load-balancing function. A smart-grid connected washing machine could delay the start of its cycle from the late afternoon until after 11 P.M., when the marginal cost of electricity is cheaper. However, the resulting emissions reductions would not be observable using the current practice of annual emission factors. The program's effect could be observable through a slight reduction in overall GHG emissions produced to meet a given level of annual electricity demand (expressed through a reduction in the annual regional emission factor). Yet, this reduction would be diluted by aggregate regional energy consumption. The real effect of the program on emissions caused by activities within the community would not be measurable. Based on the example from the UK, this could be in the range of a 20 to 33 percent reduction in GHG emissions per unit of time-shifted demand.

Some local governments have taken steps to improve the precision of electricity emission factors they use. New York City created its own emission factors for electricity consumed in the city based on data from the New York Independent System Operator and Consolidated Edison (New York City Office of Long-Term

Planning And Sustainability 2010).[11] However, these are still annual emission factors. The city will not be able to precisely measure the GHG emissions effects of programs that time-shift electricity demand.

While utilities have improved the geographic resolution of their emission factors, they have made fewer advances to increase the temporal resolution for their emission factors. No guidelines exist to create hourly or subhourly emission factors. However, utilities currently possess the real-time data on owned and purchased generation, transmission, and consumption necessary to produce the data. The growth of smart-metering technology, capable of supporting time-of-day electricity pricing,[12] may support the development to use time-of-day emission factors. Pricing GHG emissions through a mechanism such as cap-and-trade will increase the cost of fossil-fuel generation and further motivate the need for time-of-day emissions accounting.

3.5 New Methods for Accurately Measuring the Effects of Transportation Policies

Moving toward higher resolution data in the transportation sector is more challenging. Commonly employed methods rely on annual average daily traffic volumes, multiplied by roadway segment lengths and an annual scaling factor. This method has neither the spatial nor the temporal resolution to demonstrate changes in emissions resulting from improvements in vehicle or system efficiency, or to attribute changes in observed emissions to a specific policy. Annual average daily traffic, like most activity-based travel methods, relies on VMT to express quantity. However, VMT is a measure of distance and cannot be spatially or temporally explicit. It is not possible to describe miles traveled at a point in time or point in space. Higher resolution travel data will require a new metric to express vehicle activity.

Modal emissions models have two key inputs, vehicle hours operating (VHO) and vehicle specific power (VSP). The VSP data are classified into one of many bins that describe vehicle engine load. The VSP data are temporally independent, and can be spatially explicit. The VHO adds the dimension of time to the function, from a second to over a year; VHO represents the duration a vehicle engine operates at different VSP bin profiles.

Researchers have found that modal emissions models, such as the U.S. EPA's MOVES,[13] are more precise in accounting for congestion, road grade, and other factors that can affect vehicle engine load but not average speed. Existing macro-level models do not capture the full impact of traffic flow efficiency and its impact on fuel consumption (California Transportation Commission 2010, 54). Using a modal emissions model such as MOVES will allow policymakers to measure the GHG reduction effects of congestion reduction policies. Barth and Boriboonsomsin (2008) found that a microscale modal emissions model that is sensitive to second-by-second variations of fuel consumption and emissions is more appropriate for measuring emissions from congestion than are existing regional VMT-based emissions inventory models. Song, Eisinger, and Niemeier (2009, 14) find that MOVES "should be more responsive to variations in traffic dynamics and roadway congestion levels" than VMT-based models.

3.6 Using New Methods to Measure Policy Effectiveness and Validly Attribute Emissions

The methods required to quantify potential GHG reductions for a given level of policy effort and to measure the potential effectiveness of policies are one and the same. Without the ability to forecast the potential effectiveness of policies that the local government might implement, researchers cannot measure their authority in GHG terms. In the following sections, we outline new methods to determine policy effectiveness and quantify authority in the transportation sector, where past measurement challenges have been greatest.

In implementing the next generation of measurement methods, researchers and practitioners should be cognizant of factors that delay adoption in practice, such as complexity and cost. While the state of the art in modeling shows promise in forecasting GHG emissions from transportation, there is a large gap between these advanced models and the models employed in practice. In the implementation process for California's SB 375, MPOs self-assessed how their models responded to the various strategies that an MPO might choose to pursue under SB 375 implementation. At the time of the survey, no region had a model that was reasonably sensitive to all policies or factors that an MPO might choose to pursue (Regional Targets Advisory Committee 2009a).

3.7 New Approach to Valid Ex-post Emissions Measurement for Transportation

Past travel behavior research has often focused on the relationship between a policy and metrics such as VMT, trip generation, parking demand, or modal split. These metrics are directly observable, whereas travel decision making can be observed only through costly travel diaries and similarly cumbersome methods. Researchers use statistical methods to infer how a policy affects aggregate individual travel behavior, as expressed through the metric. Researchers face greater challenges in describing these individual behavioral effects than in describing the aggregated metric. Describing these behavioral effects necessitates sufficient control variables and observations to make statistically valid inferences.

Advancements in computing power and data-collection technologies will support the proliferation of advanced statistical models capable of describing how policies affect individual travel behavior. To translate these behavioral changes into emissions, researchers must describe the following:

$$\text{Policy}_A \rightarrow \sum \Delta \text{ Individual Travel Behavior}_\alpha \rightarrow \begin{cases} \Delta \text{Vehicle Specific Power}_{(x,y)} \\ \Delta \text{Vehicle Hours Operating}_{(x,y)} \end{cases} \xrightarrow{\text{yields}} \Delta \text{GHG}_{(x,y)}$$

The function uses a modal emissions framework to assess emissions changes at a specific geographic location (x,y) for a discrete period of time. The geographic location (x,y) may be inside or outside of the jurisdiction that implemented Policy$_A$. The result, spatially and temporally explicit GHG, has its limitations. Though this metric is necessary to measure GHG emissions from vehicles, it is vehicle-centric and does not describe the movement of persons through space and time or accessibility. Researchers will want to capture the full effects of Policy$_A$ on individual travel behavior, including changes in the utilization of non-GHG emitting modes to accomplish trip making.

3.8 Collection and Use of Panel Data to Make Valid Inferences for Transportation

A new, robust data-collection approach is needed both to facilitate a sufficient sample size of travel observations and to make data produced in any study useful to other studies. Existing ex-post data-collection methods do not support the approach outlined in the previous section. Existing methods produce cross-sectional data, which describe observed policy effects in multiple places, or time series data, which describe changes in time for a single place. A combination of cross-sectional and time series data is needed for new measurement approaches capable of meeting current travel behavior and GHG measurement needs. This multi-dimensional data, or panel data, should describe changes in vehicle operations, local conditions, exogenous factors, and policy treatments—and other variables for many places over time.

Such an approach will likely necessitate a standardized ex-post measurement methodology, with common requirements for control variables, data quality, and reporting formats. This approach will significantly expand on existing parking and trip-generation methodologies for Institute of Transportation Engineers studies. At a minimum, input variables will describe the area being studied, the policy or policies being implemented in that area, the observed results in terms of individual behavior expressed as travel activity, and associated emissions changes.

Once a standardized ex-post measurement method is in place and sufficient observations are available, researchers can then apply robust statistical models capable of disentangling policy effects from other observable trends in the data. Panel data allow researchers to control for variations in local conditions, external policy effects, and different policy treatments to describe the observed statistical relationship between a policy and its GHG effects.

It is likely that robust evaluation models will be necessary to process panel data and describe statistical relationship of policy effectiveness. These statistics include, but are not limited to:

- Mean, central tendencies, and variance (distribution) of the expected GHG[14] reduction impacts of Policy$_A$.
- Relationship of $\Delta GHG_{(x,y)}$ attributable to Policy$_A$ to variables external to the policy, such as local incomes, urban form, fuel prices, area rents, local economic activity.
- Relationship of $\Delta GHG_{(x,y)}$ attributable to Policy$_A$ to several intensive and extensive policy variables (such as level of implementation, geographic area effected, level of pricing, percent of population effected by policy)
- Covariance of $\Delta GHG_{(x,y)}$ attributable to Policy$_A$ to ΔGHG emissions attributable to Policy$_B$, and groups of policies to other groups of policies.

As the input data-collection and processing methods are standardized, researchers can then take steps to automate some steps of the process. Automation will make the comprehensive policy and program evaluation more accessible, for use in a wider array of ex-post measurement applications, which will increase the number of available observations.

4. CONCLUSION AND NEXT STEPS

We have set forth a framework for local GHG measurement that meets many current and future local GHG emissions measurement needs. Increasing the spatial and temporal resolution of measurement data can assist in more precisely measuring policy effects. Employing a new ex-post evaluation framework using panel data can strengthen our ability to make valid ex-post conclusions about how a policy affected GHG emissions. Ex-post data on policy effectiveness, combined with knowledge on how that policy is sensitive to local conditions, other policies, and an extensive and intensive range of applications, is essential to improving the accuracy of GHG forecasts and ex-ante quantifications of emissions for a given level of policy effort used to attribute emissions to local governments. Policymakers seek this information in implementing policies to reduce greenhouse gas emissions.

We stress that while we have introduced a framework, or rubric, for under-standing local GHG through the lens of authority and policy effort, we caution the reader away from the notion that any of the methods we have outlined are a per-manent solution for local GHG measurement. The field of GHG emissions mea-surement is evolving with the introduction of new methods and sources of data that can improve measurement precision. In conclusion, we fully expect that future measurement methods and boundary definitions will expand on our framework to meet these current and future measurement needs.

NOTES

1. Such as the Local Government Operations Protocol (California Air Resources Board, 2008) and World Resources Institute (2004).
2. There are six internationally recognized GHGs. Some inventories include CO_2 only or CO_2, CH_4, and N_2O only. Complete inventories include CO_2, CH_4, N_2O, HFC, PFC, and SF_6. Each GHG has a different global warming potential, and multi-gas inventory totals are usually expressed as CO_2-equivalence or CO_2E.
3. In some cases, a national inventory may include Scope 2 emissions, but the IPCC guidelines only account for scope 1 emissions.
4. California Air Resources Board (2008).
5. These sectors include buildings and other facilities, streetlights and traffic signals, water delivery facilities, wastewater facilities, port facilities, airport facilities, vehicle fleet, transit fleet, power generation facilities, and solid waste facilities.
6. Transit Investment for Greenhouse Gas and Energy Reduction.
7. AB 32: California's Global Warming Solutions Act of 2006 establishes the state's goal to reduce GHG emissions to 1990 levels by 2020. California's Executive Order S-3-05 establishes a goal of 80 percent below 1990 levels by 2050.
8. Metropolitan planning organizations commit to transportation projects and policy through their regional transportation plans. Local governments commit to land-use strategies through the regional housing allocation plans and updates to city and county general plan land-use elements.
9. Section 209 of the Clean Air Act grants California the right to exceed federal emis-sion standards. Any U.S. state is free to adopt the California standards, but not to adopt its own.
10. CO_2, CH_4, and N_2O are produced in the combustion process. SF_6 emissions may result from the transmission network. Emissions of HFCs and PFCs are typically not asso-ciated with electricity production and distribution.
11. Recently published guidelines will facilitate the transition to utility-specific emission factors. Utilities can use the Climate Registry's (2009) Electric Power Sector Protocol to create a utility-specific annual emission factor that is more accurate than a regional emission factor.
12. Time-of-day pricing introduces an incentive for conservation at times when it is most needed, during peak hours and system emergencies.
13. This stands for MOtor Vehicle Emissions Simulator.
14. Note that while changes in GHG emissions is necessary for climate change policy, this is one of many performance outcomes that can be measured and modeled. Other outcomes include changes in travel behavior and other policy impacts (co-benefits).

References

Barth, Matthew, and Kanok Boriboonsomsin. 2008. "Real-World Carbon Dioxide Impacts of Traffic Congestion." *Transportation Research Record: Journal of the Transportation Research Board* (Transportation Research Board of the National Academies) 2058:163–71.

California Air Resources Board. 2008. *Local Government Operations Protocol.* Los Angeles: California Climate Action Registry.

California Air Resources Board. 2010. "Proposed Regional Greenhouse Gas Emission Reduction Targets for Automobiles and Light Trucks Pursuant to Senate Bill 375." Available at: http://arb.ca.gov/cc/sb375/staffreport_sb375080910.pdf; accessed August 9, 2010.

California Transportation Commission. 2010. "2010 California Regional Transportation Plan Guidelines." Available at: http://www.catc.ca.gov/programs/rtp/2010_RTP_Guidelines.pdf; accessed June 2010.

Cambridge Systematic. 2009. *Moving Cooler: An Analysis of Transportation Strategies for Reducing Greenhouse Gas Emissions.* Washington, DC: Urban Land Institute.

Climate Registry. 2009. *Electric Power Sector Protocol.* Los Angeles: Climate Registry.

Deakin, Elizabeth, G. Harvey, R. Pozdena, and G. Yarema. 1996. *Transportation Pricing Strategies for California: An Assessment of Congestion, Emissions, Energy and Equity Impacts.* Sacramento: California Air Resources Board.

Ewing, Reid, Keith Bartholomew, Steve Winkelman, Jerry Walters, and Don Chen. 2008. *Growing Cooler: The Evidence on Urban Development and Climate Change.* Washington, DC: Urban Land Institute.

Ganson, Christopher. 2008. "The Transportation Greenhouse Gas Inventory: A First Step Toward City-Driven Emissions Rationalization." UCTC Research Paper No. 879, University of California Transportation Center.

Granade, Hannah Choi, Jon Creyts, Anton Derkach, Philip Farese, Scott Nyquist, and Ken Ostrowski. 2009. *Unlocking Energy Efficiency in the U.S. Economy.* McKinsey. Available at: http://www.mckinsey.com/en/Client_Service/Electric_Power_and_Natural_Gas/Latest_thinking/~/media/McKinsey/dotcom/client_service/EPNG/PDFs/Unlocking%20energy%20efficiency/US_energy_efficiency_full_report.ashx; accessed August 2010.

Intergovernmental Panel on Climate Change. 2006. *2006 IPCC Guidelines for National Greenhouse Gas Inventories.* Hayama, Japan: Institute for Global Environmental Strategies.

Kennedy, Christopher, Julia Steinberger, Barrie Gasson, Yvonne Hansen, Timothy Hillman, Miroslav Havránek, Diane Pataki, Aumnad Phdungsilp, Anu Ramsaswami, and Gara Villalba Mendez. 2010. "Methodology for Inventorying Greenhouse Gas Emissions from Global Cities." *Energy Policy* 38(9): 4828–37.

Larsen, H. N., and E. G. Hertwich. 2009. "The Case for Consumption-Based Accounting of Greenhouse Gas Emissions to Promote Local Climate Action." *Environmental Science and Policy* 12(7): 791–98.

New York City Office of Long-Term Planning And Sustainability. 2010. *Inventory of New York City Greenhouse Gas Emissions.* New York. Available at: http://www.nyc.gov/html/om/pdf/2010/pr412-10_report.pdf; accessed August 14, 2010.

Ramaswami, Anu, Tim Hillman, Bruce Janson, Mark Reiner, and Gregg Thomas.2008. "A Demand-Centered, Hybrid Life-Cycle Methodology for City-Scale Greenhouse Gas Inventories." *Environmental Science and Technology* 42(17): 6455–61.

Randolph, John, and Damian Pitt. 2008. "Blacksburg Energy and Greenhouse Gas Emissions Inventory." Report to the Mayor's Task Force on Sustainability and Climate Change, Sustainable Blacksburg Steering Committee, and Virginia Tech Committee on Energy and Sustainability, Blacksburg, VA.

Real Time Carbon. 2009. "Real Time Carbon Project Methodology." Available at: http://www.realtimecarbon.org/resources/RealtimeCarbonMethodology.pdf; accessed September 21, 2010.

Real Time Carbon. 2010 . "Carbon Now." Available at: http://www.realtimecarbon.org/; accessed September 20, 2010.

Regional Targets Advisory Committee. 2009a. "MPO Self-Assessment of Current Modeling Capacity and Data Collection Programs." Available at: http://www.arb.ca.gov/cc/sb375/rtac/meetings/050509/mpoassessmentupdate.pdf.

Regional Targets Advisory Committee. 2009b. Recommendations of the Regional Targets Advisory Committee (RTAC) Pursuant to Senate Bill 375, California Air Resources Board, Sacramento, CA.

Shoup, Donald. 2005. *The High Cost of Free Parking.* Chicago: APA Planners Press.

Shoup, Donald. 2006. "Cruising for Parking." *Transport Policy* 13(6): 479–86.

Song, Bai, Douglas Eisinger, and Deb Niemeier. 2009. "MOVES vs. EMFAC: A Comparative Assessment Based on a Los Angeles County Case Study." *TRB 88th Annual Meeting Compendium of Papers DVD*. Washington, DC: Transportation Research Board.

Transportation Research Board. 2009. *Driving and the Built Environment: The Effects of Compact Development on Motorized Travel, Energy Use, and CO2 Emissions.* Vol. Special Report 298. Washington, DC: National Research Council of the National Academies.

U.S. Environmental Protection Agency. 2010. *eGRIDweb Application.* Washington, DC: U.S. Environmental Protection Agency.

Vaca, Erin, and J. Richard Kuzmyak. 2005. "Parking Pricing and Fees." In *Traveler Response to Transportation System Changes,* by Transit Cooperative Research Program, Richard H. Pratt, editor. Washington, DC: Transportation Research Board.

World Resources Institute. 2004. "The Greenhouse Gas Protocol: A Corporate Accounting and Reporting Standard ," rev. ed. World Business Council for Sustainable Development. Available at: http://www.ghgprotocol.org/files/ghgp/public/ghg-protocol-revised.pdf.

CHAPTER 24

THE EVOLVING ROLE OF COMMUNITY ECONOMIC DEVELOPMENT IN PLANNING

KAREN CHAPPLE

1. INTRODUCTION

THE subfield of community and economic development (CED) addresses efforts to enhance local economies in order to increase wealth, income, and employment, as well as to improve local quality of life. As is implicit in its title, CED is primarily concerned with the normative question of who benefits from economic development—that is, how planning and policy can improve the capacity of disadvantaged local residents to participate in the mainstream economy. Such economic opportunity is not inherent in local economic growth, but comes out of intentional actions and relationships that connect marginalized populations, communities, and places to economic activity (Giloth 2006).

The field of CED emerged out of the convergence of the fields of economic development and community development in the 1970s. As waves of economic restructuring and government spending cutbacks hit cities, local interest in economic development increased. At the same time, community development sought to expand its domain from the "bricks and mortar" development that had been its focus. Thus, CED came late to urban planning; as late as the 1960s, no U.S. planning school taught local economic development (though regional planning dealt in part with economic issues); and few municipal planning departments connected their work to economic development goals and methods (Teitz 2008). Likewise, mainstream planners had little regard for community development, which had essentially splintered off into social welfare after the Progressive Era.

In many ways, the late entry of the subfield created an uneasy relationship between CED and planning. Physical planners had long taken growth for granted. Since economic growth was exogenous to population models and land-use plans, planning needed only to accommodate it, not foster it. Adding the onus of economic development to planning presented new challenges. A planning conversation that had previously been about how to guide growth had to shift to how to redistribute the benefits of growth—or even deal with decline. This, in turn, forced planners to address topics—poverty, race, empowerment—that were a little uncomfortable, particularly given past failures such as urban renewal. Even the conventional tools of planning—subdivision development, growth management, eminent domain—seemed a little blunt in the face of the new social and economic issues that planners faced. Raising the question of who benefits also brought new political attention to planning, creating a climate in which political exigencies often outweigh criteria of efficiency and equity (Dewar 1998; Wolman 1996).

The challenge of integrating CED into planning, though potentially present in many political contexts, is particularly acute in the United States because of its liberal governance mode. Even as the subfield of CED was crystallizing out of the 1960s War on Poverty, the public sector was increasing its reliance on extra-governmental actors to carry out policies and programs. The gradual retrenchment of the welfare state in the 1970s and 1980s was accompanied by the outsourcing of functions to both the market and nonprofit sectors (Smith and Lipsky 1993). Arguably, this framework of state-market-nonprofit relationships created a set of local institutions more responsive to the needs of disadvantaged constituents. Yet, it has meant that the service delivery system for CED programs is largely separate from the local government apparatus for planning. Plus, with little left of the labor-management social bargain of the 1950s, much less the social safety net, the growing income inequality in the United States creates much more of a need for CED than in other advanced industrial countries.

In this chapter, I begin with an overview of the economic context that has forced the launch and growth of CED. I then examine practices at the heart of today's CED, the core toolkit for planners entering the subfield. Since no field is without its ongoing controversy, the next section outlines a number of debates that, despite years of experimentation, have not yet been resolved. A final section examines issues on the horizon for this ever-evolving and emergent practice.

2. CONTEXT

Various forms of CED existed in the United States and other industrializing countries in the nineteenth century, though economic development and community development remained separate domains. Early efforts at infrastructure development—particularly roads and canals—were meant to foster economic growth; for instance, the 1808 Gallatin Plan explicitly linked transport investment to growth prospects for the United States (Goodrich 1958). Local and state governments in the United States—unlike their counterparts in Europe—played an aggressively entrepreneurial role in attracting and helping to subsidize economic development (Sbragia 1996). In contrast, community development conventionally finds its roots in the efforts of pioneers, mainly women, who sought to tackle poverty directly in the slums of New York and Chicago in the last quarter of the nineteenth century (Wirka 1996). The settlement house movement attempted to assuage the worst excesses of urban industrial capitalism by bringing new immigrants into the American mainstream.

But it was the demise of the labor–management social bargain that fueled the rise of the joint subfield as we know it today (Osterman 1999). After World War II, the United States emerged as the world's dominant economic power, with a huge internal market and high and rising labor productivity. Led by manufacturing growth, the oligopolistic U.S. economy maintained labor peace by sharing the productivity "dividend" among its high- and low-skilled workers. The result was rising living standards and income equality—as well as high expectations for the economy.

After 1970, profound changes occurred, with much debate about their causes. Whether due primarily to the 1973 collapse of the Bretton-Woods system of monetary controls, the rise of international competition in manufacturing, the sectoral shift toward information technology and low-wage service industries, or the influx of women into the workforce, what was clear was that the postwar boom was over and a period of rapidly increasing income inequality had begun. From 1979 to 2005, income growth for the poorest households grew by only 1.3 percent pretax, while income for the top fifth grew 75 percent and households in the top 1percent saw their income triple over these years, up by 200 percent pretax (Mishel, Bernstein, and Allegretto 2006).

Though globalization and technology indeed appear to be the main culprits, the situation in U.S. cities was more complicated than suggested by the images of the "giant sucking sound" of free trade (as labeled by presidential candidate Ross Perot) and the rise of "symbolic analysts" to replace manufacturing jobs (Reich 1991). Service sectors never experienced the productivity growth of manufacturing, meaning that instead of sharing the dividend, firms obtained profits and bolstered investor confidence by cutting labor costs. Large-scale labor force detachment and discouragement was one result. Cyclical fluctuations (in 1979–81, 1990–93, and 2001–2) exacerbated structural shifts, with plant closures as the most immediate impact.

But most important, differences in local and regional abilities to respond to restructuring magnified conditions of inequality. Overall, there was an acceleration of local shifts in population and industrial production from the Northeast and Midwest (Rustbelt) to the South and West (Sunbelt), which left older regions, particularly those specialized in manufacturing, vulnerable. Federal policies underwrote the inefficient extension of infrastructure into the suburbs and subsidized business relocation, ignoring sunk costs in infrastructure and housing in the shrinking cities left behind (Dreier, Mollenkopf, and Swanstrom 2004). Within metropolitan regions, the older inner cities and suburbs found themselves ill-equipped to reconfigure their obsolete sites and compete for new businesses.

Meanwhile, local fiscal stress also constrained the opportunity space for cities. An era of federal program devolution and fiscal federalism had begun under Richard Nixon. From the 1970s on, the federal government consolidated its categorical grant program into larger block grant programs (such as the Community Development Block Grant [CDBG] program) administered by the states. The increase in state discretionary powers over policy direction and program implementation was in theory to increase program efficiency and responsiveness, but in practice was accompanied by unfunded mandates that many cities struggled to meet. Meanwhile, a national citizens' tax reform movement (most notoriously, Proposition 13 in California) limited the ability of cities to raise more revenue through the property and sales taxes they depend on.

At the same time, a new program and policy apparatus was slowly emerging to address inequality through both community and economic development. Already, largely in response to the social upheavals of the mid-1960s, Lyndon Johnson had expanded the government's role in social welfare from education to health care to economic opportunity generally. Community development, which had been largely the domain of political advocacy groups following Saul Alinsky, suddenly became the focus of federal funding through Model Cities and the array of programs around it. By the 1970s, a parallel world of nonprofit and local governmental agencies had emerged. Moreover, as cities targeted particular neighborhoods for poverty alleviation efforts, and community development corporations (CDCs) emerged to provide economic opportunity (and soon, housing), the community development field took on more of an economic focus. As the decade saw a parade of federal programs that attempted to mitigate the effects of economic shocks—from the direct employment subsidies under CETA, to project subsidies under UDAG—city governments created organizational vehicles to manage them, and thus built local capacity and leadership. In academia, policy and planning programs began cobbling together a new CED curriculum, building on development studies and social policy courses (Teitz 2008).

With this CED infrastructure in place, the subsequent decades of government retrenchment were difficult, but not devastating. The budget cuts of the Reagan era, followed by the further erosion of the social safety net in the '90s and '00s, were met by new capacity and expansion in the third sector (Salamon 2003). Less hampered by bureaucratic silos, the new organizations further bolstered the connection between community and economic development. Part of the integration was by necessity. Community-based organizations (CBOs) and CDCs lost funding for social programs and organizing, and sought to move beyond "bricks and mortar" housing development into programs that built community economic capacity or even a profit-making double bottom line (Stoutland 1999). Simultaneously, economic development organizations gained interest in endogenous approaches, turning inward to local entrepreneurial capacity (Eisinger 1988). Though the ongoing CED activity hardly compensated for the government cutbacks—just for instance, funding for job training declined 75 percent from 1978 to 2000 (Giloth 2004a)—it did indicate that organizational seeds planted in earlier decades had come to fruition.

Also at this point, the trajectory of the subfield in the United States began to depart definitively from that in other countries. Although the growth of the nonprofit sector in advanced industrialized countries paralleled that in the United States, its role has varied. In social democracies, where the welfare state stayed largely intact, the nonprofit sector has complemented the public sector, while the advent of neoliberalism in other countries has meant that nonprofits substituted for government, in some cases competing with the private sector and tightening budgets (Anheier and Salamon 2006). Only developing countries see a significant share of nonprofit activity devoted to development, and owing to the strong role of the state in many countries, only a small share of nonprofits provide services (Anheier and Salamon 2006). For the most part, functions related to community and economic development have remained within government, and though new interest in "workfare" programs linked some social programming to economic development, the two areas largely have stayed separate.

Just as CED has (arguably) come of age, its domain is shifting. There continues to be a need to develop long-term strategies to help communities and individuals deal with rising income inequality, disinvestment, and restructuring. However, issues of community economic stability and family economic security are no longer contained within the kinds of impoverished neighborhoods that the War on Poverty targeted. Instead, the increasing suburbanization of poverty shifts the policy focus from core urban areas to the entire metropolitan region (Berube and Frey 2002). Likewise, with the very stability of the middle class at stake, the need for economic development programs has extended well beyond households under the poverty line.

3. THE STATE OF THE ART IN COMMUNITY AND ECONOMIC DEVELOPMENT

Given the political stakes in CED, the programs that predominate may serve political purposes as much as—or more than—CED goals. Nevertheless, there are clearly successful CED practices today that are "investing in people through place" via strategies that foster job opportunities, build assets and wealth, and improve neighborhood economies and quality of life (Giloth 2007). Decades of experience with solely place- or people-focused programs have shown that conceptualizing CED as an either-place-or-people proposition falls short (Crane and Manville 2008). Place-based programs targeting disadvantaged neighborhoods, such as enterprise zones, fail to benefit local residents consistently, while people-based approaches such as human capital development promote individual mobility at the expense of community goods, resulting in inefficient use of land and inequitable distribution of amenities. A more comprehensive approach targets individuals through jobs and asset-building approaches, but recognizes that investment in place makes economic benefits more accessible and provides the local public goods, both services and community, that improve life chances for neighborhood residents. Robert Giloth (2006, 6) has characterized this approach as "neighborhood saturation": "It is about how people-focused interventions and relationships attain neighborhood saturation so that the immediate environment of family-strengthening opportunities and behaviors is transformed."

As a hybrid of economic development and social policy, CED usually remains administratively separate from planning, and to a much greater extent, its implementation occurs outside of government agencies. The landscape of CED actors cuts across geographies and sectors: it includes municipal city halls and community development, planning, redevelopment, and social service agencies; stand-alone CBOs, CDCs, and community development financial institutions (CDFIs); local labor and faith-based organizations; government- or business-led economic development organizations (such as economic development corporations or chambers of commerce); and their counterparts at county, state, and federal levels. An influential private-sector support industry includes site-location consultants, bond counsel, redevelopment lawyers, economics consulting firms, and others. Given this crowded field of stakeholders, the public sector often ends up following the lead of private and nonprofit sector actors even as it takes credit for positive impacts.

The following examines some of the practices at the heart of the CED subfield today. This is not meant to be a comprehensive description. Rather, it selects the proven approaches that are continuing to evolve. Largely left out are legacy CED programs that may continue out of inertia or political concerns, but are not particularly effective, such as enterprise zone programs or reverse commuting programs to improve access to jobs (U.S. Government Accountability Office [GAO] 2006; Roder and Scrivner 2005). Other approaches have matured better. Specifically, this chapter chronicles various efforts to support existing businesses (the endogenous development approach); the rise of intermediaries in workforce development; asset-building programs; the scaling up of CDCs and CDFIs; various commercial revitalization efforts; the equitable development movement; and regional community organizing networks.

3.1 Endogenous Development

A new emphasis on endogenous development, generated in part by the realization that globalization was diminishing the opportunities for new "smokestacks" to chase, has framed the rise of CED (Teitz 1994). Endogenous development (also called autonomous or demand-side economic development) is the idea of "development from within," targeting businesses sometimes in specific neighborhoods but more commonly throughout a city or region (Bingham and Mier 1993; Eisinger 1988). After difficult postrecession recoveries in the early 1980s, the prospects for recovery through external investment declined. A growing perception that new small firms were acting as engines of innovation and job growth, though hotly disputed, supported the idea of endogenous development (Birch 1987; Harrison 1994; Saxenian 1994).

Localities, regions, and states have widely adopted such strategies, creating programs for the support of small enterprise, developing loan funds and other sources of capital, initiating business incubators, seeking out new markets or assisting with exports, and declaring small business a key element of their economic development (Blakely 1989). One of the most popular approaches is building cluster initiatives that link related businesses to organizational resources, identifying existing local businesses that have either developed as a group organically or show potential for evolving into a cluster. Though demand-side approaches are most common at the higher levels of government (e.g., see Eisinger 1995), they have also permeated CED practice due in large part to the influence of Michael Porter (1995).

Building on his work on competitive advantage and location, Porter put forth an argument that inner cities could compete if, with the help of government deregulation, they took advantage of their convenient location, integrated better with regional clusters, met emerging local demand, and put local underutilized human capital to work. Porter's work elicited a vigorous critique from CED veterans, who argued that Porter was ignoring previous decades of work, underestimating the barriers to economic development, and overestimating private-sector capacity to address complex inner city issues (Boston and Ross 1996). Despite the objections, Porter's work likely helped chain stores recognize the potential of core locations and created the policy momentum that resulted in the New Markets Tax Credit. Yet, a recent study by Porter's own nonprofit spinoff suggests that only a small handful of cities have been able to attract inner-city retail growth, ironically mostly due not to deregulation and better information about markets but to aggressive public-sector involvement and/or an influx of immigrants (Coyle 2007). Though the idea of new markets has attracted retailers, there is little evidence that core locations have competed successfully within other types of regional clusters, as Porter suggested they could, with the possible exception of health care.

Yet, endogenous strategies will likely persevere, albeit in different forms, over coming decades. The new awareness of the importance of intervention in support of small local business left a legacy of programs that seem to have become more effective over time, although systematic evaluation is rare (Markusen and Glasmeier 2008). A sampling of program outcomes suggests generally positive assessments. For instance, there are over 500 microenterprise development organizations in the United States providing technical support and loans largely targeted to the disadvantaged (Edgcomb and Klein 2005). Despite concerns about the efficiency of their operations, these programs have yielded a positive economic return on investment, income gains that can raise families out of poverty, and firm survival rates comparable to the rest of the economy (Edgcomb and Klein 2005; Servon 2006). Though there is little evidence of the effectiveness of revolving loan funds, they seem to have a catalytic effect particularly when targeted at projects unable to compete for market loans (see, for instance, U.S. GAO 2004 on brownfields redevelopment loans). A growing number of programs, from traditional loan programs to entrepreneurial support networks to public markets, also assist minority-owned or ethnic entrepreneurship (Hum 2006; Morales 2009). Despite concerns that such businesses are overly prone to failure or exploitation, there is some evidence that these businesses hire disadvantaged local residents who otherwise might not be employed, and particularly if accompanied by some higher education, can lead to upward mobility (Bates 1997; Boston 2006; Boyd 1990).

3.2 Targeting Individuals: Human Capital Development and Asset Building

A growing number of CED strategies target the individual capacity for self-sufficiency through participation in the labor market and/or the accumulation of assets. Both types of policy approaches are becoming more sophisticated, focusing not just on how to get a job or start saving but also on how to build a career and wealth. Both also are beginning to look beyond individual economic outcomes to link programs to community economic development.

   Though economists have long shown the importance of human capital for economic growth, it is only recently that CED practitioners have begun to demonstrate how to effectively link workforce development to economic development. Many initiatives have sought to meet both workforce and economic development goals simultaneously, but multiple contradictions complicate efforts to link the two. First, workforce and economic development goals and styles typically differ. Workforce development typically works in a long-term framework to improve the capacity of disadvantaged residents to participate in the economy. In contrast, economic development is primarily concerned with increasing jobs and the tax base—in other words, generating a quantitative increase in output—through efficient and productive use of resources. Most of government's business assistance programs are responding to demand from businesses that wish to start up, relocate, or expand and as such are short term and ad hoc (following the "shoot anything that flies, claim anything that falls" philosophy [Rubin, 1988]). Second, workforce development needs to argue for attracting high-growth industries that offer many jobs paying self-sufficiency wages, yet economic development to create regional competitive advantage typically entails developing industries that offer high-skill, high-wage jobs.

Nevertheless, numerous workforce intermediaries, with the Center for Employment Training (CET), Project QUEST, and the Wisconsin Regional Training Partnership (WRTP) among the most documented, have succeeded at meeting some economic development goals as well, such as job and wealth creation (Giloth 1998, 2004a; Harrison and Weiss 1998; Melendez 1996). Most of these programs adopt sector initiatives, targeting specific industry sectors in order to create a win-win situation by restructuring employment practices in a way that is beneficial to both employers and low-wage workers (Marano and Tarr 2004). A recent set of evaluations (e.g., Chapple 2005; Elliott et al. 2001; Zandniapour and Conway 2003) has shown that these and other workforce-development intermediaries have significant and positive impacts on the employability, wages, and upward mobility of their participants. Though evaluations are only just beginning to address the benefits for employers systematically (e.g., Aspen Institute Workforce Strategies Initiative 2005), these initiatives are seen as demand-responsive—that is, linked to firms, sectors, and clusters in the regional economy, and thus able to facilitate economic development. For instance, the WRTP arguably improves the productivity of its partner firms (Dresser and Rogers 1998), and CET employers benefit from ready access to a trained workforce (Melendez 1996). However, there seem to be several shortcomings (Fitzgerald 2006). Sector initiatives work well only with certain industries: the most consistent successes have occurred in health care and manufacturing. These sectors are unique in that they have difficulty with recruitment and retention (owing to the difficulty of advancement), feature heavy union involvement, and typically have a supportive corporate culture. Further, they are not rapidly growing sectors, generating jobs and wealth.

More recently, new programs have tried to address long-term upward mobility through career-ladder initiatives. Program experiments take several different forms, from increasing the pay of existing jobs, to creating new tiers within occupations, to using education and training to advance workers into occupations with better pay (Fitzgerald 2006). The idea of career-ladder initiatives is to outline the skill sets that lead to a progression of occupations and thereby solve two labor market failures: the problem for employers of recruiting and retaining qualified workers (particularly in high-turnover, low-wage industries like health care), and the difficulty for workers of gaining more responsibility and wages within a given sector. Typically, these models are built around the community college system and begin with remedial education. Yet, the most thorough evaluation of these programs, by Fitzgerald (2006), cautions that they are unlikely to be widely replicated without serious employer interest in reorganizing the workplace, as well as the complete realignment of the job-training system. It seems that many initiatives fail to solve either labor market failure (retention or advancement), perhaps because job training is not enough to foster upward mobility.

Though programs that support employment generally have positive outcomes and tend to reinforce long-term labor market attachment, they do not necessarily help families get ahead. Several factors make it difficult for wage earners to retain their income: for instance, program benefit cliffs may penalize families that increase their income by denying subsidies for child care, housing, or other work supports, and reliance on payday and refund anticipation loans may make it impossible to get ahead (National Center on Child Poverty 2004). Moreover, chronic asset poverty— lacking the accumulated wealth to help subsidize education, housing, or other costs of living—makes it even more difficult to save. Data on asset poverty suggest that more than one-fifth of households—and a disproportionate share of minority families—are asset poor, double the rate of income poverty (Corporation for Enterprise Development 2009). Even when poverty is declining, as in the 1990s, asset poverty has continued to increase. Arguably, the use of work supports to alleviate poverty has meant a focus on accommodating (and regulating) the labor market rather than addressing pervasive racial and income inequality (Oliver and Shapiro 1995, Piven and Cloward 1971).

Individual development account (IDA) programs have emerged as the most direct way to build assets, catalyzed in part by the research of Michael Sherraden (1991). Growing rapidly, from just four programs in 1994 to 500 in 2005, IDA programs offer matched savings accounts that can be used to develop wealth via purchasing a home, obtaining higher education, or starting a small business (Corporation for Enterprise Development [CFED] 2005). The best programs not only provide a small match (a few thousand dollars) toward a savings account but also offer financial literacy training, advice on repairing credit, and job-search assistance. The one systematic evaluation of the program to date (in Tulsa) has shown long-term (four-year) positive impacts on home ownership rates and com-pletion of nondegree educational courses (Abt Associates 2004). Although the housing crisis of the late 2000s has cast doubt on the viability of home ownership as a wealth-building strategy, IDA advocates point out that IDA clients are unlikely to go into foreclosure and might be protected from housing market volatility by diversifying their asset portfolios (CFED 2009).

Building assets for individuals can, under certain circumstances, lead to CED outcomes more generally. When new home or business ownership leads to improve-ments (e.g., occupying a vacant structure, renovating a building, or building a suc-cessful business), positive externalities result: the changes attract new investment and improve the quality of life for existing residents. This raises the question of how the community can retain the benefits of asset building—that is, the households who have become more affluent and wish to leave the community, or the success-ful businesses that want to relocate to more affluent areas. Several programs, most notably the Dudley Street Neighborhood Initiative, have built incentives to stay into their asset-building programs—for instance, by using shared-equity models, which cap the gains from selling an asset, or require reinvestment of profit in the community (Weber and Smith 2003).

3.3 Revitalizing the Neighborhood

The idea of neighborhood revitalization finds its origins in the settlement house movement, but did not really take off until the War on Poverty. In Robert Kennedy's "Marshall Plan," community development corporations would play a major role in rebuilding housing, public facilities, and parks, with job set-asides for local residents and opportunities for local business ownership. Revitalization is asset building writ large: community reinvestment builds up neighborhood markets and land values, and thus helps to protect and grow family assets. Lowering crime, improving schools, and supporting home improvements all contribute to stimulating asset appreciation and neighborhood markets, but in terms of CED, it is the CDCs, CDFIs, and other community development intermediaries (such as the Local Initiatives Support Corporation or LISC) that have become the major vehicles for neighborhood commercial revitalization.

Thirty years after Kennedy helped launch the CDC movement in low-income communities, it had arguably become a "community development industry system" (Yin 1998). There are over 3,300 urban CDCs in the United States, 40 percent of which were launched after 1986 (Melendez and Servon 2007). Over time, the diversity of both their funding sources and activities has increased (Melendez and Servon 2007). Though housing remains the predominant activity of CDCs, the majority also engage in other revitalization work such as commercial real estate development, commercial district revitalization, business assistance, social services, and job training.

The almost 700 CDFIs range from national banks and credit unions, to community development intermediaries, to small loan funds and venture capital providers, all with the mission of supplementing the conventional lending system with financial products and counseling targeted at low-income individuals and communities (CDFI Data Project 2003). This development finance industry has doubled in size in the last decade owing largely to the establishment of the CDFI Fund in 1994, which provides capital to CDFIs both directly and indirectly through investments from mainstream banks (CDFI Data Project 2003; Benjamin, Rubin, and Zielenbach 2004). The CDFIs support an array of financial services for both businesses and individuals, such as IDAs, checking accounts, home loans, microloans, and business loans. But perhaps their largest impact has been through the intermediaries such as LISC and the Enterprise Foundation that focus their efforts on building the capacities of CDCs and other CBOs. Intermediaries can provide the riskiest project financing to CDCs and thus enable their borrowing from other banks, while training CDC staff to manage projects (Benjamin, Rubin, and Zielenbach 2004; Liou and Stroh 1998). There is much more demand for CDFI services than they can accommodate, as well as a growing need to capitalize new CDFIs in underserved areas.

Intermediaries also help attract investors to low-income neighborhoods via projects funded by tax credit programs like the Low Income Housing Tax Credit (LIHTC) or New Markets Tax Credit. In general, tax credit programs have had varying impacts on community economic development, with few quantifiable impacts on local income or employment (Chapple and Jacobus 2009). With over 1 million housing units built, the LIHTC has become the de facto affordable housing program in the United States; since over one-fifth are built by nonprofit developers, the program has helped build CDC capacity (Schwartz and Melendez 2006). The worst performer, in nearly all evaluations, is the federal government's Empowerment Zone program (as well as related state programs), which has had no greater success in reducing unemployment or poverty or creating jobs and businesses than comparison areas without zone designation (California Budget Project 2006; Dowall, Beyeler, and Wong 1994; U. S. GAO 2006; Oakley and Tsao 2006; Rich and Stoker 2007; Wilder and Rubin 1988). Though only preliminary results are available on the New Markets Tax Credit, it seems to be an inefficient vehicle, with the funding going to private intermediaries swamping the benefit to recipients (U.S. GAO 2007). One of the most effective tax credit programs is the Historic Preservation Tax Credit, which has had strong positive impacts and multiplier effects despite its small scale (Mason 2005).

For a variety of reasons, including the growing awareness of "new" markets, shifts in consumption habits, a resurgence of historic preservation, and the "back-to-the-city" movement of young professionals, local governments and CBOs have become increasingly proficient at strengthening neighborhood retail. Different strategies employed include commercial real estate development projects supported by the public sector through direct financing or various tax incentives; "market-led" development strategies that rely on market research and promotion to attract new retailers to underserved areas; and coordinated commercial revitalization programs that combine business attraction with "softer" activities such as safety and cleanliness efforts, consumer marketing, business assistance, and smaller scale improvements to the physical infrastructure (Chapple and Jacobus 2009). Of these strategies, only commercial district revitalization strategies, such as LISC's CDC commercial revitalization programs or the National Historic Preservation Trust's Main Street program, have a demonstrably positive effect on retail revitalization (Carlson 2003; Seidman 2004). Less is known about the effectiveness of public-led commercial development and market-led retail attraction strategies (Chapple and Jacobus 2009). No matter which approach is adopted, leveraging public investment seems to be key. Commercial district revitalization programs are also the most promising in terms of improving neighborhoods, perhaps because they focus on quality-of-life issues such as crime and safety.

3.4 Organizing the Community—and the Region—for Job Quality

Arguably the most dynamic form of community and economic development at present is occurring in the form of community organizing for economic justice.

Decades of community battles over redevelopment projects and gentrification have built local organizing capacity and political savvy. Supported in part by labor- and faith-based organizations, which have refocused their approach at the community level, these activities have helped to connect marginalized groups and neighborhoods to economic opportunity, particularly (but not exclusively) in strong-market regions. Advocates argue that these efforts add up to a regional equity movement, a new "social movement regionalism" promoting more equitable development patterns (PolicyLink 2003; Pastor, Benner, and Matsuoka 2009).

The new economic-justice movement evolved from dual roots: a response to the thirty-year advent of globalization, capital mobility, devolution, and neoliberalism; but facilitated by local community development capacity. The deindustrialization and "u-turn" of America (as so aptly labeled by Harrison and Bluestone 1990) weakened the labor movement, and a search for new approaches resulted in new union coalitions with faith-based and other community organizations. Two parallel strategies emerged: the movement to improve job quality at the municipal level, best represented by the living-wage coalitions that have passed laws in over 140 cities (see Fairris et al. 2005); and the movement to ensure that the local community received some of the benefits of real estate development, whether via linkage policies, first-source agreements, or community benefits agreements. The focus on making development accountable for its impacts brought new advantages to the labor movement: the institutionalization of environmental review processes had built community capacity to participate in the development-approval process, and communities already routinely mobilized to protest development. Though many communities were not motivated or prepared to work for organized labor, the neighborhood lens created a new space for joint mobilization.

Linkage policies, first-source agreements, and local hire ordinances stem from the slow-growth movement of the 1980s. Linkage policies, enacted in a handful of cities across the country, tie large-scale commercial development to its negative effects, requiring compensating side payments, most frequently for housing but sometimes also for other social needs, such as employment training, daycare centers, and social service funding (Molina 1998; PolicyLink 2002; Smith 1989). Much more common are local hiring ordinances, which typically mandate that publicly funded developments and businesses (over a certain size threshold) reserve a certain percentage of jobs for local residents. Local hire ordinances are sometimes accompanied by first-source employment programs, which help employers meet their percentage local hiring goal by referring qualified local job seekers to them in a timely manner. In practice, these policies have not had a substantial impact on community and economic development, either because they are not implemented widely (as in the case of linkage) or because they affect mostly construction jobs (as in the case of local hire).

Community benefits agreements (CBAs) descend from these policies and, though also not widespread, tend to affect community and economic development more directly because of the targeted nature of benefits. The CBAs are legally enforceable contracts negotiated between a prospective developer and community representatives. The CBA exacts community economic-development commitments from the developer (e.g., local hires at living wages, affordable housing units, neighborhood amenities) in exchange for the community's support of its proposed development (Gross, LeRoy, and Janis-Aparico 2005). The CBA tends to focus on job quality, perhaps in part because the landmark Staples Center CBA in Los Angeles was rooted in a growing union–community coalition. Negotiated in almost fifty development projects across the United States, these CBAs are increasingly found in weaker markets like Albany and Pittsburgh, in addition to strong market coastal regions (Meyerson 2006; Salkin 2007). Though critiqued for not being inclusive and transparent (since some community groups may be left out at the negotiating table), the general principle of a contractual agreement (rather than a citywide exaction policy) seems to be withstanding the test of time (Salkin 2007).

Though many of these economic-justice movements focus on the specific community impacts of development projects, their proponents are using the region as their strategic arena to organize their constituents (Pastor, Benner, and Matsuoka 2009). Over time, strategies are spreading across the country through the regional networks of national organizations, many faith based, such as the Gamaliel Foundation, the PICO National Network, the Industrial Areas Foundation, and the Association of Community Organizations for Reform Now. Ultimately, however, their success at creating community economic development seems to depend on their ability to exercise power at higher levels of government—for instance, by obtaining federal authorization for local-hire ordinances in infrastructure projects (Swanstrom and Banks 2009; Weir and Rongerude 2007). In the absence of a federal employment policy that boosts job quality, this kind of multilevel organizing is proving critical to leveraging federal resources for CED.

4. ONGOING DEBATES IN THE FIELD

Though a comparatively young field, CED has already undergone several decades of policy experimentation and learning. Yet, several major debates remain unresolved. First, despite a prolific literature on the effectiveness of different economic development approaches, CED practice, at least at a municipal level, seems forever wed to a "smokestack chasing" approach (Rubin 1988). Second, the neoliberal-era push for more market-based CED has left many organizations confused about their mission. And third, a concurrent push for accountability has suggested that CED policy may not be very effective at shifting private-sector behavior. The following briefly examines each debate in turn.

The inward gaze of the postindustrial era brought about new awareness of the potential for endogenous or demand-side development, which was followed first by calls for more sustainable, or at least environmentally sensitive, economic development, and then by a focus on human capital development (or the "creative class"; Eisinger 1988; Fitzgerald and Leigh 2002; Florida 2002; Teitz 1994). There is mixed evidence that these so-called waves of economic development have actually occurred on the ground, though examples of each abound (Eisinger 1995; Fitzgerald and Leigh 2002; Florida 2008). In practice, cities, counties, and states still rely heavily on the use of tax incentives and bidding wars to attract businesses, despite evidence that most job growth comes from existing, not new, businesses (Markusen and Nesse 2007; Kolko and Neumark 2007). Even the movement to improve urban quality of life in order to retain "creatives" is more about attracting new business than developing endogenously. Since much CED practice occurs outside official economic development agencies (though often with agency financial or tactical support), a dual system of economic development may even be working at cross-purposes. How these two systems can become better aligned is not clear, since the political considerations driving the bureaucracy of economic development are not likely to lessen (Dewar 1998).

The last few years have seen the advent of a more market-based CED. Attempts to introduce market logic into the field have met with mixed results. Despite initial enthusiasm about social enterprises, or nonprofits with a revenue-generating sideline, they may stray too far to have a real impact on CED and seem to thrive only when the economy is strong (Giloth 2004b; Shuman and Fuller 2005). That even the best CDFIs yield fewer profits than mainstream financial institutions should suggest the limits of the market in some areas (Benjamin, Rubin, and Zielenbach 2004). As described above, the efforts of intermediaries to restore markets (or find "new markets") in low-income communities through better information have largely proved ineffective, except in new immigrant neighborhoods (Chapple and Jacobus 2009). Perhaps the most successful market-based community development programs have been those that introduce new products and services, such as savings accounts or healthy food, into underserved communities. But the recent financial crisis has shown that catalyzing markets may be less about stimulating and deregulating the market than about connecting disadvantaged communities to mainstream market alternatives through a combination of education and accessibility strategies. For example, financial deregulation created bank interest in low-income home ownership via high-risk loans, but loans brokered by the nonprofit housing industry, which came with mandated financial literacy counseling, have been much less likely to be foreclosed (Immergluck 2009).

Are CED policies and programs even effective? Evaluating these interventions has proved difficult, and there is little systematic information about what works. Evaluation questions extend beyond the technical difficulties of determining whether policy interventions are effective to the meta-issue of what CED is trying to accomplish. Economic development processes may have several different outcomes, and the question is which is the goal of interest, and for whom (Reese and Fasenfest 2004)?

Take the simple case of a successful business-attraction policy that results in employment growth. New jobs mean lower unemployment, higher local income, less poverty, and more demand for goods and services. These outcomes are easy to understand, measure, document, and convey to voters. But even if local politicians can take credit for job growth, what is the local economic development benefit? The new jobs do not necessarily go to local unemployed or impoverished residents, particularly if they require high educational levels. Most likely, most of the new jobs will be taken by in-migrants to the area (as shown by Bartik 1991), and the remaining will go to the most qualified local job applicants. Moving down the job chain, their jobs may be taken by underemployed locals; only as job vacancies move down the chain will the unemployed finally benefit. Meanwhile, the new area residents may put pressure on local housing prices, making housing less affordable. Though they purchase new goods and services locally, this multiplier spending may create low-wage jobs that require new public subsidies (e.g., for health care) to support, while generating profits for nonlocal owners. The policy has met its CED goals of creating new jobs and expanding the tax base, but because of new expenditure needs, it is unclear whether there is a net benefit, and if so, whether it has reached disadvantaged local residents.

Another issue is how to understand the impacts of a specific CED project, in terms of both the extent of the impacts and the role of public policy. A new supermarket development developed by a CDC in a low-income neighborhood might bring new jobs and sales tax revenue (direct impacts), new businesses nearby (indirect impacts), and a new community identity that attracts new residents and investors (neighborhood impacts). These direct and indirect impacts are readily measurable, but other effects are often too intangible or long term to quantify or identify. First-order outcomes might be followed by hard-to-measure second-order outcomes, creating opportunities that only later are the basis of a tangible benefit: for example, work experience for locals that gives them confidence to apply to college, or new community capacity to manage real estate development.

Moreover, largely because of the lack of local area data and resources for program evaluation, few CED evaluations ascertain whether the impact would have happened without the intervention. Though such studies are possible through matched-pair comparisons of neighborhoods, only studies of enterprise zones systematically employ quasi-experimental designs with control neighborhoods—and even these studies may be tainted by selection bias, since the neighborhoods that have obtained public investment often are the best off or most organized to start with. In the absence of data on the effectiveness of policies and programs, successful CED may be attributed to any number of factors, such as overall economic growth, shifts in economic activity between neighborhoods or groups, or increased efficiency of local firms or organizations. Is it problematic if CED is a zero-sum game, transferring growth from one place to another without directly impacting economic growth in the aggregate? Economists would argue that any policy that results in a more efficient spatial distribution of goods and services, particularly the shift of jobs from low-unemployment to high-unemployment areas (as might happen via CED policy), will increase output and create social benefits (Bartik and Bingham 1995). Political scientists might add that even if CED is zero sum in economic terms, it creates net political gain (Reese and Fasenfest 2004; Wolman 1996).

In the end, does the set of programs and policies that constitute community economic development make a difference in how the market behaves? The quick answer is that the scale of these programs is so small relative to the size of the national economy that they probably only change firm behavior at the margin, with minimal impacts on aggregate indicators of distress. Much more powerful are the various economic development incentives that cities and states offer—an estimated $50 billion per year—but even those do not have significant impacts on firm decision making about hiring and location (Peters and Fisher 2004). Just as the market finances good and bad projects, CED funding goes to both successes and failures. Perhaps the better metric by which to judge CED programs and projects is whether they have better connected marginalized groups and places to economic activity. Few would question that at least some have benefited.

5. Issues on the Horizon

The field of community and economic development faces some large challenges in the coming years. Although advanced capitalism is taking different forms across the globe, it will undoubtedly continue to leave some groups and places behind. Different forms of CED have emerged in many countries, with some notable successes, such as microenterprise development. But the lessons of the field in the United States, where it continues to expand in scale and scope, are likely to be relevant to all countries dealing with the ups and downs of the business cycle.

CED emerged in part to deal with the challenges of concentrated poverty, itself a legacy of government housing and transportation policy (Dreier, Mollenkopf, and Swanstrom 2004). But the nature of poverty in the United States is gradually evolving. Increasing income inequality at the national level has meant a decline in middle-income families and an increase in both low- and upper-income families. Spatially, this has manifested itself as a growing share of high-poverty neighborhoods in the suburbs and increasing diversity in both low- and high-income neighborhoods (Galster et al. 2005). These new configurations strain the social safety net and complicate CED. The growing ranks of the working poor need a different set of programs—for example, wage subsidies, health care, and food stamps—from the bread and butter of CED. Investing in people through place is not so simple in an environment that is both diverse and dispersed; CED's reach, its web of relationships and actions, must become much broader in order to connect households throughout the region to economic opportunity. To support a metropolitan CED, the federal government will need to revisit the poverty-based funding criteria it uses for many of its programs, instead developing a set of place characteristics related to economic security more broadly.

If CED were to broaden its scale and scope, it would need greater organizational and financial capacity. Many of the community organizations that have innovated in CED are the legacy of Johnson-era interventions, from the Economic Opportunity Act to Model Cities, that built community capacity for a coordinated attack on inner-city poverty. Though many of these CDCs have now come of age, they are not fully prepared for twenty-first-century community economic development struggles. Not only are they disproportionately concentrated in older central cities, but also they tend to focus more on housing and commercial development than on the community organizing and leadership development skills that are increasingly important to leverage resources at the federal level.

It is also unclear how an expansion of CED programs would be financed. In a climate of government retrenchment and devolution, charitable foundations stepped up to fund many of the most successful policy experiments of previous decades, in the hope of a federal role in disseminating and scaling up best practices. Though this model has worked for some high-profile programs (e.g., the Harlem Children's Zone) or bipartisan policies (e.g., IDAs), other worthy candidates for funding, such as commercial-corridor revitalization programs, never seem to gain a constituency.

One alternative to the foundation pilot–government expansion model is collaboration among foundations in order to reach scale. On a global scale, the collaborations between charitable initiatives like the Bill and Melinda Gates Foundation and the Clinton Global Initiative have the potential to make an impact. In CED, one example is the Casey Foundation's National Fund for Workforce Solutions, which has twenty-two sites and some 300 funders involved. The fund is a national venture-capital pool that invests in and supports local pools that in turn invest in workforce partnerships that better align workforce funding with employer needs.

As its subfields have grown increasingly specialized, urban planning has become more of a conglomerate than a field, with its components cemented together but also in competition (Teitz 2008). Yet CED, given the lessons it has learned, has much to offer its sister fields—and vice versa. Unlike traditional land-use planning, it has experimented much more with organization, gaining new resilience from its reliance on the third sector and caution from its experiments with markets. For its very survival, it has learned to connect to different issue areas and policy venues—as, for instance, labor activists target the federal transportation bills for quality jobs. The next generation of CED programs will flourish best if they contribute to other planning goals, such as creating sustainable urban development patterns. If CED can help reduce greenhouse gas emissions—for instance, by aligning community development finance better with regional transportation planning—urban planning may finally overcome its reluctance and embrace CED.

REFERENCES

Abt Associates. 2004. *Evaluation of the American Dream Demonstration*. Available at: http://www.abtassociates.com/reports/Final_Eval_Rpt_8-19-04.pdf.

Anheier, H. K., and L. M. Salamon. 2006. "The Nonprofit Sector in Comparative Perspective." In *The Nonprofit Sector: A Research Handbook*, edited by W. W. Powell and R. Steinberg, 89–114. New Haven, CT: Yale University Press.

Aspen Institute Workforce Strategies Initiative. 2005. *Business Value Assessment for Workforce Development Organizations Handbook*. Washington, DC: Aspen Institute.

Bartik, T. J. 1991. *Who Benefits from State and Local Economic Development Policies?* Kalamazoo, MI: W.E. Upjohn Institute for Employment Research.

Bartik, T. J., and R. D. Bingham. 1995. "Can Economic Development Programs Be Evaluated?" Working paper 95–29. Kalamazoo, MI: W.E. Upjohn Institute for Employment Research. Available at: http://www.upjohninst.org/up_workingpapers/29/.

Bates, T. 1997. *Race, Self-Employment, and Upward Mobility: An Illusive American Dream.* Baltimore, MD: Johns Hopkins University Press.

Benjamin, L., J. S. Rubin, and S. Zielenbach. 2004. "Community Development Financial Institutions: Current Issues and Future Prospects." *Journal of Urban Affairs* 26(2): 177–95.

Berube, A., and W. Frey. 2002. "A Decade of Mixed Blessings: Urban and Suburban Poverty in Census 2000." Washington, DC: Brookings Institution.

Bingham, R. D., and R. Mier, eds. 1993. *Theories of Local Economic Development.* Newbury Park, CA: Sage.

Birch, D. 1987. *Job Creation in America.* New York: Free Press.

Blakely, E. J. 1989. *Planning Local Economic Development.* Newbury Park, CA: Sage.

Boston, T. D. 2006. "The Role of Black-owned Businesses in Black Community Development." In *Jobs and Economic Development in Minority Communities: Realities, Challenges, and Innovation*, edited by Paul Ong, 11–75. Philadelphia: Temple University Press.

Boston, T. D., and C. L. Ross. 1996. "Location Preferences of Successful African American-Owned Businesses in Atlanta." *Review of Black Political Economy* 24(2–3): 337–57.

Boyd, R. L. 1990. "Black and Asian Self-Employment in Large Metropolitan Areas: A Comparative Analysis." *Social Problems* 37 (2): 258–74.

California Budget Project. 2006. "California's Enterprise Zones Miss the Mark." California Budget Project. Accessed at: http://www.cbp.org/pdfs/2006/0604_ezreport.pdf.

Carlson, N. 2003, October. "A Road Map to Revitalizing Urban Neighborhood Business Districts." New York: Local Initiatives Support Corporation.

CDFI Data Project. 2003. "Community Development Financial Institutions: Providing Capital, Building Community, Creating Impact." Available at: http://www.cfed.org/enterprise_development/CDFIData/; accessed January 2004.

Chapple, K. 2005. "Promising Futures: Workforce Development and Upward Mobility in Information Technology." Monograph 2005–01, Institute of Urban and Regional Development, University of California, Berkeley.

Chapple, K., and R. Jacobus, R. 2009. "Retail Trade as a Route to Neighborhood Revitalization." *Urban and Regional Policy and Its Effects*, vol. 2, edited by M. A. Turner, H. Wial, and N. Pindus. Washington, DC: Brookings Institution and Urban Land Institute.

Corporation for Enterprise Development. 2005. "Assets: An Update for Innovators." Newsletter no. 2, Corporation for Enterprise Development, Washington, DC. Available at: http://www.cfed.org/think.m?id=113&groupid=assets&clusterid=1.

Corporation for Enterprise Development. 2009. *Assets & Opportunity Special Report: Net Worth, Wealth Inequality and Homeownership during the Bubble Years.* Washington, DC: Corporation for Enterprise Development, Washington, DC. Available at: http://www.cfed.org/specialreport/a_o_special_report.pdf.

Coyle, D. M. 2007. "Realizing the Inner City Retail Opportunity: Progress and New Directions, An Analysis of Retail Markets in America's Inner Cities." *Economic Development Journal* 6(1): 6–14.

Crane, R., and M. Manville. 2008. "People or Place? Revisiting the Who versus the Where in Community Economic Development." Working paper, Lincoln Institute of Land Policy, Cambridge, MA.

Dewar, M. 1998. "Why State and Local Economic Development Programs Cause So Little Economic Development." *Economic Development Quarterly* 12(1): 68–87.

Dowall, D. E., M. Beyeler, and S. Wong. 1994. *Evaluation of California's Enterprise Zone and Employment and Economic Incentive Programs.* Berkeley, CA: California Policy Seminar.

Dreier, P., J. Mollenkopf, and T. Swanstrom. 2004. *Place Matters: Metropolitics for the Twenty-first Century.* Lawrence, KS: University Press of Kansas.

Dresser, L., and J. Rogers. 1998. "Networks, Sectors, and Workforce Learning." In *Jobs and Economic Development*, edited by R. Giloth, 64–84. Thousand Oaks, CA: Sage.

Edgcomb, E. L., and J. A. Klein. 2005. *Opening Opportunities, Building Ownership: Fulfilling the Promise of Microenterprise in the United States.* Washington, DC: Aspen Institute/FIELD.

Eisinger, P. B. 1988. *The Rise of the Entrepreneurial State: State and Local Economic Development Policy in the United States.* Madison: University of Wisconsin Press.

Eisinger, P. B. 1995. "State Economic Development in the 1990s: Politics and Policy Learning." *Economic Development Quarterly* 9(2): 146–58.

Elliott, M., A. Roder, E. King, and J. Stillman. 2001. *Gearing Up: An Interim Report on the Sectoral Employment Initiative.* Philadelphia: Public/Private Ventures.

Fairris, D., D. Runsten, C. Briones, and J. Goodheart. 2005. *Examining the Evidence: The Impact of the Los Angeles Living Wage Ordinance on Workers and Businesses.* Los Angeles: Los Angeles Alliance for a New Economy.

Fitzgerald, J. 2006. *Moving Up in the New Economy: Career Ladders for U.S. Workers.* Ithaca, NY: Cornell University Press.

Fitzgerald, J., and N. G. Leigh. 2002. *Economic Revitalization: Cases and Strategies for City and Suburbs.* Thousand Oaks, CA: Sage.

Florida, R. 2002. "The Economic Geography of Talent." *Annals of the Association of American Geographers* 92(4): 743–55.

Florida, R. 2008 *Who's Your City?: How the Creative Economy Is Making Where to Live the Most Important Decision of Your Life.* New York: Basic Books.

Galster, G., J. C. Booza, J. Cutsinger, K. Metzger, and U. Lim. 2005. "Low-Income Households in Mixed-Income Neighborhoods: Extent, Trends, and Determinants." Report prepared for the U.S. Department of Housing and Urban Development, Washington, DC.

Giloth, R., ed. 1998. *Jobs and Economic Development.* Thousand Oaks, CA: Sage.

Giloth, R., ed. 2004a. *Workforce Intermediaries for the Twenty-first Century.* Philadelphia: Temple University Press.

Giloth, R. 2004b. "Social Enterprise and Urban Rebuilding in the United States." In *Entrepreneurship: A Catalyst for Urban Regeneration*, edited by the Organization for Economic Co-Operation and Development, 135–53. Paris, France: OECD.

Giloth, R. 2006. "Whither Community Economic Development?" Unpublished paper.

Giloth, R. 2007. "Investing in Equity: Targeted Economic Development for
   Neighborhoods and Cities." In *Economic Development in American Cities: The
   Pursuit of an Equity Agenda,* edited by M. I. J. Bennett and R. Giloth, 23–50. Albany,
   NY: State University of New York Press.

Goodrich, C. 1958. "The Gallatin Plan after One Hundred and Fifty Years." *Proceedings of
   the American Philosophical Society* 102(5): 436–41.

Gross, J., G. LeRoy, and M. Janis-Aparicio. 2005. "Community Benefits Agreements:
   Making Development Projects Accountable." Available at: http://www.goodjobsfirst.
   org/pdf/cba2005final.pdf.

Harrison, B. 1994. *Lean and Mean: The Changing Landscape of Corporate Power in the
   Age of Flexibility.* New York: Basic Books.

Harrison, B., and B. Bluestone. 1990. *Corporate Restructuring and the Polarizing of
   America.* New York: Basic Books.

Harrison, B., and M. Weiss. 1998. *Workforce Development Networks: Community-Based
   Organizations and Regional Alliances.* Thousand Oaks, CA: Sage.

Hum, T. 2006. "NYC's Asian Immigrant Economies: Community Development Needs
   and Challenges." In *Jobs and Economic Development in Minority Communities,*
   edited by P. Ong and A. Loukaitou-Sideris, 17–212. Philadelphia: Temple University
   Press.

Immergluck, D. 2009. *Foreclosed: High-Risk Lending, Deregulation, and the Undermining
   of America's Mortgage Market.* Ithaca, NY: Cornell University Press.

Kolko, J., and D. Neumark. 2007. *Business Location Decisions and Employment. Dynamics
   in California.* San Francisco: Public Policy Institute of California.

Liou, Y. T., and R. C. Stroh. 1998. "Community Development Intermediary Systems in the
   United States: Origins, Evolution, Functions." *Housing Policy Debate* 9(3): 575–94.

Marano, C., and K. Tarr. 2004. "The Workforce Intermediary: Profiling the Field of
   Practice and Its Challenges." In *Workforce Intermediaries for the Twenty-first Century,*
   edited by R. Giloth, 93–123. Philadelphia: Temple University Press.

Markusen, A., and A. Glasmeier. 2008. "Overhauling and Revitalizing Federal Economic
   Development Programs." *Economic Development Quarterly* 22(2): 83–91.

Markusen, A., and K. Nesse. 2007. "Institutional and Political Determinants of Incentive
   Competition." In *Reining in the Competition for Capital,* edited by A. Markusen, 1–42.
   Kalamazoo, MI: W.E. Upjohn Institute for Employment Research.

Mason, R. 2005. *Economics and Historic Preservation: A Guide and Review of the
   Literature.* Washington, DC: Brookings Institution.

Melendez, E. 1996. *Working on Jobs: The Center for Employment Training.* Boston:
   University of Massachusetts-Boston, Gaston Institute.

Melendez, E., and L. J. Servon. 2007. Reassessing the role of housing in community-based
   urban development. *Housing Policy Debate,* 18(4): 751–83.

Meyerson, H. 2006. "No Justice, No Growth; How Los Angeles Is Making Big-time
   Developers Create Decent Jobs." *The American Prospect* 17(11): 39–43.

Mishel, L., J. Bernstein, and S. Allegretto. 2006. *The State of Working America 2006/07.*
   Ithaca, NY: Cornell University Press.

Molina, F. 1998. *Making Connections: A Study of Employment Linkage Programs.*
   Washington, DC: Center for Community Change. Available at: http://www.commu-
   nitychange.org/shared/publications/downloads/ccc_making.pdf.

Morales, A. 2009. "Public Markets as Community Development Tools." *Journal of
   Planning Education and Research* 28(4): 426–40.

National Center on Child Poverty. 2004. *State Policy Choices: Supports for Low-Income Working Families*. New York: NCCP.

Oakley, D., and H-S.Tsao. 2006. "A New Way of Revitalizing Distressed Urban Communities? Assessing the Impact of the Federal Urban Empowerment Zone Program." *Journal of Urban Affairs* 28(5): 443–71.

Oliver, M., and T. M. Shapiro. 1995. *Black Wealth/White Wealth A New Perspective On Racial Inequality*. New York: Routledge.

Osterman, P. 1999. *Securing Prosperity: The American Labor Market: How It Has Changed and What to Do About It*. Princeton, NJ: Princeton University Press.

Pastor, M. Jr., C. Benner, and M. Matsuoka. 2009. *This Could Be the Start of Something Big: How Social Movements for Regional Equity Are Reshaping Metropolitan America*. Ithaca, NY: Cornell University Press.

Peters, A., and P. R. Fisher. 2004. "The Failures of Economic Development Incentives." *Journal of the American Planning Association* 70(1): 27–38.

Piven, F. F., and R. Cloward. 1971. *Regulating the Poor: The Functions of Public Welfare*. New York: Pantheon.

PolicyLink. 2003. *Equitable Development Toolkit*. Available at: http:\\www.policylink.org\edtk.

Porter, M. E. 1995. "The Competitive Advantage of the Inner City." *Harvard Business Review*, May/June, 55–71.

Reese, L. A., and D. Fasenfest. 2004. Introduction. In *Critical Evaluations of Economic Development Policies*, edited by L. A. Reese and D. Fasenfest, 1–20. Detroit, MI: Wayne State University Press.

Reich, R. 1991. *The Work of Nations*. New York: Vintage Books.

Rich, M. J., and R. P. Stoker. 2007. "Governance and Urban Revitalization: Lessons from the Urban Empowerment Zones Initiative." Paper prepared for Conference on a Global Look at Urban and Regional Governance: The State-Market-Civic Nexus, Emory University, the Halle Program on Governance and the Department of Political Science, January 18–19.

Roder, A., and S. Scrivner. 2005. *Seeking a Sustainable Journey to Work: Findings from the National Bridges to Work Demonstration*. Philadelphia: Public/Private Ventures.

Rubin, H. 1988. "Shoot Anything that Flies, Claim Anything that Falls: Conversations with Economic Development Practitioners." *Economic Development Quarterly* 2(3): 236–51.

Salamon, L. M. 2003. *The Resilient Sector: The State of Nonprofit America*. Washington, DC: Brookings Institution Press.

Salkin, P. E. 2007. "Community Benefits Agreements: Opportunities and Traps for Developers, Municipalities, and Community Organizations." *Planning and Environmental Law* 59(11): 3–8.

Saxenian, A. 1994. *Regional Advantage: Culture and Competition in Silicon Valley and Route 128*. Cambridge, MA: Harvard University Press.

Sbragia, A. M. 1996. *Debt Wish: Entrepreneurial Cities, U.S. Federalism and Economic Development*. Pittsburgh, PA: University of Pittsburgh Press.

Schwartz, A., and E. Melendez. 2006. "Beyond Year 15: Responses to the Expiration of the LIHTC." Working paper, New School Community Development Research Center, New York.

Seidman, K. 2004. *Revitalizing Commerce for American Cities: A Practitioner's Guide to Urban Main Street Programs*. Washington, DC: Fannie Mae Foundation.

Servon, L. J. 2006. Microenterprise Development in the United States: Current Challenges and New Directions. *Economic Development Quarterly* 20:351–67.

Sherraden, M. 1991. *Assets and the Poor: A New American Welfare Policy.* Armonk, NY: M.E. Sharpe.

Shuman, M., and M. Fuller. 2005. "The Revolution Will Not Be Grant-Funded." *Shelterforce.* Available at: http://www.nhi.org/online/issues/143/revolution.html.

Smith, M. P. 1989. "The Uses of Linked Development Policies in U.S. Cities." Pp.35–53 in *Regenerating the Cities: The UK Crisis and the U.S. Experience,* edited by Michael Parkinson, Bernard Foley, and Dennis Judd. Manchester, UK: Manchester University Press.

Smith, S. R., and M. Lipsky. 1993. *Nonprofits for Hire: The Welfare State in the Age of Contracting.* Cambridge, MA: Harvard University Press.

Stoutland, S. E. 1999. "Community Development Corporations: Mission, Strategy, and Accomplishments." In *Urban Problems and Community Development,* edited by R. F. Ferguson and W. T. Dickens, 193–240. Washington, DC: Brookings Institution Press.

Swanstrom, T., and B. Banks. 2009. "Going Regional: Community-Based Regionalism, Transportation, and Local Hiring Agreements." *Journal of Planning Education and Research* 28(3): 355–67.

Teitz, M. B. 1994. "Changes in Economic Development Theory and Practice." *International Regional Science Review* 16:101–106.

Teitz, M. B. 2008. "Planning and Economic Development: An Uneasy Partnership." Clarkson Lecture, State University of New York, Buffalo, October 29.

U.S. Government Accountability Office. 2004. *Brownfield Redevelopment: Stakeholders Report That EPAâ€™s Program Helps to Redevelop Sites, but Additional Measures Could Complement Agency Efforts.* Report GAO-05-94. Washington, DC: GAO.

U.S. Government Accountability Office. 2006. *Empowerment Zone and Enterprise Community Program: Improvements Occurred in Communities, but the Effect of the Program Is Unclear.* Report GAO-06-727. Washington, DC: GAO.

U.S. Government Accountability Office. 2007. *New Markets Tax Credit Appears to Increase Investment by Investors in Low-Income Communities, but Opportunities Exist to Better Monitor Compliance.* Report GAO-07-296. Washington, DC: GAO.

Weber, R. N., and J. L. Smith. 2003. "Assets and Neighborhoods: The Role of Individual Assets In Neighborhood Revitalization." *Housing Policy Debate* 14(1–2): 169–92.

Weir, M., and J. Rongerude. 2007. "Multi-Level Power and Progressive Regionalism. Building Resilient Regions." UC-Berkeley Institute of Urban & Regional Development Working Paper 2007–15. Available at: http://www.iurd.berkeley.edu/publications/workingpapers.shtml.

Wilder, M. G., and B. M. Rubin. 1988. "Targeted Redevelopment through Urban Enterprise Zones." *Journal of Urban Affairs* 10(1): 1–17.

Wirka, S. 1996. "The City Social Movement: Progressive Women Reformers and Early Social Planning." I In *Planning the Twentieth-Century American City,* edited by M. C. Sies and C. Silver, 55–75. Baltimore: Johns Hopkins University Press.

Wolman, H. [with D. Spitzley]. 1996. "The Politics of Local Economic Development." *Economic Development Quarterly* 10(2): 115–50.

Yin, J. S. 1998. "The Community Development Industry System: A Case Study of Politics and Institutions in Cleveland, 1967–1997." *Journal of Urban Affairs* 20(2): 137–57.

Zandniapour, L., and M. Conway. 2003. *SEDLP Research Report No. 3: Gaining Ground: The Labor Market Progress of Participants of Sectoral Employment Development Programs.* Washington, DC: Aspen Institute.

CHAPTER 25

HOUSING: PLANNING AND POLICY CHALLENGES

LISA K. BATES

1. THE STATE OF HOUSING PLANNING

THE problems associated with urban housing are well known: persistent shortages of low-cost housing and the isolation of households who need those units; economic, social, and fiscal inequities across metropolitan areas; and overinvestment in new, high-cost single-family housing development while older, urban neighborhoods decay. Yet in a market-dominated economy, with most housing produced by the private sector, the role of planners is not to actually manipulate the housing stock but to be part of a complicated market-state interaction. Planners' tools for meeting anticipated shelter needs are indirect—creating general plans, regulations, and incentives and disincentives—and piecemeal, with limited public provision of and subsidies for housing.

While the state role in providing housing is limited, we also expect housing to achieve social outcomes beyond simply providing shelter. Housing is "home," the locus of stable family life, a vehicle for wealth building, and a location for accessing neighborhood opportunities. However, the current system for housing planning is inadequate for, and in some ways actually counterproductive to, meeting both shelter needs and the broader set of public goals for housing. This chapter assesses the role of public-sector planning in housing, and argues for more of one, considering planning's strengths as an analytic, strategic, and communicative activity. Through comparisons of the United States and the UK, I consider activities along a spectrum of state-market roles that might address the serious problems for housing in urban neighborhoods.

Some critical housing problems stem from weak and indirect planning; others from active, but misguided, planning actions. In the market context of the United States, the role of planning is at the margins; the provision of housing is largely determined by the independent decisions of developers and households within a land-use system that is not based on projected shelter needs. In the UK, the shift away from government-constructed units and toward deregulation in the finance sector means that addressing housing-supply problems has led to rethinking of planning for land and the appropriate role for private landlords and developers (Barker 2004; Clapham 1996). There are significant and persistent problems in each of these contexts, with similar difficulties arising from different circumstances. Particularly in the United States, the fiscal and political realities of planning result in imbalances in supply and demand, particularly for affordable housing units. Decisions to make land available for housing are influenced by political and fiscal considerations, such as the objections of current residents to new development or a preference for nonhousing development that increases the tax base. These factors may be more influential than observed supply shortages and needs for housing. Although homeownership is still heavily subsidized, there has been a substantial reduction in the government's provision of public housing units and subsidies for low-income housing.

As the social safety net for housing has been retracted over three decades in the United States, a disjointed set of subsidy programs has left low-income households with inadequate shelter in many locations. The U.S. nonprofit sector struggles to assemble funding and land to provide some units, though not nearly enough to meet existing needs. In the UK, nonprofit housing associations are evolving as primary actors in the social housing sector, but many low-income households are moving into the private rental sector as the government reduces support for social housing. Finally, when planners have attempted large-scale strategies in urban housing markets, such as urban renewal (in the United States) and regeneration (in the UK), the interventions have often had limited effects or have created unanticipated problems. In the United States, decades of federal policy and planning that respond to certain political demands have created, maintained, and exacerbated segregation by race and income in American metropolitan areas, with low-cost housing concentrated in low-opportunity neighborhoods (Quigley 2000; von Hoffman 2009) In a fragmented political system with a limited state role, planning has not been able to implement its strengths: comprehensiveness and a view of the geographic scale of impacts.

In this chapter, I consider what the field of planning could offer in terms of a more effective state role in the housing market. Planning has a unique perspective among policy fields in its comprehensiveness, future orientation, and awareness of space and place. Tiesdell and Allmendinger (2005, 63) describe four functions of planning in the housing market: market shaping through plans that communicate information about future development; regulating with land-use and environmental controls; stimulating some kinds of development activity with subsidies and incentives; and building capacity by developing public–private partnerships or creating networks among actors. Considering this full range of potential actions, I argue that planners could have greater influence on housing market outcomes and in meeting shelter needs.

Employing a rational strategic model, planners can offer three distinct areas of advantage. First, planners are able to work in dynamic systems, providing plans as strategic frameworks that can adapt to changing contexts. These plans shape the market by signaling to development actors. Second, a rational policy formulation that considers many alternatives and potential outcomes is possible owing to planners' knowledge of the interconnections among places, along with an understanding of the range of market reactions to policy. Finally, by understanding the housing market as a social construction as well as an economic activity space, planners can use communicative action in moving toward implementation of policies. Political problems may cause as much difficulty in rational planning for housing needs as do problems of understanding market function. Throughout this chapter, I pay particular attention to ongoing attempts to deal with the repercussions of urban and housing policies/planning—including the exacerbation of segregation and the concentrations of poverty, sprawl, and an overheated market—within a context of limited resources and limited direct manipulation of housing with planning tools.

2. THE CONTEXT OF HOUSING PROVISION AND PLANNING

This section first describes the context of housing policy and planning in a market-dominated system. The provision of affordable housing includes a combination of supply- and demand-sideapproaches that result in a patchwork of programs rather than a strong safety net. The regulatory function of planning is important for determining how much and what kind of new housing is produced.

2.1 Ad hoc Solutions to Problems of Affordable Housing

As the state production for housing has fallen out of favor, and subsidies are shifted to households rather than housing units, a piecemeal and indirect system for producing the needed units has emerged (Quigley 2000). With a disjointed set of ad hoc solutions on the supply anddemand sides, shelter challenges are persistent. In

2008, nearly 18 million American households were severely cost burdened—that is, they spent more than half their monthly income on housing, constraining their spending on other necessities like food and health care (Joint Center for Housing Studies 2008). Only one-quarter of eligible renter households received housing subsidy assistance, and the number of units available for and affordable by very and extremely low income households has been shrinking (Joint Center for Housing Studies 2008). While many advocates call for housing assistance to become a federal entitlement (Freeman 2002; Bratt, Stone, and Hartman 2006), subsidies for low-cost housing needs have shrunken in real dollars during the first decade of the twenty-first century. In the United States, subsidies have shifted from supplying public housing to supporting renters with a demand-side subsidy. Substantial numbers of public housing units were demolished under the HOPE VI program. In contrast, in Britain, while the supply of social housing has contracted substantially since 1980 (from one-third to one-fifth of the housing stock), starting in the later 1990s, nonprofit housing associations evolved to take over ownership and management of rental stock from local council authorities, bringing an increase in new capital investment (Pawson 2006).

In the United States, most rental housing support is via vouchers that increase tenants' purchasing power. Quigley (2007) reports that after 2000, rental vouchers and certificates increased from two-thirds to three-quarters of HUD's support for housing, while support for project-based assistance was decreased by 20 percent (Quigley 2007, 8–9).[1] Many economists argue that all housing subsidies should be converted into vouchers (Olsen 2008) or even simple transfers of income (Glaeser and Gyourko 2008). Katz and Turner (2007), writing in conclusion to a Joint Center on Housing Studies symposium on "Revisiting Rental Housing," call the shift to demand-side rental assistance one of the major accomplishments of the federal housing policy, as it allows households mobility outside of government-supplied housing. However, as subsidized and other low-cost units are lost in the market, households face increasing difficulty finding housing even with voucher support (Turner 2003).

The rental housing supply in many areas, particularly the affordable rental supply, is inadequate to meet needs. In places where new rental housing construction is ongoing, it largely replaces older units (which make up much of the low-cost housing inventory in the central city).[2] The U.S. Low Income Housing Tax Credit expands the supply of affordable housing by subsidizing private investment in rental construction, but with expiring rent restrictions, it does not provide a permanent supply of affordable units. Schwartz and Melendez (2008) have studied policy tools for extending the life of LIHTC affordability, concluding that states can successfully create requirements and incentives for maintaining units beyond the initial period.

Problems for renter households go beyond just supply shortages. Rental housing is often seen as a distant second-best situation, owing to its relative instability and lack of asset building. Without significant social housing supplies, based on Briggs's (2005) findings, renters continue to reside on untenable legal ground, with landlords who are abusive or exploitive, and remain vulnerable to gentrification-caused rent increases. Apgar (2004) suggests that there is still considerable work to be done in making rent a "pathway to economic and social opportunity." Low-cost rental housing is clustered in disadvantaged neighborhoods, and there is a large body of research concluding that the neighborhood environment has nontrivial effects on individual behavior, ultimately affecting socioeconomic mobility.[3] This research on neighborhood effects underpins the mixed-income housing development strategies and housing mobility programs that direct poor households to more advantaged neighborhoods. Whether these programs create significant changes for the households is unclear; it seems that most achieve only limited socioeconomic advancement (Katz and Turner 2001; Popkin et al. 2000; Imbroscio 2008). A limited supply of affordable housing in low-poverty suburban locations makes it difficult to implement a housing mobility program on any large scale (Polikoff 2006).

There are both social and policy preferences for homeownership, evident in such programs as the U.S. home mortgage interest deduction on federal income taxes and Britain's Right to Buy program that moved many social renters into homeownership. The U.S. Department of Housing and Urban Development (HUD) prescribes affordable lending goals to Fannie Mae and Freddie Mac to encourage low- and moderate-income and minority homeownership, and the Community Reinvestment Act encourages lending in formerly redlined areas to attempt to close the gap in homeownership rates between whites and people of color. While homeownership offers more stable residence along with opportunities to access advantaged neighborhoods and to build assets through home equity, homeowners also face challenges (McCarthy, VanZandt, and Rohe 2001).[4] Boom-and-bust cycles in the housing market are increasingly global, as economies and financial systems become more intertwined. Changes in the financial sector—particularly, the explosive growth in subprime mortgage lending after 2000—make the bust that started in 2007 more severe than past cyclical downturns (Fishbein and Woodall 2006; Wheaton and Nechayev 2006). Observers assessing the asset-devaluation risk have proposed using financial instruments to decouple the shelter and investment functions of homeownership—allowing owners to sell future equity gains to raise cash or renters to invest in the house price index, for example (Smith, Searle, and Cook 2008). In the absence of such innovations, the sharp rise in mortgage defaults that started in 2007 triggered a worldwide financial systems crisis. The downturn has had major effects on the construction industry, consumer spending, and the financial markets, and the concentration of subprime loans in lower income, minority neighborhoods means that the crisis compounds distress in the urban core.[5]

2.2 Regulatory Functions of Planning

The uneven geographic distribution of lower cost housing units is not merely a market phenomenon; it is also planned and enforced through zoning and subdivision requirements (Downs 1988, 2001). Planning in the United States is typically organized within political jurisdictions, with very limited coordination of land use across municipal boundaries. Land-use controls are not created based on a projection of metropolitan-wide sheltering needs, as suggested above, but largely on fiscal conditions in a locality. Planners engaging in fiscal zoning prefer "profitable" land uses, including high-value single-family home construction, rather than face the negative fiscal impacts that may arise from multifamily construction and low-cost housing generally. With a fiscal imperative, it becomes difficult to consider regional coordination or meeting overall sheltering needs rather than maximizing the benefit to the locality.

In some areas, residential construction generally is very limited, leading to price inflation at all levels. Glaeser and Gyourko (2008) note that local land-use regulations lead to shortages of a wide range of housing types owing to either outright prohibition of development or to the additional costs imposed by meeting regulations put in place to minimize localities' fiscal burdens. A National Association of Home Builders (2007) study. conducted for the U.S. Department of Housing and Urban Development, found that the overwhelming majority of communities studied had regulatory requirements that exceeded standards for health and safety, which they termed unnecessary barriers to affordable housing. The most common means of exclusionary regulation was excessive lot size. This study echoes work by Glaeser and Gyourko (2008), which found large increases in the cost of development in areas with extensive regulations.[6]

Regulation can also be used to incorporate affordable housing in a metropolitan area. Even without an expansion of social housing, inclusionary or "fair share" housing requirements can have a significant impact in creating affordable housing throughout metropolitan regions—that is, requiring new residential construction to include some units affordable to low- and moderate-income households.[7] In the UK, national planning guidelines allow localities to include "Section 106" required affordable housing in new developments. However, the impact of these regulations has been limited. Monk, Short, and Whitehead (2005), in reviewing Section 106, found that developers most often were able to negotiate lower production of affordable units than were called for in plans. Despite setting targets, local planning authorities feared appeal by developers and community resistance to mixed-income and tenure development, resulting in an overall shortage of affordable units. The most widely known U.S. inclusionary zoning statute is in Montgomery County, a suburb of Washington, D.C., where the program has created over 11,000 units affordable to moderate-income families, although production has slowed significantly in recent years (Brown 2001). Mandates that localities plan for affordable housing in Florida, California, New Jersey, and Oregon have achieved only begrudging eventual acceptance and have yet to meet their compliance goals (Hoch 2007; Bollens 2003). Goetz, Chapple, and Lukermann (2003) and Hoch (2007) report that without support by public officials, requirements are merely symbolic and include no implementation strategies.

3. A Strategic Planning Framework
for Housing

The fact that urban planning is characterized by a focus on space and place, a future orientation, and a comprehensive view gives planners tools for analyzing the problems of providing housing to meet both shelter and social and economic goals. While we plan, develop, and indeed live in housing locally, Maclennan (2009) argues that the effects of problems in the housing market scale up and down beyond their initial impact. That is, local housing problems affect metropolitan areas, regions, and national economies. Excessive concentration in real estate industries owing to unchecked growth can destabilize a region's economy when there is a downturn. When individuals have inadequate housing, thereby limiting their opportunities and the development of human capital, there is an overall economic impact (Belfield 2008). Planning analysis can incorporate scales from individual to neighborhood to region; it can also address the scope of housing's importance beyond shelter to include its broader impact on individual socioeconomic mobility, neighborhood vitality, and economic stability.

The potential to really plan for housing needs is far greater than simply regulating land availability and use. In order to achieve the public goals associated with housing, planners can employ strategic analysis of the housing market and unmet needs. Strategic analysis begins with information and projections as a basis for considering long-term goals with short-term development actions. Subsequently planners can develop strategies, make decisions about the desirability of projected outcomes, and encourage market conditions favorable to reaching policy goals.

In Anglo-American planning systems, plans may not have absolute authority in themselves, but planners can act to shape the market and achieve housing goals. Strategies for meeting overall housing goals would include projecting needs and preferences as the basis for policy formulation, setting short-term development activities, and creating adaptable plans. In a framework of strategic choice, such as the one advocated by Wenban-Smith (2002), the planner can influence the market provision of housing through attention to land availability. Planners need to understand the housing market and its actors, not only as rational economic agents who act and react to policies but also as a social process that can be facilitated by communicative action.

3.1 Projections and Policy

Housing demand that arises from needs for shelter (as opposed to purely investment) are relatively predictable. Planners are in position to monitor the housing inventory across types, tenures, sizes, and prices, and also to consider the location of housing alongside economic development needs, the infrastructure, and other public services. Planners can provide demographic projections of household growth, which predict future needs for housing, especially if combined with preference studies, as described in Myers and Gearin (2001) and Myers and Ryu (2008), which anticipate changes over twenty years. In the UK, Barker's (2004) report for the Office of the Deputy Prime Minister (ODPM) called for attention to the supply of housing, which it found was overly limited owing to local land-use restrictions, slow response to demand by producers, and decreased public investment in social housing (see also Bramley 2007).

Given that housing markets are not bounded by political jurisdictions, such projections of supply-and-demand conditions should be made at the metropolitan level, not just the local. Planning in Great Britain includes regional-level analyses incorporated into requirements for fifteen- to twenty-year productions of new housing—plans that require coordination of needs and land uses. In contrast, in the United States, the availability of land for housing development is mainly controlled locally. With each municipality trying to maximize its own welfare in a zero-sum game, the overall market fails to meet the range of shelter needs in the region. Anthony Downs (1988, 1993, 2001) has argued strenuously that planners need to pay attention to the implications of land-use planning that controls housing development, as that planning affects a wider region than its jurisdictional boundaries. Comprehensive, regional thinking is of acknowledged importance in areas such as transportation or watershed management (Wheeler 2002); housing planners should also be working at the scale of the wider market.

Projections show how current trends may play out in the future. However, projections do not and should not set policy. The continuation of a trend may result in further inequity, shortages of some types of housing, sprawl, jobs–housing spatial mismatch, or other undesirable outcomes. Planners and other decision makers need to consider the goals for providing housing of different types, prices, and in different locations in light of, but not dictated by, projected demand and likely unmet needs. Determining these goals will involve planners' forging a consensus on desirable outcomes.

3.2 Plans Shape the Market Continuously

Planners outline the policy goals and the short-term actions that lead to long-term realization of those goals through plans. Plans provide signals about when and where land will be available for housing, along with other development and the extension and upgrading of the public infrastructure. However, plans for future development have limited immediate impact on the overall housing stock, which is built up over a long period of time; and planners have to accommodate population growth mostly with existing housing, yet with only a very limited amount built to suit today's needs. Housing strategies need to recognize the changes in the market and population as "a continuous and iterative process" (Wenban-Smith 2002, 38).

While projections are useful tools for developing these strategies, as conditions change, the plans must be adaptable to the new circumstances. Hopkins (2001) calls for plans that recognize that the future is not perfectly predictable and so can maintain options for actions in the future rather than providing a false sense of certainty. Recognizing that places are connected in the market, a strategic planning model would include monitoring conditions regionally. Is a surplus of new, greenfield development leading to a decline in older areas? Are regulations restricting the amount of housing, leading to price inflation? Planners should be ready to respond to unforeseen opportunities, economic shifts, and other housing market conditions—whether it is gentrification in a neighborhood or constriction in the global mortgage market. Should plans adjust the rate at which peripheral land is rezoned for residential development? Is there a need for the public sector to increase support for brownfields remediation? Can incentives be shifted to foment desired development? Can infrastructure or schools planning be coordinated with changing housing conditions? As the market changes in response to current plans and policies, the planner's projections must adjust to update actions and even revise long-term goals.

4. Unintended Consequences: Planning to Anticipate Change

American housing policymaking is largely a matter of addressing the consequences of past programs that themselves were touted as solutions to urban problems. The demolition of high-rise public housing, for example, was necessitated by the very federal production policies that concentrated poor minorities in these isolated high rises; the challenge of the geographic concentration of affordable rental is also related to subsidized production programs that incentivize their location in low-income neighborhoods. Furthermore, many of these subsidized units have been and continue to be lost to the affordable inventory as time limits on rent restrictions expire (Schwartz and Melendez 2008). The problems of implementing the HOPE VI public housing transformation program—for example, the great difficulty many residents have in relocating—are a further result of preexisting programs, which implicates the administration of the housing choice voucher program as deficient. Significant resources are channeled to ongoing attempts to ameliorate the repercussions of past policies that maintained and exacerbated segregation, subsidized sprawl, and restricted the supply of housing generally.

These policies failed in being comprehensive and in understanding how the market operates in its entirety—as a metropolitan-wide structure of interconnected segments. Rothenberg et al. (1991), using economic analysis, demonstrated how unintended consequences of various housing programs are actually predictable, given an understanding of how market segments interact. In order to maximize intended effects, planners need to understand how the housing market functions at several geographic scales—metropolitan, citywide, and neighborhood level.

A critical concept is the submarket; neighborhoods vary in housing quality and prices, and these smaller market segments both have internal dynamics and interact with other segments. Galster and Rothenberg (1991) provided a graphical analysis of the relationships among submarkets, showing how demand and supply in each affects the others. Watkins (2008, 168) writes, "clearly, it is difficult to effectively and strategically target resources at neighborhood or sub-regional levels without a sound understanding of spatial linkages between localities and likely spillover effects." An important research agenda emerges that is eminently practical: determining how local housing markets work, and how they respond to interventions, not only at one place and one time but also dynamically in a system of spatially delimited submarkets. Bourassa and Hoesli (1999, 2003); Jones, Leishman, and Watkins (2003); and Maclennan (1992; Maclennan and Tu 1996) describe submarkets as spatial areas based on different access to the CBD, housing types, and demographics. Jones, Leishman, and Watkins (2003) look at migration among neighborhoods to see how people react and respond to changing market conditions and incentives. Jones, Leishman, and Watkins (2003, 2004; Jones and Leishman 2006) have produced extensive work on the operationalization of housing submarkets using hedonic price indices for small spatial areas and migration linkages. Bates (2006) argues that understanding housing market geography at this micro level is as important for planners as understanding neighborhoods defined by social or political relationships. A more developed model of urban housing markets lends itself to assessing policies and planning interventions by predicting how suppliers and demanders would respond to market conditions and, by mapping the market, where those changes would take place (Bramley, Leishman, and Watkins 2008).

4.1 Revitalization Planning in an Interconnected Urban Housing Market

Revitalization strategies attempt to change the supply of housing—particularly the supply of decent quality housing—and to reshape the conditions for investment in an area. Urban planning can provide a strategic framework for revitalization activities that considers market-wide ramifications of program spending. The amounts disbursed over the last forty years to localities for community development, housing, and economic development in distressed areas are staggering given the current state of American cities;[8] Grigsby et al. (1987, 5) wrote in the mid-1980s of the "lengthy record of failure" of these efforts. Teaford (2000) concluded that urban renewal had only a limited impact on private development. Evaluators have also noted some negative consequences of revitalization, such as gentrification and displacement (Kennedy and Leonard 2001; Varady and Raffel 1995; Stegman 1979). Revitalization can have positive and negative impacts on nearby neighborhoods— the demolition of blighted public housing through HOPE VI may reduce crime and raise property values of nearby areas (Zielenbach 2003), but it also requires the relocation of large numbers of households, which may disrupt the social and economic fabric of the neighborhoods (Smith 2002).

In the face of continued urban neighborhood decline, planners have struggled to prioritize public spending in an environment of diminished resources. They have experimented with different models, from slum clearance to community development to public–private partnerships and market-based approaches. Some strategies call for a "triage" of the lowest quality neighborhoods, some for intensive investment in just a few neighborhoods, and others for preventing or fomenting "tipping" to maximize policy impact (Goetze and Colton 1980; Temkin and Rohe 1996; Quercia and Galster 2000).

Imbroscio (2008, 122) suggests several problems with these approaches to inner-city revitalization: faulty development models in the urban renewal program or empowerment zones; underfunding in Model Cities; a focus on downtowns at the expense of neighborhood development (e.g., UDAG); and a failure to properly target funding (e.g., CDBG). Some programs suffered from all of the above. The efficacy of place-base revitalization may call into question program implementation and policy design problems, rather than a fundamental flaw in the basic concept of neighborhood revitalization.

Community revitalization strategies are often based on a classification of neighborhoods, with policies and programs designed to match the conditions in each category. For example, Philadelphia's Neighborhood Transformation Initiative used a set of physical, social, and economic variables to designate six types of neighborhoods, with strategies for each quality level, including reclamation for the lowest quality areas. Similar approaches have been taken in Camden (New Jersey), Baltimore, Detroit, Richmond, and other distressed U.S. cities, as have areas in Great Britain's Housing Market Renewal program. Grigsby et al. (1987) point out that the policy of ranking neighborhoods based on housing quality and providing revitalization funding only to some is not, in fact, a strategy for stabilizing neighborhoods within a dynamic, interconnected urban area. Targeting neighborhoods as discrete units imagines that effects will be contained within the boundaries of these neighborhoods when, in fact, changing conditions in one neighborhood shift the relative positions of the entire array of neighborhoods as places for housing investment. Impacts of revitalization spill over into nearby areas, and to areas in the same housing submarket.

Planners working on urban revitalization need to link their plans and strategies more closely with the housing markets—that is, demand conditions and available supply. One example of this type of linked analysis is produced by The Reinvestment Fund in Philadelphia, which provides detailed spatial housing market analyses for cities.[9] However, the analyses are still not well linked to analysis of policy effects across submarkets. In the UK, housing market analysis and revitalization planning (commonly called "regeneration") have become more closely coordinated. The Office of the Deputy Prime Minister (ODPM) and the Scottish Executive provide guidelines for local planners conducting area-wide analyses that define submarkets. Guidelines for the Housing Market Renewal program, for example, require considering positive and negative impacts of the policy in the targeted and nearby areas and at different spatial scales (Office of the Deputy Prime Minister [ODPM] 2006).

Planners measure the displacement effects of regeneration, defined not only as the displacement of residents as a result of demolition or gentrification but also by how much demand for new housing in the target area is shifted away from existing developments in the targeted area, from the immediate vicinity, and from the locality (ODPM 2006, 8). The analysis also determines whether those shifts create negative externalities for nontargeted areas—for example, an area's tipping into deterioration owing to diminished demand. In the United States, such an undertaking—a national inventory of housing supply, shelter needs, and guidelines requiring planning reform—may be politically unfeasible. Nevertheless, given the long history of negative repercussions from place-targeted revitalization intervening in the housing market, planners and funders of these programs would do well to carefully analyze local housing market conditions and explore the links among neighborhoods that could confound the effects of a well-intentioned policy.

4.2 Analysis of the Effects of Inclusionary Housing

A second application of housing submarket analysis in planning is in the assessment of potential impacts of dispersing poverty by providing affordable housing in high-income neighborhoods. There is an extensive literature on the impact on house prices of nearby subsidized or affordable housing, since many NIMBY ("not in my back yard") concerns are prompted by fears of declining property values. Researchers continue to work on refining their models to ascertain the conditions under which affordable or subsidized housing may affect nearby property values, being careful to consider whether different submarkets have different price responses (see reviews by Nguyen 2005 and Koschinsky 2009). Nguyen's review (2005) finds "various effects on property values due to the structure of affordable housing units/sites, characteristics of the host neighborhood, compatibility between the affordable housing site and host neighborhood, and clustering of affordable housing units." Sophisticated studies (Galster et al. 2003; Ellen et al. 2001; Ellen and Voicu 2006) account for the historical trajectory of values in a neighborhood, casting further doubt on the claim that subsidized properties have negative price impacts.[10] Koschinsky (2009) further separates unsubsidized from subsidized rental properties, and accounts for building type as well as neighborhood land use in spatial models. As it stands, the title of Galster and colleagues' 2003 book, *Why Not in My Backyard?* summarizes the current assessment that the introduction of nonclustered, well-designed affordable housing is not detrimental to neighborhood property values.

4.3 The Social and Political Consequences of Housing Policies

Of course, analysis of the unintended consequences of housing policies should include social and political factors as well as economic. Watkins (2008) notes that not only economists but also other disciplines are needed to describe housing policy outcomes that are "messy" owing to social, cultural, political, and institutional factors. Freeman and Botein (2002) list four feared impacts of integrating affordable housing: declining property values, racial tipping, the concentration of poverty, and increased crime. Rosin's (2008) account of increased crime in a Memphis suburb after a public housing development was demolished, published in *The Atlantic*, drew intense criticism for its depiction of holders of housing vouchers as disrupting their new neighborhoods (Briggs et al. 2008). As Freeman and Botein (2002) find, thorny methodological problems make it difficult to discover strong empirical evidence for social disruption caused by the proximity of subsidized households. However, the publicity and political fallout from stories of the "migrating ghetto" make it difficult to promote housing mobility strategies.[11] Other researchers, notably Imbroscio (2006, 2008) have criticized the mobility approach for failing to acknowledge that some residents of poor neighborhoods would prefer a "housing choice" of staying in the central city—an option that requires community development and urban revitalization rather than resident dispersal. He further argues that the mobility strategy dilutes the minority, working-class, and progressive political power that is currently concentrated in the urban core (Imbroscio 2006). Imbroscio's strongly worded critiques point to the need for assessing the full spectrum of ramifications when housing policy is used to deconcentrate urban poverty—something more comprehensive planning could accomplish.

5. COMMUNICATIVE ACTION IN PLANNING FOR HOUSING

In a highly localized system, political conflict concerning housing developments can be a significant barrier to rational planning. Actors in the housing market—developers, financers, agents, and builders, along with local government—produce a culture with norms and standard operating procedures, share information, and consider ideas within a network of often conflict-ridden relationships, not just as rational economic actors (Healey and Barrett 1990). Downs (2001) goes so far as to indict the lack of affordable housing in new growth areas as an issue of democracy: some residents' views and desires, particularly those of high-income residents, are more valued than those who need affordable housing. Planners can convey research results on the limited impacts of affordable housing, but they may not be accepted by the public.

Planners' tools for working within a market system to direct the provision of housing, therefore, need to include not only rational approaches to gathering information and considering alternative policies but also different approaches to communicative action. These are useful in a context where goals are not agreed upon, such as when there are conflicts over the amount and location of affordable housing. Christensen (1985) suggests that framing, persuasion, and consensus building are responses to conditions of value conflict. Forester (1988 demonstrates the power of language and attention shaping to planners' work in contentious situations. Given limited authority over housing development, skills of persuasion and consensus building are crucial for reaching goals. A communicative agenda for housing planning could address two areas of research: understanding the culture of the development network and how its behavior might be shaped by communication from planners; and assessing communicative approaches to creating the political support for more inclusionary housing.

5.1 Overcoming Barriers to Revitalization: Beyond Market Obstruction

In areas of decline, where development activity is limited, planners may try to stimulate the market by designating a revitalization area, providing subsidies, and assisting with land assembly, among other activities. In order to target these activities, planners need to provide more than technical justifications to the decision makers. Plans for redevelopment will be carried out largely by the private sector, and further action may be needed to encourage investment. Healey (1998) argues that planners can improve the outcomes of "catalytic projects" for urban regeneration through stakeholder involvement in policymaking to achieve consensus and buy-in for key projects.

The development industry may present an obstacle to the revitalization effort if planners do not recognize how key actors understand the market and their roles in it. In illuminating the decision culture of the development industry, research offers possibilities for how communication can improve prospects for housing planning. Healey (1991) argues that planners need to understand the social processes of development, using rhetoric and imagery to persuade actors to invest in a new and possibly risky area. Furthermore, planning for regeneration might require what she calls "reconstituting the locale"—overcoming a neighborhood's negative reputation by improving the environmental quality, infrastructure, and other public services to increase confidence by development actors and reset the standard operating procedures to include revitalizing projects. Similarly, in an area with low levels of development activity and demand, the response to a stimulus policy may be slow and weak if the local development community is not prepared to respond to incentives. By studying the institutions and cultures, Guy and Hennebery (2000, 2413) conclude that we can add to our knowledge of a housing market as "dynamic, deeply contextual, and contingent on the particular aims and objectives of development actors."

Revitalization planning can also face political opposition. While observers conclude that significant improvements in neighborhood indicators are observed only in areas with high spending levels per poor resident (Galster et al. 2005), revitalization funding is often spread around city council districts or neighborhoods to maintain the illusion of fairness. Thomson (2008) finds that, in cities with a strong district-based council or with neighborhoods that are closely identified with a racial or ethnic group, it is more difficult to target revitalization activities in a strategic spatial plan. Similarly, Downs (2001) makes the argument that, with funds targeted based on political appeasement, rather than a rational scheme for maximizing efficacious use, revitalization funding will be relatively useless. Planners working in cities with more technical decision-making institutions, or a strong city manager with limited political fallout, may be more effective at implementing housing plans.

5.2 Making the Case for Inclusive Neighborhoods: Communicative Action in Practice

Housing mobility and poverty deconcentration programs have gained extensive support from researchers, but their effects are often mixed for participants who "move to opportunity." The obvious problem in the widespread implementation of housing mobility programs for the poor is a severely inadequate supply of low-cost housing in low-poverty areas. Fully implementing a mobility strategy or inclusionary zoning tools requires more than an understanding of housing market or social impacts. It also calls for a communication and political strategy on the part of planners. The housing shortage is the result of a basic problem in planning practice: a lack of efficacy in achieving integrative goals and an excess of efficacy of exclusionary goals. Planners have problems responding to the claims of existing residents, particularly those Fischel (2001) calls "Homevoters," who are primarily concerned with protecting property values (Downs 1988, 1993).[12] In response to NIMBYism at the local level, and others' reluctance to enact inclusionary zoning models, planners and advocates are beginning to employ proactive campaigns to increase support for development of affordable housing. They use different issue frames as a narrative device that tells the audience how to think about an issue (as in Rein and Schon's "framing devices") and, concomitantly, what should be done about it (Rein and Schon 1996).

Several organizations in the United States—such as Fannie Mae's Homes for Working Families, The National Association of Homebuilders' Housing for Hometown Heroes, and statewide organizations in Illinois, Pennsylvania, Minnesota, and North Carolina, among others—have created sophisticated campaigns that frame the issue of affordable housing in terms that maximize the potential audience and minimize the points of opposition. The messages of these campaigns are tailored to the issues raised by residents and political leaders when considering affordable housing; they use the techniques of framing the issue to shift the discussion of housing away from its negative associations and toward the concept of "housing choice." The American Planning Association has adopted a policy statement on housing that echoes many of these themes as a way for planners to address housing locally (American Planning Association 2006). The framing campaigns, which are based on extensive findings of public opinion research, can give planners and public officials tools for addressing the opposition to developing affordable housing at the local level. But these campaigns need to be better analyzed to determine how broad and effective they can be. Messaging techniques may soften public opinion on expanding homeownership opportunities, but by failing to address critical housing needs, they may inadvertently exacerbate the problems for those with the greatest needs. Holtzman (2006) argues that the main risk of sending the new message on housing is that resources will become skewed toward the middle class rather than the needy. Additionally, there are questions about the effectiveness of communications strategies generally: How powerful is framing in influencing the planning and political process? Are media campaigns effective in changing public opinion about a controversial topic? And if not, what kinds of communication might be effective? Even if the new message on affordable housing is generally well received, it may not change the response to a concrete proposal for subsidized or low-cost housing. Briggs (2003) makes a distinction between effective communication—telling the story and setting the frame—and the power to influence decision making. Planners will need to organize, in the sense described by Briggs, as motivating people to act on what matters to them (Briggs 2003, 7). In order to bring developments to fruition, the planner has to become an organizer, moving beyond issue framing to mobilization of supportive residents. It remains to be seen whether there exists the political will to address housing problems in a concerted manner; Dreier (2006) suggests it will take a generation of persistent reframing and mobilization before there is widespread support for HUD programs or housing interventions generally.

6. CONCLUSIONS

The stated goal for housing policy in the United States—to achieve "a decent home and a suitable living environment for all Americans"—has meant not only meeting basic shelter requirements but also setting far-reaching social and economic goals. Housing is linked to lofty goals of racial and economic integration and to creating vibrant, stable neighborhoods. For individuals, housing is not only shelter but also the psychological and emotional "home," as well as a source of socioeconomic mobility. Housing is seen as a foundation of the national economy, an investment, and the primary wealth-building tool for most American families.

At the same time, while we expect housing to help us meet public objectives, we have limited public planning for housing. We spend relatively little on housing for low-income families, and many resources are expended to counteract the negative consequences of past urban housing policies. Housing planning as a local function is largely indirect via land-use regulations, with weak tools for ensuring an adequate supply of a range of housing options. Planners' limited tools for responding in a timely manner to anticipated shelter needs, along with the fiscal and political realities of planning for a range of shelter needs, result in imbalances in supply and demand. The problems left unresolved include a persistent shortage of low-cost housing, the isolation of households who need those units, the fiscal inequities across metropolitan areas where central cities bear a disproportionately large tax burden, and overinvestment in high-cost single-family housing development.

Even within a context of limited resources and limited direct power over housing markets, there are significant opportunities for planning research to have a real opportunity to meet persistent housing challenges. We need clear thinking on public objectives and the expectation for housing to create individual and community benefits. Creating effective programs that address both shelter needs and social goals require solid research on market and nonmarket interactions and repercussions. With improved understanding of economic, social, and political phenomena, future policies may be able to avoid some of the unintended consequences we deal with today. Further investigation of the potential for communicative strategies to improve the implementation of programs is also important. Producing consequential research on housing needs and policies may push planners toward a better understanding of the potential of their role as state actors to shape and manipulate the market.

NOTES

1. In 2007, U.S. demand-side subsidies totaled $24 billion, while supply-side subsidies totaled $7.4 billion. This accounting does not include tax credits administered by the IRS in the Low Income Housing Tax Credit program, which make up an additional $4.1 billion (Quigley 2007).
2. The Joint Center for Housing Studies reports that in the Northeast, one unit is lost for every three new units constructed; in the Midwest, the ratio is one lost to two new units; and in the fast-growing West, two units are lost for every three newly built.
3. A number of authors have reviewed the research on educational attainment, sexual behavior, childbearing, crime, substance abuse, and employment (Brooks-Gunn, Duncan, and Aber 1997; Ellen and Turner 1997; Mayer and Jencks 1989; Haurin, Parcel, and Haurin 2002; Galster 2003, 2007). Further studies suggest

that social networks, institutions, employment availability, and the stigma of poor neighborhoods also affect individual socioeconomic mobility (Wilson 1987; ; Briggs 1997,1998; Wacquant and Wilson 1993; Kain and Singleton 1996; Ferguson 1991; Orfield and Gordon 2001; Preston and McLafferty 1999; McLafferty and Preston 1996; Holzer 1991; Ihlanfeldt and Svoqvist 1998). Galster and Killen (1995) define geography of opportunity as the effects the neighborhood has on an individual's expectations for the future, with poor neighborhoods creating both a perception and a reality of limited opportunities for education, work, and socioeconomic advancement.

4. Because homeowners have a much longer tenure in their homes than renters (13 years compared to 2.5 years), neighborhoods with high homeownership rates are more stable in terms of population and property values (Rohe, McCarthy, and Van Zandt 2000; Rohe and Stewart 1996). Children of homeowners are more likely to complete high school, find employment, and have higher earnings (Harkness and Newman 2002). Housing stability may even provide a buffer against the problems of a distressed neighborhood (Aaronson 2000).

5. The problem of increased foreclosures in areas with high rates of subprime lending is related to a conspicuous absence of mainstream lenders in low-income and minority neighborhoods (Immergluck and Wiles 1999).

6. This regulatory environment builds upon a history of policy that created and exacerbated segregation by race and income. These practices included FHA mortgage insurance redlining, slum clearance and the construction of large-scale public housing projects, race-restricted covenants in Sundown suburbs, and exclusionary zoning practices (Quigley 2000; Loewen 2005). Discrimination in lending, steering and blockbusting by real estate agents, and racially stratified employment contributed further (Jargowsky 2003).

7. Based on construction trends from 1980 to 2000, Rusk estimates that 3.5 million units of "workforce housing" would have been built with IZ requirements of 15 percent affordable units in developments of more than ten units (Rusk 2005).

8. A truncated list includes the 1966 Model Cities program of the Great Society, which allocated $1.2 billion for its first three years (in 1966 dollars); the Community Development Block Grant, first authorized in 1974, currently disbursing $4 billion annually; the complementary (albeit short-lived) UDAG funded up to $675 million per year during the 1970s.

9. The organization has supplied its "market value analysis" for Philadelphia, Camden (New Jersey), and Baltimore based on neighborhood indicators, linking the assessment to a set of policies designed for those conditions.

10. These models incorporate new techniques in spatial econometrics to account for autocorrelation among nearby properties, now recognized as a serious problem in hedonic regression studies (Can 1990; Can and Megbolugbe 1997).

11. Williams (2006) describes additional journalism on the topic of poverty deconcentration, citing editorials referring to an "untidy wave of need" and suggesting that when poor public housing residents arrive, "homies" are sure to follow.

12. NIMBYism ("not in my back yard") arises when potential developments are perceived to impact quality or life and/or property values (Schively 2007).

REFERENCES

Aaronson, Daniel. 2000. "A Note on the Benefits of Homeownership." *Journal of Urban Economics* 47(3): 356–69.

Adams, David, Craig Watkins, and Michael White, eds. 2005. *Planning, Public Policy and Property Markets.* Oxford: Blackwell.

American Planning Association. 2006. *Policy Guide on Housing.* Adopted by the Board of Directors April 23, 2006. Available at: http://www.planning.org/policy/guides/pdf/housing.pdf; accessed November 20, 2011.

Apgar, William. 2004. "Rethinking Rental Housing: Expanding the Ability of Rental Housing to Serve as a Pathway to Economic and Social Opportunity." Joint Center for Housing Studies Working Paper Series W04-11. Cambridge, MA: Harvard University Press.

Barker, Kate. 2004. "Review of Housing Supply. Delivering Stability: Securing our Future Housing Needs." Report to Office of the Deputy Prime Minister, London, UK. Available at: www.barkerreview.org.uk; accessed November 20, 2011.

Bates, L. K. 2006. "Does Neighborhood Really Matter?: Comparing Historically Recognized Neighborhoods With Housing Submarkets." *Journal of Planning Education and Research* 26(1): 5–17.

Belfield, Clive. 2008. "Preschool Education and Human Capital Development in Central Cities." In *Urban and Regional Policy and Its Effects,* Vol. 1, edited by M. A. Turner, H. Wial, and H. Wolman, 155–80. Washington, DC: Brookings Institution Press.

Bollens, Scott A. 2003. "In Through the Back Door: Social Equity and Regional Governance." *Housing Policy Debate* 13(4): 631–57.

Bourassa, Steven C., and Martin Hoesli. 1999. *The Structure of Housing Submarkets in a Metropolitan Region.* Geneva: Ecole des Hautes Etudes Commerciales,Universite de Geneve. Available at: http://www.hec.unige.ch/recherches_publications/cahiers/1995-1999/99.15.pdf; accessed November 20, 2011.

Bourassa, Steven C., and Martin Hoesli. 2003. "Do Housing Submarkets Really Matter?" *Journal of Housing Economics* 12(1): 12–28.

Bramley, Glen. 2007. "The Sudden Rediscovery of Housing Supply as a Key Policy Challenge." *Housing Studies* 22(2): 221–41.

Bramley, G., C. Leishman, and D. Watkins. 2008. "Understanding Neighbourhood Housing Markets: Regional Context, Disequilibrium, Sub-Markets and Supply." *Housing Studies* 23(2): 179–212.

Bratt, Rachel G., Michael Stone, and Chester Hartman, eds. 2006. *A Right to Housing: Foundation for a New Social Agenda.* Philadelphia: Temple University Press.

Briggs, Xavier de Souza. 1997. "Moving Up versus Moving Out: Neighborhood Effects in Housing Mobility." *Housing Policy Debate* 8(1): 195–234.

Briggs, Xavier de Souza. 1998. "Brown Kids in White Suburbs: Housing Mobility and the Many Faces of Social Capital." *Housing Policy Debate* 9(1): 177–219.

Briggs, Xavier de Souza. 2003. "Organizing Stakeholders, Building Movement, Setting the Agenda." Working paper, Community Problem-Solving Project at Massachusetts Institute of Technology, Cambridge, MA.

Briggs, Xavier de Souza. 2005. "Politics and Policy: Changing the Geography of Opportunity." In *The Geography of Opportunity: Race and Housing Choice in Metropolitan America,* edited by William Julius Wilson and Xavier de Souza Briggs, 310–39. Washington, DC: Brookings Institution Press.

Briggs, Xavier de Souza; Peter Dreier, et al. 2008. "Memphis Murder Mystery? No, Just Mistaken Identity." *Shelterforce.* Online, available at: http://www.shelterforce.org/article/special/1043/.

Brooks-Gunn, Jeanne, Greg J. Duncan, and J. Lawrence Aber, eds. 1997. *Neighborhood Poverty: Context and Consequences for Children.* New York: Russell Sage Foundation.

Brown, K. D. 2001. *Expanding Affordable Housing through Inclusionary Zoning: Lessons from the Washington Metropolitan Area.* Washington, DC: Brookings Center on Urban and Metropolitan Policy.

Can, Ayse. 1990. "The Measurement of Neighborhood Dynamics in Urban House Prices." *Economic Geography* 66(3): 254–72.

Can, Ayse, and Isaac Megbolugbe. 1997. "Spatial Dependence and House Price Index Construction." *Journal of Real Estate Finance and Construction* 14:203–22.

Christensen, Karen S. 1985. "Coping with Uncertainty in Planning." *Journal of the American Planning Association* 51(1): 63–73.

Clapham, David. 1996. "Housing and the Economy: Broadening Comparative Housing Research." *Urban Studies* 33(4–5): 631–47.

Downs, A. 1988. "The Real Problem with Suburban Anti-Growth Policies." *Brookings Review* 6(2): 23–29.

Downs, A. 1993. "Reducing Regulatory Barriers to Affordable Housing Erected by Local Governments." In *Housing Markets and Residential Mobility,* edited by G. T. Kingsley and M. A. Turner, 255–82. Washington, DC: Urban Institute Press.

Downs, Anthony. 2001. "How City Planning Practices Affect Metropolitan-Area Housing Markets and Vice Versa." Report to the Millennial Housing Commission, Washington DC. Available at: http://govinfo.library.unt.edu/mhc/papers.html.

Dreier, Peter. 2006. "Labor's Love Lost? Rebuilding Unions' Involvement in Federal Housing Policy." *Housing Policy Debate* 11(2): 327–92.

Ellen, Ingrid Gould, Michael H. Schill, Scott Susin, and Amy E. Schwartz. 2001. "Building Homes, Reviving Neighborhoods: Spillovers from Subsidized Construction of Owner-Occupied Housing in New York City." *Journal of Housing Research* 12(2): 185–216.

Ellen, Ingrid Gould, and Margery Austin Turner. 1997. "Does Neighborhood Matter? Assessing Recent Evidence." *Housing Policy Debate* 8(4): 833–66.

Ellen, Ingrid Gould and Ian Voicu. 2006. "Nonprofit Housing and Neighborhood Spillovers." *Journal of Policy Analysis and Management* 25(1): 35–52.

Ferguson, Ronald F. 1991. "Paying for Public Education: New Evidence on How and Why Money Matters." *Harvard Journal on Legislation* 28(2): 465–98.

Fischel, W. A. 2001. *The Homevoter Hypothesis: How Home Values Influence Local Government Taxation, School Finance, and Land-Use Policies.* Cambridge, MA: Harvard University Press.

Fishbein, Allen J., and Patrick Woodall. 2006. *Exotic or Toxic: An Examination of the Non-traditional Mortgage Market for Consumers and Lenders.* Washington, DC: Consumer Federation of America.

Forester, John. 1988. *Planning in the Face of Power.* Berkeley, CA: University of California Press.

Freeman, Lance. 2002. "America's Affordable Housing Crisis: A Contract Unfulfilled." *American Journal of Public Health* 92(5): 709–12.

Freeman, Lance, and Hilary Botein. 2002. "Subsidized Housing and Neighborhood Impacts: A Theoretical Discussion and Review of the Evidence." *Journal of Planning Literature* 16(3): 339–78.

Galster, George. 2003. "Investigating Behavioral Impacts of Poor Neighborhoods: Towards New Data and Analytical Strategies," *Housing Studies* 18(6): 893–914.

Galster, George. 2005. "Consequences from the Redistribution of Urban Poverty During the 1990s: A Cautionary Tale." *Economic Development Quarterly* 19:119–25.

Galster, George. 2007. "Should Policymakers Strive for Neighborhood Social Mix? An Analysis of the Western European Evidence Base." *Housing Studies* 22(4): 523–46.

Galster, George C., and Sean P. Killen 1995. "The Geography of Metropolitan Opportunity: A Reconnaissance and Conceptual Framework." *Housing Policy Debate* 6(1): 7–43.

Galster, George, and Jerome Rothenberg. 1991. "Filtering in a Segmented Model of Housing Markets." *Journal of Planning Education and Research* 11:37–50.

Galster, George C., P. A. Tatian, A. M. Santiago, K. L. S. Pettit, and R. E. Smith. 2003. *Why Not in My Backyard?* Piscataway, NJ: Rutgers University Press.

Galster George C, C. Walker, C. Hayes, P. Boxall, and J. Johnson. 2005. "Measuring the Impact of Community Development Block Grant Spending on Urban Neighborhoods." *Housing Policy Debate* 15(4): 903–34.

Glaeser, Edward L., and Joseph Gyourko. 2008. *Rethinking Federal Housing Policy: How to Make Housing Plentiful and Affordable.* Washington, DC: AEI Press.

Goetz, Edward G. 2003. *Clearing the Way: Deconcentrating the Poor in Urban America.* Washington, DC: Urban Institute Press.

Goetz, Edward, K. Chapple, and B. Lukermann. 2003. "Enabling Exclusion: The Retreat from Regional Fair Share Housing in the Implementation of the Minnesota Land Use Act." *Journal of Planning Education and Research* 22(3): 213–25.

Goetze, Rolf, and Kent W. Colton. 1980. "The Dynamics of Neighborhoods: A Fresh Approach to Understanding Housing and Neighborhood Change." *Journal of the American Planning Association* 46(2): 184–94.

Grigsby, William, Morton Baratz, George Galster, and Duncan Maclennan. 1987. *The Dynamics of Neighborhood Change and Decline.* London: Pergamon.

Guy, Simon, and John Henneberry. 2000. "Understanding Urban Development Processes: Integrating the Economic and the Social in Property Research." *Urban Studies* 37(13): 2399–416.

Harkness, Joseph, and Sandra J. Newman.2002. "Homeownership for the Poor in Distressed Nieghborhoods: Does This Make Sense?" *Housing Policy Debate* 13(3): 597–630.

Haurin, D., T. Parcel, and R. Haurin. 2002. "Does Home Ownership Affect Child Outcomes?" *Real Estate Economics* 30:635–66.

Healey, P. 1991. "Urban Regeneration and the Development Industry." *Regional Studies* 25(2): 97–110.

Healey, P. 1998. "Building Institutional Capital through Collaborative Approaches to Urban Planning." *Environment and Planning Part A* 30(9): 1531–46.

Healey, Patsy, and S. Barrett. 1990. "Structure and Agency in Land and Property Development Processes: Some Ideas for Research." *Urban Studies* 27:87–104.

Hoch, Charles. 2007. "How Plan Mandates Work: Affordable Housing in Illinois." *Journal of the American Planning Association* 73(1): 86–99.

Holzer, Harry. 1991. "Spatial Mismatch Hypothesis: what has the evidence shown?" *Urban Studies* 28(1): 105–22.

Holtzman, D. 2006. "Managing the Message: Telling Stories That Support Affordable Housing." *Shelterforce.* Online 146. Available at: http://www.nhi.org/online/issues/146/managingthemessage.html; accessed November 20, 2011.

Hopkins, Lewis D. 2001. *Urban Development: The Logic of Making Plans.* Washington, DC: Island Press.

Ihlandfeldt, Keith R., and David L. Sjoqvist. 1998. "The Spatial Mismatch Hypothesis: A Review of Recent Studies and Their Implications for Welfare Reform." *Housing Policy Debate.* 9(4): 849–92.

Imbroscio, David. 2006. "Shaming the Inside Game: A Critique of the Liberal Expansionist Approach to Addressing Urban Problems." *Urban Affairs Review* 42(2): 224–48.

Imbroscio, David. 2008. "United and Actuated by Some Common Impulse of Passion: Challenging the Dispersal Consensus In American Housing Policy Research." *Journal of Urban Affairs* 20(2): 111–30.

Immergluck, Daniel, and Marti Wiles. 1999. *Two Steps Back: The Dual Mortgage Market, Predatory Lending and the Undoing of Community Development.* Chicago: Woodstock Institute.

Jargowsky, Paul. 2003. *Stunning Progress, Hidden Problems: The Dramatic Decline of Concentrated Poverty in the 1990s.* Washington, DC: Brookings Institution Press.

Joint Center for Housing Studies. 2008. *The State of the Nation's Housing.* Cambridge, MA: Harvard University Press.

Jones, C., and C. Leishman. 2006. "Spatial Dynamics of the Housing Market: An Inter-Urban Perspective." *Urban Studies* 43(7): 1041–59. .

Jones, C., C. Leishman, and C. Watkins. 2003. "Structural Change in Urban Housing Markets." *Environment and Planning Part A* 35:1315–26.

Jones, C., C. Leishman, and C. Watkins. 2004. "Migration Linkages Between Urban Housing Submarkets: Theory and Evidence." *Housing Studies* 19(2): 269–83.

Kain, J., and K. Singleton. 1996. "Equality of Educational Opportunity Revisited." *New England Economic Review,* May/June, 26–40.

Katz, Bruce J., and Margery Austin Turner. 2001. "Who Should Run the Housing Voucher Program? A Reform Proposal." *Housing Policy Debate.* 12(2): 239–62.

Katz, Bruce J., and Margery Austin Turner. 2007. "Rethinking U.S. Rental Housing Policy." Joint Center for Housing Studies Working Paper RR07–10, Harvard University.

Kennedy, Maureen, and Paul Leonard. 2001. *Dealing with Neighborhood Change: A Primer on Gentrification and Policy Choices.* Washington, DC: Brookings Institution Press.

Koschinsky, Julia. 2009. "Spatial Heterogeneity in Spillover Effects of Assisted and Unassisted Rental Housing." *Journal of Urban Affairs* 31(3): 319–47.

Loewen, James M. 2005. *Sundown Towns: A Hidden Dimension of American Racism.* New York City: The New Press.

Maclennan, Duncan. 1992 *Housing Search and Choice in a Regional Housing System: New Housing in Strathclyde.* A report to the Housing Research Foundation for the Scottish House Builders Federation, University of Glasgow.

Maclennan, Duncan. 2009. "Housing Policies: Devolved or Disunited?" Presentation at International Sociological Association Conference, Housing Assets Housing People, September 2, 2009, Glasgow, Scotland.

Maclennan, Duncan, and Yong Tu. 1996. "Economic Perspectives on the Structure of Local Housing Systems." *Housing Studies* 11(3): 387–407.

Mayer, Susan E., and Christopher Jencks. 1989. "Growing up in Poor Neighborhoods: How Much Does it Matter?" *Science* 243(4897): 1441–45.

McCarthy, Geroge, Shannon VanZandt, and William M. Rohe. 2001. "The Economic Benefits and Costs of Homeownership: A Critical Assessment of the Research." Working Paper No. 01–02, Research Institute for Housing America, Washington, DC.

McLafferty, S., and V. Preston. 1996. "Spatial Mismatch and Employment in a Decade of Restructuring." *Professional Geographer* 48:420–31.

Monk, Sarah, Christina Short, and Christine Whitehead. 2005. "Planning Obligations and Affordable housing." In *Planning, Public Policy and Property Markets*, edited by David Adams, Craig Watkins, and Michael White, 185–208. London: Blackwell.

Myers, Dowell, and Elizabeth Gearin. 2001. "Current Housing Preferences and Future Demand for Denser Residential Environments." *Housing Policy Debate* 12(4): 633–59.

Myers, Dowell, and SungHo Ryu. 2008. "Aging Baby Boomers and the Generational Housing Bubble: Foresight and Mitigation of an Epic Transition." *Journal of the American Planning Association* 74(1): 17–33.

National Association of Home Builders. 2007. Study of Subdivision Requirements as a Regulatory Barrier. Research Center report to HUD Office of Policy Development and Research. Available at: http://www.huduser.org/portal/publications/commdevl/subdiv_report.html.

Nguyen, Mai T. 2005. "Does Affordable Housing Detrimentally Affect Property Values? A Review of the Literature." *Journal of Planning Literature* 20(1): 15–26.

Office of the Deputy Prime Minister. 2006. "Assessing the Impact of a Housing Market Renewal pathfinder intervention: Displacement issues." Available at: http://www.communities.gov.uk/documents/housing/pdf/144086.pdf .

Olsen, Edgar O. 2008. "Getting More from Low Income Housing Assistance." Discussion Paper 2008–13. The Hamilton Project, Brookings Institution, Washington, DC.

Orfield, Gary, and Nora Gordon. 2001. *Schools More Separate: Consequences of a Decade of Desegregation.* Cambridge, MA: Harvard University Press.

Pawson 2006. <<please supply biblio info for your text cite>>

Polikoff, Alexander. 2006 *Waiting for Gautreaux: A Story of Segregation, Housing, and the Black Ghetto.* Evanston, IL: Northwestern University Press.

Popkin, Susan J., Larry F. Buron, Diane K. Levy, and Mary K. Cunningham. 2000. "The Gautreaux Legacy." *Housing Policy Debate* 11(4): 911–42.

Preston, Valerie, and Sara McLafferty. 1999. "Spatial Mismatch Research in the 1990s: Progress and Potential." *Papers in Regional Science* 78:387–402.

Quercia, Roberto G., and George C. Galster. 2000. "Threshold Effects and Neighborhood Change." *Journal of Planning Education and Research* 20:146–62.

Quigley, John M. 2000. "A Decent Home: Housing Policy in Perspective." *Brookings-Wharton Papers on Urban Affairs.* 53–88.

Quigley, John M. 2007. <<please supply biblio info for text/note cite>>

Rein, M., and D. Schon. 1996. "Frame-Critical Policy Analysis and Frame-Reflective Policy Practice." *Knowledge and Policy* 9(1): 85–105.

Rohe, William M., George McCarthy, and Shannon VanZandt. 2000. "The Social Benefits and Costs of Homeownership: A Critical Assessment of the Research." Working Paper no. 00–01. Research Institute for Housing America, Washington, DC.

Rohe, William M., and Leslie M. Stewart. 1996. "Homeownership and Neighborhood Stability." *Housing Policy Debate* 7(1): 37–81.

Rosin, Hanna. 2008. "American Murder Mystery." *The Atlantic*, July/August. Available at: http://www.theatlantic.com/magazine/archive/2008/07/american-murder-mystery/6872/.

Rothenberg, Jerome, George C. Galster, Richard V. Butler, and Ronald Pitkin. 1991. *The Maze of Urban Housing Markets: Theory, Evidence, and Policy.* Chicago: University of Chicago Press.

Rusk, David. 1995. *Cities without Suburbs.* Washington DC: Woodrow Wilson Press.

Schively, C. 2007. "Understanding the NIMBY and LULU Phenomena: Reassessing Our Knowledge Base and Informing Future Research." *Journal of Planning Literature* 21(3): 255–66.

Schwartz, Alex, and Edwin Melendez. 2008. "After year 15: Challenges to the Preservation of Housing Financed with Low-Income Housing Tax Credits." *Housing Policy Debate* 19(2): 261–94.

Smith, Robin E. 2002. "Housing Choice for HOPE VI Relocatees." Report by the Urban Institute. Available at: http://www.urban.org/url.cfm?ID=410592.

Smith, Susan J., Beverley A. Searle, and Nicole Cook. 2008. "Rethinking the Risks of Home Ownership." *Journal of Social Policy* 38(1): 83–102.

Stegman, Michael A. 1979. "Neighborhood Classification and the Role of the Planner in Seriously Distressed Communities." *Journal of the American Planning Association.* 45(4): 495–505.

Teaford, Jon C. 2000. "Urban Renewal and Its Aftermath." *Housing Policy Debate* 11(2): 443–65.

Temkin, Kenneth, and William Rohe. 1996. "Neighborhood Change and Urban Policy." *Journal of Planning Education and Research* 15(3): 159–70.

Thomson, Dale E. 2008. "Strategic, Geographic Targeting of Housing and Community Development Resources: A Conceptual Framework and Critical Review." *Urban Affairs Review* 43:629–62.

Tiesdell, Steve, and Philip Allmendinger. 2005. "Planning Tools and Markets: Towards an Extended Conceptualization." In *Planning, Public Policy and Property Markets*, edited by David Adams, Craig Watkins, and Michael White, 56–76. London: Blackwell.

Turner, M. A. 2003. "Strengths and Weaknesses of the Housing Voucher Program." Congressional testimony to Committee on Financial Services, Subcommittee on Housing and Community Opportunity, United States House of Representatives, June 17, 2003.

Turner, Margery Austin, Howard Wial, and Harold Wolman, eds. 2008. *Urban and Regional Policy and its Effects.* Washington, DC: Brookings Institution Press.

Varady, David P., and Jeffrey A. Raffel. 1995. *Selling Cities: Attracting Homebuyers Through Schools and Housing programs.* Albany: State University of New York Press.

von Hoffman, Alexander. 2009. "Housing and Planning: A Century of Social Reform and Local Power." *Journal of the American Planning Association* 75(2): 231–44.

Wacquant, Loic .J. D., and W. J. Wilson. 1993. "The Cost of Racial and Class Exclusion in the Inner City." In *The Ghetto Underclass: Social Science Perspectives*, edited by W. J. Wilson, 25–42. Newbury Park, CA: Sage.

Watkins, C. 2008. "Microeconomic Perspectives on the Structure and Operation of Local Housing Markets." *Housing Studies* 23(2): 163–77.

Wenban-Smith, Alan. 2002. "A Better Future for Development Plans: Making 'Plan, Monitor and Manage' Work." *Planning Theory and Practice* 3(1): 33–51.

Wheaton, William C., and Gleb Nechayev. 2006. "Past Housing "Cycles" and the Current Housing 'Boom': What's Different This Time?" Available at: http://econ-www.mit.edu/files/1760.

Wheeler, Stephen M. 2002. "The New Regionalism: Key Characteristics of an Emerging Movement." *Journal of the American Planning Association* 68(3): 267–78.

Williams, Rhonda Y. 2006. "Race, Dismantling the 'Ghetto,' and National Housing Mobility: Considering the Polikoff Proposal." *Journal of Law and Social Policy* 1(1). Available at: http://www.law.northwestern.edu/journals/njlsp/v1/n1/4/.

Wilson, William J. 1987. *The Truly Disadvantaged: The Inner City, the Underclass and Public Policy.* Chicago: University of Chicago Press.

Zielenbach, Sean. 2003. "Assessing Economic Change in HOPE VI Neighborhoods." *Housing Policy Debate* 14(4): 621–56.

CHAPTER 26

CITIES WITH SLUMS

VINIT MUKHIJA

WE live in the *Century of the City* (Pierce and Johnson 2008). Most likely in 2007, with urbanization levels peaking in the developed world but gradually increasing in most developing countries, a majority of the world started living in urban areas. In part spurred by this demographic transition, international development planning is moving from its conventional emphasis on agricultural productivity and rural subsistence to a greater focus on cities and regions as the engines of economic growth (World Bank 2009). Another reason for the renewed interest of development planners and policymakers in cities is the unexpected rise in urban poverty. A key indicator that has caught the attention of scholars and practitioners is the magnitude and increase in the number of "slum dwellers." According to the United Nations, almost a billion people now live in urban slums (UN-Habitat 2003). It is also accepted that the number of slum dwellers "increased substantially during the 1990s" (UN-Habitat 2003, 14). Most, but not all, of these slum dwellers live in cities of the developing world. Furthermore, the United Nations urban planning nodal agency—UN-Habitat—projects that without dramatic changes in urbanization patterns or sharp increases in the supply trends of formal housing, by about 2030–35 there could be almost 2 billion slum dwellers with inadequate infrastructure and substandard housing conditions (UN-Habitat 2003, xxv). Around that time, the majority of the world's poor will also be living in urban areas. In response, the United Nations has launched a global campaign for "Cities without Slums."

There is no consensus on what constitutes a slum, and this makes the UN's data and projections somewhat suspect. The United Nations, like many other public agencies, assumes that insecure tenure, substandard housing (structural quality and overcrowding) and poor infrastructure conditions (inadequate access to safe water and sanitation) define a slum (UN-Habitat 2003, 2007). It is, nonetheless, difficult to operationalize these attributes in a consistent manner for different cities across the world. Moreover, the word *slum* can be counterproductive because of its history of adverse policy implications and pejorative connotations. Like Alan Gilbert (2007, 697), I worry that the use of the terminology of slums—"with all its inglorious associations"—risks perpetuating and reinforcing the discredited policy response of urban renewal and slum clearance. Most housing researchers agree that slum clearance, ostensibly meant to help the poor, invariably reduces the supply of centrally located affordable housing (Abrams 1966). The UN's well-intentioned but poorly titled campaign of "Cities without Slums" has provided new impetus to the dangerous possibility of slum clearance. Contrary to a policy emphasis on clearance, scholars like Lisa Peattie (1994) emphasize the need for cities to preserve and increase housing that the poor can afford. If such housing is referred to as slums, and it usually is, then instead of cities without slums we need cities with slums.

Modern urban planning can trace its roots to the nineteenth-century tenements and slums of London, New York, and other Western cities (Hall 1995). Urban planners remain keenly interested in decent affordable housing for its importance as a basic human need and its contribution to the health and well-being of individuals and families (Martinez et al. 2008; Turner 1976; Turner and Fichter 1972). Housing construction is also an important economic sector with positive multiplier effects (Burns and Grebler 1977). Housing is often a site for work, particularly in developing countries, and also a location for accessing employment, services, and amenities (Peattie 1987; Rodwin 1987). It is likely that planners' involvement and efforts to address poor housing conditions will get a renewed sense of urgency, owing to the scale and extent of the housing inadequacies reported by the United Nations. The eternal quest for a better quality of housing for the poor is likely to persist as an important arena of intervention by urban planners in the twenty-first century.

My aim in this chapter is to share an appreciation of the necessity and diversity of slums, and to discuss the debates in planning literature about the appropriate policy responses for improving slum housing conditions. Planners and scholars mostly agree that there are two key avenues for policy action. First, increase the affordable supply of formal or regulated housing, and thus reduce the pressure for the formation of new slums. Second, increase private investment in existing substandard housing to improve their quality. Scholars, however, disagree on how to achieve these objectives. For example, there are differences in what proactive lessons planners can learn from slums and the informal housing strategies of the poor, and on the appropriate role for governments in the housing sector. Similarly, researchers debate the best strategies for attracting private investment in slum upgrading. The conventional wisdom based on the seminal work of John Turner (1963, 1967, 1968, 1976) and Hernando de Soto (1989, 2000) supports security of tenure and the legalization of private property rights to facilitate investment. The contrarian literature, however, suggests that there are additional possibilities and there is a need to be wary of the displacement of low-income renters. My own research supports the advantages of multiple policy approaches and the responsibility of urban planners to increase the range of viable options. However, before I elaborate on the planning debates, in the next section I begin with a short discussion of the contentious terminology of slums. It is followed by an appreciation of the diversity and the "incremental development" logic of slums in section three. The discussion on planning and policy responses follows in section four and reiterates the need for cities with slums. In the conclusion I recap the arguments and briefly dwell on the critical role of public participation in slum-upgrading decisions.

1. The Problematic Language of Slums

The term *slum* often evokes dystopian images of disorder, crime, and immorality (Davis 2004, 2006). In the ecological tradition of urban studies, slums have also been equated with a cancerous growth that is malignant and likely to spread to other neighborhoods of the city (Stokes 1962). Thus, it is hardly surprising that removing slums has been an attractive and dominant policy option. Moreover, many slums are centrally located on land that has the potential to be redeveloped for more valuable and profitable land uses. The imperative to eradicate slums also received a boost with the modernist credo in physical determinism and the presumed importance of well-designed housing in human development. Consequently, in the mid-twentieth century, slum clearance and urban renewal programs were prevalent worldwide in both developed and developing countries. But slum clearance did not help the poor. It was far easier to demolish substandard housing than to construct new housing. Almost universally, the programs reduced the stock of available housing, not just affordable housing. As Charles Abrams (1966, 126) pithily observed, "In a housing famine there is nothing that slum clearance can accomplish that cannot be done more efficiently by an earthquake."

The sociologist Herbert Gans (1962) has emphasized the importance of language and names in public policy. He provocatively claimed that if the neighborhoods of slum clearance and urban renewal in the United States had been called urban villages instead of slums, policymakers would not have received adequate public support for their redevelopment plans. Aware of the possibilities and dangers of slum clearance, many scholars and sensitive observers try to avoid using the terminology of slums, even though the alternatives—squatter settlements, informal settlements, spontaneous settlements, irregular settlements, illegal subdivisions, illegal cities, shadow cities, gray cities, and the like—are also less than satisfactory (Fernandes and Varley 1996; Gilbert 2007; Neuwirth 2005). These terms focus less on the substandard housing and living conditions but try to emphasize the different origins and legality of settlements. The alternative names are equally imprecise, and there is a lack of consensus regarding the ideal language. Their chief virtue might be that they are considered less pejorative than *slum*. For example, even the Kenya's Central Bureau of Statistics in its census of slums prefers to use the terminology of "informal settlements" (Gulyani and Talukdar 2008).

Similarly, with a colleague, I have previously argued that appellations like slums can be misleading, prejudiced, and detrimental (Mukhija and Monkkonen 2007). Generic labels like "slum" can be misleading because they are likely to hide far more than they reveal about the distinct qualities and needs of their neighborhoods. They are prejudiced because they invariably raise negative connotations about the residents of these places. Finally, they can be detrimental because they emphasize not just the otherness but also the inferior status of some urban neighborhoods, and this makes it more difficult to integrate them with the rest of the city. But we also acknowledged that such names, although controversial, have the ability to capture public attention and galvanize policy action. Until a more nuanced language is developed, the moniker of "slum" might be as good or bad as its alternatives. Urban planners, nonetheless, must recognize and be alert that the terminology of slums inevitably comes with the risk of slum clearance, and they must ensure that clearance is a policy of last resort. In addition, planning researchers must help policymakers recognize the heterogeneity and underlying logic of slums and the necessity of a range of policy options for improving living conditions within slum neighborhoods.

2. THE DIVERSITY AND LOGIC OF SLUMS

As the policy idea of slum clearance gained currency in the middle of the last century, scholars started questioning the universally negative views of slums. One line of research challenged the negative stereotype of slum residents as an underclass with little interest or capacity for progress, and explained the value of slums as an important low-cost housing option (Abrams 1966; Gans 1962; Jacobs 1961; Peattie 1968; Turner 1963, 1972). It is likely that their work helped thwart the enthusiasm for slum clearance. A second, but related, avenue of inquiry questioned the implicit homogeneity of slums in public policy. It suggested a distinction between real slums and apparent slums, and its key contribution was to explain the diversity of slums. Consequently, two kinds of slums started to emerge in the literature: good (*slums of hope*) and bad (*slums of despair*). Charles Stokes (1962) was the first to explicitly make these distinctions and use the terminology while contrasting inner-city slums in the United States with squatter settlements in developing countries. But John Turner and William Mangin, who had been working and conducting research in Lima, Peru, more comprehensively explained the underlying logic of the so-called slums of hope (Mangin 1967; Mangin and Turner 1968; Turner 1972, 1976).

2.1 Slums of Hope and Despair

Housing and living conditions in the slums of hope, scholars like Turner and Mangin argued, gradually improve. These good slums, they suggested, tend to be at the periphery of cities and are characterized by regular layouts that follow a grid-iron plan (Mangin and Turner 1968). Their origins, Turner suggested (1967), can be traced to squatting through organized land invasions of the kind he observed in Peru. Although security of tenure was tenuous for squatters, the invasions provided an opportunity for households with modest incomes to become upwardly mobile homeowners. This was their chief virtue. As more research was conducted, it became apparent that all squatter settlements were not on the urban periphery or based on gridiron layouts. Many were more centrally located but on hillsides—like some of the Brazilian *favelas*—and other precarious locations (Perlman 1976). The possibility of homeownership, nonetheless, made these neighborhoods distinct from inner-city tenements of rental housing. Subsequent researchers questioned the assumption of organized land invasions being prevalent, particularly in Africa and Asia, and suggested that with rising land costs, market-based illegal subdivisions for moderate-income households were more common (Angel et al. 1983; Baross and van der Linden 1990; Payne 1989). These commercially driven, illegal subdivisions—pirate settlements—are known by different names in various parts of the world, including *barrios pirata, colonias, gecekondus, katchi abadis*, and the like (Ward 1982, 1991; Tokman 1984).

Initially, both organized squatter settlements and illegal subdivisions look like shantytowns or slums with poor housing and infrastructure conditions, but with time many of these communities transform into thriving neighborhoods. Some researchers suggested that, in addition to the economic differences, there are also social differences among the owners of slums of hope and renters of slums of despair. For example, Alejandro Portes (1971, 243) argued that aspects like trust, social solidarity, community orientation, and the strong "we-feeling" affect the prospects for collective action and successful upgrading of the slums of hope. Urban planners and architects interested in more functional explanations, however, point to the regular layouts and the inherent possibility of "incremental development" as explanations.

In contrast to the informal incremental development process in squatter settlements and illegal subdivisions, the formal or conventional process typically starts with land-use planning (Baross and van der Linden 1990). Planners rezone agricultural land at the urban periphery as residential. Subsequently, public agencies install infrastructure to service the raw land. Private developers build new housing units to the requisite standards and norms, and sell them to homebuyers. The buyers pay developers through mortgages and occupy the ready-to-move-in, fully serviced houses. This stylized account is illustrated in table 26.1. The incremental development strategy (also shown in the table), ingeniously inverts the conventional process and helps lower the initial entry-cost of homeownership. This model of housing development can be found in most developing countries. Although

Table 26.1 Comparison of Conventional and Incremental Housing Processes

Step	Conventional housing process	Incremental development process
1.	Planning	Occupancy
2.	Infrastructure provision	Housing construction
3.	Housing construction	Infrastructure provision
4.	Occupancy	Planning

Source: Based on Baross and van der Linden 1990.

there is no institutionalized-land use planning involved in incremental develop-ment, the process starts with the entrepreneurship and planning of land brokers, or land invaders. They locate and subdivide land without the necessary planning approvals or permits. Households that occupy the subdivided lots build their hous-ing incrementally and gradually. They may start with a single room and gradu-ally expand and improve the dwelling, wall by wall, room by room, and floor by floor. The home-expansion or improvement process might be through self-help, or most likely self-managed with the help of subcontracted labor. For infrastructure, communities must mobilize and convince their political representatives or local governments. Typically, the final step in the consolidation process is official recog-nition. If all goes right, the informal neighborhoods are regularized and eventually included in formal city documents and plans.

This hopeful model of incremental development, its supporters argue, sug-gests that slums in the form of organized squatters or illegal subdivisions can be the basis for a radical, affordable-housing–driven approach of urbanization "from below" (Turner 1976, 1978). The model of cities with slums, however, faces numerous challenges (Burgess 1978). First, incremental development comes with incremental consumption and interim living conditions that would be considered substandard. Politicians and policymakers usually find it difficult to condone and actively sup-port such living conditions. Existing laws might not allow such approaches (Larson 2002). Second, the incremental development model is predicated on an affordable supply of land. Evidence, however, suggests that land is becoming more expen-sive, lot sizes are shrinking, and consolidation is more difficult (Angel et al. 1983; Baross and van der Linden 1990). As the supply of land becomes more constrained or expensive, squatters are forced to occupy more and more precarious positions. Third, contrary to the conventional wisdom, research has demonstrated that slums of hope have renters, too (Gilbert 1983; Gilbert and Varley 1991; Gulyani and Talukdar 2008; Kumar 1996), and they risk being displaced because of higher rents owing to infrastructure upgrading. Fourth, neoliberalism and a greater emphasis on cost recovery may have made it less likely for governments to assist in the incre-mental development process through infrastructure provision (Baken and van der Linden 1993; Eckstein 1990). Without public funding for adequate infrastructure, slums of hope can become slums of despair.

If organized squatting on the periphery and illegal subdivisions are the proto-typical slums of hope, then crowded inner-city tenements are the proverbial slums of despair. These slums and their renters, as Oscar Lewis infamously argued, are deeply linked to a "culture of poverty" (Lewis 1961). With land supply getting con-strained in most cities, it is likely that illegal subdivisions have slowed down and the existing so-called slums of despair are getting denser with more overcrowd-ing. As a consequence, more complex, and likely desperate, patterns of squatting and slum settlements are emerging. For example, Cairo may have over a million people living in makeshift dwellings on inner-city rooftops (Shaath and Kamel 2004). Similarly, Mumbai has thousands of squatters on inner-city sidewalks. These desperate slums, nonetheless, provide the very poor with a foothold in the economy and opportunities to access employment. Susan Eckstein (1990), based on her research in Mexico City, argued that inner-city residents may have bet-ter economic opportunities than peripheral residents. Her research showed that inner-city slums were the sites of intense economic activity and upward mobility. Many slum dwellers had made extensive investments in their homes, including mezzanine lofts within their structures. She claimed that, owing to the central city's locational advantage and better access to infrastructure, informal economic activities and job opportunities are better for inner-city residents. For the poor, these slums are also indispensable and often their best hope for survival.

Such complexities and overlaps suggest that the original conception of slums of hope and slums of despair as a duality is simplistic and limited. Policymakers need an alternative classification or framework to appreciate the rich diversity of housing and living conditions in slums. Previous attempts focused on classifying existing housing and infrastructure conditions and on the legal origins of settle-ments. They were criticized for their narrowness and for their inability to cap-ture the likelihood and possibilities of incremental development and upgrading in slums (Burgess 1985; Mukhija 2002). Ideally, a framework for comprehending slums should also include attributes of the larger social, economic, and institutional con-text. These variables are also likely to affect the upgrading paths of slums. But a comprehensive framework can easily get too complex and contingent on expensive surveys, data collection, and analysis. Planners must face the challenge of finding a simple yet robust classification system for understanding and conveying the rich-ness and diversity of slums.

3. Planning Responses and Options

One of the key contributions of past researchers was to demonstrate that indis-criminate slum clearance was a counterproductive strategy that invariably hurt the poor. They were also instrumental in shifting housing policy from a focus on clearance to an emphasis on increasing supply and upgrading existing housing. Turner and his colleagues suggested that squatter settlements were a potential solution to the housing shortage. They argued that the incremental development process inherent in popular responses to the lack of affordable housing was a creative approach to balance affordability and housing standards, and policymakers could support the process and learn from it. Policymakers, however, were both reluctant and unsure about how to explicitly support squatting. Squatting and illegal subdivisions, nonetheless, were often ignored and tolerated across the developing world. They were, however, rarely supported proactively.

A more explicit and proactive policy response to the logic of incremental development was the widespread introduction of sites and services schemes in the 1970s (Dunkerley 1983; Sanyal 1987). Sites and services provided beneficiaries with small lots of land and minimal infrastructure services, with the expectation that both housing and infrastructure would improve gradually. Sites and services, however, also ran into familiar problems. High land costs made the strategy more difficult to implement in most primary cities. To keep projects affordable, sites had to be made smaller and the initial package of services had to be further reduced or eliminated (Angel et al. 1983; Baross and van der Linden 1990). Most notably, projects in Hyderabad, Pakistan, achieved success with this approach, but were rarely replicated (Siddiqui and Khan 1994). It is likely that the biggest hurdle facing site and services projects is the lack of political support (Peattie 1994). Because sites and services take time to consolidate or upgrade, most politicians remain wary of supporting such projects. They are keen to avoid the risk of being accused of developing slums by their middle-class constituents. Sites and services projects were also affected by the growing criticism of project-oriented approaches in the late eighties and nineties (Malpezzi 1994). The World Bank led international efforts to move housing strategies away from an emphasis on projects to a focus on institutional reform and market-based approaches (World Bank 1993; Jones and Ward 1995; Mukhija 2001; Pugh 1994b).

By the early to mid-nineties, there was a broad consensus on the necessity of regulatory reform, particularly the need to reduce minimum standards to increase access to affordable housing (Dowall 1992; Pugh 1994a). But intellectual and ideological differences persist on whether governments should intervene in the housing sector through project-oriented approaches that provide housing for the poor. There are also different opinions on how to reduce the standards. The conventional approach supports fully constructed housing units through smaller unit sizes, with an emphasis on improved access to housing finance. The recent successes in Mexico illustrate this approach (UN-Habitat 2005). The alternative point of view prefers reductions that preserve prospects for incremental development and larger units in the future (Baken and van der Linden 1993; Mukhija and Monkkonen 2006; Payne 2001a; Ward 1991). It sees shelter microfinance playing an important role in facilitating future upgrading and incremental development (Ferguson 1999, 2003). Like the sites and services projects, the alternative approach faces similar challenges of increasing land costs and lack of political support. Nonetheless, some contemporary examples of state-assisted self-help can be found in Honduras, Nicaragua, and El Salvador (UN Millennium Project 2005).

Even though there is consensus on the necessity of attracting private investment to existing slums and neighborhoods with poor housing conditions, successful upgrading based on this approach remains challenging. The best strategy for attracting private investment is also an area of scholarly disagreements. The conventional wisdom championed by the Peruvian Economist Hernando de Soto (1989, 2000), and endorsed by luminaries like Madeline Albright, supports the legalization of slum housing, particularly squatter settlements and illegal subdivisions, through private property rights. De Soto and other advocates of the property rights approach build on Turner's work and argue for legal empowerment and security of tenure through individual titles (Friedman, Jimenez and Mayo 1988; Jimenez 1983; Malpezzi and Mayo 1987). Such titles, they claim, provide slum dwellers and squatters with the best form of security of tenure. Security of tenure allows slum dwellers to invest their savings in their homes without being worried about the persistent threat of demolition. Moreover, the titles can be used as collateral to access relatively low-cost bank loans for home improvements. To paraphrase de Soto, legal title can unlock the "dead capital" of slum housing.

Critics, however, claim that the argument is too simplistic (Doebele 1987; Durand-Lasserve and Clerc 1996; Razzaz 1993; Varley 2002). First, banks in developing countries are unlikely to lend to modest-income households on the basis of their housing as collateral. Property-based collateralized lending is not widespread in developing countries and is typically limited to individuals with higher incomes. Second, critics argue, the legalization argument underestimates the difficulties inherent in legalizing individual titles by ignoring the likely competing landownership claims of neighbors, customary landowners, private landowners, and multiple government agencies. Scholars like Geoffrey Payne (2001b) suggest that if individual title cannot be used for accessing bank loans, and if they are difficult to administer, policymakers should consider alternative forms of de facto and de jure legalization. These other options can include customary titles, collective leases, use rights or concessions, and long-term moratoriums or guarantees against demolition. These unconventional tenure forms might also be more amenable to be structured in ways that can protect the rights of tenants and resist their displacement. At the same time, they provide security to slum dwellers that their homes will not face demolition. Payne (2001b) shares the example of titles in Namibia that are designed to start as collective use–based titles and subsequently become freehold individual titles.

Third, along similar lines, critics have suggested that legalization-based approaches are not the only avenue for making slum dwellers feel that their housing investments are secure. Bill Doebele (1987), one of the first to challenge the conventional wisdom, argued that instead of security of tenure squatters need the perception of security of tenure. In addition to alternative tenure forms discussed above, he suggested that public investments in infrastructure and amenities in slums can also help create a perception of security of tenure. Public investments serve as an indicator to residents that their neighborhoods are stable and state-sponsored demolition drives are unlikely (Diacon 1997; Ahmed and Sohail 2003; Imparato and Ruster 2003). Research also indicates that infrastructure, particularly access to water, can provide more than a perception of security of tenure. Paul Strassmann (1984) has documented how water service makes it easier for households to engage in construction activities. Infrastructure improvements, however, are likely to be correlated with higher rents, which can adversely affect tenants. Addressing gentrification is always difficult. In theory, citywide infrastructure and improvement programs can help minimize the likelihood of higher rents and displacement. Citywide programs can also provide opportunities for structuring cross-subsidies for the poor. But implementing citywide programs is easier said than done. To protect tenants, cities might have to consider rent-stabilization measures along with infrastructure improvements. Alternatively, gradual improvements in infrastructure, with slow increases in rents, may be better for tenants. In a related strategy for slowing gentrification, Surabaya's slum-upgrading program—Kampung Improvement Program (KIP)—prevented four-wheeled vehicles access to the interiors of low-income neighborhoods (UN Millennium Project 2005).

The slow pace of progress, however, can frustrate policymakers and lead to redevelopment-based solutions. In both Mumbai and Bangkok, planners have been trying an unconventional approach for attracting investment from market-based private developers to redevelop slums (Mukhija 2003). In the Mumbai's "Slum Rehabilitation Scheme," slum dwellers were required to approve redevelopment projects, but in Bangkok's "land sharing" program, they did not have a choice. In both cities, governments increased the allowed density and intensity of development on slum sites as incentives for investors. Their strategy, however, is different from the classic urban renewal and slum-clearance model. It mandates on-site replacement housing for slum dwellers—both owners and tenants. The additional permitted density makes it possible for the replacement housing to be cross-subsidized by the sale of the market-rate housing. Because tenants (but not subtenants) are equally eligible as owners, they are not affected disproportionately by gentrification, either. In Mumbai, the policy also allowed for cooperatives of slum dwellers to act as private developers. The slum dwellers' cooperatives were even allowed to build more market-rate housing than private developers as an incentive (Mukhija 2003).

Progress on such projects, however, is usually slow. The feasibility of the redevelopment and cross-subsidy strategy depends on high real estate prices. High prices are likely to be limited to central locations and subject to fluctuations in market values. Temporary housing for slum dwellers is also difficult to arrange. Most important, unlike conventional slum upgrading, redevelopment is capital intensive and access to adequate capital is often a bottleneck. In Mumbai, the sluggish pace of redevelopment has tempted policymakers to try to redevelop the central slum of Dharavi without the consent of slum dwellers. It is unclear and difficult to foresee how these efforts will proceed. But it is likely that if redevelopment is pushed against the wishes of the slum dwellers, it will adversely affect them.

Predictably though, grassroots groups have started mobilizing to protest and resist these efforts, and make sure that Dharavi's residents are not overlooked in the process (Patel and Arputham 2008).

4. CONCLUSION

According to the United Nations, there are over a billion slum dwellers and there are likely to be 2 billion in a little more than a generation's time. The UN's slum census has led to provocative works like Mike Davis's *Planet of Slums* (2004, 2006). The census is also mobilizing policymakers across the world. The United Nations, too, has launched a campaign for "Cities without Slums." But there is a risk of this renewed attention on slums. It is possible that slum clearance will return as a dominant policy alternative, and the poor will pay the price. The international projections also indicate that the number of poor will eclipse the rural poor by about 2035. It is likely that they will live in slums. As Lisa Peattie (1994, 136) has argued, "in a world in which there are lots of poor people, we are going to need lots of housing that they can afford; that this housing will be known as slums; that we can improve its livability and even respectability by some kinds of interventions; but that to focus on the standards for the housing itself is going to cause nothing but pain to the low-income family." This chapter reiterates her argument for "slums" and affordable housing options for the poor.

Urban planners will have their task cut out. They will need to forge a better understanding of the diversity of slums and their living conditions. They will also have to convey this appreciation to politicians and other policymakers. Ideally, planners will develop a better language for slums as well. Most important, they will need to secure additional resources and develop better ways for improving the living conditions within slums. There are few success stories of successful upgrading. Planning researchers need to seek them out, carefully document them, analyze the strategies, and synthesize policy options. Past experience, nonetheless, suggests that there is no holy grail of slum upgrading. Even though the conventional wisdom supports an emphasis on individual property rights, the evidence does not sustain the advice.

Although, or perhaps because, significant progress has not been achieved in slum upgrading, there is a growing clamor for scaling up with more comprehensive or complex strategies of upgrading. The lack of adequate resources and the growing need for upgrading are going to make it difficult to implement comprehensive strategies. Planners and policymakers will need to focus on developing strategic options—conventional and unconventional forms of tenure, new development rights, infrastructure investments, public amenities, and so on—and let slum dwellers democratically choose on the basis of their needs and demands. The recent Brazilian experiments with participatory decision making convincingly demonstrate the viability of this approach (Abers 1998; Cabannes 2004; Fung and Wright 2001). Such participatory approaches may become the norm, and planners will have to find institutions for coordinating the varied preferences of thousands of slum dwellers in their cities. The pace of progress is likely to be slow, but that might be a better alternative than cities without slums.

REFERENCES

Abers, Rebecca. 1998. "From Clientelism to Cooperation: Local Government, Participatory Policy, and Civic Organizing in Porto Alegre, Brazil." *Politics and Society* 26(4): 511–37.

Abrams, Charles. 1966. *Man's Struggle for Shelter in an Urbanizing World.* Cambridge, MA: Massachusetts Institute of Technology Press. Repr.1996 as *Housing in the Modern World.* London: Faber and Faber.

Ahmed, Noman, and Muhammad Sohail. 2003. "Alternate Water Supply Arrangements in Peri-urban Localities: Awami (People's) tanks in Orangi Townships, Karachi." *Environment and Urbanization* 15(2): 33–42.

Angel, Sholomo, Raymond Archer, Sidhijai Tanphiphat, and Emiel Wegelin. 1983. *Land for Housing the Poor.* Bangkok: Select Books.

Baken, Robert-Jan, and Jan van der Linden. 1993. "'Getting the Incentives Right': Banking on the Formal Sector. A Critique of Current World Bank Thinking on Low-income Housing Delivery in Third World Cities." *Third World Planning Review* 15(1): 1–22.

Baross, Paul, and Jan van der Linden. 1990. *The Transformation of Land Supply Systems in Third World Cities.* Aldershot, UK: Avebury.

Burgess, Rod. 1978. "Petty Commodity Housing or Dweller Control? A Critique of John Turner's Views on Housing Policy." *World Development* 6(9–10): 1105–33.

Burgess, Rod. 1985. "Problems in the Classification of Low-Income Neighborhoods in Latin America." *Third World Planning Review* 7(4): 287–305.

Burns, Leland, and Leo Grebler. 1977. *The Housing of Nations: Analysis and Policy in a Comparative Framework.* London: Macmillan.

Cabannes, Yves. 2004. "Participatory Budgeting: A Significant Contribution to Participatory Democracy." *Environment and Urbanization* 16(1): 27–46.

Davis, Mike. 2004. "Planet of Slums." *New Left Review* 26(1): 5–34.

Davis, Mike. 2006. *Planet of Slums.* New York: Verso.

de Soto, Hernando. 1989. *The Other Path: The Invisible Revolution in the Third World.* New York: Harper and Row.

de Soto, Hernando. 2000. *The Mystery of Capital: Why Capitalism Triumphs in the West and Fails Everywhere Else.* New York: Basic Books.

Diacon, Diane. 1997. *Slum Networking, an Innovative Approach to Urban Development.* Coalville, UK: Building and Social Housing Foundation.

Doebele, William. 1987. "The Evolution of Concepts of Urban Land Tenure in Developing Countries." *Habitat International* 11(1): 7–22.

Dowall, David. 1992. "The Benefits of Minimal Land Development Regulation." *Habitat International* 16(4): 15–26.

Dunkerley, Harold. 1983. *Urban Land Policy: Issues and Opportunities.* Oxford: Oxford University Press.

Durand-Lasserve, Alain, and Valerie Clerc. 1996. "Regularization and Integration of Irregular Settlements: Lessons from Experience." Working paper no. 6, Urban Management Programme, Nairobi.

Eckstein, Susan. 1990. "Urbanization Revisited: Inner-city Slum of Hope and Squatter Settlement of Despair." *World Development* 18(2): 165–81.

Ferguson, Bruce. 1999. "Micro-finance of housing: A Key to Housing the Low or Moderate Income Majority?" *Environment and Urbanization* 11(1): 185–200.

Ferguson, Bruce. 2003. "Housing Microfinance—A Key to Improving Habitat and the Sustainability of Microfinance Institutions." *Small Enterprise Development* 14(1): 21–31.

Fernandes, Edesio, and Ann Varley. 1996. *Illegal Cities: Law and Urban Change in Developing Countries*. London and New York: Zed Books.

Friedman, Joseph, Emmanuel Jimenez, and Stephen K. Mayo. 1988. "The Demand for Tenure Security in Developing Countries." *Journal of Development Economics* 29(2): 185–98.

Fung, Archon, and Erik Olin Wright. 2001. "Deepening Democracy: Innovations in Empowered Participatory Governance." *Politics and Society* 29(1): 5–41.

Gans, Herbert. 1962. *The Urban Villagers: Group and Class in the life of Italian-Americans*. New York: Free Press of Glencoe.

Gilbert, Alan. 1983. "The Tenants of Self-help Housing: Choice and Constraint in the Housing Market of Less Developed Countries." *Development and Change* 14(3): 449–77.

Gilbert, Alan. 2007. "The Return of the Slum: Does Language Matter?" *International Journal of Urban and Regional Research* 31(4): 697–713.

Gilbert, Alan, and Ann Varley. 1991. *Landlord and Tenant: Housing the Poor in Urban Mexico*. New York: Routledge.

Gulyani, Sumila, and Debabrata Talukdar. 2008. "Slum Real Estate." *World Development* 36(10): 1916–37.

Hall, Peter. 1995. *Cities of Tomorrow: An Intellectual History of Urban Planning and Design in the Twentieth Century*. Oxford: Blackwell.

Imparato, Ivo, and Jeff Ruster. 2003. *Slum Upgrading and Participation: Lessons from Latin America*. Washington, DC: World Bank.

Jacobs, Jane. 1961. *The Death and Life of Great American Cities*. New York: Random House.

Jimenez, Emmanuel. 1983. "The Magnitude and Determinants of Home Improvement in Self-help Housing: Manila's Tondo Project." *Land Economics* 59(1): 70–83.

Jones, Gareth, and Peter Ward. 1995. "The Blind Men and the Elephant: A Critic's Reply." *Habitat International* 19(1): 61–72.

Kumar, Sunil. 1996. "Landlordism in Third World Urban Low-income Settlements: A Case for Further Research." *Urban Studies* 33(4–5): 753–82.

Larson, Jane. 2002. "Informality, Illegality, and Inequality." *Yale Law and Policy Review* 20:137–82.

Lewis, Oscar. 1961. *The Children of Sanchez: Autobiography of a Mexican Family*. New York: Random House.

Malpezzi, Stephen. 1994. "Getting the Incentives Right. A Reply to Robert-Jan Baken and Jan van der Linden." *Third World Planning Review* 16(4): 451–66.

Malpezzi, Stephen, and S. K. Mayo. 1987. "Use Cost and Housing Tenure in Developing Countries." *Journal of Development Economics* 25(1): 197–220.

Mangin, William P. 1967. "Latin American Squatter Settlements: A Problem and a Solution." *Latin American Research* 2(3): 65–98.

Mangin, William P., and John F. Turner. 1968. "The Barriada Movement." *Progressive Architecture*, May, 154–62.

Martinez, Javier, Gora Mboup, Richard Sliuzas, and Alfred Stein. 2008. "Trends in Urban and Slum Indicators Across Developing World Cities, 1990–2003." *Habitat International* 32(1): 86–108.

Mukhija, Vinit. 2001. "Enabling Slum Redevelopment in Mumbai: Policy Paradox in Practice." *Housing Studies* 16(6): 791–806.

Mukhija, Vinit. 2002. "An Analytical Framework for Urban Upgrading: Property Rights, Property Values and Physical Attributes." *Habitat International* 26(4): 553–70.

Mukhija, Vinit. 2003. *Squatters as Developers? Slum Redevelopment in Mumbai.* Aldershot, UK: Ashgate.

Mukhija, Vinit, and Paavo Monkkonen. 2006. "Federal Colonias Policy in California: Too Broad and Too Narrow." *Housing Policy Debate* 17(4): 755–80.

Mukhija, Vinit, and Paavo Monkkonen. 2007. "What's in a Name? A Critique of Colonias in the United States." *International Journal of Urban and Regional Research* 31(2): 475–88.

Neuwirth, Robert. 2005. *Shadow Cities: A Billion Squatters: A New Urban World.* New York: Routledge.

Patel, Sheela, and Jockin Arputham. 2008. "Plans for Dharavi: Negotiating a Reconciliation between a State-driven Market Redevelopment and Resident's Aspirations." *Environment and Urbanization* 20(1): 231–42.

Payne, Geoffrey. 1989. *Informal Housing and Land Subdivisions in Third World Cities: A Review of the Literature.* Oxford: Center for Development and Environmental Planning.

Payne, Geoffrey. 2001a. "Lowering the Ladder: Regulatory Frameworks for Sustainable Development." *Development in Practice* 11(2–3): 308–18.

Payne, Geoffrey. 2001b. "Urban Land Tenure Policy Options: Titles or Rights?" *Habitat International* 25(3): 415–29.

Peattie, Lisa. 1968. *The View from the Barrio.* Ann Arbor: University of Michigan Press.

Peattie, Lisa. 1987. "Affordability." *Habitat International* 11(4): 69–76.

Peattie, Lisa. 1994. "An Argument for Slums." *Journal of Planning Education and Research* 13: 136–43.

Perlman, Janice. 1976. *The Myth of Marginality: Urban Poverty and Politics in Rio de Janiero.* Berkeley/Los Angeles: University of California Press.

Pierce, Neal, and Curtis W. Johnston. 2008. *Century of the City: No Time to Lose.* New York: Rockefeller Foundation.

Portes, Alejandro. 1971. "The Urban Slum in Chile: Types and Correlates." *Land Economics* 38(3): 187–97.

Pugh, Cedric. 1994a. "Housing Policy Development in Developing Countries: The World Bank and Internationalization, 1972–1993." *Cities* 11(3): 159–80.

Pugh, Cedric. 1994b. "The Idea of Enablement in Housing Sector Development: The Political Economy of Housing for Developing Countries." *Cities* 11(6): 357–71.

Razzaz, Omar. 1993. "Examining Property Rights and Investment in Informal Settlements: The Case of Jordan." *Land Economics* 69(4): 341–55.

Rodwin, Lloyd. 1987. *Shelter, Settlement, and Development.* Boston: Allen & Unwin.

Sanyal, Biswapriya. 1987. "Problems of Cost-recovery in Development Projects: Experience of the Lusaka Squatter Upgrading and Site/Service Project." *Urban Studies* 24(4): 285–95.

Shaath, Randa, and Nadia Kamel. 2004. *Randa Shaath: Under the Same Sky, Cairo.* Rotterdam: Witte de With and Barcelona: Fundacio Antoni Tapies.

Siddiqui, Tasneem, and M. Azhar Khan. 1994. "The Incremental Development Scheme." *Third World Planning Review* 16(3): 277–91.

Stokes, Charles J. 1962. "A Theory of Slums." *Land Economics* 38(3): 187–97.

Strassmann, W. Paul. 1984. "The Timing of Urban Infrastructure and Housing Improvements by Owner Occupants." *World Development* 12(7): 743–53.

Tokman, K. B. 1984. "Ankara: Procedures for Upgrading and Urban Management." In *Low-Income Housing in the Developing World: The Role of Sites and Services and Settlement Upgrading,* edited by G. K. Payne, 89–107. Chichester and New York: John Wiley.

Turner, John. 1963. "Dwelling Resources in South America." *Architectural Design* 37:360–93.

Turner, John. 1967. "Barriers and Channels for Housing Development in Modernizing Countries." *Journal of the American Institute of Planners* 33(3): 167–81.

Turner, John. 1968. "Housing Priorities, Settlement Patterns, and Urban Development in Modernizing Countries." *Journal of the American Institute of Planners* 34(6): 354–63.

Turner, John. 1972. "Housing as a Verb." In *Freedom to Build: Dweller Control of the Housing Process,* edited by J. F. Turner and R. Fichter, 148–75. New York: Macmillan.

Turner, John. 1976. *Housing by People: Towards Autonomy in Building Environments.* New York: Pantheon.

Turner, John. 1978. "Housing in Three Dimensions: Terms of Reference for the Housing Question Redefined." *World Development* 6(9–10): 1135–45.

Turner, John, and Robert Fichter. 1972. *Freedom to Build: Dweller Control of the Housing Process.* New York: Macmillan.

UN-Habitat. 2003. *The Challenge of Slums: Global Report on Human Settlements 2003.* London and Sterling, VA: Earthscan (for United Nations Human Settlements Programme).

UN-Habitat. 2005. *Financing Urban Shelter: Global Report on Human Settlements 2005.* London and Sterling, VA: Earthscan (for United Nations Human Settlements Programme).

UN Millennium Project. 2005. *A Home in the City.* Task Force on Improving the Lives of Slum Dwellers. London and Sterling, VA: Earthscan (for United Nations Development Programme).

Varley, Ann. 2002. "Private or Public: Debating the Meaning of Tenure Legalization." *International Journal of Urban and Regional Research* 26(3): 449–61.

Ward, Peter. 1982. *Self-Help Housing—A Critique.* London: Mansell.

Ward, Peter. 1991. *Colonias and Public Policy in Texas and Mexico: Urbanization by Stealth.* Austin, TX: University of Texas Press.

World Bank. 1993. *Housing: Enabling Markets to Work.* Washington, DC: World Bank.

World Bank. 2009. *World Development Report 2009: Reshaping Economic Geography.* Washington, DC: World Bank.

CHAPTER 27

THE PUBLIC FINANCE
OF URBAN FORM

JOHN I. CARRUTHERS

FOR nearly forty years, dating at least to the 1974 publication of the Real Estate Research Corporation's (RERC) report, *The Costs of Sprawl*, a foundational assumption in the field of urban and regional planning has been that there is a substantive connection between urban form and public finance. The thinking is straightforward: owing to the cost of extending infrastructure and services over large areas, urban sprawl—defined for present purposes as the kind of low-density, spatially expansive pattern of land use (Carruthers and Úlfarsson 2003, 2008) that is now ubiquitous throughout the United States (Glaeser and Kahn 2004)—is more expensive to support than high-density, compact alternatives (Frank 1989; Altshuler and Gómez-Ibáñez 1993; Burchell 1998). This seemingly straightforward, intuitively appealing premise occupies a rarefied place in planning research and practice alike and, perhaps for that reason, has been subject to little scrutiny during a period in which the field and its knowledge base have blossomed.

The neglect is troubling for a number of reasons. To begin with, the very practice of urban planning has been vulnerable to criticism, especially from economists—well versed in public finance but often less so in land-use planning and appropriate metrics spatial analysis—who have raised concerns about the legitimacy of the assumption (Ladd 1998) and, by extension, the many regulatory frameworks grounded in it (see, for example, DeGrove 1984, 1992, 2005). Moreover, the lack of empirical work leaves unanswered vital questions regarding the costs of growth itself versus the costs associated with the character of the development that results from it. It also leaves unanswered another set of questions centered on which services are relevant and to what extent; little is known about the relative influence of urban form across different types of spending, making it near impossible to come up with concrete best practices, much less any sort of holistic framework wherein public finance and land-use related decisions are addressed as one. Finally, there is no evidence whatsoever on how the constant quality of services—that is, the final output produced at the same level of spending—is influenced by urban form. Entirely unknown is the extent to which actual outcomes, such as crime rates, graduation rates, and/or traffic flow, are mediated by land-use patterns. The bottom line is that the connection between urban form and public finance deserves to be much better understood, especially given its central position in the logic of urban and regional planning.

Toward that end, this chapter provides an overview of what is known about the relationship and sets out an analytical framework—with both theoretical and empirical components—for further inquiry into it. The specific objectives are three: (i) to review previous research in a way that integrates work from fields as disparate as public economics and urban design into a cohesive whole; (ii) to illustrate how to adapt traditional models of public finance to incorporate land use, plus to reflect the kind of strategic interaction that local governments regularly engage in when making both spending and regulatory decisions; and (iii) to suggest directions for future research in this essential area. Overall, the chapter is meant to serve as a starting point for more active engagement among planners on the matter—and as a way forward for those looking to examine a relationship has, for too long, been taken for granted.

2. Extant Theory and Evidence

As noted at the onset, the publication of *The Costs of Sprawl* (RERC 1974) represents at least the nominal origin of the contemporary debate over the nature and extent of the relationship between urban form and public finance.[1] The report's often-contested findings center on an "internally consistent" set of estimates of the direct cost of alternative development patterns (high-density versus low-density) that were used to show that low-density sprawl is as much as twice as expensive to support. These findings had an almost immediate impact: as Altshuler (1977, 207) wrote in a review for the *Journal of the American Institute of Certified Planners*:[2] "*The Costs of Sprawl* has become one of the most widely—and uncritically—cited sources in the planning literature." The commentary goes on to highlight the "fragility" of the main conclusions, a theme subsequently taken up by Windsor (1979) who, in an analysis of the same data with a different set of assumptions, went so far as to damn the report as "misleading." Whatever its merits, the downfall of *The Costs of Sprawl* is that it relied on a highly stylized analysis that was oversensitive to its main assumptions and that did not do a good enough job of considering mediating factors apart from density (Altshuler and Gomes-Ibañez 1993). Its legacy is nonetheless interesting because it pushed wide a positive/normative rift—how things are versus how they "ought to be"—in urban and regional planning that remains a constructive source of tension to this day. What remains of the report's afterglow illuminates the field's continuing need to be self-reflexive and more critically aware of its core epistemology.

To that point, an often—and perhaps conveniently (Richardson and Gordon 1993)—overlooked truth is that, at its core, land-use planning is market regulation—namely, land-market regulation. Generally speaking, regulation is justified from an economic standpoint when markets produce inefficient or otherwise undesirable outcomes in the form of market failures and/or socially unacceptable inequities.[3] The first zoning laws, for example, were developed for the purpose of separating industrial and residential land uses in the interest of public health—that is, in an effort to address externalities that occur as a result of people living in locations with poor environmental quality owing to adjacent industrial activity (Fulton 1999). Similarly, some of the original growth-control frameworks were developed as pragmatic responses to the overwhelming pressure of rapid population growth. Communities—beginning (most visibly) with Petaluma, California[4]—implemented development-permitting caps and related policies because they were unable to keep pace with the demand for new infrastructure, schools, and other capital facilities (Kelly 1993; Porter 1997). Over the years, though, a number of economists have actively criticized zoning and most forms of growth control for being redistributive and, as a corollary, they have raised pointed questions about whether or not the benefits of land-use planning outweigh its social costs (see Fischel 1990 for a review). In the context of public finance, the need for policies focused on urban form is thought to turn on the interest of managing tax dollars responsibly because high-density, compact development is understood to be less expensive to support. Yet, there is so little concrete evidence of this that conclusions drawn from it are essentially articles of faith.

This is a critical shortcoming and, going forward, the field of urban and regional planning needs to engage and play a more active role in addressing it. Toward that end, there are two overarching, "upper-level" questions to be answered, one positive and one normative: Is there, in fact, a relationship between urban form and public finance? And, if so, is the relationship substantive enough to bother with? As outlined in the following paragraphs, there is some theory and evidence that informs the first question but very little that informs the second. And, there is virtually none at all that informs the many and varied "lower-level" questions that trail directly from these initial two questions. In sum, there is great uncertainty surrounding the relationship between urban form and public finance—questions abound, and they need to be answered in certain, objective terms.

What *is* certain is that urbanization has grown progressively less dense and more spread out, or more sprawllike, worldwide in recent decades (see Nechyba and Walsh 2004; Bogart 2006; Bruegmann 2005; Glaeser and Kahn 2004; Carruthers et al. 2010, forthcoming) because of a core set of factors: population growth, rising incomes, and falling commuting costs. These factors form the center of the modern economic theory of urban land use,[5] jointly credited to Alonso (1964), Muth (1969),

and Mills (1971)—and together they explain nearly all of the interregional variation in urbanized land area across the United States (Brueckner and Fansler 1983;
McGrath 2005). Even still, other, more nuanced factors, market failures, also play a
role. In particular, the failure of development to internalize (i) the benefits of open
space, (ii) the social costs of traffic congestion, and (iii) the full cost of the services
that it requires have contributed to inefficient patterns of land use (Brueckner 2000,;
Brueckner and Helsley 2011) . Each of these is important to understanding patterns
of urbanization, but the third is fundamental because it suggests that new development would be more dense if it were forced to account for the full cost of the infrastructure and other services needed to support it—or, in other words, that public
subsidies may actively encourage sprawl. On this front, both theoretical (Brueckner
1997; McFarlane 1999) and empirical (Pendall 1999) analyses show that impact fees,
which attempt to correct for the problem, promote more compact land use. So, even
though urban form is largely owed to factors of human ecology, it is also shaped by
complex market failures, including at least one of which is linked to public finance.

   The main reason for the connection is that public goods and services, like their
private counterparts, are subject to economies and diseconomies of scale (Knaap
and Nelson 1992). In particular, other things being equal, if returns to scale are
increasing (decreasing) expenditures are expected to be less (greater) at high (low)
densities and large (small) city sizes. The nature of public-sector production is
addressed in detail in the coming section, which sets out a theoretical framework
for evaluating it, but before getting to that, there are two silos of empirical research
to be reviewed: physical planning/engineering-style analyses similar in approach
to *The Costs of Sprawl*; and econometric analyses that make use of the kind of
public finance models developed in the next sections.[6] Though not exhaustive, the
summary gives an overview of the existing research and, in so doing, helps illustrate why the relationship between urban form and public finance is so tenuous.

   Subsequent physical planning/engineering-style analyses have generally confirmed that denser, planned development is less expensive to support than sprawl,
but with some important caveats: urban form is complex and multifaceted, so it
is difficult to strictly isolate a single characteristic like density, which is tied to
public finance, and generalize from there; and whatever savings are gained via
urban form may be quite small unless they are gathered systematically as part of a
broader planning effort. Windsor's (1979) analysis, a revision of that presented in
The Costs of Sprawl, demonstrated that the location-specific savings that the RERC
attributed to density mainly had to do with the clustering of a specific number
of homes and it indicated that, on a wider scale, clustered development separated
by stretches of open space—or as it is often called, "leapfrog development"—may
actually be more expensive to support. Several years later, Pieser (1984) explored
the cost of major infrastructure within "planned" and "unplanned" development
by comparing two such communities outside of Houston, Texas. In the planned
community, which was developed as a cohesive whole instead of in a piecemeal
manner, there were indeed cost savings, but these were small—on the order of just
1 to 3 percent of total costs—so the evidence does not provide much support for

land-use planning as a vehicle to minimize the cost of public services. This same general conclusion is reinforced by Speir and Stephenson's more recent (2002) analysis of water and sewer costs associated with alternative development patterns, which found that dispersed development is more expensive to support, and also that shifting the expense from the public sector to the private sector may be easy to do. Here again, the evidence indicates that there is a connection between urban form and public finance, but that the connection may not be substantive enough to by itself justify regulation implemented in the name of public finance, especially if households have strong preferences for living in low-density environments, as some analysts (Mieszkowski and Mills 1993; Gordon and Richardson 1997) suggest, and therefore are willing to pay more to have their services delivered at lower densities. Finally, an analysis by Hopkins, Xu, and Knaap (2004) found that there are substantive savings to be gained in wastewater treatment systems if their development is closely coordinated with other planning activities. As a set, these results provide only modest support for land-use policy as a fiscal tool and illustrate that the relationship is clearly a complicated one that must be carefully addressed.

Taken at face value, econometric analyses—which in a nutshell involve regressing the value of service expenditures on all factors thought to matter, including land-use metrics—have produced decidedly mixed results. An early (and very coarse) study by Elis-Williams (1987) of school expenditures in the United Kingdom found evidence that the cost of education per student decreases with the size of the school and increases with the distance students live from the schools. The analysis, which is framed in the type of location allocation tradition endnoted above, is described as "coarse" because its findings rest primarily on results obtained from a series of simple, bivariate regressions. Even so, it is important because of its focus on both economies of scale in and the spatial dimensions of public services. A bit later, work by Ladd and Yinger (1991) and Ladd (1992, 1994, 1998) came up with a U–shaped relationship between the number of people per square mile of county land area and the per capita spending; thereby concluding that high-density areas are ultimately more, not less, expensive to support. This finding is attributed to the "harshness" of the urban environment, which increases the difficulty of delivering services in a cost-effective way. An often-ignored aspect of this work, however, is that it, in fact, has absolutely nothing to do with land use: density is measured using county land area, which may approximate land use in some locations, like New York City, but not in others, like expansive Maricopa County, where Phoenix is located.[7] Studies of land-use patterns, which measure density via estimates of developed land area, by Carruthers (2002) and Carruthers and Úlfarsson (2003, 2008) have found evidence that density lowers the cost of many services. These analyses have their own shortcomings, though. In particular, they are extremely general and serve only to illustrate that there does seem to be a relationship between urban form and the cost of certain services (education, parks and recreation, police protection, and roadways); and to draw broad parameters around its scale of the relationship; they address the positive question posed above, but barely even scratch the surface of the normative question. Similarly, the most recent econometric analysis of how urban form influences public service expenditures (Hortas-Rico and Solé-Ollé 2010) found that low-density development in Spain costs more to support than compact alternatives; but here again, the authors close by emphasizing that the results provide evidence of a relationship but say nothing of its fiscal impact. Finally, note that although econometric analyses have produced mixed results,[10] these contradictions are, in fact, owed more to differences in the questions motivating the work and data involved than to on-the-ground outcomes. Additional research using more refined behavioral models of public finance and spatially explicit data is needed.

It bears emphasizing that the research just described represents the sum total— with perhaps a few oversights[8]—of what is known (as opposed to believed) about the relationship between urban form and public finance. Since so little concrete evidence exists, it is more than a bit surprising that the relationship stands as such a fundamental assumption in the field of urban and regional planning. While there does seem to be a connection, almost nothing is known about the nature or extent of it, so there remains a great need to strengthen the field's knowledge base by further exploring it. But criticizing the shortcoming is not enough: having reviewed the extant theory and evidence, the next step is to set out an appropriate analytical framework—a behavioral model of public finance—for adding to it.

3. A Behavioral Model of Public Finance

To reset the discussion, there are two main ways in which urban form may matter to public finance: via returns to scale in the process of producing public goods and services, and via a mediating influence related to the kind of "harshness" of urban environments that was alluded to above. The analytical framework for getting at these relationships originates from a study by Bradford, Malt, and Oates (1969) concerning the rapid expansion of local government spending that occurred in the middle part of the twentieth century. The authors began by noting that, between 1948 and 1966, spending by local governments increased at a precipitous rate of almost 9 percent annually.[9] They further noted that some of this increase was attributable to the great wealth accumulated during that period and the corresponding evolution of household preferences, but they also questioned whether incompetence, misfeasance, static production technology,[10] and/or various environmental conditions were contributing. From this point of departure, Bradford, Malt, and Oates (1969) suggested a two–stage public-sector production function:

$$s = f(L, K, X), \tag{1}$$

where s represents an intermediate output toward the delivery of a service, L represents labor, K represents capital, and X represents other inputs. The intermediate output is government activity (effort put toward public education, police and fire protection, parking enforcement, parks and recreation), but it is the final output (graduation rates, levels of crime and property loss, number of citations issued, fun afternoons at the playground) that residents actually experience:

$$\tilde{s} = f(s, P, C, \varphi). \tag{2}$$

Here, $\tilde{s}$ represents a final output of a service, or what residents actually get in return for their tax dollars, and it is a function of s, the intermediate output; P, the size of the population served; C, a vector of environmental conditions; and φ, other unobservable factors. This setup is very different from traditional models based on the theory of the firm and profit maximizing behavior, which generally speaking are encapsulated by traditional production function shown in (1). What this two-stage production function says is that, when local governments channel resources (labor, capital, and other inputs) toward the production of public services, the outcome depends not only on production technology but also the size of the population served, environmental conditions, and other mediating factors. If urban form does, in fact, matter to public finance, two environmental conditions in particular— density, say δ, and the spatial expanse of development, say π— belong in the vector C.

Duncombe and Yinger (1993) elaborated on this framework and developed it into an operational model of public finance that has since been used in numerous analyses. First, assuming that local governments attempt to minimize costs, the cost function associated with the first-stage production function is:

$$e_s = f(s, W). \tag{3}$$

In this equation, e represents government expenditure, the total cost of production; s again represents government activity, the intermediate output; and W represents a vector of input prices. Put simply, expenditure on service s depends on how much of it is being produced, plus the prices of the inputs needed to produce it. Next, the second-stage cost function is defined by taking the inverse of equation (2) in order to obtain the solution for s—that is, $s = f^{-1}(\tilde{s}, P, C, \varphi)$—and then substituting the result of that operation into equation (3):

$$\tilde{e}_s = f\left[f^{-1}(\tilde{s}, P, C, \varphi), W\right]. \tag{4}$$

This cost function indicates that expenditure $\tilde{e}_s$, on the final output $\tilde{s}$, the actual service that residents receive, depends on an array of factors, including environmental conditions (where δ and $\pi \in C$) in addition to production technology. Equation (4) is key because it shows exactly how urban form might matter to public finance: specifically as a mediating factor that weighs on returns to scale in the production process. Finally, the average cost function that emerges is as follows:

$$\tilde{\tilde{e}}_s = f\left(\tilde{S}, W, P, C, \varphi\right). \tag{5}$$

All notation remains the same except that, this time, the hat above $\tilde{e}_s$ denotes per capita expenditure and $\tilde{S}$ represents a vector of service outcome measures, which may be endogenous to $\hat{\tilde{e}}_s$ depending on how the analysis is structured (see also Andrews, Duncombe, and Yinger 2002; Duncombe, Miner, and Ruggiero 1995; Dunncombe and Yinger 2000). Details on specifying and estimating equation (5) are provided in the next section, after a few remaining aspects of the framework have been discussed.

As stated, the usefulness of this two-stage framework rests in its ability to get at returns to scale[11] in various dimensions of the process of producing public goods and services (see Duncombe and Yinger 1993, 53–56). In particular, there are three interconnected dimensions of scale in public production, all of which may be estimated: (i) service quality, the final output; (ii) government activity, the intermediate output; and (iii) population, the number of people served.[12] The first dimension, returns to quality scale, is the change in per capita expenditure that results from a change in the final output after holding population and environmental conditions constant—it is analogous to the technical returns to scale in private-sector production, or the average cost curve slopes downward, then upward, as output increases. The next dimension, second-stage returns to scale, is the relationship between the intermediate output and the final output or, in other words, a rate of efficiency registering how well government activity translates into desired public-service outcomes. As shown in equation (2) the final output depends on the intermediate output plus population and environmental conditions, so this is a relationship that varies from place to place. The third dimension, returns to population scale, is the relationship between the intermediate output and the number of people served, holding environmental conditions, including urban form, constant; it registers the degree of congestion and is equal to zero if the good is a pure (noncongestible) public good. Each of these relationships may be measured empirically—albeit with different degrees of difficulty—but only the third results from estimates based on equation (5). Even still, knowing that—and how—the three work together is critical to understanding exactly why measures of urban form, an environmental condition, may belong in an average cost function.

Last, recent theoretical and empirical advances in public finance (see Brueckner 2003 and Revelli 2005 for detailed reviews) have revealed a preponderance of spatial spillovers in public spending:

$$e_i = f\left(e_j, Z_i\right), \tag{6}$$

where per capita spending on public services in jurisdiction i, e_i, depends on per capita spending on public services in surrounding jurisdictions j, e_j, plus a vector of local characteristics, Z_i. The function is described as a "spatial reaction function" (Brueckner 2003, 177) because it results from jurisdiction i's calculated response to the spending of proximate jurisdictions.[13] Although spillovers can take different forms—and much research is aimed at determining the nature of the government behavior that produces them—it is good enough to treat them as a composite for present purposes because the implication is that equation (5) requires an additional term, $\hat{\tilde{e}}_{sj}$, the so-called spatial lag of $\hat{\tilde{e}}_{sj}$:

$$\hat{\tilde{e}}_{si} = f(\hat{\tilde{e}}_{sj}, \tilde{S}_i, W_i, P_i, C_i, Z_i, \varphi_i).\tag{7}$$

The implementation of this function, including data and estimation techniques, is taken up in the next section.

4. An Empirical Example

The modeling framework just described is illustrated by using it to analyze per capita expenditure on education by local governments in all 3,075 counties[14] of the continental United States during the 2002 fiscal year (U.S. Bureau of Commerce 2005). To begin, figures 27.1 and 27.2 present maps, by quintile, of the spending

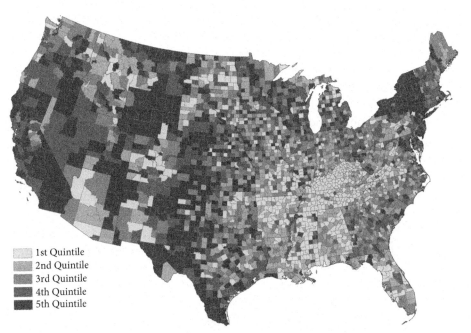

1st Quintile
2nd Quintile
3rd Quintile
4th Quintile
5th Quintile

Figure 27.1 Per Capita Spending on Education, FY 2001–2002

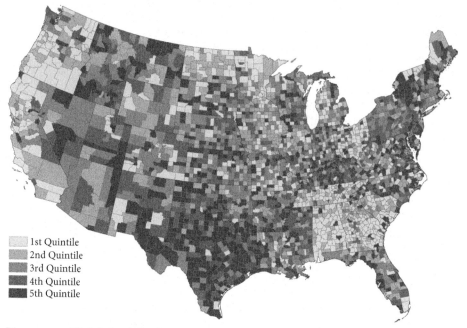

1st Quintile
2nd Quintile
3rd Quintile
4th Quintile
5th Quintile

Figure 27.2 High School Graduation Rate, 2002

variable, an aggregate that captures educational spending by all school districts located (headquartered) within each county, in the 2001–2002 fiscal year and the high school graduation rate in 2002. The spending map reveals two important patterns: expenditures are clustered by both state and region, including, in the latter case, in a way that spills across state lines. The state pattern means that state-level effects need to be included in an empirical specification of equation (7) in order to account for unobserved factors common to all counties located within the same state;[15] in practice, these can be dealt with by using either fixed effects or random effects. As important, the regional pattern highlights the spillovers that occur as a result of strategic interactions among local governments—expressed by the spatial reaction function—and it is striking how apparent they are, even at such an aggregate level: spatial relationships that are not confined by state boundaries are clearly visible, playing out across the nation. A failure to account for this pattern of spatial dependence would produce a misspecified model that ignores a key behavioral mechanism and, ultimately, gives biased and inefficient estimates (for helpful overviews, see Anselin 1988, 1992, 2002).

Next, even a quick comparison of figures 27.1 and 27.2 reveals that spending is not always correlated with outcomes: some of places at the high end of the spending scale are at the low end of the outcome scale—California stands out in this regard, for example. This is an indication that, as the modeling framework suggests, high levels of intermediate output do not necessarily translate directly into high levels of final output. As shown in equation (7) the spending observed in individual counties, $\hat{\tilde{e}}_{si}$, is explained by: $\hat{\tilde{e}}_{sj}$, spending in proximate counties; $\tilde{S}_i$, the final output;

W_i, the cost of labor to the government; P_i, the population served; C_i, environmental conditions; and Z_i, various other characteristics of the county, including fiscal and geographic factors. The question is: are the density of development, δ_i, and the spatial expanse of development, π_i, among the environmental conditions that explain the discrepancy between the two maps?

This is resolved by first collecting relevant data, then using that data to estimate an empirical implementation of equation (7) using both fixed effects and random effects. The specification of the model originates from early work done by Bradford, Malt, and Oates (1969), Bergstrom and Goodman (1973), and Borcherding and Deacon (1972); the choice of specific variables is based on subsequent work done by Ladd and Yinger (1991); Ladd (1992, 1994); Kelejian and Robinson (1992, 1993, 1997); Duncombe and Yinger (1993, 2000); Duncombe, Miner, and Ruggiero (1995); Andrews, Duncombe, and Yinger (2002); Carruthers and Úlfarsson (2003); Solé-Ollé and Bosch (2005); and Solé-Ollé (2006). The data is described in table 27.1, which lists the source, units of measurement, and descriptive statistics for each of the continuous variables involved in the exercise. All explanatory variables (except the spatially lagged version of the dependent variable) are lagged in time to 1997; this was done in part because the land-use data from the USDA's Natural Resources Inventory (see Carruthers and Úlfarsson 2008 for complete details), which is is used for the two measures of sprawl—δ_i and π_i—is available only up until that year. Moreover, the time lag makes good practical sense given how the public planning process works because there is generally a substantial delay between when expenditure decisions are made and when they are carried out. In order to be consistent, 1997 values of variables collected from decennial census data were estimated by using a time-weighted average of 1990 and 2000 values.

Applying this dataset to equation (7) results in the following fixed effects (8a) and random effects (8b) models of per capita spending on education, written in matrix form:

$$\hat{e}^* = \beta \cdot \omega \cdot \hat{e}^* + \Sigma + V \cdot \Gamma + \upsilon, \tag{8a}$$

and

$$\hat{e}^* = \beta \cdot \omega \cdot \hat{e}^* + V \cdot \Gamma + \upsilon + \varsigma, \tag{8b}$$

where the "*" in $\hat{e}^*$ indicates that per capita total direct expenditure is in natural log form (Carruthers and Úlfarsson 2003, 2008) and so is its spatial lag, $\omega \cdot \hat{e}^*$; the Σ in (8a) represents a vector of state-level fixed effects, including one for Washington, D.C.; V represents a vector of explanatory variables that collects the balance of the right-hand side of equation (7); ω represents a 3,075 × 3,075 ($n \times n$) row-standardized weights matrix that describes the spatial connectivity of the data set; β represents an estimable spatial autoregressive parameter describing the (aggregate) outcome of interaction among proximate jurisdictions; Γ represents a vector of estimable parameters on the explanatory variables; the υ represents a stochastic error term; and the ς in (8b) represents a random state-level error component. The

Table 27.1 Source, Units, and Description of Continuous Variables

Variable	Source	Units	Descriptive Statistics				
			Mean	Median	Maximum	Minimum	Standard Deviation
Per Capita Spending on Education	COG, REIS	$	1,447.88	1,357.02	6,935.84	0	483.12
High School Graduation Rate	NCES	%	0.92	0.94	2.80*	0	0.13
Average Government Wage	REIS	$	27,614.64	26,528.16	61,626.56	14,534.40	5,840.15
Population	REIS	#	88,072.3	24,506	9,206,538	78	310,352.4
Population Change	REIS	%	0.06	0.05	0.77	-0.39	0.08
Density	NRI, REIS	#	2.49	2.04	64.26	0.04	2.61
% Developed	NRI, COG	%	0.09	0.04	1.00	0.00	0.13
Median Housing Value	Census	$	85,634.15	76,521.00	759,966.00	5,174.65	45,962.78
% Housing <1940	Census	%	0.20	0.16	0.61	0.00	0.13
Per Capita Municipalities	COG	# (1,000s)	0.30	0.17	4.09	0.00	0.38
Per Capita Income	REIS	$	22,716.03	22,051.55	78,125.29	5,498.18	5,131.32

Variable	Source	Unit					
% White	Census	%	0.86	0.92	1.00	0.05	0.16
% <5 Years Old	Census	%	0.10	0.10	0.18	0.06	0.01
Average Household size	Census	#	2.66	2.62	5.38	0.83	0.23
% Property Tax	COG	%	0.79	0.82	1.00	0.16	0.16
Per Capita Federal Revenue	COG, REIS	$	79.38	45.70	5,038.61	0.00	163.14
Per Capita State Revenue	COG, REIS	$	1,033.36	953.99	7,415.72	0.00	439.59
Per Capita Long–term Debt	COG, REIS	$	1,917.46	1,072.07	12,2810.20	0.00	4,950.10
County Land Area	COG	# (1,000s ac)	616.00	396.00	12,841.00	10.00	836.00
Employment Ratio	REIS	%	0.38	0.37	2.93	0.08	0.14

Notes: COG is the U.S. Bureau of Commerce's Census of Governments; REIS is the U.S. Bureau of Economic Analysis Regional Economic Information System; NCES is the U.S. Department of Education's National Center for Education Statistics; NRI is the U.S. Department of Agriculture's National Resources Inventory; Census is the U.S. Census Bureau; NCES is the National Center for Education Statistics. All dollar values are expressed in 2002 constant dollars; zero values are excluded from the capital facilities, education, fire protection, housing and community development, libraries, natural resources, parks and recreation, roadways, sewerage, and solid waste calculations; * in a few cases, the number of people receiving diplomas outnumbers the number of 12-graders.

weights matrix was created using the center of each county's population—a point, calculated using census tract level data, identifying where people are concentrated rather than the geographic center, to identify neighbors: each county i is related to all counties j having population centers located within 50 miles of its own population center or, in the 65 cases where the distance is greater than 50 miles, to a single nearest neighbor.

Before moving on to the estimation results, note that the behavioral underpinning of the model says that proximate counties are influenced by each other, so $\omega \cdot \hat{e}^*$ is endogenous to $\hat{e}^*$, and, therefore, equations (8a) and (8b) cannot be properly estimated using ordinary least squares (OLS). That is, because per capita spending in county i depends on per capita spending in counties j and the other way around, there is a "chicken or egg" problem that needs to be resolved by choosing an appropriate estimator. The most straightforward approach is a spatial two-stage least squares (S2SLS) strategy (see Kelejian and Prucha 1998) that involves first regressing $\omega \cdot \hat{e}^*$ on V and $\omega \cdot V$, the spatial lag of V, to produce predicted values of the endogenous spatial lag and then using the predicted values in place of the actual values in equations (8a) and (8b). Like the alternative approach, maximum likelihood (ML) estimation, this least squares strategy yields efficient, unbiased parameter estimates, even if spatial error dependence is present (Das, Kelejian, and Prucha 2003). Some recent examples of other work in the area of public finance that use the S2SLS estimator as opposed to, or alongside, an ML estimator include Esteller-Moré and Solé–Ollé (2001), Revelli (2002, 2003), Baicker (2005), and Solé-Ollé (2006).[16]

The S2SLS estimation results are listed in table 27.2, which shows the fixed effects estimates in the left-hand panel and the random effects estimates in the right-hand panel; all state-level effects have been suppressed from the table. For clarity, the core of the modeling framework is listed first and each explanatory variable—or set of variables—is identified according to the notation in equation (7). Almost all variables are statistically significant at a 95 percent confidence interval—assuming two-tailed hypothesis tests—and the adjusted R^2 values show that the models explain about 20 percent and 25 percent, respectively, of the cross-national variation in per capita spending on education.

Working down through the variables and back and forth between the two models, the estimation results reveal the following. First, in the core of the model, as expected, the spatial lag of per capita spending on education, the graduation rate, and the average government wage are all statistically significant and positive, other things being equal: spending is correlated across geographic space owing to strategic interaction among local governments; better outcomes, in the form of higher graduation rates, cost more to achieve; and the expense of hiring public employees matters. Population and population change do not come in as statistically significant in either model.

Second, several environmental conditions make a difference: the density of development is statistically significant and negative, as urban planners argue, in both models; the spatial expanse of development (the percent of county land area

Table 27.2 S2SLS Estimates of Per Capita Education Spending Model with Fixed Effects and Random Effects

	Fixed Effects		Random Effects	
	Est.	t–value	Est.	t–value
Constant	4.0074 ***	5.94	3.3476 ***	5.97
Core Model				
Spatial Lag ($\omega \cdot \hat{\tilde{e}}_j^*$)	0.2265 ***	2.39	0.3854 ***	4.46
Final Output—High School Graduation Rate ($\tilde{S}_i$)	0.3547 ***	7.08	0.3622 ***	7.42
Average Government Wage (W_i)	0.0140 ***	5.36	0.0086 ***	4.33
Population (P_i)	−0.0007 n/s	−0.29	0.0017 n/s	0.63
Population Change	−0.0188 n/s	−0.17	−0.1301 n/s	−1.25
Environmental Conditions (C_i)				
Density (δ_i)	−0.0129 ***	−3.26	−0.0190 ***	−4.81
% Developed (π_i)	0.0365 n/s	0.45	0.2101 ***	2.69
Median Housing Value	0.0009 ***	3.21	0.0007 ***	3.08
% Housing < 1940	−0.0826 n/s	−0.84	0.0898 n/s	1.13
Municipalities per Capita	0.1281 ***	4.62	0.0883 ***	3.56
Per Capita Income	−0.0036 ***	−2.32	−0.0029 ***	−2.01
Demographic Conditions (Z_i)				
% White	0.0539 n/s	0.84	−0.0271 n/s	−0.51
% < 5 Years Old	6.3090 ***	8.53	4.7684 ***	7.51
Average Household Size	−0.2117 ***	−5.13	−0.1412 ***	−3.48
Sources of Revenue (Z_i)				
% Property Tax	0.3880 ***	5.00	0.1235 ***	2.53
Per Capita Federal Revenue	0.0513 n/s	1.19	0.0621 n/s	1.55
Per Capita State Revenue	0.2849 ***	14.13	0.2187 ***	13.78
Per Capita Long–term Debt	−0.0008 n/s	−0.62	−0.0021 n/s	−1.66
Geographic Factors (Z_i)				
County Land Area	0.0152 n/s	1.43	0.0047 n/s	0.51
Employment: Population	0.1878 ***	3.30	0.1179 ***	2.19
Metropolitan Indicator	−0.0109 n/s	−0.60	0.0107 n/s	0.57
Micropolitan Indicator	0.0126 n/s	0.73	0.0139 n/s	0.79
N		3,075		3,075
Adjusted R²		0.22		0.24

Note: All hypothesis tests are two-tailed; *** denotes significant at a 99% confidence interval; ** denotes significant at a 95% confidence interval; * denotes significant at a 90% confidence interval; n/s denotes not statistically significant.

that is developed, holding land area constant) is positive, again as planners argue, but only significant in the random effects model; housing value,[17] a measure of wealth and also of the strength of the property tax base, is significant and positive; municipal fragmentation is significant and positive; and per capita income is significant and negative. The negative sign on per capita income may seem surprising, but it is not given that median housing value is also included; somewhat paradoxically, other things being equal, low-income communities often require greater levels of educational spending because of various extra demands placed on the education system (Downs 1994, 1999).

Third, two demographic conditions make a difference: the proportion of the population less than five years old, which captures the influence of young families, is positive; and the average household size is negative. Fourth, the sources of revenue that are relevant are property tax reliance and state funding—debt tends to be associated with infrastructure and other capital facilities, and so does funding from the federal government (Carruthers and Úlfarsson 2003, 2008). Last, the only geographic factor that plays a part in the models is the ratio of employment to population, and the variable's positive influence might be due to the tax base or perhaps due to the need for greater spending in places where higher proportions of the population—typically middle- and upper-class segments—have pulled out, leaving more needy segments behind.

What do the estimates listed in table 27.2 show, and how, if at all, do they extend knowledge related to the two questions articulated earlier in this chapter —Is there a relationship between urban form and public finance; and if so, is the relationship substantive enough to bother with? On the one hand, the estimates show that urban form does belong in a conventional (Bradford, Malt, and Oates 1969; Bergstrom and Goodman 1973; Borcherding and Deacon 1972) model of public spending. The example also illustrates how to operationalize a two-stage public-sector production function (Duncomb and Yinger 1993) using land-use metrics that are explicitly spatial—a seemingly obvious detail that nonetheless remains absent from many analyses of local government finance. On the other hand—and here is the fine point of it—the estimates in table 27.2 do little to inform the two "upper-level" questions that this chapter has attempted to draw attention to. They do suggest that there is a relationship between urban form and public finance, but only in the most general sense; and they, like the rest of the existing pool of research, say nothing concrete about its extent. So, even as the example presented here, which is in fact state of the art, illustrates how to carry out an analysis that aims at addressing the positive and normative questions related to the connection between urban form and public finance, it also illuminates just how much work remains to be done if the this key assumption is ultimately to be understood as well as it needs to be. Toward that end, the remaining section outlines several key steps that should be taken—ideally, by researchers from within the field of urban and regional planning who, after all, know and understand the questions that need to be addressed best—if the relationship is to maintain its standing as a guiding principle of, and credible rationale for, land-use planning.

5. Research Directions

Having reviewed the pool of existing theory and evidence on the connection between urban form and public finance, and having developed and operationalized an econometric model for evaluating it, the remaining task of this chapter is to set out some directions for future work in this essential area of planning research. As suggested throughout, researchers from within urban and regional planning—trained in public finance, land-use planning, and appropriate methods of spatial analysis—are perhaps best positioned to carry out this work. And, it seems (to the present author at least) that the field owes it to itself to take the lead on deepening the knowledge base related to one of its foundational assumptions rather than leaving the task to members of other disciplines who may not understand the issue in quite the same way. There is a great need for additional and more refined research, and this need presents an opportunity to advance urban and regional planning as the kind of scientific, evidence-based enterprise it needs to be in order to fulfill the many and complicated demands that will be placed upon it during the twenty-first century. Toward that end, there are a number of paths that should be pursued.

Foremost, the existing theory behind the connection between urban form and public finance—which at present turns (loosely) on the concept of economies of scale—is in need of strengthening. Ideally, this should be done in a way that articulates the process of producing public goods and services as a spatially explicit endeavor and that connects public finance to the specific goals of urban and regional planning. A similar sort of reengagement has happened over the past two decades regarding the connection between land use and transportation planning; two obviously interconnected branches of the field are now commonly addressed as one, but that was not always the case. Similarly, if land-use planning and public finance are to be coordinated in any sort of enduring way, the manner in which planners think about them must be refined. This requires that greater attention be given to the specific nature of the connection between the two and that the connection be more formally articulated in planning theory. It is not enough to rely on simple logic—that "denser is cheaper"—no matter how straightforward or intuitively appealing the premise: Why, exactly, is high-density, compact development less expensive to support than low-density, expansive alternatives? In what ways? And how do these expectations enter into the theory and practice of "planning in the public domain"? (see Friedmann 1987).

Of course, public finance does ultimately play out across geographic space—space that is filled, to a greater or lesser extent, with physical development and the infrastructure that supports it. Yet, for as simple as it seems (for example, Glaeser [2007, 5] writes that "conceptually, cities are the absence of space between people and firms"), the task of characterizing urban form in consistent, objective ways has proved enormously difficult (see Talen 2003; Song and Knaap 2008) and the challenge of doing so remains the single largest barrier to research aimed at evaluating its connection to the cost of public services. In the present context, what is needed, in particular, are quantitative measures of urban form that can be brought into the kind of econometric models of public spending described in the preceding sections. Finding innovative and meaningful ways of measuring urban form using geographic information systems and other approaches—here again work by Song and Knaap (2003, 2004) and Song (2005) is especially instructive—is fundamental to characterizing and evaluating the spatial arena and its impact on the cost of public goods and services.

In his classic work *Good City Form*, Lynch (1981) sets out a normative theory for evaluating the built environment that involves seven specific criteria: vitality, sense, fit, access, control, efficiency and justice. The framework is mentioned here to underscore the inherent complexity of development itself—the breadth of its purpose and meaning (see Batty 2007) and to highlight the basic point that public finance, if connected to urban form, is indeed an especially good filter for judging it. Questions about the interface between spending and criteria like vitality and efficiency, to name just two, drive at the heart of community well-being and quality of life: does the built environment serve the best interests of its inhabitants? If not, there is good reason to mobilize public policy to reshape it. But the fact remains that planners and other policymakers do, as a practical matter, require a basis for discriminating among development outcomes—after all, if some are not preferable to others, why plan in the first place? (Talen and Ellis 2002)—and public finance lends itself to the task in a natural way. Circling back to the initial point of this section, Lynch's framework (1981) seems a natural starting point for thinking about a more holistic theory wherein urban form and public finance are addressed jointly.

Last, the single biggest shortcoming of all of the econometric work that has been done so far—including that presented here, plus other analyses by the author (Carruthers 2002; Carruthers and Úlfarsson 2003, 2008)—is that it is exceptionally general in nature. There is little to be gained from additional research that relies on data aggregated to the county level, so going forward, work should focus on delving deeper into the spending patterns of actual jurisdictions and, if possible, even individual service districts within them. In the end, getting precise answers to the kinds of questions raised in this chapter may require opening the books of communities and carefully examining what is spent within them and where.

6 Summary and Conclusion

This chapter has provided an overview of what is known about the relationship between urban form and public finance, and has set out an analytical framework— with both theoretical and empirical components—for further inquiry into it. The specific objectives were to: (i) to review previous research in a way that integrates work from fields as disparate as public economics and urban design into a cohesive whole; (ii) illustrate how to adapt traditional models of public finance to incorporate land use, plus to reflect the kind of strategic interaction that local governments regularly engage in when making both spending and regulatory decisions; and (iii) suggest some key directions for future research in this essential area. Overall, the chapter serves as a starting point for more active engagement among urbamn planners on this set of issues and as a way forward for those looking to examine a relationship that has, for too long, been taken for granted. Whatever specific path is taken, the bottom line is that much work remains to be done: very little is known about this critical set of issues.

Notes

1. There were, in fact, a number of other studies prior to *The Costs of Sprawl*, and these are summarized in Frank (1989).
2. Now entitled the *Journal of the American Planning Association.*
3. Lee 1981 provides a good discussion of land-use planning as a response to market failure. Note that an inequitable outcome is not a market failure—indeed, the market economy commonly yields an unequal distribution of resources, and it is explicitly structured to do so—so a second, very thorny issue that planners as regulators are commonly faced with is evaluating the acceptability of inequitable outcomes and making appropriate regulatory decisions (in the public domain) based on their conclusions.
4. Others, including Ramapo, New York, came before Petaluma, but Petaluma is generally considered the origin of the growth-control movement (see Kelly 1993).
5. See Fujita (1987) for a detailed exposition.
6. A third important—but somewhat less relevant for present purposes—silo of research is composed of Lösch-style (1954) location analyses that address the optimal placement of central facilities; see, for example, Mulligan (1991, 2000); Farhan and Murry (2006).
7. To clarify this point, New York City is 303.31 square miles in size, and in 2000, 297.53 square miles of its territory, or 98.98 percent, was classified as urbanized by the U.S. Census Bureau, while Maricopa County is 9,203.14 square miles in size and 846.61 square miles of its territory, or 9.10 percent, was classified as urbanized. Using land area as opposed to urbanized—or some other measure of developed land—area introduces a degree of measurement error that renders comparisons between the two places meaningless: 26,402.88 people per square mile in New York City versus 325.015 people per square mile in Maricopa County if land area is used, compared to 3,522.25 versus 26,915.75 if urbanized area is used. The New York City measurements are almost identical, but the urbanized density of Maricopa County is nearly eleven times its territorial density. For this reason, it is absolutely critical that land-use oriented analyses must rely on some measure approximating actual land use in order to yield sound conclusions.
8. See the 1998 report helmed by Burchell 1998, *The Costs of Sprawl Revisited*, for a comprehensive review.
9. From $13.4 billion to $60.7 billion; in 2006, local governments across the United States—counting all 89,476 counties, boroughs, municipalities, townships, school districts, and special districts—spent more than $1.5 trillion, an increase of $400 billion from five years before.

10. In the theory of the firm, "production technology" refers to how firms go about producing outputs—in other words, the blend of capital, labor, and material inputs in the firm's production function. Baumol (1967, 415) argued that the technological structure of local governments forced "progressive and cumulative" increases in the cost of providing services.

11. In production, increasing (or decreasing) returns to scale exist if a doubling of inputs more than (or less than) doubles outputs, and economies (or diseconomies) of scale correspond to decreasing (or increasing) average costs or, equivalently, increasing (or decreasing) returns to scale.

12. Each of these dimensions of scale can be described mathematically by taking derivatives of equation (4).

13. The original contribution is Case, Rosen, and Hines (1993); additional contributions in the area of spatial interaction among governments have come from Kelejian and Robinson (1992, 1993, 1997); Brueckner (1998); Revelli (2001, 2002, 2003); Baiker (2005), and Solé-Ollé (2006)

14. The actual number of county equivalents is slightly greater, owing to a number of independent cities such as Baltimore, Maryland; St. Louis, Missouri; and cities throughout Virginia. These were integrated with appropriate counties when the data were compiled because some data—from the U.S. Bureau of Economic Analysis (2006b) Regional Economic Information System, for example—is not available at that level, but the entire surface of the continental United States is still represented in the data set.

15. The state fixed effects capture various unobserved state-specific factors that influence public spending patterns. For example, some, but not all, states encourage local governments to impose development-impact fees and/or face severe spending limits imposed through legislative referenda, as with California's Proposition 13.

16. In practice, all of the spatial variables were calculated in GeoDa (Anselin 2003; Anselin, Syabri, and Kho 2006) and then imported into stata with the rest of the data, where the two-stage least squares (2SLS) regressions were run using panel settings to identify the states as cross-sections for fixed effects and as clusters for white-adjusted standard errors.

17. A more sophisticated analysis might treat housing value as endogenous (see Crane 1990), especially if it employed micro data.

REFERENCES

Alonso, W. 1964. *Location and Land Use: Toward a General Theory of Land Rent.* Cambridge, MA: Harvard University Press.

Altshuler, A. A. 1977. "Review of the Costs of Sprawl." *Journal of the American Institute of Certified Planners* 43:207–209.

Altshuler, A. A., and J. A. Gómez-Ibáñez. 1993. *Regulation for Revenue: The Political Economy of Land Use Exactions.* Cambridge, MA: Lincoln Institute of Land Policy.

Andrews, M., W. Duncombe, and J. Yinger. 2002. "Revisiting Economies of Size in American Education: Are We Any Closer to a Consensus?" *Economics of Education Review* 21: 245–62.

Anselin, L. 1988. *Spatial Econometrics: Methods and Models.* Boston: Kluwer Academic Publishers.

Anselin, L. 1992. "Space and Applied Econometrics." *Regional Science and Urban Economics* 22:307–16.

Anselin, L. 2002. "Under the Hood: Issues in the Specification and Interpretation of Spatial Regression Models." *Agricultural Economics* 27:247–67.

Anselin, L. 2003. *GeoDa 0.9 User's Guide.* Spatial Analysis Laboratory, University of Illiniois, Urbana-Champaign, IL.

Anselin, L., I. Syabri, and Y. Kho. 2006. GeoDa: An Introduction to Spatial Data Analysis." *Geographical Analysis* 38:5–22.

Batty, M. 2007. *Cities and Complexity: Understanding Cities with Cellular Automata, Agent-based Models, and Fractals.* Cambridge, MA: MIT Press.

Baumol, W. J. 1967. "Macroeconomics of Unballanced Growth: The Anatomy of Urban Crisis." *American Economic Review* 57:415–26.

Baicker, K. 2005. "The Spillover Effects of State Spending." *Journal of Public Economics* 89:529–44.

Bergstrom, T. C., and R. P. Goodman.1973. "Private Demands for Public Goods." *American Economic Review* 63:280–96.

Bogart, W. T. 2006. *Don't Call it Sprawl: Metropolitan Structure in the Twenty-first Century.* New York: Cambridge University Press.

Borcherding, T. E., and R. T. Deacon. 1972. "The Demand for the Services of Non-Federal Governments." *American Economic Review* 62:891–901.

Bradford, D. F., R. A. Malt, and W. E. Oates. 1969. "The Rising Costs of Local Public Services: Some Evidence and Reflections." *National Tax Journal* 22:185–202.

Brueckner, J. K. 1997. "Infrastructure Financing and Urban Development: The Economics of Impact Fees." *Journal of Public Economics* 66:383–407.

Brueckner, J. K. 1998. "Testing for Strategic Interaction Among Local Governments: The Case of Growth Controls." *Journal of Urban Economics* 44:438–67.

Brueckner, J. K. 2000. "Urban Sprawl: Diagnosis and Remedies." *International Regional Science Review* 23:160–71.

Brueckner, J. K. 2003. "Strategic Interaction Among Governments: An Overview of Empirical Studies." *International Regional Science Review* 26:175–88.

Brueckner, J. K., and D. A. Fansler.1983. "The Economics of Urban Sprawl: Theory and Evidence on the Spatial Sizes of Cities." *Review of Economics and Statistics* 65:479–82.

Brueckner, J. K., and R. W. Helsley. 2011. "Sprawl and Blight." *Journal of Urban Economics* 69:205–13.

Bruegmann, R. 2005. *Sprawl: A Compact History.* Chicago: University of Chicago Press.

Burchell, R. W. 1998. *Transportation Cooperative Research Program Report 39: The Costs of Sprawl—Revisited.* Washington, DC: National Academy Press.

Carruthers, J. I. 2002. "The Impacts of State Growth Management Programs: A Comparative Analysis." *Urban Studies* 39:1959–82.

Carruthers, J. I., S. Hepp, G. J. Knaap, and R. N. Renner. Forthcoming. "The American Way of Land Use: A Spatial Hazard Analysis of Changes Through Time." *International Regional Science Review.*

Carruthers, J. I., S. Lewis, G. J. Knaap, and R. N. Renner. 2010. "Coming Undone: A Spatial Hazard Analysis of Urban Form." *Papers in Regional Science* 89:65–88.

Carruthers, J. I., and G. F. Úlfarsson. 2003. "Urban Sprawl and the Cost of Public Services." *Environment and Planning Part B* 30:503–22.

Carruthers, J. I., and G. F. Úlfarsson. 2008. "Does 'Smart Growth' Matter to Public Finance?" *Urban Studies* 45:1791–823.

Case, A. C., H. S. Rosen, and J. R. Hines. 1993. "Budget Spillover and Fiscal Policy Interdependence: Evidence from the States." *Journal of Public Economics* 52:285–307.

Crane, R. 1990. "Price Specification and the Demand for Public Goods." *Journal of Public Economics* 43:93–106.

Das, D., H. H. Kelejian, and I. R. Prucha. 2003. "Finite Sample Properties of Estimators of
    Spatial Autoregressive Models with Autoregressive Disturbances." *Papers in Regional
    Science* 82:1–26.

DeGrove, J. M. 1984. *Land, Growth, and Politics.* Washington, DC: APA Planner's Press.

DeGrove, J. M. 1992. *The New Frontier for Land Policy: Planning and Growth
    Management in the States.* Cambridge, MA: Lincoln Institute of Land Policy.

DeGrove, J. M. 2005. *Planning Policy and Politics: Smart Growth and the States.*
    Cambridge, MA: Lincoln Institute of Land Policy.

Downs, A. 1994. *New Visions for Metropolitan America.* Washington, DC: Brookings
    Institute Press.

Downs, A. 1999. "Some Realities about Sprawl and Decline." *Housing Policy Debate*
    10:955–74.

Duncombe, W., J. Miner, and J. Ruggiero. 1995. "Potential Cost Savings from School
    District Consolidation: A Case Study of New York." *Economics of Education Review*
    14: 265–84.

Duncombe, W., and J. Yinger. 1993. "An Analysis of Returns to Scale in Public Production,
    with an Application to Fire Protection." *Journal of Public Economics* 52:49–72.

Duncombe, W., and J. Yinger. 2000. "Financing Higher Student Performance Standards:
    The Case of New York State." *Economics of Education Review* 19:363–86.

Elis-Williams, D. G. 1987."The Effect of Spatial Population Distribution on the Cost of
    Delivering Local Services." *Journal of the Royal Statistical Society A* 150:152–66.

Esteller-Moré, Á., and A. Solé-Ollé. 2001. "Vertical Income Tax Externalities and Fiscal
    Interdependence: Evidence From the U.S." *Regional Science and Urban Economics*
    31:247–72.

Farhan, B., and A. T. Murray. 2006. "Distance Decay and Coverage in Facility Location
    Planning." *Annals of Regional Science* 40:279–96.

Fischel, W. 1990. "Do Growth Controls Matter? A Review of Empirical Evidence on the
    Effectiveness and Efficiency of Local Government Land Use Regulation." Lincoln
    Institute of Land Policy, Cambridge, MA.

Frank, J. 1989. *The Costs of Alternative Development Patterns: A Review of the Literature.*
    Washington, DC: Urban Land Institute.

Friedmann, J. 1987. *Planning in the Public Domain: From Knowledge to Action.* Princeton,
    NJ: Princeton University Press.

Fujita, M. 1987. *Urban Economic Theory: Land Use and City Size.* Cambridge, UK:
    Cambridge University Press.

Fulton, W. 1999. *The Guide to California Planning.* Point Arena, CA: Solano.

Glaeser, E. L. 2007. "The Economics Approach to Cities." Working paper no. 13696.
    National Bureau of Economic Research, Cambridge, MA.

Glaeser, E. L., and M. E. Kahn. 2004. "Sprawl and Urban Growth." In *Handbook of Urban
    and Regional Economics*, edited by J. V. Henderson and J. F. Thisse. Netherlands:
    North-Holland.

Gordon, P., and H. W. Richardson. 1997. "Are Compact Cities a Desirable Planning
    Goal?" *Journal of the American Planning Association* 63:95–106.

Hopkins, L. D., X. Xu, and G. J. Knaap. 2004. "Economies of Scale in Wastewater
    Treatment and Planning for Urban Growth." *Environment and Planning Part B:
    Planning and Design* 31:879–93.

Hortas-Rico, M., and A. Solé-Ollé. 2010. "Does Urban Sprawl Increase the Costs of
    Providing Local Public Services? Evidence from Spanish Municipalities." *Urban
    Studies* 47:1513–30.

Kelejian, H. H., and I. R. Prucha. 1998. "A Generalized Spatial Two-Stage Least Squares Procedure for Estimating a Spatial Autoregressive Model with Autoregressive Disturbances." *Journal of Real Estate Finance and Economics* 17:99–121.

Kelejian, H. H., and D. P. Robinson. 1992. "Spatial Autocorrelation, A New Computationally Simple Test with an Application to Per Capita County Police Expenditures." *Regional Science and Urban Economics* 22:317–31.

Kelejian, H. H., and D. P. Robinson. 1993. "A Suggested Method of Estimator for Spatial Interdependent Models with Autocorrelated Errors, and an Application of a County Expenditure Model." *Papers in Regional Science* 72:297–312.

Kelejian, H. H., and D. P. Robinson. 1997. "Infrastructure Productivity Estimation and its Underlying Econometric Specifications: A Sensitivity Analysis." *Papers in Regional Science* 76:115–31.

Kelly, E. D. 1993. *Managing Community Growth: Policies, Techniques, and Impacts.* Westport, CT: Praeger.

Knaap, G. J., and A. C. Nelson. 1992. *The Regulated Landscape: Lessons on State Land Use Planning From Oregon.* Cambridge, MA: Lincoln Institute of Land Policy.

Ladd, H. F. 1992. "Population Growth, Density, and the Costs of Providing Public Services." *Urban Studies* 29:273–95.

Ladd, H. F. 1994. "Fiscal Impacts of Local Population Growth: A Conceptual and Empirical Analysis." *Regional Science and Urban Economics* 24:661–86.

Ladd, H. F. 1998. "Land Use Regulation as a Fiscal Tool." In *Local Government Tax and Land Use Policies in the United States: Understanding the Links,* edited by H. F. Ladd.. Cambridge, MA: Lincoln Institute of Land Policy.

Ladd, H. F., and J. Yinger. 1991. *America's Ailing Cities: Fiscal Health and the Design of Urban Policy.* Baltimore: Johns Hopkins University Press.

Lee, D. 1981. "Land Use Planning as a Response to Market Failure." In *The Land Use Policy Debate in the United States,* edited by J. de Neufville. New York: Plenum.

Lösch, A. 1954. *The Economics of Location.* New Haven, CT: Yale University Press.

Lynch, K. 1981. *Good City Form.* Cambridge, MA: MIT Press.

McFarlane, A. 1999. "Taxes, Fees, and Urban Development." *Journal of Urban Economics* 46:416–36.

McGrath, D. T. 2005. "More Evidence on the Spatial Scale of Cities." *Journal of Urban Economics* 58:1–10.

Mieszkowski, P., and E. S. Mills. 1993. "The Causes of Metropolitan Suburbanization." *Journal of Economic Perspectives* 7:135–47.

Mills, E. S. 1971. *Studies in the Structure of the Urban Economy.* Baltimore, MD: Johns Hopkins University Press.

Mulligan, G. F. 1991. "Equality Measures and Facility Location." *Papers in Regional Science* 70:345–65.

Mulligan, G. F. 2000. "Resolving Location Conflict with Standardized Space-Cost Curves." *Professional Geographer* 52:50–60.

Muth, R. F. 1969. *Cities and Housing.* Chicago: University of Chicago Press.

Nechyba, T. J., and R. P. Walsh. 2004. "Urban Sprawl." *Journal of Economic Perspectives* 18:177–200.

Pendall, R. 1999. "Do Land Use Controls Cause Sprawl?" *Environment and Planning Part B* 26:555–71.

Peiser, R. B. 1984. "Does It Pay to Plan for Suburban Growth?" *Journal of the American Planning Association* 50:419–33.

Porter, D. 1997. *Managing Growth in America's Communities.* Washington, D C: Island Press.

Real Estate Research Corporation. 1974. *The Costs of Sprawl: Environmental and Economic Costs of Alternative Residential Development Patterns at the Urban Fringe.* Washington, DC: Environmental Protection Agency.

Revelli, F. 2001. "Spatial Patterns in Local Taxation: Tax Mimicking or Error Mimicking?" *Applied Economics* 33:1101–07.

Revelli, F. 2002. "Testing the Tax Mimicking Versus Expenditure Spill-Over Hypotheses Using English Data." *Applied Economics* 14:1723–31.

Revelli, F. 2003. "Reaction or Interaction? Spatial Process Identification in Multi-Tiered Government Structures." *Journal of Urban Economics* 53:29–53.

Revelli, F. 2005. "On Spatial Public Finance Empirics." *International Tax and Public Finance* 12:475–92.

Richardson, H. W., and P. Gordon. 1993. "Market Planning: Oxymoron or Common Sense?" *Journal of the American Planning Association* 59:347–52.

Solé-Ollé, A. 2006. "Expenditure Spillovers and Fiscal Interactions: Empirical Evidence From Local Governments in Spain." *Journal of Urban Economics* 59:32–54.

Solé-Ollé, A., and N. Bosch. 2005. "On the Relationship Between Authority Size and the Costs of Providing Local Services: Lessons for the Design of Intergovernmental Transfers in Spain." *Public Finance Review* 33:343–84.

Song, Y. 2005. "Smart Growth and Urban Development Patterns: A Comparative Study." *International Regional Science Review* 28:239–65.

Song, Y., and G. J. Knaap. 2003. "New Urbanism and Housing Values: A Disaggregate Assessment." *Journal of Urban Economics* 54:218–38.

Song, Y., and G. J. Knaap. 2004. "Measuring the Effects of Mixed Land Uses on Housing Values." *Regional Science and Urban Economics* 34:663–80.

Song, Y., and G. J. Knaap. 2008. "Quantitative Classification of Neighborhoods: The Neighborhoods of New Single-family Homes in the Portland Metropolitan Area." *Journal of Urban Design* 12:1–24.

Speir, C., and K. Stephenson. 2002. "Does Sprawl Cost Us All? Isolating the Effects of Housing Patterns on Public Water and Sewer Costs." *Journal of the American Planning Association* 68:56–70.

Talen, E. 2003. "Measuring Urbanism: Issues in Smart Growth Research." *Journal of Urban Design* 8:195–215.

Talen, E., and C. Ellis. 2002. "Beyond Relativism: Reclaiming the Search for Good City Form." *Journal of Planning Education and Research* 22:36–49.

U.S. Bureau of Commerce. 2001. *1997 Compendium of Government Finances.* Census of Governments. Washington, DC: U.S. Government Printing Office.

U. S. Bureau of Commerce. 2005. *2002 Compendium of Government Finances.* Census of Governments. Washington, DC: U.S. Government Printing Office.

U. S. Bureau of Economic Analysis. 2006a. "Gross State Product." Available at: http://bea.gov/bea/regional/gsp.

U. S. Bureau of Economic Analysis. 2006b. "Regional Economic Information System." Available at: http://bea.gov/bea/regional/reis.

U.S. Census Bureau. 2000, 1990. Summary File 3. Available at: www.census.gov.

U.S. Department of Agriculture. 2001. *1997 National Resources Inventory.* On CD-ROM. Fort Worth: National Cartography and Geospatial Center.

Windsor, D. 1979. "A Critique of the Costs of Sprawl." *Journal of the American Planning Association* 45:279–92.

CHAPTER 28

CITY ABANDONMENT

MARGARET DEWAR AND
MATTHEW D. WEBER

URBAN planning typically focuses on growth. Planners review, encourage, manage, guide, and control real estate development. Urban planners address the externalities associated with development and advise on infrastructure investments that support development. Few planners work in places where no development is occurring, and little literature exists on the processes and politics of "undevelopment," the gradual dismantling of a city due to lack of investment. Urban planning as a field has had little to say about what cities should become following extensive population and employment loss, disinvestment, and abandonment, or how planners can operate when no development is possible. The American Planning Association's Planning Books featured only two publications during 2009 that could be useful for a planner working in such a setting (Bonham, Spilka, and Rastorfer 2002; Mallach 2006). The "Green Book," a manual for local planning, provides little specifically to help a planner working where no development is likely (Hoch, Dalton, and So 2000; Hack et al. 2009). "In the face of widespread poverty and shrinking fiscal resources, planners generally focus on economic revitalization," wrote the authors of the third edition, in a consistent focus on encouraging growth, "which may include a range of programs—from housing rehabilitation to small business loans to employment programs" (Hoch, Dalton, and So 2000, 9). The 2009 edition pointed to ways that planning approaches could apply where significant population decline had occurred—involving widespread citizen participation, reuse of surplus public property, and the leveraging of assets—nearly always with the aim of building anew (Hack et al. 2009, 71–72, 88, 146). With a focus on revitalization, chapters analyzed the impact of targeting resources in blighted neighborhoods, comprehensive planning in the South Bronx, and renewal of Washington, D.C.'s neighborhoods (Galster 2009; Shapiro 2009; Wagner 2009). The titles of books that focus on planning and community development in disinvested areas of U. S. cities communicate that the agenda is development and renewal—*Rebuilding Urban Neighborhoods* (Keating and Krumholz 1999), *Reviving America's Forgotten Neighborhoods* (Bright 2003), *Renewing Cities* (Gittell 1992), *Rebuilding the Inner City* (Halpern 1995)—although little opportunity for redevelopment may exist, as the content of such books often acknowledges.

The challenge confronting the field of urban planning is that numerous formerly industrial cities in North America and Europe in particular contain vast areas where almost no prospects for development exist. As Beauregard (2009) shows, among the fifty largest central cities in the United States, nine experienced persistent loss of population between 1950 and 2000—Baltimore, Buffalo, Cincinnati, Cleveland, Detroit, Philadelphia, Pittsburgh, St. Louis, and Washington, D.C. New Orleans lost population in every decade from 1960 through 2000, and Milwaukee lost from 1970 through 2000. Many other smaller cities have also experienced long-term, sustained population decline. Central cities in Germany, Italy, Great Britain, and elsewhere in Europe, Japan, and other parts of the world also exhibit persistent population loss and disinvestment (Rieniets 2005, 24; Oswalt and Rieniets 2006). The old industrial cities of northern England, such as Manchester and Liverpool; Glasgow, Scotland; and cities in the former East Germany, such as Leipzig, have experienced the scale of disinvestment that characterizes formerly industrial cities in the United States. These cities have generally lost one-third to three-fifths of their peak populations (Oswalt and Rieniets 2006, 152–56).

Some parts of these cities attract population, especially near assets such as waterfronts and cultural venues. Political leaders, business leaders, and planners continue to recruit and manage growth in those places. However, the job for urban planning in large sections of these cities is to find ways to manage depopulation and disinvestment in ways that achieve goals other than encouraging or managing growth, such as improving the quality of life for the people who remain, slowing the loss of tax base, improving environmental sustainability, or reducing the costs of public services.

The purpose of this chapter is to assess the state of knowledge about how urban planning can comprehend and address the issues facing cities with extensive residential disinvestment and abandonment. The sections that follow discuss three related topics. First, why does planning so rarely address issues facing the most abandoned areas of cities except to encourage growth and redevelopment? Second, how can planners think about or understand the causes of widespread urban abandonment? Third, how can planning address widespread abandonment? Two principles—efficiency and equity—offer guidance for planners' interventions. Although urban planning as a field has considerable understanding of why cities lose employment and population and why abandonment occurs, planners could make much more progress in envisioning the future for heavily abandoned areas of cities that have little prospect for growth.

1. WHY DOES PLANNING SO RARELY ADDRESS HEAVILY ABANDONED AREAS OF CITIES?

Strong forces mitigate against planning's attention to abandoned areas and decline. Land development and economic development projects are vital to local elected officials' need for publicity, a reputation for making things happen, and material benefits to distribute such as jobs and contracts in order to ensure reelection (Elkin 1987). In the city's functioning as a "growth machine," those who participate most in local affairs have the most to gain or lose from land-use decisions (Logan and Molotch 1987). The "growth machine" functions in part by creating a seemingly value-free ideology that defines growth as good for all in a city. Thus, development boosters use metaphors such as the "city as a diseased body" to lead all involved to the same conclusion: that the city must act to "renew," "revitalize," and "cure" the disease (Wilson 1996). Political and administrative attention goes where the land development action is within the city, not to abandoned areas or areas experiencing disinvestment with no new development. Mayors chase development such as sports stadia and casinos that have little if any benefit for neighborhoods where abandonment is occurring (Eisinger 2000). Members of the "growth machine" employ planners, whether in the public or the private sector, so planners' attention focuses on the growth agenda.

Moreover, as population and employment loss proceeds, many fiscally strained cities cut their planning departments to the point where they cannot address the issues facing the cities' expanding areas of abandoned neighborhoods. When they do plan in such areas, the focus is on redevelopment, on transitioning from old, obsolete uses to new development. In Detroit, for example, the prospect of Empowerment Zone funding in 1994 led to a strategic plan for creating economic opportunity, sustaining families, and restoring and upgrading neighborhoods in some of the highest poverty areas of the city (City of Detroit 1994; Bockmeyer 2000). Foundation support made possible a citywide plan in the late 1990s, the Community Reinvestment Strategy (City of Detroit 2010). The city council adopted a master plan of policies in 2009 that was the work of the city's planning staff; it built on the Community Reinvestment Strategy and laid out redevelopment possibilities for all parts of the city, regardless of how disinvested (City of Detroit 2009).

In the sections of cities that experience the most abandonment, community development corporations (CDCs) often become the de facto planning offices. The CDCs usually have broad community development aims and engage in a range of activities. However, their emphasis is nearly always on developing housing and commercial and industrial real estate (Vidal and Keating 2004), and they often need to create development plans in order to obtain the resources to carry out these projects. Their financial model also depends on real estate development fees (Ash et al. 2009; Vidal 1997). However, where little demand for land or housing exists, a focus on development does not provide enough guidance for improving the quality of life of remaining residents and transitioning to a new kind of place, likely with more vacant land.

When urban planners and others suggested planning for the loss of population in the past, their experience revealed the difficulty they encountered in altering the growth agenda and in countering low-income and minority residents' suspicions that city officials would again attempt urban renewal. During the 1970s, several city officials called for "rightsizing" cities, planning for population decline, rather than allowing disinvestment and abandonment to take its course. In 1973, the chair of Philadelphia's City Planning Commission proposed that the city take areas of North Philadelphia through eminent domain and hold the property while relocating residents to other parts of the region. The proposal was met with intense protest from African-American residents (Kleniewski 1986). In St. Louis, Missouri, in 1974, a consulting firm advised the Planning Commission to consider designating some areas of the city as "depletion areas" for applying "a no growth policy until firm market and adequate public resources are available" (Pratter 1977, 84). A newspaper report on the recommendations stimulated a "wild debate" (87) around several misconceptions: that the depletion policies would apply throughout the predominantly black section of the city, city officials would purposely neglect those areas, city departments would withdraw public services from the areas, and housing code enforcement would drive people from their neighborhoods. The city administration distanced itself from the actual recommendations, which focused on planning for land use in the context of population loss and disinvestment while providing protections for residents affected by neighborhood abandonment (Pratter 1977). In New York City, in 1976, Roger Starr, administrator for the city's Housing and Development Administration, argued for accepting that the South Bronx and Brownsville would lose substantial population and advocated planning for it. His proposals elicited intense opposition from city officials and others (Starr 1976; Cooper-McCann 2010). In Cleveland, Ohio, Norman Krumholz, director of the City Planning Commission during the 1970s, tried to persuade the city's political leadership to plan for a future without growth, but, he said, they did not want to hear it (N. Krumholz, pers. comm., October 2, 2009; see also Swanstrom 1985).

The political pressures that bring attention to most abandoned areas come late in the disinvestment process, long after city planning functions have been cut so much that they have little capacity. The interest comes from community development intermediaries and foundations seeking to ensure that their investments have impact on affordable housing development and revitalization of commercial areas (Ash et al. 2009; Vidal and Keating 2004, 133), from city officials facing budget crises (Starr 1976; Cooper-McCann 2010), and from residents with ideas about better ways to address nearly empty areas of the city.

To address the issues involving abandoned areas of cities, planners need to understand why large areas of abandoned and vacant property exist in so many cities. The next section reviews the frameworks of thinking that explain this phenomenon.

2. WHY DOES WIDESPREAD ABANDONMENT OCCUR?

Many factors lead to abandonment. Some exist within neighborhoods. Others originate from outside. Some affect the supply side of the market, others the demand side. Most work in combination with other factors. Moreover, abandonment does not merely result from these many factors; it also causes further abandonment. This complexity makes abandonment difficult to capture concisely. Consequently, researchers and theorists use numerous lenses to understand and describe abandonment. This section reviews several approaches, starting at the individual decision to abandon housing and gradually broadening the view to encompass forces of the larger political economy.

At the smallest scale, understanding widespread abandonment starts with understanding the decision of an individual property owner to abandon a particular structure. In the prototypical case, abandonment occurs when the cost of maintaining and operating a structure exceeds its value, and other uses of the property are not financially viable. This has inspired significant research into the role that maintenance expenditures play in abandonment. Indeed, early models held that abandonment of housing is inevitable because the quality of dwellings declines and the cost of maintaining them increases throughout their lifetime (Ratcliff 1949; Muth 1969; Sweeney 1974; Quigley 1979). At some point, under this view, dwellings become too expensive to maintain and are abandoned. Accordingly, widespread abandonment occurs because neighborhoods comprise dwellings of roughly the same age and quality that decline at roughly the same rate.

Empirical research has not supported the view that housing abandonment is inevitable. Rydell (1970), for example, showed that maintenance costs stabilize as a home ages and generally are not high enough to make abandonment a rational choice. Indeed, "the difference...between adequate and inadequate maintenance may be only a few hundred dollars a year. By contrast, the consequences of some forms of under-maintenance may be immediate and severe, reducing the attractiveness of a dwelling or making it uninhabitable" (Grigsby et al. 1987, 43). Thus, inadequate maintenance typically costs owners more in loss of building capital and rental income than it saves (Stegman 1972; Grigsby and Rosenburg 1975). Accordingly, abandonment is not inevitable but depends on other factors, such as market demand for a property.

Another focus of research related to the decision to abandon property is the role of property taxes. White (1986) and Arsen (1992), for example, find that high property tax rates are significant causes of residential abandonment. Similarly, Scafidi et al. (1998) present an empirically supported model of residential abandonment that shows that abandonment occurs when property taxes, fines, and other liens exceed the property's market value.

This research may help planners to act proactively to address imminent abandonment, but in terms of understanding the abandonment process, it fails to answer the question of why so many properties have collectively declined in value, moving entire neighborhoods from vibrancy to decay to abandonment. Answers to this question diverge significantly but fall into three broad categories: ecological, subcultural, and political economy (Temkin and Rohe 1996).

2.1 Ecological Approaches

Ecological approaches to neighborhood change focus on the neighborhood as part of a larger socioeconomic system. These approaches include Burgess's concentric zone model, Hoyt's sectoral model, economic models built around the filtering process, and neighborhood life-cycle models.

Burgess (1925/2007) drew from theories of plant ecology to model the urban development process. He depicted a system where lower status racial and ethnic groups and nonresidential uses push outward from a central business district (CBD) to invade surrounding neighborhoods, in much the way that plants invade new territories and come to dominate them. These invasions cause the next higher status residents to move farther out from the CBD, effectively invading the surrounding neighborhoods. This process continues, ultimately establishing a series of concentric zones radiating from the CBD. The highest status zones, farthest from the CBD, are home to the newest and most expensive housing. The zone surrounding the CBD, by contrast, has aging and obsolete structures, and serves as the receiving ground for new migrants and industrial expansion. Under this model, widespread abandonment occurs when immigration slows or ends and the central business district stops expanding. Under these circumstances, "the inner zones…lose a portion of their justification for being. With need diminished the ultimate fate of the worst structures is abandonment" (Sternlieb et al. 1974, 322).

Homer Hoyt's (1939) sectoral model inverts the causal processes that Burgess theorized. Rather than a system that pushes outward from a central business district, Hoyt understood the process of urban development as driven by the "pull" of development on the urban fringe. The middle class moves out of the city as better housing becomes available on the periphery, leaving older housing behind. As in the concentric zone model, if fewer people move into the housing left behind than move out, abandonment occurs.

Modern economic theories of abandonment build on Hoyt's insights to develop a more complex model of the abandonment process. The economic approach rests in part on the understanding that factors other than the need for shelter drive demand for dwelling units. Dwelling units offer a bundle of "housing services" that include the size and quality of housing units, environmental and aesthetic amenities (e.g., air quality, access to parks, tree cover), public services (e.g., school quality, public safety, social services), consumer conveniences (e.g., access to retail stores and services of various kinds), ease of access to transportation routes and jobs, and more. Collectively, these factors define dimensions of housing quality. Economists use differences in quality to divide the housing market into a variety of submarkets. Units within a submarket are close substitutes for each other, but poor substitutes for units in other submarkets. (Grigsby et al. 1987; Rothenberg et al. 1991). Consumers are thought to maximize their utility subject to their income constraints through choice of housing within a submarket. In a static economy this would lead to an equilibrium where people settle into the dwellings with the bundle of housing services that offers them the most "utility" at their income levels.

But local economies are not static. New and better housing built on the urban fringe renders older housing in the central city less appealing. New highways make previously remote housing and business locales more accessible. Employment opportunities change in number, kind, quality, and location. Average family size changes. Preferences for styles and types of housing shift. Incomes change. Homes age and deteriorate. These and many other factors lead to changes in both the demand for housing of different kinds and the housing services that homes in different neighborhoods deliver. The result may be that entire neighborhoods decline in relative or absolute quality, such that they move from their original submarket to a lower quality submarket. When this occurs, higher income residents seeking a higher quality submarket may move out of the neighborhood, while lower income residents seeking to take advantage of the lower prices that houses in the neighborhood now command may relocate there. This is the beginning of a "succession" or "filtering" process (Grigsby et al. 1987; Rothenberg et al. 1991). The quality of housing declines during this process as successive homeowners and landlords have less income to invest. This decrease in housing quality leads to a further decline in the value of property, and a new round of lower income tenants moves in. Unless changes interrupt the process, it leads to a downward spiral that ends in abandonment.

The geographic separation of housing by income structures this process as a neighborhood-based phenomenon. When declining and abandoned property concentrates in a particular area, the social and physical effects of those conditions also concentrate there. A recursive process often develops where abandoned housing negatively affects the surrounding neighborhood through spillover and contagion effects, and declines in neighborhood quality lead to further abandonment. (See, for example, Hillier et al. 2003; Accordino and Johnson 2000; Odland and Balzer 1979.) Likewise, many point to the rise in deviant social behavior that they assert accompanies a concentration of very low income residents in a geographic area as an important cause of decline and abandonment (Grigsby et al. 1987; Andersen 1995). As Andersen (1995, 74) explains:

> When succession has gone so far that a comparatively large share of the residents have social problems, the economy of the properties is affected by loss of rental incomes. Revenues drop because some of the residents cease paying rents, because the turnover of tenants increases, and because some of the dwellings may be vacant for longer or shorter periods. At the same time, the wear and tear on the property increases because the residents are less inclined to take care of the

dwellings. At this point, there is little likelihood of reversing the process, and abandonment will begin to occur.

Thus, a common theme in research on abandonment is that early interventions may forestall decline, but if delayed too long, decline reaches a tipping point where the process is difficult to stop (Stegman 1972; Sternlieb and Burchell 1973).

The inevitability of decline is a common theme in stage theories of neighborhood change. These theories posit that neighborhoods progress through a series of stages that lead from initial construction to abandonment, much as the life cycle of organisms leads from birth to death. Different theorists divide the stages differently. Hoover and Vernon (1959), for example, posit five stages, while Birch (1971) posits six. For some of these theorists, a "renewal" stage follows abandonment, although renewal seems more an article of faith than a theory, as these theorists do not clearly specify the causes of renewal.

Anthony Downs articulated the most influential of the stage theories, the neighborhood life-cycle theory (Real Estate Research Corporation 1973; Downs 1976), in several reports for the U.S. Department of Housing and Urban Development. Downs posits that neighborhoods progress through five stages in their life cycle, from "healthy" after their birth (Stage 1); to "incipient decline" as lower income and lower status residents begin to move into the neighborhood (Stage 2); to "clear decline" as housing prices fall, mortgage financing costs increase, and increasing demands for public services go unmet (Stage 3); to "accelerating decline," where population has fallen, poverty has increased, and many buildings stand vacant (Stage 4); to "abandoned," where the few remaining residents are impoverished and most buildings are dilapidated, empty, or have been demolished (Stage 5). While the term "neighborhood life cycle" conveys a sense of the inevitability of decline, Downs allowed that neighborhoods could move in either direction along his life-cycle continuum (Downs 1981, 64). However, he also emphasized that reversing a decline requires early action. Some have blamed Downs's life-cycle theory for accelerating neighborhood decline, arguing that it led lenders and others to walk away from distressed neighborhoods (Metzger 2000; Roberts 1991), while others vigorously dispute this characterization (Downs 2000; Galster 2000; Temkin 2000).

2.2 Subcultural Approaches

The ecological focus on forces outside a neighborhood that determine its fate gave rise to a countermovement that highlights the social relationships within neighborhoods. Most of this literature addresses the neighborhood practices and characteristics that stave off decline. Thus, strong social networks, participation in neighborhood institutions, a sense of attachment to and identity with the neighborhood, and other aspects of social capital make residents both willing and able to resist the forces that might otherwise lead residents to decide to move out of a neighborhood (Warren and Warren 1977; Ahlbrandt 1984; Varady 1986; Committee for Economic Development 1995; Stegman and Turner 1996; Vidal 1997). Moreover, community organizing and other techniques can tap political resources that bring new investment to a neighborhood.

For those interested in the causes of abandonment (rather than revitalization), this literature teaches that the absence of a sufficiently strong subculture of neighborhood solidarity and organizing allows the forces of decline to take hold within a neighborhood. Nonetheless, timing is as important in the subcultural approach as in the others. Late interventions must cope with a lack of confidence in the neighborhood and severely diminished social and physical assets on which to build. Indeed, Temkin and Rohe (1996, 168) see strong social fabric as a necessary condition of revitalization: "Unfortunately, many cities have areas that have declined beyond the point that community organizing, no matter how well intentioned, is likely to succeed. These are areas where crime and fear of crime are high, employment opportunities are scarce, and physical decay abounds." Thus, subculturalists, like others, acknowledge that neighborhoods reach tipping points beyond which the social fabric is so badly damaged that neighborhood-based efforts to resist decline cannot succeed. Decay and abandonment become almost inevitable.

2.3 Political Economy Approaches

A third approach to neighborhood change identifies the larger political economy as explanation for widespread abandonment. Thus, suburbanization beginning in the 1940s and the economic restructuring of the 1970s and 1980s moved jobs and people out of historically industrial cities, particularly in the heavily industrial Midwest and Northeast. The scale of this loss was too vast for any neighborhood-level strategy to counteract. Biased practices such as blockbusting in the 1960s and 1970s, redlining of neighborhoods through mortgage lending and insuring of homes, and fraud and abuse in federal mortgage insurance ensured that losses caused by these structural forces concentrated in minority and low-income neighborhoods and that minority households could not move to predominantly white suburbs. In the last fifteen years, subprime and other high-risk mortgage lending has served a similar function. All of these have accelerated the disinvestment in certain areas of cities, especially where African Americans lived or were moving in (Temkin and Rohe 1996; Boyer 1973; Immergluck 2009; Crump et al. 2008).

David Harvey (2001) and others argue that the disinvestment many cities have experienced is inherent in the capitalist system. "Any explanation of neighborhood 'decline' must account for the shifting flows of capital investment and disinvestment," note Smith, Caris, and Wyly (2001, 501). Capitalism's drive to increase rates of profit in the production process leads to "crises of overaccumulation," when owners have more capital than they can profitably invest in the production process. A solution is investment in the built environment, but this solution succeeds only temporarily. Harvey (2001, 247) describes the difficulty this creates due to the fixed and durable character of real estate: "Capitalist development has to negotiate . . . between preserving the values of past capital investments in the built environment and destroying these investments in order to open up fresh room for accumulation." Urban abandonment is one expression of such destruction.

In some cities, abandonment is a temporary condition before reinvestment occurs. This happens when disinvestment creates a "rent gap" (the difference between property values in a deteriorated neighborhood and potential property values if the neighborhood is completely redeveloped to achieve its current "highest and best use"). The promise of high returns on investment can thus remake an abandoned neighborhood through gentrification (Smith, Caris, and Wyly 2001). However, few abandoned neighborhoods in cities with major loss of their industrial base meet the rent-gap profile. Employment growth in these cities has not been substantial enough to drive up demand for middle-class housing in disinvested areas near downtown (Berry 1999).

The economic restructuring since the mid- to late-1970s is both a cause of widespread abandonment in some cities and a reason to expect abandonment will continue. Many older industrial regions in the United States and Europe experienced a substantial decline in their manufacturing base commencing in the 1970s, and a concomitant loss of wealth and people. These losses heralded a new phase of capitalist development often termed "post-Fordist" (Amin 1994). The term connotes a globally dispersed network of specialized suppliers and manufacturers that serve a highly segmented, global consumer market through a flexible system of production. Those cities that transitioned to the new economy became hubs in the global "space of flows" that link capital with sites of production and consumption (Castells 2002; Sassen 2005). Many regions that grew in the era of Fordist mass production, however, have yet to find their place in the new economy. For the central cities of these regions, little prospect exists for economic growth to overcome the Fordist-era legacy of vacant industrial buildings and obsolete and abandoned homes. Indeed, maintaining what they have seems challenge enough. Consequently, widespread abandonment is a continuing problem that planners and others must address.

What ways of thinking can help planners address these abandoned areas? The next section addresses this question.

3. Why and How Should Planners Address Widespread Disinvestment and Abandonment?

Thirty-five years ago, U.S. Congressman Henry Reuss, chair of the House of Representatives Committee on Banking, Finance and Urban Affairs, declared, in words that resonate in 2012, that the transition of America's cities to smaller size would be difficult and would "require creative management of shrinkage on the part of city leaders, who will have to make hard choices on how the physical space within city boundaries is to be used, and where scarce resources should be concentrated" (U. S. House 1977, vii). Others agreed. Planners "will have to begin to learn how to plan for static and declining cities," said Herbert Gans (1975, 306–307), to engage in "cutback planning," to "develop a viable and functioning city under conditions of decline."

Discussion of how to address the challenges facing cities under conditions of population loss and extensive property abandonment has occurred in two eras. From the mid-1970s through the early 1980s, planners and others debated how cities should handle these issues, instigated in part by the substantial abandonment in the South Bronx in New York City and in St. Louis, Missouri (Starr 1976; Pratter 1977). Since the early to mid-2000s, a new discussion has developed that rarely reflects awareness of the earlier ideas and lessons, inspired in part by the "Shrinking Cities" project of the German Federal Cultural Foundation (Oswalt 2005, 2006) and the attention brought to policy concerns by the National Vacant Properties Campaign founded in 2003 in the United States (National Vacant Properties Campaign 2010).

The existing literature from both eras relies on principles of efficiency and equity to offer planners ways of thinking that can guide actions for such planning in cities with extensive disinvestment and abandonment.

3.1 Efficiency in Land Use and Housing

Disinvestment results in uneven patterns of occupancy and abandonment. Some areas eventually become heavily abandoned; others experience substantial disinvestment and will become the next areas of abandonment; and some experience little decline in property conditions. Continued population loss, however, means that declining neighborhoods likely will not experience increases in demand for housing. The efficiency perspective argues, first, that planners and policymakers should guide decline so as to empty some areas while assuring greater density in neighborhoods that may remain viable. Because of greater consolidation of housing, retail and services could remain viable and increase amenities for nearby residents. In the words of Heilbrun (1979, 424), "The economic argument for neighborhood consolidation is...property value gains in conservation areas can be expected to exceed losses in clearance areas. The resulting net gain in value...reflects an increase in the productivity of local resources used to provide housing and other neighborhood services."

Second, planners should work to contain blight and disinvestment and prevent its spread into intact neighborhoods. Disinvestment "infects" other properties owing to negative externalities (Wallace and Wallace 1990). An abandoned structure influences property owners' views about the prospects for the area and lowers property values nearby, furthering decline (Mallach 2006, 8).

How could city leadership accomplish this? Discussions about the merits of "triage" raged from the mid-1970s through the early 1980s, as cities sought to adjust to population decline. Triage meant choosing to focus most resources on neighborhoods showing signs of decay but that interventions could save, withdrawing resources from areas with extensive disinvestment, and providing a few resources to areas still intact (Baer 1976; Kleniewski 1986; Downs 1976; Thompson 1977; Rybczynski 1995). In the "healthy" neighborhoods, those with no deterioration and considered desirable places to live, Downs (1976) recommended, community development spending should aim to produce "high-visibility" effects that could include planting trees, repairing curbs and streets, and putting in new sidewalks and streetlights. In "very deteriorated" neighborhoods, those with many empty homes and poor building maintenance, and those with extensive abandonment and vacant land, community development resources should address the needs of the low-income residents—for employment or health services, for instance—but should not attempt to upgrade the areas physically. In the "in-between" areas (with beginning decline but considerable amounts of good-quality housing, or with decline well under way with home and land prices falling and mortgages difficult to obtain), community development efforts should focus on major public and private upgrading to stem the disinvestment and encourage reinvestment.

Some of those assessing the effects of neighborhood decline suggested that people remaining in the most disinvested areas should move to other neighborhoods. "If the city is to survive with a smaller population," wrote Roger Starr (1976, 92), who had served as administrator of New York City's Housing and Development Administration, "the population must be encouraged to concentrate itself in the sections that remain alive." City programs and federal aid could not save all neighborhoods so a solution could involve giving "money for relocation expenses in the communities to be emptied" (Thompson 1977, 73).

During the 2000s, discussions over policy focused on "targeting" neighborhoods. Targeting meant deciding where interventions had the most chance of successfully preventing further disinvestment and stimulating renewal, and then placing disproportionate resources there. Targeting resources in certain areas would have greater impact and be more efficient than scattering these across a city (Thomson 2008). The positive externalities of concentrated public investment can inspire property owners to invest with the belief that their investments will not be lost and that property values will not continue to fall. In 1999, Richmond, Virginia, officials decided to target the distribution of their Community Development Block Grant and HOME dollars in a small number of neighborhoods, rather than spreading the funds across the city, until the investments stimulated self-sustaining, private market activity in those areas. The intermediary, the Local Initiatives Support Corporation, targeted its investments in the same places. After considerable public consultation, community development staff selected as targets six neighborhoods that had experienced the most disinvestment in the city or that showed significant signs of decline. An evaluation of the results after five years showed that the investments had notable positive effects on home prices in the targeted areas. Much larger positive effects occurred when a block had received at least $30,000 in total invest-ments over the five years, suggesting that private investment increased significantly above a threshold of public investment even in these most distressed areas of the city (Accordino, Galster, and Tatian 2005; Galster, Tatian, and Accordino 2006).

Foundations and national intermediaries began to make investment decisions in targeted areas before the results of the Richmond program appeared (Ash et al. 2009, 28; Neighborhood Progress 2010). The areas they chose were often very large compared to the smaller ones targeted successfully in Richmond. This raised ques-tions about whether the public and other investments could reach the thresholds (whether Richmond's $30,000 per block or a larger or smaller figure) needed to inspire private investment.

Another approach classifies areas by their conditions and their assets and iden-tifies varied ways to address issues in each area (Mallach 2006, chap. 17). Different strategies are appropriate in different types of areas. City officials need to act early and strategically to stem abandonment if they seek the best chance of their efforts succeeding in preventing extensive disinvestment.

These approaches often continue to focus on redevelopment. In cities where disinvestment has led to large amounts of vacant land with continuing popula-tion loss and little demand for property, however, the need is for reinvention, not redevelopment. New kinds of land uses can potentially find a place in the city. These require vacant land—farming, deconstruction, composting, natural areas enhancement, ecological solutions that enhance the experience of the natural environment—and benefit remaining residents as well as people living outside the disinvested areas (Cleveland Land Lab 2008; Geisler et al. 2009; Nassauer and VanWieren 2008).

3.2 Efficiency in Public Service Delivery

Cities that lose large amounts of population and employment also lose tax base and property tax revenue. Therefore, thinking about efficiency also involves perspec-tives on ways to adjust public services. Per capita service costs rise as abandon-ment increases, in part because public institutions cannot adjust staffs quickly in response to lower demand for services. The inability to restructure service delivery and infrastructure investment quickly leads to budget crises, but over time, cities with declining populations often consolidate services and try to make better use of employees and facilities (Muller 1977). Even after adjustments in the city's staff, service delivery may be less efficient in areas with high levels of vacancy than in denser areas because the same extent of land area needs servicing. Infrastructure built for a larger population still requires maintenance (Rybczynski and Linneman 1999; Rybczynski 1995).

Checkerboard clustering of population and clearing of nearly empty areas can keep average costs of public service delivery lower, Thompson (1977, 69) argued. "Why run police cars and fire trucks farther than necessary? Why spread out the trash collection? Why make buses stop more often than need be?…Clustering shortens utility lines."

Clustering of population can enhance property tax revenues as well. Planned neighborhood consolidation, although not necessarily as a Thompson's checkerboard with alternating patches of dense neighborhoods and empty areas, can result in higher property tax revenues because of higher property values in the consolidated areas (Heilbrun 1979).

As cities have worked to address these issues, however, the complexity of restructuring services and reducing infrastructure investments has become apparent, and no city has successfully "rightsized" services and infrastructure investment (for example, Hoornbeek and Schwarz 2009). In figuring out how to manage the reductions in service to nearly empty areas of the city, department managers, budget officers, and others looking for ways to reduce expenditures need to consider numerous questions: How much of a service's cost is fixed and therefore not avoided with cuts in service? Approximately 80 percent of infrastructure costs can be fixed costs, meaning that average cost per customer rises as use declines and that cutting services to nearly empty areas has only a small effect on a city's budget (Herz 2006, 11). Past analysis showed that declining cities had higher fixed costs (current capital expenditures, long-term debt, and pension fund liabilities) than growing ones (Muller 1975, 75). How much have city departments already reduced services in those abandoned areas so that making decisions about cuts will not realize further savings? For instance, code enforcement that responds to complaints occurs rarely in areas where few people live, so a decision to cut code enforcement in those areas does not save money. How much of the cuts in service to one area will lead to reallocation of resources to improve services in other parts of a city—and therefore provide no cost savings? Cuts in police protection in one area, for instance, do not lead to reductions in costs because other parts of the city need additional police services. What services must the city continue to provide to prevent negative externalities for others in the absence of the service? For instance, lack of trash collection in heavily abandoned areas could lead to accumulation of garbage and increase in the rat population that then affect nearby, more occupied areas. What expenditures would city departments need to make to reduce infrastructure investment? For instance, conversion of a road from paved to gravel will require an initial investment, although less than the cost of repaving and ongoing maintenance. It may also require purchase of new equipment for providing other services such as snow removal and garbage collection. What services and infrastructure should the city provide to areas that are becoming more rural than urban? For instance, can residents wheel garbage containers to the end of a block rather than receiving curbside service, just as rural residents may wheel garbage to the end of a long driveway? Can residents receive water service through wells and septic systems? Can gas lines be removed rather than replaced and savings in infrastructure investment used to help remaining residents convert to other ways of heating homes? (Holst 2007; Koziol 2004; Hoornbeek and Schwarz 2009; E. Scorsone, pers. comm., September 22, 2009; Schiller and Siedentop 2006; Herz 2006).

City officials in Youngstown, Ohio, have made progress in considering these questions. Thus far, most adjustments to services resemble those in any city seeking to reduce costs. For instance, police patrol cars now have one officer rather than two, and the city has contracted out garbage collection to a private company using funds from a fee residents pay for collection. Rather than focus on restructuring services in nearly empty areas, city officials have offered incentives to residents of those areas to move to denser neighborhoods so that eventually city departments can cut all services in the most vacant areas. No one had accepted the incentive as of October 2009 (W. Davignon, pers. comm. with University of Michigan urban planning students, October 20, 2009; J. Williams, pers. comm. with University of Michigan urban planning students, October 19, 2009).

In Detroit, Michigan, in contrast, the head of a new Office of Restructuring suggested that delivery of public services needed to take account of land use and solicited analysis of possible cost savings from restructuring service delivery and infrastructure investment in the most vacant areas of the city. The mayor abolished the office within a year, however, and the future implementation of such efforts remained uncertain (Anderson 2010).

3.3 Equity

Urban disinvestment and abandonment disproportionately affect poor and minority populations. Therefore, the pursuit of efficiency in land use, housing, and public service delivery in cities with extensive disinvestment and abandonment can affect those residents the most. The challenge for urban planners becomes how to assure equity in this context.

Equity can be defined in many different ways (see Marcuse, this volume). Equity of outcome implies that addressing extensive abandonment should result in better situations for the least advantaged. Equity of process implies that plans should reflect residents' views about what the less populated city can become. Fainstein (2000, 468) argued that "a theory of a just city values participation in decision making by relatively powerless groups and equity of outcomes" (see also Sandercock 1998; Thomas 2008). This implies that the remaining residents of the heavily abandoned sections of cities should have opportunities to participate in making decisions about whether to stay or to move to denser neighborhoods.

In Cleveland, Ohio, in 1975, the City Planning Commission articulated a goal that reflected concern about equity of outcomes in the context of widespread residential disinvestment. As Krumholz, Cogger, and Linner (1975, 298) pointed out, in Cleveland "disinvestment is the rule and investment the exception." The Planning Commission stated the goal of planning in such a context: "Equity requires that locally-responsible government institutions give priority attention to the goal of promoting a wider range of choices for those Cleveland residents who have few, if any, choices" (Cleveland City Planning Commission

1975, 9). Working toward this goal meant providing a range of alternatives and opportunities so that individuals could decide their own needs and priorities, the plan stated. The Commission would rely on an "income strategy" instead of a "service strategy" to enable individuals to have the means to choose goods and services that they saw as meeting their needs. The plan emphasized equity over efficiency while recognizing the need for efficient use of city resources. Institutions needed to change; the plan pointed to the role of "laws, customs and practices" of institutions that continued to reinforce inequity. The goal would guide the Commission's priority setting, and analyses would focus on who paid and who benefited from policies and programs. The Commission would advocate on behalf of those "less favored by present conditions" while clarifying opposing interests from those with more resources (Cleveland City Planning Commission 1975, 9–10).

During the 1970s, opponents of triage articulated the case for equity. Neighborhood decline and disinvestment is not a "natural" process or an inevitability, they said. It often resulted from federal, state, and local policies that encouraged suburbanization and restricted the choices of minority race residents as well as from the decisions of public and private actors within the city, such as cuts in fire and police protection and redlining by financial institutions and insurance companies (Wallace and Wallace 1990; Medoff and Sklar 1994). Therefore, policies could change to reinforce neighborhoods and reverse decline, at least to some extent (although major forces of suburbanization and racism left city officials, acting alone, little chance to reverse disinvestment). Decisions to accept disinvestment in certain areas for efficiency reasons would speed the process of decline, to the detriment of the poor, elderly, and minority residents. "Triage destroys communities" that would not necessarily have to become abandoned places (Marcuse, Medoff, and Pereira 1982).

Neighborhood redevelopment, coupled with organizing and led by community-based organizations and residents, can reinforce even the most disinvested neighborhoods (Medoff and Sklar 1994; Kravitz 1977; Rooney 1995). "Nehemiah [affordable housing built through church-based neighborhood organizing] is the flip side of what the city did…the counterpart of everything that Roger Starr said you have to take out," stated one of the community organizers from the South Bronx (Rooney 1995, 235). Further, planned reduction in density could prevent the destruction of entire neighborhoods. In dense cities, the thinning out of housing could improve the quality of life (Marcuse, Medoff, and Pereira 1982).

The discussion through the mid- to late 1970s of shutting down abandoned areas, argued Weiler (1983, 173 [italics in original]), "was not so much the closing down of deteriorated neighborhoods for the sake of their unfortunate residents, who might humanely be guided and relocated to so-called better housing and economic opportunities…as it was a process of acquiring inner-city land for some *future* use and dispersing its unneeded inhabitants." Planned shrinkage sounded to many like urban renewal in a new guise (Kleniewski 1986). Indeed, a recent report from the Philadelphia Office of the Controller recommended "neighborhood clearance" in the most blighted areas in order to promote future development (Philadelphia Office of the City Controller 2005, 226–32).

In the late 2000s, discussion of ways to advance equity in large abandoned sections of cities differs from the arguments of the 1970s and early 1980s. Disinvestment and abandonment have proceeded to such an extent in many formerly industrial cities that few continue to argue that organizing and redevelopment can recreate viable neighborhoods everywhere. Planned reductions in density could apply only in areas that still have some density. A vantage point twenty-five or more years after some of these discussions shows that indeed gentrification has occurred in some places and investment in low and moderate income housing in others, made possible by organizing, strong community development systems, and governmental programs such as the Low Income Housing Tax Credit (Walker and Weinheimer 1998; Vidal and Keating 2004). However, disinvestment has proceeded so far in many areas that the "neighborhood" no longer exists. The few residents are poor and minority race; the homeowners are usually elderly. Renters live in housing in poor condition. A significant share of the remaining structures await demolition.

Urban planning scholarship has not yet addressed how to assure just processes and outcomes in heavily abandoned areas of cities without redevelopment. Several guidelines emerge from the definitions from Krumholz, Cogger, and Linner (1975) and Fainstein (2000). First, the few remaining residents of heavily abandoned areas and the residents of areas experiencing disinvestment should have choices about their futures. In the nearly empty areas, residents should be able to stay if they wish with adequate services, or they should be able to choose to leave. If they stay, city services need not remain the same as before—for instance, residents may need to take a garbage cart farther than their front curb for trash pickup—but services should enable them to stay. If they wish to leave, they should receive assistance in finding other rental housing, in transitioning to elderly housing, or in trading the home they own for another in a denser area. In sections experiencing considerable disinvestment, stronger areas should receive reinforcement to prevent spread of blight as much as possible. In these areas, organizing and community development corporations' work can help prevent some disinvestment, get derelict structures demolished quickly, and encourage reuse of vacant land in ways that improve quality of life and reinforce property owners' confidence. Second, residents should have a role in deciding the future of the places where they live. When they are not suspicious about a new round of urban renewal, residents of places with extensive property abandonment have many suggestions about how to address abandonment without rebuilding, and they agree that they need to accept a less dense city. In a heavily abandoned area of northwest Detroit, residents suggested many new uses but little new development for the vacant land (Doherty et al. 2008). Finally, any policies should aim to ensure that people living in areas of high disinvestment are left at least as well off as before.

4. THE FUTURE OF PLANNING IN THE CONTEXT OF ABANDONMENT

Planning theory and research have only begun to address issues of how planning can and should address either cities with shrinking populations (Hollander et al. 2009) or cities with widespread property abandonment following major and extended loss of population and employment. For many cities, especially in the United States and Eastern Europe, planning in the context of extensive disinvestment and abandonment is the major planning issue.

Urban planning research would do well to tackle several unaddressed issues related to planning in the context of decline and abandonment. As research addresses these issues, additional questions will arise. First, what enables city officials and others to accept that a city is smaller and to identify ways to adjust while assuring a good quality of life? In other words, what enables city officials and residents to embrace Gans's "cutback planning" (1975)? When do growth coalitions weaken so that accommodation of population decline can at least coexist with the pursuit of growth? How stable is political leaders' commitment to a future as a smaller city, and what reinvigorates growth coalitions to reject this notion? How do property owners, community development corporations, developers, and other interests use the planning process to benefit or prevent harm from cutback planning?

Second, what participatory processes can lead to Fainstein's "just city" (2000) for the residents most affected by disinvestment and abandonment? What processes can lead to outcomes that both city officials and the residents of these areas can endorse (Schatz 2008)? What can resolve conflicts between the interests of residents who remain in otherwise abandoned areas and public officials' interest in cutting costs and services? How can planning processes in such areas avoid creating another phase of urban renewal?

Third, how can planners craft visions of the future that demonstrate the possibilities, other than new development, for a smaller city (Popper and Popper 2002)? What possibilities exist for envisioning a more environmentally sustainable city, for instance (Schilling and Logan 2008; Cleveland Land Lab 2008)? How do planners and other public officials ensure adequate physical and social control over abandoned land?

Fourth, residents adapt to population loss and abandonment (Armborst, D'Oca, and Theodore 2008). How can planners identify and enable those efforts, building on residents' uses of vacant land for expanded yards, community gardens, and woodlots, for instance? How does planning encourage residents' innovations? How does planning interfere with these? What do such changes mean for planners' traditional uses of zoning and regulation?

As Congressman Henry Reuss stated thirty-five years ago, "The transition to a smaller size..., above all, will require a vision of how our cities can be transformed into better places to live and work even as they become smaller" (U.S. House, 1977, p. vii). While planners have focused on growth in the intervening years, they have left much work undone in envisioning such future cities. This fact offers exciting prospects for future developments in urban planning.

References

Accordino, J., and G. T. Johnson. 2000. "Addressing the Vacant and Abandoned Property Problem." *Journal of Urban Affairs* 22(3): 301–15.

Accordino, J., G. Galster, and P. Tatian. 2005. *The Impacts of Targeted Public and Nonprofit Investment on Neighborhood Development.* Richmond: Federal Reserve Bank of Richmond.

Ahlbrandt, R. S. 1984. *Neighborhoods, People, and Community.* New York: Plenum Press.

Amin, A. 1994. *Post-Fordism: A Reader, Studies in Urban and Social Change.* Oxford: Blackwell.

Andersen, H. S. 1995. "Explanations of Decay and Renewal in the Housing Market." *Journal of Housing and the Built Environment* 10:65–85.

Anderson, J. 2010, May. "Draft Assessment of Potential Reorganization." Office of Reorganization, City of Detroit.

Armborst, T., D. D'Oca, and G. Theodore. 2008. "Improve Your Lot!" In *Cities Growing Smaller,* edited by S. Rugare and T. Schwarz, 47–64. Cleveland: Kent State University's Cleveland Urban Design Collaborative.

Arsen, D. 1992. "Property-Tax Assessment Rates and Residential Abandonment—Policy for New York City." *American Journal of Economics and Sociology* 51(3): 361–77.

Ash, C., P. Dieter, A. Fang, D. Groves, X. Li, E. Luther, and M. Pinto. 2009. *Growing Stronger: A Plan for the Future of Detroit's Community Development Corporation System.* Ann Arbor: Urban and Regional Planning Program, University of Michigan, Ann Arbor. Available at: http://sitemaker.umich.edu/urpoutreachreports/all_reports &mode=single&recordID=2946211&nextMode=list; accessed September 25, 2009.

Baer, W. C. 1976. "On the Death of Cities." *Public Interest* 45:3–19.

Beauregard, R. A. 2009. "Urban Population Loss in Historical Perspective: United States, 1820–2000." *Environment and Planning A* 41:514–28.

Berry, B. J. L. 1999. Comment on E. K. Wyly and D. J. Hammel's "Island of Decay in Seas of Renewal: Housing Policy and the Resurgence of Gentrification"—Gentrification Resurgent? *Housing Policy Debate* 10:783–88.

Birch, D. L. 1971. "Toward a Stage Theory of Urban Growth." *Journal of the American Institute of Planners* 37:78–87.

Bockmeyer, J. 2000. "A Culture of Distrust: The Impact of Local Political Culture on Participation in the Detroit EZ." *Urban Studies* 37:2417–40.

Bonham, J. B. Jr., G. Spilka, and D. Rastorfer. 2002. *Old Cities/Green Cities: Communities Transform Unmanaged Land.* Planning Advisory Service Report 506/507. Chicago: American Planning Association.

Boyer, B. D. 1973. *Cities Destroyed for Cash: The FHA Scandal at HUD.* Chicago: Follett.

Bright, E. M. 2003. *Reviving America's Forgotten Neighborhoods: An Investigation of Inner City Revitalization Efforts.* New York: Routledge.

Burgess, E. W. 1925/2007. "The Growth of the City: An Introduction to a Research Project." In *The City Reader,* 4th ed., edited by R. T. LeGates and F. Stout, 150–57. Routledge Urban Reader Series. London: Routledge.

Castells, M. 2002. "The Space of Flows." In *The Castells Reader on Cities and Social Theory,* edited by I. Susser, 314–66. Malden, MA: Blackwell.

City of Detroit. 1994. "Jumpstarting the Motor City with New Ideas, New Relationships, and New Technologies for the Detroit Empowerment Zone." Application submitted to the U.S. Department of Housing and Urban Development. Office of the Mayor, Detroit, MI.

City of Detroit. 2009. "City of Detroit Master Plan of Policies Revision." Planning and Development Department, Detroit, MI. Available at: http://www.detroitmi.gov/ Portals/o/docs/planning/planning/MPlan/MPlan_%202009/Executive%20Summary. pdf; accessed June 12, 2010.

City of Detroit. 2010. "1997 Community Reinvestment Strategy." Planning and Development Department, Detroit, MI. Available at: http://www.detroitmi.gov/Departments/ PlanningDevelopmentDepartment/Planning/LongRangeandCommunityPlanning/1997 CommunityReinvestmentStrategy/tabid/2084/Default.aspx; accessed June 12, 2010.

Cleveland City Planning Commission. 1975. "Cleveland Policy Planning Report." Cleveland, OH.

Cleveland Land Lab. 2008. *Re-Imagining a More Sustainable Cleveland: Citywide Strategies for Reuse of Vacant Land.* Cleveland: Kent State University's Cleveland Urban Design Collaborative.

Committee for Economic Development. 1995. *Rebuilding Inner-City Communities: A New Approach to the Nation's Urban Crisis.* New York: Committee for Economic Development.

Cooper-McCann, P. 2010. "Rightsizing Detroit: Looking Back, Looking Forward." Senior honor's thesis, College of Literature, Science, and the Arts, University of Michigan, Ann Arbor.

Crump, J., K. Newman, E. S. Belsky, P. Ashton, D. H. Kaplan, D. J. Hammel, and E. Wyly. 2008. "Cities Destroyed (Again) for Cash: Forum on the U. S. Foreclosure Crisis." *Urban Geography* 29:745–84.

Doherty, K., L. Morris, T. Parham, S. Powers, E. Schumacher, and B. Wessler. 2008. "A Land Use Plan for Brightmoor." Urban and Regional Planning Program, University of Michigan, Ann Arbor. Available at: http://sitemaker.umich.edu/ urpoutreachreports/housing_community_development__h_/da.data/2408151/ ReportFile/final_bookopt.pdf; accessed July 7, 2010.

Downs, A. 1976. "Using the Lessons of Experience to Allocate Resources in the Community Development Program." In *Recommendations for Community Development Planning,* edited by A. Downs, 1–28. Chicago: Real Estate Research Corporation.

Downs, A. 1981. *Neighborhoods and Urban Development.* Washington, DC: Brookings Institution Press.

Downs, A. 2000. Comment on J. T. Metzger's "Planned Abandonment: The Neighborhood Life-Cycle Theory and National Urban Policy." *Housing Policy Debate* 11(1): 41–54.

Eisinger, P. 2000. "The Politics of Bread and Circuses: Building the City for the Visitor Class." *Urban Affairs Review* 35:316–33.

Elkin, S. L. 1987. *City and Regime in the American Republic.* Chicago: University of Chicago Press.

Fainstein, S. S. 2000. "New Directions in Planning Theory." *Urban Affairs Review* 35(4): 451–78.

Galster, G. C. 2000. Comment on J. T. Metzger's "Planned Abandonment: The Neighborhood Life-Cycle Theory and National Urban Policy." *Housing Policy Debate* 11(1): 61–66.

Galster, G. C. 2009. "Richmond's Neighborhoods in Bloom." In *Local Planning: Contemporary Principles and Practice,* edited by G. Hack, E. Birch, P. Sedway, and

M. Silver, 199–204. Washington, DC: International City/County Management Association.

Galster, G., P. Tatian, and J. Accordino. 2006. "Targeting Investments for Neighborhood Revitalization." *Journal of the American Planning Association* 72:457–74.

Gans, H. J. 1975. "Planning for Declining and Poor Cities." *Journal of the American Institute of Planners* 41:305–307.

Geisler, N., S. Greenstein, C.-C. Hu, C. Minthorn, and M. Munsell. 2009. *Adversity to Advantage: New Vacant Land Uses in Flint.* Urban and Regional Planning Program, University of Michigan, Ann Arbor. Available at: http://sitemaker.umich.edu/urpoutreachreports/environment___land_use__e_&mode=single&recordID=3158560&nextMode=list; accessed January 31, 2010.

Gittell, R. J. 1992. *Renewing Cities.* Princeton, NJ: Princeton University Press.

Grigsby, W. G., and L. Rosenburg. 1975. *Urban Housing Policy.* New York: APS Publications.

Grigsby, W., M. Baratz, G. Galster, and D. Maclennan. 1987. "The Dynamics of Neighborhood Change." *Progress in Planning* 28:1–76.

Hack, G., E. Birch, P. Sedway, and M. Silver. 2009. *Local Planning: Contemporary Principles and Practice.* Washington, DC: International City/County Management Association Press.

Halpern, R. 1995. *Rebuilding the Inner City: A History of Neighborhood Initiatives to Address Poverty in the United States.* New York: Columbia University Press.

Harvey, D. 2001. *Spaces of Capital: Towards a Critical Geography.* New York: Routledge.

Heilbrun, J. 1979. "On the Theory and Policy of Neighborhood Consolidation." *Journal of the American Planning Association* 45:417–27.

Herz, R. 2006. "Buried Infrastructure in Shrinking Cities." Paper presented at symposium, Coping with City Shrinkage and Demographic Change–Lessons from around the Globe, March 30–31, Dresden, Germany. Available at: http://www.schader-stiftung.de/docs/herz_presentation.pdf; accessed September 22, 2009.

Hillier, A. E., D. P. Culhane, T. E. Smith, and C. D. Tomlin. 2003. "Predicting Housing Abandonment with the Philadelphia Neighborhood Information System." *Journal of Urban Affairs* 25(1): 91–105.

Hoch, C. J., L. C. Dalton, and F. S. So. 2000. *The Practice of Local Government Planning,* 3rd ed. Washington, DC: International City/County Management Association Press.

Hollander, J., K. Pallagst, T. Schwarz, and F. J. Popper. 2009. "Planning Shrinking Cities." *Progress in Planning* 72:223–32.

Holst, A. 2007. "The Philadelphia Water Department and the Burden of History." *Public Works Management and Policy* 11:233–38.

Hoornbeek, J., and T. Schwarz. 2009. *Sustainable Infrastructure in Shrinking Cities: Options for the Future.* Cleveland: Kent State University's Cleveland Urban Design Collaborative. .

Hoover, E. M., and R. Vernon. 1959. *Anatomy of a Metropolis: The Changing Distribution of People and Jobs Within the New York Metropolitan Region.* Cambridge, MA: Harvard University Press.

Hoyt, H. 1939. *The Structure and Growth of Residential Neighborhoods in American Cities.* Washington, DC: Federal Housing Administration.

Immergluck, D. 2009. "The Foreclosure Crisis, Foreclosed Properties, and Federal Policy." *Journal of the American Planning Association* 75:406–23.

Keating, W. D., and N. Krumholz, eds. 1999. *Rebuilding Urban Neighborhoods: Achievements, Opportunities, and Limits.* Thousand Oaks, CA: Sage.

Kleniewski, N. 1986. "Triage and Urban Planning: A Case Study of Philadelphia." *International Journal of Urban and Regional Research* 10:563–79.

Koziol, M. 2004. "The Consequences of Demographic Change for Municipal Infrastructure." *German Journal of Urban Studies* 44(1). Available at: http://www.difu.de/publikationen/the-consequences-of-demographic-change-for-municipal.html; accessed November 10, 2011.

Kravitz, A. S. 1977. "The Other Neighborhoods—Building Community Institutions." In *How Cities Can Grow Old Gracefully*, 91–96. U. S. House, Committee on Banking, Finance and Urban Affairs, Subcommittee on the City. Washington, DC: U. S. Government Printing Office.

Krumholz, N., J. Cogger, and J. Linner. 1975. "The Cleveland Policy Planning Report." *Journal of the American Institute of Planners* 41:298–304.

Logan, J. R., and H. Molotch. 1987. *Urban Fortunes: The Political Economy of Place.* Berkeley: University of California Press.

Mallach, A. 2006. *Bringing Buildings Back: From Abandoned Properties to Community Assets.* Montclair, NJ: National Housing Institute.

Marcuse, P., P. Medoff, and A. Pereira. 1982. "Triage as Urban Policy." *Social Policy* 12: 33–37.

Medoff, P., and H. Sklar. 1994. *Streets of Hope: The Fall and Rise of an Urban Neighborhood."* Boston: South End Press.

Metzger, J. T. 2000. "Planned Abandonment: The Neighborhood Life-Cycle Theory and National Urban Policy." *Housing Policy Debate* 11(1): 7–40.

Muller, T. 1975. *Growing and Declining Urban Areas: A Fiscal Comparison.* Washington, DC: Urban Institute.

Muller, T. 1977. "Service Costs in the Declining City." In *How Cities Can Grow Old Gracefully,* 119–31. U. S. House, Committee on Banking, Finance and Urban Affairs, Subcommittee on the City. Washington, DC: U. S. Government Printing Office.

Muth, R. F. 1969. *Cities and Housing: The Spatial Pattern of Urban Residential Land Use.* Chicago: University of Chicago Press.

Nassauer, J., and R. VanWieren. 2008. "Vacant Property Now and Tomorrow: Building Enduring Values with Natural Assets." Sea Grant, Michigan, Genesee Institute, Genesee County Land Bank, School of Natural Resources and the Environment, University of Michigan. Available at: http://www-personal.umich.edu/~nassauer/Publications/Vacant-property-now-tomorrow_Secure.pdf; accessed March 2, 2010.

National Vacant Properties Campaign. 2010. Web page. Originally sourced at: http://www.vacantproperties.org/; accessed January, 31, 2010.

Neighborhood Progress. 2010. "Strategic Investment Initiative." Available at: http://www.neighborhoodprogress.org/cnppsii.php; accessed March, 2, 2010.

Odland, J., and B. Balzer. 1979. "Localized Externalities, Contagious Processes and the Deterioration of Urban Housing: An Empirical Analysis." *Socio-Economic Planning Sciences* 13(2): 87–93.

Oswalt, P., ed. 2005. *Shrinking Cities: Vol. 1: International Research.* Ostfildern-Ruit, Germany: Hatje Cantz Verlag.

Oswalt, P., ed. 2006. *Shrinking Cities: Vol. 2: Interventions.* Ostfildern-Ruit, Germany: Hatje Cantz Verlag.

Oswalt, P., and T. Rieniets, eds. 2006. *Atlas of Shrinking Cities.* Ostfildern-Ruit, Germany: Hatje Cantz Verlag.

Philadelphia Office of the Controller. 2005. *Philadelphia: A New Urban Direction,* 2nd ed. Philadelphia: Saint Joseph's University Press.

Popper, D. E., and F. J. Popper. 2002. "Small Can Be Beautiful." *Planning* 68(7): 20.

Pratter, J. S. 1977. "Strategies for City Investment." In *How Cities Can Grow Old Gracefully*, 79–90. U. S. House, Committee on Banking, Finance and Urban Affairs, Subcommittee on the City. Washington, DC: U. S. Government Printing Office.

Quigley, J. M. 1979. "What Have We Learned About Urban Housing Markets? In *Current Issues in Urban Economics*, edited by P. M. Mieszkowski and M. R. Straszheim, 388–426. Baltimore: Johns Hopkins University Press.

Ratcliff, R. U. 1949. *Urban Land Economics*. New York: McGraw-Hill.

Real Estate Research Corporation. 1973. *HUD Experimental Program for Preserving Declining Neighborhoods: An Analysis of the Abandonment Process*. San Francisco: Real Estate Research Corporation, Public Affairs Counseling.

Rieniets, T. 2005. "Global Shrinkage." In *Shrinking Cities: Vol. 1: International Research*, edited by P. Oswalt, 20–34. Ostfildern-Ruit, Germany: Hatje Cantz Verlag.

Roberts, S. 1991. "A Critical Evaluation of the City Life Cycle Idea." *Urban Geography* 12: 431–49.

Rooney, J. 1995. *Organizing the South Bronx*. Albany, NY: State University of New York Press.

Rothenberg, J., G. C. Galster, R. V. Butler, and J. R. Pitkin. 1991. *The Maze of Urban Housing Markets: Theory, Evidence, and Policy*. Chicago: University of Chicago Press.

Rybczynski, W. 1995. "Downsizing Cities." *Atlantic Monthly* 276(4): 36–38, 46–47.

Rybczynski, W., and P. Linneman. 1999. "How to Save Our Shrinking Cities." *The Public Interest* 135:30–44.

Rydell, P. C. 1970. *Factors Affecting Maintenance and Operating Costs in Federal Public Housing Projects*. New York: Rand Corporation.

Sandercock, L. 1998. *Toward Cosmopolis: Planning for Multicultural Cities*. New York: John Wiley.

Sassen, S. 2005. "The Urban Impact of Economic Globalization." In *The Urban Sociology Reader*, edited by J. Lin and C. Mele, 230–40. London: Routledge.

Scafidi, B. P., M. H. Schill, S. M. Wachter, and D. P. Culhane. 1998. "An Economic Analysis of Housing Abandonment." *Journal of Housing Economics* 7(4): 287–303.

Schatz, Laura. 2008. "Is the Role of the Planner Changing in Shrinking Cities? A Comparison of Findings from Youngstown, Ohio, and Sudbury, Ontario." Paper presented at the Joint ACSP-AESOP conference, July 7–11, Chicago.

Schiller, G., and S. Siedentop. 2006. "Preserving Cost-Efficient Infrastructure Supply in Shrinking Cities." In *SASBE2006, 2nd CIB International Conference on Smart and Sustainable Built Environments*, Shanghai, November.

Schilling, J., and J. Logan. 2008. "Greening the Rust Belt: A Green Infrastructure Model for Right Sizing America's Shrinking Cities." *Journal of the American Planning Association* 74(4): 451–66.

Shapiro, J. 2009. "Strategic Planning for Community Transformation." In *Local Planning: Contemporary Principles and Practice*, edited by G. Hack, E. L. Birch, P. H. Sedway, and M. J. Silver, 258–61. Washington, D C: International City/County Management Association Press.

Smith, N., P. Caris, and E. Wyly. 2001. "The 'Camden Syndrome' and the Menace of Suburban Decline." *Urban Affairs Review* 36:497–531.

Starr, R. 1976. "Making New York Smaller." *New York Times Magazine*, November 14, 32–33, 99–102, 104–8.

Stegman, M. 1972. *Housing Investment in the Inner City: The Dynamics of Decline—A study of Baltimore, Maryland, 1968–1970.*" Cambridge, MA: MIT Press.

Stegman, M., and M. A. Turner. 1996. "The Future of Urban America in the Global Economy." *Journal of the American Planning Association* 62:157–64.

Sternlieb, G., and R. W. Burchell. 1973. *Residential Abandonment: The Tenement Landlord Revisited*. New Brunswick, NJ: Center for Urban Policy Research, Rutgers University.

Sternlieb, G., R. W. Burchell, J. W. Hughes, and F. J. James. 1974. "Housing Abandonment in the Urban Core." *Journal of the American Planning Association* 40(5): 321–32.

Swanstrom, Todd. 1985. *The Crisis of Growth Politics: Cleveland, Kucinich, and the Challenge of Urban Populism*. Philadelphia: Temple University Press.

Sweeney, J. L. 1974. "A Commodity Hierarchy Model of the Rental Housing Market." *Journal of Urban Economics* 1:288–323.

Temkin, K. 2000. Comment on J. T. Metzger's "Planned Abandonment: The Neighborhood Life-Cycle Theory and National Urban Policy." *Housing Policy Debate* 11(1): 55–60.

Temkin, K., and W. Rohe. 1996. "Neighborhood Change and Urban Policy." *Journal of Planning Education and Research* 15:159–70.

Thomas, J. M. 2008. "The Minority-Race Planner in the Quest for a Just City." *Planning Theory* 7(3): 227–47.

Thompson, W. R. 1977. "Land Management Strategies for Central City Depopulation." In *How Cities Can Grow Old Gracefully*, 67–78. U. S. House, Committee on Banking, Finance and Urban Affairs, Subcommittee on the City. Washington, DC: U. S. Government Printing Office.

Thomson, D. E. 2008. "Strategic, Geographic Targeting of Housing and Community Development Resources: A Conceptual Framework and Critical Review." *Urban Affairs Review* 43:629–62.

U. S. House of Representatives, Committee on Banking, Finance and Urban Affairs, Subcommittee on the City. 1977. *How Cities Can Grow Old Gracefully*. Washington, DC: U. S. Government Printing Office.

Varady, D. P. 1986. "Neighborhood Confidence. a Critical Factor in Neighborhood Revitalization?" *Environment and Behavior* 18:480–501.

Vidal, A. 1997. "Can Community Development Re-Invent Itself? The Challenges of Strengthening Neighborhoods in the 21st Century." *Journal of the American Planning Association* 63:429–38.

Vidal, A C., and W. D. Keating. 2004. "Community Development: Current Issues and Emerging Challenges." *Journal of Urban Affairs* 26(2): 125–37.

Wagner, J. 2009. "Renewing Washington's Neighborhoods." In *Local Planning: Contemporary Principles and Practice*, edited by G. Hack, E. L. Birch, P. H. Sedway, and M. J. Silver, 261–66. Washington, DC: International City/County Management Association Press.

Walker, C., and M. Weinheimer. 1998. *Community Development in the 1990s*. Washington, DC: Urban Institute.

Wallace, R., and D. Wallace. 1990. "Origins of Public Health Collapse in New York City: The Dynamics of Planned Shrinkage, Contagious Urban Decay and Social Disintegration." *Bulletin of the New York Academy of Medicine* 66:391–434.

Warren, R., and D. Warren. 1977. *The Neighborhood Organizer's Handbook*. Notre Dame, IN: University of Notre Dame Press.

Weiler, C. 1983. "Urban Euthanasia for Fun and Profit." In *Neighborhood Policy and Planning*, edited by P. L. Clay and R. M. Hollister, 167–77. Lexington, MA: Lexington Books.

White, M. J. 1986. "Property Taxes and Urban Housing Abandonment." *Journal of Urban Economics* 20:312–30.

Wilson, D. 1996. "Metaphors, Growth Coalition Discourses and Black Poverty Neighborhoods in a U.S. City." *Antipode* 28:72–96.

CHAPTER 29

THE CHANGING CHARACTER OF URBAN REDEVELOPMENT

NORMAN FAINSTEIN AND SUSAN S. FAINSTEIN

THE precedent for post-World War II efforts at redeveloping urban spaces was set by Baron Georges-Eugène Haussmann in nineteenth century Paris (Harvey 2003). Three aspects of his approach to urban transformation were particularly influential: adaptation of the city's form to the efficiency requirements of a modern economy; destruction of the existing built environment so as to have a clean slate on which to draw the new configuration ("creative destruction"); and production of luxurious residential buildings to provide desirable quarters for the rising bourgeoisie. Although a century later modernity was defined by different transportation modes and residential tastes, the method of clearing land in order to deal with perceived obsolescence was based on assumptions similar to Haussmann's: that it was necessary to create a new city to respond to new economic circumstances.

In the first years after World War II, redevelopment policy was responding primarily to wartime destruction and housing shortages in Europe, while in the United States blight caused by decades of failure to invest in central cities was the principal stimulus. As time passed, technological change and global economic restructuring, resulting in deindustrialization of old manufacturing centers, became dominant impetuses. Eventually the Haussmann precedent was supplanted, and there was a move away from demolition and toward rehabilitation, preservation, and adaptive reuse as redevelopment strategies. Across the political spectrum recognition grew that physical redevelopment alone could not address the causes of urban decline.

Analysts on the left called for increased attention to social disadvantage, involvement of affected communities in the planning process, and the integration of physical planning with social assistance, educational improvement, and job provision. This viewpoint, however, had limited impact within the mainstream, where neoliberal (i.e., market) ideology triumphed. Fiscal constraints on government loosened public control over redevelopment activities, and the concept of using public resources to leverage private investment with the goal of promoting economic growth prevailed. In both Europe and the United States, public–private partnerships became the principal vehicle for urban redevelopment efforts. In areas with high revenue potential, profit-making developers collaborated with public officials in development projects; in schemes where no private developer showed interest, nonprofit organizations (community development corporations [CDCs] in the United States, housing associations and philanthropic organizations elsewhere) participated. Even though the methods used at the beginning of the period no longer predominated, the overarching objective of economic expansion remained fixed in place.

This chapter outlines briefly the theoretical approaches to analyzing redevelopment. It then examines the policies that have been adopted in more than sixty years of public intervention within the already built environment, the role played by different social interests in affecting this intervention, the consequences it has had for population groups, and its causes rooted in the historical transformation of the global political economy. The focus is on the United States and Western Europe, but the policies followed in many developing countries have been imitative of those adopted in the West (Ward 2000). In particular, the method of slum clearance and new construction, while fading in the West, remains dominant elsewhere.[1]

1. Explaining Urban Redevelopment

The forces framing the definition of urban decline and the solutions implemented have changed over time. New technologies—especially the dominance of automobile, truck, and air transport in a world of cities previously built for railroads and ships—have made some places obsolete and others centers of growth. Globalization and the related institutional structure, scale, and dynamics of the economy have transformed the components of economic competitiveness. Politics in its broadest sense has reflected the changing balance of power among social classes, the roles played by race and migration, and the fall of communism. Ideas, in terms of major ideological currents as well as in more specific conceptions of "the urban problem" and of the part that redevelopment programs might play in mitigating it, have likewise mutated.[2]

While the list of explanatory elements could be elaborated at great length, we also can see from the perspective of the second decade of the twenty-first century that the variables have been organized by a smaller set of social science paradigms— systems of ideas that embody analysis of both factual evidence and the values and goals that should guide policies and programs. Three approaches have dominated the discussions of redevelopment, as well as many other policy arenas.[3]

The first is pluralism. *Pluralist theory* assumes that government is largely autonomous from economic and social organization. While economic and social hierarchies are present in every social system, political divisions are cross-cutting, and economic power is balanced by democratic institutions. Policy is the result of political coalitions of interest groups, and it is strongly shaped by leaders chosen through elections. Pluralism is at its strongest in identifying the roles of multiple actors in shaping policy, and in explaining variations among cities within the same national systems. It fails, however, to account for the elements in market economies and in social structure that produce recurring outcomes that favor dominant social groups.

Regime theory attempts to overcome the indeterminacy that pluralist theory would lead us to expect but that is not actually reflected in policies and programs. It stresses the ways that urban governing elites come to power through specific assemblages of interest groups with roots deep in social structure and it indicates that every local regime in a market society is strongly influenced by the hierarchies and dynamics of capitalism. For regime theorists, policy options are always limited by social structure, while social structure is itself a critical resultant of economic forces. Regime theory has been at its strongest in classifying the typical array of social forces that shape politics and the real, but limited, variations among governments that have produced different policy mixes. Because its field of study has been mainly city governments, it has been most useful in explaining common and differing elements at that institutional level—for example, why New York City has built so much social housing and, unlike Chicago, has chosen to maintain it rather than "dispersing the poor" in the name of "providing opportunity." It does not, however, specify the national and super-national forces that have shaped urbanism and public policy interventions across time and place.

For those kinds of explanations we must rely on a third paradigm, *structural theory*. Structural explanations lodge the object and character of redevelopment policy within the global political economy. Regardless of local factors, structural theorists emphasize the universal social forces produced by capitalism (and when it mattered, state socialism as well). Thus, global competition within capitalist markets produces the need for continuous economic growth. The tensions—and crises— that result from it define the urban problematic everywhere, while the balance of power among social classes on a national and global scale shapes local outcomes. For structuralists, the content of redevelopment policy can be directly linked to the stages of postwar capitalism. According to this analysis, the end of the cold war and ensuing dominance of neoliberal ideologies are critical factors that explain the convergence of U.S. and European redevelopment policy in the most recent period.

We attempt to draw on the strengths of all three paradigms. In the next section, when we discuss the evolution of policy, we are most cognizant of factors stressed by pluralist and regime theories. When we try to connect the global and the local and to look toward the future, we find structural explanations most helpful. By being self-conscious about our theoretical assumptions, we hope to provide a picture that balances the specific and the general.

2. Strategies and Their Advocates

The Case of the United States

In the United States,[4] the 1949 Housing Act sparked a wave of efforts at redeveloping central cities. At the time, policymakers perceived the problem as a failure of investment following years of depression and war, along with the siphoning off initially of residents, then of businesses, to the rapidly growing suburbs. Wooing back the middle class became a principal goal (Wilson 1966). It was widely believed that successful competition with the suburbs required aggregating and clearing large tracts of land so that developers would not be hindered by multiple owners and nonconforming uses. The main promoters of this strategy were property owners with interests in the central business district—groups labeled in the scholarly literature as the growth machine (Logan and Molotch 1987) or the pro-growth coalition (Mollenkopf 1983). Pittsburgh's Allegheny Conference (Sbragia 1990) set the model for subsequent organizations: the Vault in Boston, SPUR in San Francisco, Cleveland Tomorrow, and others. Holding a nostalgic vision of downtown as the center of regional activities patronized by a free-spending middle class, they pushed for clearing away what they regarded as marginal businesses and encroaching areas of low-income residence.

A different set of groups had as their main concern the rehousing of poor people in higher quality buildings. Led by social reformers associated with Roosevelt's New Deal, they sought the development of public housing on the land vacated through demolition under the urban renewal program (Plunz 1990; Harloe 1995; Schwartz 2006). They did not dispute business interests about the necessity of ridding cities of tenement buildings; rather, their disagreement was on the ultimate ends of the program. Both groups also agreed on the need for comprehensive planning (Altshuler 1965). However, local real estate boards, joined together in the National Association of Housing and Real Estate Boards (NAHREB), proved to be a potent lobbying force. They strongly opposed using federal money to lower the price of housing, fearing that it would undercut their profits. The resulting compromise led to limiting availability of public housing to the very poor, locating it in the least desirable parts of cities, and designing it according to spartan standards (Cleaveland 1967; Gelfand 1975). While the modern apartments created represented a physical improvement over the tenements vacated, they carried with them a social stigma, based on the assumption that tenants were receiving charity because of personal failure.

Associated with urban renewal in terms of redefining the city to fit the modern era, highway construction drove massive divisions into the hearts of cities. A group of industries (automobile, rubber, oil, construction, etc.) lobbied the national government for highway funds and lent support to local transportation planners (Caro 1974). Ironically, given their negative effects on the urban fabric, big-city mayors enthusiastically promoted the building of urban expressways under the federal interstate highway program (Gelfand 1975). The mayors had identified traffic congestion as a principal deterrent to businesses and customers availing themselves of their old downtowns; they saw the new highways, along with parking garages, as the instrument by which suburbanites would choose to patronize the central business district but failed to foresee their role in siphoning off commerce and population.

During the 1950s and into the 1960s, the set of programs outlined above proceeded with relatively little modification. They failed, however, to stop the continued outward suburban exodus of the white middle class, and many of the cleared sites remained empty for lack of interested investors. In the meanwhile, the great migration of African Americans from the southern states, which accelerated during subsequent decades, radically changed the demographics of northern and midwestern cities (Sugrue 1996; Self and Sugrue 2002). Then, in the mid-1960s, communities that faced the threat of evisceration, and which interpreted the displacement caused by redevelopment programs as a deliberate effort to rid city centers of people of color, began to rebel. Their cause was reinforced by intellectuals who regarded urban renewal as, in Jane Jacobs's phrase, "the sacking of cities" (Jacobs 1961/1993, 6). Academic critics from the right accused the urban renewal authorities of interfering with market processes (Anderson 1964). But the strongest attacks were from the left, which interpreted renewal programs as vehicles for class and racial domination.

Thus, Herbert Gans (1962) documented the destruction of Boston's West End in his *Urban Villagers*; Jane Jacobs (1961/1993) ridiculed the "radiant garden city beautiful" in *The Death and Life of Great American Cities*; and Clarence Stone (1976) found the power structure behind the reconstruction of Atlanta. In a magnum opus that traced the erosion of social commitment in the face of American economic and political realities, Robert Caro (1974) depicted not only the damage actually effected in New York City over the decades by master builder Robert Moses but also his thwarted plans to cross Manhattan with great, elevated expressways and to transform that island into a manifestation of Le Corbusier's prewar *Plan Voisin* for the right bank of the Seine (Fishman 1982, 205 ff.).

For a period, city governments, while not giving up on downtown regeneration, broadened their approaches to redevelopment. On the ground, protesters succeeded in blocking renewal schemes and planned highway construction in a number of places (Fellman 1973; S. Fainstein and Fainstein 1974). In response to social unrest, programs associated with Lyndon Johnson's War on Poverty focused on the most deprived neighborhoods. The federal Office of Economic Opportunity sponsored programs directed toward "soft" services like health care and job training in poor communities and had strong participatory mandates (Marris and Rein 1967). The Model Cities program provided for the melding of physical and social programs and included requirements for planning involvement by citizens of affected neighborhoods (Frieden and Kaplan 1975). After the 1968 election of Richard M. Nixon, however, and especially after his 1972 reelection, these redistributive endeavors faded away. In 1974, the Housing and Community Development Act eliminated both Model Cities and urban renewal and largely switched housing assistance to a rent-subsidy program known as Section 8 (later renamed Housing Opportunity Vouchers).

City governments faced with fiscal crises turned their attention fully to economic development. They responded to the drying up of federal funds by using their available resources to leverage private investment. Some federal dollars continued to flow their way through the Community Development Block Grant (CDBG) and the Urban Development Action Grant (UDAG) programs; they could call on their own capital budgets for infrastructure that supported new projects; and most significantly, they could use a variety of tax and regulatory relief devices to lower development costs (S. Fainstein and Fainstein 1986). These included tax abatements and credits for contributing to economic development, historic preservation tax credits, low-income housing tax credits, industrial revenue bonds, business incubators, tax increment financing (TIF),[5] and zoning bonuses.[6]

Rather than, as under the earlier urban renewal program, designating land for development and then waiting for bidders, governmental agencies initiated or responded to interest from developers and did not proceed until a deal was in place. While cities could still resort to eminent domain so as to assist developers who were looking for cleared land, they mainly retreated from large-scale displacement of existing residents and businesses. Comprehensive neighborhood renewal plans gave way to project planning, and the scope of ambition became limited. The mega-projects of the earlier period, while not altogether disappearing, became much fewer in number (Altshuler and Luberoff 2003), while construction of new public housing diminished to almost nil.

The years from the middle 1970s until the 1990s, despite the reduced level of direct governmental redevelopment expenditure, nevertheless encompassed a significant turnaround in the trajectory of American cities (Frieden and Sagalyn 1990). As cities were abandoned by manufacturers and shipping companies, former industrial and port sites were available for reuse and frequently became havens for artistic communities or entertainment districts. Those cities like New York, Boston, San Francisco, and Chicago, where the economic base was successfully converted from dependence on manufacturing to finance, advanced services, and culture, began to see population growth and new flows of investment (S. Fainstein and Fainstein 1982; Sassen 2001). The discourse of urban decline switched to one of urban renaissance (Beauregard 2003), and in many of these cities, fears of gentrification replaced alarm over abandonment. Increasing income inequality along with the heightened demand for space by business and affluent households meant that in well-located neighborhoods, particularly those with architectural amenities, middle-class families pushed out poor residents and small service businesses saw their premises taken over by boutiques and upscale eateries.

The withdrawal of the federal government from oversight of redevelopment efforts, combined with the strikingly different economic trajectories of individual cities, meant that there was huge variation among places. Old industrial centers (e.g., Gary, Detroit, Cleveland, Buffalo, Schenectady, Worcester) continued on the path of decline, while coastal and Sunbelt cities, as well as a few in the Midwest, grew. Even as interregional disparities diminished, intrametropolitan difference increased. City governments used a variety of strategies to encourage revitalization, often many simultaneously. "Smokestack chasing," whereby governments woo industry through offering packages of incentives, was prevalent throughout this period (Fisher and Peters 1998). However, programs in which localities sought to nurture home-grown entrepreneurship began to take hold (Eisinger 1988), fostered by neighborhood economic development corporations and business improvement districts, or BIDs.[7]

The composition of development coalitions changed. Some of the elites of the preceding decades lost interest in urban schemes as their businesses decentralized (e.g., department stores), were acquired by nonlocal conglomerates, or had their management replaced by outsiders relatively unconcerned with the local environment (Strom 2008). Property developers, tourism interests, and sports team owners, however, remained or became prominent actors. Some cities had much more active community-based organizations than others. In places that had vigorous CDCs— for instance, in New York's South Bronx or Newark, New Jersey—these organizations built substantial amounts of housing for low-income households (Bratt and Rohe 2007; Rubin 2000). In cities where, at least for a time, progressive administrations took office (e.g., Burlington, Chicago, San Francisco, Santa Monica), programs were put into place that linked downtown development to affordable housing or public amenities by requiring developer commitments (Clavel 1986).

Beginning in the 1990s, mega-projects once again became common (Diaz Orueta and Fainstein 2008), at least until the recession of 2008–09. They typically differed from their predecessors in that they minimized displacement by being located on obsolete industrial and port lands rather than intruding into residential areas; as Altshuler and Luberoff (2003) put it, they were intended to do no harm. Usually developed under the auspices of public–private partnerships, they frequently involved mixed uses and catered to the needs of office-based businesses, tourism, and leisure services. Financing typically came from a number of sources, including state and local governments, tax-free bonds, and private lenders. Growth and competition rather than the removal of slums and blight defined the planning agenda in line with the dominant neoliberal ideology (Swyngedouw, Moulaert, and Rodriguez 2004). The marketing of an urban identity based on the commodification of culture and the construction of sports venues became a fundamental element in the design of projects (Hoffman, Fainstein, and Judd 2003). Renowned architects ("starchitects") often added an aura of glamor to the efforts (McNeill 2009; Del Cerro 2007).

Although movements against these kinds of operations were not wholly absent (Gotham 2007), they were not as intense as those of decades earlier (Hamel, Lustiger-Thaler, and Mayer 2000). In many cases, the project was successfully sold as promoting economic development from which all would benefit (Lehrer and Laidley 2008). The publicity and editorial support generally surrounding these projects obscured the extent to which they diverted public funds from schemes of broader, longer term benefits. Since relatively few people were directly injured, it was difficult to mobilize opposition, especially when subsidies to developers were provided off-budget in the form of tax forgiveness.

The European Case

Local growth machines of the American variety did not promote development schemes within European cities (Harding 1995; Strom 1996).[8] Instead, under the much more centralized governments of Western European states, national policy drove urban rebuilding. Right after the war, with the threat of communism to the east and the pressure of social democratic parties within, central governments adopted legislation that financed massive construction of social housing—government or housing association–owned buildings with below-market rents. These new edifices went up on emptied inner-city land—vacated by wartime bombing or postwar demolition—on urban peripheries, and in satellite cities. Along with the goal of providing replacement housing for the working class, governments made population deconcentration a priority. The extent of governmentally supported housing was so large that its placement essentially reshaped European metropolises, greatly increasing their area and reducing population densities within the core.

Unlike in American cities, high-rise construction characterized the edge rather than the center, and the economic elite largely clung to their inner-city residences. As a consequence, Europe did not have the kind of "inner city problem" characteristic of the United States but instead had patches of substandard housing and obsolete factories scattered throughout metro areas along with areas of upper-class habitation. Retail also did not decentralize at anything like the American rate, so that centrally located shopping districts continued to attract customers. Furthermore, the level of car ownership substantially lagged America's; extensive road building awaited another generation and did not tear through cities; and population was more concentrated at mass transit nodes. Thus, between the war's end and the 1970s, both the context and the strategies for redevelopment in Europe were markedly different from those in the United States.

After 1975, however, fiscal crises and changing ideologies pushed European countries, at varying speeds, toward the American model. The general crisis that had afflicted capitalism in the mid-1970s led, in Europe as well as the United States, to a tightening of national welfare expenditures and efforts to induce the participation of private capital in redevelopment. Large-scale industrial job losses, arising from increased reliance on technology, exporting of work to cheaper production sites, and the rise of competitors in the newly industrializing countries generated a stronger concern with economic growth as a generator of employment. At the same time, the power of trade unions and left-wing parties was diminishing along with the size of their working-class base (Gorz 1983), while the move of large proportions of the population into white-collar occupations stimulated increased demand for home ownership. At the end of the 1980s, the fall of communism, and somewhat later of the Western European Communist Parties, meant the end of a counter-ideology that had goaded governments into competing for the allegiance of workers.

During the 1980s, the public–private partnership arrived in Europe (Heinz 1993; Judd and Parkinson 1990). In the absence of local growth coalitions, the impetus for entrepreneurial partnerships largely came from the government side, and the public sector exerted more control over them than in the U.S. case. Also, European governments were generally more reluctant than their U.S. counterparts to grant tax benefits to property investors. The extent to which businesses received subsidies for development activities and the form that they took varied considerably from country to country. The UK, under the leadership of Prime Minister Margaret Thatcher, came closest to the American approach. She established urban development corporations (UDCs) and enterprise zones that provided tax forgiveness, as well as cheap land and loosened regulation within these districts. Local authorities in areas without UDCs enticed developers with free land, training programs for workers, and incentive zoning. The Right-to-Buy program moved council housing (i.e., publicly owned housing) into the hands of owner occupants, thereby encouraging private investment in the housing stock, but at the cost of dramatically reducing the supply of affordable dwellings (Harloe 1995).

While other countries were less inclined that the UK to fully embrace the private market as the solution to all redevelopment problems, they nonetheless moved away from large-scale construction of social housing. Increasingly, the problem areas of cities came to be the places where social housing was constructed in the immediate postwar years. Now these apartment blocks, which were hastily built to relatively low standards, no longer seemed the solution to crumbling structures and homelessness. Moreover, where they had originally attracted large segments of the population, they became increasingly residualized—home to those who had no other choices, particularly to poor immigrants (Harloe 1995).

As noted above, considerable variation existed among European countries, and the UK constituted an extreme case in its commitment to wholesale privatization. The Dutch example, in contrast, points to the types of actions pursued by nations that still maintained a large social welfare sector and considerable commitment to egalitarian aims. In the Netherlands, nonprofit housing associations (HAs) were the principal builders and owners of social housing during the postwar period.

In 1995, the national government withdrew its ongoing direct subsidies to the HAs, providing them with one-time grants, but continued to expect them to be agents of urban regeneration. At the same time, the government remained committed to providing rent supplements to households within social housing so that they could afford rising rent levels in buildings owned by the now financially independent HAs. The HAs consequently became much more like profit-making firms, the difference being that they reinvested all their revenues in regeneration programs and were committed to providing units for low-income households (Van der Veer and Schuiling 2005; Priemus 2006). Their approach to urban regeneration went beyond renewal of the housing stock to achieving social diversity and increasing owner occupation. Thus, a mix of tenure types, income and ethnic groups, and housing structures became the model for a regenerated neighborhood, but at the cost of reducing the total supply of affordable housing.

In the Netherlands, as in other European countries, the thrust toward population deconcentration characteristic of the postwar years gave rise to a fear that central cities would lose their primacy. Increasingly, the American model of middle-class families with children moving out to the suburbs took hold, leaving the inner city to young adults, retirees, and immigrants. An effort to satisfy the desire for homeownership within the urban core responded to the trend toward outmigration. Regulatory changes encouraged small businesses to move into central areas, while firms requiring large amounts of space occupied new high-rise developments on the urban edge (Bruijne et al. 2002). Regional planning thus went through a number of phases in the sixty years after World War II, moving from deliberate deconcentration, to a concept of the compact city, to the most recent model of the multinodal metropolis (Faludi and van der Valk 1994; Hall and Pain 2006). Redevelopment of central areas and peripheral, postwar residential districts constituted part of this strategy, under which each node would encompass a broad range of activities and be strongly connected by rail and highway.

The Netherlands represents a northern European model that is more redistributive and more planning oriented than the approaches used elsewhere on the continent.[9] Aspects of it, however, are not exceptional, particularly the move toward reconstituting areas with significant concentrations of social housing so that populations are more heterogeneous and contain higher proportions of homeowners. While Dutch redevelopment planning reveals perhaps a greater concern with social inclusion than is the case in other European countries, it nonetheless also is directed at enhancing economic advantage within the competitive global economic marketplace. Public–private partnerships became the vehicle for the development of office complexes on the urban periphery, especially around Schipol Airport and Amsterdam Zuidas (South Axis), as well as along the Amsterdam waterfront, where office towers and tourist facilities replaced disused docks and warehouses.

The breakdown of support for mass-produced social housing, fiscal constraints on the state, pressures for gentrification, and competition for investment provided the political and economic context in which changes occurred throughout the European continent. Variations among countries existed in the extent to which social concerns accompanied the drive for economic growth that asserted itself everywhere.

3. Global Political Economy and Local Redevelopment

Both the object and the character of redevelopment reflect the state of urbanism in a particular place and time and the balance of social forces associated with it. Thus, as we have shown, urban conditions and programs were very different in the United States and Western Europe for a rather long time after World War II. Put in the starkest terms, the United States invested most of its resources in owner-occupied, single-family homes on what had been agricultural land, with a secondary commitment to redeveloping city centers for the automobile. The construction of social housing took a back seat, was concentrated in a relatively few big cities, and was commonly sited so as to channel the residential choices of the poor and to segregate African Americans.

In Western Europe, city centers, cathedrals, town halls, and other public structures were rebuilt, often just as they were before the war, in a compact, public-transit pattern. Social housing, most of it located in large projects, went up in old industrial districts and in the expanding urban periphery. A distinctly "communist" model also emerged in Eastern Europe with proportionately more emphasis on huge housing projects and far less on commercial districts and city life (Andrusz, Harloe, and Szelenyi 1996).

With the benefit of historical hindsight, we can see that these postwar decades constituted what has often been called a Fordist (or modernist) stage of advanced world capitalism outside of the Soviet bloc—one marked by reindustrialization, a compact among classes ("corporatism"), a commitment to the welfare state, and the relative economic insulation of the United States and Western European nations from both the Second (communist) and Third (developing) Worlds. World migration was limited and managed by nations with labor shortages; the advanced capitalist states of the West dominated global trade.

During the 1970s, all of this began to change dramatically in ways that would create a new political–economic force field for urban redevelopment (Castells 2000a, 2000b). We have noted some of these changes already in discussing redevelopment strategies and convergences among Western countries. In the remainder of the chapter, we will schematically describe the emergent, post-Fordist political economy.

While global transformation cannot strictly be reduced to a handful of dimensions, it is nonetheless helpful to think about a set of forces that have reshaped the world over the last three or four decades, and how the new global terrain, in both a figurative and a literal sense, creates contemporary local patterns of urban development and redevelopment.

The Rise of Neoliberalism

This movement was rooted in the contradictions and tensions associated with the world economic restructuring of the 1970s (Harvey 2005; Brenner and Theodore 2004). The "crisis" resulted from a combination of factors, including a rebellion by the upper classes against the increasing equality engendered under Fordism (with its strong trade unions, socialist parties, and welfare state); the spread of industrialism to East Asia; the aging of manufacturing plants in Europe and America; and to be sure, the dramatically rising price of energy effected by OPEC in alliance with the global petro-chemical industry.[10] The political response to "stagflation" was sharpest in the United States and Britain (and, as we have said, better resisted in Western Europe), first taking the form of deregulation and then of full-fledged neoliberalism with its monetary policy, privatization, and roll back of "welfarism" and unionism. Rather quickly, the thriving industrial heartlands of the two continents were transformed into rustbelts, with governments left to solve the urban problems of "redundant" workers, brownfields, and recent migrants (North Africans and Turks in Europe, southern blacks in America) for whom there were no jobs with the right "skills matches."

Neoliberal responses to the specific challenges took longer to surface on the European continent, even as key institutional structures were being established within the European Union and, by the 1990s, through a single currency and a banking system dominated by German monetarism. Equally important, if perhaps less apparent at the time, was the rise of finance capital, increasingly free of regulation and capable of creating lucrative (if risky) investment opportunities in Western urban development projects and in Third World manufacturing, the latter speeding up the process of industrial obsolescence and simultaneously disciplining labor through global competition.

Finally, and by no means the least consequential aspect of the neoliberal turn, was the glorification of individualism and of consumption. It was no surprise that self-realization through home ownership and freedom through auto-motion put increasing pressure on social collectivism, whether in the form of public housing or mass transit. The fall of the Berlin Wall and soon thereafter of the whole system of state socialism not only further legitimized neoliberal policy and culture but also opened vast investment markets to capital and eliminated a troublesome alternative model of urban and social organization.

The Delegitimization of Urban Utopias

A second dimension in the changing character of urban redevelopment was the delegitimization of urban utopias. Much of the assault on grand plans had started during the 1960s, in the response of academics to the urban redevelopment projects of the United States and Western Europe, with their utopian claims of not just urban but also social rebirth (Scott 1998). They gave rise to opposition on the ground and inspired a critical academic literature in planning, sociology and political science that quickly became dominant. A founding father of modern town planning, Daniel H. Burnham, might as well have turned over in his grave and announced that it was now best to "make *only* little plans."[11]

By the mid-1970s, American cities had been racked by citizen mobilization, racial conflict, and large-scale riots. The effect on planners and intellectuals concerned with social justice was to destroy the utopian vision of urban physical transformation as the way to address social inequality and political instability. The real applications of earlier utopian ideas in "comprehensive planning" were identified mainly as programs for "Negro removal" and the gentrification of valuable central-city spaces.[12] Likewise, Marris and Rein (1967) showed the internal contradictions and limits of extant schemes for government-sponsored social reform, such as the War on Poverty. Nor was the answer an alternative plan for the good or just city. With faith lost in grand visions and their proponents, planning "from above" was countered with a political program from below—a program of community control, black power, and bureaucratic enfranchisement.[13] Progressive planners and like-minded professionals became advocates for the poor, for persons of color, and for inner-city neighborhoods (Hoffman 1989). The "advocacy planning" that Paul Davidoff championed as early as 1965, and which was reformulated a few years later by Norman Krumholz as "equity planning," became *the* progressive paradigm for planning as social reform (see Krumholz and Forester 1990). Others on the neo-Marxian left, including Manuel Castells (1977) and David Harvey (1973), dismissed planning altogether, redefining the "urban question" as a crisis of capitalism that could be resolved only through class conflict, social restructuring, and possibly revolution.

During the 1980s, a European "new left" rather like that of the United States without its racial dimension grew in strength. This left strongly opposed top-down planning, a unitary conception of social citizenship, and utopian plans for urban redevelopment (see, inter alia, Hajer 1989; Mouffe 1992). Its radicalism centered on democratic processes and a "communicative rationality" that would empower multiple publics. Compounding the loss of faith in a unitary vision was the vista across the iron curtain. State socialism in its economic stagnation and dreary urbanism had long ceased to be a vibrant counter-model. Rather, it seemed to show the future of the planned society taken to scale. Its collapse in the decade of the 1990s demonstrated to most observers that a fully planned society was not sustainable. Thus was the final nail driven into the coffin of utopianism in Western thought about the city.

Migration

A third dimension of change in the global political economy has had a profound effect in reshaping urban terrains and national responses to them. Initially, in the 1960s, several dynamics generated immigration flows into the developed countries: "guest worker" programs that imported foreign labor into Western Europe; decolonization of former colonial subjects and their movement to the former metropoles; and loosening of immigration quotas after 1965 in the United States. But it was first the post-Fordist restructuring of capitalism in the late 1970s and then the demise of the Soviet empire after 1989 that unleashed a level of worldwide migration not seen for a century (for the U.S., see Alba and Nee 2003; Massey 2007; for Europe, see Musterd 1998).

New migration from developing countries in Asia and Latin America reconfigured the racialized pattern of settlement in the United States and repopulated many central cities and older suburbs. The previously clear spatial–political pattern of poor, black central cities, prosperous white suburbs, and black–white conflict became ever more complicated, while the overall number of people in poverty grew. An emergent pattern of urban trenches (Katznelson 1981) now more closely resembled the 360 degree battlefields of Iraq and Afghanistan than the clearly demarcated and linear WW I Western Front that gave trench warfare its deservedly bad name. Among cross-cutting cleavages were social class differences (in both initial conditions and rates of economic mobility); legal status (of the nearly 39 million foreign-born Americans in 2008, about a third were undocumented); ethnic differences among immigrants; splits in the "black" population among African Americans, Africans, Afro-Caribbeans, and black Hispanics; and not least, the dramatic transformation of city–suburb coloration and economic differences. As the twenty-first century moved on, more than half of the "minority" population was suburbanized, but inequality increased dramatically among suburban jurisdictions, and some entered the ranks of the poorest municipalities in America. At the same time, gentrification was changing the class and racial composition of many urban cores (N. Fainstein and Fainstein 2009).

If immigration helped defuse the American urban crisis, in Western Europe it seemed to contaminate cities with urban problems that Europeans had earlier regarded as limited to the United States. Country after country found itself severely challenged by varying combinations of immigrant economic disadvantage, demands for cultural recognition and national pluralism (commonly with a nativist counterattack), the allegiances of some second- and third-generation Muslim immigrants to anti-Western radicalism (and ocassionally terrorism), and the resentment of native workers faced with low-wage foreign competitors on their home soil. Across Western Europe, immigrant and domestic differences were racialized by political elites, even when the in-migrants were "white" former residents of Eastern Europe. Housing estates and precincts with immigrant concentrations (e.g., the eastern and South Bank boroughs of London or the northern and eastern suburbs [*banlieues*] of Paris) were stigmatized as ghettoes. The media emphasized immigrant criminality and residential segregation supposedly approaching American levels. Whatever the actual facts, and there was much evidence that most immigrants were being effectively assimilated and were not living in segregated ghettos (Freeman 2007), public views were often otherwise. The "immigrant problem" was accordingly transformed into a widespread perception of the failure of welfare-state programs, of the dangers of social housing, and of a general fragmentation of national communities. The policy response so far has been contradictory at best, sometimes involving demands for total assimilation and heavy policing and, at other times and places, for creative new community development programs, neighborhood diversity, and political pluralism. Whatever the final outcome, it is clear that immigration has further undermined faith in the old programs of social and physical redevelopment and has fractured political solidarity in many European states.

Uncertainties in the Coming World Political Economy

The current uncertainty encompasses a range of factors, including continued population movements, new patterns of settlement, and the political response to them; the availability and cost of energy; changes in the environment, and ongoing economic crisis—the list is long. Whatever its character, the emergent pattern of urbanism is bound to form the problematic of redevelopment. We can identify two forces that have shaped cities in the recent past that need to be carefully examined. The first is globalization and a new international division of labor in which global cities are centers of organization and control, while goods production occurs in many places and shifts in ascendancy are frequent (Held et al. 1999; Sassen 2001). We now take capital mobility for granted as the defining determinant of world economic structure, along with its concomitant pattern of investment, disinvestment, and redevelopment. It today seems almost inevitable that cities like Detroit and Buffalo will continue on their downward spirals of de-industrialization, population loss, and poverty, while New York, Frankfurt, London, Chicago, and Singapore will remain control centers for finance capital. But we should remember that as recently as 1970, New York City was projected to steadily decline in economic power and population, transformed into a "sandbox" where the poor would be contained and play (Sternlieb 1971). Today, New York has the greatest population in its history, is a prime site for commercial real-estate investment, provides residences to wealthy households from around the nation and, indeed, the world, and has never been more vibrant. Will we make the same errors, for better and worse, in naively extrapolating current trends in production and settlement into the future?

The second force affecting the trajectory of cities derives from the role of real estate in world capitalism. The banking crisis that began in 2007 and the subsequent sharp contraction in real estate values brought again into focus what David Harvey (2005) has described as the secondary circuit of capital. Duringthe post-Fordist epoch real estate has provided a vehicle for bringing a return on capital through a positive cycle of investment and property appreciation, such that the cost of the built environment became a proportionately and increasingly more expensive factor of worldwide production. The crisis of 2007–09 revealed the way in which real property has for more than two decades provided fictitious collateral in a securitization process that permitted enormous debt leverage and the availability of relatively cheap loans for further real estate investment (and price inflation); it also facilitated consumer debt of all kinds that drove expansion in the United States, the UK, and to a somewhat lesser extent Western Europe (Immergluck, 2009; Gotham 2009). Then, what had seemed like an inevitable and monotonic increase in real estate prices, and hence in the desirability of property investment, proved to be vulnerable to imminent collapse. The question today is whether the "secondary circuit" will become fully reestablished, or whether increased government regulation and the experience of collapse itself will make real estate a less robust mode of capital accumulation. The implications of the answer for redevelopment are enormous, given disinvestment trends already long under way in some places and the use of private investment through a variety of partnership vehicles to effect urban redevelopment.

In Conclusion

We see, therefore, that programs for urban redevelopment rest within a field of forces that connects local conditions with global transformations. Even while each metropolitan area and neighborhood presents a set of distinctive characteristics and practices (Murie and Mustard 2004), broad ideological currents, transnational economic institutional practices, and widely adopted policy models impose a certain uniformity everywhere. The set of stages through which most redevelopment programs have concurrently passed reflects these global pressures, at the same time as local politics and specific outcomes differ.

Notes

1. This was especially true in China. See Wu, Xu, and Gar-On Yeh (2007); Ma and Wu (2005).
2. With regard to this last factor, we should note the importance of emulation. At regional, national, and international levels, redevelopment policy has shown itself to be subject to the fashions of the day, ranging from making city centers "automobile friendly" to building high-rise new downtowns and social housing estates, to, most recently, transit-oriented development and attracting the "creative class." Emulation has also been apparent in oppositional movements and alternative models of urbanism, calling at various times for racial integration, community control, and the right to the city.
3. For excellent essays on theoretical approaches and a review of the vast literature on the subject, see Judge, Stoker, and Wolman (1995) and Davies and Imbroscio (2009).
4. There is a vast literature on American urban redevelopment. See especially Altshuler (1965); Altshuler and Luberoff (2003); Beauregard (2003); Caro (1974); Cummings (1988); S. Fainstein et al. (1986); S. Fainstein (2001); Friedland (1983); Hoffman, Fainstein, and Judd (2003); Judd and Parkinson (1990); Logan and Molotch (2007); Logan and Swanstrom (1990); Mollenkopf (1983); Parkinson, Foley, and Judd (1988);

Rosenthal (1980); Squires (1989); Stone (1976, 1989); Stone and Sanders (1987); Swanstrom (1985); Wilson (1966); Zukin (1982, 1991, 1995, 2010).

5. Under TIF, revenue bonds support the redevelopment of a designated district and are repaid by the increase in property taxes coming from that area as a consequence of redevelopment (see Weber 2003).

6. Developers could gain additional floor space in return for contributing to a public amenity.

7. BIDs are organizations of property owners in a commercial district who agree to a special tax that then goes only to support investment within the district. While the largest BIDs operate in downtown areas, they increasingly also provide support for neighborhood shopping streets (Hoyt 2005; Mitchell 2001).

8. For studies of redevelopment programs in Western Europe see, inter alia, Ambrose (1986); Ambrose and Colenutt (1975); Ball et al. (1985); Barnekov, Boyle, and Rich (1989); Brenner and Theodore (2004); Brindley, Rydin, and Stoker (1996); Corbridge, Martin, and Thrift (1994); Del Cerro (2007); Hall (1998, 2002); Harloe and Lebas (1981); Healey (2007); Hoffman, Fainstein, and Judd (2003); Judd and Parkinson (1990); Logan and Swanstrom (1990); Marcuse and van Kempen (2000); Newman and Thornley (1996, 2005); Parkinson, Foley, and Judd (1988); Pickvance (1976); Salet and Gualini (2007); Saunders (1979); Savitch (1988).

9. Costa Esping-Andersen (1990) identifies "three worlds of welfare capitalism"—liberal, conservative-corporatist, and socialist. The Netherlands and Scandinavia fall into the latter category, although since the beginning of the global financial crisis in 2007 they have increasingly retreated from this model.

10. On the left, this was an "urban crisis" and a "fiscal crisis of the state." On the right, the problem was seen quite differently—as a lack of entrepreneurship and insufficient investment resulting from union power, high wages, a bloated welfare state, and an overregulated private sector.

11. Burnham (according to Hall 1988, 174) said just the opposite in 1907: "Make no little plans. They have no magic to stir men's blood and probably themselves will not be realized. Make big plans. Aim high in hope and work. Remembering that a noble, logical diagram once recorded will not die."

12. An excellent history of the entire period, but especially of events in Boston and San Francisco, may be found in Mollenkopf (1983). See also Gans (1968).

13. See, inter alia, Fainstein and Fainstein (1974); Needleman and Needleman (1974); and Fainstein et al. (1986).

References

Alba, Richard, and Victor Nee. 2003. *Remaking the American Mainstream*. Cambridge, MA: Harvard University Press.

Altshuler, Alan. 1965. *The City Planning Process*. Ithaca, NY: Cornell University Press.

Altshuler, Alan, and David Luberoff. 2003. *Megaprojects*. Washington, DC: Brookings Institution Press.

Ambrose, Peter. 1986. *Whatever Happened to Planning?* London: Methuen.

Ambrose, Peter, and Bob Colenutt. 1975. *The Property Machine*. Harmondsworth, Middlesex, UK: Penguin.

Anderson, Martin. 1964. *The Federal Bulldozer*. New York: McGraw-Hill.

Andrusz, Gregory, Michael Harloe, and Ivan Szelenyi, eds. 1996. *Cities after Socialism.* Oxford: Blackwell.

Ball, Michael, V. Bentivegna, M. Edwards, and M. Folin. 1985. *Land Rent, Housing and Urban Planning.* London: Croom Helm.

Barnekov, Timothy, Robin Boyle, and Daniel Rich. 1989. *Privatism and Urban Policy in Britain and the United States.* Oxford: Oxford University Press.

Beauregard, Robert A. 2003. *Voices of Decline,* 2nd ed. New York: Routledge.

Bratt, Rachel G., and William M. Rohe. 2007. "Challenges and Dilemmas Facing Community Development Corporations in the United States." *Community Development Journal* 42(1): 63–78.

Brenner, Neil, and Nik Theodore, eds. 2004. *Spaces of Neoliberalism. Urban Restructuring in North America and Western Europe.* Oxford: Blackwell.

Brindley, Tim, Yvonne Rydin, and Gerry Stoker. 1996. *Remaking Planning.* London: Routledge.

Bruijne, Dick, Doreen van Hoogstraten, Willem Kwekkeboom, and Anne Luijten. 2002. *Amsterdam Southeast.* Bussum, Netherlands: Thoth Publishers.

Caro, Robert. 1974. *The Power Broker: Robert Moses and the Fall of New York.* New York: Knopf.

Castells, Manuel. 1977. *The Urban Question.* Cambridge, MA: MIT Press.

Castells, Manuel. 2000a. *The Rise of the Network Society,* 2nd ed. Oxford: Blackwell.

Castells, Manuel. 2000b. *End of Millennium,* 2nd ed. Oxford: Blackwell.

Clavel, Pierre. 1986. *The Progressive City.* New Brunswick, NJ: Rutgers University Press.

Cleaveland, Frederic N. 1967. *Congress and Urban Problems.* Washington, DC: Brookings Institution Press.

Corbridge, Stuart, Ron Martin, and Nigel Thrift. 1994. *Money, Power and Space.* Oxford: Blackwell.

Cummings, Scott, ed. 1988. *Business Elites and Urban Development.* Albany, NY: State University of New York Press.

Davies, Jonathan S., and David L. Imbroscio, eds. 2009. *Theories of Urban Politics.* Los Angeles: Sage.

Del Cerro, G. 2007. *Bilbao: Basque Pathways to Globalization.* Amsterdam: Elsevier.

Diaz Orueta, Fernando, and Susan S. Fainstein. 2008. "The New Mega-projects: Genesis and Impacts." *International Journal of Urban and Regional Research* 32(4): 1–8.

Eisinger, Peter K. 1988. *The Rise of the Entrepreneurial State.* Madison, WI: University of Wisconsin Press.

Esping-Andersen, Gosta. 1990. *The Three Worlds of Welfare Capitalism.* Princeton, NJ: Princeton University Press.

Fainstein, Norman, and Susan S. 2009. "Social Equity and the Challenge of Distressed places." In *Megaregions,* edited by Catherine Ross, 191–218. Washington, DC: Island Press.

Fainstein, Susan S. 2001. *The City Builders,* 2nd ed. Lawrence, KS: University Press of Kansas.

Fainstein, Susan S., and Norman I. Fainstein. 1974. *Urban Political Movements.* Englewood Cliffs, NJ: Prentice-Hall.

Fainstein, Susan S., and Norman I. Fainstein. 1982. "Restoration and Struggle: Urban Policy and Social Forces." In *Urban Policy under Capitalism,* edited by Norman I. Fainstein and Susan S. Fainstein, 9–20. Beverly Hills, CA: Sage.

Fainstein, Susan S., and Norman I. Fainstein. 1986. Epilogue. In *Restructuring the City,* rev. ed., edited by Susan S. Fainstein, Norman I. Fainstein, Richard Child Hill, Dennis Judd, and Michael Peter Smith, 283–88. New York: Longman.

Fainstein, Susan S., Norman I. Fainstein, Richard Child Hill, Dennis Judd, and Michael Peter Smith. 1986. *Restructuring the City,* rev. ed. New York: Longman.

Faludi, Andreas, and Arnold van der Valk. 1994. *Rule and Order: Dutch Planning Doctrine in the Twentieth Century.* Dordrecht, Netherlands: Kluwer.

Fellman, Gordon. 1973. *The Deceived Majority.* New Brunswick, NJ: Transaction.

Fisher, Peter S., and Alan H. Peters. 1998. *Industrial Incentives.* Kalamazoo, MI: W.E. Upjohn Institute for Employment Research.

Fishman, Robert. 1982. *Urban Utopias in the Twentieth Century.* Cambridge, MA: MIT Press.

Freeman, Gary. 2007. "Immigrant Incorporation in Western Democracies." In *Rethinking Migration,* edited by Alejandro Portes and Josh DeWind, 122–48. New York: Berghahn.

Frieden, Bernard J., and Marshall Kaplan. 1975. *The Politics of Neglect.* Cambridge, MA: MIT Press.

Frieden, Bernard J., and Lynne B. Sagalyn. 1990. *Downtown, Inc.* Cambridge, MA: MIT Press.

Friedland, Roger. 1983. *Power and Crisis in the City.* New York: Schocken.

Gans, Herbert J. 1962. *The Urban Villagers.* New York: Free Press.

Gans, Herbert J. 1968. *People and Plans.* New York: Basic Books.

Gelfand, Mark I. 1975. *A Nation of Cities.* New York: Oxford University Press.

Gorz, André. 1983. *Farewell to the Working Class.* Boston: South End Press.

Gotham, Kevin. 2007. *Authentic New Orleans: Tourism, Culture, and Race in the Big Easy.* New York: New York University Press.

Gotham, Kevin. 2009. "Creating Liquidity out of Spatial Fixity: The Secondary Circuit of Capital and the Subprime Mortgage Crisis." *International Journal of Urban and Regional Research* 33(2): 355–71.

Hajer, Maarten A. 1989. *City Politics: Hegemonic Projects and Discourse.* Aldershot, Hants, UK: Avebury.

Hall, Peter. 1988. *Cities of Tomorrow.* Oxford: Blackwell.

Hall, Peter. 1998. *Cities in Civilization.* New York: Pantheon.

Hall, Peter. 2002. *Cities of Tomorrow,* 3rd ed. Oxford: Blackwell.

Hall, Peter, and Kathy Pain. 2006. *The Polycentric Metropolis.* London: Earthscan.

Hamel, Pierre, Lustiger-Thaler, and Margit Mayer, eds. 2000. *Urban Movements in a Globalising World.* London: Routledge.

Harding, Alan. 1995. "Elite Theory and Growth Machines." In *Theories of Urban Politics,* edited by David Judge, Gerry Stoker, and Harold Wolman, 35–53. London: Sage.

Harloe, Michael. 1995. *The People's Home: Social Rented Housing in Europe and America.* Oxford: Blackwell.

Harloe, Michael, and Elizabeth Lebas, eds. 1981. *City, Class and Capital.* London: Edward Arnold.

Harvey, David. 1973. *Social Justice and the City.* Baltimore: Johns Hopkins University Press.

Harvey, David. 2003. *Paris: Capital of Modernity.* New York: Routledge.

Harvey, David. 2005. *A Brief History of Neoliberalism.* Oxford: Oxford University Press.

Healey, Patsy. 2007. *Urban Complexity and Spatial Strategies.* London: Routledge.

Heinz, Werner, ed. 1993. *Public Private Partnership — Ein neuer Weg zur Stadtentwicklung?* Stuttgart: W. Kohlhammer.

Held, David, Anthony McGrew, David Goldblatt, and Jonathan Perraton. 1999. *Global Transformations.* Stanford, CA: Stanford University Press.

Hoffman, Lily M. 1989. *The Politics of Knowledge*. Albany: State University of New York Press.

Hoffman, Lily M., Susan S. Fainstein, and Dennis Judd, eds. 2003. *Cities and Visitors*. Oxford: Blackwell.

Hoyt, Lorlene. 2005. "Planning Through Compulsory Commercial Clubs: Business Improvement Districts. *Economic Affairs* 25(4): 24–27.

Immergluck, Dan. 2009. *Foreclosed*. Ithaca, NY: Cornell University Press.

Jacobs, Jane. 1961/1993. *The Death and Life of Great American Cities*. New York: Modern Library.

Judd, Dennis, and Michael Parkinson, eds. 1990. *Leadership and Urban Regeneration*. Newbury Park, CA: Sage.

Judge, David, Gerry Stoker, and Harold Wolman, eds. 1995. *Theories of Urban Politics*. Newbury Park, CA: Sage.

Katznelson, Ira. 1981. *City Trenches*. Chicago: University of Chicago Press.

Krumholz, Norman, and John Forester. 1990. *Making Equity Planning Work*. Philadelphia: Temple University Press.

Lehrer, Ute, and Jennifer Laidley. 2008. "Old Mega-Projects Newly Repackaged? Waterfront Redevelopment in Toronto." *International Journal of Urban and Regional Research* 32(4): 786–803.

Logan, John, and Todd Swanstrom, eds. 1990. *Beyond the City Limits*. Philadelphia: Temple University Press.

Logan, John, and Harvey Molotch. 1987. *Urban Fortunes*. Berkeley, CA: University of California Press.

Ma, L. J. C., and Fulong Wu, eds. 2005. *Restructuring the Chinese City* . London: Routledge.

Marcuse, Peter, and Ronald van Kempen, eds., 2000. *Globalizing Cities*. Oxford: Blackwell.

Marris, Peter, and Martin Rein. 1967. *The Dilemmas of Social Reform*. New York: Atherton.

Massey, Douglas S. 2007. *Categorically Unequal: The American Stratification System*. New York: Russell Sage.

McNeill, Donald. 2009. *The Global Architect*. New York: Routledge.

Mitchell, Jerry. 2001. "Business Improvement Districts and the 'New' Revitalization of Downtown." *Economic Development Quarterly* 15(2): 115–23.

Mollenkopf, John. 1983. *The Contested City*. Princeton, NJ: Princeton University Press.

Mouffe, Chantal, ed. 1992. *Dimensions of Radical Democracy*. London: Verso.

Murie, Alan, and Sako Musterd. 2004. "Social Exclusion and Opportunity Structures in European Cities and Neighborhoods." *Urban Studies* 41(8): 1441–59.

Musterd, Sako, ed. 1998. *Urban Segregation and the Welfare State*. London: Routledge.

Needleman, Martin L., and Carolyn Emerson Needleman. 1974. *Guerillas in the Bureaucracy*. New York: John Wiley.

Newman, Peter, and Andy Thornley. 1996. *Urban Planning in Europe*. New York: Routledge.

Newman, Peter, and Andy Thornley. 2005. *Planning World Cities*. New York: Palgrave Macmillan.

Parkinson, Michael, Bernard Foley, and Dennis Judd, eds. 1988. *Regenerating the Cities: The UK Crisis and the U.S. Experience*. Manchester, UK: Manchester University Press.

Pickvance, Chris, ed. 1976. *Urban Sociology*. New York: St. Martin's.

Plunz, Richard. 1990. *A History of Housing in New York City*. New York: Columbia University Press.

Priemus, Hugo. 2006. "Regeneration of Dutch Post-war Urban Districts: The Role of Housing Associations." *Journal of Housing and the Built Environment* 21:365–75.

Rosenthal, Donald B., ed. 1980. *Urban Revitalization*. Beverly Hills, CA: Sage.

Rubin, Herbert J. 2000. *Renewing Hope within Neighborhoods of Despair*. Albany: State University of New York Press.

Salet, Willem, and Enrico Gualini, eds. 2007. *Framing Strategic Urban Projects*. London: Routledge.

Sassen, Saskia. 2001. *The Global City*, 2nd ed. Princeton, NJ: Princeton University Press.

Saunders, Peter. 1979. *Urban Politics*. London: Hutchinson.

Savitch, H. V. 1988. *Post-industrial Cities*. Princeton, NJ: Princeton University Press.

Sbragia, Alberta. 1990. "Pittsburgh's 'Third Way': The Nonprofit Sector as a Key to Urban Regeneration." In *Leadership and Urban Regeneration*, edited by Dennis Judd and Michael Parkinson, 51–68.. Newbury Park, CA: Sage.

Schwartz, Alex F. 2006. *Housing Policy in the United States*. New York: Routledge.

Scott, James C. 1998. *Seeing like a State*. New Haven, CT: Yale University Press.

Self, Robert, and Thomas Sugrue. 2002. "The Power of Place: Race, Political Economy, and Identity in the Postwar Metropolis." In *A Companion to Post-1945 America*, edited by Roy Rosenzweig and Jean-Christophe Agnew, 20–43. Cambridge, MA: Blackwell.

Squires, Gregory, ed. 1989. *Unequal Partnerships*. New Brunswick, NJ: Rutgers University Press.

Sternlieb, George. 1971. "The City as Sandbox. Is the Inner-City Doomed?" *The Public Interest* 25(Fall): 14–21.

Stone, Clarence. 1976. *Economic Growth and Neighborhood Discontent*. Chapel Hill, NC: University of North Carolina Press.

Stone, Clarence. 1989. *Regime Politics*. Lawrence, KS: University Press of Kansas.

Stone, Clarence, and Heywood Sanders., eds. 1987. *The Politics of Urban Development*. Lawrence, KS: University Press of Kansas.

Strom, Elizabeth. 1996. "In Search of the Growth Coalition." *Urban Affairs Review* 31(4): 455–481.

Strom, Elizabeth. 2008. "Rethinking the Politics of Downtown Development." *Journal of Urban Affairs* 30(1): 37–61.

Sugrue, Thomas J. 1996. *The Origins of the Urban Crisis*. Princeton, NJ: Princeton University Press.

Swanstrom, Todd. 1985. *The Crisis of Growth Politics*. Philadelphia: Temple University Press.

Swyngedouw, E., F. Moulaert, and A. Rodríguez. 2004. "Neoliberal Urbanization in Europe: Large Scale Urban Development Projects and the New Urban Policy." In *Spaces of Neoliberalism. Urban Restructuring in North America and Western Europe*, edited by Neil Brenner and Nik Theodore, 195–229. Oxford: Blackwell.

Van der veer, Jeroen, and Dick Schuiling. 2005. "The Amsterdam Housing Market and the Role of Housing Associations." *Journal of Housing and the Built Environment* 20:167–81.

Ward, Stephen V. 2000. "Re-examining the International Diffusion of Planning." In *Urban Planning in a Changing World*, edited by Robert Freestone, 40–60. New York: Routledge.

Weber, Rachel. 2003. "Tax Increment Financing in Theory and Practice." In *Financing Economic Development*, edited by Sammis B. White, Richard D. Bingham, and Edward W. Hill, 53–69. Armonk, NY: M.E. Sharpe.

Wilson, James Q., ed. 1966. *Urban Renewal*. Cambridge, MA: MIT Press.

Wu, Fulong, J. Xu, and A. Gar-On Yeh. 2007. *Urban Development in Post-reform China: State, Market, and Space*. London: Routledge.

Zukin, Sharon. 1982. *Loft Living*. Baltimore: Johns Hopkins University Press.

Zukin, Sharon. 1991. *Landscapes of Power*. Berkeley, CA: University of California Press.

Zukin, Sharon. 1995. *The Cultures of Cities*. Oxford: Blackwell.

Zukin, Sharon. 2010. *Naked City*. New York: Oxford.

CHAPTER 30

GENDER, CITIES, AND PLANNING

BRENDA PARKER

1. INTRODUCTION

> "But what of the men and women, the boys and girls to inhabit this beautiful city?"
>
> —"City Planning for Girls," 1928

THIS chapter takes an expansive view of urban planning. It looks back in order to see forward, and makes visible some of the marginalized voices and spaces in academic planning. In particular, I posit that gender (among other themes) has remained a persistent omission in most mainstream histories and narratives of urban planning (for some exceptions, see Shimson-Santo 2000; Spain 2001a, 2001b; Leavitt 2003; Fainstein and Servon 2005; Fenster 2005). By calling attention to the ways that feminists "make" and "write" the city across time and space, I argue for an inclusive and invigorated vision of city building.

To do so, I first reflect on female and feminist interventions in the early industrial North American city. In this movement, women envisioned not only the city beautiful but also the "city social," where comprehensively served communities, neighborhood leadership, and greater equality were potent and possible (Hayden 1982; Wirka 1996, 1998; Spain 2001b). Specifically, they addressed material concerns related to homes and housing, health, and urban politics. I recall this activism, not to romanticize the past or suggest a stable, unitary, or exclusive feminism, but to argue that both diverse feminist efforts and these themes remain critical to contemporary planning scholarship. As cities have been ravaged by neoliberal austerity compounded by a global recession, we need to revisit what it means to build cities and for whom. We also need to understand the diverse spaces, places, and processes in and through which inequalities are produced. Such a task involves planning practitioners, activists, citizens, and academics, as feminists and radical planners have well articulated. Here, I focus mainly on academic planning because how we "write" the city deeply informs how we "make" the city, including what spaces are designed and built, what problems are made pressing, and what voices and bodies are deemed important. I outline the importance of feminist material analyses focused on urban politics and planning, home and housing, and health. These analyses—along with other critical approaches—not only make gender and urban inequalities visible but also help us better comprehend and transform cities.

2. Early Feminist Materialism: Women "Make" the Modern North American City

For urban planners, the early modern North American and European city offers one starting point for a material feminist analysis of the city. In a time of tremendous urban tumult and unbridled capitalism, material feminists in the late 1800s capitalized on the ideological associations between women and home and motherhood to launch a "municipal housekeeping" agenda that transformed urban spaces, services, and politics. By arguing that the city was an extension of the home, and drawing upon their maternal subjectivities, women legitimated their presence as activists and agents of change in the public sphere (e.g., Marston 2004; Hayden 1984/2002; 2001b). This pathbreaking work was not only an important achievement that helped set the stage for later feminist work in cities, but it also helped lead to the development of urban planning as a field.

In the 1800s, material feminists directly engaged with urban politics, housing, and health in cities that were seen as crowded, corrupt, and incorrigible. They drew upon "naturalized" maternal and moral authority to challenge corruption in the political sphere and advocate for urban services. Motivated in part by anxieties about sexuality and changing gender norms, female reformers provided shelter, domestic training, and "moral supervision" for the newly arriving single working-class women.[1] They addressed poverty, racism, segregation, and the squalor of housing for immigrants—the latter an engagement that preceded urban planner's interest in housing reform by sixty years (Wirka 1996; Spain, 2001b). With regard to health, they lobbied for food safety, built public baths, and shed light on unsanitary urban conditions. They enacted early forms of environmental activism, advocating for garbage incineration instead of landfills even as this endangered business profits (Wirka 1996; Flanagan 1996; Spain 2001b).

Because racism so marked the urban landscape, African-American women and white women worked separately in their reform efforts, providing segregated services such as housing to European immigrants and black migrants from the South. African-American female reformers often had the additional burden of combining waged and unwaged labor and helping black individuals and communities manage and survive in racist cities and workplaces (Collins 1990; Gilmore 2007).

Often motivated by moralism and operating within raced, gendered, heterosexist, and classed ideologies and practices, early material feminists nonetheless addressed the "everyday" and material needs of many urban residents. Material feminists—so labeled by Dolores Hayden—of various classes, races, and ethnicities reimagined urban spaces and urban lives based on creativity, collectivity, and care. Chores and children were shared responsibilities (Collins 1990; Hayden 1980, 1984/2002). On occasions, they critiqued capitalism and the corruption of urban politics and argued that women's household labor should be compensated. As Spain (2001b, 12–13) argued, "Male professionals built grand boulevards and civic monuments in search of the City Beautiful. Female volunteers built the places of everyday life, the neighborhood institutions without which the city is not a city." And while club men protected the interests of business, club women (often informed by maternal subjectivities) proposed public solutions that considered the well-being of a wider range of residents, including children (Marston 2004).

Although their influence was eventually constrained by masculinist practices, female reformers and feminists transformed the city and the state. These women held influential policymaking positions in city, state, and national government, helping institutionalize the field of urban planning and construct the welfare state. For example, Jane Addams's extensive advocacy helped institutionalize sanitation as a core component of city planning. Catherine Bauer—an activist, journalist, and planner—led a reform movement that inspired progressive, federal housing programs within the Public Works Administration beginning in 1933 (Spain 2001a; Radford 1996). Women reformers (in a movement still relevant today) critiqued the City Beautiful and City Functional movements, arguing instead for City Social, which would integrate social services into physical design and prioritize neighborhood self-determination and community organization leadership (see Wirka 1996).

They also engaged in feminist "praxis," theorizing about space, cities, and inequality while meeting the practical needs of urban residents and considering the policy implications of their research. They critiqued political economy approaches that ignored the domestic sphere (Sibley 1995; Hayden 1984/2002; Marston 2004; Spain 2001b). However, gendered anxieties and power relations gradually led to a decline in women's political leadership. As Hayden (1984/2002, 47) argues, "Women had asserted a direct political challenge to their seclusion in the home by demanding a homelike city. Yet many men preferred to promote better government by men as defenders of women and children in the home rather than to accept direct female power."

Similarly, action-oriented feminist urban scholars within the burgeoning Chicago Sociology School were segregated into the School of Social Service Administration. These scholars collected data on tenement housing and developed sophisticated and sensitive sociospatial theories related to race, equality, and the housing markets in the early 1920s. This work contained structural analyses, pointed to the importance of "use" and "exchange" values, demonstrated how racism created housing submarkets, and included policy suggestions such as state intervention in the housing market (Sibley 1995). However, Robert Park and Ernest Burgess, academic contemporaries in Chicago, devalued this work as biased and unsophisticated. Park and Burgess, whose human ecology theories indelibly imprinted the field of urban planning, missed and "dismissed" the role of gender relations in constructing the urban landscape, as well as the contributions of feminist scholars (Sibley 1995; Spain 2001a). This exclusion has persisted in urban planning, even as feminists since the 1970s have begun to "rewrite" the city.

3. FAST FORWARD 100 YEARS: FEMINIST URBAN SCHOLARS "REWRITE" THE CITY

The concerns of urban material feminists related to gender, space, and social inequality reemerged among urban planning scholars in the 1970s, in a context of de-industrialization, urban inequality, and the rise of second-wave feminism. An important task of early feminist urban scholars was to make women's experiences visible in the city. Tivers (1985), for example, documented the daily lives of mothers in London, highlighting the spatially and economically constrained lives of urban women with young children. A special issue of the feminist journal *Signs* (1980), funded by the U.S. Housing and Urban Development (HUD) Administration, raised a number of theoretical and practical questions related to women, gender, and the city. Similar special issues appeared in the *International Journal of Urban and Regional Research* (1978) and *Antipode* (1984).

Articles in these journals focused on specific issues such as transportation and housing design that affected urban women, while also formulating and drawing upon theoretical feminist arguments about the andocentric nature of urban form; about the myriad roots of women's oppression in cities; and about the relationship between capitalism and patriarchy and its urban manifestations (e.g., Gittell and Shtob1980; Hayden 1980; Markuson 1980). For example, Markusen (1980, S23) challenged Marxist renderings of urban form by arguing that urban space that was dominated by single-family detached homes separated from workplaces was "as much the products of patriarchal organization of household production as the capitalist organization of waged work" that offers advantages for men but poses contradictions for capitalism. Leavitt and Seagert (1990) explored how residents of abandoned buildings in Harlem, primarily black and female, formed "community households" based on reciprocal social relations and community. They used this study to deepen theoretical understandings of community and communication among urban planners.

These efforts expanded the types of spaces, subjects, and syntheses that could be a part of planning scholarship, and they accompanied broader interest in urban social planning. Planning scholars exposed women's historical roles as reformers, organizers, and volunteers in cities, which had been previously unacknowledged (Hayden 1980; Birch 1983; Wilson 1991; Wirka 1996, 1998; Spain 2001b). They demonstrated how historical efforts to "control" and "plan" the disorderly city were linked to patriarchal impulses to control sexuality, women, and female bodies (Boyer 1983; Wilson 1991; Wirka 1998; Hooper 1998; Sandercock 1998). In a related conversation, feminists debated whether cities were historically or currently sites of constraint or freedom and liberation for women, including with regard to their sexuality (Gittell and Shtob 1980; Wolff 1985; Wilson 1991, 1992). These studies not only made women and gender visible, they also exposed richer and diverse processes of historic and contemporary city building.

While initial contributions by feminist urban scholars were commonly about women, there was an evolving sophisticated analysis of gendered sociospatial and temporal relations. Geography became a critical strategy for understanding how women's experiences were spatially constituted and differentiated, and how the built environment reflected and reinforced social relations, including those related to gender (McDowell 1982; Hanson and Pratt 1995; McDowell 1999). A significant body of literature emerged that analyzed gender and the spatial form of cities. Feminist urban planners and geographers argued, for example, that ideological divisions between the private and public (gendered as feminine and masculine) were inscribed in the suburban-urban form of cities, and that urban architectural design reflected masculinist power and bias (see England 1991; Spain 1992; McDowell 1999).

Responding in part to critiques from black feminists and feminists from the Global South in the 1980s and 1990s, northern feminist urban scholars also began to explore the multiple and intersecting identities and power relations surrounding women's lives. In "A Gender Agenda," Sandercock and Forsyth (1992) argued that urban planning theory needed to take the diversity of women's experience seriously, and an edited volume sought to "rewrite" planning history with attention to multicultural roots (Sandercock 1998). For example, Gilbert (1999) challenged a "generic" theory of urban women's spatial entrapment. She argued that race and racism played a critical role in determining whether spatial "boundedness" and place-based networks were enabling or constraining for working-class women. Similarly, Bondi (1999) contributed to understandings of gender and gentrification with an empirical analysis of how class and spatialized income inequality differently structured women and men's experiences related to gentrification. A parallel strand of scholarship theorized the ways that sexuality and sexual difference shaped women and men's experiences in cities and the production and organization of urban space (Adler and Brenner 1992; Binnie and Valentine 1999; Knopp 1990, 1998).

Feminist planners are now more apt to think about "difference" in complex ways. For example, recent studies carefully probe the ways that age, ability, gender, race, and other factors shape differing perceptions and experiences surrounding fear and safety. For instance, elderly women are the least likely to be victimized by crime in cities, but they express strong feelings of fear (Pain 2001). Like much of the work in feminist urban planning and geography, these studies take apart public and private binaries with regard to violence and fear, unveiling the myriad spaces around the world where varied forms of gendered violence (from war to domestic abuse) are produced, avoided, and experienced (Pain 2001; Whitzman 2007a). Furthermore, postcolonial and feminist planning scholars have articulated the deep differences in people's experience in cities and nations throughout the Global North and Global South. Importantly, they have also shown how colonial and global relations of violence and power have deeply shaped the terrain of gender and broader urban inequalities around the world (see Sandercock 1998; Miraftab 2006, 2009).

Gendered analyses of urban life and form have explored not just the experiences of men and women in urban space but also the production and reworking of masculinities and femininities (see Berg and Longhurst 2003). McDowell (1997) reflected on the changing nature of urban economies in industrialized countries and the complex ways of "doing gender" among workers in the financial sector of London. In a different study (2004), she focused on white working-class masculinities in Britain in the wake of urban restructuring and the feminization of work. Parker (2008) has explored the masculine, classed, and racialized subjectivities embedded in popular policy narratives about idealized urban "creative class" workers. Within the field of community development, Stall and Stoecker (1998) suggest that certain reified community organizing techniques can be coded as "masculine," while others are more common to women and might be seen as feminine.

How do contemporary feminist planners think about women and gender? Most clearly, feminists deconstruct simplistic categories of women and gender, thinking through multiple axes of cultural and material "difference" in cities related to age, ability, and sexuality, (e.g., Fincher and Jacobs 1998). With regard to urban scholarship, this means repositioning traditional forms of critique andanalysis. Feminists scholars have moved beyond (exoticized and eroticized) studies of the racialized or sexualized "other" to probe, for example, the spatialized reproduction of "heteronormativity" (Hubbard 2008), and the performativities of whiteness and activation of heritage in *Cities of Whiteness* (Shaw 2007). Simultaneously, feminist urban scholarship has challenged the stability and continuity of gendered and social identities and power relations (McDowell 1999; Berg and Longhurst 2003;

Lysaght 2002; Valentine 2007). For example, Lysaght (2002) examines how performances of and relationships between dominant and subordinate masculinities are spatially contingent in Belfast and are linked to fear of violence. Overall, there remains an emphasis on not just mapping different forms of oppression but also on comprehending the ways of doing "contingent" and "discontinuous' identities in part through clash, controversy, discord, and dispute (Valentine 2007; Jarvi, Kantor, and Cloke 2009, 92). Theories of resistance, insurgent planning, and collective mobilization have helped us better understand gender, sexuality, difference, and power in cities around the world (see Fincher and Jacobs 1998; Knopp 1998; Anderson 1998; Miraftab 2009).

Resistance and insurgence, however, are more than collective mobilization; they are also a set of embodied practices. For example, Klodawsky (2006) describes how homeless women use cleanliness as a way to eliminate bodily markers of homeless status and associated vulnerabilities to violence and public shame. Embodied practices and embodiment are now a central concern in feminist geographic work. The concept of embodiment acknowledges that "our awareness is profoundly influenced by the fact that we have a body, which is shaped by connections and larger networks of meanings at multiple scales" (Cresswell, 1999, 175–78). Thinking about the city in connection with the body, Grosz (1998) argues that the body has an active role the production and transformation of urban space, and that cities and bodies mutually define and constitute each other. Interestingly, feminist planning scholars have not engaged as much as other urban scholars with embodiment studies. Too often, bodies in planning literature are seen as normatively male and cities are seen as disembodied space. This oversight is important, as urban scholars point out the many ways that mundane urban experiences, such as riding a crowded bus, are embodied "fleshy" experiences (Jarvis, Kantor, and Cloke 2009) Depending on one's gender, race, sexuality, or other factors, this embodied experience might involve harassment and fear, which can be mediated by planning for better security and ample transit space.

What has emerged from feminist urban planners and scholars is a highly sophisticated and diverse body of research related to the city. Through this work, we have a better understanding of space and gender relations as mutually constituted and challenged in cities. Rather straightforwardly, Bondi (2005, 1) argues that "[g]ender is an integral, ubiquitous and taken-for-granted aspect of urban life. It is an influential dimension of urban identities, an axis of urban inequalities, and it animates the everyday practices that characterize and constitute cities and city life." It is attentive to the intersecting and intertwined cultural and material dimensions of identity and power and to embodied and emotional practices and experiences. Feminist urban scholarship draws upon multiple theoretical persuasions and an expansive range of methodologies, including spatial analysis of health and care access utilizing geographic information system (GIS) technologies; in-depth urban ethnographies; qualitative interviews and case studies; and sophisticated analysis of gender-based community patterns (e.g., McDowell 2004; Roy 2003; McLafferty 2005; Crane 2007).

The spectrum of feminist and gender research on the city is both distinct and diffuse with regard to gender. There is an abundance of research and instructional texts that specifically analyze gender and intersecting identities and power relations in the city. Urban planners have specifically explored gendered differences in mobility and transit patterns, as well as the transportation needs of low-income women and mothers (Blumenberg 2004; Polk 2004; Wekerle 2005b; Crane 2007). They have argued that traditional community development theories do not account for the ways that women organize and build community (Stall and Stoecker 1998). As I discuss later, they have also engaged critically with themes related to gender and housing (e.g., Leavitt 1993; Hayden 1982, 1984/2002; Feldman and Stall 2004). In most of this literature, gender means "gender" (at times in complex ways, at times it focuses on women) and is a specific category of analysis.

In other literatures, gender references a way of thinking critically and spatially about cities, as well as difference, that is informed by a legacy of urban feminist scholarship. In this way, feminist urban planning scholars may not engage directly or most prominently with issues related to men, women, masculinity, femininity, gender identity, or sexuality. This choice may be a conscious discursive move to avoid naming or essentializing, or it may be that gender is not the central focus of their scholarship but, rather, is integrated and diffused within it. Fainstein (2005, 120) suggests that this type of integration is positive, and that an overemphasis on gender differences can "undermine the progressive egalitarian aims that originally inspired feminist thinkers."

Other feminist planners have raised concerns about this diffusion. Rahder and Ahtilia (2004) note a decline in explicit research and curriculum on gender and feminism in planning. They inquire as to whether feminism is being *transformative* (so fully integrated as to be invisible) or being *appropriated* within planning. They argue that subsuming difference (including gender) within a broader discourse on diversity and pluralism could reflect not only a backlash against feminism but also an overall weakening of social justice commitments. Their concerns are echoed in a recent study on gender and planning. Burgess (2008) interviewed thirty-four local authorities in Britain, and found a profound lack of awareness, and even hostility, toward gender equality issues. Those interviewees (mainly women) who did champion gender equality in local authorities did not hold positions of power and influence. Similarly, Petrie and Reeves (2005) argue that UK policies toward generic equality have marginalized women and gender issues, and Whitzman (2007b) finds that feminist efforts in planning may fail due to inaccurate perceptions that gender equality has already been achieved.

In this way, conducting intersectional research on multiple forms of difference and power in cities remains critical. However, so, too, does understanding particular gendered structures of power:

> We must not lose sight of the fact that the specific social structures of patriarchy, heteronormativity, oralism and so on that so preoccupied feminists of the 1970s still matter. As such, this article ends with a call for feminism and specifically feminist geography, to reengage with questions of structural inequalities and

power, while at the same time retaining a concern for theorizing the relationship between multiple categories and structures. (Valentine 2007, 19)

In summary, there is a rich collection of urban scholarship that reflects feminist sensibilities and analyses, yet more work remains in the field of urban planning. In *Cities and Gender*, Jarvis, Kantor, and Cloke (2009) articulates several dimensions of feminist perspectives on the city: They challenge binaries; engage with complexity and intersectionality; challenge andocentric and occidocentric views of the city; probe the production of gendered spaces; blur the separation of spheres such as reproduction, consumption, and production; and emphasize everyday life in the city. It is this final point—the emphasis on everyday, that I will use to bring us full circle—to early feminist interventions in the city, to feminist materiality, and to some "silences" and spaces for engagement with regard to gender, inequality, and planning.

4. Contemporary Material Matters: Urban Politics and Planning, Home/ Housing, and Health

In this section, I revisit how feminists make and write the city. Drawing upon the new feminist materialism, I argue for refined and reinvigorated material gendered analyses of the city that center on justice and ethical practice. These accounts are particularly necessary in urban planning, where feminist and gender awareness are declining or limited, and where feminist planning practice may be resisted (Rahder and Ahtilia 2004; Petrie and Reeves 2005; Burgess 2008). I then suggest three integrated themes for further exploration: home/housing, urban politics, and health. These themes align with the historic interventions of female reformers in the city and offer opportunities to bridge theory and practice.

The everyday lives of residents and the gritty sociospatial injustices of the early modern city mortified and mobilized material feminists in the Progressive Era. These were also central to early feminist urban scholars of the 1970s and 1980s, who revealed the gendered nature of the everyday. As suggested above, this latter scholarship was shaped by and within historical materialism theories, but it critiqued Marxist geography for relegating other forms of oppression to a narrow framework focused on class and capitalism (Markusen 1980; MacKenzie 1985). Current feminist theories, analyses, and practices now work to avoid the moralizing, racist, or other marginalizing tendencies of early female reformers and to think about gender, equality, and justice in integrative and inclusive ways.

Cities remain sites of tremendous diversity, social activism, and global exchange. Yet they are deeply bifurcated, serving as home to the very wealthy and the very poor. In the United States, real wages have been declining for over twenty years, poverty is increasing, and the size of the middle class has declined. In some U.S. cities, the unemployment rate of African-American men is perilously high (Levine 2003). Racialized segregation and poverty persist: Latino and African-American residents constitute 60 percent of the poor, and women are more likely than men to live in poverty (Goetz 2003; U.S. Census Bureau 2011). Globally, women and girls constitute around 70 percent of the poorest people (UN Women 2011). Women of all incomes around the world continue to conduct the majority of "caring" work, and they must manage this paid and unpaid labor with sparse support from the state (Gilmore 2007; Perrons et al., 2006; Jarvis 2005; Jarvis and Pratt 2006; Wekerle 2000).

Within this context, contemporary feminist materialism retains a focus on the everyday and recognizes the spatial and structural dimensions of inequality, such as race, class, and gender, which remain critical in shaping opportunities and life circumstances in cities (McDowell 2004). The politics of "redistribution" are also central to material feminist urban geographers (see Fraser 1995; Bondi and Rose 2003). However, feminist materialism also incorporates theories of self, agency, discourse, and difference (see Naples 2003). Materialist feminists are attentive to the performative, fluid, and contradictory nature of identities and the necessity of unpacking both symbolic and discursive sexism and heteronormativity, along with intersecting related political, spatial, and social inequalities (see McDowell 1999; Hesford 1999). Thus, recognition is incorporated along with redistribution (Fraser 1995).

Insights from "the new feminist materialism" (e.g., Haraway 2004; Alaimo and Hekman 2008), particularly the emphasis on "material-discursive" and the materiality of the body, can help expand and refine feminist urban material planning scholarship. New feminist materialists argue that the "postmodern" feminist focus on deconstruction and discourse may have turned the "discursive pole into the exclusive sources of the constitution of nature, society, and reality" (Alaimo and Hekman 2008, 2). Haraway (2004) uses the formula "material-discursive" to recognize the importance of discourse while reasserting the materiality of bodies, of nature, of lived experience, and of nonhuman and human interfaces. However, embodiment studies and the new feminist materialism often fail to engage directly with social justice and political transformation (Johnson 2008) and too infrequently the material-discursive are considered together in urban planning.

Taking historical inspiration from the material feminists, I argue that sophisticated groundings in contemporary feminist "materiality" can inform and underpin ethical praxis related to gender and the city. They can help planning scholars understand intersecting forms of inequality and specific structures of power. Specifically, I suggest a material-discursive approach to understanding and engaging with three sites (urban politics and planning, homes/housing, and health) where gender and other urban inequalities are reproduced, contested, and embodied.

4.1 Gender, Urban Politics, and Planning

Much of the urban literature has failed to expose or interrogate gender relations as a constitutive aspect of urban politics, planning, and redevelopment (for some exceptions, see Brownill 2000; Sandercock and Forsyth 1992; Clarke, Staeheli, and Brunell 1996; Gilbert 1999; Parker 2008; Wekerle 2009, 2005b; Kern and Wekerle 2008). On one hand, this problem is rooted in an inclusive feminist rendering of "the political." In this way, a range of community activities (which cross supposed divisions of public and private, and cannot be sequestered into definitions of "informal" or "formal") comprise urban politics (See Brownill and Halford 1990; Staeheli 2003; Staeheli and Mitchell 2004; Stall and Stoecker 1998). From this perspective, a range of feminist research related to gentrification, child-care activism and provision, and homelessness can be seen as engaging with and remaking the field of urban politics, writ large.

On the other hand, there is a voluminous geographic body of scholarship related to urban politics, urban planning, and urban redevelopment. This work has produced multiple theories for and approaches to comprehending urban politics, including urban regime theory, regulation theory, and more recently, theories of "new urban politics" and neoliberalism. Corresponding activities in cities involve the construction and dissemination of policies, ideologies, and discourses about the city; the allocation of material resources; and the decisions and discourses of developers (to name a few), many of which are gendered in constitution and effect.

The representation and voice of women, of feminist perspectives, and of other marginalized groups remains a serious problem in urban governance and planning. In the United States and Canada, women make up 20 percent or less of elected city officials (Woodsworth 2005; Center for American Women in Politics 2010). Around the world, women (especially from diverse groups) participate at much lower rates than men in municipal decision making and growth politics. Furthermore, developers (urban power brokers) are disproportionately white males (Turner 1995; Fainstein 2001; Fincher 2004; Kern and Wekerle 2008; Miraftab 2006; Parker 2008, forthcoming). This lack of representation is consequential, even if it is agreed that there is no single female standpoint and that including women does not guarantee other forms of representation (see Brush 2003; Whitzman 2007b). Women do not make the decisions that affect them and others, and a diversity of voices and perspectives (including feminist ones) is excluded.

> Women are not present to add a range of female experiences to gender "neutral" policies, they are absent from posts to sponsor special concerns legislation effectively, and we seldom see them in leader positions and so continue to lack models who challenge our assumptions about gender and leadership. All of this combines into greatly diminished influence potential and tenuous access to important avenues of power....In circular fashion, the absence of women as political leaders contributes to the continued absence of women as political leaders. (Duerst-Lahti and Verstegen 1995, 220–21)

But there are also broader "gender and governance" problems in urban politics and planning. First, the terrain of urban politics and planning is construed and practiced in masculine and narrow ways (Tickell and Peck 1996; Beck 2001; Parker 2008, forthcoming). As at the turn of the twentieth century, design and development are prioritized over the social and citizen realm. The latter was recently labeled the work of "frustrated housewives," according by one city councilor (Beck 2001). Furthermore, the tight circuits of like-minded, elite, urban players help reinforce certain logics and rationales that subvert potential challenges from disenfranchised or different viewpoints. Those outside of the dominant gender norm or those occupying minority subject positions are particularly pressed to conform to the overarching rationales. To do otherwise involves confronting both gender and political norms and risking the disciplinary effects of further marginalization (Parker forthcoming). Ananya Roy's (2003, 108) definition of masculinity is instructive here:

> Masculinist power implies much more than the power exercised by men; instead it indicates the construction of the idealized subject-citizen, a regulatory fiction whose presence delimits the field and agenda of politics.

Arguably, as long as governance is constrained to an emphasis on design and development, the barriers that frame these activities in masculine ways and exclude women from leadership and participation in these arenas will also prevent them and other marginalized groups from participating in policymaking. This situation points to a broader gender and governance problem. Women's limited presence in leadership is a product of the andocentric organization of both capitalism and governance, and it involves questions not only about "presence" and "absence" but also about what rules women have to follow, who will take them seriously, how to have access without the capacity to transform the apparatus, and what the reproduction of masculinity and femininity and power differentials are within these institutions (Brush 2003). These issues are even more salient for minority women, who are doubly marginalized. As Sue Ellen Charlton (1989, 20) has argued, this creates a political dilemma: "Why should women clamor for inclusion in institutions that can never really be ours?"

Many forms of progressive, critical, and insurgent planning incorporate and parallel feminist concerns, as does a broader emphasis on social justice and equity within the planning field. Feminist and gender-focued planning in academia and in cities has led to innovative theoretical approaches and an array of successful programs and initiatives (e.g., Snyder 1995; Roy 2001; Fainstein 2005; Whitzman 2007b). However, feminism and gender-related efforts often are marginalized or met with hostility and indifference within planning (Shimson-Santo 2000; Rahder and Ahtilia 2004; Petrie and Reeves 2005; Whitzman 2007a; Burgess 2008).

In addition, many planning theories and practices show too little concern for gender and/or feminist principles. Communicative planning, for example, too often ignores the broader social, economic, and "power" contexts; in practice, can be used to co-opt insurgent movements or perpetuate hegemonies; pays scant attention to social theories such as feminism; needs to engage with a broader understanding of the public and possibilities for participatory dialogue; and is inappropriate or insufficient for a wide range of planning contexts and actors (e.g., Huxley and Yifchatel 2000; Roy 2001; Miraftab 2009). Popular planning initiatives, such as New Urbanism and "creative class" economic development strategies, perpetuate gender and other inequities; may fail to be inclusive; reify masculinist, racialized, and elite subject positions; and devote critical urban resources to gentrification (see Markovich and Hendler 2006; Peck 2005; Parker 2008). Similarly, theories of neoliberalism have become an important mode of "reading" the urban political landscape within critical urban planning and geography (e.g., Hackworth 2007; Leitner, Peck, and Sheppard 2007; Peck, Theodore, and Brenner 2009; Purcell 2009; Gunder 2010). However, gender is but a quiet chime in the cacophonous literature on urban neoliberalism (Hubbard 2004; Wekerle 2009, 2005b; Baldauf 2006; Kern and Wekerle 2008; Parker 2011, forthcoming). This may be a central omission if we consider the somewhat scant but provocative scholarship on the subject. For example, Hubbard (2004) argued that neoliberal policies and urban revanchism are closely bound up with reassertion of masculinity and control of women's bodies. Meanwhile, women's burdens of home, care, and justice work in cities have intensified under global neoliberalism (Nagar et al. 2002; Gilmore 2007; Parker forthcoming). Other studies explore feminist activism surrounding neoliberalism (e.g., Lind 2000, 2005; Wekerle 2005a) and the ways that neoliberal politics and ideologies delegitimize gender and race-based claims (Brodie 2005; Davis 2007; Wilson 2009).

4.2 Gender, Homes/Housing, and the City

Over ten years ago, Domosh (1998, 278) argued that urban scholars "have not moved much beyond the front door in our analysis of the home." Here, she reminds us that urban planners and geographers have long been scholars and advocates of the issue of housing. However, we hold more limited understanding of the relations, ideologies, and emotions both surrounding and within the home (see Shimson-Santo 2000; Domosh and Seager 2001; Marston 2004; Blunt and Dowling 2006). These dimensions are important in contemporary urban life and planning.

Feminist urban planners and architects have analyzed gender, women, and housing. In the 1980s, Hayden (1980, 1984/2002) famous critiqued gendered and classed architecture and housing policy in the United States. Wright (1981) and Birch (1985) also published important books about the relationship between housing and idealized images of women. Scholars continue to draw from a range of historic and geographic contexts to present feminist engagement with housing, care work, and neighborhood design. Hayden (1984/2002, 232) has argued that "no country has yet created an urban fabric and an urban culture to support men and women on equal terms as citizens and workers." Housing for low-income women (and related politics and activism) remains a critical area for feminist urban scholarship. Williams (2004), Feldman and Stall (2004), and Leavitt (1993) have documented women's historic and contemporary roles in public-housing activism in cities such as Baltimore, Chicago, and Los Angeles. These multiscalar studies not only assert women's agency but also suggest how bodies, households, and states are linked together in material-discursive ways, reflecting and contesting gendered and racial ideologies and practices.

Recent critical scholarship has begun to explore the gendered and intersectional cartographies of home and homelessness. This work challenges the "falsity of the visual" (e.g., the stereotypical male panhandler) in thinking about gendered homelessness; exposes and interrogates the growth in visibly homeless women; and argues for a more theoretically sophisticated investigation of gender and scale, as well as the complex and paradoxical meanings and bodily and discursive representations related to having a home or house. These studies also call for policy responses to and engagement with this issue (Klodawsky 2006; May, Cloke, and Johnsen 2007). Similarly, urban feminist planners and geographers have extensively explored home and housing as a "link between materiality and sociality" (McDowell 1999), thinking through not only housing design, identities, and gender (e.g., Hayden 1984/2002) but also the gendered and sexualized sociospatial relations surrounding urban processes such as gentrification (Knopp 1990; Bondi 1999; Kern 2007; Cahill 2010). Although not exploring gender issues in detail, Karsten (2003) has explored the activities, challenges, and perspectives of families managing child care and work in gentrified urban areas and their implications for urban planners.

Extensive feminist scholarship unveils the varieties of paid and unpaid labor and provisioning that occur in urban households. Such provisioning includes paid and unpaid labor surrounding child care; production of material goods for sale; bartering and exchange of skilled labor; and paid and unpaid sex work (see, for example, Gibson-Graham 2006, 1996/2006; Cameron and Gibson-Graham 2003; Jarvis and Pratt 2006; Pavlovskaya 2004). This labor contributes to diverse, alternative, and multiple urban economies and raises questions about how cities might be repositioned vis-à-vis global capitalism in more liberatory ways (see Gibson-Graham 2006; DeFilippis 2004). Feminist urban scholars have elaborated on how diverse urban households negotiate child care and paid labor, drawing upon embodied practices and "gendered moral rationalities" (McDowell et al. 2005; Perrons et al. 2006; also Jarvis 2005; Jarvis and Pratt 2006). They show how the widespread practice of hiring domestic laborers to care for middle-class children creates new gender, class, and racia tensions and inequalities in households and cities (Gregson and Lowe 1994; England 1997; Goldstein 2003; McDowell 2007). Planners and policymakers have engaged with these issues in only small part, arguing for living-wage laws and enhanced regulation and protection of child care and day laborers.

Other themes surrounding homes and cities suggest the need for further work. For example, Ruthie Gilmore (2007, 239) argues that "the contemporary working-class household is a site saturated by the neoliberal racial state." In this way, particular households are not only subject to the regulatory and punitive dimensions of neoliberalism (such as work requirements and incarceration) but also absorb the consequences of this abdication of social supports and the privatization of social reproduction by cities and states (Katz 2001; Marston 2004; Brodie 2005; Parker forthcoming). As feminist urban scholars, we know too little about how low-income urban households, which are often led by women, are navigating an urban terrain shaped by neoliberalism and its resulting recession.

Households are not simply subject to state policy; they also are agents of urban change. In a critique of gender-blind urban theory, feminist urban planner Daphne Spain (2001a) reminds us that transformations in homes and in women's lives were central to change the shape of the North American urban landscape after World War II (this happened in conjunction with a broader range of political-economic changes). More recently, Buzar, Ogden, and Hall (2005) argue for the need to further illuminate the changing demographics and trends in the household and their effects on urban space. In developed countries, these include, but are not limited to, plummeting marriage rates, smaller household size, frequent changes by individuals in their household arrangements, increases in interracial marriage, and related changes in social networks, social practices, and consumption patterns (to name a few). This knowledge would help planners respect and recognize the important roles played by women, families, and households (rather than autonomous masculine "rational agents") in "making" cities, and would illustrate the diverse and relational needs of people in cities. For example, in his study of the behavior of female commuters, Crane (2007) acknowledges that we do not understand *why* this behavior occurs and what kinds of households and personal dynamics are involved.

Homes and houses remain preeminent sites of social reproduction, where gender, class, and other social relations are learned, reproduced, contested, and reworked (LaReau 2003; McDowell 1999; see also Jarvis, Pratt, and Wu 2001). Particularly as feminist planners seek to apprehend intersecting power relations in cities, and in light of decades of neoliberal policies compounded by a global recession, understanding the daily strategies and practices surrounding social reproduction is critical. This will aid not only radical and insurgent planning efforts to create more just cities, and give voice to marginalized spaces and actors, but also more "mainstream" planning efforts aimed at planning for and meeting the infrastructure needs of a diverse citizenry. In addition, neoliberal policies and technological changes have lifted restrictions and furthered the extensions of markets and marketing, as well as media, into households. In some cases, this expands the opportunities for local and global awareness, of feminist and social justice activism, and of the presentation and engagement with alternative gendered and other identities. On the other hand, markets and media often have vested interests or subtle tendencies toward reproducing gendered and racial ideologies. For example, marketing to children deeply reinforces gender and racial stereotypes, and the popular media present contradictory, unrealistic, and regressive images of women's actions and bodies in what feminist cultural scholar Susan Douglas labels "enlightened sexism (2010).

4.3 Gender, Cities, and Health

As described above, feminist urban scholars have been attuned to processes of embodiment, but less frequently have engaged with themes of gender, cities, and health (but see, for example, Timander and McLafferty 1998; McLafferty and Grady 2004). In "Whither Gender in Urban Health?," Frye, Putnam, and O'Campo (2008) invite urban health scholars to engage feminist geography and sociospatial theories to understand gendered aspects of health, disease, and mortality in cities. In this area, insights from the "new feminist materialism" could be drawn upon to explore how biology, environment, urban restructuring, bodies, discourses, subjectivities, and space work together to shape different gender, racia, and class health trajectories in cities and neighborhoods. For example, in what complex ways might we understand the higher incidence rates of breast cancer among white women in Chicago neighborhoods, when mortality rates are three times higher among black women, especially in particular neighborhoods? How might material-discursive geographical studies on race, gender, and segregation engage with findings that racial discrimination and perceptions of racial discrimination are correlated with higher blood pressure, anxiety, depression, and lower birth rate for pregnant mothers (Collins et al. 2004; Williams, Neighbors, and Jackson 2008)?

Other research by urban planners suggests that spatial form, spatial equity, and environmental change quality interact with gender, race, class, and other factors to affect the health of individuals and communities. For example, urban form and limited food availability may be related to obesity and poor health, with low-income and/or racialized communities often being at particular risk (Wrigley 2002; Short and Guthman 2007; Raja et al. 2010). The prevalence and implications of obesity (as a discourse and material experience) are embodied, raced, classed, and gendered (see Guthman and DuPuis 2006). For example, women are more likely to be obese and are positioned differently from men with regard to biology, social caregiving roles, and body image discourses. Race, gender and spatial urban form also matter with regard to environmental justice, climate change, and health. As Pulido (2000) argues, whites have historically secured cleaner environments by moving away from older industrial urban cores, contributing to contemporary patterns of environmental racism. Furthermore, when environmental and climate disasters occur around the world, women and children are up to fourteen times more likely to die than men. The socially constructed roles of women make them more vulnerable, and men and boys receive preferential treatment during rescue and relief efforts (Kiwala, Masaud, and Ngena 2009). These problems are deeply related to planning practice and they suggest opportunities for feminist planning interventions to redress urban inequality.

Emphasizing materiality and integrating health with households and urban politics (undercutting the arbitrary separation I have imposed upon them here), it is possible to see other research avenues. For example, under neoliberalism, women bear intensified triple burdens of reproduction, production, and community work (Brodie 2005; Nagar et al 2002; Gilmore 2007). It has been argued that cities have become incubators of neoliberal experimentation and harsh policies (while abdicating social supports in favor of development), resulting in social tensions and inequality. However, with some exceptions, feminist urban scholars have not extensively explored the gendered effects of these policies and their associated burdens on households and health. My own interviews with African-American low-income mothers revealed significant stress and neglect of personal health for financial and time reasons (Parker forthcoming). My data also showed that the growth in neoliberal policies in one city (e.g., welfare reform, privatization, social service cuts) paralleled intensified racial disparities in infant mortality for particular populations. A range of other sites and practices, such as the incarceration of men and women, environmental inequities, resource depletion, in which bodies, health, urban/state policies, and households and gender come together in painfully bodily material-discursive ways exist for analysis by urban feminist planners and geographers.

5. Conclusion

In the past 100 years and certainly before, feminists have transformed cities in important and dramatic ways. In the early stages of modern city building, feminists and female reformers imagined cities and planning in comprehensive ways. Feminist versions of "city building" merged the social, political, and physical, and helped improved the lives of countless urban inhabitants. While often still marginalized, contemporary feminist urban planning scholarship traverses theoretical, empirical, and activist terrain in order to understand and improve the lives of men and women in cities. This terrain has become simultaneously more sophisticated, more inclusive, and more nuanced. Feminist urban planners now work to uncover and understand multiple and intersecting urban power relations. They actively pursue various avenues toward urban social justice, and recognize and respect multiple ways of "doing" diffuse and distinct urban scholarship. While feminists have often focused on gender, they also explore and bring into focus a wide range of inequalities and marginalized voices in cities.

In this chapter, I have reviewed some of the historical contributions of feminist urban scholarship, and I have pointed to three productive areas for elaborated and intertwined research and improved planning: gender and urban politics and planning processes; gender and the home/housing; and gender and health. I have argued for a continued (and reinvigorated) emphasis on intersectionality and materiality, with the inclusion of insights from the "new feminist materialism." This feminist materiality is decoupled from restrictive versions of structuralism; attentive to embodiment; encompasses intersectionalities; and focuses on the everyday. Importantly, feminist materialism is not singular or exclusive, but can work in conjunction with other approaches and theories, helping inform and promote more robust and just forms of city building.

NOTE

1. In the minds of many reformers, the specter of prostitution always loomed. See Wirka (1998), who provides an interesting discussion about the simultaneously moralistic, patriarchal, and feminist impulses embedded in the actions and texts of early female reformers.

REFERENCES

Additon, H. 1928. "City Planning for Girls." *Social Service Review* 2(2): 234–62. [Also cited in Wirka (1998)]

Adler, S., and J. Brenner. 1992. "Gender and Space: Lesbians and Gay Men in the City." *International Journal of Urban and Regional Research* 16:24–34.

Alaimo, S., and S. Hekman, eds. 2008. *Material Feminisms*. Bloomington, IN: Indiana University Press.

Anderson, K. 1998. "Sites of Difference: Beyond a Cultural Politics of Racial Polarity." In *Cities of Difference*, edited by R. Fincher and J. Jacobs, 201–25. New York: Guilford.

Bauldauf, A. 2006. "Always Already Gone: Cities, Women and the Politics of Disappearance." *Analog abaldauf*, October 8.

Beck, S. 2001. "Acting as Women: The Effects and Limitations of Gender in Local Governance." In *The Impact of Women in Public Office*, edited by S. Caroll, 49–67. Bloomington, IN: Indiana University Press.

Berg, L., and R. Longhurst. 2003. "Placing Masculinities and Geographies." *Gender, Place, and Culture* 10(4): 351–60.

Binne, J., and G. Valentine. 1999. "Geographies of Sexuality: A Review of Progress." *Progress in Human Geography* 22(2): 175–87.

Birch, E. 1985. "From City Worker to City Planner: Women and Planning, 1890–1980." In *The American Planner: Biographies and Recollections*, edited by D. Krueckeberg, 396–427. New York: Methuen.

Blumenberg, E. 2004. "Engendering Effective Planning: Spatial Mismatch, Low-Income Women, and Transportation Policy," *Journal of the American Planning Association* 70(2): 269–81.

Blunt, A., and R. Dowling. 2006. *Home*. New York: Routledge.

Bondi, L. 1999. "Gender, Class and Gentrification: Enriching the Debate." *Environment and Planning Part D: Society and Space* 17(3): 261–82.

Bondi, L. 2005. "Gender and the Reality of Cities: Embodied Identities, Social Relations and Performativities." Institute of Geography Online Paper Series; GEO-005.

Bondi, L., and D. Rose. 2003. "Constructing Gender, Constructing the Urban: A Review of Anglo-American Feminist Urban Geography." *Gender, Place and Culture* 10:229–45.

Boyer, C. 1983. *Dreaming the Rational City: The Myth of American City Planning*. Cambridge, MA: MIT Press.

Brodie, J. 2005. "Globalization, Governance, and Gender: Rethinking the Agenda for the Twenty-First Century." In *The Global Resistance Reader*, edited by L. Amoore, 244–56. New York: Routledge.

Brownill, S. 2000. "Regen(d)eration: Women and Urban Policy in Britain." In *Women and the City*, edited by J. Darke, S. Ledwith, and R.Woods, 11–40. Houndmills, UK: Palgrave.

Brownill, S., and S. Halford. 1990. "Understanding Women's Involvement in Local Politics: How Useful Is a Formal/Informal Dichotomy?" *Political Geography Quarterly* 9(4): 396–413.

Brush, L. 2003. *Gender and Governance*. Walnut City, CA: Altamira.

Burgess, G. 2008. "Planning and the Gender Equality Duty – Why Does Gender Matter?" *People, Place & Policy Online* 2(3): 112–21.

Buzar, S., P. Ogden, and R. Hall. 2005. "Households Matter: The Quiet Demography of Urban Transformation." *Progress in Human Geography* 29(4): 413–36.

Cahill, C. 2007. "Negotiating Grit and Glamour: Young Women and Urban Economic Restructuring." City & *Society* 19(2): 202–31.

Cameron, J., and J. K. Gibson-Graham. 2003. "Feminising the Economy: Metaphors, Strategies, Politics." *Gender, Place, and Culture* 10(2): 145–58.

Center for American Women in Politics. 2010. "Facts on Women in Local Office." Available at: http://www.cawp.rutgers.edu/fast_facts/levels_of_office/local.php; accessed November 2010.

Charlton, S. E. 1989. "Female Welfare and Political Exclusion in Western European States." In *Women, the State, and Development*, edited by S. E. Charlton, J. Everett, and K. Staudt, 18–35. New York: State University of New York Press.

Clarke, S., L. Staeheli, and S. Brunell. 1996. "Women Redefining Urban Politics." In *Theories of Urban Politics*, edited by D. Judge, G. Stoker, and H. Wolman, 205–27. London: Sage.

Collins, J., R. David, A. Handler, S. Wall, and S. Andes. 2004. "Very Low Birthweight in African American Infants: The Role of Maternal Exposure to Interpersonal Racial Discrimination." *American Journal of Public Health* 94(12): 2132–38.

Collins, P. 1990. *Black Feminist Thought. From: Knowledge, Consciousness, and the Politics of Empowerment*. Boston: Unwin Hyman.

Crane, R. 2007. "Is There a Quiet Revolution in Women's Travel? Revisiting the Gender Gap in Commuting Patterns." *Journal of the American Planning Association* 73: 298–316.

Creswell, T. 1999. "Embodiment, Power and the Politics of Mobility: The Case of Female Tramps and Hobos." *Transactions of the Institute of British Geographers* 24(2): 175–92.

Davis, D. 2007. "Narrating the Mute: Racializing and Racism in a Neoliberal Moment." *Souls* 9(4): 346–60.

DeFilipis, J. 2004. *Unmaking Goliath: Community Control in the Face of Global Capital*. London: Routledge.

Desena, J., and R. Hutchinson, eds. 2008. *Gender in an Urban World*. Bingley, UK: Emerald Group.

Domosh, M. 1998. "Geography and Gender: Home Again?" *Progress in Human Geography* 22(2): 276–82.

Domosh, M., and J. Seager. 2001. *Putting Women in Place*. New York: Guilford.

Douglas, S. 2010. *Enlightened Sexism*. New York: Henry Holt.

Duerst-Lahti, G., and D. Verstegen, eds. 1995. *Gender, Power, Leadership, and Government*. Ann Arbor, MI: University of Michigan Press.

England, K. 1991. "Gender Relations and the Spatial Structure of the City." *Geoforum* 22(2): 135–47.

England, K. 1993. "Suburban Pink Collar Ghettos: The Spatial Entrapment of Women?" *Annals of the American Association of Geographers* 83(2): 225–42.

England, K. 1997. "Domestic Distinctions: Constructing Difference among Paid Domestic Workers in Toronto." *Gender, Place and Culture* 4(3): 339–59.

Fainstein, S. 2001. *The City Builders*. Lawrence, KS: University Press of Kansas.

Fainstein, S. 2005. "Feminism and Planning: Theoretical Issues." In *Gender and Planning: A Reader*, edited by S. Fainstein and L. Servon, 120–40. New Brunswick, NJ: Rutgers University Press.

Fainstein, S., and L. Servon, eds. 2005. *Gender and Planning: A Reader*. New Brunswick, NJ: Rutgers University Press.

Feldman, R., and S. Stall. 2004. *The Dignity of Resistance: Women's Residence Activism in Chicago Public Housing*. Cambridge, UK: Cambridge University Press.

Fenster, T. 2005. "Right to the Gendered City." *Journal of Gender Studies* 14(3): 217–31.

Fincher, R. 2004. "Gender and Life Course in the Narratives of Melbourne's High-Rise Housing Developers." *Australian Geographical Studies* 42(3): 326–39.

Fincher, R., and J. Jacobs, eds. 1998. *Cities of Difference*. New York: Guilford.

Flanagan, M. 1996. "The City Profitable, The City Livable: Environmental Policy, Gender and Power in Chicago." *Journal of Urban History* 22(2): 163–90.

Fraser, N. 1995. "From Redistribution to Recognition? Dilemmas of Justice in a 'Post-Socialist' Age." *New Left Review* 212:68–93.

Frye, V., S. Putnam, and P. O'Campo. 2008. "Whither Gender in Urban Health?" *Health & Place* 14:616–22.

Gibson-Graham, J. K. 1996/2006. *The End of Capitalism (As We Knew it)*. London: Blackwell.

Gibson-Graham, J. K. 2006. *A Postcapitalist Politics*. Minneapolis, MN: University of Minnesota Press.

Gilbert, M. 1999. "Place, Politics, and the Production of Urban Space: A Feminist Critique of the Growth Machine Thesis." In *Urban Growth Machine: Critical Perspectives Two Decades Later*, edited by A. Jonas and D. Wilson, 95–108. Albany, NY: State University of New York Press.

Gilmore, R. 2007. *Golden Gulag: Prisons, Surplus, Crisis, and Opposition in Globalizing California*. Berkeley, CA: University of California Press.

Gittell, M., and T. Shtob. 1980. "Changing Women's Roles in Volunteerism and Reform in the City." *Signs* 5(3): S57–68.

Goetz, E. 2003. *Clearing the Way: Deconcentrating the Poor in Urban America*. Washington, DC: Urban Institute.

Goldstein, D. 2003. *Laughter out of Place: Race, Class, Gender, and Violence in a Shantytown*. Berkeley, CA: University of California Press.

Gregson, N., and M. Lowe. 1994. *Servicing the Middle Classes: Class, Gender, and Waged Domestic Work in Contemporary Britain*. New York: Routledge.

Grosz, E. 1998. "Body-cities." In *Places through the Body*, edited by H. Nast and S. Pile, 31–38. London: Routledge.

Gunder, M. 2010. "Planning as the Ideology of (Neoliberal) Space." *Planning Theory* 9(4): 298–314.

Guthman, J., and M. DuPuis. 2006. "Embodying Neoliberalism: Economy, Culture, and the Politics of Fat." *Environment and Planning Part D: Society and Space* 24: 427–48.

Hackworth, J. 2007. *The Neoliberal City*. Ithaca, NY: Cornell University Press.

Hanson, S., and G. Pratt. 1995. *Gender, Work, and Space*. New York: Routledge.

Haraway, D. 2004. "Otherwordly Conversations, Terran Topics, Local Terms." In *The Haraway Reader*, edited by D. Haraway, 125–50. New York: Routledge.

Hayden, D. 1980. "What Would a Non-Sexist City Be Like? Speculations of Housing, Urban Design, and Human Work." *Signs* 5(3): S170–187.

Hayden, D. 1982. *Grand Domestic Revolution: A History of Feminist Designs for American Homes, Neighborhoods and Cities*. Cambridge, MA: MIT Press.

Hayden D. 1984/2002. *Redesigning the American Dream: Gender, Housing, and Family Life*. New York: W.W. Norton.

Hesford, W. 1999. *Framing Idenitities: Autobiography and the Politics of Pedagogy*. Minnepolis: University of Minnesota Press.

Hooper, B. 1998. "The Poem of Male Desires: Female Bodies, Modernity." In *Making the Invisible Visible: A Multicultural Planning History*, edited by L. Sandercock, 227–54. Berkeley, CA: University of Califorina Press.

Hubbard, P. 2004. "Revenge and Injustice in the Neoliberal City: Uncovering Masculinist Agendas." *Antipode* 36(4): 665–86.

Hubbard, P. 2008. "Here, There, Everywhere, The Ubiquitous Geographies of Heteronormativity." *Geography Compass* 2(3): 605–58.

Huxley, M., and O. Yiftachel. "New Paradigm or Old Myopia? Unsettling the Communicative Turn in Urban Planning." *Journal of Urban Planning and Educational Research* 19(4): 333–42.

Jarvis, H. 2005. *Work/Life City Limits: Comparative Household Perspectives*. Basingstoke, UK: Palgrave Macmillan.

Jarvis, H., P. Kantor, and J. Cloke. 2009. *Cities and Gender*. London: Routledge.

Jarvis, H., and A. Pratt. 2006. "Bringing It All Back Home: The Extensification and 'Overflowing' of Work. The Case of San Francisco's New Media Households." *Geoforum* 37(3): 331–39.

Jarvis, H., A. C. Pratt, and P. Wu. 2001. *The Secret Life of Cities: The Social Reproduction of Everyday Life*. Harlow, UK: Prentice-Hall.

Johnson, L. 2008. "Replacing Gender? Reflections on 15 Years of Gender, Place, and Culture." *Gender , Place, and Culture* 15(6): 561–74.

Karsten, L. 2003. "Family Gentrifiers: Challenging the City as a Place Simultaneously to Build a Career and Raise Children." *Urban Studies* 40:2573–84.

Katz, C. 2001. "Hiding the Target: Social Reproduction in the Privatized Urban Environment." In *Postmodern Geography: Theory and Praxis*, edited by C. Minko, 93–112. London: Blackwell.

Kern, L. 2007. "Reshaping the Boundaries of Public and Private Life: Gender, Condominium Development, and the Neoliberalization of Urban Living." *Urban Geography* 28(7): 657–81.

Kern, L., and G. Wekerle. 2008. "Gendered Spaces of Redevelopment: Gender Politics of City Building." *Gender in an Urban World*, edited by J. DeSena and R. Hutchinson, 233–62. Bingley, UK: Emerald Group.

Kiwala, L, A. Masaud, and C. Ngena. 2009. "Climate Change Is Not Gender Neutral." *Urban World* 1(2): 27–30.

Klodawsky, F. 2006. "Landscapes on the Margins: Gender and Homelessness in Canada." *Gender, Place, and Culture* 13(4): 365–81.

Knopp, L. 1990. "Some Theoretical Implications of Gay Involvement in an Urban Land Market." *Political Geography Quarterly* 9(4): 337–52.

Knopp, L. 1998. "Sexuality and Space: Gay Male Identity Politics in the United States." In *Cities of Difference*, edited by R. Fincher and J. Jacobs, 149–76. New York: Guilford.

LaReau, A. 2003. *Unequal Childhoods: Class, Race, and Family Life*. Berkeley, CA: University of California Press.

Leavitt, J. 1993. "Women under Fire: Public Housing Activism in Los Angeles." *Frontiers: A Journal of Women Studies* 13(2): 109–30.

Leavitt, J. 2003. "Where Is the Gender in Community Development?" *Signs* 29(1): 207–31.

Leavitt, J., and S. Saegert. 1990. *From Abandonment to Hope: Community Households in Harlem.* New York: Columbia University Press.

Leitner, H., J. Peck, and E. Sheppard, eds. 2007. *Contesting Neoliberalism: Urban Frontiers.* New York: Guilford.

Levine, M. 2003. "Two Milwaukees." Report prepared by the University of Wisconsin-Milwaukee Center for Economic Development, Milwaukee, WI.

Lind, A. 2000. "Negotiating Boundaries: Women's Organizations and the Politics of Restructuring in Ecuador." In *Gender and Global Sestructuring: Sightings, Sites and Resistances,* edited by M. Marchand and A. Runyan, 161–75. New York: Routledge.

Lind, A. 2005. *Gendered Paradoxes: Women's movements, State Restructuring, and Global Neoliberalism.* University Park, PA: Pennsylvania State University Press.

Lysaght, K. 2002. "Dangerous Friends and Deadly Foes—Performances of Masculinity in the Divided City." *Irish Geography* 35(1): 51–62.

MacKenzie, S. 1985. "A Socialist Feminist Perspective on Gender and the Environment." *Antipode* 16:3–10.

Markovich, J., and S. Hendler. 2006. "Beyond "Soccer Moms:" Feminist and New Urbanist Critical Approaches to Suburbs." *Journal of Planning and Education Research* 25 (4): 410–27.

Markusen, A. 1980. "City Spatial Structure, Women's Household Work, and National Urban Policy." *Signs* 5(3; Suppl.): S22–44.

Marston, S. 2004. "A Long Way From Home: Domesticating the Social Production of Scale." In *Scale and Geographic Inquiry: Nature, Society, and Method,* edited by E. Sheppard and R. McMaster, 170–91. London: Blackwell.

May, J., P. Cloke, and S. Johnson. 2007. "Alternative Cartographies of Homelessness. Rendering Visible British Women's Experiences of 'Visible' Homelessness." *Gender, Place, and Culture* 14(2): 121–40.

McDowell, L. 1982. "Towards an Understanding of the Gendered Division of Urban Space." *Environment and Planning Part D* 1(1): 59–72.

McDowell, L. 1997. *Capital Culture: Gender at Work in the City.* London: Blackwell.

McDowell, L. 1999. *Gender, Identity, and Place: Understanding Feminist Geographies.* London: Polity Press.

McDowell, L. 2004. *Redundant Masculinities: Employment Change and White Working Class Youth.* London: Blackwell.

McDowell, L. 2007. "Spaces of the Home: Absence, Presence, New Connections and New Anxieties." *Home Cultures* 4(2): 129–46.

McDowell, L., D. Perrons, C. Fagan, K. Ray, and K. Ward. 2005. "The Contradictions and Intersections of Class and Gender in a Global City: Placing Working Women's Lives on the Agenda." *Environment and Planning Part A* 37: 441–61.

McLafferty, S. 2005. "Women and GIS: Geospatial Technologies and Feminist Geographies." *Cartographica* 40(4): 37–45.

McLafferty, S., and S. Grady. 2004. "Prenatal Care Need and Access: A GIS Analysis." *Journal of Medical Systems* 28(3): 321–33.

McLafferty, S., and B. Tempalski. 1995. "Restructuring and Women's Health: Implications for Low Birthweight in New York City." *Geoforum* 26(3): 309–23.

Miraftab, F. 2006 "Feminist Praxis, Citizenship and Informal Politics: Reflections on South Africa's Anti-Eviction Campaign." *International Feminist Journal of Politics* 8(2): 194–218.

Miraftab, F. 2009. "Insurgent Planning: Situating Radical Planning in the Global South." *Planning Theory* 8:32–51.

Nagar, R, V. Lawson, L. McDowell, and S. Hanson. 2002. "Locating Globalization: Feminist (Re) Readings of the Spaces and Subjects of Globalization." *Economic Geography* 78(3): 257–84.

Naples, N. 2003. *Feminism and Method: Ethnography, Discourse Analysis, and Activist Research*. New York: Routledge.

Pain, R. 2001. "Gender, Race, Age and Fear in the City." *Urban Studies* 38: 899–913.

Parker, B. 2008. "Beyond the Class Act: Gender and Race in the Creative Class Discourse." In *Gender in an Urban World*, edited by J. DeSena and R. Hutchinson, 201–32. Bingley, UK: Emerald Group.

Parker, B. 2011. "Material Matters: Gender and the City." *Geography Compass* 5(6): 443–47.

Parker, B. Forthcoming. *Gendering Urban Neoliberalism: A Feminist Exploration of Masculinities and Markets*. Athens, GA: University of Georgia Press.

Pavlovskaya, M. 2004. "Other Transitions: Multiple Economies of Moscow Households in the 1990s." *Annals of the Association of American Geographers* 94(2): 329–51.

Peck, J. 2005. "Struggling with the Creative Class." *International Journal of Urban and Regional Research* 29(4): 740–70.

Peck, J., N. Theodore, and N. Brenner. 2009. "Postneoliberalism and its Malcontents." *Antipode* 41(6): 1236–58.

Polk, M. 2004. "Influence of Gender on Daily Car Use and Willingness to Reduce Car Use in Sweden." *Journal of Transport Geography* 12(3): 185–95.

Perrons, D., C. Fagan, L. McDowell, K. Ragan, and K. Ward, eds. 2006. *Gender Divisions and Working Time in the New Economy. Changing Patterns of Work, Care, and Public Policy in North America and Europe*. Cheltenham, UK: Edward Elger.

Petrie, P., and D. Reeves. 2005, June. "Women in the Planning Profession: Making the Built Environment Better." Presented at International Women's Policy Research Conference.

Pulido, L. 2000. "Rethinking Environmental Racism: White Privilege and Urban Development in Southern California." *Annals of the Association of American Geographers* 90(1): 12–40.

Purcell, M. 2009. "Resisting Neoliberalization: Communicative Planning or Counter-Hegemonic Movements." *Planning Theory* 8:140–65.

Radford, G. 1996. *Modern Housing for America: Policy Struggles in the New Deal Era*. Chicago: University of Chicago Press.

Rahder, B., and C. Ahtilia. 2004. "Where Is Feminism Going in Planning? Transformation or Appropriation?" *Planning Theory* 3(2): 107–16.

Rahder, Barbara L., and Kelly O'Neill. 1998. "Women and Planning: Education for Social Change." *Planning Practice & Research* 13(3): 247–65.

Raja, S., L. Yin, J. Roemmich, C. Ma, L. Epstein, P.Yadav, and A. Ticoalu. 2010. "Food Environment, Built Environment, and Women's BMI: Evidence from Erie County, New York." *Journal of Planning and Education Research* 29(4): 444–60.

Roy, A. 2001. "A Public Muse: On Planning Convictions and Feminist Contentions." *Journal of Planning and Education Research*, 21(2): 109–26.

Roy, A. 2003. *City Requiem: Calcutta: Gender and the Politics of Poverty*. Minneapolis: University of Minnesota Press.

Saegert, S. 1980. "Masculine Cities and Feminine Suburbs: Polarized Ideas, Contradictory Realities." *Signs* 5(3): S96–111.

Sandercock, L., ed. 1998. *Making the Invisible Visible: A Multicultural Planning History*. Berkeley, CA: University of California Press.

Sandercock, L., and A. Forsyth. 1992. "A Gender Agenda: New Directions for Planning Theory." *Journal of the American Planning Association* 58:49–59.

Shaw, W. 2007. *Cities of Whiteness*. Oxford: Blackwell.

Short, A., and J. Guthman, J. 2007. "Food Deserts, Oases, or Mirages? Small Markets and Community Food Security in the San Francisco Bay Area." *Journal of Planning Education and Research* 26(3): 352–64.

Shimson-Santo, A. 2000. "Home, Memory and Beyond." *Critical Planning* 7:380–50.

Short, J. R. 2006. *Urban Theory: A Critical Assessment*. London: Palgrave.

Short, A., and J. Guthman. 2007. "Food Deserts: Oases or Mirages?" *Journal of Planning Education and Research* 26(3): 252–64.

Sibley, D. 1995. "Gender, Science, Politics, and Geographies of the City. *Gender, Place, and Culture* 2(1): 37–50.

Snyder, Mary Gail. 1995. "Feminist Theory and Planning Theory." *Berkeley Planning Journal* 10:91–106.

Spain, D. 1992. *Gendered Spaces*. Chapel Hill, NC: University of North Carolina Press.

Spain, D. 2001a. "What Happened to Gender Relations on the Way From Chicago to Los Angeles?" *City and Community* 1(2): 155–69.

Spain, D. 2001b. *How Women Saved the City*. Minneapolis: University of Minnesota Press.

Staeheli, L. 2003. "Women and the Work of Community." *Environment and Planning Part A* 35:815–31.

Staeheli, L., and D. Mitchell. 2004. "Spaces of Public and Private: Locating Politics." In *Spaces of Democracy*, edited by C. Barnett and M. Low, 147–60. London: Sage.

Stall, S., and R. Stoecker. 1998. "Organizing for Community or Community Organizing? Gender and the Crafts of Empowerment." *Gender and Society* 12(6): 729–56.

Tickell, A., and J. Peck. 1996. "The Return of the Manchester Men: Men's Words and Men's Deeds in the Remaking of the Local State." *Transactions of the Institute of British Geographers* 21:595–616.

Timander, L., and S. McLafferty. 1998. "Breast Cancer in West Islip, New York: A Spatial Clustering Analysis with Covariates." *Social Science and Medicine* 46(12): 1623–35.

Tivers, J. 1985. *Women Attached*. London: Croom Helm.

Turner, R. 1995. "Concern for Gender in Central City Development." In *Gender in Urban Research*, edited by J. Garber and R. Turner, 271–89. London: Sage.

UN Women. 2011. "Women, Poverty, and Economics." Available online at: http://www.unifem.org/gender_issues/women_poverty_economics/.

Valentine, G. 2007. "Theorizing and Researching Intersectionality: A Challenge for Feminist Geographers." *Professional Geographer* 59(1): 10–21.

Wekerle, G. 2000. "Women's Right to the City." In *Democracy, Citizenship and the Global City*, edited by E. Isin, 203–17. London: Routledge.

Wekerle, G. 2005a. "Domesticating the Neoliberal City: Invisible Genders, Food and the Politics of Place." In *Women and the Politics of Place*, edited by A. Escobar and W. Harcourt. Blomsfield, CT: Kumarian Press.

Wekerle, G. 2005b. "Gender Planning in Public Transit: Institutionalizing Feminist Policies, Changing Discourses and Practices." In *Gender and Planning: A Reader*, edited by S. Fainstein and L. Servon, 275–96. New Brunswick, NJ: Rutgers University Press.

Wekerle, G. R. 2009. "Gender and the Neoliberal City: Urban Restructuring, Social Exclusion and Democratic Participation." In *Urban Sociology in Canada*, edited by H. Hiller. Toronto: Oxford University Press.

Whitzman, C. 2007a. "Stuck at the Front Door: Gender, Fear of Crime and the Challenge of Creating Safer Space." *Environment and Planning Part A* 37:2715–32.

Whitzman, C. 2007b. "The Loneliness of the Long-distance Runner: Long-term Feminist Planning Initiatives in London, Melbourne, Montréal and Toronto." *Planning Theory and Practice* 8(2): 205–27.

Williams, D., H. Neighbors, and J. Jackson. 2008. "Racial/Ethnic Discrimination and Health: Findings From Community Studies." *American Journal of Public Health* 98:S29–37.

Williams, J. 2000. *Unbending Gender: Why Family and Life Conflict and What We Can Do About It*. New York: Oxford University Press.

Williams, R. 2004. *The Politics of Public Housing: Black Women's Struggles Against Urban Inequality*. London: Blackwell.

Wilson, E. 1991. *The Sphinx in the City: Urban life, the Control of Disorder, and Women.* Berkeley, CA: University of California Press.

Wilson, E. 1992. "The Invisible Flaneur." *New Left Review* 191:90–110.

Wilson, D. 2009. "Racialized Poverty in the U.S.: Toward a Refined Racial Economy Perspective." *Professional Geographer* 61(2): 139–49.

Wirka, S. 1996. "The City Social Movement: Progressive Women Reformers and Early Social Planning." In *Planning the Twentieth-Century American City*, edited by M. Sies and C. Silver, 55–75. Baltimore: John Hopkins University Press.

Wirka, S. 1998. "City Planning for Girls: Exploring the Ambiguous Nature of Women's Planning History." In *Making the Invisible Visible: A Multicultural Planning History*, edited by L. Sandercock, 150–62. Berkeley, CA: University of California Press.

Wolff, J. 1985. "The Invisible Flaneuse; Women and the Literature of Modernity." *Theory Culture and Society* 2(3): 37–46.

Woodsworth, E. 2005. Making Space for Women in Cities. *Focus on Space (Winter 2005)*. Vancouver, B.C: Newsletter produced by the Social Planning and Research Council of B.C.

Wright, G. 1981. *Building the Dream: A Social History of Housing in American*. New York: Pantheon.

Wrigley, N. 2002. "Food Deserts in British Cities: Policy Context and Research Priorities." *Urban Studies* 39:2029–40.

Young, I. Marion. 1990. *Justice and the Politics of Difference*. Newark, NJ: Princeton University Press.

CHAPTER 31

FRONTIERS IN LAND USE AND TRAVEL RESEARCH

MARLON G. BOARNET

1. INTRODUCTION

PLANNING studies of land use and travel date to the dawn of the U.S. Interstate Highway era beginning in the 1950s, but the modern interpretation, which seeks to use land for specific environmental, health, or community quality-of-life goals, dates to the 1980s. The literature now has scores of papers on the topic and several literature reviews (for reviews, see, e.g., Badoe and Miller 2000; Boarnet and Crane 2001, chap. 3; Brownstone 2008; Crane 2000; Ewing and Cervero 2001, 2010; Handy 2005; Heath et al. 2006; and Henderson and Bialeschki 2005). This chapter summarizes the standard approach to studying land use and travel behavior, planning's unique contribution, and the gaps in our knowledge and needed next steps.

The purpose of this chapter is twofold: to summarize what has been done to date, and to articulate the key issues that should be the focus of planning research going forward. To foreshadow the conclusion, three topics are reviewed that move land use and travel behavior research forward, none of which has received much attention in the voluminous literature of the past three decades.

1. The empirics of land use—travel behavior research and the theory supporting empirical analysis will both have to move beyond current "reduced form" approaches. The canonical method for studying this topic has been to regress a measure of individual travel behavior on individual or household demographic

characteristics and land use measures. This leaves almost no role for examining how land is developed, or why a city's or neighborhood's urban form develops in a particular way. Yet such a question is a fundamental (some might say *the* fundamental) land-use planning issue. Broadening the analysis to consider policy and plan development will be necessary to better understand questions pertaining to both the interaction of individual location choice and travel, and the endogeneity of city development patterns to residents' travel preferences.

2. The transportation literature has focused on forecasting travel impacts, in part based on land-use patterns, and then using those forecasts of future travel to assess policy impact or compliance. As an example, virtually all discussions of land use and travel in relation to greenhouse gas emissions follow a "forecast and allocate" approach, where future forecasts of travel are allocated to geographic areas for the purpose of determining policy impact or policy compliance. In contrast, there has been relatively little emphasis on retrospective evaluations of land use–transportation policies. Yet credible project evaluation is a necessary prerequisite to local innovation, and the United States is entering a period when local land use and transportation innovation should be encouraged. Program evaluation methods to assess the travel impacts of land use change should be a high research priority.

3. Economic social welfare analysis of land use–travel behavior initiatives is almost completely lacking. In place of benefit-cost analysis, advocates on both sides have offered less formal assessments of the social cost of land-use change. Opponents of compact development typically argue that Americans, and persons throughout the world, prefer low-density living, and that any policies that encourage compact development will result in substantial utility decreases and hence large social-welfare costs (see, e.g., Moore, Staley, and Poole 2010). On the other side of the debate, proponents of compact development argue that there are large, often unmeasured benefits of compact development (e.g., Winkelman and Bishins 2010) or that the American preference for low-density living is a misinterpretation made possible in part by substantial local government interference in the land market (e.g., Levine 2006). On net, we know little about preferences for particular neighborhood types. We know even less about whether such preferences are fixed or malleable. If a person moved from a suburb to a compact development, would the individual adapt his or her concept of desirable living and travel patterns? Yet understanding such questions at the nexus of psychology and the built environment, and refining cognitive measures to inform such questions, are fundamental to moving the debate about benefits and costs from disagreements about opinions to questions of measurement and analysis.

The rest of this chapter is organized as follows. Section 2 provides some historical background on land use–travel behavior research. Section 3 describes the methods of land use–travel behavior research. Section 4 describes the distinction between reduced-form and more structural analyses of land use and travel, and discusses implications for empirical analysis. Section 5 summarizes the results of the literature, with a focus on the magnitude of the association between land use and vehicle miles traveled (VMT). Section 6 discusses the distinction between local and regional (metropolitan-scale) land use–travel relationships. Section 7 discusses the need to build a program evaluation tradition in land use–travel behavior research. Section 8 closes with a discussion of controversies, challenges, and future research directions in this literature, making the case for the research agenda introduced at the beginning of this chapter.

2. HISTORICAL BACKGROUND

With the passage of the National Defense and Interstate Highway Act of 1956, the U.S. Congress approved construction of 41,000 miles of interstate highways and allocated $25 billion to be expended between 1957 and 1969, amounting to possibly the largest single infrastructure project in history at that time (U.S. Department of Transportation n.d.; also see Baum-Snow 2007; Rose 1990). That massive commitment to a new highway system required a way to predict travel flows that would assist with roadway capacity design. The four-step model was invented for that task. Issues of congestion management, air quality, and environmental externalities were either future considerations not yet voiced or, in the case of congestion, tangential policy concerns amid the optimism of the unprecedented national highway project.

The four-step model is based on trip origin and trip destination data aggregated to zones. For commute trips, *trip generations* are typically predicted as a function of the number and characteristics of residents in a zone, and *trip attractions* are forecast as a function of the number and characteristics of jobs at workplaces in a zone. In the second step, trip generations and attractions are connected to predict zone-to-zone trip flows. This second step typically uses a gravity model, predicting trip flows as a function of trip generations and attractions and an inverse function of the *travel cost* (often called impedance) between zones. In urban areas with multiple travel modes (i.e., highways and transit), the mode split is estimated based on relative time and money costs of trips via different modes. (This is the third step in the model.) As a fourth (and final) step, zone-to-zone trips for each mode are loaded onto a network, often using algorithms that route trips over minimum time or minimum cost paths. If particular network links are congested, changing travel costs, the model may iterate back to the point where travel costs are incorporated in the first three steps.[1] For a more complete description of the four-step model, see, for example, Johnston (2004) or Ortuzar and Willumsen (2001).

The four-step model had little behavioral content, and little need for behavioral content. The task at hand was to forecast peak-hour highway flows, and the model, while crude, performed that task acceptably well. But the highway-building era was brief, lasting from the late 1950s to the early 1970s in the United States. Once the network was built, attention turned to other policy problems that have more behavioral content. Congestion and air quality have been increasingly important foci for transportation policy during the past four decades, and the attention given to questions of climate change and energy now often rivals discussions about congestion management and criteria pollutants.[2] As those issues moved transportation from an engineer's focus on infrastructure construction to the social scientist's focus on behavior and policy, the modern land use–travel behavior literature emerged.

Beginning in the 1980s, planners hypothesized that the spatial distribution of trip origins and destinations could be used not only to forecast travel flows but also as a policy tool.[3] If land-use plans placed trip origins and destinations closer together, might persons drive less? In succession, this idea was articulated in the form of jobs–housing balance (Cervero 1986, 1989), transit-oriented development (Calthorpe 1993), and the transportation elements of the New Urbanism and neotraditional design (Duany and Plater-Zyberck 1991; Kelbaugh 1989; and Friedman, Gordon, and Peers 1994); and then the large explosion of land use–travel studies presaged by the early 1990s research of, for example, Ewing, Haliyur, and Page (1995); Frank and Pivo (1995); and Cervero and Kockelman (1997). The goal shifted from forecasting travel to influencing travel, and as such it became necessary to conceptualize travel as the outcome of a host of decisions made by travelers. In short, it became necessary to understand travel as a behavioral problem.[4]

Contemporaneously, the advent of geographic information systems (GIS) allowed researchers to construct detailed land-use measures at specific locations, and such data were paired with individual household travel-diary data to test the hypothesis that individual, or household, travel is influenced by land-use patterns. That hypothesis-testing literature, with microdata matched to GIS measures of land use, has been the focus of planning's travel behavior scholarship for the past two decades.

3. METHODS

In most land use–travel behavior studies, a travel behavior variable is regressed on independent variables that include sociodemographic characteristics and measures of land use.[5] The most common source for travel data is a travel diary, either for a metropolitan area or from a national or statewide survey. (The U.S. National Household Travel Survey includes a travel diary and was most recently conducted in 2001 and 2009.) Common dependent variables include trip generation, mode choice or trip generation for different modes, and vehicle or person miles of travel.

The typical form of a land use–travel behavior regression is shown below. For the seminal applications of this regression approach, see Hanson and Hanson (1981) and Vickerman (1972).

$$\text{Travel-Behavior-Variable} = \beta_0 + \textit{Land-Use-Variables}\boldsymbol{\beta_1}$$
$$+ \textit{Sociodemographic-Variables}\boldsymbol{\beta_2} + u \qquad (1)$$

Where Travel-Behavior-Variable = a measure of individual or household travel, *Land-Use-Variables* = a vector of built environment variables, *Sociodemographic-Variables* = a vector of individual characteristics, the β terms are scalars or vectors of coefficients (with coefficient vectors shown in bold), to be estimated, and u = the regression error term.

The intended policy target informs the dependent variable. Attention has recently shifted from trip generation (as in, e.g., Boarnet and Sarmiento 1998 or Crane and Crepeau 1998) to distance traveled, either by walking (e.g., Boarnet, Greenwald, and McMillan 2008), bicycling (e.g., Krizek and Johnson 2006 or Dill and Voros 2007), or automobile (e.g., Ewing et al. 2008). Trip capture—the fraction of trips that are wholly contained within a small geographic area—has also emerged as a dependent variable (e.g., Khattak and Rodriguez 2005; Greenwald 2006; and the Transportation Research Board's active project, NCHRP 8–51, "Enhancing Internal Trip Capture Estimation for Mixed-Use Developments," whose final report was not yet available at the time this chapter was written).

The land-use variables have traditionally been defined as the "D" variables, after language first used by Cervero and Kockelman (1997). The original "three D's" (Cervero and Kockelman 1997) were density, diversity, and design. Destination accessibility and distance to transit are often added as fourth and fifth "D variables." All of the land use (or "D") variables are typically measured either with census data; agency data on, for example, parcel level land-use patterns; or data that can be derived from geographic information systems.

Density is most commonly population density (persons per land area) or housing unit density. Employment density measures are sometimes also included. Diversity is land-use mix—in particular, the mix of commercial and residential land uses. Two land-use mix measures have become most commonly accepted—an entropy index (e.g., Cervero 1989 or Frank and Pivo 1995) and a dissimilarity index (e.g., Kockelman 1997 or Cervero and Kockelman 1997). The entropy index measures how evenly land uses (e.g., commercial and residential parcels) are spread across a larger geographic area. The dissimilarity index measures land-use mix at a finer grain by measuring how adjacent (or abutting) land uses are the same or different.[6] For a discussion and assessment, see Krizek (2003a) or Hess, Moudon, and Logsdon (2001). Design is typically interpreted to mean the street pattern, and is now commonly measured by block size and by the proportion of intersections that are four-way (the latter to indicate the grid orientedness of the street pattern), as in, for example, Frank et al. (2005). Destination accessibility is most commonly operationalized as a gravity measure of access to employment throughout the metropolitan area, and so measures accessibility to jobs across an area larger than the local neighborhood. Destination accessibility could also be constructed as a gravity measure of access to specific travel destinations, such as shopping opportunities. Distance to transit is simply distance (either straight-line or street-network distance) to the nearest transit station. Often, rail and bus transit are treated as distinct transit opportunities measured by distinct distance variables.

Constructing these land-use variables requires that the travel-diary survey data be matched to specific locations, using a geographic information system (GIS). The most common method, by far, is to measure land uses around the travel-diary respondent's place of residence (e.g., Boarnet and Sarmiento 1998; Crane and Crepeau 1998; Handy, Cao, and Mokhtarian 2006; Rodriguez, Khattak, and Evenson 2006; Frank et al. 2006). A few authors have discussed the need to measure land use near other locations, such as the workplace (e.g., Boarnet 2004 for a discussion and Chatman 2003 for an example of implementation), and such analyses would likely require theoretical grounding in trip chaining to understand how land-use patterns away from home influence the combination of trips into chains.

The geographic scale for the land-use variables typically approximates a walkable neighborhood—often an approximately ¼ mile area or a unit of geography such as a census block group or transportation analysis zone (e.g., Crane and Crepeau 1998; Handy, Cao, and Mokhtarian 2006; Rodriguez, Khattak, and Evanson 2006; Frank et al. 2006; Boarnet, Greenwald, and McMillan 2008). Only a few studies have experimented with varying the scale of geography (e.g., Handy 1993 or Boarnet and Sarmiento 1998), and recent results suggest that attention to land-use measures at the regional or metropolitan level is important, as will be discussed in section 6.

The sociodemographic variables are typically treated as control variables. There are a set of "usual suspect" demographic variables that correlate with travel behavior and that are included as independent variables: number and ages of children, gender, employment status and ages of adult household members, number of cars per licensed driver in the household (or other measures of vehicle availability), income, education level, race/ethnicity, and immigration status of the household or household members. Among these variables, vehicle availability is often considered endogenous to the travel-behavior decision, and so may be modeled separately (as in, e.g.., Kain and Fauth 1976 or Bhat and Guo 2007). Some studies include measures of attitudes as additional controls beyond sociodemographic characteristics (e.g., Handy, Cao, and Mokhtarian 2006; Boarnet, Joh, et al. 2011), but there is some debate as to whether attitudes may be endogenous to travel behavior if, for example, persons adjust their attitudes toward travel based on the travel options available or the choices they habitually make.

Land use–travel behavior regressions of the sort shown in equation (1) often require nonlinear estimation techniques. Trip generation is now analyzed using count regression techniques such as negative binomial regression (see, e.g., Cameron and Trivedi 1998 for a description of negative binomial regression and, e.g., Boarnet, Joh, et al. 2011, Chatman 2008, or Joh et al. 2009 for applications).

Distance traveled, for vehicles, has been analyzed via ordinary least squares (OLS), which is acceptable if the data are not censored at zero. However, in many one- or two-day travel diaries, it is possible for as much as 20 to 25 percent of the respondents to report no car travel during the diary period.[7] In such cases, and for modes of travel such as walking, where left-censoring can be even more common, techniques such as tobit regression should be used (e.g., Boarnet, Greenwald, and McMillan 2008).

Because the land-use variables are often measured for units of geography that approximate a neighborhood, several households can share the same values for the land-use characteristics. In such cases, least squares standard errors are inconsistent and can be underestimated, leading to too frequent rejections of the null hypothesis. For a description of this problem and a suggested solution, see Moulton (1990). Most land use–travel behavior studies now correct for this phenomenon either by using cluster-corrected standard errors (e.g. Moulton 1990) or by using hierarchical linear modeling (as applied in, e.g., Ewing et al. 2003).

4. Efforts to Move from Reduced Form to Structural Models of Land Use and Travel Behavior

The regression in equation (1) is a reduced-form relationship, reflecting the hypothesis that land use is associated with travel behavior. The underlying behavioral structure of how land use might be associated with travel is missing from equation (1).[8] The literature has discussed three ways in which the reduced-form relationship in equation (1) can be expanded into a more structural, and hence more behavioral, understanding of the land use–travel behavior link. Each is discussed below.

4.1. Land Use as a Determinant of Travel Costs

Land use influences travel behavior by influencing the cost of travel, either by placing origins and destinations closer together (i.e., compact development) or by changing the time it takes to travel between places. Most often, land-use and associated transportation infrastructure investments influence both travel distances and travel speeds. Crane (1996a, 1996b) developed a microeconomic demand-theory treatment of land use and travel behavior, and Boarnet and Crane (2001) suggested a relatively simple formalization of that theoretical relationship.[9] Boarnet and Crane (2001) posited that travel speed and trip distance are functions of land use in a model estimated with individual travel data. This is shown below with a composite "travel price" variable representing all land-use influences on the cost of travel.[10]

$$\text{Travel-Price} = \alpha_0 + \text{Land-Use}\alpha_1 + v \tag{2a}$$

$$\text{Travel-Behavior} = \beta_0 + \beta_1\text{Travel-Price} \\ + \text{Sociodemographic-Variables}\beta_2 + u \tag{2b}$$

Boarnet and Crane (2001) noted that if the vector of sociodemographic variables includes the individual's income, then the reduced form of the model in equations (2a) and (2b) is a microeconomic demand function, where quantity demanded (travel, in this case) is a function of prices, income, and sociodemographic "taste" or "preference" variables. This follows a long tradition that views travel as a derived demand (see, e.g., Small 1992 or Small and Verhoef 2007). Substituting equation (2a) into (2b), one recovers equation (1), illustrating how the typical regression of the sort shown in equation (1) is a reduced form of a structural system with more behavioral content.

Boarnet and Crane (2001) experimented with different methods of estimating the system of equations in (2a) and (2b). They found that mixed-land use (as proxied by the fraction of land in commercial use near a survey subject's residence) was negatively associated with car travel speeds, and in turn slower car travel speeds were associated with fewer automobile trips taken by the individual. Both Zegras (2004) and Chatman (2008) adopted similar approaches that relate land use to travel cost. Zegras (2004) used travel times between zones and so did not have an analog to the estimate of individual travel speed in Boarnet and Crane (2001). For a discussion of the advantages and disadvantages of different travel time and speed measures, including the concern that travel time is endogenous to individual travel choices, see Zegras (2004). Chatman (2008), in a study of travel-diary data in the San Francisco–San Jose and San Diego metropolitan areas in California, obtained results that were in part similar to Boarnet and Crane (2001). Specifically, Chatman (2008) found that transportation network load density was negatively associated with car travel speed, but Chatman (2008) did not find an association between car travel speed and vehicle miles traveled.

These more structural models hypothesize that land use influences travel, at least in part, by changing one or both of the two components of the time cost of travel—travel distances and travel speeds. Individual trip distances and speeds are both choice variables, which complicates the analysis. Trip distance is a function of the chosen destinations and routes, and trip speed is influenced by decisions about when to travel, which determine whether travel occurs during congested times. Both Boarnet and Crane (2001) and Chatman (2008) modeled speed and distance as endogenous variables. The studies by Boarnet and Crane (2001) and Chatman (2008) give evidence that more compact development slows car travel speeds, and that reductions in auto travel are in part due to the reduction in car travel speeds that are associated with more dense, urbanized environments.

This structural approach has not become popular in the broad literature on land use and travel behavior. Partly this may be methodological, as the endogenous measures of travel price require good instruments, which can be difficult to find given available data. Possibly lack of attention to models as in (2a) and (2b) reflects the fact that such models offer insight into *why* and *how* land use influences travel, while the literature has revolved more around questions of *whether* and *by how much* land use influences travel. The questions about whether and by how much land use influences travel can be answered with reduced-form hypothesis tests of the sort shown in equation (1). Furthermore, no scholars have suggested that the results of a reduced form such as equation (1) might be biased owing to inattention to the more structural approach in equations (2a) and (2b). Instead, the question of biased statistical inference has been focused more on a different behavioral margin—whether persons choose their residence location in part based on how they wish to travel. For that reason, efforts to examine more behaviorally grounded regression analyses of land use and travel have focused on residential location choice, which in this literature has been called *residential selection*.

4.2. Residential Selection

In the early 1990s, Cervero (1994) uncovered suggestive evidence that persons might choose where to live based in part on how they wish to travel. He surveyed residents of transit-oriented developments (TODs) in California and found that among those TOD residents who commuted by rail, 42.5 percent had been rail commuters before they moved to their existing residences. Cervero (1994, 177) stated, "Part of the high incidence of rail usage among station-area residents, then, could be due to the fact they have a proclivity to patronize rail transit, whether due to habit, personal taste, or happenstance." An implication is that the effect of land use on travel is not wholly causal, as persons might sort into particular locations (e.g., compact developments, TODs) based on how they wish to travel. Boarnet and Sarmiento (1998) noted that this would imply that land-use variables are endogenous to both desired and actual travel patterns, and they corrected for this using instrumental variables.

Since then, the literature on residential selection has grown substantially. Cao, Mokhtarian, and Handy (2009) reviewed the literature, noting that virtually every study that attempted to control for the possible endogeneity of household location found that econometric controls for residential selection did not change the sign or significance of the land use–travel behavior association. In some cases, the magnitude of the land use–travel effect was attenuated after econometrically controlling for residential selection. The association between land use and travel appears to be partly causal and partly persons sorting (or choosing) residential locations that match their travel preference. Yet the question of endogeneity of land use through residential location remains important.

The most theoretically complete treatment of residential selection is to model location choice coincident with a model of travel behavior. Bhat and Guo (2007) estimated a joint model of household residential location and car ownership for households in Alameda County in the San Francisco Bay Area. Brownstone and Golob (2009) estimated a joint model of vehicle ownership and vehicle use, accounting for endogeneity of the single land-use variable in their model—residential density—by estimating a recursive system of equations that assumes that households first choose their residential location and then, conditional on residential location, choose the number of vehicles and the amount of driving. Given that residential location influences travel in part through the choice of vehicle ownership (e.g., Bento et al. 2005; Brownstone and Golob 2009; Kain and Fauth 1976), a full model may require equations to explain residential location choice, vehicle ownership, and travel (i.e., vehicle use for car travel). The first two equations—residential location choice and vehicle ownership—would require discrete choice regression models, and the nonlinearity inherent in such models makes simultaneous estimation complex. Partly for that reason, simpler approaches, such as instrumental variables and the occasional use of natural experiments (i.e., Boarnet, Day et al. 2005 and Boarnet, Anderson et al. 2005, for walking to school) have been more common in this literature. Some recent research has suggested that a rich set of sociodemographic variables can reduce bias associated with residential selection (e.g., Handy, Cao, and Mokhtarian 2006; Cao, Mokhtarian, and Handy 2009; Brownstone 2008).

4.3. The Endogeneity of Policies, Plans, and Urban Development Patterns

For all the attention to residential location, there are larger, possibly more systemic, elements of endogeneity that have received less attention in the land use–travel literature. Policy and plan development, and the resulting impacts on urban form, have received relatively little attention compared to the large number of studies on the association between urban form and travel. Presumably, cities that pursue compact development reflect the preferences of their residents, and so policy development may be endogenous to preferences about travel behavior. Portland, Oregon—possibly the nation's best example of a sustained planning effort designed to produce a more compact, transit-oriented urban form—may be attracting residents in part because of that policy stance (Portland and Elite Cities 2010). But to what extent are policy regimes a product of the preferences of current residents? With the exception of Levine's (2006) detailed discussion of zoning as an impediment to more compact development, there has been little study of plan formation or the question of whether cities build land use–travel environments to suit the preferences of residents. Notably, Levine's (2006) analysis of zoning argues the converse—that cities build low-density development despite the possibility that residents may prefer higher density.

More intriguingly, if persons move from an auto-oriented to a compact (or more transit-oriented) urban form, might their preferences about travel change? How stable are travel preferences? McFadden (2007), in discussing cognitive aspects of travel behavior, suggested that persons might take their cues about the desirability of consumer options from available interpersonal comparisons. Friends or social networks might provide hints about how we might expect to benefit from particular purchases. If true, McFadden suggested that transportation may be shaped by imitative behavior.[11]

Taking that logic one step further, it seems reasonable to assume that a Montana resident who drives hundreds of miles weekly may happily shift to transit use if she moved to San Francisco. The change in both the physical environment and the behavior of friends and neighbors might make transit use—unthinkable to our Montana resident before the move—seem like a sensible choice. The question is not just how a change in land use would influence choices but also whether preferences about travel can be influenced by changes in the environment and changes in social networks. If our Montana resident previously opposed transit use, even in transit-oriented environments, but then upon moving to San Francisco found that she underappreciated the joys of taking buses and trains, then welfare calculations based on the a priori (before move) preferences of the Montana resident would be incorrect. Questions of preference formation and preference stability, and the link to both individual welfare and policy formation, are fundamental to social welfare analyses. Yet very little is known whether persons' preferences toward travel are malleable, and if so, in what ways and how much.

5. RESULTS

Early attempts to summarize the literature on land use and travel behavior focused mostly on hypothesis testing. Is there or is there not an association between land use and travel, and if so is that association causal? Examples of this type of summary include Crane (2000). Recent attention has shifted from hypothesis tests to magnitudes, and that is where we focus. Policy activity related to climate change regulations requires that regulating agencies develop estimates of the magnitude of impact, if any, that land use has on travel. Much of that recent literature has focused on VMT, a proxy for greenhouse gas (GHG) emissions.[12] The literature on VMT and land use has pursued three distinct approaches to summarizing research for the purposes of estimating the impact of land use on VMT: meta-analyses or other broad summaries of the literature, summaries of studies judged to be of high methodological quality, and forecasts from land use–travel models.

The most commonly cited reviews in this literature are by Ewing and Cervero (2001, 2010). In the 2001 article, Ewing and Cervero synthesized summary elasticities based on an exhaustive literature review, while in the 2010 article Ewing and Cervero used meta-analysis techniques, averaging elasticities from several studies while weighting each elasticity by the sample size used in the study. Ewing and Cervero (2001, 2010) analyzed several dependent variables, including trip generation, mode choice, and VMT. Here, we focus on VMT, the dependent variable that currently has the most policy interest. The elasticities of VMT reported by Ewing and Cervero (2001) were in the range of -.03 to -.05 for density, diversity, and design and -.20 for destination accessibility. The results of the Ewing and Cervero (2010) meta-analysis were broadly similar.

Meta-analyses have several pros and cons. A meta-analysis can take results from several smaller case studies and help generalize to a larger population. Also, meta-analyses can average out statistical fluctuations in particular studies. With that said, there are concerns about meta-analyses and about meta-analyses in land use–travel in particular. First, meta-analysis is valid if the data for the several studies are different draws from the same population, and in the land use–travel literature it is unclear that such a condition is satisfied (Brownstone 2008). Second, most of the elasticities used in meta-analyses are calculated at sample averages, and for nonlinear regression specifications (e.g., negative binomial or discrete choice models) that is inappropriate. A preferred approach would be to calculate the elasticity for each observation (using the sample data) and then average the individual elasticities over the full sample (Brownstone 2008). Often, the data required for such an exercise are difficult to obtain as researchers may not respond with such detailed data, data may have been lost, or the time involved would be substantial.

Another common critique of meta-analysis is that the technique combines findings from studies of differing methodological quality. Some authors (e.g., Crane 2000) have argued that in the land use–travel literature methodological concerns are important enough that any summary should first sort based on which studies adopt sound methodologies and then interpret the results. Brownstone (2008), in a background paper for a National Academy of Sciences/National Research Council (NAS/NRC) study committee, echoed that sentiment, suggesting that the methodologically sound studies in this topic area are those that: (1) use disaggregate travel data (for individuals or households), (2) correct for residential self-selection (the possibility that persons might choose to live in neighborhoods that support their desired travel behavior), (3) are based on data from geographic areas larger than a metropolitan area (ideally the entire United States or at least statewide data), and (4) have a rich set of individual (or household) sociodemographic control variables. Following that advice, the NAS/NRC study committee on "Relationships Among Development Patterns, Vehicle Miles Traveled, and Energy Consumption" used a small number of studies to inform their estimate of the elasticity of VMT with respect to land use variables (National Research Council 2009). This method of choosing studies (usually a small number) that are judged to be methodologically sound can be considered a second approach to summarizing the results of the broader literature.

Three studies, in particular, informed the NAS/NRC (National Research Council 2009) report. Bento et al. (2005) used data from the 1990 Nationwide Personal Transportation Survey (NPTS) to study land use–travel behavior links in 114 metropolitan areas in the United States. They constructed several measures of metropolitan-area urban form, including measures of population centrality, jobs–housing balance, city shape, road density, population density, and rail supply. Bento et al. (2005) found that the magnitude of the elasticity of VMT with respect to most of the urban-form variables was typically less than 0.07, meaning that a 100 percent change in an urban form variable typically resulted in less than a 7 percent reduction in VMT. Bento et al. (2005) examined the effect of taking a representative household and changing all land-use variables from Atlanta's values to Boston's values, and found a reduction in VMT of 25 percent. They interpret this as implying that the effect of multiple land-use variables is additive (although possibly not strictly so), and that changing several land-use variables produces a VMT reduction effect that is larger than changing any one land-use variable singly.

Brownstone and Golub (2009) used data from the California sub-sample of the 2001 National Household Travel Survey (NHTS) and obtained an elasticity of VMT with respect to population density of -.12. Brownstone and Golub (2009) estimated the elasticity for each observation in their data set, using a land use–travel regression corrected for residential selection and then using the regression coefficient for density and values for each individual in the data set, averaging the elasticities over the full sample to deal with nonlinearity. Similar studies by Bhat and Guo (2007); Fang (2008); and Chen, Gong, and Paaswell (2008) led to the NAS/NRC (National Research Council 2009) conclusion that the elasticity of VMT with respect to population density is in the range of -.05 to -.12 and that the effect of several land-use variables changing simultenously implies a VMT elasticity of -.25 (based on Bento et al. 2005).

The decision between selecting studies based on methodological criteria and using meta-analysis is not necessarily a clear either/or choice. As an example of a middle ground, Ewing and Cervero (2010) first selected studies based on methodological criteria and then applied meta-analysis. The Ewing and Cervero (2010) criteria include some of the same standards that Brownstone (2008) emphasized, such as prioritizing studies that used disaggregate data. This may help explain why the elasticities from reviews that filter based on methodology (e.g., Boarnet and Handy 2010; Spears, Boarnet, and Handy 2010; and Handy, Tal, and Boarnet 2010a, 2010b, all discussed more later) are similar to the elasticities obtained by the meta-analysis in Ewing and Cervero (2010).

A third approach, summarized by Rodier (2009), examines the results from land use–travel forecasting models. Unlike the regression (or hypothesis testing) literature, forecasting models give results that are not behavioral tests based on data but, instead, are simulations of scenarios based on calibrations that are often derived from tests on data. The behavioral quality of the scenario depends on the underlying estimates and assumptions built into the forecasting tool, and it is important to emphasize that the results that Rodier surveyed are simulations, not behavioral tests. Still, Rodier's findings are illuminating and are similar to the results from the hypothesis testing literature.

Rodier (2009) examined several forecasting scenarios from several large MPOs. Each MPO ran land-use scenarios for future time windows and then calculated reductions in vehicle travel. Rodier (2009) reports that typical model results showed that land use alone would reduce vehicle kilometers traveled (VKT) by 0.5 to 1.7 percent during time horizons ten to forty years into the future. The land-use policies were not quantified as percent changes, but instead were departures from base case (or business as usual) scenarios. Yet, the generally small impact of land use alone is similar in spirit to the small elasticities for single land-use variables from the studies summarized above. Rodier found that land-use policies plus increases in transit service reduced VKT by 2 to 6 percent over a tweny-year time horizon and that combinations of land-use, transit supply, and pricing policies produced the largest VKT reductions: 14.5 percent after ten years and 24 percent at the forty-year time horizon. The basic message is that land use, by itself, has generally small impacts on VKT reduction, but the impacts are somewhat larger when land use is coupled with pricing policies (e.g., congestion pricing, mileage fees, parking pricing) and increases in transit supply. More generally, this illustrates an understudied question, as the literature gives little information about how different classes of policies, such as land use, pricing, and travel demand management, may interact to produce impacts that could be larger than the sum of the parts. Presumably, compact development patterns might enhance the travel impact of demand management or pricing policies, and vice versa, yet few studies have examined this question. A recent exception is Guo, Agrawal, and Dill (2011), who found interactions between land use and pricing in a pilot experiment in Portland, Oregon. Further studying such interactions is a ripe area for future research.

6. Local versus Regional Land Use–Travel Relationships

Neighborhood-level land-use variables, usually measured for a ¼ or ½ mile radius area or similarly sized geographies, typically have a smaller magnitude of association with travel behavior than do regional land-use variables such as variables that measure access to employment weighted across an entire metropolitan area.[13] Boarnet, Handy, and co-authors summarized the elasticity of VMT with respect to land-use measures, focusing on selected studies that used individual or household travel data; included a comprehensive set of household characteristics as control variables; often controlled for residential selection; and yielded statistically significant land-use coefficients in the regression models (Boarnet and Handy 2010; Spears, Boarnet, and Handy 2010; Handy, Tal, and Boarnet 2010a, 2010b). The elasticity of VMT with respect to neighborhood land-use variables (population density, land-use mix, and street network connectivity) is from -.02 to -.12, with one instance (for street network connectivity) of an elasticity of -.19 (Boarnet and Handy 2010, Spears, Boarnet, and Handy 2010; Handy, Tal, and Boarnet 2010a). The elasticity of VMT with respect to regional access to employment (usually an inverse-distance–weighted gravity variable calculated over a metropolitan area) is in a range from -.05 to -.25, and the median elasticity of VMT with respect to regional employment in the studies reviewed by Handy, Tal, and Boarnet (2010b) is -.20. This result—that regional accessibility has a larger association with VMT than neighborhood land-use variables—is common in the literature and is similar to the findings from the literature review and meta-analyses of Ewing and Cervero (2001, 2010).[14]

The importance of regional accessibility for VMT is related to the importance of long trips for VMT. Table 31.1 summarizes the cumulative distribution of VMT by trip length nationally (from the 2001 National Household Travel Survey) and for the five-county Los Angeles area (from both the 2001 National Household Travel Survey and the 2001–2002 Southern California Travel Survey). For both Los Angeles and the United States, about 40 percent of VMT is from trips that are 30 miles or longer. This fact is at odds with the neighborhood-level focus of, for example, the New Urbanism and related planning ideas over the past two decades. While there is no inherent tension between neighborhood-level land-use planning and regional accessibility to jobs and activity centers, the rhetoric of some planning practice, especially the New Urbanism or the more neighborhood-focused aspects of Smart Growth, is often focused more on the neighborhood than on the metropolitan region. Relatedly, the land use–travel behavior literature has sometimes studied only nonwork travel (e.g., Boarnet and Crane 2001, especially the empirical work in chap. 5), in part motivated by the increasing share of nonwork trips as a fraction of all trips. Yet more recently, the policy discussion surrounding climate change and greenhouse gas emissions has elevated the importance of VMT as a measure of travel behavior, and for VMT long trips (and hence, presumably commute trips) matter disproportionately. This shift to a focus on VMT necessitates a rebalancing

Table 31.1 Vehicle Miles of Travel (VMT) by Trip Distance, Metropolitan Los Angeles and National, 2001

	2001 Southern California Travel Survey, metro Los Angeles 5-county area	2001 NHTS, L.A. CMSA sub-sample	2001 NHTS, National sample
Trip Length (Miles)	Cumulative Percent of VMT	Cumulative Percent of VMT	Cumulative Percent of VMT
< 30	59.27	63.16	59.53
>= 30	40.73	36.84	40.47

Source: Author's calculations (with assistance from Gavin Ferguson, Steve Spears, and Douglas Houston), 2001–2002 Southern California Travel Survey and 2001 National Household Travel Survey.

of planning's attention to the two geographic levels of the neighborhood and the metropolitan region, with regional land-use measures receiving more policy attention than has been the norm.

An implication of the importance of regional accessibility for VMT is that policy activity that seeks to leverage land use in the service of greenhouse gas emission reduction (such as California's SB 375) should focus on the regional pattern of transportation access, including land-use planning and policies (e.g., pricing) that influence access throughout a metropolitan area. The link between transportation infrastructure and employment location is an especially fruitful area for future focus. Recent research has established that highways are an important determinant of employment location in urban areas, clarifying what had long been a "chicken and egg" question: Do highways cause decentralization in urban areas or do highways simply follow the spatial footprint of metropolitan areas that are decentralizing for other reasons?[15] Baum-Snow (2007) used the 1947 plan for the U.S. National Highway System to instrument the as-built post-1956 U.S. Interstate Highway System, controlling for the joint causality between highway location and urban development and isolating the influence of highways on urban decentralization. Baum-Snow's (2007) results imply that, had the Interstate Highway System not been built, his sample of U.S. central cities would have had population growth of 8 percent from 1950 to 1990, instead of the actual population decline of 17 percent during that time period in his sample of central cities.

The influence of individual highways on urban growth has been confirmed by recent quasi-experimental control-group matching studies. Chalermpong (2004) found that the 17-mile Interstate 105 freeway, opened in south-central Los Angeles County in 1993, increased employment growth in a surrounding one-mile corridor by from two to three times what would have otherwise occurred, using causal inference from a quasi-experimental design that compared census tracts within a mile of the new freeway to a set of control tracts chosen to be as similar as possible to the experimental tracts based on selected characteristics. Funderburg et al. (2010) found that the 51-mile network of toll roads built in Orange County in the 1990s increased employment within a mile of the new highways by a similar magnitude—about two to three times 1990 levels. On net, major transportation infrastructure investments appear to be a powerful determinant of urban development patterns, and particularly employment location.

One argument against using land-use planning as a climate change policy tool is that neighborhood elasticities are small, suggesting small impacts even if those impacts are causal (see, e.g., Brownstone and Golob 2009; Brownstone 2008). Yet the pattern of regional accessibility has a larger association with VMT, and transportation infrastructure appears to be a tool that helps shape the pattern of employment location. This suggests that the planning process should include a prominent role for regional, metropolitan-scale, integrated land use—transportation planning, including the programming, financing, siting, pricing, and operation of transportation infrastructure. Neighborhood planning is still important, but if the policy focus is greenhouse gas emissions, metropolitan-scale planning is even more important.

7. THE NEED FOR A MORE ROBUST PROGRAM EVALUATION TRADITION IN LAND USE–TRAVEL RESEARCH

In California, Senate Bill (SB) 375 requires that metropolitan planning organizations (MPO) document how their transportation plans (which can include combinations of infrastructure investment, travel-demand management, or land use), when combined with the allocation of state-mandated affordable housing shares to local governments, will meet targets for greenhouse gas (GHG) emission reduction in 2020 and 2035. California is a good example of what will likely become the dominant approach in the United States and internationally, requiring that land-use plans be integrated into climate change policy. Because climate change policy inherently requires an assessment of how current actions will affect future emission levels, forecasting models have come to dominate the land use–transportation part of the climate change policy process. Yet that overlooks the important role for program evaluation in supporting policy innovation.

A forecasting approach is inherently top-down. Policymakers work with modelers to anticipate particular policy approaches. Those approaches are then modeled. Astute modelers will work hard to include a broad range of policies in their tools, and most advanced models now have prominent roles for land use, pricing, and travel demand management. The behavioral underpinnings of such models pose a technical challenge, but the point here is not a technical modeling question but instead the concern that relying overly much on forecasting models can dampen policy innovation. What if a locality wanted to establish a pedestrian mall as part of a greenhouse gas emission policy, or offer city-based subsidies for purchasing hybrid vehicles? What if a city reduced the parking supply in a downtown business district, or launched a public relations campaign to encourage commuters to use alternatives to the car? In concept, some of these policies could be modeled, but in general these policies would likely cover too small a geography or would be too non-standard to be well incorporated into current forecasting models. The risk is that local governments might feel constrained to choose from among a menu of policies that are well modeled and supported by higher level planning entities—MPOs or states—reducing innovation and possibly contributing to the sentiment that the policy regime is top-down and not respective of local control. Program evaluation is necessary both to allow a serious assessment of policy innovation and to permit a more open, experimental, bottom-up approach to transportation policy.

The basics of program evaluation are simple, and are adapted from classic research design. The program should be provided to a treatment group, but not provided to a control group. If membership in the treatment and control group is effectively random, then simple comparisons of an outcome variable for both groups before and after the intervention will give a measure of the program's impact on those receiving the "treatment." Mathematically, if the outcome variable is Y, with an average value of $\overline{Y}^{T=1}$ for the treatment group and $\overline{Y}^{T=0}$ for the control group, the impact of the program with random assignment is

$$impact = \left(\overline{Y}_{after}^{T=1} - \overline{Y}_{before}^{T=1} \right) - \left(\overline{Y}_{after}^{T=0} - \overline{Y}_{before}^{T=0} \right).$$

In nonexperimental settings, control groups can be chosen by matching methods to be similar to the treatment group. See, for example, Shadish, Cook, and Campbell (2002); Dehejia and Wahba (1999); and Rosenbaum and Rubin (1983) for discussions For recent applications, see, for example, Boarnet, Anderson, et al. (2005); Funderburg et al. (2010); Holzer, Quigley, and Raphael (2003); or O'Keefe (2004).

The primary barrier to a program evaluation approach to travel behavior has been the inability to collect before-and-after data. Travel data are difficult and expensive to collect. Travel diary surveys—typically conducted about once every ten years owing to the complexity and the cost—have long been the only source of high-quality data on individual travel. Without researchers being able to quickly and inexpensively collect before-and-after travel data, program evaluation was a pipe dream and cross-sectional hypothesis tests (which could then be used to calibrate forecasting models) were essentially all that could be done. The advent of geographic positioning system (GPS) data and the ability to use such data to track travel hold the promise of changing that reality.[17] In concept, travel data can be collected by a host of modern technologies, from providing study subjects with GPS tracking devices to using the location technology available in many cell phones or other hand-held computing devices. This makes it possible to consider tracking travel behavior before and after a broad range of land-use changes or program evaluations, in ways that would not have been feasible before the advent of location-aware technologies.

Several research questions still must be resolved. Capturing and processing GPS or similar data poses computational challenges, discussed in, for example, Miller (2010). Privacy issues are an important concern, but on this point, note that social science researchers are increasingly using geocoded, location-specific data in a broad range of topics not limited to land use and travel behavior, and protocols to safeguard subject confidentiality are required by federal funding agencies and universities. Choosing sample frames from which to obtain experimental and control groups will be conceptually thorny at times. Some land use–transportation projects might clearly affect nearby residents—transit-oriented development (TOD) might be such an example. A program evaluation of a change in transit-proximate land use might choose nearby residents as a treatment group and persons distant from the project but who are otherwise similar as a control group. Yet, because persons travel across the landscape, this simple dichotomization into treatment and control supersets may be too simplistic. What if persons distant from the station area are induced to travel to the station and change their trip-making by the land-use change? More generally, changes in land use can influence persons who both live nearby and who live in more distant locations. Assessing how that informs pre-program decisions about treatment and control groups should be an active area of research.

The point, though, is not to belabor the needed research, but to call for an increased focus on program evaluation that, incrementally, can build up a set of methodological tools and approaches and simultaneously a database on the travel impact of particular programs. Such evaluation traditions are standard in many areas of social policy, including job training, education, and health, and in many ways transportation has lagged in being overly reliant on cross-sectional hypothesis tests and forecasting models.[18] A necessary precursor to unleashing greater innovation in land use–transportation planning is an ability to credibly evaluate the effects of such programs, and that research agenda should be aggressively pursued by scholars in planning and related fields.

8. CONTROVERSIES, RESEARCH GAPS, AND NEXT STEPS

The literature on land use and travel behavior has so far focused almost exclusively on two questions: (1) hypothesis tests regarding the association between the built environment and travel, and related debates about the causality of any such association; and (2) the magnitude of the associations. Data limitations have led to a literature that is almost exclusively cross-sectional, requiring that debates about associations, causality, and even magnitude become debates about measurement and econometric specification. Amid that background, a long line of studies has consistently found associations between land-use variables and travel, and the magnitudes of those associations fall into relatively stable ranges, even allowing for the diversity of econometric methods used. (See, e.g., the studies summarized in Ewing and Cervero 2010; Boarnet and Handy 2010; Spears, Boarnet, and Handy 2010; and Handy,Tal, and Boarnet 2010a, 2010b.)

Given that, what policy advice flows from the land use–travel behavior literature? While the question of causality cannot be definitively answered with only cross-sectional data, the preponderance of the evidence, theory, and common sense all argue that there is a causal relationship (see, e.g., National Research Council 2009 for a similar conclusion). Given the stability of the magnitudes of elasticities summarized in section 7, it is sensible to focus on regional accessibility. Such a focus requires a more prominent role for metropolitan-level research and planning than has typically occurred in the often neighborhood-focused land use and travel literature. Lastly, most everything we know about land use and travel is averages for large (often metropolitan) areas, and exploring variations in those impacts across different locations and types of places is an important task going forward.

Yet the most challenging task in the land use–travel behavior literature will be to move from a relatively narrow focus on land use–travel relationships in isolation to a substantially broader and more contextual research agenda. In that regard, the three research gaps highlighted in the introduction to this chapter are fundamental.

Land use–travel research should expand to consider the many markets, policies, plans, and choices that collectively contribute to urban form and the built environment. While that sounds daunting, the incremental steps needed to make progress on such an agenda have already been explored. Land use–travel researchers should refine location choice models, and consider not only the choice of residential location but also the workplace location.[19] Integrating location and travel, often thought to be the frontier of an expanded research agenda, should only be the beginning. Planners should study the relationship between plans, land-use regulations, development patterns, individual preferences, and the interplay between markets and governance processes more closely. There is much work to be done here, and the insights offered by Levine (2006) should only be a beginning. How do plans influence infrastructure decisions and land-use change? In a world of variegated preferences for living and travel patterns, do different cities or neighborhoods specialize in different built environments, and if so, to what extent do persons move to such cities? On net, how well does a fragmented, decentralized system of land-use governance and transportation planning, programming, and finance both match individual preferences for living patterns and account for effects that are external to private markets? There is a rich literature in local public finance and political science that can lay the groundwork for addressing these questions, and both the theory and the empirics of land use–travel behavior research should work to more aggressively embed that study within the context of the city as an arena where factors that include the political, geographic, social, economic, and design interact.

As a separate, but related, research agenda, planners should build a program evaluation tradition in transportation research. The tools of program evaluation will be necessary both to expand our knowledge and to allow rigorous assessment of policy innovation. The steps needed for a policy evaluation tradition are discussed in section 7.

Lastly, planning scholars should do more to understand the costs and benefits of different land use–transportation policies. A particularly glaring gap is the lack of knowledge about how personal utility varies across different neighborhood types. Absent sound data or clarifying theory, the field has been left with rhetoric. Some persons have argued that departures from low-density living will dramatically reduce the utility of persons who prefer lower densities (e.g., Moore, Staley, and Poole 2010), while others argue that the revealed preference for different (often low-density) living patterns does not reflect an unconstrained market choice (e.g., Levine 2006). Getting better insight into such debates will be fundamental for any welfare analysis or cost-benefit assessment of land use–transportation policies. Planners have studied survey results about housing and land-use preferences in relation to travel choices (e.g., Handy et al. 2008; Levine and Frank 2007; Levine, Inam, and Torng 2005). Such work should be expanded to include insights from decisions that individuals or households make in housing and related location-choice markets.

Planners might combine theoretical insights from early urban economics (e.g., Fujita 1989; Wheaton 1977) with cognitive research on preferences about living patterns. Simple urban land-use models yield conditions under which persons will consume more land as their incomes increase (Fujita 1989; Wheaton 1977), and more recent work has suggested how the provision of place-based amenities can alter that result (Brueckner, Thisse, and Zenou 1999). One approach would be to develop survey methods that could elicit information about how persons trade off land consumption (i.e., residential lot size), transportation access, and place-based amenities to get insights into the structure of land use–travel preferences. Such research might also be combined with revealed preferences about travel choices and the capitalization of access and amenities into property values. The goal would be to support welfare analyses of changes in land use, living patterns, and transportation access and choices.

All of these research objectives will require a broad base of theory, data, and empirical methods. Planning research on this topic should move beyond the relatively single-minded theoretical grounding in economic demand theory to incorporate theories of government, institutions, and individual preference formation. Data should expand not only to include location-based (i.e., GPS) travel information but also data on plans, land-use regulation, infrastructure, and development patterns, in addition to survey or qualitative case study information on government policies, development decisions, and individual attitudes. The empirics of this field will have to expand beyond a relatively tight focus on regression analysis to include a broad range of empirical tools sufficient to illuminate the broader context. All the while, planners should note that this need not imply an agenda to study everything all at once but, instead, a call to link land use–travel research to the context of planning, cities, and the human experience.

Travel has always been the lifeline of cities, intimately bound up with the economic and social fabric of urban life and the lived experience of different places. The narrow focus of the land use–travel behavior literature has served it well in allowing the development of specific methods, approaches, data resources, and empirical results, but continuing that narrow focus would ignore the extent to which travel must be studied in the context of the broader urban experience. Broadening to embrace that context, while retaining an ability to build incrementally on theories and empirical tests, will be the challenge facing the next generation of land use–travel behavior researchers.

Notes

A substantially similar version of this chapter appeared in the *Journal of the American Planning Association* as Boarnet (2011) and is reproduced here with permission.

1. More advanced models iterate back to the land-use allocations (e.g., zonal allocations of residents and jobs) that drive the four-step model. See, e.g., Waddell (2002) or Hunt and Abraham (2003) and Putman (1983) for an early example.

2. Criteria pollutants are the six pollutants regulated by the U.S. Environmental Protection Agency as part of the National Ambient Air Quality Standards (NAAQS). Those six pollutants are ozone, particulate matter, carbon monoxide, nitrogen oxides, sulfur dioxide, and lead. See U.S. EPA, "Six Common Air Pollutants," http://www.epa.gov/oaqps001/urbanair/, accessed May, 2011. The phrase "criteria pollutants" is often used to distinguish the six NAAQS pollutants from greenhouse gas emissions, and I follow that general convention here.

3. The antecedents of the modern focus on land use as a transportation policy tool are, however, arguably as old as the field of urban planning. For a discussion, see Zegras (2010). As with most ideas, the focus on land use as a prescriptive transportation policy tool is not so much wholly new in the past two decades, but it has substantially increased. My interpretation is that the transportation field, in the broad, was more reactively focused on forecasting travel flows before the 1980s and that the increasing emphasis since then on land use as a determinant of travel behavior differs in magnitude, method, and intended policy application from the role of travel models in the first two to three decades of the U.S. Interstate Highway era.

4. Daniel McFadden, with co-authors at times, pioneered a behavioral treatment of travel behavior based on discrete-choice models derived from a random utility framework. See, e.g., Domencich and McFadden (1975), McFadden (2001), and McFadden (2007). McFadden won a Nobel Prize in Economics (technically, the Bank of Sweden Prize in Economic Sciences in Memory of Alfred Nobel) in 2000 for his contributions to the development of discrete-choice econometrics, but the computational complexity of the models and the sparseness of individual travel data—both especially daunting in the late 1960s and 1970s when discrete-choice models were first developed—reduced the use of choice-based, micro-data models in practice. The modern land use–travel behavior literature has moved beyond the four-step model's decidedly nonbehavioral approach by focusing on individual data, but as is discussed in section 4 of this chapter, the typical land use–travel behavior research approach does not incorporate the full range of behavioral choice suggested by, e.g., McFadden's work, nor has the literature agreed on how best to address the full range of behavioral aspects of transportation.

5. Here we use the term "land use" to refer to all measures of the built environment, not just those measures that might strictly relate to zoning and land-use arrangements, but also measures of infrastructure, development patterns, the spatial arrangement of all aspects of the built environment, and design treatments and aesthetics.

6. Entropy indices are calculated as shown below:

$$Entropy = \Sigma_j \frac{\left(P_j x \ln\left(P_j\right)\right)}{\ln(J)}$$

where P_j = the proportion of land in the "jth" land use type, and "J" is the number of land uses.

The dissimilarity index can be calculated as

$$Dissimilarity = \Sigma_j^K \Sigma_i^8 \left[\frac{X_i/_8}{K} \right]$$

where K = number of developed grid cells in the larger geographic area, "j" indexes grid cells, and "i" indexes the eight grid cells that abut (or border) a grid cell when units are divided into a rectangular grid, with $X_i = 1$ if abutting grid cells have differing land uses.

7. As an example, approximately 24 percent of the households in the subsample of the 2000–2001 California Statewide Household Travel Survey analyzed in Heres-Del-Valle and Niemeier (2011) took no car trips on the survey day. Approximately 19 percent of the households in the Southern California Association of Governments 2001–2002 travel diary for the five-county metropolitan Los Angeles area reported no car travel during the diary period, per Boarnet, Houston, et al. (2011).

8. The distinction between structural and reduced-form models is common in economic analysis. Structural models allow statistical estimation of the underlying behavioral parameters, while reduced-form models statistically estimate relationships that do not reflect the underlying economic structure but that, nevertheless, may be useful to analyze particular policy questions. For a discussion, see econometrics textbooks such as Davidson and McKinnon (1993, chap. 18); Johnston and DiNardo (1997, chap. 9); or Gujarati (2003, chap. 19).

9. For a recent discussion of demand theory applied to land use and travel behavior, and a suggested method to use path choice to identify land-use effects, see Crane and Guo (2011).

10. As before, the coefficients are scalars or vectors as appropriate, with coefficient vectors shown in bold.

11. McFadden's (2007) example suggested that votes on transportation projects might be shaped by imitative behavior, with persons being influenced by, for example, a small group of vocal opponents of congestion pricing. Yet, the generalization to travel behavior is straightforward. If most of your acquaintances drive three blocks rather than walk, maybe that makes you more likely to view driving three blocks as a sensible choice?

12. GHG emissions are not directly linked to VMT. In general, GHG emissions measurement would require information about tailpipe emission factors, driving behavior including both VMT and characteristics that influence emissions such as speed and acceleration/deceleration, and vehicle fleet composition. VMT is often currently used as a proxy variable, understanding that while GHG emissions are correlated with VMT, characteristics of the vehicle fleet and driving behavior also influence GHG emissions.

13. Handy (1993) popularized the distinction between neighborhood and regional land-use measures applied to travel behavior.

14. See Naess (2011) for a similar result—namely, that metropolitan-level land-use variables are more important than neighborhood-level variables for car travel, based on data from Copenhagen.

15. For a discussion of this question and the debate on the causal role of highway infrastructure in U.S. urban development patterns, see Boarnet and Haughwout (2000).

16. See, e.g., Card and Krueger (1994) and Dehejia and Wahba (1999, 2002) for general discussions of quasi-experimental control group matching methods.

17. For an overview of the potential for locationally aware technologies and other data sources to transform social scientific analyses of behavior in space, see Miller (2010).

18. The before-and-after treatment-control group studies that have appeared in the land use–transportation literature have more often evaluated the effect of transportation infrastructure changes on land-use patterns. See, e.g., Cervero, Kang, and Shively

(2009); Chalermpong (2004); or Funderburg et al. (2010). Some studies of travel behavior have examined travel changes before and after residential moves (e.g., Krizek 2000, 2003b; Handy, Cao, and Mokhtarian 2005), but such studies are not evaluations of transportation infrastructure changes, as is suggested here, but, rather, studies of travel changes coincident with residential relocations. The program evaluation approach advocated here is better exemplified by the Boarnet, Anderson, et al. (2005) before-and-after study of travel changes associated with the California Safe Routes to School program or the Krizek, Barnes, and Thompson (2009) study of travel changes associated with new bicycle infrastructure.

19. Integrated land use–transportation modelers are already working hard on this question. See, e.g., the discussions of UrbanSim and the PECAS model in, respectively, Waddell (2002) and Hunt and Abraham (2003).

References

Badoe, Daniel, and Eric J. Miller. 2000. "Transportation–Land Use Interaction: Empirical Findings in North America and Their Implications for Modeling." *Transportation Research Part D* 5(4): 235–63.

Baum-Snow, N. 2007. "Did Highways Cause Suburbanization?" *Quarterly Journal of Economics* 122:775–805.

Bento, Antonio M., Maureen L. Cropper, Ahmed Mushfiq Mobarak, and Katja Vinha. 2005. "The Effects of Urban Spatial Structure on Travel Demand in the United States." *Review of Economics and Statistics* 87(3): 466–78.

Bhat, Chandra R., and J. Y. Guo. 2007. "A Comprehensive Analysis of Built Environment Characteristics on Household Residential Choice and Auto Ownership Levels." *Transportation Research Part B* 41(5): 506–26.

Boarnet, Marlon G. 2004. "The Built Environment and Physical Activity: Empirical Methods and Data Resources." Background paper prepared for the Transportation Research Board-Institute of Medicine panel on "Does the Built Environment Influence Physical Activity? Examining the Evidence," Transportation Research Board of the National Academies, Washington, DC. Available online at: http://trb. org/downloads/sr282papers/sr282Boarnet.pdf.

Boarnet, Marlon G. 2011. "A Broader Context for Land Use and Travel Behavior, and a Research Agenda." *Journal of the American Planning Association* 77(3): 197–213.

Boarnet, Marlon G., Craig Anderson, Kristen Day, Tracy McMillan, and Mariela Alfonzo. 2005. "Evaluation of the California Safe Routes to School Legislation: Urban Form Changes and Children's Active Transportation to School." *American Journal of Preventive Medicine* 28(2, Suppl.): 134–40.

Boarnet, Marlon G., and Randall Crane. 2001. *Travel by Design: The Influence of Urban Form on Travel.* New York: Oxford University Press.

Boarnet, Marlon G., Kristen Day, Craig Anderson, Tracy McMillan, and Mariela Alfonzo. 2005. "California's Safe Routes to School Program: Impacts on Walking, Bicycling, and Pedestrian Safety." *Journal of the American Planning Association* 71(3): 301–17.

Boarnet, Marlon, Michael Greenwald, and Tracy McMillan. 2008. "Walking, Urban Design, and Health: Toward a Cost-Benefit Analysis Framework," *Journal of Planning Education and Research* 27:341–58.

Boarnet, Marlon G., and Susan Handy. 2010. *Draft Policy Brief on the Impacts of Residential Density Based on a Review of the Empirical Literature.* Sacramento, CA:

California Air Resources Board. Available at: http://arb.ca.gov/cc/sb375/policies/
policies.htm; accessed August 14, 2010.

Boarnet, Marlon G., and Andrew F. Haughwout. 2000. "Do Highways Matter? Evidence
and Policy Implications of Highways' Influence on Metropolitan Development."
Refereed discussion paper of the Brookings Institution, Center on Urban and
Metropolitan Policy, August, Washington, DC. Available at: http://www.
brookings.edu/~/media/Files/rc/reports/2000/08metropolitanpolicy_boarnet/
boarnet.pdf.

Boarnet, Marlon G., Douglas Houston, Gavin Ferguson, and Steven Spears. 2011.
"Land Use and Vehicle Miles of Travel in the Climate Change Debate: Getting
Smarter than Your Average Bear." In Climate Change and Land Policies, edited by
Yu-Hung Hong and Gregory Ingram, 158–87. Cambridge, MA: Lincoln Institute of
Land Policy.

Boarnet, Marlon, Kennth Joh, Walter Siembab, William Fulton, and Mai Nguyen. 2011.
"Retrofitting the Suburbs to Increase Walking: Evidence from a Land Use–Travel
Study." Urban Studies 48(1): 129–59. [doi: 10.1177/0042098010364859]

Boarnet, Marlon G., and Sharon Sarmiento. 1998. "Can Land Use Policy Really Affect
Travel Behavior?" Urban Studies 35(7): 1155–69.

Brownstone, David. 2008. "Key Relationships Between the Built Environment and VMT."
Draft paper prepared for Transportation Research Board panel on "Relationships
Among Development Patterns, Vehicle Miles Traveled, and Energy," Available at:
http://onlinepubs.trb.org/Onlinepubs/sr/sr298brownstone.pdf.

Brownstone, David, and Thomas Golob. 2009. "The Impact of Residential Density on
Vehicle Usage and Energy Consumption." Journal of Urban Economics 65:91–98.

Brueckner, Jan, Jacques-Francois Thisse, and Yves Zenou. 1999. "Why Is Central Paris
Rich and Downtown Detroit Poor? An Amenity-Based Theory." European Economic
Review 43:91–107.

Calthorpe, Peter. 1993. The Next American Metropolis: Ecology, Community, and the
American Dream. New York: Princeton Architectural Press.

Cameron, A. Colin, and Pravin K. Trivedi. 1998. Regression Analysis of Count Data.
Cambridge, UK: Cambridge University Press.

Cao, Xinyu, Patricia Mokhtarian, and Susan L. Handy. 2009. "Examining the Impacts
of Residential Self-Selection on Travel Behavior: A Focus on Empirical Findings."
Transport Reviews 29(3): 359–95.

Card, D., and A. Krueger. 1994. "Minimum Wages and Employment: A Case Study of the
Fast-Food Industry in New Jersey and Pennsylvania." American Economic Review
84:772–93.

Cervero, Robert. 1986. Suburban Gridlock. New Brunswick, NJ: Center for Urban Policy
Research Press.

Cervero, Robert. 1989. "Jobs-Housing Balance and Regional Mobility." Journal of the
American Planning Association 55:136–50.

Cervero, Robert. 1994. "Transit-Based Housing in California: Evidence on Ridership
Impacts." Transport Policy 1(3): 174–83.

Cervero, Robert, Junhee Kang, and Kevin Shively. 2009. "From Elevated Freeways to
Surface Boulevards: Neighborhood and Housing Price Impacts in San Francisco."
Journal of Urbanism 2(1): 31–50.

Cervero, R., and K. Kockelman. 1997. "Travel Demand and the 3Ds: Density, Diversity
and Design." Transportation Research Part D 2(3): 199–219.

Chalermpong, Saksith. 2004. "Empirical Study of the Economic Spillovers of Interstate
105 in Los Angeles County." Transportation Research Record 1864: 94–102.

Chatman, Daniel G. 2003. "How Density and Mixed Uses at the Workplace Affect Personal Commercial Travel and Commute Mode Choice." *Transportation Research Record* 1831:193–201.

Chatman, Daniel G. 2008. "Deconstructing Development Density: Quality, Quantity and Price Effects on Household Travel." *Transportation Research Part A* 42(7): 1009–31.

Chen, Cynthia, Hongmian Gong, and Robert Paaswell. 2008. "Role of the Built Environment on Mode Choice Decisions: Additional Evidence on the Impact of Density." *Transportation* 35:285–99.

Crane, Randall. 1996a. "Cars and Drivers in the New Suburbs." *Journal of the American Planning Association* 62:51–65.

Crane, Randall. 1996b. "On Form Versus Function: Will the New Urbanism Reduce Traffic, or Increase It?" *Journal of Planning Education and Research* 15:117–26.

Crane, Randall. 2000. "The Influence of Urban Form on Travel: An Interpretive Review." *Journal of Planning Literature* 15(1): 3–23.

Crane, Randall, and Richard Crepeau. 1998. "Does Neighborhood Design Influence Travel? A Behavioral Analysis of Travel Diary and GIS Data." *Transportation Research Part D: Transport and Environment* 3:225–38.

Crane, Randall, and Zhan Guo. 2011. "Toward a Second Generation of Land-Use/Travel Studies: Theoretical and Empirical Foundations." In *Oxford Handbook of Urban Economics and Planning*, edited by Nancy Brooks, Kieran Donaghy, and Gerrit Knaap, 522–44. New York: Oxford University Press.

Davidson, Russell, and James G. MacKinnon. 1993. *Estimation and Inference in Econometrics*. New York: Oxford University Press.

Dehejia, R., and S. Wahba. 1999. "Causal Effects in Nonexperimental Studies: Reevaluating the Evaluation of Training Programs." *Journal of the American Statistical Association* 94:1053–62.

Dehejia, R., and S. Wahba. 2002. "Propensity Score Matching Methods for Nonexperimental Causal Studies." *Review of Economics and Statistics* 84:51–161.

Dill, Jennifer, and Kim Voros. 2007. "Factors Affecting Bicycling Demand: Initial Survey Findings From the Portland Region." *Transportation Research Record* 2031: 9–17.

Domencich, Thomas A., and Daniel McFadden. 1975. *Urban Travel Demand: A Behavioral Analysis*. Amsterdam: North Holland.

Duany, Andres, and Elizabeth Plater-Zyberk. 1991. *Towns and Town-Making Principles*. New York: Rizzoli.

Ewing, Reid, Keith Bartholomew, Steve Winkelman, Jerry Walters, and Don Chen. 2008. *Growing Cooler: The Evidence on Urban Development and Climate Change*. Washington, DC: Urban Land Institute.

Ewing, Reid, and Robert Cervero. 2001. "Travel and the Built Environment: A Synthesis." *Transportation Research Record* 1780:87–114.

Ewing, Reid, and Robert Cervero. 2010. "Travel and the Built Environment: A Meta-Analysis." *Journal of the American Planning Association* 76(3): 265–94.

Ewing, Reid, Padma Haliyur, and G. William Page. 1995. "Getting Around a Traditional City, a Suburban Planned Unit Development, and Everything in Between." *Transportation Research Record* 1466:53–62.

Ewing, Reid, Tom Schmid, Richard Killingsworth, Amy Zlot, and Stephen Raudenbush. 2003. "Relationship Between Urban Sprawl and Physical Activity, Obesity and Morbidity." *American Journal of Health Promotion* 18(1): 47–57.

Fang, Hao Audrey. 2008. "A Discrete–Continuous Model of Households' Vehicle Choice and Usage, with an Application to the Effects of Residential Density." *Transportation Research Part B* 42:736–58.

Frank, Larry, and Gary Pivo. 1995. "Impacts of Mixed Use and Density on Utilization of Three Modes of Travel: Single-Occupant Vehicle, Transit, and Walking." *Transportation Research Record* 1466:44–52.

Frank, L. D., J. F. Sallis, T. L. Conway, J. E. Chapman, B. E. Saelens, and W. Backman. 2006. "Many Pathways to Health: Associations Between Neighborhood Walkability and Active Transportation, Body Mass Index, and Pollutant Emissions." *Journal of the American Planning Association* 72(1): 75–87.

Frank, L. D., T. L. Schmid, J. F. Sallis, J. E. Chapman, and B. E. Saelens. 2005. "Linking Objectively Measured Physical Activity with Objectively Measured Urban Form: Findings from SMARTRAQ." *American Journal of Preventative Medicine* 28(2S2): 117–25.

Friedman, Bruce, Stephen P. Gordon, and John B. Peers. 1994. "Effect of Neotraditional Neighborhood Design on Travel Characteristics." *Transportation Research Record* 1466:63–70.

Fujita, Masahisa. 1989. *Urban Economic Theory: Land Use and City Size.* Cambridge, UK: Cambridge University Press.

Funderburg, Richard, Hilary Nixon, Marlon G. Boarnet, and Gavin Ferguson. 2010. "New Highways and Land Use Change: Results From a Quasi-Experimental Research Design." *Transportation Research Part A* 44:76–98.

Greenwald, Michael J. 2006. "The Relationship Between Land Use and Intrazonal Trip Making Behaviors: Evidence and Implications. *Transportation Research Part D* 11(6): 432–46.

Gujarati, Damodar. 2003. *Basic Econometrics*, 4th ed. New York: McGraw-Hill.

Guo, Zhan, Asha W. Agrawal, and Jennifer Dill 2011. "Are Land-Use Planning and Congestion Pricing Mutually Supportive? Evidence from a Pilot Mileage Fee Program in Portland, OR." *Journal of the American Planning Association* 77(3): 232–50.

Handy, Susan L. 1993. "Regional versus Local Accessibility: Implications for Nonwork Travel." *Transportation Research Record* 1400:58–66.

Handy, Susan L. 2005. "Smart Growth and the Transportation—Land use Connection: What Does the Research Tell Us?" *International Regional Science Review* 28(2): 146–67.

Handy, Susan, Xinyu Cao, and Patricia Mokhtarian. 2005. "Correlation or Causality Between the Built Environment and Travel Behavior? Evidence from Northern California." *Transportation Research Part D: Transport and Environment* 10(6): 427–44.

Handy, Susan L, Xinyu Cao, and Patricia Mokhtarian. 2006. "Self-Selection in the Relationship Between the Built Environment and Walking: Empirical Evidence from Northern California." *Journal of the American Planning Association* 72(1): 55–74.

Handy, Susan, J. Sallis, D. Weber, E. Maibach, and M. Hollander. 2008. "Is Support for Traditionally Designed Communities Growing? Evidence from Two National Surveys." *Journal of the American Planning Association* 74(2): 209–21.

Handy, Susan, Gil Tal, and Marlon G. Boarnet. 2010a. *Draft Policy Brief on the Impacts of Network Connectivity Based on a Review of the Empirical Literature.* Sacramento, CA: California Air Resources Board. Available at: http://arb.ca.gov/cc/sb375/policies/policies.htm; accessed May 2011.

Handy, Susan, Gil Tal, and Marlon G. Boarnet. 2010b. *Draft Policy Brief on the Impacts of Regional Accessibility Based on a Review of the Empirical Literature.* Sacramento, CA: California Air Resources Board. Available at: http://arb.ca.gov/cc/sb375/policies/policies.htm; accessed May 2011.

Hanson, Susan, and Perry Hanson. 1981. "The Travel-Activity Patterns of Urban Residents: Dimensions and Relationships to Sociodemographic Characteristics." *Economic Geography* 57(4): 332–47.

Heath, G. W., R. C. Brownson, J. Kruger, R. Miles, K. E. Powell, and L.T. Ramsey. 2006. "The Effectiveness of Urban Design and Land Use and Transport Policies and Practies to Increase Physical Activity: A Systematic Review." *Journal of Physical Activity and Health* (3, 1 Suppl.): S55–S76.

Henderson, K. A., and M. D. Bialeschki. 2005. "Leisure and Active Lifestyles: Research Reflections." *Leisure Sciences* 27(5): 355–65.

Heres-Del-Valle, David, and Deb Niemeier. 2011. "CO_2 Emissions: Are Land Use Changes Enough for California to Reduce VMT? Specification of a Two-Part Model with Instrumental Variables." *Transportation Research Part B* 45(1): 150–61.

Hess, Paul Mitchell, Anne Vernez Moudon, and Miles G. Logsdon. 2001. "Measuring Land Use Patterns for Transportation Research." *Transportation Research Record* 1780: 17–24.

Holzer, Harry J., John M. Quigley, and Steven Raphael. 2003. "Public Transit and the Spatial Distribution of Minority Employment: Evidence from a Natural Experiment." *Journal of Policy Analysis and Management* 22(3): 415–41.

Hunt, J. D., and J. E. Abraham. 2003. "Design and Application of the PECAS Land Use Modeling System." Working paper, University of Calgary. Available at: http://people.ucalgary.ca/~jabraham/Papers/pecas/8094.pdf; accessed May 23, 2011.

Joh, Kenneth, Marlon G. Boarnet, Mai Nguyen, William Fulton, Walter Siembab, and Susan Weaver. 2009. "Accessibility, Travel Behavior, and New Urbanism: Case Study of Mixed-Use Centers and Auto-Oriented Corridors in the South Bay Region of Los Angeles, California." *Transportation Research Record* 2082: 81–89.

Johnston, Jack, and John DiNardo. 1997. *Econometric Methods*, 4th ed. New York: McGraw-Hill.

Johnston, Robert A. 2004. "The Urban Transportation Planning Process." In *The Geography of Urban Transportation*, 3rd. ed., edited by Susan Hanson and Genevieve Giuliano, 115–40. New York: Guilford.

Kain, John F., and Gary R. Fauth. 1976. "The Effects of Urban Structure on Household Auto Ownership Decisions and Journey to Work Mode Choice." Research Report R76–1, Department of City and Regional Planning, Harvard University, Cambridge, MA.

Kelbaugh, Douglas S., ed. 1989. *The Pedestrian Pocket Book: A New Suburban Design Strategy*. New York: Princeton Architectural Press.

Khattak, Asad J., and Daniel Rodriguez. 2005. "Travel Behavior in Neo-Traditional Neighborhood Developments: A Case Study in USA." *Transportation Research Part A* 39(6): 481–500.

Kockelman, Kara M. 1997. "Travel Behavior as a Function of Accessibility, Land Use Mixing, and Land Use Balance: Evidence From the San Francisco Bay Area." *Transportation Research Record* 1607:116–25.

Krizek, Kevin. 2000. "Pretest-Posttest Strategy for Researching Neighborhood-Scale Urban Form and Travel Behavior." *Transportation Research Record* 1722:48–55.

Krizek, Kevin J. 2003a. "Operationalizing Neighborhood Accessibility for Land Use-Travel Behavior Research and Regional Modeling." *Journal of Planning Education and Research* 22(3): 270–87.

Krizek, Kevin J. 2003b. "Residential Relocation and Changes in Urban Travel: Does Neighborhood Scale Urban Form Matter?" *Journal of the American Planning Association* 69(3): 265–81.

Krizek, Kevin J., Gary Barnes, and Kristin Thompson. 2009. "Analyzing the Effect of Bicycle Facilities on Commute Mode Share over Time." *Journal of Urban Planning and Development* 135(2): 66–73.

Krizek, Kevin J., and Pamela Jo Johnson. 2006. "Proximity to Trails and Retail: Effects on Urban Cycling and Walking." *Journal of the American Planning Association* 72(1): 33–42.

Levine, J. 2006. *Zoned Out: Regulation, Markets, and Choices in Transportation and Metropolitan Land Use*. Washington, DC: RFF Press.

Levine, Jonathan, and Lawrence Frank. 2007. "Transportation and Land-Use Preferences and Residents' Neighborhood Choices: The Sufficiency of Compact Development on the Atlanta Region." *Transportation* 34(2): 255–74.

Levine, Jonathan, Aseem Inam, and Gwo-Wei Torng. 2005. "A Choice-Based Rationale for Land-Use and Transportation Alternatives: Evidence from Boston and Atlanta." *Journal of Planning Education and Research* 24(3): 317–30.

McFadden, Daniel. 2001. "Disaggregate Behavioral Travel Demand's RUM Side: A 30-Year Retrospective." In *Travel Behavior Research: The Leading Edge*, edited by David Hensher, 17–64. Oxford: Elsevier.

McFadden, Daniel. 2007. "The Behavioral Science of Transportation." *Transport Policy* 14: 269–74.

Miller, Harvey J. 2010. "The Data Avalanche is Here. Shouldn't We Be Digging?" *Journal of Regional Science* 50(1): 181–201.

Moore, Adrian T., Samuel R. Staley, and Robert W. Poole. 2010. "The Role of VMT Reduction in Meeting Climate Change Policy Goals." *Transportation Research Part A:* 44(8): 565–74. [doi:10.1016/j.tra.2010.03.012]

Moulton, Brent R. 1990. "An Illustration of a Pitfall in Estimating the Effects of Aggregate Variables on Micro Unit." *Review of Economics and Statistics* 72(2): 334–38.

Naess, Petter. 2011. "New Urbanism" or Metropolitan-Level Concentration: A Comparison of the Influences of Metropolitan-Level and Neighborhood-Level Urban Form Characteristics on Travel Behavior." *Journal of Transport and Land Use* 4(1): 25–44.

National Research Council. 2009. *Driving and the Built Environment: The Effects of Compact Development on Motorized Travel, Energy Use, and CO2 Emissions*. Committee on Relationships Among Development Patterns, Vehicle Miles Traveled, and Energy Consumption. Washington, DC: National Academies Press.

O'Keefe, S. 2004. "Job Creation in California's Enterprise Zones: A Comparison Using a Propensity Score Matching Model." *Journal of Urban Economics* 55:131–50.

Ortuzar, Juan de Dios, and Luis G. Willumsen. 2001. *Modelling Transport*, 3rd ed. Chichester, UK: John Wiley.

"Portland and 'Elite Cities': The New Model." 2010. *The Economist,* April 15. Available at: http://www.economist.com/node/15911324; accessed Jun 22, 2011.

Putman, Stephen. 1983. *Integrated Urban Models: Policy Analysis of Transportation and Land Use*. London: Pion.

Rodier, Caroline. 2009. "A Review of the International Modeling Literature: Transit, Land Use, and Auto Pricing Strategies to Reduce Vehicle Miles Traveled and Greenhouse Gas Emissions." Paper presented atannual meeting of the Transportation Research Board, January, Washington, DC.

Rodríguez, D., A. J. Khattak, and K. R. Evenson. 2006. "Can New Urbanism Encourage Physical Activity? Comparing a New Urbanist Neighborhood with Conventional Suburbs." *Journal of the American Planning Association* 72(1): 43–56.

Rose, Mark H. 1990. *Interstate: Express Highway Politics, 1939–1989*. Knoxville: University of Tennessee Press.

Rosenbaum, P., and D. Rubin. 1983. "The Central Role of the Propensity Score in Observational Studies for Causal Effects." *Biometrika* 70:41–55.

Shadish, W. R., T. D. Cook, and D. T. Campbell. 2002. *Experimental and Quasi-Experimental Designs for Generalized Causal Inference.* Boston: Houghton Mifflin.

Small, Kenneth A. 1992. *Urban Transportation Economics.* Chur, Switzerland: Harwood.

Small, Kenneth A., and Erik T. Verhoef. 2007. *The Economics of Urban Transportation.* London and New York: Routledge.

Spears, Steven, Marlon G. Boarnet, and Susan Handy. 2010. *Draft Policy Brief on the Impacts of Land Use Mix Based on a Review of the Empirical Literature.* Sacramento, CA: California Air Resources Board. Available at: http://arb.ca.gov/cc/sb375/policies/policies.htm; accessed September 2010.

U.S. Department of Transportation, n.d. Highway history. Available at: http://www.fhwa.dot.gov/infrastructure/50interstate.cfm; accessed July 24, 2010.

Vickerman, Roger W. 1972. "The Demand for Non-Work Travel." *Journal of Transport Economics and Policy* 6(2): 176–210.

Waddell, P. 2002. "UrbanSim: Modeling Urban Development for Land Use, Transportation and Environmental Planning." *Journal of the American Planning Association* 68(3): 297–314.

Wheaton, William C. 1977. "Residential Decentralization, Land Rents, and the Benefits of Urban Transportation Investment." *American Economic Review* 67(2): 138–43.

Winkelman, Steve, and Allison Bishins. 2010. "Planning for Economic and Environmental Resilience." *Transportation Research Part A* 44(8): 575–86. [doi:10.1016/j.tra.2010.03.011]

Zegras, P. Christopher. 2004. "Influence of Land Use on Travel Behavior in Santiago, Chile." *Transportation Research Record* 1898:175–82.

Zegras, P. Christopher. 2010. "The Built Environment and Motor Vehicle Ownership & Use: Evidence from Santiago de Chile." *Urban Studies* 47 (8): 1793–817. [doi: 10.1177/0042098009356125]

PART IV

WHO PLANS, HOW
WELL, AND HOW
CAN WE TELL?

A. PLANNING AGENTS

CHAPTER 32

THE CIVICS OF URBAN PLANNING

CARMEN SIRIANNI AND JENNIFER GIROURD

1. INTRODUCTION

THE city in nineteenth-century America, especially after the Jacksonian revolution in the 1830s, was a cauldron of active and often quite contentious citizen engagement through a broad range of political clubs, neighborhood groups, and other civic associations. Typically dramatized in and over public space, civic action nonetheless tended to have little systematic control of the overall dynamics of growth, transportation, housing, and related issues (Ryan 1998; Bridges 1984; Einhorn 2001). Municipal reformers in the late nineteenth century, and especially during the Progressive Era (1890–1920), attempted to limit the corruption and inefficiency of local party machines by substituting professional planning and administration in ways that sidelined local citizen input. A large, representative city council, it was believed, could secure sufficient democratic legitimacy (Fox 1977; Teaford 1984; Peterson 2003); the burgeoning initiative process (in 500 cities by 1920) could provide a direct democratic voice city wide (Goebel 2002); and urban settlements and the social centers movement could provide for broad public deliberation, education, and inclusion (Mattson 1998; Lissak 1989). The "urban renewal" programs beginning after WWII were largely in the hands of redevelopment commissions that had very limited citizen input, especially among poor, working-class, and minority communities—the very communities that were often razed in the quest for more efficient use of downtown commercial space and new highway systems, not to mention what became less euphemistically termed "Negro removal." The

result was not just a net loss of low-income housing and increased racial segregation but also the decimation of once vibrant communities rich in civic relationships and social capital (Fullilove 2004; Jacobs 1961; Gans 1962).

From the 1960s onwards, however, the "civics" of urban planning has become
enriched through new community organizing models, community development
corporations, citywide systems of neighborhood representation, and various participatory tools (e.g., community visioning, participatory geographic information
systems [GIS]) that enable citizens to work deliberatively and collaboratively with
professional planners, even as they challenge narrow professional models. In this
sense, the civics is not limited to the third sector or to civil society, but draws in
various institutions (public agencies; nonprofits; business, trade, and professional
associations; universities) to planning and implementation (Fishman 2000), often
under the rubric of coproduction. In the process, the participatory democracy
of the 1960s has been revised and transformed in ways that make its core ideals more pragmatic and sustainable (Sirianni and Friedland 2001). Civic innovation, to be sure, occurs unevenly in the context where some urban regimes and
growth machines have far more leverage than others in resisting participation,
inclusion, and independent citizen power (DeLeon 1992; Logan and Molotch 2007;
Stone 1993, 2006; Weir 1999; Purcell 2000); core cities vary in capacity to develop
effective state legislative coalitions with surrounding suburbs (Weir, Wolman, and
Swanstrom 2005); and changes in federal policy often leave poorer communities
"swimming against the tide" (O'Connor 1999). Thus, the new civics of planning,
while responding creatively to changes in federal policy and to the increasing complexity of public problems (Innes and Booher 2010; Booher 2008), and while an
essential component of effective long-term strategies (Sirianni 2009), has hardly
resolved the challenges posed by urban/suburban inequality (Oliver 2001, 2010;
Macedo et al. 2005) and sustainable development (Portney 2003; Mazmanian and
Kraft 1999).

In this chapter, we first sketch the major models that emerged in the United
States at various points over the past half-century, tracking the shifts from the
origins of citizen participation in planning, problems of control and degree of decision-making power, and professionalization and institutionalization, to the more
current potential and challenge of coordination across a range of stakeholders and
associations. Innovation in many other countries, while proceeding within diverse
national urban policy regimes, local political cultures, and reform timetables,
shares much with U.S. models in terms of the underlying pressures to engage publics actively, as well as in emerging best practices, which tend to be shared across
international boundaries (Briggs 2008; Avritzer 2009; Baiocchi 2005; Baiocchi,
Heller, and Silva 2008). In the second part of the chapter, we examine some of the
core tools and practices, as well as persistent challenges in developing appropriately
robust systems for engaging active publics in urban planning. As will become evident in this discussion, the civics of urban planning remains diverse, combining
broad streams of contestation and collaboration and many action repertoires and
collaborative governance tools.

THE CIVICS OF URBAN PLANNING   671

2. Civic Innovation in Urban Planning since the 1960s

During the 1960s, claims for greater participation in public life exploded across many sectors as civil rights, student, women's, and environmental movements generated vocabularies and practices of engagement, as well as networks of activists, that spilled over into urban politics and planning (Mollenkopf 1983; Sirianni and Friedland 2001; Frost 2001; Polletta 2002). Some of the major federal urban programs were designed with at least tacit understanding that citizens would make further claims for voice, and planners and other officials adjusted to the reality on the ground when it became clear that the legitimacy of plans—and thus the likelihood of their implementation — was contingent on some degree of meaningful public input.

2.1 Community Action and Model Cities

In 1964, as part of his war on poverty, President Lyndon Johnson launched the Community Action Program (CAP), which was to be developed and administered at the local level with the "maximum feasible participation" of its residents. This emphasis on participation, which set a precedent for much subsequent legislation, derived from two key sources. First, despite the lack of direct legislative input by civil rights and poor people's organizations for mandated participation, imposing new programs on the poor without their having a say in them was clearly no longer feasible by the mid-1960s. The civil rights movement had simply progressed too far for the president's advisers to imagine that they could fashion a new form of welfare colonialism or white paternalism for the poor. Whatever the legislative wording or administrative policy, citizen participation would have appeared on the agenda in any war on poverty or any inner-city development initiative, and conflict over its meanings would have been inevitable (Marris and Rein 1982; Peterson and Greenstone 1977).

Second, the president and his advisers fully recognized that the language of participation and community resonated with deep American traditions of self-help, local initiative, and Jeffersonian democracy. The language and strategy of community action were designed to fit a set of political opportunities and constraints. An appeal to community could legitimate action in terms that did not have to confront racial divisions directly. Self-help contrasted favorably with welfare. Community Action could appear boldly imaginative, yet without either massive budget outlays or an ambitious full-employment strategy—neither likely from Congress—and could build a constituency for further efforts. Community Action could also be used to move around the entrenched urban power structure and racialized welfare agencies to open opportunities for minorities, even as its stated mission of forging new forms of collaboration among the poor, city officials, and private social welfare agencies resonated with the norms of American pluralism (Kramer 1969; Marris and Rein 1982; Quadagno 1994).

Established in cities across the country, Community Action agencies generated a good deal of controversy because many did take on entrenched power structures as they tried to claim a seat at the pluralist table, and because they had to develop legitimate mechanisms of fair representation within the community itself—for example, by an individual's poverty status or by local organizations' claims to represent poor and ethnic minorities (Greenstone and Peterson 1973). Furthermore, these agencies faced a whole host of challenges associated with building new administrative and program capacities, including ones designed to integrate the planning of community health, human services, and early education with economic and physical development. These liabilities of newness, manifest especially under tight pressure to show success at the federal level, helped lead to the demise of the Community Action Program, as Head Start, neighborhood health centers, and Legal Services were given separate bureaucratic homes by the early 1970s (Sirianni and Friedland 2001), although nearly 950 community action agencies covering 96 percent of U.S. counties have managed to maintain and even expand their organizational infrastructure and state and national networks through federal community service block grants created in 1981 and other sources of funding (Nemon 2007).

Federal support for Community Action, and a variety of other programs that grew around it, promoted the development of new forms of social capital. For all its problems and controversy, Community Action turned out to be a vast incubator for involving new neighborhood actors, teaching participatory skills, and spurring local self-help. It stimulated local association building, forged broader networks, and laid the foundations for new forms of collaboration between local groups, city departments, and nonprofit social service agencies. Thousands of affiliated civic organizations grew up around the community action agencies nationwide. Leadership training was an implicit and sometimes an explicit goal, and tens of thousands of new community leaders emerged. Neighborhood women, who traditionally performed much of the everyday community caretaking, gained relatively equal access to board positions allocated to the community and filled a disproportionate number of staff positions in neighborhood centers. Much of this effort took place more slowly and less visibly than the political drama surrounding Community Action, and often followed upon initial stages of conflict and confrontation. Viewed from the level of city politics in the late 1960s, Community Action may often have appeared to have been captured by the dynamics of political and racial struggle. At the grassroots level, however, it was almost always much more, and poor people demonstrated time and again that they were primarily interested in participating pragmatically to solve problems in their communities and families (Sirianni and Friedland 2001; Naples 1998; Zigler and Muenchow 1992; Marshall 1971).

The shift away from Community Action had actually begun earlier, when President Johnson announced his Model Cities program in 1966 for the newly created Department of Housing and Urban Development (HUD). But a mandate for "widespread citizen participation" remained, and despite intentions of reigning participation into city agency frameworks, officials yielded to well-organized local pressure and accommodated or even encouraged engagement through preexisting community action agencies. While HUD remained ambivalent about how much participation there should be, local administrators improvised in response to citizen demands for "partnership" and their own commonsense concerns about outcomes that could legitimate programs in citizens' eyes. Local administrators also improvised to develop means of conflict resolution among the many contending claims of community groups. And HUD's chief adviser on citizen participation, Sherry Arnstein (1969) strongly criticized programs where participation remained ritualistic and manipulative and was able to get approval for advisory guidelines and best practices for all Model Cities, as well as a technical assistance fund to build citizen capacities. Municipal agencies confronted well-organized and militant community leadership in perhaps 20 to 30 percent of cities. As one review of programs in fourteen states concluded, Model Cities "*has* mobilized an extraordinary degree of resident participation in the formation and execution of plans to attack the deep-seated problems of slum neighborhoods—despite the difficulties of organizing participation in the initial year" (Sundquist 1969, 118; see also Brown and Frieden 1976; Kaplan 1970).

Model Cities reached beyond social service agencies to a broad range of municipal services and for the first time established extensive participation in land-use planning, such as housing demolition and construction, transportation routes and freeway construction, industrial site preparation, school building, and rezoning. Model Cities took up issues of community and economic development and brought homeowners into the process. While it encouraged the participation of the poor, hence ensuring some confrontation with existing agencies, it required conflict resolution on a Model Cities plan as a condition for continued support. Model Cities also laid the basis for a set of strategic choices that would prove significant in the coming years. In cities where citizens deeply distrusted municipal authorities, their representatives on the City Demonstration Administration—sometimes known as the Community Development Agency—often refused to give their federal dollars to existing local agencies and instead set up independent community development corporations. Citizens also began to conclude that they needed formal powers decentralized to neighborhood associations so that they could have a legitimate neighborhood government with normal political processes of representation, and so that they could take up a full range of issues more systematically, "rather than dancing a new jig for each different federal program tune" (Aleshire 1972, 438). Local citizens and staff, in effect, voted with their feet as they "soon discovered that careful exploration of the labyrinths of the federal government was a poor investment of their time," and that other strategies for community development and neighborhood governance were available to them (Brown and Frieden 1976, 484; see also Haar 1975).

2.2 Community Development Corporations

The neighborhood and tenants rights movements of the 1970s spurred the growth of local community development corporations (CDCs), assisted, to be sure, by another federal program—the Special Impact Program of the 1966 revision to the Economic Opportunity Act—and especially with critical investments by the Ford Foundation (Peirce and Steinbach 1987; Rohe 2009). While the Reagan administration (1981–88) massively cut back federal budgets for housing and decimated the administrative capacities of HUD, the "community development field" (Ferguson and Stoutland 1999) had by then ripened to the point where an institutional infrastructure (Local Initiatives Support Corporation, Enterprise Foundation, Development Training Institute, Centers for Community Change, state- and city-wide associations of CDCs, community development financial institutions, local voluntary and nonprofit groups) and new policy tools (Low-Income Housing Tax Credits, Community Reinvestment Act) would catalyze further growth to approximately 2,000 CDCs by 1990, 3,600 by 1998, and some 4,600 by 2005 (National Congress for Community and Economic Development [NCCED] 2005). These local nonprofit development corporations and their various intermediaries and partners would henceforth become a more or less permanent part of the civic landscape of urban planning in many cities.

While many CDCs still arise from the efforts of local community groups, institutionalization and diversification of CDC activities are evident over time (Stoutland 1999). Housing remains the core activity, but a growing percentage of CDCs have become active in commercial development, and a good number are involved in providing venture capital, loans, and technical support for local entrepreneurial activity. Some are part of networks collaborating in workforce development. Others have created industrial parks composed of dozens of businesses and retail stores, sometimes employing hundreds of or even several thousands of people. Still others are involved in developing and coordinating family services, such as day-care cooperatives that provide licensing, training, and networking for in-home providers and link these to home renovation programs so that providers can improve their facilities and meet all code requirements for safety. In some cities, CDCs mobilize thousands of volunteers for urban reforestation, landscaping, weatherization, and home repair projects, and more are becoming partners in environmental health and justice, community agriculture, and climate action partnerships (Shutkin 2000; Lee 2005; Deitrick and Ellis 2004; Corburn 2009; Sirianni and Sofer 2011).

An increasing number of community development projects have incorporated into their work the asset-based community development approach (Kretzmann and McKnight 1993). This approach distills five key sets of assets that even the poorest communities possess, and that can be systematically mapped and mobilized in new ways to support an internally focused, relationship-driven process of community development. These include (1) the capacities of individuals, (2) the work of associations, (3) the resources (not current outputs) of local institutions public, private, and nonprofit, (4) land as physical space, and (5) monetary values and exchanges, including the purchasing power and preferences of local residents. This approach also derives from a trenchant critique of a deficit model of communities and professional model of intervention, which saw residents primarily as clients with deficiencies in need of outside professional remedy and often convinced local leaders to denigrate their own community and broker its defects for grants-in-aid, rather than recognize and build upon its strengths and capacities to act as citizens. A substantial number of community foundations, state extension services, local United Ways, settlement houses, healthy community coalitions, environmental justice partnerships, and national foundations funding health and human service reforms have undergone training and have incorporated elements of the asset-based approach into their work (Sirianni 2009; Sirianni and Friedland 2001; Green, Moore, and O'Brien 2006; Medoff and Sklar 1994).

While the trend has clearly been toward professionalization, a good number of CDCs engage in some form of community organizing and advocacy or affiliate with local grassroots groups that mobilize neighbors in a range of self-help and community building activities (Robinson 1996; Gittell and Vidal 1998; Sirianni and Friedland 2001; NCCED 2005). Local political culture and urban regime type, as well as competition with other forms of neighborhood representation, such as faith-based community organizing and neighborhood associations (Weir 1999; Orr 2007; Warren 2001; Wood 2002; Goetz and Sidney 1994; Marwell 2007; Sirianni 2009), shape the challenges that professional planners must confront when deciding which civic actors to admit to the planning table and on what terms. Those critics (e.g., Stoecker 1997) who view CDCs as disorganizing their communities by accommodating themselves to capital markets, dampening confrontational organizing, and encouraging victim blaming have not been able to offer viable alternative models for sustaining this broad range of activities of interest to community actors and planners alike (Bratt 1997; Keating 1997; Bratt and Rohe 2004). Nor indeed have such radical critics provided viable models for sustaining confrontational mobilizing as a genuine alternative for empowering communities. Much more certainly can be done to enhance the civic capacities of CDCs and other neighborhood-based nonprofits (Smith 2010; Smith and Lipsky 1993) and to strengthen various other policy tools for addressing urban poverty and democratizing urban and regional planning (Weir, Wolman, and Swanstrom 2005). But CDCs will remain central components of any viable strategy.

2.3 Citywide Neighborhood Association Systems

Model Cities and Community Action programs, as noted above, spurred the further development of neighborhood associations, existing in some cities for decades. These associations became more or less permanent fixtures in the landscape of planning, often demanding a seat at the table to review (and sometimes veto) specific projects, formulate neighborhood-wide plans, and even become part of citywide systems of neighborhood representation. Citywide systems have taken a variety of forms but have a number of traits in common, as the classic study, *The Rebirth of Urban Democracy* by Berry, Portney, and Thomson (1993) analyzed. They cover all neighborhoods, not simply poor or minority neighborhoods targeted for community development or other funding. Strictly nonpartisan by ordinance, the neighborhood associations cannot directly mobilize resources or dedicate their media to partisan campaigns for city council or mayor. They have extensive two-way information channels with city hall and multiple points to exercise voice, though they tend to be most effective on local land-use issues and least effective on citywide issues such as metropolitan transit, downtown development, and school reform. They have staff paid by the city, though many also raise other funds as incorporated nonprofits.

Perhaps most important, these neighborhood participation systems accommodate, complement, and even encourage a wide range of other forms of independent citizen organizing and self-help. Indeed, the existence of multiple organizational forms increased the vitality of participation in the seventy participatory projects in the Berry (1993) study, and other citywide neighborhood association and planning designs building upon them, such as Seattle (Diers 2004; Sirianni 2007), have made partnerships among an array of types of local neighborhood-based groups essential to the official neighborhood planning process, which is part of the comprehensive plan. Independent groups initiate action more often, but the neighborhood systems and district councils play a strong role in the outcome (Berry, Portney, and Thomson 1993). They work with the Sierra Club, Audubon Society, and other local environmental groups, such as watershed associations; with senior and youth organizations, CDCs, local Leagues of Women Voters and United Ways; and with many informal self-help efforts. They have established community mediation projects, "good neighbor plans," crime watches, sustainability and open space projects, watershed restoration, and climate action (Sirianni and Sofer 2011). Despite the fact that there have been conflicts among some types of civic organizations, such as neighborhood associations and CDCs (Goetz and Sidney 1994), citywide systems have had a clear impact on trust building within neighborhoods and with government officials and have helped to develop a sense of community at every income level. Importantly, studies have shown that they neither coopt nor supplant various independent forms of citizen action (Berry, Portnoy, and Thomson 1993).

All of these developments represent substantial learning and refinement beyond the initial designs implemented in the mid-1970s, and they have enhanced governance capacities in these cities (Sirianni 2009; Johnson 2002; Ozawa 2004; Kathi and Cooper 2005; Musso et al. 2006; Punter 2003; Thomas 1986). Well-structured citywide systems show significantly greater impacts of face-to-face democracy on *individual* citizen learning, measured by indices of political information, sense of political efficacy, and broad community perspectives beyond narrow neighborhood boundaries, which the Tufts University team (Berry, Portnoy, and Thomson 1993) used to compare these cities to comparable communities lacking citywide systems. And learning was especially noteworthy for low-income groups. Indeed, in three core study cities of Portland, St. Paul, and Dayton, the participation system produced a responsiveness bias in their favor. This by no means eliminates the challenges of generating greater equity and reducing participation biases within official systems of neighborhood representation, but cities have innovated in various ways to help spur greater inclusiveness of representation and fairer processes of deliberation (Fung 2004; Sirianni 2009).

3. Tools and Practices of Citizen Engagement in Urban Planning

In this section, we cluster some of the more important tools and practices for engaging city residents and civic associations collaboratively with professionals in urban planning systems. Needless to say, there exists a variety of practices that are more ritualistic than substantive, or that remain stuck in earlier decades when just getting open public hearings and access to information were big achievements. There is no one ideal model, no universally recognized set of best practices, no comprehensive toolbox. None of the tools and practices we review are without their challenges, and thus the question of organizational and policy learning at the city level and across organizational fields remains critical (Sirianni and Friedland 2001; Light 1998), as well as the choice of appropriate mixes and the use of political judgment within specific political and bureaucratic cultures and urban regimes (Sirianni 2009). Some key challenges that arise in new forms of civic planning involve issues of trust, inclusivity, norms of communication, and reciprocal accountability. Innovations in this field include participatory processes such as deliberative forums and relational organizing, as well as drawing upon technical tools such as GIS mapping to help address collaboration across different actors (governmental, professional, and local) with diverse and often conflicting preferences and types of knowledge.

3.1 Generating Trust Deliberatively and Relationally

Planning, of course, is a highly complex process with innumerable points of possible contention based on divergent interests, unequal power, asymmetrical distribution of costs and benefits, and the clash of professional and local perspectives and cultures. Citizens often mobilize against planning agencies, comprehensive plans, and specific projects, especially when they do not have a seat at the table or see their concerns adequately addressed, and some will mobilize contentiously even when reasonable efforts have been made to include them in the process. Given the complexity of planning, the diversity of interests and publics, and the traditions of independent citizen organizing, this is inevitable. The challenge is to engender sufficient levels of trust so that citizens can work collaboratively with professional planners to generate high-quality, workable plans with broad democratic legitimacy and capacity for implementation—indeed, when appropriate, to engage citizens in coproduction as an essential feature of implementation (Sirianni 2009; Boyte 2005; Alford 2009).

There are at least two general and potentially complementary ways of generating democratic trust in planning: public deliberation and relational organizing, broadly conceived. Deliberative democracy now has a solid foundation in political theory, with appropriate qualifiers and contingencies built into the theory to allow for considerable variation, self-correction, and learning (Fung 2004; Gutmann and Thompson 2004; Gastil and Levine 2005; Jacobs, Cook and Delli Carpini 2009). Public deliberation can take a variety of forms in urban planning. One increasingly common form is community visioning, which is generally an open and inclusive process of ordinary citizens and/or organized stakeholders who meet periodically over a period of months to forge a common vision of the future that can guide and motivate specific initiatives, some of which might be taken by civic, nonprofit, and business actors, and others by government, though often in partnerships of one form or another (Moore, Longo, and Palmer 1999; Ames 1998; National Civic League 2000). Study circles, another growing form of citizen dialogue, are small, diverse groups of eight to twelve participants each that meet over a period of weeks or months to deliberate about some critical public issue (crime, race, growth, budgets). In community-wide study circle designs, hundreds or even several thousand citizens might become engaged through circles (Walsh 2007; Leighninger 2006). Planning charrettes among lay citizens (including youth) and professional planners (Sagedy and Johnson 2004; Sirianni and Schor 2009), brainstorming (Sanoff 2000), and issue forums (housing, transportation) within an integrative neighborhood planning design (Sirianni 2007) are still other forms of open public deliberation that have been utilized to share knowledge, discuss options and alternative scenarios, and generate trust among those who may come to the table with diverse interests and perspectives. Deliberation, in short, has substantial capacity to generate trust, even when it also challenges established power and authority (Warren 1999), whether of elected officials, city planning agencies, or downtown businesses and growth coalitions.

While such forms of public deliberation are critical to opening up the planning process beyond professional planners and a narrow group of favored stakeholders, they are typically not enough to generate sufficient trust on specific details, complex interaction of parts, or difficult trade-offs, nor are they sufficient over the longer run, as new information becomes available, unforeseen obstacles and opportunities arise, and implementation drags out long beyond the deliberative forums, no matter how well designed. Relational organizing thus becomes a critical component. One approach, pursued by independent faith-based organizing groups (Industrial Areas Foundation, Gamaliel Foundation, and PICO) that organize for power but have evolved beyond the original Alinsky tradition, employs a well-structured set of practices, such as one-on-one campaigns and house meetings, to build relationships within and across core member congregations and other organizations (unions, CDCs, community health centers), and then extends these methods—sometimes in conjunction with contestation—into collaborative efforts with local businesses, banks, school systems, housing and health agencies, and other potential partners (Warren 2001; Wood 2002; Shirley 1997; Osterman 2002).

Relational organizing can also be sanctioned by city agencies working with neighborhood associations and various other civic organizations, and even designed into the heart of official planning processes. In Seattle, for instance, the role of neighborhood district coordinators in the department of neighborhoods is to facilitate relationship building within and across local neighborhood councils, business district associations, and a panoply of other civic, community development, and environmental organizations—themselves often pursuing relational and asset-based organizing of one sort or another. During neighborhood planning, which began in 1994 as part of the comprehensive plan process, the role of the project managers within the neighborhood planning office, and then neighborhood development managers during the initial phases of implementation, was based on a relational mode of trust building (Sirianni 2007, 2009). In the participatory budgeting innovations in Porto Alegre in Brazil (Baiocchi 2005; Avritzer 2009), now extended across hundreds of cities and internationally, deliberative forums often cannot function well without side conversations and other trust-building strategies by local activists and public officials alike. The communicative turn in planning theory (Forester 1989, 1999; Innes 1995; Innes and Booher 2010) increasingly recognizes that professional planners have a normative as well as practical responsibility to help generate optimal degrees of comprehensibility, sincerity, legitimacy, and truth through communicative practice (Habermas 1984) if complex planning and public problem solving with citizens is to succeed. Informal conversations around the edges and in the interstices of formal public deliberations, but according to democratic norms of respect for all participants, play a critical role in collaboration (Lee 2007, forthcoming; Baiocchi 2005), and city agency investments in staff development to enable relational trust building are essential to a robust civics of urban and environmental planning (Sirianni 2009).

3.3 Usable Tools and Street Science

To engage effectively in urban planning, citizens need authorization and scope to utilize local knowledge (Lindblom and Cohen 1979; Geertz 1983; Fischer 2000). Effectiveness, of course, is not guaranteed by local knowledge itself, or by the very act of resistance to inadequate professional paradigms, but by the extent to which the various actors in the scientific, regulatory, planning, public health, and community sectors learn to generate trust through mutual interrogation and negotiation of their various methodologies, and come to view each other as genuine "co-producers of expertise" and "street science" (Jasanoff 2004; Corburn 2005). For expertise to become a shared resource often requires investments in data systems that are sophisticated yet usable by the public, as well as professional planners and other experts capable of code switching.

Good planning support systems can integrate multiple types of information, and are flexible and user friendly. Ideally, they allow citizens and their professional partners to (1) select appropriate analysis and forecasting tools from an intelligent digital toolbox that helps users identify the most appropriate methodologies and tools for particular problems; (2) link the analytic and projection tools to appropriate local, regional, or national stored data systems; (3) run appropriate models to determine the implications of alternative policy choices and different assumptions about present and future; and (4) instantaneously view the results graphically in the forms of charts, maps, and video/sound displays that can enhance citizen understanding. Such planning support systems can facilitate a genuine process of collective design based on rich democratic social interaction (Klosterman 2001; Kwartler and Bernhard 2001; Sieber 2006).

There now exists a wide array of such tools, often based on interactive maps and geographic information systems (GIS), that support open group decision making and networks of citizens and multi-stakeholder collaboratives generating, interpreting, and utilizing such data to build trust—including trust in data from multiple and self-interested sources—and to reach workable consensus to guide common action. These tools are generally referred to as participatory GIS (PGIS) or public participation GIS (PPGIS; Sieber 2006; Criag, Harris, and Weiner 2002) and have been utilized in a broad array of urban settings in the United States (Sawicki and Peterman 2002; Elwood and Leitner 2003; Mantay and Ziegler 2006) and around the globe, north and south (McCall 2003). While there are many barriers to the effective use of such tools by community groups rooted in unequal resources and asymmetrical power relations with professionals and state actors, some of these can be reduced significantly with adequate funding by government and networks of supportive nonprofit and university intermediaries (Sawicki and Craig, 1996; Elwood and Ghose 2004; Elwood and Leitner 2003; Elwood 2002; Sieber 2006, 2007; Sawicki and Peterman 2002). An emerging next generation of such tools of public information can promote "collaborative transparency" and "empower information users themselves to provide and pool much of the essential data," and will have user interfaces that "become much more interactive and customized," and thus revisable at a much faster pace (Fung, Graham, and Weil 2007, 152). Crowd-sourcing through Web 2.0 tools also promises to expand the array of opportunities to engage networks of citizens and planners as collaborative problem solvers and co-designers (Brabham 2009), even laying the foundations for a new model of "collaborative democracy" (Noveck 2009). In the United States, the open government plans being generated by each federal agency under the Obama administration, and directly inspired by this vision of collaborative democracy, provide wide scope for the further elaboration and diffusion of such tools and their creative melding with other forms of face-to-face deliberative, trust-building, and networked forms of participatory planning (Sirianni et al. 2010).

3.4 Ensuring Adequate Inclusiveness

There are numerous sources of participatory bias in almost all systems of citizen participation, from neighborhood associations and faith-based community organizing to social democratic labor movements and revolutionary peasant movements. In the United States, levels of education and income tend to shape who participates in politics and civic life generally (Verba, Schlozman, and Brady 1995; Skocpol 2004). A range of well-known factors tend to skew participation in neighborhood associations and similar place-based organizations: homeowners have a financial investment in their homes and tend to have longer ties to the neighborhood; younger people are more mobile and tend to have fewer children in the schools; small business owners tend to be outnumbered and seen as outsiders; educated people attend more often and speak more confidently at community meetings; recent immigrants, especially those with limited English-language skills, often feel intimidated and unwelcome, or are deeply distrustful of the state as a result of their own homeland experiences and/or current immigration status; and some cultural styles of discourse, such as storytelling, tend to be less privileged than others, such as rational argumentation (Berry, Portney, and Thomson 1993; Skogan 2006; Crenson 1983; Goetz and Sidney 1994; Young 2000; Polletta 2002).

While none of these biases in participation is likely to be radically reduced without other social policies that enhance equality, they can often be addressed in a relatively effective manner that increases inclusion in the process of planning and hence legitimacy among residents and city planning agencies. In the community policing program in Chicago, significant investment in media advertisement and other forms of outreach, as well as training of community organizers to work in (and often recruited from) disadvantaged communities, had a significantly equalizing impact on levels of participation in monthly beat meetings among blacks and whites, but less so among Latinos (Skogan 2006); and well-trained beat facilitators had a demonstrated impact in reversing some common racial and class biases in the choice of projects and the quality of problem solving within some beats (Fung 2004). In Seattle's neighborhood planning, a stakeholder analysis and other outreach initiatives required of the neighborhood planning coalitions that were eligible for planning support brought in new groups that would otherwise have been left out and impacted the types of projects chosen, at least in some neighborhoods (Sirianni 2007). These kinds of methods are increasingly utilized in a broad range of cities (Berke, Godschalk, and Kaiser 2006, 265–86). Likewise, city planning agencies can become more energetic in building long-term relationships with ethnic and minority group organizations and nonprofit service agencies to ensure a more inclusive participation in neighborhood planning and implementation, though traditional neighborhood associations often push back against efforts that might seem to admit staff-based organizations on an equal footing or unbalance the number of groups participating from any one neighborhood within a larger planning area (Sirianni 2009; Diers 2004; Goetz and Sidney 1994). In addition, the more sophisticated the planning support tools, such as GIS, required to do good planning work, the greater investment in training, staff support, and networks of nonprofits and universities become to ensure that participatory tools do not further enhance inequality (Sieber 2006; Craig and Elwood 1998).

3.5 Reciprocal Accountability

Participation is often driven by the desire for democratic accountability to citizens by elected officials and administrators, as well as sufficient autonomy for citizens to make decisions and engage in coproduction. Yet planners have many reasons to mistrust citizen participation, since citizens often act in ways that display inadequate knowledge and technical competence, narrowly self-serving or short-term interests, and racial, class and other prejudices (Yang 2006; Fung 2004). Indeed, as March and Olsen (1995, 153) argue in their fertile discussion of developing political accounts, "A prolonged combination of citizen power with citizen exemption from accountability introduces intolerable elements of irresponsibility into a democratic polity." Thus, some way of ensuring reciprocal accountability or "360-degree accountability" (Behn 2001, 52) between planners and citizens or, more correctly, among all relevant actors in the accountability environment, is essential for effective and sustainable civic engagement in planning.

To address this problem, planning designs at the city level and beyond have employed various features of "accountable autonomy" (Fung 2004) and "multiple, simultaneous accountability" (Weber 2003), in addition to various forms of accountability in "democratic networked governance" (Esmark 2007; Sørensen and Torfing 2005, 2007). Essentially, these concepts permit expanded scope for civic actors to make decisions and to engage in coproduction and multiple forms of collaboration, but within a framework where they are accountable to other partners, and especially to relevant government authorities, elected by the larger polity or serving as administrators of statutes passed by democratic legislatures. The policy design of community policing and local school councils in Chicago provides resources and support in the form of training, feedback, trouble shooting, networking on best practices with others across the city, and templates for iterative problem solving and for developing beat plans and school improvement plans. But the local beat meetings and school councils are required to report on their performance and are often informed of corrective action that ought to, or in some cases *must*, be taken if the grant of autonomy is to continue (Fung 2004). In Seattle, neighborhood planning included an especially ambitious design for 360-degree accountability. Neighborhood planning groups were accountable to the neighborhood planning office for demonstrating sufficient inclusiveness in visioning and planning; to all residents, business, and property owners in a planning area for adequately publicizing plans, generating feedback for revisions, and holding open meetings and surveys for validation; to an interdepartmental team of city agencies who reviewed plans for technical feasibility and cost; and to the city council for the final say on adoption and approval. The mayor and city councilors also conducted walking tours to assess the relative degree of consensus within the neighborhoods (Sirianni 2007).

4. Conclusion

While civic engagement in urban planning has generally been extended and enriched in the decades since the 1960s, cities vary considerably on how they design civic engagement into planning processes (Fagotto and Fung 2006; Innes and Booher 2010; Kathi and Cooper 2005; Johnson 2002; Burby 2003; Ozawa 2004; Punter 2003; Berry, Portney, and Thomson 1993), whether and how states mandate such participation (Brody, Godschalk, and Burby 2003), and how much collaboration becomes embedded in governance culture (Healey 2006). All civic designs in complex environments are imperfect and thus contested—by academic researchers, professional practitioners, civic groups, growth coalitions, and local residents—in normative terms (inclusiveness, power balancing, genuine engagement by grassroots citizens, equitable outcomes), as well as instrumental ones (relative effectiveness across a range of goals, appropriate expertise, efficient use of time and resources). The civic sector itself is constituted by diverse types of organizations operating in larger fields rife with issues of ecological competition as well as complementarity (Baum 1996; Ferguson and Stoutland 1999; Marwell 2007), thus requiring planning professionals to utilize complex judgment in combining democratic practice with professional expertise in a way that secures optimal legitimacy and reciprocal accountability (Sirianni 2009). The civics of the city have never been easy (Ryan 1998), though many innovations of recent decades enable urban planning to become far more democratic than when Progressive Era paradigms were first put in place.

References

Aleshire, R. 1972. "Power to the People: An Assessment of Community Action and Model Cities Experience." *Public Administration Review* 32:428–43.

Alford, J. 2009. *Engaging Public Sector Clients: From Service Delivery to Co-production.* London: Palgrave Macmillan.

Ames, S. C., ed. 1998. *A Guide to Community Visioning.* Chicago: APA Planners Press.

Arnstein, S. 1969. "Eight Rungs on the Ladder of Citizen Participation." *Journal of the American Institute of Planners* 25:216–24.

Avritzer, L. 2009. *Participatory Institutions in Democratic Brazil*. Baltimore: Johns Hopkins University Press.

Baiocchi, G. 2005. *Militants and Citizens: The Politics of Participatory Democracy in Porto Alegre*. Palo Alto, CA: Stanford University Press.

Baiocchi, G., P. Heller, and M. K. Silva. 2008. "Making Space for Civil Society: Institutional Reforms and Local Democracy in Brazil." *Social Forces* 86:911–36.

Baum, J. A. C. 1996. "Organizational Ecology." In *Handbook of Organization Studies*, edited by S. Clegg, C. Hardy, and W. Nord, 77–114. London: Sage.

Behn, R. D. 2001. *Rethinking Democratic Accountability*. Washington, DC: Brookings Institution Press.

Berke, P. R., D. R. Godschalk, and E. J. Kaiser, with D. A. Rodriquez. 2006. *Urban Land Use Planning*, 5th ed. Urbana, IL: University of Illinois Press.

Berry, J., K. Portney, and K. Thomson. 1993. *The Rebirth of Urban Democracy*. Washington, DC: Brookings Institution Press.

Booher, D. 2008. "Civic Engagement as Collaborative Complex Adaptive Networks." In *Civic Engagement in a Networked Society*, edited by K. Yang and E. Bergrud, 111–48. Charlotte, NC: Information Age Publishing.

Boyte, H. C. 2005. "Reframing Democracy: Governance, Civic Agency, and Politics." *Public Administration Review* 65:536–46.

Brabham, D. C. 2009. "Crowdsourcing the Public Participation Process For Planning Projects." *Planning Theory* 8:242–62.

Bratt, R. G. 1997. "CDCs: Contributions Outweigh Contradictions, A Reply to Randy Stoecker." *Journal of Urban Affairs* 19:23–28.

Bratt, R. G., and W. M. Rohe. 2004. "Organizationl Changes Among CDCs: Assessing the Impacts and Navigating the Challenges." *Journal of Urban Affairs* 26:197–220.

Bridges, A. 1984. *A City in the Republic: Antebellum New York and the Origins of Machine Politics*. New York: Cambridge University Press.

Briggs, X. de S. 2008. *Democracy as Problem Solving*. Cambridge, MA: MIT Press.

Brody, S. D., D. R. Godschalk, and R. J. Burby. 2003. "Mandating Citizen Participation in Plan Making: Six Strategic Planning Choices." *Journal of the American Planning Association* 69:245–65.

Brown, L., and B. Frieden. 1976. "Rulemaking by Improvisation: Guidelines and Goals in the Model Cities Program." *Policy Sciences* 7:455–88.

Burby, R. J. 2003. "Making Plans That Matter: Citizen Involvement in Government Action." *Journal of the American Planning Association* 69:33–49.

Corburn, J. 2005. *Street Science: Community Knowledge and Environmental Health Justice*. Cambridge, MA: MIT Press.

Corburn, J. 2009. *Toward the Healthy City: People, Place, and the Politics of Urban Planning*. Cambridge, MA: MIT Press.

Craig, W. J., and S. Elwood. 1998. "How and Why Community Groups Use Maps and Geographic Information." *Cartography and Geographic Information Systems* 25:95–104.

Craig, W. J., T. M. Harris, and D. Weiner, eds. 2002. *Community Participation and Geographic Information Systems*. London: Taylor and Francis.

Crenson, M. A. 1983. *Neighborhood Politics*. Cambridge, MA: Harvard University Press.

Deitrick, S., and C. Ellis. 2004. "New Urbanism in the Inner City." *Journal of the American Planning Association* 70:426–42.

DeLeon, R. E. 1992. *Left Coast City: Progressive Politics in San Francisco, 1975–1991*. Lawrence: University Press of Kansas.

Diers, J. 2004. *Neighbor Power: Building Community the Seattle Way*. Seattle: University of Washington Press.

Einhorn, R. L. 2001. *Property Rules: Political Economy of Chicago, 1833–1872.* Chicago: University of Chicago Press.

Elwood, S. 2002. "GIS and Collaborative Urban Governance: Understanding Their Implications for Community Action and Power." *Urban Geography* 22:737–59.

Elwood, S., and R. Ghose. 2004. "PPGIS in Community Development Planning: Framing the Organizational Context." *Cartographica* 38: 19–33.

Elwood, S., and H. Leitner, H. 2003. "GIS and Spatial Knowledge Production for Neighborhood Revitalization: Negotiating State Priorities and Neighborhood Visions." *Journal of Urban Affairs* 25:139–57.

Esmark, A. 2007. "Democratic Accountability and Network Governance: Problems and Potentials." In *Theories of Democratic Network Governance*, edited by E. Sørensen and J. Torfing, 274–96. Basingstoke, UK: Palgrave Macmillan.

Fagotto, E., and A. Fung. 2006. "Empowered Participation in Urban Governance: The Minneapolis Neighborhood Revitalization Program." *International Journal of Urban and Regional Research* 30:638–55.

Ferguson, R. F., and S. E. Stoutland. 1999. "Reconceiving the Community Development Field." In *Urban Problems and Community Development*, edited by R. E. Ferguson and W. T. Dickens, 33–75. Washington, DC: Brookings Institution Press.

Fischer, F. 2000. *Citizens, Experts, and the Environment: The Politics of Local Knowledge.* Durham, NC: Duke University Press.

Fishman, R., ed. 2000. *The American Planning Tradition: Culture and Policy.* Washington, DC: Woodrow Wilson Center Press.

Forester, J. 1989. *Planning in the Face of Power.* Berkeley: University of California Press.

Forester, J. 1999. *The Deliberative Practitioner: Encouraging Participatory Planning Processes.* Cambridge, MA: MIT Press.

Fox, K. 1977. *Better City Government: Innovation in American Urban Politics, 1850–1937.* Philadelphia: Temple University Press.

Frost, J. 2001. *An Interracial Movement of the Poor.* New York: New York University Press.

Fullilove, M. T. 2004. *Root Shock: How Tearing Up City Neighborhoods Hurts America, and What We Can Do About It.* New York: Random House.

Fung, A. 2004. *Empowered Participation: Reinventing Urban Democracy.* Princeton, NJ: Princeton University Press.

Fung, A., M. Graham, and D. Weil. 2007. *Full Disclosure: The Perils and Promise of Transparency.* New York: Cambridge University Press.

Gans, H. J. 1962. *The Urban Villagers.* New York: Free Press.

Gastil, J., and P. Levine, eds. 2005. *The Deliberative Democracy Handbook: Strategies for Effective Civic Engagement in the 21st Century.* San Francisco: Jossey-Bass.

Geertz, C. 1983. *Local Knowledge: Further Essays in Interpretive Anthropology.* New York: Basic Books.

Gittell, R., and A.Vidal. 1998. *Community Organizing: Building Social Capital as a Development Strategy.* Thousand Oaks, CA: Sage.

Goebel, T. 2002. *A Government by the People: Direct Democracy in America, 1890–1940.* Chapel Hill, NC: University of North Carolina Press.

Goetz, E., and M. Sidney. 1994. "Revenge of the Property Owners: Community Development and the Politics of Property." *Journal of Urban Affairs* 16:319–34.

Goetz, E., and M. Sidney. 1995. "Community Development Corporations as Neighborhood Advocates: A Study of Political Activism of Nonprofit Developers." *Applied Behavioral Science Review* 3:1–20.

Green, M., H. Moore, and J. O'Brien. 2006. *When People Care Enough to Act.* Toronto: Inclusion Press.

Greenstone, J. D., and P. E. Peterson. 1973. *Race and Authority in Urban Politics: Community Participation and the War on Poverty.* New York: Russell Sage.

Gutmann, A., and D. Thompson. 2004. *Why Deliberative Democracy?* Princeton, NJ: Princeton University Press.

Haar, C. 1975. *Between the Idea and the Reality: A Study in the Origin, Fate, and Legacy of the Model Cities Program.* Boston: Little, Brown.

Habermas, J. 1984. *The Theory of Communicative Action.* Boston: Beacon Press.

Healey, P. 2006. *Collaborative Planning: Shaping Places in Fragmented Societies.* New York: Palgrave Macmillan.

Innes, J. E. 1995. "Planning Theory's Emerging Paradigm: Communicative Action and Interactive Practice." *Journal of Planning Education and Research* 14:183–89.

Innes, J.E. 1996. "Planning through Consensus Building: A New View of the Comprehensive Planning Ideal." *Journal of the American Planning Association* 62:460–72.

Innes, J. E., and D. E. Booher. 2010. *Planning with Complexity: An Introduction to Collaborative Rationality for Public Policy.* New York: Routledge.

Jacobs, J. 1961. *The Death and Life of Great American Cities.* New York: Random House.

Jacobs, L. R., F. L. Cook, and M. X. Delli Carpini. 2009. *Talking Together: Public Deliberation and Political Participation in America.* Chicago: University of Chicago Press.

Jasanoff, S., ed. 2004. *States of Knowledge: The Co-production of Science and Social Order.* New York: Routledge.

Johnson, S. R. 2002. "The Transformation of Civic Institutions and Practices in Portland, Oregon, 1960–1999." Ph.D. diss., Portland State University, Portland, OR.

Kaplan, M. 1970. *The Model Cities Program.* New York: Praeger.

Kathi, P. C., and T. L. Cooper. 2005. "Democratizing the Administrative State: Neighborhood Councils and City Agencies." *Public Administration Review* 65: 559–67.

Keating, D. 1997. "The CDC Model of Urban Development: Response to Randy Stoecker." *Journal of Urban Affairs* 19:29–33.

Klosterman, R. E. 2001. "The What If? Planning Support System." In *Planning Support Systems: Integrating Geographic Information Systems, Models, and Visualization Tools,* edited by R. K. Brail and R. E. Klosterman, 23–84. New York: ESRI Press.

Kramer, R. 1969. *Participation of the Poor: Comparative Community Case Studies in the War on Poverty.* Englewood Cliffs: Prentice-Hall.

Kretzmann, J. P., and J. L. McKnight. 1993. *Building Communities from the Inside Out.* Chicago: ACTA Publications.

Kwartler, M., and Robert N. Bernhard. 2001. "Community Viz: An Integrated Planning Support System." In *Planning Support Systems: Integrating Geographic Information Systems, Models, and Visualization Tools,* edited by R. K. Brail and R. E. Klosterman, 285–308. New York: ESRI Press.

Lee, C. 2005. "Collaborative Models to Achieve Environmental Justice and Healthy Communities." In *Power, Justice, and the Environment: A Critical Appraisal of the Environmental Justice Movement,* edited by D. N. Pellow and R. J. Brulle, 219–49. Cambridge, MA: MIT Press.

Lee, C. W. 2007. "Is There a Place for Private Conversation in Public Dialogue: Comparing Stakeholder Assessments of Informal Communication in Collaborative Regional Planning." *American Journal of Sociology* 113:41–96.

Lee, C. W. Forthcoming. "Accounting for Diversity in Collaborative Governance: An Institutional Approach to Empowerment Reforms." In *Varieties of Civic Innovation:*

Deliberative, Collaborative, Network, and Narrative Approaches, by Carmen Sirianni and Jennifer Girouard. Nashville, TN: Vanderbilt University Press.

Leighninger, M. 2006. *The Next Form of Democracy*. Nashville, TN: Vanderbilt University Press.

Light, P. C. 1998. *Sustaining Innovation: Creating Nonprofit and Government Organizations that Innovate Naturally*. San Francisco: Jossey-Bass.

Lindblom, C. E., and D. K. Cohen. 1979. *Usable Knowledge: Social Science and Social Problem Solving*. New Haven, CT: Yale University Press.

Lissak, R. S. 1989. *Pluralism and Progressives: Hull House and the New Immigrants, 1890–1919*. Chicago: University of Chicago Press.

Logan, J. R., and H. L. Molotch. 2007. *Urban Fortunes: The Political Economy of Place*, 2nd ed. Berkeley, CA: University of California Press.

Macedo, S. et al. 2005. *Democracy at Risk: How Political Choices Undermine Citizen Participation and What We Can Do About It*. Washington, DC: Brookings Institution Press.

March, J. G., and J. P. Olsen. 1995. *Democratic Governance*. New York: Free Press.

Mantay, J., and J. Ziegler. 2006. *GIS for the Urban Environment*. New York: ESRI Press.

Marwell, N. P. 2007. *Bargaining for Brooklyn: Community Organizations in the Entrepreneurial City*. Chicago: University of Chicago Press.

Marris, P., and M. Rein. 1982. *Dilemmas of Social Reform: Poverty and Community Action in the United States*, 2nd ed. Chicago: University of Chicago Press.

Marshall, D. R. 1971. *The Politics of Participation in Poverty*. Berkeley, CA: University of California Press.

Mattson, K. 1998. *Creating a Democratic Public: The Struggle for Urban Participatory Democracy during the Progressive Era*. College Park: Pennsylvania State University Press.

Mazmanian, D., and M. Kraft, eds. 1999. *Toward Sustainable Communties: Transition and Transformation in Environmental Policy*. Cambridge, MA: MIT Press.

McCall, M. K. 2003. "Seeking Good Governance in Participatory GIS: A Review of Processes and Governance Dimensions in Applying GIS to Participatory Spatial Planning." *Habitat International* 27:549–73.

Medoff, P., and H. Sklar. 1994. *Streets of Hope: The Fall and Rise of an Urban Neighborhood*. Boston: South End Press.

Mollenkopf, J. 1983. *The Contested City*. Princeton, NJ: Princeton University Press.

Moore, C. M., G. Longo, and P. Palmer. 1999. "Visioning." In *The Consensus Building Handbook*, edited by L. Susskind, S. McKearnan, and J. Thomas-Larmer, 557–90. Thousand Oaks, CA: Sage.

Musso, J. A., C. Weare, N. Oztas, and W. E. Loges. 2006. "Neighborhood Governance Reform and Networks of Community Power in Los Angeles." *American Review of Public Administration* 36:79–97.

Naples, N. 1998. *Grassroots Warriors: Activist Mothering, Community Work, and the War on Poverty*. New York: Routledge.

National Civic League. 2000. *Community Visioning and Strategic Planning Handbook*. Denver: National Civic League.

National Congress for Community and Economic Development. 2005. *Reaching New Heights Trends and Achievements of Community-Based Development Organizations*. Washington: NCCED.

Nemon, H. 2007. "Community Action: Lessons From Forty Years of Federal Funding, Anti-Poverty Strategies, and Participation of the Poor." *Journal of Poverty* 11:1–22.

Noveck, B. S. 2009. *Wiki Government: How Technology Can Make Government Better, Democracy Stronger, and Citizens More Powerful*. Washington, DC: Brookings Institution Press.

O'Connor, A. 1999. "Swimming Against the Tide: A Brief History of Federal Policy in Poor Communities." In *Urban Problems and Community Development*, edited by R. F. Ferguson and W. T. Dickens, 77–138. Washington, DC: Brookings Institution Press.

Oliver, J. E. 2001. *Democracy in Suburbia*. Princeton, NJ: Princeton University Press.

Oliver, J. E. 2010. *The Paradoxes of Integration: Race, Neighborhood, and Civic Life in Multiethnic America*. Chicago: University of Chicago Press.

Orr, M., ed. 2007. *Transforming the City: Community Organizing and the Challenge of Political Change*. Lawrence, KS: University Press of Kansas.

Osterman, P. 2002. *Gathering Power*. Boston: Beacon.

Ozawa, C. P., ed. 2004. *The Portland Edge: Challenges and Successes in Growing Communities*. Washington, DC: Island Press.

Peirce, N., and S. Steinbach. 1987. *Corrective Capitalism: The Rise of America's Community Development Corporations*. New York: Ford Foundation.

Peterman, W. 1999. *Neighborhood Planning and Community-Based Development: The Potential and Limits of Grassroots Action*. Thousand Oaks, CA: Sage.

Peterson, J.A. 2003. *The Birth of City Planning in the United States, 1840–1917*. Baltimore: Johns Hopkins Press.

Peterson, P., and J. D. Greenstone. 1977. "Racial Change and Citizen Participation: The Mobilization of Low-Income Communities Through Community Action." In *A Decade of Federal Antipoverty Programs*, edited by Robert Havemann, 241–78. New York: Academic Press.

Polletta, F. 2002. *Freedom Is an Endless Meeting: Democracy in American Social Movements*. Chicago: University of Chicago Press.

Portney, K. E. 2003. *Taking Sustainable Cities Seriously: Economic Development, the Environment, and Quality of Life in American Cities*. Cambridge, MA: MIT Press.

Punter, J. 2003. *The Vancouver Achievement: Urban Planning and Design*. Vancouver, BC: University of British Columbia Press.

Purcell, M. 2000. "The Decline of the Political Consensus for Urban Growth: Evidence from Los Angeles." *Journal of Urban Affairs* 22:85–100.

Quadagno, J. 1994. *The Color of Welfare: How Racism Undermined the War on Poverty*. New York: Oxford University Press.

Robinson, T. 1996. "Inner-city Innovator: The Non-Profit Community Development Corporation." *Urban Studies* 33:1647–70.

Rohe, W. M. 2009. "From Global to Local: One Hundred Years of Neighborhood Planning." *Journal of the American Planning Association* 75:209–30.

Ryan, M. 1998. *Civic Wars: Democracy and Public Life in the American City during the Nineteenth Century*. Berkeley, CA: University of California Press.

Sagedy, J. A., and B. E. Johnson. 2004. *The Neighborhood Charrette Handbook*. Louisville, KY.: University of Louisville.

Sanoff, H. 2000. *Community Participation Methods in Design and Planning*. Hoboken, NJ: John Wiley.

Sawicki, D. S., and W. J. Craig. 1996. "The Democratization of Data: Bridging the Gap for Community Groups." *Journal of the American Planning Association* 62: 512–23.

Sawicki, D. S., and D. R. Peterman. 2002. "Surveying the Extent of PPGIS Practice in the United States." In *Community Participation and Geographic Information Systems*, edited by W. J. Criag, T. M. Harris, and D. Weiner, 17–36. London: Taylor and Francis.

Shirley, D. 1997. *Community Organizing for Urban School Reform.* Austin, TX: University of Texas Press.

Shutkin, W. A. 2000. *The Land That Could Be: Environmentalism and Democracy in the Twenty-First Century.* Cambridge, MA: MIT Press.

Sieber, R. E. 2006. "Public Participation Geographic Information Systems: A Literature Review and Framework." *Annals of the Association of American Geographers* 96: 491–507.

Sieber, R. E. 2007. "Spatial Data Access by the Grassroots." *Cartography and Geographic Information Science* 34:47–62.

Sirianni, C. 2007. "Neighborhood Planning as Collaborative Democratic Design: The Case of Seattle." *Journal of the American Planning Association* 73:373–87.

Sirianni, C. 2009. *Investing in Democracy: Engaging Citizens in Collaborative Governance.* Washington, DC: Brookings Institution Press.

Sirianni, C., L. B. Bingham, K. Emerson, A. Fung, B. Israel, S. R. Smith, et al. 2010. "Partnering with Communities: Perspectives from Scholarship." National Workshop on Federal Community-Based Programs, Brookings Institution, April, Washington, DC.

Sirianni, C., and L. A. Friedland. 2001. *Civic Innovation in America: Community Empowerment, Public Policy, and the Movement for Civic Renewal.* Berkeley, CA: University of California Press.

Sirianni, C., and D. Schor. 2009. "City Government as Enabler of Youth Civic Engagement." In *Policies for Youth Civic Engagement*, edited by James Youniss and P. Levine, 121–63. Nashville, TN: Vanderbilt University Press.

Sirianni, C., and S. Sofer. 2011 "Environmental Organizations." In *The State of Nonprofit America*, 2nd ed., edited by Lester M. Salamon. Washington, DC: Brookings Institution Press.

Skocpol, T. 2004. "Civic Transformation and Inequality in the Contemporary United States." In *Social Inequality*, edited by Kathryn M. Neckerman, 729–67. New York: Russell Sage Foundation.

Skogan, W. G. 2006. *Police and Community in Chicago: A Tale of Three Cities.* New York: Oxford University Press.

Smith, S. R. 2010. "Nonprofits and Public Administration: Reconciling Performance Management and Citizen Engagement." *American Review of Public Administration* 40:129–52.

Smith, S. R., and M. Lipsky. 1993. *Nonprofits for Hire: The Welfare State in the Age of Contracting.* Cambridge, MA: Harvard University Press.

Sørensen, E., and J. Torfing. 2005. "The Democratic Anchorage of Governance Networks." *Scandinavian Political Studies* 28:195–218.

Sørensen, E., and J. Torfing, J. 2007. *Theories of Democratic Network Governance.* Basingstoke, UK: Palgrave Macmillan.

Stoecker, R. 1997. "The CDC Model of Urban Redevelopment: A Critique and an Alternative." *Journal of Urban Affairs* 19:1–22.

Stone, C. N. 1993. "Urban Regimes and the Capacity to Govern: A Political Economy Approach." *Journal of Urban Affairs* 15:1–28.

Stone, C. N. 2006. "Power, Reform, and Urban Regime Analysis." *City and Community* 5: 23–38.

Stoutland, S. 1999. "Community Development Corporations: Mission, Strategy, and Accomplishments." In *Urban Problems and Community Development*, edited by R. F. Ferguson and W. T. Dickens, 193–240. Washington, DC: Brookings Institution Press.

Sundquist, J., with D. Davis. 1969. *Making Federalism Work: A Study of Program Coordination at the Community Level*. Washington, DC: Brookings Institition Press.

Teaford, J. C. 1984. *The Unheralded Triumph: City Government in America, 1870–1900*. Baltimore: Johns Hopkins University Press.

Thomas, J. C. 1986. *Between Citizen and City: Neighborhood Organizations and Urban Politics in Cincinnati*. Lawrence, KS: University Press of Kansas.

Verba, S., K. L. Schlozman, and H. Brady. 1995. *Voice and Equality: Civic Voluntarism in American Politics*. Cambridge, MA: Harvard University Press.

Walsh, K. C. 2007. *Talking about Race: Community Dialogues and the Politics of Difference*. Chicago: University of Chicago Press.

Warren, M. E., ed. 1999. *Democracy and Trust*. New York: Cambridge University Press.

Warren, M. R. 2001. *Dry Bones Rattling: Community Building to Revitalize American Democracy*. Princeton, NJ: Princeton University Press.

Weber, E. P. 2003. *Bringing Society Back In: Grassroots Ecosystem Management, Accountability, and Sustainable Communities*. Cambridge, MA: MIT Press.

Weir, M. 1999. "Power, Money, and Politics in Community Development." In *Urban Problems and Community Development*, edited by R. F. Ferguson and W. T. Dickens, 139–92. Washington, DC: Brookings Institution Press.

Weir, M., H. Wolman, and T. Swanstrom. 2005. "The Calculus of Coalitions: Cities, Suburbs, and the Metropolitan Agenda." *Urban Affairs Review* 40:730–60.

Wood, R. L. 2002. *Faith in Action: Religion, Race, and Democratic Organizing in America*. Chicago: University of Chicago Press.

Yang, K. 2006. "Trust and Citizen Involvement Decisions: Trust in Citizens, Trust in Institutions, and Propensity to Trust." *Administration and Society* 38:573–95.

Young, I. M. 2000. *Inclusion and Democracy*. New York: Oxford University Press.

Zigler, E., and S. Muenchow. 1992. *Head Start*. New York: Basic Books.

CHAPTER 33

URBAN INFORMALITY

THE PRODUCTION OF SPACE AND PRACTICE OF PLANNING

ANANYA ROY

THE geography of the slum has long haunted urban planning. Designated as the "informal space," the slum represents the "unplanable" city that lies beyond the sphere of regulations, norms, and codes. Such informal spaces are viewed as either dismal concentrations of poverty, a tangible manifestation of economic marginality, or as alternative and autonomous urban orders, patched together through the improvisation and entrepreneurship of the urban poor. In both cases, the informal city is understood as the "other" of the planned and formal city. In this chapter, I examine contemporary understandings of the informal city and situate them in a broader history of ideas. I also put forward a conceptual framework for the study of urban informality, one that runs counter to mainstream conceptualizations of the "unplanable" city. I start with AlSayyad's (2004) provocation that it is the "formal" rather than the "informal" that requires explanation. How and why are certain land uses and settlement patterns designated as formal by the state while others are criminalized and maintained as "informal"? Such a question is particularly urgent since, in many instances, the "formal" may not be in conformity with master plans and legal codes and yet by earning the sanction of the state, it has considerably more spatial value than the "informal." It is in and through such differentiated urban geographies that social hierarchies of class, race, and ethnicity are consolidated, maintained, and negotiated. Elite informalities are rapidly converted into a formal spatial order, while subordinate groups are forced to exist in what, following Yiftachel (2009), can be understood as "blackened spaces" of exclusion or, at best, "gray spaces" of ambiguous legal standing. This production and regulation of space, then, is also the production and regulation of social difference. While such selective stigmatization by the state takes place in many different regional contexts and in many different spheres—for example, in the regulation of labor markets—in this chapter I focus on the ownership and use of property, paying attention to the splintered landscapes of spatial value that mark the metropolitan regions of the Global South.

1. Two Views of Urban Informality

The widespread urbanization of the twenty-first century has been accompanied by a revived interest in the informal city. However, the rediscovery of informality is marked by sharply contrasting perspectives and paradigms. One of the most prominent is Mike Davis's (2006) apocalyptic account of "a planet of slums." For Davis (2006, 14–15), informal urbanization is a stark manifestation of "overurbanization" or "urbanization without growth," which in turn is "the legacy of a global political conjuncture—the worldwide debt crisis of the late 1970s and the subsequent IMF-led restructuring of Third World economies in the 1980s." Davis thus designates this world system as "a planet of slums," a warehousing of the "surplus humanity" released by de-proletarianization and agricultural deregulation in hazardous and miserable forms of urban settlement. Such also is the rhetoric of the United Nations, which has made "cities without slums" one of its key initiatives. It is thus that Gilbert (2007, 697) has lamented that the "the new millennium has seen the return of the word 'slum' with all of its inglorious associations."

Davis's work is part of a substantial genre of research that traces the formation of a "new urban marginality," not only in the Third World but also in Europe and the Americas. While in the 1970s researchers undermined the "myth of marginality" (Perlman 1977), arguing that the informalized poor were integrated into the labor markets, social life, and political systems of the city, they are now making the case for the "reality of marginality" (Perlman 2004). Wacquant's work (1996, 1999, 2007), for example, documents the emergence of an "advanced marginality" that is linked to the "territorial stigmatization" faced by residents of marginalized spaces: the ghetto, the *banlieue*, the *favela*. Similarly, Auyero (2000) charts the emergence of the "hyper-shantytown." Such research is united in its emphasis on the connections between such "advanced marginality" and the hollowing out of economies and welfare states through neoliberal capitalism. The "hyper-shantytown" is thus produced by "hyper-unemployment" (Auyero 1999), a systematic process of de-proletarianization and labor informalization. While the theorists of "advanced marginality" acknowledge the poverty-targeting efforts of the state (for example, in Brazil, the upgrading of *favelas* through the provision of services), they insist that such programs are minor palliatives in the face of a massive structural crisis. In particular, they argue that the communities of the urban poor are now overwhelmed by violence: the violence of state repression, the symbolic violence of stigma and discrimination, and the material violence of poverty and unemployment (Perlman 2004). In short, yesterday's "slums of hope" are today's "slums of despair" (Eckstein 1990).

It is important to note that Davis's argument is not only about economic marginality but also about a new political configuration—what he calls the "law of chaos" (Davis 2004). With the hollowing out of formal labor markets, the urban poor, he notes, are rarely organized and mobilized in collective fashion. Rather, they are fragmented and atomized by vectors such as religion and ethnicity. Davis's lament rehearses a much older argument presented by dependency theorists. For example, in the seminal text, *The City and the Grassroots*, Castells (1983) presents an ambitious theory of urban social movements. Studying both formal political organizations and the mobilizations of informal squatter communities, Castells acknowledges the central role of politics in the transformation of the capitalist city, but also analyzes the limits of such politics. In particular, he designates the populist politics of squatter communities as a symptom of the "dependent city," a "city without citizens." He argues that while squatters mobilize to secure access to land, services, jobs, and at times even tenure, they are simultaneously co-opted into systems of political patronage. Thus, they are clients rather than citizens, disciplined subjects of urban populism rather than active agents of structural change. Similarly, Davis's global slum is a space of violence but not of social transformation. It is worth quoting at length:

> What is clear is that the contemporary megaslum poses unique problems of imperial order and social control that conventional geopolitics has barely begun to register. If the point of the war against terrorism is to pursue the enemy into his sociological and cultural labyrinth, then the poor peripheries of developing cities will be the permanent battlefields of the twenty-first century. . . . Some templates are obvious. Night after night, hornetlike helicopter gunships stalk enigmatic enemies in the narrow streets of the slum districts, pouring hellfire into shanties or fleeing cars. Every morning the slums reply with suicide bombers and eloquent explosions. If the empire can deploy Orwellian technologies of repression, its outcasts have the gods of chaos on their side. (Davis 2004, 15)

In sharp contrast to this framework is one that celebrates the informal city, viewing it as an embodiment of the entrepreneurial energies of the "people's economy." A key interlocutor is Hernando de Soto. De Soto's arc of work, from *The Other Path* (1989) to *The Mystery of Capital* (2000), presents the informal sector as an "invisible revolution" (the subtitle of *The Other Path*), a grassroots uprising against the bureaucracy of state planning. As Bromley (2004) notes, this "other path" is also meant to be the alternative to the political radicalism of the Shining Path, the guerilla movement that waged a class war in Peru, de Soto's home and the setting for *The Other Path*. In *The Mystery of Capital*, de Soto (2000) extends his arguments about the "people's economy" by arguing that the poor are "heroic entrepreneurs." He insists that the poor already possess considerable assets and he estimates that such assets amount to $9 trillion, far exceeding any transfers of aid and assistance that can be directed to them: twenty times the direct foreign investment in the Third World since the Berlin Wall fell and more than forty-six times as much as the World Bank has lent in the last three decades. The cause of poverty is not the lack of assets but, rather, that the poor are relegated to the informal sector in their ownership and use of such assets, a system that de Soto calls "legal apartheid." Thus, Bromley (2004) rightly notes that de Soto's work most closely hews to the ideas of Friedrich von Hayek and its depiction of the state as a bureaucratic obstacle to economic freedom.

Such ideas are compatible with a broader milieu of populist concepts that present the practices of the poor as an alternative to top-down planning. For example, in his influential vision for the "end of poverty," Sachs (2005) outlines a global Keynesianism that promises to take developing countries up the ladder of modernization through investments in physical and human capital. It is against this vision that William Easterly (2006) presents a provocative counter-vision. Critiquing Sachs as a Planner, Easterly condemns these new modernizations as Big Western Plans—neocolonial forms of utopian social engineering that are bound to fail and that will possibly do more harm than good. Easterly contrasts Planners with Searchers, with the grassroots and self-help activities that are incremental, efficient, effective, and accountable. His idea is pithy: that "the poor help themselves" (Easterly 2006, 27) and that they do so through "economic freedom," which is "one of mankind's most underrated inventions" (72). Perhaps his most powerful argument against planning is this: that "the rich have markets, the poor have bureaucrats" (165). In other words, Easterly calls for the liberation of the poor from the bureaucratic chains of international aid and state planning. He argues that the poor are Searchers and that, left to their own devices, they can craft and run systems of great entrepreneurial energy.

A planet of slums where the poor are warehoused in spaces of violence and an entrepreneurial economic order where the poor are able to help themselves are two fundamentally opposed interpretations of contemporary urbanism. Yet, they are marked by a common theme—that of "urban informality as a way of life." Many of these conceptualizations view this way of life as an alternative urban order, one opposed to the planned and formal city.

2. URBAN INFORMALITY AS A WAY OF LIFE?

In a 2004 essay, AlSayyad presents the idea of "urban informality as a way of life." His title refers to the classic 1938 essay by Wirth, "Urbanism as Way of Life." AlSayyad argues that today urban informality is a generalized urban condition. He thus notes that as Wirth had once studied the sociology of the urban condition, so it is possible today to analyze the "forms of social action and organization" associated with urban informality (AlSayyad 2004, 7). AlSayyad's argument resonates with diverse conceptualizations of urban informality. Davis (2006, 178), for example, states that "informal survivalism" is "the new primary mode of livelihood in a majority of Third World cities." Similarly, Bayat (2007, 579) argues that informality is the "habitus of the dispossessed." While Davis views such a habitus as characterized by anomie or extremism, Bayat argues that informality is best understood as "flexibility, pragmatism, negotiation, as well as constant struggle for survival and self-development." In earlier work, Bayat (2000), working in the context of Middle Eastern cities, outlines the repertoire of tactics through which urban "informals" appropriate and claim space. According to him, this "quiet encroachment of the ordinary" by subaltern groups creates a "street politics" that shapes the city in fundamental ways. Bayat's analysis is similar to Michel de Certeau's (1984) conceptualization of the "practice of everyday life" as a set of tactics that can undo the oppressive grid of power and discipline. While planners and rulers seek to create and enforce the "economy of the proper place" through strategies of rule, everyday and commonplace tactics refuse this discipline. In similar fashion, Simone (2006) presents the African city as "a pirate town," where urban residents develop forms of everyday practice that allow them to operate resourcefully in underresourced cities. This is a context of crisis, where "production possibilities" are severely limited; but this is also a context where "existent materials of all kind are to be appropriated" (Simone 2006, 358). While Simone does not use the term "informality," his analysis suggests that he is describing practices that can be designated as such:

> African cities are characterized by incessantly flexible, mobile, and provisional intersections of residents that operate without clearly delineated notions of how the city is to be inhabited and used....These conjunctions become an infrastructure—a platform providing for and reproducing life in the city. (Simone 2004, 407–408)

Such conceptualizations of "urban informality as a way of life" pay special attention to how the informal emerges as a response to the lack of "stable articulations" of "infrastructure, territory, and urban resources" and becomes a "generalized practice" of "countering marginalization" (Simone 2006, 359). In doing so, they signal that the informal is an alternative urban order, a different way of organizing space and negotiating citizenship. For example, in his work on South Asian cities, Chatterjee (2004, 38) makes a distinction between "civil" and "political" societies. Civil society is bourgeois society and, in the Indian context, an arena of institutions and practices inhabited by a relatively small section of people able to make claims as fully enfranchised citizens. By contrast, political society is the constellation of claims made by those who are only tenuously and ambiguously rights-bearing citizens. Chatterjee (2004, 41) writes that civil society, "restricted to a small section of culturally equipped citizens, represents in countries like India the high ground of modernity." But, "in actual practice, governmental agencies must descend from that high ground to the terrain of political society in order to renew their legitimacy as providers of well-being." The "paralegal" practices and negotiations of this political society is for Chatterjee the politics of much of the people in most of the world.

Chatterjee's work echoes that of Appadurai (2002), who finds in the political actions of Mumbai's slum dwellers a form of "deep democracy"—the ability of the poor to negotiate access to land, urban infrastructure, and services. While Castells (1983) designated the "dependent city" as a "city without citizens," Appadurai (2002, 26) argues that the urban poor of Mumbai are "citizens without a city": a "vital part of the urban workforce" and yet with few of the amenities and protections of urban living. In particular, Appadurai draws attention to the technologies of auto-planning that are used by federations of the urban poor. These forms of "countergovernmentality," as Appadurai calls this, indicate the appropriation of the planner's toolkit by poor and informal communities. It is also in this sense that Benjamin (2008, 719) has made the case for "occupancy urbanism" and the crisis it poses for global capital: "Poor groups, claiming public services and safeguarding territorial claims, open up political spaces that appropriate institutions and fuel an economy that builds complex alliances...locally embedded institutions subvert high-end infrastructure and mega projects." Thus, "'occupancy urbanism' helps poor groups appropriate real estate surpluses via reconstituted land tenure to fuel small businesses whose commodities jeopardize branded chains. Finally, it poses a political consciousness that refuses to be disciplined by NGOs and well-meaning progressive activists and the rhetoric of 'participatory planning.'"

This is the mega-slum, repositioned as an "occupancy of terrain." More broadly, it is the recognition of what Gibson-Graham (2008, 614) has titled "diverse economies" or "projects of economic autonomy and experimentation." Particularly interested in the "social economy," Gibson-Graham celebrates "squatter, slum-dweller, landless and co-housing movements, the global ecovillage movement, fair trade, economic self-determination, the relocalization movement, community-based resource management, and others" (Gibson-Graham 2008, 617). This is of course much more than "urban informality as a way of life"; this is the assertion of such forms of informality as ingredients of a "postcapitalist" order.

Such assertions are a far cry from Davis's "laws of chaos," but they also demand critical scrutiny, especially in their claims of an autonomous, alternative, informal urban sphere. In an echo of Easterly's division between Planners and Searchers, this framework presents the informal city as a way of life that exists in sharp contrast to, or at least in exclusion from, the planned, formal city. But it is a framework that tells us little about how the very categories of formal and informal are constructed, maintained, and deployed. Thus, AlSayyad (2004, 25) notes that what requires explanation is not so much informality as a way of life as does "formality" as a "new mode" of urbanism—one that "was introduced to organize urban society only in the 19th century." In the following section, I build on this observation to pay closer attention to constructions of the formal and informal.

3. The Informal State

The term "informal" can be traced to the work of Keith Hart and the International Labor Organization (ILO) in the early 1970s. While modernization theory struggled to explain how a "marginal mass" was not absorbed by industrialization, Hart showed that such forms of marginality and informality were structural features of urban economies. Writing in the context of Accra, Hart (1973, 61, 68) identified a "world of economic activities outside the organised labor force" carried out by an "urban sub-proletariat." Hart designated these activities as "informal." At more or less the same time, the ILO (1972, in Kanbur 2009) defined the "informal sector" as the activities of "petty traders, street hawkers, shoeshine boys and other groups 'underemployed' on the streets of big towns, and includes a range of wage-earners and self-employed persons, male as well as female." Hart's conceptualization of informality has been commonly interpreted as "the relationship of economic activity to intervention or regulation by the state" (Kanbur, 2009, 5). This is an accurate interpretation of his work. In a reflection on his 1973 paper, Hart (2006, 25) notes that, following Weber, he had argued "that the ability to stabilise economic activity within a bureaucratic form made returns more calculable and regular for the workers as well as their bosses. That stability was in turn guaranteed by the state's laws, which only extended so far into the depths of Ghana's economy." Informal work lay outside this realm of calculable and stable transactions and was thus erratic, with low returns. In many ways, this argument is a precursor to one later put forward by dependency theorists: that the state maintains the informal economy in unregulated form in order to subsidize a system of global capital accumulation (Portes, Castells, and Benton 1989). Indeed, a whole generation of research, much of it produced in Latin America, was to explode the "myth of marginality" (Perlman 1977) and show how informal work and habitat were integral parts of the capitalist city. But Hart also went further. Unlike later interpretations of the "informal sector," he "did not identify the informal economy with a place or a class or even whole persons" (Hart 2006, 25). Instead, he argued that many of Accra's residents sought to forge a multiplicity of livelihoods and income opportunities—in other words, that informality was a generalized condition, a way of life, if you will. Yet, Hart's analysis presents challenges to both the dependency narrative of informality and more populist celebrations. His cautionary note is as valid today as it was in 1973:

> Socialists may argue that foreign capitalist dominance of these economies determines the scope for informal (and formal) development, and condemns the majority of the urban population to deprivation and exploitation. More optimistic liberals may see in informal activities, as described above, the possibility of a dramatic "bootstrap" operation, lifting the underdeveloped economies through their own indigenous enterprise. Before either view—or a middle course stressing both external constraint and autonomous effort—may be espoused, much more empirical research is required. (Hart 1973, 88–89)

Hart's conceptualization of informality is a useful starting point. At the very least, it shifts attention from the informal as the "unplanable" to the role of the state in regulating the formal and the informal. Here, two issues, both also articulated eloquently by Meagher (1995, 259, 279) are crucial: that it is necessary for a conceptual shift "from informality represented as a marginalized sector to 'informalization' conceived as a wider economic response to crisis," and that such a process of "informalization" does not happen "outside the state" but, rather, is a "socio-economic restructuring instigated by the state." Thus, in our edited volume, *Urban Informality*, Nezar AlSayyad and I (Roy and AlSayyad 2004) argue that the urban informality is not a distinct and bounded sector of labor or housing but, rather, a "mode" of the production of space and is a practice of planning. Let me explain.

The splintering of urbanism does not take place at the fissure between formality and informality but, rather, in fractal fashion *within* the informalized production of space. A closer look at the metropolitan regions of the Global South indicates that informal urbanization is as much the purview of wealthy urbanites and suburbanites as it is of squatters and slum dwellers. These forms of informality, which are fully capitalized domains of property, are no more legal than are squatter settlements and shantytowns. But they are expressions of class power and can thus command infrastructure, services, and legitimacy in a way that marks them as substantially different from the landscape of slums. Most important, they come to be designated as "formal" by the state, regularized and regulated, while other forms of informality remain unregularized and unregulated. My research in Calcutta (Roy and AlSayyad 2004) shows that the differential value attached to what is "formal" and what is "informal" creates an uneven geography of spatial value, a patchwork of valorized and devalorized spaces that is, in turn, the frontier of expansion and development. Informalized spaces are reclaimed through urban renewal while formalized spaces accrue value through their legitimacy. It is in this sense that the informal city is wholly planned and that informality is a practice of planning. For example, in Indian cities, informality is inscribed in the ever-shifting relationship between what is legal and illegal, legitimate and illegitimate, authorized and unauthorized. This relationship is both arbitrary and fickle and yet is the site of considerable state power and violence. Thus, Ghertner (2008) notes that almost all of Delhi violates some planning or building law, such that much of the construction in the city can be viewed as "unauthorized." He poses the vital question of why some of these areas are now being designated as illegal and worthy of demolition while others are protected and formalized. How and why is it that the law has come to designate slums as a "nuisance" and the residents of slums as a "secondary category of citizens," those that are distinguished from "normal," private-property-owning citizens? Ghertner (2008, 66) notes that "developments that have the "world-class" look, despite violating zoning or building by-laws, are granted amnesty and heralded as monuments of modernity." Such differentiation, between the informal and the informal (rather than between the legal and the paralegal), is a fundamental axis of inequality in urban India today. While elite "farmhouses" on the edges of Delhi are allowed to function legally as appendages of the agrarian land laws, squatter settlements throughout the city are criminalized and violently demolished. Indeed, against Davis it may be argued that the urban catastrophe of the twenty-first century is the sprawling farmhouse and condominium suburbs of the Global South—resource-greedy landscapes of wealth that have been legalized and protected by the state.

Similarly, Holston (2007, 228) notes that Brazilian cities are marked by an "unstable relationship between the legal and illegal." While it may seem obvious and apparent that the urban poor are engaged in an informal and illegal occupation of land, much of the city itself is occupied through the "misrule of law": "Thus in both the wealthiest and the poorest of Brazilian families we find legal landholdings that are at base legalized usurpations" (Holston 2007, 207). What is the relationship between planning and this sanctified "misrule of law"? Who, then, is authorized to (mis)use the law in such ways as to declare property ownership, zones of exception, and enclaves of value? The democratization of urban space in Brazil, Holston (2007, 204) argues, is a process by which the urban poor have learned to use the law and legitimize their own land claims—"they perpetuate the misrule of law but for their own purposes."

A powerful conceptualization of this idea of urban informality comes in the work of Yiftachel (2009, 88–89). Writing in the context of Israel-Palestine, Yiftachel presents the concept of "gray spaces," "those positioned between the 'whiteness' of legality/approval/safety, and the 'blackness' of eviction/destruction/death." He notes that these spaces are tolerated and managed, but "while being encaged within discourses of 'contamination,' 'criminality' and 'public danger' to the desired 'order of things.'" Yiftachel is particularly interested, as I am, in analyzing the manner in which the state formalizes and criminalizes different spatial configurations:

> The understanding of gray space as stretching over the entire spectrum, from powerful developers to landless and homeless "invaders," helps us conceptualize two associated dynamics we may term here "whitening" and "blackening." The former alludes to the tendency of the system to "launder" gray spaces created "from above" by powerful or favorable interests. The latter denotes the process of "solving" the problem of marginalized gray space by destruction, expulsion or elimination. The state's violent power is put into action, turning gray into black. (Yiftachel 2009, 92)

Such processes are evident not only in the Global South but equally in the Global North. The seminal work of Peter Ward (1999) demonstrates how, in the *colonias* of Texas, the working poor come to be housed in the liminal space of "extra-territorial jurisdictions." These *colonias* are privately developed and sold—and thereby tolerated by the state—and yet criminalized and excluded from utilities, services, and legal protection by virtue of their fragile construction. Similarly, Klein (2007b) argues that, in the United States, the deregulation of political economies is tied to the deregulation of space. She shows how, in the last decade, there has been the emergence of a parallel, privatized disaster infrastructure that caters exclusively to the wealthy and the "chosen." This is a world, as Klein notes (2007a, 420), where the wealthy can opt out of the collective system, where the idea of the public interest loses all meaning, and where the city becomes a "world of suburban

Green Zones…as for those outside the secured perimeter, they will have to make do with the remains of the national system."

I am interested in an additional dimension of informality: how the informalization of space is also the informalization of the state. While it has been often assumed that the modern state governs its subjects through technologies of visibility, counting, mapping, and enumerating, in *City Requiem, Calcutta*, I argue that regimes of rule also operate through an "unmapping" of cities (Roy 2003). This is particularly evident on the peri-urban fringes of Calcutta where forms of deregulation and unmapping have allowed the state considerable territorialized flexibility to alter land use, deploy eminent domain, and acquire land. In particular, it has been possible for the state to undertake various forms of urban and industrial development—for example, through the conversion of land to urban use, often in violation of its own bans against such conversion. In other words, the state is not only an arbiter of value but also an informalized entity that actively utilizes informality as an instrument of both accumulation and authority. Such planning regimes function through ambiguity rather than through rigidity. However, such ambiguity is a sign of a strong, even authoritative state, rather than one that is weak or unsure of its power. An example of these types of state power is provided by Ong (2006) in her analysis of neoliberal forms of government. She shows that sovereign rule often uses zoning technologies to create zones of exception. Such invocations of exception produce a "pattern of noncontiguous, differently administered spaces of graduated or variegated sovereignty" (Ong 2006, 7). It is this uneven geography of spatial value, the fractal geometry of regulated and deregulated space, that is the landscape of urban informality.

4. THE POLITICS OF THE INFORMAL CITY

Much of the urban growth of the twenty-first century will take place in the cities of the Global South. It is therefore tempting to make the case for a "Southern urbanism," one characterized by "urban informality as a way of life," the "habitus of the dispossessed." But as I have already argued, urban informality is not the ecology of the mega-slum; rather, it is a mode of the production of space and a practice of planning. Not surprisingly, the dynamics of urban informality vary greatly from context to context. Thus, in this concluding section, I sketch two contrasting pathways of the informal city, in Brazil and India. Each can be understood to stand in for a broader trajectory—Latin American cities and South/Southeast Asian cities. However, the issue at hand is less the generalizibility of these specific cases and more the insights they provide for an analysis of the heterogeneity of "Southern urbanism."

Brazil has become famous as the home of the "right to the city" movement. While the Brazilian constitution of 1988 set the stage for a unique brand of participatory democracy, it is only through a long social struggle that the "right to the city" was institutionalized in the City Statute of 2001. The statue constructs a new legal-political paradigm for urbanism, which involves the democratization of access to land and housing in Brazilian cities, as well as the democratization of the process of urban management. It establishes a set of collective rights, including the right to urban planning, the right to capture surplus value, and the right to regularize informal settlements. In particular, it intervenes in the uneven geography of spatial value by seeking to change the ways in which space produces value and functions both as a commodity and as a public good. It is thus that the City Statute conceptualizes a "social function" of property, making it possible for municipal governments to share in the surplus value generated by real estate development (Caldeira and Holston 2005). Opponents of the City Statute have sought to characterize these instruments as a confiscation of private property rights or as "just another tax." But the Instituto Polis (n.d., 30–31), based in Sao Paulo, boldly provides a counter-argument: "What really occurs in our cities…is the private appropriation (and in the hands of the few) of real estate appreciation that is the result of public and collective investments, paid by everyone's taxes. This private appropriation of public wealth drives a powerful machine of territorial exclusion, a monster that transforms urban development into a real estate product, denying most citizens the right to benefit from the essential elements of urban infrastructure." This is, as Fernandes (2007, 207) notes, an ambitious new "project of the city," translating into spatial terms the "social project" proposed by Henri Lefebvre.

While it remains to be seen how the City Statute is actually implemented, what is important is that it forces a new set of urban meanings on the informal city. It can be argued such meanings have roots in a distinctive urban politics—what Holston (2007, 4) has called "insurgent citizenship," a citizenship that "asserts right-claims addressing urban practices as its substance." Holston (2007, 4) argues that this politics emerges from the auto-constructed peripheries of the urban working poor, where since the 1970s members of this social class "became new citizens not primarily through the struggles of labor but through those of the city." Such rights-based struggles are not necessarily radical; indeed, they often produce and reinforce propertied paradigms of citizenship. Nevertheless, Brazil's City Statute represents a distinctive configuration of city, state, and regulation.

In sharp contrast to such rights-based politics is the case of Indian cities. Here, the turn of the twenty-first century has been marked by the violent expansion of the frontier of urbanization, a making way and making space for the new Indian urban middle class through the smashing of the homes and livelihoods of the rural-urban poor in Delhi, Mumbai, Bangalore, and Calcutta. These new forms of urbanism seek to remake Indian cities as "world class" cities—those that are globally competitive with other Asian successes, such as Shanghai, Singapore, and Dubai. With this in mind, in Calcutta, the government has sought to displace peasants and sharecroppers from agricultural land in order to accommodate special economic zones, foreign investment, and gated suburban developments. In Delhi, "slum clearance" has been carried out through a set of judicial rulings that seek to assert a "public interest" (Bhan 2009). In Mumbai, evictions were starkly evident in the winter of 2004–2005. Acting on a bold report by the global consulting firm McKinsey & Company, the city put into motion "Vision Mumbai." A cornerstone of this vision is a world-class, slum-free city, promoted by an elite nongovernmental organization (NGO), Bombay First. In a matter of weeks, government authorities had demolished several slums, rendering 300,000 people homeless. The demolitions came to be known as the "Indian tsunami." The urban poor of Mumbai were quite literally being erased from the face of the world-class city. Vijay Patil, the municipality officer who led the demolitions, stated that it was time to turn Mumbai into the "next Shanghai," and to do so "we want to put the fear of the consequences of migration into these people. We have to restrain them from coming to Mumbai" (BBC News, February 3, 2005). "How can you ask people to stop coming to Mumbai? This is a democracy," noted urban analyst Kalpana Sharma (BBC News, February 3, 2005). Particularly striking about the Vision Mumbai demolitions is that they carried neither the promise nor the pretense of resettlement and rehabilitation. Indeed, the United Nations Special Rapporteur on adequate housing, Miloon Kothari, sharply criticized Mumbai at the UN Commission on Human Rights, noting that the city had effectively criminalized poverty and violated all expectations of humane resettlement (Khan 2005).

Advocacy groups have argued that the "slum" is vital to the functioning of Indian urbanism—that, for example, Dharavi, Asia's largest slum at the heart of Mumbai, is "a million-dollar economic miracle providing food to Mumbai and exporting crafts and manufactured goods to places as far away as Sweden" (Echanove and Srivastava 2009). But such devalorized spaces are now being rapidly reclaimed in India. Dharavi is also a particularly important urban "asset" (Tutton 2009), at the intersection of the city's infrastructural connections. Mukesh Mehta, the architect who is leading the redevelopment plan, argues that Dharavi could be India's "Canary Wharf" (Tutton 2009). Today, nineteen consortiums from around the world are vying to claim and redevelop the "only vast tract of land left that can be made available for fresh construction activities" at the heart of the city (Singh 2007). Such forms of urban renewal are bolstered, in Indian cities, by the emergence of the forms and structures of middle-class rule. Framed as good governance, these self-organized initiatives seek to reform government, improve service delivery, and assert the rights and needs of middle-class neighborhoods. Many of them are "protection of place" associations that thereby initiate and mobilize the evictions and demolitions of slums and squatter settlements. Baviskar (2003), in the context of Delhi, has rightly labeled these forms of urban governance a "bourgeois environmentalism," one that asserts the rights of "consumer-citizens" to "leisure, safety, aesthetics, and health" and devalues the citizenship of those who are poor and propertyless.

But a new urban politics is now afoot in Indian cities. It seeks to challenge, even blockade, the ferocious redevelopment that has been under way. In the Calcutta metropolitan region, squatters, sharecroppers, and peasants have mobilized to block development projects that displace the rural-urban poor, making it impossible for the state to deploy its power of eminent domain. In Mumbai, the brutal vision of a world-class city is contested by the National Alliance of Peoples Movements (NAPM). Since the Vision Mumbai plan had sought to remake Mumbai in the image of Shanghai, the NAPM has framed the "Shanghaification of Mumbai" as primarily an issue of rights: whether the urban-rural poor have a "right over urban space" (Patkar and Athialy 2005): "In Mumbai, 60 per cent live in the slums. Shouldn't they have a right over 60 per cent of the land in Mumbai?"

The social movements in India signal a heterodox reconstruction of the informal city and its practices of planning. They seek to assert the social function of property and to insist upon a right to the city. A similar confrontation, albeit put forward on very different terms, also marks the case of the Brazilian City Statute. In important ways, such politics reveals the logic of urban informality: the making and unmaking of spatial value. Various state practices and technologies are implicated in this differentiated production of spatial value. Some are more visible than others, such as the demolition of slums and squatter settlements. But there are many others: tools of enumeration and mapping; the zoning of land uses; the provision of infrastructure; the use of eminent domain to confiscate property for a public purpose. Applied in flexible and selective fashion, they ensure the planned production of urban informality.

References

AlSayyad, N. 2004. "Urban Informality as a Way of Life." In *Urban Informality: Transnational Perspectives from the Middle East, Latin America, and South Asia*, edited by A. Roy and N. AlSayyad, 7–30. Lanham, MD: Lexington Books.

Appadurai, A. 2002. "Deep Democracy: Urban Governmentality and the Horizon of Politics." *Public Culture* 14(1): 21–47.

Auyero, J. 1999. "'This Is a Lot Like The Bronx, Isn't It?': Lived Experiences of Marginality in an Argentine Slum." *International Journal of Urban and Regional Research* 23:45–69.

Auyero, J. 2000. "The Hyper-Shantytown: Neoliberal Violence(S) in the Argentine Slum." *Ethnography* 1:93–116.

Baviskar, A. 2003. "Between Violence and Desire: Space, Power, and Identity in the Making of Metropolitan Delhi." *International Social Science Journal* 55(175): 89–98.

Bayat, A. 2000. "From 'Dangerous Classes' to 'Quiet Rebels': The Politics of the Urban Subaltern in the Global South." *International Sociology* 15(3): 533–57.

Bayat, A. 2007. "Radical Religion and the Habitus of the Dispossessed: Does Islamic Militancy Have an Urban Ecology?" *International Journal of Urban and Regional Research* 31(3): 579–90.

Benjamin, S. 2008. "Occupancy Urbanism: Radicalizing Politics and Economy Beyond Policy and Programs." *International Journal of Urban and Regional Research* 32(3): 719–29.

Bhan, G. 2009. "'This Is No Longer The City I Once Knew': Evictions, The Urban Poor and the Right to the City in Millennial Delhi." *Environment and Urbanization* 21(1): 127–42.

Bromley, R. 2004. "Power, Property, and Poverty: Why De Soto's 'Mystery of Capital' Cannot Be Solved." In *Urban Informality: Transnational Perspectives from the Middle*

East, Latin America, and South Asia, edited by A. Roy and N. AlSayyad, 271–88. Lanham, MD: Lexington Books.

Caldeira, T., and J. Holston. 2005. "State and Urban Space in Brazil: From Modernist Planning to Democratic Interventions." *Global Assemblages: Technology, Ethics, and Politics as Anthropological Problems*, edited by A. Ong and S. Collier, 393–416. Cambridge, UK: John Wiley and Blackwell.

Castells, M. 1983. *The City and the Grassroots*. Berkeley, CA: University of California Press.

Chatterjee, P. 2004. *The Politics of the Governed: Reflections on Popular Politics in Most of the World*. New York: Columbia University Press.

Davis, M. 2004. "Urbanization of Empire: Mega Cities and the Laws of Chaos." *Social Text* 22(4): 9–15.

Davis, M. 2006. *Planet of Slums*. New York: Verso.

De Certeau, M. 1984. *The Practice of Everyday Life*, translated by S. Rendall. Berkeley, CA: University of California Press.

de Soto, H. 1989. *The Other Path: The Invisible Revolution in the Third World*. London: I.B. Taurus.

De Soto, H. 2000. *The Mystery of Capital: Why Capitalism Triumphs in the West and Fails Everywhere Else*. New York: Basic Books.

Easterly, W. 2006. *The White Man's Burden: Why the West's Efforts to Aid the Rest Have Done So Much Ill and So Little Good*. New York: Penguin Press.

Echanove, M., and R. Srivastava. 2009. "Taking the Slum out of "Slumdog." *New York Times*, February 21. Available at: http://www.nytimes.com/2009/02/21/opinion/21srivastava.html.

Eckstein, S. 1990. "Urbanization Revisited. Inner-City Slum of Hope and Squatter Settlement of Despair." *World Development* 18:165–81.

Fernandes, E. 2007. "Constructing the 'Right to the City' In Brazil." *Social and Legal Studies* 16(2): 201–19.

Ghertner, A. 2008. "Analysis Of New Legal Discourse Behind Delhi's Slum Demolitions." *Economic and Political Weekly* May 17, 57–66.

Gibson-Graham, J. K. 2008. "Diverse Economies: Performative Practices for 'Other Worlds.'" *Progress in Human Geography* 32(5): 613–32.

Gilbert, A. 2007. "The Return of the Slum: Does Language Matter?" *International Journal of Urban and Regional Research* 31(4): 697–713.

Hart, K. 1973. "Informal Income Opportunities and Urban Employment in Ghana." *Journal of Modern African Studies* 11(1): 61–89.

Hart, K. 2006. "Bureaucratic Form and the Informal Economy." In *Linking the Formal and Informal Economy: Concepts and Policies*, edited by B. Guha-Khasnobis, R. Kanbur, and E. Ostrom, 21–35. New York: Oxford University Press.

Holston, J. 2007. *Insurgent Citizenship: Disjunctions of Democracy and Modernity in Brazil*. Princeton, NJ: Princeton University Press.

International Labor Organization. 1972. *Incomes, Employment and Equality in Kenya*. Geneva: ILO.

Instituto Polis. n.d. *The Statute of the City: New Tools for Assuring the Right to the City in Brazil*. Available at: http://www.polis.org.br/obras/arquivo_163.pdf.

Kanbur, R. 2009. "Conceptualising Informality: Regulation and Enforcement." Working paper 2009–11, Department of Economics and Applied Management, Cornell University, Ithaca, NY.

Khan E. 2005. "UN Flays India for Slum Demolition." Radiff News. Available at: http://in.rediff.com/news/2005/mar/30un.htm; accessed January 20, 2008.

Klein, N. 2007a. *The Shock Doctrine: The Rise of Disaster Capitalism*. New York: Metropolitan Books.

Klein, N. 2007b. "Rapture Rescue 911: Disaster Response for the Chosen." *The Nation*, November 19. Available at: http://www.thenation.com/article/rapture-rescue-911-disaster-response-chosen.

Meagher, K., 1995. "Crisis, Informalization and the Urban Informal Sector in Sub-Saharan Africa." *Development and Change* 26(2): 259–84.

Ong, A. 2006. *Neoliberalism as Exception: Mutations in Citizenship and Sovereignty*. Durham, NC: Duke University Press.

Patkar, M., and J. Athialy. 2005. "The Shanghaification of Mumbai." Countercurrents. org. Available at: http://www.countercurrents.org/hr-athialy110805.htm.

Perlman, J. 1977. *The Myth of Marginality*. Berkeley, CA: University of California Press.

Perlman, J. 2004. "Marginality: From Myth to Reality in the Favelas of Rio de Janeiro." In *Urban Informality: Transnational Perspectives from the Middle East, Latin America, and South Asia*, edited by A. Roy and N. AlSayyad, 105–46. Lanham, MD: Lexington Books.

Portes, A., M. Castells, and L. Benton. 1989. *The Informal Economy*. Baltimore: Johns Hopkins University Press.

Roy, A. 2003. *City Requiem, Calcutta: Gender and the Politics of Poverty*. Minneapolis: University of Minnesota Press.

Roy, A., and N. AlSayyad, eds. 2004. *Urban Informality: Transnational Perspectives from the Middle East, Latin America, and South Asia*. Lanham, MD: Lexington Books.

Sachs, J. 2005. *The End of Poverty: Economic Possibilities for our Time*. New York: Penguin.

Simone, A. 2004. "People as Infrastructure: Intersecting Fragments in Johannesburg." *Public Culture* 16(3): 407–29.

Simone, A. 2006. "Pirate Towns: Reworking Social and Symbolic Infrastructures in Johannesburg and Douala." *Urban Studies* 43(): 357–70.

Singh, S. 2007. "Dharavi Displacement Project." Civil Society. Available at: www. civilsocietyonline.com.

Tutton, M. 2009. "Real Life 'Slumdog' Slum to be Demolished." CNN travel news. Available at: http://edition.cnn.com/2009/TRAVEL/02/23/dharavi.mumbai.slums/index.html.

Wacquant, L. 1996. "The Rise of Advanced Marginality: Notes on Its Nature and Implications." *Acta Sociologica* 39:121–39.

Wacquant, L. 1999. "Urban Marginality in the Coming Millennium." *Urban Studies* 36: 1639–47.

Wacquant, L. 2007. *Urban Outcasts: A Comparative Sociology of Advanced Marginality*. Cambridge, UK: Polity Press.

Ward, P. 1999. *Colonias and Public Policy in Texas: Urbanization by Stealth*. Austin: University of Texas Press.

Wirth, L. 1938. "Urbanism as a Way of Life." *American Journal of Sociology* 44(1): 1–24.

Yiftachel, O. 2009. "Theoretical Notes on 'Gray Cities': The Coming of Urban Apartheid?" *Planning Theory* 8(1): 88–100.

CHAPTER 34

CITIZEN PLANNERS: FROM SELF-HELP TO POLITICAL TRANSFORMATION

VICTORIA A. BEARD

1. INTRODUCTION

THIS chapter is about the work of citizen planners. For much of the last century, our understanding of planning practice and planning thought has been dominated by a conceptualization of planning as a professional, technical practice carried out by agents of the state. In this understanding, planning is practiced by trained architects, engineers, economists, politicians, and, more recently, trained professional city planners. Often ignored in this conceptualization is the influence that ordinary citizens have in shaping the urban environment (Evans 2002). One area where the role of citizen planners is clearly visible is the Global South, where the vast majority of urban residents live outside of formal planning and regulatory frameworks, in so-called squatter, informal, or popular settlements (Davis 2006). State planners, as well as the market, have largely ignored these urban spaces because they perceive neither opportunity for profit nor political imperative promoting intervention. Yet, such settlements are growing at an unprecedented rate, a situation in which ordinary citizens—acting from necessity, concern, or creative impulses—are impelled to assume the mantel of planners and protectors of the public good.

In the Global North, too, the citizen planner is taking on an expanded role in shaping the urban environment. In the North, the physical spaces or communities where citizen planners work are often not as clearly defined as in the Global South, where citizen planners usually focus on a territorial-based community or contiguous human settlement. Communities where citizen planners of the North appear are sometimes defined by location, but often are communities with a collective experience or cause related to racial or ethnicity identity, social class, gender, or sexual orientation.[1] In both the Global North and Global South, however, citizen planners often fill gaps overlooked by the state and the market (Sandercock 1998; Douglass and Friedmann 1998). For example, a citizen planner might work on a specific problem such as air quality or access to affordable housing, or an issue of social justice. In such a context, the citizen planner is likely to work outside the state or private sector, in the "third sector" comprising community-based, non-profit or nongovernmental organizations.

This chapter draws primarily on examples from the Global South in describing the activity of citizen planners, ranging from participation in self-help efforts to the more politicized struggles for broad social and political transformation. Using as a theoretical starting point Friedmann's (1987) broad conceptualization of planning as the link between knowledge and action in the public domain, the chapter reviews contributions from research on collective action and social movements as a foundation for understanding the breadth of the activities undertaken by citizen planners. Next, the chapter provides examples of three distinct modes of planning commonly practiced by citizen planners: community-based, covert, and radical planning. The chapter concludes with a critical discussion of the efficacy of these efforts, including the cost in terms of time and resources; the problems of elite capture, representation, and adherence to democratic principles; and the relationship of the citizen planner to the state.

2. Theoretical Foundations for Citizen Planners

John Friedmann (1987) was the first planning scholar to conceptualize planning as the link between knowledge and action in the processes of societal guidance and in the processes of social transformation in the public domain. Friedmann's term *societal guidance* refers primarily to the work of the state planner on behalf of the public good. When he refers to the process of *social transformation*, he is describing agents outside the state engaging in "political practices of system transformation" (Friedmann 1987, 38). Friedmann describes the inherent conflict between these two types of planning:

> Planners engaged in these two practices are necessarily in conflict. It is a conflict
> between the interests of a bureaucratic state and the interests of the political

community. The bulk of public planning, of course, is related to societal guidance and includes both allocative and innovative forms. The pressure for system-wide transformation is intensified when, in the course of a system-wide crisis, the legitimate authority of the state declines, and the state itself is so weakened that it can no longer successfully repress the radical practices of the political community. (38–39)

Friedmann makes a significant contribution to planning thought and practice by connecting planning as societal guidance to the social reform tradition in planning, and by connecting planning as social transformation to the social mobilization tradition. Although this conceptual broadening of our understanding of legitimate planning practice laid the theoretical foundation for our understanding of the work of citizen planners, and particularly those in direct conflict with state planning, it also created a false dichotomy. In this chapter, the work of the citizen planner is explained within the context of a more nuanced set of practices, including community-based, covert, and more overt radical or insurgent planning. In understanding these practices, we can gain much from the contributions of recent research on collective action and social movements (Beard and Basolo 2009).

2.1 Collective Action

Since the citizen planner is often working without a formal position, a title, or support from the state, scholarly work on collective action has much to contribute to our understanding of his or her practice. Citizen planners work for a nongovernmental organization, a community-based organization, or individually as activists or volunteers. In any case, their work requires collective action. That can range from a citizen planner mobilizing a community for physical improvements (for example, planning, building, and maintaining a drainage system to reduce seasonal flooding) to mobilizing the community to achieve redistribution of power and broad structural change (for example, more control over the planning process, the distribution of resources, and planning outcomes).

The citizen planner works collectively with other citizens in a process of deliberation, prioritization, decision making, implementation, and ultimately evaluation. Thus, the dilemmas faced by the citizen planner are the same as those found in collective action more generally (Beard and Dasgupta 2006). A common dilemma arises from the individual's inherent lack of incentive to contribute to a public good or service. It is theorized that public goods and services can receive inadequate resources because an individual who does not contribute nevertheless will benefit, thus creating the "free rider" problem. A second dilemma that plagues collective action is the difficulty of controlling individual use of resources. It is theorized that each individual will tend to overuse resources until ultimately the shared resources are destroyed, as describe in Hardin's (1968) "tragedy of the commons."

Recent work on collective action challenges the earlier formulations of these dilemmas. Ostrom (1990, 2005), for one, recognizes that individuals have agency to create agreements, institutions, and systems of management with the capacity to evolve and prevent tragic outcomes. Her empirical work, a series of case studies, demonstrates that a "group of principals who are in an interdependent situation can organize and govern themselves to obtain continuing joint benefits when all face temptation to free-ride, shirk, or otherwise act opportunistically" (Ostrom 1990, 29). That is precisely the challenge encountered by the citizen planner who organizes citizens to find planning solutions with continuing joint benefit. Ostrom's more recent work focuses on how norms and rules affect the management of public goods and common pool resources (Ostrom 2005). Significant challenges for the citizen planner are to work within a set of norms or to establish new rules that not only protect the integrity of the planning process but also its resources from elite capture (Dasgupta and Beard 2007).

Much of the research on collective action that has focused on the management and use of common-pool natural resources (e.g., Agrawal 2001; Baland and Platteau 1996; Ostrom 1990) has general applicability to the work of the citizen planner. Agrawal (2001) aggregates this work, identifying five areas of "facilitating conditions" for successful governance of common pool resources. One area comprises the characteristics of the resource system; for example, does the resource system have well-defined boundaries? In planning, that leads to the question of whether or not the planning process and planning outcomes have clearly defined boundaries. Research on common-pool natural resources also examines group characteristics. In planning, that raises questions about the size of the community, the composition of subgroups, ethnic heterogeneity, inequality, and whether or not the population has shared interests. Another area is the relationship between the resource system and group characteristics (i.e., the relationship between benefits of planning and group characteristics). A fourth area identified by Agrawal (2001) as relevant for managing common-pool resources is institutional arrangements; for example, do the institutions in place have the power to create and enforce rules of conduct? A fifth area is the relationship between the resource system and institutional arrangements. For the citizen planner, the question here would be whether or not an institution is appropriate to handle a particular planning problem. For example, does a nongovernmental organization have the technical knowledge and institutional capacity to plan a system of water distribution? Does a particular community-based organization have the capacity to address issues related to crime and public safety? Finally, the last area Agrawal (2001) is concerned with is the external environment, such as a community's relationship to the state and external markets. An area not dealt with in Agrawal's work, and an area that is critical to the work of the citizen planner, is the significance of broader social structures and power relationships.

2.2 Social Movements

Social movements, while a form of collective action, differ in significant ways from the collective action research discussed above. Social movements are by definition politically oppositional because they challenge the status quo. Whereas a significant subset of the collective action research, in focusing on governance and management of natural resources, tends to emphasize cooperative arrangements, the research on social movements emphasizes the problem of unequal power relations and the struggle for structural change. Social movements research also differs from the collective action research previously discussed in its greater emphasis on urban issues—for example, the leftist political party (PT) in Porto Alegre, Brazil, and the urban barrio movement in Latin America and the Philippines (Abers 2000; Friedmann 1989; Shatkin 2000). Social movements research therefore tends to have more relevance for the citizen planners working in urban areas.

McAdam, Tarrow, and Tilly (2001) describe the five main elements of the classic model used to analyze a social movement. The first element is the broad process of social change occurring in a political, cultural, and economic environment. The second element is the combination of political opportunities and constraints that individuals confront. Third is the form of the organization or associational space where, at a politically opportune time, the mobilization takes place. The fourth element is framing: the act of translating grievances into a way that connects people and makes them optimistic about their participation in the movement. Fifth are repertoires of contention, a term used to describe the strategies or tactics that people use in social movements. McAdam, Tarrow, and Tilly (2001, 42) underscore a number of limitations of this model: (1) it tends to focus on static relationships and individual movements; (2) it is too derivative of the American political experience in the 1960s; and (3) it places too much emphasis on the beginning phases of social movements.

The authors address these weaknesses by proposing a more dynamic model based on three micro-mechanisms. The first is an "analysis of small-scale causal mechanisms that recur in different combinations with different aggregate consequences in varying historical settings." The authors define such mechanisms as "a delimited class of events that alter relations among specified sets of elements in identical or closely similar ways over a variety of situations." Further, the authors identify processes as important and define them as "regular sequences of such mechanisms that produce similar (general more complex and contingent) transformation of those elements." Finally, they identify episodes, defined as a "continuous stream of contention including collective claims making that bears on other parties' interests" (McAdam, Tarrow, and Tilly 2001, 24).

Drawing on this model, in the context of the citizen planner, a mechanism might be a forced relocation of poor urban residents and the recognition of an opportunity to stake a collective claim to land tenure. The process would be community-based planning; for example, an effort to bring out and inform residents, a series of deliberative meetings reaching agreement about priorities, and decision making about a course of action. The episode would be the oppositional action taken in response to the threat; in this example, returning to the location from which people were evicted and reconstruction of housing units at night; or thousands of protesters physically overwhelming the courts or financial districts.

In order to analyze and understand the work of the citizen planner who seeks to challenge the status quo, one should consider the relevance and the interrelationship of (1) the elements of the classic social movements model; (2) the McAdam, Tarrow, and Tilly (2001) revised model; and (3) the broader socio-historical and political context.

3. THE PRACTICE OF CITIZEN PLANNING

This section describes three modes of citizen planning practice: community-based planning, covert planning, and radical planning. It provides specific examples of how the citizen planner in the Global South has used these three modes. The modes of practice represent broad areas, in each of which a citizen planner uses different techniques, is engaged in a fundamentally different relationship with the state, and has different objectives, ranging from addressing the gaps in material well-being to broad social and political transformation.

3.1 Community-Based Planning and Self-Help Movements

With the rise of civil society in the Global South, the social and political spaces available to the citizen planner engaged in community-based planning have both expanded and diversified. In community-based planning, ordinary citizens plan on behalf of their local communities, sometimes collaborating with other state, nonstate, and private-sector actors. In the Global South, such planning often seeks to provide basic infrastructure or services, or to create and distribute public goods. Sometimes the state encourages or simply ignores community-based planning because having citizens provide for themselves reduces political and fiscal pressures on the state. Since the 1960s, community-based planning has often been characterized in terms of community self-help efforts (Hirschman 1984; Peattie 1968; Turner and Fichter 1972). Examples include upgrades of informal settlements, owner-built housing, and, more recently, community-driven development and micro-finance.

An early and well-known example of the intersection of community-based planning and the self-help movement is the Kampung Improvement Program (KIP) in Indonesia. Under political pressure, Jakarta's city government started the program in 1969 (Holod and Rastorfer 1983). The main objective of the program was to raise the low standard of living in Jakarta's poor urban settlements. Like many capital cities in the developing world, Jakarta experienced a massive population increase in the 1960s and 1970s as a result of both natural population growth and the influx of rural migrants. In the absence of affordable housing, rural migrants settled in informal, unserviced, and crowded settlements. In these extensive settlements, urban sanitary services—indoor plumbing, sewage disposal, piped water, and solid waste removal—were virtually nonexistent. The dense settlements mostly consisted of one- to two-story structures separated by narrow footpaths. The lack of basic infrastructure combined with the residential density created dangerous health and environmental conditions.

In response to this urban environmental crisis, the Jakarta municipal government decided the most appropriate and cost-effective option was the "sites and services" approach implemented through KIP. In its early iterations, the program was implemented as a top-down, uniform formula for urban services (Holod and Rastorfer 1983). The difficulty was that the formula assumed uniformity in the physical settlements, as well as uniformity in the patterns of user behavior. Partly as community members' response to these early programmatic limitations, and partly because of the nature of community organization in Indonesia, the program became increasingly participatory.

While participation varied across settlements, depending on the attitude of the local civil servant responsible for the program's administration, later phases of the program did generate impressive examples of citizen planning in which local residents made significant decisions about the planning and maintaining of services. Citizen planners decided on what infrastructure was needed and where it should be located. They devised a system for regular maintenance and collecting user fees. It is important to note that KIP was conceived and then implemented for decades in an extremely tightly controlled political environment where open critiques of the state and local government were not tolerated. Yet, the program allowed citizen planners autonomy and control over their immediate environments because they were perceived as agents furthering the state's agenda for social and economic development—and not as fomenting any sort of political critique or social movement.

The KIP program and the other community-based planning and self-help efforts implemented during the same period were forerunners of the World Bank's fastest-growing strategy for delivering development assistance: community driven development, or CDD (Mansuri and Rao 2004). Like its predecessors, CDD is an approach to international development that gives control to the citizen planner. It is assumed that CDD empowers the poor because well-designed efforts "are inclusive of the poor and vulnerable groups, build positive social capital, and give [the poor] greater voice both in their community and with government entities" (Dongier et al. 2002, 304). The World Bank uses CDD in rural and urban areas to address diverse needs including, but not limited to, the provision of basic infrastructure, nutrition programs for mothers and infants, and access to financial resources and services. Currently, the World Bank's CDD portfolio is approximately $2 billion a year (World Bank 2009). This level of resource allocation underscores the large international development agency's growing interest in the work of the citizen planner.

3.2 Covert Planning

In some cases, citizen planners recognize the need for broad structural or political change to facilitate effective planning at the local level. To achieve that change is particularly complicated in restrictive political environments where public participation and political action are tightly controlled. In such nonliberal, nondemocratic political contexts, citizen planners often turn to covert planning, defined as planning that, on the surface, appears nonconfrontational, but that works in subtle, undetected ways to transform power relationships.

The understanding of covert planning builds on Scott's (1986) description of everyday forms of resistance and Kerkvliet's (2005, 5) description of everyday politics. Scott's (1986, 5) work in this area responds to accounts of the long history of class struggle that, in his view, are "systematically distorted in a state-centric direction." Scott makes the argument that scholarly work on peasant rebellion has been overly focused on large-scale insurrections, leaving the smaller, seemingly less significant forms of resistance largely unnoticed. Yet these smaller and subtler actions may, over time, have a greater cumulative impact. Among everyday forms of resistance Scott includes foot dragging, false compliance, pilfering, feigned ignorance, slander, arson, and sabotage (Scott 1986, 6). Kerkvliet (2005) also describes a similar set of behaviors as everyday politics. Covert planning is akin to everyday resistance and everyday politics in its sense that the cost of overtly challenging authority outweighs the potential gain; however, covert planning differs from Scott's and Kerkvliet's formulations because it is a collective, deliberate, and sustained effort to make small, incremental changes.

Covert planning either ostensibly supports the state's agenda or, alternatively, exists undetected by the state's radar. One example of covert planning is when citizens in a squatter settlement worked collectively to upgrade the settlement and in the process realize that their effort has had the (possibly unintended) effect of facilitating greater land tenure security (Beard 1999). In this case, as the community was mimicking the state-sponsored upgrading program, the citizens eventually became aware of how their improvements to the community's physical appearance and the local investments in the built environment had resulted in de facto land tenure rights (Beard 1999). Moreover, the collective action necessary to carry out the upgrading program was a social learning process through which the community gained valuable organizational skills. The combination of the physical improvements and the community's newly acquired organizing skills made it much more difficult for the state to force relocation.

Covert planning also has been used in the Global South to address gender inequality and empower women. Scheyven (1998, 235) argues that, in contexts where women are tightly controlled as in the Solomon Islands, subtle strategies can be more effective than confrontational ones. These strategies range from pragmatic improvements in women's material welfare to political resistance. According to Scheyven, the strategies and goals of Western feminists—for example, their radical approaches to achieving equal rights and legislative changes—are often not appropriate in non-Western contexts and so fail to address the immediate needs and priorities of women there. Moreover, women in the Global South have clearly expressed their desire to set their own development agendas. Scheyven's work (1998, 249) describes the benefits of the subtle strategies employed in the two development efforts she studied:

> Subtle strategies can result in a strong undercurrent of change without being confrontation; so they do not attract unnecessary attention and opposition to the change which is taking place. As long as potential antagonists are not alerted to the degree of change occurring, women are able to continue with their work largely undeterred by dissonant husbands, church leaders or village elders. Adopting subtle strategies for change can mean that women can better plan for their own development, while facing a minimum of interference from those with more power who may otherwise have wanted to undermine their efforts.

She explains how such strategies are particularly effective in contexts where traditional values and men's control over women are being challenged. In such a situation, overt strategies could raise widespread opposition that would destroy the modest initiatives that nevertheless, over time, could lead to profound changes.

Another example of covert planning from Indonesia is the development of a community library in a squatter settlement (Beard 2002). The story of the library has to be understood in the context of the residents' extreme social and physical insecurity based on the absence of legal land tenure, seasonal flooding of a river in their community, and most residents' low-wage employment in the informal sector. The community was surrounded by similar squatter settlements with the same land tenure problem, and the state had periodically attempted to relocate households from the neighboring settlements.

The citizen planners who planned the library had experience with a diverse array of social and economic development programs, many of them promoted by the central government. However, some efforts had been started by the city's local government and the citizen planners themselves had started others. Notably, the programs initiated by local residents were often similar to or complemented the state-sponsored programs. For example, the health-care clinic for the elderly, which was begun by citizen planners, was modeled after the mother and child health-care clinic (Posyandu), a well-known state program. As a result, the citizen planners' clinic was never perceived as a challenge to the state's authority.

In the case of the library, the citizen planners were members of the youth group—young community activists—that planned, implemented, and maintained the library, an initiative that complemented the state's programs to improve educational outcomes and eradicate illiteracy. The community library came into being through a long, incremental process. First, the youth group—local citizen planners—organized a tutoring program in which the older children tutored younger children and also operated a reading room where young people exchanged books. Before proposing the library, the youth group sought consensus among its members. It then moved to gain consensus among community leaders. With its broad support thus established, the library was allocated space in the community office. Eventually the library obtained a small, outside grant and support from the state. The library was managed successfully during the final years of the Suharto administration.

In late 1997 and early 1998, Indonesia was severely affected by the Asian economic crisis, which resulted in months of inflation and devastated households living on the economic margin. On May 12, 1998, four Indonesian university students participating in a public demonstration were killed by Indonesian security forces (Bird 1999, 29). That event, violent attacks on ethnic Chinese and the university student's occupation of the National Assembly building, culminated in massive demonstrations (Siegel 1998). During this period of upheaval, some of the citizen planners responsible for the library began collectively to publicly articulate their dissatisfaction with the administration and to demonstrate in support of political reform (*reformasi*). Similar demonstrations were widespread and they helped force the resignation of former President Suharto and subsequent consolidation of the pro-democracy and political reform movements in Indonesia. When the citizen planners of the library moved from using covert strategies for social transformation to making overt demands for political reform, they switched from covert planning to radical planning (Beard 2003).

3.3 Radical and Insurgent Planning

Different from community-based planning or covert planning, radical planning challenges power relations overtly and seeks broad structural change. At its core, radical planning is about emancipation from oppression and about empowerment (Friedmann 1987, 1992). According to our understanding of social movements, radical planning requires that the citizen planner frame grievances in ways that makes participants feel optimistic about the possibility of achieving a positive outcome. According to Friedmann, radical planning begins with a critique of the present situation and then helps citizens mobilize a response to that critique (Friedmann 1987, 303). In contrast to covert planning, radical planning is overtly oppositional.

Scholars have focused on radical planning from different perspectives. Sandercock (1998) describes radical planning in terms of a series of small, localized actions in diverse contexts. Rangan (1999) argues against limiting radical planning to opposition only against the state, and also asserts that the state itself is capable of radical action. Harvey (1999, 2000) argues against conceptualizing radical planning in a single operational scale (i.e., the local level) and instead favors radical planning at multiple scales. Holston (1995, 2008) and Miraftab (2009) focus on the importance of insurgency, insurgent citizenship, and insurgent planning, particularly in the context of the neoliberal economic and political, hegemonic structures in the Global South.

An example of radical planning can be found in the Sierra Madre del Norte region of Oaxaca, Mexico. The *pueblos*, or villages, in this mountainous region are governed by an indigenous structure known as *usos y costumbres*. Each village elects a president and board annually. The president and the board are responsible for outlining the main development projects the community will undertake. The projects are funded by the village's hometown associations in Oaxaca City, Mexico City, and the United States, which collect dues from their members and host social and cultural events to raise the funds (Beard and Sarmiento 2010). Acknowledging the economic importance of these remittances, the Mexican national government introduced the 3 for 1 Migrant Program in 2002. This program matches funds that hometown associations remit to Mexico for community development and poverty alleviation. After a project has been approved by the state, every dollar remitted is tripled. In a comparative study of three villages in Oaxaca, Mason and Beard (2008) found that two of the communities chose to participate in the program, but one community refused the program in order to preserve local autonomy.

The citizen planners of the nonparticipating village refused the program because they distrusted the state. They were apprehensive that the state would waste the community's time and resources and ultimately destroy their ability to control local planning. Residents viewed the state as an ineffective and unreliable distributor of public resources. As one citizen planner put it (Mason and Beard 2008, 256),[2]

> With the budget and the resources that the government would give us for a half kilometer of paved road, we are able to build a whole kilometer. They would buy the worst materials and hire the cheapest contractor and then pocket the rest of the money, and leave us with a shorter road.

According to another resident, the local–state relations are "game" where preferential treatment and resources are granted in exchange for political support. For example, when a new dental clinic was built in the community, part of the financing was given in exchange for votes in support of a candidate for state office.

On the basis of on these experiences with the state, the community decided to refuse participation in the 3 for 1 Migrant Program, but instead to maintain complete control over their local planning, including project selection, decisions about how remittances were spent, and the means by which projects are implemented. They also chose to focus their time and resources on broader collaborative efforts with nineteen neighboring communities on larger projects, such as a drainage system that would serve the community and its neighbors. Community leaders were aware of the power of remittances to improve residents' well-being, but more importantly, they were aware of the political power of remittances. Their refusal to participate in the state's 3 for 1 Migrant Program and preserve their independence from state government is, in the broadest interpretation, a demand for bureaucratic and political reform and incipient radical planning effort.

Miraftab (2009) argues that insurgent planning differs from radical planning. Her work presents the Anti-Eviction Campaign (AEC) in South Africa as an example of insurgent planning practice (see Miraftab 2006, 2009; Miraftab and Wills 2005; and this volume). The anti-eviction movement, which began in South Africa in 2001, comprises citizen planners working through civic groups from the anti-Apartheid movement (Miraftab 2006, 197). Despite social divisions within the movement owing to racialized distinctions bequeathed by Apartheid, the movement has successfully halted numerous evictions and efforts by the state to cut off urban services to residents in the townships. According to Miraftab (2006, 199),

> The AEC engages in a range of programs, with both short- and long-term goals of securing access for the poor to shelter and basic services. Its strategies stretch from informal negotiations, capacity building, and action research; to mass mobilization and protests, sit-ins and land invasions; to defiant collective actions such as reconnection of disconnected services by so-called "struggle plumbers and electricians" and relocation of evicted families back to their housing units.

Analyzing insurgent planning from the perspective of the Global South, Miraftab (2009, 45–46) argues that planning must decolonize its imagination in order to move away from understanding cities in the Global South as failures or in terms of what they are not. She identifies three characteristics that distinguish insurgent planning from radical planning: (1) insurgent planning transgresses distinctions between public and private, as well as formal and informal; (2) it "destabilizes normalized relations of dominance and insists on citizens' right to rebel, and to determine their own terms of engagement"; and (3) it is imaginative in terms of efforts toward alternatives to neoliberalism. In summary, insurgent planning is more directly concerned with history, particularly the history of colonialism and domination in the Global South, and with citizens' rights, and it is counter-hegemonic.

4. Conclusion

In this volume (Chapter 38), Miraftab states "Planning as an exclusive activity undertaken by formally trained and professionalized planners is increasingly questioned no only in theory but also on the ground through the social spatial production of cities, neighborhoods, and urban livelihoods that occurs through direct grassroots action." This chapter sought to move beyond a narrow understanding of the planner as a professional practitioner working on behalf of the state or private interests, and to underscore the variety, magnitude, and importance of planning practice as carried out by regular citizens on behalf of collective local interests. Such work is particularly visible in the Global South because of the sheer pace of urbanization there and the number of people consequently living outside of formal planning and regulatory frameworks. In this context, citizen planners are filling important gaps left by the state and the market. The work of citizen planners ranges from delivering basic services and infrastructure to citizens mobilizing for broad social, economic, and political transformation.

The chapter uses as its theoretical starting point Friedmann's conceptualization of planning as the link between knowledge and action in the public domain. Friedmann's work is significant particularly because of its documentation of the terrain of planning thought, ranging from planning as societal guidance to planning as social transformation. Responding to that conceptualization, the chapter describes the work of the citizen planner in terms of a more diverse and nuanced set of practices, including community-based planning, covert planning, and more radical and insurgent forms of planning. Because much of citizen planning involves collective action, these modes of planning practice are informed by recent theoretical contributions from research on collective action and social movements (Beard and Basolo 2009). Indeed, it can be argued that many of the problems faced by the citizen planner are the same problems that plague collective action more generally.

The chapter describes three distinct modes of citizen planning. The first is community-based planning or self-help movements. The chapter illustrates this with an example from the Kampung Improvement Program (KIP) in Indonesia. Then the chapter describes covert planning, by which in nondemocratic, highly restrictive political environments the citizen planner seeks to transform power relationships in subtle, non-confrontational ways. Covert planning is illustrated by the upgrading of an informal settlement to secure de facto land tenure rights, the subtle efforts to address women's inequality in the Solomon Islands, and a community library that evolved over time into a forum for radical planning. Finally, the chapter discusses radical and insurgent planning. Different from covert planning, radical and insurgent planning is openly oppositional. A description of a community's refusal to collaborate with the state is an incipient example of radical planning in Oaxaca, and a description of the anti-eviction campaign in post-Apartheid South Africa is an example of insurgent planning. The reader should note that a citizen planner could employ a variety of modes of planning practice in diverse sequences. That is, community-based planning could evolve into covert or radical planning, and the opposite is also true.

There are a number of points to note about the examples provided to illustrate the work of the citizen planner. Almost all of these efforts, regardless of the particular mode of planning practice, initially focused on meeting basic material needs. However, depending on the level at which the citizen planner is or becomes politicized, the degree to which she or he addresses power relationships and structural inequality varies. Of particular importance in that regard is the relationship between the citizen planner and the communities in which he or she is embedded, and the state. The political context defines both the opportunity structures and the barriers that the citizen planner must contend with. The more restrictive the political context and the more repressive the state, the more difficult it is for the citizen planner to influence power relationships and structural problems.

Certain limitations were not explicitly addressed in the chapter's examples of citizen planning. One limitation is the cost to the citizen and the community (Beard 2007). As mentioned above, most citizen planning starts as a way to address failure by the state and private sector to adequately provide for basic human needs. Citizen planning consumes valuable and scarce resources. This is particularly burdensome for the poor and the near poor. Furthermore, those favoring an expanded role for citizen planners assume that they can achieve a more democratic planning process and more and equitable planning outcomes; however, there is scant empirical evidence to support those claims. Moving the planning process away from an overly bureaucratic and corrupt state does nothing to ensure that elite capture will not occur at the local level. Citizens enter into the planning process with unequal access to power, resources, and various types of knowledge and experience. Moreover, most of the control mechanisms to prevent local elites from unduly influencing the planning process and using resources for their self-interest are informal. We need a better understanding of elite capture at the local level and mechanisms and institutional options available to protect citizen planning from perverse outcomes.

Another challenge for the citizen planner is whether and how to transcend the local level. For citizen planners to be effective and remain relevant, they need to be able to work across operational scales and effectively engage state planners. Thus, it is also important for planning scholars to explore the educational and informational needs of citizen planners. For example, what, if any, formal professionalization would be useful to a citizen planner? Is there a specific set of skills needed by citizen planners? Given the projected urban population growth rates, the persistence of poverty globally, and the growing number of people living outside of formal planning and regulatory frameworks, the citizen planner will be increasingly influential in shaping the world's cities into the foreseeable future.

NOTES

1. Another arena of the work of citizen planners is exemplified by the Bus Riders Union that unites diverse low-income people from different communities around Los Angeles who use mass transit.
2. In one of the communities studied, participation in the state program involved them in the faulty construction of infrastructure. This problem has damaged relations among hometown association members and has lessened the willingness of migrants to contribute to the hometown association.

REFERENCES

Abers, R. N. 2000. "Inventing Local Democracy: Grassroots Politics in Brazil." Boulder, CO: Lynne Reinner.

Agrawal, A. 2001. "Common Property Institutions and Sustainable Governance of Resources." *World Development* 29(10): 1649–72.

Baland, J. M., and J. P. Platteau. 1996. "Halting Degradation of Natural Resources: Is There a Role for Rural Communities?" Oxford: Oxford University Press.

Beard, V. A. 1999. "Navigating and Creating Spaces: An Indonesian Community's Struggle for Land Tenure." *Plurimondi* 1(2): 127–45.

Beard, V. A. 2002. "Covert Planning for Social Transformation in Indonesia." *Journal of Planning Education and Research* 22(1): 15–25.

Beard, V. A. 2003. "Learning Radical Planning: The Power of Collective Action." *Planning Theory* 2(1): 13–35.

Beard, V. A. 2007. "Household Contributions to Community Development in Indonesia." *World Development* 35(4): 607–25.

Beard, V. A., and A. Dasgupta. 2006. "Collective Action and Community-Driven Development in Rural and Urban Indonesia." *Urban Studies* 43(9): 1–17.

Beard, V. A., and C. S. Sarmiento. 2010. "Ties That Bind: Transnational Community-Based Planning in Southern California and Oaxaca." *International Development Planning Review* 32(3–4): 207–24.

Beard, V. A., and V. Basolo. 2009. "Commentary: Moving Beyond Crisis, Crossroads, and the Abyss in the Disciplinary Formation of Planning." Journal *of Planning Education and Research* 29(2): 233–42.

Bird, J. 1999. "Indonesia in 1998: The Pot Boils Over." *Asian Survey* 39(1): 27–37.

Dasgupta, A., and V.A. Beard. 2007. "Community Driven Development, Collective Action and Elite Capture in Indonesia." *Development and Change* 38(2): 229–49.

Davis, M. 2006. *Planet of Slums*. London: Verso.

Dongier, P., J. Van Domelen, E. Ostrom, A. Rizvi, W. Wakeman, A. Bebbington, S. Alkire, T. Esmail, and M. Polski. 2002. "Community-driven Development." In *A Sourcebook for Poverty Reduction Strategies*, edited by J. Klugman, 1:301–31. Washington, DC: World Bank.

Douglass, M., and J. Friedmann, eds. 1998. *Cities for Citizens: Planning and the Rise of Civil Society in a Global Age*. West Sussex: John Wiley.

Evans, P., ed. 2002. *Livable Cities? Urban Struggles for Livelihood and Sustainability*. Berkeley: University of California Press.

Friedmann, J. 1987. *Planning in the Public Domain: From Knowledge to Action*. Princeton, NJ: Princeton University Press.

Friedmann, J. 1989. "The Latin American Barrio Movement as a Social Movement: Contribution to a Debate." *International Journal of Urban and Regional Research* 13(3): 501–10.

Friedmann, J. 1992. *Empowerment: The Politics of Alternative Development*. Cambridge, MA: Blackwell.

Hardin, G. 1968. "The Tragedy of the Commons." *Science* 162(3859): 1243–48.

Harvey, D. 1999. "Frontiers of Insurgent Planning." *Plurimondi* 1(2): 269–86.

Harvey, D. 2000. *Spaces of Hope*. Berkeley: University of California Press.

Hirschman, A. O. 1984. *Getting Ahead Collectively: Grassroots Experiences in Latin America*. New York: Pergamon.

Holod, R., and D. Rastorfer. 1983. "Kampung Improvement Programme: Ongoing since 1969." In *Architecture and Community*, edited by R. Holod and D. Rastorfer, 211–21. New York: Aperture. Available at: (http://www.archnet.org/library/documents/one-document.jsp?document_id=6153; accessed July 15, 2009.

Holston, J. 1995. "Spaces of Insurgent Citizenship." *Planning Theory* 13:35–52.

Holston, J. 2008. *Insurgent Citizenship: Disjunctions of Democracy and Modernity in Brazil*. Princeton, NJ: Princeton University Press.

Kerkvliet, B. J. T. 2005. *The Power of Everyday Politics: How Vietnamese Peasants Transformed National Policy*. Ithaca, NY: Cornell University Press.

Mansuri, G., and V. Rao. 2004. "Community-based and -driven Development: A Critical Review." *World Bank Research Observer* 19(1): 1–39.

Mason, D. R., and V. A. Beard. 2008. "Community-based Planning and Poverty Alleviation in Oaxaca, Mexico." *Journal of Planning, Education and Research* 27(2): 245–60.

McAdam, D., S. Tarrow, and C. Tilly. 2001. *Dynamics of Contention.* Cambridge, UK: Cambridge University Press.

Miraftab, F. 2006. "Feminist Praxis, Citizenship and Informal Politics: Reflections on South Africa's Anti-Eviction Campaign." *International Feminist Journal of Politics* 8(2): 194–218.

Miraftab, F. 2009." Insurgent Planning: Situating Radical Planning in the Global South." *Planning Theory* 8(1): 32–51.

Miraftab, F., and S. Wills. 2005. "Insurgency and Spaces of Active Citizenship: The Story of Western Cape Anti-eviction Campaign in South Africa." *Journal of Planning Education and Research* 25(2): 200–17.

Ostrom, E. 1990. *Governing the Commons: The Evolution of Institutions for Collective Action.* Cambridge, UK: Cambridge University Press.

Ostrom, E. 2005. *Understanding Institutional Diversity.* Princeton, NJ: Princeton University Press.

Peattie, L. R. 1968. *The View from the Barrio.* Ann Arbor, MI: University of Michigan Press.

Rangan, H. 1999. "Bitter-sweet Liaisons in a Contentious Democracy: Radical Planning Through State Agency in Postcolonial India." *Plurimondi* 1(2): 47–66.

Sandercock, L. 1998. *Towards Cosmopolis: Planning for Multicultural Cities.* Hoboken, NJ: John Wiley.

Scheyvens, R. 1998. "Subtle Strategies for Women's Empowerment: Planning for Effective Grassroots Development." *Third World Planning Review* 20(3): 235–53.

Scott, J. C. 1986. "Everyday Forms of Peasant Resistance." In *Everyday Forms of Peasant Resistance in Southeast Asia*, edited by J. C. Scott and B. J. T. Kerkvliet, 5–35. London: Cass.

Shatkin, G. 2000. "Obstacles to Empowerment: Local Politics and Civil Society in Metropolitan Manila, the Philippines." *Urban Studies* 37(12): 2357–75.

Siegel, J. T. 1998. "Early Thoughts on the Violence of May 13 and 14, 1998 in Jakarta." *Indonesia* 66:74–108.

Turner, J. F. C., and R. Fichter, eds. 1972. *Freedom to Build: Dweller Control of the Housing Process.* New York: Macmillan.

World Bank. 2009. Available at: http://web.worldbank.org/WBSITE/EXTERNAL/ TOPICS/EXTSOCIALDEVELOPMENT/EXTCDD/0,,contentMDK:20250804~menu PK:535770~pagePK:148956~piPK:216618~theSitePK:430161,00.html;accessed June 10, 2009.

CHAPTER 35

....

THE REAL ESTATE
DEVELOPMENT
INDUSTRY

IGAL CHARNEY

1. INTRODUCTION

....

MOST fundamentally, the role of the real estate development industry is to config-
ure the shape of the built environment. This industry is concerned with the supply of an essential product for the entire population (dwellings) and the smooth
functioning of the economy by constructing commercial and industrial properties
(offices, shops, hotels, and factories). Numerous and seemingly separate and unrelated actions performed by various agents are responsible for producing and reproducing the built environment, and the overall spatial configuration and design of
real estate properties eventually determine how the landscape of cities and towns
will look. Despite its central position in enhancing our understanding of cities, "real
estate has not gained popularity as a topic in urban studies. The topic has been left to
real estate economists who are mostly interested in developing models as guides for
diversification of real estate portfolios" (Haila 1998, 57). The bulk of scholarship is
in the hands of economists and real estate analysts; on the other hand, geographers,
sociologists, historians, and urban planners only rarely have looked closely into
this industry. Planners, for instance, will greatly benefit from understanding the
workings of the industry that eventually restructures urban landscapes. Without
a doubt, planning and development are intimately linked, as development is mediated through planning regulations and planning has to acknowledge and even follow the logic of the development industry. Insights from these reciprocal relations
are essential for reading and interpreting the process of urban development.

This chapter reviews the dimensions of specific importance for those who study and plan cities. The first section provides a brief overview of the real estate development industry. In the second section, a review of principal approaches used to study the real estate industry is presented. The focus of the third section is on development rhythms, known as building cycles, which encapsulate the unevenness of development over time. Next, the issue of spatial scales is explored. Traditionally, real estate has been considered highly dependent on particular spaces; more recent studies point to its growing delocalized dimensions. The final section examines the workings of the core agents in the development process—real estate developers.

2. The Real Estate Development Industry: A Brief Overview

To the casual observer, the development industry involves the production of fairly simple and standardized products. Nevertheless, the makeup and functioning of the development industry is highly complex, as it involves the skill and expertise of many professionals, among them development firms, financial institutions, construction firms, landowners, planners, architects, brokers, and local government officials. As such, development does not simply react to demand expressed by different users; instead, demand is met through numerous actions taken by the different agents involved in the development process. By and large, the act of development comes after the completion of market research about matters such as patterns of growth, land-use regulations, financing alternatives, and prospective buyers/tenants. This is not necessarily so in times of prosperity and real estate booms; then, speculative development, development without significant commitment to buying or renting the finished properties, may be of greater importance than market demand.

In her study of real estate development in New York and London, Susan Fainstein (1994) touches on the uniqueness of the development industry. As in manufacturing, the development industry yields a tangible product. Unlike major industrial corporations, development firms to a great extent do not produce in mass or operate on a global or even a national scale. Agents in the real estate development industry are geared to small-batch production and a high level of subcontracting. As in the film industry, big development firms do not set up permanent facilities around the world but, instead, use temporary field offices for specific projects. The development industry is also similar to agriculture in its cyclical nature, its susceptibility to market glut, and its close relations with governments. The real estate industry depends heavily on public-sector decisions on investment in infrastructure, tax policy, and regulation of construction. These dimensions and complexities make comparisons with other industries somewhat difficult.

In terms of assets or revenues, firms in the real estate industry are generally of moderate size, and they are not considered household names like GM, WalMart, McDonald's, or CocaCola. Most of them are unknown on the national scale, and only the most flamboyant (e.g., Donald Trump), or those that have built recognizable landmarks, enjoy a widespread reputation (e.g., Ghermezian Brothers and their West Edmonton Mall). The development industry is made up of numerous small and private firms that form the bulk of the industry, as their areas of operation are largely limited to specific products and to certain locations. This is clearly seen from a look at popular corporate rankings. In the most popular ranking, Fortune 500/1000, the category of real estate as a separate industry is missing. In the Forbes Global 2000 list, which includes public companies, Brookfied Asset Management is the top-ranked real estate company (ranked 301 in 2011). Firms under this category are largely engaged in owning and managing real estate portfolios and only a few have significant corporate segments that actually engage in real estate development. For example, the developer of the world's tallest skyscraper, Burj Khalifa (previously, Burj Dubai), Emaar Properties, is ranked 1,317.

3. THINKING REAL ESTATE

Research on real estate development has taken diverse approaches. The neoclassical approach, with its focus on the demand-and-supply aspects of real estate development, dominated until about 1970. From the late 1960s and early 1970s, another set of approaches emerged and was employed to analyze real estate development. Scholars, drawing on the writings of Marx, became interested in the logic of capitalist accumulation as a major factor dominating the production of real estate properties. The monolithic "forces of capitalism" were unpacked in the 1980s by institutional approaches, which attempted to bring together structure and agency.

3.1 Neoclassical Approaches

Researchers relying on neoclassical approaches have studied real estate development by focusing on market forces. Neoclassical approaches used the demand-supply equilibrium concept in attempts to explain how real estate markets work. Efforts have been made to explain economic mechanisms, primarily price adjustments, which shape real estate markets (Rosen 1984; Hekman 1985; DiPasquale and Wheaton 1992; Fisher 1992; Keogh 1994; Mills 1995; McDonald 2007).

According to the neoclassical perspective, in a market economy exchange takes place on the basis of prices determined by the interaction of supply and demand.

In the case of real estate, rent is the price a tenant pays for occupying a particular space. The interaction of demand for real estate and the supply of rental properties determine rent levels. Price is determined by demand, and supply follows, rather than influences, demand (J. Harvey 1987). Agents engaging in the development process are assumed to act in unison, collectively providing development at the right time and reacting automatically to the structure of demand (Bourne 1976). Consumers and producers alike seek to maximize utility and profitability, and in doing so they are unhampered by social, legal, or local constraints.

Apart from rationality and profit maximization, several other assumptions are incorporated in the demand-supply model. Perfect competition, for example, relies on a simplification of real estate markets by assuming that products are homogeneous, that there are large numbers of buyers and sellers, and that actors have perfect information.

According to the neoclassical approach, the intensity of real estate development is shaped by one or more land value gradients. Transportation lines, which converge at one location, give rise to what has been referred to as the *peak land value intersection* (PLVI). As a result of maximum accessibility, land values at the PLVI are the highest in a city that has a single dominant center. Demand for space results in soaring land costs, which reflect the potential value of the land if built upon to the maximum allowable extent (Ford 1994). In these locations, the cost of land is the major component in real estate development. Capital is substituted for land, as large amounts of capital are invested in the erection of more intensive land uses to compensate for high land values (Bourne 1967). In this case, large-scale office buildings are the predominant real estate properties because of financial calculations emphasizing maximum return on investment (Willis 1995).

The notion of a perfectly functioning market has been heavily criticized (D. Harvey 1973). The real estate market is ubiquitous, and there is no formal organized marketplace, central agency, or institution, where prices are quoted and publicly witnessed. Instead of a large number of buyers and sellers, there are relatively few with sufficient finance to invest; therefore, financial institutions and real estate investment companies dominate the property market. Another criticism of neoclassical models argues that changes in income and business conditions, and difficulties obtaining up-to-date knowledge, may prevent the pursuit of maximum profits. Studies indicate that the high cost of land is not necessarily the reason for large-scale buildings. In the case of Houston, for example, high-rise office buildings were erected in the downtown even though land costs were only a small fraction of the total development costs (Feagin 1988).

Contrary to the tenets of some of the neoclassical approaches, the supply of buildings is relatively inelastic, and changes in the building stock and location are slow owing to the durability of buildings and the small proportion of real property of any type coming onto the market at any one time (D'Arcy and Keogh 1997). The property market is, therefore, in a constant state of disequilibrium. Nor do the actors who supply the market necessarily respond to demand, as posited in the simple demand–supply relationship. Various factors, such as taxation, national interest rates, and government policy and subsidies, determine the framework of supply. Developers are not a homogeneous entity but, rather, multiple agents with different interests (Beauregard 1993; Pratt 1994). Finally, development often occurs speculatively, only remotely related to actual demand. Development booms may be related to a great expansion of money supply, as was the case in the 1920s (Willis 1995) and more recently in the 1980s (Ball 1994; Fainstein 1994) and 2000s.

3.2 Political Economy Approaches

David Harvey's work (1978, 1982, 1985) on the circuits of capital and the role of investment in the production of the built environment has provided the theoretical framework for a political economy approach, which focuses on the supply of capital as the driving force of real estate development. Harvey's initial argument suggests that, in the long run, in the absence of profitable investments in the primary (manufacturing) circuit of capital accumulation, capital will flow into the secondary circuit, where capital is deployed in the production of the built environment. Harvey's contribution to understanding real estate development is important in other respects. He acknowledges the important role of the state in facilitating real estate development. The different levels of the state (federal, intermediate level, and local) provide the conditions for the continuous process of real estate production. At the local level, government regulation is needed for the speculator-developer to function (D. Harvey 1985).

Harvey discusses the nature of uneven spatial development of the built environment on different spatial scales, implying that uneven development is an essential condition for capital circulation in capitalist economies. In addition, his idea of capital switching paves the way for the notion of spatial switching. Harvey acknowledges that capital can flow from one place to another (D. Harvey 1985). This switching between circuits/sectors and places is a crucial practice of real estate companies. After research on the sources for real estate investment in Houston in the 1970s and 1980s, Feagin (1987, 182–83) suggests that "financial institutions, both those inside Texas and those outside, channeled much surplus capital from a variety of sources into Houston real estate."

Recognition of the real estate sector as an independent or nearly independent sector of the economy, which requires its own analysis, led to an emerging research agenda within the political economy approach (Feagin 1987; Haila 1991; Beauregard 1994; Leitner 1994; Fainstein 1994). In a preliminary outline, Haila (1991) argues that the real estate sector has an "intrinsic dynamic" rather than being externally driven by the switching of capital between different circuits of accumulation. This dynamic shapes investment patterns in real estate assets and is based on the internal characteristics of real estate properties, namely, tradability, divisibility, and mobility. Real estate assets are tradable; they are bought and sold in the market like other types of financial assets (D. Harvey 1982). Although properties cannot be traded in small units like stocks, they can be divided because the ownership of properties can be shared by a number of investors/partners. In addition, the real estate sector is segmented into commercial and residential subsectors, and into distinctive property types, such as office, industrial, and retail (Charney 2001; Beauregard, 1994, 2005).

The political economy approach emphasizes issues of land ownership and rent as core elements in explaining the production of the built environment (D. Harvey 1982, 1985; Haila 1988, 1991). Instead of the assumption built into neo-classical landuse models, Marxist interpretations suggest the possibility of power in the hands of a few landowners and also that land has a monopolistic character. Harvey argued that there are "monopoly privileges inherent in any form of private property in land" (1985, 102); and Logan and Molotch (1987, 23) considered land markets "inherently monopolistic." This enables landowners to manipulate or control the land market by charging monopoly rent. In this line of thinking, cities that experience decline and deterioration turn to real estate development as a tool to extract value. Here, the role of the state is important as it has developed mechanisms to make the built environment more flexible and responsive to the investment criteria of real-estate capital redevelopment efforts, making obsolescence "a neoliberal alibi for creative destruction, and therefore an important component in contemporary processes of spatialized capital accumulation" (Weber 2002, 532).

The major critique of the political economy approach revolves around its high degree of generalization and abstraction. More specifically, the relation between the general conception of the structuring dynamics of the development process and individual agents' specific interests and strategies remains to be established. Much more attention must be paid to the ways individual firms and agents interrelate, and how various economic and political factors that govern their strategies are incorporated into a structure-agency framework (Healey and Barrett 1990). Also, the impossibility of documenting some assertions such as flows from the primary to secondary circuit (Feagin 1987; Beauregard 1991, 1994) has attracted criticism (Ball 1994).

3.3 Institutional Approaches

Unlike the proponents of the political economy approach, who emphasize structural formations of the capitalist system, advocates of institutional approaches argue that it is essential to understand institutional forms, relationships, and practices of the real estate sector. The starting point is the institutional articulation of the sector and the patterns of networks and relationships among agents. This results in an institutional map of the development industry (Healey 1992b). As Healey and Barrett (1990, 93) argue:

> Much more attention needs to be given to the way individual firms and agents interrelate in the negotiation of particular development projects and how, through these transactions, land and property "markets" are constituted and built environment investment decisions made.

Healey (1992a) provided expositions on institutional approaches to the real estate industry. She argues that the focus of institutional approaches is primarily on identifying the type and composition of agents involved in the real estate development process and revealing the interests and strategies they adopt. The nature of the relationships that arise between actors, their actual roles, and the relative influence they enjoy in the negotiation of particular projects is analyzed in turn. Healey (1992a) presents an institutional model of the real estate development process that takes into account the complexity of the events and agencies involved in the process, and the diversity of forms it may assume under different conditions. On the theoretical level, "the critical issue here is to make the connection with the social relations expressed in the prevailing mode of production, mode of regulation, and ideology of society within which development is being undertaken" (Healey 1992a, 37).

This approach focuses on agents and differs from the neoclassical and the Marxist views in being concerned with the details of how the development process takes place, rather than making generalizations and engaging in abstractions. Agents are not treated as homogeneous entities, but are clearly differentiated. Here, real estate developers are among the most important agents in the development industry, and their interactions and bargaining with planners who administrate development have a prominent impact on development outcomes. Developers conceive projects, often when others are unaware that any opportunities are available. They are considered not just passive actors in the development process but also proactive agents who make things happen (Marriott 1967; Logan and Molotch 1987; Haila 1991; Fainstein 1994). By and large, city planners working for a local municipality are either gatekeepers who aim at stopping unwanted development and/or city advocates who promote those projects that they and local decision makers consider beneficial for the city.

Institutional scholars have noted how developers interact with other intermediaries in the development process. The extensive attention given to the state is in contrast to the neoclassical literature, which ignores or downplays the role of the state in the supply-demand model, and to the Marxist literature, which regards the state as a mediator of capital flows between the primary and secondary circuits without providing analyses of the state's specific role.

Dissatisfaction with structural and/or agent-based analyses of the real estate markets has led scholars to suggest that what is needed is a "thick" understanding of how the real estate industry works:

> dynamic, deeply contextual and contingent both on the particular aims and objectives of development actors, and on a shifting market framework which may enable or constrain development strategies. It further acknowledges the interrelationships between structure and agency whereby one layer of agency can become, in another context, the next layer of structure and so on. Such an approach reconnects the social and the economic as interrelated facets of the urban development process, and allows us to explore how the property "market" or perhaps more correctly "markets," are "constructed by competing design,

development and investment actors at local, national and global levels over time." (Guy and Henneberry 2000, 2413).

What we need is a "thick" rather than "thin" understanding of functional interdependence in property markets, one in which the specifics—the contexts—are made explicit. (Beauregard 2005, 2432)

In sum, institutional approaches reject the "mechanistic and deterministic interpretation of the world" (Guy and Harris 1997, 130), suggesting a more nuanced view of the complexity of the real estate industry. This view has generated critique that argues that this type of explanation lacks a "grand theory" that transcends context and specificity (Hopper 1992). Nonetheless, the importance of the specific context cannot be discarded; instead, "the production of space is captured best as the complex articulation between structure and agency, which is always in motion" (Gottdeiner 1994, 200).

4. DEVELOPMENT RHYTHMS

The workings of the real estate development industry are characterized by its cyclical behavior. Economists and financial analysts have been those who examined this feature of the real estate industry. Those engaged in urban planning have paid fairly little attention to this feature. The reliance of real estate development and redevelopment on timing has major impact on the ability to steer urban development toward making development not linear but, rather, advancing in leaps of different size.

Development cycles form because of an inherent time lag between detection of demand, start of development, and delivery of the final product to the market. During boom periods, leaps are large and development penetrates into areas remote from familiar and established locations. Bold moves that are risky and signify pioneering thinking will be initiated or strengthened during such periods. In recessionary times, though, development and redevelopment are of more conservative spatial scope. This behavior is basically related to the risk exposure that developers and investors are willing to take. During upturns these agents are more risk-loving since they are captivated by the market (Fainstein 1994).

Research has focused on commercial development, especially office development cycles, which are linked to patterns of economic growth and recession. The neoclassical explanation for office development cycles is related to the market's inability to "clear" in a short period of time. The market must remain soft or tight for several years before rents change and supply or demand reacts. Hence, the length of a cycle is considerably longer than it takes to plan and complete office buildings (Barras and Ferguson 1985; Wheaton 1987). In this context, the major macroeconomic variables

identified as shaping development patterns are GDP and service sector employment (D'Arcy, McGough, and Taolacos 1999; Wheaton, Torto, and Evans 1997).
The notion of equilibrium made some researchers suggest a synchrony of spatially-
diverse building cycles (Easterlin 1968; Gottlieb 1976). Convergence on an upper
spatial scale, the global dimension, was emphasized following the 1980s cycle, which
was unprecedented in its magnitude. During this cycle, parallel boom-bust patterns
were a worldwide phenomenon, making it the first global real estate cycle (Renaud
1997). It was observed that property development cycles acquired global similarities
so they tended to coincide in major world cities (Ball, Morrison, and Wood 1996;
Lizieri and Finlay 1995). Not surprisingly, the price of land in the 1980s in central
New York and London "appeared increasingly unrelated to the conditions of the
overall national economy.... The central areas of these cities have become part of an
international property market" (Sassen 1991, 186–87). This circumstance helped to
inflate rents and contributed to further office development in these cities.

   This worldwide rhythm was associated with several changes occurring in the
previous few decades. First, the rapid growth in service sector employment necessitated satisfactory workplaces. This was a major incentive for the construction of
higher quality office buildings on a much grander scale, particularly in the 1980s
(Ball 1994). Second, the contemporary characteristics of the financial sector massively influenced the intensity and volatility this global cycle. The foremost triggers
of this cycle were widespread financial deregulation on the national level, global
mobility of capital, and closer links between financial and property markets—all
of which facilitated the formation of international property markets (Beitel 2000;
Coakley 1994; Haila 1998; Renaud 1997). Finally, as the size and the scope of development intensified, real estate firms operating on a global scale emerged (Beauregard
and Haila 1997; Fainstein 1994).

   Evidence of global convergence in building cycles notwithstanding, regional
and local factors are discernible. Supply-side and place-specific considerations,
such as capital availability and distinct institutional and political capacities, are
crucial elements in explaining the cyclical development patterns. In examining
office construction cycles in downtown areas of major U.S. cities over a twenty-five
year period (early 1960s to mid-1980s), Leitner (1994) illustrates how local circumstances interacted with wider financial and political trends to produce office development patterns that were place-specific. Despite the trend toward convergence in
the timing of office construction cycles in different cities, individual cities continued to show differences, attributable to the articulation of national and international
tendencies with city-specific characteristics. In downtown Houston, for example,
office development during the late 1970s and early 1980s was tied to the oil boom
and Houston's image as a "hot" city for property investment (Bateman 1985; Feagin
1987, 1988). Huge oversupply of office space and the collapse of oil prices ended
in a period of relatively little office construction. In San Francisco, on the other
hand, office development in the 1960s and 1970s was linked to its role as a major
financial center. During the 1980s,, fierce competition from other West Coast cities
for investment capital, combined with local growth-control initiatives, limited the

scale of office development (Godfrey 1997; Leitner 1990). A study of office-building cycles in Canadian cities revealed regional diversity (Charney 2003). While Toronto experienced an exceptional office boom in the 1980s, Calgary's office boom was in the 1970s; the growth of Ontario's economy in the 1980s, and the escalation of oil prices in the 1970s help explain these differences. Overall, the patterning of real estate development cycles entails marked spatial dimensions, which in turn reflect an explicit regional and urban diversity.

5. LOCAL CONTINGENCIES

By definition, real estate development happens in specific places. Unique development trajectories, different power brokers, and of course specific regulatory environments determine the workings of the development industry. The importance of the "local" has preoccupied the literature in an era when global forces seem dominant. Still, spatial uniqueness has been recognized as an important component in economic performance, as specific conditions in localities have facilitated the creation of competitive advantage (D. Harvey 1989; Amin and Thrift 1992; Swyngedouw 1992). As Healey notes, "in a world where integrated place-bounded relationships are pulled out of their localities…the qualities of place seem to become more, not less, significant" (Healey 1998, 1531). Traditionally, the real estate development industry is known for its spatial specificities: it is largely a "local" business, although some components of this sector exceed the local realm (Logan 1993; Bryson 1997). This means that development was initiated, planned, built and even financed by agents who resided in the same area or the same region where development took place. More recent evidence show that real estate is turning into a less local business; architects, developers, and financiers from outside the city/region/state are involved in real estate development, making real estate increasingly "delocalized" or "deterritorialized" (Sassen 1991; Knox 1993; Beauregard and Haila 1997; Edgington 1996; Haila 1998, 2000; McNeill 2009). Nonetheless, the "inherently speculative nature of the industry places a significant premium of local knowledge" (Wood 2004, 137), thus reinforcing its parochial and fragmented features.

Attachment to specific places brings about what Cox and Mair (1989, 142) term "local dependence": "a relation to locality that results from the relative spatial immobility of some social relations, perhaps related to fixed investments in the built environment or to the particularization of social relations." In addition to premises, physical infrastructure, and appropriate labor skills, local conditions include knowledge of the place and relations of trust with a network of agents. The structure of relations among social agents is crucial in confronting issues of historical and spatial specificity. These specific relations are related to the particular characteristics of place, which are not stationary but evolve over time (Ball 1986; Pryke 1994). These relations are not easily transferable and may even be permanently fixed. All of this may contribute to profitability and serve to differentiate one location from another. To the extent that the firm cannot reconstitute these profitable conditions elsewhere, locations for that firm assume a degree of spatial non-substitutability, locking industries onto certain trajectories. These may increase over time as local advantages accumulate (Cox 1993).

Information and knowledge concentrated in well-defined territories have been important inputs into the production and circulation of capital (Storper 1997; Malecki 2000). Storper (1997, 21) underlines territorialized activities that are "rooted in assets that are not available in many other places and cannot easily or rapidly be created or initiated in places that lack them." Real estate development and investment may be considered as such. Assets for agents involved in this sector include information and knowledge. Agents have to establish a presence in a place through multiple interactions with different mediators such as real estate professionals, the local business community, and local power brokers. Before office development takes places, for instance, suitable zoning bylaws have to be in place and a permit has to be issued by a particular municipality. Above all, knowledge of the particular characteristics of the market has to be acquired, analyzed, and interpreted. "Being there" gives real estate development firms their edge. Nevertheless, structural conditions may reduce the importance of local constraints during upswings of the building cycle and shift the emphasis to local knowledge in less prosperous periods.

Local relations between developers and local planners, for instance, and presence in a place have to be constantly nurtured. Defending and enhancing the local settings becomes a major goal, and firms may intervene directly in local economic development and create conditions that will benefit them (Cox and Mair 1988; Haila 1991). This practice is time-consuming and expensive, so it tends to intensify over time, making local knowledge in specific places a valuable asset. Experience and local networks minimize the cost of doing business and determine the capacity and ambition to move to new territories or the decision to stay in accustomed settings.

6. Real Estate Developers

As suggested earlier in this chapter, real estate developers are among the most important agents in the development industry. The developer's practices "fuse" structural conditions such as building cycles and the agency's perceptions. In the cycle's recovery phase, the developer perceives opportunities when the picture of the future is not clear. As recovery turns into expansion and the market becomes crowded, some developers leave the specific market to look for greener pastures that offer higher potential profits (Whitehead 1996). Other authors have noted that the developer's behavior is not always based on rationality, but on belief, faith, and wishful thinking. Fainstein (1994, 18) asserts that developers "do not merely react to an objective situation, but operate within a subjective environment partly of their own creation." She then suggests that "Because personal rewards are not wholly tied to the ultimate profitability of projects, individuals...often succumb to wishful thinking." The important role of real estate developers in the 1980s building cycle made Beauregard (1994, 730) conclude that "city building is less and less responsive to human need and more and more driven by entrepreneurial fervor."

With regard to the British real estate sector, Marriott (1967, 24) argued:

> The developer is like an impresario. He is a catalyst, the man in the middle who creates nothing himself, maybe has a vague vision, and causes others to create things. His raw material is land and his aim is to take land and improve it with bricks and mortar so that it becomes more useful to somebody else and thus more valuable to him.

Different organizations assume the role of development, ownership, and investment for income-producing purposes: developers/entrepreneurs, construction companies, financial institutions, and landowners. These agents use distinct types of capital in the development process (Bryson 1997). Real estate firms are most likely to be developers; their major line of business is real estate, particularly development and retention of properties. Financial institutions are also key agents in this business. Financial institutions like banks, life insurance companies, and pension funds have a major stake in real estate: they occupy large amounts of office space and hold office buildings as part of their investment portfolios. Life insurance companies, for example, collect money from policy holders and invest it in different channels. They prefer investment channels that are safe for the long term. Real estate, in the form of mortgage loans or as equity investment, is such a channel.

The advantage of developers lies in the combination of capital and expertise. They have a sufficient capital base to initiate development and the ability to raise additional capital. Developers retain equity in properties, but in addition they must run the risk of not leasing in full the property under construction; and unless a considerable amount of space is leased before construction starts, it is considered speculative development (lenders are reluctant to finance this type of development). The major incentive for developers is to obtain the development profit, which is the difference between the initial outlay for a project and its value upon completion. In addition, developers who own their properties collect rent and enjoy capital appreciation.

Because the property market is spatially segmented and developers may possess different motivations for engagement in the development process, different developers will have different operational spaces. These operational spaces depend on capital resources. The optimization of capital usage involves spatial literacy: familiarity with the settings in which they operate through presence in specific settings. This enables the acquisition of local intelligence, shared by a small group of people. For smaller developers the relative spatial immobility of social relations and the dependence on specific municipalities and power centers are more significant than they are for large and powerful developers. The limited operational territory of small developers is partly a result of limited equity and a finite leverage capacity (Charney 2001; Guy, Henneberry, and Rowley 2002). But even larger developers tend to limit their operations to certain locations in the metropolitan market.

7. CONCLUSIONS

It is not surprising that the real estate development industry in itself has not come to occupy an important position in urban planning. Urban scholars preferred to study social, political, and cultural issues, leaving the real estate sector to its "natural" experts, namely, mainstream economists and real estate practitioners. The latter represented the practical side of research, that is, how research could be conducive to developers, financiers, analysts, and governments making the "right" decisions.

A less implicit but no less important outcome of studying real estate is enhancement of knowledge of urban processes. In other words, the development industry reveals mechanisms of production and reproduction in urban settings, which eventually define the shape of cities. The impact of the real estate development industry on cities cannot be underestimated, and it requires closer examination by urban scholars. The interdisciplinary situation of real estate reveals:

> [a] startling gap between the consideration and the characterization of property by urban researchers (whether geographers, sociologists, political analysts or economists) and that of property analysts (applied economists, financial analysts and valuers). The former have given surprisingly little attention to the property business, while the latter have attended only to property and have not connected with wider urban debates. (Guy and Henneberry 2004, 223)

The purpose of this chapter has been to map selected dimensions of the real estate development industry, moving beyond the somewhat reductionist views represented by mainstream economists and real estate practitioners. For that purpose, the chapter considered three major dimensions acknowledged by urban scholars, and hence analyzed rather extensively in the literature. The first is its volatility. This feature is best represented by boom-bust cycles leading to great heights and sizable troughs. Second, unlike many other industries that have taken advantage of globalization, the development industry has remained largely local and perhaps even parochial. Third, contrary to the extravagant nature of some of its most celebrated developers, small firms make up the bulk of this industry: large-scale developers are an exception. Taken together, these dimensions are important to urban planners who need to incorporate their implications into their working practices.

REFERENCES

Amin, A., and N. Thrift. 1992. "Neo-Marshallian Nodes in Global Networks." *International Journal of Urban and Regional Research* 16:571–87.

Ball, M. 1986. "The Built Environment and the Urban Question." *Environment and Planning Part D: Society and Space* 4:447–64.

Ball, M. 1994. "The 1980s Property Boom." *Environment and Planning Part A* 26:671–95.

Ball, M., T. Morrison, and A. Wood. 1996. "Structures Investment and Economic Growth: A Long-Term International Perspective." *Urban Studies* 33:1678–706.

Barras, R., and D. Ferguson. 1985. "A Spectral Analysis af Building Cycles in Britain." *Environment and Planning Part A* 17:1369–91.

Bateman, M. 1985. *Office Development: A Geographical Analysis.* London: Croom Helm.

Beauregard, R. 1991. "Capital Restructuring and the New Built Environment af Global Cities: New York and Los Angeles." *International Journal of Urban and Regional Research* 15:90–105.

Beauregard, R. 1993. "The Turbulence of Housing Markets: Investment, Disinvestment, and Reinvestment in Philadelphia, 1963–1986." In *The Restless Urban Landscape,* edited by P. L. Knox, 55–82. Englewood Cliffs, NJ: Prentice Hall.

Beauregard, R. 1994. "Capital Switching and the Built Environment." *Environment and Planning Part A* 26:715–32.

Beauregard, R. 2005. "The Textures of Property Markets: Downtown Housing and Office Conversion in New York City." *Urban Studies* 42:2431–45.

Beauregard, R., and A. Haila. 1997. "The Unavoidable Incompleteness of the City." *American Behavioral Scientist* 41:327–41.

Beitel, K. 2000. "Financial Cycles and Building Booms: A Supply Side Account." *Environment and Planning Part A* 32:2113–32.

Bourne, L. S. 1967. "Private Redevelopment of the Central City: Spatial Processes of Structural Change in the City of Toronto." Ph.D. Dissertation, Department of Geography, University of Chicago.

Bourne, L. S. 1976. "Housing Supply and Housing Market Behavior in Residential Development." In *Social Area in Cities: Spatial Processes and Form,* edited by D. Herbert and R. Johnson, 111–58. London: John Wiley.

Bryson, J. R. 1997. "Obsolescence and the Process of Creative Reconstruction." *Urban Studies* 34:1439–58.

Charney, I. 2001. "Three Dimensions of Capital Switching Within the Real Estate Sector: A Canadian Case Study." *International Journal of Urban and Regional Research* 25: 740–58.

Charney, I. 2003. "Unpacking and Repackaging Regional Diversity: Office-Building Trajectories in Canada." *Environment and Planning Part A* 35:231–48.

Coakley, J. 1994. "The Integration of Property and Financial Markets." *Environment and Planning Part A* 26:697–713.

Cox, K. 1993. "The Local and the Global in the New Urban Politics: A Critical View." *Environment and Planning Part D: Society and Space* 11:433–48.

Cox, K., and A. Mair. 1988. "Locality and Community in the Politics of Local Economic Development." *Annals of the Association of America Geographers* 78: 307–25.

Cox, K., and A. Mair. 1989. "Urban Growth Machines and the Politics of Local Economic Development." *International Journal of Urban and Regional Research* 13: 137–46.

D'Arcy, E., and G. Keogh. 1997. "Towards a Property Market Paradigm of Urban Change." *Environment and Planning Part A* 29:685–706.

D'Arcy, E., T. McGough, and S. Tsolacos. 1999. "An Econometric Analysis and Forecasts of the Office Rental Cycle in the Dublin Area." *Journal of Property Research* 16:309–21.

DiPasquale, D., and W. Wheaton. 1992. "The Markets for Real Estate Assets and Space." *Journal of American Real Estate and Urban Economics Association* 20:181–98.

Easterlin, R. A. 1968. *Population, Labor Force and Long Swings in Economic Growth.* New York: National Bureau of Economic Research.

Edgington, D. W. 1996. "Japanese Real Estate Investment in Canadian Cities and Regions." *Canadian Geographer* 40:292–305.

Fainstein, S. S. 1994. *The City Builders: Property, Politics and Planning in London and New York.* Cambridge, MA: Blackwell.

Feagin, J. R. 1987. "The Secondary Circuit of Capital: Office Construction in Houston, Texas." *International Journal of Urban and Regional Research* 11:172–92.

Feagin, J. R. 1988. *Free Enterprise City: Houston in Political-Economic Perspective.* New Brunswick, NJ: Rutgers University Press.

Fisher, J. D. 1992. "Integrating Research on Markets for Space and Capital." *Journal of the American Real Estate and Urban Economics Association* 20:161–80.

Ford, L. R. 1994. *Cities and Buildings: Skyscrapers, Skid Rows and Suburbs.* Baltimore: Johns Hopkins University Press.

Godfrey, B. 1997. "Urban Development and Redevelopment in San Francisco." *Geographical Review* 87:309–33.

Gottdeiner, M. 1994. *The Social Production of Space.* Austin, TX: University of Texas Press.

Gottlieb, M. 1976. *Long Swings in Urban Development.* New York: National Bureau of Economic Research.

Guy, S., and R. Harris. 1997. "Property in a Global Risk Society: Towards Marketing Approach." *Urban Studies* 34:125–40.

Guy, S., and J. Henneberry. 2000. "Understanding Urban Development Processes: Integrating the Economic and the Social in Property Research." *Urban Studies* 37:2399–416.

Guy, S., and J. Henneberry. 2004. "Economic Structures, Urban Responses: Framing and Negotiating Urban Property Development." In *City Matters: Competitiveness, Cohesion and Urban governance,* edited by M. Boddy and M. Parkinson, 217–34. Bristol, UK: Policy Press.

Guy, S., J. Henneberry, and S. Rowley. 2002. "Development Cultures and Urban Regeneration." *Urban Studies* 39:1181–96.

Haila, A. 1988. "Land as a Financial Asset: The Theory of Urban Rent as a Mirror of Economic Transformation." *Antipode* 20:79–101.

Haila, A. 1991. "Four Types of Investment in Land and Property." *International Journal of Urban and Regional Research* 15:343–65.

Haila, A. 1998. "The Neglected Builder of Global Cities." In *Transformation in Cities: Social and Symbolic Change of Urban Space,* edited by O Kalltorp, I. Elander, O. Ericsson, and M. Franzen, 51–64. Aldershot, UK: Ashgate.

Haila, A. 2000. "Real Estate in Global Cities: Singapore and Hong Kong as Property States." *Urban Studies* 37:2241–56.

Harvey, D. 1973. *Social Justice and the City.* London: Edward Arnold.

Harvey, D. 1978. "The Urban Process under Capitalism: A Framework for Analysis." *International Journal of Urban and Regional Research* 2:101–31.

Harvey, D. 1982. *The Limits to Capital*. Oxford: Blackwell.

Harvey, D. 1985. *The Urbanization of Capital: Studies in the History and Theory of Capitalist Urbanization*. Baltimore: Johns Hopkins University Press.

Harvey, D. 1989. *The Condition of Postmodernity: An Inquiry into the Origins of Cultural Change*. Oxford: Blackwell.

Harvey, J. 1987. *Urban Land Economics: The Economics of Real Property*. London: Macmillan.

Healey, P. 1992a. "An Institutional Model of the Development Process." *Journal of Property Research* 9:33–44.

Healey, P. 1992b. "Urban Regeneration and the Development Industry." In *Rebuilding the City: Property-Led Urban Regeneration*, edited by P. Healey, S. Davoudi, and S. Tavsanoglu, 3–13. London: Spon.

Healey, P. 1998. "Building Institutional Capacity Through Collaborative Approaches to Urban Planning." *Environment and Planning Part A* 30:1531–46.

Healey, P., and S. M. Barrett. 1990. "Structure and Agency in Land and Property Development Processes: Some Ideas for Research." *Urban Studies* 27:89–104.

Hekman, J. S. 1985. "Rental Price Adjustment and Investment in the Office Market." *Journal of the American Real Estate and Urban Economics Association* 13:32–47.

Hopper, A. J. 1992. "The Construction of Theory: A Comment." *Journal of Property Research* 9:45–48.

Keogh, G. 1994. "Use and Investment Markets in British Real Estate." *Journal of Property Valuation and Investment* 12:58–72.

Knox, P. L. 1993. "Capital, Material Culture and Socio-Spatial Differentiation." In *The Restless Urban Landscape*, edited by P. L. Knox, 1–34. Englewood Cliffs, NJ: Prentice Hall.

Leitner, H. 1990. "Cities in Pursuit of Economic Growth: The Local State as an Entrepreneur." *Political Geography Quarterly* 9:147–70.

Leitner, H. 1994. "Capital Markets, The Development Industry and Urban Office Market Dynamics: Rethinking Building Cycles." *Environment and Planning Part A* 26:779–802.

Lizieri, C., and L. Finlay. 1995. "International Property Portfolio Strategies." *Journal of Property Valuation and Investment* 13:6–21.

Logan, J. 1993. "Cycles and Trends in the Globalization of Real Estate." In *The Restless Urban Landscape*, edited by P. L. Knox, 35–54. Englewood Cliffs, NJ: Prentice Hall.

Logan, J., and Molotch, H. 1987. *Urban Fortunes: The Political Economy of Place*. Berkeley: University of California Press.

Malecki, E. 2000. "Creating and Sustaining Competitiveness: Local Knowledge and Economic Geography." In *Knowledge, Space, Economy*, edited by J. R. Bryson, P. W. Daniels, N. Henry, and J. Pollard, 103–19. London: Routledge.

Marriott, O. 1967. *The Property Boom*. London: Hamish Hamilton.

McDonald, J. F. 2007. *Urban Economics and Real Estate: Theory and Policy*. Malden, MA: Blackwell.

McNeill, D. 2009. *The Global Architect: Firms, Fame and Urban Form*. New York: Routledge.

Mills, E. S. 1995. "Crisis and Recovery in Office Markets." *Journal of Real Estate Finance and Economics* 10:49–62.

Pratt, A. C. 1994. *Uneven Re-Production: Industry, Space and Society*. Oxford: Pergamon.

Pryke, M. 1994. "Urbanizing Capitals: Towards an Integration of Time, Space and Economic Calculation." *Money, Power and Space*, edited by S. Corbridge, N. Thrift, and R. Martin, 218–54. Oxford: Blackwell.

Renaud, B. 1997. "The 1985 to 1994 Global Real Estate Cycle: An Overview." *Journal of Real Estate Literature* 5:13–44.

Rosen, K. T. 1984. "Toward a Model of the Office Building Sector." *Journal of the American Real Estate and Urban Economics Association* 12:261–69.

Sassen, S. 1991. *The Global City: New York, London and Tokyo*. Princeton, NJ: Princeton University Press.

Storper, M. 1997. "Territories, Flows, and Hierarchies in the Global Economy." In *Spaces of Globalization: Reasserting the Power of the Local*, edited by K. Cox, 19–44. New York: Guilford.

Swyngedouw, E. A. 1992. "The Mammoth Quest:' "Globalization,' Interspatial Competition and the Monetary Order: The Construction of New Scales." In *Cities and Regions in the New Europe: The Global-Local Interplay and Spatial Development*, edited by M. Danford and G. Kafkalas, 39–67. London: Belhaven.

Weber, R. 2002. "Extracting Value From the City: Neoliberalism and Urban Redevelopment." *Antipode* 34:519–40.

Wheaton, W. C. 1987. "The Cyclic Behavior of the National Office Market." *Journal of the American Real Estate and Urban Economic Association* 15:281–99.

Wheaton, W., R. Torto, and P. Evans. 1997. "The Cyclic Behaviour of the Greater London Office Market." *Journal of Real Estate Finance and Economics* 15:77–92.

Whitehead, J. C. 1996. *The Midas Syndrome: An Investigation into Property Booms and Busts*. Vancouver, BC: University of British Columbia.

Willis, C. 1995. *Form Follows Finance: Skyscrapers and Skylines in New York and Chicago*. New York: Princeton Architectural Press.

Wood, A. 2004. "The Scalar Transformation of the U.S. Commercial Property-Development Industry: A Cautionary Note on the Limits of Globalization." *Economic Geography* 80:119–40.

CHAPTER 36

THE POLITICS OF
PLANNING

J. PHILLIP THOMPSON

Politics is the practice and study of how to bring about unity, order, and create community—among individuals and groups with conflicting views—for the purpose of taking collective action. Differences among groups are perpetual; unity, order, and community are continuous challenges, are never assured, and stand as social achievements. Politicians shape processes for deciding what we are going to do in the future and defining with others who "we" are. Democracies organize political participation around the principle of equal individual rights, such as the right to vote. Since consensus among voters is rare, democracies make decisions by majority rule and enforce them by government. Democratic politics has been described as the mediation, or working relationship, between individuals (and groups) seeking rights and the rights of the government (or institution) that founds and conditions these rights (Howard 2002). Cities and states in the United States are on both sides of this division; at times they govern citizens, at times they advocate against higher levels of government for their own rights. Because the United States is a large and diverse nation of more than 310 million people, more than 80 percent of whom live in urban (mainly suburban) areas, urban politics is a broad and complex subject.

Democracies, like other political systems, have their own particular difficulties. The idea that citizens are treated as equals is more of an ideal or aspiration—or some say, a deception—than reality. The related idea that political majorities are free from group prejudices that marginalize minorities on an ongoing basis is also, in the United States, mainly an unrealized ideal. Rev. Martin L. King Jr. once said in relation to "the dream of a democratic society" that, "many Americans would like to have a nation which is a democracy for white Americans but simultaneously a dictatorship over black Americans" (Honey 2011).

For these and similar reasons, some political observers make a distinction between real and idealistic conceptions of politics (Geuss 2008). Real politics focuses on power: who is included and excluded in political groups, who benefits from political actions, and who manipulates whom. Real politics also takes a critical stance regarding arguments about legitimacy, meaning the justifiably right and wrong things to do; these arguments are examined in a social context rather than reified into so-called timeless or universal principles. Idealistic versions of politics come in at least two forms. One is the *rational-scientific*, and it assumes that citizens make political decisions based on narrow sets of clearly defined self-interests. This view ignores the power an elite can have over an oppressed subject (ex-felons, women, Muslims, immigrants), and it also contradicts the social nature of human beings. Many people do not know why they hold the beliefs they were taught, and no one is fully aware of the biases of his or her own culture and language (Pitkin 1972). Another, the idealistic *rational-ethical* approach, assumes that agreement can be reached among unequal groups on what rationally and ethically constitutes fairness, or justice, or freedom, without overcoming power differentials (Rawls 1971).

The idea that planning is an apolitical technical profession is a farce that has been associated historically with the rational-scientific view and also with governance by wealthy, well-educated elites (Low 1991). Plans produce winners and losers, making their creation a political act. Just as important, planners are often involved in implementation of projects and policies after they have been approved through formal political processes and their plans are then underlined by the force of government. Whereas earlier planners often hid their politics, today planners sometimes claim to be political while avoiding the contingency of politics in action. The rational-ethical view of the theorist John Rawls and his followers, for example, is apolitical in that they argue that principles for ordering just societies can be devised outside of the context of actual political struggle.

Once we take power differentials into account in politics and planning, and once we examine the manipulation of political discourse by powerful elites, we might think of politics and planning as having two realms. One, typically more powerful, is formal, legal, official, bureaucratic, civic, statistical, and abstract (ideal). The other tends to be informal, unofficial, situational, sometimes hidden or even illegal, often novel and creative, and seldom academic (Scott 1998). Real politics and "real" planning invariably involve both formal and informal realms and the power struggles between them (Flyvbjerg 1998). Discourse about cities often tracks this divide, particularly with discussion of "functional" or "normal" places and institutions, on the one hand, and "marginal" neighborhoods and institutions, on the other (Venkatesh 2006). It is no accident that this divide parallels that of race: the places inhabited by "good people" versus the places populated by poor blacks and "others" (Katz 1993).

In the late 1990s, Robert Beauregard (1996) described cities as, "the locus of unending struggle around the distribution of the costs and benefits of growth and decline." He argued that planning was beginning to move away from the modernist approach that initially articulated an "organic" city and sought to balance interests and tame the excesses of capital. The direction of movement among practicing planners, he said, was "to flee the problems of society" by planning for the prosperous—with scant attention to those outside "the loop." The direction of planning academics was increasingly toward postmodern cultural critiques that included, "the abandonment of critical distance for ironic commentary, the embracing of multiple discourses and the rejection of totalizing ones, a skepticism toward master narratives and general social theories, a disinterest in the performativity of knowledge, the rejection of notions of progress and enlightenment, and a tendency toward political acquiescence" (Beauregard 1996).

He argued that planning should not reject modernism entirely or unconditionally embrace postmodernism; planners should instead maintain a focus on the city and the built environment as a way of retaining relevancy and coherence, and they should maintain modernism's commitment to political reform and to planning's meditative role within the state, labor, and capital. He also mentioned that planning needed to open itself up to "a multiplicity of communities and cultures" (Beauregard 1996). Planning continues to grapple with these issues. Many recent theorists in planning have encouraged planners to pay more attention to politics, to attach themselves to social movements, and to maintain and develop "social justice" frameworks for cities (Fainstein 2009; Marcuse 2009). This is a tall order, particularly if planners are to do this without replicating the elitism, totalizing, idealistic, and sometimes racist tendencies of modernist planning and politics. I will return to these themes later, but first I turn to urban political science and its relevance to urban planning.

1. THE URBAN POLITICAL PROCESS

Urban political science in the early 1950s argued that city politics was dominated by elites, often by business and civic leaders working behind the scenes (Elkin 1987). Political machines were seen as rule by European ethnic working-class elites, with machine bosses doling out benefits to community supporters in exchange for their political support (Bridges 1984). By the late 1950s, pluralism displaced elite theory as the dominant explanation of the urban political process. Pluralists held that the mayors and other officials mediate between competing private interests, none of whom either wins or loses entirely (Dahl 1961). Pluralists described the political process as transparent—anyone could see who went into City Hall and what they got. Pluralism came under disrepute for its inability to explain why some groups (such as real estate interests) won benefits more consistently than others, and for its failure as to why certain groups never got into City Hall—an especially spectacular failure in the 1960s, when across the country black communities that had been locked out of the political system erupted in urban insurrections (Katznelson 1973/1976).

Race and power analysis then took hold in urban politics, as elites came to be understood as white union bosses, white-led universities, and other powerful white-dominated institutions, in addition to the business leaders traditionally considered the elite. Race and power analysts argued for grassroots empowerment and structural change, and some argued for revolution (Cloward and Piven 1974). Pluralism, as well as and race and power analysis, was largely displaced by (or integrated into) regime theory in the late twentieth century (Stone 1993). Regime analysts held that city governments have to produce results, yet local governments lack enough resources to do so on their own, so they seek well-resourced private partners to help them produce things. Regime theorists focused principally on development projects and the strategies used to attract and retain private businesses.

Yet, depending on the desired outcomes and the capacities needed to achieve them, the private side of "public–private" partnerships could just as easily be civic and community groups (Stone 1993). Had this latter suggestion been extended to studies of how community groups (including informal groups such as gangs) and government in poor communities develop political relationships to produce things—such as neighborhood peace—urban political science might have been led down a more "postmodern" (and more interesting) path. Nonetheless, regime analysis is a more flexible theory than either elite or pluralist theory in that it allows for various kinds of elite or anti-elite regimes depending on the goals of political leaders and the types of resources assembled (Stone 2004).

Regime theory proved itself better than previous urban theories in enabling analysts to conceptualize the role of the private sector in political processes in cities. Yet, regime analysis is lacking in important respects. It gives little attention to the role of ideology and culture in politics, but it does adequately address Robert Dahl's observation that as politics moves from the local to the national level, democratic participation declines and power increases, thus the risk of evisceration of democracy by resource-rich interest groups at the national scale (Fainstein 2009). This latter theme has received renewed attention with the decline of many large cities, such as Detroit. The structure of U.S. government (federalism) greatly limits political choices, policy, and planning at the city level (Frug and Barron 2008). Cities in the United States are not fully self-governing units; they are legal creations of state governments. Although cities are granted powers through state home-rule provisions, those provisions vary and some cities have far more autonomy than others. Cities are also constrained by the powerful rural bias of the U.S. Senate. The United States is still governed by a structure created hundreds of years ago under entirely different circumstances (Pierson and Hacker 2010).

2. RACE, CAPITALISM, AND AMERICAN POLITICAL DEVELOPMENT

Culture is a powerful force in politics because it helps to establish group identities—who is with "us" and who "we" are against. Analyzing politics simply in terms of demographics, parties and elections, and deal making between business and politicians is limiting, in that it does not illuminate how these interests and identities are constructed in the first place nor how they are legitimated (or not) through culture. Michael Rogin, in his work on political spectacle in the United States, wrote:

> American imperial spectacles display and forget four enabling myths that the culture can no longer unproblematically embrace. The first is the historical organization of American politics around racial domination....The second is redemption through violence, intensified in the mass technologies of entertainment and war. The third is the belief in individual agency, the need to forget both the web of social ties that enmesh us all and the wish for an individual power so disjunctive with everyday existence. And the fourth is identification with the state, to which is transferred the freedom to act without being held to account that in part compensates for individual helplessness but in part reflects state weakness as well. (Dawson 2011, 177)

Political culture, as suggested by Rogin, emerges from history and interprets it in a way that empowers some groups and policies and marginalizes others. Debates over taxes, for example, easily and routinely invoke both longstanding historical myths about which groups are deserving (e.g., the admirable rich create jobs for others) and undeserving (e.g., the poor, especially blacks, are lazy and ignorant) and they often invoke the quasi-religious faith many Americans put in the doctrine of "free markets" (Connolly 2008). As they simplify and distort reality and history, the myths of any political culture are contested and full of contradictions.

The political culture of the United States—one-time slavocracy and self-proclaimed leader of the free world—has always been fraught: a settler state established by Christian evangelicals and expanded through genocide, conquest, and expulsion of indigenous peoples and Mexicans; a nation that built itself on the back of imported African slaves, and enacted postemancipation state laws that segregated blacks until the mid-1960s; a country significantly shaped by a Congress that through WWII was dominated by the southern Democratic bloc elected from districts where black voting was suppressed, often violently. Through the 1980s, the nation waged a vigorous "cold war" against Soviet and Chinese socialist influence, including the Korean and Vietnam wars. Though often silenced in the dominant political narratives, throughout this history the forceful opposition movements from abolitionism, populism, the labor movement, the civil rights and women's movements, the anti-war movement, and the environmental movement, to immigrant rights and gay rights activism today, contested these policies and expanded and redefined democracy (Marone 1998). This history of contestation forms the backdrop of American culture wars and informs the contradictory thinking about politics, policy, and planning.

Modernist planning played an important role in developing America's current political geography. It was a legitimating apparatus for racialized state–capitalist development. Large-scale development plans that in effect maintained and extended race and class segregation were defended as politically neutral embodiments of reason and technological achievement that "would banish conflict and bring order and freedom" (Scott 1998). In practice, however, modernist urban renewal programs, mainly advocated by downtown business interests, led to the demolition of 1,600 black neighborhoods across the country for the ostensibly neutral and rational purpose of "eliminating blight."

Once residents' homes were demolished, "planners had control over the directions in which people could move, and the spaces they would occupy. Their thinking was guided by explicit concepts…of hiding and marginalizing the poor. Their tools included using highways, massive buildings, parking lots, and open space as barriers; eliminating connecting streets to inhibit travel in and out; and housing people in public housing projects that were cut off from the flow of the city" (Fullilove 2004, 64). Urban renewal led to black protests (a highway project through the middle of West Oakland, California, a black community, was the cause for the formation of the Black Panther Party) and "race riots," accelerating white flight from cities and triggering fiscal imbalances that drive city development priorities (seeking ever more favorable climates for business relocation) to this day. Following the riots, many planners began to take up issues of inequality, in terms of both who benefits from development and who participates in the creation of plans and development projects (see Fainstein and Fainstein, this volume).

Urban renewal took place at the same time (1950s–60s) that the federal government provided massive subsidies for the development of suburbs and highway systems (Thompson 2006). African Americans and Latinos were not only largely excluded from the new suburbs, they were excluded from the federally financed jobs that built them (Hill 1985). Black advocates had long pleaded with labor unions to racially integrate so as to build a strong social democratic majority in the United States, in support of both economic and racial justice (Thompson 2006). Labor unions in construction, often white ethnic in cities, opted instead to form coalitions with large real estate developers and white ethnic political machines to advocate greater spending on development projects, including urban renewal projects (Goldberg and Griffey 2010). Their alliances became known in urban political science as "urban growth machines."

However, labors' short-term successes produced their longer term demise. As white workers, including construction workers, moved to the suburbs and proudly declared themselves "middle class," cities became increasingly majority minority and began to elect black mayors. These mayors were less interested in appeasing white labor unions than the black businesses that helped them get elected and that hired black workers (voters). Black (and Latino) leaders also resented the building trades' tendency to support any development project that promised their members jobs, regardless of its effect on low-income minority communities. As the construction trade unions weakened in cities, businesses took advantage of their decline to do more construction nonunion. A parallel process took place in manufacturing across the country: companies took advantage of labor unions' inability to win strong union support in the South (going back to labor's rejection of an alliance with black civil rights advocates), where most African Americans reside. Many manufacturers moved to the South to avoid the unions, and many others left the United States altogether (Harrison 1984). Labor, lacking strong minority support, was unable to win legislation to constrain manufacturers.

Corporate power rose steadily in the midst of the intense racial division coming on the heels of the 1960s. Absent a strong labor–black coalition joining race and class issues, blacks and white workers went in different directions. The rising black vote in the North, the threat of urban disorder, and international embarrassment following televised repression of civil rights protests left Democrats in the White House in the 1960s little choice but to support civil rights and expanded social welfare programs. However, this price cost the national Democratic Party the support of disgruntled white voters (especially in the South), who resented Democratic Party support for civil rights legislation.

This divide caused a realignment in national politics, as southern whites moved en masse to the Republican Party. The turning point was the late 1970s. When black political mobilization produced thousands of black elected officials who argued strenuously in Congress, state houses, and city councils for greater funding for the urban poor, Republicans—and eventually conservative Democrats hoping to reposition the Democratic Party to the right—attributed high taxes and big government bureaucracy to the burden of providing welfare programs, particularly those aiding minorities (Kinder and Sanders 1995). Sensing political disarray, corporations greatly expanded their political lobbying and successfully rode the racialized anti-tax, anti-government fervor to pressure both parties to support reductions in government regulation and taxes (Pierson and Hacker 2010).[1]

With increased power and money, corporate lobbyists then pushed for legislation to weaken labor unions and programs serving poor urban communities. Some unions in areas that suffered fewer cuts, such as education and health care, still maintained much of their power. Concentrated in urban areas, these public-sector labor unions were also increasingly populated by minorities and became major advocates for urban programs and civil rights. Beginning late in 2010, Republican activists initiated a national campaign to weaken public-sector labor unions in states where Republicans control the state legislatures (Cauchon 2011). The anti-labor attacks have significant implications for democratic political theory. For much of the twentieth century, labor unions were considered to be the major counterforce to corporate power in politics. Pluralist defenders of U.S. democracy had long argued that labor unions' organizational power effectively countered the concentration of wealth among corporate elites, and thereby reconciled capitalism with democracy (Schattschnieder 1975). That power balance has now changed decidedly in favor of large corporations.

The rise in corporate political influence, and the radically conservative political agenda that the corporations successfully promoted (low taxes on individual wealth, limited government), is largely responsible for a spectacular rise in income inequality. In a 2010 study of income in New York City, for example, the Fiscal Policy Institute reported that 44 percent of all household income accrued to only 90,000 households—less than 1 percent of the population (Parrott 2011). Growing income and wealth inequality has affected cities and community development in important ways. Gentrification of neighborhoods near the financial core in successful "global cities" such as New York, Chicago, Atlanta, San Francisco, and Boston has displaced large numbers of low-income minorities, producing resentment not unlike that of urban renewal decades earlier. Another effect is that low-income housing development became hitched to growth in corporate profits via the federal tax credit program that provides corporations with tax relief for their investment in low-income housing. Ironically, as tax breaks for corporations lowered the revenue available for government programs such as affordable housing, the tax credits proliferated. This had the political effect of encouraging self-policing by community housing advocates to not criticize the corporations and banks needed to finance their housing programs. It was in this atmosphere of labor union decline and a lull in community advocacy against finance corporations that the mortgage foreclosure crisis ripened and finally exploded in 2008.

The dramatic growth in corporate power was made possible by aggressive business political organizing, but it was necessarily facilitated by manipulations of cultural beliefs, particularly white racial resentment toward minorities during and following the 1960s. Racial resentment is an important dimension of economic dynamics that is often overlooked by theorists who make category mistakes between race and class. The political theorist Nancy Fraser, for example, says that race is at heart about "recognition." The "recognition dimension corresponds to the status order of society, by socially entrenched patterns of cultural value...." Class, on the other hand, she maintains, is about distribution, which "corresponds to the economic structure of society, hence to the constitution, by property regimes and labor markets, of economically defined categories of actors" (Fraser and Honneth 2003). The urban political theorist Susan Fainstein similarly says that race, like religion, gender, ethnicity, and culture, "as a political formula...gives rise to demands for language autonomy and acknowledgement of particular customs such as holiday celebrations or styles of communications" (Fainstein 2010).

Both of the above statements are misleading. Economic oppression has never been a secondary aspect of African-American struggles. Slavery, the original racial formation, was a property regime and defining feature of U.S. labor markets; it was simultaneously a status order. It is misleading to frame slavery and segregation (the southern property regime following slavery) as fundamentally about class, even though slavery and segregation were economic structures, because white workers were not slaves or segregated into the bottom rungs of the economy. To the contrary, whiteness mattered to workers of European descent precisely because it enabled them to escape blacks' fate (Nelson 2001; Olson 2004).

The concept of race is diluted beyond recognition when it is stripped of its economic content and becomes mainly a cultural demand for particular holiday celebrations or the acceptance of language particularities (Ebonics). Moreover, wealth compounds over time under capitalism, especially in the absence of a robust social wage, so that wealth accumulated from slavery now measures many trillions of dollars. Similarly with racial segregation, the economic impact of post-WWII housing discrimination alone is estimated at nearly $500 billion (Yinger 2005). As suggested by Rogin earlier, the very popularity of free-market individualism among white Americans, with its built-in dismissal of history and social responsibility, conveniently dismisses these claims of blacks—that is part of its appeal. The concept of race, if it is to be meaningfully connected to what blacks have experienced and argued over during the last few hundred years, inextricably weaves together property and status. Separating the two, much less defining race as mainly about cultural status, is a category mistake that has political consequences. We can see one consequence in Fainstein's political analysis. She argues that,

> In the United States distributional issues are especially salient because social citizenship has not yet been won. Justice requires dampening of sentiments based on group identity, greater commitment to common ends, and identification of institutions and policies that offer broadly appealing benefits.... The inherently divisive character of identity politics cuts across the building of such institutions and therefore is largely self-defeating. For distribution to proceed, recognition is a pre-requisite, but that recognition needs to involve shared commitments, not rivalry. (Fainstein 2009)

Fainstein seems to believe that programs and institutions associated with "distribution" and "broadly appealing benefits" are somehow free of rivalry and identity politics. She does not tell us precisely what kind of political formations do not involve an identity politics—an "us" versus a "them"—or exactly which institutions are committed to "common ends" over "group" ends. Certainly government is not neutral and inclusive, while it excludes noncitizen taxpayers, ex-felons (a large proportion of the black male population), and those unable to navigate often deliberately cumbersome voter registration requirements, from voting. Unions and universities are also not very inclusive.

Pretending there is such a thing as an inclusive nonidentity politics, or all-inclusive policies, puts a veil over politics. It is substituting a utopian ideal for the reality of politics. This is not to say that there can never be greater unity, or that new and broader group affiliations cannot emerge, but rather that unity is conditional, incomplete, and temporary. There will not be "a dampening of sentiments based on group identity" so long as humans are social beings.

If more equal distribution, or some other goal, requires "shared commitments," how are they to be arrived at so as to be "shared"? After all, equality is one of those idealistic concepts (like democracy, freedom) that can never be applied uniformly and whose actual meaning is determined by politics—and hence is subject to power. Fainstein says that her notion of "recognition" is a "pre-requisite" for unity. But why would anyone accept this? By the authority, one must presume, of logic. Yet, is there only one logical way to arrive at solidarity? (Pitkin 1972). Is politics like natural science, so that once the underlying mechanical dynamics are discovered, we can reliably follow a single formula to achieve a desired result? Perhaps this kind of approach informs Fainstein's claim to know what justice "requires," even though standards for justice vary greatly across groups and nations. It seems to me as though Fainstein's argument is leading us back to master narratives and master planning, but now it's a master planning of politics. I do not think this way of thinking about politics can succeed, for all the reasons that master planning could not succeed.

An alternative to telling groups what is required for them to do to achieve a socially just city (or nation, or world) is to try to determine how and whether a social justice orientation can offer a superior means of solving problems of urgent concern to groups. That is, to broaden the theories of social justice from a set of moral requirements into the realm of innovation and practical experimentation to determine how, and which, social justice values help advance solidarity, movement building, and progressive planning in cities. Far from suppressing difference, I think that moving social justice theorizing closer to practice will demonstrate the importance of dealing directly with race and finding ways to implement equitable solutions to divisive problems as a path toward building broader interracial unity. Take, for example, the issue of increasing the efficient use of energy. Environmental advocates have stressed the importance of reducing urban sprawl by increasing urban density, increasing use of mass transit, and retrofitting buildings to increase their energy efficiency (Sierra Club n.d.; Orr 2002). Race has not figured as a prominent social justice value for many of those concerned about energy efficiency and carbon reduction. Yet, urban sprawl is itself largely a product of white flight from cities "invaded" by minorities, middle-class flight of all races from failing schools, high levels of crime and unemployment, and physical blight in inner cities. In short, sprawl is largely a race problem. Any serious attempt to reverse urban sprawl in favor of building more dense—and, by necessity, highly racially integrated—cities must politically address these interrelated economic and social/cultural problems that make up the substance of the race issue. Rather than dampening urban black community concerns about failing schools and mass incarceration in their neighborhoods, encouraging suburbanites to enter these same neighborhoods (without counterproductively displacing poor current residents out of the city), requires, I suspect, taking these issues on and incorporating them into the environmental agenda (Freeman 2006). If environmentalists do so, reducing sprawl may well broaden its appeal beyond environmental activists and policy specialists to include minority and low-income community activists in cities.

Drilling down to the mechanics of retrofitting buildings for energy efficiency exposes similar race issues. Government and utility-financed energy retrofit programs tend to take as their mental image buildings in good condition and occupants able to financially maintain their buildings. The energy finance programs generally do not make funds available for buildings requiring basic improvements prior to energy retrofits, such as removing asbestos and lead (so as not to cause cancer or poisoning), or replacing "knob and ball" wiring (so as not to cause fire). These problems are concentrated in low-income minority neighborhoods for reasons having to do with poverty and longstanding housing discrimination (Energy Programs Consortium 2004). By not taking these problems into account, government and utility-company energy retrofit programs will reduce energy costs for wealthier and whiter communities while leaving low-income minorities less able to take advantage of these government subsidies. Hence, energy efficiency programs could become new sources of racial inequality, following in the path of earlier discriminatory housing programs. Alternatively, a portion of the income from energy savings could be channeled by government and utilities to pay for basic repair and improvement of buildings with preexisting problems in poor communities. If environmentalists hope to broaden the cause of carbon reduction in low-income communities of color, something like this will need to emerge.

There are similar dynamics at work on the employment side of energy efficiency. At a time of high unemployment in the construction industry, the unionized building trades view energy-efficiency retrofits as an important opportunity for their members "on the bench" to get jobs. However, black and Latino communities with high levels of unemployment also view energy retrofits as an important source of jobs in their communities. Because of a long history of discrimination within the building trade unions, minorities are poorly represented in the trades. Since public money is being used to finance energy retrofits across the country, both sides believe they deserve the retrofitting jobs. The construction trades have lobbied government to make all publicly financed retrofit work union, while minority communities have opposed or been ambivalent about union demands because of the unions' traditional reluctance to train and place minority workers on the job. In this situation, asking either unemployed white construction workers or unemployed black workers to hold back on their particular group ends (give up jobs for another group) for a "common end" of solidarity is unlikely to succeed.

What is needed, similar to Fainstein's call for a realistic utopia, is a new framework—one of job-rich "green cities" requiring the rebuilding of infrastructure across multiple sectors—that would provide unimagined opportunities for both sets of workers and would not dampen their group ends so much as to redirect them into a transformative political and policy process. Yet, what is equally needed is a "just transition" to the new green city that provides a framework and process *right now* for white and black workers to not only reach their particular demands but also to supercede them. The building trades themselves are inching toward such a framework. They take into account two factors. One is that the residential building sector is largely nonunionized, and white workers are mainly seeking jobs working on (higher paying, traditional) large commercial or public buildings. Second, it takes many years (often five or more) to become a trained professional construction worker such as an electrician, and nearly half of unionized white construction workers are near retirement.

A "just transition" might be for black workers to support unionization in all construction (including the residential sector), while white workers support

integrating the construction trades—beginning with putting black workers immediately on the job in the residential sector, but with a clear path to expanding blacks'
share of traditionally better paying commercial/public building jobs. Overarching
all of this would be the hopeful and transformative prospect of a unifying black–
white struggle for expansion of city rebuilding across the board (transportation,
water, etc.) to build green cities. The national leadership of the building trades is
supporting this approach, which remains highly controversial within the unions
(Grabelsky and Thompson 2010).

Despite the seemingly broad and beneficial appeal and benefit of energy efficiency programs, the above examples show that they can be implemented in either
highly discriminatory or highly equitable and transformative ways. How they are
implemented matters as much as the goal itself of making cities green and prosperous. What is needed is for actors with knowledge of local conditions to act creatively
in finding ways to overcome divisive racial and class problems. These practical
innovations can be critiqued and evaluated, replicated and improved upon, and
from this we can breath life into social justice categories or put them into repose.
We will return to this theme later.

3. PLANNING AND THE FIGHT FOR
THE FUTURE OF CITIES

I argued above that race supplied a social base for anti-labor, pro-business ascendency, although it did so with the acquiescence of labor. Urban planning has taken
a beating in the process, as planning is often associated with big government, if
not socialism (Allmendinger 2009). Yet, leaving planning to the market, a refrain
heard often since conservative ascendency in the 1980s, fundamentally undermines
citizens' capacity to participate meaningfully in democracy, imperiling democracy
itself. This can readily be seen in three important areas: planning for the future;
increasing transparency in complex economic and social environments; and standards and distribution.

Markets, by their very nature, cannot plan for society, and mainstream economic theory offers no insight on how government should plan for society
(Galbraith 2008). The many public goods needed for a prosperous future for the
whole society—education, scientific research, infrastructure, health care, and environmental protection—require planning and investment even if their value is not
readily quantifiable or if unrestricted and uncompensated public assess is useful
for their success. A second problem with leaving planning to business is that the
complexity of modern societies and "markets" provides ample room for deception,
crime, and social and environmental degradation. Mainstream economic theory

holds that for a market to function efficiently, there must be competition among producers, choices among commodities, and transparency (perfect information) so that purchasers can assess what they are buying.

These conditions do not apply for major goods in the United States. Major goods involve far too much complexity and require expert knowledge to compare options. Few people know how to (or can) shop for doctors, prescriptions, and hospitals, much less for medical approaches (for example, traditional homeopathic versus osteopathic). Homeowners likewise have few if any options to choose from among energy suppliers. There are few choices among food suppliers (many of whom own multiple retail chains). A few big firms, oligopolies, dominate these sectors. How they operate has less to do with supply–demand curves than with government policy. Oligopolies deploy ample resources to influence public policy, and more to influence private behavior (through advertising) to protect their positions. Given the complexity in these areas, the ability of oligopolies to weaken government regulation has been an invitation to fraud and consumer deception. As complexity increases, and the power of corporations increases, the need for competent government oversight and planning also increases.

Leaving planning to the market also has major implications for standards and distribution. Government redistributes wealth not only through tax policy but also through contracts with private parties, through public infrastructure (such as public parks that raise real estate values), and historically through coerced labor exploitation. Whether we are a nation of a few rich and many poor, shaped like a pyramid, or a nation of a few rich and a few poor, shaped like a football, is an issue of public policy. Left alone, capitalism distributes wealth upward: those with more to invest earn a larger share of the return. The effects of our pyramid distribution structure are readily felt in nonwealthy cities and neighborhoods—deteriorating infrastructure, failing schools, and large populations of ex-felons.

A reasonable question to ask is, who are the forces that might want, and be able, to fight for socially just cities and contest privatized planning (or nonplanning)? Because eighteen of the twenty largest U.S. cities have majority nonwhite populations, I will point to some of the problems in cities that many nonwhite groups are focused on as a way of orienting social justice theorizing toward issues that might ignite the interest and commitment of minorities. Following the civil rights movement, city politics was a key outlet for black frustration at the national level, but it has since become an immense disappointment. The U.S. pattern of decentralized government, combined with intermediary associations such as community boards and nonprofit organizations, allowed blacks a form of limited autonomy (self-government).Yet, as mentioned earlier, cities lack the resources and the power of states and especially the federal government. Black mayors did not have the resources to deal with unemployment, the lack of affordable housing, and failing schools. Cities also had weaker voting power relative to the white suburbs (Beauregard 1996).[2] Even after the election of an African-American president in 2008, poor minority neighborhoods have experienced little improvement. Frustration with poor results of democracy in addressing conditions in their communities has led low-income black voters to significantly withdraw from voting (Thompson 2006). Black voting in the 2010 mid-term elections, for example, dropped 43 percent from their 2008 level during the presidential race. Latino turnout dropped 40 percent, while white turnout decreased by only 30 percent (Minnite 2010). Given their lack of progress, blacks' loss of faith in the formal political process is predictable.

Political theorist Ian Shapiro suggests that if minorities have no hope of changing the majority, they might engage in rebellion or, failing that, crime (Shapiro 2011). But in the United States, minority despair takes other forms as well, including demands for separation, depression and other stress-related diseases, internalized anger, and withdrawal from politics.[3] In the past, African Americans have responded to marginalization in the nation's formal politics and discourse by building protest movements and organizing internal self-help institutions, such as the black church (Shelby 2005; Hahn 2009). It is the power of such efforts in the past that expanded the reach of democracy and social welfare programs in the 1960s. A cardinal mistake in urban politics at this moment would be to fixate on formal politics while not paying attention to informal movement building within black communities.

By the same token, there has been little examination of the attitudes of whites and Asians who deliberately choose to live in inner cities and take active roles in improving the neighborhoods. Like the white abolitionists and anti-slavery radical Republicans of the 1850s, these contrarian groups hold out critical hope for a less racially polarized and brighter future for cities. Indeed, the lack of geo-political analysis of recent trends in cities left political scientists (not to mention planners) unable to anticipate the political appeal of Barack Obama among the white and Asian urbanites, especially among young urban voters. Obama overwhelmingly won the urban vote 70/28 in big cities, 59/39 in small cities, and he overwhelmingly won the youth vote.

A second important issue is immigration. Today, urban race issues are less frequently black–white and increasingly black–white–Latino–Asian. The majority of immigrants are from Latin America and the Caribbean. They tend to work at the bottom of the economy in the places traditionally occupied by African Americans, and this leads to some competition and enmity. More significantly, immigrants are mostly politically disenfranchised. Although legal immigrants are permitted (and may be required) to serve in the military, and pay taxes, with few exceptions they cannot vote in city and state elections. Historically, by contrast, when immigrants were mainly from Europe, noncitizens often did vote in nonfederal elections (Hayduk 2006).

Denying voting rights to legal immigrants (and ex-felons) in cities has revenue implications for cities. In New York, Los Angeles, and Miami, for example, between 35 and 40 percent of the population is legal immigrants who pay taxes, but they cannot vote in city and state elections that determine where tax revenues are spent. This means that immigrants may not get their fair share of public investment; but, often overlooked, it means that voting citizens who live near immigrant enclaves are also disadvantaged—the effect of their vote is diluted since many of their immigrant neighbors cannot vote in city or state elections. Thus, heavily immigrant cities are themselves significantly disenfranchised and are likely to be shortchanged in state budget battles. This is in essence, at least in my view, a form of voter suppression. The discrepancy between immigrants' claim on services and their weak role in formal political struggles may lead to the perception that immigrants do not contribute their to city's efforts to pay for services; or it could alternatively lead to a renewed and broader racial struggle for civil rights and equity for cities. In any case, it is an important problem seldom discussed in formal channels.

4. PLANNING FOR SOCIAL JUSTICE, OR WHAT?

If urban planning is not a rational science of ordering physical objects in urban space, then what is its purpose and claim to legitimacy? One answer, discussed earlier, is that planners should advocate utopian social justice visions for cities that are not so far-fetched as to be unrealizable. Planning can then attach itself to widespread values such as democracy, the common good, or equality (equity). As suggested in the discussion of energy efficiency above, I believe there is some value to this approach, as it positions planning as something different from private development and it encourages planners to consider what these broader values might mean in practice. Still, having a general social justice orientation does not answer what social justice means in practice. The social justice criteria provided by Fainstein, for example, may be a useful "universal" framework for comparing practice across cities within the categories she selected, but it is not clear whether her list (or anyone else's) is adequate for addressing key problems in a particular city—that is, "universal" frameworks emerging out of academic discourse are not really universal.

It is also not clear that advocates for a social justice orientation for planning have broken with rational actor models of society and politics. Rational actor models assume that actors are capable of purposive action, that they are in control of their bodies, and that they are autonomous relative to other people and their environment (Joas and Knobl 2009). Taking the first point, purposive action implies a kind of means → ends schema. I argued earlier that suppressing minority demands or dissent is a bad means for building broad unity. I gave the example of how construction unions, in trying to build solidarity with minorities, created a new win-win direction of action by meaningfully addressing both their own and the minority groups' demands for jobs.

The lesson is that the means → ends concept of social change is problematic: the choice of means (supporting black demands for jobs now instead telling blacks to wait until unemployed white workers got jobs, or vice-versa) will, if pursued into the future, fundamentally change the nature of the union and the scope of the union's politics (their ends)—such as to include advocacy for funding remediation of dangerous preexisting building conditions in minority neighborhoods. Along these lines, numerous social theorists and anthropologists have argued that humans form identities not only early in life through socialization but also during periods of "self-transcendence" brought about through extraordinary situations: religious rituals, confrontations with death or shame, moments of collective ecstasy, political confrontation, and the like. I suspect that Martin Luther King Jr., a black Baptist minister as well as an activist, was well aware of the transformative potential of white labor's joining in the rituals of civil rights protest (singing, praying, holding hands in marching) when he told the Illinois AFL-CIO that, "The resolution of our differences can be found in the struggle that must be opened to obtain fuller security in the affluent society" (Honey 2011). A similar transformation is in process for some of the building trades in the context of action, "in the struggle."

The second aspect of the rational actor model is that actors have control over their bodies. It is obvious that sometimes we do not, such as when laughing or crying. But we are often not aware of the degree to which we are visually attracted or repulsed by certain types of bodies or things—deemed ugly or beautiful, dangerous or comforting, through our cultural upbringing (Hymes 1995). I (a male African American) have regular warm and cordial conversations with many white colleagues, but when they see me walking toward them on the street, they often step away and literally fail to recognize me. I do not think this is intentional behavior on the part of any of my colleagues; I believe they would be embarrassed if I pointed this behavior out. When addressing issues like housing, living in close proximity to "the other," feelings and behavior often emerge that actors themselves didn't know they had or were capable of. How to handle these issues is an open question in need of research and practical experimentation; it is definitely not settled by agreeing on general principles of social justice.

A third aspect of the rational actor model is that actors are autonomous decision makers who decide things according to their (usually material) self-interest. This is the argument for why workers of all races and ethnicities, for example, should embrace the logic of uniting together to fight their employers and raise their common wages. Noting how white workers in the American South rejected such logic when it came to blacks, many Marxists accused them of having "false consciousness." But, if we have learned anything about race at all, it is that such consciousness is not "false"; it is how consciousness works.

Writing in 1931, the black scholar and activist W. E. B. Dubois wrote,

> Throughout the history of the Negro in America, white labor has been the black man's enemy, his oppressor, his red murderer....Socialist and Communists explain this easily: white labor in its ignorance and poverty has been misled by the propaganda of white capital, whose policy is to divide labor into classes, races and unions and pit one against the other. There is an immense amount of truth in this explanation....But white American Laborers are not fools. And with few exceptions the more intelligent they are, the higher they rise, the more efficient

they become, the more determined they are to keep Negroes under their heels. (DuBois 1995, 589)

Martin L. King Jr. often made the point that what he was after was not deseg-regation but genuine racial integration that cannot be legislated: "True integration will be achieved by true neighbors who are willingly obedient to unenforceable obligations" (King 1986, 124). King believed that a social revolution, a revolution of values and in social living, was required before meaningful (nonsuperficial) politi-cal solidarity could be achieved. How to achieve such social solidarity is an open question, of obvious relevance to planning, that is not at all resolved by professing agreement with general social justice principles.

Rejecting these three aspects of the rational actor model, as theorists in the pragmatic vein encourage, has significant implications for politics and planning. It asserts that we do not know where social justice concepts or aspirations will lead and will only learn in the flow of practice. It elevates the role of practicioners, and of reflection on practice, in developing theories on democracy, equality, race, and cities. It opens a role for planning, if as a discipline it bridges categorical justice imperatives with the contingency and creativity of action, as a leader in using les-sons from social practice to shed new light on key problems and concepts in build-ing democratic, equitable, and racially inclusive cities of the future.

NOTES

1. In 1971, 175 firms had registered lobbyists in Washington, D.C. By 1982, 2,500 firms did. Corporate political action committees (PACs) expanded from 300 in 1976 to over 1,200 by 1980. In the mid-1970s, labor and corporate PACs spent evenly; by 1980, labor PACs contributed less than 25 percent of PAC contributions, down from half six years earlier. Corporate PACs expanded their funding fivefold in the same period; see Schattschnieder (1975); Pierson and Hacker (2010).
2. This fact is often hidden by the language of free housing markets and consumer choice; Freund (2007).
3. The psychiatrist and public health scholar Jonathan Metzl has produced a study showing that the mental health profession pathologized black anger and resistance to oppression, coining a term "protest psychosis," applied specifically to blacks. This approach was strongly supported by pharmaceutical companies, which increased sales of anti-psychotic drugs to treat the "illness"; see Metzl (2009).

REFERENCES

Allmendinger, P. 2009. *Planning Theory.* New York: Palgrave McMillan.
Beauregard, R. 1996. "Between Modernity and Postmodernity: The Ambiguous Position of U.S. Planning." In *Readings in Planning Theory,* edited by S. Campbell and S. Fainstein, 213–33. Malden, MA: Blackwell.
Bridges, A. 1984. *A City in the Republic: Antebellum New York and the Origins of Machine Politics.* New York: Cambridge University Press.

Cauchon, D. 2011. "Poll: Americans Favor Union Bargaining Rights." *USA Today*, Feb. 22.

Cloward, R. A., and F. F. Piven. 1974. *The Politics of Turmoil*. New York: Pantheon.
   Connolly, W. 2008. *Capitalism and Christianity, American Style*. Durham, NC: Duke
   University Press.

Dahl, R. A. 1961. *Who Governs?: Democracy and Power in an American City*. New Haven,
   CT: Yale University Press.

Dawson, M. 2011. *Not in Our Lifetimes: The Future of Black Politics.*. Chicago: University
   of Chicago Press.

DuBois, W. E. B. 1995. "The Negro and Communism." In *W.E.B. Dubois: A Reader*, edited
   by D. L. Lewis. New York: Henry Holt.

Elkin, S. L. 1987. *City and Regime*. Chicago: University of Chicago Press.

Energy Programs Consortium. 2004. Available at: http://www.energyprograms.org/
   wp-content/uploads/2011/10/07_2004_0407_WRAP_Background.pdf.

Fainstein, S. 2009. "Planning and the Just City." In *Searching for the Just City*, edited by P.
   Marcuse, J. Connolly, and J. Novy. New York: Routledge.

Fainstein, S. S. 2010. *The Just City*. Ithaca, NY: Cornell University Press.

Flyvbjerg, B. 1998. *Rationality and Power*. Chicago: University of Chicago Press.

Fraser, N., and A. Honneth. 2003. *Redistribution or Recognition?: Politicial-PhilosophicCal
   Exchange*. New York: Verso.

Freeman, L. 2006. *There Goes the Hood: Views of Gentrification from the Ground Up*.
   Philadelphia: Temple University Press.

Freund, D. 2007. *Colored Prosperity: State Policy and White Racial Politics in Suburban
   America*. Chicago: University of Chicago Press.

Frug, G., and D. Barron. 2008. *City Bound: How States Stifle Urban Innovation*. Ithaca,
   NY: Cornell University Press.

Fullilove, M. T. 2004. *Root Shock: How Tearing Up City Neighborhoods Hurts America
   and What We Can Do About It*. New York: Ballantine Books.

Galbraith, J. 2008. *The Predator State*. New York: Free Press.

Geuss, R. 2008. *Philosophy and Real Politics*. Princeton, NJ: Princeton University Press.

Goldberg, D., and T. Griffey, eds. 2010. *Black Power at Work*. Ithaca: Cornell University
   Press.

Grabelsky, J., and J. P. Thompson. 2010. "Emerald Cities in the Age of Obama: A New
   Social Compact Between Labor and Community." *Perspectives on Work* 13(2): 15–19.

Hahn, S. 2009. *The Political Worlds of Slavery and Freedom*. Cambridge, MA: Harvard
   University Press.

Harrison, B. 1984. "Regional Restructuring and 'Good Business Climates': The Economic
   Transformation of New England Since WWII." In *Sunbelt/Snowbelt: Urban
   Development and Regional Restructuing*, edited by L. Sawyers and W. K. Tabb. New
   York: Oxford University Press.

Hayduk, R. 2006. *Democracy for All: Restoring Immigrant Voting Rights in the US*.
   New York: Routledge.

Hill, H. 1985. *Black Labor and the American Legal System*. Madison: University of
   Wisconsin Press.

Honey, M., ed. 2011. *"All Labor Has Dignity."* Boston: Beacon Press.

Howard, Dick. 2002. *The Specter of Democracy*. New York: Columbia University Press.

Hymes, S. N. 1995. *Race, Culture, and the City: A Pedagogy for Black Urban Struggle*.
   Albany, NY: State University of New York Press.

Joas, H., and W. Knobl. 2009. *Social Theory: Twenty Introductory Lectures*. New York:
   Cambridge University Press.

Katz, M. B. 1993. "Reframing the 'Underclass Debate.'" In *The "Underclass Debate: Views from History,"* edited by M. B. Katz. Princeton, NJ: Princeton University Press.

Katznelson, I. 1973/1976. *Black Men, White Cities: Race, Politics and Migration in the United States 1900–30, and Britain, 1948–68.* Chicago: University of Chicago Press.

Kinder, D. and L. Sanders. 1996. *Divided by Color: Racial Politics and Democratic Ideals.* Chicago: University of Chicago Press.

King, Martin Luther J. 1986. "The Ethical Demands of Integration." In *A Testiment of Hope,* edited by J. Washington. New York: HarperCollins.

Low, N. 1991. *Planning, Politics, and the State: Political Foundations of Planning Thought.* Cambridge, MA: Hyman.

Marcuse, P. 2009. "From Justice Planning to Commons Planning." In *Searching for the Just City: Debates in Urban Theory and Practice,* edited by P. Marcuse, J. Connolly, J. Novy, et al. New York: Routledge.

Marone, J. 1998. *The Democratic Wish.* New Haven, CT: Yale University Press.

Metzl, J. A. 2009. *The Protest Psychosis: How Schizophrenia Became a Black Disease.* Boston: Beacon.

Minnite, L. C. 2010. "An Analysis of Who Voted (and Who Didn't Vote) in the 2010 Election." Project Vote Research Memo. New York: Project Vote.

Nelson, B. 2001. *Divided We Stand: American Workers and the Struggle for Black Equality.* Princeton, NJ: Princeton University Press.

Olson, J. 2004. *The Abolition of White Democracy.* Minneapolis: University of Minnesota Press.

Orr, D. 2002. *The Nature of Design.* New York: Oxford University Press

Parrott, J. 2011. "As Income Gap Widens, New York Grows Apart." *Gotham Gazette.* Available at: http://www.gothamgazette.com/article/economy/20110118/21/3452.

Pierson, P., and J. Hacker. 2010. *Winner Take All Politics.* New York: Simon and Schuster.

Pitkin, H. 1972. *Wittgenstein and Justice: On the Significance of Ludwig Wittgenstein for Social and Poltiical Thought.* Berkeley, CA: University of California Press.

Rawls, J. 1971. *A Theory of Justice.* Cambridge, MA: Harvard University Press.

Schattschnieder, E. E. 1975. *The Semisovereign People: A Realist's view of Democracy in America.* Hindsdale, IL: Dryden.

Scott, J. C. 1998. *Seeing Like a State: How Certain Schemes to Improve the Human Condition Have Failed.* New Haven, CT: Yale University Press.

Shapiro, I. 2011. *The Real World of Political Theory.* Princeton, NJ: Princeton University Press.

Shelby, T. 2005. *We Who Are Dark.* Cambridge, MA: Harvard University Press.

Sierra Club. n.d. "New Research on Population, Suburban Sprawl, and Smart Growth." Sierra Club white paper. Available at: www.sierraclub.org/sprawl/whitepaper. population.asp.

Stone, C. 1993. "Urban Regimes and the Capacity to Govern: A Political Economy Approach." *Journal of Urban Affairs* 15(1): 1–28.

Stone, C. N. 2004. "It's More Than the Economy After All: Continuing the Debate About Urban Regimes." *Journal of Urban Affairs* 26(1): 1–19.

Thompson, J. P. 2006. *Double Trouble: Black Mayors, Black Communities, and the Call for a Deep Democracy.* New York: Oxford University Press.

Venkatesh, S. 2006. *Off the Books: The Underground Economy of the Urban Poor.* Cambridge, MA: Harvard University Press.

Yinger, J. 2005. *Closed Doors, Opportunities Lost: The Continuing Cost of Housing Discrimination.* New York: Russell Sage Foundation.

B. MAKING GOOD PLANS

CHAPTER 37

READING THROUGH A PLAN: A VISUAL THEORY OF PLAN INTERPRETATION

BRENT D. RYAN

1. INTRODUCTION

WHILE not every planner will create a plan during his or her professional career, many planners read plans on a regular basis.[1] In whatever form they may be issued, plans continue to constitute the major printed currency of the planning profession, perhaps because the public continues to see plans as meaningful expressions of future intentions for a place. The regular issuance of plans is one of the few consistencies in a profession that has seen a variety of changes during the past hundred years, and the continuing importance of plans means that their creation remains a critical responsibility of the planner. Much professional training in planning hinges on providing nascent planners with skills to develop the ideas contained within the plans and plan documents that communicate and promote those ideas. Generating plans is perhaps the central creative act of the planning profession, the act that "gave planning its name" (Neuman 1998, 216).

While plans are arguably the "planner's most important product" (Alexander 2002, 191), an important corollary of this creative process—plan interpretation and the interpretation of planning ideas contained in plans—is less examined. Planners may read plans often, but the understanding or interpretation of plan content seems to be treated by the profession as something that is either too obvious or too unimportant to require explicit discussion. This interpretational shortage is unfortunate because plans communicate much more than their recommendations' "plain sense" (Mandelbaum 1990, 350). Recommendations are only one aspect of a rich variety of content and meaning that may be found reading through a plan.

Plans are also ideological artifacts—vessels for larger intellectual concepts that are likely to have emerged before a given plan and are likely to survive it as well. Plans also interpret these intellectual concepts, and may even constitute a critical contribution to their development. Plans may be seen as cultural artifacts whose content and appearance shed light on the society that produced them, and on the larger cultural artifact (the city or region) treated by the plan. Finally, plans are historical artifacts that occupy a place in the lives of the planning profession; the plan's subject neighborhood, city, or region; and the society(s) that produced the plan. Beyond "plain sense," a discerning reader may discover a panoply of readings and meanings in each and every plan.

This chapter calls for planners to "read through" plans, not simply to grasp their essential ideas or means of implementing those ideas but also to perceive additional meanings: first, a plan as an *idea vessel* with a place in a larger intellectual sphere; second, a plan as a *statement on the social and political values* of its time; and third, a plan as a *part*, albeit small, *of the history of the planning profession, of the life of cities, and of society*. Plans are the major intellectual projects published within the planning profession, and they deserve nothing less than to be read through for all their meanings.

A first proviso: this chapter will privilege spatial plans, not because of any inherent spatial bias but because the history of planning, up to the present day, has privileged and continues to privilege spatial plans. These plans still capture much of the public's imagination and interest in planning and planning history, from historical accounts of the field's origin (e.g., Smith 2006), to major citywide planning efforts today (e.g., Kreyling et al. 2005). Though land use and spatial planning are hardly the only threads of planning practice or planning thought (Campbell and Fainstein 2003 provide a complete survey), I will read plans issued in the land-use and spatial traditions as representatives, albeit imperfect, of the larger universe of plans.

A second proviso: this chapter will examine the interpretation of plans, not their evaluation nor their implementation. Understanding the multiple meanings and concepts contained within plans is a very different enterprise from deciding whether the ideas contained within the plans conform to a notion of "goodness" or not, or from understanding the degree to which a plan or plan idea has been realized (see chapters by Hoch and Hopkins, this volume).

2. HISTORIES OF READING(S)

Much like the city itself, a plan may be read in multiple ways depending upon the reader's perspective. Thus, the history of plan readings is as diverse as those individuals who have taken an interest in the city or in the planning profession. The literature on plan reading is not numerous, but it reflects diverse planning perspectives that bear mention.

Unsurprisingly, most planning practitioners and theorists have a vested interest in the profession's healthy function, leading to more concern for plan evaluation than plan reading. Many evaluation scholars read plans to ascertain whether they conform to norms of good planning and to understand how to plan better next time. Plan evaluation's purpose as "an approach to making better plans" is stated baldly by Baer (1997). Other authors interested in plan evaluation include Talen (1996), Hopkins (2001), Hoch (2002), Alexander (2002), Waldner (2004), Evans-Cowley and Gough (2009), and Berke and Godschalk (2009). Each establishes varying criteria to judge plan quality. These criteria are standards for improving professional effectiveness, as well as city and society, broadly considered.

Implementation is a particular interest of some plan evaluators. Implementation is a challenge (Pressman and Wildavsky 1973), and plan implementation is infrequent and incomplete even in fertile planning contexts (Ryan 2006). But implementation is important to those who believe in planning. Talen (1996) sees implementation as central to evaluation, such that the "analysis of planning documents" is discounted as merely that "form of evaluation that takes place prior to implementation." She argues that evaluating plan quality but ignoring implementation is "difficult to champion" (1996, 250). This perspective incompletely assesses the value of reading plans that are no longer available or appropriate for implementation, however. It also overvalues plans that are available but may not merit implementation. Plan quality may be only lightly connected to plan implementation, just as plan content may be only lightly connected to plan quality. Despite her skepticism of plan study unconnected to implementation, Talen does describe two threads of plan reading: "detailed assessments of what are deemed to be 'model' plans," and "discourse analysis (and) deconstruction" readings (Talen 1996, 250). Both of these threads constitute important reading trajectories and I will examine them briefly.

The planning profession is only slightly over one hundred years old, and histories of planning began to emerge only in the 1960s. Reps's (1965) "history of city planning" is actually more a history of ambitious urban visions in the preprofessional era; what is generally considered the beginning of American planning, the period between the Chicago World's Fair and the 1909 Plan of Chicago, marks the end of Reps's study. Reps lauds Burnham's work, noting the plan's "elaborate and beautifully printed volume...intimate familiarity with the details of the city...and long and carefully prepared" implementation section (519). For Reps, the plan *document* is inseparable from the plan's *ideas*: both are monumental and admirable. The 1909 Chicago Plan was early and seminal, and it has received notice in almost every history of planning. One of the most recent studies (Smith 2006), written just before the plan's centennial, is generally admiring, though Smith, unlike Reps, separates the plan document from the plan ideas. Even as he notes the document's "disciplined gorgeousness" (90) Smith recognizes that the plan may "neglect the needs of humane urban living" (96). This study is a paradigmatic "detailed assessment"

(Talen 1996, 250), providing much information on the Chicago Plan's historic context, but providing little additional ideological or theoretical perspective on the plan. Abbott's (1991) assessment of Portland plans is similarly neutral.

Burnham and Bennett's plans may be well known, but other historical perspectives on plan documents are few in number, most likely because few plan documents are perceived as having impacted the city as significantly as the 1909 plan did. (Cerdá's 1867 *eixample* plan for Barcelona is another plan perceived in a similar positive light today, though this plan idea was not published in an equivalent document.) Another such study, Keating and Krumholz's 1991 equity critique of downtown plans from the 1980s is animated not by any perceived historical significance of the plans examined but by the authors' view of downtown plans as proxies for the larger neoliberal turn of planning during the era. Implementation and visual quality are irrelevant in the face of these plans' "flawed" ideas that "ignored and aggravated" urban problems (1991, 150).

In 1990, an interesting if incomplete dialogue occurred in the pages of the *Journal of the American Planning Association*. Two authors, one a planning theorist and the other a planning practitioner, were asked to comment on Philadelphia's recently issued *Plan for Center City*, almost in the form of a literary criticism or book review. The first author, planning theorist Seymour Mandelbaum's "Reading Plans" (1990) makes several points of interest, though they had little to do with the particular content of the plan (which was, after all, yet another of the neoliberal downtown plans decried by Keating and Krumholz [1991]). Mandelbaum argues that the "plain sense" of the plan is of little interest outside of the act of interpretation, and that plan interpretation in turn moves far beyond a plan's plain sense. He then provides an effective if dispiriting explanation for the shortage of literature on plan reading: plan readers are few and far between, and most readers either read because they have to or because they are interested in a small portion of the plan. He also provides a framework for plan interpretation, noting that a plan may be read as a "policy claim," a "design opportunity," or a "story." Given that the plan is an urban design study, the second interpretation occupies the most space. The author concludes somewhat wistfully that the planners seem to think they have far more control over the larger forces influencing Philadelphia than he feels they actually do. The plan may thus be interpreted as an exercise in futility and obfuscation. He calls for an improved public plan-reading process, something that may have seemed unrealistic at the time but that has in fact arrived with the explosion of online commentary on seemingly every possible topic in the twenty-first century.

Much planning theory since 1990 has focused on planning as a discursive enterprise requiring adequate, equal, and coherent communication between diverse entities and individuals (Innes and Booher 2010). Communicative theorists have, therefore, taken an interest in the plan as a means of improving communication (Healey 1993; Khakee 2000). Given that a plan is by definition a communicative device, it is fair to demand that a plan contribute to this improvement. Methods for assessing such improvements are emerging as plans prioritize the improvement of communication through participation in planning processes

(Northeastern Illinois Planning Commission [NIPC] 2005, 266–69). Judging plans on this basis alone, however, underexamines not only the plan's degree of implementation, as Talen (1996, 250) noted, but runs the risk of defining planning as little more than an exercise in communication. Amid the plethora of voices, the concepts delivered by plans seem to be diminished in meaning.

3. TOWARD A VISUAL THEORY OF PLAN INTERPRETATION

Plans are not only textual but also visual objects: maps, figures, and illustrations were central to Burnham's plan and have remained such to the present day within the traditional land-use and urban design core of planning. Mandelbaum's plan reading hinted that literary criticism might offer one approach to plan reading, but given the visual trajectory of plans, visual interpretation may offer another equally valid reading mode. Paintings are a long established means of visual expression, and their interpretation has long been a field of study by art historians. Just as paintings communicate visually, so do plans. How might a theory of art interpretation inform a theory of plan interpretation?

Planning scholars do not seem to have looked previously to art history or visual studies for a theory of plan interpretation. Perhaps this is because much planning scholarship has stemmed more from a policy (i.e., textual) origin than from a design (e.g., visual) origin; or because planning scholars have had little interest in the perspective that might be provided by a visual-studies–based plan interpretation. Those planning scholars with a visual background who have formulated theories or practices of visual interpretation have had little interest in the plan. Beginning with Lynch, whose studies of planning's visual aspect (1960, 1972, 1981) almost never mention plans per se, subsequent visually oriented works (Cullen 1971; Hosken 1972; Clay 1973; Nelson 1977; Jacobs 1984) have examined the city, not the plan. This literature may be thought of as theorizing "how to look" rather than "how to read." Within planning, the seeming subjectivity of visual interpretation has long alienated social scientists from designers (Dagenhart and Sawicki 1992), and the differences are far from finding resolution (Lilley 2000, 15–16). This chapter will not attempt to effect a reconciliation, but it will argue that a theory of plan interpretation derived from art history offers a robust and effective means of reading through a plan on multiple levels.

This theory begins with Panofsky's (1939) landmark *Studies in Iconology*. In this work, Panofsky describes three "strata" or "meanings" in art, which he related through an imaginary narrative of a man raising his hat in the street. Panofsky identified this action as having three meanings. The first meaning was *factual*: he recognized the "plain sense" of the event (a man raising his hat) as corresponding to "certain objects (and actions) known to me from practical experience" (3–4). It was also *expressional*, in that Panofsky could recognize the emotional content of the event through relatively subtle clues that allowed him to discern the hat-raiser's sincerity (recognizing expressional content would presumably have permitted him to recognize an insincere or ironic version of the same event).

Panofsky calls the second level of meaning *conventional*, in which he recognized the event as being particular to the society and time in which the event occurred. He observes "that to understand [the event's] significance…I must be familiar…with the more-than-practical world of customs and cultural traditions particular to a certain civilization" (Panofsky 1939, 4).

Lastly, Panofsky recognizes an even deeper, *intrinsic* meaning to the hat-raising event. This relatively insignificant action, he concludes, constituted part of a much larger portrait not only of the man's individual personality but also of what could be called his "philosophy," his "way of viewing things and reacting to the world," which could be understood by "co-ordinating a larger number of similar observations and by interpreting them in connection to our general information as to the gentleman's period, nationality, class, intellectual traditions, and so forth" (Panofsky 1939, 5).

Panofsky then translates the meanings derived from everyday experience into the world of art. He calls these *primary* or "natural subject" meanings; *secondary* or "conventional subject matter" meanings; and *intrinsic* or "content" meanings (Panofsky 1939, 5–8). To understand how these levels of meaning might apply to a work of art, let us examine a completely imaginary painting—say, from the Italian fifteenth century.

Our imaginary painting shows a male human figure, almost naked except for a cloth around his waist, standing against a stone wall. The figure is standing at the end of the wall, near the center of the canvas. The figure is pierced with arrows and appears to be in great pain. Where the wall ends, one can see a landscape beyond. In the distance on a hill is a castle. The canvas comprises approximately half figure-against-wall and half landscape. Against the wall, to the figure's right, grows a small tree; and within the frame of vision of the painting, this tree is located approximately opposite the castle on the other side of the canvas. The canvas is painted in vivid, quick strokes, giving it a slight lack of detail and a sense of urgency.

A primary reading of this painting tells us exactly what is described above. One instantly and unconsciously recognizes the figure as human, the wall as a wall, and the landscape, castle, and tree as well. One can also instantly discern the figure's pain, and with a little study, one discerns the composition of the overall painting. The primary reading, in other words, reveals the identity of forms, objects, and events in the work and their spatial arrangement in the painting. Panofsky called these primary elements *pre-iconographical motifs*, since the primary reading provides no meaning beyond simple identification, or "plain sense."

With additional knowledge and insight—say, a general knowledge of fifteenth-century painting—we may perform a secondary reading that provides the meaning of these motifs, allowing us to recognize the painting as a depiction of the martyr-dom of St. Sebastian. The painting is not exact, since our knowledge tells us that St. Sebastian was martyred by being tied to a tree, not against a wall, as in the paint-ing. The significance of the small tree and the castle are as yet unclear. One may identify the painting landscape as being recognizably Mediterranean from the veg-etation and climate depicted therein. Some of the motifs from the primary reading have become recognizable. Panofsky calls recognizable motifs *images*, and their combinations, *stories* or *allegories*. These secondary readings are "iconographical in the narrower sense of the word" (Panofsky 1939, 6) since particular meanings of the painting (though not all) are revealed.

Let us imagine that one examines further the life of the painter and his society. Applying this additional knowledge to the painting permits a tertiary or intrinsic reading, clarifying the painting's meaning further. One may find, for example, that the painter took substantial liberties with martyrdom themes in the later period of his life, explaining the anomalous and otherwise inexplicable wall. The rapid style of the painting was also typical of the painter's late period, when his health was failing and precision was impossible. This does not explain the composition, which marks a distinct change from paintings completed before this one, and which indicates a marked growth in the painter's sense of symmetry and perspec-tive. Nor does it elucidate the meaning of motifs such as the tree or the identity of the castle.

Providing additional intrinsic meanings for such a painting would be the work of art historians. If the painting was important, art historians would wish to understand what the castle represented, perhaps to reveal new information about the painter's life experiences or interests. The tree might arouse similar interest at the secondary level (what does it say about the allegory of St. Sebastian?) and at the intrinsic level (what might it tell us about the painter, about this period, or about fifteenth-century Italian society?).

Let us imagine what an analogous theory of plan interpretation might look like. Plans also have primary or literal meanings. The "plain sense" of a spatial plan conveys, first, a set of analyses or studies of a neighborhood, city, or region. These studies include both raw data and interpretations of this data. A plan then conveys future intentions for the subject area based on these interpretations, and it detail the actions, scope, cost, methods, and so on by which both the analyses and intentions were derived. While not every piece of information in a plan, nor every interpretation, can or should be accepted as fact, the content of a plan does represent a certain factual level of meaning. In other words, one accepts plan infor-mation, true or not, as being what it purports to be. I call this first level of meaning in a plan *factual meaning*.

A plan also has additional meanings that require additional knowledge to per-ceive and interpret. All plans are influenced by political, social, economic, and physical contexts, though this influence is seldom spelled out explicitly. A plan reflects of these interrelated contexts at the same time as it may potentially influ-ence them. Understanding a plan's many contexts, and applying those contexts to one's understanding of the content of a plan, provides a *contextual meaning*. A contextual meaning may not be explicit, or it may be obvious. An explicitly stated sustainability plan, for example, must by necessity be understood as part of the larger socioeconomic–political concept of sustainability existing at the time of the plan's creation.

Although some meanings may be available to a contemporary reader, additional meanings may only be discerned with the perspective of elapsed time in different settings: the history of a city's plans; the history of a city; the life of the plan author; or the history of the society that produced the plan. Even as a well-informed fifteenth-century observer of Italian paintings could not view a contemporary painting in historical perspective, a contemporary plan reader cannot understand the *temporal meaning* of a plan without the perspective provided by time and the observations and findings of other plan readers. An epithet like "innovative" or "groundbreaking," which gives great meaning to a plan, has fuller meaning with the passage of time.

4. Reading through Three Plans

The remainder of this chapter attempts to contribute to an ordered, learnable mode of plan reading by examining three very different plans. The plans describe different-size cities (small, large, very large) during different periods of the past eighty years (1930s, 1960s, 2000s). All are physical, spatial plans, and they do not purport to be a sample but rather illustrate how the visual theory of plan reading described above may be applied to plans from both the past and present day.

The Comprehensive City Plan for Dubuque, Iowa (John Nolen, 1931 and 1936)

A Factual Reading

The document, entitled a *Ccomprehensive City Plan* (Nolen), was published in September 1936. The plan appears attractive and high-quality (figure 37.1). It is brief—only 48 pages—but hardbound and printed on fine paper, and is well illustrated with photographs, street plans, and maps. It contains two special drawings: a foldout "public buildings and grounds plan" on vellum paper, and a large (24 by 48-inch) detached folding map of the city and vicinity (figure 37.2). The latter is labeled the "Master Plan" and is "one of a series of maps plans and reports [*sic*] comprising the city plan."

The author, John Nolen, well known as a "pioneer" of the planning profession (Hancock 1960) and a landscape architect, was nationally known by the time he

Figure 37.1 The cover of John Nolen's 1936 *Plan for Dubuque* is cheerful and even cartoonish. It shows a portion of the plan's waterfront vision, effectively marketing one of the document's principal ideas.

was hired for the plan in 1930. His dramatic recommendations are conveyed by the cover, which shows proposals for the city's downtown (figure 37.1). This decision—to reveal one of the plan's primary concepts on its cover—displays confidence in the drama of the plan ideas and a desire to convey the scale of the changes being proposed. The plan thus succeeds in communicating an important message before it is even opened.

The plan explains a small city's problems and the proposals to solve them. It is easy to understand because the map is the sole piece of information needed to understand the plan ideas, making the document a sort of appendix, providing additional explanations. The document spends little time on the plan's formulation, history, rationale, and methodology; Nolen clearly did not feel a need to explain his decisions. "Survey" and "diagnosis" are mentioned as methods that

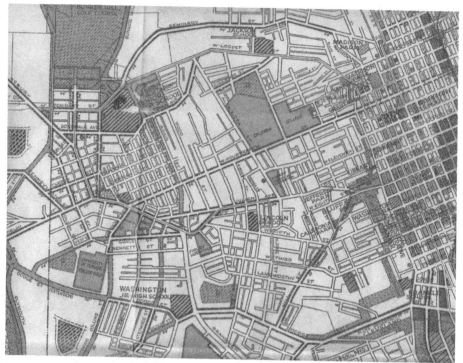

Figure 37.2 A section of Nolen's master plan map for Dubuque. The plan leaves the existing city mostly alone, but widens the streets leading to as-yet-undeveloped suburban areas.

led to recommendations, but are otherwise left unexplained—even the plan's time frame is not mentioned. This conveys a sense of confidence and expertise on the author's part, but also a methodological secrecy that is at odds with the plan's welcoming cover.

The plan, primarily concerned with traffic flow and with open space, uses 19 of its 48 pages to present solutions to these problems. It contains a great deal of local information, but both the problems and the proposals are presented, or framed, as standard, local manifestations of problems afflicting cities across the United States. Nolen is concerned that the city layout is inadequate both for automobile transportation and for meeting the necessary standards of recreation and education. Numerous statistical tables demonstrate substandard transportation and amenity levels.

The plan does not resolve these problems within the existing city. Constrained by hilly topography and by the existing street network, the city's fabric makes large-scale restructuring challenging, and the plan is therefore enthusiastic about developing outlying areas, where roadways and open space can be optimized. The plan suggests regional parkways and open spaces throughout the peripheral area, most of which actually lie beyond the city's political boundary. Apart from some widened streets to better access suburban areas, the existing city except downtown is unaltered. The plan does not project changes to the residential areas making up the rest of the existing city. The plan's tacit message is that the existing, pre-automobile-era city is inadequate, and that improved living requires suburbanization. To address the dysfunctional mix of commerce and industry downtown, the plan proposes new public buildings and reorganizes railroad and industrial land along the river, multiplying the city's industrial area many times over.

A Contextual Reading

This reading requires reflection on at least the outline of larger scale events occurring both inside and outside of cities and planning at the time of publication. Mainstream urban texts like Hall (1988), Fogelson (2001), Schaeffer (1988), Mumford (1961), Scott (1969), and Isenberg (2005) illustrate the plan's consistency with urban development and planning trends of the time. In 1936, the U.S. was in the midst of the Great Depression, when downtown development stagnated and industrial production slowed. Midwestern cities like Dubuque, Iowa, were heavily dependent upon industry and suffered particularly badly, but automobile ownership and suburbs expanded despite the crisis.

A contextual reading shows that the plan is both pragmatic and utopian, promoting some existing socioeconomic and physical trends while recommending the reversal of others. The plan acknowledges the reality of suburbanization through its parkway recommendations, and simultaneously denies the reality of industrial decline by proposing dramatic infrastructural shifts downtown. This dual accommodation was likely a pragmatic decision on Nolen's part. Dubuque perhaps commissioned the plan because it felt the twin pull of suburbanization, which drew people away from the city, and decline, which left many central-city areas abandoned. Both suburban and central-city constituencies doubtless demanded attention from the city administration, and planners such as Nolan may have been asked to provide solutions to both populations and both problems (sprawl and decline).

A contextual reading also indicates and identifies odd geographical and topical lacunas in the plan. It displays little interest in the form of the suburban settlements that its proposed parkways would generate. Nor does it display interest in the dilapidated older areas of housing that must have constituted much of the city. The easiest explanation is that Nolen had no time or budget for solutions for these areas. Yet the civic center hints that detailed proposals may have been of greater interest to the plan framers, or to the planner, than others, leaving issues like older housing suppressed or ignored. Understanding the reasons for these lacunae requires further research.

A Temporal Reading

The Dubuque plan was published over seventy years ago, and a temporal reading of the plan may be challenging because it demands a comprehensive understanding not only of Dubuque but also of cities and planning in the United States more broadly. The former is likely to be difficult for readers located outside of the Dubuque area, yet local knowledge is particularly important for a temporal reading. Without access to local information, it is difficult to know, for example, whether Dubuque issued plans before or after this one. An Internet search reveals at least one master plan dating from the late 1990s (City of Dubuque 2008). But understanding the plans that lie between requires additional research that most readers will not have the time or interest to undertake.

Instead, it is much easier to discern the degree to which the plan ideas were implemented. Aerial photographs available on the Internet indicate that much of the plan's vision seems to have been realized, particularly along the waterfront and in parkways at the city's edge. It is harder to know whether the plan played a direct role in these changes, but it seems that both pragmatic and utopian aspects of the plan were in part realized. However, contemporary aerial photographs also show that much suburban settlement occurred that was not directly portrayed in the plan, confirming the lacuna observed in the contextual reading.

A temporal reading tells us that the plan may have been both utopian and pragmatic because it lay between two eras of urban growth and two approaches to urban planning. The 1930s and the Depression occured between periods of explosive urban growth, motivated by industry and technology, and urban decline and suburban expansion, motivated by the automobile and by technological and economic changes. The plan both did and did not foresee these changes. Some proposals, such as the union railroad station or civic center, are holdovers from Beaux-Arts planning and are merely smaller versions of those produced in the 1909 *Plan of Chicago*. These ideas were dated if not obsolete by 1936, though perhaps they were more current when the Dubuque plan was written in 1930–31. Other ideas, such as the extensive parkways lacking any outline for suburban growth, seem naïve if not irresponsible. Yet the plan may also have been well timed. The Depression marked the beginning of a fertile period for public planning, and the plan's timing may have enabled the city to take advantage of these policies over the ensuing decades, permitting realization of the plan's ideas. The plan was itself conceived at the very beginning of the Depression, so explicitly taking advantage of federal funds was likely not Nolen's intention. Thus, the plan's timing may have been more due to luck than to anything else.

The plan's brevity seems inconsistent with today's understanding of city planning as a complex enterprise requiring significant data gathering and public review. Nolen was clearly accepted as an expert who had little apparent accountability to citizens, although the plan's preface shows that formal plan approval took five years. Yet the plan's brevity and efficiency are also refreshing. Its ideas are clear and confident, and they are attractively presented and bold in scope, even if they are not locally derived or innovative. The plan exudes confidence, reflecting its well-known consultant and well-trodden recommendations. Perhaps this self-assuredness encouraged implementation of the plan. It is a boilerplate Depression-era plan that confronts only some of what one now considers the full range of plan responsibilities (where is equity for example?). Yet, this conceptual familiarity may also have encouraged implementation by the small-town government of Dubuque.

Master Plan 1964 City of Newark, New Jersey (Newark Central Planning Board, 1964)

A Factual Reading

Newark's *Master Plan* is a large document—11 by 11 inches—printed in inexpensive paperback (Newark Central Planning Board 1964). The plan cover (figure 37.3) is a military green that reveals little about its contents or intention, and its back cover is similarly blank. The publication format and design provide the plan with an air of economy and reticence. Neither welcomes the reader nor encourages him or her to peruse the plan. Unlike the welcoming, almost cartoonish cover of the Dubuque Plan, Newark's reveals little to the casual reader except its officialdom. The document is substantial in length—126 pages— and is well illustrated. Its only special feature is an interior folding map in color showing proposed land uses. Unlike the Dubuque Plan, where the term "plan" refers both to the document and to a proposed physical design represented by a large map, "plan" here refers only to the document itself.

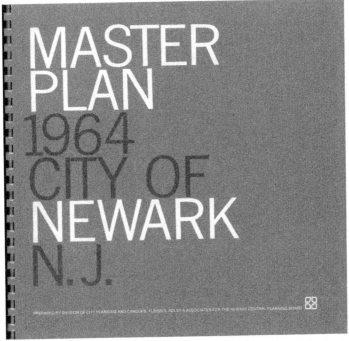

Figure 37.3 The cover of the Newark 1964 *Master Plan* is reticent, revealing nothing about the plan's content but listing a bewildering variety of authors. It unfortunately conforms to stereotypes of this era's planning being authoritative and even inhumane.

The plan is illustrated with numerous black and white photographs, color maps, and the occasional site plan. Photographs show both typical scenes in the city and signs of progress. Images of children playing, busy department stores, and flowers blooming are intermingled with documentation of concrete pipes and construction sites. The latter clearly represent the implementation of projects, though they are not keyed to actual plan recommendations. A few photographs refer specifically to existing problems like traffic congestion. The overall effect of these photographs is confusing. Are they meant to show that Newark is already a successful place (why then would one need a plan?), that progress is already under way (again, why would one need a plan?), or that the city is full of problems (thus requiring a plan).

The plan features several maps (figure 37.4). Each is topical, showing a facility inventory (schools, parks, etc.) and suggestions for the future location of new facilities. These maps are at least partially future oriented, but they are abstract and diagrammatic, showing the city at a small scale and indicating little about the nature or need for these facilities. The reticent plan graphics sharply contrast with the almost childlike clearness of the Dubuque plan, requiring that the Newark plan reader actually read the text in order to understand the plan. Given the length and unwelcoming appearance of the document, this makes the plan's suggestions more difficult to perceive. Mandelbaum (1990, 35) noted ruefully that "no one reads" most plans. The same may have been true for the Newark plan.

If one does read the text, one finds it to be both an inventory and a proposition for new facilities and land uses. The plan emphasizes an "analysis of the potential...for growth," (Page 13) showing growth to be a central concern. Yet, the plan states that Newark is likely to grow only marginally over the next twenty years. It also concludes that employment and housing will increase if the city keeps pace with the region. The plan seems to be attempting to persuade us that the city will grow instead of shrink, but its own statistics inform us of the opposite—population, employment, and housing had been declining for decades in 1960s Newark. A reader alert to this fact will no doubt wonder how the plan proposes reversing a decades-long decline.

Further reading of the plan is not reassuring. It inventories and projects different conditions of land use, "traffic and transportation," "community facilities" (parks, schools, etc.), and public buildings, with maps of existing and forecasted facilities. Each is treated differently; land use is significantly reconfigured, but many public buildings are closed, while open space and roadways are increased dramatically. The overall impression is somewhat confusing. If the city is not growing, why are large-scale changes needed? The plan does not provide an answer to this question—the need for large-scale change is assumed. Clearly, there is no single vision for the city in this plan. Instead, the *Master Plan* is an aggregation of different change projections that seem to have little relationship to each other.

Why might this be? Perhaps the plan is intended for disparate audiences, like parks officials or traffic engineers. But then why contain these within a single

TYPE OF FACILITY	Existing to be Retained	Proposed Facility (tentative)
County Parks	▨	
City Parks	▲	▵
School Recreation Facility	●	
Public Housing Facility	◐	

Parks & Recreation Plan
CITY OF NEWARK, N. J. / MASTER PLAN, 1964
PLANNING CONSULTANT: CANDEUR FLEISSIG ADLEY & ASSOCIATES

Figure 37.4 Newark's "Parks and Recreation Plan" within the 1964 plan shows eight new parks (visible as green triangles) but does not specify the size, nature, or rationale for these facilities. In a declining city unable to expand, the plan spends more time inventorying existing facilities than projecting new ones.

document? The nature of the plan makes the *Master Plan* seem like a fiction. Again, this could not be more different from the Dubuque Plan, which was a single, comprehensive urban design. The authoritative, difficult-to-read master plan is unmasked as a collection of inventories and projections for different sectoral audiences. The plan is divided, and it is also confronting a conundrum: how to plan in a city that is not growing and may decline. The plan does not settle this conundrum successfully, and it is difficult to imagine how it might do so. The document does not seem to project either significant change or a vision for that change.

A Contextual Reading

A contextual reading is eased by the relatively recent date of the plan, the large size of the city, and the well-known circumstances of the time. The 1960s were a time of great difficulty for older cities, including Newark, and the plan was issued amid these troubles. Things would get worse: Newark had race riots in 1967 in which over twenty people were killed and millions of dollars in property destroyed (National Advisory Commission on Civil Disorders 1968, 56–69). As the plan stated, Newark's population, income, jobs, and housing were all in free-fall during the 1960s. The city was in the midst of a severe crisis.

In 1964, major federal programs were in full swing to construct interstate highways and reconstruct "blighted" areas. This indicates why certain types of change but not others are projected in the plan. Federal money was available for highways and public facilities, and the plan indicates that Newark intended to take advantage of those funds. The plan itself may have been issued in order to take advantage of funds or even provide a rationale for federal spending.

The clinical, dry appearance of the plan is ironic. Newark was in the middle of tumultuous change: the staid plan masks a troubled place with economics, population, race, and infrastructure dramatically intermingling. In context, one can see that these events, like the suburbanization and industrial decline of Dubuque, were independent of the Newark *Master Plan*. The plan is clearly uncertain about how to address this change. It simultaneously projects change that is plan independent (highways), suggests change that is unlikely to occur (population stability and economic recovery), and ignores other change that is happening (racial change, poverty, and inequality). The plan confuses topic (growth or decline?), message (change? how?), and content (what kind of plan?), leading one to seriously question what the planners were really thinking, which ideas they felt responsible for, and which ideas they really believed in. The plan appears inadequate to confront the deeply troubled context of the city.

A Temporal Reading

Newark and other older cities underwent substantial changes in racial composition, economic vitality, and population in the decades after 1964. The authoritative appearance of Newark's *Master Plan* masks not only confusion but stunningly inaccurate forecasts. The city changed dramatically and for the worse (Tuttle 2009). The city's population declined from 405,220 in 1960 (page 111) to 281,402 in 2006 (U.S. Department of Commerce 2010), rather than the 406,000–416,000 growth projected by the plan. Employment declined even more sharply: manufacturing fell from the 75,000–80,000 cited in the plan to only 17,627 in 1995 and 11,000 in 2005, a far cry from the plan's most pessimistic projection of 66,000. The plan's projected Newark—economy restored, population stabilized, and city reborn—did not come to pass.

The Newark *Master Plan* may not be a complete failure—additional research could track whether particular facilities were perhaps constructed as the plan recommended. However, the plan does not seem to have fulfilled its larger purpose of showing Newark's "most appropriate course of development for the next 15–20 years" (Page 3). One can sympathize with the planners charged with projecting the future of a declining city. Caught in a bind, of either projecting additional decline or of forecasting improvement, planners opted for the latter, politically acceptable solution. That the plan could not confront the severe urban problems of mid-twentieth-century America is not totally the fault of planners who may have been politically unable to speak the truth or intellectually incapable of understanding it. But the plan's distinct lack of connection to reality speaks volumes about the larger changes that the planning profession, and the conception of the master plan, underwent around 1970 (Friedmann 1971; Neuman 1998, 208). In retrospect, the Newark *Master Plan* is not only a tombstone for industrial Newark but also for the "master planning" model that was so closely linked to the infrastructure and neighborhood transformations shown in the plan.

2040 Regional Framework Plan (Northeastern Illinois Planning Commission, 2005)

A Factual Reading

The *Framework Plan*, authored by the Northeastern Illinois Planning Commission (NIPC 2005), is actually two plans: a softbound document with 279 pages (Figure 37.5) and a separate summary document with only seventeen pages, and a compact disc with "the full plan text." The summary plan is clearly meant to increase access to the rather unwieldy full plan in something of the same manner as *Wacker's Manual* (Moody 1915) democratized the Plan of Chicago (Smith 2006, 123–25). Both the long and short plan documents contain a detachable "regional framework" map (Figure 37.6), but neither document mentions the existence of the other in its text, and the publication date (2005) of the plans is hard to locate. Both documents are available on the Internet (2009) in PDF format, but were no longer available online by mid-2011 for reasons that will be explained below.

The length of the full plan raises serious readability questions. Three hundred pages is a serious commitment of time and energy for any reader, and such great length does not make the plan accessible to a wide public audience. Was the plan intended as a technical document for a specialized audience? The summary document indicates that NIPC recognized the unreadable nature of the full plan even as they published it. Why is the plan so long? Doubtless a large volume of information was required to treat Chicago's extremely large, sprawling metropolitan area. Perhaps the plan document was designed as a lexicon, to be consulted episodically but never intended to be read in full, as Mandelbaum suggests for other plans (1990, 350–51). Another, less optimistic possibility is that the plan is simply verbose, containing more information than it needs to communicate. The plan summary proves that the plan's ideas can be discerned in

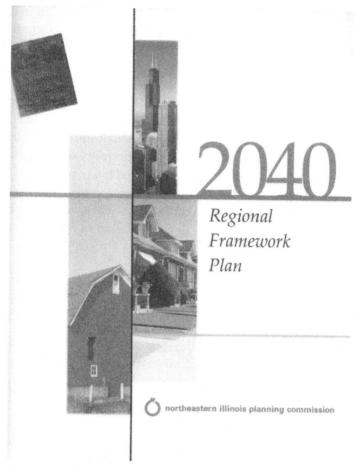

Figure 37.5 NIPC's 2005 Framework Plan for the Chicago region shows city, (prewar) suburb, and farm on its cover. Is this a description, a prescription, or both? Interestingly, auto-oriented postwar suburbs, probably the majority of the region's built environment, are not shown.

only seventeen pages and a framework map. This indicates that the full plan may be superfluous.

A dedicated reader who pores through the longer document will find that the plan is clearly organized and conveys its structure quickly. An "executive summary" is followed by two brief chapters (9 and 10 pages) explaining methodology and reiterating central ideas. A subsequent much longer chapter (almost 70 pages) explains these ideas in detail. After two more brief chapters with additional methodology and some institutional issues, the second half of the plan (almost 130 pages) discusses implementation. The plan framers clearly wish the reader to understand the plan's ideas, since these ideas repeated three times in the plan (and again in the summary plan). But implementation is the plan's focus, seemingly more important than the plan ideas themselves. Why was NIPC particularly concerned with

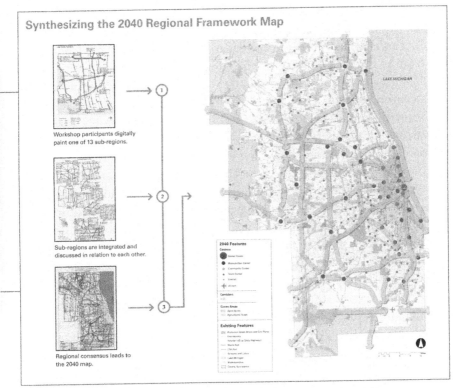

Figure 37.6 The NIPC plan's projected regional future aggregates ideas derived from community meetings and outreach. The resulting "regional framework" seems little different from today's region. This may be a reassuring scenario to citizens weary or cautious of change, but it is also an unlikely one given the explosive sprawl of the past six decades.

implementation? Whatever the reason, the plan's wildly different chapter lengths convey a sense that NIPC inconsistently valued its content. These inconsistencies do not make the document any easier to read and they hint at an equally inconsistent planning process.

The central plan ideas ("centers, corridors, and green space") propose a spatial structure for the Chicago region. While the genesis of these ideas is not stated, the plan describes a four-year public outreach process that included hundreds of participants. This extensive public process diffuses and democratizes the authorship of the plan ideas, implying that many of them were generated by the public. Yet NIPC itself must have generated some of the ideas; implementation details, for example, are unfamiliar to the public and require technical expertise to conceive. Ultimately, the authors do not claim authorship of the plan ideas, but they take responsibility for them by publishing them under NIPC's name.

The plan ideas are stated as prescriptions. Yet their prescriptive nature is ambiguous, since they are also described as existing conditions in northeastern Illinois. Since the plan ideas already exist to some extent, the plan seems to propose a rearrangement of existing spatial features rather than new or unknown features. The plan, for example, identifies 292 "centers." Is this an existing number of centers (in 2005), or is it the ideal number in 2040 (the "buildout date" of the plan)? One may assume the latter, but cannot be sure. This confusion between description (of what already is) and prescription (for what should be) applies to each of the plan's central concepts. The only plan prescription that is clearly differentiated from existing conditions is the arrest of suburban sprawl in the region's outermost areas and its preservation as agricultural space. The distinctively prescriptive nature of this idea indicates that it was a favorite of the plan authors.

The plan's core ideas are clearly stated, but the distinction between the plan's recommended future and a "no-build" or no-plan future is ultimately confusing. That is, the plan's projected future appears little different from what would occur in its absence. Does the plan really matter, then? The plan does not acknowledge or address this existential question, except if one reads the plan's publication as an assertion that "planning matters!" The plan's interest in implementation is also not aided by the confusion between prescription and description. Fuzzy plan recommendations argue against rather than for implementation. Why spend effort implementing something that might happen anyway?

A Contextual Reading

Because the plan is more or less contemporary to the time of writing (2005 and 2011), a contextual reading demands little historical knowledge. Both the excessive length and the tepid content of the plan reflect the framers' desire to satisfy a large, diverse, and fractious constituency. The plan exists in a time when public outreach is a required and necessary part of the process, and planning is seen as a complex effort involving public input and consensus building (Arnstein 1969; Forester 1989; Healey 1992). Consensus in a large, diverse setting is difficult to achieve, and strong recommendations are apparently even more difficult, as the plan indicates. Otherwise, the plan is consistent with contemporary planning wisdom. Each of the plan's ideas, like "promote livable communities" and "promote walking and bicycling as alternative modes of travel", are familiar concepts that are advocated at a nationwide level by many individual planning practitioners and academics under the smart-growth banner (Burchell, Listokin, and Galley 2000; see chapters by Talen and Song, this volume). Smart growth is in turn consistent with the architectural and planning movement of New Urbanism (Duany, Plater-Zybeck, and Speck 2001). Critics of both movements describe them as deeply conservative (Southworth 2003), and NIPC's framework plan is certainly conservative.

This conservatism may have resulted from method as much as ideology. Charged with producing a spatial strategy for a large metropolitan region, NIPC doubtless felt the need to build consensus and satisfy a wide range of constituencies. A lengthy plan is less likely to be read, but it is more likely to contain something for everyone. A plan with uncontentious recommendations is less likely to offend sensitive parties and to build a wider support base. Without speculating too far as to the effect of public participation on plan recommendations, the plan's extensive public outreach probably pushed it toward conservative, uncontentious recommendations rather than dramatic spatial and regional shifts à la Burnham and Bennett. Outreach resulted in a bigger plan with many more participants, but it also produced a less interesting plan.

The weak recommendations of the plan contrast with its energetic implementation. But why do weak recommendations require significant action? Under ordinary circumstances they would not. However, if the true goal of the plan is not to implement recommendations but to sustain interest in regional-scale planning, this focus becomes more understandable. By creating a framework plan, NIPC also rationalizes its own existence. The existence of a plan with weak recommendations but strong implementation creates a strong rationale for NIPC to exist as the implementer. This is particularly valuable in an era of widespread fiscal crisis in state government and of skepticism in "big government" more broadly. NIPC did not totally succeed—it was merged with the region's transportation agency in 2007 in a cost-saving operation—but one of the new agency's first decisions was to formally adopt the NIPC-authored framework plan (NIPC 2007, 4)

A Temporal Reading

Even though the NIPC plan is near-contemporary, enough events have occurred subsequently to allow us to perform a temporal reading of the document. Although the new Chicago Metropolitan Agency for Planning (CMAP) adopted NIPC's plan upon its absorption of that agency in 2007, CMAP began its own regional planning process in September 2007 (CMAP 2011, 28). This resulted in the issuance of the second Chicago-area regional plan in five years, *GO TO 2040*, in October 2010. This latter document, apart from any individual merits that it may have, is a full-scale replacement—an obliteration, even—of the NIPC plan, evidently for political purposes. The NIPC plan's current (2011) online unavailability makes more sense, for the plan became obsolete within five years of its issuance. In this sense, NIPC's plan timing, coming directly before its institutional author's dissolution, could not have been worse. We can thus read the NIPC plan's concentration on implementation as both futile and poignant: with all its detail, the plan ignored the one thing—institutional politics—that would be its Achilles' heel.

Both the NIPC and its successor plan were written in a time when economic, environmental, and social trends were reactivating central cities, revitalizing existing town centers, and pushing riders toward mass transit. Since at least 1980, the middle class has been returning to Chicago, making it a very attractive place to live by the early twenty-first century (City of Chicago 2002, 2.9). The plan's pro- "center" attitude and pro- "open space" approach are consistent with the larger history of late-twentieth-century trends that benefited existing cities and to some extent mitigated sprawl. The NIPC plan profits from those trends and uncritically accepts and advocates them in turn.

The framework plan may also be read as a tentative return to "master planning" in the wake of the disastrous changes of the 1960s (e.g., Hall 1980, 56–86), an era when such enterprises had been broadly discredited (Friedmann 1971). This return to master planning is consistent with larger shifts in the planning profession (Neuman 1998). One can imagine that NIPC might want their plan to avoid alienating suspicious or mistrustful constituents by speaking softly with uncontentious ideas. The plan seems to have achieved consensus, and there was little criticism or even discussion of the plan when it was issued—but this quiet return of the master plan was achieved at the expense of the plan's creativity.

5. READING LESSONS

Perhaps the most salient conclusion to be drawn from the factual readings is how information may be found in diverse aspects of a plan document. Our factual readings drew conclusions from such seemingly superficial features as the document design to unarguably important features like plan recommendations. Planners are trained to analyze recommendations more than graphic design, yet in each case the latter was deeply communicative. Each of the plans' covers, for instance, mirrored the clarity and intensity of the plans' recommendations. In our three cases, it was fair to at least partly judge a plan by its cover. But ultimately our factual reading depended on carefully looking at the plan— both document appearance and plan graphics—carefully reading it and examining and understanding the relationship between graphic features and text. In each of cases, the reading revealed aspects of the plan and the plan framers that were not readily apparent.

Our contextual readings informed us that each of our plans conformed strongly to social, economic, and political forces of the time, as well as to contemporary urban design and planning conventions. None was a "groundbreaking" plan when compared with its peers or with professional practice of the time. In this sense, each plan is what a planner of the time might have predicted the plan would contain—no surprises! Contextual conformance confirms that plans cannot be isolated from their settings and that plan recommendations are as much a product of contemporary urban conditions, social norms, and professional conventions as they are of plan-specific "survey and diagnosis," to use Nolen's words. And if every plan is a product of its time, should one look for plan quality only in its skillful execution of contemporary concerns (parkways in 1936, highways in 1964, outreach in 2005), or perhaps also in its degree of innovation—that is, its introduction of concepts, aims, or methods that have not previously appeared in plans? Innovation is highly valued in design, but it occupies little space in contemporary planning discourse. Yet innovative ideas do occasionally occur in plans (Ryan 2006, 48–49, 60). Further exploration of the occurrence and value of innovation in plans and planning is badly needed.

Much as Panofsky observed in painting, our temporal plan readings show that plans have changed dramatically over time, reflecting changes in practice that are not visible through contextual readings. Just as the contextual readings indicated consistency with contemporary plan norms, many of the changes in the planning profession evidenced by the three plans are consistent with current assessments of planning history. Our plan-reading sample, for example, while admittedly small and imperfect, may be interpreted as illustrating a shift from a planning profession governed by expert designers, to one governed by remote "out of touch" technocrats, to one governed by humble and sincere, if uncompelling, communicators. This reading is consistent with the "master narrative" of planning presented in histories of the field (e.g., Hall 1988), as well as with current planning theory (e.g., Innes and Booher 2010).

However, temporal readings also permit plan readings that differ from the conventional wisdom. Nolen's plan, for example, seems eager to communicate, almost to advertise, its recommendations. This is very far from the stereotype of the remote master architect that one may derive from plans like Burnham and Bennett's. Nolen may have been a paradigmatic expert planner, but his plan is much more concise, and readable, than the NIPC plan. Temporal readings provide perspective on both the present and the past. The differences between Nolen's plan and NIPC's, for example, provoke thought about the meaning, perhaps even efficacy, of the communicative ideal currently dominating planning theory. If a concise, accessible plan provided by an expert planner (who was also a designer) is "bad," does this in turn make NIPC's plan "good"? Hardly. We have seen that the latter plan is both unwieldy and uncommunicative, although process based.

Temporal plan readings are both diachronic in nature, permitting the present to be seen as the current end of a linear narrative, and kairological (Zukin 2010, 101), permitting the present to exploit the past without directly acknowledging it. In this fashion, NIPC alludes to the glory of Chicago's Burnham and Bennett-era planning while simultaneously evading the negative connotations that would come from any such direct comparison. Temporal plan readings, like Panosfky's intrinsic readings of art, permit us to discern the meaning of plans in the fullest sense currently available to us. The examples above are only the beginning of a variety of interpretations that may be derived from even a small plan sample, and many more insights await those planreaders interested in conducting temporal readings of plans.

Any discussion of plan reading is remiss without mentioning the transformative changes that will occur in the coming decades as the mode of presenting and sharing information shifts from the printed to the electronic word. Will the plan, as a series of printed pages, become obsolete, or will it, as is more likely, shift to being primarily digital? The NIPC plan takes some early steps in this direction: it is available online, and the summary version of the plan is in part published as digital media (a compact disc). Yet other communicative aspects of the plan already seem dated in 2011, including the long outreach period preparatory to publication of the "final" plan. Perhaps in the future advanced social media techniques will permit both instant and constant popular feedback on planning ideas, resulting in a perpetually shifting series of public imperatives. Is the plan, a set of fixed ideas for the future, even relevant in a time when our collective desires change almost by the second? This question is not easy to answer, but it does seem likely that plan reading will become ever more common even as plans promise to change beyond recognition. These welcome changes will transform the planning profession, but whether they will transform the face of our cities remains to be seen.

ACKNOWLEDGMENTS

Thanks to Ann-Ariel Vecchio for her careful editing and to Rachel Weber and Randy Crane for the invitation that generated this chapter.

NOTES

This chapter first appeared in substantially similar form as Ryan (2011). Permission from the *Journal of the American Planning Association* to reuse is gratefully acknowledged.

1. Not all plans are identical. In fact, they are diverse; not only are plans issued by a variety of entities, with public planning departments making up only a small fraction of these, but they treat a wide range of topics and spaces.

REFERENCES

Abbott, C. 1991. "Urban Design in Portland, Oregon, As Policy and Process: 1960–1989." *Planning Perspectives* 6(1): 1–18.

Alexander, E. R. 2002. "Planning Rights: Toward Normative Criteria for Evaluating Plans." *International Planning Studies* 7(3): 191–212.

Arnstein, S. R. 1969. "A Ladder of Citizen Participation." *Journal of the American Planning Association* 35(4): 216–24.

Baer, W. C. 1997. "General Plan Evaluation Criteria: An Approach to Making Better Plans." *Journal of the American Planning Association* 63(3): 329–44.

Berke, P., and David Godschalk. 2009. "Searching for the Good Plan: A Meta-Analysis of Plan Quality Studies." *Journal of Planning Literature* 23(3): 227–40.

Burchell, R. W., D. Listokin, and C. C. Galley. 2000. "Smart Growth: More Than a Ghost of Urban Policy Past, Less Than a Bold New Horizon." *Housing Policy Debate* 11:821–79.

Campbell, S., and Susan Fainstein.2003. *Readings in Planning Theory,* 2nd ed. London: Blackwell.

Chicago Metropolitan Agency for Planning (CMAP). 2011. *GO TO 2040.* Available at: http://www.cmap.illinois.gov/2040/download-the-full-plan; accessed August 15, 2011.

City of Chicago. 2002. "A Quality Place to Live: The Residential Sector." *The Chicago Central Area Plan: Preparing the Central City for the 21st Century.* Chicago: City of Chicago Department of Planning and Development.

City of Dubuque. 2008. *A Guide to the Dubuque Comprehensive Plan*. Dubuque: City of Dubuque Planning Services Department. Available at: http://www.cityofdubuque.org/DocumentView.aspx?DID=284; accessed October 14, 2010.

Clay, G. 1973. *Close-Up: How to Read the American City*. New York: Praeger.

Cullen, G. 1971. *Townscape*. Oxford: Architectural Press.

Dagenhart, R., and David Sawicki. 1992. "Architecture and Planning: The Divergence of Two Fields." *Journal of Planning Education and Research* 12(1): 1–16.

Duany, A., E. Plater-Zyberk, and J. Speck. 2001. *Suburban Nation: The Rise of Sprawl and the Decline of the American Dream*. New York: North Point.

Evans-Cowley, J. S., and Meghan Zimmerman Gough. 2009. "Evaluating New Urbanist Plans in Post-Katrina Mississippi." *Journal of Urban Design* 14(4): 439–61.

Fogelson, R. 2001. *Downtown: Its Rise and Fall, 1880–1950*. New Haven, CT: Yale University Press.

Forester, J. 1989. *Planning in the Face of Power*. Berkeley, CA: University of California Press.

Friedmann, J. 1971. "The Future of Comprehensive Urban Planning: A Critique." *Public Administration Review* 31(3): 315–26.

Hall, P. 1980. *Great Planning Disasters*. Berkeley, CA: University of California Press.

Hall, P. 1988. *Cities of Tomorrow: An Intellectual History of Urban Planning and Design in the Twentieth Century*. New York: Blackwell.

Hancock, J. 1960. "John Nolen: The Background of a Pioneer Planner." *Journal of the American Planning Association* 26(4): 302–12.

Healey, P. 1992. "Planning Through Debate: The Communicative Turn in Planning Theory." *Town Planning Review* 63:143–62.

Healey, P. 1993. "The Communicative Work of Development Plans." *Environment and Planning Part B* 20:83–104.

Hoch, C. J. 2002. "Evaluating Plans Pragmatically." *Planning Theory* 1(1): 53–75.

Hopkins, L. D. 2001. *Urban Development: The Logic of Making Plans*. Washington, DC: Island Press.

Hosken, F. P. 1972. *The Language of Cities: A Visual Introduction to the Form and Function of the City*. Cambridge, MA: Schenckmann.

Innes, J. E., and David E. Booher. 2010. *Planning with Complexity: An Introductive to Collaborative Rationality for Public Policy*. London: Routledge.

Isenberg, A. 2005. *Downtown America: A History of the Place and of the People Who Made It*. Chicago: University of Chicago Press.

Jacobs, A. 1985. *Looking at Cities*. Cambridge, MA: Harvard University Press.

Keating, D., and Norman Krumholz. 1991. "Downtown Plans of the 1980s: The Case for More Equity in the 1990s." *Journal of the American Planning Association* 57(2): 136–52.

Khakee, A. 2000. "Reading Plans as an Exercise in Evaluation." *Evaluation* 6(2): 119–36.

Kreyling, C., M. Scimmenti, G. Gaston, R. Hutcheson, R. Hardison, A. Gaffney, and Nashville Design Center. 2005. *The Plan of Nashville: Avenues to a Great City*. Nashville, TN: Vanderbilt University Press.

Lilley, K. D. 2000. "Mapping the Medieval City: Plan Analysis and Urban History." *Urban History* 27(1): 5–30.

Lynch, K. 1960. *The Image of the City*. Cambridge, MA: MIT Press.

Lynch, K. 1972. *What Time Is This Place?* Cambridge, MA: MIT Press.

Lynch, K. 1981. *Good City Form*. Cambridge, MA: MIT Press.

Mandelbaum, S. J. 1990. "Reading Plans." *Journal of the American Planning Association* 56(3): 350–58.

Moody, W. D. 1915. *Wacker's Manual of the Plan of Chicago: Municipal Economy.* Chicago: Henneberry.

Mumford, L. 1961. *The City in America.* New York: Harcourt, Brace & World.

National Advisory Commission on Civil Disorders. 1968. Kerner Commission. *Report of the National Advisory Committee on Civil Disorders.* New York: Bantam.

Nelson, G. 1977. *How to See: A Guide to Reading Our Manmade Environment.* Boston: Little, Brown.

Neuman, M. 1998. "Does Planning Need the Plan?" *Journal of the American Planning Association* 64(2): 208–20.

Newark Central Planning Board. 1964. *Master Plan 1964 City of Newark, New Jersey.* Newark: Newark Central Planning Board.

Nolen, J. 1936. *Comprehensive City Plan for Dubuque Iowa.* Dubuque: City Planning and Zoning Commission.

Northeastern Illinois Planning Commission. 2005. *2040 Regional Framework Plan.* Chicago: Northeastern Illinois Planning Commission.

Northeast Illinois Planning Commission. 2007. *NIPC Plans and Policies: Legacy Report.* Chicago: Northeast Illinois Planning Commission. Available at: http://www.cmap. illinois.gov/documents/20583/674d1b2f-7512–410a-ada7-c8dd61c6fbf5; accessed August 15, 2011.

Panofsky, E. 1939. *Studies in Iconology: Humanistic Themes in the Art of the Renaissance.* New York: Harper and Row.

Pressman, J., and Aaron Wildavsky. 1973. *Implementation.* Berkeley, CA: University of California Press.

Reps, J. 1965. *The Making of Urban America: A History of City Planning in the United States.* Princeton, NJ: Princeton University Press.

Ryan, B. 2006. "Incomplete and Incremental Plan Implementation in Providence, Rhode Island, 1960–2000." *Journal of Planning History* 5(1): 35–64.

Ryan, B. 2011. "Reading Through A Plan: A Visual Interpretation of What Plans Mean and How They Innovate." *Journal of the American Planning Association* 77(4): 309–27.

Schaeffer, D., ed. 1988. *Two Centuries of American Planning.* Baltimore: Johns Hopkins University Press.

Scott, M. 1969. *American City Planning since 1890: A History Commemorating the Fiftieth Anniversary of the American Institute of Planners.* Berkeley, CA: University of California Press.

Smith, C. 2006. *The Plan of Chicago: Daniel Burnham and the Remaking of the American City.* Chicago: University of Chicago Press.

Southworth, M. 2003. "New Urbanism and the American Metropolis." *Built Environment* 29(3): 210–26.

Talen, E. 1996. "Do Plans Get Implemented? A Review of Evaluation in Planning." *Journal of Planning Literature* 10(3): 248–59.

Tuttle, B. R. *How Newark became Newark: The rise, fall, and rebirth of an American city.* New Brunswick, NJ: Rutgers University Press.

U.S. Department of Commerce. 2010. *Newark (City) QuickFacts.* Bureau of the Census. Available at: http://quickfacts.census.gov/qfd/states/34/3451000.html; accessed October 14, 2010.

Waldner, L. S. 2004. "Planning to Perform: Evaluation Models for City Planners." *Berkeley Planning Journal* 17:1–28.

Zukin, S. 2010. *Naked City: The Death and Life of Authentic Urban Places.* Oxford: Oxford University Press.

CHAPTER 38

PLANNING AND CITIZENSHIP

FARANAK MIRAFTAB

CITIZENSHIP is a contested and old notion, dating to the ancient Greeks and Romans, whose meaning has shifted across different eras and contexts. In its modern conceptualization, citizenship marks the rights, expectations, and responsibilities associated with membership in a political community framed by the nation-state. Citizenship catalyzes debates on important questions that mediate the relationship between the state and citizens: What are the rights of citizens (in civil, political, and socioeconomic terms)? How are those rights fulfilled (through legal and extra-legal, formal and informal means)? Whose responsibility is it to fulfill those rights (individual citizens, private- and public-sector organizations and institutions)?

These questions critical to the creation and maintenance of the modern state also are significant for planning, defined here as a field of action. A key function of the planning profession is mediation between conflicting needs and between the competing claims placed on society's natural, social, and economic resources. Traditionally, the state, moderating among actors with competing agendas, has been the primary employer of planning professionals. Whether to achieve colonization, development, modernization, or neoliberalization, the state has relied on planners' technical and discursive skills. In the last three decades, however, with the demise of the developmental state in the Global South and the welfare state in the Global North, there have been profound shifts in the definition of the state's responsibilities and obligations vis-à-vis the citizens. The state's role has been reconfigured as many of its responsibilities have been shifted to its citizens, to civic organizations, and to private businesses. Planners now lend their technical and discursive abilities to a broader range of actors beyond the state.

The shifts in relationships between state, civil society, and capital that have revived debates on citizenship also have important implications for planning praxis. The questions before us in this chapter are: How do planning theory and practice articulate with the project of citizenship? How does planning respond to the shifting conceptualization of citizenship and state–citizen relations? The chapter traces the shifts in conceptualizations of citizenship and the relevant shifts in the conceptualization of planning, particularly progressive planning. I argue that the goals and objectives of planning practice are complicated by their formulation on a contested terrain of citizenship. As progressive planning aims to achieve a just society (see Fainstein 2010), it is essential for it to engage with the expanded focus of the citizenship debate, from formal rights to justice and from representative to participatory democracy.

That engagement should lead progressive planners to recognize and reflect on certain nuanced differences between participatory planning and insurgent planning. Whereas participatory planning enlists citizens to participate in decisions through professional planners and formalized, often bureaucratized, structures of participation, "insurgent" planning occurs when citizens act directly through self-determined oppositional practices that constitute and claim urban spaces. Insurgent planning is a contested field of interaction among multiple actors including, but not confined to, professional planners, who determine the arenas of action to address the specific forms of oppression.

1. Citizenship Debates

Cities and citizenship are intricately connected. For the ancient Greeks and Romans, citizens were privileged free men who lived in the protected city; subjects were slaves who worked the land outside the city and its forts. The city protected citizens against aggressors and the wars that took defeated populations as slaves. City citizenship then was a marker of privileged membership in a political community, the *polis*.

Ever since the classical period, the privileges associated with citizenship have been the subject of important political and philosophical debates. These fiercely contested debates have sought to (re)define the meanings and privileges attached to citizenship both in theory and in practice. The contemporary debate on citizenship engages with the liberal democratic notions shaped during the modern era to transform historical social hierarchies. The eighteenth-century revolutions, in particular the French Revolution, mark an important point of departure for the ensuing citizenship debates in Western liberal democracies. The motto "Liberty, equality, fraternity" for all asserted a universal but individualized ideal of citizenship. Societies were to be ruled not by allegiance to kings and feudal lords but by social contracts that sovereign and rational citizens made, exchanging individual freedom to a state in exchange for representation and equal treatment before the law (Rousseau 1762/ 1968). This modern construction of citizenship as a social contract that mediates between individual citizens and the state departs in important ways from the earlier notions. It is the nation, as opposed to the city, that defines citizens' privileged membership in a political community whose populace is ruled as equals with political rights and duties.

The modern era's notion of citizenship canceled the old hierarchies that subordinated subjects to citizens; yet it created new social hierarchies that draw much of the contemporary critique of liberal citizenship. Perhaps the best summary of the principles that guide liberal democratic citizenship is carried out by T. H. Marshall. In his often-quoted essay on citizenship and social class, he defines citizenship as "a status bestowed on those who are full members of a community. All who possess the status are equal with respect to the rights and duties with which the status is endowed" (1950/1977, 92). He divides citizenship rights into three categories of civil, political, and social rights, which he describes as arising in sequence from the eighteenth to the nineteenth to the twentieth century. The eighteenth century was preoccupied with citizens' civil rights and with creating courts that guarantee those rights, making all men equal before the law. All individual members of a national community were equally protected and punished before the law.

The main preoccupation of the nineteenth century was with citizens' political rights and the establishment of the parliament and other representative structures where, by virtue of political membership in a nation-state, all were to enjoy representation, to elect and be elected. The right of representation that marks most of the citizenship debates and struggles of the nineteenth century constructed the representative practices and institutions in place today in the Western liberal democratic societies. The twentieth century's principal gain, Marshall argues, was citizens' social rights as embodied in welfare policies and as guaranteed by state welfare agencies that protect citizens from economic uncertainties. In Marshall's view, citizens use their universal civil and political rights and the legal and representative structures set in place during the eighteenth and nineteenth centuries to achieve social rights that address their basic socioeconomic needs. In this liberal formulation of citizenship, above, citizenship is a set of universal rights for citizens that have developed in progression from civil to political to social. As such, citizenship operates through a democratic social contract by which the state grants and guarantees rights to citizens, and citizens agree to a set of duties and obligations.

These important principles of citizenship as constituted through a liberal democratic social contract have been critically examined by much of the contemporary social science literature. Sociologists like Giddens (1982) critiqued the evolutionary account of citizenship rights as cumulative, developing in an almost linear progression where one form of rights led to the next (also see Friedmann 2002). Moreover, critics assert, assuming social rights to be an outcome of representative politics conceals the class interests of the bourgeoisie in stabilizing capitalism through its welfare policies (Mann 1987), as well as the larger social movements beyond representative politics. It is pointed out that the social rights achieved in the twentieth century were the outcome of larger union struggles and socialist movements, not merely of political citizenship and representative politics (Turner 1990). Bryan Turner's analysis of citizenship coming from above and from below pushed the critique of liberal citizenship further by pointing out its top-down and formal bias (Turner 1990). Articulating different forms of citizenship emerging from above and below and through the public or the private sphere, he points out that liberal democratic conceptualizations capture only the processes that take place from above and through public realms.

Feminists have mounted fierce critiques of a formal, state-centered and top-down understanding of citizenship (Lister 1997; Yuval-Davis 1997). They uncover the hollowness of the modern era's promise of inclusion and universal political rights when women are excluded from formal structures of political representation. Moreover, feminist scholars and political theorists have redefined the arena of politics, expanding it from the formal parliaments and representative structures dominated by men to include women's informal political activism in neighborhoods and residential communities (Jelin 1990; Staheli and Cope 1994; Kaplan 1997; Tripp 1998; Hassiem 1999; McEwan 2000; Miraftab 2006). Stressing the plurality of forms of politics, feminists argue that the formalist notions of politics and political citizenship by default render women's citizenship invisible. Articulating the notion of informal politics as an equally important realm where citizens negotiate their rights vis-à-vis the state, feminists have made important inroads in the citizenship debate, opening it to alternative interpretations.

2. DECENTERING THE STATE IN CITIZENSHIP DEBATES

In the last three decades, the debate about citizenship has been reinvigorated. Since the late 1980s, the global restructuring of capitalism and the emergence of neoliberal modes of governance have privatized social risk—undermining the responsibilities of the state for public well-being in favor of the free market and a shift of that burden to the citizens. Concomitantly, we have seen the rise of social movements not only among marginalized populations that were never included in the universal promises of liberal citizenship but also among newly disenfranchised citizens who have responded to the erosion of the welfare state in Western liberal democratic societies by taking on the effort to recover their rights. The 1990s experiences of liberal democracies shaped in post-socialist Eastern Europe and in post-Apartheid South Africa have been revealing. In post-socialist Eastern Europe, citizens attained civil and political rights, but lost many of their socioeconomic entitlements and rights—for example, to social housing. In post-Apartheid South Africa, on the other hand, the black population gained recognition of full civil, political, and social rights through their new constitution, but could not access newly attained basic social rights like decent shelter and fundamental urban services, as demonstrated by the large number of evictions occurring between 1996 and 2006.[1]

In such contexts, the last three decades have exposed the disjunctures between civil, political, and social rights, and we have witnessed an unraveling and restructuring of the project of liberal citizenship. From both the left and the right of the political spectrum and in both theory and practice, we see a move away from the state-centered notion of citizenship that lies at the core of liberal citizenship.

Conservatives, for example, highly vocal in the critique of a state-centered citizenship, undermine the liberal social contract that guarantees social rights through welfare policies by insisting instead on broader citizens' responsibilities and obligations that relieve those of the state. This formulation celebrates active citizens: individualized, self-reliant, responsibible, and in need of no government assistance, since they have only themselves to praise or blame for their social welfare. Conservatives' arguments that justify shrinking the state's responsibilities toward its citizens as a way to promote active citizenship are rejected by their critics (Kearns 1992; Ong 2003) as promoting the production of "neoliberal subjects." Though the progressive left also calls for decentering the state in the expectations of citizenship, its point of departure is an opposing set of social commitments. The progressive left's advocacy of a citizen-centered citizenship does not sidestep the state's responsibility for its citizens' welfare but, rather, calls for a more inclusive notion extending beyond the state to include the participation of a range of actors that ensures the actuality of rights (see Kabeer 2002; Cornwall 2002; Gaventa 2002).

As delineated by contributors to the special issue of *Institute of Development Studies Bulletin* (Gaventa 2002) on citizenship, these alternative conceptualizations articulate citizenship not as a given but as a practice. Their inclusive formulation of citizenship stresses the importance of people's actions and their everyday practices to secure abstract rights. The authors decenter the state by highlighting the limitations of the formal rights the state grants: inscriptions of rights by state institutions and laws are necessary and can facilitate the citizens' struggle, but in and of themselves those are insufficient to ensure rights in practice; they cannot be materialized without citizens' practices on the ground. Accounting for the complexity of entangled formal and informal processes results in a nuanced analysis revealing the range of agents beyond the state who act to achieve the civil, political, and socioeconomic rights promised to citizens. Such an alternative, inclusive perspective views citizenship not as an object such as a bundle of laws or decrees but as a process constructed both as a process from above through legal and institutional arms of the state and from below through citizens' everyday actions both formal and informal. Citizenship is articulated as practices that generate "new sources of laws" (Holston and Appadurai 1999, 20).

3. CITIZENSHIP FROM BELOW

To better understand this emerging notion of citizenship as practices grounded in civil society, I offer two observations from the field: one from the Western Cape, South Africa, and the other from the Midwest of the United States. Elsewhere (Miraftab 2006, 2009), I have published a detailed case study of South Africa's Western Cape Anti Eviction Campaign (AEC), a grassroots movement that resists the eviction orders of the local state and private banks so as to help the poor to keep the roofs over their heads. The AEC also asserts poor residents' rights to basic urban services by reconnecting those that the municipal government or private sector disconnects for nonpayment. The AEC practices expose the hypocrisy of the post-Apartheid state in granting constitutional rights to shelter and basic services, yet issuing eviction orders to those unable to pay for rent or utilities. It is important to recognize how this contradiction reflects the country's larger paradox of simultaneous political liberation and economic neoliberalization (Miraftab 2008). In the country's political liberation, the 1996 constitution granted citizens universal civil, political, and socioeconomic rights; at the same time, the adoption by the state of the neoliberal Growth Employment and Redistribution (GEAR) policy privileged the private sector's growth over equity and realignment of the skewed property ownership patterns wrought by Apartheid. As a result, many South African citizens were left unable to enact their constitutionally inscribed rights to shelter and basic services. Their constraint this time is accomplished not through racial categorization but because the contemporary free-market economy has marginalized them economically.

The AEC case study, however, reveals not only the inadequacy and unwillingness of the state to deliver on the constitution's promise of universal post-Apartheid citizenship but also the potent capacity of the poor and their organizations to feed, to dress, to shelter, to make their voices heard—in short, to participate in governing their lives, communities, and city. In the AEC movement we see how poor black South African citizens rely on their own innovative practices to enact their recently obtained constitutional right to shelter and basic services. Using formal legal rights, they construct through their own, often extra-legal or illegal actions the meaning of inclusive and universal citizenship in post-Apartheid society. To realize their citizenship rights fully, campaign activists use both sanctioned channels (invited spaces of citizenship) and defiantly innovative, oppositional practices (invented spaces of citizenship). Their flexible actions are not confined by the legal parameters of formal citizenship (for details, see Miraftab 2006 and 2009).

The current conditions of post-Apartheid South Africa cast a harsh light on the limitations of constitutionally inscribed rights, revealing how distinctive citizenship rights cannot simply be bundled together, with one leading to and guaranteeing another, nor can the legal rights of citizens guarantee that those rights will materialize in citizens' lives. Formal political and civil rights of citizenship are necessary, but for marginalized populations they are not sufficient to provide tangible rights to shelter and basic services. In the South African case, while the majority citizens' political citizenship has expanded, their substantive conditions of life have not improved. Indeed, some data demonstrate that for the poor and those that Apartheid categorized as nonwhite, substantive conditions have worsened (see Terreblanche 2002).

Another example similarly illuminates the limitations of a state-centered understanding of citizenship as a formal status and set of rights granted by the state. This example comes from the experience of immigrants in the United States, many of them undocumented, whose access to food, shelter, and education improves despite, not because of, their status vis-à-vis the state. In an economically distressed, rural town of the Midwestern United States, the corporation Cargill recruits an immigrant labor force for its meatpacking plant. The town's formal politics of citizen participation in governance—for example, through an all-white and native-born city council—are exclusionary. The town's immigrants, however, are fashioning new forms of citizenship that afford them remarkable inclusion in public institutions and in public spaces. In a town that until not long ago was kept all white by the brutally racist practices of sundown towns, today we see high residential integration, with almost every block racially integrated;[2] high homeownership rate among Mexican immigrants,[3] with many of them joining the local landlord class; a multilingual education system in that has adopted a dual-language program with students receiving half their education in Spanish; and a notable presence of immigrants in public space—through cultural identity celebrations (e.g., Mexican Independence Day or Africa Day) and through numerous multiracial soccer teams playing in outdoor fields (for an expanded discussion and details see Miraftab forthcoming and 2011).

In my ethnographic study of community change in this Midwestern town, I have witnessed the importance of informal politics and innovative everyday practices and struggles through which subordinate groups renegotiate their social spatial and interracial relations. The gains listed above were not decrees granted by the town's unsupportive local government. Rather, these are gains built from below by the efforts of immigrants and their allies through their everyday practices and informal politics. For example, the adoption of a dual-language school program resulted from a tireless door-to-door campaign by residents and teachers to convince parents in both Spanish- and English-speaking families of the value of multilingual education.[4]

The foregoing examples are not meant to romanticize either the hardship of immigrant workers in the Midwestern meatpacking industry or the plight of homeless families in South African townships. Rather, the aim is to unbundle the understanding of citizens' substantive citizenship from the state's legal and formalist citizenship project. The case studies illuminate the disjuncture between formal and substantive rights and the inadequacy of a state-centered analysis. In the South African case, township residents with full formal citizenship rights must fight against evictions that contravene their constitutional right to shelter; in the Midwest, a rural town's undocumented immigrants achieve home ownership and the security of shelter despite their undocumented status vis-à-vis the state. It is evident in these examples that neither the source of citizenship nor the benefits it should embody are solely the grant of the state, but arise from the practices that citizens embark on to make a meaningful difference in their lives and livelihoods. The access to shelter achieved by the Anti Eviction Campaign or by the Midwestern immigrants is gained not through legal and formal entitlements but through claims-making struggles on the ground.

4. CITIZENSHIP RIGHTS AND JUSTICE

An important question for planning scholarship in the emerging debates on citizenship concerns the relationship between rights and justice, and specifically the caveat not to conflate the two. Rawls's theory of justice as fairness (1971), which builds on the liberal notions of the social contract, helped planning scholarship to recognize how equal rights and equal treatment of unequal citizens are not fair and do not lead to a just outcome. While urban dwellers may have equal rights to choose their residential locations, spatial inequalities persist—a recognition that prompts not only the state's redistributive policies but also several streams within a progressive planning movement, including advocates of equity planning (Krumholz 1994; Krumholz and Forester 1990) and guerrillas in the bureaucracy (Needleman and Needleman 1974). Feminist scholars of citizenship and political philosophy like Iris Young (1990) have further deconstructed the assumed unity of rights and justice. The project of justice, Young argues, is broader than individualized rights and fair treatment. To reach a just outcome we need to recognize self-determined and group-based forms of oppression. The mantra of "no redistribution without recognition" highlights the failure of welfare policies that may satisfy beneficiaries' rights as individuals yet through stigma oppress them as a group. Recognition of group-based differences has been most influential in the progressive planning debates on multicultural cities (Sandercock 1998a, 2003; Milroy 1992; Harwood 2005).

Such understanding of justice as encompassing more than abstract universal rights has shifted the core attention of the citizenship debate and practice from representation to self-determination. Disentangling abstract rights and substantive justice focuses on the value of citizens' self-determined experiences of oppression and justice, and hence validates their direct action. That change in perspective ultimately privileges participatory democracy over representative democracy.

In current debates about citizenship, direct participation and control are framed as insurgent citizenship. The term, coined by Holston (1998) and introduced to planning scholarship by Sandercock's insurgent historiographies (1998b), sheds light on the spatial struggles and practices of those that the false promises of universal citizenship exclude. Whether among "minoritized" populations of the Global North or marginalized residents of the Global South, *insurgent citizenship* refers to democratic practices where citizens do not relegate the defense of their interests to others—be they politicians, bureaucrats, or planners—but take the matter into their own hands. Through insurgent citizenship practices, grassroots groups assert their right to the city and take control of the necessities for decent life. Insurgent citizenship practices do not excuse the state from its responsibilities; rather, they hold the state accountable through means beyond the state-sanctioned channels of citizen participation. The practice of insurgent citizenship is not confined to invited spaces of citizenship such as the Senate, the municipal councils, the planning commission's community hearings, citizen review boards, and nongovernmental organizations (NGOs). Such citizenship practices occur as well in self-determined invented spaces where citizens participate through direct action, often with oppositional practices that respond to specific contexts and issues (Miraftab 2006, 2009). Examples are grassroots organizations and activities such as South Africa's AEC reconnecting households' water services and returning evicted families to their homes; Argentinean *workers* reclaiming abandoned industries; Berkeley's homeless appropriating and using the People's Park (Mitchell 2003); or Chicago's Anti Eviction Campaign (Southside Solidarity Network) that stopped housing evictions. Grassroots actions that do not stop at the limits of formal rights but go beyond them to make decisions and act across invented and invited spaces of citizenship are insurgent practices of citizenship (see Miraftab 2006).

This claiming of rights, as Mark Purcell (2003) explains, should be understood not in the limited formal and legalist sense but in the radical Lefebvrian sense of the right to appropriate (and therefore to use) and the right to participate (and therefore to produce) urban space. From this perspective, the urban landscapes of most cities of the Global South are indeed the material and spatial evidence of citizens' asserting their right to the city—not simply through legal means and bureaucratic channels but also through insurgent practices by which people produce their shelter, appropriate urban spaces, and use the city to secure a livelihood.

In curious ways, as Holston (2008) points out, the insurgent practices of *favela* residents and squatters once again uphold the city, not the nation, as the political community to which citizens claim membership in and assert their rights to. Residents of squatter settlements, *favelas*, and townships take charge of urban spaces. They make their own living space and livelihood not because of but often despite the state's institutions and laws. The insurgent citizenship practices of such subordinate groups offer an alternative challenging the assumption that the state is "the only legitimate source of citizenship rights" (Holston 1998, 39).

In the social contract that governs liberal democratic societies, citizens as individuals delegate their rights to others—political representatives, bureaucrats, and/or technical experts—to act in their best interests. In contrast, disadvantaged and marginalized citizens who recognize the inadequacy of formal rights turn to direct participation to achieve justice. They do not hand the advocacy of their interests to others but, rather, directly take part in decisions that affect their lives and shape binding decisions.[5] Participatory democracy inspired by the Lefebvrian understanding of "the right to the city" (1996) consequently promotes a form of citizenship that is multicentered and has multiple agencies, including the citizens and their direct social actions. This insurgent form of citizenship has important implications for planning scholarship.

5. Decentering the State: The Participatory Turn in Planning

How do planning scholarship and practice engage with the changing terrain of citizenship—a social, political, and spatial terrain on which the planning profession has established its enterprise? That is the question I turn to for the remainder of this chapter. I organize my reflection around two key observations.

First, since the 1970s, we have witnessed a decentering of the state in the practices of professional planners. The unraveling of the liberal social contract discussed here with respect to citizenship is reflected in the shifts within planning scholarship and practice. The lean state has neither the resources nor the will, in its agenda of public welfare or infrastructure developments, to hire planners. Consequently a range of other nonstate actors have become the employers of professional planners (Douglass and Friedmann 1998). Consulting firms and corporations set the agendas for urban and regional development decisions, as do the NGOs and nonprofit groups that try to create alternative plans and proposals to bridge the gap left by the state's restructured activities. Today, multiple actors set the agenda for and define the meaning of professional planners' practices. The state is no longer the sole legitimating source for planners' activities.

Second, this move away from a state-centered bureaucratic enterprise has expanded the definition of planning. As the private sector and civil society organizations and their members have taken over many of the public sector's responsibilities, the plurality of planning protagonists has made planning, more fiercely than ever before, a site for contestation by actors with contrasting interests and commitments. Now, not only the actions and decisions by powerful corporate interests or affluent hometown associations but also the actions undertaken by disenfranchised and marginalized communities are visible and legitimated as de facto planning. Planning as an exclusive activity undertaken by formally trained and professionalized planners is increasingly questioned not only in theory but also on the ground through the social and spatial production of cities, neighborhoods, and urban livelihoods that occurs through direct grassroots action.

The examples described earlier in this chapter may illuminate these points. In the Midwestern rural town we discussed, for instance, there were no professional planners or planning agencies, nor was there any formal political structure that represented the interests of the minorities and immigrants independent of their citizenship status as naturalized, documented, or undocumented. Nevertheless, the socioeconomic gains of the town's minority, foreign-born residents were evident, and they arose from the group's everyday practices to assert their right to the city and a dignified livelihood—not from the state's decrees or programs formulated by professional planners. Their substantive gains were achieved as the immigrants and their native allies took on the challenges of homeownership, dual-language education, and a multicultural use of public space. Similarly, in the Cape Town example, the development of and access to housing and neighborhood services by township residents took place outside the realm of formal planning. This well-documented reality holds for the poor populations of most Third World cities.[6] Worldwide, citizens participate in insurgent practices of citizenship that create their urban landscapes and are legitimated not necessarily or only through law but through everyday use and persistent claims they make for the production of those spaces.

Such on-the-ground observations have drawn planning scholars and practitioners to expand their understanding of planning beyond their own professional practices. Planning practitioners find themselves increasingly entangled with communities' collective actions and everyday livelihood strategies in responding to the state's failure to fulfill its citizenship promises. In this context, planning can no longer afford to be the sole prerogative of professional planners, even given their acceptance of participatory planning.

The emerging conversation within progressive planning, inspired by grassroots insurgent practices of citizenship, offers growing support for the notion of insurgent planning practices (Friedmann 2002; Sandercock 1998b; also see Miraftab, Perera, Roy, and Yiftachel in the special issue of *Planning Theory* on insurgency and informality 2009). Insurgent planning departs in radical ways from the guiding principles of participatory planning. Participatory planning, as understood and practiced in the last three decades, is guided by the assumption that representative democracy works to the best interests of all those with equal citizenship rights, including disadvantaged groups. To the contrary, insurgent planning is guided by an understanding of citizenship as a practice constructed from below through citizens' direct action for the development of their self-determined political community.

Participatory planning that rests on fundamental principles of liberal representative democracy can achieve only as much as the liberal project of citizenship can. The unfulfilled promises of participatory planning derive from the limitations of liberal democratic citizenship and the fallacy that rightful processes alone can reach just outcomes. A growing critical stance within planning reveals the inadequacy of participation through representative and formal institutionalized channels. This literature exposes how, in a neoliberal context, participatory planning serves as an alibi for elitist, private-sector–driven decisions (Angotti 2008; DeFilippis 2001; Mayer 2003; Miraftab 2003).

Reflecting on decades of participatory planning and the failure of both the liberal democratic notion of citizenship and its representative channels to deliver on the promise of justice, many planning scholars stress the need for citizens' direct action (e.g., Freidmann 1988; Beard 2003; Sandercock 1998b; Irazabal 2008; Leavitt 1994; Miraftab 2009). Progressive planning increasingly recognizes the need to move beyond the confines of formal rights as the project of justice. Such a move brings planning to encompass a range of insurgent practices of citizenship that occur outside the formal structures of representation by disenfranchised citizens. This is planning that values direct and self-determined spaces of action and does not confuse representation and participation. Progressive planning in the twenty-first century needs to move beyond participatory planning to recognize, nourish, and promote an expanded and insurgent notion of planning. It is this turn that is pregnant with possibilities for a more just understanding of planning, both as an ideal and as a realm of action.

6. CONCLUSION

Planning, a field that is so closely linked to the construction of the modern state, reflects the contested terrain of citizenship. As a profession, planning has been a creation of the modern state and is deeply shaped by the core liberal democratic values of representative democracy as beacon for freedom and equality. In this chapter tracing the debates on citizenship as theory and practice that mediate the relationship between the state and citizens, I have highlighted the crisis of the liberal social contract as the fallacy of its promises of equality and freedom are increasingly exposed. We have seen marginalized communities increasingly take the realization of their rights and the fulfillment of their needs into their own hands through social movements and insurgent practices of citizenship. They do not necessarily consign the production, use, and control of urban space to others, be it politicians, bureaucrats, or planners, but take charge and through direct action appropriate the city and its resources.

In the 1970s and 1980s, the emphasis on negotiation and collaboration among multiple actors brought to the center of the planning profession a new set of methodologies and understandings that marked a participatory turn in both planning scholarship and practice. A few decades into this participatory and inclusive turn in planning, we need to critically engage its core guiding values and methodologies. In the twenty-first century, just as the understanding of citizenship has shifted from a formalist top-down decree to a set of practices grounded in civil society, so has the understanding of planning as a set of state-sponsored activities changed to acknowledge a set of practices undertaken by multiple and contesting actors.

Progressive planning in the twenty-first century needs to engage with a more nuanced understanding of rights and justice and a clearer perspective on the fundamentally distinctive principles of representative and participatory democracy.

These insights highlight the need to recognize, value, and nourish citizens' insurgent practices that may fall outside or even against formal or state-sanctioned participatory channels.

As structural and institutional forces seek to stabilize oppressive relationships through inclusion, progressive planning in the twenty-first century has the moral obligation to critically reflect on methodology by which the state is decentered and its citizens are included in both citizenship and planning. If it is to promote social transformation, progressive planning's imperative must be to move beyond a misconceived celebration simply of inclusion to a conceptualization of insurgent planning. Insurgent planning practices pierce the veneer of participation and inclusion to pursue substantive forms of justice.

ACKNOWLEDGMENTS

I am most grateful for the insightful comments and suggestions made by Rachel Weber on the earlier versions of this chapter. This chapter has also benefited from a discussion held by participants and panelists (Angotti, Harwood, Marcuse, Sandercock) at a 2009 ACSP roundtable I organized on planning and citizenship.

NOTES

1. Data on the exact number of evictions by category or region are unavailable; however, the Municipal Services Project and the Human Science Research Council (HSRC) report that between 1994 and 2002, nearly 2 million South Africans have been evicted from their homes because of service nonpayments (see McDonald and Smith 2004). In addition, the cost-recovery strategies have led to extensive cutoffs of water to disadvantaged households. In the former substructures of Cape Town and Tygerberg, for example, 75,418 households had their water cut off for nonpayment of water bills in 1999 and 2000 alone (2004,1474).
2. In 2000, the white-Hispanic index of dissimilarity for Beardstown was 57.6 compared to 62.1 for Chicago; 63.2 for Los Angeles–Long Beach; and 66.7 for New York (see Diaz McConnell and Miraftab 2009).
3. My survey in Beardstown (Miraftab 2009) indicates 40 percent homeownership among Spanish-speaking immigrants. The 2000 U.S. census data indicate 49.7 percent homeownership among Hispanics nationwide.
4. Beardstown is the only rural school in Illinois with a dual-language program. As of November 2008, in Illinois there were eighteen schools and nationwide there were 335 schools with dual-language programs (also see Paciotto and Delany-Barmann 2011).
5. Participatory budgeting as practiced in Puerto Alegre is the most well known example often used to describe the distinction between representative and participatory

democracy when, at the scale of a city, residents directly take part in a city's budget allocation (Abers 2000).

6. More than two-thirds of Third World cities are developed through the spontaneous, unplanned activities that Holston (2008) conceptualizes as insurgent urbanization. Eighty-five percent of Third World urban residents "occupy property illegally" (Davis 2004, 6). Moreover, in the labor markets of many Third World economies, formal employment channels have only a minor role. Worldwide, the informal economy has grown as a percentage of nonagricultural employment, by the 1990s reaching 43.4 percent in North Africa, 74.8 percent in Sub-Saharan Africa, 56.9 percent in Latin America, and 63 percent in Asia (Beneria 2003, table 4.2, 111).

References

Abers, R. N. 2000. *Inventing Local Democracy: Grassroots Politics in Brazil.* Boulder, CO: Lynne Rienner.

Angotti, T. 2008. *New York for Sale: Community Planning Confronts Global Real Estate.* Cambridge, MA: MIT Press.

Beard, V. 2003. "Learning Radical Planning: The Power of Collective Action." *Planning Theory* 2(1): 13–35.

Beneria, L. 2003. *Gender, Development and Globalization: Economics as if People Mattered.* New York: Routledge.

Cornwall, A. 2002. "Locating Citizen Participation." *Institute of Development Studies Bulletin* 33(2): 49–58.

Davis, M. 2004. "Planet of Slums." *New Left Review* 26(March-April): 5–34.

DeFilippis, J. 2001. "The Myth of Social Capital in Community Development." *Housing Policy Debate* 12(4): 781–806.

Diaz McConnell, E., and F. Miraftab, F. 2009. "Sundown Town to 'Mexican Town': Newcomers, Old Timers, and Housing in Small Town America." *Rural Sociology* 74(4): 605–29.

Douglass, M., and J. Friedmann, eds. 1998. *Cities and Citizens.* New York: John Wiley.

Fainstein, S. 2010. *The Just City.* Ithaca, NY: Cornell University Press.

Freidmann, J. 1988. *Life Space and Economic Space: Essays in Third World Planning.* New Brunswick, NJ: Transaction.

Friedmann, J. 2002. *The Prospect of Cities.* Minneapolis: University of Minnesota Press.

Gaventa, J. 2002. "Exploring Citizenship, Participation and Accountability." *Institute of Development Studies Bulletin* 33(2): 1–11.

Giddens, A. 1982. *Profiles and Critiques in Social Theory.* London: Macmillan.

Harwood, S. 2005. "Struggling to Embrace Difference in Land-Use Decision Making in Multicultural Communities." *Planning Practice and Research* 20(4): 355–71.

Hassiem, S. 1999. "From Presence to Power: Women's Citizenship in a New Democracy." *Agenda* 40: 6–17.

Holston, J. 1998. "Spaces of Insurgent Citizenship." In *Making the Invisible Visible: A Multicultural Planning History,* edited by L. Sandercock, 37–56. Berkeley, CA: University of California Press.

Holston, J. 2008. *Insurgent Citizenship: Disjunctions of Democracy and Modernity in Brazil.* Princeton, NJ: Princeton University Press.

Holston, J., and A. Appadurai. 1999. "Cities and Citizenship." In *Cities and Citizenship,* edited by J. Holston, 1–19. Durham, NC: Duke University Press.

Irazabal, C. 2008. "Citizenship, Democracy and Public Space in Latin America." In
     *Ordinary Places/Extraordinary Events: Citizenship, Democracy and Public Space in
     Latin America*, edited by C. Irazabal, 11–34. New York: Routledge.
Jelin, E. 1990. "Citizenship and Identity: Final Reflections." In *Women and Social Change
     in Latin America*, edited by E. Jelin, 184–207. London: Zed Books.
Kabeer, N. 2002. "Citizenship, Affiliation and Exclusion: Perspectives From the South."
     Institute of Development Studies Bulletin 33(2): 12–23.
Kaplan, T. 1997. *Crazy for Democracy: Women in Grassroots Movements*. New York:
     Routledge.
Kearns, A., 1992. "Active citizenship and Urban Governance." *Transactions of the Institute
     of British Geographers N.S.* 17:20–34.
Krumholz, N. 1994. "Dilemmas in Equity Planning: A Personal Memoir." *Planning
     Theory* 10(11): 45–56.
Krumholz, N., and J. Forester. 1990. *Making Equity Planning Work: Leadership in the
     Public Sector*. Philadelphia: Temple University Press.
Leavitt, J. 1994. "Planning in the Age of Rebellion: Guidelines to Activist Research and
     Applied Planning." *Planning Theory* 10(11): 111–29.
Lefevbre, H. 1996. "The Right to the City." In *The Blackwell City Reader*, edited by G.
     Bridge and S. Watson, 367–74. Oxford, UK: Blackwell.
Lister, R. 1997. "Citizenship: Towards a Feminist Synthesis." *Feminist Review* 57(Fall): 28–48.
Mann, M. 1987. "Ruling Class Strategies and Citizenship." *Sociology* 21:339–54.
Marshall, T. H. 1950. *Citizenship and Social Class and Other Essays*. Cambridge, UK:
     Cambridge University Press.
Mayer, M. 2003. "*The Onward Sweep of Social Capital: Causes and Consequences for
     Understanding Cities, Communities and Urban Movements.*" *International Journal of
     Urban and Regional Research* 27(1): 110–32.
McDonald, D., and L. Smith. 2004. "Privatising Cape Town: From Apartheid to
     Neoliberalism in the Mother City." *Urban Studies* 41(8): 1461–84.
McEwan, C. 2000. "Engendering Citizenship: Gendered Spaces of Democracy in South
     Africa." *Political Geography* 19:627–51.
Milroy, B. M. 1992. "Some Thoughts about Difference and Pluralism." *Planning Theory*
     7(8): 33–38.
Miraftab, F. 2003. "The Perils of Participatory Discourse: Housing Policy in Post-
     Apartheid South Africa." *Journal of Planning Education and Research* 22(3): 226–39.
Miraftab, F. 2006. "Feminist Praxis, Citizenship and Informal Politics: Reflections on
     South Africa's Anti-Eviction Campaign." *International Feminist Journal of Politics*
     8(2): 194–218.
Miraftab, F. 2008. "*Decentralization and Entrepreneurial Planning.*" In *Planning and
     Decentralization: Contested Spaces for Public Action in the Global South*, edited by
     V. Beard, F. Miraftab, and C. Silver, 21–35. New York: Routledge.
Miraftab, F. 2009. "Insurgent Planning: Situating Radical Planning in the Global South."
     Planning Theory 8(1): 32–50.
Miraftab, F. 2011. "Faraway Intimate Development: Global Restructuring of Social
     Reproduction." *Journal of Planning Education and Research* 31(4): 392–405.
Miraftab, F. Forthcoming. "Emerging Transnational Spaces: Meat, Sweat and Global (re)
     Production in the Heartland." *International Journal of Urban and Regional Research.*
     [doi: 10.1111/j.1468-2427.2011.01070.x]
Mitchell, D. 2003. *The Right to the City: Social Justice and the Fight for Public Space.*
     New York: Guilford.

Needleman, M. L., and C. E. Needleman. 1974. *Guerrillas in the Bureaucracy: The Community Planning Experiment in the United States*. New York: John Wiley.

Ong, A. 2003. *Buddha in Hiding: Refugees, Citizenship, and the New America*. Berkeley, CA: University of California Press.

Paciotto, C., and G. Delany-Barmann. 2011. "Planning Micro-level Language Education Reform in New Diaspora Sites: Two-way Immersion Education in the Rural Midwest." *Language Policy* 10(3): 221–43.

Perera, N. 2009. "People's Spaces: Familiarization, Subject Formation and Emergent Spaces in Colombo." *Planning Theory* 8(1): 51–75.

Prucell, M. 2003. "Citizenship and the Right to the Global City: Reimagining the Capitalist World Order." *International Journal of Urban and Regional Research* 27(3): 564–90.

Rawls, J. 1971. *A Theory of Justice*. Cambridge, MA: Belknap, Harvard University Press.

Rousseau, J. J. 1762/1968. *The Social Contract*. New York and London: Penguin.

Roy, A. 2009. "Why India Cannot Plan Its Cities: Informality, Insurgence and the Idiom of Urbanization." *Planning Theory* 8(1): 76–87.

Sandercock, L. 1998a. *Towards Cosmopolis: Planning for Multicultural Cities*. London: John Wiley.

Sandercock, L. 1998b. "Framing Insurgent Historiographies for Planning." In *Making the Invisible Visible: A Multicultural Planning History*, edited by L. Sandercock. Berkeley, CA: University of California Press.

Sandercock, L. 2003. *Cosmopolis II: Mongrel Cities in the 21st Century*. London: Continuum.

Staheli, L., and M. Cope. 1994. "Empowering Women's Citizenship." *Political Geography* 13(5): 443–60.

Terreblanche, S. J. 2002. *A History of Inequality in South Africa, 1652–2002*. Pietermaritzburg: University of Natal Press.

Tripp, A. M. 1998. "Expanding "Civil Society": Women and Political Space in Contemporary Uganda." In *Civil Society and Democracy in Africa: Critical Perspectives*, edited by N. Kasfir, 84–107. London: Frank Cass.

Turner, B. S. 1990. "Outline of a Theory of Citizenship." *Sociology* 24(2): 189–217.

Yiftachel. O. 2009. "Theoretical Notes on `Gray Cities': the Coming of Urban Apartheid?" *Planning Theory* 8(1): 88–100.

Young, I. 1990. *Justice and the Politics of Difference*. Princeton, NJ: Princeton University Press.

Yuval-Davis, N. 1997. "Women, Citizenship and Difference." *Feminist Review* 57(Fall): 4–27.

CHAPTER 39

PLAN ASSESSMENT: MAKING AND USING PLANS WELL

LEWIS D. HOPKINS

Do plans work? The claim that plans are useful in urban development is fundamental to the planning profession. It is important to consider carefully the claims for plans and the arguments and evidence that back these claims. The frame for assessing plans is of broader significance because it can also be used to assess the usefulness of other public policy instruments.

The focus here is on understanding what work plans do and whether the ways in which plans are made and used matter. These questions are distinct from whether a plan proposes a beautiful, efficient, equitable, or sustainable city. Evaluating whether particular patterns of development (e.g., compact cities), actions (e.g., building transit), or policies (e.g., separating land uses) are desirable is largely separable from determining whether plans are useful in achieving those goals. Such evaluations depend on concepts of the good—good city form (e.g., Lynch 1960), welfare economics (e.g., O'Flaherty 2005), human capabilities (e.g., Nussbaum 1995; Sen 1993), or sustainability (e.g., Gunderson and Holling 2002). These concepts can be evaluated before or after outcomes are realized, in either case being separable from whether plans will help or did help in achieving those outcomes.

The distinction between evaluating an outcome proposed in or resulting from a plan and assessing whether making or using a plan played a role in achieving that outcome was emphasized in the strategic choice approach of Friend and Jessop (1969) and clarified in Faludi and Mastop (1982). The approach taken here assumes that the evaluation of good outcomes is largely separable from, though not entirely independent of, the question of whether plans work to influence outcomes.

First, a frame for assessing plans is used to identify various approaches that have been proposed in the literature and to identify researchable questions. Second, claims for planning are used to organize the questions that have been considered in research on plans. A sample of the literature reveals the range of explanations, arguments, and evidence brought to bear. The conclusion identifies questions for which evidence and arguments provide useful guidance on how to make and use plans well and questions that remain open or contested.

1. A Frame for Assessing Plans

Figure 39.1 presents an overall frame for assessing plans. Six observable phenomena invite explanations of attributes of or relationships among these phenomena that can be used to justify claims that plans work well. The *planning situation* is the context in which planning activities occur, including the institutional context and the general state of the world. All of what occurs is situational, so the figure should be interpreted as the situation having an initial state that evolves through levels in the frame. *Planning processes* are all the activities that happen as planners and constituents create plans, including both formal and informal activities. *Plans* are time- and place-limited collections of information about intentions, related actions, possible futures, and plausible outcomes.

Decisions are commitments to actions by persons or organizations with authority or capability to make credible commitments. *Actions* are changes that occur in the state of the world, including tangible changes in regulations and investments in construction or changes in places of residence or work. *Outcomes* are attributes or qualities of the state of the world as expressed, for example, by indicators. These indicators may be tied to intentions (goals) or to attributes of interest that are not the focus of intended change.

These phenomena, which are extracted from a more fully elaborated ontology of planning phenomena (Hopkins, Kaza, and Pallathucheril 2005) and the relationships among them, are sufficient to explain and keep track of various concepts of plan assessment. From figure 39.1, we can identify two perspectives on assessing plans: making plans well and using plans well. These perspectives account for the wide range of concepts in the literature on assessing the value of plans (Alexander and Faludi 1989; Baer 1997; Faludi 2000; Hopkins 2001; Innes and Booher 1999; Talen 1996a, 1996b) as elaborated below.

The literature on making plans well focuses on relationships among planning situations, plan-making processes, and plans, but also includes process effects—claims that good processes will increase the likelihood that plans will be used and, therefore, influence decisions and actions. Planning processes also affect future planning situations, and this relationship is often identified as a positive side effect:

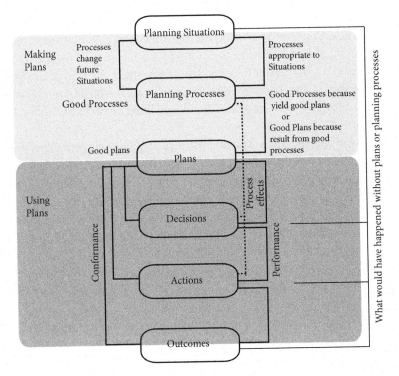

Figure 39.1

good processes modify the planning situation, creating a better situation in which to do future planning. There are also claims that plans are good because they were made using good processes and claims that processes are good because they yield good plans. These claims generally rely on direct claims for what constitutes a good plan or a good process, often without strong empirical backing. The claims about good processes are often contingent on appropriateness to a planning situation. In addition, claims are made about processes and plans independent of their relationships to each other. For example, good processes are ethically good independent of whether they yield better plans or outcomes.

The literature on using plans well includes two approaches: conformance (Alexander and Faludi 1989) and performance (Mastop and Faludi 1997). These approaches can also be applied to assessing other public policy instruments. The conformance approach asks whether decisions, actions, or outcomes conform to the content of the plan. For example, we can ask whether a city council made zoning decisions consistent with its plan, development actions were consistent with the plan, the resulting land-use pattern was consistent with the plan, or accomplished goals were consistent with the plan.

The performance approach, in contrast, tracks relationships from plans, to decisions, to actions, to outcomes in order to assess how well a plan helps decision makers decide what to do to accomplish their intentions. Performance investigations rely on explanations of how a plan affects decisions. It is not sufficient in the performance approach simply to look at the correlation of plan content with decisions, actions, or outcomes. For example, one explanation is that a plan provides legal backing for zoning decisions by protecting decision makers from legal challenges of arbitrary action and thus influences the decisions they make. Careful tracking of mechanisms of effects provides a basis for claiming that the decisions, actions, or outcomes would not have occurred without the plan (Calkins 1979).

All of these perspectives and approaches depend on deductive argument, empirical evidence, or both. Empirical evidence may rely on, and in that sense test, deductive arguments. Deductive arguments may or may not depend on empirical evidence. For example, an argument that planning processes should be deliberatively democratic might be backed only by deductive claims from ethics. Or, the argument might be backed by an explanation that deliberative democracy increases the likelihood of good solutions, fair solutions, or solutions that are carried out. This explanation can be subjected to empirical investigation. Bryson (1991) argues that scholarship on plans should focus on this latter combination of argument and evidence.

Dryzek's (2007, 250) assessment of deliberative democracy research applies at least as well to research on whether plans work:

> The empirical findings are quite capable of discomforting theorists, just as theorists are quite capable of discomforting empirical researchers. Deliberative democracy is not a hypothesis that can be falsified, nor is it a model, but rather a project, to which theorists, researchers, citizens, and activists alike can contribute.

Planning research should clarify, challenge, and refine claims about how plans work. In what circumstances do what kinds of plans made and used in what ways help us to achieve intentions? Donaghy and Hopkins (2006) argue, based on Miller (1987), that we can create argument and evidence to help cope with the world even if a "complete general theory of planning is impossible" (Mandelbaum 1979, 1).

2. Claims for Making Plans Well

Claims for making plans well can be organized into two general categories. A first category of research focuses on claims that procedural rationality, public participation, consensus building, or other planning processes yield better plans, influence the use of plans, or influence future planning situations. A second category of research focuses on claims about the characteristics of good plans, such as that plans should be comprehensive.

2.1 Do Plan-making Processes Affect Plans?

Planning processes could matter because of their effects or their inherent properties. Processes could affect the quality of resulting plans, the use of resulting plans, or future planning situations. Processes could also be assessed directly—that is, as having better or worse characteristics independent of their effect on resulting plans. A particular version of the latter is the "as if" argument for operational processes that are argued to be equivalent to the standards of Habermas's ideal speech situation or to the ideal rational decision-making procedure. All of these beg criteria with which to assess the effects of or inherent quality of processes. These criteria include better solutions, higher success rate in achieving intended actions, greater capabilities to accomplish future planning, means criteria such as democracy or justice, and comparison of expected results to those of ideal processes.

Research on these questions builds on the psychology of problem solving and group processes (e.g., Arkes and Hammond 1986; Krantz and Kunreuther 2007), the political science of collective choice including deliberation (e.g., Hurley 1989; Rosenberg 2007) and aggregation of preference (e.g., Ordeshook 1992), and the sociological concerns about power (e.g., Lukes 1974) and community formation (e.g., Putnam 1993). Most planning scholars build on only one of these disciplines, but the results are largely complementary rather than contradictory. For example, discussions of collaborative planning (e.g., Healey 2007) subsume problem solving, collective choice, learning, and community formation.

Building on psychology, planning scholars investigated particular procedures and the effects on plans and the use of plans. Claims about creativity (innovation) and search imply that working with different alternatives should yield better solutions. Several experiments (Brill et al. 1990; Hopkins 1973; Trybus and Hopkins 1980) have shown that human judgments (often seen as qualitative skills) complement analytical methods (often seen as quantitative or computer methods). One of the complementarities is that analytical and judgment methods generate different kinds of differences among alternatives. The standard of solution quality in these studies is after-the-fact ordering of discovered solutions (Hopkins 1984). Other experiments suggest that the ability of humans to express preferences valid for use in analytical methods of choice among alternatives is highly suspect, at best (Lai and Hopkins 1989, 1995).

Collaboration in cognitive psychology focuses on ways in which a group can improve solution quality relative to an individual (social cognition), which overlaps with the concept of deliberation in political science. While the benefits from the availability of more ideas and the potential of interaction among minds have been demonstrated (e.g., Sniezek and Henry 1989), the risks of group reinforcement of low-quality ideas are high (Kaza 2006; Sunstein 2003; Tetlock 2005). If the argument that public participation improves plans is based on the collaborative gains of social cognition, then the design of participation processes should consider these results. For example, analytical methods are good complements to human judgment because they tend to counter individual and group biases in generating alternatives (Andrews 1992; Brill, Chang, and Hopkins 1982) and in forecasting effects and futures (Andrews 2002).

Participation procedures should also acknowledge interactions between potential social cognition gains and conflicts among preferences and interests. Collaborators with different perspectives and experiences may be more likely to contribute different knowledge and proposals; they may also be more likely to hold different preferences and interests (Andrews 2002; Forester 2006; Willson, Payne, and Smith 2003).

Attributes of process have been shown to affect not only plan content but also accomplishment of intended actions. With a focus on project planning by lead organizations, Bryson et al. (1990) found that the effectiveness of problem-solving activity varied with the degree of conflict and that outcomes achievement and satisfaction increased with increases in problem-identification effort. Burby (2003) found that participation by a larger number of types of stakeholder groups increased the number of hazard-mitigation measures included in a plan and the proportion of those measures actually implemented. As with most empirical studies, the variables and framing can be challenged. Why, for example, does inclusion of more mitigation measures equal a better plan? Empirical evidence will, however, build from such approximations that complement each other while inviting revision of theoretical explanations.

It is also important to distinguish between using participation as a means to achieve goals rather than as a source of collaborative problem solving.

> Getting often-neglected stakeholders into the planning process provides planners with an important tool for increasing their political effectiveness without being overtly political. Many of the issues planners address in comprehensive plans, such as hazard mitigation, lack publics that have the same degree of appreciation of the problem as planners. By involving stakeholders, planners can increase public understanding of these issues and persuade potential constituency groups of the need for action. (Burby 2003, 44)

This interpretation is more consistent with the "leadership for the common good" approach of Bryson and Crosby (1992) than with the psychology of collaborative problem solving. One of Bryson and Crosby's exemplar cases is the intentional effort of local civic leaders to create regional government institutions, which resulted in the Twin Cities Metropolitan Council in Minnesota. Engaging others in these cases is a means to achieve an established idea, perhaps with modifications, not a means of figuring out what to do.

Consensus building seeks to combine mechanisms of collaborative problem solving and conflict resolution through careful selection of a limited number of stakeholder participants in an intensive, facilitated, interactive process (Susskind and Cruikshank 2006). Consensus building focused on consent to act does not require agreement on reasons for acting and thus does not require agreement on values and preferences other than willingness to participate in the process. The role of the planner is to facilitate process skillfully rather than to achieve a priori policy objectives. Common descriptions of consensus-building procedures, however, include the task of advocating the resulting agreement to the larger constituencies necessary to accomplish the agreed-on change. Thus, the process recognizes a corollary subsequent task of leadership for the common good. The consensus-building approach and its fit to these particular kinds of planning situations have been extensively demonstrated through application cases (Innes 1996, 1998, 2004; Innes, Connick, and Booher 2007; Susskind, McKearnan, and Thomas-Larmer 1999).

Currently common practices in comprehensive planning and regional visioning often claim to be based on consensus-building practices, but the differences undermine these claims. Rather than identifying a small group of stakeholders willing to work intensively at finding actions with broad consent as prescribed for consensus building, the regional visioning exercises involve large groups undertaking highly structured tasks under extreme time restrictions that provide little opportunity for true interaction, discovery, or argument. The conventional regional process includes a large public meeting with hundreds of people at tables of eight or ten, perhaps a few months of meetings by distinct task groups, and often another large meeting. The tasks are tightly framed and artificially distinct from the conflicts and problems facing participants. These procedures are not consistent with consensus-building practices just described and cannot draw on consensus-building cases to justify the effectiveness of these processes.

These visioning processes may instead serve functions of leadership for the common good. One of the salient successful examples is that of Chattanooga, Tennessee, in which the visioning exercise was the initiation event for a civic-leader coalition (Bunnell 2002). The description of the Envision Utah process by Briggs (2008) emphasizes its use in an iterative, intentional effort to influence and lead public attitudes.

The recent literature in deliberative democracy (e.g., Rosenberg 2007) also addresses collaborative processes through questions familiar to planning scholars. One useful distinction for planning is the difference between deliberations that enable future communication but are separate from decision making and deliberations that are focused on achieving a decision. In situations of deep difference or high conflict, the first may be useful as a precursor to the second by helping to discover modes of successful communication. This process would be distinct from the consensus-building processes in which participation is motivated by reaching a decision. In the frame of figure 39.1, the primary objective becomes that of influencing future planning situations rather than making a decision. Consensus building sufficient to enable action on one issue does not depend on removing the underlying differences of legacy, identity, or interests (Sandercock 2004). Sustaining these differences is useful for adaptation in the face of future challenges in future planning situations, and is thus a means to influence future planning situations.

Direct action built on conflict can achieve changes different from what would result from consensus building alone. The civil rights movement in the United States is one salient example, in which action in the streets, political arenas, and the courts played complementary roles. Cases in the planning literature of conflict and change through direct action demonstrate that desirable outcomes are, in some cases, dependent on direct action (Angotti 2008; McGurty 2007; Reardon 1998).

There are three distinguishable functions of group processes: collaborative problem solving, accomplishing goals that require collective action, and conflict resolution as a particular form of collective choice. Assessments of the effectiveness of planning processes must make clear how each of these tasks is being considered and acknowledge that a planning process may incorporate all three. Recent efforts to grasp these three aspects suggest that it can be done and that the evidence and arguments for each do not yield direct contradictions.

With a pertinent title, *Democracy as Problem Solving*, Briggs (2008) describes a kind of civic capacity to create change that can include episodes of collaborative problem solving, leadership for the common good, visioning exercises to enlarge a coalition, and consensus building. His cases show that focusing on only one of these tasks misses the larger conception of how change occurs.

> There was no single instance wherein a multistakeholder "table" of consensus building produced a grand design for problem solving. Multiple decision points, connected by pressing concerns, the institutions that evolved to address them, and informal as well as formal bargaining defined progress. (Briggs 2008, 304)

Cases of metropolitan strategy making in Europe as interpreted by Healey (1997, 2007) and stories of planning in the United States by Bunnell (2002) are similarly rich in iterative episodes of collaboration, consensus building, leadership, coalition building, and accomplishment.

2.2 Do Planning Processes Affect Planning Situations?

Planning processes are also claimed to change the attitudes and relationships among participants (Innes and Booher 1999). In the Atlanta visioning project, Helling (1998) found that participants became part of new social networks. Elkin (1987) argues that local land-use disputes are particularly effective in bringing additional citizens into the deliberative processes of democracy because of the increased concern about changes in their immediate neighborhoods and increased confidence that they know something about the situation. Briggs (2008, 303) observes that leading actors

> have interests in specific *outcomes* (unlike professional mediators or other true neutrals), but they invest significant resources—time, money, talent, reputation, and more—in improving the decision-making process (the classic role of the facilitator), too. That investment in process is an investment in better governance, not just in winning a particular outcome.

In other words, improving the context of the next planning situation may be a side effect of leadership with a priori objectives, but it is not an unintended side effect.

Planning processes affect plan content, the likelihood of plan implementation, and ensuing planning situations. These processes include planners acting with normative intent about both objectives and process. We have very little evidence, however, of the details of planning-process differences that matter in creating these effects. Further, much of the evidence we do have comes from experiments or cases that focus on projects or single-decision events, not on plans intended to help choose what to do now in relation to possible future actions and to communicate this information to others who might benefit from knowing our intentions and expectations. We now turn to assessing plans as a product of these processes.

2.3 What Are the Attributes of a Good Plan?

A frequent agenda of the planning profession is the establishment of norms for procedures, content, and goals for good plans and the institutionalization of these norms through legislative mandates. Two familiar examples are the claims that plans should be comprehensive and that government mandates should require such plans. Such claims beg two kinds of assessments. First, what evidence exists to justify these norms about good plans? Second, do mandates or advocacy of these norms affect the content of plans?

The plan-quality literature generally takes as a given norms of what attributes good plans should have without direct recourse to specific arguments or evidence for these norms (Baer 1997; Berke and Godschalk 2009; Kent 1964). Best practices are taken from embedded experience and practices in the profession. This basis can be seen as a survival-of-the-fittest argument that these norms have survived and evolved in practice and therefore are the norms that work for practitioners. Challenges to such norms will come primarily from assessments of whether such plans work, which will be considered in the section below on using plans well.

A recent framing of plan-quality assessment (Berke et al. 2006) organizes the scope of criteria developed in the literature. Building on their own previous work and on Hopkins (2001), they structure attributes into two major categories—internal and external. Their internal criteria are issues and vision statement, fact basis, goal and policy framework, and plan proposals. Plan proposals include spatial designs, development-management proposals, and monitoring and evaluation, focusing on the effectiveness of these elements in communicating and explaining content. Their external criteria are to "encourage opportunities to use plans, create clear views and understandings of plans, account for interdependent actions in plan scope, and reveal participation of actors" (Berke et al. 2006, 72).

Hopkins (2007) proposed specific graphic devices for including in maps the reasoning behind land development policy proposals and displaying in maps the relationships among interdependent actions while acknowledging the uncertainty about future decisions of others. He provides, however, only a few anecdotes as evidence that these devices are effective.

The systematic empirical research on plans focuses on whether plans have the attributes claimed to be good and whether context or process variables affect the likelihood of plans having these attributes. Berke and Godschalk (2009) conducted a meta-analysis across a set of plan-quality studies that follow the general approach developed over the last decade with their colleagues (Brody 2003; Burby et al. 1997). Such meta-analyses are valuable in refocusing research activity. Berke and Godschalk were not able to identify any strong generalizations from their analysis, with the possible exception that mandates affected plan content. They were, however, able to demonstrate the importance of further refining research designs and considering questions of measure validity.

Norton (2008) presents a carefully constructed plan-quality analysis. The object of study is plans, distinguished carefully from development programs, the latter

being the legally enforceable actions for which a plan provides guidance and backing. Identification of specific audiences—local development-program actors (e.g.,
city council), developers and residents, and judges of legal challenges—justifies the
interpretation of plans as communicative policy acts. This case also distinguishes
substance (policy focus) from mechanism (analytical quality). The application to
Genesee County, Michigan, townships raises implementation difficulties of external validity of measures (Are we measuring the phenomena we want to be measuring?), but yields a few suggestive results. For example, plans are more likely to
include analysis of actions over which the plan-making agency has authority.

The effect of mandates on plans has been investigated in several instances.
Burby and colleagues (1997) provide evidence that state mandates on natural-
hazard plans do increase local plan quality and that local plans influence local
commitment, albeit indirectly through knowledge of the natural hazards creating
the political demands for action. Hoch (2007) found that local governments tried to
meet the mandate in Illinois requiring a plan for affordable housing while resisting
the enactment of policies that would achieve the intent of the state mandate. Hoch
argues that the mandated plans do, however, focus attention on the state-mandated
goals. Pendall (2001) found that municipalities in Maine submitted plans under a
voluntary but state-supported system, but that only half of these plans were consistent with state goals. These studies demonstrate that it is important to distinguish
between the success in getting plans made from the success in achieving through
local action the substantive goals of the state mandate.

Normative claims of the planning profession do not appear to have expected
effects on plans. Berke and Conroy (2000) found that comprehensive plans explicitly framed in terms of sustainability did not include a larger scope of sustainability
content than plans not framed in terms of sustainability. Talen and Knaap (2003)
investigated regulations rather than plans and found little evidence of smart-
growth principles in zoning ordinances and subdivision ordinances in Illinois.

The plan-quality literature is a sustained project that is building an approach
to describing the attributes of good plans and suggests circumstances in which
such attributes are likely to occur. In a few instances (e.g., Burby 2003), the plan-
quality literature has been linked to planning-process questions to suggest that
how plans are made affects their quality.

3. CLAIMS FOR USING PLANS WELL

Questions about using plans well can be organized around three frequent claims:
conformance, performance, and net benefit. Plans should be implemented as evidenced by the future's conforming to the content of the plan. Plans should perform by communicating useful and usable information to intended audiences so

as to influence decisions and actions. Plans are worth making because they yield improvements in outcomes sufficient to justify the costs of making them.

3.1 Conformance

The conformance claim can be expressed in at least two ways, depending on how the plan is intended to work (Hopkins 2001). First, an agent making a plan should implement that plan by making the decisions and taking the actions called for in the plan. This claim applies to plans intended to work as agendas, policies, designs, legal backing, or visions of physical outcomes. Second, agents making plans should achieve the goals of their plans regardless of uncertainty about the future state or actions of others. This claim applies to plans intended to work as strategies or as visions with respect to goals. There is surprisingly little empirical research on the conformance of actions to plans in either of these ways, probably because of the significant difficulties encountered by those who have tried.

Alterman and Hill (1978) is the classic example of conformance research. They looked at a two-stage implementation process in Israel, from outline plan to detailed plan to building permit. The planning regime in Israel at that time was intended to be hierarchically regulatory, so these results are an assessment of the regulatory persistence of a plan as a design. Whether the 66 percent conformance they found is high or low—that is, whether it suggests that plans matter or not—is difficult to interpret or generalize because it is not easy to attribute the result to the effects of the plans. More important, they identify particular attributes of plans and planning situations that might affect conformance—in particular, flexibility, which they define as whether the intended use is specified broadly or narrowly. It is not clear what we learn from observing that a plan more broadly stated is more likely to result in conformance than one that is more narrowly stated.

This difficulty in achieving useful results continues to plague empirical investigations of conformance. Brody, Highfield, and Thornton (2006) investigated compliance with development plans in Florida by comparing wetland-alteration permits with proposed land-use patterns. Levels of conformance were not related to whether a plan included development policies expected to improve conformance. Patterns of nonconformance were consistent with development dynamics: development inconsistent with plans occurred at the edges of prior development where land prices were lower.

Talen (1996a) looked at conformance to goals. Her argument is that the success of spatial plans should not be based on conformance of specific locations of parks because these actions are only means to achieve goals. She tested whether accessibility to parks after a plan becomes more like the accessibility goals sought by the plan. For the Pueblo Colorado case, the results are inconclusive. The attempt, however, sets out the potential and difficulties of the goals-conformance approach. As Talen points out, if a plan proposes specific locations of parks that embed multiple goals, such as transportation nodes, visual relationships, or environmental opportunities, as well as accessibility, then assessing accessibility itself misses the function of the plan (working as a design) in identifying a set of actions that jointly achieve multiple goals. If, however, a plan is expressed in measurable goals distinct from specific actions (working as a vision), then goals conformance can be used to discover what sorts of goals or implementation have greater degrees of success in particular circumstances.

Johnson (1996) carried out an in-depth study of the 1929 Regional Plan of New York and Environs. He is clear that conformance is insufficient to attribute outcomes to the influence of plans for at least two reasons: proposals included in the plan might have happened anyway, and proposals included in the plan might already have been and continue to be included in other plans as well. Johnson reported the major projects that were accomplished and considered the percentage of accomplishment. He also considered how the difference between forecasted futures and realized futures might appropriately invite modifications of proposed projects. Nonetheless, his major conclusion was that it is extremely difficult to attribute outcomes to the influence of plans without even more extensive investigation of the historical trajectory of each project proposal.

In summary, the conformance approach, whether applied to actions or to goals, has been inconclusive about the effectiveness of plans even if we accept conformance as useful evidence of whether plans work. The additional difficulty of tracing the effect of a plan brings us to the performance approach.

3.2 Performance

The fundamental claim of the performance approach is that plans communicate to an audience and, through that communication, affect decisions, actions, and outcomes. Expressing the claim in this way distinguishes the effect of plans from the effect of regulations, which are enforceable. Performance assessment of plans must somehow evaluate whether people use the information in them. There are at least two ways to do so. First, we could trace the use of information in decision-making processes. Second, we could compare behaviors before and after information is available to infer whether the information affected decisions.

The direct audiences for local spatial plans in the United States are planning commissions, city councils, development companies, neighborhood organizations that may oppose development, and the courts (e.g., Norton 2008). These audiences include not only the agents of the municipality making a plan but also other municipalities that may be adjacent or competing. I know of no systematic investigation of the use of plans by plan commissions or city councils. Norton (2005), as part of a larger study, provides percentages of staff who report use of plans when making decisions, but not in a way that enables us to assess plan effectiveness. Kent (1964) made a compelling case for the use of a plan by a city council. Although his argument was based on personal experience, his claims are normative rather than empirical. Casual empiricism indicates that planning staff in many places use the content of plans to present arguments for zoning cases to planning commissions and city councils. It is accepted as best practice and supported by the legal framework within which such decisions might be challenged. There is a difference, however, between the question of whether use of plans yields better zoning decisions and that of whether zoning decisions backed by plans can more successfully meet legal challenges.

Norton (2008) articulated the assessment of plans as legal backing for regulations. This backing relies on communicating the backing not only to plan commissions and city councils but also to judges. His empirical investigations, however, focus on plan quality as discussed earlier, not on the effectiveness of plans as legal backing. The question of plans as legal backing could be investigated through case law, leading to a complex variation of influence across states in the extent to which plans carry weight in legal decisions.

Do plans affect other plans? Waldner (2008) found that regional plan policies affected local plan policies but not local regulations. In most cases, a planning professional involved at the regional level was later involved in a county plan through providing services from the regional agency to a county, becoming a consultant to a county, or moving to a new job with a county agency. The mechanism of influence was through people rather than aspects of plan quality, and the influences on planning were different from the influences on regulations. This investigation was framed with a presumption that plans should be consistent across levels, and it implies that one way to achieve this is to share planning staff.

An alternative view sees plans as interacting, but not necessarily as consistent or hierarchical. Wies (1992) used game theory to explain which organizations joined in a common freeway plan and which defected to their own plans. Schaeffer and Hopkins (1987) and Knaap, Hopkins, and Donaghy (1998) used game theory to explain circumstances in which developers and infrastructure providers would choose to plan and the implications for testing these explanations empirically. Kaza and Hopkins (2009) argue that plans are in some circumstances more effective in achieving intentions if shared strategically with particular audiences.

These formulations frame specific tests for the effects of plans. Is the plan taken as new information? Are actions consistent with the plan taken as expected? These effects can be assessed by testing whether land values or developer actions change once a plan is known and whether land values or developer actions change when an action is taken consistent with a plan. A credible plan that presents new information should change the behavior of those aware of it. If actions taken are consistent with an already known plan, then neither land values nor developer actions should change.

Knaap, Ding, and Hopkins (2001) showed that land values around proposed light-rail stations in the Portland metropolitan region increased after release of the plans. Thus, the plan influenced expectations, revealed in price changes. These price increases in turn affect the pattern of land development in intended ways by discouraging development at lower densities that would be costly to change later and by encouraging development at higher densities. That is, the plan was working as a strategy to overcome the problems of irreversibility, interdependence, and indivisibility (Hopkins 2001), and players were motivated to use the information in the plan even though it was someone else's plan. McDonald and Osuji (1995) found similar anticipation effects. Hanley and Hopkins (2007) used a simulation model to compare sewer-extension policies as explanations of the historical pattern of residential development southwest of Portland. The results suggest, though not conclusively, that the sewer provider followed its plan and that residential developers had found that plan credible. Note that in all these cases the effects are explicitly based on information in plans, not on regulations or other mediating, implementing actions.

Immergluck (2009) found similar information effects over time as expectations became increasingly clear for the Atlanta Beltline project, but he concluded that, in this case, the price effects induced unintended and undesirable speculative transactions and gentrification. This result should remind us that plans can be effective— that is, influence action and outcomes—even if those outcomes may be unintended and undesirable. External-validity questions about whether the effects of plans are indeed desirable remain an important but separable question (Hopkins 2001).

A different approach to performance asks whether plans are worth making because they yield improvements in outcomes sufficient to justify the costs. Krueckeberg (1969, 1971) looked at plan-making efficiency by comparing inputs (e.g., staffing) and outputs (planning-document products) across metropolitan planning agencies. Helling (1998) suggests that we should think about costs in relation to effects of plans. Her estimate of $4.4 million as the cost of the Atlanta 2020 visioning project included as a significant component the opportunity cost of time spent by participants. Tangible effects of the plan were difficult to identify. Even if we include the social network building benefits of the plan-making process, $4.4 million is high enough to raise the question of whether benefits have been sufficient to justify the cost.

By tackling a more tightly defined planning task, Hopkins, Xu, and Knaap (2004) found that hypothetical plans that would avoid irreversibility, indivisibility, and interdependence costs in providing and operating sewer capacity in Metropolitan Chicago over decades of growth could yield net present-value gains of $170 million. This estimate has many limitations and does not consider positive or negative effects other than construction and operating costs of sewer systems. The implication of this limited evidence, however, is that plans can yield benefits that would make them worth making.

Conformance research, despite careful formulations in qualitative and quantitative studies, has been inconclusive in providing useful insights on whether and in what circumstances plans are effective. Performance research appears to have greater potential through case-study investigations of great detail and through observation of the effects of information. Much too little evidence is available about costs and benefits of plans. The evidence there is leaves open the possibility that plans are worth making.

4. Conclusions

What do we know about whether plans are useful, based on what evidence and arguments? What more would we like to know? Several research designs are now well established and several relatively focused questions have attracted sufficient scholarly attention to yield useful results. The questions are now more focused so that new conversations can emerge.

4.1 We Think We Know That...

- Planning processes affect plans in their content and likelihood of implementation. Collaboration as social cognition and conflict resolution affects plan content, and participation by stakeholders affects the likelihood of implementation.
- Planning processes affect planning situations through learning by participating individuals and creation of new social networks. Such results have been some of the most easily attributed effects, although these are usually side effects of primary claims for planning processes.
- The ability to score plans by plan quality provides a procedure through which to test the effects of processes on plans and plans on implementation. Some plans have plan-quality attributes claimed to make them good, but this research approach has had limited success in showing that such plans work better than other plans.
- Mandates affect plan content more than they affect plan use. Those making mandated plans are more likely to meet the letter of the mandate than to achieve the intent of the mandate.
- Norms in the planning profession do not necessarily appear in plans in practice. Salient norms and rhetoric are much less apparent in observed plans and regulations.
- Conformance research has generated inconclusive results. The problem of attributing effects to plans limits the effectiveness of such research designs in assessing whether plans work.
- Performance research designs through in-depth case studies and inference of information use have generated useful results about situations in which plans work. Performance appears to have greater potential than conformance for future research.

4.2 We Would Like to Know...

The following questions are organized as three "big questions." Each big question is elaborated through examples of "little questions," which are attempts to move toward researchable questions. These questions build on things we think we know as described above.

- What operational details of planning processes affect the content and use of particular kinds of plans? In designing processes of collaboration, what are the trade-offs between focusing on claims of consensus and acknowledging differences in interests and aspirations? What are the trade-offs between focusing on collaboration as collective choice (or conflict resolution) and social cognition? What procedures for metropolitan-scale collaborarion might show more success than recent extrapolations from consensus building?
- What attributes of plans increase the value added from using plans in particular circumstances? What should the functional, geographic, institutional, and time-horizon scopes of plans be? What events should trigger revisions of plans? What combination of plans, based on what planning activities and relationships to other plans, is efficient for a city? A metropolitan region? A voluntary organization? A community initiative? Is the value added from a particular plan greater than its costs?
- In what ways can plans add value in the face of nonhierarchical institutional systems and uncertainty? What are the trade-offs in effectiveness of plans between acknowledging in a plan that futures are unknown and presenting proposals decisively in an attitude of certainty? What are the trade-offs between achieving a priori plan consistency and using inconsistent plans to interact effectively? How can uncertainty and interaction among organizations be represented in plans?

Framing sustainable research conversations will require identifying and overcoming the impediments to posing focused, researchable questions. These impediments include devising research designs that effectively link theory and methods to available or obtainable data.

REFERENCES

Alexander, E. R., and A. Faludi. 1989. "Planning and Plan Implementation: Notes on Evaluation Criteria." *Environment and Planning Part B: Planning and Design* 16(2): 127–40.

Alterman, R., and M. Hill. 1978. "Implementation of Land Use Plans." *Journal of the American Institute of Planners* 44(3): 274–85.

Andrews, C. J. 1992. "Spurring Inventiveness by Analyzing Tradeoffs: A Public Look at New England's Electricity Alternatives." *Environmental Impact Assessment Review* 12: 185–210.

Andrews, C. J. 2002. *Humble Analysis: The Practice of Joint Fact-Finding.* Westport, CT: Praeger.

Angotti, T. 2008. *New York for Sale: Community Planning Confronts Global Real Estate.* Cambridge, MA: MIT Press.

Arkes, H. R., and K. R. Hammond, eds. 1986. *Judgment and Decision Making: An Interdisciplinary Reader.* Cambridge, UK: Cambridge University Press.

Baer, W. C. 1997. "General Plan Evaluation Criteria: An Approach to Making Better Plans." *Journal of the American Planning Association* 63(3): 329–44.

Berke, P. R., and M. M. Conroy. 2000. "Are We Planning for Sustainable Development? An Evaluation of 30 Comprehensive Plans." *Journal of the American Planning Association* 66(1): 21–33.

Berke, P. R., and D. R. Godschalk. 2009. "Searching for the Good Plan: A Meta-Analysis of Plan Quality Studies." *Journal of Planning Literature* 23(2): 227–40.

Berke, P. R., D. R. Godschalk, E. J. Kaiser, and D. A. Rodriguez. 2006. *Urban Land Use Planning,* 5th ed. Urbana, IL: University of Illinois Press.

Briggs, X. de S. 2008. *Democracy as Problem Solving: Civic Capacity in Communities Across the Globe.* Cambridge, MA: MIT Press.

Brill, E. D., Jr., S. Y. Chang, and L. D. Hopkins. 1982. "Modeling to Generate Alternatives: The HSJ Approach and an Illustration Using a Problem in Land Use Planning." *Management Science* 28(3): 221–35.

Brill, E. D., Jr., J. M. Flach, L. D. Hopkins, and S. Ranjithan. 1990. "MGA: A Decision Support System for Complex, Incompletely Defined Problems." *IEEE Transactions on Systems, Man, and Cybernetics* 20(4): 745–57.

Brody, S. D. 2003. "Are We Learning to Make Better Plans? A Longitudinal Analysis of Plan Quality Associated with Natural Hazards." *Journal of Planning Education and Research* 23(2): 191–201.

Brody, S. D., W. E. Highfield, and S. Thornton. 2006. "Planning at the Urban Fringe: An Examination of the Factors Influencing Nonconforming Development Patterns in Southern Florida." *Environment and Planning Part B: Planning and Design* 33: 75–96.

Bryson, J. M. 1991. "There Is No Substitute for an Empirical Defense of Planning and Planners." *Journal of Planning Education and Research* 10(2): 164–65.

Bryson, J. M., P. Bromiley, and Y. S. Jung. 1990. "Influences of Context and Process on Project Planning Success." *Journal of Planning Education and Research* 9(3): 183–95.

Bryson, J. M., and B. C. Crosby. 1992. *Leadership for the Common Good: Tackling Public Problems in a Shared-Power World.* San Francisco: Jossey-Bass.

Bunnell, G. 2002. *Making Places Special: Stories of Real Places Made Better by Planning.* Chicago, IL: APA Planners Press.

Burby, R. J. 2003. "Making Plans that Matter: Citizen Involvement and Government Action." *Journal of the American Planning Association* 69(1): 33–49.

Burby, R. J., P. J. May, P. R. Berke, L. C. Dalton, S. P. French, and E. J. Kaiser. 1997. *Making Governments Plan: State Experiments in Managing Land Use.* Baltimore: Johns Hopkins University Press.

Calkins, H. W. 1979. "The Planning Monitor: An Accountability Theory of Plan Evaluation." *Environment and Planning Part A* 11(7): 745–58.

Donaghy, K. P., and L. D. Hopkins. 2006. "Coherentist Theories of Planning Are Possible and Useful." *Planning Theory* 5(2): 173–202.

Dryzek, J. S. 2007. "Theory, Evidence, and the Tasks of Deliberation." In *Deliberation, Participation, and Democracy: Can the People Govern?*, edited by S. W. Rosenberg, 237–50. New York: Palgrave Macmillan.

Elkin, S. 1987. *City and Regime in the American Republic.* Chicago: University of Chicago Press.

Faludi, A. 2000. "The Performance of Spatial Planning." *Planning Practice and Research* 15(4): 299–318.

Faludi, A., and J. M. Mastop. 1982. "The IOR School—The Development of a Planning Methodology." *Environment and Planning Part B: Planning and Design* 9: 241–56.

Forester, J. 2006. "Making Participation Work When Interests Conflict: Moving from Facilitating Dialogue and Moderating Debate to Mediating Negotiations." *Journal of the American Planning Association* 72(4): 447–56.

Friend, J. K., and W. N. Jessop. 1969. *Local Government and Strategic Choice: An Operational Research Approach to the Processes of Public Planning.* London: Tavistock.

Gunderson, L. H., and C. S. Holling, eds. 2002. *Panarchy: Understanding Transformations in Human and Natural Systems.* Washington, DC: Island Press.

Hanley, P. F., and L. D. Hopkins. 2007. "Do Sewer Extension Plans Affect Urban Development? A Multiagent Simulation." *Environment and Planning Part B: Planning and Design* 34(1): 6–27.

Healey, P. 1997. *Collaborative Planning: Shaping Places in Fragmented Societies.* London: Macmillan.

Healey, P. 2007. *Urban Complexity and Spatial Strategies: Towards a Relational Planning for Our Times.* London: Routledge.

Helling, A. 1998. "Collaborative Visioning: Proceed with Caution! Results from Evaluating Atlanta's Vision 2020 Project." *Journal of the American Planning Association* 64(3): 335–49.

Hoch, C. 2007. "How Plan Mandates Work: Affordable Housing in Illinois." *Journal of the American Planning Association* 73(1): 86–99.

Hopkins, L. D. 1973. "Design Method Evaluation: An Experiment with Corridor Selection." *Socioeconomic Planning Sciences* 7: 423–30.

Hopkins, L. D. 1984. "Evaluation of Methods for Exploring Ill-Defined Problems." *Environment and Planning Part B: Planning and Design* 11:339–48.

Hopkins, L. D. 2001. *Urban Development: The Logic of Making Plans.* Washington, DC: Island Press.

Hopkins, L. D. 2007. "Using Plans and Plan Making Processes: Deliberation and Representations of Plans." In *Engaging the Future: Using Forecasts, Scenarios, Plans, and Projects,* edited by L. D. Hopkins and M. A. Zapata, 283–313. Cambridge, MA: Lincoln Institute of Land Policy.

Hopkins, L. D., N. Kaza, and V. G. Pallathucheril. 2005. "Representing Urban Development Plans and Regulations as Data: A Planning Data Model." *Environment and Planning Part B: Planning and Design* 32(4): 597–615.

Hopkins, L. D., X. Xu, and G. J. Knaap. 2004. "Economies of Scale in Wastewater Treatment and Planning for Urban Growth." *Environment and Planning Part B: Planning and Design* 31: 879–93.

Hurley, S. L. 1989. *Natural Reasons: Personality and Polity.* New York: Oxford University Press.

Immergluck, D. 2009. "Large Redevelopment Initiatives, Housing Values and Gentrification: The Case of the Atlanta Beltline." *Urban Studies* 46(8): 1723–45.

Innes, J. E. 1996. "Planning through Consensus Building: A New View of the Comprehensive Planning Ideal." *Journal of the American Planning Association* 62(4): 460–72.

Innes, J. E. 1998. "Information in Communicative Planning." *Journal of the American Planning Association* 64(1): 52–63.

Innes, J. E. 2004. "Consensus Building: Clarification for the Critics." *Planning Theory* 3(1): 5–20.

Innes, J. E., and D. E. Booher. 1999. "Consensus Building and Complex Adaptive Systems: A Framework for Evaluating Collaborative Planning." *Journal of the American Planning Association* 65(4): 412–23.

Innes, J. E., S. Connick, and D. Booher. 2007. "Informality as a Planning Strategy: Collaborative Water Management in the CALFED Bay-Delta Program." *Journal of the American Planning Association* 73(2): 195–210.

Johnson, D. A. 1996. *Planning the Great Metropolis: The 1929 Regional Plan of New York and Its Environs*. London: Spon.

Kaza, N. 2006. "Tyranny of the Median and Costly Consent: A Reflection on the Justification for Participatory Urban Planning Processes." *Planning Theory* 5(3): 255–70.

Kaza, N., and L. D. Hopkins. 2009. "In What Circumstances Should Plans Be Public?" *Journal of Planning Education and Research* 28(4): 491–502.

Kent, T. J. (1964). *The Urban General Plan*. San Francisco: Chandler Publishing Co.

Knaap, G. J., C. Ding, and L. D. Hopkins. 2001. "The Effect of Light Rail Announcements on Price Gradients." *Journal of Planning Education and Research* 21(1): 32–39.

Knaap, G. J., L. D. Hopkins, and K. P. Donaghy. 1998. "Do Plans Matter? A Framework for Examining the Logic and Effects of Land Use Planning." *Journal of Planning Education and Research* 18(1): 25–34.

Krantz, D. H., and H. D. Kunreuther. 2007. "Goals and Plans in Decision Making." *Judgment and Decision Making* 2(3): 137–68.

Krueckeberg, D. A. 1969. "A Multivariate Analysis of Metropolitan Planning." *Journal of the American Institute of Planners* 35:319–25.

Krueckeberg, D. A. 1971. "Variations in the Behavior of Planning Agencies." *Administrative Science Quarterly* 16:192–202.

Lai, S.-K., and L. D. Hopkins. 1989. "The Meanings of Tradeoffs in Multi-Attribute Evaluation Methods: A Comparison." *Environment and PlanningPart B: Planning and Design* 16(2): 155–70.

Lai, S.-K., and L. D. Hopkins. 1995. "Can Decision Makers Express Multiattribute Preferences Using AHP and MUT? An Experiment." *Environment and Planning Part B: Planning and Design* 22(1): 21–34.

Lukes, S. 1974. *Power: A Radical View*. London: Macmillan.

Lynch, K. 1960. *The Image of the City*. Cambridge, MA: MIT Press.

Mandelbaum, S. J. 1979. "A Complete General Theory of Planning is Impossible." *Policy Sciences* 11:59–71.

Mastop, H., and A. Faludi. 1997. "Evaluation of Strategic Plans: The Performance Principle." *Environment and Planning Part B: Planning and Design* 24:815–32.

McDonald, J., and C. I. Osuji. 1995. The Effect of Anticipated Transportation Improvements on Residential Land Values." *Regional Science and Urban Economics* 25(3): 261–78.

McGurty, E. 2007. *Transforming Environmentalism: Warren County, PCBs, and the Origins of Environmental Justice*. New Brunswick, NJ: Rutgers University Press.

Miller, R. W. 1987. *Fact and Method: Explanation, Confirmation and Reality in the Natural and the Social Sciences*. Princeton, NJ: Princeton University Press.

Norton, R. K. 2005. "More and Better Local Planning: State-Mandated Local Planning in Coastal North Carolina." *Journal of the American Planning Association* 71(1): 55–71.

Norton, R. K. 2008. "Using Content Analysis to Evaluate Local Master Plans and Zoning Codes." *Land Use Policy* 25: 432–54.

Nussbaum, M. 1995. "Human Capabilities, Female Human Beings." In *Women, Culture, and Development: A Study of Human Capabilities*, edited by M. Nussbaum and J. Glover, 61–104. Oxford: Oxford University Press.

O'Flaherty, B. 2005. *City Economics*. Cambridge, MA: Harvard University Press.

Ordeshook, P. C. 1992. *A Political Theory Primer.* New York: Routledge.

Pendall, R. 2001. "Municipal Plans, State Mandates, and Property Rights: Lessons from Maine." *Journal of Planning Education and Research* 21(2): 154–65.

Putnam, R. D. 1993. *Making Democracy Work: Civic Traditions in Modern Italy.* Princeton, NJ: Princeton University Press.

Reardon, K. M. 1998. "Enhancing the Capacity of Community-Based Organizations in East St. Louis." *Journal of Planning Education and Research* 17(4): 323–33.

Rosenberg, S. W., ed. 2007. *Deliberation, Participation and Democracy: Can the People Govern?* New York: Palgrave Macmillan.

Sandercock, L. 2004. "Towards a Planning Imagination for the 21st Century." *Journal of the American Planning Association* 70(2): 133–41.

Schaeffer, P. V., and L. D. Hopkins. 1987. "Planning Behavior: The Economics of Information and Land Development." *Environment and Planning Part A* 19:1221–32.

Sen, A. 1993. "Capability and Well-Being." In *The Quality of Life,* edited by M. Nussbaum and A. Sen, 30–53. Oxford: Oxford University Press.

Sniezek, J., and R. Henry. 1989. "Accuracy and Confidence in Group Judgment." *Organizational Behavior and Human Decision Processes* 43:1–28.

Sunstein, C. R. 2003. *Why Societies Need Dissent.* Cambridge, MA: Harvard University Press.

Susskind, L. D., and J. L. Cruikshank. 2006. *Breaking Robert's Rules: The New Way to Run Your Meeting, Build Consensus, and Get Results.* Oxford: Oxford University Press.

Susskind, L. D., S. McKearnan, and J. Thomas-Larmer, eds. 1999. *The Consensus Building Handbook: A Comprehensive Guide to Reaching Agreement.* Thousand Oaks, CA: Sage.

Talen, E. 1996a. "After the Plans: Methods to Evaluate the Implementation Success of Plans." *Journal of Planning Education and Research* 16(2): 79–91.

Talen, E. 1996b. "Do Plans Get Implemented? A Review of Evaluation in Planning." *Journal of Planning Literature* 10(3): 248–59.

Talen, E., and G. J. Knaap. 2003. "Legalizing Smart Growth: An Empirical Study of Land Use Regulation in Illinois." *Journal of Planning Education and Research* 22(4): 345–59.

Tetlock, P. E. 2005. *Expert Political Judgment: How Good Is It? How Can We Know?* Princeton, NJ: Princeton University Press.

Trybus, T. W., and L. D. Hopkins. 1980. "Humans versus Computer Algorithms for the Plant Layout Problem." *Management Science* 26:570–74.

Waldner, L. 2008. "Regional Plans, Local Fates? How Spatially Restrictive Regional Policies Influence County Policy and Regulations." *Environment and Planning Part B: Planning and Design* 35:679–700.

Wies, K. 1992. "Cooperative Strategy in Regional Transportation Planning: Planning the Lake-Will North Expressway." PhD dissertation, University of Illinois at Chicago.

Willson, R. W., M. Payne, and E. Smith. 2003. "Does Discussion Enhance Rationality? A Report from Transportation Planning Practice." *Journal of the American Planning Association* 69(4): 354–67.

Name Index

Subject Index

....

National Civic League, 678
National Conference on City Planning and the
    Problems of Congestion, Washington, D.C.,
    1909, 358–359, 392, 398
National Congress for Community and Economic
    Development (NCCED), 674, 675
National Defense and Interstate Highway Act of
    1956, 636
national emissions inventory, 458
National Fund for Workforce Solutions, 494
National Grid Balanced Mechanism Reporting
    Services, UK, 469
National Historic Preservation Act, 1966, 181
National Historic Preservation Trust's Main Street
    program, 488
National Household Travel Survey, U.S., 637, 646, 648
National Park Service, 181
National Planning Conference, 359
national planning culture, 93
National Research Council (NRC), 441, 645, 646, 652
National Vacant Properties Campaign, 573
nation building, 200
Nationwide Personal Transportation Survey (NPTS),
    645–646
natural disasters, 209
    Bangladesh as capital for, 227
earthquakes, 222–223
    Hurricane Katrina, 209, 220, 223–225, 226, 230,
    268
Natural Resources Defense Council, 362, 365
Natural Resources Inventory (USDA), 549
Nature Conservancy (TNC), 426
negative discrimination, 149
Negro Family, The Case for National Action, The (U.S.
    Dept. of Labor), 276
neighborhood associations, 675–677, 681
neighborhood district coordinators, 679
neighborhood life-cycle theory, 570
Neighborhood Progress, 575
neighborhood revitalization, 487–488, 510
neighborhood saturation, 482
neighborhoods, inclusive, 514–515
Neighborhood Transformation Initiative,
    Philadelphia, 510
Neighborhood Unit urban design, 399–400
neoclassical approaches, to the real estate industry,
    724–726
neoclassical economics model, 71–73
neoliberalism, 598, 619
Netherlands
    planning culture in Rotterdam, 89–92
    urban redevelopment in, 595–596
Network on European Communications and
    Transport Activities Research (NECTAR), 167
Newark Central Planning Board, 773, 776, 777
Newark, New Jersey, 1964 Master Plan, 773–777
New Deal era, 49, 50, 401, 590
*New Exploration: A Philosophy of Regional Planning,
    The* (MacKaye), 130

new institutional economics, 72, 76
New Jersey
    community revitalization strategies in Camden,
    510
    Mt. Laurel I and II cases, 275
New Markets Tax Credit, 483, 487–488
New Orleans, Louisiana
    early public health issues in, 396
    Hurricane Katrina, 209, 220, 223–225, 226, 230,
    268
    reasonable expectations and social justice, 153
New Right ideology, 56–57
New Towns Movement, England, 109
new urban ecology, 131
New Urbanism, 111, 132
    air quality and, 439
    gender issues and, 621
    smart growth and, 230, 780
    travel behavior and, 637, 648
New Urbanists, 353
    and sustainability, 129, 130, 132
    smart growth development and, 422, 423, 424, 429
"new urban marginality", 692
new urban politics theory, 619
New York City
    abandonment in South Bronx, 566, 573, 578
    after 9/11, 222, 230
    air quality in, 443, 446
    art and culture in, 381, 382, 385, 386
    blackouts of 1969 and 1977 in, 218
    Central Park, 109
    Committee on the Congestion of Population, 392,
    397, 398
    conformance assessment of plans in, 813–814
    density and land-use patterns in, 543
    distribution of outputs issue in, 145
    early public health issues in, 396
    electricity emissions in, 469–470
    families and culture of poverty concept, 268
    feminist urban scholars in Harlem, 613
    Harlem Children's Zone, 494
    immigration issues in, 752–753
    income inequality in, 746
    1929 Regional Plan of New York and Environs,
    813–814
    during 1975 fiscal crisis, 220
    Penn Station preservation, 183
    population loss and disinvestment planning in, 566
    public health issues in, 394, 405
    public housing in, 268
    public plazas in, 277
    redevelopment of Times Square, 275, 382
    Regional Plan for New York, 247
    transportation and accessibility, 169
    urban design successes in, 277
    urban redevelopment in, 591, 601
    zoning issues in, 269
New York City Housing and Development
    Administration, 574

CPSIA information can be obtained at www.ICGtesting.com
Printed in the USA
BVOW09s1024131016

464888BV00004B/9/P